Seraffyn's
European
Adventure

By the same authors

Richard Blagborne

Seraffyn's
European Adventure

by

Lin and Larry Pardey

W·W·NORTON & COMPANY
New York / London

All photographs by Lin and Larry Pardey unless otherwise indicated

Copyright © 1979 by Mary Lin and Lawrence F. Pardey
Published simultaneously in Canada by George J. McLeod Limited,
Toronto. Printed in the United States of America.

All Rights Reserved

First Edition

Library of Congress Cataloging in Publication Data

Pardey, Lin.
Seraffyn's European adventures.

1. Seraffyn (Cutter) 2. Sailing—Europe.
I. Pardey, Larry, joint author.   II. Title.
GV822.S39P38   1979   797.1′24   78–32032
ISBN 0–393–03231–0

This book was set in Janson and Perpetua
Manufactured by Haddon Craftsmen, Inc.
Designed by Jacques Chazaud

1 2 3 4 5 6 7 8 9 0

Contents

Preface

~~~~~

Cruising, like the rest of life, has its different paces, its different moods, its highs and lows. During the first three years of our cruising life we sailed almost fifteen thousand miles. We spent our time learning to live free of schedules, learning to know our boat, ourselves, and the seas around us. During the next two and a half years, the ones covered by this book, we voyaged less than six thousand miles. We saw a completely different world and we came to marvel at the variety of opportunities our life on *Seraffyn* opened to us.

Acknowledgements

Besides the people who went to a lot of trouble to provide the information that appears in Appendix B, we would like to thank Mike Hope, Chris Field, and Phil Lum who took some of the photographs used in this book.

Our appreciation goes to people like Tom Nibbea, Jonathon Blair, Bruce McElfresh, and Tom Smith at National Geographic, who helped us learn to use a camera with more success. And to Julia Stansby and Irene Khor, who helped with the typing of the manuscript. Thanks also to Humphrey and Mary Barton, who edited the first half of Seraffyn's *European Adventure* in Malta, making helpful suggestions. It was at their insistence that Larry and I stopped dropping our anchor and started letting it go. John Dodd, Jim and Ann MacBeth, Peer Tangvald, and Brian Merrill each read parts of this manuscript in rough typewritten form and made very useful suggestions that we know improved it. Eric Swenson, Eleanor Crapallo, Richard Whittington, Dick Rath, John Delves, Shelley Heller, Linda Moran, and the crew of *Boating* magazine gave us their kind assistance in New York, and Shiela Waygood handled our mail and photographic problems in England. Patience Wales and the staff of *Sail* magazine helped us locate information when we needed it. Without these helping hands it would have been a lot harder to coordinate this book, especially since we have been cruising on as we wrote it.

Some people we'd especially like to remember here are the members and staff of the Parkstone Yacht Club in England and the Alborg Yacht Club in Denmark, plus all of those other people we met and shared wonderful moments with but just couldn't mention because of the limited spaces on these pages.

Finally, we'd like to thank the thoughtful people we have never met who took the time and effort to write us letters saying, "We enjoyed your first book, when do we get to read the sequel?" People like Dennis Walsh, Tor Christiansen, Bob and Sandy Levesque, and many others. We hope they are not disappointed.

Seraffyn's European Adventure

CHAPTER 1

Dragons and the Sea

S t. George had his dragon, I had the Atlantic. We had built *Seraffyn* strong enough to sail almost anywhere. We'd cruised from California along Mexico's west coast to Costa Rica and Panama, north through the Caribbean and past the Florida Keys to the Chesapeake, wandering along like gypsies for three years, singing, swimming, playing, and occasionally working. Always there'd been land within three or four hundred miles of our tiny floating home. So as the time came closer for our plunge across the forty-two hundred miles of North Atlantic that blocked our path to England, I kept telling myself, "It's nothing different, Lin, just a few more days at sea than usual."

Larry had none of these concerns. He'd been sailing since he was a kid. He'd made two passages across the Pacific on an eighty-five-foot schooner. He'd been skipper on a fifty-three-foot charter boat in Newport Beach, California, for two years, and had raced competitively in his home port of Vancouver, British Columbia, for five. He was a sailor who loved every mood of the sea. Seasickness? Larry didn't know what the word meant. The only thing in the sailing world that bothered him was being becalmed in our engineless boat near heavy shipping. The Atlantic would be a relief after the crowds of shipping we'd met in the Straits of Florida. So Larry looked forward to the crossing, dreaming of the other side long before we cast off our mooring lines.

Forty-two hundred miles! The North Atlantic! Storms! No land for twenty or thirty days! Each thought filled me with apprehension. I'd had almost no sailing experience before I met Larry. My father had owned a fourteen-foot lapstrake sloop until I was five years old, but then we'd had to sell it because the family was leaving Michigan to move to California. Each summer after we arrived in Los Angeles, we would make a one-day pilgrimage to Newport Beach, ninety miles from our home. We'd play on the yellow sands, intimidated by the roaring Pacific. We'd eat our picnic lunch of fried chicken and potato salad. Then would come the event my dad had waited for. He'd walk across the narrow peninsula, my brother Allen by his side, pay for one hour's rent of a sixteen-foot sloop, prepare it for us, and we'd step aboard and skim down Newport Bay, dad's face turned upward toward the dirty, battered sails, excitedly telling Allen, "Trim the jib, duck, watch the boom." Mom and my baby sister Bonnie would try to sunbath on the tiny foredeck. I'd look at dad with admiration. He was happy, king of his world, thoughts of house payments, a car that needed new tires, a job filled with petty conflicts far behind him. Then twenty minutes later he'd glance at his watch and the dream would vanish. He'd say, "Got to head back, take us much longer to beat up the bay."

So we'd set to work short-tacking past the glowing white yachts tied in front of luxury homes, through moorings filled with gray and blue swordfish boats, their fantastic bow platforms stretching twenty feet ahead of them. Dad would time his hour to the second, handing the painter on the rental boat to the dock man with reluctance, and all three of us kids would rush past him as he gazed at the seemingly unobtainable world that that battered rental boat represented. Now came *our* favorite event of the day. Mom would buy each of us kids the treat only Newport Beach offered, a frozen chocolate-covered banana on a stick. Then sticky, wind blown, sandy, and tired, we'd hunt up the car, scramble inside, and head for home. As mom, Bonnie, Allen, and I slowly nodded off to sleep, dad would wistfully say, "Nice sail, wasn't it?"

By the time I was fourteen I'd become like most teenage girls. A day on the beach with the folks? Wouldn't be caught dead, not when I could be chasing around with some girlfriends chattering about boys. So sailing for me was a memory of the one day a year when my dad was king.

I met Larry accidently when I was twenty. He invited me for an afternoon's sail. I couldn't resist and two hours later I was in a world neither my dad nor I had ever dreamed of. We powered over a glassy sea in the fifty-three-foot ketch, the throb of a diesel engine beneath our feet, huge white glowing sails over our heads. I fell in love that day: with the laughing blue-eyed Larry; with the sheen of white sails, varnished wood, and creaking blocks; and with the same dream I'd noticed once a year in my father's eyes, the dream of far-off lands, of freedom and tranquility.

Two weeks later I was working with Larry, learning to help him build the twenty-four-foot cutter he planned to cruise in. My every thought turned to boats: lumber, nails, varnish, sails, sailing. When I drove to visit my folks once or twice a year I'd spent half the day talking boats with dad who was saving up to buy his own day sailer. I don't think my folks really believed Larry and I would sell out, move all our remaining worldly possessions onto our beamy little turtle shell of a boat, and sail off "forever." In fact, I didn't believe it myself until the day we launched *Seraffyn,* three and a half years from when she entered my life.

With six years of Larry's patient training behind me, fifteen thousand miles of sailing and countless hours spent reading every cruising book I could find, I was still apprehensive about the Atlantic. Gordon Yates, a friend we'd made while cruising in Mexico, used to say, "If you're not afraid, you just don't know the facts." I knew I'd occasionally be seasick. That was no problem, just a nuisance. But would I have enough food on board? Had I found enough books to read? Would I hate being at sea for weeks on end?

By the time we cast off our mooring lines, I'd used up every worry I could think of and, as usually happens, the Atlantic crossing turned into a daily affair, each morning different from the one before, each day filled with easy companionship. Some good weather, some bad. Some fabulous sailing, some frustrating as hell. We'd had to beat most of the last twelve-hundred-mile leg from the Azores to Falmouth, England. But as Larry said, "If it's this much work, it must be worthwhile." We'd sailed into Falmouth the night before and let go our anchor. I cried in Larry's arms, thrilled with the dragon I'd slain. I'd done it. There was still twenty gallons of fresh water in our tanks, lots of good food left hidden away in various lockers. Both of us were healthy and unbelievably happy. I knew then that I'd stood my test of fire.

Love the sea? Not really. I didn't trust it enough. Love sailing? With Larry, yes! Love cruising? Yes, completely!

As we climbed into bed together for the first time in three weeks, Larry kissed me and teased away my tears. "Just think, Lin, tomorrow we get four months' worth of mail from home. Then there's the whole of Europe to explore."

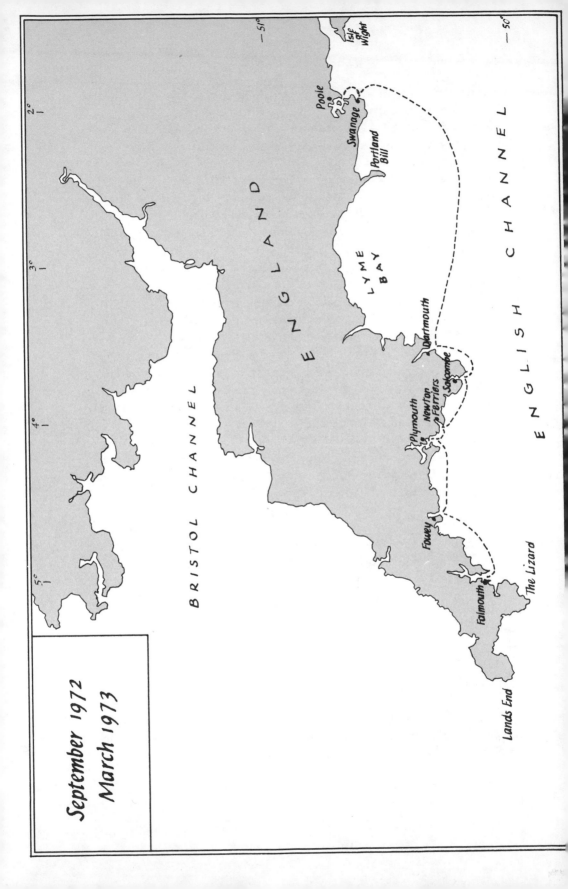

September 1972
March 1973

ENGLAND

BRISTOL CHANNEL

ENGLISH CHANNEL

LYME BAY

Isle of Wight

Poole

Swanage

Portland Bill

Dartmouth

Salcombe

Newton Ferriers

Plymouth

Fowey

The Lizard

Falmouth

Lands End

CHAPTER 2

~~~

Falmouth for Fun

An early-morning sun glowed through our portholes. *Seraffyn* dipped to a passing wake. Larry roused me by crawling out of our double sleeping bag. It took me some time to remember where we were —Falmouth! No more ocean passages for a while; just lovely day hops ahead, no matter which way we chanced to go!

Larry called to me as he slid the companionway hatch open. "Hurry, Lin, come see them. They're everywhere!" Larry sounded like a kid let loose at the zoo.

I crawled out of the warm down bag and immediately knew we were in England. It was cold! I pulled on woolly socks, jeans, and a sweatshirt at the same time as I tried to climb through the small companionway into the main cabin, and whacked the back of my head soundly. But I barely felt it in the excitement of my first daylight glimpse of the Old World.

The first sight of any port in daylight after a nightime entry is a bit magical. But Falmouth is in a class by itself. They were all around us—boats like *Seraffyn*, boats we'd read about in books by Uffa Fox and Peter Pye. Not fifty yards away was the transom of *Victory*, a seventy-year-old Falmouth oyster dredger, her hull looking just like ours, but without a cabin. Her bowsprit was fourteen feet long at least, seven feet longer than ours. Instead of the tall Bermuda-rigged mast we had, hers was short and stout with all the gear of a big gaff sail. Not far from *Victory* lay two other oyster dredgers, one red, the other turquoise and black.

Larry's coffee started to perk, filling the boat with a homey aroma. But we ignored it as a fleet of swans came alongside. I'd never seen a

The swans of Falmouth kept us fascinated.

wild swan, and to have one followed by six speckled cygnets not two feet from our floating home was irresistible. We pulled the drop boards out, I grabbed some stale bread, and we scrambled on deck. The swans knew a pair of suckers when they saw one, and started preening their feathers for us when our last piece of bread was gone. I was rummaging for something else to feed them when the forty-foot Customs boat came alongside.

Clearance was more a matter of being welcomed by the smiling officials than paperwork. Even our still-plentiful stock of duty-free liquor caused no problem since the English rule, which we'd read in Reed's *Almanac,* is that any yacht owned by a member of a recognized foreign yacht club may carry as much spirits and liquor as would "be reasonably consumed on board during the intended length of stay."

"The holding ground is poor here. Besides, the yacht club always has a mooring free for transatlantic sailors," the Immigration officer called as he left after finishing a cup of coffee.

So as soon as we'd cleaned up, we set sail toward the Royal Cornwall Yacht Club. A handsome twelve- or fourteen-foot varnished launch set off from the shore as we tacked through the club moorings.

"You the *Seraffyn*?" the young curly-haired launchman called as he approached. "Follow me. Thank God you're here; your post has filled our safe."

Over the chonk, chonk, chonk of his little Stuart Turner engine Leslie introduced himself to us. He handed up a mooring pennant and said, "Grab your shower kit. Hot water's on and the secretary is waiting."

We climbed into his launch, laden with fresh clothes and the unavoidable sailbag full of dirty laundry that every cruiser seems to have after a passage. Leslie gave us a running commentary in heavily accented West-country English. Then Larry started to say, "You Englishmen . . ." He got no further. Leslie drew himself up to full height and, fuming with regional pride, announced, "I'm not *English*, I'm *Cornish*!"

The door of the hundred-fifty-year-old gray stone home, now used by the yacht club, was flung open as we climbed the steps from the landing. A formidable-looking gray-haired woman approached us and announced, "Welcome to England! Now, do you wish to shower first or read your post?" Before either of us could say a word, she answered, "No, if you start on that pile of letters you'll never have time for a shower. You, up the stairs; men through the bar." She grabbed our sack of laundry, shoved it in a corner of the foyer, and steamed majestically off into the nether regions of the clubhouse.

"God, that shower felt good," Larry sighed when we met at the foot of the stairs forty-five minutes later. "That's one of the treats of cruising. If you could have a hot shower anytime you wanted, you'd never appreciate them at all."

Mrs. Muirhead, the club secretary, must have been listening for us. She hustled into the foyer, finally introduced herself, and said, "When you wrote four months ago, you said some of your post might contain important documents, so I put it all in the safe. Had to take the cash box out three weeks ago to make room for your things." I laughed inwardly when I remembered our letter politely asking the secretary to put our mail in a safe place. The important documents I had been referring were only travelers check receipts.

Mrs. Muirhead led us to a small round table piled six inches deep with letters. Then she went on, "Arnold Gee over there has bought you lunch and promised not to disturb you until you've read your post."

So Larry and I sat down and began opening almost a hundred letters as we devoured a chicken and ham salad without even noticing it. We read how my father's knee had healed perfectly, long before we read the letter telling how he had broken it in a boating accident. We had unexpected checks from articles we'd written during our previous winter in the Chesapeake Bay, greetings and news from friends, "When are you coming home?" from parents. Not one bill. That's why mail calls are such a treat for us.

It was at least three hours before we were sure we'd read everything. I stood up and stretched and the man who'd bought us lunch came over. Arnold Gee was a sixty-five-year-old sailor we came to know well. He had twinkling gray eyes, set in a completely bald round head, and a charming English manner that fitted perfectly with the Old World atmosphere of the gray-carpeted, bay-windowed clubhouse.

"Now come into the bar and meet some sailors," he insisted.

The first sailor was Mayne, the Irish bartender who worked as a fisherman during the winter. Mayne poured Larry his first draft Guinness. Then he asked the question that we were to answer a hundred times during our cruise in England: "Why did a North American build an English boat?" We looked at *Seraffyn,* sitting proudly on her mooring in front of the club's lawn, and Larry answered, "*Seraffyn*'s designer, Lyle Hess, tried to combine the best of both worlds, the seakeeping ability of the long-keeled English cutters with the room and stability of the beamy American bottom."

I broke in, "I think he succeeded. We averaged a hundred miles a day for the whole forty-two-hundred-mile voyage and made several runs of a hundred forty miles a day between Bermuda and the Azores in a twenty-four-foot boat." And so the afternoon evaporated as Arnold and Mayne introduced us to a dozen more sailors.

As it grew dark, Larry asked Mayne for the location of a self-service laundry and the name of the best restaurant in town. Mayne called a cab after explaining we could drop our laundry at a little shop just up the lane where they would wash and dry it for us at no extra charge. "That's great," Larry replied. "Now for a good dinner ashore. Lin deserves one after cooking aboard for the past twenty days."

As soon as we entered the carpeted foyer of the Green Lawns Hotel a hostess came to escort us to the sitting room. She took our order for drinks and handed us a menu. A waiter arrived soon with my sherry and Larry's Irish whiskey. He took our pâté order for starters, then chateaubriand for two, grilled tomatoes, and chef's oven-sauteed potatoes, to be followed with English raspberry trifle and a cheese board. We lounged in the overstuffed chairs sipping our drinks and had just finished when our waiter reappeared, "Your table is ready." He escorted us to a spot overlooking the lights of Carrick Roads and we found a salad-like display with fresh pâté and toast waiting for us surrounded by polished silver and crystal. Almost an hour later, after one last nibble at a delicious round stilton cheese, our waiter escorted us to another lounge full of comfortable couches where coffee and tea were served. Although that dinner cost us nearly twenty dollars, we didn't mind at all. We'd spent nothing during three weeks at sea, and the food, wine, and service were excellent.

As we walked through the yacht club that evening, Mayne stopped us and introduced two more local sailors. Frank and Irene Jarrett invited us to come to their home for dinner the next evening. Then Frank said, "Last club race of the season is Sunday. Care to go?"

"Sure," Larry answered. "Will you two crew for us? Can we get a rating in time for the race?"

Frank looked a bit surprised and said, "I was thinking of finding a crew spot for you. Sure you want to take your boat out racing so soon?"

"Why not?" Larry replied. "We've got a great spinnaker."

So after a meeting time was set, Frank borrowed a club member's dinghy and rowed us home since the club launch had stopped running hours before.

We climbed between our last set of clean sleeping-bag sheets, tired and happy but reluctant to go to sleep. "All the talk about English reticence must be a myth," I told Larry as we reviewed our list of invitations from only one day ashore.

By Saturday noon, two days later, we were tired of answering letters. So when we noticed some men hauling up a fifteen-foot-long jackspar to set a topsail on the oyster boat nearest us, Larry yelled, "Where are you headed?" The oysterman and his crew yelled, "Regatta day—starting line is off the yacht club. Come on, set your sails and join us." The oystermen looked disappointed as we hoisted our triangular sail. Although *Seraffyn*'s sister ship had been designed with a gaff rig, we had decided against one for cruising because Larry was concerned that I wouldn't be able to handle the running backstays and gaff. We were under way in minutes and reached alongside the smallest of the oyster dredgers, the twenty-two-foot *Magdelena*. Her owner yelled over, "Tea and sticky buns after the regatta at the Flushing Yacht Club on the quay over there." He pointed toward the opposite shore and then tacked to run down to the starting line. Over twenty engineless dredgers beat across the line, high peaked gaffs sheeted in amazingly flat. Each carried a flying jib, and under that, a long, overlapping staysail. How they flew under their massive spread of canvas! We watched them overtake IOR boats to windward in the Force 3 winds. I turned to Larry and said, "So much for modern yacht design." But Larry answered, "The oyster boats must be sixty percent ballast, no interior, no engines. Besides, with those large open cockpits, they couldn't even be out in winds over Force 7."

When we joined the finishing get-together for the strong milky tea the club was serving with sugar-coated sweet rolls, Arfie Trenier,

The only modern thing on these workingboats are their well-cut synthetic sails.

Magdelena's owner, told us how one of the oyster dredgers had sunk during the previous season's last race. "Was blowing Force 7. She was on a broad reach inside the bay, bit of a gust hit her off the shore and that was all. Sank like a stone. Lucky a local yachtsman was watching only a few feet away in his power launch. Grabbed the six crewmen as they popped to the surface. One fellow came to the surface sole first, his hip waders full of air. Probably saved him, 'cause he couldn't swim. Couple of local divers had the boat off the bottom a week later. No damage. Nothing the water could hurt in an oyster boat. No engine, no electrics. Lost a few pair of shoes, though." At 1730, Mayne appeared from the Royal Cornwall Yacht Club to join in the more serious drinking that was going on now that the club could officially open its bar. He told us how thirty-four of the thirty-nine oyster boats still afloat in the Falmouth estuary actually were used to dredge oysters in the winter. "Good catch can make a man a hundred pounds a week.

Evelyn is flying a borrowed starcut spinnaker with two knots tied into its head.

George Glasson is dried out on the shore of Flushing Creek opposite the town of Falmouth.

Not bad when you consider how little maintenance these boats need compared to a normal powered fishing boat. Then you consider the dragging hours are limited by local law to 9 A.M. to 3 P.M. Man goes sailing to work, sails while he's working, sails home from work, and is sitting feet up in front of his fireplace by dark. Then when the oyster season has closed, he has a good boat to race, and the races have a cash prize. Yup, fifteen pounds to the first boat today. *George Glasson*, the turquoise and black dredger over there, has been in the same family for three generations."

The next morning we had *Seraffyn* in "race trim" when Irene and Frank arrived one hour before the 1300 starting time. All "race trim" meant was "dinghy off, spare water jug in the dink." I set out lunch as Larry showed our crew what strings went where. We were soon off the mooring and on our way toward the harbor entrance. The starting line was between the two guardian castles built during the 1400s at each side of the entrance to the Falmouth estuary. It was to be a pursuit race, each boat starting separately according to its rating, smallest boats first. That way the winner was the first boat to cross the finishing line. Larry suggested we try out our spinnaker before hand since it was to be a downwind start. Frank let out a happy shout as he watched our thirty-two-foot-wide, thirty-four-foot-high, bell-shaped spinnaker fill. "Never seen a spinnaker that big on anything but a forty-footer," he commented as a light gust hit us on the beam and sent Irene and me scrambling after sandwiches and coffee mugs.

Because *Seraffyn* is a cutter with a bowsprit, her spinnaker can have a very wide foot and still carry no penalty on most race rating systems. Although we were mainly a cruising boat, we'd decided to buy a spinnaker when we first set off, and we were glad we had. We rarely used it at sea, but when we were day-hopping along coasts with diurnal wind patterns, that 1,050-square-foot spinnaker sometimes made the difference between spending a night at sea or getting our anchor down before dark. When we were sailing alone, we made it a rule to get the spinnaker down before the winds reached fifteen knots. But when there was a chance to join some club's local racing we carried extra crew, so we flew that spinnaker as long as it was possible.

We roared across the starting line with that blue and white balloon dead before us, one minute behind a Folkboat. We soon overtook the four smaller boats in the ten-knot breeze. Before we reached the first mark our crew was handling the boat like champs. Irene constantly trimmed the mainsheet as if she'd been racing on *Seraffyn* for seasons. Frank helped Larry get in the spinnaker and set the genoa. I tightened the staysail using our windward sheet winch. I kept glancing over my shoulder as the larger boats slowly gained on us. I was a bundle of excitement as we reached around the mark, Mr. and Mrs. Muirhead only feet to windward in their thirty-foot Sparkman and Stephens sloop *Jemalda*. A gust hit us and I slid down the cockpit and landed across the tiller. *Seraffyn* headed straight at *Jemalda*. Larry yelled, "Get off the tiller!" straining against my weight. I struggled to extricate myself—and we cleared *Jemalda* with only inches to spare. What a disaster it would have been if we'd hit the commodore's boat! Larry and I were still a bit shaken as we roared toward the Helford River with the front of the fleet. Our crew worked silently and competently, easing and tightening sheets as we worked the puffs that came off the shore. The close-quarter sailing was an exciting change from our usual life of cruising alone, and sometime during that long reach we were near enough to two other racers to hear someone say, "If that funny little cruising boat wins, I'm going to protest its rating."

Our competitor needn't have worried. As we worked back toward the entrance of the river for the beat home, we saw some of the local boats shortening sail. But we didn't take notice and put our side decks under water as we cleared the point. By the time we'd dug out our lapper (a 110 percent genoa) dropped our big genoa and staysail, and gotten under way again in the short choppy tidal sea, we were almost the last boat in the fleet. When we finally beat across the finishing line in twenty-five knots of wind an hour later, Mrs. Muirhead called, "Come aboard for tea."

The first thing she said as we climbed out of the club launch onto *Jemalda* was, "Real light-wind flyer you've got there. Wouldn't have minded you beating us to the mark if we hadn't seen the crop of goose barnacles hanging under your stern."

On September 30, 1972, the English cruising season was officially over, but the days, although getting shorter, were often sunny. We were preparing to sail eastward after three wonderful weeks in Falmouth when a Swedish couple arrived in an International Folkboat and picked up the mooring next to us. We met them in the clubhouse an hour later and soon the four of us were in the local fish-and-chips

Sunday sailors on Falmouth estuary.

shop trading sailing stories. Ingrid and Khristan Lagerkrantz had left
Sweden that spring after graduating from the university, and were
headed for Yugoslavia via Spain and Portugal. Ingrid had her degree
as a police psychologist and Khris was an anthropologist. He hoped to
write his master's thesis on the people of the Dalmatian Islands. The
conversation turned to a discussion of their twenty-five-foot boat.

"Sure she's a bit limited in space," Khris told us. "But I could never
afford to go to Yugoslavia to live and roam and study in the islands for
a year any other way."

Ingrid added, "We've got a good big bed. Khris has promised to fix
up the galley for me. When we get where it's warmer, we'll be able
to live on deck much of the time so our space will be doubled."

We've met several other people cruising on Folkboats, both
wooden ones and the slightly more roomy fiberglass version. Some of
them add a masthead lightweather genoa to the standard three-quarter
rig, then use an outboard motor or long sculling oar during calms (see
Appendix B). The boats are minimal for a couple, but as the Lager-
krantzes agreed, "Our Folkboat is good and seaworthy. And we'd
rather be a bit cramped some days than working at a desk in Sweden
full time."

We woke up the next morning to our tiny traveling alarm's amazingly loud buzz. It was 0625, time for the maritime weather forecast.
We argued about who was going to climb out of the warm bunk and
turn on the radio. England has one of the best maritime weather
forecast systems we've come across. Updated reports, consisting of a
general weather synopsis, a forecast for each of twelve areas of the
British Isles, and finally actual reports from twelve shore stations, are
broadcast four times daily on the longwave band. Wind direction,
visibility, and sea state are given. We found these reports amazingly
accurate, although sometimes we heard forecasts like "Force 2 to 3
southeast with possible increase to 5 or 6; chance of gales later" and we
figured the weather man was covering himself against future complaints.

The morning forecast was for light offshore winds. So I dug out the
tidal charts that are like a Bible for sailors in English waters. Wouldn't
pay to leave before the tide turned fair at noon. We poked our heads
out to say good-bye to Khris and Ingrid who were setting sail for
sunny Spain, four hundred miles south, then clambered back into the
still-warm bunk.

~~~~~

CHAPTER 3

A Cruise in Company

An English single-handed sailor we'd met in the Azores, Brian Crai-gie-Lucas, said, "I've cruised on three continents now and the south coast of England still beats them all, especially if you cruise it out of season." He'd given us his rubberband-bound *Shell Guide to the South Coast of England* and we thumbed through it as we cleared the entrance to the River Fal with our lapper and mainsail set to catch the northerly breeze. The guide showed a tiny fishing port called Mevagissey, just up the coast from Falmouth, but like half the man-made ports of England, it dried out at low tide. To visit it we would have had to lie up against a seawall since we weren't equipped with legs or bilge keels like so many English boats. Instead, we set our course for Fowey (pronounced Foy), twenty miles east.

Fowey's narrow entrance would have required some tricky sailing as we tacked in, but the two-knot incoming tide flushed us quickly through. A tiny city, built all of gray stone and topped by black slate roofs, nestled along the river, backed by steep green hills. If the cars were removed from the waterfront, Fowey would have looked the same as it had three hundred years ago. We were anxious to go ashore to explore but couldn't find a clear spot to anchor. Our harbor chart and the *Shell Guide* showed a ferry crossing, but we watched for five or ten minutes as we reached up and down the four-hundred-yard-wide river and saw nothing that looked remotely like a ferry. So we let go our anchor, furled our mainsail, bagged our jib, and launched the dinghy. A husky fisherman rowed alongside in a fourteen-foot skiff. "Ya can't anchor here! You're in my way! I'm the ferry," he proclaimed.

I looked at the hundred feet of clear water all around us. "Surely you can row past us," I replied.

"Nope," the ferryman growled, "Law says this is the ferry lane and you got to get out of it."

Larry noticed me getting ready to explode and whispered, "Lin, we're guests here; let's not argue." So, while the ferryman stood watching from his oar-powered fourteen-foot ferryboat, we unfurled the mainsail, weighed our anchor, and set off. We found another clear spot a quarter mile upriver and set our hook, furled the sail, and started to climb into our dinghy. A powered launch came chugging alongside before we'd cast off. "See that mooring over there?" the young boatman said, pointing to a green can about a hundred fifty feet away. "That's the tugboats' mooring. You won't want to anchor here."

By this time I was getting uptight, but again Larry signaled to me and said, "Surely a hundred fifty feet is enough clearance for any tug that would work on a river this small."

The boatman shrugged his shoulders and pointed upriver to where a green tug was just coming into view, a three-hundred-foot ship on a tow line. We couldn't believe our eyes—that tug must have been one hundred fifty feet long! We didn't need any more urging. "Come on, let's sail somewhere else," I said impatinetly. Larry was just about ready to agree when a rubber dinghy buzzed up, driven by the inevitable Seagull outboard motor. "Follow me!" the yachtsman in it yelled, "I've been watching your problem and I know where there's a good clear spot for you." David Burnett introduced himself, then waited while we again weighed anchor, set our mainsail, and got under way. We followed him through the moorings, crowded with local fishing boats, tour boats, and decomissioned yachts, past a glorious hundred-twenty-foot ketch and, sure enough, right in the middle of the crowded moorings was a clear spot just large enough to allow us to anchor with a scope of three to one. We let go our anchor right where David suggested. Then we invited him on board. David went off to get his wife Chris, and returned for drinks. He was a ship's master on holiday in his thirty-foot twin-bilge-keeled yacht. He must have noticed us glancing uneasily around, for he kept reassuring us, "Don't worry, you really can stay here. I know this harbor well." Dark fell while we all chatted and, besides, we thought it wise to be around in case any of the returning fishermen claimed our spot. We never did get ashore that day.

There was an hour and a half of flood tide when we finally roused ourselves the next morning. The wind was light. "Come on," Larry urged, "let's use the tide to go upriver and see where that big ship came from."

We drifted slowly upriver, using our sail power to stay in the center of the four-fathom-deep channel as the incoming tide did most of the work. Around the first bend, out of sight of the peaceful little city, lay a noisy commercial dock covered with china clay heaps. Two large ships were loading there and two more ships lay tied bow and stern to big mooring buoys. They took up over a third of the river's width. It started to rain just as we reached the point on the river where the shoals and oyster beds began. We donned wet-weather gear as *Seraffyn* was caught by the turning tide and began her trickle downstream. I watched the rain running off our decks and got a bright idea. Now would be a good time to give our decks the scrubbing they needed. I rushed below and squirted dish soap into a bucket, then took my dish scrubber, a Golden Fleece pad, and set to work. I rubbed the teak in a circular motion and the rain did the rinsing. Soap suds ran down our topsides as I scrubbed and we drifted within yards of a fisherman cleaning his nets at his mooring. The fisherman glanced our way, then gave a questioning look at me. Larry shrugged his shoulders and said, "Nesting urge, happens every year about this time."

I had the decks glowing by the time the tide carried us back past the sheep-spotted hills and commercial docks to the anchorage. Every stain from buttered popcorn feeds, fried chicken, and spilled wine lifted right off the teak decks and cockpit sole with the help of lots of dish soap and some light scrubbing.

The rain slowed to a drizzle as we moored up, then had lunch. So Larry rowed me into Fowey to shop for some dinner treat, then set off to look at an old shipyard across the way. I left my yellow oilskins in the Fowey Yacht Club locker room and wandered over the slippery cobbled roads, past vine-covered fishermen's cottages to the center of town. Tiny tea shops and tourist stores were almost deserted now. Only the local bakery was alive, its Georgian window filled with cakes and raisin buns. I was drooling over them and trying to decide which ones Larry would like best when a very tall fellow came purposefully toward me, towing a brown-haired girl behind him. "Hello there," he said in the wonderful accent Americans associate with England. "Lovely yacht you have. Where have you sailed from?" I was puzzled.

I hadn't noticed him on the dock when we came ashore. In fact, there had been absolutely no one around. But I answered, "Falmouth, yesterday."

"No," he interrupted, "I mean, where did you come from originally? Where did you buy her?"

So I told him we'd built *Seraffyn* ourselves in California.

He asked me, "Will you join us for a cup of tea and hot scones? I'm Ted Welstead; this is my crew, Jonquil." I finally had to ask, "How did you know I was from *Seraffyn*?"

Ted laughed as he said, "Easy, you're wearing well-worn seaboots." Ted and Jonquil were on the homeward leg of a month's cruise in Ted's thirty-seven-foot Buchanan-designed sloop *Quinag*. "We've moored up just astern of you," Jonquil explained. "Join us for dinner."

I showed them the package containing a nice Scottish beefsteak I'd bought for dinner and Jonquil, in the practical manner we came to know well, said, "Good idea. I'll buy a steak for Ted and myself and we'll grill them together on *Quinag*."

We separated and I hunted up Larry, which wasn't very hard as he was being treated to a drink at the yacht club bar by another of *Seraffyn*'s new admirers.

Over a very companionable dinner that evening the four of us agreed to a casual cruising race eastward. Ted's home port and our immediate goal were the same, Poole Harbor. We had mail and money waiting for us there. Brian Cooke, another sailor we'd met in the Azores, was a bank manager near Poole and had suggested that he and his wife handle our post for us.

So we got under way early the next morning after consulting the tide tables and watched as Ted and Jonquil lifted their anchor. They soon gave up trying to tack out in the three-knot breeze and powered past us, yelling, "Got to make a phone call by 1400. Meet you at the yacht club in Plymouth." Twenty minutes later they were hull down as we worked to pick up each puff of wind. Although it was the middle of October, the day seemed warm until a cold breeze filled in from astern. I piled into two more sweaters while we started gaining on *Quinag* as if she were standing still. We flew into Plymouth just minutes behind her, and stood clear as Ted picked up a visitor's mooring smartly under sail. Then we sailed in and anchored.

Ted yelled over, "Lost our gearbox. Guess we'll have to look for help. Seems serious." Ted spent most of the afternoon looking for a mechanic. "It's all right for you to say, 'Forget the motor, sail without it.' You two have been doing it for years," he told us that evening.

By morning a strong southerly wind was making the anchorage in front of the yacht club unsafe. The forecast was for gale-strength winds. Larry yelled across to Ted, "I'm sailing up the river to find a quiet anchorage. I'll come back and help you if you need it."

Ted shook his head, "Be a challenge to get out of here."

Running along the coast of England with our working jib on the spinnaker pole.

The wind was now Force 6, directly onto the forty-foot-high rocky cliffs under the clubhouse. Our two moorings were only a hundred yards from the cliffs. We watched *Quinag* maneuver out perfectly, Jonquil at the helm, Ted handling the sails. Then we set out. In tandem we ran upriver, fighting a two-knot ebb. An hour later we anchored near the famous River Tamar Railway Bridge, designed by Brunell.

Ted and Jonquil rowed over to have lunch with us and Larry said, "If you can sail out of a tight spot like that, you can sail anywhere. Why put up with a halfway repair job here. Take *Quinag* to Poole and give that gearbox a proper overhaul this winter."

Ted now readily agreed, "I'm not going to let an engine ruin the last of a good holiday. I'll do it without power."

And so we wandered onward in company, joining each other after the day's sail or whiling away the stormy days, visiting pubs or chattering in one boat or the other. Ted regaled us with stories of the Royal Air Force. He'd signed out after nine years as a pilot and was looking for work with a commercial airline so he could have more free time for *Quinag.* He had a hundred questions for us—he too hoped to cruise off someday. We matched him question for question about England.

We loved the southwest coast of England and sailed up each river that had enough water for the two boats. We hid from storms two or three days at a time in the Tamar River, then the river at Salcombe. One rainy, windy day Larry and I donned our wet-weather gear for a walk ashore. We were anchored a mile upriver from the village, so we landed on a tiny shingle patch next to some heavy woods and pulled the dinghy clear of the high-water mark. Then we scrambled through the woods until we came to a bramble hedge, the last of its berries long since turned to seed. Larry searched along the hedge to find a hole. He helped me through, holding the bigger branches out of my way, and then I helped him. Then hand in hand, chatting about nothing in particular, we strolled up the grass-covered hill toward a distant gate. Something made me turn my head. Standing not a hundred yards from us, slowly pawing the ground and snorting, was the biggest, blackest bull I've ever seen close up. I jerked Larry's hand and pointed. He didn't pause. He dragged me along, running as best he could in bulky wet-weather gear. We headed for the nearest hedge and literally dove through the first hole we saw. We came out the other side slightly scratched and breathing like runners from the four-minute mile. Then Larry found a place to look over the six-foot-high hedge and let out a wonderful peal of laughter. "Bull never moved an inch. Couldn't, Lin. He's chained to a big stake." Then Larry set to work pulling brambles from my hair.

Two weeks later, we approached the entrance to the River Dart. Ted and Jonquil waved good-bye. They had a fair wind and tide for home, and commitments. We had no schedule and we didn't want to miss the home of England's famous naval college. Besides, friends we'd met along the way had told us that the seawall in front of Dartmouth town was a perfect place to dry out. After almost four years of constant sailing we were beginning to be tormented by a loud clicking sound when we lay at anchor. We'd traced the sound to our gudgeons and pintals. They had worn and become sloppy. So Larry wanted to remove the rudder, bore out the gudgeons, and insert nylon bushings to stop the gradual wearing of bronze against bronze.

The tide was against us, flowing out of the narrow entrance of the River Dart at four knots. So we found a shallow spot, near a tiny old stone water mill perched on the steep shore, and let go our anchor. That evening's weather forecast was for the usual easterly winds, the same winds we'd been beating against for most of the past two weeks, so we lay comfortably in the lee of the land all night.

I was first on deck in the morning. A small fishing boat was headed into the river and I waved. The fisherman yelled, "Want a crab?" I called back, "How much do they cost?" He came carefully alongside and insisted, "Go get your biggest cooking pot." I looked at the beautiful live crabs crawling out of boxes and around the fisherman's heavily booted feet and Larry was almost instantly on deck with our eight-quart stewing pot. The fisherman picked up one crab after another, then finally settled on one that could just be squeezed into the pot if he held the claws under the crab. "That's enough for the two of you; give me five shillings." The fisherman didn't wait for our thanks but putted off with our sixty cents while we let our delicious-looking four-pound friend loose in our big plastic washbasin. Then we prepared to sail in with the tide.

CHAPTER 4

~~~~~

Of Rudders and
Surveys and Ladies

As we short-tacked past the old verandaed buildings of the Royal Dart Yacht Club, Larry asked me to set our Canadian ensign. I climbed aft of the boom gallows and reached up to hook the flag onto its grommet on the backstay. Larry called a regulation "Ready about," then brought *Seraffyn* up into the wind. I snapped the lower hook of the flag in place and moved clear of the boom as *Seraffyn* paid off on the other tack. Then I let out a shriek, "Come about quick!" A big hunk of my long unruly hair had gone into the double mainsheet block. Some very quick work on Larry's part saved me from being scalped, and we continued up the otherwise beautifully placid river, stray black hairs hanging from the block.

There's nothing quite like meeting an old cruising friend in a new port. As soon as we spotted *Mouette* I rushed below to start a pot of fresh coffee and Larry yelled, "Hey, Brian, come on over for breakfast. How long'd your trip from the Azores take?"

Brian Craigie-Lucas was alongside as soon as we'd set our anchor. Over sausages and eggs we thanked him for the *Shell Guide*. Then Brian reached into his pocket and presented us with two unpolished whale's teeth. "Your friend, Anton, in Horta, came running down to the harbor to give these to you the day you were leaving. You didn't hear him calling, so he gave them to me in case I saw you somewhere in England," Brian told us as he dug into his breakfast. Brian is over six feet tall and on the thin side. I always worried that he wasn't getting enough to eat. Yet when we'd been invited for dinner on board *Mouette* in the Azores, Brian had served us a plentiful, tasty meal. Brian had made a single-handed voyage to the Cape Verde Islands in thirty-five-year-old *Mouette.* Her engine had had a broken crankshaft when he bought her, so Brian sold the engine and did without. Now he was waiting for fair winds for the voyage up channel to his home on the Hamble river. "Most frightening part of any voyage," Brian told us, "so much shipping, bad visibility, tides. Have to stay awake for at least twenty hours to keep a lookout past Portland Bill and St. Albans. Be glad when it's over." (See Appendix B for details on *Mouette.*)

When Larry mentioned wanting to dry out, Brian grabbed our tide tables from the shelf. "Get her next to the wall by noon, then you'll have most of the afternoon to work," he said.

I was really concerned about this idea of laying our five-and-a-quarter-ton pride and joy against a stone wall, then letting her dry out. It was okay for Brian tell us not to worry. He'd been sailing around these waters for thirty years and as he said, "I've never once paid to haul *Mouette.* Why should I spend money when I can dry her out for free?"

Larry wasn't concerned either because he'd used a tidal grid at his yacht club in West Vancouver. But when we sailed across the river an hour later and tied to the iron guardrail posts lining the edge of the main street in Dartmouth, I rushed around like a nervous clucking hen. I watched as the tide rushed quickly out and *Seraffyn's* keel nestled into the hard sand bottom. Larry tied her so she leaned against three fenders, a line from her mast secured to the iron posts, a long bow and stern line and two springs holding her in position. Slowly *Seraffyn's* bowsprit lowered as the water ebbed away. I tried to find work to keep me busy, but each time *Seraffyn* wiggled or squirmed during the two hours it took for the tide to flow out from under us, I'd yell out, "Sure she won't fall?"

"Come on, be logical," Larry kept saying. "There's the whole town of Dartmouth holding her up on one side, and a twelve-inch-wide, three-thousand-pound lead keel trying to stay in one place. How can she go anywhere?" When I climbed on deck, looked overboard, and saw less than a foot of water around us, I realized Larry was right. But I still walked around on deck light-footed.

We had a cup of tea in the cockpit as the last of the water rushed away. Larry glanced up at the iron post right above our heads and joked, "Sure would be funny if some dog decided to use that particular post." He wasn't laughing when, not more than five minutes later, a spotted mongrel did just that. Larry was prancing around like a whirl-

Seraffyn's full-length keel and outboard rudder make her easy to haul, and now we found her easy to lay against a seawall for a quick scrub and rudder repairs. Our CQR anchor has lived in this position for forty thousand miles and never caused a problem.

ing dervish, screaming at the top of his lungs, trying to avoid that dog's yellow stream. His shouts cut short the dog's activities and a few buckets of sea water washed away the evidence.

Outboard rudders make sense for a cruising boat. Ours was off in less than ten minutes. The harbormaster came by as Larry was inspecting the wear on our manganese bronze gudgeons. He charged us twenty-five pence a day for using the town hard. So the complete slippage bill for the job came to seventy-five pence, or $1.80 for three days. If we'd had an inboard rudder we'd have had to be lifted by a travel lift or gone on a ways car with enough room below it to drop the rudder and shaft. Our outboard rudder had two other major advantages. We'd been able to fit the least expensive, simplest homemade type of self-steering gear. And if our rudder was ever damaged at sea we could get at it to work on it.

We scrubbed the slime off *Seraffyn*'s bottom, and Larry searched around town until he found a machine shop that could make the nylon shoulder bearings he wanted. We turned in after an early dinner, weary from the day's work. Normally we sleep with our heads toward *Seraffyn*'s bow, feet under the bookshelf that is attached to the bulkhead between the forepeak and main cabin. But *Seraffyn* was lying bow down at an angle of six or eight degrees because of the shape of her forefoot and keel. So I changed the bedclothes around and our feet pointed toward the bitts and chain locker. It was quite comfortable, and since I had finally gotten over worrying about leaning against the quay with no water around us, we both fell asleep quickly. At about two in the morning the tide started slowly to lift *Seraffyn*'s bow. A fishing boat plowed up the river and its wake caused *Seraffyn* to thump loudly twice. Larry was up like a shot. He threw the bedclothes off, and by force of habit rushed toward the foot of the bunk to climb out and see what was happening. He collided soundly with the bits and got caught in the chain locker, his heart pounding so loudly I could hear it. Finally he realized we'd been sleeping wrong way round, unscrambled himself from the chain locker, and found the companionway. *Seraffyn* lay perfectly calm. But it took a shot of brandy before Larry was calm enough to sleep again.

Many interesting people stopped to chat with us as we worked just below the sidewalk on Dartmouth's riverfront. One couple came by and said, "Hello. Know you're busy, but how about joining us in the park to share our picnic lunch?" Instead, we invited them on board and

I added tea and fruit to their spread of sandwiches and cheese. Nigel and Jan Hudson had saved all they could by working at several jobs in Australia. They'd sold everything they owned and, at about twenty-five years of age, set off with ten thousand Australian dollars (about thirteen thousand U.S. dollars) to look for a yacht to live on. They'd had an adventurous journey starting first in Singapore then leading across Asia, through the Himalayas, across Turkey, around the Mediterranean, and finally to England. They'd traveled by hitchhiking, bus, train, airplane, and foot. Now they owned a tiny old Austin estate wagon which they used as a caravan. After much consideration, they'd decided that a Vertue-class twenty-six-foot sloop would be a practical cruising boat. Nigel and Jan had come to Dartmouth to look at a nine-year-old Vertue that was advertised for four thousand pounds (about nine thousand U.S. dollars). Two days after our picnic lunch, they asked us to take a look at the boat they liked. We looked it over and agreed that it would be a fair buy if it passed survey.

"Survey?" Nigel replied. "Why should I pay seventy dollars for someone to look at a boat for me? I know enough about boats to look her over myself. Don't worry, I'll be careful before I spend my money."

Larry shook his head and explained, "I built my own boat and spent ten years repairing other people's boats, and I'd still employ a surveyor. That way a disinterested person would be double-checking it for me. He wouldn't be prejudiced by having fallen in love with some beautiful but possibly rotten old classic. He might catch all sorts of things I'd miss. Besides, I've rarely heard of a good surveyor who couldn't save you at least the cost of his fee when it came to negotiating the final price."

Jan and Nigel went away that evening discussing Larry's words. They came back the next day and told us they'd made an offer for the Vertue, subject to survey. They'd refused to use the local surveyor suggested by the owner's agent and instead hired one from out of town. We watched the surveyor at work the next day and he was good. His hammer and awl searched everyplace you might expect to find trouble. He pulled every sail from its bag. He climbed the mast, carefully removed several fastenings from the hull and pieces of ceiling from the boat's interior. Then he gave Nigel and Jan a typed list of all the defects he'd found and suggested a reduced offer. After the surveyor left, Nigel told us, "Best seventy dollars I ever spent. I learned seventy bucks' worth just watching him survey the boat. There's about three thousand dollars' worth of repairs needed to get the boat seaworthy. Won't buy it unless the owner either lowers the price or pays for the repairs."

Negotiations fell through on the Vertue, but we kept in touch with Nigel and Jan as they wandered around England for four months more looking for the perfect small cruising boat. Then they headed back to Australia and a year later wrote us, "We've started building our own twenty-eight-footer. Seems there are no cheap good small boats to be had anywhere in the world."

After three days we sailed *Seraffyn* away from Dartmouth's town quay, anchored, and rowed ashore with a bag of dirty laundry. We put our clothes in the coin-operated machines and Larry suggested a cup of tea. The closest tea shop had a window full of delicious-looking fat pills and we were soon digging into a plate of tea cakes and raisin buns. A diminutive gray-haired, sixty-five-year-old lady trundled in, flower-print dress covered by a tidy handknit sweater, white gloves immaculate. She set her large shopping bag down next to the window table and ordered tea from the smiling waitress, who addressed her as "Mrs. Smith." I whispered to Larry "Perfect English lady," as Mrs. Smith carefully removed her gloves and skillfully poured tea.

We went back for our laundry and the next time we saw Mrs. Smith was an hour later at the town quay. She was dressed from head to toe in baggy black oilskins with knee-high seaboots. She dragged an Avon dinghy through the thirty-feet of mud between quay and water, and rowed out to an antique-looking sloop. Larry and I were stopped in our tracks by this transformation, and rowed by her boat on the way home.

"Hello there," Esther Smith yelled. "You must be off that little Canadian yacht. Come on board." We gladly accepted and explored *Essex Breeze*, a 1930 Alfred Milne–designed thirty-two-foot sloop. Although someone had shortened the original ten-foot bowsprit on *Essex Breeze*, they'd never touched the magnificent thirty-foot-long boom. Esther had a fire roaring in her tiny coal-burning stove when we came below.

"I'm the worst sailor in Dartmouth," she proudly announced. Then she told us her story. "I always wanted to learn to sail, ever since I was a tiny girl, but my father wouldn't hear of it. And then when I got married my husband told me, 'Sailing isn't for ladies.' Well, my husband died when I was fifty-five so I hired a man to look after our farm for a few months, then I bought this sailboat. I figured I didn't have much time at my age to learn to sail properly. I just had to go out and *sail. Essex Breeze* has taken good care of me. But I always warn everyone to stay out of my way."

We both were enchanted by Esther, and before we left that evening we'd planned an exploratory sail upriver in company. Larry rowed me over to *Essex Breeze* the next morning, and rowed home to get *Seraffyn* under way. Esther and I had a great time running before the strong, fluky winds with the tide under us. Then without warning that six-inch-diameter, solid-pitchpine, thirty-foot-long boom came whistling by, clearing the top of my head by inches. I'd heard it coming. Most booms are quiet until they reach the end of the jibe. Esther's enormous boom gained so much velocity as it flew across a seventy- or eighty-foot arc that it actually started whistling, just like a dive bomber. I must have looked startled when I turned to where Esther was complacently steering upriver, tiller under her seaboot. "Oh yes," she chirped. "Should have said 'Jibe ho,' shouldn't I."

We anchored four miles farther upriver, near the shipyards at Galmpton, and Larry moored *Seraffyn* alongside. Clad in oilskins, the three of us climbed into our six-foot eight-inch pram *Rinky Dink* for a row ashore and a tromp through the drizzle and woods. I suggested dinner on board *Seraffyn* when we came back, and Esther excused herself for a few moments. When I set the hot beef stew on the table, Mrs. Smith from the tea room sat next to Larry, gloves on the settee, a garnet brooch on her shoulder.

Once again a pile of mail lay ahead of us. We were also almost out of money. Brian Cooke had both waiting for us in Poole. We'd sent some checks ahead to him and asked him to open a checking account for us (current account in English). But now we had less than twenty-five dollars on board, and although Poole was only about eighty miles east of us, easterly gales were blowing through the whole of the English Channel. In desperation I walked into a branch of Brian's bank in Dartmouth and asked for the manager. He laughed at my concern and explained the exceptional services offered by the National Westminster Bank of England. An account in any branch of that bank is good in any other branch with only ten minutes' delay. Although it's handier to have a checkbook from your own branch, it's not necessary.

He also told us about the most convenient way to handle money we'd ever run into—Eurochecks. Once our account was established, our bank manager would issue each of us with a Eurocard. This card would have our name, account number, and special check-cashing number. By presenting this card to any participating bank in any European country, plus twenty-four other countries, like Malta, Lebanon, Turkey, or Egypt, we could cash a check for thirty pounds each day. The National Westminster Bank would guarantee these checks as long as our special number was on the back. During the next four years of cruising in fourteen countries, we've had no need for travelers checks. All of our banking was done through our British External Account. (Any European bank can arrange Eurochecks for you.) Meanwhile, the Dartmouth bank manager gave us thirty pounds in cash and we rushed off, rich again, to buy a steak for dinner.

Easterly winds were followed by dense fog, then more easterly gales. We were tired of sitting in the River Dart. We'd rigged up a workable heater by lashing a big pot lid as a reflector in the back of

Brian and Sheena Cooke were a constant source of help during our stay in England. We'd first met Brian in Horta as he sailed the fifty-six-foot *British Steel* home from the 1972 Observer Single-handed Transatlantic Race. This photo was taken on board *British Steel* just before the race. *Mike Hope*

our Primus one-burner stove, but rain and wind kept us confined inside the boat too much. So we asked Brian Craigie-Lucas to watch *Seraffyn* for a day, and after filling and lighting our kerosene anchor light, we hitchhiked to Poole and spent the night with Brian Cooke and his wife Sheena. Brian took the morning off and showed us a safe and inexpensive marina in Poole where we could spend the winter tied to a dock with electricity and water available. Then we hitchhiked back to Dartmouth. It was dark when we arrived at the river. But we could easily spot *Seraffyn* because that little anchor light with its half a cup of oil was still burning, thirty-six hours after we'd lit it.

For three weeks the gales blew. We'd spend our mornings on board writing, then we'd wander around visiting new friends. Some afternoons we'd read books to while away the time. We had all sorts of plans for the winter months when we would hopefully be tied alongside a quay; meanwhile, we sat and waited for the weather to clear, getting up to catch each weather forecast. One day the rains let up, but the wind was still reported as gale force easterly for the Channel. When the sun came out Larry said, "Come on, let's you and me sail around the river again. At least we won't be sitting around moping all day." I pulled on my warm jacket and joined him on deck, still in short temper after three weeks of wishing for fair winds.

"Come on, Lin, get that mainsheet cleated and haul in the jib," Larry yelled from forward, as he secured the anchor. He came aft and took the tiller from me. "Ease the main," he called. I turned to ease the mainsail. "The outhaul needs tightening" was his next command. "Free the telltale," he called.

I blew up. "Stop bossing me around," I yelled. "I can sail this boat as well as you can!"

Larry merely let go of the tiller and walked away. "Do it then!" *Seraffyn* beat down on the boats moored ahead. I took hold of the tiller, brought her about, got the jib in on the other tack, and sat smugly steering close-hauled toward the boats on the other side of the channel.

"Not bad," Larry commented as he came on deck with a hot mug of coffee, "but you're pinching."

I pulled the tiller toward me.

"I'd come about now if I were you, Lin. . . . Too quick. . . . You're too far off the wind. . . . Why don't you watch your telltale?" Larry's criticisms fell on me like stinging shots of hail as my silent temper grew blacker and blacker.

When I finally tried, I found I could even handle *Seraffyn's* sixteen-foot-long spinnaker pole. But it was more difficult than we liked so Larry has since designed a much easier arrangement.

I tacked to clear the stern of a sloop moored near the shore. I was so angry by this time I couldn't see straight. Then the jib sheet got in an override on the winch. I bashed the back of my hand as I cleared the snarl up, balancing on one leg, the other stretched behind me, foot on the tiller. Still, Larry sat on the cabin top issuing commands— "Shouldn't have come through the wind so quickly. Jib sheet wasn't cleared before you tacked."

I finally let go. "I'm never going to sail with you again if you don't shut up right now!" I yelled so loud a cormarant flew squawking from the boat near us. In seven years together, I'd only once before screamed at Larry. He almost fell over and his shocked look set me laughing. "Now get to the end of the bowsprit where I can't hear your silly comments," I told him. He went meekly and sat at the forward end of the bowsprit while I short-tacked through the mooring-filled river, past the narrows in front of Agatha Christie's summer home, past the bend at Galmpton, tack on tack. Without Larry's nagging, I soon set my own pattern for each tack. I never missed a move, as I planned how to get the jib in before I needed to use the winch. An hour later I turned and ran downriver right to our mooring spot, let go the anchor, furled the sails, then glared at Larry.

He came back from his perch of exile and wrapped his arms around me. "That's the first time you've really taken charge and sailed this boat yourself, Lin. You did a hell of a job. Anytime you want to be in charge from now on, tell me and I'll play flunky."

CHAPTER 5

To Find
a Winter Haven

Another 0630 weather forecast of heavy fog sent me back into the warm sleeping bag. "Come on, Larry, dream up something to do today." He yawned, wrapped his arms more tightly around me, and sighed, "Just have to spend the day in bed, I guess."

The three-knot ebb of the tide past our anchor chain and stem gurgled and boiled. *Seraffyn* sounded as though she were under way. I listened to the water rushing past and thought of the three weeks we'd been anchored in Dartmouth waiting for fair weather. Portland Bill, with its tidal race and one of the heaviest concentrations of shipping anywhere in the world, lay between us and Poole. Each time there had not been reports of easterly gales there had been reports of fog. Not only did we feel it was wise to wait for a fair wind, we also wanted a twenty-four-hour period with good visibility. We'd feel like sitting ducks if we became becalmed in the English Channel. Twice we'd doubted the weather forecasts we heard on the radio, and twice we'd set sail, only to run into a sheet of fog rolling and boiling at the river's mouth. Each time we'd turned back to anchor and wait some more. I was bored. November. Days getting shorter and shorter. Cold. I wanted to settle someplace for the winter where we could get ashore without rowing, and Dartmouth didn't have room at its marina. Besides, we needed a new mainsail and Larry had a good idea. "I'll ask around till I find a sailmaker who's overworked, then ask if I can work for him in exchange for the materials for our new sail. That way I'll learn something about sailmaking and I can finish our mainsail to my own specs." Dartmouth had no sailmaker.

We read until lunchtime, propped against the hull in our forward

Seraffyn's Sony casette stereo works off a six-volt dry-cell battery, the same type we use for our quarter-mile flashlight. The battery gives us power for 100 to 150 hours of music.

Filling the tea kettle is easy with *Seraffyn*'s gravity-fed day tank water system. No pumps to rebuild, no parts to replace. Headroom under the skylight is 5' 6" and under the two hatches its 5' 9", enough for Larry.

The table slides out easily from under the cockpit and seats four.

bunk, then got up and dressed to share a big lunch. Fog rolled past our port lights. We couldn't see the boat on the next mooring although it was less than a hundred feet away.

Larry got out our cribbage board and beat me at another series, best of three games. We heard the buzz of an outboard. Someone yelled, "Pardeys, you there?" Larry knocked the cards off the table in his rush to open the companionway hatch. He yelled "Over here" into the thick whiteness.

Henry North appeared through the fog. "Thought you might like a ride around the moors. Grab your boots and come with me." We'd met Henry with his long gray beard, flying brown hair, and perpetual Harris-tweed, elbow-patched jacket when we'd dried *Seraffyn* out. But we'd only chatted casually with him as he worked on one or the other of the three small charter boats he owned.

"Best put on an anchor light," Henry suggested. "I've told my wife to expect you for dinner." We putted across the river then scrambled into Henry's old car, shoving boat gear out of the way. Henry inched slowly through fog-shrouded Dartmouth, then up the long steep hill past the naval college. When we reached the moors, visibility improved until we could see a mile ahead over the moss- and fern-covered rolling hills. A few shaggy dripping ponies huddled in a tiny valley by the road side, a small remnant of the herd of wild Dartmoor horses.

We rode across mile after mile of gray and brown soggy desolation until suddenly the hulking gray walls of Dartmoor prison rose through the gloom. Henry's great-great-grandfather had captured many of Napoleon's soldiers who'd later perished in this infamous fortress. So Henry was able to give us a running commentary of heroic escape attempts and prison stories. We turned into the courtyard of a slate-roofed pub and parked. Henry led us through the leaded-glass door and we were greeted by the roar of an open fire that sent flickers of light across black leather seats and red carpets. We snacked on tiny hot pies filled with beef and onions while Henry chatted on. "This is where the prison warders have hung out for the past three hundred years." After exhausting his collection of prison stories, Henry pointed at some hunting prints on the wall. "Always preferred punt-ing myself. My dad built a special boat. When you got in it, the gunwale was almost level with the river. Had a real cannon of a shotgun bolted on the deck. I'd lay in it among the reeds of the river till a flight of ducks landed. Then I'd let fly. That gun could take thirty sitting ducks at a shot."

We reluctantly left the warmth of the pub to drive on to a wood. We followed Henry through the damp grass and birch trees until we were at the top of a small rise. "You're standing on a fortress from the Bronze Age," he announced. Henry and his father had dug at this site and uncovered Bronze Age tools and household utensils. "Come on, let's get back to the house," Henry called as he turned to go back to the car, "I've got lots there to show you."

When we arrived at Henry's hundred-fifty-year-old rambling house, perched on a ridge a thousand feet above the River Dart, there wasn't the slightest chance of getting the car into the garage—it was filled to overflowing with boat gear. Three sailing dinghies littered the tiny lawn. We'd just reached the door when it was flung open by a big, buxom, raven-haired woman. "Come in, come in." She led us into the cluttered entry hall, peeled our coats from us, flung them onto an already-overheaped chair. "I'm a lousy housekeeper, but then I've got an excuse. My family always had servants before," she said with a wink. "Now I'm decadent aristocracy!"

We almost tripped over two children lying next to the fire, eyes glued to the television. "Off with the moron-a-scope!" Henry roared, "we've got company." He cleared a pile of books from two chairs. The children joined in as Henry pulled one nautical antique after another from the crowded shelves. Josephine rolled a tray of drinks into the room muttering, "Neither of our families ever threw anything away. Come on, Lin, I've got something more interesting than these silly old pieces of brass to show you." We crossed the entrance hall into a large dining room filled by a magnificent mahogany table for ten. One complete side of the room was covered by a doll's house. "Forty rooms, every bit of furniture built by my father," Josephine explained as she showed me perfectly scaled, two-inch-high, plush-covered sofas, quarter-inch-high chamber pots, and miniature silver tea services. "But that's not what I want to show you." I turned reluctantly away from the thirteen-foot-long, five-foot-high doll's house.

Josephine opened the lid on a cedar-lined chest that was as long as the doll's house and almost four-feet deep. Piles of handmade lace petticoats burst from it as she burrowed deep into its interior. "All the clothes my mother, grandmother, and great-grandmother owned. Here it is! I'm sure my grandmother was exactly your size when she was young." Before I could protest, Josephine pulled my sweater over my head and began lacing me into a whalebone, blue-ribboned corset, then a wicker bustle. Over this she dropped two lace-covered petticoats. "My ancestors were Scottish lairds, had the same family of seamstresses living in the castle since 1800. Two women worked full-time making grandmama's clothes." I looked over the fine handstitching of the petticoats while Josephine dug deeper into the chest. She pulled out a white silk blouse with a high lace ruff, then a blue-and-white-striped silk skirt and waistcoat with the same tiny stitching. Soon I stood tightly laced while Josephine combed my hair smooth. I glided slowly into the drawing room, silk rustling about me, stopped just inside the door, and dropped a curtsy as best I could from memories of Scarlett O'Hara and *Gone with the Wind*. My entry was a complete success. Larry and Henry stopped talking and stared. I turned to show off my bustle and my skirt lifted a bit. Henry toasted me with his glass of whiskey, then cocked his head to one side and stated, "Magnificent, magnificent! Fits you perfectly, but those seaboots aren't quite right, are they?"

I sat on a stool at dinner, bustle behind me, skirts in a sweep around my feet. I sympathized with the ladies of 1850 as my intake of the bountious roast-lamb dinner was limited by the tightly laced corset. I climbed reluctantly back into my slacks and bulky sweater after dinner. Without the corset I was really able to dig into the lucious strawberry trifle that was served with coffee in front of the drawing room fire.

Henry took us home through the fog and we arrived just in time for the 0030 forecast. Northerly winds, Force 4 to 5, visibility improving. A wonderful day with the incredible Norths, a good forecast for the next day. We consulted our tide tables, planned for a late-afternoon departure, then got a good night's sleep.

We sailed out of the River Dart on a westerly wind less than twenty minutes after the 1800 forecast. It was dark and we could see Start Point light twenty miles southwest of us. The lights of shipping showed around the horizon. I chose the first watch, so Larry helped me set the lapper on the spinnaker pole, then went below. Wing and wing, we flew through the night. Larry had a shot of brandy, then started to pull his shoes off as I watched him through the half-open companionway. We cleared the point of Lyme Bay and the wind shifted ninety degrees without warning. Helmer, our steering vane, changed course to compensate. "How about a hand to take the pole down?" I called to Larry. He pulled on his shoes and came up. "It'll be wet when you put her on a beam reach," Larry told me as he surveyed the situation. "I'll get the pole down; you get your wet gear on."

After pulling on another sweater, then my anorak, boots, and wet-weather gear, I struggled through the companionway feeling like a kid ready for the snow. I took over from Larry, sheeted in the jib, and reset Helmer.

Seraffyn's bowsprit pointed east again. Her bow shoved aside rolls

Waterproof gloves and good foul-weather gear are a must to enjoy English winter sailing.

of water and showers of spray burst over her windward side. I was glad of my waterproof gear as I huddled against the back of the cabin trying to shield myself from the spray and cold. *Seraffyn* reached over the tide-tossed seas of Lyme Bay at over five knots. The northerly wind had thirty miles of fetch and kicked up a nasty sea. Normally I'd have left Helmer to steer and gone below to make a hot drink of tea, but now we were surrounded by heavy shipping. When I climbed on top of the dinghy I counted the lights of twenty-six ships. They stayed well clear of us and I spent most of my time trying to keep warm. Our ship's clock rang each half hour and I woke Larry eagerly when three hours had passed.

His Canadian blood must be thicker than mine because what to me had seemed like a hell of cold and wet drew comments of delight from Larry. We steered a course to clear Portland's race by seven or eight miles. Although this put us right in the shipping lanes, it kept us clear of the tidal overfalls.

As the sun rose, we saw Portland Bill looking like an island and slowly the wind died. The tide carried us east. The sun dried our decks. By noon we had our jackets and sweaters off. Larry was shirtless. The white chalk cliffs of Lulworth Cove slid slowly past us. Then, just at four o'clock, tea time, our northerly breeze came back. God, it was cold! Larry took charge and sailed us past St. Albans Head. He piled on all the clothes he could, including his wet-weather gear although there was no spray at all. I stayed warm in the cabin, passing up mugs of hot chocolate and navigating as we beat in, looking for Poole Harbor light. "What kind of sequence is that light supposed to have?" Larry asked again.

"One flash every five seconds."

"Only light anywhere near my course is a quick flasher," Larry announced.

He came below and together we studied the chart. There was a nasty-looking mile-and-a-half-long submerged breakwater shown at the entrance to Poole Harbor. Miserable thing to bump into at night. We were trying to find the buoy that marked its end. Larry went on deck and looked again, then called, "Anywhere else we can go and anchor for the night? The lights are different from the light list. Not worth taking a chance."

I studied the chart. "Do you see a red flashing light about two miles away, right on our beam?" I asked.

"There's a red flasher on what looks like a pier," Larry called down.

"Great! Head for that and drop the anchor anywhere you want. But don't go inshore of the pier. Lots of protection from this wind."

As we reached slowly in toward the Swanage pier on the dying northerly breeze I chatted with Larry through the three-quarters-closed companionway feeling only slightly guilty about being so warm as he steered with the tiller between his legs, hands in his pockets. We talked about other times we'd made a landfall after dark only to find the lights or landmarks didn't line up with the chart. Each time, we'd chosen an alternate anchorage or hove to until morning. Each time, when daylight came we'd found we'd made the right decision. (We later learned that the light on the Poole Harbor entrance buoy had been changed to a quick flasher only two weeks before.)

We spent a peaceful night anchored in Swanage, disturbed only slightly by a southeasterly swell. By morning a southerly gale was blowing and only the reef off the southern tip of Swanage protected us. We ran into Poole Harbor under the gray, lowering sky, picking our way through the shoals, and tied up at Poole Town Quay as the first squalls of rain came down.

Brian Cooke arrived minutes after our call to take us home for showers and Sheena's wonderful steak-and-kidney pie. The storm was over when Brian drove us home late that evening. We noticed ice forming on the puddles along the quay. Our breath froze in the air of *Seraffyn*'s cabin as we got ready for bed. By morning there was snow on our decks.

Larry looked out at the glistening white covering our cockpit, shook his head, and said, "Looks like time to winter."

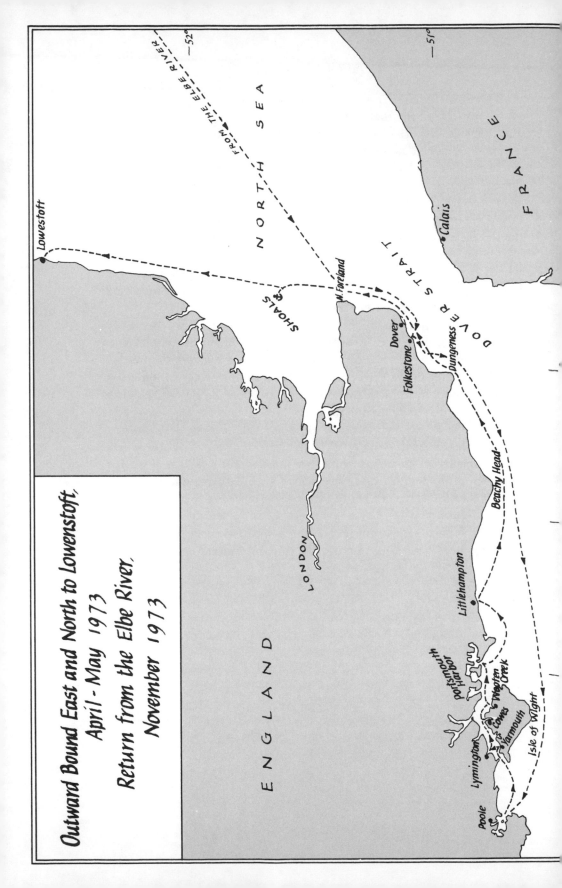

Outward Bound East and North to Lowenstoft,
April - May 1973
Return from the Elbe River,
November 1973

CHAPTER 6

~~~

Winter

Poole Town Quay—it sounds so safe and comfortable. But the name doesn't tell about a rushing five-knot current. Nor does it indicate the ten-foot rise and fall of the tide. What appeared to be husky pilings at high tide became worm-eaten scraggle-toothed monsters as the water ebbed away. We found a ten-foot-long two- by eight-inch plank and made it into a fender board. But when the wind blew strong from the east, a nasty swell ran through the channel. Then fenders popped from behind the board and lines chaffed around rusty metal securing rings so that gear had to be tended constantly. A slimy twenty-foot steel ladder was my low tide doorway to the upper world. Not twenty feet from *Seraffyn,* double-decked red buses rushed by shaking the street. Two tugs tied just ahead and often woke us with the roar of their engines and wash of their propellors.

After the quiet of river anchorages, this hustle would have been a trial but for the people we began to meet the moment we sailed in. Basil Bennet took our lines and promptly invited us to lunch at the Parkstone Yacht Club the next day. Basil could only be described as loquacious, and after overwhelming us completely with a flurry of new people, presented us to the club secretary who gave us a handwritten card that said "L & L Pardey are honorary members when ever they arrive at the Parkstone Yacht Club on board *Seraffyn.* " When we told Basil of our desire to find an overworked sailmaker, he assured us, "Should be no problem at all. Every sailmaker for miles around is overworked."

The next morning Larry left the boat early. He was back within an hour. "Found our sailmaker. His loft is only two blocks from here.

He'll come by with his girlfriend at 7 P.M. for a drink. I start work tomorrow for three weeks; then he'll help me build our new mainsail."

So our days fell into a pattern. I'd work on writing each morning while Larry went off to learn sailmaking. I'd often bring Larry a packed lunch and join in as Paul Lees told us about sails. Paul was only twenty-one but had worked two and a half years with Hood's of Lymington. He was an avid dinghy sailor and had won the National Yachting Monthly Day-Boat Championships two or three years running. As he learned sailmaking, Paul began doing repairs at home for his dinghy-sailing friends. This grew until he had to ask his mother to help with the machine work. He'd finally opened his own loft just four months previously, and he and his mother really appreciated Larry's help, especially because they didn't have to pay in cash, a commodity that is scarce in most new businesses. Paul's loft rang constantly with taped pop music. The tea kettle had a place of honor on the cluttered workbench.

"You're right about building a mainsail without battens," Paul told us as he sipped his tea. "Look at that pile of repairs. Every mainsail has ripped or chafed batten pockets." One corner of the loft was filled with a ceiling-high pile of bagged sails waiting for repairs. Larry spent most of his working day on these. He showed me headboards that were ripped loose, seams that needed restitching, weak reefing clew patches. So when it came time to build our own mainsail, Paul selected unfilled 6.5-ounce U.S.-weight Terelyne (the English brand name for Dacron) and laid it out so it would need no battens or headboard. Each seam was triple-stitched, and three rows of reefpoints were sewn in place, with the clew and tack patches strongly reinforced. Then Larry set to work using his new skills to handsew the boltrope. He handstitched every ring into the sail. The results were great. In four years not one ring or seam has needed repairs. We've also been able to hoist, lower, or reef the sail on any point of the wind, no battens or headboard to catch under the spreaders, shrouds, or lazy jacks.

"What do you think of making a genoa with a row of reef points in it?" Larry asked when Paul took the two of us to lunch at his favorite pub. "Great idea," Paul answered as he dug into his venison sausages. "That way you'll have one jib taken the place of two. Put a rope luff in—it's easier to sew a reef cringle to a rope than a wire. You'll have draft control that way, too. Want to work off that genoa now?" Larry declined the offer since our headsails still had some life left in them.

But Paul's enthusiasm set us thinking about how much space we'd save below decks by having reefpoints instead of extra sails.

As soon as Larry was finished with our sails, we decided to leave noisy Poole Town Quay and sail under the lifting bridge separating us from a huge tidal bay that contained Cobbs Quay marina. The bridge opened only four times a day, so sailing would be difficult once we were through. But Cobbs Quay had floating docks next to each boat and we could secure *Seraffyn* and not worry about tides or tugs. We used a fair tide and a light easterly breeze to sail through the bridge. Then we threaded our way up the narrow, twisting channel, nudging the muddy sides twice when we took too long to tack. I looked around at the miles of dull-brown, reed-covered tidal swamp. Cobbs Quay came into view, not a tree in sight. Two hundred deserted-looking boats were tied forlornly in the water; three hundred more were ashore for the winter, covered with tarpaulins. The low gray clouds added to the neglected, end-of-the-season mood I felt as we warped into our mooring and Larry made fast six lines to hold us in position. I went below out of the drizzle. The tide fell slowly and mud banks became my only view as I looked out the galley port light. Our little butane heater glowed bravely, but its heat didn't dispel my gloom. Larry came in as *Seraffyn*'s keel nuzzled into the soft mud below us. It was only 1600 and already dark enough to need our oil lamps.

It was extreme low tide when we got up the next morning. I couldn't believe my eyes. Mud, nothing but mud. Larry and I pulled on jeans, seaboots, two sweaters, and jackets, then climbed on deck. *Seraffyn* had made herself a nest in the mud. The floating pier next to us sat on the mud. The nearest water was twenty-five feet away where the once-wide channel was now merely a trickle. My depression became overwhelming. "We may be safe," I moaned, "but what fun is that? We're miles from everything, no people around, can't go sailing, it's cold, it's months till spring, the weather is miserable." Larry didn't look convincing when he entreated, "Come on, Lin, look at the bright side. *Seraffyn* is absolutely safe here no matter what blows up."

I was close to tears when two swans spotted us standing on the foredeck. They swam to the edge of the tiny dredged channel, then plodded toward us, sinking up to their bellies in mud. By the time they reached *Seraffyn*'s side the two normally snowy-white birds were speckled with mud, from orange beak to wingtips. Larry was quaking with laughter. I ran below to get some slices of bread as the swans begged with hissing noises. A man popped his head out from under the brown canvas cover on a deserted-looking varnished sloop moored two boats away. "It's those damn swans again," he muttered. "Don't encourage them." We turned to him in bewilderment, wondering who could dislike such glorious birds. Then the two swans spotted him and struggled through the gooey mud toward his boat. "Go away, scram!" the head growled as they approached. The two swans ignored him, waddled right up to his boat, hissing, then began to peck at his varnished rub rail. "Look at this," he called. "Not one bit of varnish left since I stopped feeding the beggars."

We walked over and watched as chip after chip of varnish came loose. Mike, who lived on the varnished sloop, introduced himself. "Come over for breakfast in ten minutes," Larry suggested.

Larry buttered toast while I scrambled eggs. "Bus is only three-quarters of a mile away, place isn't deserted, we've got neighbors. Spring's less than three months from now. London Boat Show starts this week and we've got an invite to stay with Alf Taylor in London. Gordon and Annabelle Yates will be here for a visit in four weeks. Winter is going to fly," I told Larry as we waited for Mike. "That's right," he answered. "We'll buy that little Ford Anglia and then do some exploring."

The London Boat show turned out to be a week filled with new ideas, new people. Thousands thronged the huge exposition hall, yet at each corner we'd bump into sailing friends from all parts of the world as we looked at gear from all over Europe.

We tore ourselves away from the boat show to look into visas for our summer's cruise. Sweden, Finland, Denmark, each embassy loaded us with travel brochures and said "No visas needed." The Polish Embassy was a different story: "Fill out these three forms in triplicate, bring four photos each, and pay us four pounds. Then leave your passports with us for ten days so we can decide if we can issue you a visa." We took our forms, kept our passports, and headed toward the Russian Embassy.

Few spy thrillers could have caught the oppressive atmosphere we met there—armed guards, one-way glass doors, heavy drapes, and silent watchers. "Why don't you fly to Russia," the consular officer asked us when we reached his office after a forty-five-minute wait. "I don't know of any yacht that has ever entered socialist Leningrad or Tallinn and I have no idea if it can be arranged. First, you must have a place to keep the boat. Then you'll need a pilot for your voyage up the Neva. Not an easy thing to arrange. Try our shipping company. If you can provide for the boat, I'll provide for the people."

The man at Aeroflot shipping (we've eliminated names for the protection of people who were most kind to us) was delighted by the idea of an engineless twenty-four-foot yacht trying to arrange berthage. "Our country needs visitors like you. I'll set to work immediately on this. No charge, it will be my pleasure. Call me in one week." He took *Seraffyn*'s tonnage, draft, total berthage length (which came to thirty-four feet including bowsprit and boomkin), and cargo—two curious people. "In any country but ours this would be an easy matter," the official told us, "but the Soviet Union? We're very friendly people but our officials are afraid to make unusual decisions." We left his office determined to visit Russia.

We rejoined Brian Cooke at the National Westminster Bank stand he was working on at the boat show and over lunch told him about our adventures. "I have a Polish sailing friend. Maybe you should write her. Theresa Remiszewski represented Poland in the last single-handed transatlantic race." We took her address, then set off on our two-hour drive back toward Poole.

Both of us used sheet after sheet of tissue as we sniffled from winter colds. We stopped at Brian's house to relay a message to Sheena. She took one look at Larry and all her nursing training came into play. "You're not going back to that cold, damp boat. You're climbing right into our guest bed and staying until you're well." We had no choice. We both felt like pampered children as Sheena made us a hot dinner, then tucked us in. "Come now," she admonished, "admit it, you're crazy to live on such a small boat for the winter. You could have rented a flat for eight pounds [twenty dollars] a week."

As our health improved we came to agree with her. A twenty-four-foot boat is wonderful in the tropics, or even for three or four weeks on a winter cruise. But it *is* too small to winter in. We talked of having a boat big enough to heat with a coal-burning stove. Later, when we were given clean bills of health we went to visit Fiona and Hank who were wintering in Lymington on their fifty-seven-foot cutter. *Senta* was a magnificent yacht built in San Francisco by Lester Stone—teak and mahogany, a huge main saloon, central heating. We found that Fiona and Hank had the same complaints we did. "Never going to spend another winter on a yacht in England. It's just too damp. Everytime you go out you have to walk miles to get anywhere. Get wet and come below and then the cabin sole gets wet. Have to keep everything closed up all the time. Never enough space to spread out. Be cheaper and more comfortable to put the boat on a mooring, rent a flat, and live ashore. Boats are for sailing, not sitting in port." Hank and Fiona had the right to say this. They'd sailed from California and raced and cruised through most of Europe. We left *Senta* with our plans for a bigger boat, complete with coal-burning heater, shelved for a while.

Theresa Remiszewski replied within a week. "Come to Gydnia, be a guest of our sailing club." We called our friend at Aeroflot shipping. "I have it," he said happily. "There's a Telex from Tallinn giving you berthage for the yacht *Seraffyn* and a pilot." So we took a flying trip to London. Theresa's letter got immediate results. Our passports were stamped by the Polish Embassy and returned in ten minutes. The Russian visas were still a problem. "It will take at least three weeks," the Russian consul-general told us, but he then assured us our telegram from Tallinn would solve all problems. So we left our passports and returned to *Seraffyn*.

Winter was flying. Days were growing perceptibly longer. The sun poked its head out at least four days a week. To spice up February, Annabelle and Gordon Yates arrived. We'd first met the Yateses in Baja California two months after our cruising life started. They'd sailed from San Diego on their thirty-two-foot trimaran. We spent wonderful days with them, meeting in scattered rendezvouses from La Paz to Acapulco. We'd get together to share fish recipes and rum punches while we discussed and solved all the world's problems. Then the Yateses turned north to sell *Amøbel* while we headed south toward Panama. We met again in Florida where they were living on an English twenty-two-foot Westerly Cirrus. After three years of cruising the Bahamas and Florida Keys, they'd decided they needed a slightly bigger boat so their grandchildren could come and visit for a few weeks. Now they were bound for Denmark to take possession of a brand-new Great Dane 28 (see Appendix B). For three days Gordon and Annabelle stayed in a rooming house a street away from us and we used our rickety old car to explore all the boatyards and marinas within thirty miles. We talked late into the night and their visit was like a tonic.

As spring grew closer, we set to work on *Seraffyn*'s refit. Larry was busy doing some alterations to the cockpit, so I sanded the starboard bulwark and waterway, dusted it, got out the paint, and started to put it on. I'd removed the ventilator that leads into our chain locker so I could paint around it more easily. With atrocious luck and no small amount of clumsiness, I knocked over the half liter of white paint. Then I let out a shriek as half of it poured down the ventilator hole and the other half ran in a stream down the bare teak decks. "Larry! Get me some kerosene, quick! Rags! Paper towels! Rush!" He came forward to see what was causing the ruckus, looked down at the mess quite calmly, and said "Excuse me." Then he walked off the boat. I ran for kerosene, took one look into the varnished chain locker with its liberal dose of white paint, scrambled back on deck, poured kerosene on the teak, and started rubbing. Just then Paul Lees and his girlfriend Vicky arrived. "Where is Larry?" Paul asked. I looked up from my frantic work and pointed toward the end of the pier two hundred yards away where Larry was yelling at a flock of seagulls. "What is he doing?" Vicki asked. I guiltily answered, "Shouting at the gulls instead of me."

The white paint wiped easily off the varnish of the chain locker. But in spite of scrubbing with a gallon of kerosene, spots of it still decorate the teak deck four years later.

~~~

CHAPTER 7

I'd Rather Go
to Sea

I stood at the helm, foghorn in hand. Larry rowed *Seraffyn,* making about one knot. The tide was just beginning to ebb as we approached the closed Poole Town bridge. I blasted the required signal with the horn when we were within a quarter mile of the bridge, then went forward as Larry suggested, to make sure our anchor was ready to let go if a sudden change of current threatened to drag us into danger.

There was a clanging of bells from the bridge control tower. Red lights flashed to stop the Sunday traffic. Guard gates fell into position and slowly the bridge formed a vee, then split in two. Larry kept up a strong, steady rhythm with our fourteen-foot oar and *Seraffyn* moved majestically forward. A back eddy around the bridge structure slowed our progress. The line of waiting cars quickly grew longer. People climbed out of their cars to stand in the sunshine and see what was causing the holdup. The bridgekeeper climbed down from his tower to see where we were. *Seraffyn* stood almost stationary under the bridge, Larry sweated against the oar, yet we made only inches against the back eddy. The bridgekeeper climbed back into his tower. "Get that bloody mast out from under my bridge," he called through a loudspeaker, "you're holding up half of Dorset County." That seemed to do the trick. The ebbing tide caught us at last and we burst free. I hoisted our mainsail to catch the tiny breeze that whispered along the quay. *Seraffyn* heeled lightly, then we skimmed away from the bonds of winter.

We sailed through the deepwater channel of Poole Harbor with Leslie Dyball, the sixty-six-year-old treasurer of the Parkstone Yacht

Club, on board, enjoying the warmth of early spring. Leslie seemed to make up his mind as we short-tacked back toward the club later that afternoon, "If you come back to England next summer, will you crew for me on *Chough* in the two-man Round-Britain Race?" he asked Larry.

"If things work out, I'd love to," Larry answered, and his attitude made me sure things *would* work out.

We hauled and painted *Seraffyn* at the ever-helpful Parkstone Yacht Club, disposed of our rattletrap car, had farewell dinners with wonderful winter friends. Then, laden with stores, we set off for the Baltic on the fourth year of our cruise. A dozen people had come to see us leave and yell good wishes. We set our lapper and mainsail, then reached out of the Poole Town Quay with a fair tide under us. I waved until we couldn't make out any faces while Larry steered through the intricate maze of buoys and stakes marking the shoal patches. "That's the one thing wrong with our way of life," I told Larry when I finally went below to start lunch. "You meet wonderful people who invite you into their lives. Then before you know it, it's time to leave."

"Maybe that's good," Larry answered. "We stay just long enough to learn the good things about people and we leave before they learn our faults or we learn theirs."

We came abeam of Brownsea Island castle just as my soup was ready to serve. "How about dropping the hook for lunch?" Larry suggested. I readily agreed and went forward to douse the lapper. And so ended the first leg of our Baltic cruise, although we hadn't cleared Poole Harbor and were less than three miles from where we'd started.

Brownsea Island is a one-mile-square bird sanctuary nestled just inside Poole Harbor's entrance. Once the home of royalty, it is now under the National Trust and a summer tourist spot. A small pond and swamp attracts migrating birds from all of Europe. We launched *Rinky* and rowed ashore after lunch. The caretaker met us at the ferry landing. "I'm sorry," he told us, "the island is closed to visitors until the first of May."

I was disappointed and my face obviously showed it since the caretaker asked, "Can't you come back in a month. It's only a short sail across the bay."

"We're leaving England, bound for Denmark," Larry replied. With that the caretaker seemed to notice *Seraffyn* with her Canadian flag lifting to the breeze. He asked, "Did you sail across the Atlantic?" We talked about sailing as the caretaker took us on a short tour of the main buildings. He was a keen dinghy sailor and the idea of crossing oceans under sail intrigued him. Then he remembered some work he had to do. "I must go back, but if you promise not to bother the peacocks, you can go for a walk on your own. Have a pleasant afternoon and good sailing when you leave."

Larry and I strolled hand in hand across the green meadows dotted with golden daffodils. We lay on the sun-warmed grass while a flock of glistening blue, green, gold, and brown peacocks strolled within four feet of us to investigate. We walked on, the calls of ten or twenty different species of birds echoing over the trees. When we reached the shore on the far side of the island, low tide had exposed miles of gray-brown mud dotted with tidal pools. Right on the edge of the bank we noticed an old man walking, head down, stooping to pick up something he tossed into the battered bucket he carried. I ran over to him to ask, "What are you catching?"

"Must be the people off the yacht anchored at the castle," he commented as he showed Larry and me a pile of oysters, cockles, and tiny twirled shellfish I didn't recognize. "These are winkles; ever had one?" He showed us how to remove the meat from the thumb-sized twirls. "Hang a bucket of these overboard for two days. That'll get the sand out. Then eat them as they come."

Larry was more interested in the oysters. "Aren't they polluted? Who owns them?" The fisherman had a twinkle in his eye when he answered, "The townfolk think they're polluted. But my family and I've been eating these oysters for years. No sewers around here, tide sweeps up the channel bringing fresh water twice a day to keep them clean. Wouldn't eat the oysters you'd find next to the town, though. No one owns these oysters, all strays from the commercial oyster beds upriver." We found a plastic bag in the tide line, then worked alongside the fisherman for a few minutes to see how he spotted the mud-colored oysters. Then we worked back toward the landing as the tide slowly began to cover the shoals. We had three dozen three-inch oysters, forty or fifty cockles (clams), at least a hundred winkles, muddy shoes, and soaked pantlegs by the time we reached our dinghy. The sky had clouded over and the wind was rising. We rowed out to *Seraffyn* and I climbed on board to start our cabin heater while Larry shucked the oysters in the dinghy. Then we turned on our stereo and feasted on a tossed salad with blue-cheese dressing, oysters on the half shell, then cheddar and stilton cheese on biscuits, all washed down with a bottle of white Spanish wine. Outside, the wind whistled through the rigging, wavelets slapped against our bow and *Rinky*'s clinker hull chattered to the tide.

Two lazy days later the sun came back and we set sail with the ebbing tide. The winds were light so we missed the fair tide into the Solent. It took us three hours to make two miles through Hurst Narrows against the three-and-a-half-knot ebb. When we reached the tiny port of Yarmouth, we tried to beat through the entrance but just couldn't beat the tide. We anchored outside the harbor and three hours later, when the tide was slack, we set our sails again, lifted anchor, and worked into the harbor, Larry steering, me on the foredeck warning him when I could see the rocks getting close to the surface. We secured between two pilings eight hours and seventeen miles from Brownsea. An engine would have made it easier, but nowhere near the fun. Besides, what did time matter to us? We had all the food we could use for two or three months, enough money for eight months, and our only scheduled date was on our Russian docking permit, on the first of August.

We spent a week in Yarmouth, riding bicycles through the hills of the flower-covered Isle of Wight. On Friday the thirteenth of April, I took the laundry ashore even though it would have been a lovely day for sailing. As I said to Larry, "You may not be superstitious, but I am. It's bad luck to start a voyage on a Friday." As I rowed back at noon with a load of groceries, Larry greeted me with "Come on, let's forget your superstitions and just take a day sail across to Lymington."

I agreed with him after I looked out onto the Solent. It was twinkling with sunshine, ruffled by a six-knot northerly. Lymington was in view about five miles to windward. I stowed my gear and we set off, lunching as we sailed. We easily found the entry marks and began to tack up the river to Lymington Town. Within minutes we ran aground on the east side of the river. "Friday the thirteenth," I called to Larry as he laid out our kedge anchor. "Just didn't tack soon enough," he called back. We beat upriver as soon as we were free, and four tacks later hit the mud and stuck again. "Don't say it," Larry mumbled as he climbed back into the dinghy to lay out the kedge. As soon as he dropped the anchor I bent to the winch handle and whispered "Friday the thirteenth" as I worked to winch us free again.

We tied up at the Royal Lymington Yacht club and the dockmaster took *Rinky* around behind the main pier to the dinghy dock. We called Alf Taylor and said, "Come join us for the weekend." We'd spent several days basking in Alf's warm hospitality during the previous winter, using his home as a base while we explored London. Now we were glad we could reciprocate in our own way.

Alf arrived from London early the next morning and we were soon skimming down the river. He relaxed against the lifelines and surveyed *Seraffyn* as we ran dead before the wind. "Boat looks great, but what have you done with your dinghy?" Alf asked.

Larry and I both looked behind us and said in unison, "*You* forgot *Rinky!*" Alf roared with laughter while we hardened in the sheets to beat back upchannel. "Friday the thirteenth," I muttered as we tacked well inside the marks. "Nope," Larry answered, "it's Saturday today. Blame that one on forgetfulness."

With *Rinky* once again trailing docilely behind us, we spent the next two days wandering through the Solent. We visited Cowes, tacked up the Medina River almost to Newport, then ran down with the tide. With Alf on board telling us about the scenery we passed, it was special fun. Alf was amazed by *Seraffyn*'s light-air performance. He took the helm to work her upriver and couldn't believe it when she just about sailed herself, even without the self-steering vane connected. He thought the vane was magic and, like most newcomers to self-steering vanes, started to grab the tiller each time "Helmer" reacted to a windshift. Before the weekend was over he'd decided to sell his own twenty-six-foot sloop and ask Lyle Hess to design him a thirty-two-foot *Seraffyn* for his retirement home.

At the end of the weekend we sailed up Wooten Creek to take Alf to his ferry. The tide was falling but we had an introduction to Jack Whitehead, the figurehead carver who lived up the creek. Our Royal Cruising Club guide and our Admiralty chart both showed six feet of water in front of the Wootten Yacht Club at low tide. But they were wrong. Inside the mouth of the river, just past the ferry dock but a hundred fifty yeads short of the club moorings, we ran aground. Before we had a chance to consider kedging off, *Seraffyn* began to tilt. We knew the tide had about seven feet to fall and, while there was still a thin sheet of water over the tidal flats, Larry rowed Alf and his dufflebag ashore. When Larry came back, he said, "I met the club's dockmaster. He told me the British Railway Ferry has made this pool silt up over the last two years." The club was trying to get the railway to

Aground in Wootten Creek.

provide a dredger to clear the pool (we heard two years later that they had succeeded and the Wootten Creek Yacht Club had again become a favorite cruising man's weekend retreat, complete with water).

Meanwhile, the water ebbed away until there was mud in every direction for at least three hundred yards. Twenty mooring buoys sat on the mud in front of the club like colored balloons. On one of the moorings a twin-keeled "mud duck" showed her stuff, settling evenly into the mud. But *Seraffyn* lay on her bilge, tilting at a forty-five-degree angle. Larry assured me there was nothing to worry about. "*Seraffyn* is built stout enough, and the bilge stringer is taking any extra strains. It would be nice to have legs, though, like the Falmouth oyster boats do." So, after joking about our situation and remembering when a friend in Falmouth had said "Only man who never ran aground, never went anywhere," we both took books onto the "upper deck" and lay in the sun waiting for the water to return.

About three hours later a thin sheet of water came creeping toward us. *Seraffyn* began to lift so Larry said, "Come on, Lin, let's row up the river and meet Jack. There's four more hours of rising tide. We can sail off this evening." We piled fifty feet of chain and our CQR anchor into the dinghy, rowed it out, then dropped the anchor and set it by shoving its bill into the mud with the dinghy oar.

We drifted up the tree-lined river, Larry occasionally taking a pull on one oar or the other, the tide doing the rest of the work. Two miles later, we landed at Jack Whitehead's stretch of beach. A garden full of spring vegetables lined the gravel path that led toward a wooden

After this figurehead was completed, Jack and Doris Whitehead were invited to supervise its installation on the *Falls of Clyde* in Honolulu, Hawaii.

cottage. A stocky, thick-armed carver worked in a rough, open-fronted shelter built under a tree in front of the cottage. His hammer and chisel gouged large chips of elm from the nine-foot-high block that was just beginning to take the shape of a buxom woman. We produced our letter of introduction from Monk Farnham, a New York sailor, and it brought forth a warm invitation from Jack—"You're just in time for tea." He yelled up toward the cottage "Two more for tea," then took us to see the fifteen figureheads he was restoring for the Cutty Sark museum with the help of a partner and one son. Jack had lived on the Isle of Wight most of his life and had started work as a shipwright with Uffa Fox in Cowes. One day there had been a call for scrolled trail-boards and Jack had done the carving. One thing led to another and within two years Jack was so busy he had to turn down jobs even though he had two people working with him. "The only other full-time figurehead carver I know of lives near Mystic Seaport, Connecticut," Jack told us while his wife Doris served fresh scones and home-made preserves. The nine-foot figurehead he was now carving would eventually grace the *Falls of Clyde*, a iron square-rigger being restored in Honolulu.

Jack urged us to stay another day as he walked with us down to our dinghy. When we told him about *Seraffyn* lying on her side in the mud, he said, "There's real soft mud in front of the yacht club. Move over there and she'll settle upright when the tide's out." Since the man Larry had met at the yacht club when he rowed Alf ashore had said the same thing, we decided it was worth a try and invited Jack and his wife to join us for breakfast.

We rowed *Seraffyn* across to a club mooring before we went to bed. I woke up slowly, dreaming I was falling. Larry came awake almost at the same moment. I clung to him as he grabbed the edge of the bunk. *Seraffyn* tilted first ten degrees, then fifteen, and within ten minutes, forty-five degrees. We tumbled unceremoniously out of the bunk and onto the sextant locker, Larry on top, me hysterical with giggles. "Guess local advice doesn't work when you've got a twelve-inch-wide keel," Larry said as he helped unzip our double sleeping bags. We climbed into the two quarter berths, laughing over the problems of living at such an extreme list, then slept separately for the rest of the night.

We sailed out of the river into the Solent after a lazy company breakfast of pancakes, maple syrup, and eggs. Portsmouth lay only eight or ten miles ahead. Sun warmed our decks, the stereo played soft music, our genoa and mainsail panted slightly in the five-knot breeze. *Rinky* chuckled along behind, tugging at the end of her twenty-five-foot, three-eighths-inch nylon painter.

We reached Portsmouth as the tide was rushing out the narrow entrance. We tried beating in, but the northerly wind slowly grew lighter. "Let's sail out of the channel and anchor on the shoals till the tide turns," Larry suggested. The chart showed eight feet of water at low tide on the large area just outside the big ships' channel, so I readily agreed. We reached off and the tide swept us seaward as we slowly edged out of the three-mile-long big ships' channel. The wind began to die, *Seraffyn*'s forward motion slowed to a trickle, and the tide carried us sideways at three knots.

Larry looked downtide and saw a buoy directly on our beam. "We're going to hit that buoy," he said, working to catch a breeze. "No," I said, "we'll clear it." A stray puff filled our genoa. "You're probably right, Lin, we'll miss it," he said as *Seraffyn* trickled forward. That buoy grew from toy size until it rushed toward us, nine feet high and eight feet around, red and rusty. All the time we kept debating,

"We're going to hit it, we're not, we are." Then, all of a sudden, we looked at each other and said, "We're going to hit it." Larry had the presence of mind to grab the two fenders that lay on the cockpit floor. He dropped them between *Seraffyn's* topsides and that ugly fairway buoy just as we hit it beam-on at over three knots. *Seraffyn* shuddered to a stop. I was thrown off my feet as the tiller swept wildly across the cockpit. Larry yelled, "Grab the dinghy painter!" But it was too late. *Seraffyn* slid slowly off one side of the buoy and floated downtide. The dinghy went around the other way. For a split second we stopped, dinghy on one side of the buoy, *Seraffyn* on the other. The painter stretched until it was half its normal size. Then *Seraffyn* won the tug of war. The dinghy flew around the buoy, flipped five feet into the air, landed upside down, then followed *Seraffyn* downstream. "Get ready to drop the anchor," Larry said as he pulled the dinghy alongside and lifted her gunwale high enough to reach the oars that, fortunately, were still inside. At his shout I let the anchor go. It found bottom at twenty feet and *Seraffyn* quickly turned to face the rushing tide. *Rinky's* upside-down pram bow caught the tide full on and acted like a paravane. The dinghy submerged and tugged fiercely six inches below the surface, trapped air and buoyancy tanks fighting to float her up. We

It was three hours before the tide slacked enough for us to right *Rinky Dink.*

tried to winch the dinghy alongside, but couldn't against the force of that tide. Larry carefully inspected *Seraffyn,* expecting to find at least a cracked plank or split frame. He looked wonderfully relieved when he announced, "Only damage is cosmetic." So there we sat for two hours, trying to look nonchalant as afternoon fishermen and sailors powered past us staring at *Rinky*'s white submerged bottom and the three-foot strip of red paint *Seraffyn* carried as a souvenir of our encounter with a fairway buoy.

Portsmouth is a naval harbor. You can tell that from the moment you work through the narrow fortress-guarded entrance. Gray-painted vessels from the size of rowboats to four-hundred-foot-long supply ships line its shores and anchorages. But nestled among the drydocks and warehouses we could see the masts of *Victory,* Nelson's flagship during the Napoleonic wars. She was the reason we'd come. Now we'd have a chance to see how Horatio Hornblower had lived as a midshipman. We'd be able to understand what C. S. Forester had written about how six-inch-thick hemp anchor cables took up half of one deck on a ship of the line. But first we had to find a place to moor. We looked over our detail chart. Every spare space seemed to be marked "Anchorage Forbidden." We spotted Camper and Nicholson marina and sailed alongside only to be told that one night would cost us twelve dollars. "No thanks," we replied, sailing off. The next marina had a mooring for the night at only two dollars, but said we had to clear off by 0800 as they were launching several boats then and needed the mooring. It was late so we tied up for the night and were under way at 0800. We sailed alongside a line of empty mooring stakes in an area that our charts marked as "numerous yacht moorings." Just as we were about to moor up, a launch rushed out from shore and the man on board yelled, "Can't tie there, navy only." We luffed *Seraffyn*'s jib and waited for him to come closer. "Where can we moor?" He pulled his naval cap down more securely, shrugged his shoulders, and said, "How should I know? But you can't moor here." Then he turned his launch toward shore.

"Come on, let's go to sea. No tourist attraction is worth all this hassle," I said to Larry and he agreed. We noticed a semi-empty marina up a small creek just inside the entrance to the harbor. "One more try?" Larry asked, glancing over at the yards and topmasts of *Victory.* "Okay, but if that one's a hassle too, let's call it quits."

There were only twenty boats tied in a marina built for a hundred fifty. We moored alongside the first float we came to, loosely furled our sails, then I set off to meet the uniformed man who was approaching us. I met him halfway. "Can't moor here," he said. Then I asked, "Can we at least use your phone to call the harbormaster and ask where we can anchor?"

"No problem," he said. "Come along." After fifteen minutes of phoning, he turned to me and said, "No place you can anchor; can't tie here either."

I stomped back toward the boat. Larry was talking to a tall, husky man who'd just sailed in astern of us. He introduced me to David Williams, then asked, "What did you find out?"

"Same old nonsense," I started. "Can't stay, no anchoring allowed in the harbor area. Might be room at the yacht club seven miles from here." David interrupted. "What's the problem?" Tears came to my eyes as I described the trouble we were having finding a place to moor so we could see the *Victory*. "Just wait here," David said. Then he turned and walked off toward the offices. His wife Pippa invited us on board for a cup of tea and shortbread cookies, then told us, "I'm from Canada, too. I hope David can help you." David was back before we'd finished one cup. He asked for our harbor chart, made an X on it, and said, "As soon as we've finished tea, you'd best sail over. You're expected. Good safe moorage, stay as long as you like."

We thanked David profusely as he helped us cast off our lines, then we sailed two miles up the harbor, past mothballed naval ships and the two-hundred-year-old teak ship of the line *Foudroyant*. Three uniformed men gave us salutes as we approached the floating docks X'd on our chart. As they took our mooring lines, the most gold-encrusted of the three told us, "Welcome to Whale Island Naval Artillery School. Come up to my office and I'll give you a pass for the main gate. Showers over here, make yourself at home."

We set sail four days later after a day-long visit to *Victory*. The hospitality at Whale Island had been in top British tradition. We'd had to fight hard to keep the bosun from dressing *Seraffyn*'s boom gallows completely in ropework, and we'd learned how to make a proper turks head. As we cleared the harbor Larry said to me, "I don't like your complaining to other people, especially with tears running down your face. But I must admit you chose the right man to gripe to. I was talking to the officer who took our lines that first day and he asked me, 'How long have you known Admiral Williams?'"

CHAPTER 8

~~~~~~

Of Fogs and Fires

We wandered eastward, sailing into each harbor on England's south coast. Spring's changeable weather was a trial for the best of BBC's weather forecasters, so we weren't too surprised when we sailed into a heavy fog just off Dungeness, the narrowest, most crowded part of the English Channel. But we were worried. We'd left Newhaven at 1600 with a fair wind, fair tide, and fair-weather forecast bound directly for Lowestoft, one hundred seventy miles northeast. A light but steady southeasterly breeze had carried us along past Beachy Head and the marker on the shore that indicated exactly zero longitude. As dark fell we could easily see the powerful navigation lights set along the shores and on light ships throughout the funnel-shaped, shoal-encumbered Channel. We'd stayed close to shore to avoid the constant stream of shipping that throbbed steadily through the twenty-mile wide Straits of Dover. The wind increased slowly and drew ahead until we were working northeast, almost close-hauled with only the staysail and mainsail pulling us at four knots. I'd stood the midnight to 0300 watch. A sailing jacket and one sweater had been enough to keep me warm and comfortable. My watch had flown as I took bearings on various lights, confirming our position each hour. Twenty minutes before the end of the watch I'd decided to tack offshore so we'd have more clearance rounding Dungeness. I brought *Seraffyn* onto the other tack, set Helmer, and after taking a careful look around, went below to start some water warming for hot tea.

I woke Larry at 0255, then went on deck to take a final check. A mile ahead a line of green navigation lights marched southward. I went below and, since Larry was almost dressed, began to strip. "Hot chocolate waiting for you on the stove. You'll have to tack within five or ten minutes," I said, climbing into the still-warm sleeping bag.

Larry clambered sleepily through the companionway, a mug of hot chocolate in his hand. "My God," he shouted, "we're going to hit that ship!" I felt him shove the helm to leeward. *Seraffyn* came about so quickly I almost fell out of the bunk as she heeled away on the new tack. I scrambled free of the bedclothes and looked toward the row of ships that now marched along on our beam. Larry was shaken and angrily said, "You let us get too damn close to the shipping lane."

It took a few minutes before Larry calmed down. "Lin, you didn't say 'We're heading toward the shipping lanes and need to tack within ten minutes or we'll hit a ship.' I climbed on deck completely unaware and there were ships' lights, looking as if they were only yards away."

We talked about changing watches as I brewed a cup of hot chocolate to replace the one Larry had spilled in his rush to tack. On a racing boat or any sailboat without self-steering, there's no problem. The helmsman waits at the tiller for the next watch to arrive, then he points out the situation before going below. But with a windvane on a cruising boat, the man on watch usually comes below to wake someone who is fresh out of a warm sleeping bag, groggy and trying to force himself awake. Then it becomes necessary to explain the complete situation to the new watchkeeper before he climbs on deck and is startled by the unexpected.

Larry, placated by the steaming, fragrant cup of chocolate, kissed me goodnight. I climbed into the sleeping bag in the windward quarter berth and secured the lee cloth in place. When he called me at 0600 we were shrouded in fog. A stiff easterly breeze kicked up a short chop but didn't seem to move the heavy damp whiteness. "Nothing I hate worse than fog," Larry told me while he studied the chart. Although Larry had sailed in the Pacific Northwest for several years and knew something about fog conditions, this was my first experience. I could hear the horns of shipping around us. I could imagine the surf on the shore we were steadily approaching. I stood on deck trying to will the fog away. Then Larry came up and said, "Chart shows two fathoms of water within a hundred yards of the shore, six fathoms a quarter mile off. I suggest we ease sheets just a bit and slant in toward the south side of Dungeness. Once we see the land, we'll know what the visibility really is. If it's less than a quarter mile, we'll anchor till the fog clears. It's a sand bottom so the anchor will hold in spite of the seas.

We'll be uncomfortable if we have to anchor, but it'll be safer than bumbling around out here without being able to see anything."

I looked around at the four-foot chop as I helped ease the sheets. "How about getting the lead line ready to use?" Larry suggested as he took a reading off our dependable little Negus taffrail log, then went below to advance our position. Ten minutes later we spotted the beach and identified a huge gray building that corresponded with the hydroelectric plant shown in our *Shell Guide*. I took a sounding, swinging the lead line as far ahead as I could; "Four and a half fathoms." Larry went below for the chart and plotted our position. "Here's where we are. Visibility is a bit over a quarter mile. Nearest deepwater harbor is Dover, about twenty miles north. There are three big pilot buoys with bells marked on the chart between here and Dover. So if we tack along this point till we spot the Dungeness lighthouse, then reach off and keep a careful DR, we should be able to pick our way from buoy to buoy. If we miss one, there's less than eight fathoms of water everywhere, so we can anchor."

I studied the chart with Larry and what had looked like a frightening situation turned into an adventure. His plan kept us well away from the worst danger, the shipping lanes. So we tacked eastward and found the end of Dungeness with its lighthouse. I set a course for the first buoy then pored over the tide charts and tables. Larry called down a log reading when he had the lighthouse abeam. He steered by hand to keep *Seraffyn* exactly on course. I carefully figured an average speed for the tide, allowing for a bit of leeway, then showed Larry the chart with my figures to double-check our navigation. After fifteen minutes I asked for a log reading. "We're making five knots through the water, tide is pushing us at around two knots, so watch for the buoy in twenty minutes," I told Larry as I heated a pot of coffee and some toast.

We were almost abeam of the buoy before we spotted its dim gray outline through the whirling fog. We could have missed it. We were almost a quarter mile to windward of the black-and-white-striped buoy. We had allowed too much for leeway. We eased our sheets still more and ran down to within fifty feet of the buoy, read the name stenciled on its side, took a new log reading, and set off on our treasure hunt for the next buoy. Two hours and two buoys later, the huge walls of Dover's breakwater broke through the fog, right when they should have. I gave Larry a hug and kiss, saluted our tiny spinning taffrail log, then climbed below and lit the stove, dreaming up a tasty lunch menu to serve as soon as we set our anchor. Larry eased our sheets to run into the harbor and *Seraffyn* flew through the water at over five knots. But a four-knot current and heavy overfalls slowed our progress to a crawl. Larry called down to me, "Man in the signal station on the breakwater end has just changed the black cones. What's this new pattern mean?" I brought the *Pilot* book on deck and we thumbed through it until we found the signal: "Do not leave harbor." Larry looked pleased when he said, "Must be warning shipping about us." I laughed at the idea of our twenty-four-footer stopping the traffic out of Dover's harbor.

Then we both heard it at the same time, pushing up behind us. Something sounded like a cross between an airplane, a vacuum cleaner, and a waterfall. Seconds after we first heard the roar, a huge hovercraft burst through the fog, radar scanner scanning, water foaming at its base. It was past us in seconds and disappeared through the fog at the mouth of the harbor. We followed it at our infinitely slower pace, bucking and weaving through the overfalls.

We blessed the quiet and safety we found inside the foggy harbor. A pilot boat directed us to the small-craft anchorage, an area that was unfortunately exposed to the swell caused by the easterly wind. We anchored, furled our sails, and climbed below out of the fog and drizzle, then closed our canvas companionway cover and settled into the warm cabin to eat lunch. Although *Seraffyn* rolled a bit, we were safe and I agreed when Larry said, "If I had to do all my sailing in the English Channel, I'd give up the sport. Always a threat of fog, extremely heavy shipping, strong tides, choppy sea, changeable weather, cold winds, cold water. No wonder so few English wives enjoy sailing."

Spring came back the next day and we used a light westerly breeze and the strong tide to continue north across the shoals of the sunlit Thames estuary. We often had so little wind that only the tide moved us along. As soon as the tide started to turn against us, we'd work over to a shoal patch and anchor. Since the shoal we chose at 2100 had only six feet of water over it at low tide, we felt safe from shipping with our kerosene anchor lamp burning, although we were anchored ten miles from the nearest land. The wind stayed light, the sea was smooth. We spent a quiet night and were under way with the first of the fair tide before daybreak. By midmorning a fresh warm southerly breeze set us running past the low sandy Suffolk coastline, and we tied in front of the Royal Norfolk and Suffolk Yacht Club at Lowestoft before dark.

The next morning we placed a call to the Russian Embassy in London. Every time we'd entered a port during the previous weeks we'd called to ask, "Are our passports stamped with the visas we need to sail *Seraffyn* into a Russian port?" The secretary had come to recognize our voices. As soon as we rang through this time he said, "Yes, you've finally succeeded. If you come to our embassy at ten o'clock two mornings from now, the consul will sign your permits and return your passports."

We took a train to London the next morning, spending the afternoon exploring the mammoth halls of the British Museum. After an evening of wandering around London, we took a room at an inexpensive hotel and the next morning set off for the Russian Embassy. As we walked past a newstand, I noticed huge headlines on the morning papers: "Espionage, Russian Diplomats Expelled from Britain." When we reached the embassy, everything was in confusion. The only face we recognized from our six previous visits was that of the secretary. He looked up from a mass of papers he was sorting and muttered, "Yes, you must be here for your visas." Then he turned and went into an adjoining office. We were motioned in almost immediately. Papers and boxes cluttered the usually neat consular room. A strange man sat behind the desk waiting for us. After introductions he said, "I'm sorry, but the signatures on your permit to enter the Soviet Union are no longer valid. I must write to Moscow to get a decision as to whether I should authorize your visas. Please return in three weeks." Larry and I both protested, "But we plan to sail from England this week." The new consular official shook his head. "It is beyond my power to authorize people to enter my country by any means other than on a recognized carrier. I'm sorry Mr. ——— is no longer with us. Only he had permission to sign your visas."

We watched our hopes of being the first yachtsmen to sail into Russia fade away. After ten minutes of discussion we took our passports and asked to have all of our visa documents forwarded to the Russian Embassy in Helsinki.

We took the afternoon train back to Lowestoft, lamenting all the way about our lost chance. "What if Mr. ——— had decided to sign those permits last week. Wouldn't it have been fantastic to sail up the Neva River right into the heart of Leningrad?" But we consoled ourselves with thoughts of the five other countries that would fill our summer.

We had heard rumors about the extremely high cost of food in Scandinavian countries. Members of the Royal Norfolk and Suffolk Yacht Club who had been to Denmark in the recent past confirmed the rumors. So we spent several days buying all of the stores we could fit on board. I filled my lockers with extra quantities of canned meats, especially steak-and-kidney pies, stewing steak with gravy, and chunky chicken in cream sauce, useful specialty items we've found only in English countries. We ordered two cases of duty-free liquor at the usual low price of about two dollars a bottle for Scotch, and we filled our butane tank. Then we wandered around the waterfront and rivers of Lowestoft waiting for an easterly gale to blow itself out.

A mile from the sea, on a deepwater canal lined with timber yards and warehouses, we found the once magnificent one-hundred-forty-foot schooner *Heartsease*. She had been built at the turn of the century as a racing yacht to compete for the Kaiser's Cup. Her newest owners, Caroline and Gordon, from Australia, welcomed us on board. We toured the luxurious staterooms designed during an era when labor was cheap and yachts like this had full-time crews of eight or ten

Our major storage lockers are under the two quarter berths with a third one under the head of the forward bunk. Together they hold almost thirty cases of canned goods.

professionals. Each stateroom was paneled in a different wood. The main bathroom had a full-size, three-foot-deep porcelain bathtub surrounded by African mahogany. The main saloon was paneled in bird's-eye maple from parqueted floors to shoulder height. From there up, the bulkheads were covered in pink striped satin. Unfortunately, the spars and rigging from *Heartsease* had been sold off during the years. Her huge lead ballast keel had been removed during World War II and made into bullets. She had been tied to the canal side and used as a floating houseboat. Now Gordon and Caroline dreamed of restoring *Heartsease* to her former glory. They had bought her for less than twenty thousand dollars, but were beginning to realize the immensity of the task ahead. Although the teak hull was basically sound, she needed a ballast keel, spars, and rigging. Also, the decks leaked, the houses leaked, the engines were inoperable, and the costs for the simplest items for a boat of such size were far beyond what Gordon had imagined when he first became involved. "Just to haul and scrape her, the cheapest shipyard around here wants eight hundred pounds," he told us during one of several visits we exchanged. Before we sailed from Lowestoft, Gordon and Caroline told us they had decided to go back to Australia and sell some more of their property to continue their project. We really sympathized with their problem. They had fallen for a romantic, but impractical, dream.

We came back from spending yet another afternoon in the cozy overstuffed chairs of the reading room in the friendly yacht club. The easterly wind whistled through our rigging for the fifth day and rain spattered on our decks. Larry lit the small butane heater, then trimmed the wicks on our three oil lamps, filled them, and polished the lenses while I cooked dinner. After eating, we lounged back on the two settees, feet up, listening to the rain on deck while we had a last cup of tea. "How about a game of cribbage?" Larry asked. I got the board and cards and, for once, came out on top in the three-game series. While we were playing, the rain increased to a downpour. It bounced off the cabin top so hard that large drops of it pushed through the half-inch opening under our skylight hatch. So Larry got up and closed the skylight.

We shed our clothes in *Seraffyn*'s warm main cabin, then I followed Larry into our forepeak bunk. When Larry blew out the oil lamp, we noticed the red glow from our heater. Larry molded himself warmly to my body. "Should shut the heater, uses a lot of butane." I couldn't bear the thought of climbing out of his arms. "It won't hurt to leave it burn just this one time."

We both woke up with headaches at dawn. Larry climbed over me and got aspirins and water for us. He used the loo bucket, standing up, then came back into the bunk. A few minutes later I climbed out and went into the main cabin where I sat down on the loo. I remember standing up and closing the bucket lid, but that's all. Larry heard me fall on the cabin sole. He rushed out of the bunk, shoved the sliding hatch open in spite of the drizzle, then lifted me off the floor. "You were like a limp sack of potatoes when I tried to carry you into the forward bunk. Your face was gray," he told me as soon as I regained conciousness. I only remember the dreadful worried feeling I had when I came to.

Both of us felt terrible, nauseous and headachy. I had a bad bruise on my chin. We realized we'd almost poisoned ourselves by having an unvented fire on board with too little air circulation. I'd been affected more drastically because carbon monoxide sinks and I'd sat down in the main cabin while Larry hadn't. We'd been okay in the forepeak because we were near the chain locker with its three-inch ventilator and open chain pipe.

We rowed into the clubhouse to have lunch and mentioned our episode to one of the members. "Even if your gas heater had been vented, you could have been in trouble. Last year, someone heard a baby crying on board one of the twenty-six-foot charter boats tied at the side of the canal. They went to investigate. The boat was all closed up, but not locked. When they opened the hatch, the investigators found four dead people sitting around the table with a half-eaten dinner set out. The remains of a charcoal fire smouldered in the stove with its one-and-a-half-inch flue. The baby was in the forepeak, right next to the open chain pipe. That's why it was still alive."

Our frightening experience and this sobering story made us realize that any fire in a closed area such as a boat is dangerous. To prevent loss of oxygen and the buildup of carbon monoxide, you need cross ventilation even if you have a smoke stack. After this, we kept a quarter berth ventilator and the skylight open every time we used our cabin heater.

The day we finally set off to cross the North Sea it was raining. Reports were for the wind to veer from the east to the southeast. Our course to the Limfjord in Denmark was northeast. "Come on, Lin. If

Once the wind is over Force 5, *Seraffyn's* sail plan moves all inboard. Here we are on a close reach in winds of Force 9, carrying reefed staysail and double-reefed main.

we wait for perfect conditions we'll spend the whole summer here in Lowestoft." So we set off on the first of May 1973, after one last dash to town for ice and fresh vegetables. We had a fair tide under us as we cleared the high breakwaters. The wind was just north of east. We set our yankee, staysail, and mainsail to work north-northeast, hard on the wind. By nightfall, we had the lights of Great Yarmouth far astern. The wind increased until we took the yankee in and tied two reefs in the mainsail. Despite the Force 6 or 7 winds our motion was comfortable enough so that even I enjoyed the thick stew I had remembered to prepare before we left port. I'm sure if I'd had to prepare a meal from scratch, my perennial seasickness would have reared its ugly head. I dug out our North Sea charts before climbing into the bunk and raising the lee cloth. Then I watched Larry transferring our position from the coastal chart to the much smaller scale one we'd use for our four-hundred-fifty-mile North Sea crossing.

All that night and the next day we beat onward, making almost four knots through the water on a course that pointed just east of north on our chart. By dark our second night at sea we could see lights where nothing showed on our charts but deep water. Larry kept a careful watch as we neared the lights, and when he woke me for my watch, told me, "I sure made a stupid mistake. Those are oil-rig lights. Yet when I studied our DR track it showed us twenty miles to windward of the nearest rig. So I went over all our DR, then checked the tide charts. Finally figured out I've been subtracting the variation instead of adding it." Larry was pretty unhappy about his mistake and went on to tell me about a professional delivery skipper, a man with hundreds of thousands of miles under his belt, who'd made the same mistake. Unfortunately, the delivery skipper hadn't realized his error until he'd run the heavy-displacement, sixty-five-foot power yacht up on a sand shoal at ten knots.

Larry rummaged under our forward bunk cushion until he found an old chart. He cut the small inner compass rose off it. "From now on, if there is no magnetic rose inside the compass rose on a chart, we'll place this one at the correct variation. Then we'll check our course. When you can actually see the variation, there's much less chance of making an error." We later covered a small compass rose with clear plastic and put it right next to our dividers ready for instant use.

We carried on north through the oil rigs, and during Larry's second night watch, when *Seraffyn* was close to one of the huge platforms, we almost hit an unlit six-foot-high black buoy. Larry called me from my bunk and pointed at the heavy buoy pumping in the six-foot seas. The buoy was obviously used for mooring supply ships that came to service the rigs, and Larry commented, "I'm surprised the oil people are allowed to set unlit buoys. The rig is shown on the chart, but no mention is made of buoys or dangers. Could have taken our bowsprit off if we'd hit it."

By morning the wind lightened and veered. We were able to set our whole mainsail. After we'd untied the reefpoints, Larry hoisted the sail and I couldn't believe my eyes. From the reefpoints up our brand-new sail was grimy gray. We've since washed that sail in hot soapy water, but nothing has taken the stains out. Friends have suggested that the stains were caused by industrial pollution carried from the Ruhr Valley in Germany by the strong easterly winds. Others say the stains are from diesel exhaust fumes off the oil-rig generators. But we'll never know.

By afternoon our third day out, we were close-reaching slowly along on an almost flat sea with fog surrounding us. A few times that night we saw ships' lights and were able to estimate that we had one-mile visibility. We have aluminum foil rolled inside all the hollow sections of *Seraffyn*'s thirty-eight-foot-high wooden mast and the captains of two ships have told us that our picture on a radar screen looks like that of an eighty-five-footer. That's probably why ships never came near us during any foggy periods.

For three days we drifted through the fog toward Denmark, the wind slowly veering to the west. On the fourth morning, a large trawler broke through the fog and came within a hundred yards of us, then slowed down to match our speed. "Want a fish?" the captain called over the loud hailer. One of the crew held up a fish that was as long as me. I laughed and shook my head no. The captain called back, "Want anything else?" Larry shouted at the top of his lungs, "Can you confirm our position?" The men on the trawler tried to hear him over the throb of their engines, but couldn't. Larry went below and got a chart. He wrote POSITION on the back of it in big letters with a marking pencil. Then he came on deck and held up our "live reckoning" sign. The trawler's radar scanner started to rotate and minutes later the captain called back our latitude and longitude. Then the captain yelled, "Good sailing," and the *Boston Invader* steamed off into the fog.

We were fifteen miles north of our DR after three and a half days with no sights. The nearest land was still over a hundred miles from us. But with a confirmed position we were able to ease sheets even more, and by the next morning as we sailed out of the fog bank into the sun, Denmark's low sandy shore lay before us. Larry shot the sun and his LOP confirmed our latitude. We were ten miles north of the entrance to the Limfjord. We set the lapper on our sixteen-foot-long whisker pole and skimmed toward the harbor at the fjord's entrance, never once expecting the wonderous cruising that lay ahead.

September 15, 1972
June 4, 1974

CHAPTER 9

~~~~

Sailing
Through a Farm

No matter how many times we make a landfall, I still have the same reaction. I get impatient to enter harbor, to go ashore and meet our first locals. So I set to work cleaning *Seraffyn*'s cabin, storing away charts and wet gear, polishing the stove top, wiping down the bunks and varnish work. Larry generally teases me about my sudden burst of energy. "You sure aren't like this when we can't see land!"

Larry seems to have different thoughts on his mind as we near port after each passage. He seems to look at the brave little boat under our feet with keen appreciation, marveling that our handiwork has carried us to the brink of yet another adventure.

I came on deck ready to help with the more demanding sail handling required to enter a harbor without an engine. We were rapidly approaching Tiburon's breakwater and both of us studied the detail chart of the old fishing port. Then Larry said, "Well, Lin, what's your plan?" All of a sudden I realized *I* had to maneuver *Seraffyn* into Tiburon. Larry had often urged me to improve my sailing skills by taking charge in close quarters, but previously I'd just let him make the decisions, then followed orders. After our tiff in Dartmouth, we'd agreed to take turns as captain. I'd forgotten this decision, but Larry hadn't. "The only way you'll get the confidence to bring *Seraffyn* alongside a crowded dock is by doing it. You can sail your dinghy anywhere. *Seraffyn* is just bigger and heavier. She'll scratch more paint off anything she hits if you don't plan right."

Now I became aware of the responsibilities of being skipper. *I* had to decide what the wind strength would be once we rounded the corner of the breakwater. *I* had to be sure we had the right sails set, that the anchor would be ready to let go if necessary, that mooring lines and fenders would be available in plenty of time.

I looked at our Canadian flag lifting to the following wind. We were running east; to get into the harbor we'd have to beat west. "Okay, Larry, let's drop the jib and set the staysail instead. This wind will feel a lot stronger when we have to beat. Besides, the staysail is easier to tack than the big jib." I issued my first command and with that decision made the whole task began to look easier. I took the helm while Larry made the sail change, then I steered for the far side of the channel in front of the breakwater so we could look inside the entrance and avoid colliding with any outgoing vessels. Then Larry hardened in the staysail while, tiller between my knees, I hauled the mainsheet in to start our beat. The harbor looked smaller than I'd anticipated, its wharfs and docks encrusted with fishing boats. But *Seraffyn* came about easily and gained on each lift of the wind. We short-tacked around several piers, through the outer harbor to the big inner harbor. Then I saw the small-boat harbor at the windward end of the mile-long maze of wharfs and piers, and chose the spot where I wanted to tie up. "We'll need mooring lines and fenders on our starboard side," I told Larry, remembering the countless times similar things he'd said to me.

Then I remembered to tell him my plan. "I'll come along that second fishing boat after I take one more tack. You be ready to take the breast line and slow us down if necessary. I'll handle the stern line. We'll be heading almost dead into the wind, so just let the sheets loose when I say." Larry teased me, "Okay, captain," then prepared the mooring lines and fenders. My plan worked. I took one long tack to the far side of the two-hundred-foot-wide harbor, then tacked over toward my chosen spot. "Let the staysail sheet go," I told Larry as I eased the mainsail sheet. The sails luffed and lost their power. *Seraffyn* began to lose her way a little too quickly, so I sheeted in the mainsail to give her just a bit more speed. Then I pulled the tiller to leeward, let the mainsheet fly, and *Seraffyn* slowly came to a stop, abeam of and one foot from that fishing boat. Larry only said two words as he stepped off to secure our mooring lines—"Nicely done." And that was more than enough for me.

Tiburon stands on a windswept beach. Brick houses huddle against the violent North Sea winds. There are no gardens or trees, only eight or ten sandy streets. The fish plant and trawlers provide Tiburon's only reason for existing, and even on this bright sunny day the village looked depressing. But the people made up for it. The harbormaster arrived as we were furling our sails and spoke enough English to explain that we needed no stamp in our passport, no cruising permit, no clearance since we'd come directly from England. He also knew the heart of a sailor because he told us, "Hot showers at the seaman's club," then pointed to a building nearby. We took our clean clothes and kits and went ashore.

A bank hugged the side of the seaman's club so we changed a travelers check before going for showers. The door of the club opened into an immaculate tiled foyer, which in turn led into a small cafe. A row of hooks lined the foyer wall. Sea jackets hung from half the hooks and below each jacket was a pair of shoes. We looked in the cafe and saw ten or twelve fishermen drinking beer in stocking feet. So we shed our shoes and set them in the line-up. We walked into the spotless cafe to find that the girl at the counter spoke some English, too. She directed us to the showers, which were as immaculate as the rest of the club. Throughout our stay in Denmark we found the same traditions. Shoes came off at the entrance. Homes, restaurants, bars, offices—all were immaculate. Even the roadsides were clean and free of the beercans and cigarette butts that adorn roads and paths of other countries.

We walked back toward the boat after showers and coffee. I glanced into a small butcher shop and couldn't believe the prices marked. I refigured the exchange rates and, sure enough, the pound of Plumrose brand Danish bacon that sold for eighty-five cents in England cost two dollars in Denmark (1973).

We left Tiburon the next day. The wind still came from the west and sailing out was easy. Then we began our meander through the beautiful Limfjord. About a hundred miles south of the Kattegat there is a chain of lakes connected by rivers and channels kept dredged to a depth of at least twelve feet cutting right across the Jutland penin-sula. Prime farming lands line the shores of the sheltered passage. Forty or fifty small man-made harbors are scattered throughout its ninety-mile length. Red brick houses and small tidy towns nestle among the trees on shore. Cows and sheep come right to the water's edge to graze. A constant breeze filters over the low rolling hills. There are numerous shoal areas, but the only really narrow part of the whole system is one two-hundred-foot-long, hundred-foot-wide passage that is carefully marked by stakes. We could have spent a whole summer wandering from one spot to another in the Limfjord, and our first port after Tiburon made us want to.

We reached into the small yacht and fishing boat harbor of Lemvig at about 1630 on Saturday the twenty-sixth of May, 1973. People were working on their boats or fishing off the pier, enjoying the warm sun and light breeze. Larry spotted one empty mooring between two small yachts. "May we tie alongside the blue sloop?" he called, hoping the man on the dock spoke English. "Yes, please do," the young, curly-haired blond called back. We sailed carefully in and were told, "Hand me your bow line. I'm Charles Madsen. You're coming to our yacht club party tonight, aren't you?" We tied our lines and Larry said, "Thank you, but we don't speak any Danish." Charles didn't hesitate, "Don't worry, after six schnapps, that won't matter. But I must rush now. I'll be back for you at seven. There will be dancing and dinner, but sailing clothes only."

Charles was right on time. The yacht club party was in full progress when we arrived. We soon discovered that almost every person under thirty in Denmark spoke enough English to carry on a comfortable conversation—after the loosening effects of a few schnapps (aquavit).

It is a Danish custom to have a shotglass filled with the colorless but potent liquor next to each guest at dinner. Throughout the meal, people catch your eye, lift their glass, and say "Skol." Then everyone at the table downs the contents of his or her schnapps glass. I'm sure a person's tolerance grows with practice, but I stumbled when I was asked to dance after only two "Skols." That's when my shrewd neighbor came to the rescue. He filled a schnapps bottle with water and shared that with me.

Charles asked me to dance. "Why did you ask two complete strangers to your great party?" I wanted to know. We whirled to the international music of the Beatles and he answered, "I figured that anyone who'd sail from Canada on a boat as small as yours had to be interesting."

It was 0200 before the party started to break up. Good-byes took another half hour. We weaved outside for the ride back to the harbor. The sky was a pink and blue glow. Although it was only 0300 when we reached *Seraffyn*, we sat and watched the sun rise before we went to bed.

Charles came sailing with us the next day as we voyaged eastward between the low green banks of the fjord. He had been an Olympic Dragon sailor until he had had a frightening accident the previous year. He'd trucked his Borenson Dragon to the site of the final Olympic trials at Kiel and set to work on the deck of his boat, preparing it for the crane that was to lift it off the trailer and put it in the water. Then Charles had made one misstep and fallen to the ground, his ankle fractured in seven places. Now he'd given up international racing but his instincts for speed were still keen. "Got a spinnaker?" he asked. Soon we were tearing down the river, spinnaker flying, our lapper set like a tall boy halfway out the bowsprit. Larry put Helmer to work when we reached the final leg of our day's sail. We skimmed over the smooth water at almost full speed, the sun glowing on our decks. I spread tuna salad on crackers to serve as hors d'oeuvres, then looked out at the two absolutely contented-looking, handsome, sun-browned

Palle and Gerda sailing in company with us.

95

men. "I've got the world by the tail" was my only thought.

In 1967, Larry had been involved in a crazy, fun project. He'd organized the North American team for the first attempt to sail across the Sahara Desert. Seventeen men from six countries sailed landyachts seventeen hundred miles from Colom Bechar in Algeria to Nouak-chott in Mauritania, accompanied by several Landrovers (see *National Geographic Magazine*, November 1967). During this expedition, Larry had become close friends with Leif Møller, one of the Danish land-yachters, and we'd kept in touch through the years. And as soon as we tied in Charles's home port of Holstebro-Struer, we called Leif in Copenhagen. He was thrilled to hear from us. "You wrote me when you left California and said you'd be in Denmark in a year. It has been five. What have you been doing all that time?" Larry answered easily, "Having fun!" By good fortune we'd called Leif two days before the European Landyacht Championships. "I'll come and get you," Leif insisted. "You'll love the DN machines we use. They make the desert machines look like Landrovers compared to an XKE Jaguar."

Charles and his friends Palle and Gerda Carlsen, who had a beauti-ful varnished 5.5 sloop moored next to us, readily agreed to watch *Seraffyn*. So off we drove, crowded into Leif's sport sedan along with his girlfriend, her two young boys, sailing gear, and parts of the two disassembled landyachts that were lashed on the rooftop.

The European Championships were being held at Leif's boyhood home of Rømo, a Danish island right next to the German border. Leif was in charge of the 1973 championships, and as soon as we drove across the long causeway leading to the island, we agreed with his choice of sites. Rømo had miles of hard-packed, flat sand beaches stretching toward the North Sea. Five feet four inches tall, goateed and sandy-haired, Leif was a ball of fire and we came to call him the "Great Dane" as we watched him organizing the rest of the regatta. With his inex-haustable supply of energy he even managed to locate and help assem-ble a spare DN for Larry to sail.

German. French, Belgian, and Dutch landyachters, some of whom Larry had sailed with seven years before, arrived and soon the small inn reserved for the competitors buzzed with sailing talk.

Land yachts can make up to seventy knots with a good breeze. Because of their low resistance, they can go four or five times the wind's speed, only slightly slower than ice yachts. Sailing on one is a new experience to a water man. Landyachters learn to keep hardening

Leif Møller explains that it's best to loosen the wheel bearings on a landyacht to get the least friction.

The landyachts hit the puddle on the homestretch at over fifty miles per hour in the twenty-knot winds.

97

in their sheets as their machines gather speed because the apparent wind rapidly moves forward until the sail must be kept flat amidships even on a broad reach. Once the machine reaches the speed of the wind, the sail flutters through the wind at each jibe with none of the force it would have on the much slower water-bound sailboat.

On the day of the main races, a cool fifteen-knot wind swept the beach. Rain during the night had left puddles, and despite planning the course to avoid them, one puddle lay like an obstacle on the home-stretch. Thirty-five machines spread out over the five-mile-long course moving at close to fifty miles an hour. Each one would hit the thin sheet of water and skid through, barely under control, spray and sand flying twenty feet in the air. The colorful sails of the landyachts and the flags for each competitor's homeland added to the wonderful spectator sport of the day. One person seemed to be enjoying it more than the rest. Tom Nibbea, an American photographer doing a story on Denmark for *National Geographic* magazine, calmly shot roll after roll of film. We came to know him well during the four-day regatta.

Tough, handsome, and dark-haired, born in New York of Italian parents, Tom had been an army photographer during the Korean War. He'd then worked with newspapers until he caught the eye of *National Geographic*. He shared his knowledge of photography with us over meals of meatballs, smoked fish, and overabundant boiled potatoes. "The only way to get good photos is to use your camera," he said. "Won't do you any good sitting in its box. Have it ready all the time. Shoot lots of film. I figure I'm doing my job if I get one good transparency out of a roll of thirty-six exposures—other professional photographers use up to six rolls of film to get one good shot. Take photos of people. People love to see people. What fun is a photo of sailing unless you see the people on the boat. Figure a way to get in close to your subject, and when you are taking action shots, bracket. That is, shoot three different exposures because, especially on the water where you get lots of reflected light, it's almost impossible to get a perfect meter reading every time." Tom kept us fascinated by tales of photographic safaris to Africa, meanders through the islands of Georgia looking for the spirit of the American South, voyages to Greenland. Now he kept a home in Copenhagen. "Come see me when you get there. I think a photo of your boat sailing past Helsingor Castle would look great for a Denmark story. Got a spinnaker? What's its color?" We told him that, yes, we had a blue-and-white-striped one. "Great," Tom said as he prepared to drive home. "It's a date. We'll take a photo of you two sailing past Helsingor with your spinnaker set, in a week or two."

We promised to call Tom and Leif as soon as we reached the island of Zealand where Copenhagen is located. Then we rode back to *Seraffyn* with new Danish landyachting friends who were going right past Holstebro-Struer.

The Limfjord provided us with one of those days of sailing that make up for all the discomforts of life on a small boat. The sun was warm enough so that in spite of the fifteen-knot northerly wind we didn't need sailing jackets even while beating to windward on the first leg of our day's run. *Seraffyn* heeled to the brisk wind, challenging the tiny white horses that had only a four-mile fetch to grow in. We'd chosen the perfect sail combination for the day, a reef in our mainsail

Sailing on the Limfjord.

and the yankee jib. Water gurgled along the channels, occasional spray flew across the foredeck, but the cockpit stayed absolutely dry. I left the housework undone and joined Larry in the cockpit. We took turns working *Seraffyn* to windward, catching each puff of wind that would give us a lift toward the channel markers leading to Aalborg. Before we became hungry for lunch we reached the beacon that marked the narrow channel and were able to ease our sheets until we were on a beam reach. I went below and boiled up coffee, mixed a tossed salad, and straightened up the boat, watching the green shores slide quickly by the port lights. We ate lunch in the cockpit, wearing swimsuits, taking turns steering through the maze of stakes marking our route. Larry reminded me about Peter Pye and his voyage on *Moonraker* through these same narrow channels. Peter had said that everyone told him it was impossible to sail through the Limfjord without going aground. After three groundings, Peter had agreed. But we were forewarned. And the stakes with broom heads of twigs were laid out more carefully than in previous years, and luckily we never touched.

A few small cargo boats passed us during the afternoon. As we neared Aalborg, some local sailboats joined us on the shining river. Despite four inches of weeds growing on her bottom *Seraffyn* kept up a speed of almost six knots, and when we reached the port at Aalborg we were reluctant to stop. But that weed was a bother.

We moored in the small harbor and, as instructed by Palle Carlsen, went into the old ship's wheelhouse that sat on the breakwater acting as restaurant and yacht club. The young bartender, also the yacht club secretary, spoke perfect English and was obviously expecting us. "Palle called. We've located a club member whose boat is a similar size to yours. His cradle is free and he's offered to come down and show you how to operate the ways car." The bartender made a phone call and an hour later a friendly man in a business suit came for us. He explained how the yachtsmen from several clubs on the Limfjord had gotten together and built a do-it-yourself shipyard. Each donated a few days a year to keep the equipment in good condition and paid a very small fee. Then each member could haul his own boat in and out of the water as often as he liked at no cost.

The equipment we saw was first-rate. The car and winch were strong enough to haul the largest yacht in the Limfjord with ease. Individual metal cradles built by members to hold their boats in the winter lined the sides of the clean yard. The cradle we'd been offered needed only a small bit of blocking to accommodate *Seraffyn*'s bottom. So the next morning we set her on the cradle and hauled her out—all by ourselves. We used sand and big brushes to remove the weed that had grown after only two months on the English antifouling paint we'd used. Then we applied a coat of the cheap paint used by the fishermen in Aalborg. And early the next morning we relaunched *Seraffyn* and stored the cradle back where it had come from. We offered the waiter at the clubhouse some money toward the upkeep of the wonderfully convenient self-run shipyard. "No thanks!" he said. "Free to guests. Only members pay." We offered him a drink, but he poured us one instead.

Two days later, when we sailed clear of the Limfjord into the sound between Denmark and Sweden, Larry and I looked back wistfully. "It's like we just sailed through a farm," Larry commented. "The same tranquility, the same warm hospitality we were treated to in Virginia."

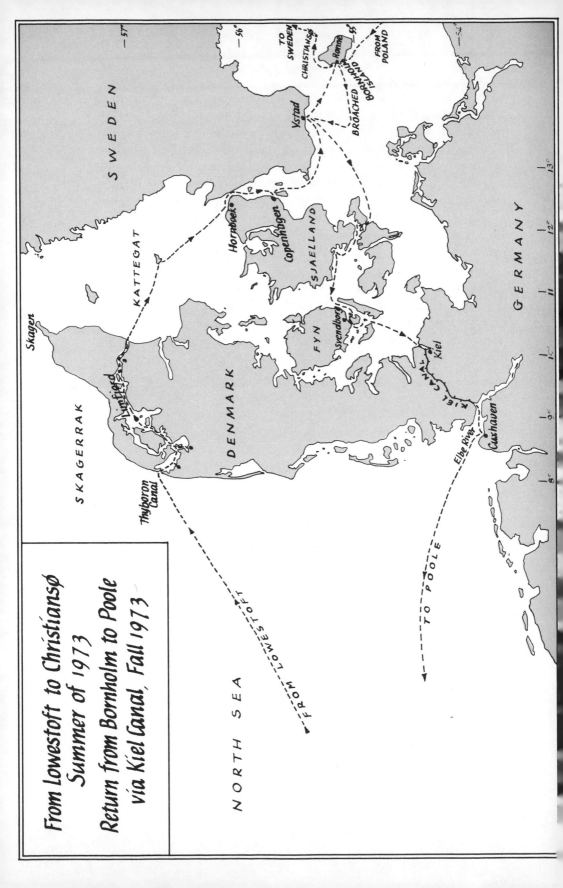

From Lowestoft to Christiansø
Summer of 1973

Return from Bornholm to Poole
via Kiel Canal, Fall 1973

CHAPTER 10

Adventures
on the Sound

We roared south through the Kattegat, all sails set. The gray clouds sifted slowly away as we approached Zealand on a broad reach. But as we drew nearer the land, the wind slowly died until we were becalmed three-quarters of a mile from the small resort harbor of Hornebek. We waited patiently for a wind, enjoying dinner in the warm flat calm. When I'd finished washing the dishes there was still no sign of a breeze. It was almost 2000 but the sun was high above the horizon.

Larry finished his brandy, decided to row in and went forward to unlash our fourteen-foot oar. I dropped the mainsail and furled it loosely in the lazy jacks, ready to use if necessary, then settled the boom in the starboard notch of the boom gallows. Larry put the oarlock and oar in the socket on the port bulwark and started rowing with a slow but steady motion, feathering the oar on the backstroke so he didn't have to lift it clear of the water. *Seraffyn* started forward. At first she tended to round toward starboard, away from the thrust of the oar, so I held the helm almost hard over. But after ten or fifteen strokes she gathered way and held a straight course with the tiller less than five degrees off center. She moved over the flat water at about a knot.

Evening strollers watched us as we moved slowly toward the high stone seawall. Our chart showed little clearance on either side of the sixty-foot-wide dredged channel for *Seraffyn*'s four-foot eight-inch draft, so Larry switched the oar from the rowing position to the sculling lock on the taffrail. We lost a bit of speed as Larry sculled instead of rowed, but *Seraffyn* became much more maneuverable.

When we could see inside the harbor, I did a double take. The three-hundred-yard-wide, five-hundred-yard-long harbor was almost filled to the brim. Larry began pulling in one direction with the sculling oar and *Seraffyn* turned in a tight 360-degree arc. This gave me time to prepare our mooring lines. When I was ready, Larry began sculling like the French fishermen do and *Seraffyn* moved forward into the crowded harbor.

We came to a stop, *Seraffyn*'s boomkin was only about twenty feet inside the entrance. But that was as far as we could go. Boats were tied five and six deep along the walls. The only open space in the whole harbor was a fifteen- or twenty-foot-wide passage from the pilot boat's mooring to the entrance.

The man on the thirty-foot motor sailer nearest the entrance helped us tie up alongside and said, "This is nothing. Wait till June twentieth when the schools let out. Then there won't be room even for you in any harbor on Zealand if you arrive after 1700." When the harbormaster came five minutes later, he also told us of the crowds he expected in two or three weeks' time. "Every yachtsman in Germany seems to head over here for the summer. So the Danes all head north to Swedish waters, the Swedes head north to Finland, and I don't know where the Finns go." This was the first harbor we'd visited in Denmark that charged us harbor dues, the equivalent of $1.50 for the night. During the rest of our Baltic cruise, only three other harbors charged us fees.

Leif Møller joined us the next morning. His unsuppressed eagerness opened our eyes. *Seraffyn* had been our home for over three years. I'd never say we'd become blasé about the world she opened to us, but it was interesting to look at our lifestyle through someone else's eyes. Although Leif was a naval architect and the head of the Danish division of Lloyd's ship surveyors, up until this time his sailing, other than land yachting, had been limited to afternoon excursions in dinghies or on friends' small weekend cruisers.

We had to be out of Hornebek harbor by 0800 so boats tied inboard of us could keep their rendezvous. Leif pitched right in, learning the ropes quickly as we reached out of the crowded harbor. Once we were under way he seemed to step back and realize that he was actually in our home. A fresh breeze filled in from the north and we set the lapper and mainsail. Then Larry put Helmer to work. I poured hot coffee and set out a plate of fresh buttered toast. Leif settled back in the cockpit and began to fire questions at us.

"Where are you headed now?"

Larry answered, "Generally north, wherever things look interesting."

"What's your schedule?"

"Haven't got any," I replied. "We have money enough to cruise until next December. Our only date before then is Tallinn in Estonia, August 10, if we can get our Russian visas finalized."

Leif thought about the idea of no schedule for a few minutes and then said, "Surely you have plans for winter? You have a job planned somewhere."

Larry told him, "We've got some ideas, no plans. I'd like to find a really first-rate shipyard somewhere here in Denmark and work building new wooden boats. I know I'd learn a lot and the Danish consulate told me Canadians can work in Denmark easily. But we'll worry about that when winter comes. Right now we've got the whole Baltic to explore." We could see that we'd given Leif something new to think about.

We took a roundabout route through the sound, skimming past the small island of Ven, an often-disputed piece of land exactly halfway between Sweden and Denmark. Then Leif pointed south to an island barely showing above water. "That's where the two countries have been considering building a bridge. All sorts of studies have been going on. Of course, the shipping lines are against the bridge—their ferries would become obsolete. But the funniest thing about it was the fight in Parliament. One M.P. said, 'I know how to save Denmark millions of kronor during the next years. We'll cancel all plans for a bridge to Sweden.' Our renegade Parliament member, Glistrup, a man who always embarrasses the government, piped up, "I know how to save even more millions. We'll plan a bridge all the way to Germany. That will cost ten times more than a bridge to Sweden. Then, to save money, we'll cancel it!' "

As we reached into the main harbor at Copenhagen, past the diminutive bronze mermaid made famous by Hans Christian Anderson and Danny Kaye, Leif told us more about living in Denmark. "We Danes pay forty-seven percent of our income in direct taxes and fifteen percent more in indirect taxes. So almost all of us have started trading labor to avoid the tax man. Carpenters build new rooms for farmers in exchange for fresh meat or produce. Everyone has a deal. That's the only way we can live so well. Denmark, Sweden, it's almost the same. Wonderfully safe places to live, but not much adventure left. Our generation is doing well. It's the people still in school I worry about. There just aren't enough challenging skilled jobs for them when they graduate. More and more young people are becoming craftsmen and artisans instead of becoming doctors and lawyers."

Our discussion of politics flourished as we ran out of Copenhagen's harbor. Leif pointed toward two huge storage tanks about four miles past the entrance. "That's the yacht club harbor. My friends are expecting you."

We could see dinghies and small cruisers sailing into the yacht club. From a distance they looked like Folkboats and Spitsgatters. Larry had often told me about the Spitsgatters of Denmark, chubby double-ended boats designed with clean simple rigs that had no backstays at all. Their rigs consisted of three wires, a forestay and two shrouds attached three-quarters of the way up the extra-stout mast. The shrouds were carried to a position about two feet aft of the mast. Larry said, "I raced against some Spitsgatters in Vancouver. They used to carry spinnakers in pretty heavy winds, but I never saw one loose its rig."

The race boats were inside the harbor before we reached the entrance, but seven boats came pouring out through the narrow entrance as we approached and rushed to meet us, foghorns blaring, shouts of "Welcome to Sundby Yacht Club" coming from Clockamaker, one of Leif's friends we'd met at the landyacht championships (and a clockmaker by profession).

We turned to Leif in surprise. "Super reception, but how did they know when to expect us?" Leif looked smug when he said, "Danish efficiency! We gave the coast guard a description of your boat and they reported each time we passed one of their observation posts—Helsingor Castle, Ven Island, each entrance to Copenhagen."

Clockamaker yelled, "I'll tow you in. Here's a line."

But the fun, confusion, and excitement made Larry rise to the occasion. "We've sailed this far, we'll sail her in. Thanks anyway."

Leif looked at Larry. "Can you? It's a terribly small entrance." Larry glanced at our chart, then at the narrow hundred-foot-long channel leading to a forty-foot-wide opening between two low stone breakwaters. Inside we could see a crowd of yachts lying stern-to at low wooden piers, bows to mooring buoys and pilings. The entrance was dead to windward. "Well," Larry commented, "if a Folkboat can do it, so can we. Besides, we've said we'll do it, so we will. Might need a few practice runs, though."

Leif shouted to his friends in Danish. Larry and I listened to some sort of argument as we reached back and forth in front of the entrance. Finally Leif laughed and translated, "Half say you can't do it. Half say you can. All of them are worried about how long you look with your bowsprit. They can't believe your hull is as short as a Folkboat." The wonderful crowd of spectators moved to the side of the channel and Larry told us, "Don't worry, absolutely no swell or sea. Worst thing that could happen is to run aground and be embarrassed." We took a practice run, short-tacking up the sixty-foot-wide channel. "The wind is slightly more favorable on the starboard tack," Larry said as we came near the rocks of the breakwater. "Let's bail out and try it again so we're on the starboard tack when we're next to the entrance. Leif, you let the mainsheet loose. Lin, you back the jib." Larry pushed the helm to windward and the backed jib quickly spun *Seraffyn*'s bow around for the run out the channel. "Come on, Larry, let's take a tow," I pleaded. "It won't hurt just this one time." But Leif was caught up in Larry's little game because he answered, "Why not try it? If Larry isn't worried, why should we be?"

We winched in the sails and took three tacks. Then came the moment of truth. Larry tacked within ten feet of the starboard breakwater end. He gave *Seraffyn* lots of time to gather way, then pulled her as close to the wind as she could go. "Leif, stand on the leeward deck and be ready to fend off that piling," Larry called as he pulled the tiller to leeward quickly. *Seraffyn*'s mainsail luffed for just thirty seconds and her five and a half tons of weight helped carry us through the breakwater's entrance. *Seraffyn* heeled to the twelve-knot breeze and Leif, with his usual sense of the ridiculous, kissed his fingertips, then tapped the top of the closest piling lightly as it slid by less than nine inches from our shrouds. "We made it!" I yelled as a blast went up from our escorts. We tacked again into the open area in front of the club and headed toward the space Leif had reserved for us. Then we ran into one of the underwater lines leading to the main mooring chains. *Seraffyn* stopped short. Larry rushed forward and let go the anchor before we drifted into any other boats. Then we launched the dinghy and warped into the pier. "Not bad," Leif said as we tied our lines. I repeated his comment, but Larry was busy analyzing how we could have sailed all the way in if only we'd tacked sooner after we'd cleared the entrance.

He didn't have long to speculate. Our reception committee moored their boats and descended on us. I exhausted our supply of eight wine glasses and eight coffee mugs, and more were borrowed from the clubhouse so we could share our duty-free whiskey with Leif's wonderful collection of yachting friends. The party moved to the buffet in the clubhouse and lasted until midnight. Danish and English mingled in the warm atmosphere, and I took time off before climbing wearily into the bunk to record my favorite comment of the evening in our logbook. I laughed to myself as I remember being told, "One of our members *circumsized* the world."

Leif spent the night at home and arrived late the next day with Tom Nibbea. Tom's reaction was typical of most people who have never been on a sailboat. He stood on the pier, stared, and then said, "You live inside that? Your boat isn't much bigger than a rowboat." We persuaded him to come on board. After he was seated in the cockpit enjoying the warm sun, a rum punch in one hand, fresh hot bread in the other, Tom began to believe we did indeed live on *Seraffyn*. "Arrangements are all made," Tom told us. "Leif has made it possible to hire a pilot boat tomorrow morning and will act as translator. Can you have your spinnaker up?" Larry glanced at the telltales lifting to a caressing breeze. "No problem. Where will we meet you?"

Tom told us to rendezvous in the pilot harbor just south of Helsingor at 0900, then left to rush and take photos of a Great Dane kennel for his Denmark story.

We didn't leave Sundby Yacht Club until almost 2100 because of one last drink with twenty different new friends. So by the time we'd cleared the harbor and headed north, it was growing dark. Leif was firmly entrenched at the helm as a soft offshore breeze carried us along on a reach. "Go catch some sleep," Larry suggested to both Lief and me. But Leif replied, "This is the first time I've ever been sailing at night." So Larry said, "Okay, call me in two hours and I'll take over."

Five hours and twenty miles later, Leif woke us both. "Helsingor Harbor just ahead." Larry glanced at his watch and told me to stay in bed if I wanted to. He climbed out of the bunk, then asked Leif, "Why didn't you call me sooner?" Leif sounded tired but content when he said, "I didn't want to miss one minute of this. It was like being in command of a magic carpet."

It was just daybreak when Larry and Leif finished furling the sails.

But it was only 0230 so everyone turned in for some sleep. The only sound in the quiet harbor came from a pair of garrulous seagulls.

I dreamed someone was throwing rocks on our decks. Larry turned in his sleep and my mind scrambled into reality. Someone *was* throwing rocks on our deck. Not only that, but our rigging was shrieking to a heavy wind. I rushed into the main cabin and pulled on my sweater and jeans. Larry was close behind me. Leif yawned in the quarter berth. The sound of rocks hitting the decks persisted and I flung open the sliding hatch and couldn't believe the strength of the wind—it was lifting dust, sand, and half-inch pebbles from the street we were tied next to. *Seraffyn*'s decks were almost covered. Each gust of wind caused a new barrage of pebbles to hit the cabin sides. I pulled the hatch closed quickly to keep as much of the debris out of the cabin as possible, but as I did Larry noticed six armed policemen approaching.

"Leif, are you sure we're supposed to be here?" Larry asked after describing the officials.

Leif climbed out of his berth and opened the canvas companionway covering. The official in the lead set off in a barrage of Danish. Within minutes all of the policemen were laughing. Leif asked us to come on deck. We shook hands with each police officer before they walked off. Leif was chuckling as he pointed to what remained of our old Canadian ensign. We'd accidently left it up during the night and the unexpected gale-force winds had torn almost two-thirds of the flag to bits. All that remained was the red inner portion and about an inch of white. Leif told us, "The NATO post saw your flag and thought you were Polish defectors looking for asylum."

Larry and I laughed at that. But all of a sudden I remembered Tom Nibbea. "We can't possibly go out in this wind to take photos," I said as I poured coffee and tea. Larry listened as more pebbles hit the deck. "If Tom shows up, we'll have to. He's gone to a lot of trouble making arrangements."

As soon as breakfast was over, we went on deck just in time to see Tom come running down the street, camera case in one hand, light meter in the other, two cameras around his neck. He was grinning from ear to ear. "Fantastic, look at those clouds, look at the color of Kronenberg Castle's roof!" We had to agree with him, but Larry did say "No spinnakers today."

So Leif and Tom departed and, as we put two reefs in our mainsail and prepared to run out of the small basin, we heard a forty-five-foot pilot boat start its diesel engine. We cleared the entrance and flew onto a white-capped sea, then hove to. The pilot boat came alongside and Leif translated back and forth for Tom, the pilot, and us. He yelled over the wind's whistle, "Deep water within eight meters of the shore in front of the castle. Wind is Force 9, current is running south about one knot. But it won't set you onshore. You sail, the pilot will stay out of your way."

So, as soon as Larry and I had finished sweeping the sand and pebbles from our cockpit, we ran south one mile past Helsingor Castle, the pilot boat clinging to our wake. Tom climbed all over the pilot boat, pointing first his camera at us, then his light meter. Then he yelled, "Okay, go the other way."

We came about and sheeted *Seraffyn*'s staysail and reefed main in until we were just five degrees off a beat and all of a sudden felt the full force of the wind. Sheets of spray flew across our sharply heeled deck. All of the sand flushed away within minutes and *Seraffyn* flew through the water with a huge bone in her teeth. Five times we beat past that castle only to turn and run back again. The pilot boat was handled superbly, sometimes ranging within ten feet of our beam but never disturbing us. Tom shot off two rolls of film, looking quite

The cover shot of *Seraffyn* passing Helsingor Castle. This was the setting for Shakespeare's *Hamlet*.

satisfied. Then an hour and a half later Leif yelled, "Meet you in the yacht harbor north of the castle. Tom wants to buy you lunch."

The pilot boat peeled away and we started the two-mile beat to the shelter of the yacht haven. It took us over an hour to beat the tide. We were soaked and tired from the hard work of sailing with such a strong wind. But Tom made up for that during a good lunch of *frikadeller* (meatballs) by saying, "Even if *National Geographic* uses one of these transparencies, I took enough really good ones to give you something exciting for your own use." He went on to tell us, "All of the best sailing photos are set-ups like we did today. The only way to get a good picture of a boat is to have a maneuverable stable motorboat to shoot from." We'd learned a tremendous amount from Tom, and he kept his promise by providing us with the photo that eventually graced the dust cover of our first book, *Cruising in Seraffyn*.

That evening the wind dropped and in the morning we set our biggest sails to head toward Sweden. Halfway there we ran completely out of wind. "Now what do you do?" Leif asked, looking toward the land which lay at least six miles away.

"Relax and enjoy it," Larry told him. And soon Leif did. Larry showed him a favorite spot of ours, lounging back against a sailbag on the sunny foredeck. We produced some of our favorite sailing books. Then I set to work doing some mending while Larry answered letters. We had dinner in the cockpit, *Seraffyn* motionless on the flat warm sea.

"How often have you been becalmed like this?" Leif asked.

We thought over our three and a half years of sailing and concluded that we'd had about a hundred hours of absolutely no wind. Leif put it right when he answered, "When you've got your home with you, a day becalmed is just like a lazy Sunday ashore."

We took a sounding at dark and found bottom at thirty-five feet. We were well clear of shipping. So we set our anchor, lit our anchor light, and set a bunk out in the cockpit for Leif. When we awoke, a light breeze was blowing across the sound and we sailed into a tiny port where Leif could catch a ferry for home and his busy work schedule. As he left, Leif called back to us, "I'm going to get a boat like yours someday. The past five days of sailing have been better for me than a month's holiday."

After he left we sat back and talked about how fortunate we were. Leif's enthusiasm had made us doubly appreciative of the joys of our floating life.

～～～

CHAPTER 11

Into the Baltic

There wasn't a ship on the horizon when we sailed from the small Swedish harbor of Ysted about three days later. Bornholm Island lay dead to windward, forty miles northeast of us. But with an absolutely flat sea and five or six knots of wind, beating was a pleasure. This was what *Seraffyn* was designed for. We set our 180-square-foot mainsail and our 369-square-foot number-one genoa. *Seraffyn* heeled about eight or ten degrees and made the sunlit sea chuckle past her sharp bow.

We headed north along Sweden's green-cliffed shore, Helmer steering, the two of us comfortably reading in the cockpit. The roar of large high-speed engines carried toward us from upwind and Larry got up and looked around. A gray launch was headed directly toward us. As it came closer, we could see seven or eight uniformed men on board. The launch carried no flag. I put up our Canadian ensign, remembering the flag incident in Helsingor. But the launch roared determinedly toward us. When it was about forty feet away, the helmsman shut down his engines and yelled in accented English, "Where are you headed?"

Larry called back, "Ronne Harbor, on Bornholm."

The helmsman answered, "Please keep moving and clear the area as soon as possible. There is a NATO exercise on and we wish to use the cliffs behind you for target practice."

We waved to let them know that we understood. Then the helmsman pulled his throttles full on and roared off seaward.

As *Seraffyn* continued chuckling along at about four knots we noticed a whole flotilla of warships massing on the horizon. Fifteen minutes later the same launch charged at us again. "Can't you get a move on?" an English naval officer yelled. "You're costing NATO thousands of pounds an hour!"

We tried to oblige by putting up our staysail. Three hundred yards away from us the NATO launch idled and gurgled as *Seraffyn* beat determinedly past the cliffs. Thirty minutes later the launch turned dead to seaward and its engines came alive as it roared off at full throttle. Then we heard the first thud of heavy artillery and felt shock-waves through the cockpit sole as each shell exploded against the peaceful green cliffs we'd passed.

We beat into Ronne, the main harbor on the Danish island of Bornholm at 0230 the next morning. The sun was up and so was the harbormaster. He helped us secure *Seraffyn* in a corner of the fishing port, then told us, "In twenty-four hours this harbor will be full because the fishing fleet will all come in for the Midsummer's Night festivities. Come see me in the morning and I'll tell you where the best things happen."

When he left, Larry and I climbed into our bunk. We tossed and turned, trying to fall asleep in the bright sunshine at 0300. Finally Larry went on deck and covered the two deadlights with a sailbag. He set another sailbag on the deadlight in the hatch. We both quickly fell asleep in the dark forepeak.

The harbormaster met us at the seaman's club at noon and bombarded us with descriptions of Midsummer's Night. Since the very best festival would be at the northeast end of the island, and since no buses ran on holidays, we decided to splurge and rent a car. When the harbormaster heard this, he insisted on calling a friend at Sveneke where the festivities would be held. "Go up there today," the harbormaster told us. "My friend is expecting you and will include you in on all activities."

We stopped at least five different times during our fifteen-mile drive across the soft green plains of Bornholm. We'd only been under way ten minutes when Larry slammed on the brakes. "Did you see that?" he asked as he put the car in reverse. I had been engrossed, watching birds flying from a reed-covered lake on my side of the car. As soon as we'd backed up a hundred or so yards I saw what Larry was so interested in. A red thatch-roofed farmhouse stood by the road, shaded by dark pine trees. Behind the house was a large red barn surrounded by piles of straw-covered thatch. Three men were busy sewing bundles of thatch on the wooden latticework that rested on the rafters of the barn's roof.

The barn's owner saw us watching from the car and came over. We greeted him, using one of the five Danish words that made up our vocabulary. But he immediately sensed that our native language was English and invited us to take a closer look. "The last time that roof was rethatched was twenty years ago," the owner told us. He went on to explain that the thatch they were using was actually reeds cut from frozen lakes during the winter. "It's hard to find men who have the skill to do a good job of thatching," he told us. "I had to engage this group a year in advance."

We kept the rented car for five days, driving from one end of Bornholm to the other. Tiny man-made fishing boat harbors dotted its shore, some of them with entrances less than forty feet wide. We made friends with two of Sveneke's fishermen, using the kind introduction of Ronne's harbormaster. And after the dancing, singing, and huge bonfire of the Midsummer's Night festival, Larry set off to watch as they hauled in their herring nets. I flopped on the backseat of the car and slept.

The next morning we drove back past the red barn and admired its new twelve-inch-thick, carefully trimmed, gold-colored thatched roof. Then we returned to Ronne and turned in our rented car. We were shocked at the sixty dollars it had cost until we considered the benefits. In a place where the cruising season is as limited as the Baltic, we had to use the time we had carefully. We would never have been able to join in the fun of Midsummer's Night, nor have come to know the central lakes and beautiful farmlands of Bornholm any other way. But if we had a larger boat, a small motorcycle or two bicycles would have been a treat and a money-saver.

Before we left Ronne harbor on June 24, 1973, everyone was telling us, "This weather is some of the best we've had in years!" We skimmed northeast along Bornholm's cliffy shores wearing only bathing suits as we passed a ruined castle clinging to the cliff tops. Then we turned and reached into the neat, grass-fringed harbor of Hammershus. Three Danish yachts and one German one lay against the seawall. We had barely secured our mooring lines and fenders when the harbormaster arrived. "Beautiful harbor you have," Larry said by the way of a greeting. The harbormaster smiled as he glanced around the peaceful scene. "Yes," he chuckled "but in every paradise there

Though we'd seen many thatched roofs in England and Denmark, this was the first time we'd had a chance to see how they were made.

These herrings would be smoked and served as Bornholmers, a fish delicacy known throughout Scandinavia.

is a snake. I have come to collect your harbor dues."

The people off the German ketch came by and, after looking through *Seraffyn,* invited us to come and share some schnapps. Werner gave us a tour of the forty-five-foot ketch he used as sailing school boat for people wanting to get their offshore sailors license. He was surprised to hear that no licensing of any kind was required of North American pleasure sailors. We discussed the relative merits of the voluntary system of sailing education available to Canadians and Americans compared with the compulsary licensing enforced in most of Europe.

One of Werner's students broke up the conversation by saying, "Enough serious talk. How about playing some music?" So Werner grabbed his accordion and a crewman came back from the galley carrying a broomstick with two pie plates nailed loosely to one end, a washbasin tacked on the side of the stick, and two nylon strings secured from the stick ends across the basin. Werner squeezed his accordion until the boat rang with the strains of a familiar-sounding polka. The crewman thumped his "devil's violin" on the cabin sole, plucking its two strings. The tins rattled and clanged in rhythm and ten of us swayed to the music. My feet itched for room to dance and I knew Larry felt the same as he put his arm around my shoulders and squeezed. We sang and listened as the sun set and rose again. Once more we had to cover our forepeak deadlights when we finally went home to get some sleep.

"Who controls Christiansø, controls the Baltic," eighteenth-century naval experts said of the two tiny islands north of Bornholm. We couldn't quite believe these miniscule dots of land had such an important place in history until we sailed into the tiny but very protected natural harbor that lay between them. The islands consisted of less than fifteen acres of land but had always been the home of fishermen, merchant sailors, and smugglers. Several years ago the Danish government declared the islands a national museum, so the beautiful yellow stone buildings with red tile roofs looked as they must have three or four hundred years ago. The 112 fishermen who now live on Christiansø are often ice- or weather-bound for three or four weeks in the winter. But in the summer their quiet island population is increased by artists who come from the mainland, attracted by the island's crystal-clear light.

Once each day from June to September a ferry full of tourists arrives and stays for three hours. But when it leaves the quiet peaceful mood of the enchanted islands returns.

On the first evening of our stay, the mayor arrived to welcome us. Mr. Jacobsen shared a glass of whiskey in our cockpit as he told us about the islands. He'd been appointed mayor five years before, and explained, "I have thirteen titles besides: justice of the peace, head of sanitation, curator, . . . and the amazing thing is, the government sends me a separate check for each job! I get eighteen dollars a year as head of sanitation, thirty-five as justice of the peace."

Our second afternoon in Christiansø we watched a handsome forty-seven-foot yawl enter the harbor flying an American flag. This was the first non-Scandinavian, non-German yacht we'd seen since we'd entered the Limfjord. The harbormaster came running down the stone pier and told the American yacht to moor in the nonexistent

The only change on Christiansø Island that is visible from the sea is the lighthouse on top of the castle.

space between us and a thirty-foot Swedish sloop. With an anchor set astern, two lines ashore, and eight people tugging, shoving, and pulling, *Puffin* was squeezed into her designated spot. We tried to help, adjusting our fenders and fending off. But none of our efforts seemed to ease the look of horror on the face of the gray-haired lady who stood staring at our protruding five-sixteenths-inch-thick solid-bronze chain plates which threatened to gouge *Puffin*'s topsides if any fender popped out of place. We've been told before that our external chainplates—standing four inches out from *Seraffyn*'s hull on channels—are unsociable, and after learning that *Puffin* had just had a complete refit, during which hundreds of dollars had been spent to give her topsides a magnificent glowing white finish, we were extra sympathetic.

As soon as *Puffin* was squeezed in and well fendered, the introductions began. The gray-haired lady broke into a beautiful twinkling smile and said, "I'm Betty Greeff. This is my husband Ed and my ten-year-old grandson Geoffrey." We also met the rest of *Puffin*'s summer crew, all New Yorkers—Pam and Bill Kellett and their thirteen-year-old daughter Allison, and Harry Anderson. Every inch of *Puffin* proclaimed the art of wooden boat building, and when Ed invited us to have a look on board we gladly accepted. *Puffin* was a Sparkman and Stevens–designed CCA ocean racer/cruiser. She'd been built for the Greeffs in 1969 by the Walstead Yacht Yard in Thruro, Denmark.

After five years of extensive racing and cruising *Puffin* needed a refit, so Ed sailed her back from New York to the yard that had built her. Walstead's took care of her during the winter while the Greeffs flew home to New York. In the spring the Greeffs and their crew of friends arrived in Denmark to find a *Puffin* that looked almost like new.

Larry was into every nook and cranny of *Puffin*, firing questions at Ed about her construction. He pointed out her varnished frames and told me, "That's locust [acacia], just like the timber we cut and stored in Virginia last year. I knew it would make good frames if we built another boat." *Puffin* was beautifully constructed of teak, mahogany, locust, and oak, bronze fastened. After hearing about the special laminating methods used by Walstead's, Larry asked Ed, "Do you think Walstead could use an extra shipwright this winter?" Ed told us about the three boats Walstead's yard planned to start and said that Mr. Walstead, like most boat builders, complained about a shortage of skilled help.

When we went on board *Seraffyn* later that afternoon, Larry said,

Puffin, owned by Ed and Betty Greeff. Length overall, 47'; load waterline, 35'; beam, 12.5'; draft, 8'; sail area, 1,048 square feet.

"Lin, I know what I want to do this winter! I want to try and get a job at Walstead's. I know I'd learn a hell of a lot about boat building there. Ed says there are cottages for rent near the boatyard. We could get one and live ashore while we did up *Seraffyn's* interior varnish." I loved the enthusiastic look Larry had and readily agreed that a winter in Denmark might prove to be a lot of fun, as long as we had a warm, cozy place to live.

Puffin lay alongside us for two days and we found once again that youngsters belong on cruising boats. Geoffrey and Allison kept everyone delighted with their observations. The morning *Puffin* was preparing to sail, Betty Greeff told us, "Yesterday after dinner we had the kids sit down and draw pictures of boats they'd like to own. Allison drew a lovely picture of *Puffin*. But Geoffrey drew one of your boat, and not too diplomatically said, 'I like *Seraffyn* because she is just the right size for a boy like me to sail by myself.'"

We waved good-bye as *Puffin* and her friendly crew powered out the narrow entrance of Christiansø then we took our towels and a book each and found a spot where we could sunbath comfortably on the warm rocks. That afternoon Larry brought up one of the problems that faced us as we cruised the Baltic. "We'd better get moving if we want to see any of the Finnish islands," he said. "I know Christiansø is beautiful, but there are only two or three months of decent weather left." Our years of casual meandering in the tropics, during which we'd often stopped for a night and stayed a month, had spoiled us. But neither of us had any desire to spend six months iced into a winter in Finland, although in retrospect that might have proved interesting.

We had coffee and cakes that evening with Mr. Jacobsen, and Larry mentioned that we planned to set sail within an hour or two. He went on to ask, "The wind is from the south so it would be quite tricky to sail out the southern entrance. Is it possible to have the bridge opened so we can sail between the islands?"

"Of course it is," Mr. Jacobsen replied. "All you have to do is ask the mayor."

So after we'd finished our coffee, Larry and I went back on board and prepared *Seraffyn*. It was 2200 and the sun was almost on the horizon as we pulled *Seraffyn* back to her stern anchor.

Mr. Jacobsen waved from the winding wheel at the end of the bridge and started turning its handle. The bridge slowly swung open and Larry pulled up our lapper, then came aft and hauled our stern anchor on board. I sheeted the lapper in and steered as *Seraffyn* gathered way. Larry had the mainsail up and pulling wing and wing as we passed the open bridge. We called good-bye to our Christiansø friends and were out onto the open sea in less than five minutes.

We set the jib on the spinnaker pole, Helmer took command, and I drew the first watch. I wore shorts and a sweatshirt and read on the afterdeck as we ran north at about four knots. At 2330 the sun set, but I still had enough light to read by. At 0130 the sun rose, a glowing gold disk over a smooth gray sea. At 0155 I woke Larry with a cup of hot chocolate. Then I climbed into the bunk and quickly fell asleep as *Seraffyn* ran steadily on toward Sweden's twenty thousand islands.

CHAPTER 12

Twenty Thousand Islands

W hen Larry was nineteen he'd fallen in love with a twenty-seven-foot Tumlaren-class sloop designed by Knud Reimers and called *Annalisa*. She'd been built by the Kungsor yard near Stockholm in 1948 for the crown prince of Denmark. By taking a bank loan, countersigned by his father, Larry had been able to buy the completely varnished sloop and for five years he raced and cruised her around Vancouver. From the time I met him, two years after he sold *Annalisa*, Larry had raved about his magnificent sloop. I'd almost grown jealous for *Seraffyn* as he described the extreme lightweight, scientific construction of the narrow, delicate Tumlaren. *Seraffyn* is twenty-four feet four inches long with a beam of nine feet, and weighs close to eleven thousand pounds. *Annalisa*, at twenty-seven feet on deck, was only six feet wide and displaced only thirty-eight hundred pounds. As we cruised north through Sweden's multitude of islands I came to appreciate the ideas behind the Tumlaren's design. She, like the much better known Folkboat class (see Appendix B), had been created for families who had protected waters to sail in. From a hundred fifty miles south of Stockolm north to Finland and east to Helsinki, a stretch of over six hundred miles, there are so many islands and anchorages that there is never a need to be more than four or five miles from land. The islands keep the seas flat with only occasional chop. Tiny villages dot the archipelagos so a family cruiser need carry only a few days' worth of supplies. But the intricate passages among the rocks and islands require boats that are handy to tack and close-winded, boats that accelarate quickly to use each puff of wind that whispers around the points and trees. These boats are built light to save money since they can only be used three or four months out of the year. We saw hundreds of them throughout Sweden and Denmark, and many are sailed without engines.

On the other hand, Swedish yachtsmen were fastinated by husky, beamy *Seraffyn* with her high lifelines, bulwarks, self-draining cockpit, and heavily stayed rig. "We don't see many real oceangoing yachts here," several sailors told us when we tied in Borgholm on Kalmar Island en route to the Stockholm Archipelago. We were moored among at least three dozen small cruisers, and *Seraffyn* did look different. One Swedish couple came by three or four times and stood whispering to each other on the dockside. I was just serving Larry a drink and so I called to them, "Do you speak English?" As we had come to expect, they answered yes. So I said, "Come have a drink with us." Breta and Walter Nathansen came on board and we soon had all our Swedish charts out as they described their favorite anchorages from Oland north to Finland. They saw my dinner set out ready to cook and left after only one hour, but pointed to their large steel ketch, moored at the far side of the harbor. "Come over after you eat," Walter insisted. "I have something I want to give you."

Two hours later we were on board the Nathansens' specially built Baltic cruiser. Walter, a Stockholm architect, explained, "The season up here is just too short for me to have a normal boat. This one has one-inch steel plating on the keel and three-quarter-inch plating at the waterline so as soon as the ice breakers clean a channel in the spring, I can set off cruising." I noticed the huge hot-water radiators everywhere in the carefully insulated accommodations.

As the evening drew pleasantly on, Walter commented, "I want you to visit my archipelago," and then he brought out a chart with a circle around a group of forty or fifty tiny islands. He'd drawn a course along the path he felt was safe for us and then a pencil line we were to follow through the island group with an *X* where he felt we could anchor comfortably. "I've written a note to our caretaker telling him to give you fresh fish and strawberries. I'll use my radio to contact my son who should be on the islands holidaying with his family."

As we sailed north, closer to the Stockholm Archipelago, we started studying the detail charts. Although each chart only covered twenty to thirty miles, some showed as many as a hundred islands and islets. The charts clearly showed every possible danger in the main channels. Lights and beacons abounded in carefully thought-out positions. But large areas of each chart were lined off and the legend on the chart explained, "These areas are not fully charted for reasons of military security." Stora Nassa, the place Walter had called "my archipelago," was inside one of these "not fully charted" areas.

It was great sailing among the gray rocky outer islands of Sweden. Evergreen trees clung to each one. Most had no inhabitants at all except for an occasional camping family with a small runabout. Others had wooden summer cottages on them. We moored at Sandhamn, the Stockholm Sailing Club's out-station, and when we raved about the wonderful weather, light breezes, and warm sunshine, several Swedes informed us, "So far this is one of the best summers in recorded history." We were also told, "Wait till you get to the Oland Islands and Finland. There are so many islands and anchorages there that if you want company at night you leave your ensign up when you anchor. But if you want to be all alone so you can go nude, you take your ensign down and no one will stop within sight of you."

We set sail from Sandhamn on one of the few blustery, cool, cloudy days we had that summer. As we tacked east, deeper into the archipelago, a light spray flew across our decks. But we didn't consider putting on wet-weather gear since the spray was fresh water and dried within minutes. That's one of the treats of Baltic sailing. Once you are north of Bornholm Island, there is so little salt in the water you can wash your hair and clothes right off the boat and feel great. Near Finland the water is almost good enough to drink. From the beginning of July until the middle of September we were surprised to find that less than three hundred miles from Arctic Circle the water was warm enough for swimming, especially on sunny days.

We followed the main shipping route north, glad to have a definite goal. Otherwise we'd have never been able to choose which channels to sail through. We reached the striped lighthouse on the third island north of Moja after two pleasant day sails and turned onto a compass course of ninety-two degrees. A warm southerly wind gave us a perfect beam reach. As soon as we'd sailed half a mile we were into the "not fully charted" area.

I stood on the foredeck holding the chart, watching for rocks while Larry kept reassuring me, "The Nathansens have been taking this route several times a year for forty years, Lin. If there were any dangers, Walter would have told us. His boat draws two feet more than *Seraffyn,* so as long as we stick to his bearings there can't be much danger."

Within a few miles the islands began to be farther apart. Fewer and fewer had trees on them. Soon the only islands in view were bare granite rocks less than fifty feet high. Our taffrail log showed we'd gone seven miles when we spotted the "island with one short tree" that marked our first course change. We skirted the island, keeping a hundred yards off as Walter's pencil line indicated. When we could lay a course of seventy degrees with the tree dead on our stern, we eased our sheets and ran for the designated four miles. Each ten or fifteen minutes Larry took a bearing over our stern, sighting on the lone tree to make sure we weren't being set off our course by a current or inaccurate steering. I practically wore Walter's chart out taking cross bearings, marking our advancing position and calculating our speed.

Fifty minutes later we resumed a course of ninety-two degrees and dead ahead of us, five miles distant, lay a cluster of islands. As they grew closer we encountered one of the most difficult problems of navigation—judging distance and height. How long is two miles, how high is 135 feet, how wide is a ninety-foot channel? Walter's archipelago covered only about four square inches on our large-scale chart. I took our dividers out and scaled this off to find forty-seven islands and several hundred rocks squeezed into an area two miles by three miles. The channel we were to run through had a spot that was less than sixty feet wide.

Seraffyn was quickly closing on the islands so I brought the chart on deck. Larry looked over my notations and asked, "Which islands do we sail between?" I went on the foredeck to search the islands for a clue, then called back, "I just can't say for sure, they all look the same to me. What do we do?"

"I'll head into the wind, you drop the jib," Larry called. "Then we'll heave to and figure this out." With her mainsail sheeted in hard, jib down in the jib net, *Seraffyn* headed close to the wind and our speed dropped from five knots to almost nothing in the twelve-knot breeze. We lay the chart out on the cockpit floor and took bearings on each end of the archipelago. The cross put us half a mile off the entrance. The two 135-foot-high rocks with only a thin ribbon of water between them *were* the ones we were supposed to sail between.

"Okay, Lin, let's set the staysail instead of the lapper. No need to sail into a strange situation at full speed. If things don't look right, we can reach back out here." So I hoisted the 104-square-foot staysail, Larry sheeted it in and eased the mainsail, and we reached along Walter's pencil line. A passage ninety feet wide appeared before us and then we were among the gray rocks, counting each one off as we turned north and wound our way toward the one island that had cabins on it. I pulled in our taffrail log as Larry checked our course on the chart. We skirted a barely submerged rock and then spotted four wooden cabins. "We round up just past this next big rock and we should be right where Walter said to anchor," Larry told me. "You take the helm. I'll get ready to anchor. Looks like close work."

We put *Seraffyn* hard on the wind for the last two-hundred-yard leg of our exciting day. Larry went forward to the leeward shrouds and we waved back at the two people who were coming toward the shore. "Larry, there's a rock ahead of us, I think," I called from the tiller. I wasn't sure; the water just seemed a slightly different color. Larry glanced quickly at the folded chart in his hand and said, "None shown here." I steered toward the center of the tiny anchorage. *Seraffyn* heeled sharply to a gust of wind. Larry looked down at the water rushing by *Seraffyn*'s channels. His face went white. He couldn't speak; he only pointed—straight down. I leaned over the side to look and went white too as I saw a rockpile slide by our bilge less than two feet below the water. If *Seraffyn* hadn't been heeled we'd have hit it, and at the four knots we were making through the water, all five and a half tons of *Seraffyn* would have hit those rocks hard! "Head into the wind," Larry shouted. When we were a hundred yards past the rock, Larry let go our anchor and *Seraffyn* came to rest with just enough room to swing in ten feet of water with fifty feet of chain out.

Larry was still quite pale; I couldn't see myself so I don't know what color I was. We furled the mainsail, then sat down and looked at Walter's chart again. I got a sudden idea and went below for a pencil. I carefully erased Walter's pencil mark and there was our rock—right under one leg of his *X!*

The two men from shore came alongside in a runabout. "Welcome to Stora Nassa. Really exciting entrance you made. We didn't think you knew where our rock was at first. But obviously you did. At least ten boats a year end up on top of it," Walter's son Thomas said. He and his cousin Hans never believed we'd missed that rock only by luck.

Thomas and Hans towed us around to the tiny dock in an almost enclosed area in front of the four cabins. As soon as we'd secured alongside, their children and wives appeared and we learned more about Stora Nassa. From the first we'd assumed that Walter Nathansen had been using English improperly when he called the islands of Stora Nassa "my archipelago." But Thomas explained that Stora Nassa had been deeded to his grandfather by the king of Sweden on the condition that it be kept as a bird sanctuary, with any structures restricted to one island only. A fisherman and his wife had been found to live on the islands year round as caretakers. Then the Nathansens built him a home plus four summer cottages and a sauna. During the main bird-breeding months, from mid-April to mid-June, no one was allowed to land on the other islands of Stora Nassa. But the rest of the year visitors were welcome if they were careful. We could see the masts of three or four other yachts moored behind various islands. In the crevices and valleys of the rocky half-mile-square main island the caretaker's wife had planted a beautiful garden with hundreds of strawberry plants. Hans sent his son for some and soon we were all sitting around, dipping fresh rosy strawberries in sugar and eating them whole.

We were immediately adopted into the summer camp atmosphere of the island. Thomas acted as activity organizer, Hans as camp comic.

Just a few of Stora Nassa's two hundred islands.

At about nine o'clock our first evening, Thomas arrived, trailed by four children and Hans. "Come on, Larry," he shouted. "Every evening every man and child on Stora Nassa runs completely around the island then dives in the water for a swim. It is a tradition."

Larry pulled on his shoes while Hans commented wryly, "Ya, it is a tradition ever since two weeks ago when Thomas dreamed it up."

The next morning Thomas, the organizer, was down to see us within minutes after Larry stepped on deck with his first cup of coffee. "Shopping day. Launch leaves at 10:30. We'll give you a tour of the inner islands on the way," Thomas told us.

We climbed into the Stora Nassa launch with Thomas, his wife, and their two children, and roared off at twenty-five knots, retracing in less than thirty-five minutes the route *Seraffyn* had taken seven hours to sail the day before. As we reached the limit of the "not fully charted" area, I commented, "Nice not to have to worry about uncharted dangers if you stray a little off your course now." Thomas laughed at my concern. "Didn't anyone tell you? Every possible danger that is within three meters of the surface is listed. It is only deep-draft vessels those charts are supposed to fool."

I related this information to Larry who was seated on my opposite side and couldn't hear Thomas over the roar of the motor. Larry commented, "That's the logic of politicians. Now all an invader has to do is use shoal-draft boats. But it's good to know so we can stop worrying about running into phantom rocks."

The closer to Stockholm we got, the greener and denser the islands became. Tour boats, cargo boats, car ferries, and pleasure craft became more plentiful. We stopped at an island with a fuel dock and grocery store on it, and watched as a small cargo boat off-loaded plastic-lined five-gallon round metal containers and then took off the same containers, only sealed and obviously full. When we asked what the containers held, Thomas proudly explained, "Five years ago the pollution in these islands within ten miles of Stockholm was so bad that swimming had to be forbidden. There are no tides to help clean up debris, so the government got down to business and introduced a law forbidding the discharge of human waste from any inhabitants of these islands. Then they arranged for the regular distribution and pickup of these toilet buckets. Yachts that are not moored near clubs or camp grounds are exempt from rules because their total pollution can be absorbed by the ecology. But everyone else has to use these buckets. It's really been

Thomas in the *Optimist* and Larry in *Rinky* run neck and neck toward the finish line.

Hans, the comedian, and his wife Gretta and two children on board *Seraffyn* after a picnic lunch.

worthwhile. Now we have clean, clear water right in the middle of Stockholm itself."

I had quite a shock when I looked at the food prices. Danish prices had been high, but Swedish ones were higher. Thomas reassured me when he said, "Wait until you reach Finland to shop. Prices are a third of what they are here." I hoped he was right because our stock of English canned foods was being steadily depleted.

We were back in Stora Nassa for a late lunch. Thomas challenged Larry to a dinghy race around the island. Larry set off in *Rinky*, Thomas in his Optimist pram. An hour later they returned, dead-running within inches of each other, laughing and taunting each other like two schoolboys. Thomas came over the line first. "I'd have done better with some local knowledge," Larry commented as soon as he tied up. He was still chuckling as he explained, "I ran into a couple of rocks."

Thomas kept our days full to the brim. Saunas, walks, shared smorgasbord meals. The day before we departed, Hans and his family joined us on *Seraffyn*, Thomas took his family in their fifteen-foot sailboat, and we all sailed to the easternmost islands of Sweden for a picnic lunch, laughing most of the time.

All of us returned to find that Breta and Walter had arrived on their steel ketch. We made fresh bread, cabbage salad, and a big pot of spaghetti and invited everyone on Stora Nassa for dinner. Larry rigged our stereo speakers on deck. I used salad plates and spoons to serve the children, while adults got dinner plates and forks. Knives had to be shared.

Larry and I prepared to sail the next morning despite the hard-to-refuse suggestions for more outings and explorations with the delightful Stora Nassans. We had a fine sendoff after Walter lined a course northward toward Finland on our chart. "Turn at the oil drum with a cross on it," he shouted as we ran off under main and lapper. Soon we cleared the tiny islands and, sure enough, two miles ahead of us stood a rock surmounted by a fifty-five-gallon drum, a wooden cross on its top. We turned northwest toward the main shipping channel and Stora Nassa, the magical family-owned archipelago, slowly faded from our view.

~~~~~~

CHAPTER 13

Thirty Thousand Islands

As Larry steered north past the last of Sweden's islands, I went below to sort out charts. Just to cruise from the south coast of England to Finland, we'd needed over fifty charts plus two *Pilot* books. If we'd had to go out and buy these charts they'd have cost us over a hundred eighty dollars in 1973. But fortunately, we've found that cruising sailors worldwide are willing to trade or loan charts. When we'd set off cruising in 1969, we'd purchased two hundred dollars' worth of charts covering the area from Newport Beach, California, to Panama. In Panama we traded with a westbound yacht for all of the Caribbean charts. And so it went. During more than nine years of cruising, we've only spent eighty to a hundred dollars more for charts we couldn't acquire by trading. During our winter in Poole we'd mentioned our sailing plans to various people and soon heard of a large power yacht fresh from a cruise of the Baltic, and we soon had the loan of all the charts we needed, plus some excellent firsthand advice.

When I brought the first of the Finnish charts on deck, Larry set Helmer steering and joined me for a look. Finnish charts are really different. Not only do they use green and yellow to show shoal water and marshes instead of the blue or gray we were used to, but because there is such an unbelievable number of islands protecting the Finnish coast, the Finnish hydrographic office hasn't tried to chart each danger or even each island. Instead, there are a large number of selected, marked routes leading to all of the inhabited islands. These routes, thin black lines threading between beacons and lighthouses, have numbers next to them which indicate the deepest vessel that can safely use them. Some say fifteen meters and are routes used by the big car ferries we saw flashing by as regularly as buses. But most of the routes we took were marked 1.8 meters or 2 meters. Since *Seraffyn* draws 1.4 meters, we were reluctant to take any route marked 1.5 or less, but we later learned that we would have been safe since the depths figured are for extreme low water.

Light winds slowed our progress across the forty miles of open water between Sweden and Finland. Already in the middle of July there was a perceptible lengthening of the time between sunset and sunrise, although the sky never lost its dusk-like glow. Larry stood the first three-hour watch and when he woke me, suggested that I heave to and wait for full daylight if I didn't spot the lighthouse marking the entrance to Marianhamina. Several lights winked, but none of their characteristics seemed to make sense. I backed the jib, tied the tiller to leeward, and *Seraffyn* lay quietly in the six-knot breeze, making absolutely no way. It was fully daylight at 0300 when Larry came on watch. Dozens of islands lay less than five miles north of us. But not a ferry was in sight and we were even more confused than we'd been during the short night. Then I spotted what looked like a patrol boat coming toward us. "That's the answer. Let's wave him down and ask where we are."

Larry wasn't too keen on that idea and suggested, "Let's try and figure this out ourselves. It's not fair to disturb other people with our problems." He poured over our chart, scanned the horizon, and read the *Pilot* book, looking for some identifiable landmark. Each island looked the same—pink granite covered with trees.

The patrol boat came directly toward us and was within fifty feet of us when a man on deck called to us in Swedish. I put up our Canadian ensign while Larry yelled, "Do you speak English?" The patrol boatman yelled back, "Is everything all right?"

"Can you confirm our position?" Larry called at the same time as I yelled, "We're lost."

The big bald Finn laughed and called back, "I'm not surprised. We've added several new navigation lights and changed all the light sequences this spring. Hold on, I'll give you a course to steer. Where are you headed?"

When we plotted in the position he'd given us, we found we had been set five miles west during the night. This surprised us because the Baltic is supposed to be tideless. But we later learned that changes in barometric pressures caused by depressions moving across Europe can cause currents up to two knots to flow through the Baltic channels.

The yacht club at Marianhamina is a tiny, bright-red wooden house heavily trimmed with white gingerbread carvings. Green trees crowd over it and less than two hundred yards away the towering rig of the iron sailing ship *Pommern* dwarfed the otherwise lofty-looking spars of *Puffin,* which had arrived two days before us after taking a completely different route north by way of Goteland and Stockholm.

The friendly yacht club manager alloted us a mooring, then hoisted a Canadian flag on the last empty guest flagpole alongside those from Germany, Sweden, Poland, and the U.S.A. The beautifully protected harbor made us feel confident about our decision to leave *Seraffyn* for a few weeks while we took a long-anticipated trip inland.

Six months before, when we'd been in London visiting various embassies, the consul for Finland had given us a pile of travel brochures. He'd asked us when we'd be in his country and when we answered "June or July," told us, "You are lucky because that's when all the Finns celebrate the long evenings by having music festivals. There's a classical music festival, one for jazz buffs, another for folk music lovers, and one for opera fans. Wonderful festivals in the nicest villages of Finland."

As we entered Marianhamina, we saw the full-rigged ship *Pommern*.

His enthusiasm was contagious. "Which one is best?" Larry wanted to know. The consul answered, "I've been to them all. It depends on what you like. But the folk festival at Kaustinen gets bigger every year." He'd given us a festival brochure and wished us a good summer in Finland.

We'd arrived in Marianhamina three days before the Kaustinen Folk Festival was to begin. We asked the yacht club caretaker to check *Seraffyn*'s doubled-up mooring lines, packed two small seabags, and discovered one of the delights of traveling in Finland. Because there are so many islands and lakes, and because roads are so hard to keep open during the long severe winters, the Finns have developed a wonderfully effective internal airline system. Low air fares, no reservations. We bought our tickets right on the plane. Flights were frequent. Our first flight to Helsinki, a distance of four hundred miles, cost us ten dollars each, and we carried out luggage on with us.

During our two-hour flight we once again debated the question of trying to get visas to visit Russia. "It's worth a try," Larry felt, so we went to the Soviet Embassy as soon as we arrived in Helsinki.

The Russian consul, a charming young man dressed in the most mod of suits, was extremely friendly. "I know we can arrange your visas. But we must rush because your port clearance is dated five weeks from today and that would be hard to change." We left feeling hopeful since the consul had been placing a call direct to Tallinn, our proposed first port of entry, when we left his office.

Once again we splurged and enjoyed the convenience of having a car for our trip to the Kaustinen festival. The drive across Finland, unhassled by concerns over bus schedules, taxi fares, and luggage, was a treat. When we arrived at the tiny farm community less than sixty miles from the Arctic Circle, the crowds that swamped the reception center glowed in their various national costumes. We located one of the thousand beds made available in the homes of local farmers. For a set fee of three dollars each we were provided with a bed, a delicious breakfast of fresh bread, fruit, and homemade cheese, and one sauna bath per day. Next to the farm we stayed at were the huge fields set aside for the thousands of people who had brought their caravans, tents, or just sleeping bags. We could hear the strains of a hundred different musicians warming up and practicing everywhere we turned.

The festival organizers had sent formal invitations to two hundred

Young and old, the music rang for sixteen hours a day

Erikke Shastamoinen, entertaining us first with his music (below) then with the music of his anvil (page 138).

folk musicians and dancers from eleven countries. Over two thousand arrived, plus fifteen thousand spectators. There were three regular exhibitions going on at all times—one in the school stadium, one in the auditorium, and one in the ski lodge, a quarter mile from the school. These cost twenty-five cents to enter. But it was the free, unscheduled sessions, put on in any convenient piece of shade or any open spot with enough room for the dancers to swing their partners, that kept our heads spinning. Larry's camera shutter seemed to click in tempo with polkas, reels, and schotisches. I wanted to rush from one end of the festival grounds to the other as I heard a new violin call out or caught the shouts of yet another Hungarian dancer. The tomtom beat of a group of young Canadian Crow Indians in full war dress was in sharp contrast to the bagpipes, flutes, and bass violins of European folksong. These wonderfully casual performances caused the shiest of performers to lose their inhibitions and sparkle as dancers and spectators from twelve or fifteen countries urged them on with whistles, shouts, and clapping.

I fell in love with accordion-playing Shastamoinen, a shaggy-haired sixty-seven-year-young Finn who was famous throughout Scandinavia for his renditions of songs and dances of northern Finland. We sat and listened, laughing at songs we couldn't understand, several times during the five-day festival. Shastamoinen noticed our obvious interest, stopped a young Finn, and, asking him to translate, questioned us for a few minutes. Then he told our friendly translator, "Tell them to come visit at my house when the festival is over. They need to see a real north man's home!"

The Polish dance group was another of our favorites. Larry happened to sit next to their translator during one performance and mentioned that my grandparents were from Poland. After the wildly beautiful performance, a musical pantomime of a fight between barbaric mountain outlaws and ax-swinging highlanders, she took us up to introduce us to the dancers. They were all amateurs from a mountain village in southern Poland. "What are you doing in Finland? How did you get here?" the Poles asked. Yet again we had the fun of watching amazed faces as we pulled out a somewhat tattered photo of *Seraffyn* and tried to explain our small magic carpet to people who had never heard of cruising.

The head of the Polish group, a tiny violin maker named Marion, thought for only a minute. "If you are sailing to Poland, you are going to come and stay with us," he said, then wrote his address on the back of a festival program.

Our heads were swimming with new sounds by the time the festival came to an end. Larry's camera had been used to the hilt. We walked around saying good-bye to friends we'd made during the five days of song and dance. Vesa-Pekka Takala, the young Finnish reporter who'd translated for Saastamoinen, searched us out only minutes before we were to climb into the car to return to *Seraffyn.* "When are you heading for Saastamoinen's?" he asked. "I'd like to ride there with you." We explained that we felt Saastamoinen's invitation had been only a spur-of-the-moment politeness. But Vesa-Pekka showed us a map drawn especially for us. So the three of us set off together over the dirt roads of northern Finland.

We had a terrible time remembering Vesa-Pekka's name, and as we came to know him better during the three-hour drive, I finally decided to tell him the nickname we had used for him during the festival. I pointed at his short leather pants, "We called you Peter Lederhausen." Vesa-Pekka nodded his tousled blond head, then repeated, "Peter Lederhausen, I like that." So the name stuck.

We pulled up at a rambling unpainted wooden house, weathered to a silver tone that glowed from among a stand of pine trees on an open meadow. A broad blue lake glistened behind it and scattered houses were in view, each the same rich silver color. An older woman was walking up the path barefoot, carrying a fifty-pound sack of charcoal lightly on her shoulder. We couldn't understand her words, but her warm smile and gestures made us feel sure we were at the right house.

Peter was kept busy translating Saastamoinen's stories as we sat two hours over what he called "a cup of coffee and a few cakes." His wife had quickly prepared a repast that definitely surpassed the bounds of "a few cakes." We marveled at the energy and hearty appearance of this woman who'd been the mother of Saastamoinen's *seventeen* children, who'd spent forty years skinning and preparing the hides of animals Saastamoinen brought back from his traps in the woods each winter. She had also looked after their twelve cows and vegetable garden at the same time. She turned aside our compliment on her fine fruit preserves and pickles by saying, "It's easy now. There are so few children about; only eight of my grandchildren and two of my children are in the house this summer." Saastamoinen took us to his tiny

soot-blackened blacksmith shop. The wooden building was far from any other dwellings and right next to the lake. He lit a fire in the brick hearth and soon had the hard coal glowing as he swayed on the huge hand bellows. He showed us some of the sharply honed sickles that made up most of his forging work, while he waited for a piece of round iron rod to heat to the proper temperature. Then he pulled the white glowing metal from the hearth with a huge set of pincers, forged and tapered it into a sweet-sounding triangle with a rhythmic pounding of his huge hammer on a much-used anvil.

Saastamoinen washed the soot from his face and arms in the lake, then regaled us with backwoods stories as we went back to his kitchen for a farewell drink.

"My attic is stuffed with liquor, must be hundreds of bottles there," he told us. "Everyone in Finland seems to think it's proper to pay a blacksmith with whiskey. Only problem is that I don't drink, not like my Canadian brother." And then he told us the gruesome story of his brother and the cat:

When my brother and I were young, I had a cat. My brother wanted that cat and I agreed to sell it to him. He took the cat, but emigrated to Canada before he ever paid me for it. Well, I knew my brother would do well in Canada, he was such a shrewd character. So I wasn't surprised when he came back to visit us here, forty years later, dressed in fancy clothes and bragging about his wealth. "You never paid me for that cat," I reminded him. My brother didn't say a word. He went back to Canada and two months later a box arrived with my brother's return address on it. I opened the box and there was a dead cat!

Saastamoinen roared with laughter over that memory. But music was his real love, and before we drove off he played his accordion for us once again. "None of this music has been written down," Sastamoinen said in response to one of Larry's questions. "Real folk music is handed down from mouth to mouth, growing, living, and changing. As soon as you write it down, it dies." His wife tapped her foot; Saastamoinen swayed and sang in his rough voice. We could well picture this kitchen during one of Finland's long, dark winter nights when it would be filled with the smell of delicious cakes and the sound of Saastamoinen's many friends as their music grew and swelled until it drove away the loneliness of a snow-filled wild northland.

When we left, Peter directed us toward the east and when Larry said, "I thought you lived south of here," Peter answered, "I do, but I'm taking you sailing."

An hour later we drove up a long winding driveway to a rambling summer cottage set on yet another of Finland's tree-lined lakes. A warm multilingual lady gave Peter the kind of greeting reserved for very welcome unexpected guests. Within a few minutes she'd extended her greeting to us. "I've got another guest you'll really enjoy. But go off sailing now and light the sauna before you do," Moya said.

Peter started the pine logs burning in the pine sauna while Larry and I rigged the Lightning-class dinghy that bobbed to a light breeze on a mooring less than two hundred feet from the summer house. We skimmed across the lake, enjoying hiking out to steady the frisky dinghy. Then, two hours later, when the sun was lower than the treetops we returned to shore and went into the steamy hot sauna. After ten minutes of sweating, we ran to the water's edge and dove into the cool, refreshing lake, then back into the sauna to sweat again. After three stints in the sauna, I scrubbed all over and washed my hair in the crystal-clear lake. My skin felt glowingly healthy as we sat on the wooden veranda with our hostess, who turned out to be a journalist. Her other guest, a young Japanese who'd come to Finland to study Russian icon painting, joined us as we snacked on cheese and cold cuts. Our dessert was a huge bowl full of tiny wild strawberries from the woods around this peaceful retreat, smothered in fresh whole cream from the cow next door.

My mind seemed to take a step backward as all of us sat there discussing the art of icon painting. Here we were, two average people,

Larry diving out of the sauna into one of Finland's thirty thousand lakes.

thousands of miles from home, hundreds of miles from the sea, among people who'd been strangers only a day before, learning about a subject we'd never heard of until a few hours ago. Yet we felt warm, welcome, and as rich as any man on earth, and I knew *Seraffyn* had opened this world to us.

We had two pleasant surprises waiting for us when we returned to *Seraffyn* in Marianhamina the next day. The first was a big brown envelope containing our mail. Brian Cooke had watched it arrive at his house in bits and pieces during our stay in Poole and suggested, "Since you are always moving, you must miss a lot of letters. How do you know where to have people write to you? How do you know if you receive all the letters people send you before you leave a place? Our yacht club always seems to have letters lying around for visitors who have already moved on. Why not use my address at the bank permanently and have all your mail sent there? Then, once a month, or when you let me know your next forwarding address, I'll send you one registered airmail package containing all your post." We'd really seen the logic in this and when that first package arrived in Marianhamina with thirty letters, all rubberbanded together, we were sold. We've used that system for five years now, and our mail, usually a headache for cruising people, has been exceptionally dependable.

The second treat was a visit to the Erickson Museum, which was in a large house on the shore next to the square-rigged *Pommern*. Fortunately, we chose a quiet day, and the museum's curator Captain Kahre (Cory), who'd sailed around the Horn over twenty times, seven times as master of a full-rigged ship, was willing to give us a personally guided tour. The lost days of sailing cargo ships came alive to us under his guidance as we stood in the wheelhouse of the late *Herzogen-Cecile*, one of the last of Erickson's square-riggers. *Herzogen-Cecile* had sunk at the mouth of the Salcombe River in southern England. Erickson, a wealthy shipowner who had survived and prospered during the switch from sail to steam, and was then already building his museum, salvaged the deckhouse of *Herzogen-Cecile* and reassembled it inside the museum building. The few remaining sails of the *Pommern* filled one room of the museum. When we looked at the mound of decaying cotton and hemp, Larry asked, "Could the *Pommern* be sailed today?" Captain Kahre proudly informed us that her hull and spars were completely ready to set to sea. "The only concession we made to make her part of this museum was to install a fire sprinkler system. But unfortunately, most of her sails have been used through the years to make hatch covers and tarpaulines for Erickson's steamships."

We added our name to the museum guest book, then left to pace once again the three-hundred-foot-long decks of *Pommern.* It took little imagination to hear the bare feet of sailors running along her decks and hear their shouts in her maze of rigging. We ran our hands over the huge drums of the revolutionary Jarvis brace winches that stood abaft the *Pommern*'s mainmast. We could well imagine Erickson's disappointment when every modern invention he added to his sailing ships, every labor-saving device he used to pare his sailing crews from fifty men down to twenty-four on the five-thousand-ton ships, still failed to make the romantic sailing ship as practical as steam.

Two views from the yard of a square-rigger. *Seraffyn* looks like a toy until Larry put the 105-mm lens on the camera for a closer view.

CHAPTER 14

≈≈≈

Never on a Friday

A light breeze ruffled the sheet that covered us in our favorite bunk, the wide cushion-filled cockpit. I got up and started the coffee and tea, then took our logbook into the rumpled cockpit bed to write in the poem my sister Bonnie had sent in her last letter.

> What matters?
> Very little.
> Only the flicker of light
> within the darkness,
> The feeling of warmth
> within the cold,
> The knowledge of love
> within the void.

Larry and I read back through our logbook, which is more like an informal dairy in which we paste favorite photos, postcards, and memorabilia, than the formal logs some sailors keep. People, places, and tiny daily adventures seemed to leap from its pages. Then Larry brought both of us into the present by saying, "Is it really July 27? We'd better move on today or we'll never see any more of Finland before our docking date in Russia."

"We can't sail today," I told him. "It's Friday! But we'd better go tomorrow because I'd like to be closer to Tallinn in case our visas do come through." We'd been in close telephone contact with the Soviet consul. Each time we spoke to him he'd sounded more hopeful. We laughed at the idea of our personal visas causing so much trouble when *Seraffyn* was already in free and clear.

"Now if we could have the two of you arrive on a registered Soviet carrier such as a bus or ship, then have your ship towed into Soviet waters, we could get you visas," the consul told us. "But I have our Moscow office working on the problem. Call me in three or four days."

His encouragement made my desire to see the home of my father's parents even greater. Larry had seen Denmark and England, the lands his ancestors came from. Now I hoped it would be my turn. Besides, we were dying to see the Hermitage and be the first post-Revolution foreign yacht to sail up the Neva.

As Larry folded the bedclothes and put the quarter berth cushions below in their places, the breeze filled in even more. The sun glowed warmly on our decks. "Lin, we've got to break this silly Friday superstition once and for all. Let's go sailing!

"But remember Lymington!" I started.

"Absolute carelessness," Larry answered.

I shrugged my shoulders, got out the chart, and stored away some dishes. Then I went on deck to hoist the mainsail while Larry cleared the spare line from the mooring buoy.

I stood at the helm while Larry hoisted the lapper, then cleared our mooring line from the buoy. *Seraffyn* slowly gathered way as I sheeted the mainsail in and Larry pulled the jib sheet. "Go to windward of the blue sloop," Larry suggested. I steered closer to the wind, but *Seraffyn* just didn't have enough speed through the water to clear the bow of the boat that had been moored a hundred feet away from us. "Fall off quick," Larry called, reaching to let the mainsheet run. I pulled the helm. *Seraffyn*'s bowsprit started to swing, and then it all happened, as if in horrible, unstoppable slow-motion. Our bowsprit went right between the shrouds of the twenty-five-foot sloop. Our bobstay hit its tow rail. *Seraffyn* stopped, slowly turned into the wind, trapped by wire and turnbuckles that grated against each other. Then hours (but really only seconds) later, slid slowly free with a ripping sound and drifted downwind, clear of the yacht club moorings.

Both of us were stunned. We got *Seraffyn* under control and then Larry said, "Take a pencil and paper over to that sloop and write a note to its owner while I reach back and forth here in clear water."

I rowed toward the sloop, concerned over the damage *Seraffyn*'s five and a half tons must have caused, and was vastly relieved to find only a twelve-inch surface scratch on the sloop's topside and a half-inch-deep nick in her toe rail. But large chips of varnish and spruce glared up at me from her white deck, so obviously *Seraffyn* had not come off so lightly. I was tied alongside, writing a note to the owner with our address, when the owner appeared. He thanked me profusely, saying, "She's just a sailing school boat so don't worry. She's been hit four or five times before this year. But not many of the culpits admit it."

His kind words didn't relieve the embarrassment Larry and I both felt as we ran out of Marianhamina. We were terribly depressed as we talked over all the possible ways we could have avoided the accident. "The real problem was that we were rushing and didn't take the time to discuss what we were going to do before we cast off the mooring line," Larry said after inspecting our bruised bowsprit. "If we'd thought for a minute or two, we'd have just cast off and drifted down-wind free of the moorings, then set our sails. But it's all talk now. I don't think we should sail on Fridays. Let's find the first anchorage we can and stop."

So only five miles later we found a cove and anchored. We were both still depressed. The skies were clouding over and turning gray.

Sailing through the Finnish Archipelago.

Larry scraped the flakes of loose varnish off the bowsprit, put on a protective coat of varnish, then went and hid in the forepeak, his nose buried in a book. I sat moping on the side deck, watching a fisherman in a small varnished runabout pull up his net at the head of the cove. He started his motor and came directly toward us. "Larry, company coming," I called. The fisherman came carefully alongside, putting tiny clean fenders over to protect his shining varnished topsides. His wrinkled, weatherbeaten face was screwed into a look of careful concentration as he thought out each word of English and said, "I have caught too many fish. You must take some for your meal or I will have to throw them away." The fisherman wouldn't stay to chat. He just handed us four flounder-like fish and putted off as we were saying our thanks.

That broke our gray mood, and after a few last comments such as "Well, the only man who never made a mistake, never did anything," and "As long as we learn from our mistakes," and . . . we set to work

Chart in hand, we weave through the islands of Finland.

planning a dinner to do justice to those lovely sweet-tasting fish.

Sailing through the Turko Archipelago on Finland's southwestern corner was different from any sailing we'd ever done before. Unlike Sweden's well-populated islands, these had only a few scattered villages on them. Trees crowded right to the water. All of the hundreds of islands we passed looked the same, and without the excellent arrangement of beacons, lights, and stakes with brush-like heads of twigs that marked isolated dangers, we'd have had a difficult time with our navigation.

A brisk northwest wind sent us roaring through the islands. It was cool enough to warrant a jacket. The sea was absolutely flat because of the islands so close to windward. Larry was engrossed in a good book on the forward bunk. So I had a lovely private morning of guiding *Seraffyn* as she seemed to prance and surge, like the living, breathing personality she had grown to be.

When we burst through a narrow channel into a patch of relatively open water, I set Helmer to steer momentarily and went below to pour a cup of tea for myself. I climbed back on deck, glanced at the chart, then looked around. I was lost! Nothing looked the same. Just before I became frantic, I looked at our compass then at the direction of the black line we were following across the chart. A wind shift had caused Helmer to steer *Seraffyn* thirty degrees off. The profusion of islands fell into order as soon as I unclutched Helmer and steered back on course.

Helsinki had been our goal when we planned our Baltic cruise during the cold English evenings. But as often happens, the realities of cruising intervened. Our tour inland, the wonderful sailing in the Turko Archipelago, delays while we restocked *Seraffyn* in the excellent and very inexpensive markets of the friendly city of Turko-Abo—all ate up the quickly flying days of the short northern summer. As the dates set on *Seraffyn*'s Russian entry permit grew closer, we found ourselves clinging even closer to villages or towns with telephones. Each two days we'd call in for a report. Each time we were told, "Your visas have not been refused; but then, they have not been approved either." Finally, two days before we'd have had to arrive in Tallinn, our first proposed Russian port, a hundred twenty miles southeast of us, the distraught young consul for the Soviet Union informed us, "The immigration department in Moscow refuses to say yes or no." We realized it was their way of telling us, "Go away. Don't bother us."

Larry and I reacted just like two children. We went home, sat in the cockpit, and pouted. "We didn't really want to visit their lousy country anyway," one of us said. But we were both deeply disappointed. If only the Soviet consul in London had not been caught spying, the visa he'd arranged would have permitted us to be the first sailing yacht to visit the Soviet Union! In a way, we'd planned on that visit to Russia as the highlight of our summer. I guess it is a case of forbidden fruit seeming sweeter. Our spirits were pretty low.

But the next morning a note was lying in our cockpit when we returned from the huge flower-filled open market in Turko's main square. It provided pleasant thoughts that turned us from griping about Soviet restrictions. When we'd arrived in Turko and tied to the park-like shore of the river that goes right through the heart of the city, we'd mailed a note to Ake and Camille Lindquist saying, "Larry and I are friends of Leif Møller of Copenhagen. Leif said we'd enjoy meeting you. If you are free, please join us for a drink on board *Seraffyn* any evening this week." We'd found that this way of responding to intro-

Seraffyn is dwarfed by the unfinished hull of a ship at the Turko-abo shipyards that line both sides of the river.

ductions people gave us worked well. We didn't feel we were putting strangers who might be too busy to entertain unknown friends on the spot as badly as if we'd just walked up and knocked on their door, or even telephoned. If they couldn't join us, or didn't want to, they were free to ignore our note. But all of our notes seemed to get immediate responses, and this time had been no exception.

"Just came back to the city and found your note. Too busy to join you today; sail out to our summer house and spend the weekend. Enclosed chart shows the spot."

We set our alarm for 0400 when we went to sleep that night. We needed a few windless hours to row *Seraffyn* out the three-mile-long river. For the past week the daytime winds had funneled upriver, and in places it was less than a hundred fifty feet wide. To make matters more difficult, just one mile downstream the river was narrowed by hulls of freighters under construction in the local shipyards. We didn't relish short-tacking all the way down river. Our early rising paid off. Larry rowed *Seraffyn* downriver in an absolute calm while I prepared him a big breakfast which we ate as we took our first southbound voyage of the summer. We'd been at 60° 30' north, only three hundred miles south of the Arctic Circle and probably as far north as *Seraffyn* would ever sail.

The Lindquists were already at their summer home, a Dr. Zhivago-ish rambling wooden building with large rooms, each dominated by huge porcelain, ceiling-high, wood-burning heaters. The house and its heaters were over a hundred years old and something of a rarity in the islands because, as Ake explained, "The reason everything in the islands looks so new is that we build of wood, then need huge fires to keep warm. So our homes and buildings often burn down. This one is standing because my parents rarely used it more than a few weeks each summer, and we do the same."

We spent two lovely days getting to know the Lindquists. Ake, the head of Lloyd's ship surveyors for Finland, was a keen racing and cruising sailor. He'd taken his Swan 43 sloop to England the previous summer and represented Finland in the Admiral's Cup races. When Larry mentioned our failure to get Russian visas, Ake, who had been to Russia many times surveying ships, told us, "Sailing boats and cruising sailors don't exactly fit in with Soviet ideology. The officials there are really concerned about letting people get any true idea of the freedoms of the outside world. Our yacht club decided to organize an overnight race out of Helsinki and contacted the Russian authorities, asking permission to race around a lighthouse that is only thirty miles south of Finland but within Russian territorial waters. It took months and piles of correspondence to get their permission. When we finally held the race, we found six Russian patrol boats sitting just off the lighthouse." Ake laughed and said, "Maybe the ships were guarding against Finnish yachtsmen defecting to Russia."

The third day there we had the first rainy weather we'd seen in our three months in the Baltic. We stayed on board, reading and writing letters, after the Lindquists commuted back to town in their runabout. The squalls let up in the evening and I was just debating what to cook for dinner when a small motorboat approached.

The dark-eyed owner, a man of about thirty, came alongside and, after introducing himself and asking where we had sailed from, said, "My sauna is hot. If you don't come and use it, the heat will go to waste." So we grabbed our towels and joined him. Three hours later he brought us back toward *Seraffyn*'s glowing anchor light, replete with the tasty smorgasbord his wife had served after the sauna.

"There it is, the first sign of winter," he told us.

"Where?" I asked.

He pointed at the stars that showed dully overhead. "When it's dark enough to see the stars again, we know that it is time to start getting our skis ready. Yes, it is an exciting time because we can start thinking of the fun of cross-country skiing."

He had a nightcap before leaving *Seraffyn*. "You should get moving, you know. You must be out of the Baltic before September 15 or you must take your boat from the water before the autumn storms come."

His words came to haunt us after we sailed away from the Lindquists' summer home. We kept planing to sail south, but we also kept meeting warm Finnish people.

We'd be sailing along, bound generally south, when another sailboat would come into view. So we'd harden up our sheets and they'd ease theirs, and soon we'd be cruising alongside each other, chatting back and forth. We met Maija and Gabor Molnar this way. They were cruising on a Dragon class with their young son. "We are sailing to a party. Come along." So we tacked alongside them, going twenty miles off our planned route to join their friends at a lovely island retreat. And another few days would slip away.

By August 16 we looked at a calendar and realized that if we wanted to see any of Poland before the September 15 date everyone kept warning us about, we'd better get moving. We sailed to Noto, one of the southernmost islands of the Turko Archipelago and filled up with sweet fresh water at the village pump. For the previous three or four weeks Larry had been complaining of itchy skin and stomach pains, and I'd definitely noticed a case of short-temperedness. By nightfall the evening we'd anchored at Noto his stomach pains were beginning to bring sweat to his forehead. He spent a terribly restless night and in the morning I rowed into the tiny village and asked if the storekeeper could call a doctor for me. The island villages all have telephones, and soon I was speaking to the woman who was the district doctor for some two hundred fifty square miles of island people. "Sounds like kidney stones, extremely painful. Give him heavy sedatives, keep him still, but don't worry as there is no danger." She contacted the local guard and then called back, "We can't send the boat for him. It's off picking up a woman who is having labor pains. Can you bring him in on your own boat?"

I carefully copied down the directions to her island clinic on Nagu, then rowed out to *Seraffyn*. Larry was in bed, tossing and turning, unable to sleep or get comfortable, uninterested in reading. I gave him the dose of codeine tablets the doctor had prescribed after I read the list of medicines we carried on board. Then after I tried to make Larry as comfortable as possible, I looked at the chart. Nagu was over forty-five miles away. The channel was mostly unlit, so it meant two days of sailing since it was afternoon by this time. In spite of the doctor's assurance, I was worried every time I looked at Larry's pale, pain-filled face. He offered to help, but when he tried to stand I knew it was one bit of sailing I'd have to handle myself.

I blessed our compact bronze Plath anchor winch as I got a hundred fifty feet of five-sixteenths-inch chain and a twenty-five-pound anchor up. I also blessed Larry's foresight in arranging the anchor so that I could hook it onto the bobstay without having to lift it on deck. Then, as I hoisted the working jib, sheeted in the mainsail, and reached past the first island on our route, I remembered our fight back in Dartmouth. Because of that argument I had finally started handling *Seraffyn* myself. Larry had encouraged me, saying, "If ever something happens to me, you'll be better prepared to take care of all of us." He'd watched to see what problems I encountered as I used *Seraffyn*'s sailing equipment and then tried to simplify anything that gave me trouble. (Before I make Larry sound like an absolute paragon of virtue, I must admit his patience sometimes wore thin and at times he sounded just like any other husband trying to teach his wife to drive.) But now I sailed *Seraffyn* with my confidence growing every minute. When I had reached over twenty-five miles to the anchorage I'd selected for the night, I rounded *Seraffyn* into the wind, let the main and jib sheets fly, released the jib halyard, and doused the jib with its downhaul, then unclutched the anchor winch and let the anchor and chain run out. I'd been conservative and anchored over a quarter mile from shore so I'd

This bronze double-action winch is made by the Plath company of Portland, Oregon.

Using the Baltic's fresh water to do the laundry.

An evening bonfire and sausage roast on Snackholm Island, just south of Noto.

have a lot of room to maneuver the next morning, but we spent a safe night.

Larry was not better the second day and I was vastly relieved when we finally sailed into the tiny bay on the island of Nagu. I anchored and went ashore to find the doctor. She had me bring Larry ashore, and after a brief examination, sent him off to a hospital on the mainland by taxi and car ferry.

I went back to *Seraffyn* and stowed her sails properly, thinking of the times Larry had said, "What good is it spending hundreds of dollars on lifejackets, emergency radios, rafts, and so on, if I don't use the best piece of safety equipment there is, a well-trained crew?"

Larry did not have kidney stones. Although the Finnish doctors cured his stomach pains, it was not until we were leaving Poland that a doctor found the real cause of his recurring problem: "Vitamin B-12 deficency. I used to see hundreds of cases during the war when flour was unavailable," the Polish doctor told us. It turned out that the high cost of meat in Scandinavia which had encouraged us to have a shipboard diet consisting mostly of canned food, combined with the fact both of us were trying to lose weight and so had avoided all bread, noodles, potatoes, and rice, had produced this deficiency. The results of a few vitamin tablets were nearly miraculous, and we became instant believers. Now, whenever we are at sea, away from the variety of fresh foods offered on shore, we take a vitamin supplement, as do many long-term cruisers.

Meanwhile the warm sunny days gave way to a northwesterly gale. Larry felt quite good, so we waited until we saw the barometer start to rise steadily and the wind to drop, then set our double-reefed mainsail and staysail and headed south, weaving our way through the southernmost of Finland's thirty thousand islands. The last lighthouse dropped below the horizon as we broad-reached swiftly along and we knew that we'd dream of returning to the "friendly archipelago" again some summer when we'd pray for another dose of the "best weather in recorded history."

CHAPTER 15

Poland and Politics

We ran across the Gulf of Finland, shaping a course that would take us well clear of the Soviet-dominated shore of Estonia. It was August 24, the northern summer was definitely fading away, and when I called Larry for his 2200 to 0100 watch, it was pitch dark with a heavy layer of scudding cloud hiding any stars.

I awoke half an hour after I climbed into the warm sleeping-bag-lined quarter berth and for a few minutes lay bracing myself against the toss and heave caused by the rising wind. Larry was pulling out navigation books, studying the chart, then going on deck only to return for another look at the chart.

I finally asked him what he was up to. "Since you're awake, how about coming on deck to see what you make of this?" Larry suggested. I struggled clear of the sheets, timing my climb out of the bunk with the roll *Seraffyn* made as another sea passed under her stern. Larry handed me my sailing jacket and came out into the cockpit. He'd taken down the mainsail while I slept and we were running under just the staysail. Helmer was steering well with two five-sixteenths-inch-diameter shock cords tied to the tiller to dampen a tendency to oversteer. The taffrail log was spinning at a rate I'd come to know meant we were moving at more than five knots.

"Look to port," Larry said. "We should be thirty-five miles from the Russian coast . . . there's not one navigation light shown on the chart for this area."

As soon as he said that, I saw what was bothering him. The loom of a huge light lit the undersides of the low clouds, just forward of our beam. It swept across the sky in a constant pattern that was unlike any navigation light we'd ever seen. Larry's search through the *Pilot* books, light lists, and charts had given no clue to this light, and with a strong northerly wind blowing, we doubted we'd been set far enough east to be in any danger. So we decided not to worry, but to keep an extra-sharp lookout.

I climbed back in the bunk and slept well until Larry called. As I pulled on my jeans and a sweatshirt, Larry told me, "Some kind of patrol ship came toward us from the east, circled about two hundred yards off, and put its searchlight on us. Then it headed due east again." He climbed on deck with me and pointed out the loom of the light we'd seen before. It was now aft of our beam. Then Larry pointed forward to where the loom of another light was just coming clear. "I'm steering a bit more to the west, just to be sure."

All that night we saw the loom of a line of very powerful lights. The next morning Larry was able to catch a glimpse of the sun with his sextant, and although the boat still surged and heeled along at over five knots, he got an accurate line of position. At noon the skies cleared and he took a noon sight. Our actual position was within two or three miles of our dead reckoning position, halfway between the Swedish island of Goteland and Russia. That evening we again saw the loom of huge lights on our port side but we didn't feel so concerned.

I had the 0100 to 0400 watch. The wind was still fresh, but had swung more to the east. *Seraffyn* roared along under just her staysail. I saw the lights of a ship approaching dead on our beam. I stood near the tiller, ready to change course if necessary. Then, exactly as Larry had described the night before, two hundred yards off the ship turned on searchlights, circled us at high speed, and headed away, due east.

The third night was the same. A patrol boat came and circled us at 0100. Lights loomed along the whole eastern horizon. By daylight our wind had decreased until we were able to set the mainsail, and by the time I served breakfast the seas were calm enough so that we could relax together in the cockpit while we reached along at five knots.

"The Russians must have had us on radar all the time. Those patrol boats never altered course when they came out and inspected us," Larry said. I ate the last peanut-butter-and-jam-covered biscuit, pondering about having to start each day without peanut butter now that we'd exhausted our supply. "I wonder if they thought we were trying to sneak into Estonia or Latvia?" Larry had no answer and we had little time to think further on the subject as we were fast approaching

Gdynia, Poland's largest Baltic port. I cleaned up inside *Seraffyn* as the high buildings of the city came into view. Larry checked our anchor and, at 1400 our third day out, we passed into the territorial waters of Poland. We'd taken two days and twenty-one hours to cover three hundred thirty miles, running most of the way under just a staysail.

We sailed past each of the six or seven basins formed by large stone breakwaters in front of Gdynia. Ferries, naval craft, and freighters filled their piers, but no one expressed the least interest in us. Then we saw the masts of several other sailing yachts and rounded the wall of the easternmost basin shown on our Admiralty chart. The submachine-gun-armed guard standing in front of a stone shed at the seaward end of the breakwater took a definite interest in us. He pointed his machine gun at our sails, then pointed the gun at the pier in front of his foot.

"I wonder if he knows that sailboats can't go directly into the wind," Larry joked uncertainly as we maneuvered *Seraffyn* toward the spot he was indicating. I hoisted our solid yellow quarantine flag to

Tied in the yacht basin at Gdynia, Poland, while a club boat practices docking under sail behind us.

show that we had no port clearance yet, then our small Polish courtesy flag. As soon as we had secured our mooring lines, the guard made a telephone call and then returned to stand on the dock beside us, his gun cradled in his arms.

We set to work putting *Seraffyn* into port order, feeling just a bit uneasy under the eye of the uniformed armed guard. Larry and I tried chatting nonchalantly as we performed the pleasant routine together, furling and tying the mainsail, stuffing the genoa into its bag, coiling the mainsheet, and tying off halyards. We'd just finished and started looking around at the wooden yachts that shared the basin with us when a line of officials came trooping down the docks.

Their warm smiles were in direct opposition to our guard's face. "Welcome to Poland," the harbormaster called as he removed his shoes before coming on board. He served as translator as the health, customs, and immigration officials presented us with about fifteen papers to be filled out. We showed them our visas and the letter from Theresa Remiszewski and the harbormaster rushed off *Seraffyn* and made a telephone call. He returned before we'd signed the last of the required forms. "Mrs. Remiszewski is not at home, but I'll contact her for you before tomorrow. I'll also call the head of our yachting association. He'll be glad to see you because you are the first Canadian yacht ever to visit Poland, and only the second yacht to come here this year. The other one was only from Sweden."

He apologetically explained that there were certain rules we had to conform to during our stay in Poland. Once we had *Seraffyn* secured to our satisfaction, we were not allowed to move her until we had cleared to leave. No guests were allowed on board until they gave their identity cards to the guard at his post. And finally, we had to leave the port before our visa expired, in twenty one days.

Since *Seraffyn* is so small and has such an open interior plan, we decided to tie our stern to a mooring buoy and have our bowsprit to the pier. Otherwise anyone—such as our omnipresent gun-totting guard—who looked down our companionway could see every move we made. We removed the dinghy and tied it alongside, scrubbed the decks down with seawater, then found an outside shower at the far end of the yacht basin. The cold water brought goose bumps out all over and I'll didn't willingly stay under its stinging spray one second after the last bit of soap was out of my hair. We wore sweaters as we ate dinner below decks that evening.

As soon as breakfast was cleared away the next morning it became obvious that the harbormaster had been busy. Petite, dark-haired, forty-three-year-old Theresa Remiszewski arrived, a bunch of flowers in one hand, a carefully wrapped packet of pastry in the other. Her sister Krystyna was with her, carrying another bunch of flowers and a bag of fruit. They had no trouble at all negotiating our bowsprit since both of them had thousands of miles of ocean sailing under their belts. Both held the rank of captain in the Polish sailing association, and worked in their spare time training other club members in offshore sailing and navigation. Each year they took a three-week-long Baltic cruise in charge of one of the club's forty-five-foot ketches. Theresa told us more about her attempt to win the 1972 single-handed transatlantic race. She'd done very well until the mast fitting holding her spreaders had started to split the hollow, unblocked wooden spar and she'd had to jury rig extra shrouds to take the strains. She'd climbed the mast alone at sea several times to do this and then completed the last eight hundred miles of the race under reduced canvas in the

Theresa Remiszewski on board *Comodor,* the yacht she sailed in the 1972 OSTAR.

forty-three-footer, still finishing in the top half of the fleet. Now she dreamed of being the first woman to circumnavigate the world single-handed and was trying to get government sponsorship for her project.

Before we had time to chat further, more people arrived, with more fruit, flowers, and pastries. We made everyone laugh by garlanding *Seraffyn*'s skylight and boom with our growing collection of bright autumn blossoms.

"How was your voyage from Finland?" one of our many guests asked. We told him about the strange lights we'd seen and the patrol boats that had inspected us. "Those were huge searchlights," the guest, a retired naval officer, explained. "The whole coast of Estonia, Latvia, and Lithuania is lined with them. There are smaller searchlights every hundred meters with machine gun towers in between. They aren't to keep you out; they are to keep Soviet people from escaping in small boats. No one is allowed to sail in those waters. The Soviets arrest any Polish fishing boat that even comes close to their territorial waters. Then our government has to intervene to get the fishermen free."

Another of our visitors went below to inspect *Seraffyn*'s interior and we noticed he was spending a long time lying on our forward bunk. Larry went in and found him reading a copy of Alexander Solzhenitsyn's *Cancer Ward*. "You can take that with you if you'd like. Lin and I have finished reading it," Larry told him. "I'd really like to have the book," our visitor said, looking at the slightly dog-eared paperback we'd bought in Finland. "It's totally banned here, but we've heard a lot about it."

"Take it then," Larry repeated.

Our guest looked very longingly at the book. "I can't take it with me. It would cause problems if someone caught me with it. But if you come to my house tonight for dinner, and if you wrap it up and put it in your wife's purse, then bring it with you. It would probably be all right. No one would stop a foreigner and insist on inspecting his wife's bag."

During our entire stay in Poland, hardly a day went by without reminders of the political restrictions of life in Poland. Hosts would check outside their apartment door before discussing anything about politics. Friends would suddenly go silent when we were walking down a street together and a passerby came close.

Meanwhile, our stream of guests continued throughout the day, more flowers turning our cabin top into a happy-looking garden.

Theresa was also fond of folk dancing and asked to know the name of the Polish dancers we'd met in Kaustinen. By that evening we had invitations to fill the next three days completely.

Theresa and her friends Julian and Margo Czerwinski came to take us for dinner our third evening. Julian was a naval captain who had been in charge of Poland's 135-foot, three-masted training schooner. Now he worked translating sailing books from English to Polish. We knew by the conspiratorial whispers that the three of them had a surprise for us. As the five of us were walking through the silent gray, partially reconstructed streets of Gdynia, past grass-covered ruins of pre-World War II buildings, Theresa finally bubbled over with the news. "We sent a telegram to your dancer friends in the mountains. They replied immediately and told us that you must come to stay with them. Marion, the leader of the Kaustinen dancers, has arranged for you to live in his brother's house for a week because both his brother and sister-in-law speak English."

Larry and I must have looked reluctant because Julian spoke up, "It is a wonderful chance for you. The mountains around Zakopane are the most beautiful in Europe. The Socialist World Folk Dance Festival will be on, and some of East Europe's best dancers will be there. Transportation will be no problem. I need a holiday and can drive you there, and act as translator, too! Theresa and Krystyna will watch *Seraffyn.*" We stopped Julian and assured him, "We think it sounds great, but are you sure we won't be inconveniencing a lot of people?"

"Poles love visitors," both Julian and Theresa insisted. So that was that.

Twelve hours later we were rambling across the coastal plains of Poland toward Lodz. The trunk of Julian's little car disgorged a magnificent lunch basket full of treats prepared by his wife Margo, who couldn't take time off from her job as an English teacher to join us. We ate the lunch under a tree by the roadside. All around us other traveling Polish families were doing the same. "Restaurants are few and far between, and then, only for very rich people," Julian told us.

Near Lodz we crossed the Vistula River and entered the small village that had been my maternal grandparents' home until just after the First World War. It stood on the flat endless-looking plain that had served as Europe's battlefield during countless wars. Julian drove slowly through the tiny farm community, its artisans mostly gone now, the streets full of chickens and geese. Then we stopped to try and get a few cold cuts to fill our basket again. The village women in their long black skirts and black shirtwaists whispered and stared as we wandered through the almost empty stores. I tried to imagine that one or another of them might have known my ancestors, or might even be a distant cousin. There were no sausages or cheese available. As we drove off, I thought, "Life sure would have been different if my grandparents hadn't emigrated."

We were fifty miles short of Krakow when Julian slowed down and questioned a bicycle-riding farmer by the roadside. "We should look for a hotel soon," Larry suggested. "There are no hotels within forty miles of here, but that's no problem," Julian told us as he turned off into the front garden of a flourishing farm. He went to the door and spoke to the husky farm wife, then came back for us. "These people have invited us to stay for the night. How many eggs do you want for dinner?"

We were given spotless linen-covered beds in a scrubbed but bare room just beside the warm kitchen with its huge wood-burning stove. The farmhouse was a rambling affair, sparsely furnished except for the main living/dining room which was filled by a lace-covered mahogany dining table. The three of us were served a dinner of six scrambled eggs each, with garden vegetables and hot honey-covered fresh bread. Then the whole farm family drifted in, along with several neighbors, and Julian was kept busy translating as our hosts asked us endless questions about "the world outside." Were the things they heard when they listened to the Voice of America really true? Could Americans really change jobs and homes anytime they wanted to? Did we have to carry identity cards at all times?

As we prepared to leave the next morning, we asked to pay for our meals and board. The farmer and his wife refused, saying, "It's not every day we have transatlantic sailors visit us." I was really glad we'd bought a supply of nylon stretch pantyhose at the suggestion of an English friend who had previously visited Communist countries. When I offered the farm wife and her eighteen-year-old daughter two pairs, the glow in their eyes showed us that these fifty-cent supermarket specials were better than money.

The mountain village of Zakopane, a favorite winter ski resort frequented by bargain-hunting Western Europeans, is beautiful. Tall stone peaks tower over the pine log houses and dark pines line the edges of grass- and sheep-covered meadows. Varnished carriages pulled by handsome light-boned horses in glowing bell-encrusted harnesses moved easily through the streets. They served as taxis, and Julian told us, "These carriages aren't for show, they are really practical. In the winter the wheels come off and are replaced with runners to make them into sleds. It's the most convenient and reliable way to get over the snowy lanes and ice-covered hills to the homes and ski lodges outside town."

Marion and his family did seem to love visitors. They made all three of us right at home, giving us a key to the house and suggestions for tours and ways to fill each day. We spent most evenings watching the carefully scheduled performances of state-sponsored dancers from Hungary, Russian, Georgia, Rumania, and eight other Iron Curtain countries, plus Austria. The costumes and dancers were professionally superb, but the festival lacked the informal spontaneity of Kaustinen. The performance I'll never forget was given by our hosts, the irrepressible Polish mountain people, or Podhale. They had a fiercely independent spirit and a delightful sense of humor that glowed through their performance. The international audience roared with laughter while our hosts danced, sang, and fiddled through a reenactment of a mountain-style wedding. The men tried to open a fifty-gallon wooden keg of beer. At first we thought it was part of the performance when they seemed to have trouble pulling the bung out of the top. But after they'd struggled on stage minute after minute, the fiddlers playing the same tune for the fifth time, the audience began to call suggestions. Finally one dancer took matters in his own hands. He gave a mighty wack with the heel of his decorated woodsman's ax, the bung disappeared into the barrel in a spray of foaming beer, and the dancers thrust their beer mugs under the flowing spout. Their jumps and whirls grew ever more daring and acrobatic as the agitated beer keg continued to foam.

During the warm autumn days we wandered through the mountains meeting friends and relatives of our hosts. Julian translated, and through him we learned the stories of men who had served as couriers and guides through the Tatra Mountains' snow- and ice-covered passes during two world wars. We became used to being offered a glass of creamy, foaming cow's milk alongside a glass of homemade brandy, no matter what time of day we arrived to visit.

Julian had to leave after five days, but we stayed on to enjoy scenes and a way of life we'd probably never see again. On the last night of

Marion and his son in their violin-making shop.

Our hosts, dancers from the Podhale folk-dancing group. These clothes are not only used for dancing, they are standard Sunday best.

Visiting the relatives of our
Tatra mountain hosts.

the festival our Polish hosts gave a party for the Russian and Austrian dance groups at a local restaurant. No one wore costumes except for the Poles, who, we learned, didn't consider their embroidery-covered natural-white-wool pants and cloaks costumes, but the normal clothes to use for evening dress.

We were seated with the Russian dancers at dinner, with Zofia, the beautiful blonde English-speaking cousin of our Polish hosts, by our side to translate. Next to her sat the Polish-to-Russian translator. Our chain of communication seemed to break down when Zofia asked us to show the Georgian dancers a photo of our little cruising boat. Their looks were both wistful and incredulous, and their questions showed that their carefully regulated way of life gave them no basis for understanding our fairytale-like wealth of freedom.

Before the dinner was half finished the Austrian musicians offered to liven up the party with some music. The wonderful strains of a Strauss waltz rang from three violins and a bass viol. The dark-eyed young Russian folk dancer seated across from me asked his translator to ask mine if I'd be willing to dance. I joined him on the empty dance floor. I had worn a pair of silk slacks and a fancy scarf top that was backless. As my handsome partner took my right hand in his and put his left arm around me, his hand touched my bare back—and shot away as if it had been burned. He blushed and put his hand lower until it reached the cloth of my trousers. That caused an even quicker reaction. Finally he put his hand firmly on my upper back where it was covered with my long hair. He nodded to the players and we glided off into a waltz. What a dancer! I was sad but slightly breathless when the music stopped after we'd danced to five or six different waltz tunes. My partner bowed to me, then asked our two translators to help him. He made me blush and glow all over when I heard his words translated. "That was wonderful! I'm fortunate to be the only man from my village who has ever danced with a beautiful American woman." Then the Poles took over on the bandstand and everyone joined in, filling the evening with song, dance, and friendly banter.

After ten days we took the train north across Poland, our bags full of handmade gifts from our mountain friends. We'd been given a packed dinner and ate it in the deserted first-class coach. By nightfall we were freezing as the rickety train rumbled over the plains. Larry found a conductor and in sign language tried to get the heater turned on. The conductor found an English-speaking student from the third-class carriage who explained, "Our law says that summer does not end until September 15. So the conductor is not allowed to turn on the heaters until September 15." It was September 14, so we pulled all our spare clothes from our bag and burrowed into them, but still we shivered and slept little that night.

Krystyna Remiszewski was manager of a large ship's chandlery in the port of Gdynia and she helped us fill *Seraffyn* with wonderful food and stores. The Polish government needs western currency and gave us a huge bonus on each dollar we spent. So all of the goods from Eastern Europe cost us far less than similar products in the West. Fine Bulgarian Reisling-type wines were thirty-five cents a bottle. Russian pink, dry champagne (a weakness of mine) cost eighty-five cents a magnum. But even better were things like the famous smoked sausages, hams, and sides of bacon from central Poland. We hung two sides of bacon in our chain locker, and by wiping them down with vinegar and water, they kept for three months and added a rich aroma to the focsle. Canned tuna and mackerel from the Soviet Union proved to be excellent, but one special treat was a case of expensive but much desired American Skippy peanut butter Krystyna located in a far corner of her warehouse. It had been ordered by some Dutch ship but never called for.

Once again *Seraffyn* settled to her lines as she filled with stores. Our Polish sailing friends urged us to try to extend our visas and stay on, at the same time saying, "You really should take your boat out of the water or leave the Baltic now as it is time for the equinotial gales." We had a hard time convincing ourselves that winter was on its way—an Indian summer gave us warm sunny days, although the nights were definitely becoming colder and longer.

We sunbathed on *Seraffyn* in the afternoon while we watched the superb boat handling displayed by the sailing club members. They maneuvered their forty-five-foot ketches in the confines of the yachting harbor completely under sail, dropping anchor and then backing them stern-to to the piers by shoving their booms to windward. The club sailors worked as a trained team on the state-owned boats. We met the owner of one of the few private yachts in Poland. The thirty-year-old boat builder told us that the cost of materials for a boat like *Seraffyn*, even after substituting items easily available in Poland, would be equal to a naval architect's complete salary for eight to ten years. He only owned a boat because he'd built it himself and had been given a large

Lin shopping in the public market of Gdynia.

pension when he lost both his legs below the knees in an industrial accident. This shocked us because we'd watched him at work, finishing the deck of a Carter-designed thirty-three-footer and seen him clamber out *Seraffyn*'s bowsprit, never once realizing his handicap existed.

Farewells are always hard and in Poland there was one further complication. Seven armed officials arrived an hour before the departure time written in our port clearance papers. Two stood guard on the dock alongside us while five came on board and looked in each locker, Larry's toolbox, the bilges. They even looked inside our oven. "Are you looking for liquor or arms or what?" Larry asked. The most ribbon-encrusted official replied, "No, we are checking for stowaways." He signed the final release paper after his crew finished their inspection. "You must leave now," he told us.

"But our friends aren't here yet. We want to say good-bye!" Larry protested.

A hurried conference ensued. "You may wait, but no one is allowed to put a foot on your boat and you must stay on board. These two guards will stay until you sail out."

Theresa, Julian, and Margo arrived, leading about ten of our Polish friends down the dock just as the five officials were leaving. We tried to exchange hugs and kisses across *Seraffyn*'s lifelines as they handed us more beautiful flowers and a lovely bag of fresh fuit. But all of us were acutely aware of the watchful guards standing at attention, their automatic rifles by their sides, less than five feet away from our farewell party.

"Please write to us as soon as you are safe for the winter," Theresa called as she helped cast off our mooring lines. We set the mainsail and lapper to catch the morning offshore breeze, and we took two extra tacks inside the breakwaters so we could exchange shouted last good-byes. The two guards rested their rifles alongside the guardpost and joined in the waves and farewell wishes as we eased our sheets and reached out of the harbor. "Dovidzania" we called out, repeating the lovely farewell word our warm Polish friends had taught us.

For a day and a half we ran wing and wing, along first the Polish, then the East German shore, the wind growing steadily fresher. "Visiting Poland made me realize how fortunate we are," Larry commented as we once again discussed the restrictions and economic problems we'd seen. "We Westerners take our freedoms for granted, especially the freedom of passports and traveling freely."

CHAPTER 16

The equinoctial gales our sailing friends from Sweden, Finland, and Poland had warned us about proved to be no myth. By the eighteenth of September 1973, the morning after we tied up in Bornholm's Ronne harbor, an easterly storm was blowing. *Seraffyn* lay comfortably in the corner of the fish haven, completely surrounded by almost a hundred Danish fishing trawlers. The wind moaned through the forest of rigging surrounding us and rain hurled down in sheets. For five days the wind blew at gale force with gusts to seventy knots.

At first we welcomed the enforced stay in port. I had mending to do. Larry was busy writing and reading. The local library had a large collection of English-language magazines. But we grew restless after our mail packet arrived at the local post office and we finished answering every letter in it.

"We're only about a hundred sixty miles from Thruro," I told Larry one evening after we'd returned from a walk decked out in full wet-weather gear plus three sweaters each. "Three good days' sailing and we'll be where we want to spent the winter."

Larry looked over my shoulder to study the chart of the natural harbor in front of Walstead's shipyard. "Looks good and safe, Lin. I'm sure we'll be able to take *Seraffyn* out of the water to revarnish her insides." We turned off the tiny butane heater we'd connected to one burner of our stove, then crawled into our Dacron-filled double sleeping bag. We quietly discussed the refit *Seraffyn* needed now that she was almost five years old. One or the other of us kept thinking of new items to add to our growing work list until we fell asleep, cuddled warmly together.

Each day the fishermen who owned the boats around us would come down from their homes in town to check their mooring lines, start their engines, and exchange news with their friends. One or the other would translate the latest weather forecast for us. On the sixth day the sky was clear and the wind did seem lighter when we opened our hatch in the early morning. By 1000 the wind was definitely lighter. The owner of the small steel yacht tied near us called, "Come listen to the forecast." He translated as a German announcer said, "Wind easterly, Force 6 to 7, decreasing to 4 or 5."

All around us the trawlers started to come to life. Their crews arrived from town shouting merrily across the water. A hundred fishing boats maneuvered out of the inner harbor, one after another. By noon there was only one trawler, the steel yacht, and ourselves left in the south end of the previously crowded harbor. "I'm not sure I want to go," I said, tapping the barometer that stood good and high at almost 1015 millibars. It didn't move. The flag on the harbormaster's office had stopped whipping and just waved gaily in the slightly gusty Force 5 east wind. Larry seemed reluctant, too. "It's dead downwind from here. Since it's about eighty-five miles to the light at Klintholm, we could leave as late as 1400 and still be sure of arriving during daylight. Let's wait another three or four hours. If the wind continues to drop, we'll set off."

I cooked up a pot of stew while I made lunch, figuring that it would be wise to have dinner ready in case the leftover seas outside were rough. At 1230 the people on the steel yacht prepared to sail. The four young Germans on board the thirty-foot *Tummler* had to get home to their jobs in Kiel. But still we were reluctant to cast off our mooring lines, although neither of us could put a finger on what was bothering us. At 1300 the last trawlermen cast off their lines and headed into the steadily calming sea. At 1400 neither of us could think of any logical excuses to stay in the harbor. We maneuvered *Seraffyn* around until she was pointing bow to the wind, then hoisted the double-reefed mainsail and staysail, cast off our doubled-up mooring lines, and reached into the center of the basin. As we tacked for the narrow entrance, the harbormaster came out of his office and called, "Good sailing." And it was good sailing as we ran wing and wing out of Ronne Harbor. The sea was calm, protected by the mass of Bornholm Island. Our small sails pulled us at top speed. We decided to eat an early dinner and really enjoyed the stew. Dark seemed to come extra early that evening as the skies clouded over and the wind began to increase. Before I went below to climb into the bunk, I helped Larry drop the mainsail, furl it, and secure the boom in the gallows. We'd already put one drop board into the companionway even though there was no spray on deck. We'd made it a rule that as soon as there was a reef in the mainsail, a drop board belonged in place. Since the first of the drop boards has its top higher than the level of our deck, water that gets into the cockpit during heavy weather can't easily find its way below decks.

Larry put our handy canvas companionway cover in place over the rest of the opening because the ever-increasing wind was cold. I was undressed down to a long-sleeve t-shirt, underpants, and socks when Larry pulled the canvas aside and said, "Hey, Bug, how about sleeping in my bunk tonight. It's on the windward side so if a bit of spray does come on board it won't get the sleeping bag wet." I was surprised at his suggestion because I prefer sleeping against the hull on the leeward side of *Seraffyn* when there is any motion. But I switched the bag across and set the lee cloth in place. One oil lamp glowed softly above the galley, swinging gaily in its gimbals as we roared off the backs of the growing seas. I squirmed around until I could lift the canvas companionway cover. I saw Larry standing in back of the boom gallows, his elbows over the stout piece of teak on which the mainboom now rested as we ran under just the staysail. Our oil-burning stern light bounced beside him, its light gleaming off his high black seaboots. He looked comfortable and warm enough in his sweater-bulged windbreaker and jeans. Our ship's bell rang four times and I secured the lashing on the lee cloth, turned over, and went easily to sleep.

How can anyone describe the horrid sensation I felt when I was thrown halfway out of the bunk? Only the lee cloth kept me from going further. *Seraffyn* made a huge whunking sound as she was hurled off the top of a breaking sea. The horrid crashing sound of flying cans, tools, books, floorboards, and dishes drowned out the rushing sound of the huge stream of water that pushed past the canvas companionway cover. We seemed to be upside down, then I was tossed just as violently back into the quarter berth. I struggled clear of the sleeping bag, sheet, and lee cloth in the solid darkness. I could only scream— "Larry, Larry!"—then my feet hit the water that sloshed fore and aft as *Seraffyn* resumed her running motion. I was standing calf-deep in water grabbing for a flashlight when Larry yelled, "I'm here. Start pumping!"

I found the bilge pump handle, inserted it in the pump, and started stroking. Floating floorboards hit my ankles, making watery-sounding thunks as they collided with the settee fronts. I had the water down three or four inches when Larry yelled, "Don't worry when the boat's motion changes." He poked his soaking-wet head past the canvas cover, "I'm going to head into the wind and heave to. Everything's all right now, Bug."

I flashed the light around the horribly littered cabin, pumping all the while. All the books from our navigation shelf were in the sink. The lenses from two oil lamps lay in shattered pieces on the drain board. Most of the tools from the locker in the starboard settee were now on top of the port quarter berth. Had I been sleeping there I'd have been hit by chisels, woodplanes, screwdrivers, wrenches—over a hundred pounds of flying sharp metal. Something kept tapping my leg. When the beam of my light picked up my toothbrush floating merrily on top of the remaining fifty or sixty gallons of unwelcome ocean that had invaded my previously tidy home, I finally broke down and started crying.

Larry hoisted the double-reefed mainsail. *Seraffyn*'s motion changed as she heeled to a gust of wind on her beam, then rounded into the wind, slowed down, and finally stopped, heeling about fifteen degrees. She began to assume the comfortable, safe-feeling motion that I knew meant we were hove to.

Larry climbed below just then. "Got to get an oil lamp burning fast. We're surrounded by fishing boats," he was saying as he took my flashlight and looked around. Then he noticed my tear-streaked face. He tugged off his dripping windbreaker, put his soggy-sweatered arms around me, and started rocking me, whispering, "It's all right now, baby, we're okay."

I realized that Larry was shivering in his wet clothes. My stockinged feet were still covered with sloshing water. "Get out of those wet clothes," I commanded, trying to catch hold of myself. I grabbed for a paper towel to wipe my tears only to get a handful of soggy paper from the towel roller. Larry took charge. "Find me some oil lamp lenses. Every one in our navigation lamps shattered when they filled with water." Our linen locker on the starboard side had stayed completely dry, so I handed Larry a fresh towel along with his new lenses. He first got a cabin light going. Then he finished pumping the bilges. "I'm sure glad we moved the bilge pump to a position inside the cabin," he commented as our Whale Gusher 10 made sucking and gurgling sounds.

The kind golden light of two oil lamps made our mess look less frightening. Larry went back on deck, retrieved and lit our running lights, then finally stripped. When I rummaged in our clothes locker I found that over half of Larry's clothes were dry but all of mine were soaked because they were on the lower shelf. I stripped too, then both of us dressed in Larry's dry warm sweaters and jeans, laughing just a bit at the luck that made me store Larry's clothes on the upper shelves of our locker. "Can you imagine me trying to get into one of your sweaters?" Larry teased. Then we started storing things somewhat back in place. A cup of hot chocolate laced with brandy tasted wonderful, and I finally convinced Larry to climb into the miraculously dry sleeping bag when he started to shiver again. "You'll have to keep a good watch on deck," Larry warned me. "There are still lots of fishing boats around, so be ready to ease the mainsheet and bear off to move clear if anything gets too close."

His shivering soon stopped and finally he told me the deckside version of our mishap. "After you went to sleep the wind increased a lot more. The seas were growing, probably because we were clear of Bornholm's lee. *Seraffyn* was going too fast even with just the staysail. I considered heaving to, but there were all of those fish trawlers heading back toward the protection of the island. I figured it would be best to run past the last of them, then heave to. So I dropped the staysail and reset Helmer to put the wind dead aft. *Seraffyn* kept running at about three knots under bare poles. Helmer held her perfectly on course. I was standing on the afterdeck, behind the boom gallows, holding on, watching that keen little steering vane do its work. There was just a low-flying spray hitting my seaboots. I didn't even once consider putting on wet gear. Then I looked astern and said to myself, 'That one is going to get me wet.' Well, the wave broke right over our stern. Next thing I knew, I was completely under, plastered against the boom gallows by a huge weight of water. Boy, did I hold on tight! I'll bet you can see fingerprints in the teak. Then my head came clear. All I could see was white foam all around, no boat all. I can just remember thinking of you trapped below before I saw one tip of one spreader break clear of the foam. Then I knew she was going to come up. The mast leapt clear and seconds later *Seraffyn* seemed to shake herself dry. The windvane took over and we were running downwind again as if nothing had happened. The amazing thing is, the vane itself was bent at least thirty degrees to port yet it could still steer the boat. God, it all happened so fast! I should have hove to and stayed on deck with our big flashlight. When I think about it now, those fishing boats would have seen us; they must have been watching, too." (See Appendix C for a further discussion of storm tactics.)

Larry finally fell asleep. *Seraffyn* rode to the steadily howling storm, laying about fifty degrees off the wind. The wind and sea seemed to increase during the next three hours. Once a sea smashed against our bow sending a heavy clatter of spray against the cabin front, but no green water came on deck. A heavy rain started, and by dawn the wind abated enough so that we felt safe in laying off toward the Swedish harbor of Ysted, fourteen miles away on a reaching course. In the gray, rain-streaked dawn we could finally assess the damage we'd sustained. Our pride and joy, a thirty-year-old copper and brass oil-lamp-lit binnacle with a four-year-old four-inch Ritchie compass, had disappeared from its wooden bracket. The one-inch-diameter bronze pipe lifeline stanchion that we lashed the blade of our fourteen-foot oar to was bent at almost forty-five degrees. The dinghy, lashed firmly to its chocks on the cabin top, had been loosened up, and closer inspection showed that one of the bronze brackets holding the chocks to the cabin top had been bent like a pretzel and its two-inch, number 14 screws pulled loose from the oak framing of the cabin top. The inside of the cabin top was cracked from the force the dinghy had exerted. Inside, the damage was minimal: a lot of dented varnish work from flying tools, several broken bottles, loads of wet clothes, and five broken oil-lamp lenses. We were glad we'd had no engine because oil or fuel from the bilges would have made matters worse. Since the only electric equipment on board was the portable radio, which had been on the windward side and stayed completely dry, we were able to get all ship's systems working in short order despite the huge amount of water that had come on board. Every bit of the damage, both inside and on deck, occurred on the port side of the boat, the side that fell into the trough of the wave.

We used our hand bearing compass to steer by. Ysted came into view by 1000, although visibility was made poor by driving rain. We reached into its almost deserted yacht basin and sighed with relief as we tied our lines securely. I pulled all our wet clothes out onto the rain-soaked decks. Larry stuffed them into sailbags and we carted them into town. The lady at the laundromat was amazed at our soggy mass of clothes, so we explained what had happened. When we returned to the small harbor, we found that she had called the local newspaper— a reporter was waiting for us. "You know, a four-hundred-ton coaster sank only seventeen miles from here yesterday evening," he told us. Then he drove us to the main harbor to see the unhappy crew of a two-hundred-ton coaster slowly moving a shattered cargo of roofing tiles to correct the seventeen-degree list their ship had assumed after being hit by a rogue wave the night before. They'd lost most of their deck cargo, and only made port with the assistance of a huge car ferry that had responded to their May Day call. The ferry had stayed carefully to windward of the coaster, giving them a lee for the eighteen-mile voyage into Ysted Harbor.

We began wondering about the thirty-foot German yacht that had left Ronne an hour before us. And to this day we don't know what happened to *Tummler* and her crew of four. "You people should know better than to sail during the equinotial gales," the reporter commented, echoing the warning we'd had from dozens of Baltic sailors. We'd ignored them all and paid the price.

CHAPTER 17

~~~~~

Looking for Work

At first we were embarrassed when a local sailing family came rushing down the wooden dock to where we were busily drying fifty pounds of assorted vegetables, all our wet-weather gear, cushions, and floorboards. The family had read of our mishap in the storm and showed us the newspaper's slightly overdramatized article with its photo of *Seraffyn*, Larry, and me tied in Ysted Harbor. But our embarrassment soon changed to pleasure when they invited us home to dinner. They were the first of several Ysted families to stop by and make sure we were healthy, secure, fed, comfortable, and well entertained. For seven more days the equinotial gales blew, sometimes accompanied by heavy rain, other times by bright sunshine. Our Swedish friends provided us with evenings at home, rides around the countryside, and an evening at the local skindiving club where we watched beautiful homemade movies of a member's expedition to dive in the Red Sea. One of the local sailors located a spare box compass in a friend's garage, and when the storm cleared we were ready to sail.

This time we listened to the weather lore Ysted's sailors offered us. All seemed to agree that for the next month or two there would be only one or two days per fortnight with strong winds, but fog might be a problem. The locals also told us that by combining the information broadcast on longwave radio by BBC in England for the North Sea and German Bight, with that on the German broadcast for the southern Baltic, we'd get a good idea of the weather. After listening to the German broadcast four or five times we began to recognize the words that meant "storm," "fog," "sunshine," and "light winds."

On Wednesday the third of October we awoke to the *brrr* of our tiny travel clock's alarm. The two weather forecasts never once mentioned any wind over Force 5. By 0700 the sun shone gaily on our dewy decks. It was nippy cold, only a few degrees above freezing, yet when we ran clear of Ysted Harbor an hour later and set full sail, I wrote in our logbook, "beautiful, beautiful sailing."

For the next week the weather remained the same. We had delightful sailing as we explored Denmark's southern islands (Great Belt). I learned to sail with gloves, three sweaters, and two pairs of pants, feeling like a kid decked out for the snow. Larry reveled in the nippy weather, consuming hot cups of coffee or chocolate as fast as I could produce them. Each day's sail ended with Larry's winter drink, a hot rum punch: one part dark rum, two heaping teaspoons of sugar, one teaspoon of lemon juice, one shake of cinnamon powder or cinnamon stick, and three parts boiling water; mix well then put a dab of fresh butter on top and serve.

We could see a heavy band of fog rolling slowly toward us as we entered the Agerso Sound late one afternoon, and we were glad when *Seraffyn* whispered slowly through the breakwaters in front of the tiny town of Karrebaeksmin. There was a bit of tide running against us as

Nippy, cold sailing as we finally sailed for southern Denmark.

water flowed out of the huge estuary behind the town, so when we dropped our anchor approximately a hundred yards south of the big pier shown on our chart, *Seraffyn* drifted slowly back, taking up the slack in her chain. The wind had died completely and the water was as flat as gravy on a plate inside the protecting arm of the breakwaters. When *Seraffyn* hit something that sounded just like rock, we didn't worry but we were quite surprised. Larry got out the lead line and dropped it overboard. At our bow there was twenty feet of water, but our stern was aground on a rock. Larry climbed into *Rinky* and sounded all around us to find a patch of clear water. Then I winched in our chain and anchor while Larry set our oar in place. *Seraffyn* easily came free of the offending rock as Larry rowed her to his chosen spot and reanchored. Then a heavy wet fog closed in and we climbed below for dinner.

Early the next day we heard the sound of a sail being dropped close astern of us. Larry opened our hatch to see three sailors maneuvering a lovely-looking R boat under jib alone. As they tacked over in the seven-knot breeze, fog swirled and coiled around them. Larry let out a great shout of warning just before they hit our rock. The wooden

The R boat crew worked hard to free the boat from the rock we'd discovered the night before.

sloop came to a sudden stop, then stuck, its waterline exposed, its crew very surprised. They started their engine but that didn't budge them. We could see they had no dinghy, so Larry rowed over and offered to help. They handed him their big kedge anchor and Larry rowed it out with two hundred feet of line, then dropped it off the stern of *Rinky*. The crew tugged on the anchor line, rocked their thirty-eight-foot boat back and forth by leaning out first from the port shrouds and then the starboard ones, and finally the R boat shot free. There really wasn't room enough for them to join us at anchor in the area clear of rocks, so they sailed alongside the town pier and Larry went with them.

He rowed home half an hour later. "I just met a fellow from the local sailing club. Seems the pier over there used to be a hundred yards longer when our chart was drawn. It collapsed about three years ago and both boats anchored a hundred yards away from what is left, or right on top of the old foundations." In all of our cruising, this was the first time we'd found an inaccuracy on any chart that affected our sailing. But the local port authorities had written to the proper hydrographic office and reports of the pier's collapse had appeared in notices to mariners.

Larry came below and poured a cup of coffee from the still hot percolator. "Egon invited us to come to his house for dinner, and we have permission to tie up next to the pier," Larry said. "Who is Egon?" I asked. "The man from the sailing club," Larry answered, as he disappeared into the forepeak with a book he was reading.

By afternoon a strong wind was blowing directly through the opening in the breakwaters. Egon was waiting for us on the pier when we lifted anchor and sailed alongside with just our staysail. "Storm coming. You'd best sail under the bridge to the yacht club," he called. This made sense since the water alongside the pier was already starting to foam and boil against the tide as the wind increased. I stayed on board, making sure our fenders stayed in place between the rugged concrete and *Seraffyn*'s white-painted topside, while Larry and Egon made arrangements to have the bridge opened. The three of us sailed easily past the open bridge, and less than half a mile upstream secured to the clean wooden pier. We found ourselves surrounded by a variety of small yachts, which seemed strange this late in the year until Egon explained. "Because of the strong currents in this estuary, very little ice ever forms on the water. So most people leave their boats afloat waiting for those special sunny days that come even in the depths of our Danish winters." By midnight when Egon brought us home from a lovely dinner, a full gale was blowing. But we couldn't have felt safer.

We walked across the bridge toward the windswept village the next day. Only one other person was on the streets, an older man limping heavily along with a cane. His hat blew off as an extra-strong gust of wind swept through the wet streets. I ran after it, enjoying the exercise after the confines of *Seraffyn*. When I caught it and brought it back, Larry was talking to the man. A heavy drizzle started. Per Gustaffsen introduced himself and pointed to a whitewashed cottage right on the quayside. "Come in and warm up," he insisted. We followed him into his foyer, shed winter coats and boots, then walked in stocking feet across the highly polished wooden floors. "Watch that door sill," Per commented as we entered his cozy sitting room. His wife greeted us warmly and soon poured out hot tea and passed a plate of shortbread-like cookies as Per told us how he'd come to limp so badly:

I've been a pilot in this port almost forty years, sometimes bringing as many as five ships a week into the harbor in every kind of weather, and sometimes we get some pretty bad seas here, what with the tide and shallow waters and wind-driven currents. Last year in the middle of a huge winter storm I got a call to go out and meet a German freighter of about five thousand tons. It was early in the morning and the snow was coming down in heavy sheets blown by forty or fifty knots of wind. The streets were covered with ice. I met the pilot boat skipper at that cafe across the street and together we went to the pier. We had to climb down the ten-foot ice-encrusted iron ladder to get to the boat. The boat was covered in ice, icicles hanging from its rigging, a sheet of ice on its deck.

As soon as we cleared the breakwaters, we started hitting some of the worst seas I've ever seen in this sound. We were taking green water right over the bridge at times. My skipper located the German ship about three miles away and brought his boat masterfully alongside the wildly swinging rope ladder they'd let down for me, but the motion of those two vessels riding alongside each other in huge seas was horrid and I had to jump at just the right moment and rush up the ladder to avoid being crushed between the boat and ship. I somehow managed to do it and climbed up the slippery rope ladder, swinging first against the ship's side and then away from it. I finally made it to the deck and a seaman was there to grab my arm. He could barely stand on the ice-covered decks. I steered that ship into the harbor, using every skill I knew, and we got her tied up.

I had a hot drink with the captain, then climbed down the icy boarding ladder to the wharf and walked the half mile home, slipping and sliding, bowing my head to shield my eyes from the wind-driven snow. I reached our doorstep, opened the door, and stepped inside. I took off my coat, removed my seaboots, and headed toward the kitchen where I could smell the coffee my wife had brewing for me. I tripped over that dammed sill, fell, and broke my hip!

The irony of the whole saga seemed to hit Per once again and he laughed loudly as he pointed to the two-inch-high polished Danish oak sill at the entrance to the room we sat in.

It was the eleventh of October when we finally sailed into the channel leading to Thruro where Walstead's shipyard lay waiting for us. I was ready to settle in for the winter. Larry called it my nesting urge, but I was really looking forward to staying in the same place for a few months. I looked forward to doing my grocery shopping in the same stores each week and coming to know who had the nicest vegetables, or where to get the spices I wanted. I needed the friendly feeling of being recognized and greeted by the local merchants and maybe joining in a coffee klatch for a bit of female talk of recipes, sewing, and homemaking. These breaks in our cruising life were a refreshing change, and after three or four months my desire to move was always stronger than ever before. As soon as we'd anchored in front of the big sheds where *Puffin* had been built, Larry rowed ashore to find out about a winter job. I was busy looking around at the four or five shuttered cottages on the point about a quarter mile away from the sheds, daydreaming about starting a fire in one of their fireplaces and spending the long winter evenings toasting my toes and marshmellows in front of the flames.

Larry was away for almost two hours, and when he returned I could sense that all was not as we'd wished. "Didn't Walstead need any help?" I asked as he secured *Rinky* and climbed on deck. Larry began, "Walstead's wants any shipwright they can find. In fact, they've been advertising for help and not getting any replies. But Denmark has just become a full member of the European Economic Common Market this month and now anyone who isn't from one of the nine countries or their trading partners can't get a work permit. They've got an American guy there who is working for free just for the experience. They don't dare hire me—the authorities are watching too closely."

I was reluctant to let go of my dream. "But there must be some way of getting a work permit," I insisted.

"I doubt it," Larry answered. "The American fellow has been trying for six weeks. But I sure would like to work here. You should see the oven and jig they have for making laminated frames quickly."

We sailed six miles to the main town of Svendborg and tried to get a work permit. We were told that we could immediately start collecting welfare as unemployable residents, but there was no way we could work in Denmark because their quota of Canadian workers was full. "Now if you were Turkish there would be no problem," they told us.

We called Leif Møller in Copenhagen and he too tried to arrange the papers. He called everyone he knew including several politicians and the chief of police. When he had no luck, we gave up.

"Let's call England," Larry finally suggested. "I know I can work there. The Parkstone Yacht Club said if we gave them warning they could probably find room to store *Seraffyn* in their shed."

When Tom Hunt answered Parkstone Yacht Club's telephone he seemed delighted to hear that we planned to spend another winter in Poole. "Come right over and have lunch with me and we'll check the tide book and decide which day to pull you out," he said. I explained that we had over five hundred miles to sail and the Kiel Canal to transit before we could join him, but we would be there in time for lunch one day soon.

Leif Møller joined us to sail from Svendborg to Kiel. We once again had a wonderful frosty Danish winter special of a day as we first beat through the southernmost of Denmark's islands past Marstal, still the home port of many Baltic sailing trading ships. Then we eased our sheets and ran toward Kiel. Leif Møllar was a delightful guest as usual, lamenting the fact that some silly-sounding bureaucratic rules were keeping us from spending the winter where we could get together frequently. But then he decided he'd find some excuse to come to England during the winter and visit us. This weighty matter taken care of, he gave us a running commentary on all we passed. The night sail up to Kiel Fjord past a myriad of shipping absolutely thrilled Leif. "Do you think they know we're here?" he asked as we tacked to avoid yet another steamer when we saw both their port and starboard running lights at the same time. "I always assume they don't," was Larry's answer.

Beating through the islands.

We anchored in front of the Kiel Yacht Club at midnight. Leif left the next morning to take a ferry home to Copenhagen and we walked to the canal control offices. "How do we get our boat through the canal? She doesn't have an engine," I asked the man at the desk. "Easy," he replied, "hitchhike!"

And, following his advice, we did "hitchhike." We got our anchor up at daybreak and sailed over to the waiting area in front of the equalizing lock at the canal entrance. Thirty or forty ships of all sizes and shapes were anchored or steaming slowly in circles waiting their turn to enter the enormous lock. Larry slowed *Seraffyn* down by heading her into the wind. I climbed clumsily into *Rinky Dink,* encumbered by all my sweaters and wet-weather gear that barely kept me as warm as I wished in the bitting breeze. Weather reports on the radio told of a snowstorm less than eighty miles north of us, and the leaden sky overhead bore signs that it might move south.

I rowed among the freighters and coasters, yelling up at the crew of the smaller ones, "What speed do you make?" Everyone answered, "Nine knots," which was the top limit in the Kiel Canal. So I rowed on. Larry had warned me of possible dangers of towing a heavy-displacement boat like *Seraffyn* at over seven knots (theoretical hull speed plus one-quarter). It could impose strains that could jerk our bitts loose, besides causing *Seraffyn* to be difficult to steer. I was becoming dubious about finding us a tow that day. The lockmaster was beginning to call ships into the lock one at a time, his voice booming over a huge loudspeaker on the top of the lockmaster's tower. Then, just as I turned up to row out to where Larry was reaching back and forth with *Seraffyn,* I heard a beautiful sound—"tump . . . tump, tump . . . tump." I immediately knew I'd found our tow. I rowed past three steel coasters and there she was—a lovely old baby-blue Danish trawler, her icy-cold single-cylinder diesel blowing perfect smoke rings out the soot-blackened smokestack as it fought against starting for one minute more. I rowed up to the forty-five-foot wooden ship, yelled to a crewman on deck, and when he came over I asked, "Will you tow me through the canal?" He was the epitome of a Danish seaman, blond, blue-eyed, husky with a laugh to match. "Tow you? Hell, we'll lift you right on deck," he said when he looked over the rail at six-foot eight-inch-long fifty-pound *Rinky* and me. But when I simply turned and pointed out to where *Seraffyn* glided back and forth pretty as a white-winged bird, Larry waving from her tiller, the Dane laughed again. "I knew there had to be a catch. But never mind, we'll tow him, too!"

So I rowed to back to *Seraffyn*. Larry and I dropped her sails, pulled the dinghy on board, and got out fenders, mooring lines, and rigged a tow cable. Our Danish tow boat steamed alongside and then, side by side, took us slowly into the lock.

Over thirty small ships and ourselves filled the lock. The captains of each went to the lockmaster's office to pay their fees as water slowly filled the lock, lifting us all about ten feet to the level of the main river system that fed the canal. Our fee came to six dollars.

There are no pilots required for the canal on ships of less than five hundred tons, and as soon as we were clear of the lock our Danish trawler captain suggested we fall back on our long tow line so there would be less chance of damage from the washes of passing ships.

Seraffyn towed well at six and a half knots, but someone had to steer her all the time. Larry seemed to stand the cold better than I did, but only by downing cups of hot chocolate did he keep from turning blue as the headwind was increased by our forward motion. Halfway

Seraffyn under tow in the Kiel Canal.

through the fifty-mile-long canal our trawler slowed down. As *Seraffyn* glided alongside, the captain called, "This is Rendsburg. My favorite restaurant is here. Do you mind if we stop and tie up for the night?" Blue-lipped Larry thought the idea was great, and as soon as we were secured to the side of the trawler next to the huge timber wharf, I began thawing him out with hot rum punch and steaming thick beef stew.

The next day we reached the lock at Brunsbuttal and tied alongside our trawler as we waited for the lock to fill with ships that came straggling slowly in. The trawler men invited us on board and I brought along two big loaves of fresh bread I'd baked as Larry steered. They produced butter, honey, and strawberry preserves as we sat next to their roaring diesel heater in the sixty-year-old trawler's forward galley and sleeping quarters. Then they explained that they were taking her to the museum at Esberg, Denmark. "She was the first Danish trawler to have an engine," the engineer told us as he proudly gave us a tour of her engine room. The rough old single-cylinder engine had a seven-foot flywheel and moved the trawler at hull speed when it was going 100 revolutions per minute. "Lovely old engine. Nothing precision about it. We can machine up any old part that needs replacement ourselves," the engineer told us. He was sad to see his little ship retire after so many years of faithful service, but admitted that a museum was a good place for her to spend her retirement.

The lock filled with forty coasters and small ships, then emptied of ten feet of water. The gates swung open and the River Elbe lay before us. Our Danish trawler friends refused payment of any kind and wished us good luck as they motored out of the lock—tump, tump, tump.

We waited half an hour tied alongside the lock wall until a customs man arrived with two cases of duty-free scotch whiskey Larry had ordered in Kiel. Then we sailed out with the last of the tide and three hours later anchored in Cuxhaven, the North Sea entrance to the Elbe River.

The evening weather report from BBC in England told of gales and snow still to the north of us, but clearing was forecast within twenty-four hours. "This time we'll take no chances. We'll wait until there is not one gale within five hundred miles of us," Larry commented as he toasted his hands over our bravely glowing butane heater.

~~~~~

CHAPTER 18

A Different Kind
of Weather

We only had to wait two days for a storm-free weather forecast. Even in Iceland the BBC reported light winds and no fog. We were really glad to be on our way because each day was perceptibly shorter, each night perceptibly colder. Besides, one stroll through the German city of Cuxhaven had given us a real fright. Food prices were the highest we'd ever seen (lamb chops were six dollars a pound, and tomatoes a dollar fifty a pound in 1973). We both like meat and fresh vegetables. With our tastes we'd have eaten up the last of our dwindling cruising funds in no time at all.

We were under way with the first of the ebbing tide bound for the notorious wintery North Sea with just enough breeze to give us steerage way. The sky was gray and streaky. A cold, damp haze cut visibility to about two miles. Shipping of all sizes, shapes, and ages chugged past us as we drifted by each marker buoy on the three-knot tide. The river traffic divided itself neatly, inbound shipping hugging the southern side of the well-marked channel, outbound traffic the north side. So we happily sailed right up the middle, taking advantage of the strongest tide, waving to the ships that passed two hundred yards on either side of us. For five hours this strategy worked perfectly. We traveled seventeen miles downriver until we were out in what looked like open water although our chart showed a maze of shoals and mud banks six hundred feet outside the channel. The shipping never thinned out, but as soon as dark fell our wind did. Then the tide began to turn against us. "Let's sail outside the channel and anchor till the tide turns fair," Larry suggested after looking at our chart. "We're right next to this buoy and there are two fathoms of water behind it for almost two hundred yards." I couldn't have agreed more. The thought of a night cuddled together in the warm bunk was much more appealing than one spent standing out in the cold and dark, steering from buoy to buoy, worrying in case a ship came too close, especially since we were barely moving. Larry looked around and said, "We'll fall off and run astern of that next ship." We eased the sheets and steered due south. The large coaster passed us, the masthead lights of the next ship were over a mile away, and the buoy that was our goal was less than two hundred yards ahead. We trickled slowly through the water, our speed dropping as the wind died even more. The green running light of the ship was joined by a red one. "They're going to hit us!" Larry gulped. I started flashing a D signal with our six-volt battery-powered quarter-mile lamp: −·· −·· −·· ("keep clear, I am maneuvering with difficulty"). The red and green lights grew steadily closer as Larry rushed to put our oar in place. The ship's masthead lights stayed right in line as Larry shoved against the oar. I kept flashing the light, swinging its beam across our sails. Larry was swearing up a storm as he worked, "Why don't they indicate they see us? They must have someone at the helm when there is such a crowd of shipping. Someone must be directing them through this channel." I could see the huge-looking ship clearly in the darkness, and when it seemed to be almost on top of us I dropped the tiller, rushed below, and grabbed the foghorn, then let out blast after blast. The ship never flashed a light or in any way acknowledged our presence. They never altered course; they never slowed down. And they only cleared our stern by what looked like fifty feet!

We were both unbelievably relieved to be out of the channel with our anchor down even though the boat rolled and bounced to the frequent wake of passing ships. I poured Larry a shot of whiskey and both of us vented our pent-up fear, calling the captain of that unknown ship all sorts of names. But as soon as we grew less tense Larry looked at our chart carefully, then said, "We were the foolish ones, Lin; we could have sailed all the way from Cuxhaven just outside the channel, clear of the shipping. There are two fathoms of water behind the buoys almost everywhere. We'd have had our own private two-hundred-yard-wide channel and we could have dropped anchor anywhere along the way. We're the ones who chose to sail without an engine. We shouldn't expect commercial shipping to stay out of our way. We've got to sail as if no one cares and no one can see us."

We set the anchor lite, hung it on the staysail stay and then slept soundly until 0300 when *Seraffyn* started to snub against her anchor chain. In our forward bunk we could hear the chain grumbling across the bottom when the wind changed direction. It served as a warning buzzer. Larry went on deck just as our alarm went off to tell us when the tide was changing. A fresh breeze blew from the east-southeast. Our course for the next hundred miles was due west. We lit our running lamps, hoisted our mainsail and lapper, and set off at five knots through the water with the fair tide under our keel increasing our speed over the bottom by three knots. There must have been some special star shining on us because our passage down the dreaded North Sea, through one of the busiest concentrations of shipping in the world, was delightful. Although it was cold and cloudy, the wind was always fair. In fact, it was always aft of the beam. When we had to alter course past the Hook of Holland and sail due south, the wind seemed happy to give us a break and within an hour it changed from east-southeast to northwest. The sea stayed almost flat. There was only a bit of morning fog, and the low clouds reflected navigation lights so we often spotted them and identified their sequences eight or ten miles sooner than we normally could have.

Three and a half days later we started to lose our wind when we were less than two miles from Folkstone Harbor in the narrowest part of the English Channel. "Let's reach in there and spend the night at anchor," Larry said. "The tide will be turning against us soon anyway. Maybe we could clear Customs in time to get real English lamb chops for dinner."

The tide was at its lowest spring ebb when we anchored a hundred yards away from the Customs house on the huge roll-on/roll-off ferry dock at Folkstone, England. We hoisted our flag and a Customs man came out of his office and yelled, "Come ashore with your dinghy and pick me up. Bring your passports." So we unlashed *Rinky* and slipped her over the side. When we rowed alongside the dock, the Customs man looked down at little *Rinky* where she bounced about at the bottom of a slime-covered forty-foot-long ladder. We could see the look of indecision on his face as he called, "Do you have much liquor on board?" Larry kept a straight face as he called back, "Only enough for our own consumption."

The Customs man looked vastly relieved and answered, "Come on up, then, no need to inspect your boat. We'll clear your papers at my office." We clambered up the ladder and went into his warm office. I glanced at the clock, "Oh, darn it, the shops will be closed in twenty-five minutes," I said. The Customs man was really sympathetic when we told him we'd had no lamb in over five months. "I'll keep your husband and passports as hostages. You run, left at the first corner, then up two streets. Tell the butcher Bill sent you," he said, opening the door for me. I ran and just caught the butcher and a green grocer and spent the two pounds I had left from the winter before. The ship's papers and our passports were cleared and stamped when I got back and the Customs officer wished us a good stay in England as we climbed back down the forty-foot ladder to the dinghy.

As we rowed back to *Seraffyn* I teased Larry, "Two cases of whiskey, one case of Russian champagne, three cases of Bulgarian wine—only enough for our own consumption!" Larry looked at me seriously, "It *is* only for our own consumption. We don't plan to sell any, and that's all the Customs people are worried about." And Larry was technically correct. We did consume it all, although we shared it with lots of friends when they came by for visits all during the long English winter.

We stayed in Folkstone only twelve hours because as soon as our alarm clock rang for the early-morning weather report we could see we had a fair wind for Poole. We ran before an ever-increasing southeast wind, each familiar landmark on England's south coast moving past us at five knots. It was the first time in five years of cruising that we'd ever sailed back through the same waters. All during the twenty-five hours it took us to run the 135 miles from Folkstone, past the Isle of Wight, right up to Poole Town Quay, one or the other of us would pipe up, "I wonder how Alf is doing. Let's call him as soon as we get in," or "Do you think Paul is still going to the same pub?" or "Won't it be fun to have another dinner at the Green Bottle?" or "Do you think Leslie still wants to go on the Round-Britain Race?" We couldn't wait to see people we now thought of as old friends, even though we'd only known them for three or four months the winter before.

We reached up Poole Harbor's now-familiar maze of channels on November 1, 1973, a warm feeling of homecoming growing inside. Poole Town Quay was almost deserted when we maneuvered alongside just astern of the two tugboats *Wendy Ann* and *Wendy Ann II*. Their captains took our lines and called, "Welcome home!" We packed our kits, clean clothes, and towels, and walked toward the bus stop past

Piplers, the local yacht chandlery. "Welcome back," Mr. Pipler called. We grabbed the first No. 2 bus that passed and rode to the Parkstone Yacht Club. "We're here to take you up on that lunch offer," Larry said as soon as we'd had a long hot shower. Tom Hunt looked up in surprise. "How did you get here so soon? Good to see you, welcome home!" And so it went.

Our winter plans seemed to make themselves. Within four days of our arrival *Seraffyn* was hauled out of the water, chocked securely among two hundred other club boats, her mast hoisted out and stored in the mast shed. We acquired a Morris 1000, a tiny gray whizz of a car we came to call Samantha. Larry was offered all the boat repair and alteration work he could handle at Cobb's Quay Marina on a contract basis. I was offered the same situation at Paul Lees's sail loft as Larry had enjoyed the previous winter, a chance to build a new sail in exchange for three mornings a week of my labor. But best of all, Paul Lees helped us find and rent a five-hundred-year-old town house, right in the middle of the quietest part of the town, only two streets away from the shops, two miles from the yacht club, and three miles away from Cobb's Quay. What a treat it was to wander through the four-story stone house with its saggy wooden floors, painted fireplaces, Elizabethan windows, and four-square staircase. We only had to pay twenty-five dollars a week for this marvel of a house because the owner was an antique dealer who used the house to store and display his collection and he worried about it if the house stood empty. It was wonderful to eat off hundred-year-old Worcestershire china, sitting on Chippendale chairs, chatting with all the friends we'd met the year before and many new ones, while around us the ghosts of a home that was built when Columbus was only twelve years old played their little tricks and refused to tell their secrets.

Our winter days fell into a comfortable pattern. Larry worked at his boat repairs ten hours a day, five days a week. I worked at the sail loft three mornings a week and spent my afternoons refitting *Seraffyn*, going over every piece of gear on her, making new covers for everything at the sail loft and putting three coats of fresh paint inside and outside *Rinky Dink*. Both of us used our spare time to write, and at least two days a month went toward the project that was to be the highlight of our next summer—the two-man Round-Britain Race.

Larry had always been fascinated by this race. "It's the only race that really tests crusing equipment and proves what kind of boats two

Leslie Dyball, commodore of the Parkstone Yacht Club and skipper of *Chough*.

people can handle well, both at sea and entering and leaving harbors,"
he told me when Leslie reiterated his desire to go on the race. It was
over a course that covered twenty-two hundred miles, starting in
Plymouth, England, going west past Ireland, north past the Outer
Hebrides and around the Shetland Islands, then south down the North
Sea to the English Channel, and ending in Plymouth. There were four
compulsory stops: Cork in Ireland, Castle Bay in the Outer Hebrides,
Lerwick in the Shetland Islands, and Lowestoft on England's east
coast. Participants had to stay exactly forty-eight hours in each of these
places. Any type of mechanical self-steering gear was allowed. The
race was held every fourth year. Leslie Dyball had asked Larry to crew
for him using his thirty-foot Sparkman and Stevens–designed half-
tonner. *Chough*, a finkeel, skeg-mounted rudder, fiberglass sloop of
moderately light displacement, was almost the exact opposite of *Seraffyn*, and Larry was curious to see what she'd be like to handle with

only one person on watch at a time. He and Leslie held long evening conferences on the equipment and stores *Chough* would need for the race. Larry helped install a Hassler self-steering gear on her, and I began to be just a little bit jealous as sixty-six-year-old Leslie and thirty-four-year-old Larry grew as excited as sixteen-year-olds preparing for their very first regatta.

Meanwhile, we began to notice a strange fact. Our pleasure in the beautiful three-bedroom stone-floored house with its often-used grand piano seemed to diminish as our freedom fund increased. At first we loved having so much room to spread out, and often dined in front of the living room fire when the dining room table was covered with *Seraffyn*'s freshly varnished hatches, blocks, and bunk boards. But I began to tire of forever leaving the one thing I needed for my downstairs projects in one of the upstairs rooms. I began to resent having to vacuum and dust five rooms when we only used two most of the time. The delight of knowing exactly where to buy each thing I needed

Our five-hundred-year-old home came complete with grand piano. Most of the house beams were originally from old ships. You can just see *Seraffyn*'s forehatch and sextant box with a fresh coat of varnish under the piano. *Peter Stevens*

in the local shops soon turned to boredom when I never saw a vegetable that was new to me and never found a sausage I hadn't tried before. The novelty of being able to go to a movie any time we wanted, or listen to live folk music at the local club, or hear a symphony orchestra soon lost their glamor when we always had to drive through the same streets to reach them. It took four and a half months of work before our cruising fund reached the minimum figure we'd set—three thousand dollars. The minute it was fifty dollars over, Larry finished up his last contract and quit working, and we knew it was time to migrate. Together we finished giving *Seraffyn* one complete fresh coat of varnish inside, from bilges to deck head including the underside of the teak decks, behind the waters tanks, inside the lockers, and under the table. We waited only until our bunk cushions arrived back from the sailmaker's glowing new in their blue imitation-leather covers. Then we moved out of the old house and back into *Seraffyn* even though she stood high and dry in the Parkstone Yacht Club shed with ten days to wait for a tide high enough to float her free.

I felt like I was coming home again. Even though we had to walk three hundred yards to use the club's toilets, we still found we loved our turtle shell of a home and longed to be under way.

All sorts of friends stopped by as we finished our refit. Leif Møller appeared unexpectedly from Denmark and stayed three delightful days. We gave farewell parties on board land-locked *Seraffyn*, our guests climbing a nine-foot ladder to join us. Then the yard crew arrived and jacked *Seraffyn* onto the wheeled launching car. She looked magnificent as she immerged from the shed, her white paint glowing brightly, her whale strip a proud royal blue, *Rinky Dink* pristine on the trolley under *Seraffyn*'s bilge. Peter and Valerie Stevens, two new Poole winter friends who had introduced us to long walks in the green rolling hills of Dorset, came by to help us restep our freshly varnished mast. On the morning of the launching rain threatened, and the Stevenses, Leslie Dyball, and Larry worked like devils to put on the last coat of antifouling paint as the tide rose up the launching ramp. Then, less than twenty minutes before the highest tide of the month, one of the few days when we could launch *Seraffyn*, the yard manager walked by and, like the voice of doom, announced, "Aren't ya going to grease her seams? She'll leak like a sieve after a dry spell like we've had the past three weeks." Larry looked at *Seraffyn*'s bright-red bottom where the seams between each plank were just visible. We couldn't see day-

During our winter refit Larry spliced up new halyards.

Then he added a coat of enamel to our topsides.

light through any of them. "She didn't leak a drop when I first launched her," Larry said with confidence. "She shouldn't leak now. Put her in the water."

I stayed below decks storing the last of our provisions as *Seraffyn* was wheeled slowly into the water. I couldn't believe my eyes as salt water shot through tight-looking seams, right across the boat. A jet of spray drummed on the bottom of the oven until I threw a dish towel over the seam. The jet quickly soaked through the towel. I pulled open a floorboard; the bilge was filling by inches every minute. I grabbed the pump handle and began pumping as fast as I could. Larry called from the dock, "Lin, come cast off the cradle lines."

I poked my head clear and yelled, "Help, we're sinking!" then rushed back to the pump. Larry jumped on deck, looked inside, and said, "Can you keep ahead of the water?" I looked up from my praying position in front of the pump. "Yes, just barely," I answered. Then Larry said, "I'll be back in three or four hours. I have to finish our new reefing lapper and deliver Samantha to Paul; then we'll be free of our car and ready to sail whenever we want. Don't worry, she'll take up quickly."

The yard men towed *Seraffyn* free of the cradle, down the half-mile-long tidal channel, and out to where a club mooring was waiting, half a mile from the clubhouse. The water was still flying three feet in the air from the seams that had been close to the electric heater we'd used while we worked inside during the cold winter days. I was really shaken to think that my safe little home could actually leak, but this was the first time in five years she had been out of the water for more than two weeks. She did take up quickly. I recorded in our logbook the strokes it took to keep the water below floorboard level:

1115 — 50 strokes every 3 minutes
1300 — 45 strokes every 4 minutes
1700 — 32 strokes every 10 minutes
1900 — 42 strokes every 26 minutes

The only problem was that Larry didn't come back in three or four hours. By the time he finally rowed home at 2100 and threw our new lapper on deck, I was close to exhaustion. I'd spent the last two hours laying on the settee, hanging my hand into the bilge so that when I fell asleep the cold salt water rising in the bilge hit my fingers. Then

I woke up with a start and began pumping madly. I was furious with Larry for leaving me alone so long on our sinking ship. But he conned his way back into my affections by saying, "I knew you could cope with almost anything, Lin, and I told the yard crew to keep an eye on you. If there had really been an emergency I could have depended on you to sail the boat on the beach or get some help. Now, you go to bed. Forget making dinner. I'll take over pumping and tomorrow I'll show you the jib you worked for. Paul says you were a great help in the loft."

So Larry did take over. He made me two of his gourmet-style peanut butter and jam sandwiches, then set the alarm for each forty-five minutes and slept in the main cabin near the pump. By the next evening we only needed to pump forty strokes every four hours. On the third day *Seraffyn* was leaking so little that we went off for a day sail on board *Chough*, which had been launched on the same tide as *Seraffyn*. We returned six hours later to find only a few gallons of water in the bilges. By the fourth day our bilges were absolutely dry.

We said our last farewells, but this time our friends in Poole just teased, "You'll be back." And somehow we knew they were right. Even though we were headed for the Mediterranean as soon as the Round-Britain Race was over, we would come back to Poole some day.

We sailed once again to Brownsea Island and spent a week wandering through the Solent while westerly winds blew. Finally, on June 3, 1974, we got a good weather report with southerly winds and we headed west toward Dartmouth to find a place where I could enjoy cruising alone while Larry came back to join Leslie for the estimated five or six weeks the Round-Britain Race would take.

~~~~~~

CHAPTER 19

A Busman's Holiday

The wind freshened as we beat south to clear Portland Bill. When water started splashing up *Seraffyn*'s sharply tilting lee deck we decided to stop admiring the shape of our pure-white brand-new lapper and try to reef it. With the lapper we'd had before we'd had to take the sail down, unhank it from the headstay, bag it, get out the working jib, unbag that, hank it on, and hoist it, then store away the lapper. Now, shortening sail was simply a matter of dropping the lapper in the jib net, tying in the reef points, retying the sheets in the reefing cringle, then hoisting the sail again.

We had to retie the reef points in our new lapper three times that first day to get the foot of the sail setting perfectly, but once we figured out the tricks, we became believers. "We'll sell our working jib to the first person who can use it," Larry said, admiring his handiwork on the tautly pulling, reefed lapper. We've since become completely converted to reefing headsails. We now have two reefs in our staysail, one in our lapper, and one in our genoa. These three reefing headsails give us a complete range of sail combinations. The alternative is an interior full of bulky, expensive sails that are nowhere near as handy.

Dartmouth was absolutely beautiful in its spring finery, flowers edging the roadsides, tourists in their summer frocks strolling along the quay. The river was full of holidaying yachtsmen, including two long-distance cruisers. Nick Skeates and a friend were Azores-bound on *Wylo,* Nick's twenty-nine-foot, forty-year-old cutter (see Appendix B for details of *Wylo*), and Dan Bowen on his sleak, T. Harrison Butler–designed wooden thirty-footer *Romadi* was bound for the Caribbean.

All of us sailed up the River Dart about five miles to Dittisham to visit a famous pub Dan knew about. I'd heard there were oysters on the mud banks in the middle of the river. It was still low tide when we anchored and Larry and I rowed over and found absolutely no oysters, but returned happy and muddy as can be with a bucket of cockles. I set the cockles to clean themselves in a pail filled with fresh salt water. Then we joined the cruising crowd at the two-hundred-year-old stone "Ferryman's" Pub on Dittisham's tree-covered shore. An old-timer played folksongs on his concertina as local fishermen and summer tourists filled the pub until there was barely room to move. We were among the last to leave, and all of us rowed back to *Romadi* where Dan boiled up a pot of tea, then brought out his guitar to continue the evening's entertainment. After we'd exhausted the usual supply of cruising sailors' standard discussions—self-steering gears, anchors, hard dinghies versus inflatables, running rigs, floor timbers, and leaking decks—we talked of voyages past and future, anchorages we'd like to visit again, storms we'd like to have avoided, and wine we dreamed of tasting.

Larry ties a reef into the lapper as the jib downhaul holds it into the jib net.

We sailed back to Dartmouth's main anchorage and spent several evenings visiting on board various yachts that were gathering for the "Old Gaffers Race." One evening as we shared some of our fresh clams on a new friend's yacht, I decided to use his marine toilet. I thought I'd turned off all the proper valves when I'd pumped the bowl clean. A half hour later our host's face took on a look of shock as he saw a stream of water running out from under the loo door. He ran into the loo, and I heard him cursing under his breath and pumping furiously. Then I heard him turning a valve. He came into the main cabin and tried to reassure me. "My fault, Lin. I should have made sure you turned off the right valves. It's happened before." The overflowing loo and soggy carpet definitely put a damper on the evening and we left shortly thereafter. "What did I do wrong?" I whispered to Larry as soon as we rowed clear. "It wasn't really your fault," Larry told me. "His head installation was poor. The hoses should have looped high above the waterline and had antisyphon valves at the top of the loops. The way he has it now, everytime anyone uses that head he has to open the valves, then pump the loo, and finally close all the valves. It's a pretty dangerous situation. If the same thing had happened when we were all on our way ashore for the evening, his boat could have filled with water and sunk. I've heard of that happening before." I looked at our blue plastic bucket and its lid with more respect after that. It had its inconveniences, but it would never sink our boat!

Henry North, with his inimitable sense of humor, joined us the day of the Dartmouth Annual Old-Gaffers Race and we sailed the course, enjoying the sight of thirty gaff-rigged sailboats, twenty-two to eighty feet long, some built before the turn of the century, topsails pulling, crews working to spread clouds of canvas to gain every inch they could on the ever-dying wind. *Dyarchy*, the husky, well-known forty-five-foot Laurent Giles cruising cutter, was queen of the day, glowing magnificently in a fresh coat of black enamel and varnish. But our fishermen friends from Falmouth walked off with the first two prizes in their open oyster dredgers, and when we joined them for beer in the Royal Dart Yacht Club after the trophies were given out, several of them said, "Bring *Seraffyn* to Falmouth. We'll keep an eye on her and make sure Lin has a good time."

Their invitation was irresistible, and on the next day we set off on an impromptu race westward, twenty-six-foot, seventy-year-old *Evelyn* taking the lead, *Seraffyn* in the center, and twenty-two-foot *Magdelena*

Elizabeth and Mary, an old Plymouth hooker, had a few worms in her deadwood so her owner hauled her on the tide and . . .

Larry helped fit a worm shoe and get her **ready** for the Old-Gaffer's Race.

Magdelena in the foreground, *Evelyn* closest to the shore. Two fine examples of seventy-year-old Falmouth oyster dredgers.

right on our heels. Each boat set its spinnaker and ran toward the
River Yealm. A heavy fog threatened and we took bearings just before
it settled over us. *Evelyn* was ahead and out of sight. The breeze grew
lighter and we dropped our spinnaker and drifted along under mainsail and genoa. We plotted our position on our detail chart and steered
a careful compass course. Then we heard the putt-putt of a small
outboard motor and looked astern to see *Magdelena* emerge slowly
from the fog. Arfie had inflated his rubber dinghy, lashed it alongside
the engineless *Magdelena*, and put the outboard motor on the inflatable.
The little three-horsepower Seagull moved five-ton *Magdelena* at over
three knots, and as he caught us Arfie called, "I know you guys are
yachtsmen. I figured you'd have a compass and chart on board. Mind
if I follow you in?" We laughed and offered to boil up a pot of tea. But
Arfie's girlfriend Sue emerged from under *Magdelena*'s tiny enclosed
forepeak with an already-brewed pot of tea she'd cooked up on a
primus stove. Arfie turned off the outboard and the four of us chatted
comfortably as we sailed through the fog side by side, until we reached
the black rocks at the entrance to the river. We tacked across the bar,
caught the first of the incoming tide, and beat upriver, sounding with
our lead lines as we went. Once anchored, we settled in to wait for the
fog to clear.

It took us another ten days to reach Falmouth even though it was
only forty-five miles away. We dawdled along, visiting each of the

Larry sailed *Rinky Dink* on the river Yealm while I got dinner ready.

beautiful anchorages and rivers we'd seen almost two years before. It was special fun feeling like old hands as we remembered the names of each headline and recognized the bar men in the pub we'd visited before. When we sailed into Falmouth there were only three days left before Larry had to take the bus back to Poole to join Leslie. Commander and Mrs. Coxwell had been told that we were coming and immediately offered us the use of a spare mooring in front of their home which they used as a sailing school. It was about two hundred yards upriver past the Royal Cornwall Yacht Club. "I just set that mooring," the jolly, twinkle-eyed commander told us, "so Lin will feel safe leaving *Seraffyn* there no matter what blows up. I'll have my nephew put a longer pennant on the pickup float so Lin can reach it more easily when she comes back from a day sail."

Larry finished attaching a boathook to the end of *Rinky*'s seven-foot-long boom. "That will make it easier for you to pick up that pennant under sail. You won't have to lie on deck to reach water level when you come back from a sail," he told me as he stored the now dual-purpose boom back in place.

When I rowed Larry across the river to the center of Falmouth on June 28, *Rinky* was full to the brim. Larry was borrowing *Seraffyn*'s 450-square-foot nylon drifter and 1,050-square-foot spinnaker to add to *Chough*'s wardrobe. He also had our new Negus taffrail log and a little whiskey from ship's stores. "Now don't be afraid to take *Seraffyn* out for a sail," he said as he climbed on the express bus. "Worst you can do is scratch her paint. She's your boat, too!"

I'm terrible at good-byes and kissed Larry self-consciously under the steady stares of the fifty holidaying British lady members of the garden club that filled the bus. "Try and win that race," I said as I turned to leave. "I'll take care of *Seraffyn*—you have fun!"

I rowed back toward the far side of the river wondering if I'd want to go sailing now that Larry wasn't there. As odd as it sounds, I didn't know whether I really liked sailing or if I went because going places and being with Larry was what I enjoyed.

No one in Falmouth gave me time to be lonely. Within hours of his departure several people had sent messages inviting me for meals, and the day after Larry left Mrs. Coxwell asked me to help collect money for raffle tickets at the fishermen's festival at Flushing, the village across the river from Falmouth. I watched the hilarious fishermen's parade, roared with laughter as several men tried to walk out a greased pole set over the water, and held my sides while the same men had a pillow fight on the grease-smeared varnished spar. I was conned into joining the ladies rowing race, and put up a very poor showing against the husky local fishermen's wives when I tried to row a four-hundred-pound dory with ten-foot oars set on tholepins. I was used to fifty-pound *Rinky* with her closed bronze oarlocks. The lady who won must have weighed a hundred sixty pounds. She made that sixteen-foot dory fly over the water, its long oars groaning on each stroke. I learned afterward that she often joined her husband to pull nets on his mackerel trawlers. With that kind of competition, I felt I had some excuse for coming in last.

The next day I sat on deck sipping a cup of morning tea, feeling free as a bird in the warm sunshine. Dean and Carolyn rowed up in their little rubber dinghy. We'd first met them in Dartmouth and they were bound for Texas in their twenty-two-foot fiberglass sloop. After I invited them on board and poured them some tea, I heard myself saying, "How about joining me for a sail upriver to see Restrounget Creek? Tide's fair." Minutes later we'd secured the rubber dinghy to the mooring, reached off the mooring, and jibed around, *Seraffyn*'s sails filled for the run downriver. I loved it. Being in charge of our lively

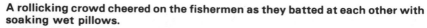

A rollicking crowd cheered on the fishermen as they batted at each other with soaking wet pillows.

little ship, I felt confident that I could make the right decisions and bring her up to the mooring at just the right speed so that my guests could easily pick up the mooring pennant. I was out sailing around Falmouth estuary with *Seraffyn* and some friend or other two or three hours every day. When Pat Daniels, a lady friend from Poole, came to join me for her one-week summer vacation, I thought nothing of saying, "Let's sail to Plymouth and help Leslie and Larry get ready for the race." The two of us had a bit of a struggle getting *Rinky* on board, but we managed, and just as we were ready to drop the heavy mooring chain, the Coxwells' six-foot four-inch nephew David James called out, "Where are you two girls going?" "To Plymouth," we shouted back, and David was soon on board, too. The three of us had a rollicking sail on a fresh northerly breeze. All doubts I had about my love of sailing were dispelled. Larry or no Larry, as a sport, sailing is great! It requires practice and careful planning, but offers a tremendous feeling of freedom and accomplishment.

We picked up one of the double moorings in outer Millbay Docks, and secured *Seraffyn* bow and stern. Then all of us walked to the inner dock where sixty-one boats were being measured and prepared for the race.

Thirty-foot *Chough* looked tiny surrounded by boats like eighty-foot *Burton Cutter*, skippered by Leslie Williams and crewed by Peter Blake; seventy-foot *British Oxygen*, the catamaran sailed by Robin Knox-Johnston and Jerry Boxall; and *Manerava*, the huge aluminum trimaran being sailed by the two Colas brothers from France.

It was just great being part of the preparations for a race like this! Pat and I did bags of laundry, spent hours shopping for stores to last Larry and Leslie twenty-five days, and turned *Seraffyn* into a steaming galley ship as we cooked up and prepacked enough food to last Larry and Leslie for five days. Brian Cooke on his lightweight fifty-foot trimaran *Triple Arrow* had to be extremely conscious of every pound he put on board his boat, and he gave Leslie a bit of ragging when we carried two cases of wine and a fly-fishing rod and reel on board *Chough*. But Leslie turned to Brian and said, "Just because we're racing doesn't mean we have to suffer, and I plan to do some salmon fishing in the Shetlands."

By the time we followed *Chough* to the starting area, on Saturday the sixth of July 1974, I was exhausted from dinner parties, race preparations, and one last private evening with Larry on *Seraffyn*. But Larry

Larry was busy helping Leslie prepare *Chough* for the race, but even so he had time to enjoy the prerace festivities. *Chip Mason*

Chough of Parkstone and her two-man crew sail out to the starting line.

362

and Leslie looked great as they posed for the cameras of the eight sailing friends who were with me on *Seraffyn*. There was a nice light breeze for the start and all sixty-one of the competitors safely cleared Plymouth's breakwaters, the multihulls showing occasional bursts of speed as puffs of wind blew through the hills of Plymouth.

As soon as we sailed back to Millbay Docks, all of my guests, including Pat, left and there I was, all alone, forty miles from Falmouth where I had a date in three days. I'd never considered single-handed sailing, but here was my chance to try it. I'd met five-foot three-inch Claire Francis who was skippering thirty-two-foot *Cherry Blossom* in this race with Eve Bonham as crew. Claire had single-handed across the Atlantic. So had five-foot two-inch Theresa Remis-zewski. If they could do it, so could four-foot ten-inch me. I sat on deck enjoying the quiet of the deserted docks, contemplating the adventure ahead of me, when a twenty-six-foot blue and white fiberglass sloop came into the dock under power. The two men on board backed between the mooring buoys that lay less than thirty feet to port of *Seraffyn*. As they secured their lines to the rings on the buoys, I called over, "Please take up real tight on your mooring lines. It's high tide now and when the tide's out these moorings have just a bit too much scope and we'll bump." The men seemed to give me the usual "who wants to take notice of a girl" look, and after chatting about the weather for a few minutes they went below decks.

I was sound asleep in our forward bank, dreaming someone was knocking. Then I woke up. Something was knocking against *Seraffyn*'s hull. I looked out the hatch. It was 0500 and just beginning to grow light. That fiberglass sloop was banging against *Seraffyn*'s port quarter, the only part of our topsides not protected by fenders. I was furious. I became an instant Women's Libber, roared on deck, grabbed two of the wire shrouds of the offending sloop, pulled them apart as hard as I could, then let them loose. *Twang!* The fiberglass sloop vibrated, making a sound like a plastic guitar breaking a string. Two heads flew out through two hatches and turned quickly. The look of confusion on their faces turned to one of definite interest. They didn't say a word, only grinned, and I could sense that something was not as it should be. I followed their gaze, looked down at myself, and realized that I was completely nude. I jumped into the cockpit and rushed below, yelling, "Get your bloody boat off my bloody boat."

I heard a few whispered comments and chuckles as the men tightened their mooring lines and their boat pulled clear. I took a book and retreated into the forward bunk, trying to calm down and regain my shattered composure while I waited for the 0630 weather forecast.

The weather forecast gave me no reason to stay in port, so I got dressed and started to remove the sail covers before my confidence ebbed away. One of the men on the next boat asked me what I was up to, and then offered, "I'll row over and help you sail clear of the mooring. Then I can row back here."

"Thanks, but I can do it myself," I replied. Then I almost wished I hadn't been such a smart aleck when I looked at the boats moored less than twenty feet on each side of *Seraffyn* and considered the careful short-tacking I'd need to sail out of the dock area. I poured another cup of tea and slowed down to think out each move I'd have to make. Then I climbed into the dinghy and removed the mooring lines that held *Seraffyn* and replaced them with long lines that I first cleated on deck, then ran through the rings on the moorings and back to *Seraffyn*, where I cleated the end. That way when I was ready to be free, I could simply cast off one end, the line would run through the mooring buoy ring, and I could gather it in once I was under way. There was a fresh southeasterly breeze blowing at an angle across the docks. I set the mainsail and sheeted it to a close-reaching position, then tied the tiller just a bit to windward. *Seraffyn* started pulling against her stern mooring. I hoisted the staysail and sheeted in. Since I had no reason not to go, I cast off the stern line. *Seraffyn* slid a few feet to leeward of the buoys and then immediately began to gather headway. I rushed forward to cast off the bow line. Its free end threatened to snag around the tip of our CQR anchor, but I gave it a quick jerk and the line slipped free. I pulled the two lines on deck as *Seraffyn* glided past the mooring buoys into open water. One easy short tack and I reached past my would-be assistant, waving nonchalantly although my heart was just falling back into its proper place. Then I eased sheets to run out of Plymouth Sound. I felt as tall as the sky and was almost convinced that single-handed sailing was the greatest sport on earth when, eight hours and thirty-five miles later, my warm sunny beam reach turned into a cold blustery beat with a backing wind. Then I began to think differently. The tide was against me as I beat the last six miles and I came to appreciate the assistance and security a sailing partner offered. By the time I picked up my mooring in front of the Coxwells' home I began to understand the problems and dangers of sailing alone, especially without an engine. But I was as proud as punch and eager to share my adventures with Larry.

The Falmouth fishermen and members of the Royal Cornwall Yacht Club kept me busy and happy as I eagerly followed Leslie and Larry's progress in both newspaper and radio reports. They quickly took the handicap lead in the race, and by the time they reached Lerwick in the Shetlands, were nine hours ahead of the nearest competition. The weather reported by most of the competitors proved that this was not the type of race I'd have enjoyed. The yachts had had to beat three-quarters of the course in Force 7, 8, and 9 winds. One after another, competitors began to drop out of the race. The multihulled entrants seemed to suffer the most; *Peter Peter,* a forty-eight-foot catamaran lost its mast, retrieved it, restepped it, and sailed another thousand miles in the race, only to lose its mast again; *John Willy,* a forty-six-foot trimaran, split up and was abandoned; *Triple Arrow,* the fifty-foot trimaran sailed by our good friends Brian Cooke and Eric Jensen, flipped over in a sudden gust of wind off Lerwick and had to be towed into harbor and righted by a crane—all in all there were twenty-one retirements in a fleet of sixty-one, almost all caused by heavy weather damage. And when Larry joined me again one month later in Falmouth, he was the glowing joint winner of the fleet handicap prize. I was anxious to hear the sea stories he'd have to tell.

"Leslie sure was one hell of a partner," was the first thing Larry told me. "The second night out of Lerwick he made three complete headsail changes all by himself in one three-hour watch; number-two genoa, working jib, finally ending up with the storm jib beating into a really rough headsea with winds gusting Force 9! Later I made him a special breakfast, scrambled eggs and corned beef hash, to celebrate his sixty-seventh birthday. Hope I've got that kind of determination when I'm fifty."

I asked Larry about the complaints I'd heard about the handicap system being faulty. "Of course it was inaccurate," he replied.

It's impossible to handicap multihulls with monohulls—there should have been two categories. But I feel we had a real victory. *Chough* was forty-sixth from the top of the fleet according to overall size, and we were the thirteenth boat to cross the finish line. The huge multihulls didn't show the speed people expected from them. *British Oxygen* was seventy feet long with a sixty-foot waterline and took ten days and four hours to sail the course. We took fifteen days

A map of *Chough's* course in the 1972 Round-Britain Race.

and twenty-two hours with only a twenty-one-foot waterline. They had three times the waterline length yet only turned in a thirty-four-percent faster time. That was probably because there was a lot of windward work in the race and multihulls are faster off the wind.

One thing I did notice was how tired people seemed to be when they finished each leg. Leslie and I were quite tired when we finished the first leg at Cork. Leslie had done a wonderful job using his local knowledge to catch each lift of the current and tides. He knew the area from Plymouth to Cork like the back of his hand, knowledge gained on seven Fastnet races. He took us right into the bays to beat the foul tides and got us the lead. But I knew that we couldn't keep it up if we didn't get more rest. So when we were in Cork, I suggested, "From now on, the man off watch should climb right in the bunk, even during the day. The man on watch should handle everything, with the windvane doing the steering: sail changes, navigation, chores. If we get more rest, we'll do great." Well, it sure worked. When we reached Lerwick, Leslie was so rested he stepped right off the boat, fly-fishing rod in his hand, and asked directions to the nearest salmon creek. The young guys on some of the other boats couldn't believe their eyes. This race proved it to me—thirty-five feet is the biggest boat two people can keep racing efficiently. *Quailo,* the fifty-four-foot boat that was successful in the Admiral's Cup, had a thirty-nine-foot-long waterline but only moved twenty-two percent faster than *Chough.* Her crews complained of being too tired to want to change big, heavy headsails halfway through the race.

I wanted to know what Larry had thought of sailing an IOR-type boat over such a long distance.

I prefer *Seraffyn* anytime, Lin. She's so much easier to steer and her motion is much more comfortable. Besides, *Chough* could never have carried the gear and stores *Seraffyn* does and done as well. Downwind with a spinnaker *Chough* was mannerly, but the minute we got near a reach with the chute, she was horrid. And on a beat in heavy conditions she pounded like hell; in fact, she shattered the sliding glass doors in the loo and threw the glasses and bottles right out of the specially designed liquor locker. But we were really pushing her hard. Leslie refused to show his boat one bit of mercy. You wouldn't believe how she could go to windward. We often had her moving at six knots and above, close-hauled! She didn't respond to self-steering as well as *Seraffyn,* but I'll say one thing—after the unbelievable pounding we gave her, I sure have more respect for a well-built fiberglass boat. The hull never gave us one worry.

For the next few days Larry and I shared sailing adventures. I learned how the thirty- to thirty-five-foot boats seemed to be the ones that could be driven hardest by their crews, and that the people on them always seemed to be the ones having parties at the rest points while the men off the fifty-footers slept. Larry shared the fun moments of the race, the bottle of champagne at the finish line, the songs and beer at tiny Castle Bay pub, and the kindness of people in each port. He told me about their trials and tribulations, such as when *Chough* sailed into a maze of gill nets off northwest Ireland and they had to waste three hours finding a way out of the mess. And the time they beat into Lerwick Harbor on a Force 9 headwind, then rested forty-eight hours while the winds blew fair, and had to leave again just as the winds backed and turned into a Force 9 headwind again. When I asked Larry if he'd go on the race again, he said, "I was thinking of asking you: if we're in England in 1978, what do you think of taking *Seraffyn* in the next Round-Britain Race? I'd buy you a good warm pair of sailing gloves. You may not be as tough as Leslie, but we'll have had ten years of two-man sailing practice by then."

Fortunately I never had to give him a definite answer since we were sailing the Pacific in *Seraffyn* when the next Round-Britain Race came around.

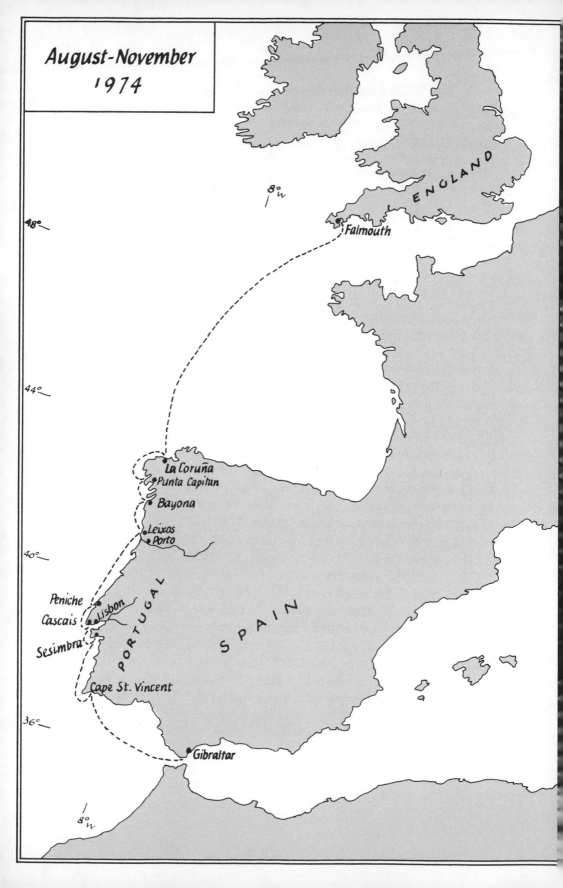

CHAPTER 20

~~~~~~

Heading for the Sun

Once again we'd reached that difficult point—we had to make a decision. The English days were warm and sunny those first weeks of August, but we remembered the fickle weather September usually brings to European waters. Both of us longed to visit Scotland with its lochs and islands, and Larry's brief stop at Castle Bay in the Outer Hebrides had made him more interested than ever before in getting to know the Scottish sailors better. Mayne, the Irish barman from the Royal Cornwall Yacht Club, added his voice to those who said we'd be sorry if we missed Ireland's wild west coast. But Dan Bowen had poisoned our minds with stories of Spanish wines, brandy, and champagne, served alongside buckets of mussels and oysters on the sun-warmed waters of Spain. We didn't have to toss a coin to make our decision; I just reminded Larry of the freezing days he'd spent working in the boatyard in Poole, coming home blue and shivering from the rain and winter wind. "I've heard there's a real shortage of yacht repairers in Gibraltar," Larry said. A quick telephone call to the Gibraltar Information Service Office and we knew that getting a work permit would be no problem. So our plans were made, and we set to work getting our international vaccination cards brought up to date, buying stores, scrubbing and antifouling *Seraffyn*'s bottom, and gathering last memories of Falmouth to take along with us.

My parents arrived from California on a three-week tour of England and drove their rented car down from London to join us for three days. One of the main drawbacks of a boat as small as *Seraffyn* is that she doesn't have room to provide a separate private stateroom for guests. So, few people can join us for longer than two or three days without feeling cramped. It was fun to show my mother the exciting antique shops in Falmouth and to take her for tea and cakes in the two-hundred-year-old Greenbank Hotel. The two of us sat by the hotel window watching Larry and dad short-tack *Seraffyn* up the river after a long day sail. We tried to cram two years of memories and family gossip into two hours.

After telling me of yet another divorce among friends in California, my mother looked at our tiny home coming to rest at the mooring across the river and said, "How do the two of you live together twenty-four hours a day in such a small home? Don't you miss your privacy? Don't you get bored with each other?" I tied to explain that the two of us were drawn closely together by the shared work required to take care of *Seraffyn* and voyage in safety and comfort. With our common interests, we never seem to run out of things to talk about—places we'd like to go, people we'd like to meet, things we'd like to do, changes we'd like to make to our floating home, things we'd like to write about. We didn't have the outside pressures caused by jobs, mortgages, and a hectic social life that steal time from the average shoreside couple. Because we couldn't easily hide from each other, we had to face our personal problems and work them out way before they grew too big to handle. We had the time to really communicate, uninterrupted by telephones or life-insurance salesmen. Despite our limited living accommodations, we'd learned to find the moments of privacy everyone needs. Larry would say, "Excuse me for a few hours, I'm going to read a book." Then he'd climb into the forepeak or lounge back against a sailbag and I'd work happily away in the main cabin or row ashore for a walk. Every year or two we'd arrange to spend three weeks or a month separate from each other. This sometimes happened naturally such as it had during the Round-Britain Race. At other times we chose a convenient meeting spot so that one or the other of us could take a trip inland to visit friends or go sightseeing while the other enjoyed having *Seraffyn* all to himself. We'd use the time learning not to take each other for granted, and I know I always came back appreciating our partnership more than ever. About once a year when we've stayed in the same harbor waiting for weather to clear, mail to arrive, or a check to be cleared, one or the other of us becomes short-tempered or generally obnoxious. But we've come to recognize this as a disease we call "port fever," and since boats are made for going places it is simply cured—we set sail and move somewhere new. Now, four years later, after we've lived on board for over nine years, we are busy scheming and planning a new boat we might build some day. As we do that, I realize that our shared projects and mutual goals are the reason we rarely get bored with each other.

After three sunny days my parents departed amid a flood of tears and good-luck wishes and we went back to our preparations. The August weather deteriorated. Rain came to mar the holiday makers fun. Strong southerly winds gave us an excuse to have more time with the Falmouth oystermen, spending delightful days racing on their rugged gaff-rigged cutters. Finally, on the morning of August 22, 1974, the depression and bad weather moved east and we rushed to buy our final stores so we could set sail that day. It was Thursday and if we hadn't gone then, we'd have been trapped by the lessons we'd learned about sailing on Friday.

At 1330 we reached clear of Falmouth and for the next three days we had headwinds varying in strength from less than two knots to more than twenty as we beat across the Bay of Biscay. We passed the time pleasantly, sharing our memories of two winters and part of a summer in England. We were going to miss the people we'd met there. "I'd become used to being able to communicate well with people. So many of the Englishmen were on our wavelength with their love of boats and sailing," Larry said as he went on deck to check for ships.

We made just over sixty miles a day along our rumbline, always close-hauled, Helmer in charge, catching each lift or heading of the fickle wind. We'd tack every time we got a definite heading, plot our position, then settle in while *Seraffyn* chewed away at the miles, heeled about twenty degrees with her deck not quite touching the water. On our fourth day out of Falmouth the wind drew to the southwest and we could finally lay our course direct for Corunna on Spain's northwest corner. Five days out the wind veered until we could ease our sheets. *Seraffyn* carried her full mainsail, staysail, and lapper, beam-reaching at five knots. Spain lay about seventy miles ahead of us and I sunbathed on deck considering a matter of relativity. Moving at her top comfortable speed of six knots, *Seraffyn* could cover a maximum of 144 nautical miles in a twenty-four-hour day, or about 165 land miles. Our average speed for over sixteen thousand miles of cruising had been 3.56 knots or eighty-five nautical miles a day (ninety-five land miles) including tacking in and out of harbors and waiting out calms. That really wasn't much until you stopped to consider that we were moving our home and all we owned, using the natural power of the wind.

At 1500 that fifth day we spotted the gray outline of Spain's hills on the horizon. The wind had freshened until we were carrying only a double-reefed main and staysail, reaching on an ever-growing easterly wind. Large waves started to march out of the Bay of Biscay. By 1800 I had a rough time holding myself in the tossing galley while I heated up a can of baked beans with another can of hot dogs poured into the same deep pot. I buttered up some bread that luckily I had baked the day before, and handed it to Larry who'd come below after setting the oil running lamps in place.

I didn't even consider eating—my stomach threatened to rebel just from the aroma of the hot baked beans. "Isn't it a bit rough?" I asked Larry, wedging myself into a corner of the settee. Larry wiped his bowl clean with a fourth slice of bread and answered, "If it gets much worse I'll heave to, but we're only thirty miles out of Corunna. In less than twenty miles we should pick up some protection from the land." *Seraffyn* lurched over one sea and a roaring sound of water shooting away from her bow resounded through our wildly moving home. "I'll go on deck and hand-steer. You climb into the bunk and get some rest so you'll be fresh to help us navigate into port. I'll call you as soon as I pick up any navigation lights."

The motion seemed to get even worse as I lay against the hull in the leeward bunk. I tried to sleep, but with little success. The cabin lamp we'd left burning ran out of oil and in the complete darkness each sound was magnified. Books on the shelf thudded, wine glasses clinked, a pot in the oven screached as it shifted, a can in the locker beneath me thumped against the wooden bunk front. I heard the hiss of passing waves, the slapping crash as our channel and chain plates hit the waves. Spray splattered against the windward cabin side; wind shrieked through our rigging. I was becoming really nervous and concerned when Larry called, "Lin, open the companionway!" I scrambled out of the bunk. "What's wrong?" I yelled over the roar of wind that filled the night.

"Everything is under control," Larry reassured me. "It's magnificent out here, but I've just picked up a light and I need you on deck to take a bearing and time the light sequence. Put on something warm under your wet-weather gear."

I lit another cabin lamp and found an extra sweater in my locker under the forward bunk. With light glowing through the cabin and my mind occupied by studying the information on our approach chart, I lost my apprehensions. I climbed over the drop board in the companionway, pushing the heavy canvas cover aside.

The sight that met my eyes *was* magnificent. Huge waves ranged toward us in even rows, their crests glowing green with turbulent phosphorescence, white spray streaking their faces. Larry steered, one hand on the tiller, the other clutching the bulwark, with the end of the mainsheet tied around his waist. *Seraffyn* roared across the face of the waves, sometimes burying her whole bowsprit in the foam that lifted from her bow. The white swinging anchor light we used as a stern lantern threw light that gleamed off our soaking decks.

"Tie the end of the jib sheet around yourself and go up next to the shrouds. The light I spotted is just on the windward side of our bow," Larry told me, giving a big grin as *Seraffyn* gathered speed from an extra-heavy gust. I passed the end of the jib sheet that was tied to my waist around two shrouds and secured it so my hands could be free. I had to shield my eyes from the spray as Larry headed *Seraffyn* up into a particularly big sea. Then I caught the flash he'd seen. Flashlight in one hand, arm around a shroud, stopwatch in the other hand, I finally figured out the beginning and end of the light sequence and timed it. It definitely was the huge light of Corunna and we were right on course. I unlashed myself from the shrouds, sat down on deck, and scooted back to the cockpit, the jib sheet dragging on the deck behind me. Larry reached over and secured my jib sheet safety line around a cleat, gave me a quick hug, and went back to steering.

Together we enjoyed the majesty of the stormy night as *Seraffyn* charged across the waves like a racehorse, averaging close to seven knots. Within another hour we could feel the huge seas swinging more toward our stern as they curled around the northern corner of Spain. Soon they began to lose their power. Within four hours of the height of our "quicky" storm the wind lost its force as it became blanketed by the hills, and within another hour we were almost becalmed.

It was 2300 when Larry said, "How about standing a watch for me?" I readily agreed, since by then we had an accurate fix on our position from two different navigational lights. *Seraffyn* moved slowly through the water on the offshore breeze. Helmer steered and I spent my time enjoyably washing dinner dishes, putting away the various small items that had been dislodged in the gale, and drying wet-weather gear as our stormy Biscay Bay farewell blow became just another memory.

In six years of cruising this had been one of only three or four times when we'd used anything like a safety harness. But *Seraffyn* had strong twenty-four-inch-high lifelines, eight-inch-high bulwarks, and a massive boom gallows frame to hang onto. And from the first day I sailed with Larry he had told me, "One hand for the ship, one hand for yourself." We'd often discussed safety harnesses and always carried two in a convenient place in *Seraffyn*. But, as a good friend once said, "You can't buy safety. You have to earn it by learning good sea habits." Safety harnesses are a great assistance if you happen to be wearing them at the right time. But in practice few people wear them every minute of the time they are at sea. Good hanging-on habits, strong and convenient handholds, and the awareness that death is only one misstep away are just as important and will stop you from falling overboard when there is an emergency that gives you no time at all to find and put on your harness. The time in the Baltic when we were suddenly broached, Larry didn't have a safety harness on—it was good hanging-on habits that saved him.

It was midmorning before we finally sailed into Corunna. We'd both had over five hours of sleep. *Seraffyn* was scrubbed and tidy inside and out. Fifteen minutes after we let go our anchor we were in the dinghy bound for shore to see if we still remembered the Spanish we'd learned when we'd cruised through Mexico and Central America two and a half years before.

CHAPTER 21

~~~~~

The Five Rias

The Club Naval at Corunna is one of the most magnificent yacht clubs we've ever been in. Marble floors, mirrored staircases, mahogany-paneled rooms. The showers were complete with an attendant to hand you a club towel at a cost of twenty-five cents. After a shower we went onto the veranda and looked over the oil-covered basin where the club members kept their boats. Three other cruising boats were tied there, and the two men off a thirty-foot Swedish yacht soon joined us. One was definitely under the weather. "What's the problem?" Larry asked. "He's suffering from the Spanish-Swedish disease," his partner answered. "Stomach trouble?" I asked. "No, it's just that a whole bottle of good brandy here costs less than a glass would at home in Sweden. He's been like that every morning for over a week now."

We all laughed except for the afflicted sailor and the hours passed quickly as we shared the club's specialty, tortillas. This was completely different from the tortillas of Mexico. Those had been pancake-like pieces of unleavened bread. A Spanish tortilla turned out to be an egg omelette filled with fried onions, potato chunks, garlic, and spices, and served chilled with salt and pepper. It became a favorite of ours.

Corunna is a big city with a busy harbor. Shopping was delightful but the harbor traffic and strong winds made our anchorage uncomfortable and we definitely didn't wish to move into the oily club basin to wait for the winds to die down, even though it was well protected. So four days after we arrived, we set sail to explore the coves and bays of the much indented coastline.

For six days God worked hard creating the earth. On the seventh he was tired and lay back to rest. He rested his hand down on the northwest corner of Spain and made five great dents. When God saw what he had done he felt sorry, so he blessed the area and made it bountiful.

So goes a legend about the coast of Galicia, and as we cruised this green hilly coast with its five great estuaries, locally called "The Rias," we came to believe the legend was true. Never have we eaten such a variety of delicious seafood, and nowhere have we found lighter, more palatable inexpensive wines. Only three small industrial cities marred the coast; most of the time we could only see small tidy fishing villages and farms.

After two hours of sailing in protected waters with a fresh northwesterly wind blowing, we came to the village of Nada. A huge gleaming power yacht was anchored in the bay just off the town's fishing boat harbor. As we circled the yacht, its name stood out proudly, carved and gold-leafed, *Arturo.* An old, tall, heavy-featured man waved and called "buenos dias" to us as we tacked in closer to shore to anchor. A police boat came rowing out: "Sorry, but you must move," the young officer said in hesitant English. When we asked why, he told us to come with him to the *commandante*'s office.

"You must move at least five miles away from here immediately," the *commandante* told us as soon as we walked into his office. "Why?" we wanted to know. We told him about the strong winds in Corunna and said how peaceful and welcoming his small port looked to us. The *commandante* only repeated, "You must move immediately."

We set sail again, grumbling more than just a little bit, and beat five miles out to the center of yet another deep fjord, when we ran into El Ferrol. We noticed an American yacht tied alongside and an English yacht next to a pier in a comfortably enclosed fishing boat basin. As we tacked by them, a sandy-haired man yelled, "Toss me a line." We set fenders and sailed carefully alongside the forty-foot *Summer Salt,* secured, and soon were chatting with Spencer and Dale Langford and their three children.

"Did you happen to see Franco?" Spencer asked. "He's supposed to be cruising around here in his power yacht. It's huge and named *Arturo.* " We remembered the lone man who'd waved and smiled at us from *Arturo*'s flower-decorated afterdeck. We didn't envy him at all as we joined in the friendly atmosphere that spreads over any group of cruising boats that happen to share the same harbor.

Pedro Lema, a local sailor who was also harbormaster and pilot for the huge shipbuilding yard at the north end of town, came by to have a chat. He invited the whole cruising crowd home to meet his wife Marisa and have a real Spanish dinner. Then he took Larry and me for a tour of the shipyard. The three of us climbed into the drydocks and up the steep boarding ladder of a 186,000-ton Swedish oil carrier that was undergoing repairs and alterations. Its captain gave us an interesting tour of the huge ship. We used its elevator to go up eleven stories from the engine room to the ship's bridge where the captain and first mate had created a small vegetable garden in planters around the electronics of the computer-like room. "I've just picked up a strange report," the radioman told the captain as we stood examining the million dollars' worth of navigation equipment around us. "A hurricane is reported heading this way. It's only six hundred miles west of us with winds to eighty-five knots." The ship's barometer was dropping steadily. The sky outside was filled with cirrostratus clouds thickening by the minute. The wind on the bridge anemometer read forty knots. We rushed back to *Seraffyn* to prepare extra mooring lines and Pedro went to check his harbor boats. Fishing boats filled the harbor. There had never been a hurricane reported this close to Europe before. By the next morning the weather had cleared but the Bristol Channel, seven hundred miles north in England, reported winds of up to one hundred miles per hour. I was glad we'd come south before September.

After a week in El Ferrol we decided to move south. Locals all told us that we had to be south of Cabo San Vicente, Portugal's southern tip, before October 25 to avoid winter and we still wanted to explore the other four "rias." "Sail to the Ria Arosa, then turn east and go past three islands, head north, and on the very last point before the end of the estuary you'll see a yellow stone grainery and a very tall line of eucalyptus trees. Anchor there. Marisa's family owns a seafood farm there. We'll take a holiday and meet you," Pedro suggested. Although he and Marisa spent an hour more telling us all of the fun things we'd do together if we sailed to Punta Capitan, we'd been convinced from the first, and so were the Langfords.

We had unremarkable sailing south past Cabo Finnisterre. The navigation lights were reliable, currents ran as we expected, and winds were light but fair. Four days of pleasant, sunny sailing later, we rounded up and anchored next to *Summer Salt*. Pedro, Marisa, and two of her brothers rowed out with two one-gallon galvanized buckets full of clams, oysters, limes, and fresh grapes. We ate them all. The party moved from *Seraffyn* to *Summer Salt* to the farmhouse, and from there to the local bar where the light-yellow local wine was served in flat white bowls instead of glasses. Marisa's eighty-year-old aunt shared stories of the family's two hundred years on this same farm. The second afternoon we all drove to the town ten miles away and bought ten large locally caught fish to barbecue that night. I just couldn't make it ashore for the party—I had an upset stomach and headache that made all my previous illnesses seem small in comparison. "I must have eaten a bad oyster at lunchtime," I moaned to Larry. He had less sympathy than usual when he replied, "Bad oyster, that's a joke. Anyone who eats five dozen oysters for one lunch deserves to be sick." So I stayed in bed feeling sorry for myself as the laughter and songs on the shore two hundred yards away from our quiet anchorage rang through the night.

It must have been 0400 when I heard shouted good-byes from the beach, then the sound of oars striking water. I was just beginning to be sure I'd survive when Larry climbed clumsily on board. His movements were a sure sign of "one too many."

"Lin, you should have seen it. The most mesmerizing thing I've ever experienced, it was almost pagan. We drank lots of homemade wine, the fish was delicious. Marisa and her family entertained us with haunting Spanish songs. We reached over our heads to grab the bunches of grapes that were ripening in the arbors. When the fires burned down real low, Marisa brought a large silver bowl from the house and filled it with some brandy-like liquor. Her brother hummed softly in the dark, strumming his guitar. Then Marisa lit the brandy and took a ladle and poured the burning liquid through the air, the flames throwing dancing shadows across her face. She caught the brandy in the wine cups and handed one to each of us, still flaming. We drank the hot liquor and its fumes went right to my head. When my cup was dry the fires had died. We stood in the darkness, only the sound of crickets and the guitar calling softly through the night."

We had a rude awakening only four hours later. *Seraffyn*'s bow dipped and bobbed violently to the waves of a near gale. She snubbed against her anchor chain and spray found its way through our open forehatch onto our bunk. I went on deck to see the rock retaining wall that fronted Punta Capitan less than a hundred yards from our stern. An unusual northeast wind blew. The nearest shore to the north lay over two miles away, and a nasty sea was starting to build.

Spencer and his family were up and preparing to move, showing signs of wear and tear from the night before. Larry really didn't want to get out of the bunk; his eyes were red indicators of what his head must have felt like. But *Seraffyn* moved a few yards closer to the rocks as she straightened out her chain. So we reefed the mainsail, set the staysail, and beat two miles to calm water and reanchored. That took just over an hour and we were both ready to climb right back into the bunk when Pedro and his irrepressible cousins appeared in a car on the road opposite our new anchorage. "Come ashore," they yelled. "We'll take you to visit a friend who has a wine shop." But not one of us had the energy to accept. "Come back in three hours, we need some more sleep," we yelled.

The fishing fleet in the village across from Punta Capitan.

The days passed quickly, and we only decided to sail on when Pedro and Marisa left to return to El Ferrol. We reluctantly waved good-bye to Punta Capitan and sailed swiftly south toward Bayona on a fresh northerly breeze.

The friendly village of Bayona nestles under a beautiful parapeted castle at the entrance to the Ria Vigo. It is one of the most popular stops on the nautical route to sunshine. Almost every European yachtsman bound for the Caribbean via the Canary Islands stops here to rest after escaping from the Bay of Biscay. The Bayona Yacht Club makes voyagers welcome, and even goes to the trouble of having an English-speaking manager. The club was enlarged and their docks modernized for the 1972 transatlantic race, but most of the dock space was filled with local yachts when we arrived, so we happily anchored out among the cruising yachts.

Wanderer III, the thirty-foot sloop which had carried Eric and Susan Hiscock for over one hundred ten thousand miles, lay looking fresh and clean in green and white, just astern of us. It was now owned by a young German couple bound for the United States. Six-foot-plus Svend Kaee had his twenty-one-foot *Optimist* nearby, with its oversize Danish flag. He rowed over to visit us in the smallest rubber dinghy we've ever seen. Svend had to lie down to row, and his feet hung over the stern. He was bound for the sun after a chilling visit to Iceland the previous year. (See Appendix B.) Two couples from Belgium, Paul and Pierrette Benoidt and Marc and Françoise Besirre, were bound for Barbados on their two French-built fiberglass sloops. They invited us for a barbecue on one of the deserted islands ten miles north of Bayona. We joined them and ate mussels pulled from the rocks at low tide and then steamed in a mixture of tomatoes, onions, and garlic.

One young English couple had arrived in Bayona just a few days before we did on a thirty-year-old, thirty-five-foot ex-racing sloop. They had fallen in love with her the first time they saw her up a river on England's south coast. She'd been built by a famous Scottish yard, designed by an artist, and her sheer was a delight to behold. So they paid the low price the owner was asking and bought her without a survey. Then the two of them, both new to sailing but full of dreams, put most of their life's savings into buying cruising equipment and stores. They set off with only a little money left, bound for the Caribbean where they heard they could earn more by doing charter work. Halfway down the Bay of Biscay their inboard rudder started to loosen up. When they reached Bayona they put the boat on the concrete ramp next to the club and waited for the tide to go down so they could check the rudder. A bit of surge kept the boat from settling close to the wall. So they put a bulk of timber between the concrete wall and the mast of the sloop with heavy padding to protect the varnish. When the boat settled and leaned its weight against the mast, the mast split open just below the deck partners. It had been made up of laminations and was rotten where someone had tacked a piece of copper over the split glue joint. A close inspection of the inboard rudder and its shaft running up through the stern timber showed that extensive repairs were necessary to both the rudder and the shaft alleyway. The rudder needed at least six feet of clearance below the keel to drop out of the hull and that couldn't be done on the concrete ramp. So the boat was shifted to the beach as soon as the mast was hoisted out. Then by setting several anchors she was held upright as the tide went out. The couple

Mussels are cultivated throughout the five rias on huge rafts built of girders. Ropes hang into the water and mussels cling to these ropes and develop until they are harvested when about two inches in length. This family had five rafts fifteen feet by forty feet long in the bay at Bayona.

dug a deep hole under the rudder and removed it. As the days passed their dream ship began to turn into a nightmare. As they tried to find some way of replacing their mast with very limited funds, Larry offered to help build a new one, but the price of decent timber was beyond their budget. When we left two weeks later, the handsome but crippled old sloop was still on the beach, rudderless and mastless. We never heard what finally happened to her and our hearts ached for the couple who could have saved thousands of dollars and weeks of worry by spending only a hundred dollars to hire a surveyor in the first place.

Another sad story was tied to the club docks. The forty-five-foot-long, almost-new aluminum French sloop had been on its way north from Portugal. Its crew of four were tired after motoring north into headseas and headwinds for two days. They arrived at the entrance to the Ria Vigo at night and spotted one of the range lights that mark the clear passage north of a group of submerged rocks. They decided they were well clear of Wolf Rocks even though no second range light came into line with the first as the chart indicated it should. "Must be out of order" was the navigator's comment. They headed into the ria and seconds later a wave lifted them beam-on onto the rocks. A second wave washed right over them. A third wave sent them clear, and it was then that they realized that one man had been washed overboard. Their flares quickly brought help from Bayona, only two miles away, but despite a careful search the man was not found until his body washed up on the beach three days later. The aluminum hull had a dent almost a foot and a half deep and five feet long in its side, and the boat had suffered some internal damage. The comment someone made at the club was particularly poignant, "Yes, that proves it, you can put an aluminum or steel boat on the rocks and it will float off again. But the whole idea of this sport is to keep off the rocks!"

We were sitting on deck early one morning, watching fishing boats leave the harbor with their trail of seagulls, when a tall Spaniard came powering out in the club launch. "Remember me?" he called in perfect English as he came alongside. Both of us shook our heads no. Then he pointed to the far side of the mooring area. There it stood, the white and blue fiberglass sloop that had swung against *Seraffyn*'s side when I was alone in Millbay Docks at Plymouth. I must have blushed from head to toe at that memory because Adriano gave a teasing smile and said, "I have some movie pictures I took of you that your husband might especially like to see!" We ate dinner at Adriano's house later that evening and his wife helped us with our faulty Mexican-accented Spanish. Since the evening was cool she'd draped the dinner table with a long quilted cover and set a small heater under the table. It glowed against our legs and felt great.

No home movie ever interested me quite as much. I glowed with delight as Adriano showed *Seraffyn* and me maneuvering out of the close confines of Millbay Dock looking completely at ease. "I wish I'd had my camera ready a few hours before I took these," Adriano said. "I'd have had even more interesting photos to share with you then." He ran the four-minute film through at least three more times just for our entertainment.

The days were growing cooler. I had jeans on more often than a bikini, and along with most of the last southern-bound cruising boats we set off for Portugal on October 1, giving Wolf Rocks an extra-wide berth.

CHAPTER 22

~~~~~

Looking for
the Portuguese Trade Winds

O nly twenty miles from the entrance of Bayona lay the notoriously
uninviting coast of Portugal. Even though there are several rivers
running out of the hills and through the coastal plains of this western-
most corner of Europe, almost all are fronted by sandbars. In the three
hundred miles from Bayona south to Cabo San Vicente, there are now
only four all-weather harbors available to ships that draw over three
feet. Three of these harbors are man-made, two of them constructed
in the last twenty years. Over ninety percent of the fishing done off
this coast is in boats that can be landed on the beach or surfed over
river bars. Yet this is the country which produced and sponsored some
of the world's most adventuresome navigators, men like Vasco da
Gama, Magellan, and Amerigo Vespucci. From this inhospitable coast
sailors have ventured into the cold, ice-laden waters of the Grand
Banks to bring home catches of cod in their handsome sailing schooners.

This coast is also known for its northwesterly wind, which usually
blows so steadily that it is called the Portuguese trade winds. But that
wind was nowhere in evidence when we left Spain. In fact, even
though the Atlantic stretched in an unbroken reach for over three
thousand miles to the west, the sea we trickled slowly over was almost
as flat as a plate.

We reached Leixos (Lay-show-ez) at 0130. Even in the dark we could
tell it was an industrial harbor. The flares of a huge fire, burning off
waste gases at a refinery, dwarfed the twenty-mile range navigation
light at the north end of the harbor. The sound of generators hummed
across the still water combined with the roar of trucks and screech of

heavy cranes. We sailed slowly past the red and green lights on the end
of the breakwater. Our harbor chart was in the cockpit, inside a clear
plastic chart case we'd been given in England. I used a flashlight to
study the details as Larry short-tacked up the channel. At first we
thought a fishing boat was busy at work in the harbor entrance, but
as we came closer to what turned out to be a light-covered barge, we
decided it was some kind of drilling platform. Someone on the platform flashed lights at us and yelled. We couldn't make out his words
over the noise of generators. A large bell rang. A horn blasted. Suddenly a huge "be-humph" resounded through both air and water.
Seraffyn's cockpit sole jumped under our feet and less than two hundred yards astern a geyser of water, mud, and rock shot fifty feet into
the air. Even though we finally found a berth at the far end of the
harbor, almost a mile away from the blasting operations being carried
out to deepen the rock bottom of the harbor entrance, we never quite
felt comfortable as the shock of underwater blasting shook our home
at unexpected intervals both day and night.

Leixos had a filthy harbor. Crude oil covered our waterline within
hours after we tied to a fishing boat in the rock-wall-enclosed inner
basin. It smelled like rotten fish at low tide and sour oil at high tide.
Normally we would have moved on immediately, but the man on the
fishing boat told us, "Come into Porto. Help us celebrate our happy
flower revolution." His description of the beauties of the town where
port wine was blended sold us on it. We rowed to the dinghy landing,
secured *Rinky*, and found the wonderful old No. 1 tram. This tiny,
electrically run wooden carriage had carried passengers along the
waterfront from Leixos to the entrance of the River Duro, then along
the riverbank to Porto, for over fifty years. It was a delightful ride, past
the swirling mud banks at the river's entrance, alongside boatyards
still repairing the wooden cod fishing schooners, past women washing
their laundry on the river's edge. Frolicking children stopped to wave
and yell to us as we rumbled quietly past. Twenty minutes later the
old-fashioned cane-seated carriage came to stop at the foot of Porto. As
soon as we stepped off into the hustle of the open market along the
riverbank, an English-speaking man appeared and said, "Because of
our revolution there are not many tourists right now. So you'll get a
warm welcome if you visit one our wine cellars on the other side of
the river." He directed us along our way and we spent the whole
morning on a slow, enjoyable guided tour of the two-hundred-year-old

wine cellar. We stood watching as men made new oaken barrels for the mellow red wine. We met the wrinkled old winetaster and shared glasses of wine with the charming, black-eyed young girl who'd given us our tour. After tasting over ten different types of port we couldn't really tell one from the other. Two relaxed and contented cruising sailors stepped out of the cool stone cellars and walked the one mile into the ancient city that climbed the hills on the north side of the river.

Everyone we met was wearing a carnation in his lapel or pinned to her blouse. All seemed to notice us and wave, then shout, "Viva Portugal!" When we came to the main plaza, a crowd was busy tearing revolution posters off marble monuments and building fronts. A young man had climbed a huge bronze statue of a general on a horse. He secured a red carnation on the general's bronze breast and worked to secure a Portuguese flag between the horse's ears as the happy crowd below laughed and shouted encouragement. We were the only foreigners in the crowd and people tried to tell us what was happening. But our Spanish, similar as it sounded to Portuguese, just didn't work. Finally, a young student came and translated. "We no longer have a dictator. Portugal is free! Now we can build a modern nation. These are all students and citizens giving a day of their time to clean the city." We watched as the crowd hosed down the plaza with fire hoses and worked to remove some of the thousands of posters and painted slogans that defaced the beautiful old stone buildings of Porto.

It is possible to sail up the River Duoro right into the heart of Porto. But after speaking to a pilot and seeing the complicated, tide-swept, shoal-encumbered shifting river entrance, we decided it was safer to stay in Leixos. Besides, we'd watched piles of refuse running down the river, dead rats included. Health authorities who'd stamped our ship's papers had warned us of reports of cholera in the city. Besides, we liked having an excuse to use the antique No. 1 tram.

We left the harbor of Leixos five days later laden with beautiful fresh vegetables and seafood from the huge public market. Prices had been extremely low (people told us it was because of the revolution). As we worked very slowly south being pulled by a one-knot current, close-reaching on a light southwesterly wind, we became convinced that the Portuguese trade winds were a myth. We spent a calm night anchored off the beach and the next day found the entrance to Aviero, a small town whose river entrance was shown in detail on our chart.

Piles of refuse float past women who are washing their clothes in the river Douro.

Below left: The young Portuguese student tried to secure his flag to the horse's ears as the crowd below cheered him on.

Below right: The beggar king celebrates Portugal's hard-earned freedom.

VIVA POR-TUGA

The bar at its entrance should have had seven feet of water at low tide, but even in the calm weather there were breakers right across the entrance. We could see no clear passage into the harbor even after reaching slowly across the entrance three times. So we continued slowly south, our big blue and white drifter pulling us along at two knots.

Our charts indicated a fishing harbor behind a point called Peniche. Although our British Admiralty *Pilot* book for the coast of Portugal did not mention this harbor, the American edition we happened to have on board gave a careful description of a new harbor with fifteen feet of water, a new breakwater, and room for up to two hundred fishing boats with good holding ground. "Let's head in there and wait for a change in the weather," Larry suggested. "I don't particularly like being out here in the shipping lanes with so little steerage way." We only had fifteen miles to go when a heavy fog settled over us. The wind died completely. We stood watches through the night, blasting our foghorn in answer to ships that passed eerily by. Occa-

We found the ends of the breakwater at Peniche after ten hours of heavy fog.

sionally the fog would clear enough so that we could take a bearing on the Peniche light and the one on the small island of Berlenga, five miles off the mainland. Then whoever was on watch would recompute our position and work to try to sail on any puff of wind that drifted by. The fog and sporadic winds persisted but we found the ends of Peniche's breakwater after taking sixty hours to cover one hundred ten miles. The fog lifted and a fresh northwesterly breeze filled in within minutes after we set our anchor amid a fleet of gaily painted fishing boats.

We rowed ashore to the small village and wandered across the peninsula, carefully investigating the wooden fishing boats under construction along the beach. We watched two men sawing frames from a huge piece of oak, using the same kind of cross saw we'd seen in museums. The building methods didn't seem to have changed in two hundred years. But the fifty- and sixty-foot-long fishing boats that resulted now sported huge Spanish-built diesel engines.

The quiet village seemed untouched by the revolution or the outside world. A stone windmill worked quietly grinding corn, its canvas sails moving ever faster as the October wind freshened. We ate dinner in the village's one restaurant that evening. There was no menu and the waitress spoke no English or Spanish. We still spoke no Portuguese. After several frustrating minutes of noncommunication, Larry had an idea. He pulled the last of our supply of Portuguese escudos from his pocket, the equivalent of three dollars, and set them in front of the waitress. She smiled, then drew first a fish on her pad, then something that resembled a pig. "Which one?" she indicated in sign language. We chose the fish. She disappeared into the kitchen and came back minutes later with a loaf of hot fresh bread, a carafe of vino verde (the local young white wine), and a chunk of fresh butter. We stalled our appetites with this and ten minutes later she emerged again, proudly carrying a platter with two huge, perfectly grilled fresh fish steaks seasoned with garlic and oregano, a mound of french-fried potatoes, and a fringe of juicy bright-red tomato slices. Dessert was a bowl of grapes and fresh fruit. As we left we wished we'd saved some escudos to give her as a tip. But our one word of Portuguese had to suffice. "Thank you" was all we could say.

I wanted to stay in Peniche longer. But when we woke up the next morning and heard a fresh northwesterly wind blowing through our rigging, I couldn't help but agree with Larry, who said, "Come on, let's

Two men use the same methods their fathers and grandfathers used to cut sawn frames from huge slabs of oak. The adze is being used to shape a keel. This is one boat-building tool that is still widely in use today. These fishing boats will work out of Peniche, using trawl nets.

set sail and use this wind." I stored things away below while Larry put a reef in the mainsail and led the staysail sheets. "Ready to flake the chain?" he called. "Okay," I answered as I climbed over the forward bunk to the chain locker. Larry cranked the chain in, our handy bronze Plath double-acting winch clicking happily. I scattered the chain as it dropped through the chain pipe so it wouldn't stay in a pile and overflow the edge of the chain locker or fall over itself and jam when *Seraffyn* heeled. When the five-fathom marker came into view, Larry called, "Come on deck, I'll hoist the main." I scrambled out into the cockpit, glad of my sweater and jeans in the Force 6 wind, and took hold of the tiller. Larry hoisted the main and I stood ready to pull in the mainsheet. Larry pulled in the last five fathoms of chain and called "Anchors up!" I sheeted in the mainsail. *Seraffyn* gathered way. Larry hooked the anchor onto the bobstay and hoisted the staysail as I jibed the boat. Then he came back and trimmed the staysail and I steered for the harbor entrance. As soon as we were clear, Larry suggested, "How about plotting a course to Lisbon. Is it possible to get another cup of coffee?"

So in the pattern that had almost become a ritual, I handed Larry the tiller and climbed below, plotted our proposed course, reheated the coffee and tea, and poured out cups three-quarters full. Then Larry sat at the helm, I perched on the companionway sill, and we chatted as Peniche dropped quickly away behind us.

What a glorious sail we had that day! The sun warmed our decks and we shed our sweaters as soon as we'd put *Seraffyn* on a dead downwind course, the staysail on the whisker pole, reefed mainsail vanged and prevented on the opposite side. When we cleared the lee of Peniche Point the ocean swell caught us. *Seraffyn* would rush down the face of the large long swells at what seemed like ten knots, then she'd slow down to climb the back of the next swell, seem to pause for a moment as she reached the crest, then surge down its face, throwing spray and foam twenty feet on either side. If we hand-steered, *Seraffyn* tried to surf off almost every wave. But if we let Helmer stay in charge she didn't, because he couldn't anticipate and give her rudder that little twitch right at the top of each wave that got her going.

Landmarks flashed by as we roared along, clocking seven knots over the bottom. But we knew that at least half a knot of that speed was due to current. By midafternoon we could see the cliffs of Cascais, marking the entrance to Lisbon, and couldn't have been happier as we shared a bottle of Portuguese wine and a plate of crackers with white farmer's cheese in the surprisingly steady cockpit.

Ahead of us a large power yacht came pounding directly into the seas, going north, spray flying right over the bridge driven by the twenty-five-knot wind. It passed close by us, rolling heavily, its motors growling and rumbling, and Larry raised his wine glass to the man at the helm and said, "I'll bet that man is looking at us and thinking, 'It's an ill wind that blows no one some good!'"

Although we thought little of that incident at the time, it had an ending almost three years later. We were at the 1977 World Half-Ton Regatta in Trieste, Italy. Larry was off *Seraffyn* crewing on the Canadian half-tonner, and I was hanging upside down varnishing under the bowsprit, when a tall, lanky West Indian came by. "I know where you were at 1530 on the twelfth of October 1974," he said to me. I had to think hard as I varnished, then I answered, "We must have been somewhere in Portugal about then."

"Yes," he answered, "You were running free, looking beautiful as can be about twenty miles out of Lisbon and I was having my guts rolled out in a sixty-five-foot motorboat, wishing I were you. I saw you salute with your glasses of wine and felt like turning and running, too." Jeff Bishop, a delivery skipper, had been taking the motorboat north to England.

We roared upriver to Lisbon, past the tower of Belem where Henry the Navigator had watched for his explorers to return. We tied in the visitors' basin just at dark. We'd sailed fifty-five miles in only nine hours including the time we'd spent maneuvering into the tight little basin. The decks had stayed dry the whole time. "What a fine little boat! Give her a bit of wind and she flies," we both agreed as we settled in to eat our dinner.

Lisbon turned out to be one of the loveliest capitals we've ever visited, rivaled only by Copenhagen. Its naval museum took a whole day of our time. Not only was the collection beautifully housed, it held some of the finest models we've seen. The carriage museum, just a quarter mile from the harbor, is definitely the most unusual we've visited. Housed in an indoor riding academy building constructed during the eighteenth century, its collection of close to fifty horse-drawn luxury carriages came from craftsmen of over four centuries. Three of the largest carriages, ornately carved and cushioned in velvet, had carried Portuguese royalty during a papal procession a hundred fifty years previously, and each had a cleverly concealed chamber pot inside for the relief of its elderly passengers.

The city was particularly quiet as there were few foreign tourists about and the local people were settling back, peacefully waiting for the promised elections. The second day after we arrived, we returned from a day of touring feeling slightly footsore. Some people were on the deck of an interesting-looking local yacht moored two boats away. "Who designed your boat?" Larry called over. José Da Veiga Ventura and Judy Kuenzle, his fiancée, introduced themselves and invited us over. Judy worked as a stewardess and José as airport manager for Pan American Airlines, and after we'd shared drinks and tours of both boats, they took us for a walk in the old city of Lisbon by night. Then we went to their apartment and cooked up a dinner together. They shared their dreams for Portugal with us and the worries they had about the growing pains their country had yet to face. "Our students are all dreamers and believe the promises the Communists make. But

The happy cook at a tiny restaurant in Lisbon fans the flame under her brazier while three-inch-long fish sizzle on top.

our small farmers and fishermen are the backbone of the economy. They don't want communism, they just want the right to own their own land or their own boat and the peace to work them," José told us. He and Judy made our stay in Lisbon pass far too quickly. They took us into the country to meet farming friends and taste the wines that city people rarely enjoy. They showed us their favorite shops. But they too warned, "You should be moving on. Winter storms will be coming at the end of October." Their warning, combined with the fact that our cruising funds were really getting low, made up our minds to move on quickly. We'd known when we left England that we had only enough freedom chips to last five months more. The one thing we didn't want to have happen was to arrive in Gibraltar flat broke and be forced to take the very first job that came along, even if we didn't like it. So after only a week in Lisbon we invited Judy and José to join us for a day sail.

They seemed to love it as the wind freshened just outside the yacht basin and we flew downriver on a beam reach under a reefed main and staysail. José directed us to an anchorage he liked near the handsome village of Cascais, ten miles outside Lisbon. Soon after we anchored, Larry rowed all of us ashore in the dinghy for dinner.

The anchorage had been quite calm when we'd left the boat three hours earlier. But when we finished saying good-bye to our new friends at the train station and walked back through the quiet streets toward the waterfront, we couldn't believe the surge and swell we saw in the anchorage. Launching *Rinky* off the concrete ramp in front of the Cascais Sailing Club was a real challenge. Larry timed the incoming three-foot surge and shoved the dinghy off the ramp. On the next surge he jumped into the dinghy and rowed clear. He waited until there was a momentary lull and rowed stern to the ramp. "Jump!" he called. I just made it into the dinghy as a large swell ran along the seawall and up the ramp, crashing against the beach. I got my trousers wet to the knees.

Seraffyn rose and fell gently to the swell that ran under her from astern. The wind still came gusting off the beach. We'd never seen anything like it, but José had told us that this was quite normal. He'd described how the formation of the headland turned the northwesterly swell around until it ran into Cascais from the south, even when northerly winds blew fresh. "Sometimes the swell is as high as ten feet," José had told us when we stood watching the local fishermen bring their twenty-five-foot-long fish-laden dories up the beach on log rollers.

We slept quite comfortably all night, so I was doubly surprised when I opened the hatch in the morning and saw eight- or ten-foot-high rollers coming into the anchorage. When *Seraffyn* was in the trough of the waves, the forty-foot pilot boat on a mooring two hundred yards astern of us disappeared from view. The twenty-knot wind kept us perfectly aligned, stern into the smooth rolling swell, so we didn't roll. But as we watched the swell becoming roaring breakers on the beach three hundred feet in front of us, we decided to forget trying to row ashore for a last bunch of fresh fruit. "Let's get out of here quick" was what I said, and within minutes we were running wing and wing into that ten-foot swell.

Five miles later the sea pattern straightened out. We had another headlong dash south on the Portuguese trades as far as Seisembra, the newest harbor on this coast. It was tiny, with room for only about

Larry carries water to *Rinky Dink* on the ramp at Peniche.

twenty fishing trawlers and maybe two yachts. Heavy gusts of wind blasted the harbor, dropping off the high cliffs and whistling through the rigging at fifty knots although the wind outside ran no more than twenty. So we spent less than forty-eight hours here before setting sail to run away from winter.

Cabo San Vicente came clear on the horizon on Tuesday the twenty-second of October. The wind was fresh and cold, laden with moisture. Clouds of fog rushed along with us, obscuring the headland, then lifting momentarily to show us the bold cliffs that marked our turning point. As we rounded the cape, heavy squalls rushed off the land, some so strong that we had to luff up when they hit or risk getting water in the cockpit over the lee deck. We anchored in the lee of the land for the night and the next morning awoke to find a warm, sunny day. "Remember what Pedro told us when we were in El Capitan?" I asked Larry as we worked to again be under way. "Yes," Larry answered, "Get past Cabo San Vincente by October 25 and you'll miss winter. He was right on."

We set every sail we could on a romping beam reach. The wind pulled aft and we set our huge blue and white spinnaker, laughing like two school kids as we scudded along at four and a half knots. "Just think—no real winter, no heater, no gloves, no three layers of sweaters." We shouldn't have laughed so loud.

A gust of wind from dead ahead collapsed our spinnaker. Helmer sent the tiller hard over to correct for the wind shift, and seconds later we were headed back the way we'd come. Down with the spinnaker, up with the lapper. We disconnected Helmer, tightened in the sheets, and reset the steering vane to head toward the straits of Gibraltar hard on the wind. Squalls began to grow in the north. By midnight we were down to storm sails and I'd pulled out our winter sailing clothes. By morning we were hove to as Force 8 squalls swept over us, kicking up a nasty sea. Rain slashed against the decks and we stayed below most of the day while *Seraffyn* lay comfortably hove to. We only glanced out once in a while to check for ships. Larry beat me again at cribbage, the cards held in place on our tilted table by a bunched-up towel. "That'll teach us to laugh at winter," he said as he warmed his hands on a cup of hot chocolate.

If I believed in weather gods I'd have said one was listening in just at that moment because soon the wind lightened and drew back to the northwest. We set sail and by nightfall were on a close reach, moving

All plain sail set in the Mediterreanean sunshine. *Ton Steen*

beautifully. The stars were out, the seas grew steadily clamer, the decks dried, and the air warmed. The current caught us.

Larry was reluctant to go below and climb into the bunk. He sat with his arm around me in the cockpit. Helmer steered and the taffrail long hummed as it counted the miles we covered. We could see our oil lamps burning through the open companionway, turning *Seraffyn*'s main cabin into a golden glow of varnished mahogany and teak. The chime on our ship's clock rang clearly over the hiss and mumble of our churning wake, eight bells. "I'm kind of looking forward to doing some work," Larry commented. "It's a good change, isn't it? Three months of work, nine months of cruising. I wonder what kind of jobs we'll find in Gibraltar."

I thought of the six and a half years we'd been cruising on *Seraffyn* and the ten years Larry and I had been together. We'd always seemed to find some way to replenish our cruising funds. Larry could do wood repairs or splice rigging. Quite often owners of large yachts wanted their boats moved across an ocean and didn't have enough spare time so paid us to deliver their yachts for them. As long as we kept our expenses low and some money in our cruising emergency fund, we always seemed to find interesting work when we needed it. "I guess having to work as we go makes our whole life more interesting. If we never had to think of earning money it would all seem too easy," I said to Larry. "I wonder where we'll moor the boat. There seem to be lots of places to go for a day sail. Hope the markets have some interesting foods." Larry took over the day dreaming, "Wonder if there'll be any cruiser races we can take *Seraffyn* in. Hope there's a good library and some English movies."

He finally went below to sleep. The lights of Trafalgar passed quickly by during the misty night prompting Larry to comment "Nelson's ghosts must be nearby" as we changed places at 0200. It was my watch when the first gray of dawn showed on the horizon. Since there were no ships around, I began tidying up inside the boat and made a cup of tea as *Seraffyn* ran smartly along. The sky turned to a rosy glow. I climbed on deck, tea in hand, and almost gasped in awe. The sun rose slowly, a majestic red globe, perfectly framed on one side by Europe, on the other by Africa. "Larry, come on deck," I called. He sleepily climbed into the cockpit. We watched in quiet warm companionship as the sun seemed to beckon *Seraffyn* toward the new adventures waiting for us in the Mediterranean.

Glossary

boom gallows: A metal and wood structure on the afterdeck that supports the main boom when it is not in use.

carlin: A fore-and-aft structural member of the deck framing.

channel: A wooden strut over which the chainplates pass so that the shrouds do not crush against the bulwarks.

drop boards: Stout wooden boards that are dropped into a slot to close off the companionway.

Force 8 to 9: Wind speeds of thirty-four to forty-seven knots.

head: See loo.

heaving to, hove to: A way of stopping the boat's forward motion so that she lies at an angle of about fifty degrees off the wind and creates a wide wake or slick water on her windward side; this action can be taken to wait for a change in the tide, to rest, or to be safe during a storm.

Helmer: The name of *Seraffyn*'s wind-activated self-steering gear.

lapper: A small genoa that just reaches aft of the mast when sheeted tight in.

lazy jacks: A set of lines secured on both sides of the boom which serve not only as double topping lifts but keep the mainsail from falling all over the cockpit and helmsman when it is dropped; usually found on gaff-rigged vessels.

loo: A marine toilet, often called a head, an object of much discussion and many bad jokes on board cruising yachts.

quay: An English name for any dock to which a ship or boat may tie.

Rinky, alias *Rinky Dink* (*Wrinkles* when she needs a paint job): The six-foot eight-inch pram-style Montgomery dinghy we use as a tender to *Seraffyn;* the dinghy was originally christened *Rubicon* but that seemed a bit grandiose.

scope: The ratio of the length of anchor chain let out to the depth of water the boat is anchoring in; a scope of five to one is our minimum for strong winds in anchorages with good holding ground (chain doesn't do you any good in the chain locker).

telltails: Twelve-inch lengths of nylon yarn that are attached to the shrouds and backstay to serve as wind direction indicators; total cost for a ten-year supply—fifty cents; cost for one electronic wind direction indicator—one hundred and fifty dollars.

wing and wing: To run with the mainsail on one side of the boat, the jib on a pole to the other side; our favorite course, dead downwind.

APPENDICES

APPENDIX A

The Idea Is Freedom

"How can the two of you live on a twenty-four-foot boat for eight years?"

"Isn't *Seraffyn* a bit small for safe extended cruising?"

"Don't you miss the comforts you could have on a thirty-five-footer?"

The only other question we've heard as often as these is "How can you afford to cruise around like you do? Where do you get the money?"

Two basic questions—size and money. The answers are simple. We chose between the physical luxuries of a big boat and the freedom of a small one.

But we're not the only people who choose to cruise in a small boat. Gordon and Annabelle Yates are now enjoying their fourth year on board twenty-eight-foot *Amøbel*. Nick Skeates is approaching Australia after three years of cruising from England on twenty-nine-foot *Wylo*. The Hiscocks sailed for ten years and one hundred ten thousand miles on thirty-foot *Wanderer III*. When we think of the cruising friends we've met in the past eight years, one fact becomes obvious. Most people who cruise away from home waters year in and year out, living on money they earn before they leave or as they cruise, have small yachts. By small we mean thirty-two feet or under. Even those with private incomes who cruise year in and year out usually choose boats around thirty-five feet on deck.

Cruising Represents Freedom—Small Boats Insure Freedom

If we had waited until we could afford a forty-five-foot yacht and all its luxuries, we might never have gone cruising. Yachts of any size are expensive. The bigger they are, the more they cost. A quick walk around any boat show will prove the difference between a twenty-eight-footer and a forty-five-footer. Then comes outfitting. During the past three years we've taken a cost survey, asking people who are currently cruising away from home for a minimum of twelve months to fill out our questionnaire. So far, thirty-eight cruisers from eight different countries have obliged. Some of these people have been cruising as long as ten years on their present boat. Every one of them listed outfitting as costing an additional twenty-five percent above and beyond the purchase or construction price of their boat, be it new or secondhand. So, if you pay sixty thousand dollars for the forty-five-footer, you'll spend an additional fifteen thousand dollars getting it ready for offshore work. If you buy a thirty-footer for thirty thousand dollars, outfitting will be seventy-five hundred. Since we are working people and have no private income, we equate money saved with time off. The difference between the outfitted forty-five-footer and the outfitted thirty-footer means starting to cruise seven years sooner, or having money for seven extra years of cruising. We are willing to give up a lot of physical luxuries for all those years of freedom.

Someone is bound to counter that statement by saying, "I'm handy with tools. I can buy a forty-five-footer built of plywood/ferrocement/fiberglass or what-have-you, and finish and outfit it myself for only twenty-five thousand dollars." If the expenses of cruising ended right after purchasing and outfitting your boat, we'd say, "Great, have at it." But they don't. The survey answers proved that cruising expenses are directly related to size. The fifteen families who cruised for over two years on boats thirty-three feet and under (five of these listed private incomes) had monthly expenditures of a hundred fifty to three hundred fifty dollars with an average of two hundred fifty dollars. The twenty-two people on boats from thirty-four to forty-nine feet (fourteen of these listed private incomes) had monthly expenses ranging from two hundred fifty to a thousand dollars a month with an average of four hundred fifteen dollars. Displacement seemed to have little effect on monthly expenses; they always related to length on deck.

Everything costs more for the larger boat. Mooring fees are charged by the foot. Cruising permits (an unhappily expanding custom) cost according to size. Hauling, gear, and equipment costs depend on boat size. And finally, human nature being what it is, tradesmen and suppliers identify with the man on a small boat. But they see a forty-five-footer and assume the owner must be rich, so *they* charge accordingly.

Can You Handle It?

Any reasonably healthy couple, no matter what their ages, can handle a forty-five-foot yacht in average conditions with the aid of an engine. As long as there are enough winches and a bit of forethought, people can sail seventy-footers alone. The Observer Single-handed Transatlantic Race proves this. But cruising year in and year out is not like taking one dash across the Atlantic, with only one harbor to enter. When a couple are cruising for pleasure they will each have to handle the boat single-handed at times, if only during night watches. They'll have to take care of the boat and themselves in storm conditions and while entering strange harbors time and time again. Since engines are not infallible, long-term-cruising people are occasionally going to be forced to short-tack into some strange harbor under sail alone. On a thirty-footer it's a pleasant challenge; on a forty-five-footer it's plain hard work.

Although we've often heard that sail area is the limiting factor as to the size of boat two people can handle, cruising has proved to us that it's in harbor that a boat's size matters. If all hell breaks loose at sea, it's not too difficult to heave to and wait it out. But when a fifty-knot squall blows through your anchorage and dislodges your ground tackle, either you or your spouse may have to set another anchor or get the first one up—quick and alone. The thirty-five-pound anchor on a twenty-eight-footer is all I'd want to handle, the seventy-five-pounder on the forty-five-footer is far beyond my (Lin's) capability, especially when the motion and emergency factors are added to the equation. Even more frightening, but an event that unfortunately happens too often when you are cruising, is when that same squall catches you lying against a dock or seawall. The chop builds up in the harbor. Your fenders start popping out of place, leaving your handsome, vulnerable topsides exposed, four inches from a grinding pier.

While you are struggling to push your boat away from the wall so you can put in another fender, consider what size boat you really want to cruise in. Our criteria for the absolute maximum size we'd enjoy is one that either of us could shove off a pier against a thirty-five-knot beam wind while the other ran to secure another mooring line or set a beam anchor. We've worked around yachts for thirteen years together and cruised for over nine. We've delivered yachts ranging from thirty-five feet to fifty-four feet, and I'm convinced that our safe limit based on harbor criteria is thirty-two feet on deck.

Often people in forty-five-footers seem to have lost the joy of sailing. Yes, they still make passages mostly under sail, but they rarely seem to go "out for a day sail." Once again, this is caused by the problem of handling the big boat. It's too much work to lift a forty-five-footer's anchor and set its sails just for a cruise around the harbor. Then, to make it worse, designers and builders of many of today's production cruising boats have sold people on the idea of forty-five-footers by saying, "You can handle it—only seven hundred square feet of sail area, less than four hundred feet in the mainsail." The boat is vastly underrigged, so it moves like a monument in anything under ten knots of wind. Not much fun for sailing. We've found that sailboats that are a joy in light winds (three to eight knots) usually have eighty to eighty-five square feet of working sail area (jib and mainsail) for every ton of weight. It's sail area that drives a sailboat. Light-weather racing machines like *Windward Passage, Ondine,* and Holland half-tonners have as much as one hundred five square feet of working sail area per ton, and this doesn't include genoas, spinnakers, and so on. At the other end of the scale is the Tahiti ketch, known for its slow passages in anything less than fifteen knots of wind. It has fifty-five square feet of canvas for each ton of weight. To get good light-weather performance on a forty-five-footer you need big sails. These sails are more than two people can easily handle. That's why thirty- to thirty-five-foot boats finished well ahead of forty-five- to fifty-footers in the last two-man Round-Britain Race and swept the fleet handicap prizes.

Safety

No boat, no matter what its size, is safe without good seamanship. The ability to make the right decision, the ability to handle the boat in all conditions, the ability to maintain your equipment so it's ready at all times—these determine a boat's safety. When it comes to storm conditions, no boat is really comfortable no matter what its size, but the man on the thirty-footer might have one advantage. Because his gear will be smaller and easier to manhandle, be it storm trysail, sea anchor, warps, he might be ready to take preventative measures sooner. Because of his boat's smaller size and generally shallower draft, the man on the thirty-footer would probably find more places of refuge available to him than the man on the forty-five-footer. Yes, the small-boat sailor will have to think twice before choosing to round the Horn or take a winter passage. He may choose to lay in port and wait out a gale the man in a forty-five-footer may challenge. But prudence and good seamanship, not the boat's size, are where safety lies.

The Question Is Comfort

Yes, I'd sometimes like the physical luxuries of a forty-five-foot yacht—an enclosed shower, a powered anchor winch, hot water, refrigeration. But from delivering big yachts we've learned that each of these items not only requires constant maintenance but seems to break down just when you want it. When you are tied up in a marina for four months trying to get repairs done, waiting out winter gales, or working to earn money for your cruise, even a forty-five-footer is a poor excuse for an apartment. The fun of cruising is going places, meeting people, making new landfalls. When you are on the move, the smallest boat is a joy.

It all comes down to deciding what comfort is. To us, it means being free to go. The reason we can afford to go is because of *Seraffyn*'s small size. By working three months each year, we can have nine months of freedom. Because of her low maintenance costs, we have the "comfort" of extra money to explore inland in the countries we visit, money to take a shoreside apartment for three or four months if a winter turns cold, wet, and miserable. We have the "comfort" of being able to buy the very best equipment for *Seraffyn*. If we want an anchor, it will cost about eighty dollars for the finest twenty-five-pound CQR. The seventy-five-pounder needed for a forty-five-foot yacht is three hundred dollars (Malta prices, 1977). Since we can afford the best equipment and can be sure *Seraffyn* is well maintained from masthead to keel, we have the mental "comfort" of confidence.

We know we can push *Seraffyn* to her sailing limit if it becomes necessary. And we are "comforted" by the knowledge that either one of us can handle her in almost any situation.

There may come a time, no matter how much we are enjoying the cruising life, when we need to move into a community ashore. Twenty-four-foot *Seraffyn* has one final advantage—she's not such a big investment that we'll have to sell her. We can put her on a mooring while we rejoin society. And there she can be used as a weekender, waiting patiently until we again get the urge to wander.

Come on, join the wonderful community of long-distance cruising people. If you have a small boat now, look it over and consider ways to make it more comfortable, seaworthy, and fun to sail. If you are trying to find a boat, don't be trapped by the glitter of the forty-five-footers. Their glamor soon palls when you are broke or covered with sweat and grease from working in the engine room trying to keep those luxuries functional, while the folks on the twenty-eight-footer astern of you are free to wander ashore or set off for an afternoon sail.

We received a letter from two of the most experienced cruising people afloat, Eric and Susan Hiscock, cruising New Zealand's waters on *Wanderer IV* (January 13, 1977). Their comments sum it up well:

> To judge by the many people we have met during our recent world voyage, I would say that it is those in the smaller vessels, simply but efficiently equipped, who get the greatest pleasure and satisfaction. (We . . . met *Wanderer III;* she came sailing into Taiohae Bay while we were there, and was the only one of many that did *sail* in.) With the small-boat people, as with ourselves still, although we now have so vast a ship, I would say that they prove the point: "It is better to travel hopefully than to arrive." The owners of larger, more sophisticated craft tend to regard their yachts as most people do cars, i.e., as a means of getting themselves from one glamor spot or tourist attraction to another in the greatest possible comfort and the least possible inconvenience, and with safety as a high priority. . . . So you see, my thoughts on this matter are much like your own.

The whole idea is freedom. Go small, go simple, go now!

APPENDIX B

The Small Boats

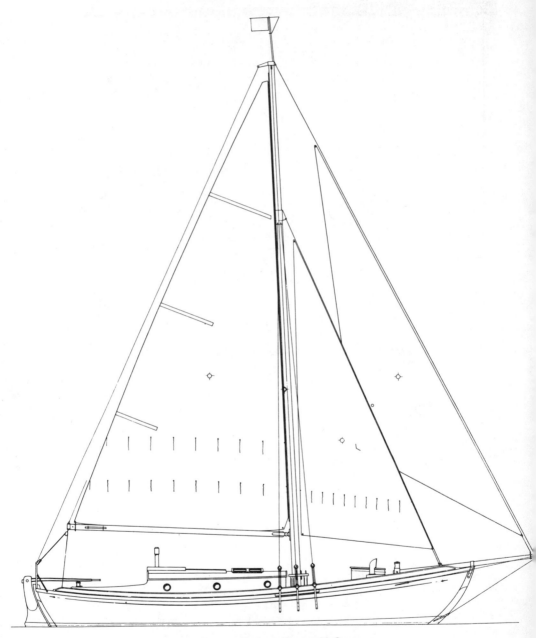

Kion Dee, sail plan. *François Graeser*

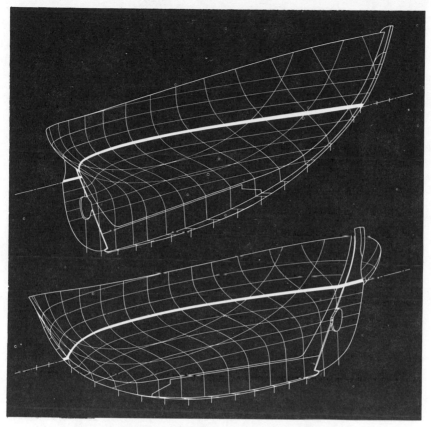

Kion Dee, hull design. *François Graeser*

KION DEE

Owned by: François and Rosemary Graeser

Designer: François Graeser N.A.
      Ch. de Bellerive 19
      1007 Lausanne, Switzerland

Built of wood by owner

Length: 26' on deck
Beam: 9' 1"
Draft: 4' 3"
Displacement: 8,000 lbs.
Ballast: 2,400 lbs.
Rig: cutter
Working sail area: 323 square feet

Maximum sail area: 440 square feet
Spars: wood
Whisker poles: alloy
Rudder: outboard
Self-steering: self-made, trim-tab type
    on main rudder
Dinghy: inflatable

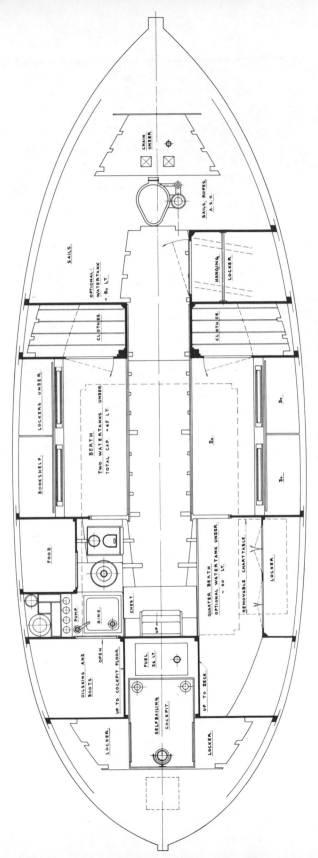

Kion Dee, interior plan, top view. *François Graeser*

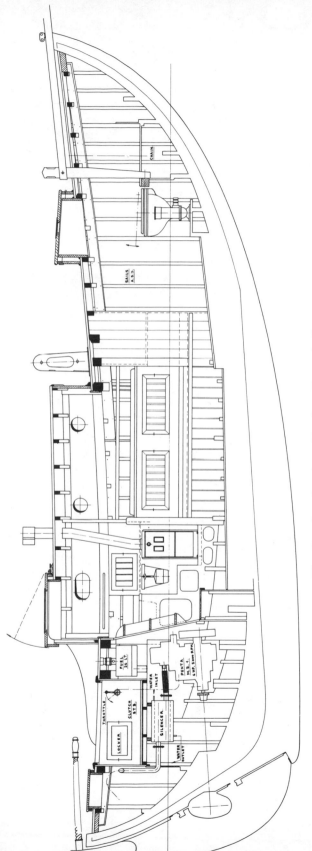

Kion Dee, interior plan, side view. *François Graeser*

François Graeser, black-bearded, six foot four inches tall, and slim, is a serious, prudent sailor with a vast technical knowledge and skill in yacht design and drafting. He is the physical opposite of his tiny, laughing, fondue-cooking wife Rosemary, and the two of them could often be seen sharing long walks ashore in Gibraltar and José Banus, Spain, where we came to know them well. François would stride along with Rosemary's legs doing two steps for each of his long ones.

Kion Dee, teak-hulled, classic-looking double-ended cutter, is our favorite cruising boat next to *Seraffyn*. She was built piece by piece by her designer who then trucked her down from Lake Zurich, Switzerland, to her natural element, salt water. The Graesers spent three years cruising Europe, covering over five thousand miles. By living, sailing, and cruising on *Kion Dee*, François tested his own design in a thorough, long-term way few cruising yacht designers can ever dream of.

Lin and I first looked over *Kion Dee* when we arrived in Gibralter. We liked her because she had small port lights; a low profile; strong sea-going deckhouse; bulwarks and teak decks for safety; lots of anchor chain; a hand-operated anchor winch; an easy-to-remove outboard rudder which facilitated a simple but effective trim-tab type windvane; a generous beam, which gave her a good motion at sea and added volume below to carry all the food, water, and spares that are vital to a cruising yacht; a long, triangular keel profile which allows her to tack with ease; good windward performance with her efficient rig; a simple hand-start single-cylinder Volvo diesel without any electrics; and oil lamps for navigation and cabin lamps. (Both *Kion Dee* and *Seraffyn* are without electrics and neither suffers from any electrolysis.)

Kion Dee's interior is very traditional for small yachts of about twenty-six feet, fine for two people who plan on a lot of ocean work and spartan cooking. The small galley with one burner and no oven is enough at sea, but for a couple living on board and cooking three meals a day, it is (in our opinion) too spartan. I also know that most couples who live on yachts these days demand a double bunk to use in port. This could be added to *Kion Dee*'s fo'c'sle.

Two of my previous keelboats were double-enders similar to *Kion Dee* and I don't have any strong feelings for or against double-enders or transom yachts for cruising. With a wide-sterned transom yacht I might want to heave-to a bit sooner than I would with a double-ender. But on the other hand, I do like the security of the wide decks aft with boom gallows, stanchions, and lifelines out in the quarters as is possible on a transom-sterned yacht. The boom gallows frame is a great place to hang onto in any kind of weather. The double-ender is harder to plank when it comes to fitting and bending the after ends of the topside planks. The transom-sterned yacht is slightly weaker in the quarters or fashion timber area. The double-ended hull form, with its similar waterline shapes fore and aft, is generally considered easier to steer and balance, although not so fast to windward as the transom-sterned yacht. I am not convinced that the double-ender is any more seaworthy than a transom-sterned yacht—both types have been pooped while running too long before heavy seas. It's simply a matter of personal preference, since both types have their good points and not-so-good points, just like two automobiles, one with rear-end drive the other with front-wheel drive.

The only drawback to a custom-designed, nonproduction yacht like *Kion Dee* is that you can't order one from Sears and Roebuck for next-week delivery. The only way to get a yacht built to your personal specifications is to build it yourself or to contract with a boatyard. The first method requires hard, meticulous work and is time-consuming. The second also takes time and is usually expensive. But the rewards are well worthwhile if you end up with a yacht like *Kion Dee*.

The *Kion Dee* under construction. *François Graeser*

The *Kion Dee* is double-planked of teak set in Resorcinal glue with double-sawn frames of acacia (locust). Her backbone is iroko, and, held by silicon-bronze fastenings, she should be good for fifty years or more. *François Graeser*

The good little ship at rest in Barcelona, Spain. *François Graeser*

The *Kion Dee* running at hull speed in the Golf de Lyons. Note the nice bulwarks and the beautiful teak decks, with plenty of space for easy sail handling. *François Graeser*

François put on the dodger so he could have headroom in the chart table–galley area. Note the boathooks which double as handrails on the cabin top.

A clean wake and a well-cut, light genoa. *François Graeser*

Kion Dee and the first mate, Rosemary.

Careened upriver to clean and paint the bottom. *François Graeser*

François is the physical opposite of his tiny, laughing, fondue-cooking wife Rosemary.

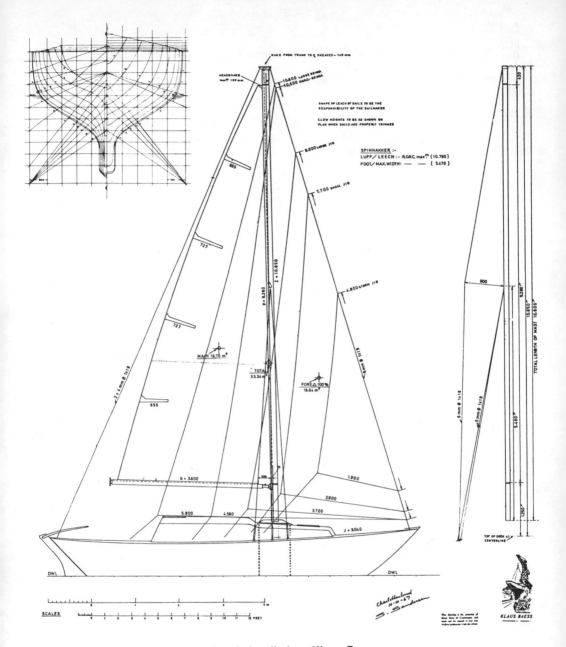

Amøbel, sail plan. *Klaus Baess*

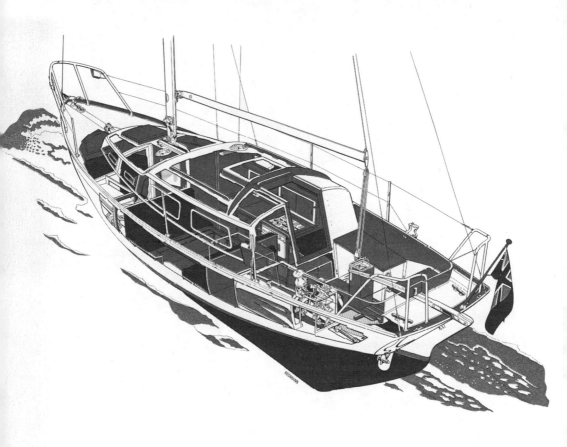

AMØBEL, Great Dane 28

Owned by: Annabelle and Gordon Yates

Designer: Aage Utson
c/o Baess Boats
21 Livjaegergade
DK 2100 Copenhagen
Denmark

Built of fiberglass by Klaus Baess, Copenhagen, Denmark

Length: 28' on deck
Beam: 8' 3"
Draft: 5' 0"
Displacement: 8,500 lbs.
Ballast: 4,000 lbs.
Rig: masthead sloop

Mainsail: 167 square feet
Jib: 166 square feet
Spars: alloy
Rudder: outboard
Self-steering: QM (cost: $300)
Dinghy: inflatable

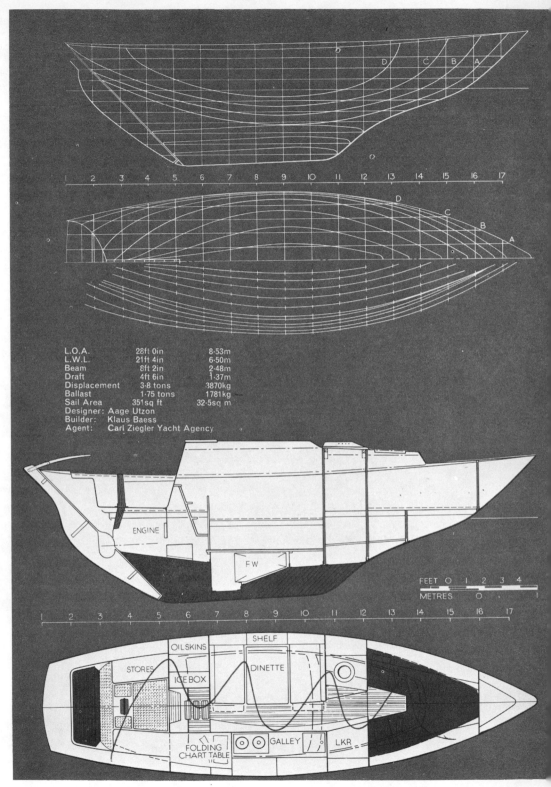

L.O.A.	28ft 0in	8·53m
L.W.L.	21ft 4in	6·50m
Beam	8ft 2in	2·48m
Draft	4ft 6in	1·37m
Displacement	3·8 tons	3870kg
Ballast	1·75 tons	1781kg
Sail Area	351sq ft	32·5sq m

Designer: Aage Utzon
Builder: Klaus Baess
Agent: Carl Ziegler Yacht Agency

Amøbel, hull design and interior plans. *Yachting World*

Nine years ago we sailed into La Paz, Baja California, in Mexico. As soon as we'd anchored, Gordon and Annabelle Yates rowed over in a black Avon dinghy. "Welcome to La Paz," they chimed and then proceeded to answer all of our questions: where to buy beer by the case, which restaurant had the best combination plate *(cielo Azul)* where to buy Mexican brandy ($1.10 a bottle). The four of us formed a fast friendship, sampling the restaurants in the evenings and sharing quantities of beer during the day while we talked of anchors, wind-vanes, Vietnam, politics, cruising Baja. Annabelle and Lin talked about how to cook shellfish and Spanish mackerel, about galley arrangements, buckets, husbands, children, and mothers-in-law. There was hardly a subject the four of us didn't tackle in the eight months we cruised the Sea of Cortez.

Gordon, a civil engineer, had designed and built his own trim-tab type self-steering gear. In Acapulco he solved Helmer's main problem, showing me how to rig a differential in my linkage between the wind-vane and trim tab. Since Acapulco, Helmer has steered *Seraffyn* beautifully for over twenty-four thousand miles. Thanks, Gordy!

Annabelle and Gordon are an unusually determined couple. They raised five children and then, at the age of fifty, were both still mentally and physically flexible enough to adapt to the rigors of small-boat cruising. They had kicked the steady job habit and gone cruising a year before we did.

We asked Gordon to write about his three boats:

First, in Las Vegas, Nevada, I built a thirty-foot Piver trimaran which later tried to capsize us twice. In 1967, we sailed from Los Angeles to within six hundred miles of Hawaii where Captain Dittler on the U.S. naval vessel *Prairie* rescued us. [The Yateses hit a freak storm and had been hove-to for several days when Captain Dittler spotted them and offered assistance, lifting the trimaran on deck and taking them to San Diego, California.] We fixed up and sailed the Mexican coast as far as Acapulco, where I lost my nerve. I had to get a good boat.

We flew to Annapolis in 1970 and bought a twenty-two-foot Cirrus, *Amøbel II.* We sailed down to, across, and around Florida and the Bahamas. The Cirrus was too small. No way could she carry enough to cross an ocean. We sold her but we are still wistful. She was so close-winded and cozy.

We flew to Copenhagen in 1973 and bought a Great Dane 28. Larry had said, "Folkboats are okay," so we got the closest boat to it with room for an engine and a head. Annabelle would not go for a "bucket and chuck it." I was too old to wait out in front of ports wishing for wind. Larry was worried about my buying a stock boat, but "time's a-wastin' " so we got it and learned "What's hidden is either not there, loose, or iron." In *Amøbel* we sailed to England, Madeira, Tenerife, Barbados, Tortola, Panama, and north to San Francisco in 1975. Our total time logged at sea in ten years is eighty-five hundred hours.

Twenty-eight-foot *Amøbel* is a fiberglass, full-keel, outboard-rudder, masthead sloop. Loaded for an ocean crossing with a ton of stuff, including two fearful old sailors, she is one inch below her scribed waterline. She has four thousand pounds of sealed-in lead ballast, with a quick, five-second roll that snaps the buttons off my shirt. She has four diesel horsepower per ton, which is what is needed to go north up the West Coast from Panama. Her galley should be at the center of motion on the port side; where it's now located, *Amøbel* can throw soup out of the pot. I think her windows should be smaller, but she dances up and over the seas and has never scooped up green water. QM self-steering rules her (cost: $300).

Gordon Yates, skipper of *Amøbel*. Phil Lum

Amøbel's owners and crew,
Gordon and Annabelle Yates.
Phil Lum

Annabelle
and her galley.
Phil Lum

A Great Dane 28 fitted out for cruising.
Note the reef points—two in the mainsail
and one in the jib—the windvane, and the
CQR anchor ready to go over if needed.
Phil Lum

In a second letter Gordon writes about *Amøbel*'s handling, anchoring, and motion at sea:

> First the good things: anchoring and docking, she works under main only, dinghy-like. She steers herself to weather under working sails or main only. I kill time waiting for dawn or the tide under main; with helm tied to weather, she tends herself on a slow beat. In a gale she slowly works to windward under deep-reefed main and self-steering. Bob Burn of GD-28 *Blue Gypsy* heaves to by sheeting his boom to weather. QM steers her downwind with main (vanged and prevented) plus poled-out jib. In a stronger wind the heavy-weather jib sheeted amidships dampens rolling. Her full keel and outboard rudder shed kelp, fishnets, and anchor rodes.
>
> Bad things: at anchor she charges about like a bull. [Because of her motion] she broke one of my ribs in the English Channel, making me tend her with one arm till Madeira. In light wind she snaps the air out of her genoa, which bugs me.

Gordon's comment about *Amøbel*'s whippy motion is a familiar complaint of owners with highly ballasted (forty-six percent for *Amøbel*) high-freeboard, high-cabined, light- to medium-displacement yachts. The lightweight hull will initially heel quickly and easily until the tremendous amount of lead jerks the heeling movement to a stop, giving the "button-snapping motion" Gordon speaks of.

The cutaway forefoot and full bow sections would probably be the cause of her restlessness at anchor. When a gust of wind hits her bow she has no depth or sharpness of forefoot to grip the water and stop her from falling off and charging around. An all-chain anchor rode can often help prevent this problem because of its weight and drag on the bottom.

If you plan on living afloat and cruising full time, your interior layout should (1) be comfortable and convenient in port, and (2) comfortable and convenient at sea. The facts are that most people who call their yacht "home" spend only ten percent of the hours in any cruising year actually sailing or at sea. *Amøbel*'s layout is good for an eight-foot two-inch by twenty-eight-foot yacht. The forward area has been converted to a double for a separate shoreside bunk that is always ready for use, if only just to lay down on to read a book for a couple of hours. You don't have to make it up each time you want to use it. If one of you wants to go to bed early, it's ready and you won't disturb anyone in the main salon. Across from the loo, Gordon and Annabelle have installed a solid-fuel central heater which is great for cool winter nights in the San Francisco Bay area where they are now cruising.

Lin and I have delivered a number of new yachts with the dinette-type table and find it great in port. At sea you need something to hold plates and cups secure, but this is true with all fixed tables. If something on the dinette table in *Amøbel* does spill, it will usually go to port or starboard, not on the eater. With the more common fore and aft table and settees, you have a fifty-fifty chance of hot soup or coffee on your lap.

The quarter berth on the starboard side would be a good sea berth with one person on watch, one in the bunk.

The Great Dane 28 is a fiberglass production boat and you can get one quickly, outfit it, and be off cruising without too much cost, too much waiting, or too much personal labor. As Gordy says, "Time's a-wastin'."

GD 28 fitted out for racing or local cruising. *Klaus Baess*

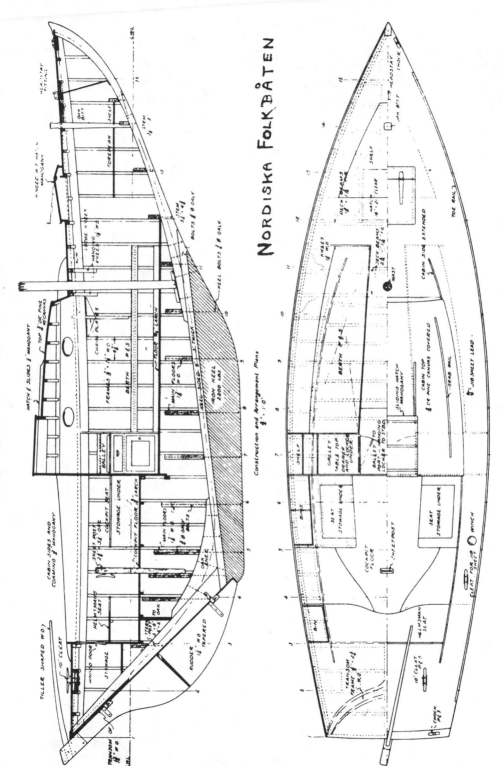

NORDISKA FOLKBÅTEN

Construction and Arrangement Plans
$\frac{3}{4}" = 1'-0"$

A Norwegian Folkboat, side and top views. *SNAME Transactions*

A Folkboat, the F-117, out cruising. *SNAME Transactions*

FOLKBOAT

Original Nordic Folkboat designed by Jac N. Iverson of Stockholm and
Tore Sunden of Gothenberg

Built of wood, various builders

Length: 25' 1"
Beam: 7' 2 1/2"
Draft: 3' 11"
Displacement: 5,000 lbs.
Ballast: 2,000 lbs.

Rig: three-quarter sloop
Sail area: 235 square feet
Spars: wood
Rudder: outboard
Dinghy: inflatable

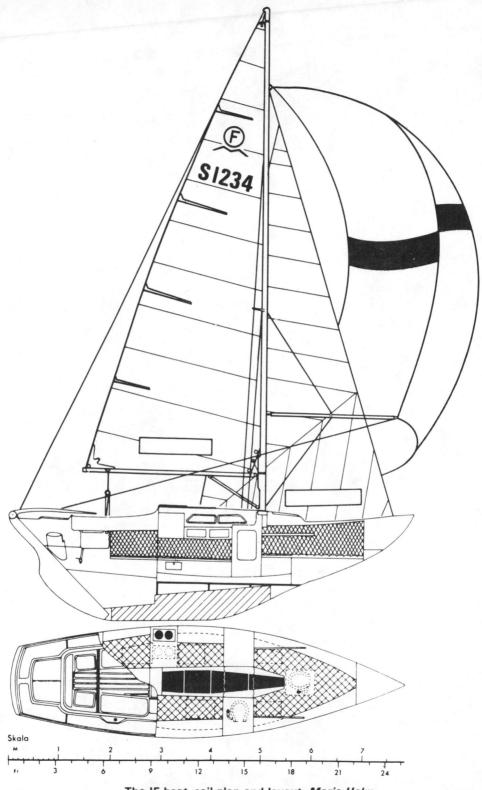

Skala

The IF boat, sail plan and layout. *Marie Holm*

IF BOAT

Designer: Jac Iverson

Built of fiberglass by: Marieholms Bruck AB
330 33 Hillerstrod
Sweden

Length: 26' 0"
Beam: 7' 4"
Draft: 4' 0"
Displacement: 4,800 lbs.
Ballast: 2,425 lbs.
Rig: seven-eights sloop

Mainsail: 160 square feet
Jib: 100 square feet
Genoa: 150 square feet
Spars: alloy
Rudder: outboard
Dinghy: inflatable

"I say, if I were young, I would get a Folkboat, a sweep, drink my beer warm, and go." We quote Gordon Yates.

The Folkboat is also my stock answer for young would-be cruisers. The Folkboat is easy to handle, it's cheap, it's easy to fit with a windvane, and with a few modifications it can be outfitted to sail the Atlantic.

Folkboats were designed in 1948 to be inexpensive. In fact, Folkboat means "people's boat" and is yachting's answer to the Volkswagen. Many of the older wooden ones can be bought quite cheaply, depending on condition. The newer fiberglass versions are reasonably priced since the Folkboat is of moderate displacement and new sailboats can be priced like beefsteak, so much a pound.

I have always liked the Folkboat since I saw *Bambi,* in the West Vancouver Yacht Club in 1959, twenty years ago. She was an original lapstrake Folkboat with low freeboard, a sweet sheer, and modest overhangs. At times I'm wistful and wish she had been for sale because somehow I would have found the money and bought her. As it was, I took ten years to get organized, build *Seraffyn,* and save some money for the insurance fund and cruising fund. *Bambi* and I could have been away at least five years earlier. But the Folkboat is a minimal cruiser for two, or three in a severe pinch. Carrying enough food and water is always a problem in a small boat, and to cruise in a Folkboat extensively you can't afford the space and weight an inboard motor takes. A small outboard, or a sweep or sculling oar will stretch your Folkboat's interior and keep the load waterline in sight. The Folkboat, with its small three-quarter rig, loses light-weather performance rapidly if she is overloaded. Most of the older wooden versions were built without self-draining cockpits. A self-draining cockpit is a necessity for extended cruising.

Bill Isreal, saved his money while working in an electronics factory and bought a secondhand wooden Folkboat, then modified it for long-distance cruising. He sailed from California, down the coast of Mexico to Costa Rica, single-handed, taking over a year for his voyage. Bill removed his Folkboat's cockpit seats and flush-decked the area aft of the cabin. This gave him enormous storage space below plus the extra stiffening and strength of full-width deck beams and decking. He remarked that the deep cockpit was not necessary for protection from wind and rain as he stayed below during rough weather, letting his windvane do the steering, and only came on his large uncluttered afterdeck to reef or change sails, or steer into harbor.

He used a three-horsepower outboard motor on a small rubber dinghy for his tender. With this tied alongside his Folkboat, he could maneuver in harbor or move along in a calm at about three knots.

Bill paid about twenty-five hundred dollars for his older lapstrake Folkboat, then spent about fifteen hundred more for his sextant, radio receiver, extra anchors, and afterdeck modifications. For four thousand dollars he had a nice mini-cruiser. Bill said he longed for a masthead, light-weather genoa to increase his sail area for light winds.

In Falmouth we met Ingrid and Khristian Lagerkrantz, a young Swedish couple who planned to sail to Yugoslavia to research Khristian's master's thesis on the anthropology of the island people. Ingrid managed to get a year off from her job as a criminologist to sail on their Swedish-built IF boat which they planned to use as both accommodation and transportation once they reached the Dalmatian coast. As Khristian said to us, "Yes, she is a small boat, but as students we could not afford to live and travel in the many islands without our little moving home." The Lagenkrantzes had sailed their Folkboat from Stockholm to Falmouth, then from Falmouth to Bayona, Spain, and from there down the coast of Portugal to Gibraltar, where we lost track of the tiny scientific sailboat. (We assume they arrived in the Dalmatian Islands although we have not heard a word since Gibraltar.)

The IF (International Folkboat) is built of fiberglass, designed by Jac Iverson, and is an attractive production yacht. It has a self-draining cockpit, a longer trunk cabin, and more living space below than the original Folkboat. No major modifications are necessary to set off cruising in an IF boat. And you can continue to enjoy it even after you return home. You can race in the IF boat fleet in your area.

In Gibraltar we met another Folkboat owned by three jolly English boys. Barry Hollis worked as a yacht rigger at Moody's Shipyard on the Hamble River, Will Keech was employed at Blake's galvanizing plant (both of these jobs showed in the fine outfitting of *Piratical Pipet*), and the third, Gordon Butler, worked as ship's accountant. All were in their early twenties and while they were in Gibraltar contracted to lay tiles in new apartments to replenish their cruising funds. The three were avid dinghy sailors who had pooled their resources to buy *Piratical Pipet* and outfit her for a total cost of twenty-nine hundred dollars (1973–74), including new spars and six new sails. Even though the little carvel-planked Folkboat was thirteen years old and they had sailed her hard down from the United Kingdom by way of northern Spain and Portugal, she looked almost like new.

The boys had changed the interior of *Piratical Pipet* completely by installing a galvanized tabernacle to replace the main bulkhead. This gave them an open, more spacious interior, allowing space for two quarter berths and a settee for the three average-sized crew. On a basically ultra-simple yacht without motor, they used oil lamps and a sculling oar with which muscular Barry could move *P.P.* at about one and a half knots. When they modified the rig from the original three-quarter sloop to masthead sloop, they "reduced the sail area for cruising." They all agreed this was their only mistake. They wished for a larger rig than the original Folkboat for the light winds they encountered. With jiffy reefing, shortening sail could have been simple. But even so, *Piratical Pipet* sailed so well in the cruiser races in Gibraltar that the boys had a few of the local IOR boats worried.

The last we heard, Gordon had acquired Barry's and Will's shares of *P.P.* and was cruising southern Spain with a girl crew. Barry was professional skipper on a sixty-one-foot American yacht and Will was last seen bound from Palma Majorca on a large charter yacht.

These three different crews on their modified Folkboats were having a great time. They were seeing and enjoying the same sights, the same beautiful harbors, the same interesting people as the crews on the large yachts anchored next to them.

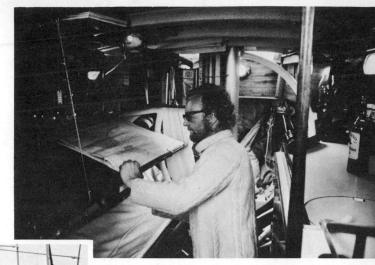

Piratical Pipit's chart table is folded down by Gordon Butler, one of *P.P.*'s three owners. The pipe tabernacle near the mast is in place of a bulkhead.

Piratical Pipit has fairly narrow side decks and a Perspex fore hatch.

Piratical Pipit is a much-modified folkboat. The carvel planking and a large cabin are the most obvious changes from the original folkboat designs. Note the combination port and starboard oil lamp on the pulpit.

Gordon with his seven-dollar "outboard motor." *Piratical Pipit*'s windvane is of the horizontal-axis, or QME, type. The Rock of Gibraltar is to starboard.

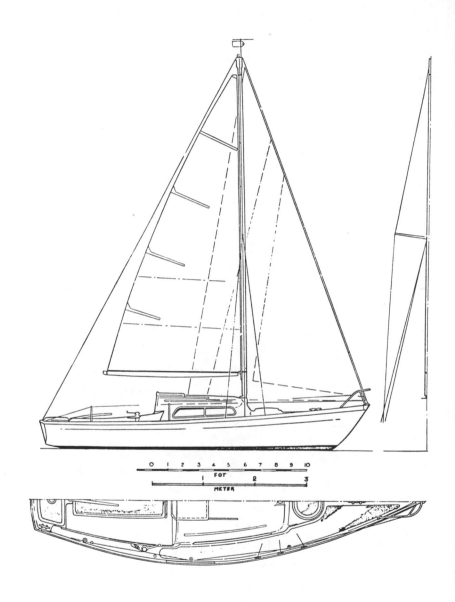

Optimist, sail plan drawing. *E. G. van de Stadt*

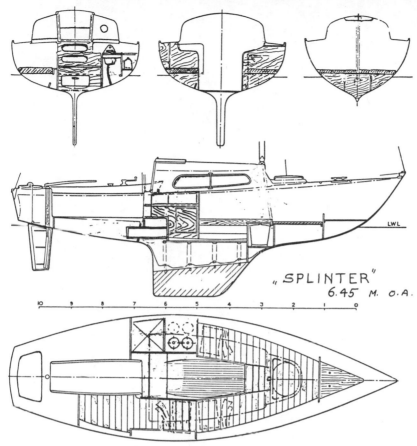

Optimist, interior views. *E. G. van de Stadt*

OPTIMIST

Owned by: Svend Kaae

Splinter class fiberglass sloop
Designer: E. G. van de Stadt
           Scheepswerf N.V.
           Zanndam, Holland

Built of fiberglass by G. Stead
                        Poole, Dorset, England

Length: 21'
Beam: 6' 3"
Draft: 3' 9"
Displacement: 1,760 lbs.
Ballast: 800 lbs.
Rig: masthead sloop
Mainsail: 90 square feet
Jib: 80 square feet

Genoa: 115 square feet
Storm jib: 45 square feet
Spars: alloy
Rudder: inboard
Self-steering: homemade, much like
    QME
Dinghy: inflatable

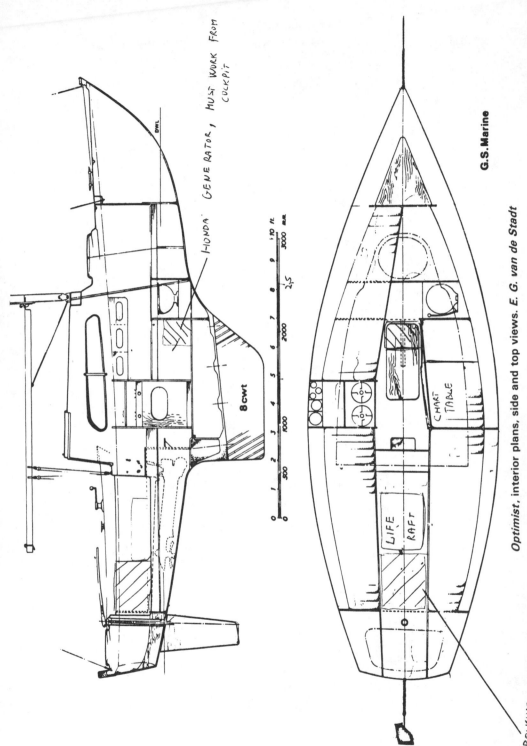

'HONDA' GENERATOR, MUST WORK FROM COCKPIT

DWL

8 cwt

POLYURETHANE FILLED BOX

LIFE RAFT

CHART TABLE

G.S. Marine

Optimist, interior plans, side and top views. E. G. van de Stadt

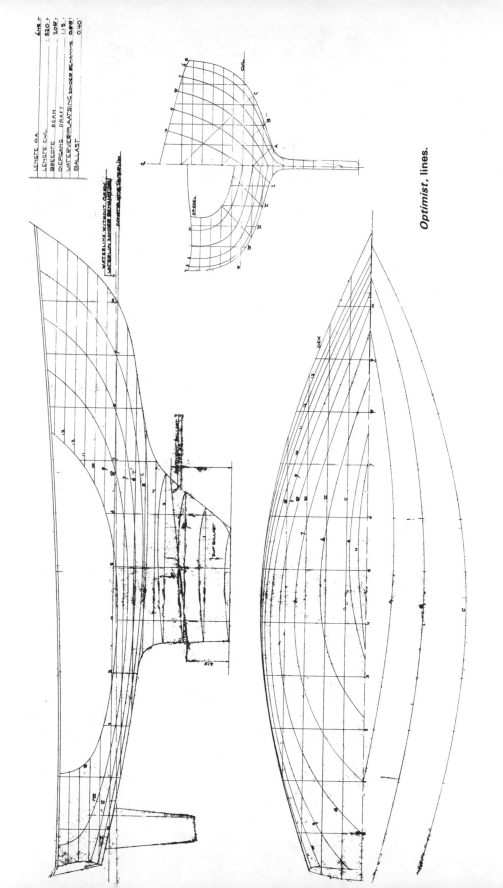

Optimist, lines.

Svend Kaae rowing his inflatible back to *Optimist*, Bayona Harbor, Spain.

Optimist is not Svend Kaae's permanent home, probably because Svend is six foot three and weighs 190 pounds and his yacht measures only twenty-one feet overall. But *Optimist*'s size has not stopped Svend from making various single-handed voyages from his home and job in Aarhus, Denmark—including a circumnavigation of Iceland and a voyage from Denmark to England, Spain, Madeira, the Canaries, the West Indies, and then a return to Denmark. In six years Svend has voyaged over twenty thousand miles on board *Optimist*.

We met Svend in Bayona, northern Spain, when he was on his way to the West Indies in 1974–75. In answer to a recent letter of ours, Svend wrote:

> I agree with you that people should stop dreaming of forty-five-foot boats and go now, provided they know the smaller boat they have. Some people I met had only sailed in sheltered waters before they started to the West Indies. Usually it went okay, but in my opinion they were too dependent on good luck in the beginning.
>
> Go simple! I prefer electric lanterns, but on *Optimist* the generator must be in the cockpit; when the battery was recharged in the middle of the Atlantic heading back from the West Indies, it got soaked and never recovered. I would have liked a Tilley storm lantern [pressure kerosene] instead of the paraffin [kerosene] anchor lantern.
>
> Overload is a problem on such a small boat. At departure from St. Thomas, U.S. Virgin Islands, with food and water for two months, the waterline was approximately ten centimeters [four inches] lower than at home. I put more weight on the starboard side because in the beginning I would sail close-hauled in the trade winds and the sailing performance was good but wet.

The return trip was full of "small" accidents. The second night (Force 5) the small genoa parted into two pieces, causing twenty hours of repairs the next four days. After three or four hundred miles in the trade winds I ran into many days with weak variable winds and Sargasso seaweed. The last was a great trouble, because a piece of it would fasten at the top front of the rudder and destroy the laminar flow, so it was impossible to sail close-hauled in Force 3 or more without running into the wind. Down with the sails, look out for sharks, swim down to the rudder (I always have a lifeline), away with the seaweed, up again, up with the sails, and the situation was okay—at least for two hours. This continued for two or three weeks. Four hundred miles east of Bermuda I read an article about thunder and lightning. Five hours later I had it (only Force 4)! I did not read the article about stormy weather.

In the middle of the Atlantic the generator got soaked and never recovered, so I used a paraffin lantern the next three weeks and battery the last five days in the Channel.

I had no wind stronger than Force 7 and a maximum headwind of Force 6, but one time (downwind) the waves were at least six meters high. I had fog southwest of the Scilly Islands, a lot of haze in the Channel, and (of course) easterly winds in the Channel. It took forty-seven days, eighteen hours, and fifty-two minutes from St. Thomas to New Haven, England.

After a month it was a little boring to sail—I had very few books —but one of the reasons for sailing directly to the Channel was to find out how I liked such a long voyage.

Single-handed sailing such as Svend does is definitely an extra risk. I personally don't recommend it, but I can appreciate a person's desire to go it completely alone. This should always remain one of man's choices, to risk his own life the way he sees fit. On the other hand, the Rules of the Road do require that a twenty-four-hour watch be kept at all times, not only to avoid collisions but to see and hear distress calls. The single-hander can't keep a twenty-four-hour watch and could possibly miss a distress flare or sail right past a dismasted yacht without seeing it. The single-hander is on his own and must be extra well prepared. Svend was, and carried

2 mainsails, 7 headsails, 2 spinnaker poles, 3 halyards for headsails. Compass in cockpit, compass on bulkhead that can be seen from bunk; Sailar receiver with D.F. and a shortwave converter from Brookes and Gatehouse. Kelvin Hughes sextant and one plastic sextant. Echo sounder, sum log and tuning fork watch. Combined

Optimist is a tiny little yacht with three reefs in the main and a large self-steering vane. *Svend Kaae*

lantern on top of mast plus lanterns in stem and stern. A 60-watt Aldis 66-amp/hour battery, Honda generator, and paraffin anchor lantern. Emergency equipment: life raft, 1-watt transmitter, (safety link) rockets, orange smoke flares, 2 fire extinguishers. Self-made windvane, 2 anchors, 50-gallon rubber water tank, 50-gallon kerosene tank, plastic containers for more water, Seagull outboard, 2 bilge pumps, radar reflector, spare rigging, and a lot of tools.

Svend also served a good apprenticeship during his sailing holidays to Aland, the Faroes, and western Norway before he set off across the Atlantic. He knew his boat's limitations, and that her gear was good. But most important, he was mentally and physically prepared for a long voyage on a small yacht.

But no matter how well prepared a single-hander is, he must be an optimist, and most of them eventually hope to find a good mate. This is when *Optimist*'s main drawback becomes obvious. She is just too small for two.

Wylo **is a masthead cutter with a large staysail. Note the battonless loose-footed main with vertical panels for less chafe on shrouds.** *Nick Skeates*

WYLO

Owned by: Nick Skeates

Designed and built by: Berthon Boat Company
Lymington, England
(1930)

Hull: wood
Length: 29'
Beam: 8'
Draft: 4' 4"
Displacement: 14,000 lbs.
Ballast: 4,000 lbs.
Rig: cutter

Mainsail: 225 square feet
Jib: 110 square feet
Staysail: 120 square feet
Spars: wood
Rudder: outboard
Self-steering: sheet-to-tiller method
Dinghy: 7' 6" sailing dinghy

Wylo's large, clean foredeck is natural pine for good footing, a safe deck for working at night. *Nick Skeates*

Nick Skeates and his boat.

WYLO   LONDON

Nick Skeates and *Wylo* are a classic example of a love affair between a young man and an older lady. When we cruised the south coast of England we met many love matches like theirs. While working as a government weights and measurements inspector Nick, who was in his early twenties, bought his 1930 twenty-nine-foot cutter and refitted her himself in 1972 for the very low price of twenty-four hundred dollars plus "a great deal of labor."

Since we met him in Dartmouth, England, he has sailed to New Zealand taking three years and going via the West Indies, Panama, and the Galapagos to the Marquesas, where he made a fantastic six-day run of a thousand miles (including one day of one hundred eighty miles), broad-reaching in Force 5 to 6 winds with all sails set and the boat self-steering at all times. *Wylo* does not have a windvane. Instead, Nick uses the cheaper but less convenient method of tiller-to-sheet steering (see John Letcher's book, *Self-Steering for Sailing Craft*, pp. 36–73). Nick usually has crew but did try single-handing from Tahiti to New Zealand.

He recently wrote us an interesting seaman-like summation of his yacht's performance:

You ask for comments on her good and bad points. Her comparatively shallow draft is a good point; I certainly would not want any more—it is actually about 4' 4". Much less than this and she'd need a centerboard to go to windward at sea. She is very full-ended and straight-sided. Thus her comparatively narrow beam extends a good proportion of her length, giving good deck space and volume below. Her full bow makes it possible to drive her hard off the wind; she never shows any signs of nose-diving. This feature also gives her a long waterline, twenty-seven feet or so, and is reflected in her good passages. A friend with a similar-size boat, but with pinched-in ends (and a similar keel profile), said his boat became "busy" at high speed and he had to reef down to self-steer properly. [We agree with Nick on this point because *Seraffyn* has fine ends and also gets busy at six knots and has to be reefed down to self-steer.]

Full ends can't be all good, otherwise all boats would have 'em. Her full bow does slow her down in a chop to windward, by comparison with a fine bow under the same conditions. This was proved by sailing in company with the boat mentioned above, but *Wylo* was faster on a reach in the same sea.

Her keel profile makes her very steady on the helm and she has never, ever refused to come about, probably due to her good cutaway forward.

Channels are handy for resting against the ways car so the whole topside can be painted in one go. The long keel makes *Wylo* easy to haul out. *Nick Skeates*

Wylo's stern view, showing her easy bilges (dead rise) and English-style boom-kin. *Nick Skeates*

Wylo's full bow. *Nick Skeates*

One bad feature is a large hole entirely through the rudder for the 17 1/2-inch propellor. This makes the rudder unnecessarily heavy to turn. It ought to be at least partly in the keel (stern post) and very possibly a quarter installation would be better; she doesn't steer going astern under power anyway.

I would like a bit more beam, giving more room inside, particularly in the main hatch area, which can become congested with a few people aboard. However, she is a surprisingly slippery boat and I fancy her narrow beam (by modern standards) may have something to do with this, also her fairly shallow draft.

Nick, like his boat, is practical. While cruising he has worked as a bus driver, yacht painter and carpenter, and writing articles for the English magazine *Yachting Monthly*.

When commenting on the cost of living and cruising on *Wylo,* Nick said, "Food can cost as little or as much as you like. Eating out is expensive, as is hauling out (use tides where possible). Engine troubles are a curse and costly, so are electrics—do without for cheapness. Labor is very expensive—do your own. Above all, keep it simple and strong. Live aboard rather than ashore when in port for economy, and sail—don't motor unnecessarily. Use what you've got, not what's in the shop."

Nick's philosophy has taken him a long way and he has had three years of fine cruising. He wrote us, "Now I have a blonde Kiwi crew who is really keen on cruising. She's done a fair bit before. I have a feeling she'll be with me for quite some time." He was right. They got married in the United Kingdom during Christmas 1977.

Nick Skeates sailing his fiberglass dinghy in Dartmouth, England, a great little tender with spars that stow in the boat.

Brian notes: "She handles very well. The fact that I can tack her up and down the [confined] Hamble River proves this. . . ." *Brian Craigie-Lucas*

Mouette at her mooring in front of the Elephant Boatyard. *Brian Craigie-Lucas*

MOUETTE

Owned by: Brian Craigie-Lucas

Designer: Peter Brett
The Pitts, Bonchurch
Ventor, Isle of Wight
England

Built of wood by Enterprise Small Rock Ferry Craft Company, 1938

Length: 32'
Beam: 8' 10"
Draft: 6' 0"
Displacement:
16,000 lbs. gross
Ballast: unknown
Rig: cutter

Spars: wood
Sails: seven in all
Rudder: inboard
Self-steering: homemade, similar to
QME
Dinghy: hard fiberglass

Brian Craigie-Lucas is one of the old school of sailors, weaned on Stockholm tar and Italian hemp. He is a reformed single-hander, and Chris, his cute, red-headed crew who has been sailing with him for the past three years, has transformed the interior of *Mouette* from bachelor's quarters to "a tidy home for two, complete with oil paintings, comfy cushions, and a mounted whale's tooth from the Azores engraved with a full-rigged ship."

When we first met Brian in the Azores (August 1972) he was sailing alone. He wore ancient high, multipatched fisherman-style boots and rowed an old rubber dinghy with patches to match the boots. His mailing address was "Yacht *Mouette*, c/o Elephant Boatyard (find me at the Jolly Roger Pub), Old Burlesdon, Hants." Now the reformed solo sailor has a new hard fiberglass dinghy and a very respectable London bank to forward his mail.

Brian bought his lovely forty-year-old *Mouette* in very rundown condition for approximately three thousand dollars in 1968, and with the practical skill of the complete sailor, started to work on her. She had a large diesel with a broken crankshaft that stole most of what is now her galley area. Brian hoisted the motor out, sold it to a passing fisherman, and has sailed ten years to date, "doing without." Then he carefully and methodically checked the hull, especially the floors and garboards which are the most likely area to give trouble in an older outside-ballasted wooden boat. The total refit of *Mouette* cost Brian five hundred pounds, which he spent mostly on new keel bolts, new garboards, and new sails. (When we met Brian in the Azores, he showed us his battenless red mainsail. He had sailed the Atlantic twice with it and never had to repair chafe or damage caused by battens. Seeing the condition of his battenless sail convinced me. Our next sail was just like his and has worked great.) Brian used heavy, reliable galvanized fittings on *Mouette*, no stainless-steel "yacht" gear. So he ended up buying and refitting his thirty-two-foot cruising home for less than forty-eight hundred dollars.

Not all sailors have the practical knowledge needed to eye up an old boat and appreciate an originally well-built, well-designed hull under the neglect and abuse of the years. Brian did, and with thousands of hours of his own labor made *Mouette* into a reliable cruiser which has taken him to the Azores, Canary Islands, Cape Verdes, Brazil, and beyond. As of 1978 *Mouette* and Brian have crossed the Atlantic six or eight times.

Brian in
the companionway
of *Mouette. Brian Craigie-Lucas*

Mouette at rest
somewhere
in Brazil. *Brian Craigie-Lucas*

Mouette, hauled out for a
refit in 1975 at Moody's
yard on the Hamble River.
Brian Craigie-Lucas

Mouette makes "a tidy
home for two, complete
with oil paintings, comfy
cushions, and a mounted
whale's tooth from the
Azores engraved with a
full-rigged ship." *Brian
Craigie-Lucas*

A recent letter from Brian gives a glimpse of the tall, quiet, prudent English sailor with "no problems":

Well, as you will have gathered I am under way again—once more to South America. This time I have a crew, believe it or not. Takes quite a lot of readjustment after single-handing for so long. We left England last June, heading for the Azores first (of course), my fifth visit. Horta is changing a bit with over thirty yachts in port at a time and more tourists on shore. But the people are as nice as ever. . . . We spent two months in the Azores, visiting San Jorge, Terceira, and San Miguel, apart from Fayal. Then headed for Madiera and Porto Santo—the latter delightful but landing sometimes awkward. After that we spent six weeks in the Canaries before heading across the Atlantic. The crossing was slow but easy, like most of the trip so far. Mostly light winds and calms so that we took forty-nine days for about thirty-three hundred miles. No problems.

Two months were spent at and around Salvador [Brazil], a wonderful cruising area. Beautiful sheltered anchorages, completely deserted except for an occasional dugout paddling by, and this within a few miles of a large city. From there we came here direct, having a heartening welcome from friends I made at a small yacht club when I was here before. We shall stay for about another two or four weeks, then go to Ilha Grande, a day's sail south and supposed to be beautiful, a sort of Brazilian south seas archipelago. I gather we can keep the boat in Brazil for six months only, and when this is up in about three months we are going down to Uruguay and Argentina. . . . As I said, it has been an easy trip so far, with no mishaps and *Mouette* has behaved beautifully as always.

In a second letter Brian gives us some information about *Mouette:*

Load waterline [is] listed as twenty-four feet but actually about twenty-five feet now. About twenty-five years ago her keel was deepened from a draft of four feet six inches to six feet. This was very nicely done with the designer's approval. At that time she was owned by a syndicate of Harley Street doctors who were keen ocean racers and the alterations were done for improved windward performance and sail-carrying ability, and also accounts partially for the difference in her load waterline. . . . I believe her racing career was fairly satisfactory although she was never designed for it. She is now cutter-rigged with a bowsprit, although originally a sloop. Under this she handles very well. The fact that I can tack her up and down the [confined] Hamble River proves this, I think. No engine and no electrics apart from dry-cell battery-operated lights to galley and compass.

Some time ago she had a fire on board and was run ashore. I have no exact details of this, but she was a complete write-off and had to have a Lloyd's Certificate of Seaworthiness before being put back on the register. I have owned her for ten years, living and cruising on her through that time.

Brian works at anything that comes along (yacht agent, jig maker, clerk, writing) to supplement a very small pension. These endeavors and an inexpensive-to-maintain yacht are the reasons he can afford his cruising habit.

Broad-reaching off the Brazilian coast. Note the windvane, fiberglass dinghy, heavy galvanized rigging, and red mainsail. *Brian Craigie-Lucas*

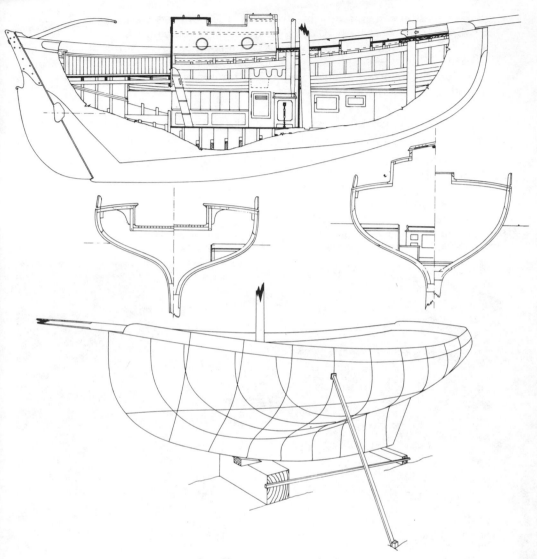

Seraffyn's lines. *Lyle C. Hess*

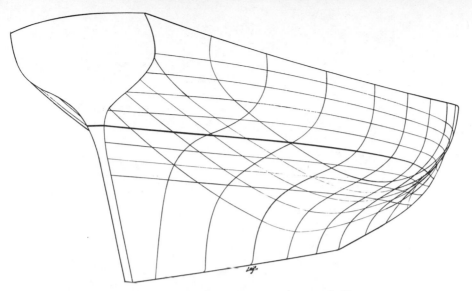

Isometric plan of our dream cutter. *Lyle C. Hess*

SERAFFYN

Owned by: Lin and Larry Pardey

Builders: Lin and Larry Pardey (launched November 1968)

Designer: Lyle C. Hess
         1907 W. Woodcrest
         Fullerton, California

Built of wood

Length: 24′ 4″
Beam: 8′ 11″
Draft: 4′8″
Displacement: 10,687 lbs.
Ballast: 2,700 lbs.
Rig: cutter
Sail area: 180 square feet in mainsail,

104 square feet in staysail,
265 square feet in working genoa
Spars: wood
Self-steering: trim tab on main rudder
Dinghy: fiberglass lapstrake pram with
    sail rig

OUR DREAM CUTTER

Designer: Lyle C. Hess
         1907 W. Woodcrest,
         Fullerton, California

To be built of wood by Lin and Larry Pardey

Length: 29′ 9″
Beam: 10′ 9″
Draft: 5′ 0″
Displacement: approximately 16,000
  lbs.
Ballast: approximately 5,500 pounds

Rudder: outboard
Spars: wood
Self-steering: trim tab on main rudder
Dinghy: fiberglass lapstrake stem
    dinghy with sail rig

Preliminary sail plan of our dream cutter. *Lyle C. Hess*

When Lin and I built *Seraffyn*, we planned to cruise six months, maybe a year. If we liked cruising, we would carry on. If anyone had said nine years ago that we would have lived on her since 1969, cruised to twenty-seven countries from California to Malaysia (February 1978), I would have answered, "She's too small to live on for so long!" We never planned it this way; we just kept looking forward to the next country, the next island, or the next sailing season—and it's been fun! The little twenty-four-footer has been adequate to live on except in cold weather.

Since we never planned on using *Seraffyn* as a long-term home, we have lately been thinking about building a boat that would have all of *Seraffyn*'s great seakeeping and sailing qualities but also a more comfortable interior, especially since we would like to cruise in colder climates. We'd like to have two tables (galley and chart table) so that both Lin and I could work on our writing at the same time. We'd like an inside sit down bath and loo, and a piano for Lin, and we've found it can be done because Yamaha produces a portable tuning fork piano for traveling bands which measures about twelve inches high, eighteen inches deep, and forty-nine inches high (nonelectric). We plan to have the piano under the foldup chart table. Anyway, that is our dream.

Lyle Hess has drawn the plans for us, and for the last two years we've been savoring the delightful experience of getting our next yacht designed just the way we want it while we enjoy cruising on board *Seraffyn*.

We haven't laid the keel yet. In fact, we're still cruising enjoyably on *Seraffyn* over eight thousand miles away from the place we'd like to build our dream ship. But we have bought a Plath hand-operated anchor winch, opening ports, prismatic deadlights, and now as we cruise the Orient, we are looking for nice long-grained quarter-sawn teak to make the decks and cabin.

The greatest problem Lin and I have is deciding to part with our child substitute, *Seraffyn*. It is almost unthinkable to sell our fine little cutter which has never disappointed us or let us down. *Seraffyn* is a "right now" cruising reality, while the new boat would be at least three years of hard work away. *Seraffyn* is small enough so that we can afford to keep her indefinitely if we decide to live ashore. We could happily use her for local cruising and racing. To justify the larger boat with its extra maintenance and extra costs, we must think very carefully. Do we want to make our home permanently on a yacht? Can we part with *Seraffyn*? Do we want to give up three years of cruising time just to gain some creature comforts? This is the dilemma. If we do decide to build, then the twenty-nine-foot nine-inch Lyle Hess–designed dream cutter will become our reality cutter.

~~~~~~

Some Thoughts
on Heavy Weather

But in running before it your vessel may go along quite comfortably and dry for a time, and then with dreadful suddenness, a sea may come over the stern and put you and your ship out of business. . . .
—Captain Voss, *The Venturesome Voyages of Captain Voss*

A few years ago *Tzu Hang* was running from Reykhavik to the northwest point of Iceland in a southwest gale. It was a dark night and the wind force 9 with a heavy sea on her quarter. *Tzu Hang* had only her storm headsail set and in order to prevent it jibing over and back again, with sudden strains on sheet, halyard, and stay, we were running with the wind on our quarter, which gave us a nice offing from the inhospitable shore. *Tzu Hang* was tearing along through the night in the conditions that she seems to like best, and I was happy and singing at the tiller, since we were going fast in the direction we wished to go. Suddenly I felt, rather than saw a monster wave breathing down my neck and coming at a slightly different angle. The next moment we were hit with a shock that felt as if a ten-ton lorry had run into us. *Tzu Hang* was knocked bodily sideways and the tiller was wrenched out of my hand and thumped against the leeward coaming at the limit of its travel. . . . *Tzu Hang*'s masts went down to the horizontal. . . .

[In another instance] *Tzu Hang* was running before a gale which I should estimate now to have been force ten or more. At no time was she running too fast, nor was she particularly difficult to steer. . . . When she pitchpoled a very high and exceptionally steep wave hit her, considerably higher than she was long. It must have broken as she assumed an almost vertical position on its face. The movement was extremely violent and quick. There was no sensation of being in a dangerous position with disaster threatening. Disaster was suddenly there.
—Miles Smeeton, *Because the Horn Is There*

It was becoming more and more difficult to hold *Joshua* before the seas because the trailing hawsers made her less and less maneuverable as the seas got bigger. She was yawing more even with the helm right down, and what I had vaguely feared eventually happened. But it was my fault, for my attention must have momentarily wandered after fifteen hours at the helm. Carried by a wave *Joshua* suddenly came beam on to the seas and when the breaker arrived it was too late. A rush of icy water hit me in the neck and the next moment *Joshua* was heeled rapidly over. The angle of heel increased steadily but not abruptly while noise became dim. Then the silence was suddenly broken by the unholy din of a cascade of objects flying across the cabin . . . three or four seconds . . . then *Joshua* righted herself.

[Later that night] the boat was running exactly stern on to a fast approaching wave, nicely curved but not excessively large, on the point of breaking . . . or maybe not breaking. . . . I was wide awake, I think I was even extra lucid at that moment.

The stern lifted as always and then, accelerating suddenly but without heeling the slightest, *Joshua* buried her forward part in the sea at an angle of about 30 degrees, as far as the forward edge of the coachroof. Half the boat was under water. Almost immediately she emerged again. . . . We had almost been pitchpoled by a slightly hesitant wave—I would not have believed it possible.

—Bernard Moitessier, *The First Voyage of the Joshua*

Our technique for the entire period of storms was to run with the prevailing wind and wave set on the starboard quarter, holding a fair course and surging down the faces of the rising swells. As the crests caught us, they would kick the stern over, and *Sorcery* would round up slightly till she luffed; then she would fly along the top of the wave. . . . Steering was never difficult in these gale conditions, but it did require some concentration and by the tenth day of real wind, everyone on board had put in many hours of heavy-weather helm time. . . . Then the freight train hit us. There was no time to react. As the starboard locker emptied onto me, the engine which had been battery charging, kicked off. I pile-drived into the amazingly white surface of the overhead, right where the cabin sole used to be: then the port lockers emptied out. Sometime in between it seemed that a wave had washed through into the forepeak, but I barely noticed it. . . . the first definite sounds that penetrated the chaos were the piercing screams from one deck, then a shout of "Man overboard! Man overboard!"

—Aulan Fitzpatrick, "360 Degree Roll Sweeps Sorcery Clean," *Sail*,

August 1976.

All Monday it was staysail only. To hold the course without flogging its 300 square feet in accidental gybes required constant attention at the helm. . . . [The wind was an estimated] Force 9, over 46 knots. . . . And so dawned the fateful morning . . . the wind had veered. We'd come over to the port gybe. . . . We remarked the abating seas; at the same time our pace diminished to eight knots. "Were we racing," I said, "We'd be upping the main." We agreed in the interest of rest and comfort to postpone this until I came on watch again at 1300. . . .

Bill had impressed me as an alert helmsman more than once the past ten days. I could see him through the companionway checking the tillermaster [electric autopilot]. . . . I read the first sentence of the first six volumes of Anthony Trollope. Then Bill shouted, "Look out. . . ."

A second to rise up, another to swing my legs off the bunk. Four seconds. Bill's next agonized cry coincided with the creaking slapping sound of a flat surface slamming water with maximum impact. . . . Even as the mast must have struck the water and *Streamer* lay like a wing-crippled swan on her side I still felt confident. . . . A second shattering smack. Then gently as the mast subsided below the surface the bunk revolved above my head. I stood calf deep in water on the cabin ceiling.

[Later Bill told me] "I'd been looking ahead. I turned around. This wall. Forty feet high. It had two crests just off the stern. I kicked tilly clear. Grabbed the wheel and pulled her off with all my weight. Three spokes. I thought she'd come back until I saw the mast hit the water. Then the second crest hit us."
—Philip S. Weld, "Five Nights Upside Down—Then Rescue for
Gulf Streamer," *Sail*, August 1976.

Seraffyn's broach as described in Chapter 16 was a classic case of running too long under bare poles.

Seven different instances, five very different types of boats. *Seraffyn* is twenty-four feet long with short overhangs and heavy displacement. *Gulf Streamer* is a sixty-foot-long lightweight trimaran. *Sorcery* is a sixty-one-foot-long light-displacement IOR racing boat. *Joshua* is a thirty-five foot double-ended heavy steel ketch. *Tzu Hang* is a forty-six-foot-long wooden canoe stern ketch. Each encountered waves that could have been disastrous, yet only two of these instances happened near Cape Horn. Smeeton's first account was near Iceland. *Sorcery* got into trouble in the North Pacific, *Gulf Streamer* in the North Atlantic, and *Seraffyn* in the Baltic. All of us got into trouble while running, with no warning and with dreadful suddenness.

Why do yachtsmen continue to run in heavy weather? It's because they are not aware of any danger. The yacht feels like it is completely under control. In some instances it is even being steered by vane or autopilot. The motion is relatively comfortable. The wind speed seems lower because you are running away from it. To round up and heave to means a definite decision, backed by action and hard work. It means setting some sort of riding sail, sea anchor, or drough. Rounding up to heave to can be frightening, especially if you have left it too long. And that's what happens. You hang on longer than is prudent, hoping the wind and sea will lay down. That's usually when disaster strikes.

Heaving to requires gear preparation before leaving port. It requires experimentation to learn the adjustment and trimming of sails and or droughs necessary to get your particular boat into the proper hove-to position. Every boat heaves to differently and the only way to learn which way works best for yours is to practice at sea in winds of gale force. Few of us choose to go out in heavy winds just to practice. It is easier to accept a pat solution like running under bare poles, with or without warps or droughs. We have been lulled into a false sense of security by other yachtsmen who have fortunately survived to write about "running with it."

In the author's notes in his book *The First Voyage of the Joshua,* Bernard Moitessier says, "The following lines are only a very incomplete testimony, and perhaps quite mistaken. Just because we have once got away without suffering damage I cannot pretend to talk like an authority on the handling of a yacht in the high latitudes of the South Pacific."

Miles Smeeton makes a similar statement in *Because the Horn Is There:* "I write of the management of a ship in heavy weather with hesitation, because my experience, although gained in many seas, is confined to one ship."

These men don't profess to be authorities on heavy weather. But their opinions, along with those of other famous yachtsmen, have been influencing us to run in heavy weather using various methods—with warps, with bare poles, with storm sails.

In Allen Villers's book *The War with Cape Horn,* he tells of sailing the grain ship *Parma* from Australia west to east around the Horn. In the roaring forties they were running with little sail set and were suddenly swept by a large wave, suffering extensive damage. The captain was the famous Ruben de Clouix. He hove the ship to and *Parma* suffered no more.

Captain Voss, another master sailor, has recommended heaving to when heavy weather is encountered, and gives details on how this can be done in vessels of all types and sizes in the appendix of his book *The Venturesome Voyage of Captain Voss.* This appendix is worth careful study and, in my opinion should be carried on board every sea-going yacht for reference.

Miles Smeeton notes in his section on heavy weather in his book *Because the Horn Is There,* "I have been unable to find in Adlard Cole's book [*Heavy Weather Sailing*] any record of a yacht incurring damage while hove to." We have hove-to on *Seraffyn.* I have lain hove-to in various boats while I was delivering them. Never once while lying hove to have we suffered any damage.

I think we should reconsider the question of storm tactics and follow the example and advice of the master sailors instead of yachts-men. We should listen to the men who spent up to nine months of every working year at sea, who often made thirty or forty trips around the Horn during their lifetimes, men who had experience on various types of sailing ships in all kinds of weather, men like Rueben de Clouix and Captain Voss.

To finish the quote that started this appendix, Voss says, "So once more I repeat my advice: be most careful in running and heave to rather a little earlier than deemed necessary by others."

The authors

BIO-
ETHICS

Rem B. Edwards/Glenn C. Graber

University of Tennessee

HARCOURT BRACE JOVANOVICH, PUBLISHERS

San Diego   New York   Chicago   Austin   Washington, D.C.
London   Sydney   Tokyo   Toronto

Dedicated to John W. Davis
A Great Friend and Department Head

ISBN: 0-15-505420-1

Library of Congress Catalog Card Number: 87-81881

Printed in the United States of America

Preface

In the philosophy department of the University of Tennessee, we have been teaching medical ethics to hundreds of students each year for more than ten years. We believe that we have learned how to do this well, and we hope that this book will permit us to share with others some of what we have learned.

In the following chapters, you will find articles that are well written as well as understandable by and informative and challenging to students who wish to know more about such topics as ethical theory, therapist–patient relations, informed voluntary consent, medical experimentation, health and disease, involuntary hospitalization and behavior control, the concept of death, euthanasia, abortion, reproductive decisions, the allocation of scarce or expensive medical resources, and many subordinate themes related to these issues. No book can be exhaustive, but we believe that these are the central issues of medical ethics.

The selections represent some of the best and most enlightening work in bioethics in recent years. We have chosen articles that will help students gain an understanding of underlying ethical principles and develop skill in critical analysis of issues, rather than articles that presuppose that these abilities are already present.

The first chapter is an introduction to ethical theory. Basic concepts in ethics and teleological and deontological moral theories are discussed, providing a foundation from which students can analyze the selections in the subsequent chapters. Each chapter ends with a Selected Bibliography, which can easily serve as a list of suggested readings.

In the detailed introductions to each of the chapters, we have introduced the articles that follow and also have tried to make a significant contribution to the understanding and clarification of the issues themselves. We have incorporated much that we have found to work well in

teaching these themes to both undergraduate and graduate students. Both the introductions and the articles are designed to provide students with the basic factual, medical, conceptual, ethical, and philosophical information needed for making intelligent judgments about these bioethical issues that so much affect our living and our dying.

Although each editor has contributed to the development of each chapter and the writing of each introduction, primary authorship has been divided as follows. Rem B. Edwards is the primary author of parts A and B of Chapter 1 and of the introductions to Chapters 2, 4, 5, 6, 7, and 8. Glenn C. Graber is the primary author of part C of Chapter 1 and of the introductions to Chapters 3, 9, and 10.

We thank Robert Audi, University of Nebraska at Lincoln, Fred Gifford, University of Illinois at Chicago, Gregory Pence, University of Alabama, Birmingham, James Wallace, University of Illinois, Urbana, and Daniel Wikler, University of Wisconsin Medical School, for their careful reviews of the manuscript. We wish to express our appreciation to the authors and publishers who have given permission for this material to be reproduced. Each editor also wishes to express to the other deep appreciation for many hours of collaboration on a most rewarding venture.

Rem B. Edwards

Glenn C. Graber

Contents

CHAPTER **10**

Allocation of Scarce or Expensive Medical Resources

CHAPTER 1

Ethical Foundations

IF THE ONLY CONCERN when facing an issue in bioethics were to get the matter settled by making some choice or other, then we could rely on emotion and arbitrary whim. However, since the actual goal is a decision that is rationally defensible and capable of being communicated to others, then decision-making must be grounded in careful and systematic reflection on fundamental values and moral principles. Ethical theory is the discipline which explores these foundational matters. Unfortunately, philosophers discuss these issues in general and abstract terms; thus connections with concrete issues in bioethics are not always easy to establish. Many of the selections in future chapters contain detailed attempts to relate specific concrete issues to fundamental principles. Ethical theory is also a discipline in which philosophers are still searching for definitive solutions, and it will not be possible here to review all the possibilities. Nevertheless, certain key concepts need to be understood, and a number of central positions in ethical theory will be identified, explained, and critically evaluated.

A. SOME BASIC CONCEPTS

Philosophers have developed certain concepts such as the following which are essential to understanding almost any ethical position and which must be incorporated into the working vocabulary of any student who takes a serious interest in ethics.

(1) *Ethics* itself may be broadly (and somewhat loosely) understood to be the domain of good and evil, right and wrong. There are many approaches to ethics. *Normative ethics* attempts to prescribe definite answers to our questions about good and evil, right and wrong. *Descriptive ethics* merely describes for us how some person, philosopher, group, or culture answers questions about good and evil, right and wrong, without necessarily endorsing these answers. *Religious ethics* either prescribes or describes how ethical questions are answered in faith by some authoritative religious tradition. *Philosophical ethics* either describes how one or more philosophers or philosophical traditions deal with ethical questions or prescribes answers to these questions based on rational examination and justification. *Metaethics* deals with the meaning of value concepts and the nature of proof or justification in ethics. This book will focus primarily on normative philosophical ethics as applied to the area of bioethics. *Bioethics* is ethical theory applied to biomedical practice or research.

In explaining the meaning of "ethics," many concepts need to be further defined. The word "good" and its correlative words "bad" or "evil"

1

are central to any ethical investigation. Philosophers have distinguished several different kinds of good and evil.

(2) An *extrinsic or instrumental good* is something which is desirable as a means to some end or goal other than itself. Most of us on reflection desire money only as an extrinsic good. We are convinced that money is a good thing; but our considered judgment is that we want it solely because of what we can *do* with it, not just for its own sake. If we could not spend it or exchange it for other objects or experiences that are desirable, we would not want it. Even the proverbial miser is no exception to this rule, though he might at first appear to want money for its own sake. He really wants it, however, merely as a means to the pleasure that it gives him to finger it or count it, and experience the sense of security that he derives just from knowing that it is there for his disposal. Similarly, medical care and medical technology are great human goods, but their value too is like that of money. They are merely means to the ends of promoting health and preventing or curing illness. In a later chapter, we shall inquire about what kinds of evils are involved in illness and what kinds of goods in health.

One extrinsic good is *better than* another if either (a) it is a more efficient means to the same end or an end of equal value or (b) it is an equally efficient means to a more valuable end. A money system is better than a barter system on grounds (a) and medical care is valued more highly than watch repair on grounds (b).

Philosophers seem to have little use for a corresponding notion of *extrinsic bad* or evil, though it might refer either to an efficient means to a bad end or an inefficient means to any end.

(3) An *intrinsic good* is something which is desirable for its own sake and not merely as a means to something else. It is an end in itself, something worth having, realizing, cultivating, and preserving just because it is what it is. Since all things exist within extended chains of causes and effects, intrinsically good things may also be

extrinsic goods if they in turn contribute to the realization of other future goods. Pleasure and autonomy may be desirable for their own sake and also contribute to the realization of other goods. This merely adds to their value; it does not detract in any way from the fact that, considered in themselves, they are desirable as ends. The notion of something desirable for its own sake is a rather abstract notion. What sorts of things have been thought to be intrinsic goods? We shall examine hedonism and pluralism as providing some important answers.

(4) An *intrinsic evil* is something which is undesirable for its own nasty sake. It is worth avoiding or eliminating just because it is what it is and not merely because of its effects. Of course, it may have further undesirable effects; but considered merely for what it is, we find it to be inherently undesirable. The practice of medicine is concerned with the avoidance and elimination of things which are regarded as undesirable in and of themselves, such as pain, death, and incapacities resulting from illness and injury. The masochist who values pain is very much like the miser who values money. He seems to value pain as an intrinsic good, rather than as an intrinsic evil; but actually he finds pain desirable merely as a means to pleasure, i.e., as an instrumental good. Unlike most of us, he derives pleasure directly from pain, just as the miser derives pleasure directly from handling and having money. If not for this abnormal capacity for enjoying suffering, it would be more obvious that the masochist too regards pain as an intrinsic evil. If he considers pain in itself and not its consequences, even the masochist would find pain to be undesirable for its own nasty sake.

(5) An *essential or primary good* is something which is desirable as a necessary condition for living almost any kind of a worthwhile life. Though different persons give different answers to the question of what things are intrinsically good, there are certain things which are desirable for the realization of almost any kind of well

being. There is nothing culturally relative about this, though the degree to which they are valued and the particular forms they take may vary from culture to culture. But everyone in every culture must have life itself and some degree of liberty, security, nutrition, basic education, basic health, etc. for well-being. These primary goods may also be classifiable as either intrinsic or fundamental extrinsic goods or as both; but that is a matter of considerable controversy.

As noted, our concepts of intrinsic good or ill are high abstractions. Most of us want to know what exactly these abstractions include. Philosophical answers to the question "What *things* are intrinsically good or bad?" may be subdivided into at least two groups—hedonistic and pluralistic theories. Later we shall see how theories of good and bad are related to our questions about right and wrong.

(6) *Hedonism* is the view that intrinsic good consists only of pleasure, or happiness defined in terms of pleasure, and that intrinsic evil consists only of pain, or of unhappiness defined in terms of pain. *Pleasures* seem to be feelings that we ordinarily like and wish to cultivate and sustain for their own sake, and *pains* are feelings that we normally dislike and wish to avoid and eliminate for their own sake. *Happiness* means many different things to different people, but in the hedonistic sense it consists of a positive surplus of pleasure over pain through an extended period of time. There would be no pain at all in perfect happiness, though happiness is seldom if ever perfect. Happiness requires time as well as pleasure, though there is no exact answer to the question of how long—an hour, a day, a season, etc. *Unhappiness* in the hedonistic sense is composed of a surplus of pain over pleasure through an extended period of time. In the second chapter of his *Utilitarianism*, John Stuart Mill characterized happiness as being "not a life of rapture; but moments of such, in an existence made up of few and transitory pains, many and various pleasures, with a decided predominance of the active over the passive, and having as the foundation of

the whole, not to expect more from life than it is capable of bestowing."

Hedonists disagree about whether pleasures and pains differ qualitatively or merely quantitatively from other pleasures and pains. Hedonism is thus a much more complicated position than may appear on the surface. *Quantitative hedonism,* such as that of Jeremy Bentham and Henry Sidgwick, is the view that there is only one quality of feeling that we call "pleasure," though individual instances of this feeling may differ from other instances in such *quantitative ways* as intensity and duration. They may also differ with respect to their causes and effects. As for causes, pleasure or happiness may have many sources. Some people may get pleasure from poetry, others from pushpin (a children's game in which one player tries to push his pin over that of another); but pleasure is pleasure no matter how we get it. As for effects, some pleasures lead to other pleasures and some to pains. Similar things are true of pain. The pain derived from a bee sting or a broken bone is exactly the same feeling as the pain derived from guilt, jealousy, rejection, grief, boredom, or what have you, according to quantitative hedonism. Instances of pain may differ from other instances in duration and intensity, may have a variety of sources or causes, and may have a diversity of effects, some painful and some not. The intrinsic value or disvalue of pleasures or pains depends entirely on their intensity and duration, and their extrinsic value or disvalue depends entirely on the quantitative pleasantness or painfulness of their consequences, according to quantitative hedonism.

Qualitative hedonism, such as that held by John Stuart Mill, does not deny that pleasures and pains may differ in intensity or duration or in their causes and effects. It adds that there are *many qualities* of agreeable feeling that we call "pleasure," not just one, and there are many kinds of feeling that we call "pain," not just one. The agreeable feeling derived from loving another person, or from intellectual activity, or creativity, or religious rapture, is not of the same

kind as that derived from having one's back rubbed, sexual arousal, eating a good meal, or sadistic torture. Similarly, there are many different kinds, not just quantities, of disagreeable feeling derived from an injection, an incision, a laceration, an infection, a broken heart, grief, or a sin-sick soul. Though quantitative considerations are relevant in assessing the value or disvalue of same-quality pleasures and pains, they are irrelevant in evaluating those differing in quality. Our reflective preferences for or aversions to pleasures or pains differing in quality may vary independently of their intensity and duration. Some pleasures may thus be better than others, though less intense and/or prolonged; and some pains may be worse than others, though less intense and prolonged. If this is true, then medical professionals who must deal with pains and who adopt professional obligations to help relieve suffering must take both quantitative and qualitative considerations into account if they hope to be effective. The best way to decide who is right in the dispute between quantitative and qualitative hedonism is to pay very careful attention to our own pleasures and pains, then to compare notes with others who have done the same.

(7) *Pluralism* is the view that there are other intrinsic goods besides pleasure or happiness defined in terms of pleasure and that there are other intrinsic evils besides pain or unhappiness defined in terms of pain. This view has been advocated by such philosophers as G. E. Moore, Hastings Rashdall, and Sir David Ross. The pluralist does not usually deny that pleasure is *one* intrinsic good or that pain is *one* intrinsic ill. He merely denies that these are *the only* intrinsic goods or evils. For the pluralist, there are *many* intrinsic goods and many intrinsic bads. Many persons have thought that one or more of the following have intrinsic worth in addition to pleasure or happiness: moral virtue, conscientiousness, rationality, knowledge, autonomy, free will, freedom of action, beauty, creativity, love, friendship, self-realization, preference or desire fulfillment, etc. Correspondingly, pluralists also

think that one or more of the following have intrinsic disvalue in addition to pain or unhappiness: moral vice, violations of conscience, irrationality, ignorance, constraints on autonomy or free will or freedom of action, ugliness, stagnation, hatred, violence, undeveloped selfhood, unfulfilled preferences or desires, etc.

There is something very fundamental or axiomatic about our human judgments of intrinsic value and disvalue. There seems to be no way to derive them logically or psychologically from other value commitments. In deciding where we stand in the hedonism–pluralism controversy, we must try procedurally to be as clearheaded and open-minded as possible on several relevant matters. First, one is not a hedonist merely because one regards pleasure or happiness as intrinsically good or pain or unhappiness as intrinsically bad. They must be regarded as *the only* intrinsic goods or ills. Next, if pleasures and pains do in fact differ qualitatively as well as quantitatively, this must be taken into account. Next, we need not accept *all* the items in our list of pluralistic goods as intrinsic goods or ills in order to qualify as pluralists. Just *one* in addition to pleasure or pain will do, and it need not appear in the list just given. Finally, we must not confuse the intrinsic worth of these pluralistic goods with their extrinsic worth. The hedonist argues that the pluralist confuses them because the pluralistic goods are enjoyable and the pluralistic evils are sources of suffering. Only the enjoyment or suffering, not the pluralistic goods or evils themselves, has intrinsic value or disvalue, according to the hedonist. The pluralist must reply that the intrinsic value or disvalue of these things is not exhausted by the fact that they are standard sources of pleasure or pain. There is still a residue of value or disvalue after all that has been taken into account.

The dispute between hedonists and pluralists may be very important for theoretical purposes, but for practical purposes it may make very little difference. Would it make any practical difference if physicians believed that physical fitness is valuable in and of itself instead of

merely contributing to overall health? The hedonist concedes that pluralistic goods, though having merely extrinsic worth, are indispensable for health and happiness, at least under ordinary conditions of life. The pluralist concedes that the pluralistic goods are extrinsic goods causing happiness while insisting that there is also a residuum of nonderivative intrinsic worth in them as such.

We must now look at some of the ways in which our views of good and evil enter into our beliefs about moral duty or obligation.

(8) *Morality* is not easily defined. In fact, there seems to be no single set of common and distinctive set of traits designated by the term. There is at best a family of sometimes shared characteristics which persons have in mind who speak of the province of the moral as opposed to the provinces of the prudential, the aesthetic, the legal, the religious, etc. Moral values and principles are thought to exemplify one or more of the following family traits, none of which may be absolutely necessary. They are (a) action-guiding rules or prescriptions, which (b) are chosen seriously, authentically, or rationally, (c) are regarded as universalizable or as applying to and valid for everyone, (d) are at least prima facie if not always supreme or overriding in relation to conflicting (e.g., prudential) prescriptions, (e) aim at the promotion of the common good or welfare of all persons or sentient beings or at least of some other persons or sentient beings, (f) aim at the prevention of harm to all persons or sentient beings, or at least to some others, (g) require treating all persons or sentient beings as ends in themselves and never merely as means (at least where avoidable), (h) may require personal sacrifice for the greater good of or rights of others, (i) must be socially teachable and institutable, (j) must be of such great importance that they are worth the price of enforcement by such negative sanctions as adverse public opinion, guilty conscience, and the police power of the state. *Moral duties or obligations* consist of action-guiding rules or prescriptions conjoined conceptually with at least some of the foregoing

family traits of morality. There are many different philosophical accounts of the precise form and nature of moral duty. Most viable theories of moral obligation are classifiable either as teleological or deontological theories.

(9) *Teleological or consequentialist ethics* asserts that the rightness or wrongness of a moral act or rule depends on the goodness or badness of its consequences. More specifically, a morally right act or rule is one which maximizes intrinsically good and/or minimizes intrinsically bad consequences or which provides and protects essential conditions for intrinsic well-being.

(10) *Deontological ethics* affirms that there is some other way of identifying right acts or justified rules besides taking account of the goodness or badness of their consequences. Extreme deontologists like Immanuel Kant deny that we need ever consider consequences in distinguishing right from wrong. Less extreme deontologists like Sir David Ross admit that we should consider consequences among other things but deny that we should ever consider consequences alone. Some nonteleological principle is always available that must also be considered, according to this more moderate position. We will later consider some of these nonconsequentialist options.

Sometimes it is mistakenly claimed that deontology is an ethics of conscience whereas teleology is an ethics of consequences. This suggests that teleologists do not have any conscience! The troubling truth is that deontologists have a deontological conscience and teleologists have a teleological conscience. Which is best justified rationally is something to be decided after a more detailed look at some of the main contenders. Even then, each of us must make this decision for himself or herself, preferably under conditions of ideal rational choice such as freedom, enlightenment, and impartiality.

(11) *Moral rules* have an important but varied place in most theories of moral obligation. Most moral theories incorporate moral action-guiding rules at at least two levels of

abstraction—ultimate norms and concrete general rules or maxims.

Ultimate norms are the most general and axiomatic principles of a moral position. They are the first principles of morality, and relative to a given system of moral belief they are so basic or fundamental that they cannot be derived logically from any other principles more basic than themselves. They are the sort of ultimate moral beliefs that Jeremy Bentham had in mind when he suggested that those principles which are used to prove all else cannot themselves be proved. In the discussion to follow, we shall identify the ultimate norms of such moral positions as Act Utilitarianism, Rule Utilitarianism, Minimizing Utilitarianism, Kantianism, Ross's Rule Deontologism, and Natural Law Theory. To give a few examples for now, the ultimate norm of Act Utilitarianism is that "we are morally obligated to perform that individual act which is likely to result in the best or least harmful consequences for the greatest number of persons or sentient beings affected by the act." In Kantian ethics, the various forms of Kant's Categorical Imperative function as ultimate norms: "Act always on that maxim (concrete moral rule) that you could will (without contradiction) to become a universal law of nature," or "Always treat persons as ends in themselves and never merely as means."

Concrete moral rules or maxims are the familiar action-guiding rules of everyday commonsense morality, though they are not perfectly identical with such since new ones may be proposed and eventually incorporated. Concrete moral rules are usually thought to be derivable in some way from the ultimate norms of a system. Some examples of some commonplace concrete rules:

Anyone in situation X ought

1. to keep promises;
2. to tell the truth;
3. to prevent harm to innocent people;
4. not to kill;
5. to prevent one's children from starving;
6. not to steal;
7. not to commit suicide;
8. to stop at red lights and stop signs;
9. to obey "Keep off the grass" signs;
10. not to give students unearned grades;
11. to save lives;
12. to prevent and relieve suffering;
13. to develop one's talents;
14. to vote in elections;
15. not to punish the innocent.

This list could be extended indefinitely. We soon will see how particular theories justify such rules, how they deal with conflicting rules, whether they make exceptions to them, how exceptions to them (or taboos against exceptions) are justified, and what sorts of exceptions are condoned.

(12) *Moral rights* are given more prominence in some moral systems than others. Moral rights are usually thought to be justified claims by an individual against society (i.e., one or more other individuals). They involve those concrete moral rules thought to be most essential, and they usually involve enforcement mechanisms or sanctions for protecting individuals in their rights against other persons. Various kinds of rights impose different sorts of duties upon other persons in relation to rights-holders. *Negative rights* involve duties not to harm or interfere. A negative right to life involves merely the duty not to kill, but not a duty to provide means necessary for the preservation of life. *Positive rights* involve providing the necessary means to those ends being protected. A positive right to life involves more than abstaining from killing. It requires providing the means necessary for the preservation of life, such as food, shelter or fundamental medical care. *Moral rights* are those positive or negative rights recognized as morally binding by a given system of moral belief and practice. *Legal rights* are those which have been codified into

positive law in some existing state or society. *Absolute rights* correlate with duties regarded as binding in all relevant circumstances and to which there are no legitimate exceptions. *Defeasible rights* correlate with prima facie duties, i.e., duties regarded as normally binding but which may be overridden by even stronger conflicting duties. *Alienable* rights are those which individuals may voluntarily waive or transfer to others. *Inalienable* rights are those which individuals either cannot or should not waive or transfer to others under any circumstances. Many contemporary philosophers seem to regard all rights as alienable, though this position is at least debatable. Traditionally, some rights, such as those to life, liberty, and the pursuit of happiness, were regarded as inalienable. An inalienable right to liberty would paternalistically prohibit persons from selling themselves into slavery. An inalienable right to life would paternalistically prohibit persons from renouncing life-saving medical treatment. Are either of these two rights truly inalienable?

We shall now examine how particular teleological and deontological moral theories deal with moral duties, rules, and rights.

B. TELEOLOGICAL MORAL THEORIES

(1) *Act Utilitarianism* has as its ultimate norm the abstract principle that "we are morally obligated to perform that individual act which is likely to result in the best or in the least harmful consequences for the greatest number of persons or sentient beings affected by the act." There may be hedonistic (Jeremy Bentham) or pluralistic (G. E. Moore, Hastings Rashdall) varieties of this, depending on one's view of the precise nature of intrinsic goods and evils. A version of Act Utilitarianism which assumes that the dispute between hedonists and pluralists makes very little practical difference has been vigorously defended recently by J. J. C. Smart. The Act Utilitarian thinks that it is always our duty, where possible, to do what is best. In those horrendous existential predicaments where it seems that only evil will come of it no matter what we do, we should try to do the least harm possible, to act in accord with the "lesser of two evils" precept. Act Utilitarianism requires that we consider long-run future consequences, the consequences for everyone affected, and probabilities. It is not enough just to take into account the immediate consequences for a few of the most directly affected individuals. For example, if a stubborn patient with a viral respiratory infection insists that a doctor prescribe an antibiotic even after the doctor has carefully explained that viruses are not affected by antibiotics, the doctor must weigh many factors in order to identify that particular course of action which is likely to have the best or least harmful consequences. The quick and easy way to get such a stubborn patient off his back might be to give him what he wants or to give a placebo and tell him the lie that an antibiotic has been prescribed. But the broad long-range consequences of lying need to be considered, as well as the consequences of overprescribing antibiotics and the character-corrupting effects for both physician and patient. Some of the medically undesirable effects of overprescribing antibiotics are now well known. When penicillin was first introduced in the early 1940's, it was effective against almost all staphylococcus infections, but today it will cure only ten percent of them. Any unnecessary use of antibiotics contributes to the evolution of resistant strains of bacteria. In a few short decades, this is likely to have very significant adverse consequences for large numbers of persons and animals as well. Once all the relevant good and bad effects have been taken into account, Act Utilitarianism usually requires rather complicated and sophisticated solutions to seemingly simple moral problems.

Moral rules and rights have an important place within Act Utilitarianism. They are a necessary part of any working morality, partly because there is often not much time available for making

complicated calculations. Also, vast eons of human experience have disclosed that when commonsense moral rules are obeyed, the best or least harmful consequences will likely follow; when they are violated, predominantly undesirable consequences usually ensue. Yet there are problems with such rules, the Act Utilitarian insists. First, in rare circumstances, one might be able to predict with reasonable assurance that the worst rather than the best consequences will follow from acting on a commonsense moral rule. For example, if we had lived in occupied France during the Second World War, we might have been awakened in the middle of the night by Hitler's SS troops making a house to house search for Jews. If we, like those who sheltered Anne Frank and her family, were hiding some of our Jewish friends in a concealed part of our attic, how should we respond to the SS officer's question "Do you know where there are any Jews?" Should we follow the rule "Tell the truth?" Should we respond "Of course, I have a number of them in my attic," or should we lie to save their lives and our own? Here an exception to the rule seems justified to avoid the worst possible outcome. The Act Utilitarian insists that all our common moral maxims have legitimate exceptions if the stakes are high enough. Second, the Act Utilitarian recognizes that our common moral rules may come into conflict with one another. Under desperate conditions of life, the rule which says we should not allow our children to starve may conflict with the rule prohibiting stealing. Or a medical professional may realize that under some circumstances the only way to obey the rule mandating that suffering be relieved is to violate the conflicting rule that requires the saving of lives. When rules conflict, the proper solution according to Act Utilitarianism is to follow that rule which is likely to have the best or least harmful consequences.

Critics have developed a number of objections to Act Utilitarianism. Before we adopt or reject the position, we should examine some of these and see if the Act Utilitarian can give a plausible response to them. They all take the general form that Act Utilitarianism has "counterintuitive" implications or applications when pushed to its limits. The presupposition is that certain commonplace moral intuitions are the final and absolutely correct court of appeal in deciding moral questions. The Act Utilitarian may reply to these criticisms either by trying to show that, when properly understood, his position is really in accord with or not much at variance with these basic intuitions or by trying to show that the intuitions themselves are wrong and unacceptable.

First of all, critics argue that Act Utilitarianism is mistaken because it implies that certain kinds of rule violations would be acceptable when done in secret, though wrong when done openly or publicly. The correct intuition, says the critic, is that if anything is wrong when done openly, it is also just as wrong and perhaps more so when done secretly. Consider this illustration. Suppose that a physician has been treating an eccentric old man for a terminal condition for some time. He is attending the old man as death approaches, and no one else is with them. Just before he loses consciousness for the last time, the old man pulls off a money belt that he has worn strapped to him, tells the doctor that it contains $50,000, and gets the doctor to promise that after his death he will give the money to his favorite charity, Charity A. Death follows shortly. If others had been present, it seems clear that the doctor should keep his solemn deathbed promise, if for no other reason than that publicity about a violation would have devastating long-term effects on the public's confidence in the important social institution of promise-keeping and would also greatly diminish public trust in physicians. Also, the promisee is now dead and (at least in this world) cannot have his expectations disappointed, as would be the case in most situations of promise-breaking. Since the promise was made in secret and now the physician is the only one who knows about it, it seems that he would be perfectly justified on Act Utilitarian grounds in not giving the money to Charity A but in giving it instead to his own choice of Charity B if he

honestly believes that Charity B generally does more good than Charity A.

The Act Utilitarian might reply to this critique in at least two ways. First, he might accept the intuition that if anything is wrong when done openly it is also wrong when done secretly, and then contend that, when certain subtle long-range effects have been considered, his position is much closer to this intuition than his critic will allow. The main undesirable effects that are relevant here seem to be character-corrupting effects on the physician himself and the long-range liabilities of that for others. Will breaking a solemn secret promise corrupt the physician's character and turn him into a chronic breaker of promises and other important rules involving secrecy? The probability of this is difficult to assess, but the Act Utilitarian seems to have little besides character-corrupting consequences to appeal to if he accepts the critic's intuition that if anything is wrong when done openly it is also wrong when done secretly. The second way out for the Act Utilitarian would be to deny the validity of this intuition. He might maintain that the following circumstances would show this intuition to have only general but not absolute validity. One week after our doctor has promised to give the dying eccentric's $50,000 to Charity A, new information is published for the first time which shows that Charity A spends eighty-five percent of its income on fundraising and providing an elaborate lifestyle for its officers, giving only fifteen percent to its beneficiaries. A similar Charity B channels eighty-five percent of its income to its beneficiaries. The eccentric old man did not know this, but the secret deathbed promise had been made. Should it be kept, or should it be violated for the sake of greater good? If we opt for the latter, we can no longer maintain that if anything is wrong when done openly it is also wrong when done secretly. (This assumes that it would be wrong to violate this promise if made openly, but it is possible that even openly made promises may be violated for the greatest good.)

A second difficulty with the Act Utilitarian position is that it may require flagrant violations of individual rights to promote the greatest happiness or well-being of the greatest number. This "society versus the individual" predicament might take many forms. Suppose that a major transplant center has a number of patients on the verge of death whose lives can be saved if they immediately receive various transplanted organs. One needs a liver, one a heart, two need kidneys, two need lungs, etc. It would seem that by violating just one patient's right to life and secretly taking his organs, at least six other lives could be saved, thus maximizing the greatest good of the greatest number.

How might the Act Utilitarian respond? First, he could note that secrecy is the key to the example. Since many people are involved in such a complex medical transfer it would be almost impossible to maintain secrecy about it, and without secrecy certain highly undesirable consequences (like getting the medical staff involved prosecuted for murder or generating massive anxiety in the community of potential patients) would surely follow. Again, he could question the urgency of any such transplant needs given the availability of medical technology and other alternatives for preserving the six other lives. If there are ways to preserve the six lives without killing anybody, surely that would be the best alternative.

Not being quite satisfied with the factual contingencies to which the Act Utilitarian appeals to save his position in the foregoing example, the critic now constructs another example to show that Act Utilitarianism would wrongfully require the sacrifice of individual rights for the greatest good of the greatest number. Suppose that a Nazi physician is in charge of a concentration camp and that he delights in playing the following sadistic game with Jewish physicians who have been incarcerated in his camp. He brings one into his clinic and tells him that if he will inject his wife with a fatal overdose of narcotics, he will allow five other Jews to be released and transported safely to some Allied country. On the other hand, if he refuses, ten Jews (including his wife) will immediately be tortured slowly to

death before his eyes. This sadistic Nazi doctor is known to have played this game many times before; and he always keeps his word, one way or the other. Wouldn't it be obviously wrong here to sacrifice one cherished individual for all the others?

In response, the Act Utilitarian might maintain first of all that this example simply shows that if the stakes are high enough, the intuition that it is wrong to sacrifice the rights of individuals for the greater good of (or to avoid greater harm to) others is simply faulty. Next, "society" or the "greatest number" is not a mere abstraction but is itself composed of definite individuals who also have rights. The choice here would seem to be between sacrificing the right to life of one person versus sacrificing the right to life of ten or fifteen other persons. The "lesser of two evils" principle would justify the former course of action; and it would be morally correct despite our preliminary intuitions to the contrary. We do not think that it is morally wrong to sacrifice the life of an unborn baby to save the life of the mother; and we would not think it to be wrong to sacrifice somewhat prematurely the life of a Siamese twin who has little chance for survival in any event to save the life of the one twin who does have a chance. However regrettable, we think it proper not to ransom the lives of present hostages to prevent the deaths of many future ones. In an ideal world, perhaps, the rights of an individual would never have to be violated for the rights of others; but unfortunately we do not live in that kind of world. We occasionally confront those distressing but inescapable existential predicaments in which we must use a person merely as a means in order to treat others as ends in themselves.

A third and perhaps more telling difficulty with Act Utilitarianism is that it seems to moralize all of life and to require us to be saints and heroes at all times. This theory seems to allow no place for supererogation, i.e., for "going beyond the call of duty." It does not merely *permit* us to choose that act which will have the best results on all occasions; rather, it makes the maximization of good or minimization of evil an absolute moral *requirement*. We are duty bound to optimal saintliness and heroism at all times if we accept Act Utilitarianism. Yet we judge that this ideal is simply too high, too demanding, too exalted. The intuition with which it comes into conflict is that morality should not be excessively demanding but should allow for a surfeit of moral achievement that goes "beyond the call of duty." This moral surfeit may be permitted and encouraged, but it should not be required. Yet Act Utilitarianism requires it.

Criticisms of Act Utilitarianism such as those we have developed have prompted some philosophers to give up on Act Utilitarianism as a lost cause. Yet they have not wanted to abandon the teleological principle that moral rightness or wrongness depends somehow on the goodness or badness of consequences. These teleologists have developed another consequentialist ethics, Rule Utilitarianism, to which we now shall turn.

(2) *Rule Utilitarianism,* as defended by such philosophers as Stephen Toulmin, P. H. Nowell-Smith, and Richard Brandt, consists of two ultimate normative principles, one dealing with justified moral rules and one with moral duty or obligation. (1) A justified moral rule is one whose consequences would be best or least harmful for everyone (or every sentient being) if everyone acted in accord with the rule. (2) We are morally obligated to act in accord with justified moral rules, even on those occasions when more good or less harm might be realized by acting in some other way. On this view, it is still the goodness or badness of the consequences that determines rightness or wrongness, but it is not the goodness or badness of the consequences of individual acts, as in Act Utilitarianism. Rather, it is the goodness or badness of everyone's acting in accord with particular moral rules on all relevant occasions.

To illustrate the difference between Act and Rule Utilitarianism, consider these simple situations. If an Act Utilitarian comes upon a sign that says "Keep off the grass" and is in a hurry to get

across, he will presumably violate the rule that says we should obey such signs if he judges that better consequences would follow from violating than obeying the rule. He knows that his one infraction of the rule will do little or no harm to the grass and that he is not a very influential person who will actually start a stampede across the lawn. The Rule Utilitarian, by contrast, would note that the wrongness of breaking the rules does not depend on the actual consequences of an individual act but on the probable consequences of everyone's breaking the rule. Now if everyone trampled the grass, the lawn would be obliterated, an eyesore would be created, and the results would be sufficiently harmful to outweigh the advantage of getting to the other side of the lawn a few seconds sooner. Duty would require that the rule be obeyed.

Again, if an Act Utilitarian drives up to a red light or stop sign and notes as she approaches that no pedestrians are nearby, that no vehicles are coming from opposite directions, and that no police are nearby, she would presumably not feel obligated to stop if it were advantageous not to do so. A conscientious Rule Utilitarian, by contrast, presumably would think it wrong not to stop even though no harm would result from the infraction and good would come of it. Wrongness again depends on the consequences of everyone's violating the rule, i.e., on probable carnage on the streets and highways, not on the likely consequences of the individual act.

Once more, if our previously discussed physician makes a solemn, secret deathbed promise to give an eccentric old man's $50,000.00 to Charity A, there would be a difference in his view of duty if he were a Rule Utilitarian. The goodness or badness of the particular act of distributing the donation would be irrelevant. Rather, duty would depend on the consequences of everyone's violating the rule that says we ought to keep solemn, secret deathbed promises. The relevant undesirable results here would be the elimination of the entire highly desirable social practice of making and keeping solemn, secret deathbed promises. For the Rule Utilitarian,

duty depends on the good or bad results of everyone's obeying or violating a relevant rule, not on those of any individual act.

Critics have found difficulties with Rule Utilitarianism. One problem is that of explaining exactly how the rules are to be formulated. Two forms of Rule Utilitarianism must be distinguished. According to *Simple Rule Utilitarianism,* all moral rules must be simple and unqualified, like the fifteen rules previously listed in definition (11) on Moral Rules. According to *Refined Rule Utilitarianism,* however, moral rules may be very complex and may have all sorts of qualifications and exceptions written into them. Consider the differences between these different formulations of moral rules relevant to our preceding examples.

A. Simple Rules	*B. Refined Rules*
1. We should obey signs that say "Keep off the grass."	1. We should obey signs that say "Keep off the grass" unless we are sure that we will do little damage and will not influence many others to disobey the sign.
2. We should stop at red lights and stop signs.	2. We should stop at red lights and stop signs except when we are sure that no one will be hurt and no police are around.
3. We should keep our solemn, secret promises made to the dying.	3. We should keep our solemn, secret promises made to the dying except when new information comes to light after the death of the promisee that likely would have altered his or her preferences.

Obviously, quite different courses of action are commended by these rules; yet they might all be justified on the Rule Utilitarian ground that everyone's acting on them would have the best or least harmful consequences for everyone. Which is the correct formulation of a justified rule?

Critics also note that the Simple Rule position is plagued by the old problem of conflicting rules. A rule which requires us to tell the truth will on occasion come into conflict with a rule that requires us to save lives, as when the SS troops ask us if we know the whereabouts of any Jews. A rule that tells us to conserve life may conflict with a rule that tells us to relieve excruciating suffering, as when only death can bring relief. The Refined Rule position attempts to avoid such conflicts by building a sufficient number of qualifications into the rules. The conflict is resolved if our rules require that we should tell the truth except when lying is absolutely necessary to save lives or that we should save lives except when the patient chooses to die to escape prolonged, excruciating, and unrelievable pain. The question remains, however, whether *sufficient* exceptions can be specified to avoid *all* conflict.

In many respects, the Refined Rule position is much closer to what most reflective people actually believe about moral rules than is the Simple Rule view. With respect to the wrongness of actively killing people, for example, most of us do not believe, after reflection, that it is always wrong to kill people purely and simply. Most of us accept a refined rule that has a number of legitimate exceptions included in the rule. How many of the following exceptions can be accepted in good conscience? We ought not actively to kill persons, except when absolutely necessary (1) in self-defense, (2) in defense of friends and loved ones, (3) in defense of any other innocent persons, (4) in a just or justified war, (5) where capital punishment is appropriate, (6) where euthanasia is appropriate, etc. The Refined Rule Utilitarian has a highly plausible explanation of how legitimate qualifications or

exceptions to rules are to be identified. They are the ones which it would be best or least harmful for everyone if everyone made those exceptions! In other words, they are universalizable or universally beneficial exceptions that it would be best for everyone in relevant circumstances to make. Notice that these are not self-serving exceptions like lying to gain an economic advantage for oneself or killing to satisfy one's private passion for revenge. The self-serving exceptions to moral rules are the objectionable ones. But these are everyone-serving exceptions that we would be willing for everyone in similar circumstances to make, and they should be written into our rules according to Refined Rule Utilitarianism. The difficulty that now arises, however, is that once all the legitimate exceptions have been incorporated into the rules, the courses of moral action commended by Refined Rule Utilitarianism turn out to be very close to (if not identical with) the courses of action commended by Act Utilitarianism. Indeed, many critics have suspected that the two positions turn out to be "extensionally equivalent"; i.e., when the rules are sufficiently developed and refined, they both commend the same courses of action. Also, what if the principle of Act Utilitarianism should itself turn out to be the rule that would have the best consequences for everyone if everyone acted upon it?

A final difficulty with Rule Utilitarianism is that unless it is very similar to Act Utilitarianism, the position seems to commit us to acting in accord with justified rules even when there is massive noncompliance with them, i.e., even when the rules are actually doing little if any good and may be gravely disadvantageous to the few who still comply with them. For example, suppose that three physicians have incorporated into a common practice and contracted to work together and share equal income from the corporation for at least three years. The rule that would appear to be most beneficial to all under these circumstances would be that each should work as hard as possible to maximize the earnings of

the practice. However, if after a few months, two of the partners decide to play golf four days a week, Rule Utilitarianism would commit the remaining conscientious partner to work as hard as possible every day, even though the freeloading partners would be getting most of the money which he earns for the practice. Of course, this might be remedied by adopting the refined rule that each partner should work as hard as possible to maximize the earnings of the practice, unless one or more of the others becomes a freeloader. Then, however, it is difficult to see how Rule would differ from Act Utilitarianism. The latter position has maintained all along that rules have legitimate exceptions when they fail to commend courses of action that maximize good or minimize harm. The Rule Utilitarian may formalize the exceptions by including them in the rules. This has the conceptual advantage that making the exception can now be said to be acting in accord with rather than in violation of the rule. But the fact remains that a maximizing exception is a maximizing exception no matter how it is packaged.

(3) *Minimizing Utilitarianism* as formulated by John Stuart Mill is a distinct form of consequentialist ethics. It involves two basic normative principles and a number of qualifying considerations. The principle of utility is its basic axiom of general axiology, or what Mill called "Teleology" or "the Art of Life." This principle affirms that it is *desirable* (and in that sense right or correct) to act so as to maximize the greatest happiness, or minimize the unhappiness, for the greatest number of persons (or sentient beings). However, *desirability* is not equivalent to *moral obligation*. The province of the moral must be distinguished from nonmoral domains of value and practice, such as prudence, law, or taste, all of which also have the principle of utility as their ideal foundation. What distinguishes moral duties from these others is that they must be (1) worth the cost of social enforcement by such negative sanctions or reinforcers as guilty conscience, adverse public opinion, or the police

power of the state and they must be (2) correlated with easily teachable and learnable action-guiding rules. Rules are very important here, but rightness and wrongness do *not* depend upon the good or bad consequences of everyone's acting on the rule, as in Rule Utilitarianism. Rather, they depend upon the probable good or bad consequences of instituting and enforcing the rules as general social practices. On this view, an act is morally *wrong* only if it violates a moral rule that is worth the cost of being instituted and enforced as a general social practice. Rule conflicts are to be resolved by direct appeal to the principle of utility.

Not everything which is desirable is thereby moral, for many desirable action-guiding rules are simply not worth the price of social perpetuation and coercive enforcement, which can be worse than the harms likely to be prevented by the rules. Many rules are simply unenforceable at any price, and for others the cost of enforced compliance would be generally worse than the rule violations themselves would be. Prudence, taste, supererogation, saintliness, etc. may all be desirable, but their action-guiding rules are either not enforceable (like prohibition) or not worth the price of enforcement. Where they are not incompatible with what is morally required, they may be morally permitted; but in these domains, the rule of liberty rather than the rule of coercive social enforcement is best or least harmful for everyone. The principle of utility itself requires that many desirable behaviors not be moral duties. They may be positively encouraged, but they go beyond the call of duty and are best left to individual interest and initiative. In Minimizing Utilitarianism, there is no moral obligation to maximize the good; for the price of forcing people to be saints and heroes, or even to be prudent, at all times is just too great to be paid. Going "beyond the call of duty," (supererogation) and doing what is best for oneself (prudence) are generally permitted and encouraged but are not morally obligatory, as they are in both Act and Rule Utilitarianism.

What then is morally required? The second normative principle of Minimizing Utilitarianism, having the principle of utility as its ultimate "test" or "foundation," identifies those concrete action-guiding rules which are judged, upon reflection, to be enforceable and serious enough to be worth the price of holding us "accountable to society" for noncompliance. The basic norm of morality: To the extent that the results are possible, we are morally required to act in accord with those concrete secondary rules which demand (a) that we avoid harm to all other persons (or sentient beings) who are affected by our behavior and (b) that we protect and/or provide for everyone else (or every other sentient being) certain minimal essential conditions of any sort of well-being whatsoever, such as life, liberty, security, basic education, and basic health, and (c) that we engage in a decent minimum of charity or benevolence (and perhaps other "imperfect obligations" such as gratitude).

Moral rights are solidly grounded in Minimizing Utilitarianism. Rights involve justified claims by all to the absence of harm and the presence of those minimal essential or primary goods which are necessary conditions for having any sort of worthwhile existence. *Justice,* the main part of moral obligation, consists in those perfect duties that protect and provide moral rights for everyone on every relevant occasion. A moral right, by definition, is anything so essential to well-being that society ought to provide and/or protect its possession by everyone (or all sentient beings), at least where possible. Where rights conflict, as they often do in an imperfect world, justice cannot be fully done. The world is just not organized properly for perfect justice, but justice must be done to the fullest extent possible. Where rights conflict, the obligatory act is the one which is likely to result in the lesser of all the evils. For example, if a physician is fully convinced that a patient is quite serious in his threats to kill another person, the patient's right to confidentiality is in conflict with the other person's right to life. The duty to warn here re-

sults from the judgment that less harm is involved in the loss of confidentiality than in the loss of life. (This conclusion is, of course, subject to dispute. The disagreement between the majority opinion and the dissenting opinion in the *Tarasoff* case which is reprinted below in Chapter II hinges in part on differences in predictions about which course of action will bring the most harm in the long run, all things considered.)

Outside the domain of justice, other "imperfect" duties are also morally required, but to a much lesser extent. Charity and gratitude are also duties, but they are required only on certain indefinite occasions when they are not too costly to the individual. A person who is never benevolent should have a bad conscience about it and be an object of moral opprobrium to his or her acquaintances, but charity would be too costly if we made it obligatory whenever requested. This would shortly reduce us all to paupers! Excessively costly generosity clearly goes beyond the call of duty, though maximizing Act and Rule Utilitarianism could require it. As saintliness, it should be encouraged; but it should not be coerced. However, after the demands of justice have been satisfied, there is still a decent minimum of altruistic endeavor that should be expected of us.

Critics will find a number of difficulties with Minimizing Utilitarianism. For one thing, it will not be patently obvious to everyone that matters of prudence or self-interest are *never* worth the price of social enforcement, i.e., that we never have *moral* duties to ourselves. In extreme instances of harm to ourselves, paternalistically minded persons might think that others are justified in interfering with our liberty or other rights for the sake of preventing even greater harms. When he considered the question of whether other persons would ever be justified in preventing us from selling ourselves into slavery, even John Stuart Mill himself endorsed strong paternalism with respect to competent adults, and he would have had no difficulty accepting weak paternalism with respect to imma-

ture and incompetent persons. Mill judged that the loss of liberty involved in preventing competent adults from selling themselves into slavery was obviously much less harmful than the loss of liberty involved in slavery itself. In extreme instances, to prevent greater harms, society might be justified in preventing persons from renouncing or waiving certain of their (inalienable?) rights. Thus some instances of paternalism might be justifiable within the framework of Minimizing Utilitarianism. The final limits of this domain of moral, socially enforceable duties to ourselves will be subject to much debate.

Another difficulty for Minimizing Utilitarianism is that we do not have available to us any definitive list of what our rights are. Of course, this is a difficulty for *any* ethical theory which takes rights seriously, but in Minimizing Utilitarianism the difficulty centers around the fact that we have no agreed-upon table of primary or essential goods that are necessary for living any sort of a worthwhile life. Sometimes the rights identified are relatively noncontroversial. Sometimes rights language is misused altogether, as when we are told in an advertisement that we have "a right to chicken done right." Sometimes, however, it is used to persuade us that something as yet unrecognized is so important that it ought to be protected or provided by society where possible on every relevant occasion. Our contemporary debate over whether there is a right to a certain decent minimum of health care for all, and what constitutes this minimum, falls more clearly within the realm of advocated rights than within the realm of recognized rights. This debate too will continue indefinitely, for it is likely that we will never have a fixed and universally recognized list of rights. To some extent, what a society can afford to recognize as a right may depend upon the available and changing resources of that society. Does everyone who needs it have a right to be provided with a new artificial heart? We will be debating that one for a long time whether we are Minimizing Utilitarians or not. The Humana Corporation is doubtless hoping

that our answer will be affirmative, most taxpayers that it will be negative!*

A final difficulty that has plagued other forms of Utilitarianism might also be a problem for Minimizing Utilitarianism. The difficulty is that Utilitarianism too readily sacrifices the rights and interests of the individual person (or animal) to the greater good of others. This seems to be rather clearly the case with Maximizing Act and Rule Utilitarianism, but it may not be true of the Minimizing variety. Perhaps it is best after all for everyone that we not institute and enforce rules that would require excessive sacrifices of individuals and individuality for the greater *good* of others. Totalitarian societies may try that, but societies that make a place for individual worth, liberty, and other rights actually are better societies. What may be required is that individuals and individuality be sacrificed on rare occasions in order to prevent even greater sacrifice of or *harm* to numbers of others. Minimizing utilitarianism requires only minimal moral encroachment on individuals and individuality where absolutely necessary for preventing even greater *harms* to other individuals. It also requires that extreme caution be used in identifying such moral predicaments, for it is so easy to be wrong about matters of such grave consequence. It cannot always be impossible, however. It all depends on whether the secondary rules that would demand such sacrifices are really worth the price of their social institution and enforcement. For example, Minimizing Utilitarianism would not legitimate a rule which says that physicians should sacrifice the life of a patient if they could thereby harvest his organs and save the lives of five other patients. If instituted and enforced as a general social practice, such a rule would cause such horrendous public anxiety, such mistrust of physicians, such avoidance of hospitals for greatly

---

*The Humana Corporation owns the hospital in Louisville, Kentucky, at which most artificial hearts have recently been implanted—at the Corporation's expense.

needed medical care, that it simply would not be worth the price.

C. DEONTOLOGICAL MORAL THEORIES

Deontological theories deny that the rightness or wrongness of an act is derived *wholly* from the goodness or badness of its consequences. It is claimed that other features of actions, which are not reducible to evaluation of consequences, make a moral difference. Consider, for example, the situation of a physician who has just confirmed a terminal diagnosis and is deciding what she should say to the patient. To tell the patient the bad news will undoubtedly cause him harm—sadness, anxiety, depression; and on this ground the physician may be tempted to withhold the information and perhaps even to tell the patient an outright lie to shield him from this terrifying news.

Most teleologists would argue against lying in this situation by appealing to the long-term consequences of such an act (How long could the pretense be kept up as the patient's illness progresses?) and/or to the society-wide effects of having all or many physicians institute a rule or practice of lying in such situations. At the most, they would insist, lying could be justified only in those rare circumstances when the harms of truthtelling decisively outweigh the benefits.

However, from the patient's point of view, this position may not be fully satisfactory. Most of us would be deeply offended at the idea that our physician would *seriously consider the possibility* of lying to us. We feel that we are *entitled* to be told the truth (about our state of health as about other matters), regardless of whether this knowledge will bring us any pleasure or other benefit. Whether it would be good for us to know this information is not the crucial moral issue. More important morally is the fact that we may *want* to know; to deny us this right, even for the benevolent purpose of sparing us from harm,

is an affront to our dignity as persons. And this reaction is not to be considered as merely one more consequence, to be added in and balanced against the other effects of the policy. Rather, it is a recognition of a wholly different type of moral consideration.

It is tempting to think of moral dignity as the sort of trait which one person might have more or less of than another and which might be augmented and diminished in certain ways. Strength is an example of a trait of this sort. Zelda might be stronger than York, but he might enhance his strength by working out, and hers might diminish as a result of a muscle-wasting disease so that by next year conditions will be reversed and York will be stronger than Zelda.

We sometimes speak of dignity in similar terms. When a dignified man is made to look foolish (e.g., by being made to fall into a mud puddle by prankish boys), we might sometimes say that he "lost his dignity" or that "his dignity was destroyed" by their prank.

But this way of talking is misleading. Moral dignity is not lost or destroyed in this episode. What he lost was his *composure;* what was destroyed was his *dignified image.* His moral dignity was *affronted* by the prank—or he might describe what was done to him as "an indignity." But his moral dignity was neither destroyed nor diminished. It is not the sort of thing that *can* be destroyed or diminished. One clue that this is the case is to note the different effects a *second* assault has on his image, on the one hand, and on his dignity, on the other hand. If one of the pranksters pushed him into the puddle a second time as he was in the process of picking himself up after the initial assault, we might say that his image was only slightly damaged this time around (since he was so muddy already). But the indignity of the second attack is as great or greater than the first—which suggests that his moral dignity was not at all diminished by the first round.

The notion of (moral) dignity is a reification. It is a (potentially misleading) way of stat-

ing moral rules of action. To remind someone that persons "have moral dignity" is to call his or her attention to moral rules which say that one ought not to treat people in certain ways. If I feel indignant about something you did to me, or I consider your action an affront to my dignity, it is not that I feel that you took something away from me or destroyed something belonging to me. My dignity is intact. The wrong you did was to fail to *respect* my dignity; i.e., you acted in ways you ought not to act.

What is the *content* of this concept? That is far from precise. The rules in question are sometimes condensed into the principle of Respect for Persons. But what sort of actions fail to show respect? (Part of the difference between the different deontological theories we shall examine below comes from how they answer this question—what sorts of affronts to dignity they focus upon.) Affronts to dignity include such acts as

- humiliating someone;
- ridiculing a person;
- deliberately causing embarrassment;
- putting someone in a position in which he is uncomfortable or in which he does not want to be;
- ignoring someone when she is calling for attention;
- taking someone for granted.

Many of the other wrongs one can do against a person *include* an affront to dignity as one element. If Xavier loses his temper with Will and strikes at him, he may cause pain and mental anguish—and perhaps lasting injury. But, in addition to these harms, he also affronts Will's dignity. And this is a basis for saying that his act was wrong, even if for some reason the other harms fail to result—e.g., because he failed to hit him when he struck out at him.

If there is a common element to affronts to dignity, it has to do with a breakdown in an established system of cooperative mutual inter-

action. Instead of treating you as a peer or a colleague engaged in a joint enterprise, I fail to acknowledge your interests or concerns and, instead, "use" you to further goals of my own.

Who comes under the protection of this rule? When we speak of respect "for persons" or of our dignity "as persons," the implication is that one must qualify as a *person* to merit this protection. We will discuss this concept at greater length in Chapter 8, where it arises in connection with questions about the status of the fetus; but suffice it for now to say that a *person* must be capable of communication and possess self-consciousness. Thus newborns are not yet persons, strictly speaking, and comatose patients are no longer persons. Some have argued that chimpanzees or porpoises could qualify as persons because of their ability to communicate.

However, we also sometimes speak of "human dignity," which suggests that one qualifies merely by being a member of the human species. Thus newborns and the comatose would qualify, but not chimpanzees or porpoises.

The rule of Respect for Dignity is a rule within a complex social system of morality. Thus the best answer to the question of whom it protects is "every member of our moral community." It is (at least in part) a matter of social decision who is included. Traits like self-consciousness or being human can be appealed to in arguments for extending the scope of the moral community to include certain beings (and, perhaps, for retracting it to exclude others), but it is only when these arguments have been *accepted* and the complex social system of a moral community is adjusted in practice that new individuals come under the protection of the rule of Respect for Dignity. Failure to respect dignity is a matter of a breakdown in moral interaction. Thus it is only after we have found reason to recognize moral duties towards chimps and dolphins and consequently to interact with them on that basis that it is possible to affront their dignity.

To beings who are not members of the moral community, we may be cruel or inhumane,

including the 1957 AMA code, have been silent on the topic, but the new 1980 AMA code recognizes that patients do have rights. If we seek guidance on truthfulness in medical communications, we will be met generally by massive silence—though, for the first time in history, the most recent AMA code explicitly commends dealing honestly with patients and colleagues.

Second, conflicts among and within codes are also a serious problem. As Hull notes, the 1953 International Code of Nursing Ethics, not included here, contained so many internal conflicts that it was significantly revised in 1973 to eliminate them. In addition to those conflicts mentioned by Hull, Jehovah's Witnesses, who refuse life-saving blood transfusions out of religious conviction, created a grave conflict between provisions requiring that life be preserved and provisions requiring that the religious beliefs of patients be respected. In the AHA's Patient's Bill of Rights, there is a conflict between the requirement that all communications concerning the patient's care be confidential and the authorization to give information without his knowledge and permission "to an appropriate person in his behalf" when it is "medically advisable." Since this is permitted without the patient's knowledge, there is a conflict with the requirement of informed consent as well. A possible conflict between codes may be found in the requirement of the 1957 AMA code that physicians "should observe all laws," which seems to exclude civil disobedience (and perhaps even efforts to change bad laws) and the requirement of the new 1980 code that physicians merely respect the law and try to change those laws which are contrary to the best interests of patients.

Third, as Hull notes, medical professionals may have other ethical commitments which conflict with those prescribed by a relevant professional code. Most physicians today who still take the ancient Hippocratic Oath have no intention of abiding by its absolute prohibition on abortion because they are convinced that there are many situations in which women have a moral right to have an abortion. (Incidentally, the prohibition of abortion and even of active euthanasia by the Hippocratic Oath was not representative of Greek medical practice generally.) The Hippocratic Oath seems to prohibit females from acquiring a medical education, requiring that medical knowledge be imparted only to males, to sons, which is quite incompatible with a moral commitment to equality of opportunity for the sexes. The Hippocratic commitment to doing what the physician thinks best for the patient (in contrast to what that patient thinks best) is often thought to involve a morally unconscionable manifestation of crass medical paternalism.

Implicit in Hull's discussion we may find some additional difficulties with reliance on professional codes. A fourth important difficulty is that the language of a code is often so vague that it gives little or no specific guidance. The category of "medical advisability" in the Patient's Bill of Rights may hide a multitude of sins, as may "using judgment" in sharing information about patients in the International Code of Nursing Ethics and the matter of keeping secret things "which ought not to be spoken of abroad" in the Hippocratic Oath. The 1980 AMA code requires that physicians "safeguard patient confidences within the constraints of the law." But this last phrase could prohibit communications about patients in any or all of the following ways, and it is not clear which: if expressly required by law; only if expressly forbidden by law; only if expressly permitted by law.

A final difficulty is that professional codes often contain provisions of professional etiquette rather than of ethics. A rule of etiquette is one designed to promote or preserve the customs, manners, and interests or well-being of members of a profession. The prohibition on advertising formerly contained in many codes for physicians and nurses may have been largely a self-serving attempt to eliminate the competition in a free enterprise system. This is now prohibited by federal courts and regulatory agencies as being incompatible with the constitutional right to freedom

of speech. The rule in the Hippocratic Oath which permits communicating of medical knowledge to medical students "but to no one else" began the long and at least partially professionally self-serving tradition of medical secrecy which is now in conflict with the ethical requirement of informed consent. Yet we still see traces of this tradition of secrecy in the practice of writing prescriptions in Latin or illegible handwriting and in the taboos against patients reading their own medical records.

B. MODELS OF THERAPIST–PATIENT ROLES AND RELATIONS

Values are built into the way relations between therapists and patients are conceived and structured from the very outset. These values are not always consciously acknowledged, though they may be or become so. Often they exist as unspoken and unrecognized presuppositions which doctors, nurses, other health care professionals, and patients bring with them into their relations with one another. When unacknowledged, they become tacit institutionalized structures which provide unexamined answers to the question of how therapists ought ideally to relate to their patients and to one another. Unexamined answers are often the wrong answers, however, and we will attempt to bring some of these into the open.

Whenever people have power over other people or sentient beings, moral problems arise. The medical setting is one in which such power relations are to be found. We need an ideal model for structuring power relations between therapists and patients. Upon examination, some models may turn out to be more acceptable morally than others. A complete model for ethically ordering therapist–patient relations would answer each of the following questions:

1. Who has and is entitled to exercise power— i.e., who makes the important decisions? Two types of decisions must be distinguished:

(a) decisions about the *ends,* goals, or values to be realized and (b) decisions about the *means* or technical medium and skills to be employed.

2. What is a "good therapist" like—i.e., what does the doctor, or nurse, or other therapist ideally do in the relationship?

3. What is a "good patient" like—i.e., what does the patient ideally do in the relationship?

4. What happens when the values of the therapist and the patient come into conflict? Are they ever entitled to say no to one another about medical matters? Though Robert M. Veatch is not explicit about this in the following article, it seems that the relevant norms might be moral standards, ideals of professional competence, legal requirements, or other values.

The selection to follow by Robert M. Veatch is a seminal article titled "Models for Ethical Medicine in a Revolutionary Age." Veatch outlines four distinct models for doctor–patient relations which he calls the Engineering, Priestly, Collegial, and Contractual models. Since Veatch's suggestions are sketchy, we shall develop the models in more detail in relation to the above four questions about the ethical ordering of power relations between patients and physicians.

The Engineering Model   In this patient-dominated model, power resides entirely with the patient, and the physician places his or her knowledge and skills entirely at the disposal of the patient for a fee. Our four questions about power distribution are answered as follows:

1. The patient has all the power and makes all the important decisions, both about the ends to be served and the important means to those ends. Here the patient is the only recognized moral agent in the relationship, and the patient bears complete moral responsibility for what happens as long as the physician does a

professionally competent job in carrying out his or her orders.

2. A "good physician" on this model is one who (a) explains to the patient the various options for dealing with the medical problem at hand and then (b) carries out the patient's wishes, no matter what they might be.

3. A "good patient" is one who (a) knows what he or she wants and (b) can give clear directives for carrying out her/his wishes.

4. Since ideally physicians keep all their personal values out of professional relations, they should not come into conflict with those of the patient. However, if a conflict of values does arise, physicians must suppress their values and yield to those of the patient. The physician is never entitled to say no to the patient but must always do what the patient wants.

The Priestly Model   In this physician-dominated model, power resides exclusively with the physician. This has traditionally been the prevailing model in medicine, though it is now being seriously challenged by new ideals of patient power and participation in the decision-making process. It answers our questions as follows:

1. The physician has all the power and makes all important decisions, both about the ends to be served and the important means to those ends. This implies that the physician is the only recognized moral agent in the relationship and bears complete responsibility for all outcomes.

2. A "good physician" is one who (a) always knows what is best for his or her patients and who (b) always does what he or she thinks best for them.

3. A "good patient" is one who (a) passively and completely accepts the authority of the physician in both valuational and technical matters and who (b) always "follows doctor's orders." (The historical dominance of this model is

revealed by the fact that the very idea of a "patient" is that of one who is acted upon, whereas an "agent" is one who acts and decides).

4. Since the values of the patient have no recognized standing or significance in this model, they must be ignored or suppressed when they come into conflict with those of the physician. The patient has no right to give directives or to say no. There is no patient right to refuse treatment in this model.

The Collegial Model   On this model, physicians and patients are equals in a number of important respects. Here our questions seem to have these answers:

1. Physicians and patients participate equally in the decisions which must be made with respect to both medical ends and means.

2. A "good physician" is one who brings equal dignity, trust, and respect into the relationship and who has common interests and goals with his or her patients.

3. A "good patient" also brings equal dignity, trust, and respect into the relationship and has common interests and goals with his or her physician.

4. Since goals are always mutual, there is never any conflict or occasion to say no. When real conflict arises, the model itself collapses.

Robert Veatch is so sensitive to the possibility of conflicting ethnic, class, economic, and other value differences that he regards this model as "a mere pipedream." In the selection in this chapter titled "Models of Nurse/Patient/Physician Relations," Richard T. Hull finds the Collegial Model to be particularly appealing for ordering relations between doctors and nurses, though not without its difficulties.

The Contractual Model   In this model, physician and patient enter into their relations as persons equally qualified to enter into mutual

agreements and equally committed to respecting the values of the other while recognizing the possibility of conflict. Here we get these answers to our questions:

1. The physician and the patient contract at the beginning of their relationship to share power and responsibility in the pursuit of mutually acceptable goals and with the employment of mutually acceptable means to medical ends. Both persons are recognized as moral agents who share responsibility for what happens.

2. A "good physician" (a) discusses medical ends and means with the patient but (b) agrees to carry out only those projects which do not violate her or his own moral values or norms of professional competency.

3. A "good patient" is one who is competent to give informed voluntary consent and refusal. Such patients take responsibility for proposing ends and choosing major means to those ends. Though power is shared, patient values are dominant because patients initiate the relationship and pay for the services rendered either directly or through such agents as insurance companies and government programs.

4. Physician and patient negotiate an agreement for only those services in which their values are in harmony. Both parties have a right to say no. Patients may refuse treatment or services, and physicians may refuse to accept a patient or may withdraw from the relationship when their own deepest values are threatened by patient demands.

Although there is an initial agreement by physician and patient at the beginning of a contractual relationship, the temporality of physician–patient encounters needs to be recognized. New agreements must be negotiated as new problems and previously unknown details emerge. There is no inherent reason why the contractual model cannot account for the dynamic features of continuing patient–physician

negotiations. Veatch insists that the idea of a contract should not be construed too legalistically but should be likened to a marriage contract or a covenant, both of which obviously involve continuing interactions and ever new understandings.

C. NURSES, TREATMENT TEAMS, PROFESSIONAL AUTONOMY

Health care today is rarely confined to interactions between two persons—physician and patient. Instead, nurses and other "ancillary" personnel of various sorts are integrally involved.

In the hospital, patients typically see their physician only a few minutes per day. Most caregiving is done by others acting to carry out doctor's orders. Even in an office visit, nurses, laboratory technicians, and assistants play a significant role. This raises such questions as What is the appropriate relationship (a) between the patient and these personnel and (b) between these personnel and the physician? Also, (c) What are the implications of (a) and (b) for the *self*-concept of the nonphysician practitioner? The same questions previously asked about the physician–patient relationship can be asked here.

(a) To what extent does the nonphysician practitioner have *power* over the patient which he or she is entitled to exercise in making significant decisions? For example, pain medications are sometimes ordered on a PRN ("as needed") basis. Does this mean that the nurse must administer them whenever the patient thinks they are needed and asks for them, or is the nurse expected to exercise professional judgment and administer the medications only when he or she considers that they are really needed? In the first situation, the power is in the hands of the patient and the nurse's status fits the Engineering Model. The nurse uses technical knowledge in determining the proper dosage and skill in administering

the drug but has no role in deciding when to administer it. In the second situation above, the nurse assumes the power. The model in force is Veatch's Priestly Model. In the selection to follow titled "Models of Nurse/Patient/Physician Relations," Richard T. Hull illustrates Veatch's Priestly, Contractual, and Collegial models as applied to the nurse–patient relationship and to the physician–patient relationship. Similar adaptations could be made for other health services personnel.

(b) To what extent should the nonphysician practitioner have decision-making power independent of the physician? The American College of Physicians' *Ethics Manual* says the following, in the section titled "The Relationship of the Physician to Other Health Professionals":

> Delegation of treatment or technical procedures must be limited to persons who are known to be competent to conduct them with skill and thoughtfulness; the physician who is primarily in charge of the patient's care must retain *ultimate responsibility* for all aspects of the patient's management. Society has identified the physician as possessing the necessary training to undertake this responsibility and has granted a specific license to exercise this authority and responsibility. This relationship is implied between patient and physician. [Our emphasis.][2]

This incorporates a Priestly Model of the nurse–physician relationship in which the physician makes all crucial decisions and the nurse's role is that of "handmaiden."

However, nurses are trained to make independent assessments of patients and develop plans for care on that basis. In an Engineering, Contractual, or Collegial Model of the nurse–physician relationship they would be given autonomy (in degrees and scopes which vary depending on the model) in decision-making and action on the basis of nursing assessments.

Hull explores some presuppositions and implications of these variations in his essay in this chapter.

(c) How are the self-concept and integrity of nonphysician practitioners affected by relationships with physicians in which the former lack autonomy? In her following article on "Integrity in Interpersonal Relationships," Christine Mitchell explores this problem. She analyzes a poignant case and examines various meanings of the concept of moral integrity and their application to dependent practice. Though she does not cast her reflections in terms of the models discussed by Veatch and Hull, it would be instructive to consider her points in terms of these structures. What model offers the greatest prospect for maximizing the nurse's integrity?

D. CONFIDENTIALITY

A rule of confidentiality is usually thought to be an essential part of ethically acceptable relations between professionals and clients, especially in medicine. Such an action-guiding rule commits medical practitioners to hold in confidence information gained about their patients during the course of providing medical care. Yet there is considerable confusion among medical professionals concerning the strength and scope of such a commitment and a corresponding confusion among patients and the general public about just how much confidentiality is to be expected from medical professionals. The extent of this confusion is amply reflected in the diverse formulations of rules of confidentiality found in professional codes of ethics for physicians, nurses, and hospitals. Consider these examples:

1. *Oath of Hippocrates* (fifth century B.C.)
   Whatever, in connection with my professional practice, or not in connection with it, I see or hear, in the life of men, which ought not to be spoken of abroad, I will not divulge, as reckoning that all such should be kept secret.

2. Thomas Percival, *Medical Ethics* (3rd edition 1849)
   Secrecy and delicacy, when required by

peculiar circumstances, should be strictly observed; and the familiar and confidential intercourse to which the Faculty are admitted in their professional visits, should be used with discretion, and with the most scrupulous regard to fidelity and honor.

3. *The Declaration of Geneva* (World Medical Association, 1948; amended 1968)

    I will respect the secrets which are confided in me; even after the patient has died.

4. *International Code of Medical Ethics* (World Medical Association, 1949)

    A doctor owes to his patient absolute secrecy on all which has been confided to him or which he knows because of the confidence entrusted to him.

5. *Principles of Medical Ethics* (American Medical Association, 1957)

    Section 9: A physician may not reveal the confidences entrusted to him in the course of medical attendance, or the deficiencies he may observe in the character of patients, unless he is required to do so by law or unless it becomes necessary in order to protect the welfare of the individual or the community.

6. *AMA Principles* (1980, Section IV)

    A physician . . . shall safeguard patient confidences within the constraints of law.

7. *Principles of Ethics* (British Medical Association, 1971)

    If, in the opinion of the doctor, disclosure of confidential information to a third party seems to be in the best medical interest of the patient, it is the doctor's duty to make every effort to allow the information to be given to the third party, but where the patient refuses, that refusal must be respected.

8. *Code for Nurses* (American Nurses' Association, 1976)

    Section 2: The nurse safeguards the client's right to privacy by judiciously pro-

tecting information of a confidential nature.

9. *ICN Code for Nurses* (International Council of Nurses, 1973)

    The nurse holds in confidence personal information and uses judgment in sharing this information.

10. *Patient's Bill of Rights* (American Hospital Association, 1972)

    Section 5: The patient has the right to every consideration of his privacy concerning his own medical care program. Case discussion, consultation, examination, and treatment are confidential and should be conducted discreetly. Those not directly involved in his care must have the permission of the patient to be present.

    Section 6: The patient has the right to expect that all communications and records pertaining to his care should be treated as confidential.

Differences Among the Rules The foregoing rules of confidentiality may differ from one another in at least three ways.

(1) Rules of confidentiality may differ with respect to *scope,* i.e., with respect to the kind and amount of information covered by the rule. For example, in #1 the Hippocratic commitment to confidentiality was not limited to the realm of professional practice but extended to that part of life that was not connected with it. In contrast, rule #3 above covers only "secrets which are confided" to the physician; but rule #4 extends to "all which has been confided . . . or which he knows." Rule #5 covers "confidences entrusted" but extends as well to observed deficiencies of character. Rule #10 includes "all communications and records." Thus there is a problem about what sorts of information fall within the scope of confidentiality commitments.

(2) Rules of confidentiality may differ with respect to *strength,* i.e., with respect to whether confidentiality is absolute or allows for exceptions. The strongest rule in our list is #4, which

requires absolute secrecy about everything; the weakest is #9, which requires only that "judgment" be used in sharing information—which suggests that a great deal of sharing may actually take place. Some rules write exceptions explicitly into the rules. In such cases, making these specified exceptions counts as acting in accord with the rule, rather than as violating it. The old AMA rule (#5) includes three exceptions: where giving out medical information is (a) required by law, (b) necessary to protect the individual, and (c) necessary to protect the welfare of society. The new AMA rule (#6) continues only the exception of requirement by law, recognizing that most states have laws which mandate reporting to the proper authorities such things as gunshot and knife wounds, venereal diseases, and child abuse, whether the patients or parents involved like it or not. The chief difference between these two provisions lies in where the locus of discretionary authority is placed. In the 1957 AMA rule, it was left to the physician to determine whether the welfare of the individual or society is threatened to a degree that justifies unauthorized disclosure. In the 1980 code, this judgment is transferred to the lawmaking and regulatory agencies of the larger society. The selections that follow include the majority and minority opinions in the famous California *Tarasoff* case, which requires psychotherapists to report threats to the life of another to proper authorities.

(3) Rules of confidentiality may differ with respect to *clarity or definiteness*. Some phraseology is very vague or ambiguous and gives little clear guidance to those who must interpret and follow the rules. For example, the notion of things "which ought not to be spoken of abroad" in #1 helps very little since we are not told what these are. In #8, the notion of "judiciously protecting information" gives little concrete guidance; and in #9 the idea of using "judgment in sharing" information gives even less, for we are not told what kind of judgment is to be used.

Considerable philosophical reflection is required to work through the various options and to formulate an ideally adequate rule of confidentiality. Can we rationally justify adopting and conforming to second-order rules such as those of confidentiality or truthfulness (soon to be discussed)? Interestingly enough, almost every option in theoretical ethics can provide a rationale for these rules. Perhaps much disagreement in ethics becomes evident only at the abstract level of ultimate justifications rather than at the concrete level of what generally ought to be done. Deontologists may commend these rules to us because they seem intuitively obvious, or because they are universalizable, or because they are involved in treating persons as ends in themselves rather than merely as means. Teleologists might commend them because they identify specific or general courses of action that might have the best or least harmful consequences.

Are there any legitimate exceptions to the rules? Although debatable, the same reasons that justify the rules themselves may also justify making some exceptions (or not making them, as the case may be). Philosophical problems about rules of confidentiality are explored in the following selection by Rem B. Edwards and in the case study dealing with "Confidentiality and Family Members."

E. COMMUNICATING THE TRUTH

In 1980, when the American Medical Association affirmed in its revised *Principles of Medical Ethics* that "a physician shall deal honestly with patients and colleagues," it officially recognized for the first time in its history a moral obligation to tell patients the truth, at least as physicians see it. Traditionally, doctors and other health care professionals have often assumed on paternalistic grounds that patients are better off if they do not know what is wrong with them or what needs to be done about it. Physicians have often withheld relevant information from their pa-

tients (and sometimes told them outright lies). Truthfulness has not had an important place in the prevailing priestly model of doctor–patient relations.

Occasionally they have brazenly advocated untruthfulness as a general policy. In "Should Doctors Tell The Truth?", an article by Dr. Joseph Collins published in *Harper's Magazine* in 1927, the author blatantly advocated lying to patients—insisting that "the art of medicine consists largely in skillfully mixing falsehood and truth" and that "every physician should cultivate lying as a fine art." In the following selection "Truth-Telling to Patients," by Labrini Moutsopoulos, the history of this policy of benevolent lying to or withholding relevant information from patients is critically reviewed.

Moutsopoulos finds at least three arguments supporting nondisclosure to patients in the relevant medical literature. It is argued first that patients will be greatly harmed by the truth. Overbearing communications may harm the patient psychologically by destroying hope and inducing anxiety, depression, and fear; and they may harm physically by destroying the will to live, or even inducing suicide, we are told. Second, patients do not want to be told the truth. Patients tend "to deny, forget, or transform 'bad news' or risk information." Third, it is often not at all clear what counts as truth. It is argued that "there is no perfect truth, all is relative, and since there is no such thing as truth, information cannot be conveyed in a perfect way." Moutsopoulos replies quite effectively to these arguments for untruthfulness.

He also examines other psychological explanations of why physicians and other health care professionals fail to communicate the truth. Some personnel are so insecure in their own attitudes toward death that they are psychologically unable to talk about such things to others. Some see the death of a patient as such a personal and/or professional defeat that they cannot admit of its possibility. Still others simply lack the com-

munication skills necessary for imparting such delicate information, though the acquisition of such skills should be an integral part of any medical education.

As Moutsopoulos suggests, a powerful case for truthfulness in medicine can be developed, even in those extreme cases where the news is very bad news. Many of the following advantages of truthfulness will apply most obviously to patients who must be told that their lives cannot be greatly prolonged, but truthfulness is an important ideal in the whole of medicine and not just in its extremities. Also, some of these advantages will apply only to selected patients; but many of them will apply to all, especially to the dying.

The Case for Truthfulness in Medicine

(1) First of all, patients should be told all that can be related about their terminal condition *so that they can make financial and other preparations for death.* Of course, they *can* make or update their wills and set their business affairs in order even if they do not know that death is drawing near, but they are *unlikely* to do so unless they are informed. Not telling them does not deny them the opportunity so much as the proper stimulus they might need for such undertakings, and the same may be said for other kinds of preparations for death which they might wish to make, such as planning their own funerals, or giving directives for organ donations, or withholding or withdrawing treatment as death approaches.

(2) Patients should be told that death is rapidly approaching *so that they can make religious preparations for death if they so desire.* Though the precise details of what this involves may vary from one religion to another, every major world religion enjoins making final religious preparations for death. This is a religious task which enormous numbers of persons take with utmost seriousness, and withholding or denying the truth in effect deprives them of their chance.

Many religious persons believe that their eternal destiny may hang in the balance; and even those physicians who doubt that anyone has an eternal destiny should not deprive patients of the incentive to make preparations if *they* see fit.

(3) Communicating the truth about terminal conditions *may prompt patients to make peace, overcome existing alienations, and make final reconciliation with family, friends, and acquaintances.* People who have lived for years in a condition of alienation from significant others may not wish to die that way. Indeed, efforts to overcome such alienation are commonplace with the dying, who seem at last able to put trivial and not-so-trivial affronts into proper perspective. Many are finally able to swallow their pride and to request and to give forgiveness. Some patients may want to set aside social barriers and inhibitions and speak *honestly* with certain people. This, too, is their right.

(4) Knowing the truth *may further enable and activate patients to make the most of what remains of their lives for their self-realization and enjoyment.* Without knowing, they will likely lack the proper stimulus to "have that last fling," to take that last journey, to paint that last picture, to write that last book or article, to see that National League team in action, or to do whatever they find rewarding.

(5) Communicating the truth *will likely built patient confidence and trust in members of the medical profession.* There has been so much systematic lying and withholding of information by health care professionals that patients do not believe half of what they are told. Trust is something which has to be rebuilt. Until physicians and other health care professionals regain a reputation for trustworthiness through systematic honesty, many patients will continue to believe in their hearts that it really does not matter what their caregivers tell them because they are not going to tell them the truth anyway.

(6) Communicating honestly with patients *will likely enable them to cooperate more fully* with their physicians and nurses in executing a therapeutic regimen, including pain management. This is extremely important even when illnesses are not terminal, but terminal illnesses also must be managed to the end. Such management can be done for better or for worse, but knowledge gives power even to dying persons.

(7) Truthfulness with terminally ill patients *may help relieve the terrible anxieties and fears of not knowing.* Patients are uncomfortably anxious and often terrified when they do not know what their problem is, what their chances are, what can be done, and what future distresses, deformities, debilities, and demises await them. It is true that bad news is also likely to be distressing, to generate at least temporary anger, fear, denial, and even depression. But this is only one side of the story. The other side is that knowledge properly imparted can assuage the wild suspicions and terrors of not knowing. Over time it can greatly assist patients in overcoming their initial anger, apprehension, denial, and despair.

(8) Truthfulness with patients *will enable patients, family members, and health care professionals to avoid the degrading and demoralizing conspiracy of lies that otherwise accompanies untruthfulness.* Most dying patients know that they are dying anyway, and the ultimate indignity at the end of life is a social conspiracy to deny them the knowledge they already have. One lie requires another to reinforce it, and all persons involved find themselves caught in a conspiracy of lies.

(9) Truthfulness is important because *it is a necessary precondition of informed voluntary consent and refusal.* This consideration will be explored in depth in Chapter 3 of this book.

Communicating Effectively

Truth should be communicated effectively, not merely told. There are many things other than deliberate lying or withholding information that may interfere with communicating the truth to

patients. Telling the truth in the alien language of medical jargon may impress patients with the erudition of doctors and nurses, but it hardly informs them. Telling the truth bluntly and unsympathetically may inform them, but it will not give hope or help to heal or develop therapeutic bonds of trust. Telling the whole truth all at once may at times be appropriate, but it may fall on deaf ears when patients are so distracted or distraught that they are incapacitated for hearing and heeding. Communicating as opposed to mere telling may take time and may have to be spread out over time (though not spread out so far that it is tantamount to withholding). In some cases, several attempts at communication spread out over several days may be necessary. This matches the process through which clinical knowledge becomes available, as initial diagnostic impressions are confirmed or altered through further clinical tests. If effective communication is to take place, two conditions must be satisfied. First, the health care professional must be willing and able to communicate. Next, the patient must be willing and able to listen. It is the task of health care professionals to find or create opportune times when these two conditions are met.

Communicating the truth adequately may involve making room for hope—sometimes hope for survival, always other kinds of hope. As for hope for survival, there are doubtless many ways of communicating this. Consider telling a patient about an illness which typically involves a 95 percent death rate in one year's time. There is not much room for hope in such statistics, but there is some. Honesty requires that the low probability of survival be communicated; hopefulness might involve indicating that these grim statistics never pick out particular persons. There is really no way to know in advance that any given individual will fall into the subclass of nonsurvivors, however large, or into the subclass of survivors, however small. Any given individual might fall into the small subclass of survivors, so there is room for hope.

What about situations in which there is a 100 percent probability of death within one year, or six weeks, or even six days? Well, there is more than one kind of hope. To a person with any probability of death, these other kinds of hope can be effectively conveyed, as Howard Brody indicates in the following selection titled "Hope."

Are there any legitimate exceptions to the rule of truthfulness? Immanuel Kant was one of the few philosophers to defend absolute truthfulness under all conditions, even when lying is necessary to save the life of another. Yet most reflective persons are willing to allow some exceptions to the rule of truthfulness. Moutsopoulos considers this problem near the end of his discussion. Though he advocates a general policy of truthful disclosure to patients, he argues on utilitarian grounds that such exceptions as the following are justified:

> when a patient directly and persistently asks his doctor not to be informed about his unpleasant condition
>
> when the patient is mentally ill or has a history of suicide in his family background

Are the above, or any of the following, exceptions justifiable? On what grounds?

> when giving placebos would likely result in reduced pain or contribute to healing
>
> when some other disease will kill the patient first
>
> when necessary to prevent immediate violence to the patient or to the medical staff or other patients (For example, a nurse working alone on a ward in a mental hospital might tell a violent and abusive patient that other staff members are nearby when they are not.)

Are there other legitimate exceptions?

There are many good reasons why health care providers should skillfully communicate the

truth as they best understand it to patients, and justifiable exceptions are few and far between. This will be made even more obvious in the fol-lowing chapter when we take a look at the ideal of informed voluntary consent.

NOTES

[1]For a variety of other codes, see *The Encyclopedia of Bioethics*, Warren T. Reich, ed. (New York: The Free Press, 1975), vol. IV, pp. 1731–1815.

[2]*Annals of Internal Medicine* 101, no. 1 (July 1984): 136.

The Hippocratic Oath

This Oath was written by members of the Hippocratic school of Greek medicine somewhere around the fourth or fifth century B.C. *It is representative only of the Hippocratic Pythagorean outlook, not of Greek medicine generally, especially in its absolute prohibition of abortion and euthanasia. Many graduating medical students still take this Oath either in its original or in a slightly modified form.*

I swear by Apollo Physician and Asclepius and Hygieia and Panaceia and all the gods and goddesses, making them my witnesses, that I will fulfil according to my ability and judgment this oath and this covenant:

To hold him who has taught me this art as equal to my parents and to live my life in partnership with him, and if he is in need of money to give him a share of mine, and to regard his offspring as equal to my brothers in male lineage and to teach them this art—if they desire to learn it—without fee and covenant; to give a share of precepts and oral instruction and all the other learning to my sons and to the sons of him who has instructed me and to pupils who have signed the covenant and have taken an oath according to the medical law, but to no one else.

I will apply dietetic measures for the benefit of the sick according to my ability and judgment; I will keep them from harm and injustice.

I will neither give a deadly drug to anybody if asked for it, nor will I make a suggestion to this effect. Similarly I will not give to a woman an abortive remedy. In purity and holiness I will guard my life and my art.

I will not use the knife, not even on sufferers from stone, but will withdraw in favor of such men as are engaged in this work.

Whatever houses I may visit, I will come for the benefit of the sick, remaining free of all intentional injustice, of all mischief and in particular of sexual relations with both female and male persons, be they free or slaves.

What I may see or hear in the course of the treatment or even outside of the treatment in regard to the life of men, which on no account one must spread abroad, I will keep to myself holding such things shameful to be spoken about.

If I fulfil this oath and do not violate it, may it be granted to me to enjoy life and art, being honored with fame among all men for all time to come; if I transgress it and swear falsely, may the opposite of all this be my lot.

Ludwig Edelstein, tr., *Bulletin of the History of Medicine,* Supplement 1. The Johns Hopkins Press, 1943. Reprinted with permission of the publisher.

Principles of Medical Ethics, 1980

American Medical Association

In July of 1980, the House of Delegates of the American Medical Association adopted this new code of professional ethics. It differs from earlier AMA codes in explicitly recognizing that patients have rights and that physicians have a duty to be honest or truthful with patients.

PREAMBLE

The medical profession has long subscribed to a body of ethical statements developed primarily for the benefit of the patient. As a member of this profession, a physician must recognize responsibility not only to patients, but also to society, to other health professionals, and to self. The following Principles adopted by the American Medical Association are not laws, but standards of conduct which define the essentials of honorable behavior for the physician.

I. A physician shall be dedicated to providing competent medical service with compassion and respect for human dignity.

II. A physician shall deal honestly with patients and colleagues, and strive to expose those physicians deficient in character or competence, or who engage in fraud or deception.

III. A physician shall respect the law and also recognize a responsibility to seek changes in those requirements which are contrary to the best interests of the patient.

IV. A physician shall respect the rights of patients, of colleagues, and of other health professionals, and shall safeguard patient confidences within the constraints of the law.

V. A physician shall continue to study, apply and advance scientific knowledge, make relevant information available to patients, colleagues, and the public, obtain consultation, and use the talents of other health professionals when indicated.

VI. A physician shall, in the provision of appropriate patient care, except in emergencies, be free to choose whom to serve, with whom to associate, and the environment in which to provide medical services.

VII. A physician shall recognize a responsibility to participate in activities contributing to an improved community.

Code for Nurses, 1973

International Council of Nurses

In 1973, the International Council of Nurses adopted this new code of ethical concepts applied to nursing. It gives very general guidelines to nurses in matters of both ethics and professional etiquette.

The fundamental responsibility of the nurse is fourfold: to promote health, to prevent illness, to restore health and to alleviate suffering.

The need for nursing is universal. Inherent in nursing is respect for life, dignity and rights of man. It is unrestricted by considerations of

nationality, race, creed, colour, age, sex, politics or social status.

Nurses render health services to the individual, the family and the community and coordinate their services with those of related groups.

NURSES AND PEOPLE

The nurse's primary responsibility is to those people who require nursing care.

The nurse, in providing care, promotes an environment in which the values, customs and spiritual beliefs of the individual are respected.

The nurse holds in confidence personal information and uses judgment in sharing this information.

NURSES AND PRACTICE

The nurse carries personal responsibility for nursing practice and for maintaining competence by continual learning. The nurse maintains the highest standards of nursing care possible within the reality of a specific situation.

The nurse uses judgment in relation to individual competence when accepting and delegating responsibilities.

The nurse when acting in a professional capacity should at all times maintain standards of personal conduct which reflect credit upon the profession.

NURSES AND SOCIETY

The nurse shares with other citizens the responsibility for initiating and supporting action to meet the health and social needs of the public.

NURSES AND CO-WORKERS

The nurse sustains a cooperative relationship with co-workers in nursing and other fields.

The nurse takes appropriate action to safeguard the individual when his care is endangered by a co-worker or any other person.

NURSES AND THE PROFESSION

The nurse plays the major role in determining and implementing desirable standards of nursing practice and nursing education.

The nurse is active in developing a core of professional knowledge.

The nurse, acting through the professional organization, participates in establishing and maintaining equitable social and economic working conditions in nursing.

SUGGESTIONS FOR APPLICATION BY NURSING EDUCATORS, PRACTITIONERS, ADMINISTRATORS AND NURSES' ASSOCIATIONS OF CONCEPTS OF THE CODE FOR NURSES

The *Code for Nurses* is a guide for action based on values and needs of society. It will have meaning only if it becomes a living document applied to the realities of human behaviour in a changing society.

In order to achieve its purpose the *Code* must be understood, internalized and utilized by nurses in all aspects of their work. It must be put before and be continuously available to students and practitioners in their mother tongue, throughout their study and work lives. For practical application in the local setting, the *Code* should be studied in conjunction with information relevant to the specific situation which would guide the nurse in selecting priorities and scope for action in nursing.

These suggestions need to be adapted, expanded and supplemented by additional items.

Code for Nurses, 1976

American Nurses' Association

In its professional code of ethics adopted in 1976, the American Nurses' Association provided guidelines to nurses concerning their obligations to patients, colleagues, and the larger society.

Point 1   The nurse provides services with respect for human dignity and the uniqueness of the client unrestricted by considerations of social or economic status, personal attributes, or the nature of health problems.

Point 2   The nurse safeguards the client's right to privacy by judiciously protecting information of a confidential nature.

Point 3   The nurse acts to safeguard the client and the public when health care and safety are affected by the incompetent, unethical, or illegal practice of any person.

Point 4   The nurse assumes responsibility and accountability for individual nursing judgments and actions.

Point 5   The nurse maintains competence in nursing.

Point 6   The nurse exercises informed judgment and uses individual competence and

Developed by the American Nurses' Association. Reprinted by permission.

qualifications as criteria in seeking consultation, accepting responsibilities, and delegating nursing activities to others.

Point 7   The nurse participates in activities that contribute to the ongoing development of the profession's body of knowledge.

Point 8   The nurse participates in the profession's efforts to implement and improve standards of nursing.

Point 9   The nurse participates in the profession's efforts to establish and maintain conditions of employment conducive to high quality nursing care.

Point 10   The nurse participates in the profession's efforts to protect the public from misinformation and misrepresentation and to maintain the integrity of nursing.

Point 11   The nurse collaborates with members of the health professions and other citizens in promoting community and national efforts to meet the health needs of the public.

A Patient's Bill of Rights

American Hospital Association

On February 6, 1973, the American Hospital Association issued this statement concerning the moral and legal rights of hospital patients. These rights place corresponding duties to patients upon hospital personnel.

The American Hospital Association presents a Patient's Bill of Rights with the expectation that ob-

Reprinted with permission of the American Hospital Association, copyright 1972.

servance of these rights will contribute to more effective patient care and greater satisfaction for the patient, his physician and the hospital organization. Further, the Association presents these

rights in the expectation that they will be supported by the hospital on behalf of its patients, as an integral part of the healing process. It is recognized that a personal relationship between the physician and the patient is essential for the provision of proper medical care. The traditional physician-patient relationship takes on a new dimension when care is rendered within an organizational structure. Legal precedent has established that the institution itself also has a responsibility to the patient. It is in recognition of these factors that these rights are affirmed.

1. The patient has the right to considerate and respectful care.

2. The patient has the right to obtain from his physician complete current information concerning his diagnosis, treatment, and prognosis in terms the patient can be reasonably expected to understand. When it is not medically advisable to give such information to the patient, the information should be made available to an appropriate person in his behalf. He has the right to know by name the physician responsible for coordinating his care.

3. The patient has the right to receive from his physician information necessary to give informed consent prior to the start of any procedure and/or treatment. Except in emergencies, such information for informed consent should include but not necessarily be limited to the specific procedure and/or treatment, the medically significant risks involved, and the probable duration of incapacitation. Where medically significant alternatives for care or treatment exist, or when the patient requests information concerning medical alternatives, the patient has the right to such information. The patient also has the right to know the name of the person responsible for the procedures and/or treatment.

4. The patient has the right to refuse treatment to the extent permitted by law, and to be informed of the medical consequences of his action.

5. The patient has the right to every consideration of his privacy concerning his own medical care program. Case discussion, consultation, examination, and treatment are confidential and should be conducted discreetly. Those not directly involved in his care must have the permission of the patient to be present.

6. The patient has the right to expect that all communications and records pertaining to his care should be treated as confidential.

7. The patient has the right to expect that within its capacity a hospital must make reasonable response to the request of a patient for services. The hospital must provide evaluation, service, and/or referral as indicated by the urgency of the case. When medically permissible a patient may be transferred to another facility only after he has received complete information and explanation concerning the needs for and alternatives to such a transfer. The institution to which the patient is to be transferred must first have accepted the patient for transfer.

8. The patient has the right to obtain information as to any relationship of his hospital to other health care and educational institutions insofar as his care is concerned. The patient has the right to obtain information as to the existence of any professional relationships among individuals, by name, who are treating him.

9. The patient has the right to be advised if the hospital proposes to engage in or perform human experimentation affecting his care or treatment. The patient has the right to refuse to participate in such research projects.

10. The patient has the right to expect reasonable continuity of care. He has the right to know in advance what appointment times and physicians are available and where. The patient

has the right to expect that the hospital will provide a mechanism whereby he is informed by his physician or a delegate of the physician of the patient's continuing health care requirements following discharge.

11. The patient has the right to examine and receive an explanation of his bill regardless of source of payment.

12. The patient has the right to know what hospital rules and regulations apply to his conduct as a patient.

No catalogue of rights can guarantee for the patient the kind of treatment he has a right to expect. A hospital has many functions to perform, including the prevention and treatment of disease, the education of both health professionals and patients, and the conduct of clinical research. All these activities must be conducted with an overriding concern for the patient, and, above all, the recognition of his dignity as a human being. Success in achieving this recognition assures success in the defense of the rights of the patient.

Codes or No Codes?

Richard T. Hull

Richard T. Hull has been on the faculty of State University of New York at Buffalo since 1967. On leave in 1979–80, he worked for M. David Lowe Personnel Services in Houston, Texas, assisting nurses and other health-related personnel in finding employment. His experiences in interviewing applicants formed the basis for a series of articles written for The Kansas Nurse, *of which this is one. He currently is an associate professor of philosophy, with a joint appointment in the Department of Medicine, at SUNY at Buffalo.*

Hull examines the functions of the 1979 American Nurses' Association "Code of Ethics" and argues that it and other codes suffer from numerous shortcomings. Professional codes of ethics (1) do not all contain the same provisions and are silent on many important topics, (2) conflict with themselves and with one another, (3) conflict with other ethical commitments, (4) are often vague and give little specific guidance, and (5) may contain much professional etiquette as well as ethics.

You have been working in a large, county-operated metropolitan hospital for just under a year since earning your cap and your first promotion has just been approved! You are to be a charge nurse on the chronic care ward, which is a sort of in-hospital nursing home for mostly elderly, senile patients who are not critically ill and who are either waiting for space to open up in a local nursing home or have repeatedly been referred back to the county hospital for treatment of ailments usually handled in house because they

From *The Kansas Nurse*, vol. 55, no. 10 (November 1980), pp. 8, 18–19, 21. Reprinted by permission of the author and the Kansas State Nurses Association.

are "management problems." As you begin to familiarize yourself with the patients, you note that although none is critically ill, many have a No Code entry written in their records, indicating that in case of cardiac or respiratory arrest the patient is not to be resuscitated. Most of these patients are to some degree senile and probably not competent to consent to such orders and you doubt that any effort has been made to discuss the matter with them. Nor is there any indication in any of the charts that the question of resuscitation has been discussed with family members, particularly since the hospital is in an area of the Sun Belt where elderly people move to retire away from their children.

You are greatly disturbed by this; but mindful of the hostility that a challenging inquiry from a nurse can provoke, particularly when coming from one who doesn't have a solid power base, you determine to be on firm footing before protesting the ethics of the practice. You decide to review your copy of the ANA Code of Ethics for Nurses (a document which you received when you joined the ANA but which you have scarcely glanced at so far), so that you can point out that the profession backs you up in your opposition to the practice. Alas! When you read the 11 points of the Code, although it contains some strong general statements about your duty to safeguard your client from unethical practice, the Code doesn't say whether the practice of No Coding is unethical or not. You expand your reading to the accompanying set of Interpretive Statements and read them very carefully; but again you do not find the specific condemnations that you seek. Where age and long-term illness are mentioned, the nurse is enjoined not to let those factors limit practice except insofar as is appropriate to the circumstances of the individual case. About the only explicit point that speaks to your type of situation occurs where the Code allows that the nurse who is personally opposed to the procedures used in a particular case is justified in refusing to participate. But this seems to land you squarely in a dilemma: you either swallow your dislike for what is being done and remain at your new post, or ask to be transferred to another ward on personal grounds and risk being labeled a malcontent early in your still vulnerable career. You seem unable to find professional backing in the Code for your opposition to the practice and wonder if maybe it is just a matter of your personal values rather than an ethically questionable practice at stake. You finally decide that you can't fight city hall, particularly if you are banished from the city and so you learn to live with the situation, occasionally "overlooking" the No Code orders and spending a lot of sleepless nights hoping for another transfer (which eventually comes).

I believe that the nurse in this hypothetical but all-too-common scenario is the victim of one of several mistaken views as to just what a professional code of ethics does and can do. The topic of this essay is an examination of those several views, but at bottom lies the question "Would nurses and/or others in the health care and medical professions be better off with codes, or no codes?"

A document published by the Committee on Ethics of the ANA in 1979 contains three sentences all the more remarkable for their juxtaposition. "The statements of the Code and their interpretation provide guidance for conduct and relationships in carrying out nursing responsibilities consistent with the ethical obligations of the profession and quality in nursing care."[1] "The Code for Nurses cannot answer all moral questions and tell the nurse what she ought to do in each particular situation. Codes can deal only with broad issues and suggest general ethical stances."[2] What is remarkable about the juxtaposition is that the first sentence appears to offer a promise that is removed by the other two. The initial promise is that the Code serves as a guide to "conduct and relationships in carrying out nursing responsibilities" that are ethical and professional, yet the pair of sentences that immediately follow make a rather weaker claim on behalf of the Code. They indicate that it should be read not as providing specific, situational directives but as only "suggestive" of ethical stances.

The foregoing comments make it surprising to find yet another view of codes in the literature. May observes that a code of technical proficiency provides a standard to which appeals can be made for peer discipline and he observes that ostracism in medicine, in the form of nonreferral to one believed an incompetent, "is probably the commonest and most effective form of discipline in (that) profession today."[3] And Davis and Aroskar note that "The requirements of the (ANA) Code may often exceed, but are not less than, those of the law. While violation of the law subjects the

nurse to criminal or civil liability, *the Association may reprimand, censure, suspend, or expel members from the Association for violation of the code.*"[4] (Italics added.)

There are thus at least three views of the Code extant in the literature: (i) the Code is intended to provide individual nurses with ethical guidance in their conduct; (ii) the Code is intended as suggesting general stances which nurses might wish to consider seriously on broad issues confronted by the profession; (iii) the Code expresses profession-wide standards that are to serve as the basis for peer discipline and quality assurance within the profession. In my role as a non-nurse observer and commentator on the profession, I want to consider each of these views and indicate what I take the arguments to be in support and in opposition of them. As one might suspect, it seems to me that each is partly right and partly wrong. I then want to offer a fourth view of the Code and the role that it can and should play. Finally, I will return to our hypothetical situation of the nurse confronted with an ethical knot and indicate how the Code might be best used to unravel it.

Earlier in this series, I criticized the view that codes provide a kind of ethical catalogue or recipe for the conduct of the professional and I am not alone in that rejection. First of all, simply by laying side by side the codes of different professions, one can easily observe that those codes commend different and sometimes conflicting courses of actions to members of different professions involved in a common case. Consider the question of confidentiality. The American Hospital Association's Patient's Bill of Rights, readily available to any patient hospitalized in an AHA-member institution, asserts that "the patient has the right to privacy concerning his own medical care program (and) to confidential communication and records."[5] A patient reading that (in 1979) might well have concluded that the facts about his case would be made known only to parties having a direct role in his treatment or care (or the accompanying record-keeping). Should the jumble of pamphlets on the lamp table of his lounge area have also contained a copy of the International Code of Medical Ethics (1949), this expectation would have been strongly reinforced. "A doctor shall preserve absolute secrecy on all he knows about his patient because of the confidence entrusted in him."[6] A small worry might have been raised in our patient if he had perused the ANA Code for Nurses (1976), reading that "the nurse safeguards the client's right to privacy by *judiciously* protecting information of a confidential nature"[7] (emphasis added) since it appears to leave the matter of disclosure somewhat up to the nurse's judgment. But he would have been reassured by the repeated emphasis in the interpretative statements on the nurse's responsibility to obtain consent for disclosure and to safeguard the information from others not involved in the patient's care. But, should our patient have then relaxed in the belief that his interests were unequivocally protected by every professional code involved, he might have been in for a rude shock. For the American Medical Association's 1957 Code qualified the physician's obligation not to breach confidence, not only when required to do so by law, but also when "it becomes necessary in order to protect the welfare of the individual or of the community."[8] What seemed clear grows murky; for just what comprised the welfare of the community (and indeed perhaps what counted as the community as well) was left up to the individual physician in cases where the law had not spoken.[9] Better read all the codes, John Q. Patient!

Nor do the problems with codes' ability to guide involved parties towards ethical conduct stem only from inter-code disparities; a given code may provide conflicting directives. The 1965 International Code of Nursing Ethics held that the nurse had a three-fold responsibility: "to conserve life, to alleviate suffering and to promote health."[10] Hunt and Arras[11] suggest that a nurse who must counsel the parents of a severely deformed newborn child may not be able to meet all

of these responsibilities. (Perhaps an awareness of the growing power of medicine to prolong the lives of such unfortunates without curing them prompted the revision of the International Code in 1973 to strike the clause concerning conservation of life and to add clauses enjoining prevention of illness and restoration of health.)[12] I have elsewhere[13] mentioned the conflict that may result from pursuing as a researcher the development of nursing's body of knowledge when the nature of a particular research problem dictates the use of either placebos or other forms of deception, or of standard double-blind techniques in which the subject is either ignorant of what is actually being done to him or is allowed to make a predictably wrong assumption. And one may well imagine conflicts between the nurse's obligation to provide services "unrestricted by considerations of . . . economic status" and the obligation to "participate in the profession's efforts to establish and maintain conditions of employment conducive to high quality nursing care",[14] which neither in itself nor in the Interpretive Statements explicitly excludes work slowdowns, stoppages and strikes under extreme conditions.

These problems of internal consistency of codes stem in part from a lack of explicit ordering principles—that is, instructions as to which principle to preserve in the face of a conflict—and in part from the inherent difficulty of formulating a set of rules both manageably finite and sufficiently encompassing to cover every torturous situation one may encounter. To be fair, it should be noted that some effort has gone towards providing that type of guidance in the ANA Interpretive Statements, as when a limit is imposed on a nurse's individual agreements with potential employers to providing practices and services which do not violate the Code. However, nothing even approaching a complete set of ordering principles is included in the Code.

Perhaps we can agree that the Code cannot stand alone as providing individual nurses with the guidance needed to ensure ethical conduct in their professional lives, in that it fails to be consistently applicable to all nursing situations and it fails to square with all the requirements of other professional codes with the same putative status as directives. Finally, there is the important point that a nurse may have other ethical commitments which conflict with those prescribed by the code. While "each client has the moral right to determine what will be done with his/her person",[15] "if a client requests information or counsel in an area that is . . . contrary to the nurse's personal beliefs, the nurse may refuse to provide these services but must advise the client of sources where such service is available."[16] This may leave a client high and dry in seeking a particular kind of legal service where the nurse who declines on the basis of a personal belief is that client's only realistic source of that service—thereby rendering that right of self-determination hollow. Nurses faced with this sort of dilemma find themselves torn between their rights as persons and their roles as representatives of the profession.

On the other hand, the view that the Code serves, rather than as a specific ethical guide, as a source of "suggestions of general stances" to be considered seriously (a sort of nurses' "Dutch uncle") seems rather insipid, inviting the amused inattention a Dutch uncle usually gets. Certainly the issues covered in the Code are ones which any nurse should consider and the stands endorsed there are worthy of serious attention. But the language of the Code is far stronger, indicating what the nurse does and must do in language that demands heeding, not merely consideration. The points at which the individual wishes or preferences of the nurse are properly to be exercised are specified explicitly and they would be so indicated rather misleadingly if the rest were also merely suggestive and ultimately up to the individual nurse. This is especially so if, as the third view holds, the Code serves as a basis for peer discipline. However, since we have argued that the Code is not sufficient as a basis for moral

behavior in every nursing situation, perhaps there is something to a view which says that one of the Code's proper functions is to suggest areas of particular concern and directions of a general sort as to the basic boundaries within which the specifics of one's decisions should fit to count as moral. There is no harm in the Code functioning to keep one morally mindful, if one also bears in mind that the Code may also be the basis for barring those who deviate from its prescriptions from future gainful employment as nurses!

This third view of the Code, that it serves as an instrument of peer regulation, fits in with the usual philosophical understanding of nursing as a profession. Jaggar[17] observes that a code of professional ethics, "like the test of professional competence, is designed by the profession itself and enforced by the use of in-group sanctions" and she counts a code as one of the defining characteristics of a profession (as a chief means for controlling continuing competence and fitness to practice). I find it interesting that codes in general are determined by those offering a particular type of service for compensation, rather than by those who pay for that service (or their representatives). Although no statement avows it explicitly, the practice of self-regulation through promulgation and enforcement of codes of ethics by members of the profession smells to the consumer of the familiar odor of paternalism. It is no surprise that the recent spectacle of a new Code of ethics for the AMA being drawn up by a panel of MD's without a single non-AMA member on it and passed at the annual convention was defended by the panel's chair, James Todd, on the grounds that nonphysicians (and presumably non-AMA physicians as well) "don't understand all the ramifications. It's like having the inmates run the institution."[18] (It's also interesting to note that the AMA physicians themselves may not have been fully understanding "all the ramifications" until now, for the new code incorporates substantial changes in acknowledging patient's rights, permitting advertising, and allows physician referrals to chiropractors—practices that were restricted and rights that were limited in the 1957 AMA Code.)

Thus, the practice of generating codes as self-regulating devices can be seen not only as conservative devices which uphold current standards embodying the best in a tradition's history, but also as devices for insulating a profession against unwanted incursions from affected parties or groups who may dissent with some of the historically or currently favored features and traditions of that profession. That this process does not wholly insulate a profession from outside influence can be seen by a political analysis of the recent changes in the AMA's Code, which reflects both the patients' rights movement, the approximate annual $1 million costs of lawsuits brought by chiropractors charging physicians with failure to provide them with referrals, and the 1979 Federal Trade Commission's ruling that the AMA's traditional ban on advertising was not in the consumer's interests because it restricted competition between physicians. Despite Todd's defense, this really doesn't look like a case of "Physician, heal thyself!"

In speculating on the causes of the rather dramatic recent changes in the AMA code and of similar changes throughout the history of various professional organizations, yet a fourth interpretation of the functions of the practice of issuing codes (particularly in a multi-professioned field such as medical and health care) occurs to me. Codes function much the same way as do platforms of political parties and candidates. Both codes and platforms serve to give the sense of common commitment in matters of principle which bind together members of the same group (profession or party) at a given point in time; they also record changes in those commitments as generations of the profession or party react to changes in other aspects of the culture with which they are involved. Viewed in this way, codes and platforms serve both as brakes on too rapid change and as records of fundamental reorienta-

tions of their groups in response to both changing powers and new demands which technology and its socialization thrust upon them.

Codes thus are to be seen, in addition to moral guides and reminders and devices for peer control, as cultural instruments of communication about what is commonly expected of the professional by peers, other professionals and consumers of their services alike. Insofar as such communication is essential to the very identity and integrity of a profession, codes are absolutely indispensible.

This communicative function is particularly well served by the ANA Code for Nurses together with its Interpretive Statements. One editor commends the Code for identifying the underlying values and beliefs, showing the breadth of the profession's social concerns, and identifying a commitment to accountability not only to professional peers but also to clients. In these respects the ANA Code is noteworthy for its "distinctiveness among codes of ethics",[19] particularly since it lacks much of the philanthropic condescension to be found in many medical codes, as noted by May.[20]

Thus, our hypothetical nurse has incompletely understood the functions of the Code of her or his profession. It should have been taken as a statement of the convenant which exists among nurses to protect and nourish the gift of knowledge and skill imparted by their teachers.

That convenant includes commitments not only to peer review of competence and its continued maintenance and to the correlative development and implementation in practice of the body of knowledge on which that practice rests; it also recognizes a commitment to organization and implementation of official mechanisms within institutions, agencies and the society at large that encourage the raising of concerns, such as troubled our nurse, without fear of reprisal. One does not protest effectively or very long armed only with a list of don'ts; one does see protest effect change when backed by the power of a professional organization. The Code thus serves as a convenant between the nurse and his/her profession, a promise of what the nurse may expect of the profession if she/he conforms to what the profession expects of the nurse.

Nursing has a fine document in the ANA Code with Interpretive Statements, a document which articulates a mature image of the professional nurse appropriate for our time. Let me suggest that the profession give attention to the question of how to make alive in the nurse's daily practice the sense of convenant which is embodied in its Code. That would be a step closer toward recapturing that image it projects for each nurse. Had that held for our hypothetical nurse, she would not still be left wondering, "Code, or no code?"

Footnotes

[1]American Nurses' Association, *Code for Nurses with Interpretive Statements* Kansas City, MO.: ANA, 1976 (Preamble). Quoted in 2, below.

[2]American Nurses' Association, *Ethics in Nursing: References and Resources* Kansas City, MO.: ANA 1979 (p. v.).

[3]William F. May, "Code, Covenant, Contract, or Philanthropy", *Hastings Center Report,* 5(6). 29–38 (December, 1975) (p. 37).

[4]Anne J. Davis and Mila A. Aroskar, *Ethical Dilemmas and Nursing Practice* New York: Appleton-Century-Crofts, 1978 (p. 14).

[5]American Hospital Association, *A Patient's Bill of Rights* Chicago: AHA, 1973.

[6]World Medical Association, "International Code of Medical Ethics", *World Medical Association Bulletin,* 1(3):109, 111 (October, 1949).

[7]ANA *Code, op. cit.,* Point 2.

[8]American Medical Association, "Principles of Medical Ethics," *JAMA,* 167:2 (June, 1958, Special Edition).

[9]The recently passed 1980 AMA Code is reported to have eliminated the clause enjoining protection of the community apart from legal restraints. See below, in 18.

[10]Quoted by Robert Hunt and John Arras, *Ethical Issues in Modern Medicine.* Palo Alto: Mayfield Publishing Company. 1977 (p. 7).

[11]*Ibid.*

[12]International Council of Nurses, "Code for Nurses (1973)," reprinted in Warren T. Reich, Editor-in-Chief, *Encyclopedia of Bioethics,* Vol. 4. New York: The Free Press, 1978. The ANA *Code for Nurses with Interpretive Statements* (1976), the AHA "A Patient's Bill of Rights" (1973), the AMA *Principles of Medical Ethics* (1957), and the WMA's International Code of Medical Ethics (1949), along with numerous other professional codes, oaths, declarations and guidelines, are all reprinted in an Appendix to this excellent source work.

[13]In Richard T. Hull, "Defining Nursing Ethics Apart from Medical Ethics," *Kansas Nurse,* 1(1):5, 8, 20–24 (p. 23).

[14]ANA Code, *op. cit.,* Points 1 and 9.

[15]*Ibid.,* Point 1.

[16]*Ibid.,* Point 1.4 in the Interpretive Statements.

[17]Alison Jaggar, "Philosophy as a Profession". *Metaphilosophy,* 6(1):100–116 (January, 1975) (p. 101).

[18]James Todd, quoted in Marjorie Sun, "AMA's New Ethics Code in Major Break from Past." *Science,* 209(4458):790–791 (August 15, 1980).

[19]*Encyclopedia of Bioethics,* Vol. 4, *op. cit.,* p. 1789.

[20]May, *op. cit.,* p. 31.

Models for Ethical Medicine in a Revolutionary Age

Robert M. Veatch

Robert M. Veatch, Ph.D., is professor of medical ethics at the Kennedy Institute of Ethics, Georgetown University. He also holds professorships in philosophy and in medicine. His training is in pharmacology and in ethics. He is the author of books in medical ethics, including Case Studies in Medical Ethics *(Harvard University Press, 1977) and* A Theory of Medical Ethics *(Basic Books, 1981).*

Veatch explores four ways in which value presuppositions are incorporated into the way in which doctor–patient relations are conceived or modeled. (1) In the Engineering Model, the patient has all the power and makes all the important decisions. (2) In the paternalistic Priestly Model, the doctor has all the power and makes all the important decisions. (3) In the Collegial Model, power is shared by the doctor and patient as social equals. (4) In the Contractual Model, preferred by Veatch, power is shared through contractual negotiation, which ideally does not violate the moral integrity of either physician or patient.

Most of the ethical problems in the practice of medicine come up in cases where the medical condition or desired procedure itself presents no moral problem. Most day-to-day patient contacts are just not cases which are ethically exotic. For the woman who spends five hours in the clinic waiting room with two screaming children waiting to be seen for the flu, the flu is not a special moral problem; her wait is. When medical students practice drawing bloods from clinic patients in the cardiac care unit—when teaching material is treated as material—the moral problem is not really related to the patient's heart in the way it might be in a more exotic heart transplant. Many more blood samples are drawn, however, than hearts transplanted. It is only by moving beyond the specific issues to more basic underlying ethical themes that the real ethical problems in medicine can be dealt with.

Most fundamental of the underlying themes of the new medical ethics is that health care must be a human right, no longer a privilege limited to those who can afford it. It has not always been that way, and, of course, is not anything near that in practice today. But the norm, the moral claim, is becoming increasingly recognized. Both of the twin revolutions have made their contribution to this change. Until this century health care could

From *The Hastings Center Report,* Vol. 2 (June 1972). Reprinted by permission of the author and publisher. © The Hastings Center, 360 Broadway, Hastings-on-Hudson, NY 10706.

be treated as a luxury, no matter how offensive this might be now. The amount of real healing that went on was minimal anyway. But now, with the biological revolution, health care really is essential to "life, liberty, and the pursuit of happiness." And health care is a right for everyone because of the social revolution which is really a revolution in our conception of justice. If the obscure phrase "all men are created equal" means anything in the medical context where biologically it is clear that they are not equal, it means that they are equal in the legitimacy of their moral claim. They must be treated equally in what is essential to their humanity: dignity, freedom, individuality. The sign in front of the prestigious, modern hospital, "Methadone patients use side door" is morally offensive even if it means nothing more than that the Methadone Unit is located near that door. It is strikingly similar to "Coloreds to the back of the bus." With this affirmation of the right to health care, what are the models of professional-lay relationships which permit this and other basic ethical themes to be conveyed?

1. THE ENGINEERING MODEL

One of the impacts of the biological revolution is to make the physician scientific. All too often he behaves like an applied scientist. The rhetoric of the scientific tradition in the modern world is that the scientist must be "pure." He must be factual, divorcing himself from all considerations of value. It has taken atomic bombs and Nazi medical research to let us see the foolishness and danger of such a stance. In the first place the scientist, and certainly the applied scientist, just cannot logically be value-free. Choices must be made daily—in research design, in significance levels of statistical tests, and in perception of the "significant" observations from an infinite perceptual field, and each of these choices requires a frame of values on which it is based. Even more so in an applied science like medicine choices based upon

what is "significant," what is "valuable," must be made constantly. The physician who thinks he can just present all the facts and let the patient make the choices is fooling himself even if it is morally sound and responsible to do this at all the critical points where decisive choices are to be made. Furthermore, even if the physician logically could eliminate all ethical and other value considerations from his decision-making and even if he could in practice conform to the impossible value-free ideal, it would be morally outrageous for him to do so. It would make him an engineer, a plumber making repairs, connecting tubes and flushing out clogged systems, with no questions asked. Even though I strongly favor abortion reform, I am deeply troubled by a physician who really believes abortion is murder *in the full sense* if he agrees to either perform one or refer to another physician. Hopefully no physician would do so when confronted with a request for technical advice about murdering a postnatal human.

2. THE PRIESTLY MODEL

In proper moral revulsion to the model which makes the physician into a plumber for whom his own ethical judgments are completely excluded, some move to the opposite extreme, making the physician a new priest. Establishment sociologist of medicine Robert N. Wilson describes the physician-patient relationship as religious. "The doctor's office or the hospital room, for example," he says, "have somewhat the aura of a sanctuary;" ". . . the patient must view his doctor in a manner far removed from the prosaic and the mundane."

The priestly model leads to what I call the "As-a syndrome." The symptoms are verbal, but the disease is moral. The chief diagnostic sign is the phrase "speaking-as a. . . ." In counseling a pregnant woman who has taken Thalidomide, a physician says, "The odds are against a normal baby and "speaking-as-a-physician that is a

risk you shouldn't take." One must ask what it is about medical training that lets this be said "as-a-physician" rather than as a friend or as a moral man or as a priest. The problem is one of generalization of expertise: transferring of expertise in the technical aspects of a subject to expertise in moral advice.

The main ethical principle which summarizes this priestly tradition is "Benefit and do no harm to the patient." Now attacking the principle of doing no harm to the patient is a bit like attacking fatherhood. (Motherhood has not dominated the profession in the Western tradition.) But Fatherhood has long been an alternative symbol for the priestly model; "Father" has traditionally been a personalistic metaphor for God and for the priest. Likewise, the classical medical sociology literature (the same literature using the religious images) always uses the parent-child image as an analogy for the physician-patient relationship. It is this paternalism in the realm of values which is represented in the moral slogan "benefit and do no harm to the patient." It takes the locus of decision-making away from the patient and places it in the hands of the professional. In doing so it destroys or at least minimizes the other moral themes essential to a more balanced ethical system. While a professional group may affirm this principle as adequate for a professional ethic, it is clear that society, more generally, has a much broader set of ethical norms. If the professional group is affirming one norm while society affirms another for the same circumstances, then the physician is placed in the uncomfortable position of having to decide whether his loyalty is to the norms of his professional group or to those of the broader society. What would this larger set of norms include?

a. Producing Good and Not Harm. Outside of the narrowest Kantian tradition, no one excludes the moral duty of producing good and avoiding harm entirely. Let this be said from the start. Some separate producing good and avoiding evil into two different principles placing greater moral weight on the latter, but this is also true within the tradition of professional medical ethics. The real difference is that in a set of ethical norms used more universally in the broader society producing good and avoiding harm is set in a much broader context and becomes just one of a much larger set of moral obligations.

b. Protecting Individual Freedom. Personal freedom is a fundamental value in society. It is essential to being truly human. Individual freedom for both physician and patient must be protected even if it looks like some harm is going to be done in the process. This is why legally competent patients are permitted by society to refuse blood transfusions or other types of medical care even when to the vast majority of us the price seems to be one of great harm. Authority about what constitutes harm and what constitutes good (as opposed to procedures required to obtain a particular predetermined good or harm) cannot be vested in any one particular group of individuals. To do so would be to make the error of generalizing expertise.

c. Preserving Individual Dignity. Equality of moral significance of all persons means that each is given fundamental dignity. Individual freedom of choice and control over one's own life and body contributes to that dignity. We might say that this more universal, societal ethic of freedom and dignity is one which moves beyond B. F. Skinner.

Many of the steps in the hospitalization, care, and maintenance of the patient, particularly seriously ill patients are currently an assault on that dignity. The emaciated, senile man connected to life by IV tubes, tracheotomy, and colostomy has difficulty retaining his sense of dignity. Small wonder that many prefer to return to their own homes to die. It is there on their own turf that they have a sense of power and dignity.

d. Truth-telling and Promise-keeping. As traditional as they sound, the ethical obligations of truth-telling and promise-keeping have retained their place in ethics because they are seen as essential to the quality of human relationships. It is

common form of this ethic. With the central point being that the individual's interests, to be legitimate, must so accord with those of other individuals as to maximize the general welfare; it is the general good that is to be served by individual choices and general policies. Where individual preferences do not conflict with the interests of others, acting under individualistic and under utilitarian ethics may not diverge. But where serving one individual's desires and wishes detracts from other's welfare, then this ethic dictates the subordination of the individual's interests and desires.

THREE MODELS OF THE PATIENT-PHYSICIAN RELATIONSHIP

Let us review three characterizations of the relationship between physician and patient that have appeared in recent medical ethics literature. These are not the only ones, but they are useful in further illustrating how those who have come to the topics of medical ethics presuppose one or another view of the nature of humanity and one or another concordant ethic. The three models we will examine are the Priestly model, the Contractual model, and the Collegial or Team model.

In the traditional religious view of humanity and its ethic, the obligations which humans have in relation to medical decision-making are few and uncomplicated. This does not mean that they may be clearly and without difficulty applied to every case in a manner which yields a clear-cut decision, but it does mean that the task of ethical assessment is simpler for the proponent of the traditional religious ethic, in that there is little or no involvement of considerations about future consequences. There is a somewhat comforting aura of finitude that surrounds the decision-making process in medicine, a sense that there are limits to what is expected of us; above given levels of wisdom and farsightedness we should not and

need not aspire. One frequently encounters among those of this persuasion the admonition that one ought not to "play God", or try to religislate morality in the light of increasing technical power.

Descriptions of the Priestly model vary according to the sympathies of the writer. One philosopher-physician, Howard Brody, writes: "In the 'Priestly Model' . . . the physician plays a role that is frankly paternalistic. The patient (who, we might say, has somehow 'sinned' by getting sick) comes for treatment, counsel, and comfort. The decision-making is placed in the physician's hands, and the patient who does not follow the doctor's orders is adding an even greater 'sin' on top of his illness . . . (A) chief sign of this model is the 'Speaking-as-a' syndrome: 'Speaking as your doctor, I feel that it is definitely time for you to undergo surgical sterilization.' The decision here is a moral, not a medical one; but the priest-doctor is presumed to have competence in both areas by virtue of his M.D. degree."[2] Clearly, this author doesn't have much patience with the priestly, paternalistic role into which doctors sometimes slip.

Insofar as the physician is relatively clear about the prescribed duties that are pertinent in a given case, insofar as the physician has the clearest understanding of the empirical possibilities and contingencies, and insofar as there is not a conflict among the relevant moral rules that do apply, the physician is probably in the best position of those involved to make a valid judgment about the course of action that is required ethically. If there appear to be conflicting rules involved in a particular case, or if that case doesn't clearly fall under any moral prescription known to the physician, his or her limited expertise as a kind of amateur theological ethicist may be insufficient to provide clear guidance. In this situation the physician, like the analog parish priest, would turn to the system of higher authorities which exist, in part, for the purpose of interpreting the moral law. But the search for higher authority is not likely to lead to the patient in this tradition.

There is another dimension to the patient-

physician relationship which is illuminated under the Priestly model. It is not uncommon that a patient's diseases or disorders are partially due to behavior which is in the patient's control. Insofar as the religious ethic contains such admonitions as "The body is the temple of the soul" and thereby enjoins humans toward circumspection and moderation in consumption of food and drugs, in sexual activity, in rest and exercise, one whose disease stems directly or indirectly from a failure to behave in accordance with these injunctions may well be seen as having sinned. For a physician who has the point of view that so characterizes the patient's disease, the analogy between his role and that of the priest may recommend itself irresistably. The patient, like the penitent sinner, suffers the pains of his wrongdoing and comes for a treatment which aims at rectifying his or her wrong as far as possible. The physician, like the priest, encounters the patient in a position of considerable potential to exert an influence that may alter the wrongdoer's ways. Even medical problems not traceable causally to the behavior of the patient are frequently viewed by patients as chastizing visitations inflicted in retribution for wrongdoing. While the analogy between physician and priest ultimately breaks down, when viewed under the scope of traditional religious ethics, it seems capable of illuminating why some feel most comfortable in the role of either patient or physician as characterized by the Priestly model.

The accompanying traditional view of the relationship of nurse to physician has been variously characterized as that of a handmaiden,[3] or a tool,[4] in the hands of the physician. The emphasis, of course, is on the nurse serving without questioning medical decisions; various reminders of this subordinate status have existed in such practices as nurses rising when physicians (and even medical students) enter the room.[5] The common sociological explanation points out that this phenomenon has as much to do with the fact that most nurses are female and most doctors have been male as it does with the fact that nurses are

not doctors. But this sociological fact receives additional explanation under the Priestly model, in that, being female, nurses are thus poor candidates for standing in a paternalistic role that appeals implicitly to a tradition in which religious authorities have been called "father" in recognition of their status as representatives of the divine masculine Personage. Finally, the metaphor involved in the very meaning of the term "nurse" (one who nurtures, as a mother), characterizes the relationship between nurse and patient beyond that involved in the notion of physician's handmaiden or tool.

A second model of the patient/physician relation described in recent literature is the Contractual model.[6] This model seeks to replace the one-sided decision-making of the paternalistic approach with a form that gives recognition to the fact that inner-directed, highly independent individuals respond better to therapeutic regimens in the choice and administration of which they have an active role.[7] The "contract" is usually an implicit understanding between the patient and the physician concerning their mutual obligations and benefits which calls for a sharing of the decision-making responsibility. Where there are significant, life-altering decisions to be made, the physician recognizes and respects the legitimacy of the patient's informed decision-making in regards to value-laden matters. Once the general goals are agreed to, the patient accedes to the physician's superiority in making the technical decisions needed to implement them. Thus, the patient does not need to be kept informed on all the technical details, but expects to be consulted on decisions involving major courses of action, even when alternatives differ significantly in the probability of the desired outcome. For example, this view would recognize the legitimacy of a patient's preference for medical or radiation treatment over that of amputation, even when the latter had the greatest chance of saving life.

An important reservation that the physician makes on the Contractual model is the right not to enter into the contract if the patient's wishes

would, if implemented by the physician, force the latter to violate his or her own moral values. Thus, a physician would not be obligated to respond positively to a patient's request for an abortion if providing one would run counter to deeply held convictions on the part of the physician; but a physician would be obligated to bow to a patient's wishes to increase the dosage of morphine for otherwise intractible pain, even if doing so increased the risk of a somewhat shortened lifespan. (There is some dispute among proponents of the Contractual view on whether a physician retains the right to withhold a standard medical service, such as abortion, on personal moral grounds if he or she represents the patient's only realistic alternative.)

The Contractual model appears to hold considerable attraction for nursing and its aspirations. First, it provides a recognition, in the principles of individualism, of the importance of providing nurses the same rights and respect captured for patients and physicians in the model. Extrapolating the model to nursing, we see that the nurse enters into a tacit agreement with both physicians and patients (or clients) in which the rights and obligations of each party are recognized and respected by the others. Nurses and physicians accept that patients have the right to determine the major objectives of medical intervention and nursing care; patients and nurses accord to physicians primary power to determine diagnoses and the details of treatment aiming at the general ends of the patient; and physicians and patients will accord to nurses primary authority in determining the details of nursing care. Second, just as physicians reserve the right not to provide even standard medical treatments to patients where providing those treatments would be morally repugnant, so the nurse would seem, on the Contractual model, to reserve the right to refuse to participate in actions that would violate strongly held personal values. Finally, insofar as the mutual agreement between all parties is to cover benefits as well as rights, nursing finds in the Contractual model and individualistic ethics a basis for negotiating improvements in compensation, working conditions and other areas of needed reform.

The final model to be considered here is one rather more closely coordinated with the image of humans as essentially social beings, whose specific obligations of a moral character arise out of a general duty to seek to maximize the welfare and happiness of the greatest number of individuals possible. As indicated earlier, the status of individual interests and desires is one of conditional legitimacy—the condition being that they not be pursued to the detriment of others. The Team model (which has been called the Collegial model by others[8]) suggests that the physician and patient, rather than seeing themselves in a relationship suggestive of bargaining and legalism, see themselves as colleagues, co-investigators pursuing the common goal of identifying and eliminating the illness and restoring the health of the patient. This is a relationship characterized by mutual trust and harmony, with an equality, if not coincidence, of value considerations. It aims at the utilitarian's maximization of welfare in its belief that, in general, individuals are better off in active, participating roles even as patients than when forced to suffer either the virtual total passivity of the patient in the Priestly model or the rather limited decision-making functions of the Contractual model. The possibilities of involving the patient as a colleague have recently been eloquently explored by Norman Cousins.[9] John Gunther[10] has also provided a moving account of how, in the special situation of parental colleagueship, the parents of a young cancer patient participated actively and constructively in the planning of his treatment. And Renee Fox[11] has recounted the active participation and contribution of patients in kidney research programs.

The potential of the Team model to transform nurse/physician relations has not received the kind of attention in the public press as has its power for the physician/patient relationship. But

it is evident that, among colleagues who accord to one another an equality of dignity and respect and who acknowledge shared responsibility and accountability for their actions, there is a greater likelihood of consensus as to mutual ends and means. This does not appeal necessarily to a consensus model of diagnostic or therapeutic decision-making, because each involved party can be accorded the right and responsibility to have primary input and final say over that portion of the case where his or her expertise is most relevant. At the same time, the mutuality of respect and the sense of common purpose which members of the team accord to one another creates an atmosphere in which the checks and balances of constructive criticism and review can operate in a wholesome and non-threatening way.

It may be that the circumstances and stage of the case will dictate that some one member of the team fulfill the role of captain, the one charged with generating the major decisions for that stage of the case. That captaincy, however, is not automatically determined by rank or title or degree, but rather by the character and stage of the case. The physician is only one member of the team, whose ascendancy comes at the points of diagnosis and interpretation, perhaps again at the point of treatment implementation. One of the chief functions of the physician, however, is to issue an accurate set of conditionals: "If you want to maximize your chances of surviving this throat cancer, then present statistics indicate you will do so only by a combination of surgery and radiation therapy; if it is more important to you to lead a relatively normal next few months than to maximize your chances of surviving five years, then radiation therapy alone is indicated", and so on. But the physician who diagnoses may be neither the one who operates nor the one who delivers radiation therapy. And in terms of planning daily postoperative care, the importance of any physician may be vanishingly small in contrast to that of the nurse, the physical therapist and the dietician. And the ultimate decision as between the conditionals offered by the physician may be made by the patient or by the patient's proxy, who thereby determines the points and times of the ascendancy of other members of the team to its captaincy. Rather than representing each of these individuals as entering into a contractual relationship that is characterized by potentially competing self-interests (as in the Contractual model), and rather than automatically deferring to the physician's authority, the Team model characterizes the mutual relationships as centering around a set of common values and goals adopted by the members of the team in consenting to participate in the joint venture.

LIMITATIONS AND RELATIVE MERITS OF THE THREE MODELS

There are several reasons why the Priestly model is the least satisfactory of the three. First, it presupposes a religious orientation that is not universal, even among believers. The system of specially appointed protectors of morality is not common to a sufficient portion of religions and religious sects to make that mode of behavior on the part of the physician comfortable for most patients. This is especially true when one is increasingly unlikely to have the same physician throughout one's life and thus unlikely to develop a sense of that individual being thoroughly knowledgeable and wise about one's needs and individual quirks. Second, the model runs counter to so many other movements and trends (e.g. the patients' rights movement) as to be something of an anachronism. Third, it is widely and increasingly perceived as derogatory and demeaning of the nurse, and even as promoting an unhealthy image of the doctor whose "status is a function of the vacuum created by the nurse's low self-esteem."[12] Certainly it is less than ideal as a model to be emulated by a profession working to improve its own image. Its major merit is to serve

as a reminder that there are patients who need a paternalistic approach, even to the point of believing that the physician is in total and complete charge.

The Contractual model, of course, will not work as well with that type of patient if he or she is forced into the position of actively processing information and deciding between alternative courses of therapy. However, it is possible to avoid this consequence by noting that it is certainly legitimate on the individualistic approach (although not very laudatory) for one to assign to a proxy (family member, friend, physician, nurse or whoever is willing to take it) the decision-making function. This is probably what goes on when a patient, confronted by a doctor who is carefully explaining the options, comes up with, "Whatever you say, Doctor." That is a patient who is attempting to contract with the physician to play according to the Priestly model's rules.

A deeper flaw of the Contractual model (stemming from its roots in individualism) is that it virtually capitulates to a kind of relativism of morals, in which each individual is his own source of morality and any one individual's ethic is as good as any other. The Contractual model does not impose any general goals for the negotiating parties; each is free to lay down his or her limits as to what services to offer or withhold on moral grounds and the patient is free to elect the least promising alternative on the basis of whim or even of a desire to end life. This model provides no incentive or even justification for the kind of counseling that can bolster a flagging spirit and transmit the resolve to seek the longer, more painful therapy which has the better chance of success. In short, the Contractual model is essentially amoral and can work well, but to the detriment of the patient. Nor is the health care professional immune to this sort of effect; provided that what the patient elects is not inherently offensive to the moral sensitivities of the physician or nurse, the latter have no basis in the model for refusing to cooperate or even for advising the patient that

they believe his choice to be ill advised. For to so object would presuppose some standard of value external to the patient's own choice-making and individualism denies that possibility.

While the Team model with the presupposition of a utilitarian ethic seems to have a remedy for many of these foregoing defects, it too is not without its problems. First and perhaps foremost, there are extraordinary interpersonal problems that can arise in seeking to implement the Team model among professionals who have been used to other approaches. Physicians seem notoriously inclined to regard the increased participation of the nurse as an usurpation of his responsibility and authority and the transfer of comprehensive functions as not a delegation but a surrender of them.[13] This potential for a sense of professional encroachment is increasingly familiar to nurses as they view the development and spread of Physician's Assistant programs, and it would seem that a precondition for the successful application of the Team model would be the successful negotiation of the division of labors and responsibilities by the prospective members of each team.[14] A second source of resistance to the team approach can be the individual nurse who may be unprepared by training and experience for the increased leadership roles, the increased responsibility and accountability that come from the shifting mantle of authority in team leadership and the increased participation of members of the team in decision-making functions. A third source of conflict in implementing the Team model is the fact that economic differences among team members may be greater than seem justified to individuals who have come to regard one another as colleagues and as increasingly equal in interprofessional status.[15] Finally, a major source of resistance may be encountered in the patient who is accustomed to conducting all negotiations through the physician. It is clear that the education and realignment of all members of the team will be a major task, and insofar as present structuring of medicine and health care delivery does not make for constancy

of association among relatively small groups, that education and retraining may well be ongoing.

The possibilities of opting effectively for the Team model seem at present rather limited, restricted to relatively small groups that are thrown into close and continual professional proximity. Where those conditions can be met, and there is successful negotiation of the many issues involving shared responsibility and accountability, it can be an enormously pleasant and rewarding form of professional interaction. The Contractual model perhaps offers the best general compromise for those who seek to avoid the Priestly model, in part because it can make provisions for at least some of the involved parties to behave towards others as described by the Priestly model, where tradition and personality type make that the most effective mode, without endorsing the general applicability of that kind of physician-centered structure. The Priestly model will continue (although perhaps with decreasing frequency) to be encountered by the nurse. The tensions between the three models are lived out by all nurses. It is hoped that this discussion will enable the nurse to recognize her situation(s) and better change them for her patient's and her own well-being.

Footnotes

[1] Charles Montagne, "Informed Consent and the Dying Patient," *Yale Law Journal* 83:1646 (July, 1974).

[2] Howard Brody, *Ethical Decisions in Medicine*. Boston: Little, Brown & Co., 1976 (p. 31).

[3] Cf. Larry Churchill, "Ethical Issues of a Profession in Transition," *American Journal of Nursing*, May, 1977 (p. 873).

[4] James Gustafson, "Mongolism, Parental Desires, and the Right to Life," *Perspectives in Biology and Medicine* 16:548 (Summer, 1973).

[5] Churchill, *op. cit.*

[6] Robert Veatch, "Models for Ethical Medicine in a Revolutionary Age," *Hastings Center Report* 2(3):5–7 (June, 1972).

[7] Rue L. Cromwell, Earl C. Butterfield, Frances M. Brayfield, & John J. Curry, *Acute Myocardial Infarction: Reaction and Recovery.* St. Louis: C. V. Mosby Co., 1977.

[8] Veatch, *op. cit.*; Brody, *op. cit.*

[9] Norman Cousins, "Anatomy of an Illness," *New England Journal of Medicine,* December 23, 1976.

[10] John Gunther, *Death Be Not Proud.* New York: Harper & Brothers, 1949.

[11] Renee C. Fox, *Experiment Perilous*. Glencoe: Free Press, 1959.

[12] Churchill, *op. cit.*

[13] Barbara Bates, "Doctor and Nurse: Changing Roles and Relations," *New England Journal of Medicine,* 283(3):129 (July 16, 1970).

[14] Shirley Smoyak, "Problems in Interprofessional Relations," *Bulletin of the New York Academy of Medicine,* 53:51–9 (1977).

[15] Veatch, *op. cit.*

Integrity in Interprofessional Relationships*

Christine Mitchell

Christine Mitchell, R.N., M.S., M.T.S., is the ethics consultant at Boston Children's Hospital and a member of the Department of Nursing, Staff Development, and Research. She received her training in nursing at Boston University and in ethics at Harvard University. Ms. Mitchell served as Vice-Chair of the American Hospital Association Special Committee on Biomedical Ethics. She is a member of the American Nurses' Association Committee on Ethics and is associate producer and narrator of the documentary film Code Gray: Ethical Dilemmas in Nursing.

Mitchell analyzes the concept of "integrity" and finds it to include elements of truthfulness, fairness, pureness, fittingness, and wholeness. She applies these to moral conflicts faced by nurses in a number of case studies. She finds that conflicts between obligations to physicians and to patients often compromise nursing integrity.

The concept of integrity is of particular importance to health professionals because it lays bare moral tensions inherent in health care which are not immediately obvious in the usual debates involving such concepts as justice, rights, utility, or the quality of life. These concepts are applied most often in an effort to discern the duties and moral obligations owed to others by health professionals. The strain and conflict which these duties cause health care workers, however, has largely gone unconsidered. Integrity, on the other hand, directs attention to the moral agency of the health professional.

Integrity is a fundamental moral concept because it intimately involves the concept of self as well as the self in relation to others. We speak of an individual, such as a nurse or physician, as having integrity and thereby express a judgment of character. We may also speak of a collective or group, such as a health care team, as having integrity, and thereby make an important observation about its unity as a community. An analysis of integrity in health care will bring to the surface moral tensions which health care workers experience in themselves, in relationships with other health professionals, and in relationships with health care institutions, which are not fully revealed in sociological and psychological analyses or even in standard medical ethical analysis. Attention to integrity, therefore, serves as a reminder that ethical conduct is linked ineluctably to the formation of moral character and community in health care as elsewhere.

It seems appropriate to begin with a brief discussion of the common usages of the word *integrity* and a categorization of the main meanings employed in ethics. This categorization will then

be applied to health care, in particular to bring to the fore the moral conflicts faced by nurses. Nurses will be the main concern because their position in the social structure of health care and the role relationships open to them are paradigmatic for non-physician health professionals. The conflicts they experience will be illustrated by a case discussion which will permit analysis of the competing and incompatible conceptions of health care which contribute to nurses' compromised integrity. . . .

I

Integrity is derived from the Latin *integritas,* meaning unimpaired condition, soundness, health, honesty, uprightness. Several different usages of the word "integrity" are evident in English language usage and literature: moral integrity, physical integrity, structural integrity, aesthetic integrity, professional integrity, and psychological integrity.[1] Of these usages, moral integrity is more germane in the context of this essay, though the other aspects of integrity are clearly related. At least five aspects of the meaning of moral integrity can be distinguished on the basis of usage in the ethics literature: truthfulness, fairness, pureness, fittingness, and wholeness.

First, integrity etymologically means *truthfulness* or honesty. Having integrity in this sense means that an individual is truthful on two levels—with others and with himself. On one level, an individual with integrity is described as one who does not lie or deceive others, but speaks instead with sincerity ([9], p. 191). For example, we speak of the integrity of businessmen when seeking to establish that they are honest and that their claims are truthful ([8], p. 114; [11], p. 210). On another level, integrity applies to individu-

als—in the sense that persons who are not honest with themselves do not have integrity ([3], p. 25n). Benefactors who are blindly convinced of their own virtuous goodness, but who are actually motivated by selfish considerations which they are unable to acknowledge to themselves, are said to lack integrity. Thus, both individuals who deceive others and self-deceptive individuals can be said to lack integrity in this sense.

Second, integrity as *fairness* refers to being unprejudiced, unbiased and impartial. Integrity in this sense is employed normatively as an ethical standard regarding obligations to treat others fairly. Furthermore, it has a self-transcendent quality in that it requires the overcoming of selfishness and partiality. Integrity as fairness means being upright, acting with probity, and strictly adhering to the moral demands of justice. It is in this sense that we speak of the integrity of a judge who regards all equally and, without favoritism, gives each individual a fair hearing.

Third, integrity as *pureness*[2] refers to being uncorrupted, undefiled, without impurities or foreign admixture. In this sense we may think of integrity as analogous to pure water wherein every drop is as consistent and as unpolluted as another. Every belief and action of an individual with integrity reflects a consistent and uncorrupted spirit. When we speak of a politician's integrity being corrupted by a bribe or the integrity of a leader being corrupted by a lust for power, we have perceived that their vows to serve the people were polluted by selfish motives. On the other hand, persons of moral integrity are consistent. They do not say one thing and do another; they do not behave in a certain manner one time and in a diametrically opposed fashion another time.

The fourth aspect of the moral meaning of integrity is *fittingness,* which emphasizes the formal requirement of interdependence and harmony among the integral parts of a unit. Integrity as fittingness is often invoked in remarks about the integrity of a person's life, where convictions, commitments, and projects all fit coherently together across the life span ([10]; [19], pp. 108–

118). We may also speak similarly of the integrity of a system, such as the judicial system with its laws, courts, and prisons, in which all of the parts fit harmoniously within the whole, thereby contributing to the unity of the system.

The fifth and most common meaning is integrity as *wholeness.* Here integrity refers to solidarity and completeness: solid in the sense of undivided, and complete in the sense of lacking nothing essential ([14], p. 26). On a personal level, one who is divided within himself cannot act with integrity. Similarly, on an interpersonal level, a group which is divided within itself, or which lacks essential elements, cannot function with integrity. There is an inherent threat to integrity in any system or chain of command with a weak link which can be pulled and pushed, drawn this way and that until it snaps, drops out, and leaves a gap, thus disabling the whole.

The foregoing discussion makes it clear that moral integrity involves a richness of meaning. Perhaps the most important feature of the concept of integrity is that it refers simultaneously to the self in terms of character and the self in relation to others as a group or community. At the simplest level, the individual with integrity is thought to cultivate an honest consciousness; to control tendencies toward unfair partiality; to develop an internally consistent and uncorrupted set of beliefs; to nurture dimensions of the self which fit together and which are fitting for a particular time, place, and profession; and finally, to manifest a wholeness and solidarity of self which signifies individuality. It is in action and in interaction, however, that individuals express their selves. Thus, in relation to others, the individual with integrity acts honestly and fairly, behaves with consistency through time, and fulfills an essential function in interdependent interaction with the parts of the whole. Finally, a group or institution may manifest an integrity which, though primarily formal, also has moral overtones. Thus the health care system may be said to have integrity if it represents itself truthfully, treats its own and others fairly, is uncorrupted and

acts with consistency, exhibits a fittingness among the component parts, and expresses a wholeness wherein all essential elements contribute to the complete system.

An examination of health care reveals that integrity is compromised at each of these levels. The individual nurse is severely handicapped in acting with integrity. Nurses' interprofessional relationships with physicians come into direct conflict with their relationships with patients. Consequently, the integrity of the whole health care system is threatened.

II

It is one thing to speak of the meaning of an ethical concept and ideal and quite another to face the concrete and the real. In order to reveal the moral strains within the health care community, a case illustrating the problem of integrity facing nurses will be used. At the outset, however, several caveats are in order. Situations, issues, and problems are rarely only moral in nature. Rather, in addition to moral considerations, a complex intermingling of psychosocial, professional, and historical factors are usually involved. This point will be evident in the analysis of the following case. Although the case could be discussed in terms of patients' rights, informed consent, quality of life, or autonomy (patient and/or professional), remarks have been restricted to those relevant to the concept of integrity. To this end, some of the case information not crucial to a discussion of integrity has been omitted.

While this case highlights the plight of the nurse, it is obvious that nurses are not the only health professionals who experience and are affected by moral conflicts involving integrity. Psychologists, various kinds of therapists, chaplains, social workers, and physicians—as well as moral agents not involved in health care—face questions of integrity. For purposes of this essay, however, only the moral predicament of the nurse will be considered. Other considerations will be sub-

ordinated to an analysis of the conflicts contributing to the nurse's compromised integrity. Although this case may tend to elicit sympathy for the nurse's position, it is the nurse's position, not the sympathy, which is significant. Regardless of any agreement or disagreement with the moral judgments made in the case, it should be evident that the nurse faces a problem of integrity partly as a result of her position in health care. Hence the crucial question becomes: How important is the nurse's integrity in health care?

* * *

Sharon Andrews was the primary nurse for two severely neurologically damaged young men— Joe and Bill. Both patients had been involved in automobile accidents and were brought to the acute care ward of the neurological unit in a large teaching hospital. Twenty-one-year-old Joe had been driving while intoxicated and had crashed into a tree. He sustained multiple lacerations and a spinal cord compression at the sixth cervical vertebra which was unrelieved by attempted surgical decompression. He was completely paralyzed except for gross motor movement of his arms and head. Although he could not speak because he was on a respirator, he was fully alert until shortly before his death.

Doctor Samuels, a neurosurgeon attending the case, instructed Nurse Andrews that Joe was not to be coded, meaning that in the event of an emergency, which was likely to occur in the unstable course of Joe's condition, no resuscitation efforts were to be made to save Joe's life. When Nurse Andrews questioned the order, the neurosurgeon said, "I don't code my quads." ("Quads" is shortened medical vernacular for quadriplegics—those who are paralyzed from approximately the neck down and are thus unable to make voluntary movements of their four extremities.) Nurse Andrews was unable to convince the physician to change this order, which he later entered in Joe's record.

The other patient was Bill, an eighteen-year-old, who had stormed out of the house following

a family argument, driven away in the car, and lost control of the automobile on a corner not far from his home. As a result of the accident, he sustained severe head and spinal cord injuries which had left him in a coma. Bill was completely flaccid, with fixed and dilated pupils, and unresponsive to all language and touch except some painful stimuli. He did not, however, have a flat electroencephalogram, which is often used as a criterion for brain death. Bill's physician did not order "no code" and Bill was resuscitated several times before the final failure to restore and sustain his heartbeat.

A comparison of the physician's and the nurse's writing on Joe's case is telling. Nurse Andrews charted the usual technical data regarding vital signs, intravenous infusions, respirator, settings, and so forth. She also wrote: "Patient extremely agitated and upset. Makes frequent attempts to attract attention. Flails arms frequently. When given pen, and a pad of paper held by the nurse, writes 'my mouth hurts.'" Doctor Samuels wrote: "NS" (meaning "normal sinus," the usual rhythm of the heart) "Awake. Intubated" (meaning that Joe was attached to a respirator to assist breathing). Three days later the nurse noted, "Is able to communicate needs by drawing letters in the air with his hand." The physician wrote, "Quadriplegic as before. No code." He wrote new orders for respiratory care designed to progressively wean Joe from the respirator. If successful, the respirator would not be reinstituted during a respiratory crisis under the no-code order. The nurse indicated that Joe did not want to be left alone. She stated that during times when he was off the respirator he flailed his arms, wildly mouthing, "Help me". The physician ordered morphine sulfate to be administered as necessary for restlessness.

In discussing this case several months after Joe's death, Nurse Andrews clearly recalled Joe's pride in those first simple words which he wrote and the nurses recognized. She said, "The letters were shaky but they were easily made out by the staff. Joe did seem rather proud of himself for that

accomplishment." And she vividly remembered his look of terror during periods of asystole when his heart would temporarily stop beating. Clearly he knew something was wrong and nothing was being done about it. Nurse Andrews told what it was like on the evening he died:

> I stayed with him until his heart finally stopped for good. He had been pretty much alert until the day before he died. He knew he was getting worse and seemed scared. His family was in and out. They knew he was going, and I guess they found it hard to stay and watch. I tried to talk to him that night, but you know how hard it is to talk to patients who don't respond at all. I don't know if he could hear me or not. After awhile I just took care of him and held his hand. I remember I kept thinking, "Joe, we could have saved your life." I think he really wanted to live. I know Doctor Samuels thinks no one would want to live that kind of life, and three-quarters of the staff felt that Joe's death was better than his being alive as a quadraplegic. Still, he tried hard to exercise and always cooperated with the cough and deep breathing routine after we told him how important it was. He didn't want to die. He fought all the medications we used to sedate him, trying to stay alert, as if fighting for his life. After awhile I don't think he trusted any of us, and you can't blame him. It's no wonder he was terrified. The funny thing is, my other patient during that time was a quad too, much worse than Joe. But he was Doctor Rossi's patient, and we coded him quite a few times. I remember, that night, looking over at Bill while I was standing at Joe's bed. And I asked myself, "Why do we keep saving his life, and we let you die?"

* * *

Nurse Andrews was morally troubled. Her integrity was compromised. This claim may be examined in the light of the meanings of integrity—integrity as truthfulness, fairness, pureness, fittingness, and wholeness.

First, the nurse was not completely truthful toward Joe. She may indeed have been hopeful in encouraging Joe to exercise and to write, to understand and to participate in the world around him. Nevertheless, it could not have been easy (if even possible) to be genuinely sincere in offering

such encouragement when she knew that she would withhold the crucial action of saving his life. Nurse Andrews, therefore, was guarded. Although integrity might require spontaneity and candor, and while she might have wished she could simply say to Joe, "Look, your doctor has written an order that means we will not try to save your life in an emergency," she was simply not that truthful. In their interactions, she was not spontaneous, but guarded, in order to prevent Joe from asking unsettling questions (such as "Am I going to die?" or "Can I depend on you to help me?"), which she felt constrained from answering fully and which would force her to face the fact that she was not completely truthful with him.

Some would say that Nurse Andrews should simply have told Joe the truth—the whole truth. After all, it is a patient's right to know the full nature and extent of his illness and the prospects afforded by health care. But is it the nurse's right to inform the patient? A tradition of respect for and deference to the physician-patient relationship, bolstered by legal rulings and institutional norms which support the primacy of that relationship, leaves the nurse who does not follow orders—particularly in a moral matter where patient and professional competency are in question—vulnerable to legal action at the worst and to severe censure from medical colleagues at the least.

Many health care professionals, including most nurses and physicians, would say: "Of course, the nurse can be honest." If Joe had asked her if he was going to die, these professionals might argue that she should have said everyone dies sooner or later; that Joe would probably die sooner than others his age because he was so seriously ill and injured; and that neither nurses nor physicians can know exactly how soon anyone will die. Nurse Andrews should have suggested, they would say, that Joe talk with his physician about this matter. Such an answer, however, is itself guarded and guileful. In fact, it is outrightly evasive and deceptive. The message is clear: "This topic is highly sensitive; don't ask me." Joe could not depend on the nurse to face the topic in a forthright manner—even though as his nurse she probably knew him better than did any other member of the health care community. Had she made such a response, the nurse would have implied that there was nothing untoward in Joe's case. She would have concealed from him the information he needed in order to ask the right questions. Joe probably did not know what a "code" is. He might not have known that every patient does not routinely receive the most extensive efforts of all health care personnel to save his life. Because the nurse could not behave and speak truthfully, she cannot be said to have acted with integrity. Paradoxically, she is kept from acting truthfully by the requirements to support the physician-patient relationship and to perform her role according to physician's orders.

It is clear that these two patients did not receive equal treatment, that the same efforts were not made to save their lives or to let them die. The nurse who participated in the resuscitation efforts for Bill and did not respond to the asystolic episodes of Joe was not nursing them both impartially. She lacked integrity in the sense of fairness. It is difficult not to be partial to the patient with a demonstrated desire to live and improve. Nurse Andrews probably wanted to help Joe, who clearly acted as if he wanted to be helped, to live, and to get better. Recognizing her moral and professional obligation to treat all patients fairly and impartially, she also sought to give Bill equally good nursing care. In the instance of nursing care to be provided during a life crisis (such as when the heart develops an irregular rhythm or stops), however, Nurse Andrews had been ordered to give nursing care to Bill and not to give nursing care to Joe.[3] Thus Bill's nursing care involved a partiality on the side of life and Joe's nursing care involved a partiality on the side of death. Furthermore, the ordered partiality was out of line with the felt partiality. Nurse Andrews violated her own sense of fairness in giving nursing care in this manner, and thereby compromised her integrity.

These events also illustrate the meaning of integrity as pureness. The nurse's position cannot

be maintained without some sort of moral schizophrenia. It might be helpful here to indicate what regularly occurs over a period of time in a nurse's professional and moral experience. Like other moral beings, the nurse has a strongly felt need to maintain coherence between what she thinks should be done and what she is doing. She must act in situations, though, in which several different physicians decide what should be done with different patients. For example, if Doctor Smith writes orders for vigorous medical management of a living fetus from an abortion which was performed too late, the nurse is expected to share underlying values, such as a belief in the "sanctity of life". Yet when Doctor Jones decides to provide minimal medical intervention for another brain-damaged and deformed infant, the nurse, in turn, must find a belief that fits the situation, perhaps a belief regarding "quality of life". She is rarely able to maintain a single set of values in her work. Different, oftentimes conflicting beliefs are needed and are collected over a period of time in the attempt to salvage some sense of integrity while caring for patients, cooperating with physicians, and functioning within the system. Thus, an incompatible mixture of beliefs becomes an essential component of the strategy to maintain at least a minimal coherence between beliefs and acts in specific instances. Along the way, however, the nurse abandons consistency across time and so sacrifices integrity as pureness.

The moral crisis involving integrity is thus best illustrated when the nurse has two similar patients at the same time whom she is expected to care for differently. As the cases are proximate and concurrent temporally, an error in moral reasoning painfully emerges. Nurse Andrews may have attempted to achieve coherence in one case by believing in the lifesaving goal for Bill and acting to give him assiduous nursing care. Similarly, she may have tried to believe in the rightness of Joe's "no code" status (as apparently three-quarters of the staff did), and to enact that belief by not taking the usual emergency measures to stimulate his heart. The inconsistency between the two beliefs and between the two actions is especially blatant when not separated by time. In this situation, the nurse is handicapped in determining how to act morally because she lacks integrity as pureness. She has a history of choosing coherence between beliefs and actions in each case sequentially, and relinquishing consistency among beliefs and actions across cases and time. Thus she cannot rally all the forces of herself scattered among incompatible beliefs and actions, and bring her integral self to bear with precision and strength upon the present moral problem caused by the orders to give different care to similar patients.

This point suggests that the nurse's integrity is compromised in the aspect of fittingness as well. Not only do her beliefs and actions not fit together coherently, but her practice does not demonstrate fittingness with her profession as a nurse—one who seeks to comfort the suffering, care for the sick, and safeguard the rights of the afflicted.[4] Moreover, attempts to diminish the inner conflict by bringing it into the open are likely to meet with recrimination, alienating the nurse from her medical colleagues, and threatening the unity and harmonious functioning of the health care community.

The nurse, then, is left divided within herself and troubled by the threat to community solidarity which would occur if she were to resolve her conflict by maintaining consistent beliefs and actions across time. The problem of integrity as wholeness deeply touches the nurse's sense of self and also involves interprofessional relations within the health care community. For example, Nurse Andrews might have sought to avoid inner conflict and maintain individual integrity by trying to change one of the orders, by finding a new belief to morally justify her different actions, by refusing to follow orders she believed to be morally wrong, or by removing herself from the situation.

The specific complexities of these alternatives are worth noting. Nurse Andrews was unable to convince Joe's physician to change the no-code order. Although she apparently complained to other physicians, they were unwilling to insert themselves, uninvited, into another physician's

(1) First of all, confidentiality in professional–client relations is desirable because it affirms and protects the more fundamental value of *privacy*. The scope of this concept extends to information about the individual which he or she regards as too personal or intimate to be disclosed to others. One of the brute but inescapable facts about human nature that we all recognize is that there are some things about ourselves, both physical and psychological, that we do not want to be revealed to others, things which are really not anyone else's business.

To identify these highly personal and private facts, we must know what kinds of information persons in general typically wish not to be disclosed to others, and we must also know the individual preferences of the person at hand. Exactly what facts about ourselves enjoy the status of private facts may vary from person to person, but we all have them. Many of them are common in the sense that all of us usually wish to safeguard the same sorts of information about ourselves. These personal facts about ourselves may be physical facts about our bodily structure, function, and condition, or mental facts about our beliefs, thoughts, feelings, attitudes, and disposition, or behavioral facts about our habits and activities. Such facts lie at the core of our identity as distinctive individuals; and in cherishing and protecting them, we may be either positively evaluating our own well-being and unique individuality or protecting ourselves from certain harms which would befall us if others knew things about us that were none of their damned business. Some of these private facts about ourselves are so secret that we will never relate them to anyone. Some of these facts we will relate to a close circle of acquaintances, including those professionals, such as doctors, nurses, lawyers, and psychiatrists, who can serve us well only if they know us well. Still others we will relate to an even wider circle of acquaintances, and there are many facts about ourselves which we will relate to anyone who wants to know and which do not fall within the realm of privacy at all. A professional commitment to confidentiality is an acknowledgment that we all have a fundamental human interest in privacy and a desire that the behavioral standards of those professionals who serve us should recognize and protect this interest.

Closely related to the positive value of privacy itself are certain disvalues which usually are generated when privacy is violated. A commitment to confidentiality in the professions must be justified in part by a concern for protecting clients against the ensuing harms of embarrassment, shame, guilt, hurt, and general unhappiness which typically follow upon violations of privacy.

(2) Confidentiality in professional–client relationships is desirable also because it affirms and protects the *social status* of the client. Although we profess to be a highly egalitarian society in which all persons enjoy equal social standing, opportunity, and respect, the disappointing reality is that many classes of persons are not allowed to enter as social equals into a variety of social transactions. Blacks and other racial minorities, women and other relatively powerless groups, homosexuals, communists, and other social outcasts, the retarded, deranged, and other handicapped persons are all often assigned an inferior social status. Consequently, they are denied the opportunities, respects, powers, and social standing that others enjoy. Furthermore, many of the conditions for which persons seek professional help are stigmatizing conditions which if publicized to others can rob clients of their social standing and spoil their social identity. To be "in trouble with the law" and seek the professional assistance of an attorney can be greatly disadvantageous socially. To suffer sufficiently from depression, anxiety, obsession, phobia, or other mental disorders to require the professional help of a doctor, psychiatrist, psychologist, minister, or other counselor is to be stigmatized, often irrevocably for life, no matter how much things have improved in the interim. Look at what happened

to Senator Thomas Eagleton, who was George McGovern's first choice for a vice-presidential running mate, when news leaked out that he had previously been treated for depression. Physical conditions may also be socially stigmatizing. If our doctors make it readily known that we suffer from AIDS or sexual herpes virus, we are no longer allowed to enter as equals into certain desirable social transactions! Cancer patients are often shunned by their fellow workers once their condition has been disclosed. Reputations may be damaged in an incredible variety of ways by the professionals who serve us unless they are pledged to confidence. What would happen to the way others view and treat us if our veterinarian broadcasts the fact that we are consistently cruel to our pets or that we are zoophiliacs who engage repeatedly in sexual activities with them? What would happen to our social standing if librarians freely publicized to others the kinds of books and magazines we read? Many professionals have the power to do us social harm if they readily disclose to others the intimate details of our lives, and we require professional confidentiality from them in order to protect our social status.

(3) Confidentiality in professional–client relations is desirable also because it is *economically advantageous* to the client. Medically stigmatized persons often find it extremely difficult to find adequate housing and to obtain and retain jobs. Cancer patients often face serious economic stigmatization after their medical problems have been disclosed. They may be fired, denied promotions, forced into early retirement, and either denied or forced to give up their group health insurance. Usually the loss of jobs is totally unjustifiable, though in rare situations, such as that of the bus driver or pilot with a grave heart condition, it may be quite proper. Professional confidentiality with respect to the details of client activities can often be extremely profitable for the client in a variety of other ways as well, not all of which are legal. The *Model Code of Professional Responsibility* of the American Bar Association requires absolute

confidentiality with respect to the *past* crimes of the client, but it also requires disclosure of the intention of the client to commit a *future* crime if the attorney knows beyond a reasonable doubt that a future crime will be committed.[1] Where does this leave the lawyer who learns of *ongoing* financial fraud which can be very advantageous economically to the client and very disadvantageous to the defrauded? Here permitted disclosure about present and future crimes will inevitably involve forbidden disclosure of past crimes! At its February 1983 meeting in New Orleans, members of the ABA considered revising their rules to allow disclosure of confidences when attorneys reasonably believe that their clients are engaged in fraudulent activities which would result in substantial injury to the financial interests of another, but the proposed revision was overwhelmingly rejected. The legal profession apparently believes that professional confidentiality that is economically advantageous to the client is of sufficient importance that it should be honored even when fraud is involved. We may or may not agree with this position, and a thorough treatment of the topic of exceptions to rules of confidentiality would have to consider this issue more carefully. It is at least possible that confidentiality which is economically advantageous to the client is sometimes justifiable and sometimes not. If we were ranking our justifications for confidentiality, we might want to rank this one somewhat lower than some of the others. We might also find, however, that the six other justifications for confidentiality would be sufficient even in the absence of economic advantage.

The situation of the veterinary profession with respect to economic advantage should be contrasted with that of the legal profession. The veterinarian's professional commitment to confidentiality is purely a moral commitment which has no legal recognition and is not supported by legal sanctions.[2] Suppose that a veterinarian has treated a valuable animal that is for sale to or has been sold to a new owner and refuses to turn over

of *Fargo v. United States* (1967) comes closer to the issue. The Veterans Administration arranged for the patient to work on a local farm, but did not inform the farmer of the man's background. The farmer consequently permitted the patient to come and go freely during nonworking hours; the patient borrowed a car, drove to his wife's residence and killed her. Notwithstanding the lack of any "special relationship" between the Veterans Administration and the wife, the court found the Veterans Administration liable for the wrongful death of the wife.

In their summary of the relevant rulings Fleming and Maximov conclude that the "case law should dispel any notion that to impose on the therapists a duty to take precautions for the safety of persons threatened by a patient, where due care so requires, is in any way opposed to contemporary ground rules on the duty relationship. On the contrary, there now seems to be sufficient authority to support the conclusion that by entering into a doctor-patient relationship the therapist becomes sufficiently involved to assume some responsibility for the safety, not only of the patient himself, but also of any third person whom the doctor knows to be threatened by the patient." [Fleming & Maximov, *The Patient or His Victim: The Therapist's Dilemma* (1974) 62 Cal. L. Rev. 1025, 1030.]

Defendants contend, however, that imposition of a duty to exercise reasonable care to protect third persons is unworkable because therapists cannot accurately predict whether or not a patient will resort to violence. In support of this argument amicus representing the American Psychiatric Association and other professional societies cites numerous articles which indicate that therapists, in the present state of the art, are unable reliably to predict violent acts; their forecasts, amicus claims, tend consistently to overpredict violence, and indeed are more often wrong than right. Since predictions of violence are often erroneous, amicus concludes, the courts should not render rulings that predicate the liability of therapists upon the validity of such predictions.

The role of the psychiatrist, who is indeed a practitioner of medicine, and that of the psychologist who performs an allied function, are like that of the physician who must conform to the standards of the profession and who must often make diagnoses and predictions based upon such evaluations. Thus the judgment of the therapist in diagnosing emotional disorders and in predicting whether a patient presents a serious danger of violence is comparable to the judgment which doctors and professionals must regularly render under accepted rules of responsibility.

We recognize the difficulty that a therapist encounters in attempting to forecast whether a patient presents a serious danger of violence. Obviously we do not require that the therapist, in making the determination, render a perfect performance; the therapist need only exercise "that reasonable degree of skill, knowledge, and care ordinarily possessed and exercised by members of [that professional specialty] under similar circumstances." Within the broad range of reasonable practice and treatment in which professional opinion and judgment may differ, the therapist is free to exercise his or her own best judgment without liability; proof, aided by hindsight, that he or she judged wrongly is insufficient to establish negligence.

In the instant case, however, the pleadings do not raise any question as to failure of defendant therapists to predict that Poddar presented a serious danger of violence. On the contrary, the present complaints allege that defendant therapists did in fact predict that Poddar would kill, but were negligent in failing to warn.

Amicus contends, however, that even when a therapist does in fact predict that a patient poses a serious danger of violence to others, the therapist should be absolved of any responsibility for failing to act to protect the potential victim. In our view, however, once a therapist does in fact determine, or under applicable professional standards reasonably should have determined, that a patient poses a serious danger of violence to others, he bears a duty to exercise reasonable care to protect

the foreseeable victim of that danger. While the discharge of this duty of due care will necessarily vary with the facts of each case, in each instance the adequacy of the therapist's conduct must be measured against the traditional negligence standard of the rendition of reasonable care under the circumstances. As explained in Fleming and Maximov, *The Patient or His Victim: The Therapist's Dilemma* (1974), ". . . the ultimate question of resolving the tension between the conflicting interests of patient and potential victim is one of social policy, not professional expertise. . . . In sum, the therapist owes a legal duty not only to his patient, but also to his patient's would-be victim and is subject in both respects to scrutiny by judge and jury" . . .

The risk that unnecessary warnings may be given is a reasonable price to pay for the lives of possible victims that may be saved. We would hesitate to hold that the therapist who is aware that his patient expects to attempt to assassinate the President of the United States would not be obligated to warn the authorities because the therapist cannot predict with accuracy that his patient will commit the crime.

Defendants further argue that free and open communication is essential to psychotherapy; that "unless a patient . . . is assured that . . . information [revealed by him] can and will be held in utmost confidence, he will be reluctant to make the full disclosure upon which diagnosis and treatment . . . depends." The giving of a warning, defendants contend, constitutes a breach of trust which entails the revelation of confidential communications.

We recognize the public interest in supporting effective treatment of mental illness and in protecting the rights of patients to privacy and the consequent public importance of safeguarding the confidential character of psychotherapeutic communication. Against this interest, however, we must weigh the public interest in safety from violent assault. The Legislature has undertaken the difficult task of balancing the countervailing concerns. In Evidence Code section 1014, it established a broad rule of privilege to protect confidential communications between patient and psychotherapist. In Evidence Code section 1024, the Legislature created a specific and limited exception to the psychotherapist–patient privilege: "There is no privilege . . . if the psychotherapist has reasonable cause to believe that the patient is in such mental or emotional condition as to be dangerous to himself or to the person or property of another and that disclosure of the communication is necessary to prevent the threatened danger."

We realize that the open and confidential character of psychotherapeutic dialogue encourages patients to express threats of violence, few of which are ever executed. Certainly a therapist should not be encouraged routinely to reveal such threats; such disclosures could seriously disrupt the patient's relationship with his therapist and with the persons threatened. To the contrary, the therapist's obligations to his patient require that he not disclose a confidence unless such disclosure is necessary to avert danger to others, and even then that he do so discreetly, and in a fashion that would preserve the privacy of his patient to the fullest extent compatible with the prevention of the threatened danger.

The revelation of a communication under the above circumstances is not a breach of trust or a violation of professional ethics; as stated in the Principles of Medical Ethics of the American Medical Association (1957), section 9: "A physician may not reveal the confidence entrusted to him in the course of medical attendance . . . *unless he is required to do so by law or unless it becomes necessary in order to protect the welfare of the individual or of the community.*" (Emphasis added.) We conclude that the public policy favoring protection of the confidential character of patient-psychotherapist communications must yield to the extent to which disclosure is essential to avert danger to others. The protective privilege ends where the public peril begins.

Our current crowded and computerized society compels the interdependence of its

members. In this risk-infested society we can hardly tolerate the further exposure to danger that would result from a concealed knowledge of the therapist that his patient was lethal. If the exercise of reasonable care to protect the threatened victim requires the therapist to warn the endangered party or those who can reasonably be expected to notify him, we see no sufficient societal interest that would protect and justify concealment. The containment of such risks lies in the public interest. For the foregoing reasons, we find that plaintiffs' complaints can be amended to state a cause of action against defendants Moore, Powelson, Gold, and Yandell and against the Regents as their employer, for breach of a duty to exercise reasonable care to protect Tatiana. . . .

Dissenting Opinion in Tarasoff v. Regents of the University of California

Justice William P. Clark

At the time he wrote this minority opinion, Justice Clark was an associate justice of the Supreme Court of California.

The dissenting view in the Tarasoff *case offered a number of reasons for not imposing an overriding "duty to warn" upon psychotherapists. Without assurances of confidentiality, (1) those requiring treatment will be deterred from seeking it, (2) patients will be inhibited from making disclosures necessary for effective treatment, and (3) the patient's trust in his therapist, so necessary for treatment, will be destroyed. Further, the duty to warn policy (4) will greatly increase the risk of involuntary civil commitment, (5) presupposes the grossly incorrect claim that psychiatrists can accurately predict violent behavior, and (6) encourages psychiatrists to further overpredict violence to avoid civil prosecution.*

Until today's majority opinion, both legal and medical authorities have agreed that confidentiality is essential to effectively treat the mentally ill, and that imposing a duty on doctors to disclose patient threats to potential victims would greatly impair treatment. Further, recognizing that effective treatment and society's safety are necessarily intertwined, the Legislature has already decided effective and confidential treatment is preferred over imposition of a duty to warn.

The issue whether effective treatment for the mentally ill should be sacrificed to a system of warnings is, in my opinion, properly one for the Legislature, and we are bound by its judgment. Moreover, even in the absence of clear legislative direction, we must reach the same conclusion because imposing the majority's new duty is certain to result in a net increase in violence. . . .

COMMON LAW ANALYSIS

Entirely apart from the statutory provisions, the same result must be reached upon considering both general tort principles and the public policies favoring effective treatment, reduction of violence, and justified commitment.

Generally, a person owes no duty to control the conduct of another. Exceptions are recognized only in limited situations where (1) a special relationship exists between the defendant and injured party, or (2) a special relationship exists between defendant and the active wrongdoer, imposing a duty on defendant to control the wrong-

doer's conduct. The majority does not contend the first exception is appropriate to this case.

Policy generally determines duty. Principal policy considerations include foreseeability of harm, certainty of the plaintiff's injury, proximity of the defendant's conduct to the plaintiff's injury, moral blame attributable to defendant's conduct, prevention of future harm, burden on the defendant, and consequences to the community.

Overwhelming policy considerations weigh against imposing a duty on psychotherapists to warn a potential victim against harm. While offering virtually no benefit to society, such a duty will frustrate psychiatric treatment, invade fundamental patient rights and increase violence.

The importance of psychiatric treatment and its need for confidentiality have been recognized by this court. "It is clearly recognized that the very practice of psychiatry vitally depends upon the reputation in the community that the psychiatrist will not tell." [Slovenko, *Psychiatry and a Second Look at the Medical Privilege* (1960) 6 Wayne L. Rev. 175, 188.]

Assurance of confidentiality is important for three reasons.

Deterrence from Treatment

First, without substantial assurance of confidentiality, those requiring treatment will be deterred from seeking assistance. It remains an unfortunate fact in our society that people seeking psychiatric guidance tend to become stigmatized. Apprehension of such stigma—apparently increased by the propensity of people considering treatment to see themselves in the worst possible light—creates a well-recognized reluctance to seek aid. This reluctance is alleviated by the psychiatrist's assurance of confidentiality.

Full Disclosure

Second, the guarantee of confidentiality is essential in eliciting the full disclosure necessary for effective treatment. The psychiatric patient approaches treatment with conscious and unscious inhibitions against revealing his inner-most thoughts. "Every person, however well-motivated, has to overcome resistances to therapeutic exploration. These resistances seek support from every possible source and the possibility of disclosure would easily be employed in the service of resistance." (Goldstein & Katz, *Psychiatrist-Patient Privilege: The GAP Proposal and the Connecticut Statute,* 36 Conn. Bar J., 175, 179; see also, 118 Am. J. Psych. 734, 735). Until a patient can trust his psychiatrist not to violate their confidential relationship, "the unconscious psychological control mechanism of repression will prevent the recall of past experiences." [Butler, *Psychotherapy and Griswold: Is Confidentiality a Privilege or a Right?* (1971) 3 Conn. L. Rev. 599, 604.]

Successful Treatment

Third, even if the patient fully discloses his thoughts, assurance that the confidential relationship will not be breached is necessary to maintain his trust in his psychiatrist—the very means by which treatment is effected. "[T]he essence of much psychotherapy is the contribution of trust in the external world and ultimately in the self, modelled upon the trusting relationship established during therapy" (Dawidoff, *The Malpractice of Psychiatrists,* 1966 Duke L. J. 696, 704.) Patients will be helped only if they can form a trusting relationship with the psychiatrist. All authorities appear to agree that if the trust relationship cannot be developed because of collusive communication between the psychiatrist and others, treatment will be frustrated.

Given the importance of confidentiality to the practice of psychiatry, it becomes clear the duty to warn imposed by the majority will cripple the use and effectiveness of psychiatry. Many people, potentially violent—yet susceptible to treatment—will be deterred from seeking it; those seeking it will be inhibited from making

revelations necessary to effective treatment; and, forcing the psychiatrist to violate the patient's trust will destroy the interpersonal relationship by which treatment is effected.

VIOLENCE AND CIVIL COMMITMENT

By imposing a duty to warn, the majority contributes to the danger to society of violence by the mentally ill and greatly increases the risk of civil commitment—the total deprivation of liberty—of those who should not be confined. The impairment of treatment and risk of improper commitment resulting from the new duty to warn will not be limited to a few patients but will extend to a large number of the mentally ill. Although under existing psychiatric procedures only a relatively few receiving treatment will ever present a risk of violence, the number making threats is huge, and it is the latter group—not just the former—whose treatment will be impaired and whose risk of commitment will be increased.

Both the legal and psychiatric communities recognize that the process of determining potential violence in a patient is far from exact, being fraught with complexity and uncertainty.[1]

In fact precision has not even been attained in predicting who of those having already committed violent acts will again become violent, a task recognized to be of much simpler proportions.

This predictive uncertainty means that the number of disclosures will necessarily be large. As noted above, psychiatric patients are encouraged to discuss all thoughts of violence, and they often express such thoughts. However, unlike this court, the psychiatrist does not enjoy the benefit of overwhelming hindsight in seeing which few, if any, of his patients will ultimately become violent. Now, confronted by the majority's new duty, the psychiatrist must instantaneously calculate potential violence from each patient on each visit. The difficulties researchers have encountered in accurately predicting violence will be heightened for the practicing psychiatrist dealing for brief periods in his office with heretofore nonviolent patients. And, given the decision not to warn or commit must always be made at the psychiatrist's civil peril, one can expect most doubts will be resolved in favor of the psychiatrist protecting himself.

Neither alternative open to the psychiatrist seeking to protect himself is in the public interest. The warning itself is an impairment of the psychiatrist's ability to treat, depriving many patients of adequate treatment. It is to be expected that after disclosing their threats, a significant number of patients, who would not become violent if treated according to existing practices, will engage in violent conduct as a result of unsuccessful treatment. In short, the majority's duty to warn will not only impair treatment of many who would never become violent but worse, will result in a net increase in violence.[2]

The second alternative open to the psychiatrist is to commit his patient rather than to warn. Even in the absence of threat of civil liability, the doubts of psychiatrists as to the seriousness of patient threats have led psychiatrists to overcommit to mental institutions. This overcommitment has been authoritatively documented in both legal and psychiatric studies. This practice is so prevalent that it has been estimated that "as many as twenty harmless persons are incarcerated for every one who will commit a violent act." [Steadman & Cocozza, *Stimulus/Response: We Can't Predict Who Is Dangerous* (Jan. 1975) 8 Psych. Today 32, 35.]

Given the incentive to commit created by the majority's duty, this already serious situation will be worsened. . . .

Notes

[1] A shocking illustration of psychotherapists' inability to predict dangerousness . . . is cited and discussed in Ennis, *Prisoners of Psychiatry: Mental Patients, Psychiatrists, and the Law* (1972): "In a well-known study, psychiatrists predicted that

989 persons were so dangerous that they could not be kept even in civil mental hospitals, but would have to be kept in maximum security hospitals run by the Department of Corrections. Then, because of a United States Supreme Court decision, those persons were transferred to civil hospitals. After a year, the Department of Mental Hygiene reported that one-fifth of them had been discharged to the community, and over half had agreed to remain as voluntary patients. During the year, only 7 of the 989 committed or threatened any act that was sufficiently dangerous to require retransfer to the maximum security hospital. Seven correct predictions out of almost a thousand is not a very impressive record.

"Other studies, and there are many, have reached the same conclusion: psychiatrists simply cannot predict dangerous behavior." (*Id.* at p. 227).

[2]The majority concedes that psychotherapeutic dialogue often results in the patient expressing threats of violence that are rarely executed. The practical problem, of course, lies in ascertaining which threats from which patients will be carried out. As to this problem, the majority is silent. They do, however, caution that the therapist certainly "should not be encouraged routinely to reveal such threats; such disclosures could seriously disrupt the patient's relationships with his therapist and with the persons threatened."

Thus, in effect, the majority informs the therapists that they must accurately predict dangerousness—a task recognized as extremely difficult—or face crushing civil liability. The majority's reliance on the traditional standard of care for professionals that "therapist need only exercise 'that reason-

able degree of skill, knowledge, and care ordinarily possessed and exercised by members of [that professional specialty] under similar circumstances'" is seriously misplaced. This standard of care assumes that, to a large extent, the subject matter of the specialty is ascertainable. One clearly ascertainable element in the psychiatric field is that the therapist cannot accurately predict dangerousness, which, in turn, means that the standard is inappropriate for lack of a relevant criterion by which to judge the therapist's decision. The inappropriateness of the standard the majority would have us use is made patent when consideration is given to studies, by several eminent authorities, indicating that "[t]he chances of a second psychiatrist agreeing with the diagnosis of a first psychiatrist 'are barely better than 50–50; or stated differently, there is about as much chance that a different expert would come to some different conclusion as there is that the other would agree.'" (Ennis & Litwack, *Psychiatry and the Presumption of Expertise: Flipping Coins in the Courtroom,* 62 Cal. L. Rev. 693, 701, quoting Ziskin, Coping with Psychiatric and Psychological Testimony, 126.) The majority's attempt to apply a normative scheme to a profession which must be concerned with problems that balk at standardization is clearly erroneous.

In any event, an ascertainable standard would not serve to limit psychiatrist disclosure of threats with the resulting impairment of treatment. However compassionate, the psychiatrist hearing the threat remains faced with potential crushing civil liability for a mistaken evaluation of his patient and will be forced to resolve even the slightest doubt in favor of disclosure or commitment.

Truth-Telling to Patients

Labrini Moutsopoulos

Moutsopoulos documents and explains the recent shift in physicians' attitudes towards truthtelling to patients, noting that surveys done in the 1950's and 1960's showed that from 69 to 90 percent of physicians preferred a policy of nondisclosure to patients, whereas by the late 1970's 97 percent favored a policy of disclosure. He refutes three standard arguments for nondisclosure: (1) that it prevents harm, (2) that patients do not want to know the truth, and (3) that there is no such thing as truth. He further develops a convincing case for a general policy of truthfulness while allowing for a small handful of legitimate exceptions. The editors have been unable to obtain biographical information about Dr. Moutsopoulos.

I propose to analyze in this paper the force of Kant's famous words: "To be truthful (honest) in

Reprinted with permission of the publisher from *Medicine and Law,* vol. 3, (1984), pp. 237–51. Copyright © 1984 by Springer-Verlag, Heidelberg. Excerpt from "Truth-Telling: Attitudes" by Robert M. Veatch adapted with permission of the Free Press, a division of Macmillan Inc. and the Kennedy Institute of Ethics, Georgetown University. From *Encyclopedia of Bioethics,* Warren T. Reich, Editor in Chief. Vol 4, pp. 1678–

all declarations is therefore a sacred unconditional command of reason, and not to be limited in any expediency . . ." [1]. Can this statement actually be translated into a 'moral policy' in medicine?

79, 1685–86. Copyright © 1978 by Georgetown University, Washington, D.C.

In this paper I argue for a moral policy of full disclosure to patients, from all medical professionals. By the term moral policy I mean that which should be done in the vast majority of cases. A moral policy will not yield coverage of all cases; therefore, exceptions or modifications of the policy are possible, but they must be justified on moral grounds rather than expediency.

I shall present arguments supporting this thesis, the arguments against it, and a mediating position. Before I proceed, I shall briefly review and analyze studies of physicians' and patients' attitudes toward truth disclosure in some instances of medical intervention.

Traditionally physicians have been guided in basic forms of ethics since the Hippocratics and the Attic philosophers [2]. Evidence in scattered historical texts shows that Hippocrates partially practiced truth disclosure in some very difficult cases with adults despite the fact that the oath states that physicians' central duty is to benefit patients.

Unfortunately, in modern medicine physicians do not always feel obligated to tell the whole truth, and many decide for their patient's future only by privately consulting the guidance of their own conscience. There have been efforts in recent years, and in the United States particularly, to reconsider physicians' attitudes towards truth disclosure, and efforts to include the patient in medical decisions. The scientific truth is not hidden any longer, as it was in ancient Egypt, where the priests (physician of that time) presented themselves as secondary gods.

In June 1979 I interviewed eight physicians and scientists from southern Europe and Middle Eastern countries. I concluded that, as a general rule, the patient in those countries does not participate in decisions about treatment. In contrast to those countries, in northern Europe (England, Sweden, and Holland) the patient is better informed about his condition and about the course of his treatment. Since research and human experimentation is almost non-existent in southern Europe and the Middle East, the notions of informed consent and the autonomy of the individual are not very well developed in the practice of medicine or research.

The situation was not very different a few years ago in the United States as well. I will review the transition from the early stage to the present stage of truth-telling.

I see this transition as a result of the maturation through the course of centuries of certain moral principles, e.g., freedom of the individual, autonomy, fidelity, self-respect, respect for others and, finally, in the medical context, care.

To care for another is to help him to maintain or establish an independent existence [3]. I agree with Hauerwas [3] that medicine is not only the cure of a particular disease but the task of maintaining the physical and psychological integrity of the individual, which, of course, cannot be maximally maintained through deception. Absence of full disclosure or deception, which might affect a patient's free decision, might create a fictional environment and a false social situation and thus has questionable ethical implications.

PHYSICIANS' ATTITUDES

The earliest study in the United States of physician attitudes about truth disclosure was published in 1953, by Fitts and Ravdin [4] who questioned 444 practicing physicians in the Philadelphia area. This early study gives us a picture of the attitudes of one homogeneous group of physicians. They reported the following practices with cancer patients: 3% *always tell,* 28% *usually tell,* 57% *usually do not tell,* 12% *never tell.*

In 1961, Oken [5] questioned 219 members of the staff of the Departments of Internal Medicine, Obstetrics-Gynecology, and Surgery of Michael Reese Hospital in Chicago; he received 193 replies. Of the total group 88% said that they usually followed a policy of nondisclosure of diagnosis containing "bad news." Data from studies show that the attitudes of American physicians changed rapidly after 1970, because physicians in the 1970s were more willing to disclose a diagnosis of terminal cancer.

Rea and co-workers [6] published a study in 1975 of 151 physicians in ten medical specialties and found that 39% expressed some degree of negativity toward informing cancer patients of their condition. Only 22% would refuse to tell a dying patient who was functioning well that he or she was terminal. Another interesting element in this study was the attempt to determine the role of the family in the decision of what should be disclosed. Of the physicians 54% would leave their options open by coordinating with the family what the patient would be told, 37% would honor the family's wishes, and only 9% would tell the patient what he wanted to know regardless of the family's decision.

The historical transition from the practice of nondisclosure is clearly demonstrated in a study by Novack and associates [7]. The investigators replicated the same questionnaire from the 1961 study [5], given to a university hospital medical staff, and gave it again in 1977 to 699 university hospital medical staff members in another university. Of 264 respondents, 97% indicated preference for telling a cancer patient his diagnosis, in contrast with physicians in 1961, when 90% of responding physicians indicated a preference for nondisclosure. This data indicated a complete reversal of medical professionals.

The respondents to the 1977 study emphasized the influence of medical schools and hospital training upon their attitudes about truth-telling. However, physicians in both studies keyed their answer to what they thought the patient wanted to know. Physicians in 1977 believed that patients would be better off emotionally with disclosure. Physicians in 1961 believed the patients would be harmed if told.

Why, then, have these attitudes changed so radically within 16 years? The answer in my view is that social changes contributed the greatest part to the change in attitude. First, therapy of many fatal diseases and the early detection of them have increased public awareness of cancer at many levels. Public figures such as Betty Ford and Happy Rockefeller spoke openly about breast cancer. Perhaps this led to lessen the stigma of cancer patients, a greater ease in talking about its reality, and a greater awareness of its signs and symptoms [7].

Other social changes that must be mentioned are the spread of the concept of individual autonomy, the declaration of human rights in many parts of the world, the work of modern moral philosophers, and finally the overall structure of a modern society, which presupposes individuality and responsibility in every aspect of human behavior. These factors combine to create a movement toward maximum informed consent in medicine, which only reflects a much greater movement toward democratic participation in society by citizens.

Moral responsibility rests upon two premises as Joseph Fletcher states [8]: first, the freedom to choose; second, knowledge about the facts about which we are to choose. However, freedom of choice and knowledge are not abstractions. These opportunities, or the lack of them, depend upon social processes which tend toward maximization or minimization of the conditions of democracy.

To be a morally responsible person in the Aristotelian sense of being praiseworthy or blameworthy [9] for a decision, presupposes that an individual must be in possession of the facts upon which the decision rests. Without the social processes that promote knowledge of the facts, individuals cannot be morally responsible. Ethics and politics cannot be divorced. Physicians can add social as well as personal insult to injury by denying freedom of choice. By denying the freedom to choose, one can cause an even greater social tragedy.

Social change processes have led to legal change. In recent years it has become, for example, a legal obligation of the physician to tell the truth to patients, and this obligation has been embodied in a Patient's Bill of Rights [10]. The bill states that a patient has a right:

(1) to informed participation in all decisions involving his health care program

(2) to a clear, concise explanation of all procedures in laymen's terms

(3) to know the identity and professional status of all those providing service

Even though social change has led to legal and ethical pressure for truth-telling to patients, there are additional important moral questions about the extent of the obligation. Does one tell the whole truth at once? Does one tell every fact?

PATIENTS' ATTITUDES

There are other studies of patients' attitudes to ward truth disclosure, but often the question is addressed in terms of the cancer patient, since the issue of truth-telling to cancer patients is one of the most debatable.

Kelly and Friesen [11] in 1950 surveyed three groups of outpatients in university-affiliated hospitals. They interviewed 100 cancer patients. They determined that 89 preferred knowing about having cancer, while 6 preferred not knowing, and 5 were not sure about it.

Since the responses of these cancer patients could be interpreted as being influenced by the patient's knowledge of his cancer [12], Kelly and Friesen asked a group of 100 noncancer patients. For that group they reported that 82 said they wanted to be told while 14 said they did not.

In a third group of 740 patients being examined in a cancer detection center, 98.5% said that they wanted to be told of the cancer diagnosis. In 1950 Branch [12] found that 88% from a noncancer group preferred to be told of their condition. Samp and Curreri [12] in 1957 found that 81% of a group made up of patients and nonpatients wanted to be told the cancer diagnosis.

R. Alfidi's study [13] was made to determine the reaction of patients to a general disclosure of complications which might result from angiographic procedures. The results of this study indicate that the majority of patients referred to the Cleveland Clinic desired this information. The most recent study on attitudes toward fatal illness [14] by Blumenfeld et al., involving 1518 normal adults in the United States, found that 82%–92% of the group wanted to be told if they had a fatal illness.

Additionally, the study compared attitudes by sex and different socioeconomic levels: 87% of women compared with 92% of men wanted to be told. A significantly smaller percentage of nonwhites, those with less education, and those of lower socioeconomic levels wanted to be told their fatal diagnosis. There are two studies of attitudes and motivations to participate in screening programs: a cancer screening program [15] and a program screening for Huntington's disease [16]. These studies show a high percentage of participants who want to know about their disease. Only one British study [17] suggests a potentially contrary conclusion. McIntosh found that, among 74 patients hospitalized in a ward for the treatment of malignant disease in a Scottish teaching hospital, 88% either knew or suspected they had a malignant tumor at admission to the ward. He reported that a great majority of those patients with diagnosed but undisclosed malignancies had no desire to increase their knowledge about their illness. The design of the study seems inadequate to me for the following reasons: first, the investigator does not mention what kind of questionnaire was given to the patients, an omission which is very important for the assessment of the study; second, the conclusion of the study rests upon the patients' observed interaction on the ward. The investigator does not explain what behavior was being observed or how the behavior was carried out. Veatch [12] finds the study of no value because the author never reports the basis of the findings that led him to the conclusion. Veatch states that it is hard to understand how the findings of this study relate to the findings of the previous studies.

Furthermore, I believe that this study is unethical for several reasons:

1. The patients had already been misinformed.

2. It deprived the patients of the opportunity to discuss and learn about their condition.

Since the patients entered a ward for the treatment of malignant diseases, it is very unlikely that they did not know or did not highly suspect the nature of their disease. Moreover, the study was conducted in a country with traditionally high cultural, educational, and medical standards. It is hard for me to believe that in Great Britain where informed consent has played a major role for years now in the patient-doctor relationship, there are patients who refuse informed participation in this relationship.

I find only one explanation for this attitude: the patients already knew about their disease when they entered the cancer center. They understood that their doctors did not want for some unexplained reasons to disclose the truth and to share with them their emotional reactions to the disclosure.

As it is a fact that there is some degree of psychological dependency on physicians, these patients felt unable to stand up for their rights. They felt they would upset their doctors if they asked more questions, because they already knew that the doctors were not open to questions. (On admission, the study reports that physicians used euphemisms such as "nasty cells," a fact which shows the physicians' intention to avoid the truth.)

Another important source that may limit truth-telling of physicians to patients is the physicians' own fear of death. Schulz, Anderman and Feifel [18, 19], found a significantly higher fear of death among physicians compared with other groups. As Veatch asserts [12], and I fully agree with him, if an individual has a high or low fear of death and then asks himself what the impact would be on another of disclosure of terminal illness, he or she may systematically misjudge the impact by appealing primarily to his own high or low fear of death.

One may clearly conclude from the reviewed studies that (a) most patients prefer to be told the truth and (b) most patients do not believe that they will be harmed if they are informed about the true nature of their illness.

Can we derive moral imperatives from studies of attitudes? Not always, because it is obvious that the majority of persons can be on occasion morally wrong. For example, the majority of Germans in 1934 may have preferred to persecute Jews. If an opinion poll had been taken, the results would doubtless have shown a bias against Jews, but opinions and attitudes do not constitute morality. In this case we find that the majority of people prefer to be treated in a manner consistent with the moral rule to tell the truth. Let us now look at the major moral arguments with regard to truth-telling.

DEBATES AMONG MORAL PHILOSOPHERS

There are two major schools of thought in ethical theory, the absolutist (or deontological school) and the utilitarian. The first school, which holds that there is no sufficient reason for any kind of lie, is represented by Kant in the philosophical analysis of deception and by Ramsey in the field of medical ethics. Kant holds that a lie always harms another; if not some other particular man, it still harms mankind generally, for it vitiates the source of law itself [1]. He argues for the truth as a sacred command of reason, limited by "no expediency."

Even a single lie would be a breach of the duty of veracity that is owed to all mankind. Ramsey [20] holds that fidelity is an absolute necessity for human interaction and, therefore, informed consent for the patient is the expression in medicine of this general truth.

Plato in the *Republic* [21] argues that the falsehood should be available to physicians only, for the good of patients, and not to laymen.

Aquinas and Augustine [22] permit certain lies that intend great good. Nevertheless, both counsel against all lies, holding them to be unnatural since they go against the very purpose of communication, which is to convey truth [23].

Aquinas makes use of the notion of "intention" to judge the morality of human statements. For example, if one planted a false statement in someone else's mind for good intentions, Aquinas may treat this as an "excusable" lie. This distinction is important, because some scholars came to regard deceptive statements not as lies, but as statements with "mental reservations."

The utilitarian position on this issue, has been elaborated and defended by many philosophers.

Bentham [24] evaluates lying by consequences. He argues that if a falsehood does not have any harmful effect, it would not constitute an offense to anybody. Despite the fact that his policy toward lying might not differ substantially from that of Kant, the justification for accepting or rejecting a particular lie or a policy differs sharply.

Sidgwick [25] argues that common sense seems to allow deception. If deception is designed to benefit the deceived person, it may sometimes be right. He would not hesitate to speak falsely to an invalid if a dangerous shock could be avoided. The way he decides whether or not a lie is allowable, is to weigh the gain of any deception against the imperilment of mutual confidence involved in all violations of truth.

Ross [26] holds a mixed utilitarian and non-utilitarian position on truth-telling. He argues that there is a *prima facie* duty to veracity, although a much greater disparity of value between the total consequences would justify us in failing to discharge our *prima facie* duty to tell the truth.

In a book published in 1891, Dr. Holmes [27] advises physicians to deceive the sick and dying patients in their own best interest, Dr. Henderson [28] supports Holmes thesis by arguing that it is impossible to convey the whole truth to patients, since perfect information can never be given on any subject to anyone. I agree with Bok [20] who says that Henderson confuses the dimensions of completeness and accuracy of information.

Joseph Fletcher [8] is a supporter of full disclosure of all information, even to patients who do not ask for it. He finds an element of degradation in the doctor-patient relationship if the medical servants, no matter how kindly the motives may be, have lied to their patients. Truth-telling is essential to any personal I-thou relationship.

This brief review of philosophical debate shows that from antiquity to contemporary life, philosophers and religious thinkers have regarded truthfulness as preferable but not always indispensable. On the other hand, ethicists who accept some justified instances of deception have the burden of defending the reasons for their positions.

DISCUSSION

Arguments Supporting "Nondisclosure"

My primary task is to *identify* and *analyze the consequences* of *following a moral policy* of maximum disclosure in the physician-patient relationship. I propose to use a method followed by some rule-utilitarians, which consists of weighing the positive and negative consequences of keeping the moral rule of truth-telling to patients against the positive and negative consequences of not keeping it. We can discern the possible negative consequences of disclosure by examining first the arguments for nondisclosure found in the medical literature.

The first and most common argument for deceiving patients by altering or withholding the truth is the argument on the basis of "prevention of harm". The proponents hold that the patient will be psychologically or physically harmed when he receives "frightening" or "depressing" news. They believe that by giving the patient the painful news, he or she may suffer a cardiac arrest or wish to commit suicide. Furthermore, they believe that by informing the patient of the fatal prognosis, the result is "taking away hope," which reduces the patients' chances for even temporary recovery.

This kind of deception is what Sidgwick [25] calls "benevolent deception." The advocates of this position argue more abstractly that disclosure of a fatal diagnosis violates the duties of beneficence and nonmaleficence by causing the patient anxiety and possibly physical harm.

The second argument for nondisclosure proceeds from the "presumption that the patient does not want the truth." The argument is usually based on the observed fact that patients deny, forget, or transform "bad news" or risk-information. The proponents are additionally critical of empirical studies that show a desire to "be told the truth" by patients or nonpatients. They point out that most patient studies deal with patients who already knew about their disease and thus had no choice to refuse a knowledge already acquired. Secondly, studies which deal with a healthy population have less value since the psychology of patients is completely different. The negative consequence of disclosure is understood to be a further variation of psychological or moral harm, i.e., depriving the patient of the "right not to know."

A third argument, the most abstract and the least persuasive of all, is the argument based on "imperfection." According to this argument there is no perfect truth, all is relative, and since there is no such thing as truth, information cannot be conveyed in a perfect way. Therefore, there is no clear distinction between true and false information in medicine. The negative consequence here is seen as the self-righteousness of the perfectionistic truth-teller that results in misery. This thesis was defended primarily by L. Henderson [28] but is a common theme among practitioners. They argue that the patients will not be able to understand the whole truth about their condition. Therefore, the physicians will not take the trouble and time to explain to their patients whatever they might understand. This theme is most frequently repeated in medical literature.

How often do these negative consequences occur? What is the empirical validity of these arguments? After an exhaustive review of medical literature on disclosure, I have found one instance where a patient suffered an acute physical or psychological reaction to the truth that led to harm, namely one case of suicide. On the other hand, in the same study there were two cases of reported suicide of patients who had not been informed of their diagnosis. As Oken [5] stated, it is not inconceivable that those two individuals would have felt better and not worse if informed. There is, therefore, literally only a shred of evidence that disclosure causes harm.

It is easy to rebut the argument about respecting the patient's "right not to know" on empirical grounds. First, no study has even been conducted to investigate whether patients desire not to be informed. Secondly, physicians do not routinely ask patients if they desire not to be informed. The burden of proof should certainly fall on those who claim to respect such an imputed right until it is known that the majority do not want "to know."

This argument sets, as Beauchamp and Childress argue [29], dangerous precedents for paternalistic behavior on the part of physicians. The greatest fallacy in the argument is that the autonomy of competent adults should not be respected, because a third party believes that patients feel they have a right not to know. On the basis of the only published studies we have, it is truly absurd to make this assumption, even though I do not doubt that there are a few patients who would espouse such a position.

The third argument based on "imperfection" is difficult to test empirically for the damage done through perfectionism and self-righteousness. There are undoubtedly a few physicians who would be cruel in their demands that patients measure up perfectionistically to tests of informed consent. One should assume that there is a small, probably statistically insignificant truth to this argument, but on any logical basis this argument is also absurd. Because complete information and complete comprehension are impossible, we are asked to conclude that erroneous information is

SELECTED BIBLIOGRAPHY

A. Professional Codes of Ethics

Annas, George J. "The Emerging Stowaway, Patients' Rights in the 1990s." In Gruzalski, Bart, and Carl Nelson, eds., *Value Conflicts in Health Care Delivery.* Cambridge, Mass.: Ballinger Books, 1982. (An examination of the AHA Bill of Rights).

Graber, Glenn C., Alfred D. Beasley, and John A. Eaddy. *Ethical Analysis of Clinical Medicine: A Guide to Self-Evaluation.* Baltimore–Munich: Urban & Schwarzenberg, 1985, pp. 77–98.

Reich, Warren T., ed. *Encyclopedia of Bioethics.* New York: The Free Press, 1978. Vol. IV, pp. 1723–815. (A large collection of professional codes).

Yeaworth, Rosalee C. "The ANA Code: A Comparative Perspective." *Image: The Journal of Nursing Scholarship* XVI, no. 3 (1985): 94–98.

B. Models of Therapist–Patient Roles and Relations

Childress, James F., and Mark Siegler. "Metaphors and Models of Doctor–Patient Relationships: Their Implications for Autonomy." *Theoretical Medicine* 5 (1985): 17–30.

Siegler, Mark. "Searching for Moral Certainty in Medicine: A Proposal for a New Model of the Doctor–Patient Encounter." *Bulletin of the New York Academy of Medicine* 57 (1981): 56–69.

Smith, Sheri. "Three Models of the Nurse–Patient Relationship." In Spicker, Stuart F., and Sally Gadow, eds., *Nursing: Images and Ideals.* New York: Springer Publishing Co., 1980, pp. 176–88.

C. Nurses, Treatment Teams, Professional Autonomy

Benjamin, Martin, and Joy Curtis. *Ethics in Nursing.* New York: Oxford University Press, 1981.

Jameton, Andrew. *Nursing Practice: The Ethical Issues.* Englewood Cliffs: Prentice-Hall, 1984.

D. Confidentiality

Appelbaum, Paul S., *et al.* "Confidentiality: An Empirical Test of the Utilitarian Perspective." *Bulletin of the American Academy of Psychiatry Law* 12, no. 2 (1984): 109–16.

Graber, Glenn C., Alfred D. Beasley, and John A. Eaddy. *Ethical Analysis of Clinical Medicine.* Baltimore–Munich: Urban & Schwarzenberg, 1985, pp. 53–72.

Siegler, Mark. "Confidentiality in Medicine: A Decrepit Concept." *New England Journal of Medicine* 307 (1982): 1518–21.

E. Communicating the Truth

Bok, Sissela. "The Ethics of Giving Placebos." *Scientific American* 231, no. 5 (1974): 17–23.

Brody, Howard. "The Lie that Heals: The Ethics of Giving Placebos." *Annals of Internal Medicine* 97 (1982): 112–18.

McNeil, Barbara J., *et al.* "On the Elicitation of Preferences for Alternative Therapies." *New England Journal of Medicine* 306 (May 27, 1982): 1259–62.

Novak, D. H., *et al.* "Changes in Physicians' Attitudes Toward Telling the Cancer Patient." *Journal of the American Medical Association* 241 (1979): 897–900.

Informed Voluntary Consent and Paternalism

OBTAINING PATIENT CONSENT HAS become a routine part of health care treatment, largely as a practical result of legal requirements. In the first of the selections to follow, the President's Commission indicates that informed voluntary consent is an ethical ideal that has gradually worked its way into the law. As an ethical rule (as we shall see later), this ideal tells us that it is wrong to perform any diagnostic, therapeutic, or experimental medical procedure on competent adults if they have not knowingly and freely consented. But the gap between ideal and practice must be bridged.

Perhaps this process has become *too much* a matter of routine. Upon admission to a hospital (and at the initial visit to many outpatient clinics), patients are often given a general consent form to read and sign. A similar process takes place before each risky and/or invasive diagnostic and treatment procedure. But, all too often, none of the parties involved has a clear understanding of what is supposed *to be accomplished* by this ritual; and, as a result, it is not likely to achieve its purpose.

The point of this chapter is to explore key ethical issues underlying the requirement of consent: What is the process supposed to accom-

plish? When should consent be sought and when (if ever) is it unnecessary? By whom should consent be obtained? *From* whom? What are the elements of a valid consent? What (if anything) is added to the notion of consent by speaking of "informed" consent? What (if anything) is added by speaking of "voluntary" consent? What is the relationship between consent and paternalism? These and related questions are the focus of this chapter.

A. TRADITIONAL MEDICAL PATERNALISM WITHOUT CONSENT

No mention was made of informed consent, or any concept like it, in the Hippocratic Oath. In sharp contrast to a policy of enlisting the patient's consent, the Hippocratic physician pledged to apply treatment regimens "for the benefit of the sick according to *my* ability and judgment." (Our emphasis.) The goal postulated here is "benefit," i.e., promoting the best interests of the patient. The assumption seems to be that professional expertise qualifies the physician to

or saves a physician from five telephone calls in the middle of the night over the next several months or years, it is a good investment of time rather than a waste of time.

4. It is futile because many people will not understand or use the information given.

Reply: Here, again, the first response is to deny the fundamental relevance of this complaint. Even if patients do not make ideal use of the information, they may still have a right to receive it. A part of what is involved in the right to informed consent is the discretion to decide how (or whether) to use the information given. Of course, a decision not based on the information available may not be an ideally autonomous choice—but, as we have seen, the right to informed consent is not limited exclusively to fully autonomous individuals nor to fully autonomous choices of reasonably autonomous individuals. Even if some competent adults will not understand or use the information given, psychological prediction is such an inexact science that it is virtually impossible to pick out those persons in advance.

There may be a threshold of irrationality below which it is appropriate for others to override the patient's decision paternalistically. Some (in particular, Drane in this chapter) argue that this threshold is relative to the seriousness of the decision to be faced, as well as to other factors. However, above that threshold, it would be a violation of the patient's consent right to deny information merely because it is not used in the way others think is most appropriate.

However, the claim made in this objection is an empirical claim. There is need for further research about the extent to which patients do understand and make use of information—and this research will not be decisive until it includes situations in which patients were informed in the gradual, supportive way we have argued for here in a process guided by principles of learning and of emotional reaction to illness. If it could be shown that, *even in such preferred situations*, information presented made little or no difference to the patients' choices, there might be reason to re-think the present requirements of disclosure. The thing to do if that were the result would be to find out what information *does* make a difference to patients' rationally autonomous choices and revise the requirements to stress these elements.

The requirement of informed consent would be shown to be morally unjustified only if it were shown that rationally autonomous choice by patients is *impossible*. To the extent that it (or its close approximation) is possible, the obligation to promote and respect it applies.

5. Patients do not really want to know.

Reply: This is another empirical claim, and one which has been decisively disproven. The essay by Labrini Moutsopoulos in Chapter 2 reviews a number of empirical studies on this issue, which show clearly that patients in general are extremely interested in knowing the truth about their health status. They are similarly interested in participating in decisions about their own health care.

NOTES

[1]David L. Schiedermayer, M.D., "The Hippocratic Oath—Corporate Version," *The New England Journal of Medicine* 314, no. 1 (January 2, 1986): 62.

[2]Alan Meisel, "The 'Exceptions' to the Informed Consent Doctrine: Striking a Balance Between Competing Values in Medical Decision-making," *Wisconsin Law Review* no. 2 (1979): 420.

[3]*In re Conroy,* 486 A.2d 1209 (N.J. 1985).

[4]*Current Opinions of the Judicial Council of the American Medical Association—1982*, John H. Burkhart, M.D., Chairman (Chicago: American Medical Association, 1982), p. 26.

[5]See Paul S. Appelbaum and Loren H. Roth, "Treatment Refusals in Medical Hospitals," in *Making Health Care Decisions: The Ethical and Legal Implications of Informed Consent,* Volume 2, *Appendices—Empirical Studies of Informed Consent* (Washington, D.C.: U.S. Government Printing Office, 1982), pp. 411–77.

The Ethical and Legal Implications of Informed Consent in the Patient– Practitioner Relationship

President's Commission for the Study of Ethical Problems in Medicine and Biomedical and Behavioral Research

The President's Commission for the Study of Ethical Problems in Medicine and Biomedical and Behavioral Research was established by Congress in 1979, began its work in 1980, and concluded in 1983. It was authorized to deal not only with the ethics of research but also with a wide range of issues such as the nature of death, decisions to forego life-sustaining treatment, genetic engineering screening and counseling, equitable access to health care, and informed voluntary consent. The commission was chaired by Morris Abram, had Alexander M. Capron as its executive director, and consisted of eleven persons from medicine, nursing, the behavioral sciences, law, and ethics.

The Commission indicates that the ideal of informed voluntary consent is essentially an ethical ideal that has come to have substantial foundations in the law. It is intended to promote the two values of personal well-being and self-determination. It applies directly to competent adults and only indirectly through proxy decision-makers to those who lack decision-making capacity. The Commission summarizes the results of relevant empirical studies that provide a foundation both in experience and in ethics for the ideal.

What is informed consent to health care, and why has it assumed such an important place in legal and ethical discussions? Is it merely a rhetorical construct, imposed halfheartedly upon medicine by the law? Or is it perhaps a token of larger changes in the relationship between patients and health care professionals, especially physicians? And why does the concept have such importance in the United States today—because of a particular cultural attachment to independence and autonomy? The growing importance of biomedicine in people's lives? Skepticism over "expertise" in many spheres? Or perhaps some combination of these and other factors?

These were among the basic issues before the President's Commission during its Congressionally mandated study of "the ethical and legal implications of the requirements for informed consent to . . . undergo medical procedures."[1] Rather than embroider the doctrine of informed consent within the confines of the case and statutory law that was its source, the Commission decided early in its study to examine the subject within the broader context of relations and communications between patients and health care professionals. It wished to see whether means could be found to promote a fuller understanding

Reprinted from the President's Commission for the Study of Ethical Problems in Medicine and Biomedical and Behavioral Research, *Making Health Care Decisions*, Vol. 1 (Washington, D.C.: U.S. Government Printing Office, 1982), pp. 1–9.

[1]42 U.S.C. § 300v-1(a)(1)(A) (1981) also instructs the Commission to study the implications of "informed consent to participation in research projects." The Commission treats issues of human research generally in its biennial reports, PROTECTING HUMAN SUBJECTS. Furthermore, although they developed initially along independent lines, *see* note 19, Chapter One *infra*, the legal rules for informed consent to treatment and to participation in research spring from common legal and philosophical ground, have had parallel courses of development, and are now basically congruent, so that a separate discussion is not required in this Report.

by patients and professionals of their common enterprise, so that patients can participate, on an informed basis and to the extent they care to do so, in making decisions about their health care.

SUMMARY OF CONCLUSIONS AND RECOMMENDATIONS

Before the Commission could consider means of improvement, it had to address the underlying theoretical issues. The ethical foundation of informed consent can be traced to the promotion of two values: personal well-being and self-determination. To ensure that these values are respected and enhanced, the Commission finds that patients who have the capacity to make decisions about their care must be permitted to do so voluntarily and must have all relevant information regarding their condition and alternative treatments, including possible benefits, risks, costs, other consequences, and significant uncertainties surrounding any of this information. This conclusion has several specific implications:

(1) Although the informed consent doctrine has substantial foundations in law, it is essentially an ethical imperative.

(2) Ethically valid consent is a process of shared decision-making based upon mutual respect and participation, not a ritual to be equated with reciting the contents of a form that details the risks of particular treatments.

(3) Much of the scholarly literature and legal commentary about informed consent portrays it as a highly rational means of decisionmaking about health care matters, thereby suggesting that it may only be suitable for and applicable to well-educated, articulate, self-aware individuals. Whether this is what the legal doctrine was intended to be or what it has inadvertently become, it is a view the Commission unequivocally rejects. Although subcultures within American society differ in their views about autonomy and individual choice and about the etiology of illness and

the roles of healers and patients,[2] a survey conducted for the Commission found a universal desire for information, choice, and respectful communication about decisions.[3] Informed consent must remain flexible, yet the process, as the Commission envisions it throughout this Report, is ethically required of health care practitioners in their relationships with all patients, not a luxury for a few.

(4) Informed consent is rooted in the fundamental recognition—reflected in the legal presumption of competency—that adults are entitled to accept or reject health care interventions on the basis of their own personal values and in furtherance of their own personal goals. Nonetheless, patient choice is not absolute.

- Patients are not entitled to insist that health care practitioners furnish them services when to do so would violate either the bounds of acceptable practice or a professional's own deeply held moral beliefs or would draw on a limited resource on which the patient has no binding claim.

- The fundamental values that informed consent is intended to promote—self-determination and patient well-being—both demand that alternative arrangements for health care decision-making be made for individuals who lack substantial capacity to make their own decisions. Respect for self-determination requires, however, that in the first instance individuals be deemed to have decisional capacity, which should not be treated as a hurdle to be surmounted in the vast majority of cases, and that incapacity be treated as a disqualifying factor in the small minority of cases.

---

[2]Robert A. Hahn, *Culture and Informed Consent: An Anthropological Perspective* (1982), Appendix F, in Volume Three of this Report.

[3]The Commission's survey of the public broke down these responses on the basis of variables such as age, gender, race, education, and income.

- Decisionmaking capacity is specific to each particular decision. Although some people lack this capacity for all decisions, many are incapacitated in more limited ways and are capable of making some decisions but not others. The concept of capacity is best understood and applied in a functional manner. That is, the presence or absence of capacity does not depend on a person's status or on the decision reached, but on that individual's actual functioning in situations in which a decision about health care is to be made.

- Decisionmaking incapacity should be found to exist only when people lack the ability to make decisions that promote their well-being in conformity with their own previously expressed values and preferences.

- To the extent feasible people with no decisionmaking capacity should still be consulted about their own preferences out of respect for them as individuals.

(5) Health care providers should not ordinarily withhold unpleasant information simply because it is unpleasant. The ethical foundations of informed consent allow the withholding of information from patients only when they request that it be withheld or when its disclosure per se would cause substantial detriment to their well-being. Furthermore, the Commission found that most members of the public do not wish to have "bad news" withheld from them.

(6) Achieving the Commission's vision of shared decision-making based on mutual respect is ultimately the responsibility of individual health care professionals. However, health care institutions such as hospitals and professional schools have important roles to play in assisting health care professionals in this obligation. The manner in which health care is provided in institutional settings often results in a fragmentation of responsibility that may neglect the human side of health care. To assist in guarding against this, institutional health care providers should ensure

that ultimately there is one readily identifiable practitioner responsible for providing information to a particular patient. Although pieces of information may be provided by various people, there should be one individual officially charged with responsibility for ensuring that all the necessary information is communicated and that the patient's wishes are known to the treatment team.

(7) Patients should have access to the information they need to help them understand their conditions and make treatment decisions. To this end the Commission recommends that health care professionals and institutions not only provide information but also assist patients who request additional information to obtain it from relevant sources, including hospital and public libraries.

(8) As cases arise and new legislation is contemplated, courts and legislatures should reflect this view of ethically valid consent. Nevertheless, the Commission does not look to legal reforms as the primary means of bringing about changes in the relationship between health care professionals and patients.

(9) The Commission finds that a number of relatively simple changes in practice could facilitate patient participation in health care decisionmaking. Several specific techniques—such as having patients express, orally or in writing, their understanding of the treatment consented to— deserve further study. Furthermore, additional societal resources need to be committed to improving the human side of health care, which has apparently deteriorated at the same time there have been substantial gains in health care technology. The Department of Health and Human Services, and especially the National Institutes of Health, is an appropriate agency for the development of initiatives and the evaluation of their efficacy in this area.

(10) Because health care professionals are responsible for ensuring that patients can participate effectively in decisionmaking regarding their care, educators have a responsibility to prepare

physicians and nurses to carry out this obligation. The Commission therefore concludes that:

- Curricular innovations aimed at preparing health professionals for a process of mutual decisionmaking with patients should be continued and strengthened, with careful attention being paid to the development of methods for evaluating the effectiveness of such innovations.

- Examinations and evaluations at the professional school and national levels should reflect the importance of these issues.

- Serious attention should be paid to preparing health professionals for team practice in order to enhance patient participation and well-being.

(11) Family members are often of great assistance to patients in helping to understand information about their condition and in making decisions about treatment. The Commission recommends that health care institutions and professionals recognize this and judiciously attempt to involve family members in decisionmaking for patients, with due regard for the privacy of patients and for the possibilities for coercion that such a practice may entail.

(12) The Commission recognizes that its vision of health care decisionmaking may involve greater commitments of time on the part of health professionals. Because of the importance of shared decisionmaking based on mutual trust, not only for the promotion of patient well-being and self-determination but also for the therapeutic gains that can be realized, the Commission recommends that all medical and surgical interventions be thought of as including appropriate discussion with patients. Reimbursement to the professional should therefore take account of time spent in discussion rather than regarding it as a separate item for which additional payment is made.

(13) To protect the interests of patients who lack decisionmaking capacity and to ensure their well-being and self-determination, the Commission concludes that:

- Decisions made by others on patients' behalf should, when possible, attempt to replicate the ones patients would make if they were capable of doing so. When this is not feasible, decisions by surrogates on behalf of patients must protect the patients' best interests. Because such decisions are not instances of personal self-choice, limits may be placed on the range of acceptable decisions that surrogates make beyond those that apply when a person makes his or her own decisions.

- Health care institutions should adopt clear and explicit policies regarding how and by whom decisions are to be made for patients who cannot decide.

- Families, health care institutions, and professionals should work together to make health care decisions for patients who lack decisionmaking capacity. Recourse to courts should be reserved for the occasions when concerned parties are unable to resolve their disagreements over matters of substantial import, or when adjudication is clearly required by state law. Courts and legislatures should be cautious about requiring judicial review of routine health care decisions for patients who lack capacity.

- Health care institutions should explore and evaluate various informal administrative arrangements, such as "ethics committees," for review and consultation in nonroutine matters involving health care decisionmaking for those who cannot decide.

- As a means of preserving some self-determination for patients who no longer possess decisionmaking capacity, state courts and legislatures should consider making provision for advance directives through which people designate others to make health care decisions on their behalf and/or give instructions about their care.

The Commission acknowledges that the conclusions contained in this Report will not be simple to achieve. Even when patients and practitioners alike are sensitive to the goal of shared decisionmaking based on mutual respect, substantial barriers will still exist.[4] Some of these obstacles, such as long-standing professional attitudes or difficulties in conveying medical information in ordinary language, are formidable but can be overcome if there is a will to do so. Others, such as the dependent condition of very sick patients or the ever-growing complexity and subspecialization of medicine, will have to be accommodated because they probably cannot be eliminated. Nonetheless, the Commission's vision of informed consent still has value as a measuring stick against which actual performance may be judged and as a goal toward which all participants in health care decisionmaking can strive.

THE COMMISSION'S PROCESS

The Commission's inquiry into the ethical, legal, and practical aspects of informed consent in health care has drawn on the expertise of leading scholars from around the country, on the existing literature, on newly commissioned empirical studies, and on testimony from health care professionals, consumers, and commentators. The Commissioners devoted five hearings to informed consent and deliberated on the subject at three additional meetings.

Over the five days of hearings, testimony was heard on the components and functions of informed consent in health care, the relationships between patients and health care professionals, ways to increase patient participation in decisionmaking, the issue of patient competence and the roles of families in health care decisionmaking,

and the education of physicians and nurses about informed consent issues. The witnesses included physicians, nurses, health care administrators, representatives of consumer groups, and professors of sociology, philosophy, history, law, and public health. In addition, the Commission convened a panel of nursing experts from all over the country to discuss these issues.[5]

The Commission also contracted for three empirical studies in order to clarify certain aspects of informed consent in practice.[6] The results of these studies are used throughout the Report to illustrate key points and to measure the extent of discrepancy between current practice and the goals for communication and decisionmaking articulated by the Commission.

Although health care is clearly a diverse enterprise, the legal doctrine of informed consent seems to operate on the implicit assumption that medical care is only concerned with invasive procedures (typically surgery). To redress the narrowness of this focus, the first commissioned study sought to determine whether and how decisionmaking and communication between patients and health care professionals varied in different health care settings according to the nature of the illness and treatments under consideration, the types of health care providers, and patient characteristics. The study was conducted through interviews and observation under the direction of Professors Charles W. Lidz and Alan Meisel of the University of Pittsburgh and of the Western Psychiatric Institute and Clinic. Two researchers observed a surgical outpatient clinic and cardiology and surgery wards in a university

---

[4]Jay Katz, *Informed Consent—A Fairy Tale?: Law's Vision,* 39 U. Pitt. L. Rev. 137 (1977).

[5]For a complete list of witnesses and consultants, see the Addendum, pp. 189-91 *infra.*

[6]Reports from the commission's own studies and a review of the empirical literature may be found in the Appendices, published as Volume Two of this Report. The focus of most of these studies has been on physicians, with very little attention paid to nurses and other health professionals who interact with patients. Where information about the roles of nonphysician professionals is available it has been included.

hospital over a period of several weeks, throughout the day and evening. After noting the routines in each setting for several days, information was gathered on almost 200 cases. In 124 of these, the encounters between patients, physicians, and nurses were observed and recorded, and semistructured interviews were conducted with all who were involved in the decision at hand, often including family members.

Much as been written about the potentially negative consequences of providing patients with full information about their conditions and treatment, especially when it leads to refusals of "medically necessary" treatment, yet only scattered anecdotal evidence of such refusals exists. The Commission's other observational study sought to determine the frequency, nature, causes, and effects of treatment refusals. It found that treatment refusals were usually triggered by too little information rather than too much. The study was conducted in three stages by Drs. Paul S. Appelbaum and Loren H. Roth of the Western Psychiatric Institute and Clinic in Pittsburgh.

In the first stage, seven wards in four different medical hospitals were studied: a medicine, a surgery, and a neurology ward in a university-affiliated teaching hospital; a gynecology ward in a university-affiliated women's hospital; an ophthalmology ward in a university-affiliated specialty hospital; and a medical and a surgical ward in a large community hospital. Each ward was visited for most of a day four times at one-week intervals, with each visit being held on a different day of the week. Information was provided by the nurse on all treatment refusals in the previous 24 hours; charts were reviewed and interviews conducted with the nurse most familiar with the case, with the staff member who elicited the refusal, and with the patient.

In the second stage, more in-depth study was made of the longitudinal course of refusals on the medical and surgical wards of the university-affiliated teaching hospital. Daily rounds were made for a three-week period of the surgery ward and

for an eight-week period on the medicine ward. One observer made rounds with house staff and conducted interviews with physicians and nurses while the other observer interviewed patients. In the third stage, a case study approach was used to follow a number of cases of treatment refusal through the end of the patients' hospitalization. Medical charts were reviewed daily, extensive initial interviews were conducted with patients and they were re-interviewed at least every other day, and in most cases a family member was interviewed as well.

In the third empirical study done for the Commission, Louis Harris and Associates conducted parallel national surveys of physicians and the public regarding their attitudes toward, experience with, and knowledge of informed consent, disclosure of information, and decisional authority in medical care. The questionnaires were designed by Commission staff in conjunction with John M. Boyle and Paul J. Brounstein of the Harris organization. Telephone interviews were conducted with representative national samples of 800 physicians and 1250 adults in the general public. According to the accepted principles for such polls, the sample sizes were sufficiently large to allow general statements to be made about the populations from which they were drawn with 95% confidence that estimates were correct to within 3%, and to permit analysis by subgroups with reasonable confidence. For the public an "area probability sample" based on random-digit dialing was used,[7] and for the physician survey a

---

[7]The public sample was stratified by region of the country and within each region by size of the community. Use of random-digit dialing ensures that unlisted telephones are surveyed. Telephone surveys may slightly overrepresent the elderly and will generally significantly overrepresent females. To avoid this latter imbalance in the sample, a quota technique was used. In addition, all responses were weighted before doing the analyses to ensure that results reflected the total population rather than the population with telephones, thereby eliminating the slight bias that arises from the fact that about 2% of the U.S. population do not have telephones.

random sample was drawn of doctors who spend the majority of their time in direct care of adult patients.[8] The response rate to both surveys was approximately 70%, which is well within (or above) the range of statistical acceptability for such surveys.

In analyzing the data from the surveys, many cross-tabulations were performed to see whether there were variations in attitudes or behavior by subgroups of the public or the physicians. For the public survey all questions concerning disclosure of information, decisionmaking, and knowledge of informed consent were examined in relation to the respondents' age, gender, race, family income, education, self-reported health status, and health insurance status, whether or not the person had ever had a life-threatening illness, and the locale where he or she usually received medical care. For the physician sample all data were examined in relation to specialty, year of graduation from medical school, type of medical school attended (public, private, or foreign, and extent of research involvement), normal location of practice (office or hospital), the proportion of patients under the physician's care who were seriously ill, the proportion who were poor, and the proportion who the physician thought could understand most aspects of their condition and treatment.

It is important to note that different empirical methods yield data that can differ in several ways. Surveys are based on self-reports about past or hypothetical situations and therefore may not be entirely accurate reflections of practice. Regarding health care, surveys are known to overstate the frequency with which information is disclosed and may present a rosier, more homogeneous picture of medical practice than an on-site investigation of the same population would.

On the other hand, although studies by qualified neutral observers provide a truer picture of a piece of the real world, they often do not permit broad conclusions to be drawn. The results of surveys are quantifiable, whereas observational studies largely yield qualitative results. The findings from these two types of studies are often complementary but they may also be divergent in some respects. (Differences between the Commission's survey and the observational studies are noted throughout the Report where relevant.)

In general, the Commission's surveys found that the relationship between physicians and patients is dynamic, that disclosures are extensive, that understanding and satisfaction are high, that decisionmaking is shared—and that patients expect their relations with physicians to have these characteristics. This was found to be especially true for office-based (as distinct from clinic- or hospital-based) settings, where doctors and patients are apparently able to establish a relationship over time. Furthermore, as might be expected, the public's experience with the health care system appears to vary depending on whether the patient is young or old, in good or poor health, and well or poorly educated. In contrast, physicians' self-reported behaviors and attitudes were relatively homogeneous. Even though the issue of informed consent has received a great deal of attention in the last decade, there was little variation among physicians by specialty, age, or nature of patients under their care.

The observational studies, on the other hand, found enormous variation in the patient-professional relationship and the decisionmaking process within various hospital settings. Such variation appears to be related to the structure in which care is delivered and the nature of patients' conditions and treatments. In these studies, it was rare for the process described in this Report as ideal to be realized in practice. Because the observational studies were conducted principally in university-affiliated teaching hospitals the findings may not be representative of all hospital care.

---

[8]The physician sample was drawn according to study specifications by the American Medical Association, which maintains files of all physicians in the country and updates them monthly. This is the most reliable source of data on the total physician population in the country.

For example, in nonteaching hospitals patients are more likely to be cared for by fewer doctors (perhaps only one) than in teaching hospitals staffed with a large number of interns and residents, thus lessening the possibility that one doctor will mistakenly assume that another doctor has talked with a patient about treatment. . . .

The Management of Medical Information: Legal and Moral Requirements of Informed Voluntary Consent

Tom L. Beauchamp and Laurence B. McCullough

Tom L. Beauchamp is professor of philosophy and senior research scholar at the Kennedy Institute of Ethics, Georgetown University. He is the author or co-author of Principles of Biomedical Ethics *(Oxford University Press, 1983),* A History and Theory of Informed Consent *(co-author, Oxford University Press, 1986),* Philosophical Ethics *(McGraw-Hill, 1982),* Medical Ethics: The Moral Responsibilities of Physicians *(Prentice-Hall, 1984), and* Hume and the Problem of Causation *(Oxford University Press, 1981). He is also chairman of the American Philosophical Association's Committee on Medicine and Philosophy and serves as the general editor of* The Critical Edition of the Works of David Hume, *now being edited and published by the Princeton University Press.*

Laurence B. McCullough is associate professor of Community and Family Medicine and of Pediatrics in the School of Medicine at Georgetown University. He holds a joint appointment in the Department of Community Dentistry and is a senior research scholar in Georgetown's Kennedy Institute of Ethics.

Beauchamp and McCullough review the major court cases involving informed voluntary consent from 1914 to 1972 and beyond. They critically examine such standards of disclosure as (1) the Professional Practice Standard, (2) the Reasonable Person Standard, and (3) the Subjective Standard. They explore conflicts between protecting patient well-being and patient self-determination. They suggest that the second objective should prevail when dealing with competent adult decision-makers and the first when dealing with others whose decisional capacities are either substantially impaired or temporarily diminished.

LEGAL REQUIREMENTS

Legal History of the Informed Consent Doctrine

The law of informed consent is still actively evolving. As the *Berkey* court noted, its early foundations are in tort law of battery, which holds that

From Tom L. Beauchamp and Laurence B. McCullough, *Medical Ethics: The Moral Responsibilities of Physicians,* © 1984, pp. 63–78. Reprinted by permission of the authors and Prentice-Hall, Inc., Englewood Cliffs, New Jersey.

an individual can be validly "touched" by another only when he or she authorizes that touching. When touching is nonauthorized, questions of liability for the causal outcome are raised. This legal doctrine of informed consent has passed through three identifiable stages in the United States, each demarcated by landmark legal decisions.

The 1914–1957 Period.   The first phase ran roughly from 1914 to 1957—a period characterized by concern about whether a patient had

given a consent that acknowledged some general description of the procedure involved. The most influential case was *Schloendorff v. Society of New York Hospitals* (1914).[1] A fibroid tumor had been removed from the abdomen of a female patient, but the patient had requested "no operation." The court cited negligence and trespass in noting that the tumor had been removed "without her consent or knowledge." Justice Cardozo . . . vigorously insisted on the patient's right to self-determination and on the liability of the physician when patients are not given the opportunity to exercise that right by consenting to treatment. Subsequent cases between 1914 and 1957 exhibit a consistent pattern of reasoning in the courts: Either a patient consented or failed to consent; a partial or incomplete consent plays no role in the court's decision. This analysis sprang from the prevalent notion at the time that consents were broad; a simple, routine disclosure was given about the procedure itself, usually without much background explanation.

The 1957–1972 Period.

The second phase involved a transition from the bare fact of consent to a concern about the quality of consent, with a special emphasis on the quality of disclosure. The *Berkey v. Anderson* case . . . was in litigation during the early days of this period, and was decided near its conclusion. In this legal environment, the term "informed consent" was born and flourished, and the legal category of "professional negligence" came to describe a wrong caused by a failure to inform *adequately.* The following aspects of the legal doctrine stabilized: As the *Berkey* court noted, battery is involved if a procedure is performed without basic disclosure as to nature and scope prior to consent (whether by omission or misrepresentation). One is bat-

tered when even simple consent is not present, or when a "consent" is vitiated by misrepresentation. Simple consent is regarded as a necessary first level of any valid consent. Negligence, by contrast, is involved when a procedure is performed with consent based on disclosure as to its nature and scope (and so there *is* simple consent), but without disclosure as to possible complications or risks of the procedure and possible alternatives to it. (Battery involves injuries as the result of intended action, whereas no intent is required in negligence.)

Thus, during the 1957 to 1972 period a more complex consent requirement emerged. It established a second level of valid consent. This conclusion is embraced by the *Berkey* court and was one important reason Dr. Anderson was found guilty of negligence. Beginning in the late 1950s, the courts began to consider informed consent a matter of professional conduct and to establish the breach of a duty to inform as negligence—not battery—therefore aligning informed consent cases with other medical malpractice cases.[2]

The courts applied this approach even in cases where there was no dispute about whether the level of disclosure was consistent with sound

---

[1] *Schloendorff v. Society of New York Hospitals,* 105 N.E. 92 (1914). Ironically, this landmark case pertained to hospital liability, and the court found neither a violation of informed consent nor even delivered its findings in terms of consent.

[2] First in 1957 with *Salgo v. Leland Stanford, Jr. University Board of Trustees,* 154 Cal. App. 2d 560, 317 P.2d 170 (1957). For legal details including explanations of the shifts discussed here, see *Trogun v. Fruchtman,* 58 Wis. 2d 596, pp. 599–600, 207 N.W. 2d 297, p. 313 (1973); Alan McCoid, "A Reappraisal of Liability for Unauthorized Medical Treatment," *Minnesota Law Review* 41 (1957): 381, 423–25; James Ludlam, *Informed Consent* (Chicago: American Hospital Association, 1978); and Alan Meisel, "Expansion of Liability for Medical Accidents: From Negligence to Strict Liability by Way of Informed Consent," *Nebraska Law Review* 56 (1977). The informed consent action in negligence has five elements: (1) the physician's *duty* to give information (under the appropriate informational standard) which is part of his professional duty of due care; (2) *breach of duty;* (3) *risk:* materialization of the undisclosed outcome or possible outcome; (4) *proximate causation:* had a plaintiff been informed of an outcome or risk he or she would not have consented; (5) damages, i.e., *actual injury.* If the plaintiff can prove the existence of all five elements, the physician is liable for medical malpractice, regardless of the skill with which treatment was provided.

medical practice—a matter at issue in *Berkey*. An important case was *Natanson v. Kline,* a 1960 Kansas case in which cobalt radiation therapy was administered after a radical mastectomy to the area where the cancer had been removed. Injuries to the chest, skin, and cartilage resulted from the radiation therapy, and the woman brought suit against her physician. The physician acknowledged that risks were inherent in the procedure, but he "failed to warn the patient of risks of (such) bodily injury." A trial court found for the physicians, but an appeals court asserted that physicians are required to disclose the nature, dangers, and probable consequences of cobalt radiation and may not substitute even *sound* medical judgment for the patient's judgment. Consequently, the appeals court judge viewed the protection of autonomy as the major purpose of informed consent and denied that the patient's medical best interests could legitimately override duties of disclosure.

Natanson not only established a category of "risks" that must be disclosed to the patient, but also established that mere consent does not shield the physician from negligence (liability for injury), even if the medical performance is good. That is, the medical practice can be flawless, but if injury results from a routine risk, and the risk was not disclosed, the physician is liable. The "consent" was invalidated in *Natanson* because the patient was not informed of those "collateral hazards" any "reasonable medical practitioner" would disclose.[3]

The Post-1972 Period.

When the *Berkey* court rejected Dr. Anderson's argument that the standards determining his disclosure obligation to the patient were set by what physicians routinely disclose about risks, it was knocking on the door of some newly emerging problems. Since 1972, several influential courts have addressed the issue of what counts as adequate disclosure, in light of the patient-centered standard established in some courts during the 1957 to 1972 period. The 1972 cases that have achieved landmark status are *Canterbury v. Spence* and *Cobbs v. Grant.*[4] Let us first briefly examine these important cases and certain problems about disclosure standards that they create. We shall then offer some reservations—mainly moral reservations—about their disclosure requirements.

Canterbury v. Spence was the first and most influential of the landmark informed consent cases in this period. This case involved a laminectomy[5] for severe back pain. Subsequent to the laminectomy, the patient fell from a hospital bed, a fall that caused major paralysis. The patient had not been warned that a laminectomy might increase the danger of paralysis as the result of such events as falling out of bed. A second operation failed to relieve the paralysis, and an appeals court held that risk of possible paralysis should have been disclosed prior to the first procedure. Judge Spottswood Robinson's opinion focused on autonomy: "The root premise is the concept, fundamental in American jurisprudence, that 'every human being of adult years and sound mind has a right to determine what shall be done with his own body.' . . ."[6] True consent was held in this case to be contingent upon the informed exercise of a choice; thus, the physician's disclosure should have provided the patient an opportunity to assess available options and attendant risks, such as paralysis. As to sufficiency of information, the court held: "The patient's right of self-decision shapes the boundaries of the duty to reveal. That right can be effectively exercised only if the patient possesses enough information to enable an intelligent choice."[7]

Cobbs v. Grant came to similar conclusions.

---

[3]*Natanson v. Kline,* 350 P.2d 1093 (1960).

[4]*Canterbury v. Spence,* 464 F.2d 772 (1972); *Cobbs v. Grant,* 502 P.2d 1 (1972).

[5]A laminectomy is the surgical removal of parts of the vertebrae, commonly including spinous processes of the vertebrae.

[6]From *Canterbury,* p. 786, quoting *Schloendorff v. Society of New York Hospitals.*

[7]*Canterbury v. Spence,* p. 786 (footnotes omitted).

The court required disclosure of "*all* significant perils pertaining to death or serious harm," and rejected the view that decisions whether to proceed with a specific therapy are solely medical determinations. The court insisted that all significant risks peculiar to a proposed procedure must be divulged, as judged by the extent to which a prudent or reasonable person in the patient's position would want to know about the risk. In this case, Dr. F. P. Grant examined Mr. Ralph Cobbs and diagnosed a duodenal ulcer. Surgery was recommended, and Dr. Grant explained the *nature* of the operation to Mr. Cobbs, but did not discuss any of several complicated *risks* inherent in the surgery itself. Mr. Cobbs consented to the operation and an apparently successful surgery was performed. But complications arose: Mr. Cobbs suffered intense abdominal pain, injuries to the spleen that necessitated a subsequent operation, and a developing gastric ulcer. All are risks inherent in surgery performed to relieve a duodenal ulcer. The court declared these events "links in a chain of low probability events inherent in the initial operation," and reasoned that Dr. Grant's failure to disclose them ran contrary to the physician's duty to disclose.

These two cases inaugurated the present period, and many courts now require disclosures as to a medical diagnosis, prognosis with and without treatment, proposed treatments, risks inherent in the treatment, and alternative treatment modes and their risks. Such disclosure requirements have met with opposition in much of the medical community. The following reaction by Dr. Robert B. Howard is typical:

> Is it good medical practice to discuss with an apprehensive, febrile, partially obtunded patient with pneumonia the possibility that the medication selected may produce an anaphylactoid reaction or may cause exfoliative dermatitis, urticaria, serum sickness, fever, hemolytic anemia, leukopenia, thrombocytopenia, neuropathy, and/or nephropathy? Must I explain all of these and present optional forms of therapy, each of which has its own list of possible side effects?
>
> I believe that such action on my part would be inappropriate and irresponsible. Yet, if I interpret correctly the recent court decisions and awards, my failure to discuss even the rarest potential adverse reactions may expose me to successful legal action if such reaction occurs.
>
> I believe that truly informed consent is an impossible goal in many, indeed most, of our daily clinical experiences. I believe that with each patient we must use our best professional judgment to guide the discussion—the disease, the patient's immediate clinical condition and intellectual capacity, and the actual probability of adverse events connected with treatment all are pertinent. Obtaining informed consent that meets strict legal requirements will solve few health care problems and will seriously impede recovery in many cases.[8]

The requirements denounced in this critique have gradually crept up on medicine, which has witnessed a shift from a beneficence-based standard of disclosure to the autonomy-based standard present in the 1972 cases. A professionally based standard of disclosure has its source in the beneficence model, while a patient-based standard of disclosure fits with the values in the autonomy model. This may be seen more clearly if we structure what we have learned about legal history in terms specific to the *standards* governing physician disclosure that we discussed previously. We make this effort not with the intent to reform the law, but rather to construct an adequate general standard for clinical practice from the moral point of view.

Standards Governing Physician Disclosure

The Professional Practice Standard. A professional practice standard was invoked by Dr. Anderson in the *Berkey* case and traditionally has been the standard of disclosure favored by physicians and others favoring the beneficence model. The professional practice standard holds that adequate disclosure is determined by the customary

---

[8]Robert B. Howard, "More on Informed Consent," *Postgraduate Medicine* 65 (January 1979): 25.

rules or traditional practices of the professional community of physicians, who are presumed to be in a privileged position to determine their patients' best interests. The physician, by reference to the perspective of medicine—specifically, by reference to the practice of physicians in general—determines the balance of harms and goods of disclosure and establishes both the topics to be discussed and the amount and kinds of information to be disclosed about each topic. The disclosure needing to be made (if any) is as much a professional decision as the physician's original diagnosis.[9] Thus, the burden of proof in most legal jurisdictions is on the patient to show that the physician's disclosure failed to conform to established standards.

Many problems, however, attend this professional practice standard for disclosure. First, as the *Canterbury* and *Cobbs* courts noted, it is unclear that customary standards for disclosure prevail in the medical profession, and in any event, the rules that would constitute the standard are not precisely formulated.[10] Hence, it is difficult to answer questions about how much consensus is necessary—and within which fields of medicine—in order to establish that a medical practice standard for disclosure does in fact exist. Moreover, if custom alone is decisive, then negligent disclosures are "acceptable" if physicians generally provide inferior information and precautions.[11] Finally, the professional practice standard neglects the patient's autonomy rights in the face of no empirical evidence that physicians make either good decisions about appropriate information or even that they have a better conception of what is in a patient's best interest than does the patient. Critics of this first standard hold that weighing the harms and goods of disclosure is not a medical skill to be measured by a professional standard; rather it is an individual value judgment reserved to the affected person alone. . . .

The Reasonable Person Standard.

In the aftermath of *Canterbury,* the reasonable person standard has emerged as a prominent legal criterion. This standard was implicitly invoked by Mr. Berkey, even though his case antedated *Canterbury.* Approximately twenty-five percent of the legal jurisdictions in the United States now accept this new criterion, while the remaining seventy-five percent still adhere to the more traditional medical practice standard. Thus, while there has been a significant shift toward a patient-based standard, that shift has yet to be accepted in the majority of legal jurisdictions.

According to the reasonable person standard, which flows from the legal principle of respect for self-determination, the physician must disclose to the patient all information relevant to a decision, as judged by what a hypothetical reasonable person would want to know. Providing material information is part of the physician's fiduciary duty of due care, and a physician's medical expertise is recognized as only one of several factors that a patient may wish to take into consideration. The relevance of a piece of information to a patient's decision is measured not by a professional judgment, but instead by the significance a reasonable person would attach to a risk in reaching a decision. If that risk would be regarded as significant, it should be disclosed. If not, disclosure is unnecessary. Therefore, in theory, a physician may be found guilty of negligent disclosure even if the physician's behavior conforms perfectly to recognized and routine professional practice (as occurred in *Natanson*).

Whatever its virtues, the reasonable person standard harbors problems. First, the concept of the "materiality" or relevance of information is

---

[9]See Marcus Plant, "The Decline of Informed Consent," *Washington and Lee Law Review* 35 (1978): 96–99.

[10]Alan Stone notes—in "Informed Consent: Special Problems for Psychiatry," *Hospital and Community Psychiatry* 30 (May 1979): 322, and "Reply," *Hospital and Community Psychiatry* 30 (September 1979): 637—that physicians are not trained uniformly in appropriate disclosures. He expresses doubt that "any such standard exists" (p. 323).

[11]See Jon R. Waltz, "The Rise and Gradual Fall of the Locality Rule in Medical Malpractice Litigation," *DePaul Law Review* 18 (1969), esp. p. 408.

only ambiguously defined in *Canterbury* and related cases, and the central concept of "the reasonable person" goes altogether undefined. Second, no specific or extensive duty of disclosure follows from such a standard; thus, from the perspective of autonomy, the "new" standard expressed in *Canterbury* may give a false sense of an advance over the older standard. Indeed, some empirical evidence suggests that in medical practice it makes no difference in physicians' behavior in making disclosures whether the medical practice standard or the reasonable person standard is operative in the relevant legal jurisdiction.[12] Finally, because application of the abstract reasonable person standard to a concrete case would require reference to specific facts of the case, an unresolved problem is how to understand what information the reasonable person would want "under the same or similar circumstances" as those of the patient. If, for example, a physician fails to disclose a remote risk of surgery, we must ask whether a reasonable person in this patient's *precise* position would have wanted to be told of the risk. But how broadly is *that* position to be described? This leads to consideration of a third standard, which has been proposed to answer this question.

The Subjective Standard.   Individual patients have different needs for information, especially if they have idiosyncratic or unique beliefs, deviant health behaviors, a unique family or personal history, or the like. Such patients require a different informational base than that required by most persons. . . . Such special circumstances are clearly relevant to the process of decisionmaking. If a physician has grounds for believing that a patient needs such information, the autonomy model strongly suggests its disclosure. By thus following the demands of this model, the reason-

able person standard is modified to a "subjective" form.[13]

The subjective standard has been rejected almost wholly by the courts,[14] largely because of the legal doctrine of proximate cause on which so many informed consent malpractice cases turn. According to the proximate cause theory, a patient cannot recover for injury unless he or she can show that the physician's negligence in disclosing information was a proximate cause of the injury. There is no causal connection in law between a physician's negligent disclosure and the patient's injury unless consent would *not* have been given had a proper disclosure been made. If a subjective approach were taken to the proximate cause issue, a patient could recover if *that particular* patient would not have consented had an adequate disclosure been made. *Canterbury* and other courts insist that this determination would be guesswork and constantly would place physicians in jeopardy of the vindictive hindsight of patients, including possible outright falsification. Hence, these courts allow only the "objective reasonable person" to be the appropriate standard.

Such *legal* arguments fail to determine whether the subjective standard is a better *moral* standard for communications in the patient-physician relationship. As we shall now see, this

---

[12]See the two studies by Faden et al., "Disclosures of Information to Patients in Medical Care" and "Disclosure Standards and Informed Consent."

[13]For legal commentary favoring this standard, see Alexander Capron, "Informed Consent in Catastrophic Disease Research and Treatment," *University of Pennsylvania Law Review* 123 (1974): 364–76; L. W. Kessenick and P. A. Mankin, "Medical Malpractice: The Right to be Informed," *University of San Francisco Law Review* 8 (1973); Marcus Plant, "An Analysis of Informed Consent," *Fordham Law Review* 36 (1968); and Leonard L. Riskin, "Informed Consent: Looking for the Action," *University of Illinois Law Forum 1975* (1975). The standard has been overtly embraced as a moral standard for medical practice by Charles Culver and Bernard Gert, *Philosophy in Medicine: Conceptual and Ethical Issues in Medicine and Psychiatry* (New York: Oxford University Press, 1982), Chapter 3.

[14]At least one court—the Oklahoma Supreme Court—has adopted a subjective approach. See *Scott v. Bradford,* 606 P.2d 554 (Okla. 1980), esp. 556 and the analysis of this case in "Note," *Tulsa Law Journal* 15 (1980): 665ff.

standard is strongly recommended from the point of view of morality.

COMPETING MODELS OF DECISIONAL AUTHORITY

Jay Katz, professor of law and psychiatry at Yale, has written extensively on problems of legal standards of disclosure and their inadequacies. He has convincingly argued that the primary problem underlying the aforementioned battles over shifting legal standards is not one that the law directly addresses or is well equipped to address. The fundamental question, he holds, is "Whose judgment is to be respected and overriding?" Katz has approached the prevailing situations in law and medicine through what he calls a "conflict between two visions": a "vision of human beings as autonomous persons and . . . deference to paternalism, another powerful vision of man's interaction with man."[15] "Autonomous persons" here refers to an individual's capacity to assume authority over his or her medical fate. This capacity law and medicine alike sometimes recognize as the patient's right to self-determination and consequent right to the fullest possible disclosure—an autonomy-based standard. "Paternalism" here means that the physician assumes authority to manage the information disclosed, without consulting the patient, on grounds of beneficence.

Katz notes that the courts have traditionally paid allegiance to this vision of humans as autonomous only to deviate from their pronouncements once the realities of medical practice and the patient's decisionmaking capacities in medical facilities are brought to the court's attention. Katz therefore sees the entire legal doctrine of informed consent—including all the standards discussed above—as little more than a symbol of the need for patient decisionmaking—a symbol having virtually no impact on how decisions are made by patients, courts, or physicians:

> The conflict created by uncertainties about the extent to which individual and societal well-being is better served by encouraging patients' self-determination or supporting physicians' paternalism is the central problem of informed consent. This fundamental conflict, reflecting a thoroughgoing ambivalence about human beings' capacities for taking care of themselves and need for care-taking, has shaped judicial pronouncements on informed consent more decisively than is commonly appreciated. The assertion of a 'need' for physicians' discretion—for a professional expert's rather than a patient's judgment as to what constitutes well-being—reveals this ambivalence. Other oft-invoked impediments to fostering patients' self-determination, such as patients' medical ignorance, doctors' precious time, the threat of increased litigation, or the difficulty of proving what actually occurred in the dialogue between physician and patient are, substantially, rationalizations which obscure the basic conflict over whose judgment is to be respected.[16]

The lengthy quotation in *Berkey* of the 1957 precedent case *Salgo v. Leland Stanford, Jr. University Board of Trustees* . . . can be used to illustrate Katz's valuable contentions. The *Salgo* court notes that *any* withholding of facts "necessary to form the basis of an intelligent consent by the patient" is a violation of a physician's duty to the patient. Having made this strong pronouncement, the court does an immediate about-face . . .: The "patient's mental and emotional condition is important and in certain cases may be crucial, and . . . in discussing the element of risk a certain amount of discretion must be employed consistent with the full disclosure of facts necessary to an informed consent."[17]

The need in many cases of physician discretion, under the ideal of a fiduciary relationship

---

[15]Jay Katz, "Informed Consent—A Fairy Tale? Law's Vision," *University of Pittsburgh Law Review* 39 (Winter 1977): 139.

[16]Ibid.

[17]*Salgo,* as quoted in *Berkey v. Anderson,* p. 72.

between patient and physician, leads the court to hold that on the one hand, an autonomy-based standard of disclosure sometimes justifiably yields to a beneficence-based standard, and on the other hand, a beneficence-based standard sometimes justifiably yields to an autonomy-based one. Moreover, the court suggests that a physician *violates a duty* and invites a malpractice suit by not providing sufficient information on which to base an intelligent choice; at the same time, the court suggests that the duty itself is *validly qualified* by the physician's professional discretion. Hence, Katz properly doubts that there can be complete consistency between "physician discretion" in the disclosure of information and "full disclosure of facts." "Only in dreams or fairy tales," he writes, "can 'discretion' to withhold crucial information so easily and magically be reconciled with 'full disclosure'."[18] *Salgo* and virtually all subsequent courts have exhibited such wishful thinking.

The law thus seems committed to two competing moral objectives. The first is that patients should be treated as autonomous, with the right to make informed decisions. The second is that it is appropriate for the physician to limit disclosure depending on the weight of the harms and goods of disclosure. When the law focuses on patient autonomy, the emphasis is on decisionmaking by patients; when the law focuses on the possible consequences of full disclosure to patients, as understood from medicine's perspective, the emphasis is on professional discretion and the avoidance of harm to patients. Physicians are to respect autonomy, but they also may validly invoke a "therapeutic privilege"—one that permits physicians on grounds of "good medical practice" not to disclose information (to the patient, anyway) if it would "seriously jeopardize the recovery of an unstable, temperamental, or severely depressed

patient."[19] Because courts must eventually evaluate a broad range of problems in managing information, they have not been able to escape confrontation with the full power of the conflict between the two models of moral responsibility. . . . Patients' rights and physicians' professional judgments compete in the courts' deliberations.

Contemporary writings in medical ethics on the purposes of informed consent requirements suffer the same problem.[20] One widely shared view is that the primary purpose of informed consent is the protection of autonomy. This description presupposes the dominance of the autonomy model of professional responsibility. However, other purposes of informed consent requirements have also been promoted, in particular the prevention of injury to patients. Informing patients of treatment increases patient cooperation and recovery and presumably avoids those treatments patients consider unjustifiably risky. This second candidate for a primary purpose conforms to the canons of the beneficence model.

There is no *a priori* inconsistency between the dual purposes of protecting autonomy and protecting from harm. But if we believe there is no deep tension between these ideals, we are indulging in the same pattern of wishful thinking reflected in *Salgo*. A direct conflict between full disclosure and physician discretion is inescapable

---

[18]Katz, "Informed Consent—A Fairy Tale?": 138 (see also 150), and "Disclosure and Consent in Psychiatric Practice: Mission Impossible?" in *Law and Ethics in the Practice of Psychiatry,* ed. Charles Hofling (New York: Brunner-Mazel, Inc., 1981), p. 93.

[19]*Natanson v. Kline,* p. 1103. For slightly different formulations, see *Sard v. Hardy,* 367 A.2d, p. 1022 and *Canterbury v. Spence,* p. 789. Even here, however, considerable uncertainty surrounds the precise conditions under which therapeutic privilege may be validly invoked, the courts having left indeterminate *how* adverse the impact of disclosed information must be and how much latitude is to be given to the physician. A typical pronouncement is "the doctor's primary duty is to do what is best for the patient. Any conflict between this duty and that of a frightening disclosure ordinarily should be resolved in favor of the primary duty." *Nishi v. Hartwell,* 473 P.2d 116, p. 119.

[20]Several basic functions, purposes, or objectives of informed consent have been distinguished in the influential article by Alexander Capron cited previously: "Informed Consent in Catastrophic Disease Research and Treatment."

in many interchanges between physician and patient. One's view as to which of these is the *primary* objective of informed consent requirements has decisive implications for several major issues about informed decisionmaking—most prominently for issues about what types and how much information ought to be disclosed if a patient might autonomously reject a physician's compelling medical recommendations and thereby cause injury through his or her autonomous choice.

Patients and physicians, no less than courts, cannot escape a struggle with the dual vision of human nature as at once autonomous and responsible, but needing the same comfort a child does when reduced in decisional capacity by the throes of worry, illness, or injury. The pattern of this problem is everywhere present in medicine, as reflected in circumstances where patients are at once socially functional but mentally ill, partially insistent and partially yielding, partially resistant and partially malleable, depressed but mentally alert, hostile and yet capitulating. The same pattern is also apparent in empirical studies of the quality of decisionmaking by patients: Studies indicate that although *some* patients carefully weigh risks and benefits (among other considerations) when making their decisions about proposed treatments, most follow either their own predispositions or a physician's recommendations, usually without a careful assessment of available information.[21]

Clinical experience also suggests that patients exhibit wide variability in their capacities to understand and appreciate information about their diagnoses, treatments, or prognoses. While some patients, like Mr. Berkey, seem capable of grasping the particular details of a diagnostic or therapeutic procedure, other patients are excessively nervous, anxious, or distracted—e.g., the older patient who is worried about the word "cancer" and its many meanings, or the adolescent patient with cancer who is obsessed with possible hair loss caused by chemotherapy. Such patients may not, at first, be capable of dealing with information about their diagnosis and treatment. The two visions of the patient's ability to make medical decisions that Katz has identified are also entrenched in the two models of moral responsibility, focused as both are on the problem of decisionmaking responsibility.

WHO SHOULD DECIDE?

Who, then, should decide—the patient or the physician? Who would be so bold as to answer this question with confident finality? Any answer would shipwreck on an infinity of qualifications and in the end would fail to provide more than general guidelines. There is no single or final answer to the question "Who should decide?" because there is no single or final solution to the larger conflict between the two models of moral responsibility. Every rational person wants decisional authority over his or her fate, but who has not known how quickly the contradictory desire to yield to professional authority manifests itself in the face of illness? Everyone wants respect, but like all fundamental moral principles, "respect for persons" can be applied in innumerable ways. One patient may be respected by demanding that he or she resist a desire to capitulate, while another may be respected by lifting the burden of decision from a wearied and tortured soul in need of rest. There can be no single, general answer, substantive or procedural, to the utterly unanswerable and all too general question, "Who should decide?" What can be hoped for instead are physicians well prepared to grapple with the question in light of the moral demands of the beneficence and autonomy models. (This conclusion must not be taken to imply either that in the final analysis the burden of decision rests with the physician or that specific criteria for appropriate

---

[21]See Meisel and Roth, "What We Do and Do Not Know About Informed Consent." Cf. also Ruth R. Faden and Tom L. Beauchamp, "Decision-making and Informed Consent," *Social Indicators Research* 7 (1980): 313–36; and C. H. Fellner and J. R. Marshall, "Kidney Donors: The Myth of Informed Consent," *American Journal of Psychiatry* 126 (1970): 1245–51.

decisionmakers can never be adduced for specific contexts. Both assumptions are clearly false.)

General policies that define the physician's responsibilities in the management of information through only one model will inevitably fail. To follow the autonomy model and emphasize only the patient's right to information overlooks clinical realities. Some patients simply are not prepared to hear the physician. Some might be harmed by too much information or poorly timed disclosures, while illness, disease, and catastrophic accidents might have a significant impact on some patients' capacities to decide. To emphasize the beneficence model exclusively is an equally flawed strategy. It can be used to so overemphasize the impact of illness, pain, suffering, and debility that no patient could qualify as autonomous; and it also fails to appreciate the variety of contexts in which physicians manage information—including, for example, genetic counseling or screening for hypertension.

If both models are accepted as the basis of the physician's responsibilities in the management of information, the following three guidelines can be justified. First, patients whose decisional capacities are substantially intact (and who qualify as autonomous) should be treated primarily in accordance with the autonomy model and a subjective standard of disclosure of information that emphasizes relatively complete disclosure. Second, patients whose decisional capacities are substantially impaired by such conditions as severe or profound mental retardation, advanced dementia, emergency situations, and the like (and whose autonomy is thus substantially reduced) should be treated primarily in accordance with the beneficence model, with its characteristic emphases on harms, goods, and the careful monitoring of information. These two guidelines are not together adequate for the full range of patients because many patients are borderline—not substantially autonomous, yet not substantially reduced in autonomy. The effective management of information can itself play a role in the process of overcoming impairments, such as those caused by temporary fear, mild depres-

sion, and anxiety. The approach to disclosure with such patients necessarily is directed by a third guideline that involves discretion in the use of both models. The impairment such patients suffer renders the autonomy model inapplicable, but psychological needs for information may nonetheless be present, and effective communication with such patients may be a crucial element in the recovery process.

Many virtues . . . play an essential role in shaping the physician's management of medical information. For example, the virtue of compassion reminds the physician that some of the information may be unpleasant, disturbing, or even frightening, while prudence plays a role in directing the sequence and timing of disclosure so that patients can absorb information in a meaningful way. Patience, too, is of critical importance, especially when dealing with compromised patients. Finally, Osler's *aequanimitas* reminds the physician that "bodily virtues" (whether to sit or stand at the patient's bedside and whether he or she touches the patient and looks at the patient directly) and "mental virtues" (the tone of voice and the balanced exercise of authority) are significant aspects of the physician's moral responsibilities in the effective communication of medical information.

These virtues jointly encourage the virtue of respectfulness. From the fact that a patient may be confused, frightened, or impaired and may have lost the capacity for autonomous decision-making, it does not follow that he or she no longer is owed the respect that all of us command. The virtue of respectfulness nowhere applies more insistently than in the management of medical information.

EXTENSIONS AND CONCLUSIONS

. . . *Berkey v. Anderson* . . . served as an introduction to the legal history of informed consent. That history raises, but insufficiently explores, questions about what a physician ought to discuss

with a patient in the process of making decisions. While a flood of malpractice cases such as *Berkey* has haunted courts and physicians in recent years, these cases have not, in our experience, profoundly altered medical practice. They have served principally to increase the volume of words in physician disclosures, as well as to increase recorded documentation of disclosure. Most legal pronouncements do not even encourage dialogue, let alone meaningful communication, between patients and physicians.

Nevertheless, if serious dialogue and communication between physician and patient were institutionalized in accordance with the *moral* analyses and arguments set out in this chapter, medical practice might be profoundly altered. The responsibilities of the physician in the management of medical information would be based in a patient-centered standard of communication. For patients whose decisional capacities are adequately intact, this approach would be understood in terms of the autonomy model and the subjective standard: The patient's values and choices would constitute the perspective from which the harms and goods of disclosure should be assessed. For patients whose decisional capacities are seriously impaired, or even absent, the approach would be understood in terms of the beneficence model and the reasonable person standard of disclosure: Medicine's objective values and the (objective) reasonable person would provide the perspectives from which the harms and goods of disclosure should be assessed. For patients whose decisional capacities are basically intact yet whose emotional state may temporarily retard the exercise of sound judgment, the physician must determine the proper balance between the demands of the autonomy model and those of the beneficence model. In reaching this conclusion, we are not rejecting the professional practice standard as a legally appropriate standard in (at least some) malpractice cases. However, we do mean to reject it as a *morally* appropriate standard of disclosure in clinical practice because of the potentially cavalier attitudes toward the patient permitted by such a standard.

Some courts have given indecisive hints in the direction of our conclusions. For example, some have suggested that a physician must render not only an accurate, comprehensible, and sufficiently comprehensive judgment as to the nature, risks, and consequences of a procedure, but also ought to discuss whether the course of treatment should be undertaken at all. The latter question requires a delicate presentation to patients of benefits and risks of particular diagnostic interventions and therapeutic alternatives, without compromising the physician's authority. That is, the physician is asked to render a professional judgment as to the *limits* of what he or she recommends and to discuss those limits realistically with patients.

Much more of an innovative nature needs to be said along these lines than has been said by physicians, courts, and writers in medical ethics. For example, we need to discuss openly how false assurances intended to encourage patients may seriously mislead them; when to disclose to a family information that is judged inappropriate for the patient; how to present information straightforwardly and clearly;[22] and the importance of unhurried, courteous, and properly timed discussions with patients. Disclosure requirements should be discussed in terms not only of what should be said but also what should be asked. The focus should be on the entire communication process, and not simply on disclosure as an obligatory recitation of some stipulated set of facts about risks, benefits, and alternatives. The problem to date with the legal history of disclosure requirements is the near absence of concern about such requirements of communication.

The goal of this chapter has been to elevate our appreciation of the physician's moral responsibilities in the management of information to a

---

[22]Variations in the way information is presented to autonomous patients have been shown to significantly influence their seemingly autonomous choices between alternative therapies. See Barbara J. McNeil et al., "On the Elicitation of Preferences for Alternative Therapies," *The New England Journal of Medicine* 306 (27 May 1982): 1259–62.

greater level of maturity, by arguing against simple resolutions of moral problems surrounding that responsibility. In the case of seriously ill and injured patients who face appreciable risks or frightening choices, the physician's commitment to the patient demands that he or she not abandon the patient to the mere formalities of contemporary legal requirements of informed consent. Let us make no mistake. The physician who deeply cares about the dignity and welfare of patients must operate with and even be trapped between the two models. Both are essential for appropriately dignified and responsible exchanges between physician and patients, and many patients cannot be treated simply in accordance with the demands of one in isolation from the other.

Moreover, we cannot reasonably expect to eliminate the fundamental conflicts arising from the two models and from conflicting legal approaches to the management of medical information. How to address the informational needs of ill, and often compromised, autonomous patients cannot be determined with confident moral generalizations. We can, however, hope to fashion a clearer vision of what it means to treat such patients both professionally and with respect. We can also insist and reinsist on the importance of the virtues and duties of truthfulness and respectfulness in medicine. The importance of discretion in the management of medical information can never excuse the physician from adopting attitudes of self-preoccupation or disrespect.

A Defense of Medical Paternalism: Maximizing Patients' Autonomy

Mark S. Komrad

Mark S. Komrad received his B.S. degree from Yale University in 1979, graduating summa cum laude and as a member of Phi Beta Kappa. He finished Duke University Medical School in 1983, AOA. In 1982 he was a fellow at the Hastings Center for Society, Ethics and the Life Sciences. Currently he is a senior resident in psychiatry at Johns Hopkins Hospital, Baltimore, with special interests in psychosomatics and conversion disorders. He teaches medical ethics at the Hopkins School of Medicine and is a member of the Hospital Ethics Committee. He is preparing to enter a career in the private practice of psychiatry and part-time academic psychiatry.

Komrad notes the importance of the principle of human self-determination or autonomy in both Kant's deontological ethics and Mill's utilitarian ethics. He defines "paternalism," suggests that there are degrees of autonomy, takes the somewhat extreme position that "all illness represents a state of diminished autonomy," and argues that a paternalism in medicine which aims at restoring the autonomy of ill patients is justified.

The physician-patient relationship is surely characterized by certain types of inequalities among the two participants. Perhaps the least disputed is the knowledge gap that separates patient and doctor. It motivates the former to seek medical attention in the first place and underlies, in part, the professional authority of the latter. This particular

asymmetry has historically been used to justify medical paternalism at the alleged expense of the patient's autonomy. Paternalism has been one of the traditional characteristics of the therapeutic relationship in medicine that distinguishes it from a mere contractual interaction of coequals, perfect mutuality, and simple negotiated claims. However, it is precisely this feature of the doctor-patient relationship that has suffered the harshest criticism lately with the advent of medical

From *Journal of Medical Ethics*, vol. 9, no. 1 (March 1983). Reprinted by permission of the author and IME Publications.

Handwritten margin note (vertical): *illness = diminished autonomy (but of which type — Mill's liberty or Kant's free will?)*

**PRESI
PATEI**

Recall t
of perso
ternalis
(Kant),
autono
This su
tions ir
a full r
should
wantin
be a de
uals w
autono
this inc
the hu
sionall
tonom
neithe
namic
examp
onmei
Howe
and d
devel
sis. Ir
*state c
on ot
thera
gitim

and v
invol
defin
less :
only
to be
be d
clear
state
are p
phys
cars

what the authors call *guidance-co-operation*. Here, the patient is far more of a participant than in the first model but is active only as a co-operator and can only partially exercise his judgment. The analogue of this relationship is that of parent and adolescent.

These three states represent only two extremes and a midpoint. The therapeutic relationship should be able to assume any combination of paternalism and autonomy along this continuous scale. Moreover, modulations along the scale should be easy and dictated by negotiation and situation. Some clinical examples where activity-passivity is the rule are anaesthesia, acute trauma and coma. Guidance-co-operation is suited to acute infection, post-operative care, etc. Mutual participation is appropriate for psychoanalysis, chronic illness and rehabilitation. The continuously shifting ratio of paternalism and autonomy is illustrated by a diabetic who enters the emergency room in ketoacidotic coma and is eventually discharged on a responsible diet and insulin regimen. This progression traces the therapeutic relationship from maximal to minimal paternalism. Generally, the most important determinant of where along this spectrum the relationship will stabilize is the degree to which the patient's autonomy is diminished at any one time and must be restored by compensatory limited paternalism.

COMPARISON WITH OTHER APPROACHES

The scheme which has been proposed here uses the maximization of autonomy as the touchstone for evaluating paternalism. It helps to reconcile the seeming disparity between autonomy and paternalism which many think cannot and should not co-exist in the therapeutic relationship. This approach is preferable to other techniques of reconciliation such as the 'reasonable man' standard (32), cost-benefit analysis (33), and the moral calculus that pits the evils of interfering with liberty against the evils spared by such interference.

The 'reasonable man' standard suffers from moral relativism that is inherently unsatisfying. It does not acknowledge that a person who has assumed the sick role is not an average, reasonable man. The cost-benefit technique can include definitions of cost, harm and benefit that are so broad as to be useless. Finally, those who utilize a moral calculus to weigh injustices suffered by the patient are in danger of presumptuousness. Gert and Culver subscribe to this technique. They submit the data showing the iniquities prevented by paternalism and caused by it, to the scrutiny of 'all rational persons': 'If all rational persons would agree that the evil prevented by universally allowing the violation would be greater than the evil caused by universally allowing it, the violation is strongly justified; if none would it is unjustified' (34). Unfortunately, the authors go on to use a presumptuous generalization of their own morality as a canon of validity. This is typified by constructions such as: 'Would any rational person believe that . . .? We think they would . . .'

SUMMARY AND CONCLUSION

Kant and Mill articulated two aspects of autonomy: will and action. The former refers to freedom of the mind which functions according to universal laws discerned by pure reason. The latter implies a liberty of action or overt behavior that is limited only by the injunction that nobody's autonomy (including one's own) may be compromised. Both philosophers insist that autonomy is not so much a right as it is a duty to pursue according to one's capabilities.

Paternalism is acting in another's interest in the absence of his or her immediate consent, although with the expectation of eventual consent. It is first cousin to autonomy since both are related to the same good of the same person. Thus, paternalism and autonomy are reciprocal. Where autonomy falters paternalism supports.

Autonomy is not universal and there are persons who have varying capacities to behave au-

tonomously. There are 'degrees of autonomy' based on capability that legitimately require compensatory 'degrees of paternalism.' One's degree of autonomy is not fixed but fluctuates in the course of human affairs. Illness can be viewed as a state of diminished autonomy and this is in fact one of the important features of the sick role in our culture. Thus, the sick constitute a group with less autonomy than when they were healthy and, as such, they require some element of paternalistic treatment. However, this is a very limited type of paternalism, designed solely to maximize the patient's autonomy. This is the only legitimate interest of medical paternalism. The patient's incapacity for autonomy as a result of his condition is the major factor determining where on the spectrum of paternalism-autonomy the therapeutic relationship must operate. Paternalism is a response to incapacity, not a negation of rights. A continuous update of the patient's autonomy-status is required to modulate the doctor's paternalism.

It is important to recognize that the doctor-patient relationship is a dynamic process. It is a journey from limited paternalism to maximal autonomy which is its *telos,* or ultimate purpose. As the patient's capacity for autonomy increases, so the physician's paternalism which nurtures that autonomy decreases. The recovery of a patient from a diabetic coma can be used to illustrate this process.

The relationship between patient and doctor is unique among the professions, not because of the knowledge gap but because of 'the special dimensions of anguish in illness' (35). Confronted with this reality, it is difficult to deny the patient's need, however slight, for a paternalism which is not a challenge to his autonomy but its champion.

ACKNOWLEDGMENTS

I am most grateful to the staff at the Hastings Center for Society, Ethics, and the Life Sciences for their valuable discussions concerning the issues raised in this paper, and for the use of their splendid resources.

This work was supported by the National Institutes of Mental Health, Medical Student Psychiatric Education Grant, MH15204; The Josiah Charles Trent Memorial Foundation Grant, 383–7078; and a student internship grant from The Hasting Center for Society, Ethics, and the Life Sciences.

References and Notes

[1]Haug E, Lavin B. Public challenge of physician authority. *Medical care* 1979; 17: 844–858.

[2]Veatch R. The generalization of expertise. *Hastings Center studies* 1973; 1: 29–49.

Kant I. *Groundwork of the metaphysic of morals.* New York: Harper and Row, 1958: 108.

[4]See reference (3): 34.

[5]Warnock M, ed. *John Stuart Mill: utilitarianism, on liberty, essay on Bentham.* New York: World Publishing, 1962: 108. Hereafter, all references to this edition will be documented in the text by page number.

[6]Beauchamp T, Childress J. *Principles of biomedical ethics.* New York: Oxford University Press, 1979: 56.

[7]Husak D. Paternalism and autonomy. *Philosophy and public affairs* 1981, Winter; 10: 35–36.

[8]Kao C. Maturity and paternalism in health care. *Ethics in science and medicine* 1976 Sept; 3: 179–186.

[9]See reference (6): 60.

[10]Dworkin G. Paternalism. In: Wasserstrom R, ed. *Morality and the law.* Belmont California: Wadsworth, 1971: 108.

[11]See reference (8): 184. Also see White A. *Paternalism* (PhD dissertation). University of Virginia, 1974.

[12]Gert B, Culver C. The justification of paternalism. In: Robison W and Pritchard M, eds. *Medical responsibility.* New Jersey: Humana Press, 1979: 2.

[13]See reference (12): 2. Other moral rules include interdictions against 'killing, causing pain (physical or mental), disabling, depriving of freedom, opportunity or pleasure, deceiving, breaking a promise, or cheating.' See also, Gert B. *The moral rules.* New York: Harper, 1975.

[14]Gert B, Culver C. Paternalistic behavior. *Philosophy and public affairs* 1976 Fall; 6/1: 45–57.

[15]See reference (14): 53.

is aware of her situation and assents to receiving an effective, low-risk treatment for a certain diagnosis, there is no reason to question her competence to consent.

Phil Randall's situation is quite different. A twenty-three-year-old veteran who has been addicted to drugs and alcohol, he is on probation and struggling to survive in college. When Phil stops talking and eating for almost a week, his roommate summons a trusted professor. By this time Phil is catatonic, but the professor manages to get him on his feet and accompanies him in a police car to the state hospital. The professor gets through to Phil sufficiently to explain the advantages of signing in as a voluntary patient. Phil signs his name to the admission form, authorizing commitment and initial treatment. His consent to this first phase of therapy is valid because Phil is sufficiently aware of his situation to understand what is happening, and he assents to the treatment. Later on, when his condition improves, another consent may be required, especially if a more dangerous treatment or a long-term hospitalization is required. The next decision will require a higher degree of competence because it is a different type of task.

Having a lenient standard of competence for safe and effective treatments eliminates the ambiguity and confusion associated with phrases like "virtually competent," "marginally competent," and "competent for practical purposes." Such phrases are used to excuse the common sense practice of holding certain decisions to be valid even though the patients are considered incompetent by some abstract standard, which ignores the specific task or type of medical decision at hand.

The same modest standard of competence should apply to a dying patient who refuses to consent to treatments that are ineffective and useless. This is the paradigm case in the refusal-of-ineffective-treatment category.

Most of the patients who would be considered incompetent to make treatment decisions under this first category are legally incompetent. Those who use psychotic defenses that impede the awareness of their situation and any decision making ability are the only other patients who fall outside the wide first criterion. Even children who have reached the age of reason can be considered competent. According to law, however, those below the ages of twenty-one or sometimes eighteen are presumed incompetent to make binding contracts, including health care decisions.

But exceptions are common. The Pennsylvania Mental Health Procedures Act (1976), for example, decided that fourteen-year-old adolescents were competent to give informed consent to psychiatric hospitalization. Adolescents are also considered competent in many jurisdictions to make decisions about birth control and abortion. I am suggesting that, for this first type of decision, children as young as ten or eleven are competent.

Authors like Alexander M. Capron, Willard Gaylin, and Ruth Macklin support a lowering of the age of competency to make some medical decisions.[5] The President's Commission also endorses a lower age of competence. The physician, however, cannot ignore the law and must obtain the consent of the child's legal guardian. But if a minor is competent or partially competent, there is good reason to involve him or her in the decision-making process.

LESS CERTAIN TREATMENTS

Standard No. 2. If the diagnosis is doubtful, or the condition chronic; if the diagnosis is certain but the treatment is more dangerous or not quite so effective; if there are alternative treatments, or no treatment at all is an alternative, then a different type of task is involved in making an informed treatment decision. Consequently, a different standard of competence is required. The patient now must be able to understand the risks and outcomes of the different options and then be able to make a decision based on this understanding.

In this setting competence means ability to understand the treatment options, balance risks and benefits, and come to a deliberate decision. In other words, a higher standard of competence is required than the one discussed above. Let me give some examples of this type of decision, and the corresponding competency standards.

Antonio Marachal is a retired steel worker who has been hospitalized with a bad heart valve. Both the surgeon and his family doctor recommend an operation to replace the valve. Mr. Marachal understands what they tell him, but is afraid of undergoing the operation. He thinks he'll live just as long by taking good care of himself. His fear of surgery may not be entirely rational, but the option he prefers is real and there is no basis for considering his refusal to be invalid because of incompetence.

Or consider Geraldine Brown, a forty-year-old unmarried woman who is diagnosed as having leukemia. Chemotherapy offers a good chance for remission, but the side effects are repugnant and frightening to her. After hearing and understanding the diagnosis, alternatives, risks, and prognosis, she refuses, deciding instead to follow a program that centers on diet, exercise, meditation, and some natural stimulants to her immune system. Objectively, the standard medical treatment is preferable to what she decides, but informed consent joins objective medical data with subjective personal factors such as repugnance and burden. In this case the objective and subjective components balance out. A decision one way or the other is reasonable, and a person who can understand the options and decide in light of them is competent.

Although ability to understand is not the same as being capable of conceptual or verbal understanding, some commentators assume that the two are synonymous in every case. Many would require that patients remember the ideas and repeat what they have been told as a proof of competence. Real understanding, however, may be more a matter of emotions. Following an explanation, the patient may grasp what is best for her with strong feelings and convictions, and yet be hard pressed to articulate or conceptualize her understanding or conviction.

Competence as capacity for an understanding choice can also be reconciled with a decision to let a trusted physician decide what is the best treatment. Such a choice (a waiver) may be made for good reasons and represent a decision in favor of one set of values (safety or anxiety reduction) over another (independence and personal initiative). As such, it can be considered an informed consent and create no suspicion about competence.

Ignorance or inability to understand, however, does incapacitate a person for making this type of decision. This is especially so when the ignorance extends to the options and persists even after patient and careful explanation. Patience and care may sometimes require that more than one person be involved in the disclosure process before a person is judged incompetent to understand. An explanation by someone from the same ethnic, religious, or economic background may also be necessary.

DANGEROUS TREATMENTS

Standard No. 3. The most stringent and demanding criterion for competence is reserved for those treatment decisions that are very dangerous, and run counter to both professional and public rationality. Here the decision involves not a balancing of what are widely recognized as reasonable alternatives or a reasonable response to a doubtful diagnosis, but a choice that seems to violate reasonableness. The patient's decision now appears irrational, indeed life-threatening. And yet, according to this model, such decisions are valid and respectable as long as the person making them satisfies the most demanding standards of competence. The patient's decision is a different type of task than the others we have considered.

A Sliding-Scale Model for Competency

Standard No. 1

Objective Medical Decisions

A. *Incompetent*
unconscious
severe retardation
small children
total disorientation
severe senile dementia
autism
psychotic defenses
  denial of self and
    situation
  delusional projection

consent

effective treatment for acute
  illness
diagnostic certainty
high benefit/low risk
limited alternatives
severe disorder/major
  distress/immediately
  life-threatening

refusal

ineffective treatment

B. *Competent*
children (10 and above)
retarded (educable)
clouded sensorium
mild senile dementia
intoxicated
conditions listed under
  #2 and #3 (A & B)

Competency Standards
Minimal Requirements:
1. *Awareness:* orientation to one's medical situation
2. *Assent:* explicit or implied

Standard No. 2

Objective Medical Decisions

A. *Incompetent*
severe mood disorders
phobia about treatment
mutism
short term memory loss
thought disorders
  ignorance
  incoherence
  delusion
  hallucination
  delirium
conditions listed under
  #1 (A & B)

consent or refusal

chronic condition/doubtful diagnosis
uncertain outcome of therapy
  for acute illness
balanced risks and benefits:
  possibly effective, but burdensome
  high risk, only hope

B. *Competent*
adolescent (16 and over)
mildly retarded
personality disorders:
  narcissistic, borderline and
    obsessive
conditions listed under
  #3 (A & B)

Competency Standards
Median Requirements:
1. *Understanding:* of medical situation and proposed treatment
2. *Choice:* based on medical outcomes

A Sliding-Scale Model for Competency (continued)

Standard No. 3

Objective Medical Decisions

A. *Incompetent*

indecisive or ambivalent
  over time
false beliefs about reality
hysteria
substance abuse
neurotic defenses:
  intellectualization
  repression
  dissociation
  acting out
  mild depression
  hypomania
conditions listed under
  #1 and #2 (A & B)

refusal → ineffective treatment ← consent

effective treatment for acute
  illness
diagnostic certainty
high benefit/low risk
  limited alternatives
severe disorder/major
  distress/immediately
  life-threatening

B. *Competent*

above legal age
reflective and self-critical
mature coping devices:
  altruism
  anticipation
  sublimation

Competency Standards

Maximum Requirements:

1. *Appreciation:* critical and reflective understanding of illness and treatment
2. *Rational decision:* based on relevant implications including articulated beliefs and values

As such, different and more stringent criteria of capacity are appropriate.

Competence in this context requires an ability on the part of the decision maker to appreciate what he or she is doing. Appreciation requires the highest degree of understanding, one that grasps more than just the medical details of the illness, options, risks, and treatment. To be competent to make apparently irrational and very dangerous choices, the patient must appreciate the implications of the medical information for his or her life. Competence here requires an understanding that is both technical and personal, intellectual and emotional.

Because such decisions contravene public standards of rationality, they must be subjectively critical and reflective. The competent patient

must be able to give reasons for the decision, which show that he has thought through the medical issues and related this information to his personal values. The patient's personal reasons need not be scientific or publicly accepted, but neither can they be purely private or idiosyncratic. Their intelligibility may derive from a minority religious view, but they must be coherent and follow the logic of that belief system. This toughest standard of competence demands a more rational understanding: one that includes verbalization, consistency, and the like. Some examples will illustrate.

Bob Cassidy, an eighteen-year-old high school senior and an outstanding athlete, is involved in an automobile accident which has crushed his left foot. Attempts to save the limb are unsuccessful, and infection threatens the boy's

7) with a number of interesting arguments. Can medical research on either humans or animals really be justified on the grounds that (1) the experimenter is merely carrying out the orders of superiors; or (2) the experimental subjects are condemned to die anyhow so we might as well get some good for humanity out of them; or (3) since the experiments are going to be performed anyway, they should be done by qualified and trained scientists so the data will be reliable; or (4) since it is right to take the lives of useless or incurable persons, it must also be right to take the lives of those destined to die for political reasons? As Dr. Ivy indicates, the Nazis also argued that their experiments on Jews, Gypsies, Poles, and Russians were justified (5) because these individuals belong to "subhuman species." Quite aside from gross errors of biological classification, should the assumption that we are justified in doing anything whatsoever we want to do to a nonhuman animal be accepted? The morality of this needs careful examination, as Bernard E. Rollin will argue in a selection to follow titled "The Use and Abuse of Animals in Research."

If the foregoing arguments for medical experimentation are not compelling, what is wrong with them? If there are better arguments for human or animal experimentation, what are they? If medical experimentation is morally permissible under certain conditions but not under others, what are they; and why are these conditions decisive? If they differ for humans and subhumans, why so, or why not? Articles in this chapter will address these issues.

B. EXPERIMENTATION ON HUMAN AND ANIMAL RESEARCH SUBJECTS

Medical experimentation is necessary for determining the natural course of diseases, testing new drugs and biochemical products, learning the effectiveness of new operations and medical technologies, discovering the comparative effectiveness of alternative therapies, identifying preventive measures, etc. Progress in medicine is not possible without medical experimentation on both human and animal research subjects.

Since the Nuremberg trials, many recommendations for the regulation of medical experimentation on human subjects have been made and enacted into law or prescribed by governmental regulatory agencies. Ethical guidelines for the conduct of research on human subjects have been expressed in the Nuremberg Code (1948), the Principles of Those in Research and Experimentation of the World Medical Association (1954), the Declaration of Helsinki (1964), the AMA's Principles of Medical Ethics (1971), and the DHEW Guidelines (1974). Details of these guidelines are examined in the following article by George H. Kieffer and in another by Robert J. Levine and Karen Lebacqz.

George H. Kieffer indicates in his "Human Experimentation" that abuses of medical experimentation on humans have not occurred merely in Nazi Germany. He cites a number of instances that have occurred on this side of the Atlantic. Kieffer describes the Phase 1, 2, and 3 trials which are involved in drug and chemical testing and examines the use of prisoners and children as research subjects.

Revisions of federal research guidelines have been issued since Kieffer's selection was written in 1978 and have made some of his comments a bit out of date. The *Code of Federal Regulations* (CFR), Title 45, Part 46 dealing with "Protection of Human Subjects" was revised as of March 8, 1983. Some of its important new provisions:

(a) Whereas earlier guidelines applied only to research directly funded by the federal government, new regulations require institutions that conduct any federally funded research to subject all research conducted by or at the institution to review in terms of these guidelines. Since virtually every research agency in the nation has some federal support funding, this brings almost

all research involving human subjects under review. [45 CFR 46.103]

(b) Current regulations require (as Kieffer recommends in his selection) that the committees which review research protocols (called "Institutional Review Boards" or "IRB's") include "at least one member whose primary concerns are in non-scientific areas; for example: lawyers, ethicists, members of the clergy" [45 CFR 46.107(c)] and "at least one member who is not otherwise affiliated with the institution." [CFR 46.107(d)] This brings a wider diversity of viewpoints to bear on the review in order "to promote complete and adequate review." [45 CFR 46.107(a)]

(c) Severe restrictions are placed on the types of research that can be conducted on prisoners [45 CFR 46.306] and children [45 CFR 46.407]. Additional safeguards require that prisoners be represented on IRB's which review research within penal institutions and that children be permitted to dissent from participation even if they are not old enough to give a legally valid informed consent or refusal and even if their parents have given consent for them to participate.

(d) To counteract patients' concern that "if the physician's request is refused, there is the danger that no treatment or only minimal treatment will be given," regulations now require that consent forms contain an explicit "statement that participation is voluntary, refusal to participate will involve no penalty or loss of benefits to which the subject is otherwise entitled, and the subject may discontinue participation at any time without penalty or loss of benefits to which the subject is otherwise entitled." [45 CFR 46.116(a)(8)]

Intrinsic and Extrinsic Goods and Ills in Medical Experimentation

A number of positive values are integral to medical experimentation, such as

(1) the pursuit and/or acquisition of new scientific knowledge for its own sake. These, or at least the enjoyment of them, may be regarded as intrinsic goods. Scientific investigators often attach great significance to the value of knowledge as such. Nazi scientists attached such great importance to the pursuit of knowledge that they inflicted unthinkable horrors on their research subjects to achieve it. There is no value-free medical experimentation, and what the Nazis did should convince us that medical researchers do not have an unlimited license to pursue knowledge, even when, as below, it has considerable utility.

(2) the instrumental use of medical knowledge in the prevention, diagnosis, management, or cure of diseases and injuries and all the distresses, deformities, dysfunctions, and demises that they might engender. Benefit to patients depends on the realization of this value. However, not all patients benefit from the experiments to which they are subjected. In what is called *therapeutic experimentation,* there is some likelihood that the knowledge gained will benefit the experimental subjects themselves. In *nontherapeutic experimentation,* there is little or no chance that those experimented upon will benefit from the knowledge acquired, although others later might.

(3) the inherent moral dignity of the research subjects (and the researchers as well, though our emphasis will be on the former). We saw in Chapter 2 that there is considerable room for disagreement about the precise analysis of "human dignity." It might consist in being rationally autonomous, in belonging to the human species, in being the subject or object of recognized moral duties, in possessing intrinsic individual worth, etc. There is also considerable room for debate about whether animal research subjects possess inherent moral dignity. Some animals, like language-using primates, actually might possess a degree of rational autonomy comparable to that of retarded human beings. Many concerned persons recognize animals as having moral standing as objects if not subjects of moral obligations and as possessing individual intrinsic

Some have seriously challenged the ethics of these protocols, especially in cases where the subject volunteers in anticipation of some useful outcome, for example, the administration of an inert substance instead of a birth control chemical. Philosopher Jonas feels that especially in the case of a sick patient, the subject is definitely wronged even when not physically harmed for the giving of placebos betrays the trust of the patient who believes that he/she is receiving treatment. Even apart from ethics, the practice of deception holds the danger of undermining the faith in legitimate treatment, the very basis of the doctor-patient contract. Clearly the prescription of placebos is intentionally deceptive and makes informed consent impossible. Even benevolent deception is not allowable because it makes a mockery of human individual freedom and dignity. Some argue, however, the prohibition against the use of placebos should not be absolute. In these instances, great care should be exerted in balancing benefits over costs.[20] Ethicist Sissela Bok suggests the following principles in trying to decide the difficult cases:[21]

1. Placebos should be used only after careful diagnosis.

2. No active placebos should be employed, merely inert ones.

3. No outright lie should be told and questions should be answered honestly.

4. Placebos should never be given to patients who have asked not to receive them.

5. Placebos should never be used when other treatment is clearly called for or all possible alternatives have not been weighed.

The whole matter of deception is especially sensitive in social or psychological experimentation. Experimentation without consent, deceit, and even compulsory participation of psychology students were commonplace before the new insistence on openness. One of the concerns here is that although no one is physically at risk, psychological damage may be done. Sociological research involving interviews and questionnaires must now meet the same review procedures as medical research. Informed consent is seen to be more important than any scientific considerations. Secret observers, researcher role-playing, and other unobstructive techniques are being seriously questioned. The main ethical criticism is the violation of the subject's privacy.[22 and 23]

It is apparent that silence sometimes is necessary in certain experiments and so is deception; but they are never desirable if they can be done without. Psychologist Perry London suggests these three questions to be answered by researchers before using deception or purposely withholding information:[24]

1. Is there any way to get the information without such a practice?

2. Is the sought-for information so valuable that it is worth misleading, debriefing, and apologizing to subjects?

3. Is there significant risk of damaging the subject's psyche so that even an explanation of the truth following the experiment will not correct the psychological harm or reduce the sense of humiliation of having been duped?

London concludes that there is far too much deceptive research going on in the psychological and social sciences.

PRISONERS AS RESEARCH SUBJECTS

The use of prisoners as research subjects has raised some of the hottest confrontations over the ethics of human experimentation. While prisoners normally do not lack the capacity to offer a reasonably informed consent, their capacity to do so voluntarily is problematical. Consequently, most states have taken steps to either completely abandon or more stringently control those activities within their boundaries. Some are calling for an outright ban on all prison research. In 1975,

the Federal Bureau of Prisons issued an indefinite moratorium on all forms of nontherapeutic research in any federal prison. Essentially, the issue returns again to that most singular anxiety, the necessity of insuring voluntary participation and obtaining informed consent. A second matter of ethics concerns the use of penitentiaries as the experimental setting; openness and public inspection are not as easily maintained under conditions which are intrinsically secretive.

In recent times prisoners formed the largest pool of potential subjects, especially for drug testing, and most drug companies had working agreements with prisons. Although the extent and nature of experimentation with prisoners cannot be determined, at least 3600 prisoners in the United States were used for drug testing during 1975 alone, according to the National Commission for the Protection of Human Subjects. Besides these tests, performed primarily by drug companies, the commission also determined that the federal government funded a number of other studies in which prisoners were used: within the Public Health Service, 124 biomedical studies and 19 behavioral projects between 1970 and 1975; the Department of Defense sponsored numerous studies for research on infectious diseases; and the former Atomic Energy Commission had supported research involving radiation of male prisoners' genitals.[25]

During the year 1975, eight states and six county and municipal prisons were used. One of the largest and most elaborate research facilities is located at the State Prison of Southern Michigan at Jackson. This is a maximum-security prison, one of the biggest penitentiaries in the United States. Of its 5000 inmates, 800 prisoners form an available pool for research in special facilities built within the walls of the prison by two of the country's largest pharmaceutical manufacturers, Parke-Davis and Upjohn. Between 1964 and 1968, over 100,000 tests on human subjects were performed here. Approximately eighty to ninety percent of all Phase I testing by drug companies has been done in prisons.

By contrast, in no country surveyed by the National Commission other than the United States were prisoners used as volunteer subjects for medical experimentation. And in fact, virtually no country except the United States conducts any clinical pharmocological studies on healthy subjects in or out of prisons. Also, unlike the United States, other countries will accept data generated from studies made in other countries. (The countries surveyed were Belgium, France, Germany, Italy, the Netherlands, Spain, Sweden, Australia, Canada, New Zealand, South Africa, the United Kingdom, Brazil, Colombia, Mexico, Peru, and Japan.)

Prison abuses of all kinds have been widely publicized. Jessica Mitford's book *Kind and Usual Punishment* on prison conditions points out that some experimentation conducted in prisons is dangerous and has little scientific value. At the Iowa State Prison, for example, the experimental induction of scurvy in eleven prisoners led to acute episodes of swollen and bleeding gums, joint swelling and pain, hemorrhaging, etc. In some, the effects proved to be irreversible (two of the prisoners later escaped). All this was done even though the cause and cure of scurvy are well known. Another example of questionable research is the infamous Tuskeegee syphilis study, where 400 black men with syphilis were not treated so the course of the disease could be followed. Here again, the etiology and cure of this affliction are well known. The list could be added to from medical literature as well as popular reporting.

However, the personal welfare of the prisoners is not the only ethical consideration. The issue of whether any nontherapeutic research should be allowed in prisons arises from several factors:

1. The subjects involved are captives of the state and are made available by the permission of the state. Does this put the state in the position to decide who is to be martyred and in the service of what cause? Society first creates the

conditions of loss of freedom and then exploits it. Prisoners, as a group, are generally held in low esteem by society and, in fact, are considered inferior by most. There can be no informed consent, according to Jay Katz (psychiatrist), when one of the parties is not free. It is far too easy to strike a bargain between unequals. If the ultimate concern with human experimentation involves personal dignity and individual inviolability, then the setting for conflict becomes real when the long and the short range interests of society, science, and progress are set up against the rights of the individual.[26]

2. The prisoner participants' position of confinement renders their consent to participate questionable; prisoners are not free agents and true consent without overt or implied coercion is impossible in prisons. In a study (McGuire, personal communication) 1200 prisoners at the Cook County Jail (Ill.) were evaluated relative to their ability to give consent. It was found that over 95 percent of them could not render adequate and informed consent. The largest share of them were pretrial detainees, hence ineligible for any state assistance or rehabilitation programs. Even basic necessities such as soap and toothpaste had to be personally furnished. Unable to come up with bond, unable to hire lawyers, and convinced they would not be defended well, they would do anything to get out or to improve their situations. At the California Medical Facility at Vacaville, research on "aversive conditioning" using the drug anectine (it creates a muscle paralysis and a sensation of suffocation) with 64 extreme-acting criminal offenders determined that 5 signed up against their will and 18 involuntarily signed because of implied pressure.

3. Research in prisons is carried on in an environment which lacks the kind of peer review or openness found in other research settings. Because such research is not in the public eye, there is the possibility of abuse even if it is unintended. Such abuse can be easily covered up if negative publicity may result.

4. The special problem of informed consent implies or even requires that information be given and that it be understood by the candidate for participation. The intellectual capacity of most prisoners disqualifies them on these grounds. Thus, unconscious motivations, psychopathologies, states of deprivation, wretched conditions and the like, all mitigate against giving free and informed consent.

It is especially this issue of voluntary informed consent that raises the greatest ethical question. Prisons, as total institutions, by their very purpose and character, make it highly questionable whether free consent to research is possible. As Patricia King, one of the commission's most adamant opponents of prisoner experimentations, expressed it: "I, personally, do not believe that theoretically one can ever remove enough of the constraints from a prison to afford self-determination because by the time you removed them all you would not have a prison."[27]

The National Prison Project of the American Civil Liberties Union filed a complaint in the U.S. District Court on behalf of seven prisoners who were involved in viral diarrhea, malaria, shigella, and typhoid experiments. The complaint asked that the court declare that "the use of prisoners in nontherapeutic biomedical experimentation of this type is unconstitutional per se because of the impossibility of truly voluntary consent.[28] Eight states have prohibited the use of state prisons for these purposes: six by departmental policy, one by moratorium, and one by legislation (Oregon). The Board of Directors of the American Correctional Association adopted this statement:

> The American Correctional Association has long viewed with concern the use of prisoners as subjects of medical pharmacological experimentation . . . It now urges that efforts to eliminate such practices be undertaken by responsible bodies at the Federal, State, and local levels . . . The authority which authorizes or permits prisoners to become subjects of human experimentation ignores his historic obligation as a

custodian to protect and safely keep those for whom he assumes legal responsibility.[29]

The use of prisoners has been stoutly defended by some. Dr. Albert Sabin (of oral polio vaccine fame) noted at the National Academy of Sciences Conference on human experimentation that basic studies on his own polio vaccine were done on prisoners. If research using prisoners was stopped, he says, "it would greatly impede medical research."[30] Dr. William N. Hubbard, Jr., president of Upjohn Company, at the same meeting stressed that meticulous care has been taken over the past 15 years at the Michigan facility to safeguard inmate welfare and rights and to ensure that the participants are true volunteers giving their informed consent. Dr. C. Joseph Stetler, president of the Pharmaceutical Manufacturers Association (representing 131 member firms), testified before a congressional subcommittee that (1) prisoners are the best subjects for Phase I testing since within that population there are the least number of variables; (2) prisoners volunteer readily to achieve financial rewards, to relieve boredom, or, in some cases, to make amends to society; and (3) all major drug research would be severely curtailed or stopped if the use of prisoners was prohibited.

The Pharmaceutical Manufacturers' Association has established the following guidelines for drug studies carried out with prisoners:

1. There must be complete freedom from coercion.

2. Adequate medical protection must be given to all research subjects.

3. Full information about the nature of the testing must be made available.

4. There should be suitable monetary compensation for participation.

5. The prisoner-subject has the right to withdraw from the experiment at any time.

6. Refusal to participate or withdrawal from an experiment should have no effect on parole eligibility.

The effectiveness of the PMA guidelines was perhaps demonstrated by this testimony before the commission where it was stated that "to the best of our knowledge, not a single prisoner has died or been permanently injured as a result of drug-firm–sponsored (Phase I) testing."[31]

Since it is universally asserted by those who defend the practice of using prisoners that the rights of the individual are being protected and that informed consent is obtained, one might inquire as to the validity of this claim. In an extensive study prepared for the commission by the University of Michigan, interviews with 181 prisoners in four prisons found 87 percent very willing to participate in research projects.[32] Commission members personally interviewed prison research participants at Jackson and were startled to find that subjects were among the best educated and intelligent at the prison (56 percent had completed twelve grades or more). They were very indignant that they might lose the opportunity to participate for several reasons: (1) they are housed in a decent environment (not in jail); (2) they get real money—up to $200 per research project as opposed to 50¢ per day with an $8 maximum per month for routine prison work; and (3) they receive good medical care.

Money, it turns out, is no less important in prisons than in the free world. A person in prison gets only the bare necessities; any extras, such as toiletries, books, magazines, snacks, art supplies, and cigarettes, must be purchased with personal funds. Money is also an important contact with the outside world. Prisoners send money home to their families; others continue to pay union dues so they have a better opportunity to work once released; and money saved can help them get started again when they get out. In addition, money is an effective "cooling" agent in prisons. Where money is freely available, there is less prison violence since the need to fight for simple amenities (e.g., cigarettes) is minimized.[33]

On the con side of the issue, in the case where prison volunteers are offered money payments, the position of pretrial detainees is extremely tenuous. In the time before sentencing,

and tendered the following recommendations in October 1976:[43]

Recommendation 1   Studies of the possible causes, effects, and processes of incarceration and studies of prisons as institutional structures or of prisoners as incarcerated persons may be conducted or supported, provided that (a) they present minimal or no risk and no more than mere inconvenience to the subjects, and (b) the requirements under recommendation (4) are fulfilled.

Recommendation 2   Research on practices, both innovative and accepted, which have the intent and reasonable probability of improving the health or well-being of the individual prisoner may be conducted or supported, provided the requirements under recommendation (4) are fulfilled.

Recommendation 3   Except as provided in recommendations (1) and (2), research involving prisoners should not be conducted or supported, and reports of such research should not be accepted by the Secretary, DHEW, in fulfillment of regulatory requirements, unless the requirements under recommendation (4) are fulfilled and the head of the responsible federal department or agency has certified, after consultation with a national ethical review body, that the following three requirements are satisfied:

(a) The type of research fulfills an important social and scientific need, and the reasons for involving prisoners in the type of research are compelling.

(b) The involvement of prisoners in the type of research satisfies conditions of equity; and

(c) A high degree of voluntariness on the part of the prospective participants and of openness on the part of the institution(s) to be involved would characterize the conduct of the research; minimum requirements for such voluntariness and openness include adequate living conditions, provisions for effective redress of grievances, separation of research participation from parole considerations, and public scrutiny.

Recommendation 4

(a) The head of the responsible federal department or agency should determine that the competence of the investigators and the adequacy of the research facilities involved are sufficient. . . .

(b) All research involving prisoners should be reviewed by at least one human subjects review committee or institutional review board comprised of men and women of diverse racial and cultural backgrounds that includes among its members prisoners or prisoner advocates and such other persons as community representatives, clergy, behavioral scientists and medical personnel not associated with the . . . research or institution. . . .

Recommendation 5   In the absence of certification that the requirements under recommendation (3) are satisfied, research projects covered by that recommendation that are subject to regulation by the Secretary, DHEW, and are currently in progress should be permitted to continue not longer than one year from the date of publication of these recommendations in the Federal Register (January 14, 1977) or until completed, whichever is earlier.

In essence, the commission said no human experimentation with prisoners is permitted unless there are compelling reasons for carrying on the research, unless voluntary participation is meticulously carried out, and unless the principle of equity is satisfied, that is, specific ethnic or racial groups are not disproportionately represented in the experimental population. The burden of proof is placed on the researcher to demonstrate compelling reasons for using prisoners for research purposes. Fairness requires more equitable distri-

bution of the research burden; however, the commission does not specify how this should be done.

Although the objective of the report was not to declare an outright ban on prison research, critics of the recommendations argue that they would probably result in a moratorium on most medical research conducted in prisons in the United States. And, indeed, HEW ruled that prisoners cannot be used at all in nontherapeutic research if it involves more than minimal risk (January, 1978).

Returning to the general question of nontherapeutic research, a number of writers have suggested various ways to strengthen protection of human subjects. Some of these are the following:

1. Examination of possible methods of compensation for subjects, who, in spite of all precautions, are harmed by the research activities; this would require a form of indemnification or insurance for subjects to cover all consequences of their participation arising unforeseeably and without negligence.[44] This policy would force a greater concern on the part of the experimenter as well as providing compensation to the participant in the event something goes awry. Fewer but more carefully run experiments may result. There are some ethical as well as practical questions here: Is consent a waiver of damage or harm? How much harm is compensable? Are economics of overall greater concern than ethical or moral issues? Are dollars to be equated with humanness or humanitarian goals?

2. Research proposed should be more carefully evaluated in advance of the actual experimentation. Perhaps limits do exist in our search for knowledge and ends do not always justify the means. The principle here could well be that an experiment is ethical or not ethical at its inception and is not determined by some later measure of success. Consider the following example: Liver biopsy is a very dangerous and potentially lethal procedure; the first several pioneer attempts resulted in death; the experimental subjects, however, were moribund patients where death was imminent. Were these experiments ethically acceptable? Does every human being have the right to be treated with decency regardless of his/her state of health? Also, there is much duplication of research in a number of laboratories. Is this necessary and could it be controlled? Should data gotten from other countries be used in the United States (see p. 205)?

3. Evaluation of the review process: Peer review is still held up as a mystical force which ensures quality in science; however, in ethical matters at least, it is no safeguard, as an earlier discussion showed (see p. 210). A way around the peer review problem is to expand local committees to include other professional and lay input (e.g., ethicists, social scientists, citizen representatives, etc.) Greater visibility could be generated by making the review process open, thus precluding dubious or clandestine procedures. There exists a need to know more about what is going on in research. A suggestion to accommodate this is to initiate a communication system among review committees out of which could evolve some common law or limits of permissibility. Furthermore, by turning to other cases of a similar kind, local committees needn't begin anew on experiments presented to them for review.

4. Information and consent: A system is needed to ensure that someone knowledgeable clearly and accurately conveys all needed information, including all hazards, to subject-participants. Many investigators leave this to subordinates, some of whom are nonmedical personnel. To protect the interests of the subject during the experiment, an intermediary person or ombudsman should be available who has free access to all information on both sides and has no vested interests in the experiment; such an individual would function to enhance the freedom of the subject, e.g., to

Bibliography

Beecher, Henry K., *Research and the Individual: Human Studies* (Boston: Little, Brown, 1970).

Goldiamond, Israel, "Protection of human subjects and patients: a social contingency analysis of distinctions between research and practice, and its implications," *Behaviorism* **4** (1976): 1–41.

Ivy, Andrew C., "Nazi war crimes of a medical nature," *Federation Bulletin* **33** (1947): 133–146.

Ivy, Andrew C., and Leo Alexander, "Medical science under dictatorship," *The New England Journal of Medicine* **241** (1949): 39–47.

Rivlin, Alice M., and Michael P. Timpane (eds.), *Ethical and Legal Issues of Social Experimentation* (Washington, D.C.: The Brookings Institute, (1975).

White, Robert R. (ed.), *Experiments and Research with Humans: Values in Conflict* (Washington, D.C.: National Academy of Sciences, 1975).

Ethical Considerations in Clinical Trials

Robert J. Levine and Karen Lebacqz

Robert J. Levine received his M.D. degree in 1958 from George Washington University School of Medicine. He completed his internal medicine residency at the Peter Bent Brigham Hospital, the National Heart Institute, and Yale–New Haven Medical Center. Currently, he is professor of medicine and editor of IRB: A Review of Human Subjects Research. *He is author of* Ethics and Regulation of Clinical Research *(Urban and Schwarzenberg, 2nd ed., 1986).*

Karen Lebacqz is professor of christian ethics at the Pacific School of Religion in Berkeley, California. She is a former member of the National Commission for the Protection of Human Subjects of Biomedical and Behavioral Research. She specializes in professional ethics and issues of liberation and justice.

Levine and Lebacqz identify and explore the application of six ethical norms for research involving human subjects: (1) good research design, (2) balance of harm and benefit, (3) competence of the investigator(s), (4) informed consent, (5) equitable selection of subjects, and (6) compensation for research-related injury.

The ethical norms established in various codes and regulations are inadequate to resolve some of the ethical problems presented by clinical trials. They are stated too vaguely to provide unequivocal answers to many specific questions. In order to remedy this situation, many commentators have proposed the development of more specific and complex regulations. We propose that a more fruitful approach would be to examine the

From *Clinical Pharmacology and Therapeutics* vol. 25, no. 5, part 2 (May 1979). Reprinted by permission of the authors and The C. V. Mosby Company.

ethical principles underlying the norms and to apply these principles to the specific problems. We apply this approach to two questions: (1) Is it ethical to select subjects for a randomized clinical trial (RCT) exclusively from Veterans Administration (VA) hospitals? (2) In the conduct of an RCT is it necessary to disclose the fact that therapy will be determined by chance? We conclude that problems of justice arise not only because of the vulnerability of patients in VA hospitals but also because of the loss of the physician-patient relationship in an RCT. However, the use of pa-

tients in a VA hospital is not always unjust; in most cases such use can be made more just through various modifications in design. We also conclude that the fact of randomization should be disclosed in any situation in which it might materially affect the prospective subject's decision, and that the values and preferences of the subjects should be taken into account in determining what information might be material. This work is only a preliminary step toward analyzing ethical issues in clinical trials. While some would challenge our conclusions, we hope that our methods will facilitate clarity about the locus of disagreement in current controversies and about the value questions that must be answered in order to set an ethical context for the conduct of clinical trials.

Most discussions of the "ethics" of research tend to concentrate on issues related to "informed consent."[15] Important though such issues are, they are neither the only nor the most important ethical considerations in the design and conduct of clinical trials.* As a simple rule of thumb, any time the words "should" or "ought" appear, an ethical question has been raised. For example, the question, "When should a clinical trial be stopped?" is an ethical question in that one cannot answer by looking only to scientific considerations. Along with scientific judgments about how many data are required in order to draw meaningful conclusions will be considerations of possible injury to subjects in the trial or injury to patients waiting for the development of new therapies. The range of ethical problems one encounters in the course of planning and conducting clinical trials is vast; it encompasses nearly all of those

presented by all research involving human subjects.

Consequently, in this paper we shall not attempt either a thorough analysis of the issues or a comprehensive survey of the relevant literature. Rather we shall begin by taking seriously several problems: When and how to stop a clinical trial, Who will be effective as a clinical trials investigator, and Patient recruitment: Problems and solutions. From these and one additional question that we propose (should subjects be compensated for injury), we suggest the dimensions of ethical dilemmas in clinical trials, namely, problems in the interpretation or application of underlying norms and principles of ethical conduct. We shall then take issues related to patient recruitment for more careful examination, in order to show how differences in interpretation of basic norms and principles affect decisions about the conduct of trials and in order to suggest possible solutions to some central ethical dilemmas.

ETHICAL ISSUES AND BASIC NORMS

Each of the questions or areas of concern mentioned above points to a range of related questions and to one or more basic norms which are commonly understood to apply to the conduct of research on human subjects.

When and how to stop a clinical trial. We begin by posing this area of concern in the form of two questions: When should clinical trials be stopped? How should clinical trials be stopped? These two ethical questions suggest a range of related questions: When should clinical trials be started? If controlled, what should be used as the control intervention? Should interventions be assigned according to a process of randomization? How should information gathered during the course of the trial affect its conduct?

This set of questions points to two basic norms identified in codes of ethics for the conduct

---

*We use the term "research," "practice," and "innovative therapy" as defined by the National Commission for the Protection of Human Subjects of Biomedical and Behavioral Research (Commission).[20, 31] For reasons elaborated elsewhere,[20] we prefer the term "nonvalidated practice" to "innovative therapy." The term "clinical trial," as used here, refers to a class of research activities designed to develop generalizable knowledge about the safety and/or efficacy of either validated or nonvalidated practices.

of research on human subjects.* The first of these is the norm of *good research design*.† This norm appears in almost all codes and regulations for the conduct of research:

> The experiment should be so designed and based on the results of animal experimentation and a knowledge of the natural history of the disease or other problem under study that the anticipated results will justify the performance of the experiment (Nuremberg 3).

> Biomedical research involving human subjects must conform to generally accepted scientific principles and should be based on adequately performed laboratory and animal experimentation and on a thorough knowledge of the scientific literature. (Helsinki I. 1).

While there are slight variations in the expression of the norm, the basic idea is constant. Research must be sufficiently well designed to achieve its purposes and must be scientifically sound; otherwise, it is not justified. What constitutes good design is, of course, a matter of some debate which is not resolved by the norm itself. But the question of when to stop a clinical trial is at least in part a question of adequate design and is thus covered in part by this norm.

---

*The normative statements cited in this paper are taken from the Nuremberg Code, the 1975 revision of the Declaration of Helsinki (both of which are reproduced in a recent book[25]), and from the Regulations of the Department of Health, Education, and Welfare (DHEW).[5] Often, normative statements contained in the Code and in the Declaration will have no parallel in Regulations. There are various reasons for this. Most importantly, the Regulations are not intended to be an ethical code. Rather, they require that an institution submit "a statement of principles which will govern the institution in the discharge of its responsibilities for protecting the rights and welfare of subjects. This may include appropriate existing codes or declarations or statements formulated by the institution itself" (DHEW, 46.106a). However, in some cases there are parallel norms stated in the Regulations. In the event of conflicts the Regulations go on to state: "It is to be understood that no such principles supersede DHEW policy or applicable law" (DHEW, 46.106a).

†As a matter of convenience, we shall use brief expressions of the ethical norms in this paper. In general, they may be translated into proper normative statements by incorporating them in suitable declarative sentences—e.g.: There should be good research design. There should be a favorable balance of harms and benefits.

But implicit in the question is also the suggestion that a trial might be stopped *before* its designated time. To the requirement for good design is added concern for the well-being of the subjects. Thus, another basic norm is brought into play, the norm that requires an identification of the consequences of action and a *balance of harm and benefit*.* The norm is expressed in codes of ethics in two common forms: First it requires that possible harms to subjects be outweighed by the benefits one expects to accrue from the research:

> The degree of risk to be taken should never exceed that determined by the humanitarian importance of the problem solved by the experiment (Nuremberg 6).

> Biomedical research involving human subjects cannot legitimately be carried out unless the importance of the objective is in proportion to the inherent risk to the subject (Helsinki I.4).

> The risks to the subject [must be] so outweighed by the sum of the benefit to subject and the importance of the knowledge to be gained as to warrant a decision to allow the subject to accept these risks . . . (DHEW, 46.102 b, 1).

Second, it requires that some harms be considered sufficient to outweigh anticipated benefits and, hence, to require stopping a trial in process:

> During the course of the experiment the scientist in charge must be prepared to terminate the experiment at any stage, if he has probable cause to believe . . . that a continuation . . . is likely to result in injury, disability, or death to the experimental subject (Nuremberg 10).

---

*This norm is often referred to as a "risk-benefit calculus." However, we prefer to state the norm in terms of balancing harms and benefits for two reasons: (1) Since "risk" means "probability of harm," it is more accurate to balance it against "probability of benefit" rather than against "benefit" per se. (2) Harms and benefits are not merely to be *calculated*; rather, they are required to be in a certain ratio or relationship to each other customarily alluded to as "favorable." A more complete discussion of the factors that should be considered in balancing harms and benefits is published elsewhere.[21]

The investigator or the investigating team should discontinue the research if in his/her or their judgment it may, if continued, be harmful to the individual (Helsinki III. 3).

Thus, research may not be initiated unless the consequences of conducting it are judged likely to produce more good than harm, and it must be terminated if certain harms appear likely, no matter what good consequences might result.

The question, When and how should clinical trials be stopped? has thus opened up a range of issues related to two basic norms: *good research design* and *balance of harm and benefit.*

Who will be effective as a clinical trials investigator? As posed, this does not appear to be an ethical question; rather, it seems to be concerned with various matters of fact: What sort of person will be effective in a certain role? However, to judge someone's performance "effective" is to make a value judgment. In order to reveal the underlying ethical content of this question, it may be reformulated: Who should be permitted or encouraged to do clinical research?

The question gives rise to a series of concerns: What training should be required of clinical trials investigators? Should they be licensed especially to do this sort of research? Should students, interns, or others in training be permitted to conduct clinical trials? What disciplines should be represented in the research team? Is it permissible for physicians to conduct clinical trials on their own patients, or must another physician always be involved?

These questions point to the basic norm that requires *competence of the investigator(s):*

The experiment should be conducted only by scientifically qualified persons. The highest degree of skill and care should be required through all stages of the experiment of those who conduct or engage in the experiment (Nuremberg 8).

Biomedical research involving human subjects should be conducted only by scientifically qualified persons and under the supervision of a clinically competent medical person. The responsibility for the human subject must always rest with a medically qualified person . . . (Helsinki I.3).

The norm requires: (1) adequate scientific training and "skill" to accomplish the purposes of the research, and (2) a high degree of professionalism necessary to "care" for the subject.

The 1975 revision of the Declaration of Helsinki and the recently developed DHEW Regulations governing research on the fetus reflect another concern for competence of the investigator:

When obtaining informed consent for the research project the doctor should be particularly cautious if the subject is in a dependent relationship to him or her or may consent under duress. In that case the informed consent should be obtained by a doctor who is not engaged in the investigation and who is completely independent of this official relationship (Helsinki I. 10).

Individuals engaged in the (research) activity will have no part in: (i) any decisions as to the timing, method, and procedures used to terminate the pregnancy, and (ii) determining the viability of the fetus at the termination of the pregnancy . . . (DHEW, 46.206a, 3).

These statements recognize the possibility that a physician-investigator performing in a dual role may have difficulty dealing with the conflicts of interest arising from this double function. They create a requirement to avoid certain situations in which the interests of research might be permitted to override the interests of the patient-subject.

Patient recruitment: Problems and solutions. At first glance, this topic—like its predecessors—seems to reflect concerns about matters of fact: What techniques are effective in attracting subjects to proposed trials? How can suitable prospective subjects be located? And so on. Once again, however, further examination reveals two basic ethical questions:

1. Whom should we select for possible involvement as subjects in a clinical trial?

2. Once they have been selected, how should we invite them to participate or be involved in the trial? These are, respectively, questions about the ethics of subject selection and of informed consent.

A norm requiring *informed consent* is well established in codes and regulations for the conduct of research:

> The voluntary consent of the human subject is absolutely essential (Nuremberg 1).

> [E]ach potential subject must be adequately informed of the aims, methods, anticipated benefits and potential hazards of the study and the discomfort it may entail (Helsinki I.9).

> Legally effective informed consent will be obtained by adequate and appropriate methods . . . (DHEW, 46.102b,3).

These expressions of the norm would suggest that patients may not be involved in a trial unless they have given informed and voluntary consent.

However, the Declaration of Helsinki makes an apparent exception to this norm (or gives it an alternative interpretation) in which the subjects-to-be are patients and the research involves a new therapeutic intervention intended to benefit them. Here, the Declaration does not make consent mandatory:

> If the doctor considers it essential not to obtain informed consent, the specific reasons for this proposal should be stated in the experimental protocol . . . (Helsinki II. 5).

The Declaration of Helsinki may be interpreted to mean that under some circumstances it would be permissible to involve nonconsenting subjects. While DHEW regulations permit no such exceptions, the regulations of the Food and Drug Administration (FDA)[4] permit the following exceptions:

> In "those relatively rare cases in which it is not feasible . . . or in which as a matter of professional judgment exercised in the best interest of a particular patient . . . it would be contrary to that patient's welfare to obtain his consent" (Section 310.102d).

The norm of *informed consent* includes not only the right to refuse participation at the outset, but is also usually interpreted to include the right to withdraw at any time:

During the course of the experiment the human subject should be at liberty to bring the experiment to an end . . . (Nuremberg 9).

> [The subject] should be informed that he or she is at liberty to abstain from participation in the study and that he or she is free to withdraw his or her consent to participate at any time (Helsinki I.9). The basic elements of . . . consent include: . . . (6) an instruction that the person is free to withdraw his consent and to discontinue participation in the project or activity at any time without prejudice to the subject (DHEW 46.103c, 6).

In general, therefore, we may say that the norm of *informed consent* requires the investigator to secure the consent of patients acts prior to their involvement and to permit them to withdraw at any time without prejudice.*

While the norm related to the involvement of particular subjects is well established—and much debated[15]—less has been said explicitly about requirements for selection of groups or individuals to invite to participate in research. Most codes appear to subsume this question under the norms of scientific design and of consent: Physician-investigators would select patients on the basis of appropriate scientific considerations, and, then, provided the subject (or his or her legal guardian) gives valid consent, the selection of that subject is deemed appropriate.†

---

*Surprisingly, there has been little debate as to whether subjects should indeed always be free to withdraw at any time; most of the debate in this area has been over interpretations of what constitutes an adequately "informed" or "voluntary" consent. The requirement that subjects should always be at liberty to withdraw without prejudice seems to be based on the assumption that the subject is always doing something for the good of others; such supererogatory acts are generally not considered mandatory. There are several alternative ways to view the role of research subject: (1) McCormick[22] has argued that participation in some sorts of research is a duty. One might extrapolate from this argument to contend that—under some circumstances—the subject might not have the freedom to withdraw. Parenthetically, McCormick would probably argue that the individual should be free to choose *when* to exercise this duty. (2) Ramsey[23] and Jonas[10] characterize research as a "joint venture" between the subject and the investigator; ideally, they may be considered "coadventurers." If one accepts this argument, the agreement to participate in research may be viewed as a form of *promise*.

In 1970, Hans Jonas[10] published an influential essay in which he argued for a "descending order of permissibility" for the recruitment ("conscription") of subjects for research. His criteria for selection related directly to the person's capacity to understand the goals of the research and to participate in it as a partner with the investigator. Accordingly, he proposed that the most suitable subjects would be researchers themselves because they had the greatest capacity to give a truly "informed" consent. He also argued that very ill or dying subjects should not be used in research even when they give consent unless the research relates directly to their own illnesses. Underlying this argument is a perception of very ill or dying subjects as peculiarly vulnerable to pressures which make their consent insufficiently free or informed. In this way, the strict concern for consent was supplemented by Jonas with a concern for the situation of the subject and the ways in which the situation might render the subject vulnerable; vulnerable subjects were afforded extra protection against selection even if they wished to be selected or to participate.

Recognition that extra protection is required for those who are vulnerable by virtue of their capacities or situations is expressed in the 1975 revision of the Declaration of Helsinki. However, the requirement established in the Declaration is precisely the opposite of what Jonas proposed: Sick persons are to be recruited as subjects of "nontherapeutic research" only when it is unrelated to their illnesses.

> Nontherapeutic Biomedical Research: The subjects should be volunteers—either healthy persons or patients for whom the experimental design is not related to the patient's illness (Helsinki III. 2).*

In several of its recent reports, the Commission has made recommendations that regulations be developed to protect the vulnerable. In general, what is being developed is a requirement not to use institutionalized subjects—e.g., prisoners[30]—or persons with limited capacities to consent—e.g., children[29]—if less vulnerable persons are available and would be suitable subjects. For example, in its report on research involving children,[29] recommendation 2 reads, in part:

> Research involving children may be conducted or supported provided an Institutional Review Board has determined that . . . (B) where appropriate, studies have been conducted first on animals and adult humans, then on older children, prior to involving infants . . . (E) subjects will be selected in an equitable manner . . .

Ethically, promises may be broken only for certain justifying reasons, not simply at the whim of the promisor. (3) Levine[16] has argued that the subject ordinarily chooses to receive an "innovative therapy" because of the good (benefit) he or she expects to derive from this choice. In some circumstances the subject may be viewed as having assumed a "reciprocal obligation" of bearing the *inconvenience* of tests necessary to prove its safety and/or efficacy. The argument that an individual who chooses to receive a benefit from society thereby incurs a reciprocal obligation to serve society by participating in research designed to validate the therapy he or she receives seems highly germane to considerations of clinical trials. It must be emphasized that this obligation is to assume a burden characterized as "mere inconvenience";[16] it is not extended to create an obligation to assume risk of physical or psychological harm.

†As noted above, however, the Declaration of Helsinki makes an exception to the rule of consent for certain patients. As might be expected, then, the criteria for selection of subjects within that group also differ from the normal consent criteria. Selection of patients to receive nonvalidated therapies is left to the discretion of the physician: "In the treatment of the sick person, the doctor must be free to use a new diagnostic or therapeutic measure . . ." (Helsinki II. 1). The assumption is clearly that selection will be based on patient need and expected benefit to the patient: "If in his judgment it offers hope of saving life, re-establishing health, or alleviating suffering" (II. 1).

---

*A strict interpretation of this principle—in the context of a document that distinguishes between therapeutic and nontherapeutic research—has the following unfortunate (and unintended) consequences: (1) All rational research designed to explore the pathogenesis of diseases would be forbidden. The Declaration would require that it be conducted only on healthy persons or patients not having the disease one wishes to investigate. (2) In a placebo-controlled drug trial, those who receive the placebo must be either healthy persons or patients for whom the experimental design is not related to the patient's illness. Problems created by the spurious distinction between therapeutic and nontherapeutic research are discussed in more detail elsewhere.[13, 19, 20]

respect the free choice of persons, patients should generally be told of the plan to randomize and should be given the choice to accept participation in the trial or to accept one of the available standard treatments. In practice, the burden of proof should rest with those who would argue that it is not necessary to inform prospective subjects that their therapy will be determined by chance; unless they can convince reasonable persons (i.e., the IRB members) that this is so, the patients should be informed of their therapy.

In sum, we do not believe that concerns for

beneficence should outweigh those of *respect for persons,* nor do we accept the interpretation that "material" facts relevant to showing such respect are limited to gross medical equivalency. We therefore hold that patients should be informed that their therapy will be selected randomly. While we have chosen some rather dramatic cases to illustrate the relevance of personal values and preferences, we consider it likely that such values and preferences will affect the relevance of many characteristics of RCTs.

Notes

[1]H. Atkins, J. L. Hayward, D. J. Klugman, and A. B. Wayte, "Treatment of Early Breast Cancer: a Report after Ten Years of a Clinical Trial," *British Medical Journal,* vol. 2, p. 423, 1972.

[2]P. V. Cardon, F. W. Dommel, Jr., and R. R. Trumble, "Injuries to Research Subjects," *New England Journal of Medicine,* vol. 295, p. 650, 1976.

[3]T. C. Chalmers, "The Ethics of Randomization as a Decision Making Technique and the Problem of Informed Consent," in USDHEW Report of the 14th Annual Conference of Cardiovascular Training Grant Program Directors. Bethesda, Md., 1967. National Heart Institute. (As cited by Fried, below, note 9.)

[4]Code of Federal Regulations, 21 CFR 310, revised as of March 29, 1974.

[5]Code of Federal Regulations, 45 CFR 46, revised as of April 1, 1977.

[6]J. L. Coulehan, S. Eberhard, L. Kapner, F. Taylor, K. Rogers, and P. Garry, "Vitamin C and Acute Illness in Navajo School Children," *New England Journal of Medicine,* vol. 295, p. 973, 1976.

[7]DHEW Secretary's Task Force on the Compensation of Injured Research Subjects, DHEW Publication OS-77-003, Washington, D.C., 1977.

[8]A. R. Feinstein, "Clinical Biostatistics. XXVI. Medical Ethics and the Architecture of Clinical Research," *Clinical Pharmacology and Therapeutics,* vol. 15, p. 316, 1974.

[9]C. Fried, *Medical Experimentation: Personal Integrity and Social Policy,* North-Holland Publishing Co., Amsterdam, 1974.

[10]H. Jonas, "Philosophical Reflections on Experimenting with Human Subjects," in P. A. Freund, (ed.), *Experimentation with Human Subjects,* p. 1, Braziller, New York, 1970.

[11]L. Lasagna, "Drug Evaluation Problems in Academic and Other Contexts," *Annals of the New York Academy of Science,* vol. 169, p. 503, 1970.

[12]K. Lebacqz, "Ethical Issues in Psychopharmacological Research," in D. M. Gallant, and R. Force (eds.), *Ethical and Legal Issues in Psychopharmacologic Research and Treatment,* p. 113, Raven Press, New York, 1978.

[13]K. Lebacqz, "Reflections on the Report and Recommendations of the National Commission: Research on the Fetus," *Villanova Law Review,* vol. 22, p. 357, 1977.

[14]K. Lebacqz, "The National Commission and Research in Pharmacology: An Overview," *Federation Proceedings,* vol. 36, p. 2344, 1977.

[15]K. Lebacqz, and R. J. Levine, "Respect for Persons and Informed Consent to Participate in Research," *Clinical Research,* vol. 25, p. 101, 1977.

[16]R. J. Levine, "Appropriate Guidelines for the Selection of Human Subjects for Participation in Biomedical and Behavioral Research," prepared for the National Commission for the Protection of Human Subjects of Biomedical and Behavioral Research, 1976.

[17]R. J. Levine, "Guidelines for Negotiating Informed Consent with Prospective Human Subjects of Experimentation," *Clinical Research,* vol. 22, p. 42, 1974.

[18]R. J. Levine, "Informed Consent to Participate in Research" (in 2 parts), *Bioethics Digest,* vol. 1, no. 11. p. 1; no. 12, p. 1, 1977.

[19]R. J. Levine, "Nondevelopmental Research on Human Subjects: The Impact of the Recommendations of the National Commission," *Federation Proceedings,* vol. 36, p. 2359, 1977.

[20]R. J. Levine, "The Impact on Fetal Research of the Report of the National Commission for the Protection of Human Subjects of Biomedical and Behavioral Research, *Villanova Law Review,* vol. 22, p. 367, 1977.

[21]R. J. Levine, "The Role of Assessment of Risk-Benefit Criteria in the Determination of the Appropriateness of Research Involving Human Subjects," *Bioethics Digest,* vol. 1, p. 1, 1976.

[22]R. A. McCormick, "Proxy Consent in the Experimentation Situation," *Perspectives in Biology and Medicine,* vol. 18, p. 2, 1974.

[23]P. Ramsey, *The Patient as Person,* Yale University Press, New Haven, 1970.

[24]J. Rawls, *A Theory of Justice,* Harvard University Press, Cambridge, Mass., 1971.

[25]S. J. Reiser, A. J. Dyck, and W. J. Curran, *Ethics in Medicine: Historical Perspectives and Contemporary Concerns,* MIT Press, Cambridge, Mass., 1977.

[26]D. D. Rutstein, "The Ethical Design of Human Experiments," in P. A. Freund (ed.), *Experimentation with Human Subjects,* Braziller, New York, 1970.

[27]L. W. Shaw, and T. C. Chalmers, "Ethics in Cooperative Clinical Trials," *Annals of the New York Academy of Science,* vol. 169, p. 487, 1970.

[28]The National Commission for the Protection of Human Subjects of Biomedical and Behavioral Research, "Identification of Basic Ethical Principles," Draft of June 3, 1976.

[29]The National Commission for the Protection of Human Subjects of Biomedical and Behavioral Research, "Research In-volving Children," Washington, D.C., Publication No. (OS) 77-0004.

[30]The National Commission for the Protection of Human Subjects of Biomedical and Behavioral Research, "Research Involving Prisoners," Washington, D.C., 1976, DHEW Publication No. (OS) 76-131.

[31]The National Commission for the Protection of Human Subjects of Biomedical and Behavioral Research, "The Boundaries between Biomedical and Behavioral Research and Accepted and Routine Practice," Draft of February 24, 1976.

[32]Veterans Administration Cooperative Study Group on Antihypertensive Agents, "Effects of Treatment on Morbidity in Hypertension," *Journal of the American Medical Association,* vol. 213, p. 1143, 1970.

[33]H. Zeisel, "Reducing the Hazards of Human Experiments through Modifications in Research Design," *Annals of the New York Academy of Science,* vol. 169, p. 475, 1970.

The Use and Abuse of Animals in Research

Bernard E. Rollin

Bernard E. Rollin is professor of philosophy, professor of physiology and biophysics, and director of bioethical planning at Colorado State University. His published papers have appeared in a wide variety of philosophical and scientific journals, and he has lectured extensively in the United States, Canada, Europe, and Australia.

Rollin identifies six types of research on animals and insists that good research must be theory-based. He argues that animal research is justified if (1) "the benefit to humans (or to humans and animals) clearly outweighs the pain and suffering experienced by the experimental animals" and if the experimentation is (2) "conducted in such a way as to maximize the animal's potential for living its life according to its nature or telos, and certain fundamental rights (are) preserved . . ." He recommends replacing animals with alternatives, reducing their numbers, and refining procedures to reduce animal suffering where these are possible.

INTRODUCTION

Thus far, we have allowed ourselves the luxury of theory, unsullied by the pressures and constraints of *realpolitik*. We have arrived at the ideal, the target in Aristotle's phrase, the yardstick against which we can measure actual practice. Certainly the significance of such an activity cannot be

underestimated; yet man and society being what they are, we cannot expect expect immediate reversal of habits and traditions entrenched by time and nurtured by expediency. What, then, can be done? Despairing of foreseeable total success, does one retire to polish and refine one's abstract theoretical model? Here we may take a clue from David Hume, the great philosophical skeptic, a thinker whose powerful arguments cast doubt on our grounds for believing in minds (including our

own), physical objects, causality, order in nature, God, science, reason, and the difference between the subjective and objective. Having done this, Hume does not reject his arguments but sets them aside and does practical ethics for, after all, one must live in the world. "Be a philosopher," he tells us, "but be first a man."

In a similar vein, we must conclude that being a philosopher does not allow us the luxury of escaping from the world, however attractive that may be. Philosophers, especially moral philosophers, can no longer justify disengagement from the mundane on the grounds that they are concerned with what ought to be, not with what is. The crystalline purity of our reasoned arguments must be sullied by an encounter with social reality. This is especially pressing in the case of the moral status of animals. An arsenal of well-wrought arguments proving conclusively that we all ought to be vegetarians or that all animal experimentation is immoral is important, as we have stressed, but will probably in and of itself make little direct difference to the total amount of suffering in the universe. It is equally important to make these arguments count in some real and efficacious way. And to do this requires that we confront in detail the existential facts of our moral situation and realistically assess the ways in which our arguments can meaningfully intersect with practice.

We must not expect our philosophical model to serve as a blueprint for immediate social change, for this expectation is as realistic as Allen Ginsberg's attempt to levitate the Pentagon. Our moral model must provide us with a yardstick to measure our moral progress. Most people who consider themselves Christians are not capable of turning the other cheek; that does not make them hypocrites. To some, our willingness to deviate from the ideal we have set up in the face of what is practically possible may appear as hypocrisy, as "selling out," as prostitution of one's ideals. But in the final analysis, the question that must always loom before us is this: Are the animals any better

off in virtue of our efforts? We must avoid contenting ourselves with serving as moral *kamikazes,* going down in a blaze of glory, yet making little difference to the outcome of the battle.

So it is to the question of animal experimentation that we now turn, where we shall attempt to adjust our theoretical model to the harsh landscape of reality. It is here that we find the greatest amount of animal suffering, and correlatively, the greatest potential for diminution of that suffering. We shall find, in the course of our discussion, that the problem is enormously complex and not amenable to simple solutions. The traditional rhetoric that has characterized the debate between proponents and opponents of research is so simplistic as to be almost meaningless. Yet, tragically, it has served as an insurmountable barrier to genuine dialogue and, even worse, as a barrier to the determination of common ground. In addition to the invective invariably hurled by both sides ("Sadistic vivisectionist"; "Bleeding heart humaniac"; "You would stop us from curing leukemia"; "You torture kittens for fun," etc.), the situation has been characterized by abysmal ignorance on both sides. Typically, opponents of animal experimentation know little about research and often discredit themselves by offering wholly implausible "alternatives" to the use of animals. By the same token, researchers have rarely thought through the moral questions associated with animal experimentation and discredit themselves with absurd claims that animals have no awareness, or really don't suffer, or that might makes right. Our problem then is to bridge these gaps of ignorance and to work towards a realistic improvement in the lot of the experimental animals, keeping always in view the ideal model we have constructed, yet not hesitating to deviate from it if the pressures of reality force us to do so. The problem of the research animal serves as a dramatic exemplar and best case for our ultimate purpose—unifying moral philosophy and current reality. Our society is not yet ready to grant legal and moral rights to animals—we must look to the best approxima-

tion of these ideals that can be actualized in our current socio-cultural context.

THE SIX SENSES OF RESEARCH

Few of us realize the extent to which animals are employed in research and testing of all sorts. In fact, the figures stagger the imagination. It is currently estimated that the total number of laboratory animals now used throughout the world annually is 200 to 225 million. The United States accounts for about 100 million of these animals as follows: 50 million mice, 20 million rats, and about 30 million other animals, including 200,000 cats and 450,000 dogs. These statistics, incidentally, indicate the true absurdity of the Animal Welfare Act, growing out of its failure to provide any protection at all for the vast majority of animals used, as rats and mice alone constitute 70 percent of the total.

Most of us tend to think of laboratory animals in terms of cancer research and the cure of disease, major areas of activity that are clearly of enormous significance in potentially bettering all of life, human and animal. As a result, most people are not too terribly concerned with the "plight" of laboratory animals and tend to see whatever suffering they do undergo as major contributions to the common good. Indeed, scientists tend to perpetuate this image of the use of research animals and, when referring to the killing of laboratory animals, even in scientific papers, tend to speak of "sacrificing" the animal. (We shall return to a detailed discussion of such language shortly.) It is revelatory for most people that most laboratory animals are in fact employed in far less noble pursuits, although no clear statistics are available to document this in any detailed way. Such activities include the toxicity and irritation testing of various consumer products, such as foodstuffs and cosmetics; teaching; extraction of products; and the development of drugs. Thus, when speaking of the question of "research or

laboratory animals," we must take great care to realize the variegated activities subsumed under that rubric. We must take care to distinguish a number of distinct activities. For convenience, we may group them into the following categories, recognizing that they represent gross oversimplifications:

1. Basic biological research, that is, the formulation and testing of hypotheses about fundamental theoretical questions, such as the nature of DNA replication or mitochondrial activity, with little concern for the practical effect of that research.

2. Applied basic biomedical research—the formulation and testing of hypotheses about diseases, dysfunctions, genetic defects, etc., that, while not necessarily having immediate consequences for treatment of disease, are at least seen as directly related to such consequences. Clearly the distinction between category one and this category will constitute a spectrum, rather than a clear-cut cleavage.

3. The development of drugs and therapeutic chemicals and biologicals: this differs from the earlier categories, again in degree (especially category two), but is primarily distinguished by what might be called a "shotgun" approach; that is, the research is guided not so much by well-formulated theories that suggest that a certain compound might have a certain effect, but rather by hit-and-miss, exploratory, inductive "shooting in the dark." The primary difference between this category and the others is that here one is aiming at discovering specific substances for specific purposes, rather than at knowledge *per se*.

4. The testing of various consumer goods for safety, toxicity, irritation, and degree of toxicity: such testing includes the testing of cosmetics, food additives, herbicides, pesticides, industrial chemicals, and so forth, as well as the testing of drugs for toxicity, carcinogenesis (production of cancer), mutagenesis (production of mutations in living bodies), and teratogenesis (production of monsters and abnormalities in embryo develop-

ment). To some extent, obviously, this category will overlap with category three, but should be distinguished in virtue of the fact that three refers to the discovery of new drugs, and four to their testing relative to human (and, in the case of veterinary drugs, animal) safety.

5. The use of animals in educational institutions and elsewhere for demonstration, dissection, surgery practice, induction of disease for illustrative purposes, high school science projects, etc.

6. The use of animals for the extraction of products—serum from horses, musk from civet cats, etc. This is not, strictly speaking, research.

It is thus quite important to be clear about which activities one is referring to when discussing "research on animals," since arguments relevant to one area will clearly not fit one or more of the others. A failure to do so on the part of many well-intentioned opponents of "animal experimentation" has traditionally led to a breakdown in communication with those who utilize animals in their activities. It is obviously necessary to discuss each of these categories separately, taking cognizance of the problems unique to each pursuit.

MORAL PRINCIPLES FOR RESEARCH: THE UTILITARIAN AND RIGHTS PRINCIPLES

Before embarking on these discussions, it is worth clarifying some basic moral presuppositions that follow from our previous discussion, and that will underlie our subsequent argument. We have argued that there is no clear-cut line between men and animals from a moral point of view, and further, that animals have moral rights following from their nature or *telos* if or even as men do. We have correlatively argued that since law rests on morality and that a key moral notion encoded in the law is the notion of rights possessed by human individuals, animals too ought to possess legal rights that protect their fundamental na-

tures. From a strictly philosophical point of view, I think that we must draw a startling conclusion: If a certain sort of research on human beings is considered to be immoral, a *prima facie* case exists for saying that such research is immoral when conducted on animals. Our reasons for saying that various kinds of research on humans is immoral is that it causes pain or infringes on freedom or violates some basic interest or right of man. Clearly then, such reasoning should be carried over to animals as well, unless one can cite a morally relevant difference that characterizes the animal, and we have already argued that such a difference is not likely to be forthcoming. Such a criterion would not eliminate *all* research on animals, even as use of that criterion has not vitiated all research on men. After all, we still do experiments on people that do not violate their right to dignity, equality, choice, and freedom from suffering. But use of that criterion would effectively curtail the vast majority of research in all of the above categories. Clearly such a position is utopian and socially and psychologically impossible in our culture. And if, as I suggested earlier, morality must deal with what is in some sense at least in part actualizable, we cannot even adopt the abolition of animal experimentation as an achievable moral goal in our socio-psychological milieu. As Kant said in another context, "ought implies can." That is, meaningfully to suggest that we *ought* to abolish our animal experimentation, legislatively or otherwise, is absurd unless this is something that *can* happen in our world—cf. abolishing war. That is not to suggest that it cannot serve as a regulative ideal or yardstick against which to measure our activities, but it is to suggest that it cannot currently be seen as a goal to be achieved.

Why not? Primarily because most of us are not prepared to sacrifice the benefits that research brings, especially in the area of disease control and treatment. Nor are we prepared to give up our faith in science as a dominant mode of dealing with reality, and the abolition of animal experimentation would essentially mean an end to

much of science as we know it. That is, our rejection of the moral status of animals in this context grows out of *utilitarian considerations,* out of considerations that suggest that more good than suffering comes out of experimentation. We have seen in the previous chapter that such an approach typifies our societal approach to decision making. We are not prepared to give up the chance to cure cancer in order to limit the suffering of mice.

This then, I think, circumscribes the arena upon which our discussion of animal research must be played out if our arguments are to have any potential effect, or point of contact with the real world, or potential for ameliorating animal suffering. For one to argue and work for the total abolition of animal experimentation is to act as a moral *kamikaze,* a suicide pilot, though the analogy breaks down insofar as the *kamikaze* had some statistical chance of making a dent in the opposition. Perhaps, as we said earlier, Allen Ginsberg's attempt to levitate the Pentagon during the Vietnam War is a better analogy. This is not, of course, to suggest that one must simply accept the *status quo;* in fact, much of our subsequent discussion will be directed precisely towards making significant changes in this monumental edifice.

One point emerges quite clearly here: If utilitarian considerations govern our acceptance of animal experimentation, it is reasonable to ask, as Bentham and Mill did, why *all* creatures capable of feeling pleasure and pain are not included in the utilitarian reckoning? It is sometimes said that they are; that research on animals benefits animals as well as humans, so that the net benefit outweighs the net cost. This may be true for certain areas of research, but a moment's reflection on our categories of research makes it quite clear that this is far from usual.

Ignoring this inconsistency, and accepting as socially inevitable the idea that human utility will always be paramount, at least in the foreseeable future, one can at least reasonably make the following demand of all our categories: *that the ben-*efit to humans (or to humans and animals) clearly outweighs the pain and suffering experienced by the experimental animals. Granted that the weighing of pleasure and pain is notoriously difficult, still we all do so daily. I judge that I will cause more total pain than pleasure by having an affair with one of my students. My colleagues judge that we will engender more pleasure than pain by sharing our meager raises equally than by rewarding one or two people at the expense of the others, and so forth. Correlatively, as we shall see, there are many cases of research in which the pain to the animals is clear and extreme, whereas the benefit to humans or animals is questionable and nebulous. Let us call this demand *the utilitarian principle.*

We may reasonably make another demand. If we are socially committed to research on animals and are prepared to embrace the utilitarian principle, we should also reasonably embrace the following dictum: In cases where research is deemed justifiable by the utilitarian principle, *it should be conducted in such a way as to maximize the animal's potential for living its life according to its nature or telos, and certain fundamental rights should be preserved as far as possible, given the logic of the research, regardless of considerations of cost.* We can call this the *rights principle.* It essentially suggests that certain aspects of the animal's nature are sacred and need to be protected against total submersion by utilitarian considerations. This in turn means that we cannot do as we see fit to a research animal, even if we have determined that the animal's use is justified by the utilitarian principle. We must avoid encroaching on the animal's fundamental interests and nature, and this in turn means that it has a right to freedom from pain, to being housed and fed in accordance with its nature, to exercise, to company if it is a social being, etc.; in short, to being treated as an end in itself, regardless of the cost. What this means in practice is this: We weigh a piece of research by the utilitarian principle. If it meets this test, it may be performed. There may be discomfort associated with such an experiment that is unavoidable—

e.g., if we are infecting the animal with a disease. The point of the rights principle is that even if the experiment is justified and does involve infringing on some aspects of the animal's nature, we are still obliged to protect the other aspects of its nature and other interests, and to do so regardless of cost. Thus, if the disease is accompanied by pain, the animal should be given analgesics.

Furthermore, I think that it is both morally required and pragmatically feasible to envision these principles incorporated into a meaningful federal Animal Welfare Act, covering all animals in all categories. This is the point of intersection between our previous chapters and our actual socio-cultural situation. Legislation must be written that insures that research be chosen (*and funded*) in accordance with the utilitarian principle and conducted in accordance with the rights principle, with animal advocates serving as guardians of the animals' rights, and as reviewers of the adherence of the research to the two principles, empowered to bring legal action to the direct benefit of the animal. Further, meaningful penalties must be provided for violators of this legislation—perhaps researchers ought to be licensed, and violation punished by loss of licensure.

It may be thought that such a suggestion is as utopian as abolishing all research altogether. Scientists will never consent to such a surrender of their freedom, especially when the scientific community has historically tended to resist all control and has tended to minimize the significance of animal suffering. This is a major objection, and we shall return to it in what follows. So now, let us review the various categories of research in greater detail, keeping in mind our previous arguments and the two principles we have distilled from them.

INTRODUCTION TO THE TESTING OF CONSUMABLES

According to regulations promulgated by the Food and Drug Administration, each new chemical or biological substance marketed for con-

sumer use—drugs, food and food additives, herbicides, pesticides—must be subjected to safety evaluation; cosmetics, shampoos, etc., are also subject to such testing, in part due to additional federal regulations, and in part due to manufacturers' desires to protect themselves from lawsuits, in case a substance should later prove to be detrimental to human health. With increasing numbers of substances being marketed, and more pressure from the consumer lobby, more and more testing is required. The primary vehicles for testing these substances are animals (*circa* 20 million per year), and the methods employed fall into a few major categories.

THE LD50 TEST

The testing of these various substances first of all requires some standard way of judging their *toxicity*, i.e., the extent to which they are poisonous. One standard measure that has been adopted is called the LD50 test, short for Lethal Dose 50 percent. The test was introduced in another context in 1927 by Trevan, who was concerned with providing a statistical solution to the problem of biological variation: that is, given a group of rats exposed to a given substance, not all the rats responded to the same dose in the same way. The LD50 indicates the amount of a substance that, when administered in a single dose to a group of animals, will result in the death of 50 percent of the group within fourteen days. (The LD100 indicates the minimum dosage that would kill *all* of the animals in the time period; the LD0 indicates the maximum dosages that would kill *none* of the animals.)

The LD50 test is thus a measure of acute toxicity, i.e., single dose or fractional doses given over a short period, typically orally, though there are also inhalant and dermal versions of the test. It by far is the most widely used test of toxicity of drugs, chemicals, pesticides, insecticides, food additives, and household substances; it is invariably the first study done in toxicity evaluation and *often the only test done.* A high percentage (no

exact figure is available) of the animals used in product and drug testing are used in LD50 tests. By the time the LD50 is determined, sixty to one hundred animals have been poisoned. A variety of federal regulations and agencies in the United States militate in favor of the use of the LD50, and procedural methodology for the test has been standardized through the Hazardous Substances Act, the Registry of Toxic Effects of Chemical Substances (or Toxic Substances List), and the Federal Insecticide, Fungicide, and Rodenticide Act. For example, the most conspicuous value listed in the Toxic Substances List is the LD50. The LD50 is also effectively required by the Interstate Commerce Commission, since a failure to supply LD50 data forces a manufacturer to treat the substance as belonging to the most toxic category, and shipping requirements become very stringent and expensive.

Given the prevalence of the test, and the number of animals who suffer in virtue of its widespread use, it is worth considering its legitimacy as a scientific device, ignoring moral considerations for the moment. Extraordinarily, one finds a wide variety of stringent criticisms directed against the test, considered as an indicator of safety evaluation for humans. In a 1968 article in *Modern Trends in Toxicology,* "The Purpose and Value of LD50 Determinations," Morrison, Quinton, and Reinert critically reviewed the literature on LD50 testing. These authors, it must be emphasized, were totally unconcerned with the moral problems surrounding the test, or with the moral status of animals—their concern was simply methodological and theoretical. The authors point out, first of all, that LD50 tests tell us only about the gross effect, all or nothing, of a given substance. That is, all we learn is that a certain dosage either kills or does not. Correlatively, LD50 results are totally unextrapolatable to *chronic* (prolonged) exposure to the substance in question. The effect in an animal of massive acute doses tells us nothing about the long-term effects of small doses. This is especially significant in light of the fact that the typical danger to humans from these substances comes from *repeated, low-*

level doses. For example, if one is evaluating a new drug, one is typically not concerned with the effects of massive doses, barring suicide attempts and major industrial accidents. Rather, one is worried about the possible long-term effect of a cumulative series of relatively small doses. One is also concerned with the *mechanisms* of toxicity, the *sites* of toxic action, and the *metabolic processes* affected by the drug, etc., none of which the LD50 deals with at all. In fact, emphasis on the LD50 figures tends to lead to a de-emphasis upon qualitative data, such as clinical signs and autopsy results. Nor do LD50 tests contribute much to design of further toxicity trials, since they are purely quantitative and consider only mortality.

Most dramatically, cross-species variation, coupled with a total failure of the LD50 to come to grips with the metabolic pathways taken by the various toxins, renders the results of animal LD50's all but meaningless *vis-à-vis* a justifiable extrapolation to human beings. Nor is this mitigated by tests across different species. Morrison *et al.* flatly assert that:

> Neither variations nor uniformity of LD50 figures in a number of laboratory animals species can assist in estimating toxicity in man (p. 4).

So without knowledge that the metabolic pathways of the substance are identical in man and test animal, we cannot draw inferences to human toxicity from LD50 studies on animals.

Furthermore, there are huge numbers of variables, typically not controlled for, that can radically alter LD50 results on test animals. Among these are species differences, genetic differences even in the same species (LD50 for the substance thiourea was 4mg/kg in Hopkins rats and 1340–1830 mg/kg in Norwegian rats), crowding conditions, sex, age, composition of diet, latent infection, caging conditions (in mice caged alone, an increase of cage size has been shown to reduce toxicity of amphetamine by 50 percent), temperature, humidity, and light. The LD50 for amphetamine in rats increases 700 percent when the rats are caged in groups of twelve, compared to when they are caged singly.

blatantly espouse such a simplistic view of science is shocking but illustrative of our thesis. As I pointed out to him, science is not just or even basically the gathering of facts. Scientific theories do not typically emerge from random data collection. The main importance of data is in the *verification* of hypotheses, not in their discovery. After all, when one considers any major scientific theory, be it the theory of gravitation, relativity, quantum mechanics, the gene, etc., one makes references to entities and processes that are unobservable, and whose discovery required imaginative leaps. Newton was certainly not the first man to be hit by a falling apple; yet it took Newton's theoretical vision to postulate gravitation!

The most superficial look at the history of science reveals that virtually no major advances were made simply by gathering data. The great scientists were guided by theory and vision, indeed, sometimes by erroneous vision, as in the case of Kepler, who sought to prove that the orbits of the planets could be related mathematically as the notes of the musical scale, thereby establishing the music of the spheres postulated by the Pythagoreans. Or let us recall Galileo, who is often said to have shown that the acceleration of falling bodies is independent of their mass and is uniform by dropping a heavy and a light object from the Leaning Tower of Pisa. In actual fact, as seen in his *Dialogues Concerning the Two Great Systems of the World*, Galileo was a good deal more ingenious than that and employed reason to establish his point. Take two five-pound weights, said Galileo, and drop them from the same height. Surely they will hit the ground at the same time. Join them by a weightless rod—surely they will still hit the ground at the same time when dropped. Shrink the rod until the two weights are stuck together. Surely they will still hit the ground at the same time. But now we have a ten-pound weight, showing that rate of fall is independent of mass.

As another example of where theory precedes data and predominates over it, consider Einstein. His world-shattering critique of Newton was not based on data or experiment unavailable to others, but rather on a conceptual analysis of the concept of simultaneity. Correlatively, when asked what he would have said if some astronomical predictions generated by the general theory of relativity had not been supported by the data gathered by Eddington, Einstein said in essence, "So much the worse for the data—the theory is correct!"

A similar account can be given about the father of genetics, Gregor Mendel. Every schoolboy knows of Mendel's famous experiments with the pea plants, which allegedly led him to the discovery of genetics. In fact, statistical analysis of Mendel's studies indicate that the probability of Mendel actually obtaining the experimental results he claimed was only .00007, or one in 14,000! In short, Mendel *knew* that the theory was correct and chose the data which met his expectations.

We know too from the history of science that in the face of theoretical commitment, recalcitrant data is easily dismissed or explained away, and that theory determines what we see. Consider Galileo's bishops, who refused to look through the telescope because they knew the moon was perfect. Suppose they would have been forced to look—would they then have been forced to admit that it was not perfect? Not at all—they simply would have said that Galileo had created an instrument that made the perfect moon look flawed. An even more dramatic example is told of Franz Anton Mesmer, the discoverer of "animal magnetism" or hypnotism. In order to illustrate the anaesthetic effects of hypnotism, Mesmer hypnotized a patient who was to undergo amputation, and the limb was removed with no visible discomfort. "Have I not proved my point," asked Mesmer triumphantly. "Not at all," replied the physicians. "The man felt pain, he just failed to show it."

The point, then, is this: Contrary to the way science is often taught and contrary to the way many researchers proceed, science is not merely fact gathering. To paraphrase the great philosopher, Immanuel Kant, "theories without data are

empty, data without theories are blind." Certainly we shall make no progress without accumulating data and facts. But those facts must not be gathered at random. They must be gathered in order to test hypotheses and theories arrived at via the creative power of thought, reason, and imagination, as the members of the Royal Society after Newton we discussed earlier ruefully discovered. . . .

SELECTED BIBLIOGRAPHY

Beecher, H. K. "Ethics and Clinical Research." *New England Journal of Medicine* 274 (1966): 1354–60.

Childress, James F. "Compensating Injured Research Subjects: I. The Moral Argument." *Hastings Center Report* 6 (December 1976): 21–27.

Greenwald, Robert A., Mary Kay Ryan, and James E. Mulvihill. *Human Subjects Research: A Handbook for Institutional Review Boards.* New York: Plenum, 1982.

Jonas, Hans. "Philosophical Reflections on Experimenting with Human Subjects." *Daedalus* 98 (1969): 219–47.

Katz, Jay, Alexander M. Capron, and Eleanor S. Glass, eds. *Experimentation with Human Beings: The Authority of the Investigator, Subject, Professions, and State in the Human Experimentation Process.* New York: Russell Sage, 1972.

Levine, Robert J. *Ethics and Regulation of Clinical Research.* 2nd ed. Baltimore: Urban & Schwarzenberg, 1986.

National Commission for the Protection of Human Subjects of Biomedical and Behavioral Research. *The Belmont Report: Ethical Principles and Guidelines for the Protection of Human Subjects of Research.* DHEW (OS) 78-0012.   *The Belmont Report: Appendix.* Vols. 1, 2. DHEW (OS) 78-0013, 78-0014. Bethesda, Md.: U.S. Government Printing Office, 1978.

Robertson, John A. "Compensating Injured Research Subjects: II. The Law." *Hastings Center Report* 6 (December 1976): 29–31.

Ryder, Richard. "Experiments on Animals." In Godlovich, Stanley, Roslind Godlovich, and John Harris, eds., *Animals, Men and Morals.* New York: Grove Press, 1972, pp. 41–82.

Schafer, A. "The Ethics of the Randomized Clinical Trial." *New England Journal of Medicine* 307 (1982): 719–24.

Singer, Peter. *Animal Liberation.* New York: Avon Books, 1975, Ch. 2.

and the scope of the task before the Committee therefore knows no bounds."

In Dr. Chisholm's statement, put very succinctly, are all of those elements of the WHO definition which led eventually to its criticism: defining all the problems of the world as "sickness," affirming that science would be sufficient to cope with the causes of physical disease, asserting that only anachronistic attitudes stood in the way of a cure of both physical and psychological ills, and declaring that the cause of health can tolerate no limitations. To say that Dr. Chisholm's "vision" was grandiose is to understate the matter. Even allowing for hyperbole, it is clear that the stage was being set for a conception of "health" which would encompass literally every element and item of human happiness. One can hardly be surprised, given such a vision, that our ways of talking about "health" have become all but meaningless. Even though I believe the definition is not without its important insights, it is well to observe why, in part, we are so muddled at present about "health."

HEALTH AND HAPPINESS

Let us examine some of the principal objections to the WHO definition in more detail. One of them is that, by including the notion of "social well-being" under its rubric, it turns the enduring problem of human happiness into one more medical problem, to be dealt with by scientific means. That is surely an objectionable feature, if only because there exists no evidence whatever that medicine has anything more than a partial grasp of the sources of human misery. Despite Dr. Chisholm's optimism, medicine has not even found ways of dealing with more than a fraction of the whole range of physical diseases; campaigns, after all, are still being mounted against cancer and heart disease. Nor is there any special reason to think that future forays against those and other common diseases will bear rapid fruits. People will continue to die of disease for a long time to come, probably forever.

But perhaps, then, in the psychological and psychiatric sciences some progress has been made against what Dr. Chisholm called the "psychological ills," which lead to wars, hostility, and aggression? To be sure, there are many interesting psychological theories to be found about these "ills," and a few techniques which can, with some individuals, reduce or eliminate antisocial behavior. But so far as I can see, despite the mental health movement and the rise of the psychological sciences, war and human hostility are as much with us as ever. Quite apart from philosophical objections to the WHO definition, there was no empirical basis for the unbounded optimism which lay behind it at the time of its inception, and little has happened since to lend its limitless aspiration any firm support.

Common sense alone makes evident the fact that the absence of "disease or infirmity" by no means guarantees "social well-being." In one sense, those who drafted the WHO definition seem well aware of that. Isn't the whole point of their definition to show the inadequacy of negative definitions? But in another sense, it may be doubted that they really did grasp that point. For the third principle enunciated in the WHO Constitution says that "the health of all peoples is fundamental to the attainment of peace and security. . . ." Why is it fundamental, at least to peace? The worst wars of the 20th century have been waged by countries with very high standards of health, by nations with superior life-expectancies for individuals and with comparatively low infant mortality rates. The greatest present threats to world peace come in great part (though not entirely) from developed countries, those which have combatted disease and illness most effectively. There seems to be no historical correlation whatever between health and peace, and that is true even if one includes "mental health."

How are human beings to achieve happiness? That is the final and fundamental question. Obviously illness, whether mental or physical, makes happiness less possible in most cases. But that is only because they are only one symptom of

a more basic restriction, that of human finitude, which sees infinite human desires constantly thwarted by the limitations of reality. "Complete" well-being might, conceivably, be attainable, but under one condition only: that people ceased expecting much from life. That does not seem about to happen. On the contrary, medical and psychological progress have been more than outstripped by rising demands and expectations. What is so odd about that, if it is indeed true that human desires are infinite? Whatever the answer to the question of human happiness, there is no particular reason to believe that medicine can do anything more than make a modest, finite contribution.

Another objection to the WHO definition is that, by implication, it makes the medical profession the gate-keeper for happiness and social well-being. Or if not exactly the gate-keeper (since political and economic support will be needed from sources other than medical), then the final magic-healer of human misery. Pushed far enough, the whole idea is absurd, and it is not necessary to believe that the organizers of the WHO would, if pressed, have been willing to go quite that far. But even if one pushes the pretension a little way, considerable fantasy results. The mental health movement is the best example, casting the psychological professional in the role of high priest.

At its humble best, that movement can do considerable good; people do suffer from psychological disabilities and there are some effective ways of helping them. But it would be sheer folly to believe that all, or even the most important, social evils stem from bad mental health: political injustice, economic scarcity, food shortages, unfavorable physical environments, have a far greater historical claim as sources of a failure to achieve "social well-being." To retort that all or most of these troubles can, nonetheless, be seen finally as symptoms of bad mental health is, at best, self-serving and, at worst, just plain foolish.

A significant part of the objection that the WHO definition places, at least by implication, too much power and authority in the hands of the medical profession need not be based on a fear of that power as such. There is no reason to think that the world would be any worse off if health professionals made all decisions than if any other group did, and no reason to think it would be any better off. That is not a very important point. More significant is that cultural development which, in its skepticism about "traditional" ways of solving social problems, would seek a technological and specifically a medical solution for human ills of all kinds. There is at least a hint in early WHO discussions that, since politicians and diplomats have failed in maintaining world peace, a more expert group should take over, armed with the scientific skills necesssary to set things right; it is science which is best able to vanquish that old Enlightenment bogeyman, "superstition." More concretely, such an ideology has the practical effect of blurring the lines of appropriate authority and responsibility. If all problems— political, economic and social—reduce to matters of "health," then there cease to be any ways to determine who should be responsible for what.

THE TYRANNY OF HEALTH

The problem of responsibility has at least two faces. One is that of a tendency to turn all problems of "social well-being" over to the medical professional, most pronounced in the instance of the incarceration of a large group of criminals in mental institutions rather than prisons. The abuses, both medical and legal, of that practice are, fortunately, now beginning to receive the attention they deserve, even if little corrective action has yet been taken. (Counterbalancing that development, however, are others, where some are seeking more "effective" ways of bringing science to bear on criminal behavior.)

The other face of the problem of responsibility is that of the way in which those who are sick, or purportedly sick, are to be evaluated in terms of their freedom and responsibility. Siegler and

Osmond [*Hastings Center Studies,* vol. 1, no. 3, 1973, pp. 41–58] discuss the "sick role," a leading feature of which is the ascription of blamelessness, of non-responsibility, to those who contract illness. There is no reason to object to this kind of ascription in many instances—one can hardly blame someone for contracting kidney disease—but, obviously enough, matters get out of hand when all physical, mental, and communal disorders are put under the heading of "sickness," and all sufferers (all of us, in the end) placed in the blameless "sick role." Not only are the concepts of "sickness" and "illness" drained of all content, it also becomes impossible to ascribe any freedom or responsibility to those caught up in the throes of sickness. The whole world is sick, and no one is responsible any longer for anything. That is determinism gone mad, a rather odd outcome of a development which began with attempts to bring unbenighted "reason" and free self-determination to bear for the release of the helpless captives of superstition and ignorance.

The final and most telling objection to the WHO definition has less to do with the definition itself than with one of its natural historical consequences. Thomas Szasz has seen the most eloquent (and most singleminded) critic of that sleight-of-hand which has seen the concept of health moved from the medical to the moral arena. What can no longer be done in the name of "morality" can now be done in the name of "health": human beings labeled, incarcerated, and dismissed for their failure to toe the line of "normalcy" and "sanity."

At first glance, this analysis of the present situation might seem to be totally at odds with the tendency to put everyone in the blame-free "sick role." Actually, there is a fine, probably indistinguishable, line separating these two positions. For as soon as one treats all human disorders—war, crime, social unrest—as forms of illness, then one turns health into a normative concept, that which human beings must and ought to have if they are to live in peace with themselves and others. Health is no longer an optional matter, but the golden key to the relief of human misery. We *must* be well or we will all perish. "Health" can and must be imposed; there can be no room for the luxury of freedom when so much is at stake. Of course the matter is rarely put so bluntly, but it is to Szasz's great credit that he has discerned what actually happens when "health" is allowed to gain the cultural clout which morality once had. (That he carries the whole business too far in his embracing of the most extreme moral individualism is another story, which cannot be dealt with here.) Something is seriously amiss when the "right" to have healthy children is turned into a further right for children not to be born defective, and from there into an obligation not to bring unhealthy children into the world as a way of respecting the right of those children to health! Nor is everything altogether lucid when abortion decisions are made a matter of "medical judgment" (see *Roe* vs. *Wade*); when decisions to provide psychoactive drugs for the relief of the ordinary stress of living are defined as no less "medical judgment"; when patients are not allowed to die with dignity because of medical indications that they can, come what may, be kept alive; when prisoners, without their consent, are subjected to aversive conditioning to improve their mental health.

ABUSES OF LANGUAGE

In running through the litany of criticisms which have been directed at the WHO definition of "health," and what seem to have been some of its long-term implications and consequences, I might well be accused of beating a dead horse. My only defense is to assert, first, that the spirit of the WHO definition is by no means dead either in medicine or society. In fact, because of the usual cultural lag which requires many years for new ideas to gain wide social currency, it is only now coming into its own on a broad scale. (Everyone now talks about everybody and everything, from Watergate to Billy Graham to trash in the streets,

as "sick.") Second, I believe that we are now in the midst of a nascent (if not actual) crisis about how "health" ought properly to be understood, with much dependent upon what conception of health emerges in the near future.

If the ideology which underlies the WHO definition has proved to contain many muddled and hazardous ingredients, it is not at all evident what should take its place. The virtue of the WHO definition is that it tried to place health in the broadest human context. Yet the assumption behind the main criticisms of the WHO definition seem perfectly valid. Those assumptions can be characterized as follows: (1) health is only a part of life, and the achievement of health only a part of the achievement of happiness; (2) medicine's role, however important, is limited; it can neither solve nor even cope with the great majority of social, political, and cultural problems; (3) human freedom and responsibility must be recognized, and any tendency to place all deviant, devilish, or displeasing human beings into the blameless sick-role must be resisted; (4) while it is good for human beings to be healthy, medicine is not morality; except in very limited contexts (plagues and epidemics) "medical judgment" should not be allowed to become moral judgment; to be healthy is not to be righteous; (5) it is important to keep clear and distinct the different roles of different professions, with a clearly circumscribed role for medicine, limited to those domains of life where the contribution of medicine is appropriate. Medicine can save some lives; it cannot save the life of society.

These assumptions, and the criticisms of the WHO definition which spring from them, have some important implications for the use of the words "health," "illness," "sick," and the like. It will be counted an abuse of language if the word "sick" is applied to all individual and communal problems, if all unacceptable conduct is spoken of in the language of medical pathologies, if moral issues and moral judgments are translated into the language of "health," if the lines of authority, responsibility, and expertise are so blurred that the

health profession is allowed to pre-empt the rights and responsibilities of others by re-defining them in its own professional language.

Abuses of that kind have no possibility of being curbed in the absence of a definition of health which does not contain some intrinsic elements of limitation—that is, unless there is a definition which, when abused, is self-evidently *seen* as abused by those who know what health means. Unfortunately, it is in the nature of general definitions that they do not circumscribe their own meaning (or even explain it) and contain no built-in safeguards against misuse, e.g., our "peace with honor" in Southeast Asia—"peace," "honor"? Moreover, for a certain class of concepts—peace, honor, happiness, for example—it is difficult to keep them free in ordinary usage from a normative content. In our own usage, it would make no sense to talk of them in a way which implied they are not desirable or are merely neutral: by well-ingrained social custom (resting no doubt on some basic features of human nature) health, peace, and happiness are both desired and desirable—good. For those and other reasons, it is perfectly plausible to say the cultural task of defining terms, and settling on appropriate and inappropriate usages, is far more than a matter of getting our dictionary entries right. It is nothing less than a way of deciding what should be valued, how life should be understood, and what principles should guide individual and social conduct.

Health is not just a term to be defined. Intuitively, if we have lived at all, it is something we seek and value. We may not set the highest value on health—other goods may be valued as well—but it would strike me as incomprehensible should someone say that health was a matter of utter indifference to him; we would well doubt either his sanity or his maturity. The cultural problem, then, may be put this way. The acceptable range of uses of the term "health" should, at the minimum, capture the normative element in the concept as traditionally understood while, at the maximum, incorporate the insight (stemming from criticisms of the WHO definition) that the

term "health" is abused if it becomes synonymous with virtue, social tranquility, and ultimate happiness. Since there are no instruction manuals available on how one would go about reaching a goal of that sort, I will offer no advice on the subject. I have the horrible suspicion, as a matter of fact, that people either have a decent intuitive sense on such matters (reflected in the way they use language) or they do not; and if they do not, little can be done to instruct them. One is left with the pious hope that, somehow, over a long period of time, things will change.

IN DEFENSE OF WHO

Now that simply might be the end of the story, assuming some agreement can be reached that the WHO definition of "health" is plainly bad, full of snares, delusions, and false norms. But I am left uncomfortable with such a flat, simple conclusion. The nagging point about the definition is that, in badly put ways, it was probably on to something. It certainly recognized, however inchoately, that it is difficult to talk meaningfully of health solely in terms of "the absence of disease or infirmity." As a purely logical point, one must ask about what positive state of affairs disease and infirmity are an absence of—absent from what? One is left with the tautological proposition that health is the absence of non-health, a less than illuminating revelation. Could it not be said, though, that at least intuitively everyone knows what health is by means of the experiential contrast posed by states of illness and disease; that is, even if I cannot define health in any positive sense, I can surely know when I am sick (pain, high fever, etc.) and compare that condition with my previous states which contained no such conditions? Thus one could, in some recognizable sense, speak of illness as a deviation from a norm, even if it is not possible to specify that norm with any clarity.

But there are some problems with this ap-

proach, for all of its commonsense appeal. Sociologically, it is well known that what may be accounted sickness in one culture may not be so interpreted in another; one culture's (person's) deviation from the norm may not necessarily be another culture's (person's) deviation. In this as in other matters, commonsense intuition may be nothing but a reflection of different cultural and personal evaluations. In addition, there can be and usually are serious disputes about how great a deviation from the (unspecified) norm is necessary before the terms "sickness" and "illness" become appropriate. Am I to be put in the sick role because of my nagging case of itching athlete's foot, or must my toes start dropping off before I can so qualify? All general concepts have their borderline cases, and normally they need pose no real problems for the applicability of the concepts for the run of instances. But where "health" and "illness" are concerned, the number of borderline cases can be enormous, affected by age, attitudinal and cultural factors. Worse still, the fact that people can be afflicted by disease (even fatally afflicted) well before the manifestation of any overt symptoms is enough to discredit the adequacy of intuitions based on how one happens to feel at any given moment.

A number of these problems might be resolved by distinguishing between health as a norm and as an ideal. As a norm, it could be possible to speak in terms of deviation from some statistical standards, particularly if these standards were couched not only in terms of organic function but also in terms of behavioral functioning. Thus someone would be called "healthy" if his heart, lungs, kidneys (etc.) functioned at a certain level of efficiency and efficacy, if he was not suffering physical pain, and if his body was free of those pathological conditions which even if undetected or undetectable could impair organic function and eventually cause pain. There could still be dispute about what should count as a "pathological" condition, but at least it would be possible to draw up a large checklist of items sub-

ject to "scientific measurement"; then, having gone through that checklist in a physical exam, and passing all the tests, one could be pronounced "healthy." Neat, clean, simple.

All of this might be possible in a static culture, which ours is not. The problem is that any notion of a statistical norm will be superintended by some kind of ideal. Why, in the first place, should anyone care at all how his organs are functioning, much less how well they do so? There must be some reason for that, a reason which goes beyond theoretical interest in statistical distributions. Could it possibly be because certain departures from the norm carry with them unpleasant states, which few are likely to call "good": pain, discrimination, unhappiness? I would guess so. In the second place, why should society have any interest whatever in the way the organs of its citizens function? There must also be some reason for that, very possibly the insight that the organ functioning of individuals has some aggregate social implications. In our culture at least (and in every other culture I have ever heard of) it is simply impossible, finally, to draw any sharp distinction between conceptions of the human good and what are accounted significant and negatively evaluated deviations from statistical norms.

That is the whole point of saying, in defense of the WHO definition of health, that it discerned the intimate connection between the good of the body and the good of the self, not only the individual self but the social community of selves. No individual and no society would (save for speculative, scientific reasons only) have any interest whatever in the condition of human organs and bodies were it not for the obvious fact that those conditions can have an enormous impact on the whole of human life. People do, it has been noticed, die; and they die because something has gone wrong with their bodies. This can be annoying, especially if one would, at the moment of death, prefer to be busy doing other things. Consider two commonplace occurrences. The first I have alluded to already: dropping a heavy brick

on one's foot. So far as I know, there is no culture where the pain which that event occasions is considered a good in itself. Why is that? Because (I presume) the pain which results can not only make it difficult or impossible to walk for a time but also because the pain, if intense enough, makes it impossible to think about anything else (or think at all) or to relate to anything or anyone other than the pain. For a time, I am "not myself" and that simply because my body is making excessive demands on my attention that nothing is possible to me except to howl. I cannot, in sum, dissociate my "body" from my "self" in that situation; my self is my body and my body is my pain.

The other occurrence is no less commonplace. It is the assertion the old often make to the young, however great the psychological, economic, or other miseries of the latter: "at least you've got your health." They are saying in so many words that, if one is healthy, then there is some room for hope, some possibility of human recovery; and even more they are saying that, without good health, nothing is possible, however favorable the other conditions of life may be. Again, it is impossible to dissociate good of body and good of self. Put more formally, if health is not a sufficient condition for happiness, it is a necessary condition. At that very fundamental level, then, any sharp distinction between the good of bodies and the good of persons dissolves.

Are we not forced, therefore, to say that, if the complete absence of health (i.e., death) means the complete absence of self, then any diminishment of health must represent, correspondingly, a diminishment of self? That does not follow, for unless a disease or infirmity is severe, it may represent only a minor annoyance, diminishing our selfhood not a whit. And while it will not do to be overly sentimental about such things, it is probably the case that disease or infirmity can, in some cases, increase one's sense of selfhood (which is no reason to urge disease upon people for its possibly psychological benefits). The frequent reports of those who have recovered from a serious

illness that it made them appreciate life in a far more intense way than they previously had are not to be dismissed (though one wishes an easier way could be found).

MODEST CONCLUSIONS

Two conclusions may be drawn. The first is that some minimal level of health is necessary if there is to be any possibility of human happiness. Only in exceptional circumstances can the good of self be long maintained in the absence of the good of the body. The second conclusion, however, is that one can be healthy without being in a state of "complete physical, mental, and social well-being." That conclusion can be justified in two ways: (a) because some degree of disease and infirmity is perfectly compatible with mental and social well-being; and (b) because it is doubtful that there ever was, or ever could be, more than a transient state of "complete physical, mental, and social well-being," for individuals or societies; that's just not the way life is or could be. Its attractiveness as an ideal is vitiated by its practical impossibility of realization. Worse than that, it positively misleads, for health becomes a goal of such all-consuming importance that it simply begs to be thwarted in its realization. The de-mands which the word "complete" entail set the stage for the worst false consciousness of all: the demand that life deliver perfection. Practically speaking, this demand has led, in the field of health, to a constant escalation of expectation and requirement, never ending, never satisfied.

What, then, would be a good definition of "health"? I was afraid someone was going to ask me that question. I suggest we settle on the following: "Health is a state of physical well-being." That state need not be "complete," but it must be at least adequate, i.e., without significant impairment of function. It also need not encompass "mental" well-being; one can be healthy yet anxious, well yet depressed. And it surely ought not to encompass "social well-being," except insofar as that well-being will be impaired by the presence of large-scale, serious physical infirmities. Of course my definition is vague, but it would take some very fancy semantic footwork for it to be socially misused; that brat next door could not be called "sick" except when he is running a fever. This definition would not, though, preclude all social use of the language of "pathology" for other than physical disease. The image of a physically well body is a powerful one and, used carefully, it can be suggestive of the kind of wholeness and adequacy of function one might hope to see in other areas of life.

Ideology and Etiology

H. Tristram Engelhardt, Jr.

H. Tristram Engelhardt, Jr., Ph.D., M.D., is professor of medicine and community medicine and member of the Center for Ethics, Medicine and Public Issues at Baylor College of Medicine. He is also adjunct professor of philosophy at the Institute of Religion and editor of The Journal of Medicine and Philosophy. *Among his recent publications is* The Foundations of Bioethics *(Oxford University Press, 1985).*

Engelhardt maintains that "illness" is a value-laden concept, incorporating the disvalues of (1) dysfunction, (2) distress, and (3) deformity. Other authorities would add (4) deadliness. Engelhardt insists that illnesses involve only those instances of these disvalues which (a) are not a part of a function deemed proper to the organism, (b) manifest themselves at an intolerable level, (c) are psychological or physiological states of the diseased organism, and (d) are not under the immediate voluntary control of the diseased organism.

A clinician reading Professor Margolis's article is likely to be somewhat shocked by the statement "Medicine is ideology." . . . Even if it should be the case that cultural prejudices play a role in judgments that homosexuality or polydactylia are diseases, it would appear that bronchogenic carcinoma and typhoid fever are unambiguously diseases, apart from any reference to particular cultures or ideologies. There appears to be a hard core of disease states the recognition of which as such is not a function of cultural inclinations, much less ideology. Moreover, this hard core seems to be quite broad, including the vast majority of infectious and metabolic diseases—in fact, all those diseases with a clear somatic basis which compromise basic human functions. Not only clinicians but also some philosophers of medicine would see Margolis's argument as a dangerous misconstrual of the nature of disease, liable to open the concepts of health and disease to redefinition at the whim of passing cultural fancy.

To guard against such cultural relativism while at the same time acknowledging the contribution of cultural expectations to the appreciation of sickness, authors have, as Margolis indicates, attempted to distinguish a domain of objective reality from a subjective domain open to cultural variance, on the basis of a distinction between disease and illness. "Disease" in such accounts would refer to an objective bedrock, the somatic alterations of basic functions, which are appreciated by the sick and by those who observe them as illnesses. In different cultures, diseases would be experienced differently (e.g., it might be one thing to experience the plague as an infectious disease and another as a pestilence sent from the deity), but there would in all cases be the same underlying pathological findings.

As a preliminary warning, one must recognize the varied linguistic usages that cluster around our interests in disease and health. One speaks of deformities, dysfunctions, disabilities,

From *The Journal of Medicine and Philosophy* 1, no. 3 (1976). Reprinted by permission of the author and the publisher, D. Reidel Publishing Company.

sicknesses, defects, complaints, and ailments, in addition to speaking of diseases and illnesses. Any sorting of such usages must be in part arbitrary or at least stipulative—including the distinction between "disease" and "illness." Further, although I will distinguish between disease and illness, I recognize that the uses in ordinary language of "disease," "illness," and "sickness" have no precise borders.

Against the background of our wide-ranging interests and talk about disease and health, I will attempt both to expand and to criticize Margolis's very useful analysis of the concept of disease. On the one hand, I will in part defend his argument that "medicine in general must subserve, however conservatively, the determinant ideology and ulterior goals of given societies, [and that] the actual conception of diseases cannot but reflect the state of the technology, and the social expectations, the division of labor, and the environmental condition of those populations." . . . In doing so, I will side against theories of disease such as those advanced by Leon Kass (1975) and Christopher Boorse (1975), who hold that one can discern the proper functions of organs apart from reference to human goals and values. On the other hand, I will hold that there is in fact not only a great deal of coincidence in human interests and, therefore, in definitions of disease and health, as Margolis contends, but that some of that coincidence is indeed essential. Thus I will also in part agree with theorists of disease such as Kass in holding that there is a basic sense of disease. I will, however, maintain that that essential core is both abstract and meager—it offers only the most general sort of guidance.

I. ILLNESSES, DISEASE STATES, AND DISEASES

To sketch out these arguments, I will employ a stipulative distinction between diseases and illnesses. I will use the word "illness" to identify a set of observables identified by the ill person or

his or her associates as pathologically (this term to be defined below) distressful, displeasing, painful, or dysfunctional; a "disease state" will indicate some observables identified by the term "illness" and, in addition, other measurements or determinations which have come to be causally associated with or have otherwise shown themselves to be good predictors of a particular illness and which set of observables is held to be explainable in terms of pathophysiological or psychopathological generalizations. Finally, I will use the word "disease" to identify those pathophysiological or psychopathological generalizations used to correlate the elements of a disease state in order to allow (1) an explanation of its course and character, (2) prediction or prognosis concerning its outcome, and (3) therapy through manipulating variables important to the course of the illness. "Illness" and "disease state" will then identify clusters of phenomena, including straightforward observables as well as scientific determinations (observations requiring some scientific acumen, e.g., a white-blood-cell count). "Disease" will identify an explanatory structure, a theory to account for disease states, including illnesses. Illnesses and, more broadly, disease states are then the explananda, the phenomena to be explained. Diseases, on the other hand, are the explanantia, the explanations of those phenomena.

I wish to identify two different universes of discourse: (1) the universe of observations we make about the world, including the illnesses of our fellowmen and ourselves; and (2) the explanations we put forward to account for the observations we make about the world, including explanations of how we are at times ill. Statements such as "I feel sick," "He looks sick," "She has a rash," "My big toe hurts," "His pulse is rapid and irregular," "He looks possessed," "He says he is in league with the devil," "When dunked in water she floats," "His white-cell count is twelve thousand per cubic millimeter," "His chest film shows a solitary nodule overlying the right seventh rib near the spine," and "There is a cat sitting in the tree" involve observations about the world. Some of these observations concern states of af-

fairs which we recognize as illnesses (e.g., "I feel sick," "He looks sick"). Depending upon our theoretical framework, we are likely to explain most or all of the illnesses we encounter as disease states, as states of ill health due to some disease process (i.e., explainable in terms of the laws of pathophysiology or psychopathology). There are, of course competing modes of explanation—"He is possessed," "She is bewitched." . . .

We impart certain presuppositions to our considerations of illnesses or states of demonic possession by virtue of how we relate those observations to particular frameworks of explanation. Moreover, some states of affairs which are not experienced as part of an illness may still be identified as part of a disease state—the apparently healthy individual who, on routine chest examination or in the course of a routine examination of his blood, is found to have bronchogenic carcinoma of the lung or leukemia. Such an individual may not feel ill or look ill. But the observations that another party makes concerning such a person identify him or her as being in a disease state because of the ways in which certain observations are related by virtue of an explanatory model (e.g., bronchogenic carcinoma or leukemia). To some extent (with slight violence to the language and by means of a partial stipulation), "disease state" can be identified with the term "syndrome": "A set of symptoms which occur together; the sum of signs of any morbid state; a symptom complex" (*Dorland's Dictionary*, 24th ed., s.v. "syndrome").

We sort out sets of observations and experiences as objects of medical concern on the basis of whether (1) we find them unpleasant, disagreeable, or distressing in the fashion we usually associate with illnesses; (2) we easily recognize them as part of a pattern of an illness (e.g., a rash on the palms of a person's hands); or (3) we find usually unperturbing, unremarkable, or unnoticed observables (e.g., the solitary nodule found on routine chest film) to be related to an illness on the basis of an explanatory account, a disease model (this corresponds to Alvan Feinstein's concept of a lanthanic [hidden] disease [Feinstein 1967, p. 145]). In particular, we identify illnesses

by virtue of our experience of them as physically or psychologically disagreeable, distasteful, unpleasant, deforming—by virtue of some form of suffering or pathos due to the malfunctioning of our bodies or our minds. We identify disease states as constellations of observables related through a disease explanation of a state of being ill.

Dorland's Medical Dictionary defines disease as "a definite morbid process having a characteristic train of symptoms; it may affect the whole body or any of its parts, and its etiology, pathology, and prognosis may be known or unknown" (24th ed., s.v. "disease"). I will use this definition of disease with one emendation to make it contrast with the meaning of "syndrome" (which I have used as equivalent to "disease state," as a set of observables). "Disease," as I will use it, will identify an explanation of a set of observables, a syndrome or disease state, by reference to laws of pathophysiology or psychopathology. Thus I am distinguishing two elements usually both identified by the term "disease": disease states and disease explanations. Taken together, they constitute our usual meaning of "disease." I am separating them to indicate in each case the different roles of cultural forces and ideologies.

When one says that values play a role in our concepts of disease, it is worth warning that many different sorts of values are at stake. Not only are there ethical values to consider, but there are also values with regard to the simplicity and elegance of conceptual models, notions of the aesthetic in human form, notions of what would constitute the good life apart from any issues of moral obligations, etc. In comparing illnesses and diseases, one can see that cultural forces play quite a different role with regard to what will count as illnesses from their role in influencing what will count as disease explanations. On the one hand, there is the judgment that a particular state of affairs involves pain, dysfunction, deformity, disagreeable sensations, loss of self-control, etc., in such a fashion that an individual's fellows would agree that he or she is ill. That is, apart from any explanation of that state of affairs, it is found to be dysfunc-

tional, or to involve pain which is not a part of a function deemed proper to the human organism (compare the pain of teething with the pain of a migraine headache), or to be in some sense deforming. There may be, in addition, further criteria for classifying states of affairs as illnesses. The point I wish to advance is that there is not one single set of criteria for calling something an illness. Thus one would call a state of affairs which led to the loss of those functions held to be proper to humans an illness, even if it involved no pain (e.g., consider an illness involving loss of vigor). On the other hand, one would term a process an illness if it involved pain, even in the absence of the loss of function, if that pain were not part of a proper human function (e.g., childbirth). Finally, we often term certain states "disease states" (even if one would not say they are states of illness or correlated with states of illness), because they involve disfigurement or deformity which we treat as pathological (e.g., vitiligo), by virtue of the character of revulsion or sympathy that the sick individual elicits, and because we hold them to be in principle amenable to a pathophysiological or psychopathological explanation. In most states of illness, these criteria overlap, so that an illness usually involves some loss of function, the presence of pain, and often some disfigurement (e.g., "She looks sick"). But they need not do so. That is, we sort things out as illnesses and disease states according to judgments bearing on what functions are proper to humans (more will be said of these judgments below), or because of pain that does not play a role in such functions, or because of judgments concerning human disfigurement and deformity. These are judgments concerning the nature of the pathos or suffering that will single out some states of affairs to be explained as pathophysiological or psychopathological phenomena rather than as simply physiological or psychological phenomena.[1]

---

[1]My choice of the scope of terms differs from that of Margolis in placing judgments with regard to function and dysfunction within the domain of illness language, not disease language; but our terminology for the most part coincides.

Illnesses and disease states, then, identify a set of phenomena associated with loss of functions held to be proper (however that is to be determined) to humans, or a state of affairs including pain that does not contribute to a proper human function, or a state which is characterized by deformity or disfigurement. Moreover, being in such states of illness or deformity places one to varying extents within what has been termed the sick role: (1) the sick person is exempted from those social responsibilities impeded by his or her illness or deformity; (2) the state of affairs is not one depending immediately upon the will of the sick individual (e.g., it cannot be simply willed away, as in the case of malingering); (3) the ill or sick person is expected to cooperate in getting well or at least staying as well as possible; and (4) the ill or sick person is expected to seek out appropriate "medical" treatment (consider the role of the priest with regard to the diagnosis and quarantine of leprosy in Leviticus 13) (Siegler 1973, p. 41). The sick role describes certain patterns of behavior associated with states of illness as well as some states of deformity and expands the meaning of being ill by giving it a social dimension.[2]

Value judgments play a different role with regard to disease explanations, including the usual roles to be played by those values which bear on choosing between explanatory models in terms of their simplicity, elegance, etc. Further, cultural expectations and values are liable to skew our patterns of discovery so that we will be more likely to consider as causes of diseases practices or states of affairs of which we disapprove (Engelhardt 1974). In particular, ideologies are likely to tempt us to explain particular phenomena as diseases in order to fit our ideological needs (e.g., drapetomania, the disease of slaves who fled the South for the North [Cartwright 1851, pp. 707–9]). Moreover, disease explanations are often favored in order to classify a state of affairs as a disease state for social or ideological reasons, to apply the sick role to those in that state (e.g., alcoholism, drug abuse, dysfunctional states in times of war [Engelhardt 1976]). But, all things considered, judgments concerning the explanatory and predictive force of different theories are likely to be more objective than judgments concerning which functions are or are not proper to humans; for, if judgments regarding proper functions are evaluative, such evaluations are central to such judgments, not just peripheral and distorting. Such value judgments would be central to our understanding of normal versus abnormal functions. Still, even if ideologies may not have an ingredient influence in disease explanations, disease explanations count as disease explanations, rather than as physiological or psychological explanations, because they are used to account for states of affairs we judge to be disagreeable, dysteleological, etc. Even if the structure of disease explanations may be fairly value free, the fact that they are disease explanations will turn on whatever values cause us to identify certain states of affairs as illnesses, that is, as proper to be explained as diseases.

II. MARGOLIS VERSUS BOORSE AND KASS

Margolis contrasts disease as "what is apt to cause a disease state or that disease state itself" with illness, "a diseased state manifest to an agent through that agent's symptoms—sensations, introspective cognition, proprioceptive awareness,

---

[2]There is no reason that all states of feeling ill need be explained as diseases or states of being sick (i.e., placed within the sick role). That is, one may simply feel ill, and yet it would be appropriate to say that one does not have a disease—"There is nothing wrong with you except that you are exhausted and hungry—you may feel ill but you don't have a disease." "Illness," however, tends to identify constellations of phenomena for which disease explanations are expected. Also, given the distinctions between illnesses and disease states on the one hand and disease explanations on the other, one can compare states of being well (i.e., feeling well) with states of being healthy (in which the latter involve an explanatory move—e.g., "What you have is a functional heart murmur about which you need not be concerned").

and the like; or, more informally and not narrowly the concern of medicine, a temporary condition of ailing (or complaint) not caused by a disease state at all" (Margolis, p. 243). From this Margolis concludes, "Plants may be diseased but never ill" (ibid.). The core question becomes then for Margolis, "What is the role of values in our deciding that certain states of affairs are states of illness, or are pathological states?" In particular, are the judgments of whether or not particular states of affairs are functional or dysfunctional, judgments which are value free or value infected?

Some individuals such as Boorse have defined illnesses as that subclass of diseases which have normative features reflected in the institutions of medical practice (Boorse 1975, p. 56) and contend that in general one can decide what is or is not a disease in terms of what is or is not dysfunctional, as a value-free fact that can be read from nature. Boorse holds, for example, that "the state of an organism is theoretically healthy, i.e., free of disease, insofar as its mode of functioning conforms to the natural design of that kind of organism. . . . And the single unifying property of all recognized diseases of plants and animals appears to be this: that they interfere with one or more functions typically performed within members of the species" (pp. 57–58). Boorse takes such judgments to be based on descriptions, not on values. He contrasts this basic notion of disease with those diseases which are also illnesses by virtue of being (1) undesirable to their bearers, (2) a title to special treatment, and (3) a valid excuse for behavior usually subject to criticism (p. 61).

Margolis writes his paper against this distinction between illness and disease and the assertion that one can identify some human functions as being normal and others as abnormal without appeal to values. In fact, Margolis appears to be espousing a position that Boorse characterizes as weak normativism: that health judgments have a "descriptive as well as normative component" (Boorse 1975, p. 51). Margolis's point is that references to norms in medicine involve grading or ranking different physiological or psychological states with regard to standards that include a judgment of merit or worth.

In particular, Margolis is arguing that one cannot, *pace* Boorse, specify the functions of animals or their organs without reference to goals or purposes. Margolis brings this out very well in pointing to what must be the conclusion of any evolutionary understanding of biology: within any population, there will be members possessing various traits enabling more or less successful adaptation to the environment in which the species for the most part, at any particular time, is found. "What is normal," as Margolis indicates, "must be construed not as a fixed point but as a range of variations, tolerated in accord with some antecedent theory of the relationship between individual organisms and the populations of which they are members, a fortiori, between individual organisms and their environment. Species variation contributes to species survival in a changing world, and individual variability may accommodate different careers in different kinds of tolerance" (Margolis, p. 246).

There are no standard environments and, as a result, no standard successful adaptations for members of a species. Views such as Boorse's tend to gloss over the important role of intraspecies variability, while at the same time imposing the survival of species as an overriding good. Given an evolutionary biology and variability within a species (not to mention the variability of environments and therefore variability as to what will be functional or dysfunctional), there is no absolute standard with regard to which one can identify an organism as healthy—"i.e., free of disease, insofar as its mode of functioning conforms to the natural design of that kind of organism" (Boorse 1975, p. 57). There is simply no single natural design. Health is not "a natural standard or norm . . . a state of being that reveals itself in activity as a standard of bodily excellence or fitness, relative to each species and to some extent to individuals, recognizable if not definable, and to some extent attainable . . . 'the well-working of the organism

as a whole, . . . an activity of the living body in accordance with its specific excellence'" (Kass 1975, pp. 28–29). There is simply not a single excellence or unambiguous function to be played by all the individuals of the species. Rather, there are variations, including aging and even special debilities, which may play their role in the overall survival of a particular species. What will count as successful function in one environment may count as disease in another.

If one attempts to define illnesses and disease as Boorse hopes to, by reference to "a generally excellent species design" (Boorse 1975, p. 68), the best that one can do is to assert that disease is a state of affairs not leading to the survival of the species in the environment in which the organism is at present usually found. Health correspondingly would be the absence of any state of affairs that would significantly decrease the survival of the species in the environment in which the organism is at present usually found. The variability maintained within a population in order to secure a wide range of potential adaptability will then be viewed as simply the price paid for future adaptability. For example, as Margolis indicates, diseases such as sickle cell anemia are the price paid for the increased survival (health!) of the heterozygote.

But this violates the concern of much of our disease and health language for the plight of individual persons. If one takes into consideration the plight of individual persons, our judgment of them as being diseased or healthy turns at least in part on their and our evaluation of the extent to which they meet particular norms of function that we set for individuals, apart from whatever service they may be "designed" to contribute, via their "disease," to the survival of the species (e.g., "genetic resistance to disease or predation often results in lowered fitness in another component" [Wilson 1975, p. 115]). Although we might be willing to accept a species-survival definition of health and disease for animals (other than our pets or domestic animals with which we emotion-

ally or financially identify), we would not accept it for our fellow humans, in that it defines disease and health without regard to the suffering of particular individuals—one of the functions of illness and disease language. We are immediately concerned with disease and illness because of their bearing on our lives, not the long-range adaptability of the species. In short, one can escape from value judgments in the process of defining disease and health only if (1) one defines diseases as departures from the usual physiological and psychological functions of members of particular species (though the usual may indeed turn out to be a disease—consider Boorse's [1975] example of tooth decay—and be experienced as an illness; also the unusual, such as extraordinary athletic abilities, may not be a disease nor experienced as an illness) and eschews any implications that such departures are good or bad, although they can still be described as painful or pleasurable, etc.; or (2) one accepts species survival as the goal (i.e., so that all judgments about disease and health simply presuppose this and no further value judgments). Otherwise, what counts as disease counts so not because of the designs of nature but because of our goals and expectations.

Boorse's criticism of Margolis and like positions must, then, turn on his distinction between diseases and illnesses, in which he wishes to hold that one can be diseased, although not ill, not in the sense of having a lanthanic disease but in the sense of being in a dysfunctional state which one in the end judges to be worthwhile.[3] Boorse suggests as an example homosexuality or other sexual deviations, which although "abnormal," might contribute to the happiness of the homosexual

---

[3]My language concerning disease and illness departs from Boorse, because for him illness is defined with reference to distress and disease with regard to the "natural design" of an organism. I, instead, distinguish illnesses and diseases as experienceable states vs. explanations of such states and disease states as phenomena associated with illnesses by either experience or inference on the basis of a disease model.

and others (Boorse 1975, p. 63). Again, Boorse must presume that one can decide whether a particular state of affairs is *sub specie aeternitatis* functional or dysfunctional. But, as Edward O. Wilson indicates, homosexuality may very well have developed because of its contribution to species survival (Wilson, p. 555). The same can be said of altruistic behavior like the suicidal acts of social insects such as bees, which sting to defend the hive and, as a result, kill themselves (Wilson, p. 121). A bee not disposed to sacrifice itself in such a suicidal act would in Boorse's terms be diseased, although not ill (i.e., refusing suicide might very well maximize that bee's own happiness). But, again, the distinction between disease and illness presupposes that either a non-environmentally dependent notion of function and dysfunction can be advanced or one avoids further value judgments by an initial value judgment through which one embraces species survival as the goal.

Although disease and health judgments depend on our value judgments, there will tend to be a great deal of coincidence in such judgments. We are likely to find general accord with respect to certain "prudential values—avoidance of death, prolongation of life, restriction of pain, gratification of desires, insuring security of person and body . . ." (Margolis, p. 251). All humans are likely to find good reasons for holding angina or sarcoma to be disease states, because they cause pain and circumscription of our goals, whether or not they have a positive or negative bearing on the survival of our species. Indeed, it may be against our interests in the survival of the species to label as diseases states such as sickle cell disease. Our definition of disease in terms of the distress of individuals may lead to diminishing our species adaptability and, therefore, our potential for survival. This is not to say that we make a mistake in deciding that sickle cell disease is a disease and should be prevented by genetic counseling, even if that were to lower the frequency of sickle cell alleles and the general adaptability of

our species, but simply that we have chosen personal goals over long-range species survival. We can find grounds for concurring concerning states being disease states because of our interest in avoiding the pain and early death associated with sickle cell disease. But these are not judgments compelled by the recognition of natural norms. Disease does not reflect a natural standard or norm, because nature does nothing—nature does not care for excellence, nor is it concerned for the fate of individuals qua individuals. Health, insofar as it is to indicate anything more than the usual functions or abilities of the members of the species, must involve judgments as to what members of that species should be able to do—that is, must involve our esteeming a particular type of function.

There is, however, one lineament of a natural norm in the definition of human health and disease—the extent to which a state of affairs augments or circumscribes our activities as free, rational agents (i.e., and thus defines human health and diseases in terms not of characteristics peculiar to humans but, rather, those integral to being a person; not all persons need to be human—consider extraterrestrial rational animals). At one level, such activities are part of the condition for giving definitions of health and disease: to decide what is functional or dysfunctional requires embracing or disavowing particular goals. Our varied definitions of disease presuppose that we are free, rational agents, able to assess our environments. Rational, free agency is presupposed in the assessment of any functions. Moreover, persons are wholes, as self-conscious agents, in such a way as Kass wants all organisms to be. So, even if there are not characteristic, typical ways for cats, dogs, or horses to be wholes (and therefore, in the end, what will count as illness for them will depend on the judgment of persons), there is one typical way for persons to be wholes—to be rational, free agents.

Any condition which would cause a member of a species capable of self-consciousness to lose

its ability to act freely and rationally would count *eo ipso* as a disease. Conditions causing mental retardation, loss of intellectual function, or disintegration of thought would be diseases in violation of this norm, natural to (i.e., essential to being) a person. This should be the guiding thread in the coincidence of our prudential values: interest in preserving our states as free, rational agents. But one should be quick to realize that any concrete specification of this norm requires value judgments as to what is a reasonable expectation, with regard to freedom of action on our part as humans, and what is an instance of *hubris*. Arguments about whether aging is a disease turn on questions of this sort (e.g., deciding what limits those persons who are humans should accept). The expansive definition of health of the World Health Organization reflects the fact that persons can have unbounded expectations with regard to freedom from limitations on their abilities. In deciding what limits to set to such expectations, one chooses the actual norms to be used in the value judgments which specify the boundaries between health and disease.

III. CONCLUSIONS

We seek clear and enduring criteria for our judgments about the world. It is no different with re-spect to our interest in health and disease. Such criteria, however, are not forthcoming from an inspection of organisms in order to see what their natural design or natural excellences are. In short, Margolis is correct. Our ideologies and expectations concerning the world move us to select certain states as illnesses because of our judgment as to what is dysfunctional or a deformity and to select certain causal sequences, etiological patterns, as being of interest to us because they are bound to groups of phenomena we identify as illnesses. Although there is a stark reality, it has significance for us only through our own value judgments, in particular through our social values. Through these, we construct a world of communal action and reaction, of planning and reflection—including the arts and sciences of medicine. To find that value judgments are core to our language of health and disease is not to deny that there are real causes of disease or real empirical factors important in maintaining health or causing disease. It is, rather, to recognize the obvious—that to speak of being ill or being well turns on our value judgments about the world. To talk about health and disease (i.e., explanations of our states of being ill or well), presupposes evaluations of ourselves and our ambience.

References

Boorse, C. "On the Distinction between Disease and Illness." *Philosophy and Public Affairs* 5 (Fall 1975): 49–68.

Cartwright, S. A. "Report on the Diseases and Physical Peculiarities of the Negro Race." *New Orleans Medical and Surgical Journal* 7 (May 1851): 691–715.

Engelhardt, H. Tristram, Jr. "The Disease of Masturbation: Values and the Concept of Disease." *Bulletin of the History of Medicine* 48 (Summer 1974): 234–48.

Engelhardt, H. Tristram, Jr. "Fear of Flying: The Psychiatrist's Role in War." *Hastings Center Report* 6 (February 1976): 21.

Feinstein, Alvan R. *Clinical Judgment.* Baltimore: Williams & Wilkins, 1967.

Kass, Leon R. "Regarding the End of Medicine and the Pursuit of Health." *Public Interest,* no. 40 (Summer 1975): 11–42.

Margolis, Joseph. "The Concept of Disease." *The Journal of Medicine and Philosophy* 1, no. 3 (1976): 238–255.

Siegler, M., and Osmond, H. "The 'Sick Role' Revisited." *Hastings Center Studies* 1, no. 3 (1973): 41–58.

Wilson, Edward O. *Sociobiology.* Cambridge, Mass.: Harvard University Press, 1975.

The Concepts of Health and Disease and Their Ethical Implications

John Ladd

John Ladd is professor of philosophy at Brown University and chairman of the Program in Biomedical Ethics. He is a former chairman of the Committee on Philosophy and Medicine of the American Philosophical Association. He has published extensively in the field of philosophy and medicine, including the book Ethical Issues Relating to Life and Death *(Oxford University Press, 1979).*

Ladd explains why "health" and "disease" are not interdefinable opposites. He identifies three positive values in "health": (1) being predisposed not to have diseases, (2) subjectively feeling well or fit, and (3) having the capacity to carry on various desirable activities.

ARE HEALTH AND DISEASE CONCEPTUALLY INTERDEFINABLE?

In the literature on health and the health care system it is generally taken for granted that health and disease are interdefinable. Indeed, there is an almost universal assumption among medical and health care practitioners, among philosophers, and in the general public that health is equivalent to and may be defined as the absence of disease. It naturally follows from this assumption that if our aim is the promotion of health, then we should try to eradicate disease, an objective that might be said to be the aim of medicine.

Let us start with the question of interdefinability. Are the concepts of health and disease logical correlatives, that is, interdefinable in the same way as "dark" and "light," "odd" and "even," or "north" and "south"? If so, then "health" might simply mean the absence of disease or, conversely, "disease" might simply mean the absence of health. For example, to say that Smith is not healthy is to say that he has a disease and to say that he is healthy is to say that he does not have any disease.

Usually, when two concepts are found to be interdefinable, it is assumed that one of the pair is more basic than the other and that through the use of a definition the less basic concept can be eliminated and replaced by the more basic one. When used for purposes of elimination and replacement a definition is usually called a *reduction*. Definitions in general, and reductions in particular, may be introduced for clarification or to link the concept being defined to another set of concepts or to a theoretical framework.

As I have already indicated, "health" might be defined as the absence of disease or "disease" might be defined as the absence of health, depending on which of these terms is thought to be more basic for purposes of reduction. Those who choose to define "health" in terms of disease generally suppose that if "health" is defined in this way, it will be possible to clarify health issues by translating them into the more objective and scientific language of medicine.[1] On the other hand, those who choose to define "disease" in terms of health are generally interested in stressing the connections between problems of disease and wider social and value questions.

It should be easy to see the implications of adopting either of these reductionist definitions. Definitions of disease in terms of health tend to be expansive, general, and all-inclusive. The focus on health reflects the point of view of the layman

and of society: They are concerned with disease only as it interferes with health. Humanistic and value concerns also loom large among those who adopt health as the basic concept. Definitions of health in terms of disease, on the other hand, tend to be restrictive, specific, and medical. By focusing on disease, the reductionist definition of "health" generally reflects the point of view of the professional medical practitioner, the scientist, and the technician.

Although philosophically unsophisticated discussions of health and disease usually do not reflect an awareness of the logical character of reductionist definitions—like M. Jourdain in Moliere's *Bourgeois Gentilhomme,* who suddenly learned that he had been talking prose all his life—it is easy for a philosopher to see that those who treat health in terms of disease and those who treat disease in terms of health are in fact speaking a reductionist language. Medicalization, as I have already observed, is based, either consciously or unconsciously, on a reductionist definition of "health" to disease; antimedicalism (e.g., the views of holistic health faddists) generally depends, consciously or unconsciously, on a reductionist definition of disease to health.

However, before committing ourselves to either one of these reductionist conceptions of health and disease, we must first ask whether the concepts themselves are in fact interdefinable. I shall argue that on closer examination we will find that the two concepts are not interdefinable, at least in the sense required for a reduction of one to the other.

The Case for the Incommensurability of Health and Disease

There are a number of arguments against the proposition that "health" and "disease" are interdefinable. A brief survey of them will help us understand some of the issues of concern here.

We might begin by noting that, etymologically, "health" and "disease" are unrelated. "Health" comes from an old English word whose cognates are "hale," "whole," and "holy." (And, of course, "healing.") We say that something is wholesome, meaning that it is conducive to health.[2] "Disease," on the other hand, comes from old French and incorporates the Latin prefix "dis," as it occurs in "disorder," "disarray," and so forth. As Dubos and others have pointed out, Greek mythology represents the two concepts by quite different personages: Hygeia and Asclepius.[3] There are also significant grammatical differences between the two words. "Health," in its ordinary usage, has no plural and, except in a manner of speaking, there are not different kinds of "health(s)." (The same grammatical peculiarity applies to "illness.") In contrast, the noun "disease" can be pluralized and there are many different kinds of diseases.

There are other significant differences between the two concepts. Health represents a general condition and, to a certain extent, an abiding condition; disease, on the other hand, reflects a specific, episodic, and often acute condition. Furthermore, "health" is also used not only specifically for good health, but also generically for a person's general bodily condition, as in one's "state of health," which may be good or bad. In this regard, "health" resembles grammatically some other generic words, like "intelligence"; such words are used to stand for both the general category and the preferred condition under that category. One is healthy when one's health is good and unhealthy when one's health is bad, just as one is intelligent when one's intelligence is high and unintelligent when one's intelligence is low.

This last consideration brings out another important difference between the concepts of health and disease. Health is a condition that allows of degrees; that is, a person can be in better or worse health,[4] one person can be healthier than another, and a person can be healthier at one time than at another time. Health embodies, as it were, a continuum of comparative degrees. Disease, on the other hand, does not allow of degrees or comparatives; one either has a disease or does not. That is not to say, of course, that a disease may

not vary in severity, distress, development, or be in remission; but one cannot have more or less of a disease, It may be better to have one disease rather than another, but better or worse cannot be predicated of the disease itself.[5]

Being Healthy Versus Being Disease-Free

Perhaps the crucial difference between health and disease is categorical, for health is a dispositional property (capacity or power), whereas disease is an actual occurrent property. Thus, being healthy means more than simply not having a disease; at the very least, being healthy means, in addition, being *predisposed* not to have diseases. It is like an ability, the ability to cast off and recover from diseases. To say that a person is healthy implies a subjunctive or counterfactual conditional of the type that asserts that if the person in question is exposed to health hazards, invasive organisms, or traumas, that person will be less likely than others to contract a disease.[6]

The category difference between health and the absence of disease may be compared to the difference between "being safe" and "not having accidents." The safety of a building or of a driver consists of more than simply not having or having had any accidents; it entails that the thing in question has certain properties that render it unlikely to have accidents in the future and under a variety of different circumstances. To be safe means that if certain events were to occur, the thing in question would still be accident-free. Furthermore, the mere having of an accident does not necessarily prove that a building or driver was unsafe. The accident might be a freak. The not having of an accident is neither necessary nor sufficient to qualify a thing as safe.

Similarly, when we speak of a person as being healthy we mean that the person has the ability or the power (or strength) to resist diseases and to overcome them easily and quickly when assailed by them.[7] When one's body is under stress, it will quickly return to normal if one is healthy. To be healthy is not only to be free from actual disease, but also free from possible diseases or, to be more exact, comparatively free from them. Healthy people are much less likely than unhealthy people to succumb to diseases in general.[8] Health, in this sense, is connected with the notion of immune responses. I shall return to the notion of health as a capacity later.

Furthermore, health is something general that is predicated of a person as a whole. When we say that Mr. Jones is healthy, we are not saying that a particular part of him is healthy; it would be absurd to ask where he is healthy, although it is not at all absurd to ask where a person's disease is.[9] In general, then, "health" is used to refer to the overall condition of the organism rather than to the condition of a specific part of it. (Insofar as a particular organ is diseased, we might, of course, say that a person is ill or unhealthy on that account. But it usually does not follow that a person with a disease is therefore unhealthy; for example, if someone has athlete's foot or even a cold, it does not follow that the person is unhealthy.) Moreover, we do not ordinarily say that a person is unhealthy simply because of a particular disability or impairment; for example, a person may be completely healthy even though blind or an amputee. The important thing is the individual's overall capacity to resist diseases in general.

All these considerations suggest that when we speak of health we are dealing with a concept belonging to a different category from the category to which the concept of disease belongs. If this is so, then it follows that the concepts are not interdefinable and that it is not logically possible in any simple way to define "health" as the "absence of disease" or "disease" as the "absence of health." The concept of health, as I have argued, means something more than the mere absence of disease; perhaps, indeed, "disease" means something more than the absence of health.[10] So far, however, we have examined only the "logical" differences between the concepts of health and disease. We must now examine some of the positive ways in which health differs from disease.

POSITIVE THEORIES OF HEALTH

There are a number of positive theories of health; most of them are very general and, like the World Health Organization definition already cited, they are vague, and not particularly helpful for an understanding of the concept of health. Among such vague definitions are metaphysical conceptions of health that are presented in a specialized framework, such as definitions of health in terms of teleological wholeness or the harmonious ordering of bodily parts and functions.

In addition to freedom from disease and the capacity to resist disease, there are two other elements in the concept of health that should be mentioned. The first is the subjective aspect of health, namely, "feeling well" and "feeling fit." The second is the capacity to carry on various activities: If one is unhealthy, one cannot swim or play tennis, one cannot work, and one cannot fulfill many of one's responsibilities. Being in constant discomfort or having a chronic pain such as arthritis or migraine headaches combine these two aspects, for these "subjective" states generally incapacitate a person's daily activities. . . .

GENERAL REMARKS ON THE CONCEPT OF HEALTH

In order to elucidate the general features of the contextualistic concept of health that I have in mind, it may be worthwhile to contrast the positive concept of health with a positive concept of disease. Since it is not possible to undertake an analysis of the concept of disease here, I shall merely make a few remarks about it.

Disease, in the sense that concerns us here, is basically a physiological concept. Thus, in *Stedman's Dictionary* we find disease defined as "an interruption, cessation or disorder of body functions, systems or organs."[11] Likewise, *The Shorter Oxford English Dictionary* defines disease (definition 2) as "A condition of the body, or of some part or organ of the body, in which its functions are disturbed or deranged."[12] We may also take note of Henrik Wulff's definition of a "disease entity" as "the vehicle of clinical knowledge and experience."[13] I shall treat the abstract term "disease" as the name of the class of specific diseases of the sort used in disease classification and diagnosis. There are many ways of classifying diseases, but the general purpose of using a "disease entity" in a particular diagnosis is to connect signs and symptoms (manifestations) with a prognosis and with a determination of how the disease in question will be affected by different sorts of treatment.

If we put together all these points, the concept of disease will emerge as a very specific concept, ordinarily referring to something locatable in some place in the body, and characteristically clinically oriented; in other words, the concept of disease is primarily a technical medical concept. As such, it may be said to be a *closed* concept as compared with the concept of health, which, if we accept the analysis presented here, is an open concept. It is unnecessary to specify in any more detail the senses in which the concept of disease is closed. Suffice it to say that disease is basically a clinical concept and, as such, it is conceptually linked to medical treatment in one way or another.

The concept of health, on the other hand, is *open* in a number of different ways. To begin with, it is multidimensional and involves a cluster of features. As a value concept, it is "open-textured," that is, the connection between its value aspects and various defining components in the concept is open—"fuzzy" to use Wittgenstein's term.[14]

INFLUENCES ON HEALTH VERSUS CAUSES OF DISEASE

The conceptual difference between health and disease may be clarified by another distinction, namely, the distinction between influences on health and causes of disease. For influences on

health, let us begin by citing the four different "fields of health" that are used by Lalonde to categorize the health problems of Canadians.[15] The four fields are: (1) *Human biology:* genetic inheritance, the processes of maturation and aging, and other things connected with the body as a complicated biological organism; (2) *Environment:* things external to the body over which the individual has little or no control, such as foods, drugs, air, water, and noise; (3) *Life-style:* matters affecting an individual's health that are controlled by the individual's decisions and habits; and (4) *The Health Care Organization:* resources available through medical practice, hospitals, and so forth. The first three fields are more important for our purposes than the last one. It should be noted in passing that Lalonde's list places what I have called "medical care" in the fourth and final category.

I use the term "influences on health" to refer to etiological factors in these three fields that contribute to health. Thus, "good stock," genetically speaking, tends to endow a person with a natural ability to resist and to overcome disease. A good environment also contributes to a healthy society (people with the ability to resist and overcome disease). Finally, a healthy life-style and healthy habits tend to make healthy people.

The term "influence" is used because no single one of these factors is necessary or sufficient to make a person (or a society) healthy. Each of these factors interacts with other factors and with unforeseeable circumstances to determine the outcome in particular cases. The term "influence" is used to suggest that we are dealing here with fuzzy concepts and open-ended categories.

What I have called "influences on health" may be contrasted with the causes of disease. The most typical causal analysis of a disease focuses on a necessary condition of the disease (e.g., a lesion or an infectious agent), such that, if that condition is removed, the disease in question will be cured or prevented. Thus, tuberculosis (TB) is caused by the presence of tubercle bacillus in the sense that the presence of the bacillus is a neces-

sary condition of having TB; it follows that, in the absence of the bacillus in one's body, one cannot have TB. That is not to say, of course, that the presence of the bacillus in one's body is sufficient to cause the disease; there are a number of other conditions that favor or mitigate against having the disease. But for medical purposes, a necessary condition is all that is required.[16]

Not all clinical diagnoses and causal analyses are as simple conceptually as infectious diseases, but I submit that the objective of medical intervention, that is, treatment, whether it be preventive or curative, presupposes a fairly simple kind of causal analysis like the one just mentioned.[17] This side of clinical medicine explains both the stunning successes of modern medicine and its disappointing failures; for it fails when it is unable to identify the necessary condition of a disease, such as the cause of certain kinds of cancer.[18]

It is easy to see that the relationship between health and disease and the other factors affecting them, such as the contribution of the environment or of life-style, is not so easy to determine. We often know, as from epidemiological studies, that there is a relationship of some kind, but that is all we know for sure. For the most part, it is impossible to use this information in an individual diagnosis. Thus, it may not be amiss to call the relationships in question "open." Two examples will illustrate this point: the relevance of nutrition and of stress to health.

In *The Role of Medicine* Thomas McKeown argues persuasively that the extraordinary decline in mortality rates in the last two hundred years is due to improvements in nutrition rather than, as is commonly thought, to the development of hygienic measures related to such things as water supplies and sewage disposal.[19] He bases his conclusion on the fact that this decline in mortality rates antedates the introduction of hygienic measures and is correlated with an earlier improvement in food supply; there is further support for his conclusion in the fact that the decline in mortality rates reflects a decline in deaths from airborne infectious diseases, notably TB, rather than

from waterborne or foodborne infectious diseases, which began to decline later. McKeown summarizes as follows:

> The appraisal of influences on health in the past suggests that we owe the improvement, not to what happens when we are ill, but to the fact that we do not so often become ill; and we remain well, not because of specific measures such as vaccination and immunization, but because we enjoy a higher standard of nutrition and live in a healthier environment. In at least one important respect, reproduction, we also behave more responsibly.[20]

The second example relates to stress. In a study of Boston middle-class families, Meyer and Haggerty observed that 21 percent of the children were positive for streptococci (from throat cultures), but only half of them had the associated clinical disease. They found that there was a definite association of both the acquisition of the streptococcus and the resulting illness with "chronic family stress." There have been many other studies that trace susceptibility to clinical disease to chronic stress in the family and on the job.[21]

There seems to be no doubt that both malnutrition and stress have an adverse influence on health, that is, the capacity to resist disease—especially in connection with infectious disease. My point is a simple one: *healthy people are less likely than unhealthy ones to get sick.* And the causes of good and ill health are largely social rather than medical. A brief list of the kind of conditions that make people unhealthy will suffice to show that the influences on health are largely social. Malnutrition (such as junk foods), smoking, obesity, and alcoholism account for most of our health problems as well as, directly and indirectly, for most of the unnecessary deaths and hospitalizations in our society. It is clear that

medical intervention is not the solution to these problems; they are, rather, social problems.[22]

SOCIAL PROBLEMS VERSUS MEDICAL PROBLEMS

The penchant for converting social problems into medical problems and for seeking medical solutions to these problems is pervasive in our society; I have referred to it as medicalization. It is, in a sense, a kind of escapism. We want quick and easy solutions: Technology is the model. For the most part, this kind of solution is what the medical establishment promises or, perhaps more accurately, is expected to deliver. In our society, we handle problems of stress by resorting to alcohol and drugs, and then we treat the resulting alcoholism and drug addiction as medical problems requiring medical treatment in pursuit of medical cures. By the same token, we handle teenage pregnancy, which is surely one of our most urgent social problems, by turning it into a medical problem and by trying to solve it through medical means (abortions) rather than addressing its basic social causes. We even consider hyperkinesis in children to be a medical problem rather than an educational or social problem.

There are many explanations for the use of medical solutions for social (and moral) problems. The social problems we face are most difficult and controversial; to solve them requires sacrifices of everyone, and at the same time requires a critical reexamination of the moral basis of our social life and of our favorite social institutions: the complex bureaucratic organizations dominated by mindless managers and vested interests. Instead of taking seriously our responsibilities for our health, as a society and as individuals, they are bypassed in the universal rat race for money, power, and prestige.[23]

Notes

[1]See, for example, Christopher Boorse, "Health as a Theoretical Concept," *Philosophy of Science* 44 (December 1977): 542–573.

[2]For further details on the etymology of these terms, see *The Shorter Oxford English Dictionary* (Oxford: The Clarendon Press, 1964).

[3]See René Dubos, *The Mirage of Health* (New York: Harper & Row, 1959), ch. 5.

[4]Aristotle, "Health Admits of Degrees." *Nicomachean Ethics* 1173a24.

[5]This is a logical point about the concept of disease, not a scientific one.

[6]In this regard, being healthy is like being strong; a person can be strong even when not exhibiting his or her strength, and a strong person can be subdued by superior force.

[7]"Health is a margin of tolerance for the inconstancies of the environment." Georges Canguilhem, *On the Normal and the Pathological,* trans. Carolyn R. Fawcett (Dordrecht, Holland: Reidel, 1978), p. 115.

[8]Epidemiological information about the spread of infectious diseases attests to the fact that healthy people are much less susceptible to them than others (e.g., TB). See Thomas McKeown, *The Role of Medicine* (London: Nuffield Trust, 1976).

[9]The same considerations hold for the words "ill" and "sick." I have not specifically discussed the terms "illness" and "sickness," which represent notions that share some of the category properties of both health and disease. However, in contrast to the latter, "illness" and "sickness" generally have subjective connotations; for example, one says: "I feel ill" or "I feel sick." I shall discuss these particular notions later.

[10]"Disease is a positive, innovative experience in the living being and not just a fact of decrease or increase. The content of the pathological state cannot be deduced, save for a difference in format, from the content of health; disease is not a variation on the dimension of health; it is a new dimension of life." Canguilhem, *On the Normal,* p. 108.

[11]*Stedman's Medical Dictionary* (Baltimore: Williams and Wilkins, 1976), p. 401.

[12]*The Shorter Oxford English Dictionary* (Oxford: Clarendon Press, 1964), vol. 1, p. 524.

[13]Henrik R. Wulff, *Rational Diagnosis and Treatment* (Oxford: Blackwell Scientific Publications, 1976), p. 66.

[14]See J. M. Brennan, *The Open-Texture of Moral Concepts* (New York: Barnes and Noble, 1977).

[15]Marc Lalonde, *A New Perspective on the Health of Canadians* (Ottawa: Information Canada, 1974).

[16]Obviously, this statement needs further qualification. The analysis of cause presents many complications, both on the philosophical and on the medical level.

[17]I do not want to say, of course, that medical diagnoses are themselves simple and straightforward. I merely want to emphasize that the logical structure of the causal analyses they involve is simple, at least relatively so. See Wulff, *Rational Diagnosis,* pp. 51–56.

[18]There are, of course, also cures that have been discovered experimentally, as in the development of new therapeutic drugs.

[19]Thomas McKeown, *The Role of Medicine* (London: The Nuffield Provincial Hospital Trust, 1976), especially pp. 61–66.

[20]*Ibid.,* p. 94.

[21]For references, see George W. Brown, "Social Causes of Disease," in David Tuckett, ed., *An Introduction to Medical Sociology* (London: Tavistock Publications, 1976), especially pp. 296 ff.

[22]For further information on these matters, see Department of Health, Education, and Welfare (DHEW), *Healthy People: The Surgeon General's Report on Health Promotion and Disease Prevention,* DHEW (PHS) Publication No. 79-550713 (Washington, D.C.: U.S. Government Printing Office, 1979).

[23]After completing this essay, my attention was called to a very interesting article: Michael H. Kottow, "A Medical Definition of Disease," *Medical Hypotheses* 6 (1980): 209–213. Dr. Kottow approaches the subject of health and disease from a slightly different point of view from mine. He distinguishes what he calls "core disease," which is a verifiable self-conscious sensation of dysfunction, from what he calls "conditioned disease," which is based on a sociocultural consensus. The essay is an attempt to avoid the problem of relativism, which I also discuss here, by connecting subjectively felt dysfunction and distress with objectively verifiable medical conditions. Dr. Kottow's concern is with the undefined area between what I call health and what I call disease.

I want to take this opportunity to express my gratitude to my old friend and colleague Sidney Cobb, M.D., from whom I have learned all that I know about preventive medicine and public health. He was the first to instruct me in the profound differences between positive health and the mere absence of disease.

The Myth of Mental Illness

Thomas Szasz

Thomas Szasz—a Hungarian-born American psychiatrist, psychoanalyst, and writer—is professor of psychiatry at the State University of New York, Upstate Medical Center in Syracuse. His essay "The Myth of Mental Illness," originally published in 1960, has, according to Science Citation Index *and* Social Science Citation Index, *been cited in more than 190 publications since 1961.*

Szasz tries to distinguish true "brain disease" from "mythical" functional "mental illness." He argues that only physical diseases are real diseases and that the extension of the concept of "disease" to include functional mental disorders is illicit. So-called mental illnesses are really nothing more than behavioral deviancies from various psychosocial, ethical, or legal norms. Psychotherapists are educators, tutors who teach deviant persons how to behave themselves, but not true medical practitioners.

At the core of virtually all contemporary psychiatric theories and practices lies the concept of mental illness. A critical examination of this concept is therefore indispensable for understanding the ideas, institutions, and interventions of psychiatrists.

My aim in this essay is to ask if there is such a thing as mental illness, and to argue that there is not. Of course, mental illness is not a thing or physical object; hence it can exist only in the same sort of way as do other theoretical concepts. Yet, to those who believe in them, familiar theories are likely to appear, sooner or later, as "objective truths" or "facts." During certain historical periods, explanatory concepts such as deities, witches, and instincts appeared not only as theories but as *self-evident causes* of a vast number of events. Today mental illness is widely regarded in a similar fashion, that is, as the cause of innumerable diverse happenings.

As an antidote to the complacent use of the notion of mental illness—as a self-evident phenomenon, theory, or cause—let us ask: What is meant when it is asserted that someone is mentally ill? In this essay I shall describe the main uses of the concept of mental illness, and I shall argue that this notion has outlived whatever cognitive usefulness it might have had and that it now functions as a myth.

II

The notion of mental illness derives its main support from such phenomena as syphilis of the brain or delirious conditions—intoxications, for instance—in which persons may manifest certain

From *The American Psychologist* 15 (1960): 113–15. Copyright 1960 by the American Psychological Association. Reprinted by permission of the publisher and the author.

disorders of thinking and behavior. Correctly speaking, however, these are diseases of the brain, not of the mind. According to one school of thought, *all* so-called mental illness is of this type. The assumption is made that some neurological defect, perhaps a very subtle one, will ultimately be found to explain all the disorders of thinking and behavior. Many contemporary physicians, psychiatrists, and other scientists hold this view, which implies that people's troubles cannot be caused by conflicting personal needs, opinions, social aspirations, values, and so forth. These difficulties—which I think we may simply call *problems in living*—are thus attributed to physicochemical processes that in due time will be discovered (and no doubt corrected) by medical research.

Mental illnesses are thus regarded as basically similar to other diseases. The only difference, in this view, between mental and bodily disease is that the former, affecting the brain, manifests itself by means of mental symptoms; whereas the latter, affecting other organ systems—for example, the skin, liver, and so on—manifests itself by means of symptoms referable to those parts of the body.

In my opinion, this view is based on two fundamental errors. In the first place, a disease of the brain, analogous to a disease of the skin or bone, is a neurological defect, not a problem in living. For example, a *defect* in a person's visual field may be explained by correlating it with certain lesions in the nervous system. On the other hand, a person's *belief*—whether it be in Christianity, in Communism, or in the idea that his internal organs are rotting and that his body is already dead—cannot be explained by a defect or disease of the nervous system. Explanations of this sort of occurrence—assuming that one is interested in the belief itself and does not regard it

simply as a symptom or expression of something else that is more interesting—must be sought along different lines.

The second error is epistemological. It consists of interpreting communications about ourselves and the world around us as symptoms of neurological functioning. This is an error not in observation or reasoning, but rather in the organization and expression of knowledge. In the present case, the error lies in making a dualism between mental and physical symptoms, a dualism that is a habit of speech and not the result of known observations. Let us see if this is so.

In medical practice, when we speak of physical disturbances we mean either signs (for example, fever) or symptoms (for example, pain). We speak of mental symptoms, on the other hand, when we refer to a patient's communications about himself, others, and the world about him. The patient might assert that he is Napoleon or that he is being persecuted by the Communists. These would be considered mental symptoms only if the observer believed that the patient was *not* Napoleon or that he was *not* being persecuted by the Communists. This makes it apparent that the statement "X is a mental symptom" involves rendering a judgment that entails a covert comparison between the patient's ideas, concepts, or beliefs and those of the observer and the society in which they live. The notion of mental symptom is therefore inextricably tied to the social, and particularly the ethical, context in which it is made, just as the notion of bodily symptom is tied to an anatomical and genetic context.[1]

To sum up: For those who regard mental symptoms as signs of brain disease, the concept of mental illness is unnecessary and misleading. If they mean that people so labeled suffer from diseases of the brain, it would seem better, for the sake of clarity, to say that and not something else.

---

[1] See Szasz, T. S.: *Pain and Pleasure: A Study of Bodily Feelings* (New York: Basic Books, 1957), especially pp. 70–81; "The problem of psychiatric nosology." *Amer. J. Psychiatry,* 114:405–13 (Nov.), 1957.

III

The term "mental illness" is also widely used to describe something quite different from a disease of the brain. Many people today take it for granted that living is an arduous affair. Its hardship for modern man derives, moreover, not so much from a struggle for biological survival as from the stresses and strains inherent in the social intercourse of complex human personalities. In this context, the notion of mental illness is used to identify or describe some feature of an individual's so-called personality. Mental illness—as a deformity of the personality, so to speak—is then regarded as the cause of human disharmony. It is implicit in this view that social intercourse between people is regarded as something inherently harmonious, its disturbance being due solely to the presence of "mental illness" in many people. Clearly, this is faulty reasoning, for it makes the abstraction "mental illness" into a cause of, even though this abstraction was originally created to serve only as a shorthand expression for, certain types of human behavior. It now becomes necessary to ask: What kinds of behavior are regarded as indicative of mental illness, and by whom?

The concept of illness, whether bodily or mental, implies deviation from some clearly defined norm. In the case of physical illness, the norm is the structural and functional integrity of the human body. Thus, although the desirability of physical health, as such, is an ethical value, what health is can be stated in anatomical and physiological terms. What is the norm, deviation from which is regarded as mental illness? This question cannot be easily answered. But whatever this norm may be, we can be certain of only one thing: namely, that it must be stated in terms of psychosocial, ethical, and legal concepts. For example, notions such as "excessive repression" and "acting out an unconscious impulse" illustrate the use of psychological concepts for judging so-called mental health and illness. The idea that chronic hostility, vengefulness, or divorce are indicative of mental illness is an illustration of the

use of ethical norms (that is, the desirability of love, kindness, and a stable marriage relationship). Finally, the widespread psychiatric opinion that only a mentally ill person would commit homicide illustrates the use of a legal concept as a norm of mental health. In short, when one speaks of mental illness, the norm from which deviation is measured is a *psychosocial and ethical* standard. Yet, the remedy is sought in terms of *medical measures* that—it is hoped and assumed—are free from wide differences of ethical value. The definition of the disorder and the terms in which its remedy are sought are therefore at serious odds with one another. The practical significance of this covert conflict between the alleged nature of the defect and the actual remedy can hardly be exaggerated.

Having identified the norms used for measuring deviations in cases of mental illness, we shall now turn to the question, Who defines the norms and hence the deviation? Two basic answers may be offered: First, it may be the person himself—that is, the patient—who decides that he deviates from a norm; for example, an artist may believe that he suffers from a work inhibition; and he may implement this conclusion by seeking help *for himself* from a psychotherapist. Second, it may be someone other than the "patient" who decides that the latter is deviant—for example, relatives, physicians, legal authorities, society generally; a psychiatrist may then be hired by persons other than the "patient" to do something *to him* in order to correct the deviation.

These considerations underscore the importance of asking the question, Whose agent is the psychiatrist? and of giving a candid answer to it. The psychiatrist (or non-medical mental health worker) may be the agent of the patient, the relatives, the school, the military services, a business organization, a court of law, and so forth. In speaking of the psychiatrist as the agent of these persons or organizations, it is not implied that his moral values, or his ideas and aims concerning the proper nature of remedial action, must coincide exactly with those of his employer. For example, a patient in individual psychotherapy may believe that his salvation lies in a new marriage; his psychotherapist need not share this hypothesis. As the patient's agent, however, he must not resort to social or legal force to prevent the patient from putting his beliefs into action. If his *contract* is with the patient, the psychiatrist (psychotherapist) may disagree with him or stop his treatment, but he cannot engage others to obstruct the patient's aspirations.[2] Similarly, if a psychiatrist is retained by a court to determine the sanity of an offender, he need not fully share the legal authorities' values and intentions in regard to the criminal, nor the means deemed appropriate for dealing with him; such a psychiatrist cannot testify, however, that the accused is not insane, but that the legislators are—for passing the law that decrees the offender's actions illegal.[3] This sort of opinion could be voiced, of course—but not in a courtroom, and not by a psychiatrist who is there to assist the court in performing its daily work.

To recapitulate: In contemporary social usage, the finding of mental illness is made by establishing a deviance in behavior from certain psychosocial, ethical, or legal norms. The judgment may be made, as in medicine, by the patient, the physician (psychiatrist), or others. Remedial action, finally, tends to be sought in a therapeutic—or covertly medical—framework. This creates a situation in which it is claimed that psychosocial, ethical, and legal deviations can be corrected by medical action. Since medical interventions are designed to remedy only medical problems, it is logically absurd to expect that they will help solve problems whose very existence have been defined and established on nonmedical grounds. . . .

---

[2]See Szasz, T. S.: *The Ethics of Psychoanalysis: The Theory and Method of Autonomous Psychotherapy* (New York: Basic Books, 1965).

[3]See Szasz, T. S.: *Law, Liberty, and Psychiatry: An Inquiry into the Social Uses of Mental Health Practices* (New York: Macmillan, 1963).

Does Madness Exist?

Michael S. Moore

Michael S. Moore is the Robert Kingsley Professor of Law at the University of Southern California and has written extensively not only in the philosophy of law and jurisprudence but also in the philosophy of science as applied to psychiatry and psychoanalysis. His most recent book is The Semantics of Judging *(Clarendon Law Series, Oxford University Press, 1987).*

Moore argues that mental illness is not a myth but "a cruel and bitter reality that has been with the human race since antiquity." He responds to the objections to mental illness offered by Szasz and other antipsychiatrists. And he offers a conservative definition of mental illness as involving the dysfunctional disvalues of irrationality and irresponsibility.

Doubtlessly the most dramatic way to combat the challenge of modern psychiatry's extended view of madness is to adopt a position exactly the opposite of that which one would combat. With a rather nice symmetry one might answer those post-Freudian psychiatrists who urge that we are *all* crazy, by saying that *no one* is crazy. Such an answer not only heightens the disagreement as much as possible, but it also relieves one from the difficult task of drawing any line between the healthy and the ill, the bad and the sick. For in such a view, there is no such line to be drawn.

Such a response is to be found in the work of the "radical psychiatrists," the most prominent and most theoretically ambitious of whom is Thomas Szasz. For over two decades Szasz and his followers have been proclaiming mental illness to be a myth. As might be expected, repetition of this mantra has hardly furthered any serious analysis about the nature of concepts like mental illness or madness, nor about their moral and legal relevance. Indeed, quite the reverse. Answers to essentially ethical and political questions about psychiatric practices or legal doctrines with regard to the mentally ill have been given by trundling out the contemporary shibboleth that mental illness is a myth, rather than in terms of the ethical and political arguments necessary for such answers. There has developed a disturbing ten-

dency to regard complicated legal issues, notably the proper place of mental illness in various legal tests (of insanity in criminal trials, of incompetency to perform various legal acts or to stand trial, the tests for civil commitment), as solved by the new truth that mental illness is but a myth anyway. Equally disturbing is the accompanying belief that problems of social policy and social justice, such as what in fact society should do with dangerous persons who have not committed any criminal acts, can be satisfactorily resolved if legislatures will but recognize mental illness for the sham that it is.

If mental illness were a myth, acceptance of such a truth would provide straightforward answers to such legal, ethical, and political questions. One would not have to muddle along in the grubby details of comparing awful prisons with almost as awful hospitals for the criminally insane. One would not have to grapple with difficult policy issues such as the rationale for punishment generally and its relation to those found not guilty by reason of insanity. For it would be instantly clear that those we call mentally ill should be punished just like anyone else if they commit a criminal act; that they should have all the rights of an accused criminal if society should seek to deprive them of their liberty, no matter how the proceeding or the place of confinement might be named; that legal tests should abolish the phrase; and, easiest of all, that psychiatrists should mind their own business and leave the law to the lawyers.

The problem is that mental illness is not a myth. It is not some palpable falsehood propagated among the populace by power-mad psychiatrists, as Szasz in increasingly strident tones has proclaimed; it is a cruel and bitter reality that has been with the human race since antiquity. This is such an obvious truism that to have stated it thirty years ago would have been an embarrassment. Since the advent of radical psychiatry and its legal entourage, however, such truths need restatement. Even more, they need restatement in a form specifically addressed to the various senses in which mental illness has been thought to be a myth. Since in my reading of the radical psychiatrists there seem to be five distinguishable points they have in mind in thinking of mental illness as a myth, the discussion will proceed by considering them seriatim.

THE MYTHOLOGY OF RADICAL PSYCHIATRY

The Myth as a Question of Ontological Status: There Is No Such Thing as Mental Illness Because There Is No Referent of the Phrase

Mental illness is a myth because, stated popularly, "There is neither such a thing as 'insanity' nor such a thing as 'mental disease.' These terms do not identify entities having separate existence."[1]

Less popularly: "It is a term without ostensive referrent [sic] and lacking any, it cannot even be said to have outlived its usefulness, because there is no reason to think that it ever had any."[2] Szasz and his psychiatric and legal followers are suspicious of mental illness as an entity or thing; when looking into their ontology they see no such thing. Three points require discussion here.

1. If the argument is that entity thinking *as such* is to be regarded with suspicion, as Szasz at times suggests, then the critique is radical indeed. As Quine has noted, "We talk so inveterately of objects that to say we do so seems almost to say nothing at all; for how else is there to talk?"[3] "Thing theory" is implicit throughout our ordinary and scientific speech, and it is simply wrong to regard it as some primitive form of speech that is replaced with a more sophisticated mode of talk with the maturity of a science. Thus, Szasz's statement that "entity thinking has always preceded process-thinking"[4] is not an accurate characterization of the development of modern science. In fact, higher-order theoretical statements characteristic of advancing science *increase* the number of entities we admit into our ontology, not *de*crease it. Forces, fields, and electrons are obvious examples.

2. If the argument is that entity thinking is scientifically legitimate, but only about those entities referred to by terms capable of *ostensive* reference (i.e., things that can be pointed at such as Nixon or St. Elizabeth's Hospital), the radical psychiatrists have a radically impoverished ontology—a nominalist ontology that would not admit the thinghood of abstract entities such as the number 2, squareness, shape, zoological species, or, more to the point perhaps, psychological states. Such a restricted ontology is characteristic neither of science nor of common understanding.

In response to this charge of nominalism, made by me in an earlier article criticizing Szasz, David Levin has urged that "the caution and skepticism of the radical (existential) psychiatrists . . . has nothing to do with a Quinean predilection for desert landscapes."[5] Yet much of the popular appeal of the "There is no such thing as mental illness" slogan stems from just this kind of nominalist understanding of what there is. When Szasz or even his more sophisticated defenders tell us that mental illness does not refer to any "specific, punctuate, somehow localizable entities,"[6] they imply that the phrase must have such a reference on pain of being a myth. This *is* a kind of nominalism about what there is that holds mental illness to a standard that could not be met by the numerous abstract terms of any theoretical science.

Indeed, in such a restrictive, nominalist ontological system physical illnesses would not exist either. For the names of physical illnesses do not refer to concrete entities: "Diseases are not things in the same sense as rocks, or trees, or rivers. Diseases . . . are not material."[7] Although diseases might be *caused* by the presence in the body of some such entity (as a cold may be caused by a virus), and although they might be associated with *symptoms* that are concrete entities (e.g., the fluid present in the sinuses), a physical illness is not (identical with) either its causes or its symptoms. The only thing one can fix as the referent of the names of various physical illnesses are states the ill are in, abstract entities incapable of being pointed at in some ostensive definition.

3. In any case, most of the things people have wanted to say about mental illness can be said without making ontological commitments to any entity, concrete or abstract, referred to by the phrase, and thus any criticism of its use based on its lack of a referent, ostensive or otherwise, is misconceived. In his essay on "Sense and Reference" Frege made famous the distinction between the sense of a term and its reference.[8] The important corollary for our purpose is that words may be used significantly (i.e., they may make good sense) and yet *not refer.* As Quine has elaborated, "Being a name of something is a much more special feature than being meaningful." Even "a singular term need not name to be significant."[9]

This is particularly evident in our use of predicates. We can say "Some dogs are white" or "Some houses are red," without making ontological commitments to (without presupposing there are such things as) whiteness or redness. Similarly, we can say "Some persons are mentally ill" without making ontological commitments to any *thing* referred to by "illness." More colloquially, denial of the existence of anything called mental illness hardly entails a denial of the existence of *persons* who are mentally ill.

In addition to describing people as being mentally ill, we also often wish to explain their behavior as being due to their mental illness. Although such statements as "He did it because of his mental illness" appear to require an entity referred to by mental illness, in fact, such explanations mean nothing more than is conveyed by "He did it because he is mentally ill"—another use of the predicate "is mentally ill" that does not require a reference to be significant.

To the extent that common and psychiatric discourse about mental illness can be paraphrased so as to avoid the hypostasis of an entity named by the phrase, then any criticism that complains that there is no such thing as mental illness is beside the point; for orthodox psychiatry and common understanding can happily agree, but still use the phrase to make significant (albeit nonreferring) statements. We often make use of the names of states, attributes, properties, and traits as if they named some things in our ontology, for economy of speech is often gained by so doing.[10] To be sure, if someone (such as Szasz) makes an issue of the ontological commitments involved in our uses of redness or illness, "the burden is of course on us to paraphrase or retract."[11] But if we can paraphrase the usage into the noncommitting use of "ill," then the phraseology is a harmless but convenient mode of speaking against which the "ontological discovery" of radical psychiatry is irrelevant.

For my own part I think this detour into ontology is a red herring. The lack of any thing one can point to as the referent of mental illness does not do orthodox psychiatry the damage Szasz and others suppose; if mental illness is a myth in this sense, it is in the good company of many other words and phrases useful in science and everyday life that have either no reference or a reference only to abstract entities. That this herring is constantly being dragged across our path is doubtless due to the immense popular appeal of the denial-of-existence idiom in the hands of a skillful polemicist. It makes psychiatry and the study of mental illness *sound* about as useful as "unicornology" and the study of unicorns.

Szasz has accused me generally of putting words in his mouth[12] and has specifically denied

that he makes this ontological version of the myth argument:

> I do not assert, as some of my critics claim, that psychiatry is not a science because it deals with non-existent things, such as "mental illness."[13]

This is hard to square with Szasz's repeated assertion of just this argument, as in:

> Psychiatry is said to be a medical specialty concerned with the study and treatment of mental illness. Similarly, astrology was the study of the influence of planetary movements and positions on human behavior and destiny. These are typical instances of defining a science by specifying the subject matter of study. These definitions completely disregard method and are based instead on false substantives . . . But suppose, for a moment, that there is no such thing as mental illness and health. Suppose, further, that these words refer to nothing more substantial or real than the astrological conception of planetary influences on human conduct. What then?[14]

In any event, perhaps Szasz and his defenders agree that "it is no part of the radical (existential) position to argue 'occamistically' that . . . there is no such thing as mental illness."[15] If so, the ontological status of some *thing* called mental illness is not really at issue here. Other types of arguments must thus be marshaled if mental illness is in some sense to be made out to be a mere myth.

The Myth as an Empirical Discovery: No One Is in Fact Mentally Ill

Often mental illness is said to be a myth, not just in the sense that it does not exist, but also in the sense that no one is in fact mentally ill. The claim, in other words, denies not just that mental illness is a name of some thing, but that mentally ill is ever truly predictable of a person. The claim is that no one is really mentally ill.

This claim that mental illness is a myth is put forward as an empirical discovery: All of those people who have been thought to be mentally ill (i.e., irrational) are in fact just as rational as you and I. Szasz makes this claim when he argues that "insane behavior no less than sane, is goal-directed and motivated," and concludes from this that we should regard "the behavior of the madman as perfectly rational from the point of view of the actor."[16] Braginsky, Braginsky, and Ring purport to have made the same "discovery" regarding schizophrenics:

> The residents who remain in "mental hospitals" are behaving in a perfectly rational manner to achieve a personally satisfying way of life—often the most satisfying of which they are capable . . . in a certain sense an individual *chooses* his career as a mental patient; it is not thrust upon him as a consequence of his somehow becoming "mentally ill." But in just what sense does the individual "choose" his career? In our view, having and maintaining the status of a mental patient is the outcome of *purposive* behavior. Furthermore, given the life circumstances of most of the persons who become and remain residents of mental hospitals, their doing so evinces a realistic appraisal of their available alternatives; it is, in short, a *rational* choice.[17]

The central thrust of this form of the argument is not to claim that mental illness and mentally ill are meaningless—their meaning is assumed to be closely connected with that of irrational—but to dispute as a factual matter that there are persons who fit the agreed-upon definition of mental illness (irrationality). In fact, however, what has been done here is not to present a discovery of new facts, overlooked by orthodox psychiatrists because of their own self-interest or whatever, but rather to stretch our concepts of rationality and purposive behavior to accommodate within their criteria facts well known to orthodox, as well as to radical, psychiatrists. The facts—the behavior of patients—are often undisputed. What is disputed is the precise nature of the criterion to be applied in judging the behavior as rational or not.

As the foregoing quotations from Szasz and Braginsky et al. make clear, the notion of rationality they employ is linked to the actor's having reasons for his actions. The relationship between an agent's being thought to be rational and his

acting for reasons is best brought out by the Aristotelian idea of a practical syllogism. When we explain an action by giving the actor's reason, we refer to a belief/desire set the contents of which fit the form of a valid practical syllogism. To act so as to satisfy *any* valid practical syllogism is to be *minimally* rational as we earlier defined that phrase. There are also, as we explored, several stronger senses of rational that impose requirements of intelligibility on desires, evidential well-foundedness on beliefs, consistency between different beliefs or different desires, transitivity of desires, and the like. We can for now put these stronger senses of rational to the side, because by and large the empirical version of the myth argument is only intended to show that the behavior of the mentally ill is rational in the minimal sense defined earlier; that is, *some* set of beliefs and desires (no matter how bizarre) is furthered by the act in question.

The crunch for even this limited attempt at making out the behavior of the mentally ill as rational comes in making more precise the nature of the beliefs and desires of mental patients in terms of which their actions are to be so adjudged. More specifically, the fudge occurs with the use of *unconscious* beliefs and desires to fill in where we all know that mental patients did not consciously guide their actions to achieve such goals in light of such beliefs. Braginsky et al. are explicit about this: "It is obvious that rational goal-directed behavior does not guarantee that the individual appreciates what he is up to."[18] Szasz's glossing over of this distinction is particularly transparent:

> In describing this contrast between lying and erring, I have deliberately avoided the concept of consciousness. It seems to be that when the adjectives "consciously" and "unconsciously" are used as explanations, they complicate and obscure the problem. The traditional psychoanalytic idea that so-called conscious imitation of illness is "malingering" and hence "not illness," whereas its allegedly unconscious simulation is itself "illness" ("hysteria"), creates more problems than it solves. It would seem more useful to *distinguish between goal-directed and rule-following behavior on the one hand, and indifferent mistakes on the other . . .* In brief, *it is more accurate to regard hysteria as a lie than as a mistake.* People caught in a lie usually maintain that they are merely mistaken. The difference between mistakes and lies, when discovered, is chiefly pragmatic. From a purely cognitive point of view, both are simply falsehoods.[19]

The fudge occurs in the shift from our judgments of rationality being based largely on the agent's conscious beliefs and objectives, to a notion of rationality by virtue of which we adjudge an action as rational if we can *posit* any set of beliefs or objectives with which we can explain the action. The problem is that it is notoriously easy to posit beliefs and desires to explain any finite sequence of the behavior of anything. Simply pick a consequence of the behavior and label it the objective, pick a set of beliefs by virtue of which it would appear likely that such a consequence would indeed ensue as a result of the behavior, and one is then in a position to adjudge the behavior as rational, relative to that objective and that set of beliefs. The shedding of leaves by a tree, the falling of stones, the pumping of blood by the heart, and the most chaotic word salad of a schizophrenic are all "rational" activities, judged by such a standard. The "action" of a tree in shedding its leaves is rational if we suppose that it desires to survive the coming winter, and believes that the only way to do this is to lower its sap level, thereby killing off its leaves. Similarly for stones, hearts, and schizophrenics.

The reason why such explanations are so easy to manufacture lies in the inherent ambiguity of behavior as a criterion for such matters. If we know by some independent means that an agent believes that action *A* will lead to result *R*, and he does *A*, we have good grounds for attributing to him a desire for *R*; if we know that he desires *R* and that he does *A*, we have equally good grounds for supposing that he believes that *A* will lead to *R*. But if we know neither his beliefs nor his desires, but only that he does *A* and that *A* does result in *R*, we have no means of singling out *R* as

his motive, for any other consequence of *A* would do as well. "There is nothing in a pure behaviorist theory to prevent us from regarding each piece of behavior as a desire for whatever happens next."[20]

Neither Braginsky's "goal-directed" nor Szasz's "rule-following" criteria are adequate here. . . . Such Wittgensteinian patter fails to distinguish between behavior that happens to have a pattern to it and behavior that has the pattern it does because the actor whose behavior it is *followed* that pattern as he acted. All sequences of behavior have patterns to them; indeed, for any finite sequence there is an infinite number of such patterns (rules) that will fit that sequence. To make rule-following into a criterion with which one can *discover* belief/desire sets, and not merely *posit* their existence, Szasz and company must tell us when an actor truly is following some rule, that is, when he actually has a belief/desire set that includes the rule in its contents.[21] The most plausible candidate as a criterion for such rule-following lies in the actor's first-person knowledge, including his extended memory.[22] But such a criterion gets Szasz back to the consciousness (or the potential for consciousness) criterion that he is so eager to abandon.

Thus Szasz can "avoid the concept of consciousness" only at the price of significance. What he fails to realize is that any behavior can be seen as rational (or as in accordance with rules of a game, or as furthering certain goals—Szasz's substitute criteria for consciousness), if one allows oneself the freedom to *invent* the beliefs and desires in terms of which the behavior is to be so viewed.

On occasion the empirical version of the myth claim is put forward without any extensive reliance on some supposed unconscious beliefs or desires of the mentally ill. R. D. Laing, in particular, explicitly disavows use of unconscious beliefs or desires in reaching his well-known conclusion that "*without exception* the experience and behavior that gets labelled schizophrenic is *a special strategy that a person invents in order to live in an unlivable situation.*"[23] Nonetheless, such studies do not show schizophrenics to be as rational as

everyone else, for the conscious beliefs such patients admittedly do have are themselves irrational beliefs; and the actions that are predicated on irrational beliefs, and actors who hold them, are, in common understanding, irrational.

This is quite clear with regard to many of Laing's reported patients. The woman who avoids crowds may be rational in so doing, *given* her belief that "when she was in a crowd she felt the ground would open up under her feet." Similarly, many of the peculiar actions of one who believes that "she had an atom bomb inside her"[24] may be rational, *given* such a belief. But the beliefs themselves are irrational, with the result that neither the agent nor the action they explain can be said to be rational. To be sure, Laing's studies of the "social intelligibility" of schizophrenic symptoms do not end with the discovery of such obvious beliefs; Laing often attempts to go further and explain how such beliefs could be formed by an individual in the patient's situation. Yet the explanation Laing typically gives—the patient "adopts" the symptom as the only response to an intolerable situation—involves reference to further beliefs that are also irrational.

A convenient example is the case of "Joan," a catatonic who was not one of Laing's patients but whose case Laing believed to afford "striking confirmation" of his views regarding schizophrenia. Joan's own subsequent avowals were used by Laing in attributing to her catatonic withdrawal a rational basis. She recalled that when she was catatonic, she "tried to be dead and grey and motionless." She thought that her mother "would like that: She could carry me around like a doll." She also felt that she "had to die to keep from dying. I know that sounds crazy but one time a boy hurt my feelings very much and I wanted to jump in front of a subway. Instead I went a little catatonic so I wouldn't feel anything."[25]

Laing finds in such statements the two typical motives for catatonic withdrawal. First, "There is the primary guilt of having no right to life . . . and hence of being entitled at most only to a dead life." Since Joan's parents had wanted a boy, and since "she could not be anything other than what

her parents wanted her to be," she sought to be "nothing," that is a passive catatonic.[26] Second, Joan's withdrawal was viewed by Laing as a defensive mechanism to avoid the loss of identity (Joan's metaphorical dying) with which she was threatened by any normal relationship with others: "One no longer fears being crushed, engulfed, overwhelmed by realness and aliveness . . . since one is already dead [by the catatonic withdrawal]. Being dead, one cannot die, and one cannot kill. The anxieties attendant on the schizophrenic's phantastic omnipotence are undercut by living in a condition of phantastic impotence."[27]

None of this would convince us that Joan or others like her were rational in effecting catatonic withdrawal (even if we were convinced that at least in her case the withdrawal was an *action* she performed for reasons at all). Her action (or nonaction) is based on a series of beliefs that are irrational, including her belief in a disembodied self, a belief in her parents' complete determination of her worth, and a belief in her own omnipotence and impotence.

It is sometimes thought that the rationality of beliefs cannot be objectively judged and that calling them irrational is simply a pejorative way of saying they are false. The conclusion in the present context would be that people like Joan are thus as rational as the rest of us, only mistaken about certain facts. [Earlier] analysis . . . was intended to forestall just such an objection. Prima facie, the most obvious way to differentiate beliefs that are irrational from those that are merely false is by looking, first, at the consistency of the belief with other beliefs of the patient, and second, at the coherence of the belief with all else the patient believes. With regard to consistency, if Joan believes both that she is omnipotent and that she is impotent, one or both of those beliefs is irrational. With regard to coherence, one must look at the influence relevant evidence would have on the holder of the belief. It is characteristic of irrational (incoherent) beliefs that their holders maintain them despite the lack of coherence with other beliefs they have. There is a "fixed" or "frozen" nature about such beliefs, in the sense that they

are not corrigible by relevant evidence. Such irrational beliefs are held with a strength (relative to other beliefs the actor has) disproportionate to the evidence known to the actor. Thus, the man "who believes very strongly that his brother is trying to poison him (in spite of appearances) and who believes, rather weakly by comparison, that Boston is north of New York, is likely to be flying in the face of the evidence and the claims that the evidence renders likely."[28] He is likely, in other words, to be irrational in his belief of his imminent poisoning.

The empirical version of the myth argument fails because it is, empirically, false. By our shared concept of what it is to be rational, the mentally ill are not as rational as the rest of the population. Only by muddling the concept of rationality have the radical psychiatrists appeared to call into question this obvious truth. Only by attributing unconscious beliefs and desires to the mentally ill for which there is no evidence, or only by referring to beliefs that are themselves irrational, can motives be found for all of the peculiar behavior symptomatic of mental illness. Neither of these moves satisfies what we usually mean by rational as applied to actions and agents. One may, of course, like Humpty Dumpty, choose to make a word like rationality mean what one pleases, but surely it is unhelpful when one does so to then present the *manufactured* match between the facts and the new criteria for the word as a discovery of new facts, previously overlooked because of the willful blindness of self-interested or power-mad psychiatrists. To do so is to manufacture one's own myths.

The Myth as a Category Mistake: Mental Illness Is Not a Physical Cause

In *The Concept of Mind,* Gilbert Ryle made popular the notion of a category mistake. His motive for using this notion was to avoid having to take a position on the ontological status of mental entities. The dualism Ryle attributed to Descartes, that is, the two-worlds view that there are minds and there are bodies, each in its own species of

existence, is difficult to maintain for all of the reasons Ryle recounts throughout the book. Yet neither form of monism—that there are only minds (idealism) or only bodies (physicalism)—seems to do justice to the way we speak of ourselves as persons. We do use mental terms such as belief, desire, or pain in apparently significant discourse, and yet when we attempt to say something about the entities to which such terms ostensibly refer, we are baffled. How do we describe a belief? What properties can we give it? Does it have physical extension? And if it has no such properties, what sort of a thing is it anyway?

Ryle sought to avoid answering these questions about the ontological status of mental entities. One kind of question we do not have to answer is a question that is not meaningful. Ryle sought a way of saying that questions of the form "Are there bodies and minds?" are not meaningful, because a category mistake has been made in conjoining a term in one category (bodies) with a term in another (minds). It is like conjoining hopes, the tide, and the average age of death to say (in the same logical tone of voice) that all three are *rising*. Ryle explicitly avoids the snare of saying that there are two species of existence (which is just dualism); he is operating on the level of language only, claiming that we use the word "exists" in two different senses when we speak of bodies and when we speak of minds.[29] Hence, a difference of linguistic categories for Ryle does not imply a difference in ontological status (nor does it exclude it).

One of the particular category mistakes that Ryle is at pains to correct throughout his book is the assumption that "there are mechanical causes of corporeal movements and mental causes of corporeal movements."[30] For Ryle this statement contains a category mistake because it is a conjunction of words in different categories—specifically, the names of the candidates for mental causes, such as belief, desire, volition, and so on, are in a different category from the kinds of words we use to label mechanical causes. Ryle later brings out this difference: He likens mental

words, such as desire or motive, to dispositions, and contrasts them with mechanical causes. His well-known example is the broken window: One way of explaining the shattering of a window is to say a rock hit it; another is to say the glass was brittle, that is, it had a tendency to break when hit by a hard object. The first form of explanation refers to a mechanical cause, the second, to a dispositional property. Ryle construes motive words such as vanity or greed similarly to words such as brittle or soluble: Such words do not cite a cause, but rather a tendency of persons or objects to behave in certain sorts of ways.

By his examples, vocabulary, and explicit citation, Szasz makes it clear that he has read Ryle with approval. Thus he begins Part I of *Law, Liberty, and Psychiatry* by quoting Ryle on the nature of myths: "A myth is, of course, not a fairy story. It is the presentation of facts belonging in one category in the idioms belonging to another. To explode a myth is accordingly not to deny the facts but to re-allocate them."[31] Mental illness is a myth, then, in the same way that other mental terms are myths: It is as improper to place mental illness in the same category with real illnesses (read as physically caused illnesses) as it is to treat belief, desire, and perception as the names of mechanical or paramechanical causes.

Szasz, in fact, makes a number of distinct uses of the doctrine of categorical differences in his attack on mental illness as a myth.

1. His primary use is to focus on mental in mental illness and to argue that mental illness is a myth because mind is a myth (and hence a sick mind is a myth).

2. He also focuses on illness, to argue that the term necessarily refers to physiochemical events going on in the body; thus, to say that a *mind* could be ill is absurd because only physical bodies can be ill (in the ordinary meaning of the word).

3. Szasz also utilizes the doctrine of category difference to inveigh against any use of the names

of particular mental illnesses, such as schizophrenia or hysteria, the argument here being
that the symptomatologies of particular illnesses illicitly conjoin words referring to behavioral tendencies with words referring to
physiological happenings in the brain, as well
as with words whose only reference is to mental experience—a clear example, for Szasz, of
a category mistake.

4. Finally, because of the categorical differences
between mind words and brain words, Szasz
appears to believe that it is logically impossible
to establish correlations between the mental
and behavioral-based syndromes we call mental illnesses and the brain events that may
cause them; hence, the scientific aspirations of
psychiatry and the medical treatment of mental illness are forever condemned to frustration
because the aspirations themselves are logically absurd.

It should be noted that the first two of these
arguments deal with mental illness in general, the
second two with the names of particular illnesses.
For clarity, it helps to keep these two discussions
separated, even though they are obviously related.
Thus, I shall proceed to discuss Szasz's use of the
doctrine of categorical differences in the foregoing four-part order. The ultimate conclusion of
all of them, it is worth emphasizing, is that mental
illness, and mental illnesses, are myths.

1. What is a sick mind? Surely a large part of
the appeal of the myth argument stems from the
difficulty one has in answering this question. One
may indeed be tempted by the radical psychiatrists' reply that only bodies can be sick and that
minds are not the sorts of things that can be either
healthy or ill. Yet a good deal of the attraction of
this argument should be eliminated once it is realized that the difficulty we have in saying anything very intelligible about what a sick mind is
stems directly from the difficulty we have in saying anything very intelligible about what a mind
is. For unless we are prepared to jettison our talk
about minds in toto—as Szasz plainly is not—

merely pointing out that mental illness has no
clearer reference than does mind itself is hardly a
sufficient basis for labeling it a myth.

Fixing the reference of mind, and mental
words generally, is notoriously difficult. Yet, in
fact, we can leave the question of reference open
and still see that in no pejorative sense is a sick
mind a myth. One may adopt any nondualistic
position on the ontological status of mental entities (the popular ones presently being logical behaviorism, which asserts that minds are
hypothetical constructs from behavior; material-
ism, which asserts that minds are [identical with]
an as yet unknown set of physiological phenomena; functionalism, which contends that minds
are functional states of physical systems; or Ryle's
own position that one may avoid the question
because it cannot be meaningfully framed). Perhaps mind and other mental terms are not even
referential in character, as has also been suggested,[32] so that we need not worry about what
sorts of things minds are. Whichever of these positions one adopts, one is immune to the kind of
criticisms Ryle directed against Cartesian dualism
(and which Szasz and others would redirect
against the supposedly dualistic assumptions inherent in the term mental illness); for in none of
them does one presuppose the existence of some
funny, nonmaterial mind substance. In none of
them need one who speaks of mental illness be
committed to "paramechanical myths" about
ghostly mind things being "injured" in some nonspatial way. Mental illness can make perfectly
good sense—as much so as mind and mind words
generally—no matter which of these general positions one takes as to the reference of mental
terms, even if the position adopted is that none of
them refer to anything.

The question "What is a sick mind?" can be
left aside in favor of a more useful question: Does
mental illness have as significant a descriptive/
explanatory use as other mental expressions? If it
does not, then "myth" is as good a pejorative label
as any; but if the phrase does have a significant
use, then no amount of Rylean exorcism as to the

phrase's supposedly ghostly referents can suffice to eliminate it from our vocabulary.

Our mentalistic vocabulary may conveniently be divided between experiential terms and those terms we use to describe and explain human actions. Thus, when we predicate "is in pain," "is feeling tired," or "is seeing an orange afterimage" of another, we are ascribing mental experiences to him; when we predicate "is murdering," "is hiding," "is trying to hide," or "wants a yacht" of another, we describe his doings as actions and explain such actions by his (mental) intentions, desires, beliefs, motives, and so on. Since the concept of mind is intimately connected with our concept of what it is to be a person, predicating mental experiences, actions, and intentions of another being is necessary not only for saying that he has a mind, but also for thinking of that being as a person.

Mental illness is used to deny that part of our mentalistic vocabulary, namely, the action/intention predicates, is as regularly or as properly applicable to the mentally ill as it is to more normal persons. This is merely a corollary of saying that the mentally ill are not as rational as the rest of us, . . . For those senses of rationality are all linked to our usage of the action/intention predicates. If an individual is irrational in the sense that his desires or beliefs are unintelligible, inconsistent, intransitively ordered, or incoherent, then the action/intention mode of explanation begins to break down. If the individual is so far gone that for some of his actions we are unable to make out any set of beliefs or desires, no matter how bizarre or inconsistent, then this mode of explanation breaks down entirely. Although no one would deny that the mentally ill have mental experiences (indeed, they may have something of a surplus), the diminished rationality of the mentally ill does entail a diminished applicability of the other part of our mentalistic vocabulary, the action/intention predicates.

If enough of the observed behavior of the same individual resists application of the action/intention predicates, we will come to regard that individual as different from most of our fellows,

different because we lack *the* form of description/explanation of his behavior by virtue of which we understand ourselves and others in daily life. To identify another being as a person fully like us, we need to be able rather regularly to see his actions as promoting desires we find intelligible in light of beliefs we find rational.

A sick mind is thus properly predicated of an individual when we are unable to presuppose his rationality to the same extent we do for others. A sick mind is an incapacity to act rationally, which, in the senses of rational used here, means an incapacity to act so as to further rational desires in light of rational beliefs.

In so using mental illness one is thus committed to no funny, nonmaterial substances that are in some nonspatial way injured or impaired. Mind and other mind terms may not refer to such paramechanistic myths, but then mental illness does not either. To say that someone's mind is ill is only to say that his capacity for rational action is diminished, that the subject himself is irrational. Since mind in Ryle's own analysis is the name of all such capacities for intelligent performances, a lack of some of them may as properly invoke mind words as may the possession of them. To the extent that one is willing to say of another, "He has a mind" (or "He is a person"), then to the same extent one should be willing to say "His mind is defective" (or "He is not fully a person"), if he in fact lacks the relevant capacities.

2. Of course, if illness meant "deviation from an anatomical or physiological norm,"[33] as Szasz believes, then *mental* illness would still make no sense—for how can a mind (or capacities for intelligent performances) deviate from physical norms? Minds cannot be normal or abnormal vis-à-vis such physiological norms, and, Szasz argues, beliefs to the contrary are simply category mistakes.

Does illness properly predicated of a person mean that that person's bodily structure is abnormal in comparison with other people's bodily structures? The first thing one wants to say is that illness was a word in the English language long before anyone knew very much about anatomy or

physiology, and thus, the meaning of the word cannot be a matter of statistical deviation from a physiological or anatomical norm (else the word would have had no use prior to knowledge of such norms and such deviations). Still, one might think that our ancestors had a different concept of illness from ours. So, to move on to contemporary thought experiments, imagine an individual possessed of a cubical stomach. This stomach, although abnormal in its physical structure, functions perfectly efficiently in digesting foods; it thus allows its owner as long a life as people with normal stomachs. Suppose further it causes him no discomfort and that it allows him to eat and drink the variety and quantity of foods available in his society. Despite the presence of an abnormal physical condition, no one would call this individual ill.

What such a thought experiment shows is that physical abnormality is not a sufficient condition of being properly adjudged ill. Is such abnormality even a necessary condition of illness? Imagine an individual who possesses a small gland common to all people. As with everyone else, this gland causes him pain, increases his chance of early death, and prevents him from eating a large number of foods. Despite the fact that this physiological condition (until corrected by surgery) is universal, I should think we would want to label the state caused by it an illness, similar to the universal illnesses from which we all might suffer after a nuclear war.

What these examples show is that being ill, even physically ill, is not the same as being in a certain physical state, even if that state deviates widely from what is normal for human beings. It is not a state in which one's bodily structure deviates from a statistical norm, as Szasz argues throughout his work.[34] Deviance from a physiological norm is in itself neither a necessary nor a sufficient condition of being ill. It is at best an indication that someone *might* be ill because some physical abnormalities are correlated with some diseases (and thus with being ill).

Saying what illness does not mean is considerably easier than saying what it does mean. Yet being ill seems to involve something like being in a state of pain or discomfort, which, if not removed, may lead to premature death, and which for its duration incapacitates the patient from certain activities thought normal in our society.[35] One might assume that such states are physically caused, but such assumptions are irrelevant to what we mean by illness. There are presumably physical causes for our being in all kinds of states, such as being a thousand miles from Paris or for being alert or angry. *Whether* there are physical causes for such states, and if so, *whether* they are manifested by abnormal physical structures, is irrelevant to whether or not one is ill, alert, angry, or a thousand miles from Paris. Merely discovering a physical deviation in no way tells us that the person whose body it is that deviates is ill. Rather, properly to predicate illness of another we need to know such things as whether he is in pain, is incapacitated, or is dying.

The reason why this has been so well camouflaged by the radical psychiatrists is that the names of *particular* illnesses, such as polio or pneumococcal pneumonia, do involve knowledge of physical causes (as discussed at the end of this section). Whether one has polio or pneumococcal pneumonia is determined in part by knowledge of the bacterium or virus involved. Yet whether one is ill (in general) is *not* determined by such causes; whether one is ill in general is determined by wholly different criteria, seemingly connected with pain, incapacitation, or hastened death.

Once one appreciates this, then the propriety of terming hysterics (mentally) ill is also evident. The activities for which one is incapacitated by a paralyzed arm do not differ a whit whether the paralysis is anatomical or hysterical; in neither case can one play baseball, tend father effectively, etc. The admittedly sincere reports of pain of a hysteric throat irritation are as good evidence that the hysteric feels pain as are such reports of one whose C fibers are really jingling with physiological pain signals due to a physically caused throat irritation. More generally, those whose capacity to act rationally is diminished because their mem-

ory, perception, reasoning abilities, or other mental faculties are impaired are incapacitated from a normal life in our society no less than is, for example, the chronic alcoholic whose short-term memory banks have been physically damaged by his long-term drinking habits (Korsakoff's syndrome).

Being in a state properly called ill, then, does not depend on one's knowing, or even in the first instance on there being, any particular physiological condition. It depends on one's being in a state characterized roughly by pain, incapacitation, and the prospect of a hastened death. There is nothing mythical about such a state, whether it be due to a broken leg or a broken home.

3. If mental illness is not a myth, that is not yet to say that psychiatry is the scientific way to go about studying it. The claim of orthodox psychiatry to scientific expertise, in other words, rests on there being not only a nonmythical subject of study (mental illness), but also scientific knowledge about it. Some of such knowledge is to be found in the diagnostic categories of orthodox psychiatry.

It is for this reason that it has been important for radical psychiatrists to attack the validity of the traditional diagnostic categories. Szasz's version of the attack is based on Ryle's category distinctions. Szasz's primary use of the doctrine of category distinctions here is as a reminder that schizophrenia, hysteria, and so on do not presently refer to known events in physiology that cause behavior. But this is undisputed and provides no grounds for saying that schizophrenia or hysteria are mere myths, or for denying that such words have a significant use. Understanding that schizophrenia is on a par with some of our other mental-conduct terms, in that we do not know whether it refers to any set of mechanical or paramechanical causes, is not to eliminate it from our vocabulary but to "reallocate it," in the language of Ryle. The syndrome we call schizophrenia may currently explain behavior only in a way analogous to explanations in terms of character traits, that is, in terms of dispositions themselves implied from the pattern of a person's prior be-

havior, and not by reference to any set of physiological conditions. Yet as Ryle points out, we engage in the same construct building when we explain the breaking of glass, or the dissolution of salt, by citing the dispositional properties of brittleness or solubility. Significant explanatory (albeit nonmechanistic) truths can be framed with all such terms, and no one goes around writing books on "the myth of brittleness" or "the myth of greediness."

Szasz, however, presses the argument to claim that schizophrenia and other terms are logically absurd in ways that brittleness is not. There seem to be two versions of the category-mistake argument here. The first is the juxtaposition of behavioral symptoms and brain symptoms in the same classificatory scheme:

> Consider, for example, general paresis. This diagnosis refers to a physiochemical phenomenon. The term does not describe any particular behavioral event. How then can we hope to bring it into a meaningful relation with other psychiatric diagnoses that refer only to behavioral events, such as hysteria, reactive depression, or situational maladjustment? It is as if, in the periodic table of elements, we would find coal, steel, and petroleum interspersed among items such as helium, carbon, and sulfur. This is the main reason the taxonomic system known as psychiatric nosology does not work.[36]

Second, at other points in his works Szasz puts forward the rather curious argument that psychiatrists cannot classify human behavior because human beings react to the classificatory labels placed upon them whereas stones, plants, and stars do not. This error is not "due to any lack of humane feeling in psychiatrists, but rather to the fallacy of thinking in terms of natural science." Such an approach ignores "the differences between persons and things and the effects of language on each." In the orthodox account of mental disease, Szasz asks: "What is the status of human action? The answer is: none. There is no such thing as action to attain a goal—only behavior determined by causes. Herein lies the fundamen-

tal error of the medical and mechanomorphic approach to human behavior and to psychiatric classification."[37]

The first of these two additional attacks on the classificatory scheme is mistaken for the reasons discussed in the following subsection: There is no logical error in supposing that mental incapacities can be *correlated* with brain events to form composite symptomatologies, even if minds are not *identical* with brains. Discussion of this will be deferred briefly. The second of Szasz's arguments here obviously has nothing to do with "the logic of classification," as Szasz sometimes terms his Rylean weaponry. The blunt fact of the matter is that in everyday life and in social science we do classify human behavior all the time, and the fact that those labeled patriotic, ambitious, greedy, or schizophrenic may not care for the label has nothing whatsoever to do with their propriety for descriptive or explanatory purposes. One might have *ethical* qualms about *telling* the subjects they are being so classified, particularly if one has the authority of a psychiatrist in a mental hospital to make the label stick; such ethical qualms, or their associated therapeutic concerns, are totally beside the point if one is judging psychiatric classifications of behavior by their logical or scientific methodology. The error, if there be any, is more akin to that of a nuclear physicist working on the atomic bomb—a mistaken sense of personal value, perhaps, but hardly a mistake in the scientific methodology of nuclear physics.

There are questions that might be raised about the diagnostic categories of psychiatry, but they are not questions of category difference. The aggregation of symptoms into particular syndromes associated with hysteria, schizophrenia, and so forth forms inductive claims whose nature is clear—as clear as the nature of the claim that people who tend to look in the mirror often also tend to feel pleased when flattered and avoid conversations in which others are praised (Ryle's partial unpacking of the character trait of vanity). There is nothing logically suspect about the inductive process by which we initially classify familiar as well as bizarre behavior into character

traits and mental diseases. Nor is there anything illegitimate in our seeking to find the hidden natures of either mental diseases or character traits in physiology.

4. The heaviest burden placed by Szasz on the category-mistake version of the myth argument comes in another of his uses of it, viz., his attempt to construct a logical chasm out of Ryle's categorical distinctions. For Szasz not only asserts that schizophrenia and other syndromes are not currently to be explained by reference to mechanical causes, but also appears to insist that such explanations cannot be given, no matter what medical discoveries might be made. Unlike physical illnesses, those syndromes we call mental illnesses cannot be caused by some set of physiological events. In this logical claim he is surely in error.

What Szasz has in mind here is the Wittgensteinian distinction Richard Peters drew between actions and movements, and between reasons and causes.[38] Physical bodies, including the physical bodies of human beings, move through space in a manner describable by physical descriptions in terms of velocities, accelerations, spatial coordinates, directions, and so on. According to Peters, such movements of the human body constitute *actions,* however, only if they are seen in the light of human conventions: The physical movements of the arm and fingers in moving wooden figures on a checkered board only constitute the action of "castling the king" in light of an intelligent agent following the rules of chess. Further, in the Peters view, only physical movements can be explained by the mechanical causes provided by the laws of physics, whereas for actions only reasons (purposive rule following) are appropriate. One neither explains the orbiting of the planets by reference to their motives nor explains why another human being castled his king by reference to his synaptic firing patterns.

While I do not think Peters's or (Szasz's) rule-following analysis is adequate as a general account of human action, but rather represents an analysis of one species of *complex* actions, this does not matter for present purposes. For Szasz

and Peters were struggling to express a thesis that might better be defended on other grounds. The thesis is the irreducibility thesis we encountered in [an earlier chapter] according to which no Intentional discourse (such as is involved in reason-giving explanations) can be reduced to the non-Intentional discourse of natural science. In numerous ways philosophers have sought to capture the striking fact that the words we apply to describe and explain the doings of *persons* differ significantly from the words we use to describe and explain natural phenomena. The analytic philosophy of the last twenty-five years has variously polarized these differences as being between actions and movements, reasons and causes, teleology and mechanism, Intentional idioms and the non-Intentional, intensional talk and extensional, the language used to describe meaningful behavior and that used to describe the inanimate, those claims known with certainty and those claims supported only by fallible, inductive inferences as in science.

In [an earlier chapter] we left open whether any of these differences justified the permanent nontranslatability of mental words to brain words that the irreducibility thesis entails. We granted only "provisional independence" to reason-giving accounts from underlying physiological accounts. Such a tentative separation of mind from brain cannot, of course, justify the belief that it is some kind of logical mistake to think that mental illness may be physically caused, as Szasz believes. And even if one grants that there is permanently, and not merely provisionally, some fundamental cleavage in one's speech and its irreducibility, that does not mean (contra Peters and Szasz) that the various mental illnesses may not be explained by reference to physiological events or any other mechanical causes. What the irreducibility thesis entails is that one cannot *identify* mental entities such as beliefs, desires, or pains with physical events, either behavioristic or physiological.[39] It does not entail that one may not *correlate* the mental experience of pain with certain physiological events (e.g., the stimulation of *c* fibers in the

brain). Nor does it entail that schizophrenia may not be correlated with some sorts of events in the brain.

None of this is to say that such correlations between the aggregations of symptoms we label as mental illnesses of various kinds and physiology do exist, for one cannot tell in advance what slices of behavior can be correlated with what slices of physiology (this is true no matter how strictly one subscribes to determinism). It is a question for empirical discovery, and logical arguments either way are not decisive. The correlations between the disposition to bleed profusely and certain chemical states of the blood (hemophilia), violent character and XYY genetic makeup, and certain addictions (dispositions to act in certain ways) and the events in physiology that cause them are still suggestive examples. Whether similar correlations can be found between, for example, schizophrenia and certain happenings in physiology[40] is a matter for painstaking research, not for the armchair guesswork more frequently found in philosophy than in medicine.

It might be argued that it is illegitimate for psychiatrists to anticipate such discoveries before they are made, by using implicitly causal disease words such as schizophrenia or kleptomania. Szasz argues, for example, that it is "faulty reasoning to make the abstraction 'mental illness' into a cause of, even though this abstraction was originally created to serve only as a shorthand expression for, certain types of human behavior."[41]

Yet this is done all the time in "real" medicine as well as in psychiatry. Clusters of symptoms are thought to be due to an underlying condition, named and treated as illnesses, well before one could identify the cause of such symptoms. Polio was a disease before one discovered its virus origin. Moreover, we say that such diseases are (causally) responsible for the cluster of symptoms; even without knowledge of the cause, and knowing only the behavioral symptoms, we still do not mean that polio *is* just the symptoms by which we diagnose it. If we had meant this prior

to knowing the causes of polio, no doctor could "ever [have] said (and many did) 'I believe this may not be a case of polio,' knowing that all of the text-book symptoms were present."[42] By polio we meant *whatever* was responsible for the symptoms doctors observed, assuming that, in time, scientific research would tell us what the "whatever" might be.

Unless one can show some good reason to suppose that the symptoms of the various mental illnesses may not be caused by some kind of events in physiology (which I have attempted to show cannot be done, at least on logical grounds), then schizophrenia and other mental illnesses are no more myths because of the lack of any presently known physical causes than was polio a myth in the absence of similar knowledge.

The Myth as a Deduction from Epistemological Relativity: We Are Equally Mad from the Epistemological Point of View of Those We Label Mad

"The quality of myth," Quine tells us, "is relative . . . to the epistemological point of view."[43] Mental illness is a myth in the interpretation discussed here, because our current epistemology, in which we have concepts like mental illness, is itself a myth—judged, of course, from another epistemological point of view, not from our own. If one subscribes to the view that there is no judging between such basic points of view, then the argument of R. D. Laing and others—that from the point of view of those we label insane we are insane—has some sting. Attribute to those we label as mentally ill an epistemology; grant that, although it differs from ours, the relative merits cannot be judged. Our labeling of others as mentally ill thus is a myth because it presupposes what it cannot have, namely, a standard of judgment applicable to those judged as well as to those judging.

Aside from Laing and his glorifying of the "schizophrenic voyage," one may perhaps find this version of the myth argument in the existential analysts. Manfred Bleuler, for example, characterizes existential analysis as treating

> the patient's utterance quite seriously and with no more prejudice or bias than in ordinary conversation with ordinary people. . . . Existential analysis refuses absolutely to examine pathological expressions with a view to seeing whether they are bizarre, absurd, illogical or otherwise defective; rather it attempts to understand the particular world of experience to which these experiences point . . . The existential analyst refrains from evaluations of any kind.[44]

It is tempting to treat this as no more than "the most promising therapeutic approach," as does David Levin.[45] The success of such therapeutic approaches is, of course, irrelevant to our epistemological concerns here. One may well be called upon to be very empathetic to the patient's point of view in therapy; one may also need such empathy to understand "the patient's world" for any purpose, therapeutic or explanatory. To make out the version of the myth argument here considered requires more, namely, that one *cannot* (not *will not*) judge the patient's point of view as "bizarre, absurd, illogical or otherwise defective."

The problem with this version of the myth argument is the premise with which it begins, namely, epistemological relativity itself. More specifically, the error of the relativists is their assumption that to have the capacity to judge another's entire system of beliefs one must have the ability to stand outside one's own beliefs. The general idea is that objective knowledge about anything requires that one have the ability to stand outside all human convention, to gape at reality unmediated by the distortions of such conventions. Since no person can do this—it is doubtful that any god could, since the idea is probably self-contradictory—the relativist concludes that there can be no objective knowledge.

Yet our capacities to judge another point of view are not hostage to our attaining this unattainable convention-free stance. We admittedly view the world, scientifically and morally, by the

imperialist epistemology

conventions involved in our society's shared set of beliefs, and we make our judgments accordingly. Yet this is no embarrassing concession for realists to make, for they are only committed to saying that we can alter those conventions to better fit the real nature of the world as we progressively experience it. The "conventions" of our shared beliefs are in effect part of our collective *theory* about how the world really is.[46] When we come across a radically different system of beliefs, following different conventions, we do not have to grant it some kind of epistemological parity. It may be an equally plausible theory, in which case we should consider it a supplement or a replacement of our own; or, as in the case of the insane, it may be a wildly implausible theory. In either case, such beliefs form a *theory* that competes with our own; to the extent a rival system of beliefs fares badly in such competition, we are perfectly entitled to judge it to be false. If it is not only false, but obviously false in the face of overwhelming evidence, it is also a "crazy" system of beliefs to adhere to, and those who adhere to it nonetheless are themselves quite properly judged to be crazy.

The relativists are hard put to disagree with the foregoing. For what could their disagreement come to? They cannot get free of their conventions in order to tell us how things really stand with competing epistemologies. Their statement that all beliefs are relative to the system of beliefs of which they are a part is, *by their criterion,* a relative statement. By the realists' criterion, on the other hand, it is not a relative statement—it is a false one.

In addition to these general philosophical difficulties, any mythicist who urges this version of the myth argument has the challenging task of showing that the beliefs of the severely disordered are sufficiently *systematic* that one could call them an epistemological point of view. For the fragmented beliefs of such human beings can only with the broadest tolerance for contradiction be cohered into much of a system at all. There is something almost cruel in Laing's glorifying of the

experience of schizophrenia into a voyage of self-discovery by someone too virtuous to adhere to the epistemology of a sick society. Such awe for the insane, typical in primitive peoples, belongs with other primitive beliefs: as myths that should no longer command our respect.

The Myth as an Evaluation Masquerading as an Explanation: The Abuse of the Normative Force of Mental Illness by Orthodox Psychiatry

Sensitivity to the normative connotations of the concepts of mental health and mental illness is, I suspect, rather widespread. When one of the psychiatrists at the annual meeting of the American Psychiatric Association some years ago loudly diagnosed a radical feminist who was disrupting the meeting as a "stupid, paranoid bitch," something other than a value-neutral explanation of her behavior was intended. The same suspicions are engendered when psychiatrists label homosexuals as mentally ill, or when mental health is used as a synonym for whatever way of life is adjudged good. The radical psychiatrists build on these kinds of examples to argue that mental illness and the predicate mentally ill are used *only* to make evaluations of others' behavior, and that these terms are particularly effective as evaluations because they are paraded as value-neutral, scientific explanations: "While allegedly describing conduct, psychiatrists often prescribe it."[47]

> The masquerading of promotive assertions in the guise of indicative sentences is of great practical significance in psychiatry. Statements concerning "psychosis" or "insanity" . . . almost always revolve around unclarified equations of these two linguistic forms. For example, the statement "John Doe is psychotic" is ostensibly indicative and informative. Usually, however, it is promotive rather than informative.[48]

It may seem curious to claim that mental illness is used like "bad" or "wrong"—that is, used to pass moral evaluations—when by our shared

notions for moral responsibility we use the same phrase to *excuse* those who are mentally ill. To attribute a harmful action to the actor's mental illness, then, cannot always be exactly the same as attributing it, say, to his "murderous personality." What Szasz *sometimes* has in mind in saying that mental illness is used prescriptively or promotively is not that moral judgments are made with such use; rather, psychiatric usage of the phrase is often promotive in the quite different sense that the capability of being morally responsible is denied. Mental illness for Szasz is evaluative often only in the sense that the term denies the personhood of those to whom it is applied: "What better way is there . . . for degrading the culprit than to declare him incapable of knowing what he is doing . . . This is the general formula for the dehumanization and degradation of all those persons whose conduct psychiatrists now deem to be 'caused' by mental illness."[49]

Although needlessly stated in inflammatory terms (as if orthodox psychiatry were universally motivated by a desire to degrade the mentally ill), Szasz here suggests a very important feature of mental illness. Insanity and mental illness mean, and historically have meant, irrationality; to be insane, or to be mentally ill, is to fail to act rationally often enough to have the same assumption of rationality made about one as is made of most of humanity. And without that assumption being made, one cannot be fully regarded as a person, for our concept of what it is to be a person is centered on the notions of rationality introduced earlier. Unless we can perceive another being as acting for rational ends in light of rational beliefs, we cannot understand that being in the same fundamental way that we understand each other's actions in daily life. Such beings lack an essential attribute of being a person. It is thus easy to appreciate that the insane historically have been likened to young children, the intoxicated, and wild beasts. . . . For lacking rationality, the mentally ill are, as Bleuler said of his schizophrenic patients, stranger to us than the birds in our gardens.

Such statements are, of course, offensive to the ears of those concerned about the moral claims and legal rights of mental patients. Yet unless radical psychiatry and its lawyerly following can show, as I have argued earlier in this chapter it has not, that those we label mentally ill are just as rational as everyone else, part of our fundamental explanatory scheme and part of our fundamental notion of personhood are not applicable to the mentally ill. This includes notions about their lack of responsibility and inability to choose and act upon their own conception of their good. If one believes (contra Szasz et al.) that there are in fact people who do not act rationally often enough for us to make the same assumption of rationality for them as we do for most of our fellows, then this evaluative force customarily attached to the use of mental illness in certain contexts is accurate enough in its reflection of how the mentally ill fit into our fundamental conceptual scheme.

Szasz at other times seems to have in mind a second kind of normative force that we do on occasion attach to mentally ill, in everyday expressions such as "That was an insane thing to do" or "That's crazy!" In such usages we may express disapproval of the agent's ends and actions, recommending that one ought not to do such things or seek such ends. Thus Szasz is also right to note that *at times* mentally ill or insane can be used as terms of general disapproval: "The difference between saying 'He is wrong' and 'He is mentally ill' is not factual but psychological."[50] Other examples with which we began this section were the spot "diagnosis" of the radical feminist and the use of "mental health" by some psychoanalysts, such as Erich Fromm, as if it were synonymous with "good."

To the extent that orthodox psychiatry uses these words in this way it is plainly abusing them. The phrase mental illness and its companions are so abused not by being applied to those who are in fact irrational, but by being applied to persons who are rational but of whose values prevailing psychiatric opinion does not approve. An action that is fully rational in each of the senses examined earlier cannot, without ignoring the meaning

of the words, be said to be insane or due to mental illness, no matter how deviant the end pursued may be. The fact that homosexuals have a preference for a sexual relationship not shared by most of the populace is hardly grounds (as the APA, with strong dissent, implicitly recognized in its delegation of homosexuality as an illness) for labeling that preference irrational (ill). Homosexuals may (sometimes, often, or always) be mentally ill, if their capacity for rational action is significantly diminished below our expectations. Such irrationality is hardly shown, however, by their unpopular sexual desires alone if those ends are pursued on the basis of rational and consistent beliefs, without conflict with other strong desires, and by relatively efficient means.

The mistake of radical psychiatry is to assume that mental illness is a myth just because the phrase can be so abused. The mistake is to assume that because words such as murder, greediness, mental illness, or even good can be used to express attitudes, kindle emotions, pass evaluations and the like, they cannot also be used at the same time as a legitimate form of explanation or description, or at different times only as a description or explanation.[51] Those moral philosophers who purported to discover another logical gulf, this time between evaluative and descriptive statements, ignored the relatively obvious fact that words used in evaluations can also be used to express descriptions. Merely because a woman may call the doctor who, through surgical error, kills her husband a murderer, despite the fact that one of the main criteria for that term's proper use is not met (viz., *intentional* killing), is not sufficient to show that "murderer" cannot have legitimate descriptive and explanatory uses.

Szasz's essential confusion here is between the *force* of a term and its *meaning*. Szasz appears to believe that if a term has an evaluative force it cannot also have some descriptive meaning. Although Szasz here has some respectable company in the emotivist moral philosophy of the 1940s and 1950s, no one, I think, takes such analyses very seriously any more. Since J. L. Austin's im-

portant work on speech acts,[52] few would believe that because a word has a conventional force—say, of condemnation—it cannot also have descriptive content. Murderer is just such a term.

Mental illness is perhaps a dangerous term because its normative force makes possible the kind of abuse mentioned earlier; but the same also can be said of many of the terms with which we describe and explain human action, such as greedy, stupid, murder, or manipulative.

In the earlier paper from which this chapter was derived,[53] I thought that Szasz himself should not be accused of making this mistake. Having read my earlier paper, Szasz now wishes to make it clear that he claims this mistake as his own. For he has recently urged at length that one of the principal difficulties with the concept of mental illness "is that although 'mental illness' is a prescriptive term, it is usually used as if it were a descriptive one."[54] From this, he concludes that "psychiatry is not a science because its practitioners are basically hostile to the ethic of truthtelling," truth telling for Szasz being linked to *descriptive* use of language only.[55]

What Szasz has failed to recognize is that no amount of haranguing about the various normative forces conventionally attached to mental illness can convince anyone that the phrase has no descriptive meaning. Needed is some independent argument to establish that there is no descriptive meaning for such phrases. Such arguments as are to be found in the literature of radical psychiatry—the four previous versions of the myth argument—are insufficient for this purpose. With their collapse must also fall this fifth and final version of "the myth of mental illness."

CONCLUSION

The disease that radical psychiatry has contracted (and that appears to be contagious, at least for those lawyers who always knew that psychiatry was pseudoscience anyway) is the temptation to regard complex legal, social, ethical, and concep-

tual problems as solved once it administers a sufficient amount of antimyth antidote. In Szasz's case in particular, it is an attempt to use the therapeutic tools of modern philosophy to dissolve the problems, not to solve them.

If indeed one believes that there is no such thing as mental illness, that those we call mentally ill are fully as rational as anyone else, only with different aims, that the only reason anyone ever thought differently was because of unsophisticated category mistakes or because of his adherence to the epistemology of a sick society, and that the phrase accordingly is only a mask used to disguise moral judgments in pseudoscientific respectability—if, in other words, one accepts the myth thesis—one will necessarily also believe that one wields an Alexandrian sword with which to cut through the knotty legal problems surrounding the treatment of the mentally ill. For once one subscribes to these versions of the myth argument a number of radical consequences for the present treatment of the mentally ill are self-evident truths to all but the uninitiated: Either the

insanity defense should be abolished and those we call mentally ill punished like anyone else, or at the very least the phrase should play no part as a separate defense; the incompetency plea should either be abolished or highly limited; those we call mentally ill should be sued for breach of contract like anyone else, not excused from their contractual obligations because of supposed incapacity to contract; no one should be civilly committed for mental illness, for the mentally ill know their own good and have the capacity to act in accordance with such a conception no less than anyone else, the state thus having no parental role to play here; anyone inside or outside a mental hospital should have the full civil rights of any citizen because he is just like any citizen. In short, one who subscribes to the myth arguments will believe that "we abolish the problem of mental illness by abolishing the concept of mental illness."[56]

This is, of course, preposterous. The mentally ill and their attendant problems will not go away this easily. . . .

Notes

[1]*Blocker v. United States,* 229 F. 2d 853, 859 (D.C. Cir. 1961) (concurring opinion of Warren Burger, present chief justice of the United States Supreme Court, quoting Philip Roche).

[2]B. M. Braginsky, O. D. Braginsky, and K. Ring, *Methods of Madness: The Mental Hospital as Last Resort* (New York: Holt, Rinehart and Winston, 1969), p. 164 (the authors are here speaking of schizophrenia).

[3]W. V. Quine, "Speaking of Objects," in *Ontological Relativity and Other Essays* (New York: Columbia University Press, 1969), p. 1.

[4]T. Szasz, *The Myth of Mental Illness* (New York: Harper & Row, 1961), p. 1.

[5]David Michael Levin, "The Concept of Mental Illness: Working Through the Myths," *Inquiry,* vol. 19(1976): 362.

[6]Ibid.

[7]L. S. King, "What Is Disease?" *Philosophy of Science,* vol. 21(1954): 199. King recognizes that "the problem . . . is the ontological status of a relationship," not the existence of concrete objects such as witches. Thus Szasz's scornful, "Mental illness thus exists or is real in exactly the same sense in which witches existed or were real" (*Ideology and Insanity: Essays on the Psychiatric Dehumanization of Man* [Garden City, N.Y.:

Doubleday, 1970], p. 21) completely misses the only ontological point at issue.

[8]G. Frege, "Über Sinn und Bedeutung," *Zeitschrift für Philosophie und Philosophische Kritik,* vol. 100(1892): 25–50. Translated and reprinted in H. Feigl and W. Sellers (eds.), *Readings in Philosophical Analysis* (New York: Appleton-Century-Crofts, 1949), pp. 85–102, and in P. T. Geach and M. Black (eds.), *The Philosophical Writings of Gottlob Frege* (Oxford: Blackwell Publisher, 1960), pp. 56–78.

[9]W. V. Quine, "On What There Is," in *From a Logical Point of View* (Cambridge, Mass.: Harvard University Press, 1953), pp. 9 and 11.

[10]See the examples by Quine in his "Speaking of Objects," in *Ontological Relativity and Other Essays,* pp. 14–15; see also his *Philosophy of Logic* (Englewood Cliffs, N.J.: Prentice-Hall, 1970), pp. 68–9.

[11]Quine, "Existence and Quantification," in *Ontological Relativity and Other Essays,* p. 100. Quine goes on to observe that "many of our causal remarks in the "there are" form would want dusting up when our thoughts turn seriously ontological."

[12]Thomas Szasz, "The Concept of Mental Illness: Explanation or Justification?" in H. T. Engelhardt and S. F. Spicker (eds.),

Mental Health: Philosophical Perspectives (Dordrecht: Reidel, 1978). Reprinted in A. L. Caplan, H. T. Engelhardt, and J. J. McCartney (eds.), *Concepts of Health and Disease* (Reading, Mass.: Addison-Wesley, 1981), pp. 459–73, quotation on p. 468.

[13]Szasz, "The Concept of Mental Illness," in Caplan et al. (eds.), p. 473.

[14]Szasz, *The Myth of Mental Illness*, pp. 1–2.

[15]Levin, "The Concept of Mental Illness," p. 361.

[16]T. Szasz, *The Manufacture of Madness* (New York: Harper & Row, 1970), p. 123.

[17]Braginsky et al., *Methods of Madness*, p. 171 (emphasis in original).

[18]Ibid., p. 171.

[19]Szasz, *The Myth of Mental Illness*, pp. 142–3 (emphasis in original). Alan Stone has some fun exposing other aspects of the illogic of this passage in "Psychiatry Kills: A Critical Evaluation of Dr. Thomas Szasz," *Journal of Psychiatry and Law*, vol. 1(1973): 23–37.

[20]A. Kenny, *Action, Emotion, and Will* (London: Routledge & Kegan Paul, 1963), p. 108. A more complete discussion of the "epistemic interdependence of belief attributions and goal attributions" will be found in Carl Hempel's "Rational Action," *Proceedings and Addresses of the American Philosophical Association*, vol. 35(1962): 5–23. Reprinted in N. S. Care and C. Landesman (eds.), *Readings in the Theory of Action* (Bloomington: Indiana University Press, 1968), pp. 281–305.

[21]For a critique of Szasz along these lines, see A. R. Louch, *Explanation and Human Action* (Berkeley: University of California Press, 1969), chap. 9.

[22]Extended memory . . . should be included here so as to make room for unconscious beliefs and desires. Yet Szasz abandons even this limitation in attempting to find strategies or goals pursued by hysterics. In addition, it is worth pointing out that such unconscious motive explanations as do satisfy this limitation do not typically render the behavior they explain *fully* rational even if they render it *minimally* rational. See P. Alexander, "Rational Behaviour and Psychoanalytic Explanation," *Mind*, vol. 71(1962): 326–41; T. Mischel, "Concerning Rational Behaviour and Psychoanalytic Explanation," *Mind*, vol. 74(1965): 71–8; H. Mullane, "Psychoanalytic Explanation and Rationality," *Journal of Philosophy*, vol. 68(1971): 413–26.

[23]R. D. Laing, *The Politics of Experience* (New York: Ballantine Books, 1967), pp. 114–15 (emphasis in original). Laing here relies on Esterson and Laing, *Sanity, Madness and the Family*, 2d ed. (Harmondsworth: Penguin Books, 1970), where on p. 26 they disavow any use of unconscious motives or beliefs to make out this thesis.

[24]Esterson and Laing, *Sanity, Madness and the Family*, pp. 75, 131.

[25]R. D. Laing, *The Divided Self* (London: Tavistock, 1960), chap. 10, pp. 191–2. The case was originally reported in M. Hayward and J. E. Taylor, "A Schizophrenic Patient Describes the Action of Intensive Psychotherapy," *Psychiatric Quarterly*, vol. 30(1956): 211–48.

[26]*The Divided Self*, p. 191.

[27]Ibid., p. 191.

[28]R. J. Ackermann, *Belief and Knowledge* (Garden City, N.Y.: Doubleday [Anchor Books], 1972), p. 33. See generally chap. 3, "Rational Belief."

[29]G. Ryle, *The Concept of Mind* (London: Hutchinson, 1949), chap. 1.

[30]Ibid., p. 22.

[31]T. Szasz, *Law, Liberty, and Psychiatry* (New York: Macmillan, 1968), p. 11, quoting Ryle, *The Concept of Mind*, p. 8. See also *The Myth of Mental Illness*, pp. 88, 93–4, where Szasz gains further theoretical support from the notion of a category mistake. In a generally perceptive review of Szasz's work, Ronald de Sousa concludes that "the basis of the contention that mental illness is a myth . . . is the philosophical doctrine of category difference between intentional behavior and natural events in the causal order of the physical sciences." de Sousa, "The Politics of Mental Illness," *Inquiry*, vol. 15(1972): 187–201. Other mythicists also base their arguments on Ryle's work. See particularly T. R. Sarbin, "The Scientific Status of the Mental Illness Metaphor," in S. C. Plog and R. B. Edgerton (eds.), *Changing Perspective in Mental Illness* (New York: Holt, Rinehart and Winston, 1969), pp. 9–31.

[32]For an explicit argument that mind words are not referential see D. Dennett, *Content and Consciousness* (London: Routledge & Kegan Paul, 1969), chap 1.

[33]Szasz, *The Manufacture of Madness*, p. 167.

[34]See *The Manufacture of Madness*. See also Szasz's *Ideology and Insanity*, p. 19: "The term 'bodily illness' refers to physiological occurrences"; and p. 23: "We call people physically ill when their body functioning violates certain anatomical and physiological norms; similarly we call people mentally ill when their conduct violates certain ethical, political, and social norms." Despite the considerable literature in the philosophy of medicine since these passages were written, Szasz clings to this by now obviously inadequate account of illness as deviation. See his "The Concept of Mental Illness," in Caplan et al. (eds.), p. 471.

[35]The ordinary language conceptions of illness and health are explored in G. H. Von Wright, *The Varieties of Goodness* (London: Routledge & Kegan Paul, 1963), pp. 50–61; and in L. S. King, "What is Disease?" pp. 193–203. The relation of illness to incapacitation is also suggested in Joel Feinberg, *Doing and Deserving* (Princeton, N.J.: Princeton University Press, 1970), pp. 253–60.

[36]Szasz, *Law, Liberty, and Psychiatry*, p. 25.

[37]All quotes are from *Ideology and Insanity*, pp. 191–6.

[38]Peters, *The Concept of Motivation* (London: Routledge & Kegan Paul, 1958). See Szasz, *The Myth of Mental Illness*, esp. p. 88, and chap. 10, for his explicit reliance on Peters.

[39]One of the reasons for this is the idea Szasz quotes from Peters: Movements "cannot be characterized as intelligent or unintelligent, correct or incorrect, efficient or inefficient." One may only describe *actions* with such adjectives (Peters, *The Concept of Motivation*, p. 15, quoted in *The Myth of Mental*

Illness, p. 171). Since one of the principal requirements for using the identity sign is that the expressions referring to the same thing be substitutable for one another without change of truth value, one cannot identify action with movements. But this argument goes only against *identifying* mental entities with physical ones; it says nothing about correlating the two and calling one the cause of the other, for there is no substitutability requirement for the names of effects and their causes.

[40] An informative summary of the recent evidence that some forms of schizophrenia may have a genetic etiology is L. L. Heston's "The Genetics of Schizophrenic and Schizoid Disease," *Science,* vol. 167(1970): 249–56.

[41] Szasz, *Ideology and Insanity,* p. 15.

[42] H. Putnam, "Brains and Behavior," in R. J. Butler (ed.), *Analytical Philosophy,* 2d ser. (Oxford: Blackwell Publisher, 1965), p. 6. Putnam uses the concept of disease as an example of a much more general point, namely, that the meaning of "natural kind" words, such as water, gold, or red (or polio) is not fixed by operational tests based on contemporary knowledge, but presupposes a hidden nature that we know with increasing precision with the advancement of science. See his "The Meaning of 'Meaning,'" in H. Feigl and M. Scriven (eds.), *Language, Mind and Knowledge,* Minnesota Studies in the Philosophy of Science, vol. 7 (Minneapolis: University of Minnesota Press, 1975), pp. 131–93.

[43] Quine, "On What There Is," in *Logical Point of View,* p. 19.

[44] Manfred Bleuler, "Researches and Changes in Concepts in the Study of Schizophrenia," *Bulletin of the Isaac Ray Medical Library,* vol. 3(1955): 42–5.

[45] Levin, "Concept of Mental Illness," p. 363.

[46] For further argument and citations, see Moore, "Moral Reality," *Wisconsin Law Review* (1982): 1061–1156.

[47] Szasz, *Law, Liberty, and Psychiatry,* p. 18.

[48] Szasz, *The Myth of Mental Illness,* p. 131.

[49] Szasz, *The Manufacture of Madness,* pp. 122–3. See also *Ideology and Insanity,* p. 204: "Most psychiatric diagnoses may be used, and are used, as invectives: their aim is to degrade—and, hence, socially constrain—the person diagnosed." Laing makes the same objection in numerous places in his work. E.g., *The Politics of Experience,* pp. 121–2.

[50] Szasz, *Law, Liberty, and Psychiatry,* p. 205. See also p. 19: "The new label 'mental illness' (and its variants) became only a substitute for the abandoned words of denigration."

[51] For a review of the passing of the emotivist and prescriptivist traditions in metaethics, see Moore, "Moral Reality."

[52] J. L. Austin, *How To Do Things With Words* (New York: Oxford University Press, 1961).

[53] M. S. Moore, "Some Myths About 'Mental Illness,'" *Inquiry,* vol. 18(1975): 259.

[54] Szasz, "The Concept of Mental Illness," in Caplan et al. (eds.), p. 459.

[55] Ibid., p. 473.

[56] F. A. Gerbode, Book Review, *Santa Clara Lawyer,* vol. 13(1973): 622. For statements of each of these positions as a result of some version of the myth argument, see T. Szasz, "Psychiatry, Ethics and the Criminal Law," *Columbia Law Review,* vol. 58(1958): 183–98; J. H. Hardisty, "Mental Illness: A Legal Fiction," *Washington Law Review,* vol. 48(1973): 735–62; Szasz, *Psychiatric Justice* (New York: Macmillan, 1965); G. Alexander and T. Szasz, "From Contract to Status via Psychiatry," *Santa Clara Lawyer,* vol. 13(1973): 537–59; R. Roth, M. Dayley, and J. Lerner, "Into the Abyss: Psychiatric Reliability, and Emergency Commitment Statutes," *Santa Clara Lawyer,* vol. 13(1973): 400–66; L. V. Kaplan, "Civil Commitment 'As You Like It,'" *Boston University Law Review,* vol. 49(1969): 14–45; A. T. Elliott, "Procedures of Involuntary Commitment on the Basis of Alleged Mental Illness," *University of Colorado Law Review,* vol. 42(1970): 231–69, esp. p. 231; B. Ennis, *Prisoners of Psychiatry* (New York: Harcourt Brace Jovanovich, 1972). American courts have begun to accept such conclusions of the myth argument. See *Lessard v. Schmidt,* 349 F. Supp. 1078 (E. D. Wis. 1972), vacated, 414 U.S. 473, 94 S.Ct. 713, 38 L.Ed.2nd 661 (1974), and *State ex rel Hawks v. Lazaro,* 202 S.E.2d 109 (W. Va. 1974), holding unconstitutional the Wisconsin and West Virginia civil commitment statutes; *United States v. Brawner,* 471 F.2d 969, 985–6, 995 (D.C. Cir. 1972), where the Court of Appeals for the District of Columbia gave more than sympathetic consideration to eliminating mental illness as an excuse in the criminal law.

SELECTED BIBLIOGRAPHY

Boorse, Christopher. "On the Distinction Between Disease and Illness." *Philosophy and Public Affairs* 5 (Fall 1975): 49–68.

———. "What a Theory of Mental Health Should Be." *Journal for the Theory of Social Behavior* 6 (April 1976): 61–84.

Caplan, Arthur L., H. Tristram Engelhardt, Jr., and James J. McCartney, eds. *Concepts of Health and Disease: Interdisciplinary Perspectives.* Reading, Mass.: Addison-Wesley, 1981.

Edwards, Rem B. "Mental Health as Rational Autonomy." *The Journal of Medicine and Philosophy* 6 (August 1981): 309–22.

Engel, G. L. "The Need for a New Medical Model: A Challenge for Biomedicine." *Science* 196 (April 1977): 129–36.

Engelhardt, H. Tristram, Jr. "Human Well-Being and Medicine: Some Basic Value-Judgments in the Biomedical Sciences." In Engelhardt, H. Tristram, Jr., and Daniel Callahan, eds., *Science, Ethics and Medicine*. Hastings-on-Hudson, N.Y.: Institute of Society, Ethics and the Life Sciences, 1976. Pp. 131–39.

––––––. "The Disease of Masturbation: Values and the Concept of Disease." *Bulletin of the History of Medicine* 48 (Summer 1974): 234–48.

Jahoda, Marie. *Current Concepts of Positive Mental Health*. New York: Basic Books, 1958.

Kass, Leon R. "Regarding the End of Medicine and the Pursuit of Health." *Public Interest* 40 (Summer 1975): 11–42.

King, Lester S. "What is Disease?" *Philosophy of Science* 21, no. 3 (1954): 193–203.

Sedgwick, Peter. *Psycho Politics*. New York: Harper and Row, 1982.

Szasz, Thomas S. *Ideology and Insanity: Essays on the Psychiatric Dehumanization of Man*. New York: Doubleday, 1970.

CHAPTER 6

Involuntary Hospitalization and Behavior Control

ARE WE EVER MORALLY and/or legally justified in depriving ill persons of their liberty and committing them to an institution for confinement and/or therapy against their wills? Legally, this has seldom been allowed in the United States if such persons are physically ill, though there are occasional involuntary quarantines and treatments for highly communicable diseases. By contrast, our laws allow mentally ill persons to be incarcerated and treated against their wills, and this is commonly done. Is the involuntary hospitalization and treatment of the mentally ill morally acceptable? Many severe critics regard these practices as morally barbaric. Even voluntary mental hospitalization and therapies are troublesome enough, as we soon will see.

Types of Mental Patients

Mental hospital patients fall into many classes. In theory, *voluntary* mental patients are those who enter psychiatric hospitalization and/or treatment voluntarily; i.e., they recognize their need for help and request it without being coerced. In psychiatry, however, things are not always as they seem. Most voluntary patients actually experience intense coercion. They are subjected to immense pressures and threats by family members, friends, and society generally unless they "sign themselves in." They do not become mental patients under ideal conditions of informed voluntary consent. Many have been temporarily hospitalized involuntarily on an "emergency" basis. Then they are persuaded to sign "voluntary" commitment papers by being threatened with such treatments as electroshock, solitary confinement ("time-out therapy"), loss of such "privileges" as having visitors or getting off the ward, or with "regular" involuntary commitment. In theory but not necessarily in practice, voluntary patients can request and receive release within 24 to 48 hours. Once they make such a request, involuntary commitment proceedings may be immediately initiated by their hospital to retain them against their wills. The courts seldom deny such requests.

Involuntary mental patients, those hospitalized and/or treated against their wills, fall roughly into two classes. *Involuntary criminal* or *forensic* patients are those who have been charged with or tried for a crime. Some forensic patients are hospitalized so that tests may be done to determine whether they are competent to stand trial. Others, found to be incompetent to

stand trial, are hospitalized to receive treatment that would restore such competency. Still others have been tried and found "not guilty by reason of insanity." Yet the innocence of this last group does not free them from involuntary institutionalization. They are merely sent to a mental hospital for indefinite detention rather than to prison for a definite term of incarceration. Critics charge that they are really worse off and that punishment parades as therapy under such conditions. These forms of involuntary commitment obviously exist primarily to serve the needs of the criminal justice system.

Involuntary civil patients have not been court committed for competency tests or restoration or tried for a crime, though many of them have actually committed crimes. In the following article by Thomas Szasz we are told that they "have not violated any criminal statutes." This is true of some such patients but not of all. Many involuntary civil patients have violated laws against indecent exposure, disturbing the peace, sexual abuse of minors, rape, assault, driving under the influence of alcohol or drugs, theft, and murder. The judgment of "dangerous" underlying their commitments is often predicated upon just such criminal behaviors, not upon the mere threat or likelihood of such. They are not prosecuted for their offenses, because someone in a position of authority has decided to process their deviancy through the mental health system rather than through the criminal justice system. When is such a decision appropriate?

Laws authorizing involuntary civil commitment vary from state to state, but the trend in recent years has been to narrow their scope of application. Formerly, persons branded as "mentally ill" could be involuntarily deprived of their liberty for such things as being a public nuisance or merely needing custody or treatment. Abuses of such permissive civil commitment laws have been horrendous. More recently, attempts have been made to develop a much stronger and narrower rationale for depriving persons of their freedom and subjecting them to treatment

against their will. Today, many if not most state laws authorize involuntary civil commitment only if persons are (1) mentally ill *and* (2) dangerous to self or others. Some statutes require that the mental illness be the *cause* of the dangerousness, but in practice mental health professionals pay little attention to such niceties. Where (3) extreme self-neglect, the inability to provide for one's safety and basic needs, is not included under the category of dangerousness to self, it may appear as an additional commitment condition. Usually, commitment statutes also require that hospitalization be (4) the "least restrictive alternative" available to meet the patient's treatment needs, i.e., that it be used only as a very last resort; but this too is often ignored in practice.

Though they are jointly necessary and sufficient, none of the foregoing commitment conditions is sufficient by itself for involuntary civil commitment. Dangerousness is clearly not enough. Such dangerous persons as former prison inmates, drunken drivers, speeders, and members of motorcycle gangs can be incarcerated only if they have been tried and convicted of a crime, but never merely because they are dangerous. "Preventive detention" is generally illegal and immoral except where there are compelling "clear and present dangers" to society. Many mentally ill persons clearly are not dangerous and have been "deinstitutionalized" or refused hospitalization because they satisfy condition (1) but not condition (2) as well. They may be a nuisance, and they may need treatment, but the law no longer recognizes these as being sufficient to justify deprivations of liberty.

A. CRITICISMS AND DEFENSES OF INVOLUNTARY CIVIL COMMITMENT

Many outspoken critics of involuntary civil commitment are unwilling to accept it even in its more recent restricted form. As the title of his

following article suggests, Thomas Szasz regards "Involuntary Hospitalization" as "A Crime Against Humanity" akin to slavery. He contends that the condition requiring mental illness can never be satisfied, as we saw in the preceding chapter. If mental illness is a myth, if no one ever is mentally ill, then none can be institutionalized on grounds that they are. Szasz believes that the concept of "mental illness" merely provides us with a medical excuse for oppressing and controlling others who are different and that it is moving us toward a world in which "the principal requirement for the position of Big Brother may be an M.D. degree." Furthermore, very few so-called mentally ill persons ever meet the dangerousness condition. In his view, those who do should not be incarcerated until they have actually committed a crime. When they do and are properly tried and convicted for it, they should be sent to jail or prison for punishment just like the rest of us. Sending them to a mental hospital for "treatment" is only punishment in disguise. Since no one is insane, the "insanity defense" should be abolished, Szasz contends.

Szasz also attacks the notion of "dangerousness" that appears in modern civil commitment statutes. The term is often undefined, and it has been applied to everything from writing bad checks and shooting at mailboxes to criticizing the President. Whether others are thought to be dangerous or not "depends on the observer's religious beliefs, political convictions, and social situation."

Recent legislation in many states limits "dangerousness" to "a high probability of imminent physical harm to self or others." Objections remain, however. Most seriously, many studies have shown that mental health professionals cannot accurately predict dangerousness, that their predictions are wrong at least 85 to 95 percent of the time. Thus, for every 5 to 15 truly dangerous persons incarcerated under such statutes, 85 to 95 nondangerous persons are unjustly deprived of their liberty. Should we accept a social policy that inevitably involves such massive misuse?

The task of predicting dangerousness which society has assigned to mental health professionals seems to be one that nobody is qualified to perform.

In her article to follow, titled "Liberty, Beneficence, and Involuntary Confinement," Joan C. Callahan examines the ethical and conceptual foundations of involuntary civil commitment. She finds that a beneficent paternalism of harm prevention comes sharply into conflict with the value of liberty. Should such paternalism ever prevail?

Callahan's answer is affirmative, but she is convinced that justifiable paternalism does not correlate exactly with current civil commitment laws. In one respect, she argues, such laws are too narrow because many nondangerous persons who are mentally ill are justifiably confinable to prevent self-caused or self-permitted harm to self. The relevant harms need not be extreme and irreversible if the patients are incompetent, for incompetent persons simply are not capable of giving informed voluntary consent to or refusal of hospitalization and treatment. Harms should not be restricted to physical injury, for we are justified in preventing a person in a manic state from squandering his financial resources. Weak paternalism with respect to incompetent persons justifiably may prevent both minor and major physical harms as well as major nonphysical harms such as financial ruin. Callahan carefully delineates the domain of incompetence, refines the concept of dangerousness, and places additional side constraints on the application of the weak paternalism which she advocates.

Callahan argues that current civil commitment laws are also too broad because they apply to persons who are perfectly competent to choose or refuse hospitalization and treatment. Our commitment laws require only that persons be mentally ill, but not that they be incompetent. The two are not coextensive, for our broad and elastic notions of mental illness allow many rationally competent persons to be classified as mentally ill. For involuntary civil commitment,

Callahan's weak paternalism requires that persons be specifically incompetent to make their own decisions about hospitalization and treatment. She recommends drastic, but much called for, changes in current laws.

B. NONINTRUSIVE BEHAVIOR CONTROL THERAPIES: PSYCHOTHERAPY AND BEHAVIOR MODIFICATION

Perry London defined "behavior control" as "the ability to get someone to do one's bidding."[1] Thus understood, behavior control may apply to oneself or to another. We may attempt to control our own behavior or that of someone else. There is nothing inherently immoral about behavior control, just as there is nothing inherently immoral about coercion and paternalism, though some forms of these may be *prima facie* wrong. There are morally acceptable forms of coercion, such as the police power of the state; and there are morally acceptable forms of paternalism, such as weak paternalism exercised over the immature and the incompetent. There are also morally acceptable forms of behavior control, such as exercising will power or rationally autonomous self-direction, and providing others with information. Behavior control, as London conceives it, consists in influencing behavior, not rigidly determining it. In the selection to follow, he examines two forms of behavior control commonly employed in psychotherapy: insight therapy and behavior modification.

Insight Therapy

London defines insight therapy as the control of behavior through information. He often calls it "talk therapy" because its method is that of talking and inducing patients to talk, combined with sympathetic listening. It is the traditional method of those forms of psychotherapy which do not employ physical intrusions, such as drugs or electroshock, into the body of the patient to influence behavior. The paradigm user of this method is the psychoanalyst trying to talk her patient on the couch out of his psychological hang-ups.

Many schools of psychotherapy employ insight therapy, varying in details of technique. They all have in common, according to London, the assumption that "motives dictate behavior." They all attempt "to lead the patient to some insight into the relationship between his motivations and his behavior, on the assumption that this insight will give him greater control. . . ." On the surface, insight therapy seems to be the most morally acceptable form of psychotherapy because it is noncoercive and its primary objective is to enhance the patient's self-control and responsibility through self-knowledge. London does not deny these objectives, though he indicates that insight therapy has its unexpected shortcomings. For one thing, it may give self-understanding, but "it is a poor means of symptom control." For another, insight therapists inescapably exert manipulative influences which they do not acknowledge. They also may keep patients in therapy indefinitely long because they refuse to employ other, more effective methods of symptom relief, such as behavior modification or drugs.

Behavior Modification

Perry London calls techniques of behavior modification "action therapies." He explains various techniques of action therapy employed on psychiatric patients: counterconditioning, extinction therapy, operant conditioning, aversion therapy, desensitization, implosive therapy, etc. Behavior modification therapies do not aim directly at internal psychological changes in motivation or insight. Rather, as London notes, "they tend to focus treatment on the (behavioral) symptoms proper without much concern over their origins or meaning." Objectionable behaviors are learned, and with proper conditioning they can be unlearned. Unlike insight therapy, behavioral therapy does not promote internal self-control

and it is deliberately manipulative. Its primary justification is that it works!

Behavior modification therapies are logically independent of traditional psychodynamic or other mentalistic psychologies. Even traditional notions of mental illness are expendable in behavior therapy. From a behavioral perspective, a patient's "real problem" is his behavior, not some underlying mental illness. Nothing more is required than, first, the identification of an unacceptable or otherwise "maladaptive" pattern of behavior to be eliminated and/or a behavioral deficiency to be promoted and, second, the development of conditioning techniques that will fix the problem. Ineffective, prolonged, and expensive talk therapies, as well as medically intrusive therapies with their unacceptable side effects, ideally are avoided by behavior modification. In practice, however, all these therapies are often combined. Patients in mental hospitals may spend one hour with a behavioral therapist, the next in group talk therapy, and the next few hours or days responding to psychotropic medication or some other physically intrusive treatment.

C. PHYSICALLY INTRUSIVE BEHAVIOR CONTROL THERAPIES: ELECTROSHOCK, ELECTROSTIMULATION, PSYCHOSURGERY, PSYCHOPHARMACOLOGY

Unacceptable behaviors, thoughts, beliefs, attitudes, emotions, desires, and volitions may be influenced or controlled by physical intrusions into the brain. Modern psychotherapy has developed a plethora of such intrusions which count as therapies. In a selection to follow, George H. Kieffer describes a number of these and explains how they work. All need to be evaluated for their ethical acceptability or unacceptability. They may be satisfied to varying degrees, and some may be

more important than others; but the following criteria may be employed to distinguish acceptable from unacceptable techniques of behavior control. A technique is preferable to the extent that

1. it is used with voluntary informed consent on competent adults;

2. its use does not infringe on basic legal and/or moral rights;

3. there is a high probability of a favorable cost/benefit ratio, using some ideal of intrinsic good and evil;

4. it enhances, or at least does not diminish, a person's capacity for rational autonomy;

5. it involves minimal physical intrusion into a person's body;

6. it does not have irreversible bad effects (Irreversible good effects are acceptable if we are confident that we can identify them.);

7. no less objectionable and less restrictive forms of behavior control are readily available;

8. its effectiveness is proven rather than experimental;

9. its monetary costs are not prohibitive.[2]

As described in following accounts, electroshock, electrostimulation, psychosurgery, and psychopharmacology should be evaluated in light of these criteria.

D. SUICIDE INTERVENTION

It is probably true both that there is such a thing as rational suicide and that in an emergency situation medical professionals should treat all suicide attempts as irrational. Even if some suicide attempts are authentic expressions of rational autonomy, time is required for other persons to determine this, especially if they are medical professionals who are called upon to intervene. In the following selection, David F. Greenberg

identifies a number of situations in which, as "the lesser of evils," it might be rational to commit suicide. Greenberg mentions "to escape the pain of an excruciating terminal illness" as well as "to prevent the enemy from obtaining secrets through torture" as possibilities.

Greenberg also argues that it would be rational for us to adopt a social policy of interference with suicide attempts and temporary emergency civil commitment to hospitalization for those who try it. Many studies show that an overwhelming majority of those who attempt suicide do not clearly want to die, that their self-harm is usually a desperate plea for some fundamental change in their life situation rather than for death, and that they will shortly express "retrospective gratitude" to those who have prevented them from doing something so grave, rash, and irreversible. Although our present civil commitment laws require both mental illness and dangerousness to self for emergency commitment to prevent suicide, Greenberg thinks that mental illness is not necessary for a policy of intervention, that temporary rashness would be quite sufficient. On the other hand, he insists that only emergency commitment for a period of not more than 24 hours is justifiable, that longer confinement is never justifiable.

While the policy suggested by Greenberg may be satisfactory for rationally competent adults, it seems unsatisfactory for persons who are both mentally ill and rationally incompetent to decide whether they want to live or die. A person suffering from severe pathological, as opposed to reactive, depression cannot usually be restored to rational competence in 24 hours. Psychotropic medication for depression often takes a minimum of three weeks to be effective. Similar problems arise for persons suffering from other forms of psychosis. Extreme and persisting irrationality is much more serious than temporary rashness and calls for a more enduring response, justifiable on grounds of weak paternalism. Further, the substantive safeguards for suicide intervention suggested by Greenberg should be observed. We should be sure that protected individuals have a right to rational suicide when restored to competency, that safeguards exist to prevent detainment of those falsely accused of being suicidal, that interventions are not excessively distressing or prolonged, and that least restrictive alternatives are employed.

Notes

[1] Perry London, *Behavior Control, 2nd ed.* (New York: New American Library, 1969), p. 3.

[2] With only slight modification, these criteria were published in Rem B. Edwards, ed., *Psychiatry and Ethics: Insanity, Rational Autonomy, and Mental Health Care* (Buffalo: Prometheus Books, 1982), p. 348.

Involuntary Mental Hospitalization: A Crime Against Humanity

Thomas S. Szasz

A biographical sketch of Dr. Szasz is given on page 281.

Szasz maintains that the involuntary civil commitment of persons with "functional" mental illnesses (who do not have real illnesses at all, in his view) is merely society's attempt to coercively control and repress deviants who have committed no crime. Thus, to incarcerate them is itself a crime, even when it is done from benevolent or paternalistic motives. In mental hospitals, punishment is disguised as therapy.

For some time now I have maintained that commitment—that is, the detention of persons in mental institutions against their will—is a form of imprisonment;[1] that such deprivation of liberty is contrary to the moral principles embodied in the Declaration of Independence and the Constitution of the United States;[2] and that it is a crass violation of contemporary concepts of fundamental human rights.[3] The practice of "sane" men incarcerating their "insane" fellow men in "mental hospitals" can be compared to that of white men enslaving black men. In short, I consider commitment a crime against humanity.

Existing social institutions and practices, especially if honored by prolonged usage, are generally experienced and accepted as good and valuable. For thousands of years slavery was considered a "natural" social arrangement for the securing of human labor; it was sanctioned by public opinion, religious dogma, church, and state;[4] it was abolished a mere one hundred years ago in the United States; and it is still a prevalent social practice in some parts of the world, notably in Africa.[5] Since its origin approximately three centuries ago, commitment of the insane has enjoyed equally widespread support; physicians, lawyers, and the laity have asserted, as if with a single voice, the therapeutic desirability and social necessity of institutional psychiatry. My claim that commitment is a crime against humanity may thus be countered—as indeed it has been—by maintaining, first, that the practice is beneficial for the mentally ill, and second, that it is necessary for the protection of the mentally healthy members of society.

Illustrative of the first argument is Slovenko's assertion that "Reliance solely on voluntary hospital admission procedures ignores the fact that some persons may desire care and custody but cannot communicate their desire directly."[6] Imprisonment in mental hospitals is here portrayed—by a professor of law!—as a service provided to persons by the state because they "desire" it but do not know how to ask for it. Felix defends involuntary mental hospitalization by asserting simply, "We *do* [his italics] deal with illnesses of the mind."[7]

Illustrative of the second argument is Guttmacher's characterization of my book *Law, Liberty, and Psychiatry* as ". . . a pernicious book . . . certain to produce intolerable and unwarranted anxiety in the families of psychiatric patients."[8] This is an admission of the fact that the families of "psychiatric patients" frequently resort to the use of force in order to control their "loved ones," and that when attention is directed to this practice it creates embarrassment and guilt. On the other hand, Felix simply defines the psychiatrist's duty as the protection of society: "Tomorrow's psychiatrist will be, as is his counterpart today, one of the gatekeepers of his community."[9]

These conventional explanations of the nature and uses of commitment are, however, but culturally accepted justifications for certain quasi-medical forms of social control, exercised

[1]Szasz, T. S.: "Commitment of the mentally ill: Treatment or social restraint?" *J. Nerv. & Ment. Dis.* 125:293–307 (Apr.–June), 1957.

[2]Szasz, T. S.: *Law, Liberty, and Psychiatry: An Inquiry into the Social Uses of Mental Health Practices* (New York: Macmillan, 1963), pp. 149–90.

[3]Ibid., pp. 223–55.

[4]Davis, D. B.: *The Problem of Slavery in Western Culture* (Ithaca, N.Y.: Cornell University Press, 1966).

[5]See Cohen, R.: "Slavery in Africa." *Trans-Action* 4:44–56 (Jan.–Feb.), 1967; Tobin, R. L.: "Slavery still plagues the earth." *Saturday Review*, May 6, 1967, pp. 24–25.

[6]Slovenko, R.: "The psychiatric patient, liberty, and the law." *Amer. J. Psychiatry,* 121:534–39 (Dec.), 1964, p. 536.

[7]Felix, R. H.: "The image of the psychiatrist: Past, present, and future." *Amer. J. Psychiatry,* 121:318–22 (Oct.), 1964, p. 320.

[8]Guttmacher, M. S.: "Critique of views of Thomas Szasz on legal psychiatry." *AMA Arch. Gen. Psychiatry,* 10:238–45 (March), 1964, p. 244.

[9]Felix, op. cit., p. 231.

especially against individuals and groups whose behavior does not violate criminal laws but threatens established social values.

II

What is the evidence that commitment does not serve the purpose of helping or treating people whose behavior deviates from or threatens prevailing social norms or moral standards; and who, because they inconvenience their families, neighbors, or superiors, may be incriminated as "mentally ill"?

1. The Medical Evidence   Mental illness is a metaphor. If by "disease" we mean a disorder of the physicochemical machinery of the human body, then we can assert that what we call functional mental diseases are not diseases at all.[10] Persons said to be suffering from such disorders are socially deviant or inept, or in conflict with individuals, groups, or institutions. Since they do not suffer from disease, it is impossible to "treat" them for any sickness.

Although the term "mentally ill" is usually applied to persons who do not suffer from bodily disease, it is sometimes applied also to persons who do (for example, to individuals intoxicated with alcohol or other drugs, or to elderly people suffering from degenerative disease of the brain). However, when patients with demonstrable diseases of the brain are involuntarily hospitalized, the primary purpose is to exercise social control over their behavior;[11] treatment of the disease is, at best, a secondary consideration. Frequently, therapy is nonexistent, and custodial care is dubbed "treatment."

In short, the commitment of persons suffering from "functional psychoses" serves moral and social, rather than medical and therapeutic, purposes. Hence, even if, as a result of future research, certain conditions now believed to be "functional" mental illnesses were to be shown to be "organic," my argument against involuntary mental hospitalization would remain unaffected.

2. The Moral Evidence   In free societies, the relationship between physician and patient is predicated on the legal presumption that the individual "owns" his body and his personality.[12] The physician can examine and treat a patient only with his consent; the latter is free to reject treatment (for example, an operation for cancer).[13] After death, "ownership" of the person's body is transferred to his heirs; the physician must obtain permission from the patient's relatives for a post-mortem examination. John Stuart Mill explicitly affirmed that ". . . each person is the proper guardian of his own health, whether bodily, or mental and spiritual."[14] Commitment is incompatible with this moral principle.

3. The Historical Evidence   Commitment practices flourished long before there were any mental or psychiatric "treatments" of "mental diseases." Indeed, madness or mental illness was not always a necessary condition for commitment. For example, in the seventeenth century, "children of artisans and other poor inhabitants of Paris up to the age of 25, . . . girls who were debauched or in evident danger of being debauched, . . ." and other "misérables" of the community, such as epileptics, people with venereal diseases, and poor people with chronic diseases of all sorts, were all considered fit subjects for

---

[10]See Szasz, T. S.: "The myth of mental illness." This volume pp. 281–84; *The Myth of Mental Illness: Foundations of a Theory of Personal Conduct* (New York: Hoeber-Harper, 1961); "Mental illness is a myth." *The New York Times Magazine,* June 12, 1966, pp. 30 and 90–92.

[11]See, for example, Noyes, A. P.: *Modern Clinical Psychiatry,* 4th ed. (Philadelphia: Saunders, 1956), p. 278.

[12]Szasz, T. S.: "The ethics of birth control; or, who owns your body?" *The Humanist,* 20:332–36 (Nov.–Dec.) 1960.

[13]Hirsch, B. D.: "Informed consent to treatment," in Averbach, A. and Belli, M. M., eds., *Tort and Medical Yearbook* (Indianapolis: Bobbs-Merrill, 1961), Vol. I, pp. 631–38.

[14]Mill, J. S.: *On Liberty* [1859] (Chicago: Regnery, 1955), p. 18.

confinement in the Hôpital Général.[15] And, in 1860, when Mrs. Packard was incarcerated for disagreeing with her minister-husband,[16] the commitment laws of the State of Illinois explicitly proclaimed that ". . . married women . . . may be entered or detained in the hospital at the request of the husband of the woman or the guardian . . . , without the evidence of insanity required in other cases."[17] It is surely no coincidence that this piece of legislation was enacted and enforced at about the same time that Mill published his essay *The Subjection of Women.*[18]

4. The Literary Evidence   Involuntary mental hospitalization plays a significant part in numerous short stories and novels from many countries. In none that I have encountered is commitment portrayed as helpful to the hospitalized person; instead, it is always depicted as an arrangement serving interests antagonistic to those of the so-called patient.[19]

III

The claim that commitment of the "mentally ill" is necessary for the protection of the "mentally

healthy" is more difficult to refute, not because it is valid, but because the danger that "mental patients" supposedly pose is of such an extremely vague nature.

1. The Medical Evidence   The same reasoning applies as earlier: If "mental illness" is not a disease, there is no medical justification for protection from disease. Hence, the analogy between mental illness and contagious disease falls to the ground: The justification for isolating or otherwise constraining patients with tuberculosis or typhoid fever cannot be extended to patients with "mental illness."

Moreover, because the accepted contemporary psychiatric view of mental illness fails to distinguish between illness as a biological condition and as a social role,[20] it is not only false, but also dangerously misleading, especially if used to justify social action. In this view, regardless of its "causes"—anatomical, genetic, chemical, psychological, or social—mental illness has "objective existence." A person either has or has not a mental illness; he is either mentally sick or mentally healthy. Even if a person is cast in the role of mental patient against his will, his "mental illness" exists "objectively"; and even if, as in the case of the Very Important Person, he is never treated as a mental patient, his "mental illness" still exists "objectively"—apart from the activities of the psychiatrist.[21]

The upshot is that the term "mental illness" is perfectly suited for mystification: It disregards the crucial question of whether the individual assumes the role of mental patient voluntarily, and hence wishes to engage in some sort of interaction

[15]Rosen, G.: "Social attitudes to irrationality and madness in 17th and 18th century Europe." *J. Hist. Med. & Allied Sciences,* 18:220–40 (1963), p. 223.

[16]Packard, E. W. P.: *Modern Persecution, or Insane Asylums Unveiled,* 2 Vols. (Hartford: Case, Lockwood, and Brainard, 1873).

[17]Illinois Statute Book, Sessions Laws 15, Section 10, 1851. Quoted in Packard, E. P. W.: *The Prisoner's Hidden Life* (Chicago: published by the author, 1868), p. 37.

[18]Mill, J. S.: *The Subjection of Women* [1869] (London: Dent, 1965).

[19]See, for example, Chekhov, A. P.: *Ward No. 6,* [1892], in *Seven Short Novels by Chekhov* (New York: Bantam Books, 1963), pp. 106–57; De Assis, M.: *The Psychiatrist* [1881–82], in De Assis, M., *The Psychiatrist and Other Stories* (Berkeley and Los Angeles: University of California Press, 1963), pp. 1–45; London, J.: *The Iron Heel* [1907] (New York: Sagamore Press, 1957); Porter, K. A.: *Noon Wine* [1937], in Porter, K. A., *Pale Horse, Pale Rider: Three Short Novels* (New York: Signet, 1965), pp. 62–112; Kesey, K.: *One Flew Over the Cuckoo's Nest* (New York: Viking, 1962); Tarsis, V.: *Ward 7: An*

Autobiographical Novel (London and Glasgow: Collins and Harvill, 1965).

[20]See Szasz, T. S.: "Alcoholism: A socio-ethical perspective.' *Western Medicine,* 7:15–21 (Dec.), 1966.

[21]See, for example, Rogow, A. A.: *James Forrestal: A Study of Personality, Politics, and Policy* (New York: Macmillan, 1964); for a detailed criticism of this view, see Szasz, T. S.: "Psychiatric classification as a strategy of personal constraint." *Ideology and Insanity* pp. 190–217.

with a psychiatrist; or whether he is cast in that role against his will, and hence is opposed to such a relationship. This obscurity is then usually employed strategically, either by the subject himself to advance *his* interests, or by the subject's adversaries to advance *their* interests.

In contrast to this view, I maintain, first, that the involuntarily hospitalized mental patient is, by definition, the occupant of an ascribed role; and, second, that the "mental disease" of such a person—unless the use of this term is restricted to demonstrable lesions or malfunctions of the brain—is always the product of interaction between psychiatrist and patient.

2. *The Moral Evidence*

The crucial ingredient in involuntary mental hospitalization is coercion. Since coercion is the exercise of power, it is always a moral and political act. Accordingly, regardless of its medical justification, commitment is primarily a moral and political phenomenon—just as, regardless of its anthropological and economic justifications, slavery was primarily a moral and political phenomenon.

Although psychiatric methods of coercion are indisputably useful for those who employ them, they are clearly not indispensable for dealing with the problems that so-called mental patients pose for those about them. If an individual threatens others by virtue of his beliefs or actions, he could be dealt with by methods other than "medical": if his conduct is ethically offensive, moral sanctions against him might be appropriate; if forbidden by law, legal sanctions might be appropriate. In my opinion, both informal, moral sanctions, such as social ostracism or divorce, and formal, judicial sanctions, such as fine and imprisonment, are more dignified and less injurious to the human spirit than the quasi-medical psychiatric sanction of involuntary mental hospitalization.[22]

3. *The Historical Evidence*

To be sure, confinement of so-called mentally ill persons does protect the community from certain problems. If it didn't, the arrangement would not have come into being and would not have persisted. However, the question we ought to ask is not *whether* commitment protects the community from "dangerous mental patients," but rather from precisely *what danger* it protects and by *what means*? In what way were prostitutes or vagrants dangerous in seventeenth century Paris? Or married women in nineteenth century Illinois?

It is significant, moreover, that there is hardly a prominent person who, during the past fifty years or so, has not been diagnosed by a psychiatrist as suffering from some type of "mental illness." Barry Goldwater was called "paranoid schizophrenic";[23] Whittaker Chambers, a "psychopathic personality";[24] Woodrow Wilson, a "neurotic" frequently "very close to psychosis";[25] and Jesus, "a born degenerate" with a "fixed delusional system," and a "paranoid" with a "clinical picture [so typical] that it is hardly conceivable that people can even question the accuracy of the diagnosis."[26] The list is endless.

Sometimes, psychiatrists declare the same person sane *and* insane, depending on the political dictates of their superiors and the social demand of the moment. Before his trial and execution, Adolph Eichmann was examined by several psychiatrists, all of whom declared him to be normal; after he was put to death, "medical evidence" of his insanity was released and widely circulated.

According to Hannah Arendt, "Half a dozen

---

[22]Szasz, T. S.: *Psychiatric Justice* (New York: Macmillan, 1965).

[23]"The Unconscious of a Conservative: A Special Issue on the Mind of Barry Goldwater." *Fact,* Sept.–Oct. 1964.

[24]Zeligs, M. A.: *Friendship and Fratricide: An Analysis of Whittaker Chambers and Alger Hiss* (New York: Viking, 1967).

[25]Freud, S. and Bullitt, W. C.: *Thomas Woodrow Wilson: A Psychological Study* (Boston: Houghton Mifflin, 1967).

[26]Quoted in Schweitzer, A.: *The Psychiatric Study of Jesus* [1913] transl. by Charles R. Joy (Boston: Beacon Press, 1956), pp. 37, 40–41.

what purpose is served by calling Eichmann insane?

psychiatrists had certified him [Eichmann] as 'normal.'" One psychiatrist asserted, ". . . his whole psychological outlook, his attitude toward his wife and children, mother and father, sisters and friends, was 'not only normal but most desirable.' . . . And the minister who regularly visited him in prison declared that Eichmann was 'a man with very positive ideas'."[27] After Eichmann was executed, Gideon Hausner, the Attorney General of Israel, who had prosecuted him, disclosed in an article in *The Saturday Evening Post* that psychiatrists diagnosed Eichmann as '"a man obsessed with a dangerous and insatiable urge to kill,' 'a perverted, sadistic personality.'"[28]

Whether or not men like those mentioned above are considered "dangerous" depends on the observer's religious beliefs, political convictions, and social situation. Furthermore, the "dangerousness" of such persons—whatever we may think of them—is not analogous to that of a person with tuberculosis or typhoid fever; nor would rendering such a person "non-dangerous" be comparable to rendering a patient with a contagious disease non-infectious.

In short, I hold—and I submit that the historical evidence bears me out—that people are committed to mental hospitals neither because they are "dangerous," nor because they are "mentally ill," but rather because they are society's scapegoats, whose persecution is justified by psychiatric propaganda and rhetoric.[29]

4. The Literary Evidence

No one contests that involuntary mental hospitalization of the so-called dangerously insane "protects" the community. Disagreement centers on the nature of the threat facing society, and on the methods

and legitimacy of the protection it employs. In this connection, we may recall that slavery, too, "protected" the community: it freed the slave-owners from manual labor. Commitment likewise shields the non-hospitalized members of society: first, from having to accommodate themselves to the annoying or idiosyncratic demands of certain members of the community who have not violated any criminal statutes; and, second, from having to prosecute, try, convict, and punish members of the community who have broken the law but who either might not be convicted in court, or, if they would be, might not be restrained as effectively or as long in prison as in a mental hospital. The literary evidence cited earlier fully supports this interpretation of the function of involuntary mental hospitalization.

IV

I have suggested that commitment constitutes a social arrangement whereby one part of society secures certain advantages for itself at the expense of another part. To do so, the oppressors must possess an ideology to justify their aims and actions; and they must be able to enlist the police power of the state to impose their will on the oppressed members. What makes such an arrangement a "crime against humanity"? It may be argued that the use of state power is legitimate when law-abiding citizens punish lawbreakers. What is the difference between this use of state power and its use in commitment?

In the first place, the difference between committing the "insane" and imprisoning the "criminal" is the same as that between the rule of man and the rule of law:[30] whereas the "insane" are subjected to the coercive controls of the state because persons more powerful than they have labeled them as "psychotic," "criminals" are

---

[27] Arendt, H.: *Eichmann in Jerusalem: A Report on the Banality of Evil* (New York: Viking, 1963), p. 22.

[28] Ibid, pp. 22–23.

[29] For a full articulation and documentation of this thesis, see Szasz, T. S.: *The Manufacture of Madness: A Comparative Study of the Inquisition and the Mental Health Movement* (New York: Harper & Row, to be published in 1970).

[30] Hayek, F. A.: *The Constitution of Liberty* (Chicago: University of Chicago Press, 1960), especially pp. 162–92.

subjected to such controls because they have violated legal rules applicable equally to all.

The second difference between these two proceedings lies in their professed aims. The principal purpose of imprisoning criminals is to protect the liberties of the law-abiding members of society.[31] Since the individual subject to commitment is not considered a threat to liberty in the same way as the accused criminal is (if he were, he would be prosecuted), his removal from society cannot be justified on the same grounds. Justification for commitment must thus rest on its therapeutic promise and potential: it will help restore the "patient" to "mental health." But if this can be accomplished only at the cost of robbing the individual of liberty, "involuntary mental hospitalization" becomes only a verbal camouflage for what is, in effect, punishment. This "therapeutic" punishment differs, however, from traditional judicial punishment, in that the accused criminal enjoys a rich panoply of constitutional protections against false accusation and oppressive prosecution, whereas the accused mental patient is deprived of these protections.[32] . . .

VII

A basic assumption of American slavery was that the Negro was racially inferior to the Caucasian. "There is no malice toward the Negro in Ulrich Phillips' work," wrote Stanley Elkins about the author's book *American Negro Slavery,* a work sympathetic with the Southern position. "Phillips was deeply fond of the Negroes as a people; it was just that he could not take them seriously as men and women; they were children."[33]

Similarly, the basic assumption of institutional psychiatry is that the mentally ill person is psychologically and socially inferior to the mentally healthy. He is like a child: he does not know what is in his best interests and therefore needs others to control and protect him.[34] Psychiatrists often care deeply for their involuntary patients, whom they consider—in contrast with the merely "neurotic" persons—"psychotic," which is to say, "very sick." Hence, such patients must be cared for as the "irresponsible children" they are considered to be.

The perspective of paternalism has played an exceedingly important part in justifying both slavery and involuntary mental hospitalization. Aristotle defined slavery as "an essentially domestic relationship"; in so doing, wrote Davis, he "endowed it with the sanction of paternal authority, and helped to establish a precedent that would govern discussions of political philosophers as late as the eighteenth century."[35] The relationship between psychiatrists and mental patients has been and continues to be viewed in the same way. "If a man brings his daughter to me from California," declares Braceland, "because she is in manifest danger of falling into vice or in some way disgracing herself, he doesn't expect me to let her loose in my hometown for that same thing to happen."[36] Indeed, almost any article or book dealing with the "care" of involuntary mental patients may be cited to illustrate the contention that physicians fall back on paternalism to justify their coercive control over the unco-operative pa-

---

[31]Mabbott, J. D.: "Punishment" [1939], in Olafson, F. A., ed., *Justice and Social Policy: A Collection of Essays* (Englewood Cliffs, N.J.: Prentice-Hall, 1961), pp. 39–54.

[32]For documentation, see Szasz, T. S.: *Law, Liberty, and Psychiatry: An Inquiry into the Social Uses of Mental Health Practices* (New York: Macmillan, 1963); *Psychiatric Justice* (New York: Macmillan, 1965).

[33]Elkins, S. M.: *Slavery: A Problem in American Institutional and Intellectual Life* [1859] (New York: Universal Library, 1963), p. 10.

[34]See, for example, Linn, L.: *A Handbook of Hospital Psychiatry* (New York: International Universities Press, 1955), pp. 420–22; Braceland, F. J.: Statement, in *Constitutional Rights of the Mentally Ill* (Washington, D.C.: U. S. Government Printing Office, 1961), pp. 63–74; Rankin, R. S. and Dallmayr, W. B.: "Rights of Patients in Mental Hospitals," in *Constitutional Rights of the Mentally Ill, supra,* pp. 329–70.

[35]Davis, op. cit., p. 69.

[36]Braceland, op. cit., p. 71.

tient. "Certain cases" [not individuals!]—writes Solomon in an article on suicide—". . . must be considered irresponsible, not only with respect to violent impulses, but also in all medical matters." In this class, which he labels "The Irresponsible," he places "Children," "The Mentally Retarded," "The Psychotic," and "The Severely or Terminally Ill." Solomon's conclusion is that "Repugnant though it may be, he [the physician] may have to act against the patient's wishes in order to protect the patient's life and that of others."[37] The fact that, as in the case of slavery, the physician needs the police power of the state to maintain his relationship with his involuntary patient does not alter this self-serving image of institutional psychiatry.

Paternalism is the crucial explanation for the stubborn contradiction and conflict about whether the practices employed by slaveholders and institutional psychiatrists are "therapeutic" or "noxious." Masters and psychiatrists profess their benevolence; their slaves and involuntary patients protest against their malevolence. As Seymour Halleck puts it: ". . . the psychiatrist experiences himself as a helping person, but his patient may see him as a jailer. Both views are partially correct."[38] Not so. Both views are completely correct. Each is a proposition about a different subject: the former, about the psychiatrist's self-image; the latter, about the involuntary mental patient's image of his captor. In *Ward 7*, Valeriy Tarsis presents the following dialogue between his protagonist-patient and the mental-hospital physician: "This is the position. I don't regard you as a doctor. You call this a hospital. I call it a prison. . . . So now, let's get everything straight. I am your prisoner, you are my jailer, and there isn't going to be any nonsense about my health . . . or treatment."[39]

This is the characteristic dialogue of oppression and liberation. The ruler looks in the mirror and sees a liberator; the ruled looks at the ruler and sees a tyrant. If the physician has the power to incarcerate the patient and uses it, their relationship will inevitably fit into this mold. If one cannot ask the subject whether he likes being enslaved or committed, whipped or electro-shocked—because he is not a fit judge of his own "best interests"—then one is left with the contending opinions of the practitioners and their critics. The practitioners insist that their coercive measures are beneficial; the critics, that they are harmful.

The defenders of slavery thus claimed that the Negro "is happier . . . as a slave, than he could be as a free man; this is the result of the peculiarities of his character";[40] that ". . . it was actually an act of liberation to remove Negroes from their harsh world of sin and dark superstition";[41] and that ". . . Negroes were better off in a Christian land, even as slaves, than living like beasts in Africa."[42]

Similarly, the defenders of involuntary mental hospitalization claim that the mental patient is healthier—the twentieth-century synonym for the nineteenth-century term "happier"—as a psychiatric prisoner than he would be as a free citizen; that "[t]he basic purpose [of commitment] is to make sure that sick human beings get the care that is appropriate to their needs . . .";[43] and that "[i]t is a feature of some illnesses that people do not have insight into the fact that they are sick. In short, sometimes it is necessary to protect them [the mentally ill] for a while from themselves. . . ."[44] It requires no great feat of imagination to see how comforting—indeed, how absolutely necessary—

---

[37]Solomon, P.: "The burden of responsibility in suicide." *JAMA*, 199:321–24 (Jan. 30), 1967.

[38]Halleck, S. L.: *Psychiatry and the Dilemmas of Crime* (New York: Harper & Row, 1967), p. 230.

[39]Tarsis, V.: *Ward 7: An Autobiographical Novel* (London and Glasgow: Collins and Harvill, 1965), p. 62.

[40]Elkins, op. cit., p. 190.

[41]Davis, op. cit., p. 186.

[42]Ibid., p. 190.

[43]Ewalt, J.: Statement, in *Constitutional Rights of the Mentally Ill, supra,* pp. 74–89, p. 75.

[44]Braceland, op. cit., p. 64.

these views are to the advocates of slavery and involuntary mental hospitalization, even when they are contradicted by facts.

For example, although it was held that "a merrier being does not exist on the face of the globe than the Negro slave of the United States,"[45] there was an ever-lurking fear of Negro violence and revolt. As Elkins put it, "the failure of any free workers to present themselves for enslavement can serve as one test of how much the analysis of the 'happy slave' may have added to Americans' understanding of themselves."[46]

The same views and the same inconsistencies apply to involuntary psychiatric hospitalization. Defenders of this system maintain that committed patients are better off in hospitals, where they are contented and harmless; "most patients," declares Guttmacher, "when they get in a [mental] hospital are quite content to be there. . . ."[47] At the same time, such patients are feared for their potential violence, their escapes from captivity occasion intense manhunts, and their crimes are prominently featured in the newspapers. Moreover, as with slavery, the failure of citizens to present themselves for involuntary psychiatric hospitalization can serve as a test of how much the currently popular analysis of mental health problems has added to Americans' understanding of themselves.

The social necessity, and hence the basic value, of involuntary mental hospitalization, at least for some people, is not seriously questioned today. There is massive consensus in the United States that, properly used, such hospitalization is a good thing. It is thus possible to debate *who* should be hospitalized, or *how*, or for *how long*—but not whether *anyone should* be. I submit, however, that just as it is improper to enslave anyone—whether he is black or white, Moslem or Christian—so it is improper to hospitalize anyone without his consent—whether he is depressed or paranoid, hysterical or schizophrenic. . . .

XI

We know that man's domination over his fellow man is as old as history; and we may safely assume that it is traceable to prehistoric times and to pre-human ancestors. Perennially, men have oppressed women; white men, colored men; Christians, Jews. However, in recent decades, traditional reasons and justifications for discrimination among men—on the grounds of national, racial, or religious criteria—have lost much of their plausibility and appeal. What justification is there now for man's age-old desire to dominate and control his fellow man? Modern liberalism—in reality, a type of statism—allied with scientism, has met the need for a fresh defense of oppression and has supplied a new battle cry: Health!

In this therapeutic-meliorist view of society, the ill form a special class of "victims" who must, both for their own good and for the interests of the community, be "helped"—coercively and against their will, if necessary—by the healthy, and especially by physicians who are "scientifically" qualified to be their masters. This perspective developed first and has advanced farthest in psychiatry, where the oppression of "insane patients" by "sane physicians" is by now a social custom hallowed by medical and legal tradition. At present, the medical profession as a whole seems to be emulating this model. In the Therapeutic State toward which we appear to be moving, the principal requirement for the position of Big Brother may be an M.D. degree.

---

[45]Elkins, op. cit., p. 216.

[46]Ibid.

[47]Guttmacher, M.: Statement, in *Constitutional Rights of the Mentally Ill, supra,* pp. 143–60, p. 156.

Liberty, Beneficence, and Involuntary Confinement*

Joan C. Callahan

Joan C. Callahan teaches ethics and political philosophy at the University of Kentucky. She has published a number of articles in these areas and is editor of Ethical Issues in Professional Life *(Oxford University Press, 1988) and co-author with James W. Knight of* Controversial Methods of Contraception *(University of Utah Press, 1988).*

    Callahan argues that, in dealing with persons who are mentally ill, a benevolent paternalism is justifiable if and only if they are mentally incompetent to make their own decisions about hospitalization and treatment. She regards her form of paternalism as one which is acceptably protective of individual liberty while not requiring unnecessary sacrifices of individual welfare. She criticizes current commitment laws by arguing (1) that many incompetent but nondangerous persons are justifiably commitable to prevent harm to self and (2) that incompetence and not mere mental illness is what is essential for involuntary commitment.

INTRODUCTION

Miss Simm is a 69-year-old voluntary patient in a county hospital. She was brought to the hospital four weeks earlier for emergency admission when she began having auditory hallucinations. She received medication and is no longer hallucinating, but she continues to be delusional and extremely lethargic. She lies in bed all day, staring into space. She will not dress or wash herself, and only occasionally leaves her room to take a meal. She now wants to go home—to a small apartment where she has lived alone for a number of years. She tells the staff that she will take better care of herself at home, but this is almost certainly not true since she was in the same lethargic and delusional state for some time prior to her admission. In spite of her lethargy and insistence on leaving, she accepts medication and other therapeutic interventions. Her diagnosis is paranoid schizophrenia, and the staff is certain that continued inpatient treatment will ameliorate her condition and will substantially increase the likelihood of her staying on anti-psychotic medication after discharge. It is uncontroversially agreed that Miss Simm is, at present, incapable of making a responsible decision regarding her need for care. But it is also agreed that Miss Simm is not an immediate danger to herself or others and that she can (with the help of a neighbor who brings her groceries) provide for her basic needs. The law requires that Miss Simm must be released as she requests, but the staff is deeply troubled.

Cases like Miss Simm's are more common than might be assumed, and they are deeply problematic because they present us with a serious moral dilemma. Moral dilemmas arise when we are forced to choose between compelling values. In cases like Miss Simm's, concern for the individual's welfare sharply conflicts with recognition of her right to choose her own courses of action. On one hand, it seems right to protect Miss Simm and to pursue her welfare as far as possible; why permit pointless suffering when we have the power to lessen it? But we also have a duty to respect Miss Simm's liberty; having the power to help does not bestow the right to interfere. Whenever we encounter a situation like this, we are involved in the problem of paternalistic interference.[1] What makes paternalism of this sort so problematic is

From the *Journal of Medicine and Philosophy* 9, no. 3 (August 1984): 261–93. Copyright © 1984 by D. Reidel Publishing Company. Reprinted by permission of the author and the publisher.

we can. In the case of Miss Simm (and of persons similarly situated) we are confronted with a person living in a state which is harmful. Her depressed and lethargic state, though not dangerous or otherwise threatening immediate substantial physical injury to her, is harmful (independent of the fact that she is confined), for it involves not only the deprivation of freedom (i.e., she is genuinely a victim of her illness), opportunity, and pleasure; she also suffers greatly—as do most mentally ill persons, although this is too rarely acknowledged in discussions of involuntary confinement (Chodoff, 1976).[26] Since her continuing in such a state is harmful to her, we have an acceptable reason (although not a sufficient one) for paternalistic interference. That is, detaining her would not be an instance of positive or promotive paternalism; it would be an instance of negative or preservative paternalistic interference. What is compelling about Miss Simm's case, however, is not that she suffers a harm which is largely avoidable, but that she suffers a harm which she cannot, because of her present degree of illness, choose freely either to suffer or to avoid. It is this combination of harm and incompetence which so distresses the psychiatric personnel caring for her, and it is this combination of conditions which is captured by the principle of paternalism offered in the first section.

Since Miss Simm is presently incompetent to decide her own needs, and she is in a harmful state, the major conditions for paternalistic interference are met in her case. *If* we can assume that the side constraints of the principle are also met, then we have the moral justification we need to detain her a while longer for her own good.[27] If this conclusion is acceptable, then it has been shown that we are justified in giving priority to beneficence over liberty in the form of involuntary confinement in at least some cases where the individual can provide for his basic needs and is not a danger to himself. Thus, the danger and safety/basic needs criteria are (jointly) too narrow and need to be amended.

The Danger and Safety Criteria as Too Broad

The principle offered in the first section has another implication for mental health law, for it has the incompetence of the intervenee as a necessary condition for the justifiability of *any* paternalistic interference with an adult. Since *parens patriae* confinement is a particular instance of paternalistic interference, it will not be justifiable to confine someone for his own good if it is not shown that the person is incompetent to make a responsible decision on his own hospitalization. Although important recent cases reveal a strong trend toward requiring a formal finding of incompetence to justify the imposition of *treatment*,[28] no such finding is generally required for the imposition of *hospitalization*. In principle, then, many statutes permit the confinement of perfectly competent individuals for their own good, and this is unacceptable.[29]

My argument is *not* that a blanket adjudication of incompetence should be made at commitment hearings. For a person may be incompetent to make a responsible self-regarding decision on protective confinement, but competent to make such decisions on questions of treatment. This is to appeal to an earlier point, viz, that interference justified on paternalistic grounds must be limited to the kinds of incompetence manifested. Also, I am not suggesting that an adjudication of incompetence is necessary for emergency confinement to protect the individual or to protect others. Emergency intervention to protect the intervenee can be justified on the basis of a strong and reasonable presumption of incompetence. And confinement for the protection of others is justifiable on very different grounds, which need not include considerations of competence.[30] What I am suggesting is that for more lengthy confinement to be justified on paternalistic grounds, it must be shown that the individual is incompetent to decide the question of his own hospitalization. Insofar as current criteria for paternalistic con-

finement include no incompetence condition, they are too broad and need to be amended immediately.[31]

CONCLUSION

My attempt here has been to develop a formal principle of justified paternalistic interference with adults and to go some way toward illuminating and applying that principle to a practical problem of considerable importance. But there are pressing questions that remain regarding justifying claims that *each* of the necessary conditions of the principle is met. We need, for example, a sound theory distinguishing harms from which people should be protected from harms rightfully permitted. And how we decide questions of competence is a particularly complicated and urgent matter. I have mentioned some common but unacceptable reasons for considering people incompetent; but positive, explicit guidelines for acceptable judgments of *de facto* incompetence to make certain self-regarding choices need to be developed to serve as justifications for adjudications of legal incompetence in these areas. And the value judgments required by the side constraints bring us into difficult territory since they involve matters like balancing harms, and reasonable people may disagree about such things even when trying to decide from the perspective of the potential intervenee. Clear guides for making these decisions, too, need to be set out. There is, then, still *much* to be done. But I think it can be

done, and, despite the thorny problems involved, that we need not conclude with authors like Morse (1982) that the practice of involuntary civil confinement needs to be abandoned. What it needs is to be practiced with infinitely more care than it too often has been practiced in the past.

The benefit of a principle like the principle of paternalism offered here is that it requires that paternalistic confinement judgments take into careful account the considerations which are morally crucial to so troubling an interference with liberty. A conscientious use of the principle will, at least, rule out morally indefensible interferences with liberty without forcing us to doom some mentally ill persons to a pointless freedom. And requiring that each of the principle's conditions is met will place a firm and needed restraint on the discretion physicians and justices have been allowed.[32]

There will always be the proverbial residue of vexing borderline cases where it is not clear, for example, that the harms of unwanted institutionalization are manifestly less than those of living in freedom. When we come to those remaining cases where agreement cannot be reached, we shall have to allow other kinds of considerations (e.g., different kinds of costs to family and society) to determine the decision.[33] My hope, however, is that a careful use of the principle defended here will lessen such cases without oversimplifying the conflict between liberty and beneficence as regards the mentally impaired.

Notes

*An earlier version of this paper was written while I was a Charlotte W. Newcombe Doctoral Dissertation Fellow. The paper has been greatly improved by the extensive comments of Raymond Martin, Tziporah Kasachkoff, and referees for this *Journal*. I have also been helped by the perceptive comments of Samuel Gorovitz, Patricia Greenspan, and Connie Rosati. What faults remain are entirely my own. The cases of Miss Simm and Mr. Drake are fictional.

[1] I use 'paternalistic interference' here to recognize that all paternalistic behavior need not be of an interfering or what is often called a 'coercive' kind (see Fotion, 1979). Also, I avoid the generally used term 'coercive paternalism' because I am (among other things) concerned about behaviors like paternalistic deception which, it might be argued, are not obviously coercive. Finally, when I use 'paternalism' or one of its cognates alone, I mean it to be elliptical for these interfering kinds

of behaviors or practices, e.g., those which ignore the known or probable self-regarding preferences of intervenees.

[2]The example comes from Gorovitz (1982).

[3]Few existing statutes avoid both objections. See Schwitzgebel (1981).

[4]It needs to be acknowledged that there are strong competing theories of justified paternalism in the literature which merit thorough consideration. Space prevents me from discussing these competitors here, but I do this elsewhere ('Paternalistic interference' [Callahan, 1982]). These views include: Dworkin (1971); Feinberg (1971); Gert and Culver (1976, 1979); Murphy (1974); Hodson (1977); Ten (1971); Bayles (1973, 1978), Carter (1977); and Regan (1973).

[5]I develop this distinction more fully in 'Paternalistic interference' (Callahan, 1982).

[6]This is recognized in *O'Connor v. Donaldson* (1975), pp. 2493–2494:

> May the State confine the mentally ill merely to ensure them a living standard superior to that they enjoy in the private community? That the State has a proper interest in providing care and assistance to the unfortunate goes without saying. But the mere presence of mental illness does not disqualify a person from preferring his home to the comforts of an institution. Moreover, while the State may arguably confine a person to save him from harm, incarceration is rarely if ever a necessary condition for raising the living standards of those capable of surviving safely in freedom.

[7]I borrow here from Gert's account of personal evil (1966, Ch. 3). Also, I shall accept Gert's notion of what counts as a reason. Gert holds that reasons for acting are certain beliefs. Thus, if I believe that having my leg amputated will save my life, or give me pleasure, or allow me to fly on my own power, I have a reason for allowing the surgery. But having my leg amputated *just because I want to* is not to have a reason. "Just because" is to fail to have a reason. This is not to say that any reason for any action will count as a good or adequate reason; I might attach an irrational weight to a desire, or I may have an irrationally held false belief. It is just to say that objective harms are those things which tend to interfere with personal wants and desires, goals and plans and are, therefore, *prima facie* undesirable.

[8]I understand disability as an absence of some capacity or loss of ability to function which any normal adult is expected to have. I realize there are problems of cultural relativity lurking here, but I have in mind basic capacities and abilities, e.g., the capacity to hear or draw inferences, or the ability to walk.

[9]Broader views of harm can be found in Hare (1972, 1976); Lucas (1966); and Stern (1970).

[10]Kleinig concludes that personal harm consists in the impairment of an individual's welfare interests. This is an attractive view which can account for instances of relatively major harm (Kleinig says, "Impairment is thus an interference which has substantial deleterious effects.") But the view will have difficulty capturing cases of minor harm.

[11]See, e.g., Murphy (1974, p. 483); Ten (1971, p. 65); Thompson (1980, p. 251); and Richards (1977, p. 219).

[12]This case is borrowed from Hodson (1977). Under my distinction, this is a case of fraternalism.

[13]This case is hauntingly captured on the video tape, *Please Let Me Die,* developed by Robert White of the University of Texas Medical Branch at Galveston (1974). If this case is controversial, consider cases of heroism (e.g., sacrificing one's life to save another), or even allowing soldiers to enter a battle.

[14]I do not believe that complete necessary and sufficient conditions for showing incompetence can be established in advance of particular cases. But relevant positive considerations might include showing that a person is so disoriented as to time and place that his request to leave the hospital is meaningless, or showing that a person's condition leads him to have irrationally held false beliefs (e.g., that his depression leads him to think that he is unworthy to live or be cared for). Much more work on such positive guidelines needs to be done.

[15]Again, *much* more needs to be said about the incompetence condition. Some interesting recent work has been done by Roth (1979) and Roth et al. (1982). But among the problems with these treatments of incompetence is a failure to distinguish clearly between necessary and sufficient conditions for incompetence, and a confusing introduction of discretion into the analysis of the concept of incompetence (see Roth, 1979, p. 1122). Space prevents me from offering more than the two limiting principles I suggest here, but I discuss the question of incompetence more thoroughly elsewhere, focussing on cognitive incompetence in 'Competence and Competents', and on volitional incompetence in 'Paternalism and Voluntariness' (both in Callahan, 1982). For another recent and helpful discussion of what should *not* count as justifying incompetence judgments see Stromberg and Stone (1983, pp. 301–302).

[16]Allen Buchanan (1978) has shown the enormous difficulties involved in making judgments of relative magnitudes of harm for another. But Buchanan's argument, though convincing as an argument against paternalistic interference with the competent, does not tell against protecting the incompetent. If we allow that paternalistic interference with the incompetent is sometimes justified, we must, however reluctantly, face the vexing problem of balancing harms to another.

[17]I put the point this way because there may be cases where a person's prior judgment can be justifiably overridden. This is because such judgments often rest on the person's forecast of what his future circumstances would be like. If his situation becomes such that it is unlikely that he accurately forecasted his future condition, then his prior judgment need not be conclusive. If, however, his judgment was based on settled values which are independent of empirical considerations (e.g., firm religious values), overriding his prior judgment will be even more difficult to defend.

[18]Livermore et al. (1968) point out that in *U.S. v. Charnizon* (1967), the defendant was found dangerous on the basis of the probability of his issuing checks on insufficient funds. Monahan (1980) mentions the same judgment being made in *Overholser v. Russell* (1960).

[19]Stromberg and Stone (1983, e.g., p. 303 and p. 305) also fail to recognize this.

[20]I am distinguishing here between mental illness and incompetence. A person may be mentally ill in some way, but com-

petent to make self-regarding choices. Further, I am not assuming that the alcoholic is either mentally ill or incompetent, even though I realize that addiction raises serious questions of competence.

[21]I am, as earlier, distinguishing between a presumption and a demonstration of incompetence. Smith may be competent and the alcoholic may be so influenced by his addiction that he is no longer competent. But we are, in general, less reluctant to forcibly intervene in Smith's case than in the alcoholic's case, and this needs to be accounted for.

[22]See, e.g., *Lessard* (1972). In *Addington v. Texas* (1979) however, the Supreme Court ruled that the criminal standard is not constitutionally required for involuntary confinement as a mentally ill and dangerous person. The Court also ruled that the standard of proof must be greater than a preponderance of the evidence. An intermediate standard (clear and convincing evidence) was held to be minimally constitutionally acceptable for involuntary civil confinement statutes.

[23]Stromberg and Stone (1983) have suggested the locution 'recent behavior' instead of 'recent overt act'. What follows is indifferent to this choice, as long as a serious threat (to include verbal and/or menacing behavior) can be interpreted as an overt act.

[24]It should be noted, however, that a study by Wenk and Emrich (1972) suggests that the best predictor of violent behavior is a previous incident of violence.

[25]Someone may take issue with my use of 'unfair' here. But my view is just that justice and utility can conflict; thus an act can be unjust but justified. This view is not novel (see, e.g., Feinberg, 1970b, p. 45).

[26]Alan Stone (1982) is exceptionally sensitive to this, as well as the tension between liberty and beneficence as regards the mentally disabled.

[27]This, of course, is a *large* assumption, made here for the sake of the argument, which is to establish formal requirements for justified paternalistic confinement. The questions involved in meeting the side constraints are, like questions pertaining to incompetence, urgent and difficult. In practice, meeting these constraints must include numerous considerations regarding conditions in the particular institution, the feasibility of less restrictive alternatives, likelihood of improvement, etc. For an excellent articulation of the difficult questions here, see Morse (1982).

[28]See, e.g., *Rennie v. Klein* (1978); *Rogers v. Okin* (1979); *In re K. K. B.* (1980); and *Roth v. Clarke* (1980). Discussions of these cases can be found in the American Bar Association's *Mental Disability Law Reporter,* 1980.

[29]This unacceptability has been noticed before. See, for example, the *Harvard Law Review,* 1977, pp. 1212–1219, and the American Bar Association's 1977, p. 90.

[30]Treatment for the protection of others is quite another matter. But this takes us into questions of behavior modification which I cannot take up here.

[31]This paper goes to press too late to incorporate a detailed discussion of the Model Commitment Law just suggested by Stromberg and Stone (1983). Although, from the perspective of the principle defended here, there are still serious inadequacies in the Model Law, Stromberg and Stone are thorough and offer the most careful (and acceptable) criteria for involuntary civil confinement I have yet seen.

[32]See Allen *et al.* (1968, p. 52) for an example:

> The hearings began at 2.00 p.m.—an hour and five minutes for 40 persons; about a minute and a half per patient! All the doctors were sworn . . . prior to testifying. As each case was called, the doctor would give the height, weight, and color of hair and eyes of the patient. These data are for the form sent to the Department of Public Safety concerning drivers' licenses. Next, the Judge would read the patient's name and state the dates of medical examination. Without pausing or looking up he would then read to the doctors, apparently from the Order of Commitment, "Is it your opinion and both of you agree that—— is a mentally ill person and needs medical care and treatment for his own welfare and protection or the protection of others and is mentally incompetent?" The doctor answered "yes" and the next case would be called in like fashion. . . . All of the proposed patients were ordered indefinitely committed and all were found to be incompetent. . . .

[33]I deal with the question of combining paternalistic and non-paternalistic reasons to justify liberty-limiting legislation in 'Legal paternalism' (Callahan, 1982).

References

Addington v. Texas: 1979, 441 U.S. 418.

Allen, R., Zenoff, E., and Weihofen, H.: 1968, *Mental Impairment and Incompetency,* Prentice-Hall, Englewood Cliffs, N.J.

American Bar Association: 1977, 'Civil commitment', *Mental Disability Law Reporter* 2, 75–126.

American Bar Association: 1980, 'Case reports', *Mental Disability Law Reporter,* 4, Numbers 1 and 2.

Bayles, M.: 1978, *Principles of Legislation,* Wayne State University Press, Detroit.

Bayles, M.: 1973, 'Criminal paternalism', in J. R. Pennock and J. W. Chapman (eds.), *Nomos XV: The Limits of Law,* Aldine-Atherton, New York, pp. 174–188.

Buchanan, A.: 1978, 'Medical paternalism', *Philosophy and Public Affairs* 7, 370–390.

Callahan, J. C.: 1982, *On Justifying Paternalistic Interference With Adults,* Ph.D. Dissertation, University of Maryland.

Carter, R.: 1977, 'Justifying paternalism', *Canadian Journal of Philosophy* 7, 133–145.

Chodoff, P.: 1976, 'The case for involuntary hospitalization of the mentally ill', *American Journal of Psychiatry* 133, 496–501.

Colyar v. Third Judicial Court for Salt Lake County: 1979, 469 F. Supp. 431 D. Utah, D.C.

Cross v. Harris: 1969, 418 F. 2d 1099, D.C. Cir.

Dworkin, G.: 1971, 'Paternalism', in R. A. Wasserstrom (ed.), *Morality and the Law,* Wadsworth, Belmont, Cal., pp. 107–126.

Feinberg, J.: 1970a, 'Crime clutchability and individuated treatment', in J. Feinberg, *Doing and Deserving,* Princeton University Press, Princeton, pp. 252–271.

Feinberg, J.: 1970b, 'On being "morally speaking a murderer"', in J. Feinberg, *Doing and Deserving,* Princeton University Press, Princeton, pp. 38–54.

Fotion, N.: 1979, 'Paternalism', *Ethics* 89, 191–198.

Gert, B.: 1966, *The Moral Rules,* Harper and Row, New York.

Gert, B. and Culver, C.: 1979, 'The justification of paternalism', *Ethics* 89, 199–210.

Gert, B. and Culver, C.: 1976, 'Paternalistic behavior', *Philosophy and Public Affairs* 6, 45–57.

Gewirth, A.: 1978, *Reason and Morality,* University of Chicago Press, Chicago.

Gorovitz, S.: 1982, *Doctors' Dilemmas: Moral Conflict and Medical Care,* Macmillan, New York.

Hare, R. M.: 1976, 'Ethical theory and utilitarianism', in H. D. Lewis (ed.), *Contemporary British Philosophy 4th Series,* Allen and Unwin, London, pp. 130–131.

Hare, R. M.: 1972, 'Wrongness and harm', in R. M. Hare (ed.), *Essays on the Moral Concepts,* University of California Press, Berkeley, pp. 92–109.

Harvard Law Review: 1974, 'Note: developments in the law—civil commitment of the mentally ill', *Harvard Law Review* 87, 1190–1406.

Hodson, J.: 1977, 'The principle of paternalism', *American Philosophical Quarterly* 14, 61–69.

In re K. K. B.: 1980, No. 51, 467 Okla. Sup. Ct.

Kleinig J.: 1978, 'Crime and the concept of harm', *American Philosophical Quarterly* 15, 27–37.

LaForet, E. G.: 1976, 'The fiction of informed consent', *Journal of the American Medical Association* 235, 1579–1585.

Lessard v. Schmidt: 1972, 349 F. Supp. 1078, E. D. Wis.

Livermore, J., Malmquist, C., and Meehl, P.: 1968, 'On the justifications for civil commitment', *University of Pennsylvania Law Review,* 117, 75–96.

Lucas, J. R.: 1966, *The Principles of Politics,* Oxford University Press, New York.

Mill, J. S.: 1859, *On Liberty,* Bobbs-Merrill, (1956), New York.

Monahan, J.: 1980, *The Clinical Prediction of Violent Behavior,* National Institute of Mental Health, Rockville, MD.

Morse, S.: 1982, 'A preference for liberty: the case against involuntary commitment of the mentally disordered', *California Law Review* 70, 54–106.

Murphy, J.: 1974, 'Incompetence and paternalism', *Archiv für Rechts- und Sozialphilosophie* 60, 465–485.

O'Connor v. Donaldson: 1975, 422 U.S. 563.

Regan, D.: 1973, 'Justifications for paternalism', in J. R. Pennock and J. W. Chapman (eds.), *Nomos XV: The Limits of Law,* Aldine-Atherton, New York, pp. 189–210.

Rennie v. Klein: 1978, 476 F. Supp. 1294, D. N.J.

Richards, D.: 1977, *The Moral Criticism of Law,* Dickenson, Encino, CA.

Rogers v. Okin: 1979, 478 F. Supp. 1342, D. Mass.

Roth, L.: 1979, 'A commitment law for patients, doctors, and lawyers', *American Journal of Psychiatry* 136, 1121–1127.

Roth, L., Lidz, C., Meisel, A., Soloff, P., Kaufman, K., Spiker, D. and Foster, F.: 1982, 'Competency to decide about treatment or research', *International Journal of Law and Psychiatry* 5, 29–50.

Roth v. Clarke: 1980, No. 79–449, B.D. Pa.

Schwitzgebel, R.: 1981, 'Survey of state commitment statutes', in A. McGarry, R. Schwitzgebel, P. Lipsett, and D. Lelos, *Civil Commitment and Social Policy: An Evaluation of the Massachusetts Mental Health Reform Act of 1970,* Department of Health and Human Services, Rockville, MD, pp. 47–83.

Steadman, H.: 1980, 'The right not to be a false positive: problems in the application of the dangerousness standard', *Psychiatric Quarterly* 52, 84–99.

Stern, L.: 1970, 'Deserved punishment, deserved harm, deserved blame', *Philosophy* 45, 317–329.

Stone, A.: 1982, 'Psychiatric abuse and legal reform: two ways to make a bad situation worse', *International Journal of Law and Psychiatry* 5, 9–28.

Stromberg, C. and Stone, A.: 1983, 'A model state law on civil commitment of the mentally ill', *Harvard Journal on Legislation* 20, 275–396.

Taylor, R.: 1973, *Freedom, Anarchy, and the Law,* Prentice-Hall, Englewood Cliffs, N.J.

Ten, C.: 1971, 'Paternalism and morality', *Ratio* 13, 55–66.

Thompson, D.: 1980, 'Paternalism in law, medicine and public policy', in D. Callahan and S. Bok (eds.), *Ethics Teaching in Higher Education,* Plenum, New York, pp. 245–275.

United States ex rel. Matthew v. Nelson: 1978, 461 F. Supp. 707, N.D. Ill.

Wenk, E. and Emrich, R.: 1972, 'Assaultive youth: an exploratory study of assaultive experience and assaultive potential of California youth authority wards', *Journal of Research in Crime and Delinquency* 9, 171–196.

Control by Information: Psychotherapy

Perry London

Perry London is professor of education in the Program in Counseling and Consulting Psychology at the Harvard Graduate School of Education. He has written extensively about values in psychotherapy, including his Behavior Control *(Harper and Row, 1969) and* The Modes and Morals of Psychotherapy *(Holt, Rinehart and Winston, 1964).*

London has defined behavior control as "the ability to get someone to do one's bidding." He examines two forms of behavior control used in psychotherapy for their ethical basis and therapeutic effectiveness. (1) Insight therapy consists in influencing behavior through information. All forms of "talk therapy" attempt to give patients insight into the relationship between their motivation and their behavior, assuming that this will give them greater control. London identifies the major problems of insight therapy. (2) Behavior modification, or "action therapy," consists in employing various conditioning techniques to alter the behavior of patients. London identifies and points out the strengths and weaknesses of various forms of behavior modification.

INSIGHT THERAPY

The basic idea that guides all insight therapies (though subject to many variations and polemics of interpretation, expansion, and detail) is that *motives dictate behavior;* this means that disordered behavior is the result of peculiarities inside the individual. To treat such disorders successfully, it is argued, the therapist must seek out the inner states that underlie the surface difficulties and, by bringing them to light, loosen the bond between them and the disordered behavior they produce. Stated differently, the therapist tries to lead the patient to some insight into the relationship between his motivations and his behavior, on the assumption that this insight will give him greater control over them than he previously had.

Insight means understanding. All the techniques of insight therapy try to lead the patient to greater understanding of himself, particularly those aspects of himself which have not been fully conscious or which he has been unable previously to face in a direct and forthright manner. As the patient himself sees it, he is trying to find out why

he acts and feels the way he does, expecting that the discovery will free him of the troubles that brought him to therapy in the first place.

In the course of the inquiry, which sometimes takes hundreds of hours spread over several years, he will probably explore not only the reasons for his original problem, but his feelings and experiences of inhibition, anxiety, guilt, hostility, anger, pleasure, competence, self-esteem, lust, sorrow, love, jealousy, and dependency in all his important interpersonal relationships and many less important ones; and he may experience these same feelings in the therapy session itself and in relation to the psychotherapist. With luck, patience, and effort, he may get rid of his symptoms, too, but he will gain self-understanding in any case.

Understanding the basis of one's own behavior, of course, makes that behavior more meaningful; thus insight therapy comes to be regarded by most of its adherents as a technique which not only frees the patient of disabling symptoms but which also, by seeking the meaning of his acts, helps to make his whole life more meaningful. This characteristic of insight therapy gives it its greatest appeal in modern times, especially in the form of existential psychotherapy, which maintains its popularity unblemished, while its actual

but only the therapist chooses the interpretations he makes of them. Whether those interpretations support or challenge the patient's behavior patterns, his acceptance of them reflects, to that extent, his acquiescence to the therapist's controlling influence.

The extent to which the patient is likely to buy the therapist's interpretations, with whatever that implies for his behavior, probably depends more on their personal relationship than on any other single factor, including the wisdom or accuracy of the interpretation. The importance of the therapeutic relationship is widely recognized by insight therapists, who ostensibly use it as a means of promoting further self-understanding rather than of promoting their interpretations. The classic device for producing a warm, friendly atmosphere in all psychotherapy is simply listening sympathetically to what the patient says. Action therapists identify sympathetic listening as one of many techniques called "reinforcement withdrawal," but its operations and effects are the same by any name. It boosts people's tendency to reveal themselves to the therapist and to change because of him. If someone expects to be derided, criticized, or condemned for exposing his thoughts, feelings, or experiences, for example, he becomes anxious and clams up. If he does reveal himself, however, and no such unpleasant result occurs, the anxiety diminishes or disappears (is extinguished) and he feels more free to open up to his listener. John Dollard and Neal Miller, then of Yale University, have pointed out that this kind of reinforcement withdrawal is a common technique of insight therapy. By simply listening to his patient without reacting negatively to what he says, the therapist avoids reinforcing the patient's anxieties about self-revelation and willy-nilly makes it easier for him to talk.

Sympathetic listening has a strong seductive effect on people in ordinary life situations as well as in psychotherapy. If it is difficult for someone to talk to people, then the more need he feels to

do so and the more he expects an unsympathetic response if he does, the more likely it is that actually unloading to an unexpectedly sympathetic listener will produce in him strong feelings of gratitude and even affection toward that person. The shrewd listener, if he chooses, may then exploit those positive feelings to get money, sex, or other largesse from his grateful "client"—and may say, in so doing, that he has not actually "done anything" to the other person. The intuitive recognition of this principle is one of the main things that sends professional confidence men after *lonely* victims who have nobody to talk to. Indeed, the ability to systematically elicit trusting and affectionate reactions is what makes them confidence men. In this connection, James H. Bryan, of Northwestern University, and I found, in an extensive interview study of American call girls, that an important motive of some girls to attach themselves to procurers, give them all the money they earn, and stay hopelessly and futilely "in love" with them despite the general shabby treatment received at their hands is that they provide a sympathetic ear. A pimp is, if nothing else, "somebody to talk to," especially for a girl who fears to discuss her work publicly, and especially in the cold and lonely hours before dawn. For many people, loneliness mostly means "not having somebody to talk to."

Most psychotherapists use sympathetic listening as a general means of fostering a good relationship with patients, but psychoanalysts make more precise use of it, in combination with their deliberate anonymity, to produce transference reactions. "Transference" is the experience of projecting onto the analyst the attributes of other people who are important in one's life and then feeling the same emotions toward him which the other people arouse. A patient may come to believe, for example, that the psychoanalyst is just like his cruel father, and then begin to feel furious and fearful toward him just as he feels toward his father. Transference occurs to some extent in any intimate personal relationship, but psychoanaly-

sis makes deliberate and ingenious use of it to help the patient expose feelings that have been frightening him and impairing his relationships with others. Once exposed, they can be analyzed and the transference resolved.

The therapist's personal anonymity helps promote the transference reaction by withholding information which would give the patient a realistic basis for evaluating and responding to him. Since the patient knows little about the analyst's life or what he is really like, the things he attributes to the analyst and the emotions he has toward him must be taken from his experience with other people. One reason Freud began sitting out of sight of his patients was to minimize the influence of his own expressive gestures and reactions on them (he also found it wearing to have to look-at and be-looked-at for many hours every day).

The Consequences and Conundrums of Control by Insight

Insight therapy has been subjected to many criticisms on both technical and moral grounds. In terms of its status as behavior-control technology, these reduce to two complementary arguments. The first says that it is an ineffective means of controlling behavior; the second that, where it does work, its effects are obtained immorally, either by seducing the patient away from his original purposes or seductively changing his purposes to fit his pecularities. Both arguments have some merit.

Insight therapy is clearly a poor means of symptom control; after almost seventy years of use, there are still few indications that uncovering motives and expanding of self-understanding really confer much therapeutic power over most troubling symptoms. Studies of therapy's effectiveness have proved equivocal, by and large. A few report fair results; others show little evidence that therapy "works" in the sense of removing symptoms. The fact that intelligent, educated, sophisticated people tend to stay in therapy for a long time anyway suggests that it works in some other sense which is not measured by most research into its effectiveness. It is here that the morality of insight therapy is challenged.

By assuming that problems of motive underlie the symptoms that bring people into psychotherapy, the insight therapist inevitably tries to move the patient toward a concern with his motivations. But it was concern with symptoms, more than with motives, that brought him to treatment in the first place. If it then turns out that the treatment of motivation fails to cure the symptom, the therapist finds himself seductively selling a somewhat different product than the patient intended to buy—understanding instead of relief.

While seduction for this purpose may be reproachable, the product may still be worthwhile, supporting the claim that insight therapy helps to resolve people's existential dilemmas even when it fails to cure their symptoms. Many patients who enter therapy at first wishing only to be free of their symptomatic difficulties later discover that "the quest for meaning," or what James Bugental calls the "search for authenticity," is really more important in their lives. In such cases, the patient is now in the position of saying that though the symptom has not been treated, he is no longer troubled by it. Here, therapy has changed the patient's needs to suit the symptom instead of curing the symptom to suit the patient's needs.

There is often little else that it can do, for the very nature of insight therapy, let alone the scientific and moral rationales of its practitioners, makes it function as a very general, nonspecific means of behavior control, which tends either to radically alter people's life styles or to leave them unaffected. A person is much more likely to change his career as a result of insight therapy than to lose a nervous tic, more likely to move away from home, shift his political position, or alter his religious convictions as a result of psychoanalysis than to give up phobias, smoking, homosexuality, or compulsive hand washing.

One patient, who entered therapy because he was afraid to drive on Los Angeles freeways, after one year of treatment divorced his wife, successfully changed careers, and radically altered some important patterns of social relationships—but still could not drive on the freeways. He considered his therapy successful, even though it never satisfied his initial purpose.

Both the assumptions and methods of insight therapy make it most effective only on broad targets. Its first assumption is that the only proper locus of behavior control is the patient himself, which means that the only proper behavior control is self-control. Second, it assumes that self-control results from expanding consciousness; and third, that consciousness can be expanded by verbal means. All the techniques of insight therapies serve these ends, at once promoting the patient's search of himself and avoiding any sharing of responsibility with the therapist for what he finds. Free association and reflection both leave the patient in control of his own activity; the therapist, by maintaining anonymity and interpreting the transference, avoids exercising undue influence on him. "Undue influence" means anything the therapist does that dictates what the patient should do, even if doing it might help cure his symptoms. The source of control is more important to the insight therapist than is the act of control. If it cannot be vested in the patient himself, he believes, then it cannot legitimately be achieved at all. And strict adherence to the ground rules of the system not only makes therapy depend entirely on consciousness-expanding methods, but demands in turn that these must work through consciousness alone, pure and unadorned, without external props such as drugs. The aim is not simply to treat the patient, but to do so without *manipulating* him.

Regarding manipulation as immoral gives insight therapists some defense against some critics. If they are selling something the patient did not originally intend to buy—self-understanding instead of symptom relief—they are still selling something of value in its own right; and the pa-

tient himself is responsible for whether or not he wants to take it. If uncovering motives does not always relieve symptoms, it is still wrong to remove symptoms by indecent means, even though they work. Finally, the quest for meaning is more important than the lust for contentment, and if the patient deliberately and meaningfully changes himself to live with his symptom, one cannot gainsay the therapy on that account. If a man loses his ability to make money, talks to a therapist because of it, and discovers that his life is made more meaningful by a new career that can never make him rich, it is naïve (or worse) to say that the treatment failed. The only control which insight therapists promote, by their lights, is self-control.

Most observers of insight therapy, on the other hand, would say that it does not work quite so purely as it pretends and that insight therapists use far more influence on their patients than they realize. There is some evidence to that effect in research reports that patients tend to identify with their therapists, gradually developing similar personal values.

It is no wonder that they should. For no matter how tentatively he approaches the patient, nor how pure his motives *not* to control or dominate, the insight therapist cannot help but address what he himself considers the most salient material presented to him. Eventually, the patient's ideas of salience must largely correspond to his or the interaction cannot continue. What is more, the inherent imbalance in the relationship, where one person is always helping and the other receiving help, makes the patient look up to the therapist as a potential authority, model, or inspiration, no matter how little he knows of the therapist's outside life. Almost inevitably, he knows plenty about the therapist's attitudes toward the things that count most in his own life, and it is those attitudes that he is most likely to absorb.

This says, in short, that control in insight therapy works by a combination of subtle suasion and benign neutrality; the one turns the patient's attention to whatever the therapist thinks impor-

tant, the other encourages him to adopt whatever attitude he thinks the therapist has. All this happens without the therapist's trying to exert control; were he to try, he might have more powerful or precise effects than he usually does.

Whether or not they wish to control their patients, at all events, insight therapists must take some responsibility for relieving symptoms as long as they hang out shingles telling symptom-ridden people to come to them for help. And it is this responsibility which their gentle techniques will not support, and with respect to which they are ill-defended, regardless how much either therapists or patients think of them. Without a good technology for symptom relief or a disclaimer of the ability to provide it, the moralistic refusal to manipulate becomes the ultimate manipulation because it is patently irrelevant grounds for keeping somebody in therapy. Suppose a doctor treated appendicitis by feeding patients bananas and, when they died, defended himself by saying it would have been wrong to feed them apples! Insight therapists are thoroughly in the business of controlling behavior, like it or not, but the stringent restrictions of their theories on their activities prevents this control from being exercised over symptoms. Allegiance to those theories leaves them useful agents of control in other respects, perhaps even in more important ones, but it paralyzes or invalidates their symptom-curing role.

It is over symptom relief in particular that action therapies have registered a legitimate complaint against insight methods. Making this their sole criterion of therapeutic success, they have built a strong competitive system, leading to a new dimension of control through information.

ACTION THERAPY

In technical procedures, action therapies fall toward the opposite pole from the insight therapies. Instead of concentrating chiefly on the motives that produced a person's symptoms, they tend to focus treatment on the symptoms proper without much concern over their origins or meaning. Instead of seating responsibility for treatment with the patient, they place it entirely with the therapist. Instead of focusing on the patient's existential concerns, they attend only to his functioning and to how his symptoms interfere with it. Instead of handling therapy as a means of aiding self-understanding, they view it as a *planned* attack on disorder in which it hardly matters whether any insight comes about. Most symptoms, they believe, are really habit patterns which, according to Hans Eysenck, the distinguished British psychologist who coined the term "behavior therapy," are learned "through a process of conditioning and capable of being extinguished through several techniques of demonstrated effectiveness in the laboratory. . . . Treatment is directed entirely to the symptoms, as distinguished from psychotherapy with its stress on hypothetical underlying complexes and disease processes."

Two of the leading expositors of action therapy are Joseph Wolpe and Arnold Lazarus, both currently at Temple University and both practitioners as well as researchers. They similarly define the field as the use of "experimentally established principles of learning" for overcoming "persistent maladaptive habits." In fact, action therapies are less critically tied to scientific theories or laboratory studies of learning than their expositors would like to believe. Even so, they are broadly based on some established principles of learning that serve as useful guidelines for planning specific therapeutic efforts. Like most practical therapists, actionists are more concerned about the value of their methods for treating people than about the scientific status or origins of those methods.

Behavior is behavior, and action therapy, as a competing system, is used for the same sets of behavior as insight therapy, differing in how it works and in what it accomplishes, not in what it attempts. Their different perspectives on human nature and psychological theory are less important than their technical differences, which

kinds of counterconditioning

reduce to a single issue: the ability to exert *precise* control over *specific* behavior problems. Action therapies assail the insight therapies as imprecise, which means lacking control power. They make relief or symptoms the main criterion for therapeutic success because it is the most visible index of ability to control behavior. By its efforts at precision, action therapy begins to meet the criteria of a true technology. What is gained or lost by having one depends on what it can do and where it leads.

Techniques of Action Therapy

There is no overstating the cardinal rule of all action therapy technique: be specific. All its methods, therefore, depend upon the same clear sequence of operations. First, define the problem precisely; next, calculate a specific way to attack it; then, do what you planned; finally, see how it worked. The problems, symptoms, or troubles (as you please) to be defined, and the ins and outs of evaluating how the treatments worked, are the same for all kinds of therapy; the actionist's specific ways of attacking them are less familiar to most people. Two of the main ones, "counterconditioning" and "extinction," are used chiefly to relieve extreme fears (phobias), anxiety, and sexual problems. A third, called "behavior shaping," or "*operant* methods," is used mostly for training desired habit patterns or skills. All of them claim pronounced effectiveness, and sometimes in very short order, like a single treatment session.

Counterconditioning means replacing one feeling or behavior with another that is antithetical to it. In treatment, this generally means replacing a useless or bad feeling with a constructive or pleasurable one. The helpless anxiety of a milquetoastish employee is turned into justified, constructive anger at an unreasonable supervisor. The relentless desire to guzzle whisky is converted to nausea at the sight of it. The obsessive preoccupation of a college sophomore over what other people think of her is exchanged for a calmly realistic recognition of what difference it makes in different situations.

There are several ways to do counterconditioning; most of them are associated with the contemporary work of Joseph Wolpe, but they originate, as he points out, in treatments reported as early as 1924.

Sexual impotence can be helped by "discriminative training," which is used almost exclusively for such problems. It consists basically of teaching a patient to recognize which sexual encounters are likely to be frightening and disabling, to tell them apart from those likely to be gratifying, and to adapt his behavior to his understanding. As Wolpe describes it, the patient is taught to attempt sexual relations *only* when "he has an unmistakable, positive desire to do so, for otherwise he may very well consolidate, or even extend, his sexual inhibition." He is taught to seek out people with whom he can be aroused in

a desirable way . . . and when in the company of one of them, to "let himself go" as freely as the circumstances allow. . . . If he is able to act according to plan, he experiences a gradual increase in sexual responsiveness to the kind of situation of which he has made use . . . [and] the range of situations in which lovemaking may occur is thus progressively extended as the anxiety potentials of stimuli diminish. . . .

For people who are easily intimidated and exploited by others, a very common complaint of psychotherapy patients, "assertive training" is the method of choice. In it, the patient is taught when and how to respond to others with (verbal) aggression, practices doing so in the therapy sessions, and applies his training in real life, reviewing and rehearsing appropriate aggression with the therapist's coaching. Assertion is not only used to teach aggression; Wolpe also uses it to facilitate "the outward expression of friendly, affectionate, and other nonanxious feelings" and for "gaining control of an interpersonal relationship by means subtler than overt assertiveness." For the latter, he takes Stephen Potter's *Gamesman-*

ship as a worthy text and recommends Potter's works unhesitatingly "to patients who seem likely to profit from reading them."

Like all counterconditioning methods, assertive training is based on the assumption that anxiety inhibits self-expression. Practicing assertion inhibits anxiety, which gives the patient greater latitude to express himself in his dealings with others.

The reduction of general, or "free-floating," anxiety is done by "conditioned avoidance" methods. Wolpe describes one, rarely used in practice, which works by subjecting the patient repeatedly to a harmless but painful electric shock. Before shocking him, the therapist tells the patient that if he finds the shock excessive, he can terminate it by saying "calm." Continued over many trials, the word "calm" becomes associated with (conditioned to) pain reduction so that merely thinking or saying it has a soothing effect. Presumably, this conditioning generalizes beyond the consulting room, so that whenever the patient is confronted with intense anxiety, he can reduce it by saying "calm."

Conditioned avoidance can also be used to reduce the pleasure of behavior patterns that patients wish to get rid of. To free a man of homosexual desires, for example, the electric shock is connected with pictures of nude males. Each time the patient is aroused by a picture, he is shocked, till eventually the pleasure of the picture is destroyed by coupling it with pain. The resulting "unlust" generalizes to real-life situations where he faces homosexual stimulation.

Extinction methods work by making head-on attacks on problems rather than by replacing old feelings with new ones. In practice, three techniques are recommended. Where the symptom is pleasant or gratifying to its perpetrator, as is common in the behavior problems of children, remove the reward; this is called "reinforcement withdrawal." Where the problem is anxiety, as in phobias, eliminate the fear, either by gently manipulating the patient's imagination with "system-

atic desensitization," or by "burning out" his capacity for neurotic anxiety with "implosive therapy."

The treatment of bedtime temper trantrums illustrates reinforcement withdrawal. When children have such tantrums, typically, they scream and rage after their parents have left the room; this brings the parents back and permits the children to stay up longer, which reinforces (rewards) their having yelled in the first place. But if the parents put the child to sleep in a leisurely fashion, leave the room, and do not return when he rages, he will gradually give up the tantrum. C. D. Williams, writing in the *Journal of Abnormal and Social Psychology,* charted changes in crying during one such treatment. On the first night of his parents' "cold turkey" treatment, the little boy in question screamed for forty-five minutes before falling asleep. On the second, he went to sleep immediately, cried for ten minutes on the third, and so forth till, by the tenth night, he neither whimpered or cried but even smiled when his parents bade him goodnight and left the room.

The most widely used, tested, and evidently successful single technique of action therapy is systematic desensitization. Originally developed by Joseph Wolpe, desensitization is a method of using imagination to dissolve anxiety, especially in phobias. It works as follows: The patient and therapist jointly compose a list of things that arouse anxiety, ranking them from least to most frightening. The patient is trained, sometimes with hypnosis, to relax deeply; then, the therapist describes the lowest ranking item on the list and asks him to imagine it vividly. If he can do so without getting upset, he is given a description of the next item and told to imagine it. When any image starts to make the patient tense, he signals the therapist, who then backs up to an earlier one. This goes on from session to session until the most frightening item finally fails to disturb the patient's relaxed state in the session and, from the evidence at hand, he is no longer troubled by the real-life fears outside of it.

Implosive therapy serves the same purpose as desensitization, but it looks dramatically different. Instead of letting the tantrum, phobia, or whatever wear itself out, this method tries to create an internal explosion (implosion) of anxiety, frightening the patient as much as possible without letting any actual harm come to him. As in desensitization, the therapist and patient decide what things are more and less anxiety-arousing, and the therapist then gets the patient to imagine them. Unlike desensitization, however, the implosive therapist starts at the top of the list, with the most frightening items; he describes them as intensively and fearsomely as he can, trying to terrify rather than soothe the patient. The principle involved is a kind of elegant distortion of the adage "Sticks and stones may break my bones, but words will never hurt me." Since phobic anxiety is, by definition, "neurotic"—that is, unrealistic—its repeated experience from mere words, where its dread consequences go unrealized, causes its extinction. Treatment is completed when the therapist can no longer frighten the patient with his scary stories. Implosive therapy was devised by Thomas Stampfl less than ten years ago and is just beginning to be widely known in psychotherapy literature.

The fact that desensitization and implosion are both used on the same types of problems and that both seem to work very well is hard to explain, since they appear to be diametric opposites, the one soothing, the other terrifying. Which is really a better technique for whom, or whether it matters, is a moot point.

Critics of implosive therapy sometimes fear that, in the hands of a sufficiently dramatic practitioner, patients may be frightened into heart attacks or into being "overwhelmed with anxiety"—that is, scared out of their wits. No such event has yet been reported, perhaps because implosive therapists are not good enough at their own game or because frightening words really don't hurt as much as people fear they will.

An increasingly popular variant of consulting-room extinction methods has therapists assigning homework to patients or going with them to confront the things that frighten them, riding together in elevators, airplanes, or subways, or giving them other live practice with experiences that help overcome their fears. In one such case, extreme claustrophobia was cured by having the patient practice staying alone in a tiny room, locked from the outside, while bound hand and foot in a zippered sleeping bag. As everyone knows who has learned any dangerous skills, people adapt to frightening circumstances if they are exposed enough to them without being hurt.

Behavior shaping is derived from the work of B. F. Skinner, who, though not a psychotherapist, has devised important training methods with promising applications to psychotherapy. Behavior shaping is used for chronic conditions which require complex changes in activity. This includes not only many symptoms of neuroses and psychoses, but behavior problems as narrow as stuttering, at one extreme, and as broad as juvenile delinquency, school failure, and general social adjustment at the other.

Two simple principles form the basis for all behavior-shaping operations. First, the principle of reinforcement, common to all action therapies, which says that an organism will learn to repeat an act for which it is rewarded and to avoid one for which it is ignored or punished. The second principle, that of learning by "successive approximation," says that complicated behavior patterns, especially "skillful" ones, are learned gradually, in small steps that come closer and closer to an optimal level of performance.

To make practical use of these principles, the therapist must know what his patient finds rewarding or unpleasant. He must have enough control over the environment so that he can provide or withhold these rewards at will, increasing them when the desired behavior increases and withholding them when undesirable behavior appears. He might also, of course, use punishment to control undesirable behavior. But punishment, unless applied with great skill, often has unexpected effects. The Skinnerian therapist, there-

fore, commonly works only with reward and need, manipulating the one to satisfy the other.

The technique requires more ingenuity and inventiveness than do any other action therapies and may take longer to work. Some impressive results have nevertheless been achieved by behavior shaping. At the University of Virginia, Bachrach, Erwin, and Mohr were able to induce a person with anorexia nervosa (a form of depresson in which food is refused) to eat and gain weight, by controlling the availability of things she found rewarding, like listening to music and chitchatting with people. Willard Mainord, at the University of Louisville, and others have used behavior-shaping methods for therapeutic groups and therapeutic hospital wards. Still others have used them to teach parents and teachers how to manage behavior problems in children. Since each unit of behavior that can be taught by behavior shaping tends to be very small, however, the method has not yet proved as effective with chronic psychotics as was originally hoped. But even here it is more promising than not. Ivar Lovaas and his collaborators at the University of California at Los Angeles have had more success in teaching schizophrenic children different intellectual and social skills than have most other workers; they have done so with supposedly hopeless cases; and they have notably succeeded in teaching nonprofessionals to perform the same therapeutic functions that Lovaas's senior team members can do—which gives behavior-shaping methods tremendous economic promise. Their profound importance for behavior control in general becomes even plainer . . . as aspects of conditioning.

Action therapies are easier to evaluate as control systems than are insight therapies because they are more explicitly designed to function as such. The techniques of action take for granted that the proper locus of behavior control belongs with the therapist. He must decide what needs to be done to help (change) the patient, and he is obliged to direct the doing. His job is to give the patient not self-control but symptom relief, which can be done by many different means, only one of which is verbal; whatever works without damaging the patient is acceptable. The expansion of consciousness is usually irrelevant, occasionally harmful, and rarely valuable for this purpose.

Skill at manipulation, anathema to insight therapy, is the moral prize beyond purchase of the actionists, whose title to exercise control is as certain to them as their responsibility for healing is clear. To them, successful manipulation is not merely a useful tactic but a moral imperative which they must satisfy to have the right to offer help at all. Therapeutic intervention in the patient's life is the goal and *raison d'être* for their activity. The ability to do so successfully demonstrates their technological promise, makes of action therapies much more than merely optimistic cook books for cooling people's anxieties or reshaping their appetites or making them happy, and anticipates the moral quandaries that all behavior technologies will sometime face.

Action therapy is not a rudely empirical enterprise with no theoretical foundations, but its emphasis on finding practical applications makes theory sometimes seem an afterthought. Advocates of action have no more mortgage than do insight therapists on the belief in cause-and-effect relationships, for example; their practical use of the idea, however, leads them to plan their therapeutic work more precisely and to judge it by standards that can be understood by everyone. In so doing, they sometimes overlook or oversimplify complexities of human nature and experience, inadvertently fictionalizing them. But these fictions are more valuable for therapeutic use than most of those available until now, for action therapies have been comparatively much more successful with many problems than insight treatments have been.

The most important fact that separates the action therapies irrevocably from all their predecessors, regardless of how much Adler, Jung, Freud, Rogers, Sullivan, and all the rest dispute among themselves, is that the actionists have

firmly linked the things they do to those they undertake to treat. One technique is best for sex, they say, another for tantrums; this for timidity and that for terror; and a third for aggression or stuttering or quietly burbling insanity. And once this claim can be put forth with any measure of its truth in evidence, then a technology has been founded, regardless of how limited it may be. This has happened in the case of action therapies not because their methods have been devised from novel theories, which they have not, or because the methods themselves are very novel, which they are not, or because they are so successful, which they sometimes are and sometimes aren't—but because they have transcended, in their multiplicity, what was hitherto the common coin of all psychotherapies, the use of language as the singular medium of communication and control. . . .

The Control of Behavior

George H. Kieffer

A biographical sketch of George H. Kieffer is given on page 196.

Kieffer examines a number of physically intrusive treatments for psychiatric problems, such as (1) electroshock or electroconvulsive therapy; (2) electrostimulation, which involves implanting activated electrodes in the brain; (3) psychosurgery, in which brain tissue is altered or destroyed for the purpose of modifying behavior; and (4) psychopharmacology, the use of psychotropic medication.

FACT AND FANTASY OF BEHAVIOR CONTROL

It has been said that the age of psychotechnology has arrived. The physical and chemical control of the mind, behavior prediction and modification have all been made possible by our new understandings of the brain and its function. It does not require much imagination to see that the power to regulate minds would raise unique ethical and moral problems about such matters as the surrender of constitutional freedoms and human dignity. The power has the potential to change our whole system of life—politics, economics, war, and more—if it is ever misused. It is a frequent occurrence to read in the daily newspapers, popular magazines, and paperbacks and see pictured in the movies the nature and force of behavioral con-

From *Bioethics: A Textbook of Issues* by George Kieffer. Published by Addison-Wesley Publishing Company, Inc. Reading, Massachusetts, 1979. Reprinted by permission of the author and the publisher.

trol technology. In Ken Kesey's *One Flew Over the Cuckoo's Nest,* a lobotomy puts a permanent halt to Randle Patrick McMurphy's heroic struggle against Big Nurse. In Michael Crichton's *Terminal Man,* Harry Benson learns to stop worrying and instead learns to love the electrical charge he gets from forty electrodes planted in his brain. David Rorvick's *Esquire* article "Someone to Watch over You" portrays a society governed by ESB (electrostimulation of the brain), as does Karen Waggoner's piece in the *Yale Alumni Magazine,* "Psychocivilization or Electroliarchy: Dr. Delgado's Amazing World of ESB." These and other plays, articles, and books convey the impression that psychotechnology has a wide range of applications to medical and social problems now or in the near future. Even Dr. Kenneth Clark, in his presidential address to the American Psychological Association in 1971, proclaimed that society was on the threshold of a new era. Biochemical intervention was called for to stabilize the moral and ethical propensities of man. No longer could

world leaders be trusted to subordinate or eliminate their negative and primitive behavioral tendencies.

The particular impression conveyed in these writings is that mass behavior control is imminent; the world will soon face the far-reaching applications and the social consequences of this awesome new power exemplified in Orwell's *1984* or Huxley's *Brave New World*. It goes without saying that control means power and behavior control means power over people. And so we might begin this discussion with the questions: How valid are these claims? Can mass control over minds lead to a world of human robots? Eating, drinking, sleeping, sex—can these all be managed on demand much like puppets on strings?

Although there has been and continues to be a large number of these predictions for the future, Dr. Eliot Valenstein, professor of psychology and neuroscience at the University of Michigan, labels such claims modern "myths." Here, . . . the popular reporting is usually distorted and oversimplified, exaggerating the degree of control possible. It is quite true that animal studies have demonstrated that brain stimulation can initiate eating, drinking, and aggression, or intensify sexual behavior and many other responses that are characteristic of a particular species. And some of these demonstrations are very dramatic. However, first impressions can be misleading, as can be the extrapolations from these to human behavior.

One of the main reasons why a mere listing of all the behaviors ever evoked by stimulation can be very deceptive is that it creates the impression that a greater amount of control and predictability exists than actually is possible. One can easily be impressed with the observation that electrodes implanted in specific brain regions of monkey brains always elicit a particular behavior—flexing a leg, opening the mouth, or change in facial expression; they can cause unlimited sexual gratification in rats if a lever is pressed or a continuation of eating even after complete satiation. However, those who have participated in the research know that electrodes placed in a given part of the brain do not always invoke a particular behavior. In a large percentage of the cases, animals do not display any specific behavior in response to stimulation even though great care and precision may have been exerted in placing the electrodes. Even in rats, where behavior is much more stereotyped than in monkeys or humans, stimulation of the same brain region produces variable results. For example, one rat may eat, another may drink, another may initiate sexual behavior, while still others will actively explore the environment searching for a reward. All of these behaviors may be evoked when the same region is stimulated in different animals. In another experiment, rats ate food pellets when a certain brain region was stimulated. However, if the food offered was first ground up, the same rats would not eat the food in this new form; instead they would drink. Nonstimulated rats would eat the food in either form.

Thus a great amount of uncontrolled variability in behavior triggered by electrostimulation of the brain has been observed in a variety of species. Such factors as the composition of the group, social rank, role of the individual in the group, its sex, and physical environment were important determiners of behavior (see Valenstein, Reference 1, for a detailed discussion of these experiments).

Experimental data clearly indicate that electrodes that seem to be in the same brain locus in different animals often evoke different behavior, and electrodes located at different brain-sites in the same animal may evoke the same behaviors. Even the often referenced work of Dr. Jose Delgado—the dramatic taming of aggression in fighting bulls—is an exaggerated claim of presumed control. What is thought to occur in this case is not pacification of the aggression center of the brain but a general motor effect. In the original experiment, electrodes were implanted in that region of the brain, the amygdala and the caudate nucleus, presumed to be the aggression-inhibition region. A charging bull was brought to a sudden stop when this region was electronically stimulated. Newer studies, however, suggest that the stimulated region of the brain controlled neck

muscle movements and the animal lost motor control of his head, leading to confusion and frustration. Under these conditions, the animal simply could not launch an effective attack. It hardly seems necessary to point out that the same stimulation will very likely disrupt almost any behavior that happened to be going on at the time, even if it was only a peaceful pleasantry occurring in a pasture.

Another set of observations which were thought to be indicative of direct brain correlates and behavior was Dr. Wilder Penfield's dramatic work at the Montreal Neurological Institute. He demonstrated that stimulation of the temporal lobes elicited auditory and visual memory. Presumably what was described by the patient was a real past event. As one patient described it: "I see my mother coming toward me; she is wearing a blue dress; she is calling my name." The patient's mother had been dead for over thirty years. From observations of this kind came the general theory of memory which suggested that every conscious experience is stored in a specific location in the brain. Stimulation of that locus would elicit recall much like opening a book to a specific page and locating a certain line. What is not generally reported in these experiments is that in many instances the patient's responses are very sketchy and abbreviated, and much of the time there is no response at all. Others who tried to duplicate Dr. Penfield's results report total failure. Even in those instances when a vivid memory is reported, it is very difficult to verify if the patient is actually reliving the past. Also, it has been determined that some of the images reported were not derived from memories of real experiences at all. Subjectivity of the patient influences response and this may change from hour to hour. A more reasonable interpretation has been put on these phenomena, namely, that these images are nothing more than evoked hallucinations; when neurons are stimulated they do something, from recalling some particular past event to manufacturing experiences which may *seem* very real.

There is little convincing evidence that elec-

trostimulation of the human brain can elicit specific and predictable behavior, not even the simple responses of hunger and thirst. What is more likely to occur is an effect on the general emotional state of the subject—feelings of relaxation, euphoria, well-being, confusion, anger, or rage. Stimulating the same region in the brains of human subjects at various times in the day may trigger completely different responses; stimulating the same region in different patients also produces varying results. Even the environment or those present in the room may determine the behavior demonstrated. It would seem that the physiological-psychological state of the total individual is of utmost importance in effecting the final response. Valenstein lists a number of other instances where, in general, the same kind of indeterminacy is shown. The point here is that behavior cannot be predicted accurately on the basis of brain anatomy alone even with precise placement of electrodes.

And these observations are exactly what one would expect in the light of what is being learned about brain function. In the first place, individual brains differ as much as individual fingerprints. Both macro- and micro-architecture of the brain have been shown to be another facet of human uniqueness. . . . Since no two brains are alike, either in terms of their gross physical dimensions or in the details of their wiring patterns, electrodes cannot be positioned so that they will elicit the same response in different subjects.

It is also thought that neuronal networks overlap one another extensively. Neurons may be part of many circuits; which circuit will be fired depends on a number of factors. Hence, implanted electrodes may trigger a variety of behaviors, depending on a number of inputs, not just that of the stimulating electrode. The behavior elicited depends on which pathway is being accorded priority at the time of the stimulation and this can be conditioned by a number of other stimuli not related to the experimental one. Many experiments have suggested that stimulation seldom produces specific goal-directed behavior;

rather, it produces a more general motivational state which itself is influenced by one's own personality and previous history. Many responses are dependent on the situation; such things as who is present, what has just happened, where the subject is located, the physiological state of the subject, and other such factors can all affect the response even though the same region is being stimulated. Lastly, response may change over time as individuals acquire new association networks from the state previously induced (in other words, the subject, or more correctly, the subject's brain, "learned" from the experimental stimulation).

Most everyone in the field of neurophysiology agrees that electricity is a very crude stimulus that has its effects by grossly disrupting neural circuits rather than by causing them to subtly reveal normal function. Electrical stimulation can be compared to a bull in a china shop, crashing here and there, disrupting neural circuits in chaotic fashion rather than directing fine control of function.

If electrical intrusions are crude, can chemical control provide a higher degree of specificity and finesse? It is thought that chemical stimulation may not violate the normal physiology of the brain to the same extent as electricity. However, the problem of diffusion of the introduced chemical over a wide neural area can occur as the chemical mixes with intercellular fluids. Diffusion can be reduced by using a chemitrode or a double-barrelled cannula. . . . Such an arrangement makes it possible to apply extremely minute quantities of a drug to specific neural sites without many of the undesirable side effects. The strategy in chemical stimulation of the brain is to either mimic or antagonize the action of the brain's own chemical transmission system. To gain an appreciation of the difficulties inherent in interpreting results from these experiments, consider that there are only six major known neurotransmitters—acetylcholine, norepinephrine, dopamine, serotonin, glutamic acid, and GABA (gamma amino butyric acid); but with these few

chemicals an infinitely large number of behaviors is possible. It is apparent that the relationship between brain chemistry and behavior cannot be simple.

Without going into detail, much the same story can be observed here as was seen with electrical control. For example, although physical aggression can be reduced by pharmacological treatment (e.g., through injecting biogenic amines such as norepinephrine or dopamine), the effects are not restricted to aggressive behavior alone. Subjects given such agents are less responsive in general and have been described as being neurologically numb. Also, the effect of any drug can vary enormously in different individuals. One need only think of alcohol and its effects on people—some fight, some sleep, others become the life of the party, while still others wax philosophical. Another factor affecting response to drugs is the internal state of the body as directed by internal rhythms; a whole new biology—chronobiology, or the study of the function of biological clocks—informs us of these varying effects. Dr. Jonathan Cole of the National Institutes of Health put the whole situation this way:

> Even if one were only attempting to control the mind of a homogeneous group of psychiatric patients with a drug with which one had considerable experience, the desired effect would not be produced in all patients and one would not be able to plan specifically that any particular effect would be produced in a particular patient. A drug designed to speed up mental processes could lead to increased activity and productivity in one person while producing an increase in frustration and aggression in another and an exacerbation of anxiety in a third.[2]

The picture of brain function that is emerging from these researches then is this: There are few areas of the brain that are concerned with the regulation of one and only one behavior and there is no single area in the brain that has complete control over any single behavior. The brain is not organized into spatially discrete units that conform to categories of behavior, as specified by the

older localization theory of brain function. More recent interpretation holds that no part of the brain by itself contains a bit of information or particular memory. The functional brain, it turns out, does not fit our labels. Even those neatly drawn diagrams of brain maps one sees in biology books are not that definitive in relating behavior to brain structure; much overlap and interdependence exist.

The one-region, one-function idea has been replaced by what neurobiologist E. Roy Jones has called the statistical configuration model. He proposes that many brain functions are distributed throughout most brain regions. For example, vast areas of the brain are involved in every thought process. Some regions may contribute more than others to certain functions. Thus, the auditory regions of the brain play the major role in hearing, motor areas have the biggest roles in muscular movement, and the like. When something is learned, according to Jones, small groups of cells do not form new connections. Rather, cells distributed in many parts of the brain learn new firing patterns corresponding to the learning. If this be true, then what is learned cannot be found in any specific brain region. Brain function, in this model, is not just a matter of the physical parts or the connections between them. The brain rhythms are at least as important as the way the brain is put together.[3] The relationship of a light bulb to an electrical circuit might describe the association between the brain parts and behavior. Just as the essence of the light bulb is not the light switch so the discrete brain regions do not control single behaviors.

The strength of the evidence linking specific brain regions to behavioral functions depends to a great extent on the sophistication of the methods used to gather data and on the completeness of the theory employed in analyzing it. Simple, rather naive, overly mechanistic theories of brain function lead to strong conclusions linking discrete areas of the brain to specific behavioral responses. Such views often include the logical fallacy that given a presumed relationship, stimulation of that region will result in a definite behavior, anything from lifting a finger to robot-like aggressive actions.

More complex (and newer) theories of brain function view this magnificent organ as an interacting complex of relationships. We are beginning to think in terms of brain circuits rather than brain centers. Each specific area participates simultaneously in a number of behavioral response circuits. Subtle functional relationships exist between structure and function which cannot be directly or easily controlled by experimental stimuli.

For all of these reasons it is considered unlikely that in the foreseeable future at least we will acquire the capacity to control specific behavior, to administer a drug, or to implant an electrode that can modify neural activity so that discrete, fine behavior can be elicited. The external stimulation of the brain using either electrical or chemical means does, though, produce less specific responses—changes in motivation, attention, or sensory sensitivity. Valenstein contends that effective education can go far in dispelling the myth of directed behavior control. But this is not to deny there are significant ethical concerns in the matter of behavior control. Rather, they are of a different sort than some of the popular literature may lead us to believe.

References

[1]Elliot S. Valenstein, *Brain Control* (New York: John Wiley, 1973).

[2]Elliot S. Valenstein (in Reference 1), p. 130.

[3]E. Roy Jones, "How the Brain Works—A New Theory," *Psychology Today* (May 1976), pp. 48, 51–52.

PHYSICAL INTERVENTION INTO THE BRAIN

Electroshock

There are at least three methods for physical intervention into the brain. These are (1) electroshock, (2) electrostimulation of the brain, and (3)

psychosurgery. They are listed in the order of severity relative to their physical intrusion into the brain, as well as the ethical issues each raises; from least to most. Each of these has as its target the alteration of some function of the subjective experience—the "mind." This assumes that subjective experiences are somehow related to specific processes taking place in the brain. It further presumes that predictable and therapeutically useful changes in mind function can be obtained through alterations of activity in the brain either through direct physical (surgical) or physiological (electrical or chemical) manipulation. On the basis of the previous discussion, these presumed relationships are open to argument on many theoretical and empirical grounds.

Perhaps one of the least understood is electroshock, also known as electroconvulsive treatment (ECT) or shock treatments. There is no general agreement on how electroshock works although it has been known for almost four decades that the induction of convulsive seizures is an effective treatment for the relief of actue psychoses. According to one theory, electrical stress to the nervous system triggers a therapeutically useful reaction—for example, it may escalate the interaction of ACTH (adrenodorticotrophic hormone) and epinephrine, elevating the production or utilization of certain neurotransmitters which regulate mood-biogenic amines such as norepinephrine. The treatment can have beneficial effects on some patients, especially the severely depressed, and is considered safe if muscle relaxants are used first. (It is known that some forms of psychotic depression may result from a deficiency in norepinephrine.) ECT is not administered as a single treatment but in a series. The typical ECT series for depression is 6 to 12 separate shocks given at two to three-day intervals. A schizophrenia series may involve 18 to 25 shocks depending on severity (and administering physician). The electricity may be applied in one of two ways: bilaterally, where the electrodes are placed on both temples resulting in both sides of the brain being shocked; or unilaterally, in which case the electrodes are placed one on the forehead and

the other on the rear of the scalp. In unilateral ECT, only one hemisphere is exposed to the shock, usually the less dominant hemisphere (as determined by right or left handedness).

A single shock consists of an electrical current of between 500 and 900 milliamperes which is approximately the energy needed to light a 100-watt light bulb. The amount of current that actually passes through the brain is about one-tenth of that; most of it travels between electrodes on the skin surface. Seventy to 150 volts powers this current. The duration of the charge varies from 0.2 to one full second. The objective is to produce the grand mal convulsions of the type demonstrated in epileptic episodes.

Patients are lightly anesthetized so that no pain is felt. They are administered succinylcholine or anectine to produce a placid paralysis; these chemicals function by detaching the motor endplates of nerves from muscles so that violent muscular contractions cannot occur that might fracture the long bones (e.g., arms and legs) of the body. Ventilation of the lungs with 100 percent oxygen is supplied during the procedure since the muscles controlling breathing are also paralyzed. The whole procedure, from start to recovery, requires a total time of three to five minutes.

Although no firm records are kept as to the number of these procedures performed, estimates range from 50,000 to 200,000 a year.[1] For what it is worth, two-thirds of all shock recipients are females. ECT enjoys almost total acceptance in the medical community and electroshock units are found in almost every psychiatric hospital or ward.

Not everyone within the profession, however, agrees that ECT is a desirable therapy; and, in fact, some are calling for its complete ban in this country. The most serious side effect is memory loss. That is not surprising since the electrodes are discharged directly over the temporal lobes, where the most recent memory is thought to be encoded. Retroactive amnesia inevitably follows treatment and in some cases, the memory loss can be long-term, even permanent. The effect of this loss can be devastating—particularly for

disturbances without interfering with performance ability of learned tasks. Lesioning of the frontal lobe tracts using a surgical knife called a leucotome was carried out on a limited number of seriously disturbed patients. Here too, calming effects were observed following the surgery. In 1936, Drs. Walter Freeman and James Watts introduced a modified precision-lobotomy technique into the United States. It has been estimated that anywhere from 40,000 to 70,000 frontal lobotomies were performed in the United States alone up to 1955.[5]

The behavioral side effects produced in animal subjects following the destruction of the frontal lobes were overlooked by these scientists; they recognized only the calming effects and the release from obsessive compulsions. In humans, the operation often resulted in a general intellectual decline which showed up as reduced ability to plan for the future. Personality changes also were sometimes reported. These included inappropriate behavior such as a lowering of moral standards and a general lack of emotional responsiveness. The latter, when especially pronounced, gave rise to the vegetative existence of some patients who had undergone this procedure and in general, caused frontal lobotomies to be tainted in the eyes of the public. In an effort to reduce the untoward side effects and to maximize benefits, psychosurgical procedures have undergone a continuous evolution in refinement. The original leucotome of Egas Moniz was a hollow shaft with a cutting wire loop which was extended through a longitudinal slit near the tip of the instrument once it was in place. The leucotome, with the cutting wire retracted, was inserted through a burr hole in the top of the skull, eased into the white fiber tracts filling the frontal lobes, and rotated. The extruded cutting wire removed a roughly spherical core of the white material. The wire loop was then retracted, the leucotome withdrawn and reinserted at a different angle and another cut was made. This sequence was repeated until a total of six lesions, three in each hemisphere, had been produced. Freeman and Watts developed the precision leucotome, a narrow-bladed, dull-edged, and blunt-pointed knife with depth gradations marked along its length. This was inserted to the desired depth through a hole in the side of the skull and with a single sweeping motion of the blade, the fiber tracts within the frontal lobes were severed. Depending on how far the leucotome was inserted, the procedure was referred to as moderate, standard, or radical frontal lobotomy. Later Freeman, over the vehement opposition of Watts introduced the infamous transorbital lobotomy (or ice-pick surgery) into the United States. In this technique, a surgical instrument much like an ice-pick was inserted through the soft tissues above either eye and hammered (using a mallet) upward through the thin bones above the eye sockets (orbits) and with a side-to-side sweep of the handle, the fibers at the lower depths of the frontal lobe were severed. . . . This procedure had several advantages: A hospital stay was not necessary; it could be (and was) done in a doctor's office; it was fast and easy to perform even by unskilled hands; and no cosmetic disfigurement of the patient resulted. The only immediate effect was two black eyes. It was because of these advantages that this technique made possible the greatest number of abuses and literally thousands of these operations were done by nonspecialists in their own offices across the country in the 1940s and early 1950s.

The procedures mentioned so far are considered *closed* because the tissue being sectioned is not directly visible. Such operations were criticized on the technical grounds that they could result in potentially lethal hemorrhages which could not be detected and the exact extent of the lesion could not be accurately controlled. In response, an *open* approach to the brain was developed in the late 1940s. In this technique, a relatively large opening is made in the skull and the brain is gently spread to expose the desired site. This technique allows direct visualization of the area to be lesioned, resulting in less damage to tissues. Several procedures have been developed to effect the lesioning. Skill in locating exactly the area for surgery has been refined, using stereotaxic instrumentation. A 3-D picture of the

brain is made, using anatomical landmarks and x-ray. The stereotaxic instrument has made it possible to produce small and precisely located lesions deep within the brain, utilizing electrocautery, thermocoagulation, cyrogenic cooling, radio-frequency energy, and ionizing radiation emitted by implanted granules of radioactive yttrium.

An almost endless variety of techniques have been applied at one time or another to most areas of the brain in attempts to alleviate this or that symptom, but in the final analysis, the technique employed makes little difference in terms of the *correction* effected. It is not necessary to make different lesions in different areas of the brain for various mental illnesses since there is little specificity between region and behavior. The benefit derived is determined largely by the quantity of brain tissue removed or destroyed. Also, the success of the procedure is largely determined by selection of the patients suffering from specific categories of mental illness. For example, for frontal lobotomy to be helpful in schizophrenia, the disorder must be the pseudoneurotic variety with obsessive thinking and hysteria, and must be of long duration with the patient exhibiting suffering. (psychopaths never benefit from lobotomy); also the patient must be genuinely desirous of assistance. Patients suffering from severe neuroses of the anxiety-tension type, or of the obsessive compulsive type with repetitive phobic or ritualistic thoughts, are considered good candidates for lobotomy since these disorders are generally intractable to all other sorts of therapy and ECT may exacerbate the symptoms.[6]

Brain surgery has also been used to control pathological aggression or uncontrollable, destructive, and violent behavior (most such individuals are also mentally retarded). The model is the dramatic taming of aggresive animals following amygdalectomy. India and Japan lead the world on the number of amygdalectomies done, especially on children. The danger associated with this procedure is that many brain areas influence multiple behaviors, not just one; thus the destruction of one region can affect other unin-

tended behaviors. Especially is this true with the region of the amygdala for this structure is involved in the regulation of a number of functions (e.g., in monkeys the region controls the "4 F's": feeding, fighting, fleeing, and sexual activity, as well as visceral and endocrine functions). It may require a long time before the secondary effects show up so they often go undetected. Also, follow-up studies on long-term effects are very difficult since baseline behavior prior to surgery is very difficult to determine as the patient is violent and uncontrollable before surgery; after surgery he/she is manageable. But the condition of the other behaviors was not (and could not) be determined because of the emotional problems. In such cases, qualitative data are lacking; hence, there is virtually no evidence that intellectual or emotional changes do occur.

With any of the procedures described there is no way at present of exactly predicting the consequences, either short or long term; consequences range all the way from complete relief, to some or little alleviation, to no effect on the symptoms, but devastating side effects, such as obliteration of personality, have been observed. Furthermore, it is a difficult problem to decide the point at which the patient's mental state cannot be improved by some as yet untried treatment that is less drastic than irreversible surgery. Psychosurgery performed on children presents a special problem. One psychosurgical team recently reported results of limbic system lesions made in 115 children, including 39 who were under age eleven. O. J. Andy, a well-known psychosurgeon at the University of Mississippi, has reported operations on a number of children six to nineteen years of age. The majority of these were institutionalized, demonstrating violent and uncontrollable behavior. Following the surgery, they became manageable. Yet, who can predict what the long term effects of this or that lesion will be? The temporal and frontal lobes and the limbic region are structures involved in a wide range of behavioral activities. The so-called Kluves-Bucy Syndrome, in which the subject loses grip of reality, directs sexual activity at a variety of objects, is

A. PREVENTION OF HARM TO OTHERS

A suicide can be devastating in its impact. Intimate survivors may feel guilty, blaming themselves for having caused the suicide or for having failed to prevent it.[12] Alternatively, they may be blamed by others.[13] These responses may, of course, take place independently of the wishes of the deceased. In some instances, however, the person suiciding may attempt to elicit guilt or blame through a suicide note.[14]

While such posthumous accusations may be injurious to a survivor's reputation or peace of mind, and may be difficult to rebut, we have no reason to assume that they are necessarily undeserved or so serious in their consequences as to justify coercive state intervention.

Other kinds of harm to survivors of suicide include financial loss to surviving dependents, which, in extreme cases, may seriously affect their life chances, and lives made more difficult for reasons other than financial.[15] Sometimes a suicide will induce intimate survivors to commit suicide.[16] Someone who suicides may also leave behind unfulfilled legal commitments (e.g., contractual obligations).

In addition to the harm to intimate survivors there may also, in some cases, be harm to society. When the suicide possesses some rare talent, all of us may be diminished by what appears to be a premature death.

Yet, even where an injury to others can clearly be identified, state intervention may not be justified, at least if the intervention is coercive. There are many areas of social life for which we provide no legal channels by which one person can seek redress for harm occasioned by another's actions. In some cases, this is because fault would be difficult to assign. In others, official enforcement would require extreme invasion of privacy and strangling regulation of our private lives. Indeed, since state intervention tends to be crude and mechanical, it is often more likely to make matters worse than better.

Significantly, much of the harm to others occasioned by a suicide involves aspects of life that seem ill-suited to legal regulation. Such harm, when it arises from other causes, does not ordinarily provide the basis for a legally recognized claim (e.g., sparing someone from experiencing grief). Often it is unclear why we should prefer the claims of the survivors who seek protection from distress to those of the potential suicide attempter, who may experience considerable unhappiness if forced to continue living.

In other cases, a basis for a legal claim may be more solidly founded. Just as a parent may be jailed for failure to make child support payments, so the child of a suicide attempter may be legally entitled to support. The difficulty here is that the cost to the person kept alive—the psychic distress of the person who wishes to die—may far exceed the harm prevented, especially when preservation of life requires long-term confinement to a mental institution. Thus, it seems clearly preferable to permit the suicide and use welfare payments to survivors to alleviate financial hardship.

The case for coercion to prevent injury to others from a suicide clearly is weak, and should not ordinarily constitute grounds for state interference with a suicide attempter. Exceptions might be made only in the very rare case when a suicide would result in extremely serious injury to others. For example, if the potential suicide is the only witness to an alibi for a defendant on trial for a serious crime, the latter might reasonably argue that his right to be absolved is sufficiently important to justify the temporary prevention of suicide until after the witness testifies.

B. Prevention of Harm to Self

Upon reflection, the claim that suicide is necessarily harmful must be rejected. We know nothing of the fate of those who kill themselves; conceivably, their souls are transported to an especially favored spot on the Isle of the Blessed. More to the point, however, it is hardly difficult to imagine circumstances where suicide, if not a positive good, would readily be recognizable as the lesser

of evils. One obvious case would be the victim who suicides to escape the pain of an excruciating terminal illness.[17] Many other possibilities can be imagined, or discovered in case histories in the suicide literature: to prevent the enemy from obtaining secrets through torture, to end a life that has become lonely and tedious, to preserve honor or reputation in the face of threatened scandal, to call attention to a political injustice or to control one's final "scene" in the theatre of life.

In other instances, however, suicide may seem clearly disproportionate to the precipitating cause. For example, suicide attempts have been attributed to feelings of intense guilt over matters that may seem to many others to be venial or totally inconsequential (*e.g.,* sexual experiences). Yet distress is subjective. The anguish of the person who finds continued life intolerable is not mitigated by another's opinion that the occasion for distress is minor. That most others might not commit suicide in a given situation indicates only that the suicidal person has experienced the situation differently. To prevent suicide in this case is to permit someone else to decide that the potential attempter is better off alive and suffering than dead and to impose that decision on the attempter. This violates the right to die when one wishes, which would seem to be a necessary part of the right to live with dignity and privacy, a right to be denied only if there were some other, overriding interest to be served by the denial. This right would mean little if it could be exercised only when consistent with others' views of what is reasonable or appropriate. While it may seem anomalous to speak of "a right to die," the infringement of this right seriously jeopardizes the right to live one's life as one wishes, and not to live it when it is no longer possible to do so as one wishes.

C. Suicide as the Product of Mental Illness

The case for benevolent coercion to prevent suicide has not rested entirely on the prevention of self-injury. Most commitment statutes specify not only that the defendant must be thought likely to be dangerous to himself if permitted to remain at liberty, but also that he be mentally ill. Sometimes it is specified that the dangerousness must be a *consequence* of the mental illness. The reason for requiring that mental illness be present presumably is that while libertarian principles might allow a sane person to engage in activity others considered self-injurious, a person who is not sane—whose mental processes are so disordered by illness as to preclude a rational choice—forfeits no valued prerogative when prevented from committing suicide, because such a person cannot meaningfully be said to have chosen to die.[18]

There are several problems with this claim. First, the diagnosis of mental illness is far from an exact science. The boundary between behavior that is merely eccentric and behavior that arises from malfunctioning of the faculties of the mind may be extremely difficult, some would say conceptually impossible, to draw.[19] This may be one cause of the wide variation in estimates of the incidence of mental illness among suicide populations.[20] The requirement that mental illness not only be present but in addition be the *cause* of the dangerousness only compounds the difficulty, since the causal element may be difficult to establish even when it is possible to achieve consensus as to the *presence* of "mental illness."

It is safe to assume that these fine points are ignored in present commitment practice. Questions of mental illness are now often decided either by lay notions of mental health or by physicians using psychiatric classifications or, perhaps, their own moral judgments concerning defendants' lifestyles.[21] In the absence of vigorous legal representation (and sometimes in the absence of the defendant as well—not all states require notification or the presence of the defendant at the commitment hearing), delicate questions of causation are likely to be brushed aside, and the working assumption made that dangerousness and mental illness imply one another.

The second problem concerns the empirical relationship between mental illness and suicide.

pose a danger of immediate suicide, even when opportunities for further attempts are not lacking.[49] For this reason, the stringent time limit on intervention would entail a sacrifice of very few lives. This feature makes the policy especially attractive. Moreover, even the small number of subsequent suicides that will continue to occur need not necessarily be considered failures of the policy, since those persons will at least have been provided a chance for reconsideration.[50]

There are several disadvantages to this policy. Some small number of individuals will die who would have changed their minds had they been held for a longer period. Others, firmly committed to suicide, will be detained for a period of some hours. This may be annoying, perhaps extremely distressing. Nevertheless, there are reasons for not being too concerned with this small number of individuals. First, their distress will come to an end in a few hours; secondly, those concerned with avoiding this delay could simply choose a time, place and method unlikely to attract attention.[51]

To reduce some of this imposition, the state might even accommodate determined attempters by granting immunity from any interference to those who register their intention to commit suicide in advance, or by providing resources for painless suicide following a short waiting period so as to be confident that only those who wish to die kill themselves.[52] Despite these provisions, however, some genuinely suicidal persons are likely to be subjected to distress, embarrassment and inconvenience because, contrary to plans, their suicide attempt has been interrupted.

A third class of individuals who may suffer from the minimal policy consists of those who are falsely identified as having been engaged in a suicide attempt or whose attempt would have had no serious consequences and who would not have gone on to a more serious attempt in the absence of intervention. These persons may incur inconvenience and some degree of stigmatization as the result of having been considered suicidal.

Nevertheless, the negative consequences of mistaken identification do not seem serious enough to constitute fatal objections to this proposal. An analogy to arrests for criminal law violations is instructive. Under the "probable cause" standard some innocent persons undoubtedly are wrongly arrested and charged. Though regrettable, the undeserved inconvenience and stigmatization are thought to be unavoidable consequences of law enforcement practices believed to be necessary to the public welfare. Our desire to minimize the unavoidable evil might, for example, lead to protection of the confidentiality of arrest records, but not to outright elimination of the power to arrest, absent an alternative procedure to handle the charging of individuals with crimes and the production of them at trial. The judgment is made that our interest in safety from crime is sufficient to warrant risking some interference with our activities through wrongful arrest.[53] On the other side of the coin, a person suspected of criminal activity cannot lawfully be taken into custody unless there is at least "probable cause" to believe that he committed the crime. Relaxation of this restriction might result in the taking into custody of some criminals who at present are free to continue preying on innocent victims, but we forfeit this potential benefit in order to remain free from arrest based on mere suspicion of involvement in criminal activity.

It is doubtful that coercive suicide prevention is as justifiable as coercive crime prevention; the social consequences of unpunished serious crime probably are much greater than those of unprevented suicide. Failing to attach legal sanctions to acts seriously harmful to the life of another, for example, may lead to vigilantism. Nevertheless, the considerable benefits to be obtained from minimal restraint of suicide attempters seem to us sufficient to justify the limited degree of interference proposed here, notwithstanding its costs for "truly" suicidal persons and for those who are not suicidal at all.

Notes

The author's views on suicide prevention policy were largely crystallized during his tenure with the Committee for the Study of Incarceration. Some of the material presented here appeared previously in an unpublished staff memorandum of the Committee for the Study of Incarceration, coauthored with Andrew von Hirsch. Comments and discussions with the Committee's Executive Director, Andrew von Hirsch, and with its members, notably Dr. Willard Gaylin and Professor Alan Dershowitz, are gratefully acknowledged. Neither the Committee for the Study of Incarceration nor the aforementioned individuals are responsible for the views expressed here. This essay is dedicated to Caleb Foote.

[1] For a brief history of the criminal prohibition of suicide and a list of states in which suicides or attempted suicides are illegal, see Schulman, *Suicide and Suicide Prevention: A Legal Analysis,* 54 A.B.A.J. 855 (1968). A list of states where the criminal law prohibits committing, aiding, assisting, encouraging or abetting suicide is contained in Litman, *Police Aspects of Suicide,* in THE PSYCHOLOGY OF SUICIDE 519, 520 (E. Shneidman, N. Farberow & R. Litman eds. 1960) [hereinafter THE PSYCHOLOGY OF SUICIDE].

[2] This has been the supposition. A recent study, however, found evidence of virtually unanimous negative attitudes toward suicide attempters on the part of the general public as well as specific occupational groups dealing with attempters. Psychiatric residents had negative attitudes more often and more intensely than other groups. Ansel & McGee, *Attitudes Toward Suicide Attempters,* 8 BULL. OF SUICIDOLOGY 22, 27 (1971).

[3] *See* text accompanying notes 54–56 *infra.*

[4] Jackson v. Indiana, 406 U.S. 715, 737 (1972).

[5] Limited information about the length of hospitalization of 138 suicidal patients admitted to a British psychiatric ward in 1946 is presented in E. STENGEL, SUICIDE AND ATTEMPTED SUICIDE 80–92, 89–91 (1964) [hereinafter STENGEL, SUICIDE]. Generalization to another country a quarter of a century later would obviously be unwarranted.

[6] *E.g.,* Dershowitz, *The Law of Dangerousness: Some Fictions About Predictions,* 23 J. LEGAL ED. 24 (1970: Dershowitz, *Psychiatry in the Legal Process: A Knife that Cuts Both Ways,* 4 TRIAL, Feb./Mar. 1968, at 29; Ervin, *Foreword: Preventive Detention—A Step Backward for Criminal Justice,* 6 HARV. CIV. RIGHTS—CIV. LIB. L. REV. 291 (1971); Foote, *The Coming Constitutional Crisis in Bail,* 113 U. PA. L. REV. 959 (1965); Tribe, *An Ounce of Detention: Preventive Justice in the World of John Mitchell,* 56 VA. L. REV. 371 (1970); von Hirsch, *Prediction of Criminal Conduct and Preventive Confinement of Convicted Persons,* 21 BUFFALO L. REV. 717 (1972). The conceptual framework of this essay on preventive confinement to stop suicide is deeply indebted to von Hirsch's work on the preventive confinement of persons considered dangerous to others.

[7] Some of the issues involved in preventive confinement to prevent danger to self were raised in Siegel, *The Justifications*

for Medical Commitment—Real or Illusory, 6 WAKE FOREST INTRA. L. REV. 21 (1969). It is testimony to the legal profession's neglect of civil commitments that the issues Siegel raised in this article have not been explored in greater depth in the several years since it appeared.

[8] Three convenient tabulations of psychiatric commitment statutes and procedures have appeared recently: S. BRAKEL & R. ROCK, THE MENTALLY DISABLED AND THE LAW (rev. ed. 1971); B. ENNIS & L. SIEGEL, THE RIGHTS OF MENTAL PATIENTS app. A (1973); Roth, Dayley & Lerner, *Into the Abyss: Psychiatric Reliability and Emergency Commitment Statutes,* 13 SANTA CLARA LAW. 400, 412–15 (1973).

[9] IDAHO CODE § 66-317(b) (1973).

[10] A recent empirical study of civil commitments in Arizona, Wexler & Scoville, *The Administration of Psychiatric Justice: Theory and Practice in Arizona,* 13 ARIZ. L. REV. (1971), illustrates the discrepancy between the provisions of a commitment statute and actual commitment procedure. The project investigators found that although the legal criteria for civil commitment required a showing of dangerousness, in some counties testifying psychiatrists did not even bother expressing an opinion as to the issue of dangerousness. At least one judge openly admitted to blatantly illegal commitments for the "benefit" of the defendant, *id.* at 3–4, and the project team suggests generally that the wording of the statute has little bearing on decision outcomes, since the law can be and is interpreted, twisted or ignored to accomplish the commitment. *Id.* at 113–17. In a few states is the wording of the relevant statute sufficiently precise as to make this at all difficult. This use of psychiatric commitment statutes suggests that they are not so much an expression of *norms,* but *resources* to be used in accomplishing the goals of those who seek commitments. For a general discussion of this way of looking at formal rules, see Johnson, *The Practical Uses of Rules,* in THEORETICAL PERSPECTIVES ON DEVIANCE 215 (R. Scott & J. Douglas eds. 1972).

Statutory differences among states in *procedure* for commitments are discussed in BRAKEL & ROCK, *supra* note 8, and in R. ROCK, M. JACOBSON & R. JANOPAUL, HOSPITALIZATION AND DISCHARGE OF THE MENTALLY ILL (1968).

[11] A. ALVAREZ, THE SAVAGE GOD 50, 69 (Bantam ed. 1973); 4 W. BLACKSTONE, COMMENTARIES ⅓ 189.

[12] Henslin, *Guilt and Guilt Neutralization; Response and Adjustment to Suicide,* in DEVIANCE AND RESPECTABILITY: THE SOCIAL CONSTRUCTION OF MORAL MEANINGS 192, 200–01 (J. Douglas ed. 1970) [hereinafter DEVIANCE AND RESPECTABILITY]. *But see* S. WALLACE, AFTER SUICIDE 268 (1973), a recent study of adjustment to suicide among widows of Boston-area men who committed suicide, which found that some widows experienced relief, rather than grief, at their husbands' deaths. *See also* Breed, *Suicide and Loss in Social Interaction,* in ESSAYS IN SELF-DESTRUCTION 188 (E. Shneidman ed. 1967) [hereinafter ESSAYS].

[13] Henslin, *supra* note 12, at 204–205.

[14]Tuckman, Kleiner & Lavell, *Emotional Content of Suicide Notes,* 116 Am. J. Psychiatry 59, 60 (1959).

[15]*See* Cain & Fast, *Children's Disturbed Reactions to Parent Suicide,* 56 Am. J. Orthopsychiatry 873 (1966); Cain & Fast, *The Legacy of Suicide: Observations on the Pathogenic Impact of Suicide upon Marital Partners,* 29 Psychiatry 406 (1966) [hereinafter Cain & Fast, *Legacy*].

[16]*See* Cain & Fast, *Legacy, supra* note 15, at 410. One commentator has observed that "suicidal efforts seem not infrequently to follow the patterns of suicidal attempts by father, mother, older brother, or older sister." Kubie, *Multiple Determinants of Suicide,* in Essays, *supra* note 12, at 455, 458; *accord,* Teicher & Jacobs, *Adolescents Who Attempt Suicide: Preliminary Findings,* 122 Am. J. Psychiatry 1248, 1257 (1966).

[17]A study of suicides in King County, Washington (Seattle), found that 70% of suicides had active physical illness; illness was considered to have contributed to 51% of the suicides. Dorpat, Anderson & Ripley, *The Relationship of Physical Illness to Suicide,* in Suicidal Behavior: Diagnosis and Management 209, 210–11 (H. Resnik ed. 1968) [hereinafter Resnik].

[18]For a typical expression of this viewpoint, see Ringel, *Suicide Prevention as a Contribution to the Re-evaluation of Human Life,* 7 Lex et Scientia 11, 14–15 (1970).

[19]*See* T. Szasz, Law, Liberty and Psychiatry 11–36 (1963); M. Pollner, "The Very Coinage of Your Brain": The Resolution of Reality Disjunctures (May 1973) (copy on file at offices of *New York University Law Review*); Blum, *The Sociology of Mental Illness,* in Deviance and Respectability, *supra* note 12, at 31; Sarbin, *The Scientific Status of the Mental Illness Metaphor,* in Changing Perspectives in Mental Illness 9 (S. Plog & R. Edgerton eds. 1969); Rosenhan, *On Being Sane in Insane Places,* 179 Science 250 (1973).

[20]Figures given [for the percentage of suicides who are mentally ill] rest largely on the definition of mental illness, however, and therefore run the gamut from as low as 20 percent to as high as 90 to 100 percent. Such a wide variation reflects the difficulty of defining and categorizing mental illness in the first place and the relative independence of suicide and present day psychiatric nosology. . . .

C. Leonard, Understanding and Preventing Suicide 273 (1967). *See also* M. Kramer, E. Pollack, R. Redick & B. Locke, Mental Disorders/Suicide 286 (1972).

[21]*See* D. Mechanic, Mental Health and Social Policy 129–31 (1969); T. Scheff, Becoming Mentally Ill ch. 5 (1969); Kutner, *The Illusion of Due Process in Commitment Proceedings,* 57 Nw. U.L. Rev. 383 (1962).

[22]Thus, Erwin Ringel states:
Any man who has given serious and scientific thought to the problem of suicide knows that death—that state of not being—is for the most part chosen under pathological circumstances or under the influence of diseased feelings, and even then I put it to you that the word choice is wrong because an overwhelming imperative compulsion renders any free choice null and void.

Ringel, *supra* note 18, at 15. According to Ilza Veith, "the act [of suicide] clearly represents an illness." Quoted in Szasz, *The Ethics of Suicide,* 31 Antioch Rev. 7, 8 (1971).

[23]Pokorny, *Myths About Suicide,* in Resnik, *supra* note 17, at 57, 62 [hereinafter Pokorny, *Myths*].

[24]A. Kobler & E. Stotland, The End of Hope 3–4 (1964). The issue of mistaken attribution of depressive psychosis has also been raised in a recent study of adolescent suicides, Jacobs & Teicher, *Broken Homes and Social Isolation in Attempted Suicides of Adolescents,* 13 Int'l J. Social Psychiatry 139 (1967). The authors criticize psychiatrically oriented diagnosticians for failure to investigate the experiences that might lead to a suicide attempt, an omission they attribute to a self-confirming assumption that suicide must be the consequence of mental pathology. *Id.* at 147–48. Their own efforts to obtain life histories for the attempters they studied suggest that, at least for adolescents, symptoms of depression may be a perfectly understandable response to their experiences.

[25]Farberow, Shneidman & Leonard, *Suicide among Schizophrenic Mental Hospital Patients,* in The Cry for Help 78, 91 (N. Farberow & E. Shneidman eds. 1965) [hereinafter The Cry for Help]. Similarly, Jacob Tuckman, Robert J. Kleiner and Martha Lavell comment:
In this study the writers were impressed with the possibility that in a number of cases the suicide could have resulted from a conscious, "rational" decision reached by weighing the pros and cons of continuing to live, although to a lesser extent unconscious factors may have been operating.

Tuckman, Kleiner & Lavell, *supra* note 14, at 62. Jerry Jacobs and Joseph D. Teicher are likewise impressed with "the matter-of-fact presentation found in suicide notes." Jacobs & Teicher, *supra* note 24, at 148.

[26]Gittleson, *The Relationship Between Obsessions and Suicidal Attempts in Depressive Psychoses,* 112 Brit. J. Psychiatry 889 (1966). This is consistent with Norman Farberow's finding that suicide attempters appear less psychologically abnormal or disturbed than suicide threateners or nonsuicidal mental patients. Farberow, *Personality Patterns of Suicidal Mental Hospital Patients,* 42 Genetic Psychology Monographs 3, 67 (1950) [hereinafter Farberow, *Personality Patterns*].

[27]Pokorny, *Myths, supra* note 23, at 64. Consequently, treatment of mental illness may lead to suicide rather than prevent it:
If psychosis is . . . an escape from intolerable stresses of reality, perhaps the partial easing of the psychotic state through medication or tranquilizing drugs brings these patients to a state of painful insight before they are able to cope with new insights.

Farberow, Shneidman & Leonard, *supra* note 25, at 91. The process is illustrated in the following tragi-comic story:
One resident whom I supervised spent a year and a half working to establish a relationship with a regressed hebephrenic woman who lived largely in a hallucinatory world of self-fulfilling fantasies in which she was a socially active debutante. Gradually she gave up these delusions as her ingenious therapist made headway. When after 18 months of painstaking work she surfaced in the world of reality, she discovered that she was fat, forty, and friendless, and made a drastic suicide attempt.

Stone, *Suicide Precipitated by Psychotherapy,* 25 AM. J. PSY-
CHOTHERAPY, 18, 22 (1971).

[28]The problem of prediction in commitments to prevent suicide is discussed in text accompanying notes 107–22 *infra.*

[29]The effectiveness of suicide prevention measures is discussed
in text accompanying notes 91–106 *infra.*

[39]*E.g.,* E. DURKHEIM, LE SUICIDE: ETUDE DE SOCIOLOGIE (1897);
H. MORSELLI, SUICIDE: AN ESSAY ON COMPARATIVE MORAL STATIS-
TICS (1882).

[31]Douglas, *The Absurd in Suicide,* in ON THE NATURE OF SUICIDE
111, 117–18 (E. Shneidman ed. 1969).

[32]Rubinstein, Moses & Lidz, *On Attempted Suicide,* 79 A.M.A.
ARCHIVES OF NEUROLOGY & PSYCHIATRY 103, 111 (1958). Characteristically, the authors of this study found:

> The patient was involved in a struggle with the persons
> important to him and sought a modification of their at-
> titudes or a specific change in his relationships with
> them. After a crisis was reached in this struggle, the pa-
> tient sought to effect these changes through a suicide
> attempt. . . . Patients sometimes told of seeking such
> changes prior to their suicide attempt, of seeking them
> through the attempt, and by still other means after-
> ward. . . .

Id. at 109. A similar conclusion was reached in a study of
suicidal behavior on the part of Irish women. Lukianowicz,
Suicidal Behavior: An Attempt to Modify the Environment, 6
PSYCHIATRICA CLINICA 171, 185 (1973). *See also* Sacks, *The
Search for Help: No One to Turn To,* in ESSAYS, *supra note* 12, at
203, 211.

[33]Weiss, *The Suicidal Patient,* in AMERICAN HANDBOOK OF PSY-
CHIATRY 115, 121 (S. Arieto ed. 1966 [hereinafter Weiss, *The
Suicidal Patient*].

[34]Rubinstein, Moses & Lidz, *supra* note 32, at 105. Similar
conclusions are reported in E. STENGEL & N. COOK, ATTEMPTED
SUICIDE: ITS SOCIAL SIGNIFICANCE AND EFFECTS 119–29 (1958)
[hereinafter STENGEL & COOK, ATTEMPTED SUICIDE], and in
STENGEL, SUICIDE, *supra* note 5, at 95–99.

Adolescents seem less successful than adults at turning a
suicide attempt to their advantage. *See* Teicher & Jacobs, *supra*
note 16, at 1249.

[35]*See* Firth, *Suicide and Risk-Taking in Tikopia Society,* 24 PSY-
CHIATRY (1961); Weiss, *The Gamble with Death in Attempted
Suicide,* 20 PSYCHIATRY 17 (1957). Edwin Lemert discusses the
relevance of risk-taking to deviance theory generally in E.
LEMERT, HUMAN DEVIANCE, SOCIAL PROBLEMS, AND SOCIAL CON-
TROL 11–12 (1967).

[36]Many suicide attempters give at least one, sometimes more
than one, clear warning of an impending suicide during the
days and weeks prior to an attempt. Delong & Robins, *The
Communication of Suicidal Intent Prior to Psychiatric Hospitalization: A Study of 87 Patients,* 117 AM. J. PSYCHIATRY 695, 699–
700 (1961); Dorpat & Ripley, *A Study of Suicide in the Seattle
Area,* 1 COMPREHENSIVE PSYCHIATRY 349, 355 (1960); Pokorny,
*Characteristics of Forty-Four Patients Who Subsequently Com-
mitted Suicide,* 2 ARCHIVES OF GEN. PSYCHIATRY 314, 315–16
(1960); Robins, Gasser, Kayes, Wilkinson & Murphy, *The

*Communication of Suicidal Intent: A Study of 134 Consecutive
Cases of Successful (Completed) Suicide,* 115 AM. J. PSYCHIATRY
724, 733 (1959); Wilson, *Suicide in Psychiatric Patients Who
Have Received Hospital Treatment,* 125 AM. J. PSYCHIATRY 752,
753 (1968); Yessler, Gibbs & Becker, *On the Communication of
Suicidal Ideas,* 3 ARCHIVES OF GEN. PSYCHIATRY 612, 613 (1960).
A problem generally encountered in such studies is that of
retrospective interpretation of the sometimes ambiguously
worded "warning."

[37]Pokorny, *Myths, supra* note 23, at 60.

[38]Tuckman & Youngman, *Assessment of Suicide Risk in At-
tempted Suicide,* in Resnik, *supra* note 17, at 190, 192–93;
Gardner, Bahn & Mack, *Suicide and Psychiatric Care in the
Aging,* 10 ARCHIVES OF GEN. PSYCHIATRY 547, 550 (1964); Ro-
sen, *The Serious Suicide Attempt: Epidemiological and Follow-
Up Study of 886 Patients,* 127 AM. J. PSYCHIATRY 764, 766,
(1970) [hereinafter Rosen, *Serious Attempt*]; Tuckman &
Youngman, *Identifying Suicide Risk Groups Among Persons At-
tempting Suicide,* 78 PUB. HEALTH REP. 585 (1963) [hereinafter
Tuckman & Youngman, *Identifying Suicide Risk Groups*].

[39]N. RETTERSTOL, LONG-TERM PROGNOSIS AFTER ATTEMPTED SU-
ICIDE 95 (1970); STENGEL, SUICIDE, *supra* note 5, at 81–84;
STENGEL & COOK, ATTEMPTED SUICIDE, *supra* note 34, at 116;
Oltman & Friedman, *Life Cycles in Patients with Manic-De-
pressive Psychoses,* 119 AM. J. PSYCHIATRY 174, 175 (1962); Pitts
& Winokur, *Affective Disorder: Diagnostic Correlates and Inci-
dence of Suicide,* 139 J. NERVOUS & MENTAL DISEASE 176, 179
(1964); Pokorny, *A Follow-Up Study of 618 Suicidal Patients,*
122 AM. J. PSYCHIATRY 1109, 1111 (1966) [hereinafter Pokorny,
Follow-Up Study]; Stengel, *Recent Research into Suicide and
Attempted Suicide,* 118 AM. J. PSYCHIATRY 725 (1962).

[40]Moss & Hamilton, *Psychotherapy of the Suicidal Patient,* in
CLUES TO SUICIDE 99, 107 (E. Shneidman & N. Farberow eds.
1957) [hereinafter CLUES TO SUICIDE].

[41]Even when manipulation is not the purpose of an attempt,
the attempt may nevertheless have the consequence of improving the attempter's social environment sufficiently to allay
further attempts. Some psychoanalytic theorizing on suicide
has emphasized aggressive elements, *e.g.,* hostility toward others redirected inward. S. FREUD, *Mourning and Melancholia,* in
14 THE STANDARD EDITION OF THE COMPLETE PSYCHOLOGICAL
WORKS OF SIGMUND FREUD 252 (J. Strachey ed. 1957) [herein-
after COMPLETE PSYCHOLOGICAL WORKS]; K. MENNINGER, MAN
AGAINST HIMSELF (1938).

If newly evoked sympathy and attention reduced the intensity
of such feelings we might expect a low repeat rate even though
there was no conscious or unconscious "appeal" element to
the original attempt. Indeed, Ronald Akers has suggested that,
from a social learning perspective, the increased attention a
suicide attempt elicits may reinforce suicidal behavior, so that,
if the attention does not resolve the crisis which precipitated
the original attempt, the attempter will be likely to repeat the
reinforced behavior. R. AKERS, DEVIANT BEHAVIOR: A SOCIAL
LEARNING APPROACH 251 (1973).

[42]KOBLER & STOTLAND, *supra* note 24, at 10.

[43]J. CHORON, SUICIDE 50 (1972), cites several studies from different countries in which 90% to 100% of rescued suicide attempters reported they were glad they had been saved. *Accord,* RETTERSTOL, *supra* note 39, at 96.

[44]Alan Dershowitz has called this line of reasoning the "Thank you, doctor" doctrine (private conversation with the author). The concept also is employed under the label "future-oriented consent" in Wexler, *Therapeutic Justice,* 57 MINN. L. REV. 289, 330–32 (1972). We shall refer to the concept in this article as the principle of retrospective gratitude.

[45]J. RAWLS, A THEORY OF JUSTICE 136–42 (1971).

[46]Thus, in Litman & Farberow, *Emergency Evaluation of Suicidal Potential,* in THE PSYCHOLOGY OF SUICIDE, *supra* note 1, at 259, 268, an example is given of a woman who claimed that her husband was living "in a dream world" and wanted him committed on grounds that he was likely to kill himself. Upon investigation it turned out that he frequently lost much of his wages gambling. The woman wanted him committed so that she could use his money to straighten out their financial affairs. Sympathetic as we might be with her plight, we would want to provide protection against the use of suicide prevention commitment proceedings to advance goals having nothing to do with suicide prevention. Even where there is no deliberate attempt to deceive or misuse statutory provisions, we still would need to be on guard against family members who are sincere but mistaken in their belief that a suicide attempt may be imminent.

[47]*See* text accompanying notes 43–44 *supra.*

[48]As defined here, then, minimal interference includes simple restraint at the scene, arrest and removal from the scene and very short-term detainment. Although we consider these together as "minimal," it ultimately might prove useful to distinguish among them and perhaps permit only the least restrictive. These distinctions need not be discussed here.

[49]Stengel & Cook, *Recent Research into Suicide and Attempted Suicide,* 1 J. FORENSIC MEDICINE 252 (1954); Shneidman, *Some Reflections on Suicide Theory and Prevention,* in PROCEEDINGS OF A SECOND TECHNICAL ASSISTANCE PROJECT CONFERENCE ON SUICIDE AND DEPRESSION 35 (1967); Weiss, *The Suicidal Patient, supra* note 33, at 121.

[50]This need not mean that we should be complacent about suicides, only that this particular coercive policy cannot be made to shoulder the burden of suicide prevention.

[51]Ordinarily this should not be too difficult. A major exception might be individuals incarcerated in total institutions where suicide, though certainly not impossible, can be made much more difficult by intensive surveillance and deprivation of materials from which weapons can be constructed. I am indebted to Andrew von Hirsch for this observation.

[52]This procedure was employed in the Greek colonies at Marseilles and Ceos. ALVAREZ, *supra* note 11, at 59.

[53]On the other hand, we become much more alarmed at more extended pretrial detention, as its disruptive effects mount rapidly when its duration begins to exceed 24 hours. It is clear that, behind the veil of ignorance, we would never accept the class bias built into current pretrial release procedures.

SELECTED BIBLIOGRAPHY

Breggin, Peter R. *Psychiatric Drugs: Hazards to the Brain.* New York: Springer Publishing Co., 1983.

Culver, Charles M., and Bernard Gert. *Philosophy in Medicine: Conceptual and Ethical Issues in Medicine and Psychiatry.* New York: Oxford University Press, 1982.

Edwards, Rem B. *Psychiatry and Ethics: Insanity, Rational Autonomy, and Mental Health Care.* Buffalo: Prometheus Books, 1982.

Feinberg, Joel. *Harm to Others.* New York: Oxford University Press, 1985.

————. *Harm to Self.* New York: Oxford University Press, 1986.

Gross, Martin L. *The Psychological Society.* New York: Random House, 1978.

London, Perry. *Behavior Control.* New York: Harper & Row, 1969, 1977.

Macklin, Ruth. *Man, Mind, and Morality.* Englewood Cliffs: Prentice-Hall, 1982.

Moore, Michael S. *Law and Psychiatry: Rethinking the Relationship.* Cambridge: Cambridge University Press, 1984.

Robitscher, Jonas. *The Powers of Psychiatry.* Boston: Houghton Mifflin, 1980.

Schwitzgebel, Robert L., and Ralph K. Schwitzgebel, eds. *Psychotechnology: Electronic Control of Mind and Behavior.* New York: Holt, Rinehart, and Winston, 1973.

Sedgwick, Peter. *Psycho Politics.* New York: Harper & Row, 1982.

Szasz, Thomas S. *Ideology and Insanity.* New York: Doubleday, 1970.

Valenstein, Elliot S. *Brain Control: A Critical Examination of Brain Stimulation and Psychosurgery.* New York: John Wiley, 1973.

CHAPTER 7

Death and Dying

This chapter will introduce a conceptual problem that has profound implications for ethical practice. What do we mean by "death" and how do we know that someone is dead? We must understand the concept of death and the criteria for applying the concept. Criteria of death like dilated pupils and absence of reflexes or pulse are signs that point to something other than themselves. What is that something? What is death itself?

In our next chapter, on abortion, the meaning of "life" becomes critical. "When are we dead?" and "When are we alive?" are correlative questions. If we can find out when life ends, presumably we can discover when life begins. If we fail at the first task, however, we might also fail at the other. Such a failure would have momentous significance for ethics and public policy.

A. DEFINITIONS OF DEATH

Many recent developments in medicine require that we carefully reexamine the meaning of "death." The miracles of modern medical technology now enable us to keep many people alive, in some minimal sense of life, who would have died readily twenty or thirty years ago. If left entirely in the hands of God, they would die; but now *we* can save them! So what is that "minimal sense" that marks the difference between life and death?

Again, our new technology of organ transplants makes it imperative that we have a clear concept of death. Most transplanted organs come from cadaverous (i.e., dead) donors, though a few come from living ones, usually from a relative of the recipient with a closely matching tissue type. It is legally and ethically unacceptable to harvest organs from cadaverous donors unless they are truly dead. But when are they truly dead?

Other considerations also call for a clear concept of death. There are enormous economic and emotional costs to family, friends, and society in medically maintaining the minimal physiological functions of persons who are questionably alive. Also, physicians need assurances that they will not be prosecuted for some degree of homicide when they "pull the plug" on such individuals. If they cannot be prosecuted for killing someone who is already dead, we need a clear notion of what constitutes being already dead. Finally, the already dead may deprive the living of access to lifesaving scarce medical resources if the former are maintained indefinitely on such equipment.

The modern problem of determining death had its counterpart earlier in concerns about premature burial. These fears were not entirely unfounded. Excavations in cemeteries reveal that approximately two percent of those buried prior

to the use of embalming in the twentieth century were buried alive, presumably in a state of what is popularly called "suspended animation."[1] Today doctors have the important social function of pronouncing death and signing death certificates, but it has not always been that way. Why and when were they given that role?

Prior to the late eighteenth and early nineteenth centuries, families, clergymen, or civil magistrates determined when death had occurred. Around the middle of the eighteenth century, physicians in France, led by Jean Jacques Winslow, undertook to convince western societies that physicians should be the official deciders of death. They argued that there would be much less chance for error and premature burial if medical professionals were in charge. Winslow, who initiated the movement, had a vested interest. Twice as a child he had awakened in a coffin about to be buried![2]

How do doctors know when death has occurred? They too must have both a clear concept of death and criteria of application. A survey of graduates from many medical schools, conducted in the late 1960's, revealed that none of the doctors could remember being instructed in medical school on how and when to diagnose death.[3] Has this changed since then? Neither doctors, lawyers, nor philosophers completely agree on what "death" means or on when death occurs. In the selections to follow, the President's Commission reviews recent developments in medicine which make it necessary for us to update our concept of "death." The major options are explained and critically examined.

There is at least this much consensus about the meaning of "death": It is the irreversible cessation of *something*. The disagreement is about that something. In pronouncing death, physicians both announce that something about a living creature has ceased functioning and predict that it is impossible to start it back up again. But what is that something? Consider these possibilities:

Death is the irreversible cessation of

(1) the functioning of all bodily cells, tissues, or organs;

(2) the flow of all bodily "fluids," including air and blood;

(3) the functioning of heart and lungs;

(4) the spontaneous functioning of heart and lungs;

(5) the spontaneous functioning of the whole brain, including the brain stem;

(6) the complete functioning of the upper or neocortical brain;

(7) the all but minimal functioning of the upper or neocortical brain;

(8) the embodied capacity for consciousness.

Which of these definitions should we enact into law as public policy?

Definition 1 may never have been seriously held by anyone. It is still important because it recognizes that different parts of the body die (i.e., become irreversibly nonfunctional) at different times. Thus it compels us to decide which part of the body is really essential for being a living person. Some cells, tissues, or organs of the body can still be functional after death has occurred. We accept the transplantation of bodily organs and tissues such as hearts, lungs, kidneys, livers, corneas, and bones from cadaverous donors; but transplanting them after they become irreversibly nonfunctional would be pointless. Something else must be the locus of life. What is it?

Definition 2 is accepted by many Jews and American Indians, as the President's Commission notes. The Commission indicates that, in the modern intensive care unit, the flow of bodily fluids may easily be maintained by machines "in the absence of almost all other life processes." Is a person with no spontaneous heart, lung, or even brain function whatsoever still alive? This option also restricts organ and tissue transplantation as severely as Definition 1. Should it be our legal definition of death? The Commission

thinks not, though it agrees that Jews and Native Americans who hold this concept should not be compelled by law to abandon it.

Definition 3 was the conventional medical notion of death until recent decades. "Chest death" has been rendered highly problematic by modern cardiopulmonary resuscitation techniques and intensive care technology. Until the recent development of CPR techniques, almost any cessation of heart and lung functions was irreversible. Now we know how to crank these organs back up again and how to maintain their functions almost indefinitely with heart/lung machines. Unfortunately, this definition implies that persons whose heart/lung functions are being maintained by purely mechanical means are still alive and that none of the "death behaviors" by others toward such patients (as identified by Robert Veatch in a following article) would be appropriate.

The President's Commission endorses the Uniform Determination of Death Act, as follows: "An individual who has sustained either (1) irreversible cessation of circulatory and respiratory functions, or (2) irreversible cessation of all functions of the entire brain, including the brain stem, is dead. A determination of death must be made in accordance with accepted medical standards."[4] Regrettably, when element (1) of the definition is strictly interpreted, it implies that persons whose heart/lung functions are being maintained purely mechanically are still living. The Commission and the numerous legislatures now adopting the Uniform Determination of Death Act may assume that this implication can be avoided simply by moving to option (2). However, as long as option (1) is permitted, this consequence cannot be avoided. Also, since (1) and (2) give very different results, it is not clear whose judgment should prevail if a doctor wants to declare death under criterion (1) while the patient's family insists that (2) is sufficient. Again, whose judgment should prevail if a transplant surgeon wants to declare death under (2) and the treating physician under (1)?

Definition 4 avoids the difficulties of 3 by requiring not merely that heart and lungs be working but that they work spontaneously, i.e., without the assistance of mechanical respirators or other devices. Many statutory definitions of "chest death" have included "spontaneous." Yet 4 has difficulties of its own.

Definition 4 implies that any person is dead who is both using an artificial heart (or a permanent pacemaker) and breathing only with the assistance of an iron lung or mechanical respirator. Even without any spontaneous heart or lung functions, such persons may be fully conscious and conversing with others. Surely they are not dead!

The heart can continue to function spontaneously for several days without spontaneous lung function, even after the brain stem has irreversibly ceased working. The life reserves of the body allow the heart to work for a time independently of any control and direction from the brain, and organs (including beating hearts) are often harvested from bodies with spontaneously beating hearts. For spontaneous breathing, however, some control and direction from the brain stem is necessary. The brain stem also integrates the activities of the major organ systems and thus maintains the functioning of the organism as a whole, as opposed to the individual organs considered in isolation. These facts, according to the President's Commission, have convinced medical professionals and most others that the brain is the locus of life.

Definition 5 requires the irreversible cessation of the spontaneous functioning of both the brain stem and the neocortical or higher brain, the primary locus of consciousness. Hopelessly comatose persons with little or no upper brain activity are still alive by this definition, as long as their brain stems continue to operate. Such persons "can not only breathe, metabolize, maintain temperature and blood pressure, and so forth, on their own but also sigh, yawn, track light with their eyes, and react to pain or reflex stimulation,"[5] but they do not have and never will have

the moral rights and standing of personhood. Personhood is achieved only at a later stage of development when the status of being "a responsible moral agent" is actually achieved. The mere potential for such is not enough. If some defective newborns probably "will never be persons," Engelhardt believes their parents should have an almost unrestricted right, and sometimes a definite duty, to decide not to save them.

Needless to say, Engelhardt's liberal view of personhood and his permissive ethic of infanticide are highly controversial. This notion of personhood will be examined in the next chapter, on abortion. In English and American common and positive law, newborn human infants definitely are persons with rights, including the right to life. A more conservative stance on infanticide which reflects this legal perspective is taken in the following article by John A. Robertson, who insists that human newborns are persons whose rights must be protected.

Robertson would not exclude any defective newborns from personhood. He agrees, however, that in certain extreme instances proxy decision-makers may allow such persons to die. He thinks that, at times, decisions to allow seriously ill newborns to die are not based upon whether doing so really would be in their best interests. The claim that it is best for the child to die often masks the fact that the decision is actually being made to benefit others, such as parents, family members, doctors, and society itself.

Except in the most extreme instances, Robertson insists, parents and other proxy decision-makers should not be allowed to refuse treatment for defective newborns. This general social policy would best protect the individual infants themselves and would best promote respect for all human life. Robertson accepts selective nontreatment only when (1) there is overwhelming suffering and (2) infants are irreversibly of greatly diminished consciousness or are comatose. He advocates the formulation and enforcement of general social policies which would

allow passive infanticide only in these limited situations and which would provide procedural safeguards that will minimize errors of overinclusion of infants who are unsuitable for nontreatment. He also advocates that society itself, i.e., the taxpayers, should help shoulder the burden for protecting the defective newborn's right to life.

In a selection to follow, the President's Commission develops in some detail ethical guidelines for proxy decision-making for seriously ill newborns. The Commission strongly disagrees with the so-called Baby Doe Regulations, issued in 1983 by the Department of Health and Human Services to implement legislation for the protection of the handicapped. These regulations were declared invalid by the Supreme Court on June 9, 1986, on the grounds that this legislation for the handicapped was not meant to extend to such situations. However, a federal law passed in 1984 attempts to bring under child abuse legislation inappropriate decisions not to treat.

The Commission recommends that the most difficult nontreatment cases be reviewed first by Ethics Committees and then, if necessary, by the courts as a last resort. Like the AMA, the Commission stresses that the primary decision-makers should be the parents and that other review bodies should become involved only if the parents make a questionable choice or are unable to make a decision at all. The Commission also reminds us that "public funds may ultimately be needed so that these children, once rescued, are not then left to drown in a sea of indifference and unresponsiveness." Again, it may cost a great deal of money to protect basic human rights.

E. ETHICS COMMITTEES

In the following selection on "Hospital Ethics Committees: Administrative Aspects," Fost and Cranford identify the numerous influences

which have resulted in the rapid proliferation of such committees in recent years. Although almost no one wants to "play God" in making decisions about the withholding or withdrawal of life-sustaining medical care, such decisions nevertheless must be made. In both pediatrics and situations where incompetent adults are suitable candidates for passive euthanasia, others must often decide. Ideally, decisions should be the most reasonable ones possible; but what procedural safeguards will best insure reasonable results?

Where tough decisions to allow others to die must be made, many factual and valuational matters are relevant. Consideration of these is best facilitated if the membership of Hospital Ethics Committees includes a diversity of both medically and ethically competent and reflective persons. Richard A. McCormick has suggested that, in reaching rational decisions about the "best interests" of those who might be allowed to die, "it has become increasingly clear that such a determination exceeds the perspective of an individual and that a group might be expected to approximate more nearly (if not always achieve) the "reasonable person standard."[11] The danger, of course, is that ethics committees will simply degenerate into mindless bureaucracies. Fost and

Cranford make suggestions about membership that will help insure valid results.

Our experience with Hospital Ethics Committees is relatively new, and Fost and Cranford identify the following unresolved problems:

(1) Should the purpose of Ethics Committees include any or all of the following functions: to improve public relations, to educate hospital staff and others, to develop policy and guidelines, to consult for active decisions?

(2) What steps should be taken to give such Committees official status with the Hospital and gain acceptance by Hospital personnel?

(3) In what way should the patient and family members be allowed to participate in the proceedings of these Committees?

(4) Should the meetings and records of the Committee be open or closed?

(5) How can the patient's right to confidentiality be protected?

(6) How, when, and why should the Committee be convened for consultations?

(7) To what extent will Committee members be legally liable for their decisions?

Notes

[1]David Dempsey, *The Way We Die* (New York: McGraw-Hill, 1975), p. 26.

[2]Marc Alexander, "The Rigid Embrace of the Narrow House: Premature Burial and the Signs of Death," *Hastings Center Report* 10, no. 3 (June 1980): 25–31.

[3]John D. Arnold et al., "Public Attitudes and Diagnosis of Death," *Journal of the American Medical Association* 206, no. 9 (Nov. 25, 1968): pp. 1949–54.

[4]President's Commission for the Study of Ethical Problems in Medicine and Biomedical and Behavioral Research, *Defining Death, A Report on the Medical, Legal and Ethical Issues in the Determination of Death,* (Washington, D.C.: U.S. Government Printing Office, 1981), p. 119.

[5]*Ibid.,* p. 35.

[6]For more details, see Cynthia B. Cohen, "'Quality of Life' and

the Analogy with the Nazis," *The Journal of Medicine and Philosophy* 8, no. 2 (May 1983): especially pp. 115–17.

[7]This is the view of the New Jersey Supreme Court in the recent *Conroy* case. See *In re Conroy,* 486 A. 2d 1209 (1985).

[8]Pope Pius XII, "The Prolongation of Life," *Pope Speaks* 4, no. 4 (1958): 393–98.

[9]Gerald Kelley, *Medico-Moral Problems* (St. Louis: The Catholic Hospital Association, 1958), p. 129.

[10]In another essay, James Rachels has come to some very similar conclusions. See James Rachels, *The End of Life: Euthanasia and Morality* (New York, Oxford University Press, 1986), pp. 96–100.

[11]Richard A. McCormick, "Ethics Committees: Promise or Peril?" *Law, Medicine & Health Care* 12, no. 4 (September 1984): 151.

an intact heart will continue to beat, despite loss of brain functions. At present, however, no machine can take over the functions of the heart except for a very limited time and in limited circumstances (e.g., a heart-lung machine used during surgery). Therefore, when a severe injury to the heart or major blood vessels prevents the circulation of the crucial blood supply to the brain, the loss of brain functioning is inevitable because no oxygen reaches the brain.

LOSS OF VARIOUS BRAIN FUNCTIONS

The most frequent causes of irreversible loss of functions of the whole brain are: (1) direct trauma to the head, such as from a motor vehicle accident or a gunshot wound, (2) massive spontaneous hemorrhage into the brain as a result of ruptured aneurysm or complications of high blood pressure, and (3) anoxic damage from cardiac or respiratory arrest or severely reduced blood pressure.[3]

Many of these severe injuries to the brain cause an accumulation of fluid and swelling in the brain tissue, a condition called cerebral edema. In severe cases of edema, the pressure within the closed cavity increases until it exceeds the systolic blood pressure, resulting in a total loss of blood flow to both the upper and lower portions of the brain. If deprived of blood flow for at least 10-15 minutes, the brain, including the brainstem, will completely cease functioning.[4] Other pathophysiologic mechanisms also result in a progressive

and, ultimately, complete cessation of intracranial circulation.

Once deprived of adequate supplies of oxygen and glucose, brain neurons will irreversibly lose all activity and ability to function. In adults, oxygen and/or glucose deprivation for more than a few minutes causes some neuron loss.[5] Thus, even in the absence of direct trauma and edema, brain functions can be lost if circulation to the brain is impaired. If blood flow is cut off, brain tissues completely self-digest (autolyze) over the ensuing days.

When the brain lacks all functions, consciousness is, of course, lost. While some spinal reflexes often persist in such bodies (since circulation to the spine is separate from that of the brain), all reflexes controlled by the brainstem as well as cognitive, affective and integrating functions are absent. Respiration and circulation in these bodies may be generated by a ventilator together with intensive medical management. In adults who have experienced irreversible cessation of the functions of the entire brain, this mechanically generated functioning can continue only a limited time because the heart usually stops beating within two to ten days. (An infant or small child who has lost all brain functions will typically suffer cardiac arrest within several weeks, although respiration and heartbeat can sometimes be maintained even longer.[6])

Less severe injury to the brain can cause mild to profound damage to the cortex, lower cerebral

---

[3]Ronald E. Cranford and Harmon L. Smith, "Some Critical Distinctions Between Brain Death and Persistent Vegetative State" 6 *Ethics in Sci. and Med.* 199, 201 (1979).

[4]H.A.H. van Till-d'Aulnis de Bourouill, "Diagnosis of Death in Comatose Patients under Resuscitation Treatment: A Critical Review of the Harvard Report," 2 *Am. J. L. & Med.* 1, 21–22 (1976).

[5]One exception to this general picture requires brief mention. Certain drugs or low body temperature (hypothermia) can place the neurons in "suspended animation." Under these conditions, the neurons may receive virtually no oxygen or glucose for a significant period of time without sustaining irreversible damage. This effect is being used to try to limit brain injury in patients by giving them barbiturates or reducing temperature; the use of such techniques will, of course, make neurological diagnoses slower or more complicated.

[6]Julius Korein, "Brain Death," in J. Cottrell and H. Turndorf (eds.) *Anesthesia and Neurosurgery*, C.V. Mosby & Co., St. Louis (1980) at 282, 284, 292–293.

structures, cerebellum, brainstem, or some combination thereof. The cerebrum, especially the cerebral cortex, is more easily injured by loss of blood flow or oxygen than is the brainstem. A 4-6 minute loss of blood flow—caused by, for example, cardiac arrest—typically damages the cerebral cortex permanently, while the relatively more resistant brainstem may continue to function.[7]

When brainstem functions remain, but the major components of the cerebrum are irreversibly destroyed, the patient is in what is usually called a "persistent vegetative state" or "persistent noncognitive state."[8] Such persons may exhibit spontaneous, involuntary movements such as yawns or facial grimaces, their eyes may be open and they may be capable of breathing without assistance. Without higher brain functions, however, any apparent wakefulness does not represent awareness of self or environment (thus, the condition is often described as "awake but unaware"). The case of Karen Ann Quinlan has made this condition familiar to the general public. With necessary medical and nursing care—including feeding through intravenous or nasogastric tubes, and antibiotics for recurrent pulmonary infections—such patients can survive months or years, often without a respirator. (The longest survival exceeded 37 years.[9])

CONCLUSION: THE NEED FOR RELIABLE POLICY

Medical interventions can often provide great benefit in avoiding irreversible harm to a patient's injured heart, lungs, or brain by carrying a patient through a period of acute need. These techniques have, however, thrown new light on the interrelationship of these crucial organ systems. This has created complex issues for public policy as well.

For medical and legal purposes, partial brain impairment must be distinguished from complete and irreversible loss of brain functions or "whole brain death." The President's Commission, as subsequent chapters explain more fully, regards the cessation of the vital functions of the entire brain—and not merely portions thereof, such as those responsible for cognitive functions—as the only proper neurologic basis for declaring death. This conclusion accords with the overwhelming consensus of medical and legal experts and the public.

Present attention to the "definition" of death is part of a process of development in social attitudes and legal rules stimulated by the unfolding of biomedical knowledge. In the nineteenth century increasing knowledge and practical skill made the public confident that death could be diagnosed reliably using cardiopulmonary criteria. The question now is whether, when medical intervention may be responsible for a patient's respiration and circulation, there are other equally reliable ways to diagnose death.

The Commission recognizes that it is often difficult to determine the severity of a patient's injuries, especially in the first few days of intensive care following a cardiac arrest, head trauma, or other similar event. Responsible public policy in this area requires that physicians be able to distinguish reliably those patients who have died from those whose injuries are less severe or are reversible. . . .

---

[7]Cranford and Smith, *op. cit.* at 203.

[8]Bryan Jennett and Fred Plum, "The Persistent Vegetative State: A Syndrome in Search of a Name," 1 *Lancet* 734 (1972); Fred Plum and Jerome B. Posner, *The Diagnosis of Stupor and Coma*, F. A. David Co., Philadelphia (1980 3rd. ed.) at 6–7.

[9]See Norris McWhirter (ed.) *The Guinness Book of World Records*, Bantam Books, New York (1981) at 42, citing the case of

---

Elaine Esposito who lapsed into coma following surgery on August 6, 1941 and died on November 25, 1978, 37 years and 111 days later.

Understanding the "Meaning" of Death

President's Commission for the Study of Ethical Problems in Medicine and Biomedical and Behavioral Research

The President's Commission is described on page 123.

The Commission describes Whole Brain, Higher Brain, and Non-Brain formulations of the concept of "death" and explains why it prefers the Whole Brain concept. The references at the end of the discussion are to the proposed Uniform Determination of Death Act, which reads as follows: "An individual who has sustained either (1) irreversible cessation of circulatory and respiratory functions, or (2) irreversible cessation of all functions of the entire brain, including the brain stem, is dead. A determination of death must be made in accordance with accepted medical standards."

It now seems clear that a medical consensus about clinical practices and their scientific basis has emerged: certain states of brain activity and inactivity, together with their neurophysiological consequences, can be reliably detected and used to diagnose death. To the medical community, a sound basis exists for declaring death even in the presence of mechanically assisted "vital signs." Yet before recommending that public policy reflect this medical consensus, the Commission wished to know whether the scientific viewpoint was consistent with the concepts of "being dead" or "death" as they are commonly understood in our society. These questions have been addressed by philosophers and theologians, who have provided several formulations.[1]

The Commission believes that its policy conclusions . . . including the [Uniform Determination of Death Act] must accurately reflect the social meaning of death and not constitute a mere legal fiction. The Commission has not found it necessary to resolve all of the differences among the leading concepts of death because these views all yield interpretations consistent with the recommended statute.

Three major formulations of the meaning of death were presented to the Commission: one focused upon the functions of the whole brain, one upon the functions of the cerebral hemispheres, and one upon non-brain functions. Each of these formulations (and its variants) is presented and evaluated.

THE "WHOLE BRAIN" FORMULATIONS

One characteristic of living things which is absent in the dead is the body's capacity to organize and regulate itself. In animals, the neural apparatus is the dominant locus of these functions. In higher

---

[1]*See, e.g.,* Robert M. Veatch, *Death, Dying and the Biological Revolution: Our Last Quest for Responsibility,* Yale University Press, New Haven, Conn., (1977) at 21–76; Douglas N. Walton, *Defining Death: An Analytic Study of the Concept of Death in Philosophy and Medical Ethics,* McGill-Queen's University Press, Montreal, Que. (1979); William C. Charron, "Death: A Philosophical Perspective on the Legal Definitions," 4 *Wash. U.L.Q.* 797 (1975); Dallas M. High, "Death: Its Conceptual Elusiveness," 55 *Soundings* 438 (1972); Paul Ramsey, *The Pa-*

From the President's Commission for the Study of Ethical Problems in Medicine and Biomedical and Behavioral Research, *Defining Death: A Report on the Medical, Legal and Ethical Issues in the Determination of Death* (Washington, D.C.: U.S. Government Printing Office, 1981), pp. 31–43.

tient as Person: Explorations in Medical Ethics, Yale University Press, New Haven, Conn. (1971) at 59–112; Stanley Hauerwas, "Religious Concepts of Brain Death and Associated Problems," 315 *Ann. N.Y. Acad. Sci.* 329 (1978).

animals and man, regulation of both maintenance of the internal environment (homeostasis) and interaction with the external environment occurs primarily within the cranium.

External threats, such as heat or infection, or internal ones, such as liver failure or endogenous lung disease, can stress the body enough to overwhelm its ability to maintain organization and regulation. If the stress passes a certain level, the organism as a whole is defeated and death occurs.

This process and its denouement are understood in two major ways. Although they are sometimes stated as alternative formulations of a "whole brain definition" of death, they are actually mirror images of each other. The Commission has found them to be complementary; together they enrich one's understanding of the "definition." The first focuses on the integrated functioning of the body's major organ systems, while recognizing the centrality of the whole brain, since it is neither revivable nor replaceable. The other identifies the functioning of the whole brain as the hallmark of life because the brain is the regulator of the body's integration. The two conceptions are subject to similar criticisms and have similar implications for policy.

The Concepts

The functioning of many organs—such as the liver, kidneys, and skin—and their integration are "vital" to individual health in the sense that if any one ceases and that function is not restored or artificially replaced, the organism as a whole cannot long survive. All elements in the system are mutually interdependent, so that the loss of any part leads to the breakdown of the whole and, eventually, to the cessation of functions in every part.[2]

Three organs—the heart, lungs and brain—assume special significance, however, because their interrelationship is very close and the irreversible cessation of any one very quickly stops the other two and consequently halts the integrated functioning of the organism as a whole. Because they were easily measured, circulation and respiration were traditionally the basic "vital signs." But breathing and heartbeat are not life itself. They are simply used as signs—as one window for viewing a deeper and more complex reality: a triangle of interrelated systems with the brain at its apex. As the biomedical scientists who appeared before the Commission made clear, the traditional means of diagnosing death actually detected an irreversible cessation of integrated functioning among the interdependent bodily systems. When artificial means of support mask this loss of integration as measured by the old methods, brain-oriented criteria and tests provide a new window on the same phenomenon.

On this view, death is that moment at which the body's physiological system ceases to constitute an integrated whole. Even if life continues in individual cells or organs, life of the organism as a whole requires complex integration, and without the latter, a person cannot properly be regarded as alive.

This distinction between systemic, integrated functioning and physiological activity in cells or individual organs is important for two reasons. First, a person is considered dead under

---

[2]Germain Grisez & Joseph M. Boyle, Jr., *Life and Death with Liberty and Justice: A Contribution to the Euthanasia Debate,* University of Notre Dame Press, Notre Dame, Ind. (1979) at 59–61.

If death is understood in theoretical terms as the permanent termination of the integrated functioning characteris-

tic of a living body as a whole, then one can see why death of higher animals is usually grasped in factual terms by the cessation of the vital functions of respiration and circulation, which correlates so well with bodily decomposition. Breathing is the minimum in "social interaction." However, considering the role of the brain in the maintenance of the dynamic equilibrium of any system which includes a brain, there is a compelling reason for defining death in factual terms as that state of affairs in which there is complete and irreversible loss of the functioning of the entire brain. To accept this definition is not to make a choice based on one's evaluation of various human characteristics, but is to assent to a theory which fits the facts.

Id. at 77.

this concept even if oxygenation and metabolism persist in some cells or organs. There would be no need to wait until all metabolism had ceased in every body part before recognizing that death has occurred.

More importantly, this concept would reduce the significance of continued respiration and heartbeat for the definition of death. This view holds that continued breathing and circulation are not in themselves tantamount to life. Since life is a matter of integrating the functioning of major organ systems, breathing and circulation are necessary but not sufficient to establish that an individual is alive. When an individual's breathing and circulation lack neurologic integration, he or she is dead.

The alternative "whole brain" explanation of death differs from the one just described primarily in the vigor of its insistence that the traditional "vital signs" of heartbeat and respiration were merely surrogate signs with no significance in themselves. On this view, the heart and lungs are not important as basic prerequisites to continued life but rather because the irreversible cessation of their functions shows that the brain had ceased functioning. Other signs customarily employed by physicians in diagnosing death, such as unresponsiveness and absence of pupillary light response, are also indicative of loss of the functions of the whole brain.

This view gives the brain primacy not merely as the sponsor of consciousness (since even unconscious persons may be alive), but also as the complex organizer and regulator of bodily functions. (Indeed, the "regulatory" role of the brain in the organism can be understood in terms of thermodynamics and information theory.[3]) Only the brain can direct the entire organism. Artificial support for the heart and lungs, which is required only when the brain can no longer control them, cannot maintain the usual synchronized inte-

gration of the body. Now that other traditional indicators of cessation of brain functions (*i.e.*, absence of breathing), can be obscured by medical interventions, one needs, according to this view, new standards for determining death—that is, more reliable tests for the complete cessation of brain functions.

Critique

Both of these "whole brain" formulations—the "integrated functions" and the "primary organ" views—are subject to several criticisms. Since both of these conceptions of death give an important place to the integrating or regulating capacity of the whole brain, it can be asked whether that characteristic is as distinctive as they would suggest. Other organ systems are also required for life to continue—for example, the skin to conserve fluid, the liver to detoxify the blood. The view that the brain's functions are more central to "life" than those of the skin, the liver, and so on, is admittedly arbitrary in the sense of representing a choice. The view is not, however, arbitrary in the sense of lacking reasons. As discussed previously, the centrality accorded the brain reflects both its overarching role as "regulator" or "integrator" of other bodily systems and the immediate and devastating consequences of its loss for the organism as a whole. Furthermore, the Commission believes that this choice overwhelmingly reflects the views of experts and the lay public alike.

A more significant criticism shares the view that life consists of the coordinated functioning of the various bodily systems, in which process the whole brain plays a crucial role. At the same time, it notes that in some adult patients lacking all brain functions it is possible through intensive support to achieve constant temperature, metabolism, waste disposal, blood pressure, and other conditions typical of living organisms and not found in dead ones. Even with extraordinary medical care, these functions cannot be sustained indefinitely—typically, no longer than several

---

[3]Julius Korein, "The Problem of Brain Death: Development and History," 315 *Ann. N.Y. Acad. Sci.* 19 (1978).

days—but it is argued that this shows only that patients with nonfunctional brains are dying, not that they are dead. In this view, the respirator, drugs, and other resources of the modern intensive-care unit collectively substitutes for the lower brain, just as a pump used in cardiac surgery takes over the heart's function.

The criticism rests, however, on a premise about the role of artificial support vis-a-vis the brainstem which the Commission believes is mistaken or at best incomplete. While the respirator and its associated medical techniques do substitute for the functions of the intercostal muscles and the diaphragm, which without neuronal stimulation from the brain cannot function spontaneously, they cannot replace the myriad functions of the brainstem or of the rest of the brain. The startling contrast between bodies lacking *all* brain functions and patients with intact brainstems (despite severe neocortical damage) manifests this. The former lie with fixed pupils, motionless except for the chest movements produced by their respirators. The latter can not only breathe, metabolize, maintain temperature and blood pressure, and so forth, *on their own* but also sigh, yawn, track light with their eyes, and react to pain or reflex stimulation.

It is not easy to discern precisely what it is about patients in this latter group that makes them alive while those in the other category are not. It is in part that in the case of the first category (i.e., absence of all brain functions) when the mask created by the artificial medical support is stripped away what remains is not an integrated organism but "merely a group of artificially maintained subsystems."[4] Sometimes, of course, an ar-

tificial substitute can forge the link that restores the organism as a whole to unified functioning. Heart or kidney transplants, kidney dialysis, or an iron lung used to replace physically-impaired breathing ability in a polio victim, for example, restore the integrated functioning of the organism as they replace the failed function of a part. Contrast such situations, however, with the hypothetical of a decapitated body treated so as to prevent the outpouring of blood and to generate respiration: continuation of bodily functions in that case would not have restored the requisites of human life.

The living differ from the dead in many ways. The dead do not think, interact, autoregulate or maintain organic identity through time, for example. Not all the living can always do *all* of these activities, however; nor is there one single characteristic (*e.g.*, breathing, yawning, etc.) the loss of which signifies death. Rather, what is missing in the dead is a cluster of attributes, all of which form part of an organism's responsiveness to its internal and external environment.

While it is valuable to test public policies against basic conceptions of death, philosophical refinement beyond a certain point may not be necessary. The task undertaken in this Report, as stated at the outset, is to provide and defend a statutory standard for determining that a human being has died. In setting forth the standards recommended in this Report, the Commission has used "whole brain" terms to clarify the understanding of death that enjoys near universal acceptance in our society. The Commission finds that the "whole brain" formulations give resonance and depth to the biomedical and epidemiological data presented in [a part of the study not reproduced here]. Further effort to search for

---

[4]James L. Bernat, Charles M. Culver and Bernard Gert, "On the Definition and Criterion of Death," 94 *Ann. Int. Med.* 389, 391 (1981).

   . . . When the respirator maintains the organism, it is questionable whether there is complete and irreversible loss of the functioning of the entire brain. But this is a question to be settled by empirical inquiry, not by philosophy. Philosophically, we answer the objection by saying that if the functioning of the brain is the factor which principally in-

tegrates any organism which has a brain, then if that function is lost, what is left is no longer as a whole an organic unity. If the dynamic equilibrium of the remaining parts of the system is maintained, it nevertheless as a whole is a mechanical, not an organic system.
Grisez & Boyle, *op. cit.* at 77.

a conceptual "definition" of death is not required for the purpose of public policy because, separately or together, the "whole brain" formulations provide a theory that is sufficiently precise, concise and widely acceptable.

Policy Consequences

Those holding to the "whole brain" view—and this view seems at least implicit in most of the testimony and writing reviewed by the Commission—believe that when respirators are in use, respiration and circulation lose significance for the diagnosis of death. In a body without a functioning brain these two functions, it is argued, become mere artifacts of the mechanical life supports. The lungs breathe and the heart circulates blood only because the respirator (and attendant medical interventions) cause them to do so, not because of any comprehensive integrated functioning. This is "breathing" and "circulation" only in an analogous sense: the function and its results are similar, but the source, cause, and purpose are different between those individuals with and those without functioning brains.

For patients who are not artificially maintained, breathing and heartbeat were, and are, reliable signs either of systemic integration and/or of continued brain functioning (depending on which approach one takes to the "whole brain" concept). To regard breathing and respiration as having diagnostic significance when the brain of a respirator-supported patient has ceased functioning, however, is to forget the basic reasoning behind their use in individuals who are not artificially maintained.

Although similar in most respects, the two approaches to "whole brain death" could have slightly different policy consequences. The "primary organ" view would be satisfied with a statute that contained only a single standard—the irreversible cessation of all functions of the entire brain. Nevertheless, as a practical matter, the view is also compatible with a statute establishing irreversible cessation of respiration and circulation as

an alternative standard, since it is inherent in this view that the loss of spontaneous breathing and heartbeat are surrogates for the loss of brain functions.

The "integrated functions" view would lead one to a "definition" of death recognizing that collapse of the organism as a whole can be diagnosed through the loss of brain functions as well as through loss of cardiopulmonary functions. The latter functions would remain an explicit part of the policy statement because their irreversible loss will continue to provide an independent and wholly reliable basis for determining that death has occurred when respirators and related means of support are *not* employed.

The two "whole brain" formulations thus differ only modestly. And even conceptual disagreements have a context; the context of the present one is the need to clarify and update the "definition" of death in order to allow principled decisions to be made about the status of comatose respirator-supported patients. The explicit recognition of both standards—cardiopulmonary and whole brain—solves that problem fully. In addition, since it requires only a modest reformulation of the generally-accepted view, it accounts for the importance traditionally accorded to heartbeat and respiration, the "vital signs" which will continue to be the grounds for determining death in the overwhelming majority of cases for the foreseeable future. Hence the Commission, drawing on the aspects that the two formulations share and on the ways in which they each add to an understanding of the "meaning" of death, concludes that public policy should recognize both cardiopulmonary and brain-based standards for declaring death.

THE "HIGHER BRAIN" FORMULATIONS

When all brain processes cease, the patient loses two important sets of functions. One set encompasses the integrating and coordinating functions,

carried out principally but not exclusively by the cerebellum and brainstem. The other set includes the psychological functions which make consciousness, thought, and feeling possible. These latter functions are located primarily but not exclusively in the cerebrum, especially the neocortex. The two "higher brain" formulations of brain-oriented definitions of death discussed here are premised on the fact that loss of cerebral functions strips the patient of his psychological capacities and properties.

A patient whose brain has permanently stopped functioning will, by definition, have lost those brain functions which sponsor consciousness, feeling, and thought. Thus the higher brain rationales support classifying as dead bodies which meet "whole brain" standards, as discussed in the preceding section. The converse is not true, however. If there are parts of the brain which have no role in sponsoring consciousness, the higher brain formulation would regard their continued functioning as compatible with death.

The Concepts

Philosophers and theologians have attempted to describe the attributes a living being must have to be a person.[5] "Personhood" consists of the complex of activities (or of capacities to engage in them) such as thinking, reasoning, feeling, human intercourse which make the human different from, or superior to, animals or things. One higher brain formulation would define death as the loss of what is essential to a person. Those advocating the personhood definition often relate these characteristics to brain functioning. Without brain activity, people are incapable of these essential activities. A breathing body, the argument goes, is not in itself a person; and, without functioning brains, patients are merely breathing

– humanist

bodies. Hence personhood ends when the brain suffers irreversible loss of function.

For other philosophers, a certain concept of "personal identity" supports a brain-oriented definition of death.[6] According to this argument, a patient literally ceases to exist as an individual when his or her brain ceases functioning, even if the patient's body is biologically alive. Actual decapitation creates a similar situation: the body might continue to function for a short time, but it would no longer be the "same" person. The persistent identity of a person as an individual from one moment to the next is taken to be dependent on the continuation of certain mental processes which arise from brain functioning. When the brain processes cease (whether due to decapitation or to "brain death") the person's identity also lapses. The mere continuation of biological activity in the body is irrelevant to the determination of death, it is argued, because after the brain has ceased functioning the body is no longer identical with the person.

what about MPD or religious conversion?

Critique

Theoretical and practical objections to these arguments led the Commission to rely on them only as confirmatory of other views in formulating a definition of death. First, crucial to the personhood argument is acceptance of one particular concept of those things that are essential to being a person, while there is no general agreement on this very fundamental point among philosophers, much less physicians or the general public. Opinions about what is essential to personhood vary greatly from person to person in our society—to say nothing of intercultural variations.

The argument from personal identity does not rely on any particular conception of personhood,

---

[5]H. Tristram Engelhardt, Jr., "Defining Death: A Philosophical Problem for Medicine and Law," 112 *Ann. Rev. Respiratory Dis.* 587 (1975); Robert M. Veatch, "The Whole-Brain Oriented Concept of Death: An Out-moded Philosophical Formulation," 3 *J. Thanatology* 13 (1975).

[6]Michael B. Green and Daniel Wikler, "Brain Death and Personal Identity," 9 *Phil. and Pub. Affairs* 105 (1980); Bernard Gert, "Personal Identity and the Body," *Dialogue* 458 (1971); Roland Puccetti, "The Conquest of Death" 59 *The Monist* 252 (1976); Azriel Rosenfeld, "The Heart, the Head and the Halakhah, *N.Y. State J. Med.* 2615 (1970).

but it does require assent to a single solution to the philosophical problem of identity. Again, this problem has persisted for centuries despite the best attempts by philosophers to solve it. Regardless of the scholarly merits of the various philosophical solutions, their abstract technicality makes them less useful to public policy.

Further, applying either of these arguments in practice would give rise to additional important problems. Severely senile patients, for example, might not clearly be persons, let alone ones with continuing personal identities; the same might be true of the severely retarded. Any argument that classified these individuals as dead would not meet with public acceptance.

Equally problematic for the "higher brain" formulations, patients in whom only the neocortex or subcortical areas have been damaged may retain or regain spontaneous respiration and circulation. Karen Quinlan is a well-known example of a person who apparently suffered permanent damage to the higher centers of the brain but whose lower brain continues to function. Five years after being removed from the respirator that supported her breathing for nearly a year, she remains in a persistent vegetative state but with heart and lungs that function without mechanical assistance.[7] Yet the implication of the personhood and personal identity arguments is that Karen Quinlan, who retains brainstem function and breathes spontaneously, is just as dead as a corpse in the traditional sense. The Commission rejects this conclusion and the further implication that such patients could be buried or otherwise treated as dead persons.

Policy Consequences

In order to be incorporated in public policy, a conceptual formulation of death has to be ame-

nable to clear articulation. At present, neither basic neurophysiology nor medical technique suffices to translate the "higher brain" formulation into policy. First, as was discussed in [a part of the study not reproduced here], it is not known which portions of the brain are responsible for cognition and consciousness; what little is known points to substantial interconnections among the brainstem, subcortical structures and the neocortex. Thus, the "higher brain" may well exist only as a metaphorical concept, not in reality. Second, even when the sites of certain aspects of consciousness can be found, their cessation often cannot be assessed with the certainty that would be required in applying a statutory definition.

Even were these difficulties to be overcome, the adoption of a higher brain "definition" would depart radically from the traditional standards. As already observed, the new standard would assign no significance to spontaneous breathing and heartbeat. Indeed, it would imply that the existing cardiopulmonary definition had been in error all along, even before the advent of respirators and other life-sustaining technology.

In contrast, the position taken by the Commission is deliberately conservative. The statutory proposal presented in [the Uniform Determination of Death Act] offers legal recognition for new diagnostic measures of death, but does not ask for acceptance of a wholly new concept of death. On a matter so fundamental to a society's sense of itself—touching deeply held personal and religious beliefs—and so final for the individuals involved, one would desire much greater consensus than now exists before taking the major step of radically revising the concept of death.

Finally, patients declared dead pursuant to the statute recommended by the Commission would be also considered dead by those who believe that a body without higher brain functions is dead. Thus, all the arguments reviewed thus far are in agreement that irreversible cessation of *all* brain functioning is sufficient to determine death of the organism.

---

[7]"Karen Ann Quinlan: A Family's Fate," May 26, 1981, *Wash. Post*, A at 1, col. 1. [Karen died on June 11, 1985.]

THE NON-BRAIN FORMULATIONS

The Concepts

The various physiological concepts of death so far discussed rely in some fashion on brain functioning. By contrast, a literal reading of the traditional cardiopulmonary criteria would require cessation of the flow of bodily "fluids," including air and blood, for death to be declared. This standard is meant to apply whether or not these flows coincide with any other bodily processes, neurological or otherwise. Its support derives from interpretations of religious literature and cultural practices of certain religious and ethnic groups, including some Orthodox Jews[8] and Native Americans.[9]

Another theological formulation of death is, by contrast, not necessarily related to any physiologic phenomenon. The view is traditional in many faiths that death occurs the moment the soul leaves the body.[10] Whether this happens when the patient loses psychological capacities, loses all brain functions, or at some other point, varies according to the teachings of each faith and according to particular interpretations of the scriptures recognized as authoritative.

Critique

The conclusions of the "bodily fluids" view lack a physiologic basis in modern biomedicine. While this view accords with the traditional criteria of death, as noted above, it does not necessarily carry over to the new conditions of the intensive care unit—which are what prompts the reexamination of the definition of death. The flow of bodily fluids could conceivably be maintained by machines in the absence of almost all other life processes; the result would be viewed by most as a perfused corpse, totally unresponsive to its environment.

Although the argument concerning the soul could be interpreted as providing a standard for secular action, those who adhere to the concept today apparently acknowledge the need for a more public and verifiable standard of death. Indeed, a statute incorporating a brain-based standard is accepted by theologians of all backgrounds.[11]

Policy Consequences

The Commission does not regard itself as a competent or appropriate forum for theological interpretation. Nevertheless, it has sought to propose policies consistent with as many as possible of the diverse religious tenets and practices in our society.

The statute set forth in [the Uniform Determination of Death Act] does not appear to conflict with the view that the soul leaves the body at death. It provides standards by which death can be determined to have occurred, but it does not prevent a person from believing on religious

---

[8]J. David Bleich, "Neurological Criteria of Death and Time of Death Statutes," *in* Fred Rosner and J. David Bleich (eds.) *Jewish Bioethics.* Hebrew Publishing Co., New York (1979) at 303–316.

[9]Telephone conversation with Richard E. Grant, Assistant Professor of Nursing, Arizona State University, July 17, 1981.

[10]Milton McC. Gatch, "Death: Post-Biblical Christian Thought" in Warren T. Reich (ed.), *Encyclopedia of Bioethics* (v. 1), MacMillan Publishing Co., N. Y., N.Y. (1976) at 249, 250; Saint Augustine, *The City of God*, Vernon H. Bourke (ed.) Image Books, Garden City, N. Y. (1958) at 269, 277; J.

David Bleich, "Establishing Criteria of Death," *in* Fred Rosner and J. David Bleich (eds.), *Jewish Bioethics*, Hebrew Publishing Co., New York (1979) at 285.

[11]Bernard Haring, *Medical Ethics*, Fides Publishers, Inc., Notre Dame, Ind. (1973) at 136; Charles J. McFadden, *"The Dignity of Life: Moral Values in a Changing Society,* Our Sunday Visitor, Inc. Huntington, Ind. (1976) at 202; Paul Ramsey, *op. cit.* at 59–112; Seymour Siegel, "Updating the Criteria of Death," 30 *Conservative Judaism* 23 (1976); Moses D. Tendler, "Cessation of Brain Function: Ethical Implications in Terminal Care and Organ Transplant," 315 *Ann. N.Y. Acad. Sci.* 394 (1978). *See also* pp. 13–14 *supra* and accompanying notes for a summary of the religious views presented to the Commission [not here included].

grounds that the soul leaves the body at a point other than that established as marking death for legal and medical purposes.

The concept of death based upon the flow of bodily fluids cannot be completely reconciled with the proposed statute. The statute is partially consistent with the "fluids" formulation in that both would regard as dead a body with no respiration and circulation. As noted previously, the overwhelming majority of patients, now and for the foreseeable future, will be diagnosed on such basis. Under the statute, however, physicians would declare dead those bodies in which respiration and circulation continued *solely* as a result of artificial maintenance, in the absence of all brain functions. Nonetheless, people who believe that the continued flow of fluids in such patients means they are alive would not be forced by the statute to abandon those beliefs nor to change their religious conduct. While the recommended statute may cause changes in medical and legal behavior, the Commission urges those acting under the statute to apply it with sensitivity to the emotional and religious needs of those for whom the new standards mark a departure from traditional practice. Determinations of death must be made in a consistent and evenhanded fashion, but the statute does not preclude flexibility in responding to individual circumstances after determination has been made. A fuller discussion of the implications of the proposed statute for decisions about the dead is presented in [the Uniform Determination of Death Act.]

Whole Brain, Neocortical, and Higher Brain Related Concepts of Death

Robert M. Veatch

A biographical sketch of Professor Veatch is given on page 51.

Veatch defends a higher brain concept of "death" and replies to the following objections to this concept, which were developed in the preceding selection by the President's Commission: (1) there is a lack of general agreement supporting it, (2) a spontaneously breathing human with irreversible loss of higher brain function would not be buried and therefore is not dead, (3) no techniques are available to measure higher brain death, and (4) adopting a higher brain concept would require adopting a "new concept" while adopting a whole brain concept would not. Veatch holds that persons are dead when their "embodied capacity for consciousness or social interaction is gone irreversibly," a condition correlated with a loss of all but minimal upper brain function. He proposes that our laws should allow us to choose our own concept of death and that a conservative whole brain concept should prevail for those who do not choose.

The organizers of this conference have chosen to contrast the *whole brain* and *neocortical* defini-

Reprinted by permission of author and publisher from Richard M. Zaner, ed., *Whole Brain and Neocortical Definitions of Death: A Critical Appraisal,* Boston and Dordrecht: D. Reidel Publishing Co., 1986. Copyright by D. Reidel Publishing Company, Dordrecht, Holland. This was originally delivered at a conference at Vanderbilt University supported in part by grants from the Tennessee Committee for the Humanities, Inc., and by The National Endowment for the Humanities.

tions of death. It is not clear how precisely they are using the terms. Presumably, to be precise, a whole brain oriented concept of death is one that measures death by the loss of all brain structure or functions while a neocortical concept of death is one that measures death by the loss of all neocortical structure or functions.

The original critique of the whole brain oriented definition of death was rooted in the point

that it seems bizarre to consider a person alive simply because some utterly trivial brain stem reflex arc happens to be intact. Surely, whatever we mean by death, so the argument goes, some brain function might be retained while still considering the human being with only that function dead. This led some to conclude that a person could really be dead if there were irreversible loss of just neocortical brain function, thus permitting one diagnosing death to ignore the extraneous brain stem reflex. Several problems arise with the neocortical position, however.

One of the first challenges came from those who realized that brain function at the cellular level might outlast organ system level function by a long period. The National Institute of Neurological Diseases and Stroke seemed to realize this when it decided to tolerate up to 0.2 microvolts of electron potential ([15], p. 983) while considering someone dead. Since EEG readings record neocortical activity, if there were any electrical activity presumably something was alive. The obvious conclusion is that cellular level function, even at the neocortical level, does not count as anything significant any more than isolated lower brain activity did. Only supercellular or system-level functions count.

Upon reflection, however, even this solution does not prove satisfactory for those of us who are convinced that the critical functions are ones that are normally associated with the neocortex. It seems possible that even some system-level neocortical functions might be considered trivial. If, for example, the critical functions were considered to be sensory, how would we assess someone who, due to a hypothetical freak accident, had an isolated section of motor cortex alive and functioning? If stimulated, that cortex would control some movement of a hand or foot, but no consciousness or conscious control would be possible. Anyone who is sympathetic with the position that moves the search for a definition of death beyond the whole brain and in the direction of the neocortex would have difficulty concluding that such a person were alive simply because he

retained some system-level neocortical motor activity. The neocortical conception of death, just like the whole brain oriented one, may be too conservative.

On the other hand, it is possible that a neocortical conception of death may be too liberal. It is at least hypothetically possible that some functions normally associated with the neocortex (what we often refer to as "higher" functions) could be replaced by other brain tissues or—at some point in the future—by computers. Surely a person walking around with a microcomputer that permitted him to think and feel, but who had no living neocortical tissue, would still be alive. (This formulation is based on a related argument in Tomlinson [10].) What we are really interested in is not the presence of neocortical activity, but the presence of certain functions that, for want of a better term, we often refer to as higher brain functions. Exactly what these functions are is open to much further debate, but they would seem to include capacity to be conscious, to think, feel, and be aware of other people. It is striking to note that these are almost precisely the functions Henry Beecher, the Chairman of the Harvard Ad Hoc Committee, referred to when identifying why he thought a person with a dead brain should be considered dead ([1], pp. 2–4).

It seems clear that when people speak of a so-called neocortical concept of death, they really have in mind a concept of death in which a person is considered dead when he or she irreversibly loses certain supercellular functions traditionally associated with the neocortical portion of the brain. Should we someday be capable of preserving those functions in the absence of the neocortex, a person retaining those functions would surely be considered alive. Thus when we speak of neocortical death it is really a short-hand for the more cumbersome phrase: death based on the irreversible loss of supercellular functions traditionally related to the neocortex. To convey that nuance, I have for some years referred to a "neocortically oriented" or "neocortically related" concept of death rather than the simpler "neocortical

death." By the same token I have tried to speak of a "whole brain oriented" concept of death rather than the simpler "whole brain death."

If, however, the term "neocortically oriented concept of death" conveys that death occurs when there is irreversible loss of all supercellular functions, but it is really plausible to hold that a person could be dead even while retaining certain supercellular neocortical functions (such as motor activity), then we need still another term. I have taken to speaking of "higher brain functions" to refer to the capacity to think, feel, be conscious, and be aware of other people, conceding that the term lacks precision. On this basis I shall contrast whole brain oriented and higher brain oriented concepts of death, leaving out of further consideration the somewhat different neocortical concept of death. I shall defend in this paper a higher brain concept. By that I mean that a person should be considered dead when there is an irreversible loss of higher brain functions, i.e., certain functions normally associated with the neocortex that include the capacity to be conscious, to think, feel, and be aware of other people.

The President's Commission consistently refers to a higher brain concept of death rather than a neocortical one. It is the Commission's rejection of that concept that I address.

A CRITIQUE OF THE PRESIDENT'S COMMISSION

In its report *Defining Death,* the President's Commission for the Study of Ethical Problems in Medicine and Biomedical and Behavioral Research ([9], p. 1) concluded that "death is a unitary phenomenon which can be accurately demonstrated either on the traditional grounds of irreversible cessation of heart and lung functions or on the basis of irreversible loss of all functions of the entire brain." With that conclusion very few people are in disagreement. That conclusion, how-

ever, finesses the really interesting philosophical and ethical question: can this unitary phenomenon of death also be demonstrated by the irreversible loss of some more limited set of so-called "higher brain" functions? It is clearly the Commission's intention to reject this possibility, although when it comes right down to it, it never offers a single argument that actually supports that conclusion. It does present three pages summarizing the higher brain position. It concludes that section, however, with a non sequitur: "Thus, all the arguments reviewed thus far are in agreement that irreversible cessation of *all* brain functioning is sufficient to determine death of the organism" ([9], p. 41). The real question today, however, is not whether this is a sufficient condition, but whether it is a necessary condition. The advocates of higher brain formulations have argued that the irreversible loss of higher brain function is also sufficient to determine the death of the organism.

As early as the early 1970s a number of people were aware that a great deal of what some people took to be essential to human existence could be lost without the destruction of the entire brain or even the loss of all brain functions. The critical scientific paper, at least for those of us involved in the Hastings Center's Death and Dying Research Group (the group which stimulated much of the philosophical and public policy reflection on this subject) was that by Brierley and his colleagues [2] in 1971. By 1973, in a paper presented at a Foundation of Thanatology symposium, I had reached the conclusion that the whole brain oriented conception of death was not sufficiently precise (published in 1975 [13]). Others seemed to be coming to a similar conclusion ([7], p. 133; [5], pp. 587–590). This was apparently sufficient for the President's Commission to treat the higher brain related formulation of a concept of death with some seriousness. They offered what I count as four points against a higher brain formulation and in favor of one more oriented toward the irreversible loss of all brain

functions. As we shall see, not one of them really counts as an argument.

1. The Lack of General Agreement

The Commission begins its discussion by reducing the higher brain formulation to one involving personhood such that loss of personhood is taken to be equated with death. The Commission then concludes that "crucial to the personhood argument is acceptance of one particular concept of those things that are essential to being a person, while there is no general agreement on this very fundamental point among philosophers, much less physicians or the general public" ([9], p. 39).

There are two problems with the Commission's discussion. First, it reduces the "higher brain" formulation to one depending upon a concept of personhood. Quite frankly the philosophical discussion of the concept of personhood over the past decade has been less than illuminating. More to the point, there is no reason to assume that clarification of the concept of personhood must be achieved in order to consider someone dead based on loss of higher brain functions. I have never in my own discussions of the concept of death made my formulation dependent upon the concept of the person. I have done so in part because of the confusion over that concept and in part because it has seemed quite possible to me that someone could have irreversibly lost personhood, whatever that may mean, and still be alive. If, for example, personhood is defined as the possession of the concept of "a self as a continuing subject of experiences and other mental states" [11], or as the possession of consciousness, reasoning ability, and self-motivated activity [16], making loss of personhood synonymous with death would make many people (such as the noncommunicative senile) dead simply because they were no longer persons while a consensus seems to exist that they should be treated as alive. I have preferred simply to avoid this thicket by attacking the definition-of-death problem without any reference to a theory of personhood. Let it be clear that I am not here attempting to avoid the difficult question of what characteristics are essential for treating someone as alive. In fact, it is precisely that question that must be answered and will be addressed below. Rather, I am claiming that that question can be dealt with without reference to the personhood debate or deciding what characteristics are essential to personhood, whatever that may mean.

The Commission seems to take the position that if there is no general agreement among philosophers (or physicians or the general public) on some concept, then it cannot be correct. The absence of consensus is surely not a sound argument against a position. In fact, there is no more of a consensus in favor of a whole brain oriented formulation than there is in favor of a higher brain oriented one. The only survey of which I am aware that would permit us to address this question seems to point to the conclusion that there is no majority support for *any* definition of death: whole brain, higher brain, or non-brain [4]. The Commission may have been meaning to argue that, since there is no consensus, the society should take the safer course and opt for the whole brain oriented concept of death so that no one may be treated as dead who could by some philosophical views be alive. If that is the Commission's position, however, it is an argument in favor of adopting a heart and lung oriented concept of death, not a whole brain oriented one.

The absence of a consensus may be a reason to be concerned about how to formulate a public policy, but not necessarily a reason for adopting the centrist alternative. I take the lack of consensus to be a good reason for adopting a more pluralistic and tolerant attitude about defining death, one that permits individuals to choose their own definition of death from among some small list of reasonable alternatives ([14], pp. 72–76; [12], pp. 316–317). However, it is wrong to conclude, as the Commission does, from the premise "There exists no consensus on a definition of death," that

This is only the first of the two higher brain formulations considered by the Commission, the personality criterion may be more acceptable to Veatch — hope

therefore "The whole brain oriented definition should be chosen."

2. The "Would You Bury a Breathing Body" Argument

The Commission's second point against the higher brain oriented formulations is equally a non-argument. The Commission points out that

the implication of the personhood and personal identity arguments is that Karen Quinlan, who retains brain stem function and breathes spontaneously, is just as dead as a corpse in the traditional sense. The Commission rejects this conclusion and the further implication that such patients could be buried or otherwise treated as dead persons ([9], p. 40).

There are several problems here. It is true that by some concepts of the person Karen Quinlan may not be a person. I say "may not be" because I, like the Commission, have doubts about what kind of empirical evidence it would take to demonstrate irreversible loss of personhood according to various concepts of personhood. Regardless, however, it is at least a mistake to consider Karen Quinlan dead according to a neocortical concept of death. The neurological evidence is clear that she retains some neocortical function ([8], p. 654). If the neocortical conception of death is one that equates death to the irreversible loss of all neocortical functions, then Karen Quinlan could not be dead by such a conceptualization any more than she could be by whole brain oriented conceptions. It is somewhat more difficult to judge whether she would be dead according to a "higher brain" conception of death. That would depend upon exactly what counted as the higher functions.

All of this may miss the point, however. The argument from our intuitions about whether we would bury someone who had lost all higher brain functions but retained spontaneous respiration is fallacious. It assumes that it is acceptable to bury people simply because they are dead—that is, corpses. Yet by any definition of death it seems

clear that some people would not be buried immediately when they become dead. I would not want to bury a person who had been pronounced dead based on a whole brain oriented concept of death if that person was still respiring on a respirator and his heart was still beating. On aesthetic grounds I would want to disconnect the respirator and let his heart stop before burial. I would also remove IVs, NG tubes, etc. The fact that we would not bury certain dead people until certain residual functions ceased is not a plausible argument against considering them dead. The fact that we would await cessation of spontaneous respiration for someone pronounced dead based on higher brain function loss is not a sound argument against the use of higher brain related criteria for death.

3. The "No Techniques Are Available" Argument

The third point made by the Commission against the higher brain oriented formulation is that "at present, neither basic neurophysiology nor medical technique suffices to translate the 'higher brain' formulation into policy" ([9], p. 40). This is an important point, one that cannot be overemphasized. It may lead to the policy conclusion that in order to pronounce people dead (based on higher brain conceptualizations of death) we must revert to the old whole brain oriented criteria. The logic of such a move is that persons will be considered dead when they lose higher brain function, but that the only way we can know for sure that higher brain function has been lost is to demonstrate that all brain function has been lost. For the past eight years I have suggested precisely this conservative policy course ([14], p. 72). It is important not to overstate the difficulty, however. If we have real doubts that Karen Quinlan has irreversibly lost higher brain functions, that would seem to have very critical implications for the decision that it is appropriate to withdraw respiratory and other medical support. If she is not dead because we cannot determine that she

has lost higher brain function, by the same token she may not be a good candidate for stopping treatment. On the other hand, if we are sufficiently convinced of irreversible loss of mental capacity (the court actually referred to loss of "cognitive, sapient function"), maybe we can be sufficiently convinced to pronounce death based on loss of those functions.

Regardless of whether we want to take the safe course and not operationalize measures to diagnose irreversible loss of higher brain function, this decision is surely not a sound argument against the position that people ought to be considered dead when it *can* be determined that they have irreversibly lost higher brain function. It may be an argument leading to the conclusion that it is not urgent for policy purposes to distinguish between higher brain and whole brain formulations, but it does not count against a philosophical position that says humans are to be treated as dead when it has been established that they have lost higher brain functions.

4. The "No New Concept" Argument

Finally, the Commission argues that adopting a higher brain oriented concept of death would be adopting a "new concept" of death and that "one would desire much greater consensus than now exists before taking the major step of radically revising the concept of death" ([9], p. 41). On its face, this is a strange point. It argues that a reason not to adopt a particular concept is that it would be new. Surely, one ought to adopt positions that are right and reject ones that are wrong regardless of whether they are new or old. Regardless of whether being new is a telling argument against a concept, the Commission's point requires a hidden premise that the whole brain oriented concept is not new.

In order to understand what is happening here some history is necessary. Since the early 1970s Alexander Capron, the Executive Director of the Commission, and I have disagreed on how to conceptualize the whole brain oriented concept

of death. For Capron, the whole brain oriented conception requires no new understanding of death, no new conceptualization. He seems to believe that throughout history people have always held that death is equated with the irreversible loss of all brain function. They have simply measured this loss by looking at heart and lung activity.

However, the historical and linguistic evidence is to the contrary. My reading of the evidence is that people have traditionally meant by death the irreversible stopping of the flowing of bodily fluids—the blood and the breath. Only on this basis can people have said meaningfully that persons with dead brains were still alive. Only on this basis would it be necessary to have statutory and common law revisions of the concept of death. Only on this basis would we have to overturn the idea that people die when their heart and lung function stops. Shifting to the idea that death means the loss of brain function even though the fluids continue to flow required a major shift in conceptualization. It is simply wishful thinking to claim that the states that, after years of often bitter struggle and debate, have adopted brain oriented definitions of death have not made an important conceptual shift in their understanding of death.

If I am correct, then adopting either a whole brain oriented concept or a higher brain oriented concept is a major step, a radical revision of the concept of death. Capron's device of claiming that the whole brain oriented concept has always been with us is implausible, even if for some reason it counts against a position that it is new.

This leads me to the conclusion that the Commission has in no way undercut the use of a higher brain oriented concept of death. It may show that there has not been any general agreement in favor of a higher brain concept (or any other concept for that matter), that we would not bury all dead persons immediately, that we may have to be overly conservative in measuring higher brain related death, and that a higher brain concept (like a whole brain related concept) is a new concept. But none of these counts against (or for) the use of a higher brain oriented concept. In

order to defend the use of a higher brain oriented concept, some additional work is necessary.

THE PHILOSOPHICAL UNDERPINNINGS OF THE HIGHER BRAIN CONCEPT

One of the most sophisticated presentations that seems to support a higher brain oriented formulation is that offered by Michael Green and Daniel Wikler in their article "Brain Death and Personal Identity" [6]. They argue that death should be equated with the loss of personal identity. To the extent that personal identity can be equated with what we are referring to as higher brain functions or what is sometimes for convenience referred to as neocortical functions, their argument is an apparent defense of higher brain or neocortical death.

While, as Green and Wikler suggest, the personal identity theory of the definition of death may have much to offer, and while their conception of personal identity seems to lead to a conclusion that is similar to mine, I find there are problems with it. Their position, in contrast to my own, does seem, contrary to their claim, to require a theory of personhood (or at least personal identity). They are therefore subject to all the criticisms that suggest that a human being who has lost personhood or personal identity may nevertheless still be alive.

Consider the case of a man (following the Green and Wikler convention, let us call him Mr. Jones) who, through a severe head trauma, had clearly and irreversibly lost all personal identity according to the criterion suggested by Green and Wikler, but after months of medical administration regained consciousness and mobility (of course, not recalling anything of his past). Such events are at least conceivable; perhaps they have actually happened. Under the Green and Wikler personal identity conception of death, we would have to say that Mr. Jones was dead; that, therefore, assuming the normal behavioral correlates of calling him dead, Mr. Jones's beneficiaries would inherit his property; that his home and assets would no longer be his; and that, if he happened to be in public office, he would *automatically* be removed. We would face some very awkward moments. What, for instance, would we call the person who gets up and walks away from the hospital bed possessing a new personal identity? Who, in fact, would name him? How would he be supported—without any assets or even disability insurance or social security?

It seems clear to me that we should concede to Green and Wikler that Mr. Jones may have lost personal identity, but surely not that a death has occurred. Even if there had been a total loss of personal identity and a new personal identity created in the same body, I am convinced that we would have no trouble concluding that no death had occurred. Death is not merely the irreversible loss of personal identity.

I have consistently maintained that death should be the name we give to the condition under which it is considered appropriate to initiate a series of behaviors that are normally initiated when we call someone dead. I have referred to these as "death behaviors." We begin mourning in ways that were not included in anticipatory grief; we may decide that certain medical interventions should only be stopped at the time of death, in which case we cease those interventions; we begin the process of reading the will; life insurance companies pay off; social security and annuity checks cease; we begin referring to the person in the past tense ("Mr. Jones was a good man" rather than "Mr. Jones is a good man"); and, if the person were President of the United States, the Vice President is automatically elevated to the Presidency. On the other hand, if we consider the person still alive, none of these behaviors is appropriate. We may engage in other behaviors—behaviors appropriate in response to a dying man or a seriously ill man, but we do not treat him as dead. We may,

hypothetical case of severe amnesia [margin annotation]

for example, anticipate the death; we may inquire about the location of a will, but not read it. If the person we consider still alive is President, we may initiate emergency procedures to have him removed from office, but we do not automatically have a new President.

Since the 1960s I have maintained that "death" is simply the name we give to the condition when these behaviors are considered appropriate. It may be that we now have to come to the conclusion that not all of them should occur at the same instant. In that case death as we know it would cease to exist. It would be replaced by a series of discrete events signalling the appropriateness of the various social behaviors. It seems, however, that society still is comfortable acknowledging a moment when all of these behaviors ought to occur. Whatever that moment is, it is not necessarily the same moment as the time when personhood, however defined, is lost, even irreversibly lost. It is not the moment when personal identity is lost, either. It surely is not the moment when all brain tissue is destroyed, as Byrne and his colleagues [3] would have us believe. That would commit us to having to measure the anatomical disintegration of all brain tissue. There is nothing illogical or unscientific about such a position, but it is both implausible and inconsistent with Judeo-Christian, Greek, and modern, secular thought. We would not even insist on the irreversible destruction of all brain function. Whatever it is that leads us to the ethical conclusion that humans should not be treated as dead, it is not the mere presence of isolated cellular activity of the brain.

The critical factors are surely functions, and they are functions at the supercellular level. What functions these are is fundamentally a nonscientific question. It must be answered by appeals to religious or metaphysical world views about when we should stop treating human bodies the way we treat living beings. Increasingly we are convinced that these functions are not respiratory and circulatory. I cannot think of any possible reason why we would assign such significance to brain stem reflex arcs. We have since 1970 excluded spinal cord reflex arcs, which are not that different. Nevertheless the position adopted by the President's Commission would force you to treat me as alive if my body had through some freak event preserved in my brain only the simplest gag reflex.

I do not want to be confused with my gagging. I would not want society to continue to treat me as if I were alive simply because my body could gag. By the same token, I would not want society to continue to treat me as if I were alive simply because my body retained some isolated perfused motor cortex capable of jerking my arm if stimulated properly. All of this leads me to the conclusion that I would want me considered dead in these circumstances. I even take it as a kind of insult that I could be confused with any of these trivial bodily capacities.

You may, at this point, press me for the underpinnings of my position. Can I give any reasons why I would want to be considered dead rather than alive in these situations? My answer is that I can, but they are reasons that are not likely to be persuasive to everyone in our pluralistic and secular society.

I, like a great many in our society, stand in the Judeo-Christian tradition. As such I maintain two things. First, I maintain that the human is fundamentally a social animal, a member of a human community capable of interacting with other humans. Second, I maintain that I am in essence the conjoining of soul and body—or to use the more modern language, mind and body. If either one is irreversibly destroyed so that the two are irretrievably disjoined, then I—this integrated entity—no longer exist. What is critical is the embodied capacity for consciousness or social interaction. When this embodied capacity is gone, I am gone. When there is no longer any capacity for consciousness, to think and feel within a human body, then I am gone. Were capacity to interact socially separable from the capacity for

consciousness, I would have a problem of deciding which is critical. But after many years of worry over that question I am forced to the conclusion that they are not separable. When this embodied capacity for consciousness or social interaction is gone irreversibly, then, and only then, do I want society to treat me as dead.

Now, however, is this simply an affirmation of a particular religious/philosophical view with which others may disagree? I am sure that it is. And the implications of that are significant. First, while my affirmation that death behaviors are appropriate when, and only when, there is an irreversible loss of embodied capacity for consciousness and social interaction reflects a particular religious/philosophical view, so does any other conceivable answer to the question of when death behavior is appropriate. The answer that death behaviors are appropriate when and only when respiratory and circulatory function ceases is surely a reflection of a strange animalistic view. Institutionalizing the circulatory and respiratory oriented concept of death would be institutionalizing a religious perspective just as surely as adopting a higher brain functions position. Moreover, institutionalizing the view that bodily integration maintained by the presence of *any* supercellular brain functions including lower brain functions is also adopting a particular religious/philosophical position. It is the position that what really counts in justifying treatment of a human as alive or dead is whether there is any capacity to integrate bodily functions—respiratory function, brain stem reflexes, and the like. That, like the heart and lung oriented conception of death, is a reflection of animalism, the view that humans are nothing more than their animal functions.

Where does that leave us? If I am correct, the President's Commission has opted for a particular theological/philosophical view—that of the animalists who give highest priority to the capacity to integrate bodily functions and who are not all that different from those who would insist that heart and lung function are what counts. They

have adopted a theological/philosophical position that is at odds with the Judeo-Christian tradition, but a theological/philosophical position nonetheless.

I am convinced that adopting the position more consistent with the Judeo-Christian tradition that affirms unity of mind and body is more plausible. I think that is sufficient reason for individuals to adopt it. It would, however, mean imposing a particular view on others—imposing it, for example, on some Jews and American Indians who apparently hold firmly to the heart–lung oriented concept of death, and to some animalists who hold firmly to the whole brain oriented concept of death. As a matter of public policy (as opposed to personal conviction) I am unwilling to do that. I have therefore advocated a position that is more tolerant. Before the President's Commission I argued that this problem should be treated just like any other question of religious/philosophical pluralism. People should be permitted to examine their own religious and philosophical traditions and adopt the positions that are most plausible to them.

Picking a definition of death, of course, has behavioral consequences. In fact, I have argued, that is the only reason the question is of significant policy concern. In matters affecting behavior, we permit only limited religious and philosophical liberty. As a society that loves liberty we will generally tolerate conscientious behaviors as well as conscientious belief whenever we can, but we must set limits.

This, however, may be much less of a problem than we imagine. We must realize that many of the practical behavioral issues can be resolved independently of the definition of death. If, for example, someone holds that death occurs when and only when the heart stops beating, he still has available to him the option of refusing medical treatment so that the heart will stop. In an extreme situation, society could even insist that such treatment be stopped against the individual's will so that the heart stops. Death could be pronounced for that individual based on his person-

ally held position that death occurs when the heart stops with virtually no social or economic implications. On the other hand, for the person who, like myself, held that death occurs at the time there is irreversible cessation of higher brain functions, death might be pronounced earlier than others in society would like. That, in itself, has virtually no policy significance, however. The alternative would be to require that such a person be considered alive until his whole brain stops. In such a case it is widely recognized that the individual (now considered alive) or his agents would have the right to refuse further treatment so that he would be dead very soon in any case.

The only real problems created by the recognition that the choice of a definition of death should be left to individual conscience would be for that very small group at the extreme who might either decide that they wanted themselves or the ones for whom they were agents considered dead when heart, lung, lower brain, and higher brain all continued to function, or the other small group at the other extreme who might decide that they wanted themselves or the ones for whom they were agents considered alive even though heart, lung, lower brain, and higher brain all had ceased to function. Here, especially when decisions are being made for other parties, the behavioral implications are so great and the deviation is so serious that society would have to place limits.

There is one objection to the pluralistic solution that needs to be addressed. It is sometimes argued that permitting individuals to choose, even within a limited range, would create confusion and administrative nightmares. The unconscious emergency room patient would be alive or dead depending upon his views, and he would be in no condition to be asked what his views are. There is a simple solution to this problem, however. As a matter of public policy we could adopt any one of the three plausible concepts of death referred to by the Commission with the proviso that individuals could opt for one of the others.

This is the way we handle related matters such as Uniform Anatomical Gift Act donations. We establish a default position and let those who are concerned opt for an alternative. In the case of the concept of death it might be acceptable to opt for the whole brain oriented position as a middle of the road option. I would prefer we opt for the higher brain oriented position for the default. The choice would not matter much if those who objected had the opportunity to opt out.

My conclusion is that the President's Commission has made two mistakes. First, it has mistakenly rejected the higher brain oriented concept of death as the most plausible. For a country that stands so close to the Judeo-Christian tradition to reject the position favored by that tradition and by most contemporary scholars within that tradition seems odd. Second, at the policy level it has missed the obvious and traditional way of resolving policy conflicts when matters of religious and philosophical variation are at stake. Permitting individuals to exercise their consciences based on their religious and philosophical beliefs would make the most sense. It would create virtually no adverse impacts on others within the society. Only in extreme cases would limits have to be placed. Those limits could easily be set. The Commission's recommendation, as it stands, manages to violate the convictions of both a conservative group of Jews and others who could be considered dead when they would want to be considered alive, and a more liberal group of Jews, Christians, and secular thinkers who could be considered alive when they would want to be considered dead. Were there a good reason to force a position onto these people against their will perhaps it could be tolerated, but there is not. Had the Commission adopted one of the positions—preferably the most plausible higher brain oriented concept—and then permitted individuals to dissent, ethical and religious freedom would have been preserved, mental anguish would have been prevented, and greater philosophical clarity would have been obtained, all at no significant social and economic costs.

References

[1]Beecher, H. K.: December 1970, "The New Definition of Death, Some Opposing Views," Paper presented at the meeting of the American Association for the Advancement of Science.

[2]Brierley, J. B.; Adam, J. A. H.; Graham, D. I.; and Simpson, J. A.: 1971, "Neocortical Death after Cardiac Arrest," *Lancet* 2, 560–565.

[3]Byrne, P. A.; O'Reilly, S.; and Quay, P. M.: 1979, "Brain Death—An Opposing Viewpoint," *Journal of the American Medical Association* 242, 1985–1990.

[4]Charron, W. C.: 1975, "Death: 'A Philosophical Perspective on the Legal Definitions," *Washington University Law Quarterly* 4, 979–1008.

[5]Engelhardt, H. T.: 1975, "Defining Death: A Philosophical Problem for Medicine and Law," *Annual Review of Respiratory Disease* 112, 587–90.

[6]Green, M. B.; and Wikler, D.: 1980, "Brain Death and Personal Identity," *Philosophy and Public Affairs* 9(2), 105–133.

[7]Haring, B.: 1973, *Medical Ethics*, Fides Publishing, Notre Dame, Indiana.

[8]*In re Quinlan.* 70 N.J. 10, 355 A. 2d 647 (1976).

[9]President's Commission for the Study of Ethical Problems in Medicine and Biomedical and Behavioral Research: 1981, *Defining Death: Medical, Legal and Ethical Issues in the Definition of Death,* U.S. Government Printing Office, Washington, D.C.

[10]Tomlinson, T.: 1984, "The Conservative Use of the Brain Death Criterion—A Critique," *Journal of Medicine and Philosophy* 9(4), 377–393.

[11]Tooley, M.: 1972, "Abortion and Infanticide," *Philosophy and Public Affairs* 2, 37–65.

[12]Veatch, R. M.: 1978, "The Definition of Death: Ethical, Philosophical, and Policy Confusion," *Brain Death: Interrelated Medical and Social Issues,* Edited by Julius Korein, The New York Academy of Sciences, New York, pp. 307–321.

[13]Veatch, R. M.: 1975, "The Whole-Brain-Oriented Concept of Death: An Outmoded Philosophical Formulation," *Journal of Thanatology* 3, 13–30.

[14]Veatch, R. M.: 1976, *Death, Dying, and the Biological Revolution,* Yale University Press, New Haven, Connecticut.

[15]Walker, A. E., et al.: 1977, "An Appraisal of the Criteria of Cerebral Death—A Summary Statement," *Journal of the American Medical Association* 237, 982–986.

[16]Warren, M. A.: 1973, "On the Moral and Legal Status of Abortion," *The Monist* 57, 43–61.

Euthanasia

James Rachels

James Rachels is University Professor of Philosophy at the University of Alabama at Birmingham. He is the author of two books: The End of Life: Euthanasia and Morality *(Oxford University Press, 1986) and* The Elements of Moral Philosophy *(Random House, 1986).*

Rachels reviews the history of our philosophical and religious attitudes toward euthanasia, critically examines the main arguments for and against euthanasia, and defends active euthanasia. He makes a proposal for legalizing active euthanasia and examines the principal arguments for and against it.

In this essay we shall discuss the major moral and legal questions concerning euthanasia. Is euthanasia morally permissible, or is it morally wrong? Should it be against the law, or should it be legal?

It would be useful if we could define at the

From *Matters of Life and Death: New Introductory Essays in Moral Philosophy,* edited by Tom Regan. Copyright © 1980 by Random House, Inc. Reprinted by permission of the author and publisher.

outset exactly what we mean by the word 'euthanasia'. But that is not an easy task. The word derives from two Greek words that mean, literally, "a good death," but we mean much more by it than that. The nearest English synonym for 'euthanasia' is 'mercy killing', which is close. Beyond that, it is hard to give a precise definition because the word is used in connection with a wide variety of cases.

I. INTRODUCTION

§1 The Central Case

Let's begin by looking at a case that illustrates perfectly what euthanasia is. (Incidentally, all the examples of euthanasia that I use throughout this essay are taken from real life.)

> Albert A., a hospital patient, was dying of cancer, which had spread throughout his body. The intense pain could no longer be controlled. Every four hours he would be given a painkiller, but over many months of treatment he had built up a tolerance for the drug, until now it would relieve the pain for only a few minutes each time. Albert knew that he was going to die anyway, for the cancer could not be cured. He did not want to linger in agony, so he asked his doctor to give him a lethal injection to end his life without further suffering. His family supported this request.

It would have been illegal for the doctor to grant this request—in fact, it would have been first degree murder—so Albert was not given the injection.

If the doctor had killed Albert, it would have been a perfect example of euthanasia. The case would have had these five important features:

1. The patient would have been deliberately killed.
2. The patient was going to die soon anyway.
3. The patient was suffering terrible pain.
4. The patient asked to be killed.
5. The killing would have been an act of mercy; that is, the *reason* for the killing would have been to prevent further needless suffering and to provide the patient with a "good death," or at least as good as it could be under the circumstances.

When all these features are present, we have the clearest possible case of euthanasia.

It is easy to find other examples of the same kind. Here is one in which the patient's request *was* granted:

> Barbara B. was a multiple amputee and diabetic in constant pain, who was told that she could live for only a few more months. She begged her husband to kill her, and he did, by electrocution. The husband was charged with murder and was convicted. On sentencing day the judge wept. Mr. B., who could have spent decades in prison, was sentenced to a year and a day. He never wavered in his opinion that he had done the right thing, and he said that his act was an act of love.

§2 Related Cases

There are many other cases in which the above five features are *not* all present to which the word 'euthanasia' is also commonly applied. For example:

> Charles C. begged to be killed after being paralyzed from the neck down in an automobile accident. The doctors ignored the request, but his brother did not. The brother brought a sawed-off shotgun into the hospital and fatally wounded him.

This case is different from the previous ones because Charles C. was not going to die soon anyway, and he wanted to be killed, not because he was in pain, but because he did not want to live as a hopeless invalid. Other people, of course, might have had a different preference. Others might prefer to live paralyzed, rather than not to live at all. But not Charles C; he preferred to die.

> Donald D. had been a jet pilot and a rodeo performer and was in the prime of life when he was severely burned over 67 percent of his body by an exploding gas line. He was grotesquely disfigured, blinded, lost the use of both his arms and legs, and was in constant horrible pain for many months as all the most sophisticated techniques of modern medicine were used to keep him alive. When rational, he would ask to be killed—specifically, he wanted an overdose of heroin. He refused to give permission for treatment, and so a psychiatrist was called in to declare him "incompetent" to withhold consent. After interviewing Donald, the psychiatrist decided that he was in fact competent. But, having won his point, Donald suddenly changed his mind and consented to further treatment. He eventually regained partial use of his limbs and went to law school.

In all the cases I have mentioned so far, the patient is conscious, at least arguably rational, and requests death. In the following case, however, the patient is not rational and makes no such request:

> Edward E., eighty-nine years old, had suffered three heart attacks, had bad kidneys, suffered various other ailments, and was hopelessly senile. He was hospitalized for his heart condition, and most of the time was only semiconscious. He was unable even to recognize members of his own family. There was no expectation of significant improvement in his condition. The attending physician instructed the hospital staff that if he should suffer another attack, nothing should be done to save him. Shortly afterwards, Edward's heart failed, no action was taken, and he died.

This is a very common sort of case, in which doctors have to decide how much is to be done to prolong lives that have become meaningless even to the patients themselves. In addition to the fact that the patient is not rational and that death is not requested, there are two other important features of this case that should be noted. First, the patient is not killed, but is merely allowed to die. And second, the reason for allowing the patient to die is not as a kindness to him. The patient is not allowed to die for his own good, since he is not suffering. Rather, he is allowed to die because it is felt that there is simply no longer any point in keeping him alive. The case of Edward E. is similar in these ways to the following case:

> Frances F. was in a permanent coma, being kept alive by machines and fed intravenously. She had suffered such severe brain damage that she could never wake up. She could be kept alive indefinitely by the use of artificial life-support systems, but if these machines were turned off she would die. The machines were turned off, and she died.

Like Edward, Frances did not ask to die, and like him, she was really unable to express an opinion in the matter. The attending physician judged that there was no point in keeping her alive—death would be neither kind nor cruel for her, since it would make no difference at all as far as *she* was concerned—so she was allowed to die.

§3 Some Distinctions

At this point I want to introduce a bit of terminology. The phrase '*active* euthanasia' is used to refer to cases in which the patient is killed, for example by being given a lethal injection. The phrase '*passive* euthanasia' refers to cases in which the patient is not killed but merely allowed to die. In passive euthanasia we simply refrain from doing anything to keep the patient alive—for example, we may refuse to perform surgery, administer medication, give a heart massage, or use a respirator—and let the person die of whatever ills are already present. It is important to note this distinction, because many people believe that, although active euthanasia is immoral, passive euthanasia is morally all right. They believe that, while we should never actually kill patients, it is sometimes all right to let them die.

In addition to the distinction between active and passive euthanasia, it is important to bear in mind the difference between voluntary, nonvoluntary, and involuntary euthanasia. *Voluntary* euthanasia occurs whenever the patient requests death. The cases of Barbara B. and Charles C. are both examples of voluntary euthanasia, since both patients asked to be killed. *Nonvoluntary* euthanasia occurs when the patient is unable to form a judgment or voice a wish in the matter and, therefore, expresses no desire whatever. The cases of Edward E. and Frances F. are both instances of nonvoluntary euthanasia; Edward was senile and only semiconscious, while Frances was permanently comatose, so neither could form a preference.

Finally, *involuntary* euthanasia occurs when the patient says that he or she does not want to die, but is nevertheless killed or allowed to die. In this essay I will not be concerned with involuntary euthanasia. My view is that it is simply murder, and that it is not justified. If a person *wants* to live on, even in great pain, and even with the

certainty of a horrible end, that is the individual's right. I believe that most people would agree with this judgment, but at any rate, I will not discuss this sort of case any further. Rather, attention will be focused primarily on voluntary euthanasia, and, to a somewhat lesser extent, on nonvoluntary euthanasia.

§4 The Main Issues

We have now looked at a number of cases and noted some of the important similarities and differences among them. Now let us return to our original question: What are we to understand by the word 'euthanasia'? Primarily it means killing someone—or letting someone die—who is going to die soon anyway, at the person's own request, as an act of kindness. This is the central case. The other cases I have described are called "euthanasia" because of their similarities to it.

In what follows we will be concerned mainly with the morality of euthanasia in the central case. The two main issues are: first, is it morally permissible to kill or let die someone who is going to die soon anyway, at the persons' own request, as an act of kindness? And second, should such killing or letting die be against the law?

Along the way I will also discuss the morality of killing, or letting die, in the other cases I have described, since many of the same problems are involved. However, it is primarily the central case that will concern us.

Let me add one word of caution: We must be careful not to confuse the question of whether euthanasia *is* against the law with the very different question of whether it *ought to be* against the law. As a matter of fact, in the United States, active euthanasia is against the law. But it does not follow from this fact that active euthanasia ought to be against the law, for it *could be* that this is an unwise law that ought to be stricken from the books. The law itself can be the object of moral criticism. Once, for example, it was against the law in the southern United States for black people and white people to eat together in restaurants.

But this legal rule was clearly a bad one, and it was changed after moral objections were raised forcefully against it. In the same spirit, we will ask whether the law prohibiting active euthanasia is a good one or a bad one, and whether it ought to be changed.

II. AN HISTORICAL PERSPECTIVE

We cannot conclude that any practice is morally right simply because people believe that it is right, or because historically the practice has been accepted. What we believe, or what our culture accepts, may be wrong. Nevertheless, in order to place our convictions in context, it is useful to reflect on the history of those beliefs and to compare them with the beliefs of people who live, or who have lived, in societies different from our own.

§5 Attitudes from the Ancient World

The people of ancient Greece took an attitude toward human life that is very different from our own. They did not believe that all human life is precious, or that it must be preserved at all costs. In Sparta, for example, it was required by law that deformed infants be put to death—this was considered better than an unhappy life for them and their parents. The approval of infanticide was not limited to Sparta; in Athens, which we consider to have been a more enlightened community, the destruction of deformed or unhealthy babies was also approved. The Athenians did not *require* that they be killed, but on the other hand there was no condemnation of the practice, either. It is worth remembering that we are not talking about a crude, backward society, but about one of the world's great civilizations, which produced some of our finest literature, art, and philosophy, as well as virtually inventing science and mathematics.

The fact that the Greeks approved infanticide is not a sign that they placed little value on human

life. They were not a murderous people, and they took a stern view of some other types of killing. In general, they did not approve of suicide: Pythagoras, Plato, and Aristotle all rejected it as a cowardly way of avoiding life's hardships and one's duties to self and state. However, all three of these philosophers thought it foolish to prohibit suicide in *every* situation, and they allowed that in cases of incurable disease accompanied by great pain, a person has the right to choose an earlier death. Unfortunately, the Greek whose views are most often remembered on this subject was not really representative. Hippocrates, sometimes counted as the "father of medicine," was the author of an oath that is still taken by new doctors; in it, the doctors pledge that "If any shall ask of me a drug to produce death I will not give it, nor will I suggest such counsel." This part of the Hippocratic Oath would not have been endorsed, without qualification, by the majority of Greek thinkers.

The Romans adopted many of the Greeks' attitudes. The Stoic philosopher Seneca, for example, wrote without apology that "We destroy monstrous births, and drown our children if they are born weakly and unnaturally formed."[1] If anything, the Romans regarded killing—in special circumstances—even more indifferently than the Greeks. The Stoic and Epicurean philosophers thought suicide an acceptable option *whenever* one no longer cared for life. The most famous statement of this attitude is by Epictetus: "If the room is smoky, if only moderately, I will stay; if there is too much smoke I will go. Remember this, keep a firm hold on it, the door is always open."[2] To those with such a frame of mind, it seemed obvious that euthanasia was preferable to a miserable, lingering death. Seneca, again, wrote:

> I will not relinquish old age if it leaves my better part intact. But if it begins to shake my mind, if it destroys my faculties one by one, if it leaves me not life but breath, I will depart from the putrid or the tottering edifice. If I know that I must suffer without hope of relief I will depart not through fear of the pain itself but because it prevents all for which I would live.[3]

§6 The Early Christian View

The coming of Christianity caused vast changes in these attitudes. The early Church was resolutely pacifist and opposed the killing of humans in *every* context. Infanticide was prohibited, for it was thought that all who are born of woman, no matter how monstrous or miserable, have immortal souls. Suicide was forbidden because one's life was viewed as a trust from God, and only God has the right to take it. Considering the nonpacifist views of most modern Christians, the reader may be surprised to learn that participation in warfare was also condemned by the early Church. The Church fathers—Lactantius, Tertullian, Origen—were in agreement on all of this. Of war, Tertullian wrote: "Can it be lawful to handle the sword, when the Lord himself has declared that he who uses the sword shall perish by it?"[4]

The Church continued to denounce infanticide and suicide, but it soon modified its position on war. A sympathetic interpretation of this change might be that Christians came to recognize a valid moral difference between killing in a just war and other forms of killing. A less sympathetic view is taken by the sociologist-philosopher Edward Westermarck, who remarked in his classic work *Christianity and Morals*:

> A divine law which prohibited all resistance to enemies could certainly not be accepted by the State, especially at a time when the Empire was seriously threatened by foreign invaders. Christianity could therefore never become a State religion unless it gave up its attitude towards war. And it gave it up.[5]

The early Church had also condemned capital punishment, which was not surprising considering the number of Church figures, including Jesus himself and St. Peter, who had been executed. But this position, too, was soon modified, bringing the Church's stance more into line with political requirements. The imposition of death by the State was said to be all right, so long as priests took no part in the proceedings.

But the Church's opposition to euthanasia continued, and under its influence, what for the Greek and Roman philosophers had been a compassionate solution to the problem of lingering, degrading death became a mortal sin. Suffering, no matter how horrible or seemingly pointless, came to be viewed as a burden imposed by God himself, for purposes known to Him, which men and women must bear until the "natural" end. This attitude prevailed throughout the Middle Ages, and was not seriously challenged until the sixteenth century.

§7 Other Religions and Cultures

But I do not want to give the impression that the prohibition of euthanasia is exclusively a Christian doctrine. Jewish law also forbids it. In fact, we find a rare consensus among rabbinic authorities on this subject. The medieval Jewish theologians were no less emphatic than their Christian counterparts: The great Maimonides, for example, wrote in the twelfth century that "One who is in a dying condition is regarded as a living person in all respects . . . He who touches him (thereby causing him to expire) is guilty of shedding blood."[6] The Islamic tradition is also uncompromising, for the Koran explicitly states that the suicide "shall be excluded from heaven forever," and voluntary euthanasia is regarded as simply a form of assisted suicide.[7] So not only Christianity but all these religious traditions conspire to withhold a merciful death to those who suffer—or, to look at things from an opposite point of view, conspire to affirm the preciousness of life even when life is most wretched.

If we turn for a moment to the experience of other cultures, we find a striking contrast. While these developing Western traditions were opposing euthanasia, most Eastern peoples were comfortably accepting it. In China, Confucian ethics had always allowed voluntary death in the case of hopeless disease, and the great Eastern religions, including Shintoism and Buddhism, took a simi-

lar attitude. In *The Dialogues of Buddha* there are described two holy men who commit suicide to escape incurable illness, and this is said to be no obstacle to their attaining "nirvana," the spiritual goal of all Buddhist endeavor. Among so-called primitive societies, there is a wide range of attitudes toward euthanasia, but it is easy to compile long lists of cultures in which the suicide or killing of those with intolerable illness is approved; one historian mentions eighteen such societies in the space of two pages.[8]

§8 Dissenters

But now let us return to our historical sketch of Western attitudes. As I said, after Christianity became a state religion, opposition to euthanasia, as well as to suicide, infanticide, and abortion, took a firm hold on the minds of almost everyone who bothered to think seriously about it. Throughout the Middle Ages, the prohibition on these practices was virtually unchallengeable. Not until 1516 do we find an important defense of mercy killing. In that year Sir Thomas More, later to be made a saint of the Church, wrote in his *Utopia* that in the imaginary perfect community:

> When any is taken with a torturing and lingering pain, so that there is no hope either of cure or ease, the priests and magistrates come and exhort them, that, since they are now unable to go on with the business of life, are become a burden to themselves and all about them, and they have really outlived themselves, they should no longer nourish such a rooted distemper, but choose rather to die since they cannot live but in such misery.[9]

Remarkably, More advocates in this passage not only that euthanasia be permitted, but that it be *urged* on the desperately ill, even when they are reluctant to accept it. This certainly seems to be going too far; I do not know of any other advocate of euthanasia who would agree with More about *that*. Nevertheless, More adds that a person who refuses euthanasia is to be cared for as well as possible.

Gradually, more and more thinkers came to believe that the prohibition on euthanasia ought to be relaxed. It was, however, a very slow movement, and those who favored the relaxation remained in a distinct minority. After Thomas More, the next notable proponent of euthanasia was Francis Bacon, credited as one of the founders of modern philosophy. A hundred years after More's *Utopia,* Bacon defined the role of the physician as "not only to restore the health, but to mitigate pain and dolours; and not only when such mitigation may conduce to recovery, but when it may serve to make a fair and easy passage."[10]

§9 Modern Secular Thought

Seventeenth- and Eighteenth-Century Thought During the seventeenth and eighteenth centuries, philosophers began to move away from the idea that morality requires a religious foundation. Although most were still theists, and God still held a prominent place in their understanding of the universe, they did not think that right and wrong consisted in following God's commandments, and they did not look to the Church as a primary source or moral guidance. Instead, human reason and the individual conscience were regarded as the sources of moral insight. This did not mean, however, that these thinkers abandoned all traditional moral views. Although they were revolutionary in their ideas concerning the *sources* of morality, often they were not so radical in their particular moral opinions. The most famous German philosophers, Kant (1724–1804) and Hegel (1770–1831), held that moral truths are known through the use of reason alone; but when they exercised their reason on such matters as suicide and euthanasia, they discovered that the Church had been right all along. A notable exception to this way of thinking was the greatest British philosopher, David Hume (1711–1776), who argued vigorously that one has the right to end one's life when he or she pleases. Hume, who was a sceptic about religion, particularly tried to refute theological arguments to the contrary.

It is one thing for a philosopher to argue that morality is separate from religion, or that the basis of morality is not necessarily religious, but it is quite a different matter for those ideas to affect popular thinking. In spite of the growing secularization of philosophical thought in the seventeenth and eighteenth centuries, in the popular mind, ethics was still very much tied to religion. The Protestant Reformation had created many churches where before there had been the one Church; and for Protestants the authority of the Church had been replaced by the individual believer's direct relationship with God. But still, people's moral duties were conceived as the outgrowth of their religious beliefs, and the purpose of the moral life was still thought to be the service of God. Then in the nineteenth century a remarkable thing happened: a philosophical movement, utilitarianism, not only captured the imaginations of philosophers but revolutionized popular thinking as well.

Utilitarianism Jeremy Bentham (1748–1832) argued that the purpose of morality is not the service of God or obedience to abstract moral rules, but the promotion of the greatest possible happiness for creatures on earth. What we ought to do is calculate how our actions, laws, and social policies will actually affect people (and other animals, too). Will they result in people being made happier, in people having better lives? Or will they result in people being made more miserable? According to Bentham, our decisions should be made on that basis, and *only* on that basis.

But Bentham did not stop when he had articulated this as a theoretical idea. He was concerned with bringing about social change and not merely with voicing a philosophy. Bentham became the leader of a group of philosophers, economists, and politicians who sought to reform the laws and institutions of England along utilitarian lines, and the social and intellectual life of people in the English-speaking countries has not been the same since. Bentham argued, for example, that in order to maximize happiness, the law should not seek to enforce abstract moral rules or meddle in the private affairs of citizens. What consenting adults

do in private is strictly their own business, and the law has no right to interfere. The law should concern itself with people's behavior only when they may do harm to others. This idea, now so familiar a part of liberal ideology, was radically new when the Benthamites first urged it on their fellow Englishmen.

The implications for euthanasia were obvious. For the utilitarians, the question was simply this: Does it increase or decrease human happiness to provide a quick, painless death for those who are dying in agony? Clearly, they reasoned, the only consequences of such actions will be to decrease the amount of misery in the world; therefore, euthanasia must be morally right. Moreover, as Bentham's famous follower John Stuart Mill (1806–1873) put it, the individual is sovereign over his own body and mind; where one's own interests are concerned, there is no other authority. Therefore, if one wants to die quickly rather than linger in pain, that is strictly a personal affair, and the government has no business intruding. Indeed, Bentham himself requested euthanasia in his last moments.

§10 Recent Developments

The utilitarian movement changed the way people think. Today, the calculation of benefits and harms is routinely accepted as a primary way of determining what is right and what is wrong. (The fact that contemporary philosophers spend so much time criticizing and arguing about utilitarianism only attests to its tremendous influence.) As a result, more and more people have come to favor euthanasia. In 1936, there was organized in England the Voluntary Euthanasia Society, with an eminent surgeon as its first president and many physicians among its sponsors. This was followed in the United States by the organization of such groups as the Euthanasia Society of America, the Euthanasia Educational Council, and the Society for the Right to Die. Advocacy of active euthanasia is no longer confined to a few figures on the fringes of academic

thought. It is publicly supported by thousands of doctors, lawyers, scientists, and clergymen (including many Catholics), as well as philosophers; and although active euthanasia is still illegal, bills are being introduced in various legislative bodies every year in an attempt to legalize it.

§11 The Position of the American Medical Association

The preceding historical sketch must be qualified in an important way. Throughout the history of our subject, most people have thought that the distinction between active euthanasia and passive euthanasia is morally important; and many of those who condemned active euthanasia raised no objection against passive euthanasia. Even when killing was thought to be wrong, allowing people to die by not treating them was thought in some circumstances to be all right. Four centuries before Christ, we find Socrates saying of a physician, with approval, ". . . bodies which disease had penetrated through and through he would not have attempted to cure . . . he did not want to lengthen out good-for-nothing lives."[11] Neither the Christians nor the Jews, in the centuries following, significantly altered this basic idea; both viewed *allowing to die,* in circumstances of hopeless suffering, as morally permissible. It was killing that was zealously opposed.

The morality of allowing people to die by not treating them has become critically important in recent years because of advances in medical technology. By using such devices as respirators, heart-lung machines, and intravenous feeding, we can now keep almost anybody alive indefinitely, even after he or she has become nothing more than a "human vegetable," without thought or feeling or hope of recovery. The maintenance of life by such artificial means is, in these cases, sadly pointless. Virtually everyone who has thought seriously about the matter agrees that it is morally all right, at some point, to cease treatment and allow such people to die. No less a figure than the Pope has concurred: as recently as 1958, Pius XII

reaffirmed that we may "allow the patient who is virtually already dead to pass away in peace."[12]

In December 1973, the American Medical Association issued a statement, "The Physician and the Dying Patient," in which it announced its official policy on euthanasia. That statement reaffirmed the traditional ban on mercy killing but also accepted the traditional view of letting die as (in some circumstances) all right. It said, in its entirety:

> The intentional termination of the life of one human being by another—mercy killing—is contrary to that for which the medical profession stands and is contrary to the policy of the American Medical Association.
>
> The cessation of the employment of extraordinary means to prolong the life of the body when there is irrefutable evidence that biological death is imminent is the decision of the patient and/or his immediate family. The advice and judgment of the physician should be freely available to the patient and/or his immediate family.

Since passive euthanasia is relatively uncontroversial, most of our attention in what follows will be given to active euthanasia.

III. ARGUMENTS SUPPORTING THE MORALITY OF ACTIVE EUTHANASIA

§12 The Importance of Argument

We come now to the most important part of our investigation. So far we have seen that there is widespread agreement that passive euthanasia is morally all right, in at least some cases, but that active euthanasia is much more controversial. We have seen that in the course of Western history, some thinkers have approved of active euthanasia, but most have condemned it. We have seen that in some other cultures, a more tolerant attitude is taken toward active euthanasia. And finally, we have examined the position of the medical establishment in our own country, according to which active euthanasia is always "con-

trary to that for which the medical profession stands," even though passive euthanasia is said to be in some circumstances all right. But, while all of this is valuable as background information, none of it directly touches the most important issue. We want to know, most of all, whether euthanasia—active or passive—*really is moral,* or whether in fact it is immoral.

How are we to go about answering this question? We cannot discover whether euthanasia is immoral simply by consulting our feelings. Our feelings may be nothing more than irrational prejudice; they may have nothing to do with the truth. At one time most people "felt" that people of other races are inferior, and that slavery is God's own plan. Our feelings about euthanasia may also be mistaken, so we cannot rely on them.

If we want to discover the truth about euthanasia, there is only one way this can be done, namely, by examining and analyzing the *arguments,* or reasons, that can be given for and against it. If cogent, logical arguments can be given in favor of euthanasia, and if at the same time the arguments against it can be refuted, then it is morally acceptable, no matter what emotions or preconceptions one might have. And likewise, if upon analyzing the arguments, we find that the strongest case is against euthanasia, we shall have to conclude that it is immoral, no matter what our feelings were previously.

This is true not only of euthanasia but of any moral matter whatever. A moral judgment—*any* moral judgment—is true only if there are good reasons in its support. If someone tells you that you ought to do something, or that a certain action would be wrong, you may ask *why* you ought to do it, or why that action would be wrong, and if no answer can be given, you may reject that advice as arbitrary and unfounded. In this way moral judgments are very different from mere expressions of preference. If someone says "I like coffee," there does not have to be a *reason;* this is merely a statement about individual tastes. And if someone else says "I don't like coffee," this is merely a statement about *different* personal tastes. There is nothing for these two to argue about, and

there is no question of who is right and who is wrong (they are both right). There is no such thing as "rationally supporting" one's like or dislike of coffee. However, when *moral* claims are being made, rational support is in order; and the truth is simply the position that has the best reasons on its side. The attempt to determine what is true in morals, then, is always a matter of analyzing and weighing up reasons. Otherwise, morality degenerates into nothing more than prejudice, propaganda, and crass self-interest, without claim on any rational person.

§13 The Argument from Mercy

Preliminary Statement of the Argument
The single most powerful argument in support of euthanasia is the argument from mercy. It is also an exceptionally simple argument, at least in its main idea, which makes one uncomplicated point. Terminal patients sometimes suffer pain so horrible that it is beyond the comprehension of those who have not actually experienced it. Their suffering can be so terrible that we do not like even to read about it or think about it; we recoil even from the descriptions of such agony. The argument from mercy says: Euthanasia is justified because it provides an end to *that*.

The great Irish satirist Jonathan Swift took eight years to die, while, in the words of Joseph Fletcher, "His mind crumbled to pieces."[13] At times the pain in his blinded eyes was so intense he had to be restrained from tearing them out with his own hands. Knives and other potential instruments of suicide had to be kept from him. For the last three years of his life, he could do nothing but sit and drool; and when he finally died it was only after convulsions that lasted thirty-six hours.

Swift died in 1745. Since then, doctors have learned how to eliminate much of the pain that accompanies terminal illness, but the victory has been far from complete. So, here is a more modern example.

Stewart Alsop was a respected journalist who died in 1975 of a rare form of cancer. Before he died, he wrote movingly of his experiences as a terminal patient. Although he had not thought much about euthanasia before, he came to approve of it after rooming briefly with someone he called Jack:

> The third night that I roomed with Jack in our tiny double room in the solid-tumor ward of the cancer clinic of the National Institutes of Health in Bethesda, Md., a terrible thought occurred to me.
>
> Jack had a melanoma in his belly, a malignant solid tumor that the doctors guessed was about the size of a softball. The cancer had started a few months before with a small tumor in his left shoulder, and there had been several operations since. The doctors planned to remove the softball-sized tumor, but they knew Jack would soon die. The cancer had metastasized—it had spread beyond control.
>
> Jack was good-looking, about 28, and brave. He was in constant pain, and his doctor had prescribed an intravenous shot of a synthetic opiate—a pain-killer, or analgesic—every four hours. His wife spent many of the daylight hours with him, and she would sit or lie on his bed and pat him all over, as one pats a child, only more methodically, and this seemed to help control the pain. But at night, when his pretty wife had left (wives cannot stay overnight at the NIH clinic) and darkness fell, the pain would attack without pity.
>
> At the prescribed hour, a nurse would give Jack a shot of the synthetic analgesic, and this would control the pain for perhaps two hours or a bit more. Then he would begin to moan, or whimper, very low, as though he didn't want to wake me. Then he would begin to howl, like a dog.
>
> When this happened, either he or I would ring for a nurse, and ask for a pain-killer, She would give him some codeine or the like by mouth, but it never did any real good—it affected him no more than half an aspirin might affect a man who had just broken his arm. Always the nurse would explain as encouragingly as she could that there was not long to go before the next intravenous shot—"Only about 50 minutes now." And always poor Jack's whimpers and howls would become more loud and frequent until at last the blessed relief came.
>
> The third night of this routine, the terrible thought occurred to me. "If Jack were a dog," I thought, "what would be done with him?" The answer was obvious: the pound, and chloroform.

No human being with a spark of pity could let a living thing suffer so, to no good end.[14]

The NIH clinic is, of course, one of the most modern and best-equipped hospitals we have. Jack's suffering was not the result of poor treatment in some backward rural facility; it was the inevitable product of his disease, which medical science was powerless to prevent.

I have quoted Alsop at length not for the sake of indulging in gory details but to give a clear idea of the kind of suffering we are talking about. We should not gloss over these facts with euphemistic language, or squeamishly avert our eyes from them. For only by keeping them firmly and vividly in mind can we appreciate the full force of the argument from mercy: If a person prefers—and even begs for—death as the only alternative to lingering on *in this kind of torment,* only to die anyway after a while, then surely it is not immoral to help this person die sooner. As Alsop put it, "No human being with a spark of pity could let a living thing suffer so, to no good end."

The Utilitarian Version of the Argument

In connection with this argument, the utilitarians should be mentioned again. They argued that actions and social policies should be judged right or wrong *exclusively* according to whether they cause happiness or misery; and they argued that when judged by this standard, euthanasia turns out to be morally acceptable. The utilitarian argument may be elaborated as follows:

1. Any action or social policy is morally right if it serves to increase the amount of happiness in the world or to decrease the amount of misery. Conversely, an action or social policy is morally wrong if it serves to decrease happiness or to increase misery.

2. The policy of killing, at their own request, hopelessly ill patients who are suffering great pain, would decrease the amount of misery in the world. (An example could be Alsop's friend Jack.)

3. Therefore, such a policy would be morally right.

The first premise of this argument, (1), states the Principle of Utility, which is the basic utilitarian assumption. Today most philosophers think that this principle is wrong, because they think that the promotion of happiness and the avoidance of misery are not the *only* morally important things. Happiness, they say, is only one among many values that should be promoted: freedom, justice, and a respect for people's rights are also important. To take one example: People *might* be happier if there were no freedom of religion; for, if everyone adhered to the same religious beliefs, there would be greater harmony among people. There would be no unhappiness caused within families by Jewish girls marrying Catholic boys, and so forth. Moreover, if people were brainwashed well enough, no one would mind not having freedom of choice. Thus happiness would be increased. But, the argument continues, even if happiness *could* be increased this way, it would not be right to deny people freedom of religion, because people have a right to make their own choices. Therefore, the first premise of the utilitarian argument is unacceptable.

There is a related difficulty for utilitarianism, which connects more directly with the topic of euthanasia. Suppose a person is leading a miserable life—full of more unhappiness than happiness—but does *not* want to die. This person thinks that a miserable life is better than none at all. Now I assume that we would all agree that the person should not be killed; that would be plain, unjustifiable murder. Yet it *would* decrease the amount of misery in the world if we killed this person—it would lead to an increase in the balance of happiness over unhappiness—and so it is hard to see how, on strictly utilitarian grounds, it could be wrong. Again, the Principle of Utility seems to be an inadequate guide for determining right and wrong. So we are on shaky ground if we rely on *this* version of the argument from mercy for a defense of euthanasia.

Doing What Is in Everyone's Best Interests   Although the foregoing utilitarian argument is faulty, it is nevertheless based on a sound idea. For even if the promotion of happiness and avoidance of misery are not the *only* morally important things, they are still very important. So, when an action or a social policy would decrease misery, that is *a* very strong reason in its favor. In the cases of voluntary euthanasia we are now considering, great suffering is eliminated, and since the patient requests it, there is no question of violating individual rights. That is why, regardless of the difficulties of the Principle of Utility, the utilitarian version of the argument still retains considerable force.

I want now to present a somewhat different version of the argument from mercy, which is inspired by utilitarianism but which avoids the difficulties of the foregoing version by not making the Principle of Utility a premise of the argument. I believe that the following argument is sound and proves that active euthanasia *can* be justified:

1. If an action promotes the best interests of *everyone* concerned, and violates *no one's* rights, then that action is morally acceptable.

2. In at least some cases, active euthanasia promotes the best interests of everyone concerned and violates no one's rights.

3. Therefore, in at least some cases active euthanasia is morally acceptable.

It would have been in everyone's best interests if active euthanasia had been employed in the case of Stewart Alsop's friend Jack. First, and most important, it would have been in Jack's own interests, since it would have provided him with an easier, better death, without pain. (Who among us would choose Jack's death, if we had a choice, rather than a quick painless death?) Second, it would have been in the best interests of Jack's wife. Her misery, helplessly watching him suffer, must have been almost equal to his. Third, the hospital staff's best interests would have been served, since if Jack's dying had not been pro-longed, they could have turned their attention to other patients whom they could have helped. Fourth, other patients would have benefited since medical resources would no longer have been used in the sad, pointless maintenance of Jack's physical existence. Finally, if Jack himself requested to be killed, the act would not have violated his rights. Considering all this, how can active euthanasia in this case be wrong? How can it be wrong to do an action that is merciful, that benefits everyone concerned, and that violates no one's rights?

§14 The Argument from the Golden Rule

"Do unto others as you would have them do unto you" is one of the oldest and most familiar moral maxims. Stated in just that way, it is not a very good maxim: Suppose a sexual pervert started treating others as he would like to be treated himself; we might not be happy with the results. Nevertheless, the basic idea behind the Golden Rule is a good one. The basic idea is that moral rules apply impartially to everyone alike; therefore, you cannot say that you are justified in treating someone else in a certain way unless you are willing to admit that that person would also be justified in treating *you* in that way if your positions were reversed.

Kant and the Golden Rule   The great German philosopher Immanuel Kant (1724–1804) incorporated the basic idea of the Golden Rule into his system of ethics. Kant argued that we should act only on rules that we are willing to have applied universally; that is, we should behave as we would be willing to have *everyone* behave. He held that there is one supreme principle of morality, which he called "the Categorical Imperative." The Categorical Imperative says;

> Act only according to that maxim by which you can at the same time will that it should become a universal law.[15]

Let us discuss what this means. When we are trying to decide whether we ought to do a certain action, we must first ask what general rule or principle we would be following if we did it. Then, we ask whether we would be willing for everyone to follow that rule, in similar circumstances. (This determines whether "the maxim of the act"—the rule we would be following—can be "willed" to be "a universal law.") If we would not be willing for the rule to be followed universally, then we should not follow it ourselves. Thus, if we are not willing for others to apply the rule to *us*, we ought not apply it to *them*.

In the eighteenth chapter of St. Matthew's gospel there is a story that perfectly illustrates this point. A man is owed money by another, who cannot pay, and so he has the debtor thrown into prison. But he himself owes money to the king and begs that *his* debt be forgiven. At first the king forgives the debt. However, when the king hears how this man has treated the one who owed him, he changes his mind and "delivers him unto the tormentors" until he can pay. The moral is clear: If you do not think that others should apply the rule "Don't forgive debts!" to *you*, then you should not apply it to others.

The application of all this to the question of euthanasia is fairly obvious. Each of us is going to die someday, although most of us do not know when or how. But suppose you were told that you would die in one of two ways, and you were asked to choose between them. First, you could die quietly, and without pain, from a fatal injection. Or second, you could choose to die of an affliction so painful that for several days before death you would be reduced to howling like a dog, with your family standing by helplessly, trying to comfort you, but going through its own psychological hell. It is hard to believe that any sane person, when confronted by these possibilities, would choose to have a rule applied that would force upon him or her the second option. And if we would not want such a rule, which excludes euthanasia, applied to us, then we should not apply such a rule to others.

Implications for Christians   There is a considerable irony here. Kant, as we have already noted, was personally opposed to active euthanasia, yet his own Categorical Imperative seems to sanction it. The larger irony, however, is for those in the Christian Church who have for centuries opposed active euthanasia. According to the New Testament accounts, Jesus himself promulgated the Golden Rule as the supreme moral principle—"This is the Law and the Prophets," he said. But if this is the supreme principle of morality, then how can active euthanasia be always wrong? If I would have it done to me, how can it be wrong for me to do likewise to others?

R. M. Hare has made this point with great force. A Christian as well as a leading contemporary moral philosopher, Hare has long argued that "universalizability" is one of the central characteristics of moral judgment. ('Universalizability' is the name he gives to the basic idea embodied in both the Golden Rule and the Categorical Imperative. It means that a moral judgment must conform to universal principles, which apply to everyone alike, if it is to be acceptable.) In an article called "Euthanasia: A Christian View," Hare argues that Christians, if they took Christ's teachings about the Golden Rule seriously, would not think that euthanasia is always wrong. He gives this (true) example:

> The driver of a petrol lorry [i.e., a gas truck] was in an accident in which his tanker overturned and immediately caught fire. He himself was trapped in the cab and could not be freed. He therefore besought the bystanders to kill him by hitting him on the head, so that he would not roast to death. I think that somebody did this, but I do not know what happened in court afterwards.
>
> Now will you please all ask yourselves, as I have many times asked myself, what you wish that men should do to you if you were in the situation of that driver. I cannot believe that anybody who considered the matter seriously, as if he himself were going to be in that situation and had now to give instructions as to what rule the bystanders should follow, would say that the rule should be one ruling out euthanasia absolutely.[16]

We might note that *active* euthanasia is the only option here; the concept of passive euthanasia, in these circumstances, has no application.

We have looked at two arguments supporting the morality of active euthanasia. Now let us turn to some arguments that support the opposite view, that active euthanasia is immoral.

IV. ARGUMENTS OPPOSING THE MORALITY OF ACTIVE EUTHANASIA

§15 The Argument from the Wrongness of Killing

Almost everyone accepts the principle of the value of human life, in one form or another. Religious people speak of the "sanctity" of life, and although nonreligious people may not like the theological overtones of the word 'sanctity', they nevertheless agree that human life is precious and ought to be protected. They all agree that it is wrong to kill people. The simplest and most obvious objection to active euthanasia, then, is that it is a violation of the moral rule against killing.

But to this the advocate of euthanasia has an easy answer. The rule against killing is not absolute; it has exceptions. People may disagree about exactly which exceptions should be allowed, but there is general agreement that there *are* exceptions. Most people would agree that it is permissible to kill in self-defense, if that is the only way to prevent someone from murdering you. Others would add that it is permissible to kill in time of war, provided that the war is just and you are observing the rules of war. Some think that capital punishment is morally permissible, as a way of dealing with vicious murderers. Others believe that abortion is a justified exception to the rule. Thus, even though killing people is *usually* wrong, it is not *always* wrong. And once this much is admitted, defenders of euthanasia can simply claim that euthanasia is one of the justified exceptions to the rule.

There are two arguments that might be given to show that euthanasia is a justified exception to the rule. First, killing is objectionable only because, in normal cases, the person who is killed loses something of great value—life itself. In being deprived of life, a person is *harmed*. In euthanasia, however, this is not true. If a dying person, whose life holds nothing but torment, says that such a life no longer has value, that surely can be a reasonable judgment. We are not doing harm by putting an end to the person's misery. So, in the special case of euthanasia we do not have the same reasons for objecting to killing that we have in the normal cases. Second, killing a person is, usually, a violation of the individual's right to life. But if a person *asks* to be killed, the killing is not a violation of individual rights. (This is a general point that applies to other rights as well. If, for example, you steal something that belongs to me, you violate my property rights; but if I ask you to take it, and you do, then you do not violate my rights.) For these reasons, saying that euthanasia is a violation of the rule against killing is not enough to prove that it is wrong.

§16 Religious Arguments

Religious people often oppose euthanasia and claim that it is immoral, but there is often nothing particularly religious about the *arguments* they use. The argument from the wrongness of killing, for example, does not require any theological assumptions. Therefore, when assessing that argument, we did not need to get into any matters of religion at all.

There are some other arguments, however, that are distinctively religious. Since these arguments do require theological assumptions, they have little appeal to nonreligious people or to religious people whose presuppositions are different. Here are three of the most popular such arguments:

a. What God Forbids   It is sometimes said that active euthanasia is not permissible simply because God forbids it, and we know that God

forbids it by the authority of either Scripture or Church tradition. Thus, one eighteenth-century religionist wrote that, in the case of aged and infirm animals,

> God, the Father of Mercies, hath ordained Beasts and Birds of Prey to do that distressed creature the kindess to relieve him his misery, by putting him to death. A kindness which *We* dare not show to our own species. If thy father, thy brother, or thy child should suffer the utmost pains of a long and agonizing sickness, though his groans should pierce through thy heart, and with strong crying and tears he should beg thy relief, yet thou must be deaf unto him; he must wait his appointed time till his charge cometh, till he sinks and is crushed with the weight of his own misery.[17]

When this argument is advanced, it is usually advanced with great confidence, as though it were *obvious* what God requires. Yet we may well wonder whether such confidence is justified. The Sixth Commandment does not say, literally, "Thou shalt not *kill*"—that is a bad translation. A better translation is "Thou shalt not *murder*," which is different, and which does not obviously prohibit euthanasia. Murder is by definition *wrongful* killing; so, if you do not think that a given kind of killing is wrong, you will not call it murder. That is why the Sixth Commandment is not normally taken to forbid killing in a just war; since such killing is (allegedly) justified, it is not called murder. Similarly, if euthanasia is justified, it is not murder, and so it is not prohibited by the commandment. At any rate, it is clear that we cannot infer that euthanasia is wrong *because* it is prohibited by the commandment.

If we look elsewhere in the Christian Bible for a condemnation of euthanasia, we cannot find it. These scriptures are silent on the question. We do find numerous affirmations of the sanctity of human life and of the Fatherhood of God, and some theologians have tried to infer a prohibition of euthanasia from these general precepts. But we also find exhortations to kindness and mercy, and the Golden Rule proclaimed as the sum of all morality; and these principles, as we have seen, support euthanasia rather than condemn it.

We *do* find a clear condemnation of euthanasia in Church traditions. Regardless of whether there is scriptural authority for it, the Church has historically opposed mercy killing. It should be emphasized, however, that this is a matter of history. Today, many religious leaders favor active euthanasia and think that the historical position of the Church has been mistaken. It was an Episcopal minister, Joseph Fletcher, who in his book *Morals and Medicine*[18] formulated the classic modern defense of euthanasia. Fletcher does not stand alone among his fellow churchmen. The Euthanasia Society of America, which he heads, includes many other religious leaders; and the recent "Plea for Beneficent Euthanasia," sponsored by the American Humanist Association, was signed by more religious leaders than persons in any other category.[19] So it certainly cannot be claimed that *contemporary* religious forces stand uniformly opposed to active euthanasia.

It is noteworthy that even Roman Catholic thinkers are today reassessing the Church's traditional ban on mercy killing. The Catholic philosopher Daniel Maguire, of Marquette University, has written one of the best books on the subject, *Death by Choice.*[20] Maguire maintains that "it may be moral and should be legal to accelerate the death process by taking direct action, such as overdosing with morphine or injecting potassium"; and moreover, he proposes to demonstrate that this view is *"compatible with historical Catholic ethical theory,"* contrary to what most opponents of mercy killing assume! Historical Catholic ethical theory, he says, grants individuals permission to act on views that are supported by "good and serious reasons," even when a different view is supported by a majority of authorities. Since the morality of active euthanasia *is* supported by "good and serious reasons," Maguire concludes that Catholics are permitted to accept that morality and act on it. At the very least, they do *not* have to assume that euthanasia is immoral because "God forbids it."

> ***b. The Idea of God's Dominion*** Our second theological argument starts from the prin-

ciple that "The life of man is solely under the dominion of God." It is for God alone to decide when a person shall live and when he shall die; therefore, we have no right to "play God" and arrogate this decision unto ourselves. So euthanasia is forbidden.[21]

The most remarkable thing about this argument is that people still advance it today, even though it was decisively refuted over 200 years ago by the great British philosopher David Hume. Hume made the simple but devastating point that *if it is for God alone to decide when we shall live and when we shall die, then we "play God" just as much when we cure people as when we kill them.* Suppose a person is sick and we have the medicine to cure him or her. If we do cure the person, then we are interfering with God's right to decide whether a person will live or die! Hume put the point this way:

> Were the disposal of human life so much reserved as the peculiar providence of the Almighty that it were an encroachment on his right, for men to dispose of their own lives; it would be equally criminal to act for the preservation of life as for its destruction. If I turn aside a stone which is falling upon my head, I disturb this course of nature, and I invade the peculiar providence of the Almighty by lengthening out my life beyond the period which by the general laws of matter and motion he had assigned it.[22]

We alter the length of a person's life when we save it just as much as when we take it. Therefore, if the taking of life is to be forbidden on the grounds that only God has the right to determine how long a person shall live, then the saving of life should be prohibited on the same grounds. We would then have to abolish the practice of medicine. But everyone concedes that this would be absurd. Therefore, we may *not* prohibit active euthanasia on the grounds that only God has the right to determine how long a life shall last. This seems to be a complete refutation of this argument.

c. *Suffering and God's Plan*

The last religious argument we shall consider is the following. Suffering is a part of life; God has ordained that we must suffer as part of his Divine plan. Therefore, if we were to kill people to "put them out of their misery," we would be interfering with God's plan. Bishop Joseph Sullivan, a prominent Catholic opponent of euthanasia, expresses the argument in this passage from his essay "The Immorality of Euthanasia":

> If the suffering patient is of sound mind and capable of making an act of divine resignation, then his sufferings become a great means of merit whereby he can gain reward for himself and also win great favors for the souls in Purgatory, perhaps even release them from their suffering. Likewise the sufferer may give good example to his family and friends and teach them how to bear a heavy cross in a Christlike manner.
>
> As regard those that must live in the same house with the incurable sufferer, they have a great opportunity to practice Christian charity. They can learn to see Christ in the sufferer and win the reward promised in the Beatitudes. This opportunity for charity would hold true even when the incurable sufferer is deprived of the use of reason. It may well be that the incurable sufferer in a particular case may be of greater value to society than when he was of some material value to himself and his community.[23]

This argument may strike some people as simply grotesque. Can we imagine this being said, seriously, in the presence of suffering such as that experienced by Stewart Alsop's friend Jack? "We know it hurts, Jack, and that your wife is being torn apart just having to watch it, but think of what a good opportunity this is for you to set an example. You can give us a lesson in how to bear it." In addition, some might think that euthanasia is exactly what *is* required by the "charity" that bystanders have the opportunity to practice.

But, these reactions aside, there is a more fundamental difficulty with the argument. For if the argument were sound, it would lead not only to the condemnation of euthanasia but of *any* measures to reduce suffering. If God decrees that we suffer, why aren't we obstructing God's plan when we give drugs to relieve pain? A girl breaks her arm; if only God knows how much pain is right for her, who are we to mend it? The point is similar to Hume's refutation of the previous

argument: This argument, like the previous one, cannot be right because it leads to consequences that no one, not even the most conservative religious thinker, is willing to accept.

Conclusion Each of these three arguments depends on religious assumptions. I have tried to show that they are all bad arguments, but I have *not* criticized them simply by rejecting their religious presuppositions. Instead, I have criticized them on their own terms, showing that these arguments should not be accepted even by religious people. As Daniel Maguire emphasizes, the ethics of theists, like the ethics of all responsible people, should be determined by "good and serious reasons," and these arguments are not good no matter what world view one has.

§17 The Possibility of Unexpected Cures

We have seen that euthanasia cannot be proved immoral by the argument that killing is always wrong, and that the most popular religious arguments against it are unsound. There is one additional argument we must now consider. Euthanasia may be opposed on the grounds that we cannot really tell when a patient's condition is hopeless. There are cases in which patients have recovered even after doctors had given up hope; if those patients had been killed, it would have been tragic, for they would have been deprived of many additional years of life. According to this argument, euthanasia is immoral because we never know for certain that the patient's situation is hopeless. *Any* so-called hopeless case might defy the odds and recover.

Those who advance this argument usually intend it as an argument against active euthanasia but not passive euthanasia. Nevertheless, we should notice that if this argument were sound it would rule out passive euthanasia as well. Suppose we allow someone to die by ceasing treatment; for example, we disconnect the artifical life-support systems that are necessary to maintain life. It *may* be that, if we had continued the treatment, the patient would eventually have re-covered. Therefore, we cannot appeal to the possibility of unexpected recovery as an objection to active euthanasia without also objecting to passive euthanasia on the same grounds.

It must be admitted that doctors have sometimes made mistakes in labeling patients as "hopeless," and so we should be *very* cautious in any given case before saying that there is no chance of recovery. But it does *not* follow from the fact that doctors have *sometimes* been mistaken that they can *never* know for sure that any patient is hopeless. That would be like saying that since some people have sometimes confused a Rolls Royce with a Mercedes, no one can ever be certain which is which. In fact, doctors do sometimes know for sure that a patient cannot recover. There may be spontaneous remissions of cancer, for example, at a relatively early stage of the disease. But after the cancer has spread throughout the body and reached an advanced stage of development, there will be no hope whatever. Although there may be some doubt about *some* cases—and when there is doubt, perhaps euthanasia should not be considered—no one with the slightest medical knowledge could have had any doubt about Alsop's friend Jack. He was going to die of that cancer, and that is all there was to it. No one has *ever* recovered from such a dreadful condition, and doctors can explain exactly why this is so.

The same goes for patients in irreversible coma. Sometimes there is doubt about whether the patient can ever wake up. But in other cases there is no doubt, because of extensive brain damage that makes waking impossible. This is not merely a layman's judgment. Some of the best minds in the medical profession have argued that, in carefully defined cases, persons in irreversible coma should be regarded as *already dead!* In 1968, the *Journal of the American Medical Association* published the report of a committee of the Harvard Medical School, under the chairmanship of Dr. Henry K. Beecher, containing such a recommendation.[24] This report spells out, in precise terms, "the characteristics of a *permanently* non-functioning brain." There are four clinical signs of brain death. First, there is no response to stimuli

that would be quite painful if felt; second, there is no movement or spontaneous breathing; third, there are no reflexes, such as swallowing or contraction of the pupils in response to bright light; and finally, there is an isoelectric (sometimes mistakenly called a "flat") electroencephalogram. It is noteworthy that all these signs may be present even while the heart still beats spontaneously, without the aid of machines. Yet the Harvard committee assures us that when these signs are present for a twenty-four-hour period, we may as well declare the patient dead.

What, then, are we to conclude from the fact that doctors have sometimes been mistaken in declaring patients hopeless? We may surely conclude that extreme care should be taken so as to avoid other such mistakes, and we may perhaps conclude that in any case where there is the slightest doubt, euthanasia should not be considered. However, we may *not* conclude that doctors *never* know when a case is hopeless. Sadly, we know that in some cases there simply is no hope, and so in those cases the possibility of an unexpected cure cannot be held out as an objection to euthanasia.

V. THE QUESTION OF LEGALIZATION

We turn now to the question of whether euthanasia ought to be illegal, which is different from the question of whether it is immoral. Some people believe that, even if euthanasia is immoral, it still should not be prohibited by law, since if a patient *wants* to die, that is strictly a personal affair, regardless of how foolish or immoral the desire might be. On this view, euthanasia is comparable to sexual promiscuity; both are matters for private, individual decision and not government coercion, regardless of what moral judgment one might make. Others take a very different view and argue that active euthanasia *must* remain illegal, even if some individual acts of euthanasia are morally good, because the *consequences* of legalizing active euthanasia would be so terrible. They

argue that legalized euthanasia would lead to a breakdown in respect for life that would eventually make all of our lives less secure. We shall consider the merits of these two arguments in §§20 and 21 below. But first, let us study something of the present legal situation respecting euthanasia.

§18 How Mercy Killers Are Treated in Court

In 1939, a poor immigrant named Repouille, living in California, killed his 13-year-old son with chloroform. The boy, one of five children in the family, had suffered a brain injury at birth that left him virtually mindless, blind, mute, deformed in all four limbs, and with no control over his bladder or bowels. His whole life was spent in a small crib.

Repouille was tried for manslaughter in the first degree—apparently the prosecutor was unwilling to try him for first-degree murder, even though technically that charge could have been brought—but the jury, obviously sympathetic with him, brought in a verdict of *second*-degree manslaughter. From a legal point of view their verdict made no sense, since second-degree manslaughter presupposes that the killing was not intentional. Obviously the jury was intent on convicting him on only the mildest possible offense, so they ignored this legal nicety. They further indicated their desire to forgive the defendant by accompanying the verdict with a recommendation for "utmost clemency." The judge agreed with them and complied by staying execution of the five-to-ten-year sentence and placing Repouille on probation.[25]

What Repouille did was clearly illegal, but the lenient treatment he received is typical of those tried for "mercy killing" in American courts. (The court regarded this as a case of euthanasia, even though it does not fit our strict definition.) Sometimes, as in the case of Robert Weskin, the jury will simply find the defendant not guilty. Weskin's mother was dying of leukemia in a Chicago hospital, in terrible pain, and Weskin took a gun into the hospital and shot her three times. He

made no attempt to hide what he had done, saying, "She's out of her misery now. I shot her." He was indicted for murder, and legally it was an open-and-shut case. But the jury refused to convict him.[26]

From a strictly legal point of view, the juries' actions in both the Repouille case and the Weskin case were incorrect. In practice, however, juries have great discretion and can do practically anything they choose. (About the only thing they can't do is convict a defendant of a *more serious* charge than is made in the indictment.) What juries choose to do depends very much on the details of the particular case. For example, if the *manner* of the killing is especially gruesome, or if the killer tries to lie his way out, a jury might not be so sympathetic:

> In one case a lawyer killed his six-month-old mongoloid son by wrapping an uninsulated electrical cord around his wet diaper and putting the baby on a silver platter to insure good contact before plugging the cord into the wall. At the trial he claimed that the child's death was an accident, and he was convicted of first-degree murder and sentenced to electrocution himself, although the sentence was later commuted to life.[27]

There have been only two occasions on which *doctors* have been tried for mercy killing in this country. In New Hampshire in 1950, Dr. Herman Sander gave a patient four intravenous injections of air and then noted on the patient's chart that he had done so. The patient, who had terminal cancer, had asked to be put out of her misery. At the trial, the defense claimed that the patient was already dead at the time of the injections—which was a bit strange, since if the woman was already dead why were the injections given? Anyway, the jury acquitted Dr. Sander. The next such trial of a physician, and the only other one in the United States to date, occurred twenty-four years later in New York. Dr. Vincent Montemareno was charged with giving a lethal injection of potassium chloride to a patient with terminal cancer. At first the prosecutor announced that the case would be tried as a case of mercy killing; Dr. Mon-

temareno, he said, had killed the patient to put her out of misery. But by the time the trial opened, the prosecutor had changed his mind and claimed that the doctor had murdered the patient for his own convenience, so that he would not have to return to the hospital later in the evening. At the conclusion of the trial the jury promptly voted to acquit.

But whatever juries may or may not do, active euthanasia is clearly against the law. The legal status of passive euthanasia is more uncertain. In practice, doctors do allow hopeless patients to die, and as we have seen, the American Medical Association officially endorses this policy when the patient or his family requests it and when "extraordinary" means would be required to keep the patient alive. The legal status of such actions (or nonactions) is uncertain because, although there are laws against "negligent homicide" under which criminal charges could be brought, no such charges have been brought so far. Here district attorneys, and not juries, have exercised their discretion and have not pressed the issue.

It makes an important difference from a legal point of view whether a case of passive euthanasia is voluntary or nonvoluntary. Any patient—except one who has been declared legally "incompetent" to withhold consent—always has the right to refuse medical treatment. By refusing treatment, a patient can bring about his or her own death and the doctor cannot be convicted for "letting the person die." It is *nonvoluntary* passive euthanasia, in which the patient does not request to be allowed to die, that is legally uncertain.

§19 The Case of Karen Ann Quinlan

There has been one famous case in which the question of nonvoluntary passive euthanasia was put before the courts. In April 1975, a 21-year-old woman named Karen Ann Quinlan, for reasons that were never made clear, ceased breathing for at least two fifteen-minute periods. As a result, she suffered severe brain damage, and, in the words of the attending physicians, was reduced to "a chronic persistent vegetative state" in which

reasons, rega
Therefore, if
better avoid t
Foot is maki
ment than wl
of the slipper

How str
the argumen
ought to be
whether lega
lead to terrib
question—a
losophers ha
then, neither
tive "scientifi
us is left to
concerning v
active euthan
I do *not* beli
general break
reasons.

First, w
anthropologi
in one contex
in different ci
mentioned, i
fective infan
guilt—but th
of other type
kind could b
ing of infant
accepted as
among the Es
of. Such evid
distinguish b
keep them se

Second,
and still is, a
example, we
what if it we
this, on the g
self-defense v
in respect for
not true, beca

she "no longer had any cognitive function." Accepting the doctors' judgment that there was no hope of recovery, her parents sought permission from the courts to disconnect the respirator that was keeping her alive in the intensive-care unit of a New Jersey hospital. The Quinlans are Roman Catholics, and they made this request only after consulting with their priest, who assured them that there would be no moral or religious objection if Karen were allowed to die.

Various medical experts testified in support of the Quinlans's request. One doctor described what he called the concept of "judicious neglect," under which a physician will say: "Don't treat this patient anymore . . . It does not serve either the patient, the family, or society in any meaningful way to continue treatment with this patient." This witness also explained the use of the initials 'DNR'—"Do Not Resuscitate"—by which doctors instruct hospital staff to permit death. He said:

> No physician that I know personally is going to try and resuscitate a man riddled with cancer and in agony and he stops breathing. They are not going to put him on a respirator . . . I think that would be the height of misuse of technology.[28]

The trial court, and then the Supreme Court of New Jersey, agreed that the respirator could be removed and Karen Quinlan allowed to die in peace. The respirator was disconnected. However, the nuns in charge of her care in the Catholic hospital opposed this decision, and anticipating it, had begun to wean Karen from the respirator so that by the time it was disconnected she could remain alive without it. (Reviewing these events, one prominent Catholic scholar commented angrily, "Some nuns always were holier than the church."[29]) So Karen did not die; and at this writing she remains in her "persistent vegetative state," emaciated and with deformed limbs and with no hope of ever awakening, but still alive in the biological sense.

It is anticipated that the Quinlan decision will set a precedent for future cases, and that the legal right to terminate treatment in such circumstances will become established. If so, then the law will not have been particularly innovative; it will only have caught up, somewhat belatedly, with medical practice, public opinion, and the best thought of the day concerning passive euthanasia. The question that will then remain is: What about *active* euthanasia? Should *it* be legalized, too?

§20 An Argument for Legalizing Active Euthanasia: The Right to Liberty

Should active euthanasia be legalized? We have already reached a number of conclusions that bear on this issue. We have seen that there are powerful arguments supporting the view that active euthanasia is morally permissible, and that the arguments opposing it are weak. If active euthanasia is moral, as these arguments suggest, why should it not be made legal? We have noted that whenever charges have been brought against "mercy killers," prosecutors have had great difficulty securing convictions. Juries have not wanted to punish genuine mercy killers, and judges have not been willing to impose heavy sentences. So if active euthanasia were legalized, it would seem little more than an official acknowledgment of attitudes that already exist in the courtroom.

However, none of this really proves that active euthanasia ought to be legalized. We need to turn now to arguments that are addressed more directly to the issue of legalization. One such argument is the "argument from the right to liberty." According to this argument, each dying patient should be free to choose euthanasia, or to reject it, simply as a matter of personal liberty. No one, including the government, has the right to tell another what choice to make. If a dying patient wants euthanasia, that is a private affair; after all, the life belongs to the individual, and so that individual should be the one to decide.

Mill's Principle This argument starts from the principle that people should be free to live their own lives as they themselves think best. But of course the right to liberty is not completely unrestricted. We should not be free to murder or

used this a
British m
thinks th
thanasia i
it should
serious pi

Many p
of their
husban
be able
what w
it be p
which
morall
rights
possibi
change
very ba
expect
This is
we mig
it. It n
likely
for the
thing
povert
genuir
societi
ual dis

The con
what vi
mercy k
ought to
wise, we
To
guish b
take. W
argumer

Th
Slope
like this
a logica
cepting
are no g
additioi

§22 How to Legalize Active Euthanasia: A Modest Proposal

Opposition to the legalization of active euthanasia comes from those who believe it is immoral, from those who fear the consequences of legalization, and from those who believe that, although it may be a fine idea in theory, in practice it is impossible to devise any workable laws to accommodate active euthanasia. This last point is important. If we wanted to legalize active euthanasia, exactly how could we go about doing it? Who should be granted the awesome power to decide when a person may be put to death? Should patients or doctors or the patient's family be allowed to decide on their own? Or should some sort of hospital committee be authorized to make the decision? And if so, exactly who should sit on such a committee? What if those who are given the power abuse it? Shall they then be liable to charges of murder? If so, then it would seem that they do not really have the power to decide; but if not, their power is unchecked and they have a license to do as they please. It is easy to think of objections to almost any proposed scheme, so it is no wonder that even those who approve active euthanasia in theory are often wary of actually legalizing it.

I want to make a modest proposal concerning how active euthanasia might be legalized so as to avoid all these problems. Before outlining this proposal, I need to make some elementary points about American law.

Individuals charged with a crime have no obligation to prove their innocence. The burden of proof is on the prosecution, and the defense may consist entirely in pointing out that the prosecution has not decisively proven guilt. If the prosecution has not discharged its obligation to prove guilt, the jury's duty is to acquit the defendant.

However, if the prosecution does establish a strong case against the defendant, a more active defense is required. Then there are two options available. The defendant may deny having done the criminal act in question. Or, while admitting to the act, the defendant may nevertheless argue that he or she should not be punished for it.

There are two legally accepted ways of arguing that a person should not be punished for an act even while admitting that the act is prohibited by law and that the person did it. First, an *excuse* may be offered, such as insanity, coercion, ignorance of fact, unavoidable accident, and so on. If it can be shown that the defendant was insane when the crime was committed or that he was coerced into doing it or that it was an unavoidable accident, then the defendant may be acquitted. Second, a *justification* may be offered. A plea of self-defense against a charge of murder is an example of a justification. The technical difference between excuses and justifications need not concern us here.

Here is an example to illustrate these points. Suppose you are charged with murdering a man, and the prosecution can make a strong case that you did in fact kill the victim. You might respond by trying to show that you did *not* kill him. Or you might admit that you killed him, and then have your lawyers argue that you were insane or that the killing was a tragic accident for which you are blameless or that you had to kill him in self-defense. If any of these defenses can be made out, then you will be acquitted of the crime even though you admittedly did kill the victim.

When such a defense is offered, the burden of proof is on the defense, and not the prosecution, to show that the facts alleged are true. The prosecution does not have to show that the defendant was sane; rather, the defendant (or the defendant's lawyers) must prove that he or she was insane. The prosecution does not have to prove that the killing was not done in self-defense; instead the defense must prove that it was. Thus it is not quite accurate to say that under American law the burden of proof is always on the prosecution. If the defendant concedes to having performed the act in question but claims an excuse or justification for the act, the burden of

proof may shift so that the defense is required to show that the excuse or justification should be accepted.

Now, my proposal for legalizing active euthanasia is that a plea of mercy killing be acceptable as a defense against a charge of murder in much the same way that a plea of self-defense is acceptable as a defense. When people plead self-defense, it is up to them to show that their own lives were threatened and that the only way of fending off the threat was by killing the attacker first. Under my proposal, someone charged with murder could also plead mercy killing; and then, if it could be proven that the victim while competent requested death, and that the victim was suffering from a painful terminal illness, the person pleading mercy killing would also be acquitted.

Under this proposal no one would be "authorized" to decide when a patient should be killed any more than people are "authorized" to decide when someone may be killed in self-defense. There are no committees to be established within which people may cast private votes for which they are not really accountable; people who choose to mercy kill bear full legal responsibility, as individuals, for their actions. In practice, this would mean that anyone contemplating mercy killing would have to be very sure that there are independent witnesses to testify concerning the patient's condition and desire to die; for otherwise, one might not be able to make out a defense in a court of law—if it should come to that—and would be legally liable for murder. However, if this proposal were adopted, it would *not* mean that every time active euthanasia was performed a court trial would follow. In clear cases of self-defense, prosecutors simply do not bring charges, since it would be a pointless waste of time. Similarly, in clear cases of mercy killing, where there is no doubt about the patient's hopeless condition or desire to die, charges would not be brought for the same reason.

Thus, under this proposal, the need to write difficult legislation permitting euthanasia is bypassed. The problems of formulating a statute, which were mentioned at the beginning of this section, do not arise. We would rely on the good sense of judges and juries to separate the cases of justifiable euthanasia from the cases of unjustifiable murder, just as we already rely on them to separate the cases of self-defense and insanity and coercion. Some juries are already functioning in this way but without legal sanction: when faced with genuine mercy killers, they refuse to convict. The main consequence of my proposal would be to sanction officially what these juries already do.

VI. CONCLUSION

We have now examined the most important arguments for and against the morality of euthanasia, and we have considered arguments for and against legalizing it. It is time to summarize our conclusions. What do the arguments show?

First, in the central case of the terminal patient who wants to be killed rather than die slowly in agony, we are led inescapably to the conclusion that active euthanasia is morally acceptable and that it ought to be made legal. The morality of euthanasia in this case is supported by such diverse ethical precepts as the Principle of Utility, Kant's Categorical Imperative, and the Golden Rule. Euthanasia here serves the interests of everyone concerned: it is a mercy to the patient, it reduces the emotional strain of death on the patient's family and friends, and it conserves medical resources. Moreover, if doctors are legally forbidden to provide a painless death to such patients at their request, it is an unwarranted restriction on the freedom of the patients; for it is *their* life, and so it is their right to decide. The arguments opposing euthanasia, both morally and legally, are not nearly so strong.

Second, in the case of the patient in an irreversible coma, we are struck by the fact that as far as *the patient's own* interests are concerned, it does

bring about death in a vacuum, so to speak; death always occurs from some specific cause.

Many patients who are dying in these ways are either comatose or heavily sedated. Such deaths do not allow for a period of conscious reflection at the end of life, nor do they permit farewell-saying, last rites, final words, or other features of the stereotypically "dignified" death.

Even less likely to match the patient's conception of natural death are those cases in which the patient is still conscious and competent, but meets a death that is quite different than he had bargained for. Consider the bowel cancer patient with widespread metastases and a very poor prognosis who—perhaps partly out of consideration for the emotional and financial resources of his family—refuses surgery to reduce or bypass the tumor. How, exactly, will he die? This patient is clearly within his legal rights in refusing surgery, but the physician knows what the outcome is very likely to be: obstruction of the intestinal tract will occur, the bowel wall will perforate, the abdomen will become distended, there will be intractible vomiting (perhaps with a fecal character to the emesis), and the tumor will erode into adjacent areas, causing increased pain, hemorrhage, and sepsis. Narcotic sedation and companion drugs may be partially effective in controlling pain, nausea, and vomiting, but this patient will *not* get the kind of death he thought he had bargained for. Yet, he was willing to shorten his life, to use the single legally protected mechanism—refusal of treatment—to achieve that "natural" death. Small wonder that many physicians are skeptical of the "gains" made by the popular movements supporting the right to die.

WHEN THE RIGHT TO DIE GOES WRONG

Several distinct factors contribute to the backfiring of the right-to-die cause. First, and perhaps the most obvious, the patient may misjudge his own situation in refusing treatment or in executing a natural-death directive: his refusal may be precipitous and ill informed, based more on fear than on a settled desire to die. Second, the physician's response to the patient's request for "death with dignity" may be insensitive, rigid, or even punitive (though in my experience most physicians respond with compassion and wisdom). Legal constraints may also make natural death more difficult than might be hoped: safeguards often render natural-death requests and directives cumbersome to execute, and in any case, in a litigation-conscious society, the physician will often take the most cautious route.

But most important in the apparent backfiring of the right-to-die movement is the underlying ambiguity in the very concept of "natural death." Patients tend to think of the character of the experience they expect to undergo—a death that is "comfortable, decent, peaceful"—but all the law protects is the refusal of medical procedures. Even lawmakers sometimes confuse the two. The California and Kansas natural-death laws claim to protect what they romantically describe as "the natural process of dying." North Carolina's statute says it protects the right to a "peaceful and natural" death. But since these laws actually protect only refusal of treatment, they can hardly guarantee a peaceful, easy death. Thus, we see a widening gulf between the intent of the law to protect the patient's final desires, and the outcomes if the law is actually followed. The physician is caught in between: he recognizes his patient's right to die peacefully, naturally, and with whatever dignity is possible, but foresees the unfortunate results that may come about when the patient exercises this right as the law permits.

Of course, if the symptoms or pain become unbearable the patient may change his mind. The patient who earlier wished not to be "hooked up on tubes" now begins to experience difficulty in breathing or swallowing, and finds that a tracheotomy will relieve his distress. The bowel cancer patient experiences severe discomfort from obstruction, and gives permission for decompression or reductive surgery after all. In some cases,

the family may engineer the change of heart because they find dying too hard to watch. Health care personnel may view these reversals with satisfaction: "See," they may say, "he really wants to live after all." But such reversals cannot always be interpreted as a triumph of the will to live; they may also be an indication that refusing treatment makes dying too hard.

OPTIONS FOR AN EASIER DEATH

How can the physician honor the dying patient's wish for a peaceful, conscious, and culminative death? There is more than one option.

Such a death can come about whenever the patient is conscious and pain-free; he can reflect and, if family, clergy, or friends are summoned at the time, he will be able to communicate as he wishes. Given these conditions, death can be brought on in various direct ways. For instance, the physician can administer a lethal quantity of an appropriate drug. Or the patient on severe dietary restrictions can violate his diet: the kidney-failure patient, for instance, for whom high potassium levels are fatal, can simply overeat on avocados. These ways of producing death are, of course, active euthanasia, or assisted or unassisted suicide. For many patients, such a death would count as "natural" and would satisfy the expectations under which they had chosen to die rather than to continue an intolerable existence. But for many patients (and for many physicians as well) a death that involves deliberate killing is morally wrong. Such a patient could never assent to an actively caused death, and even though it might be physically calm, it could hardly be emotionally or psychologically peaceful. This is not to say that active euthanasia or assisted suicide are morally wrong, but rather that the force of some patients' moral views about them precludes using such practices to achieve the kind of death they want. Furthermore, many physicians are unwilling to shoulder the legal risk such practices may seem to involve.

But active killing aside, the physician can do much to grant the dying patient the humane death he has chosen by using the sole legally protected mechanism that safeguards the right to die: refusal of treatment. This mechanism need not always backfire. For in almost any terminal condition, death can occur in various ways, and there are many possible outcomes of the patient's present condition. The patient who is dying of emphysema could die of respiratory failure, but could also die of cardiac arrest or untreated pulmonary infection. The patient who is suffering from bowel cancer could die of peritonitis following rupture of the bowel, but could also die of dehydration, of pulmonary infection, of acid-base imbalance, of electrolyte deficiency, or of an arrhythmia.

As the poet Rilke observes, we have a tendency to associate a certain sort of end with a specific disease: it is the "official death" for that sort of illness. But there are many other ways of dying than the official death, and the physician can take advantage of these. Infection and cancer, for instance, are old friends; there is increased frequency of infection in the immuno-compromised host. Other secondary conditions, like dehydration or metabolic derangement, may set in. Of course certain conditions typically occur a little earlier, others a little later, in the ordinary course of a terminal disease, and some are a matter of chance. The crucial point is that certain conditions will produce a death that is more comfortable, more decent, more predictable, and more permitting of conscious and peaceful experience than others. Some are better, if the patient has to die at all, and some are worse. Which mode of death claims the patient depends in part on circumstance and in part on the physician's response to conditions that occur. What the patient who rejects active euthanasia or assisted suicide may realistically hope for is this: the least worst death among those that could naturally occur. Not all unavoidable surrenders need involve rout; in the face of inevitable death, the physician becomes strategist, the deviser of plans for how to meet death most favorably.

Consent, Coercion, and Conflicts of Rights

Ruth Macklin

Ruth Macklin is professor of bioethics at Albert Einstein College of Medicine in New York. She received her doctorate in philosophy from Case Western Reserve University in 1968. Before assuming her present position, she was on the staff of the Hastings Center, and she is also a fellow of the Center. She has authored one book, co-edited five others, and published over 70 articles in professional journals of philosophy, law, and medicine.

Macklin focuses on the conflict between the duty of the physician to respect the refusal of life-saving blood transfusions by competent adult Jehovah's Witnesses and the duty to provide competent medical care. She examines the religious foundations of their refusal. Then she reviews a number of judicial decisions concerning Witnesses and identifies the ethical foundations for respecting their refusal. She concludes that their right to refuse should prevail.

Cases of conflict of rights are not infrequent in law and morality. A range of cases that has gained increasing prominence recently centers around the autonomy of persons and their right to make decisions in matters affecting their own life and death. This paper will focus on a particular case of conflict of rights: the case of Jehovah's Witnesses who refuse blood transfusions for religious reasons and the question of whether or not there exists a right to compel medical treatment. The Jehovah's Witnesses who refuse blood transfusions do not do so because they want to die: in most cases, however, they appear to believe that they will die if their blood is not transfused. Members of this sect are acting on what is generally believed to be a constitutionally guaranteed right: freedom of religion, which is said to include not only freedom of religious belief, but also the right to act on such beliefs.

The study will examine a cluster of moral issues surrounding the Jehovah's Witness case. Some pertain to minor children of Jehovah's Witness parents, while others concern adult Witnesses who refuse treatment for themselves. The focus will be on the case as a moral one rather than a legal one, although arguments employed in some of the legal cases will be invoked. This is an issue at the intersection of law and morality—one in which the courts themselves have rendered conflicting decisions and have looked to moral principles for guidance. As is usually the case in ethics, whatever the courts may have decided does not settle the moral dispute, but the arguments and issues invoked in legal disputes often mirror the ethical dimensions of the case. The conflict—in both law and morals—arises out of a religious prohibition against blood transfusions, a prohibition that rests on an interpretation of certain scriptural passages by the Jehovah's Witness sect.

THE RELIGIOUS BASIS FOR THE PROHIBITION OF BLOOD TRANSFUSIONS

The Witnesses' prohibition of blood transfusions derives from an interpretation of several Old Testament passages, chief among which is the following from Lev. 17:10–14:

> And whatsoever man there be of the house of Israel, or of the strangers that sojourn among you, that eateth any manner of blood: I will even

From *Perspectives in Biology and Medicine*, vol. 20, no. 3 (Spring 1977): 360–71. Copyright © 1977 by the University of Chicago Press. Reprinted by permission of the author and the publisher.

set my face against that soul that eateth blood, and will cut him off from among his people. . . .

The question immediately arises, On what basis do the Jehovah's Witnesses construe intravenous blood transfusions as an instance of eating blood? Witnesses sometimes claim that the prohibition against transfusions arises out of a literal interpretation of the relevant biblical passages, but the interpretation in question seems anything but "literal." One explanation for this is as follows: "Since they have been prohibited by the Bible from eating blood, they steadfastly proclaim that intravenous transfusion has no bearing on the matter, as it basically makes no difference whether the blood enters by the vein or by the alimentary tract. In their widely quoted reference *Blood, Medicine, and the Law of God* they constantly refer to the medical printed matter which early in the 20th century declared that blood transfusions are nothing more than a source of nutrition by a shorter route than ordinary" [1, p. 539]. Whether based on a literal interpretation of the Bible or not, the Witnesses' prohibition against transfusions extends not only to whole blood, but also to any blood derivative, such as plasma and albumin (blood substitutes are, however, quite acceptable) [1, p. 539].

This brief account of the basis of the religious prohibition has not yet addressed the moral issues involved: but for the sake of completeness, let us note two additional features of the Jehovah's Witness view—features that bear directly on the moral conflict.

The first point concerns the Witnesses' belief about the consequences of violating the prohibition: Receiving blood transfusions is an unpardonable sin resulting in withdrawal of the opportunity to attain eternal life [2]. In particular, the transgression is punishable by being "cut off": "Since the Witnesses do not believe in eternal damnation, to be 'cut off' signifies losing one's opportunity to qualify for resurrection" [3, p. 75]. A second, related feature of the Witnesses' belief system is their view that man's life on earth is not important: "They fervently believe that they are

only passing through and that the faithful who have not been corrupted nor polluted will attain eternal life in Heaven" [1, p. 539]. This belief is important in the structure of a moral argument that pits the value of preservation of life on earth against other values, for example, presumed eternal life in Heaven. Put another way, the Witnesses can argue that the duty to preserve or prolong human life is always overridden by their perceived duty to God, so in a case of conflict, duty to God dictates the right course of action.

THE ADULT JEHOVAH'S WITNESS PATIENT

Freedom to exercise one's religious beliefs is one important aspect of the moral and legal issues involved in these cases: But in addition to this specific constitutionally guaranteed right, there are other rights and moral values that would be relevant even if religious freedom were not at issue. Even in cases that do not involve religious freedom at all, the question of the right to compel medical treatment against a patient's wishes raises some knotty moral problems. The Jehovah's Witness case may prove instructive for the range of cases in which religious freedom is not at issue.

Just which rights or values are involved in the adult Jehovah's Witness case, and how do they conflict? We shall return later to the right to act on one's religious beliefs, but first let us look at other moral concepts that enter into Witnesses' moral defense. Chief among these is the notion of autonomy. Does the patient in a medical setting have the autonomy that we normally accord persons simply by virtue of their being human? Or does one's status as a *patient* deprive him of a measure of autonomy normally accorded him as a nonpatient *person*? Many medical practitioners tend to argue for decreased autonomy of patients, while some religious ethicists, a number of moral philosophers, and a small number of physicians defend autonomous decision making on the part

to keep a patient alive against the patient's wishes, it is often unclear when a person is incompetent to make important decisions. Although these observations raise the troublesome question of whether or not we are justified in treating (A) as a necessary condition of paternalistic actions, two considerations will show that (A) is satisfied in the cases with which we are concerned. The first is that severe burn victims and cervical spinal cord injury patients are typically in pain, shock, often delusional, experiencing grief, or under the stress of being in a new environment in which they have practically no control, not even over the fate of their own bodies. Second, such patients often later welcome our intervention, which suggests that something was amiss with their earlier wish to die, even from their own point of view.

This second observation points to a central criterion that we must satisfy if we are to justify intervening in such cases. The second criterion expresses the requirement that paternalistic interventions correspond as far as possible to the person's own assessment of the positive and negative results of the intervention by reflecting the deeper will of the person which would express itself were the person not under duress. This second criterion helps us to identify what the person would, if not incompetent, see as being in his or her best interests. Hence, if satisfied, it would seem to justify treating incompetent patients against their wishes:

B. The person will come to welcome the intervention.

We have good reasons for thinking that (B) is a sufficient condition for intervening in the case of the incompetent patient. When (B) applies we have evidence for claiming that the person was incompetent [viz., that (A) applies]. But more importantly, when (B) applies it reflects both the Kantian and the utilitarian moral views discussed above. If the person says that we did what the patient would have willed had he or she known enough and been able to assess clearly the pain, grief, and anxiety, what more could be asked by a

Kantian as evidence that the intervention reflected the victim's deeper will? If the patient says that the suffering was worth it and is outweighed by the happiness or pleasures that followed, what else could a utilitarian demand insofar as the utilitarian is assessing the happiness or suffering of the patient that will result from a decision to treat?[15]

Of course, more might be available: "living wills" and similar documents that request or refuse treatment in just such cases. But what if these documents were inconsistent with (B)? There are two plausible explanations for such an inconsistency. The first is that the patient is now better informed about the alternatives than he or she was when making out the "living will." This possibility brings out one serious problem with such a document: the "cool moment" reflection of a person in his or her study, kitchen, or lawyer's office may not reflect an adequate appreciation of the alternatives that the badly injured patient confronts. This specific problem with prior expressions of choice in life and death matters was recently cited by Seattle internist Dr. Norman K. Brown: "You can pass living wills around a roomful of young people and 95 percent will sign them. . . . But pass them around a nursing home and you'll get a different response."[16] The discrepancy Dr. Brown cites is just the sort that could well occur when comparing the less informed wishes of the healthy with the better informed assessments of those badly injured patients who are no longer under the duress experienced in the more acute phase of their injuries.

The second reason a "living will" may be inconsistent with a subsequent welcoming of the paternalistic treatment is that the treatment itself caused the patient to be unable not to welcome it. The starkest case would be one in which a person's brain is so reconstructed that the person is caused to welcome the reconstruction.[17] Although such a case is currently a technical impossibility, it is worth exploring what would be objectional about producing a situation that causes the patient to consent. It is not that the favorable con-

sent is predictable, since that will be true of the cases best justified on paternalistic grounds. (For example, a man who unwittingly consumes LSD and, as a result of his altered state, prepares to launch himself off the edge of a five-story apartment building for a flight over Boston will predictably come to welcome a timely intervention.) Rather, <u>the difficulty is that the brain reconstruction patient *cannot do* otherwise</u>. <u>In making the patient's subsequent rejection physically or psychologically impossible, we have removed the possibility of choice and assessment, and that is what is offensive about the imagined brain reconstruction.</u> Significantly, this explanation of our moral repugnance at such an intervention corresponds with the inadequacy of such a justification from both the Kantian and the utilitarian points of view. From a Kantian point of view, the person's will has been altered and hence the subsequent affirmation does not express the person's deeper will *at the time of treatment*. From the utilitarian point of view, the person *is not able to assess* the merits of the intervention and, hence, any postoperative assessments are without value. <u>It follows that such an intervention, even though satisfying (B), would not be justified, and, hence, a requirement in addition to (B) is needed.</u>

Ⓒ If (B) is satisfied, that is, if the patient comes to welcome the intervention, it must be the case that the patient was able to assess the intervention negatively.[18]

Although we would not be justified in intervening in cases unless (C) is satisfied in addition to (B), it is difficult to find cases that are ruled out by (C). The imaginary brain reconstruction case is one, and, perhaps, examples involving posthypnotic suggestion would constitute others. But in the cases on which we are focusing, the subsequent welcomings, if any, are not caused in this way. <u>If the burn victim or the quadraplegic is subsequently glad to be alive, there is no good reason to believe that the "will" of the person has been coerced or that the person is unable to make an assessment of what has happened.</u> These ex-pa-

tients *can* judge that the interventions should not have been performed. Hence, we may use (A), (B) and (C) to assess life-saving paternalistic interventions for burn patients or paralyzed patients who have been recently injured.

TWO TEST CASES

It will be useful to test these criteria by applying them to the following cases:

Case 1: A 25 year old married woman was admitted to a hospital having lost two-thirds of her body's blood supply from a ruptured ulcer. The woman and her husband, both Jehovah's Witnesses, had signed a document releasing the physician and the hospital from any liability that might result from the failure to administer blood. Both the husband and the wife refused to approve a blood transfusion.[19]

Case 2: A 52 year old married man was admitted semi-conscious to an intensive care unit after a suicide attempt. He had adapted to his multiple sclerosis, which had been the cause of progressive physical disability over a fifteen-year period. Three weeks prior to the suicide attempt he had become morose and withdrawn. . . . During a period when his family was gone for six hours, he ingested an unknown quantity of diazepam. In the ICU he expressed his wish to die with dignity should complications develop, stressing the meaninglessness of his life as his disability progressed. Examination revealed severe neurological deficits, but no worse than in recent examinations. Psychiatric consultation revealed that the onset of withdrawal and depression coincided with a diagnosis of inoperable cancer in his mother-in-law, with whom his wife was spending more and more time. On the night of the suicide attempt the patient's wife and two sons had left him alone for the first time to visit his mother-in-law.[20]

In Case 1 we would *not* predict that the patient would come to welcome a blood transfusion. Jehovah's Witnesses wish to live, "but not with blood transfusions,"[21] because they believe that a blood transfusion would deprive them of eternal salvation. Hence, criterion (B) is not satisfied, a

blood transfusion would be wrong on our criteria, and this is consistent with our considered moral judgment that Jehovah's Witnesses should not be compelled to receive blood transfusions for which they have not consented. In Case 2, however, the paternalistic intervention is justified because we expect that the patient would come to welcome life-prolonging interventions that may be necessary, at least once he was helped to communicate his needs to his family. That, in fact, was the outcome: "The patient had too much pride to complain to his wife about his feelings of abandonment. . . . Discussion with all four family members led to improved communication and acknowledgement of the patient's special emotional needs. After these conversations, the patient explicitly retracted both his suicidal threats and his demand that no supportive medical efforts be undertaken."[22] Applying our criteria in both cases justifies precisely what we take to be the proper course of action in each. These cases provide additional support for our confidence in the soundness of using criteria (A), (B) and (C) to justify or condemn paternalistic interventions.

THE PRACTICAL IMPLICATIONS OF THESE RESULTS

Our results to this point show that if we are to continue treating patients against their expressed wishes in cases of serious bodily injury, we must begin an investigation to insure that what we are doing is justified. Our current practices must be measured against the evidence already available, viz., whatever follow-up reports there are on patients who have been kept alive against their wishes. Every suicide by a former burn victim or cervical spinal cord victim who wished to be allowed to die raises nagging doubts about whether keeping the person alive was the right course of action, whereas every interview in which the patient is grateful is some evidence for continuing such interventions. Our current care of such patients need not change as long as there is no reasonable suspicion that we are keeping alive badly injured patients who would later only resent our interference. But follow-up work on such patients has not been thoroughly carried out.[23] To fail to begin such research into the attitudes of those we have kept alive against their wishes is to continue to rely on convenient conventions or on "hunches," and so to be willing to take the chance that what we are doing is morally wrong.

The aim of the research for which I am calling is to gain evidence that will permit us to identify those badly injured patients who are likely to welcome the medical treatments that they are currently refusing. The beginning format of such research involves interviewing patients who have been severely burned or have suffered cervical spinal cord injury to see what they think about the value of their lives and the worth of the intervention. A number of questions would need to be answered, and the following list is not intended to be exhaustive:

1. After your injury, did you consent to the medical treatments that were required to keep you alive?

2. Do you recall whether your explicit consent to or your rejection of life-saving treatment was an inner and settled conviction, or did you feel unsure?

3. If you now contracted a blood infection that could be rather easily cured but otherwise would cause you to become unconscious and to die painlessly in a matter of days, would you consent to be treated for the infection?

4. If you could return to the time of your injury and have the medical staff do precisely what you wished, in light of what you now know, would you ask to be treated for your injury or only to be treated for your pain?

5. If another person much like yourself suffered an injury as you did, and the medical staff asked your opinion on what the staff should do, what would you say?

These questions may seem psychologically distressful to ex-patients, but persons who have undergone such traumas are typically much more comfortable with these and other troublesome topics—sex, work, loneliness—than are most of us who project our own insecurities into their situations. There is, of course, nothing sacrosanct about the form of the above questions, but what must be discovered is:

Was this a patient who was able to express consent? Was consent expressed?

What was the patient's inner conviction at the time, if any?

Does the patient now generally find life worth living?

Does the patient generally think that the intervention was worthwhile?

Does he or she generally welcome it?

The answers to these questions will likely vary with the kind of injury (e.g., burn or spinal cord), the severity of the injury, the time elapsed since the injury, the time elapsed since the patient no longer needed acute medical treatment, the age of the patient, the patient's sex, the patient's race, the social supports available to the person, the person's economic status, whether or not the person has a suicidal history, whether or not the person has a drug or alcohol history, whether or not the person feels responsible for the injury, whether or not any other persons were hurt or killed, and so on. The list of potential relevant factors will be extensive, and one of the challenges of the research will be to try to identify social, personal, medical, and other factors that may allow us to isolate relevant differences among patients. Depending on the answers patients give to the questions that must be asked, further puzzles and new dead ends may be created, but there will also be some headway as well as a greater appreciation of what we in fact do in keeping such patients alive against their wishes.

This research, ideally, will lead to one of three results. (1) We may discover, for some iden-tifiable group of patients who refused treatment, that most of these patients came to welcome the intervention that they formerly refused. If these are our findings, we have justified the practice of keeping these patients alive against their wishes, and, of course, we should continue the practice of doing so. (2) We may, however, discover that some groups of patients tend to commit suicide shortly thereafter, or tend not to maintain life-prolonging therapies, or, *what is equally definitive from an ethical point of view,* condemn the medical profession for having prevented them from dying earlier. If we do uncover such widespread rejection by a group of patients, then, because we are not ethically justified in keeping alive a patient who will not likely come to welcome our intervention, we have no realistic option but to stop keeping badly injured persons in this group alive against their wishes.[24] (3) We may also discover that the few survivors of some severe injuries, most of whom we allowed to die out of compassion, welcome the treatment they previously tried to reject. If these are our findings, we have grounds for extending paternalistic treatment to all similar cases.

The results of this research are likely to be of help to medical personnel who care for badly injured patients who want to die. Some bioethicists have argued, for instance, that we should let such patients die.[25] The providers of such care clearly do not agree and they frequently keep such patients alive.[26] The bioethicists in question, in their defense of liberty, accuse the medical providers of violating the rights of patients, whereas the medical practitioners see bioethicists as outsiders who are making a very difficult job even harder. (The difficulty of the job is typified by the remark of one nurse who works with burn victims: "Twenty-four hours a day we inflict pain."[27]) In many cases, I believe, the research I am calling for will justify the medical practitioner and provide justificatory protection and even solace to persons working in some of the most difficult areas of patient care.

Whatever we discover, the results are likely to generate a complexity and controversy that will

require further conceptual work after the preliminary research is well underway. For example, suppose that a patient comes to welcome the intervention only after many years. Does this show we were right in intervening, or only that this patient has forgotten how painful the treatments, grief, and life-changes were? Or, to take a different problem, suppose 50 or 60 percent of the patients come to welcome (or reject) the interventions, rather than 80 or 90 percent? And suppose there seem to be no further relevant distinctions or categorizations we can employ that will allow us to segregate those who come to welcome (or reject) interventions from those who do not? Although we could speculate about these and other possible findings, such speculation at this point would only be a distracting form of mental gymnastics. Our findings, of themselves, will provide not only some important answers, but also new controversies.

A general objection to this approach that has been raised by some bioethicists is worth discussing before I close. Some persons may be uncomfortable treating patients against their will if one out of ten will not come to welcome the treatment, and others may be uncomfortable in failing to treat if only one out of ten will come to welcome the life-saving treatments.[28] Such discomfort, however, does not reflect the status of our moral obligations in a world in which everything is uncertain, including the outcomes of most medical protocols. If we apply the Kantian ethic and try to do our best to respect the deeper will of a person under severe duress, then we do that by intervening if the odds are very high—say nine out of ten—that we are doing what the person will welcome after the period of stress has passed. On the other hand, we fail to respect the person's autonomy if the odds are very high that the person will not come to welcome our intervention, yet we intervene anyway. So, too, acting on good but inconclusive evidence is justified on a utilitarian ethic.[29] If the odds are very high that the person will assess that the suffering is offset by the positive quality of his or her life, then we are

doing what will likely bring about the best results if we treat similar recalcitrant patients. If the odds are very high that the person will not think the treatments are made worthwhile by the subsequent quality of life, then to treat such a person is to do what will likely bring about unnecessary suffering. For anyone who still feels that we cannot act morally unless we are absolutely certain of the results, it must be pointed out that everything we do in life we do under conditions of uncertainty. The following remarks from the opening passages of Aristotle's *Nicomachean Ethics* are relevant: "Our discussion will be adequate if it achieves clarity within the limits of the subject matter. For precision cannot be expected in the treatment of all subjects alike, any more than it can be expected in all manufactured articles. . . . A well-schooled person is one who searches for that degree of precision in each kind of study which the nature of the subject at hand admits."[30] This is the general procedure we follow in medicine and elsewhere in our lives, and not to follow it in ethics would be debilitatingly irrational.

Our conclusions point to an important kind of research that must begin if we are to make headway in justifying, on some objective grounds, daily medical interventions and their omissions in cases involving burn victims and cervical spinal cord injury patients. This research, in turn, must be interdisciplinary in nature, for it requires the ability to bring into play the key conceptual and ethical points discussed above, the insight and experience to identify those features that might allow us to distinguish among relevant categories of patients, and the skill to conduct the required interviews with openness and compassion. The results of such research will, most likely, raise new questions as much as they resolve old ones. But to fail to proceed with such an investigation is to be unresponsive to the relevant conceptual and ethical considerations and, as a result, to take the chance of making life and death decisions on the basis of values and intuitions that may have little to do with the values and character of the patients in question. I hope that this essay will serve as a

catalyst for the serious work of finding out just what burn victims, quadraplegics, and others whom we have kept alive against their wishes think we have done to them, for the results of this research will put to rest many of those ethical controversies that make caring for these patients more difficult than it has to be.[31]

Notes

[1]Some writers distinguish between violations of liberty and restrictions of freedom. See, for example, Bernard Gert and Charles M. Culver, "Paternalistic Behavior," *Philosophy and Public Affairs* 6, no. 1 (1976): 45–57, especially note 4.

[2]For example, see Gordon Harper, "The Burn Unit," in Thomas Hackett and Ned Cassem, eds., *Massachusetts General Hospital Handbook of General Hospital Psychiatry* (Saint Louis: The C. V. Mosby Company, 1978), especially pp. 407–413.

[3]In this rough definition of paternalism, I follow Gert and Culver, "Paternalistic Behavior," although for another influential definition, see Gerald Dworkin, "Paternalism," *The Monist* 56, no. 1 (June, 1972): 64–84.

[4]No one insists upon aggressive treatment in cases in which survival is unprecedented, although such patients may be offered a full therapeutic regimen if they would like. See Sharon Imbus and Bruce Zawacki, "Autonomy for Burned Patients When Survival is Unprecedented," *New England Journal of Medicine* 297, no. 6 (1975): 308–311.

[5]Bruce Miller, "Autonomy and Refusing Lifesaving Treatment," *The Hastings Center Report* 11, no. 4 (August 1981), p. 27.

[6]H. Tristram Engelhardt, "A Demand to Die," *The Hastings Center Report* 4 (1975), p. 11.

[7]Arthur Dyck, "An Alternative to the Ethics of Euthanasia," in Reiser, et al., eds., *Ethics in Medicine* (Cambridge, Mass.: MIT Press, 1977), p. 533.

[8]Kant, *Foundations of the Metaphysics of Morals* (Indianapolis, Indiana: The Bobbs-Merrill Company, Inc., 1959): p. 47.

[9]Robert Nozick, *Anarchy, State, and Utopia* (New York: Basic Books, Inc., 1974), p. 31.

[10]For a relevant distinction between choices and unrealistic wishes, see Aristotle, *Nicomachean Ethics,* 1111b–1112a.

[11]Richard Brandt offers a very thorough discussion of how depression alters rational assessment in "The Morality and Rationality of Suicide," in James Rachels, ed., *Moral Problems* (New York: Harper & Row, 1971): 363–387.

[12]On utilitarian grounds, the rightness or wrongness of an act does not depend on what *actually* happens, but on what was *likely* to happen *given the evidence available to the agents at the time of action.* For more on the interpretation of utilitarianism, see B. Gruzalski, "Forseeable Consequence Utilitarianism," *Australasian Journal of Philosophy* 59 (June 1981): 163–176.

[13]John Stuart Mill, *Utilitarianism* (Indianapolis, Indiana: The Bobbs–Merrill Company, Inc., 1975), p. 10.

[14]L. H. Roth, et al., in "Tests of Competency to Consent to Treatment," *American Journal of Psychiatry* 134 (1977): 279–284, point out that competency is rarely determined as an independent variable.

[15]There may, of course, be other evidence that in specific cases will seem more important than what the ex-patient reports. For example, it might be that the patient is deceiving himself about the quality of his life but refuses to admit that deception to himself because it would be too painful psychologically. Or it might be that the patient believes that he ought to have died (perhaps he was given a blood transfusion against his religious convictions) and cannot psychologically admit that his life is so good that it justifies the suffering he went through in order to stay alive. Although in such cases the observations of others might be better evidence than the explicit report of the ex-patient about the ex-patient's assessment of whether the intervention was worth it, to rely on such third party reports would be to overlook the fact that third parties themselves have vested interests that may prevent them from correctly assessing what is worthwhile to the ex-patient. Hence, it seems that we must, at least at the start, focus on ex-patient reports as the most reliable evidence available.

[16]Matt Clark et al., "When Doctors Play God," *Newsweek,* 31 August 1981, p. 53.

[17]The problem illustrated by this example is discussed by, among others, Rosemary Carter in "Justifying Paternalism," *Canadian Journal of Philosophy* 7 (1977): 133–145.

[18]Contrast this with Rosemary Carter's criterion, *Ibid.,* p. 138, viz.: that it not be true that the act in question is causally sufficient for the subsequent consent.

[19]This first case is based on the discussion of cases of Jehovah's Witnesses in Samuel Gorovitz, et al., eds., *Moral Problems in Medicine* (Englewood Cliffs, New Jersey: Prentice-Hall, Inc., 1976), pp. 234–241.

[20]David L. Jackson and Stuart Youngner, "Patient Autonomy and 'Death with Dignity,'" *The New England Journal of Medicine* 301 (1979), p. 406.

[21]Bruce Miller, "Autonomy," p. 22.

[22]Jackson and Younger, "Patient Autonomy," p. 406.

[23]Although there has been a lot of follow-up with children, very little has been done with adults, and what has been done does not focus on what they would now wish had been done to them. For a recent study, see N. J. C. Andreasen, et al., "Psychiatric Complications in the Severely Burned," *Annals of Surgery* 174 (November 1971): 785–793.

[24]A logical alternative would be to so improve the quality of these persons' lives that they now think that their paternalistic treatments have been made worthwhile, but this option is a pipedream, especially given the current political climate.

[25]For example, Engelhardt, "A Demand to Die," pp. 9–11.

[26]"Caring for the Burned," *Life 3,* no. 3 (March 1980).

[27]*Ibid.,* p. 119.

[28]Donald Van De Veer, "Paternalism and Subsequent Consent," *Canadian Journal of Philosophy* IX, no. 4 (December 1979), p. 640.

[29]See Supra, note 12.

[30]Aristotle, *Nicomachean Ethics,* 1094b 10–25.

[31]I am indebted to comments and suggestions made by William DeAngelis, Carl Nelson, Stephen Nathanson, Sharon B. Young, and the members of the first year medical school class to whom I presented this material in the spring of 1981 at Tufts Medical School.

Ethical Issues in Aiding the Death of Young Children

H. Tristram Engelhardt, Jr.

A biographical sketch of Professor Engelhardt is given on page 266.

Engelhardt argues that passive infanticide is not only permissible but morally required when an infant is so damaged or diseased that its continued existence would be a grave injury or "wrongful life." He affirms that parents normally should make decisions about infanticide and that society should limit parents' discretion only if they refuse treatment for the child when continuing care will not be a severe burden and when it is likely that the child can "be brought to a good quality of life." Engelhardt does not view newborns as persons because they have not reached the status of being "responsible moral agents." He concludes by exploring the possibility of active infanticide.

Euthanasia in the pediatric age group involves a constellation of issues that are materially different from those of adult euthanasia.[1] The difference lies in the somewhat obvious fact that infants and young children are not able to decide about their own futures and thus are not persons in the same sense that normal adults are. While adults usually decide their own fate, others decide on behalf of young children. Although one can argue that euthanasia is or should be a personal right, the sense of such an argument is obscure with respect to children. Young children do not have any personal rights, at least none that they can exercise on their own behalf with regard to the manner of their life and death. As a result, euthanasia of young children raises special questions concern-

Reprinted from *Beneficent Euthanasia,* ed. by Marvin Kohl, published 1975 by Prometheus Books, 700 E. Amherst St., Buffalo, New York 14215, by permission of the author and publisher.

ing the standing of the rights of children, the status of parental rights, the obligations of adults to prevent the suffering of children, and the possible effects on society of allowing or expediting the death of seriously defective infants.

What I will refer to as the euthanasia of infants and young children might be termed by others infanticide, while some cases might be termed the withholding of extraordinary life-prolonging treatment.[2] One needs a term that will encompass both death that results from active intervention and death that ensues when one simply ceases further therapy.[3] In using such a term, one must recognize that death is often not directly but only obliquely intended. That is, one often intends only to treat no further, not actually to have death follow, even though one knows death will follow.[4]

Finally, one must realize that deaths as the result of withholding treatment constitute a significant proportion of neonatal deaths. For ex-

ample, as high as 14 percent of children in one hospital have been identified as dying after a decision was made not to treat further, the presumption being that the children would have lived longer had treatment been offered.[5]

Even popular magazines have presented accounts of parental decisions not to pursue treatment.[6] These decisions often involve a choice between expensive treatment with little chance of achieving a full, normal life for the child and "letting nature take its course," with the child dying as a result of its defects. As this suggests, many of these problems are products of medical progress. Such children in the past would have died. The quandaries are in a sense an embarrassment of riches; now that one *can* treat such defective children, *must* one treat them? And, if one need not treat such defective children, may one expedite their death?

I will here briefly examine some of these issues. First, I will review differences that contrast the euthanasia of adults to euthanasia of children. Second, I will review the issue of the rights of parents and the status of children. Third, I will suggest a new notion, the concept of the "injury of continued existence," and draw out some of its implications with respect to a duty to prevent suffering. Finally, I will outline some important questions that remain unanswered even if the foregoing issues can be settled. In all, I hope more to display the issues involved in a difficult question than to advance a particular set of answers to particular dilemmas.

For the purpose of this paper, I will presume that adult euthanasia can be justified by an appeal to freedom. In the face of imminent death, one is usually choosing between a more painful and more protracted dying and a less painful or less protracted dying, in circumstances where either choice makes little difference with regard to the discharge of social duties and responsibilities. In the case of suicide, we might argue that, in general, social duties (for example, the duty to support one's family) restrain one from taking one's own life. But in the face of imminent death and in the presence of the pain and deterioration of a

fatal disease, such duties are usually impossible to discharge and are thus rendered moot. One can, for example, picture an extreme case of an adult with a widely disseminated carcinoma, including metastases to the brain, who because of severe pain and debilitation is no longer capable of discharging any social duties. In these and similar circumstances, euthanasia becomes the issue of the right to control one's own body, even to the point of seeking assistance in suicide. Euthanasia is, as such, the issue of assisted suicide, the universalization of a maxim that all persons should be free, *in extremis,* to decide with regard to the circumstances of their death.

Further, the choice of positive euthanasia could be defended as the more rational choice: the choice of a less painful death and the affirmation of the value of a rational life. In so choosing, one would be acting to set limits to one's life in order not to live when pain and physical and mental deterioration make further rational life impossible. The choice to end one's life can be understood as a noncontradictory willing of a smaller set of states of existence for oneself, a set that would not include a painful death. As such, it would not involve a desire to destroy oneself. That is, adult euthanasia can be construed as an affirmation of the rationality and autonomy of the self.[7]

The remarks above focus on the active or positive euthanasia of adults. But they hold as well concerning what is often called passive or negative euthanasia, the refusal of life-prolonging therapy. In such cases, the patient's refusal of life-prolonging therapy is seen to be a right that derives from personal freedom, or at least from a zone of privacy into which there are no good grounds for social intervention.[8]

Again, none of these considerations apply directly to the euthanasia of young children, because they cannot participate in such decisions. Whatever else pediatric, in particular neonatal, euthanasia involves, it surely involves issues different from those of adult euthanasia. Since infants and small children cannot commit suicide, their right to assisted suicide is difficult to pose.

The difference between the euthanasia of young children and that of adults resides in the difference between children and adults. The difference, in fact, raises the troublesome question of whether young children are persons, or at least whether they are persons in the sense in which adults are. Answering that question will resolve in part at least the right of others to decide whether a young child should live or die and whether he should receive life-prolonging treatment.

THE STATUS OF CHILDREN

Adults belong to themselves in the sense that they are rational and free and therefore responsible for their actions. Adults are *sui juris*. Young children, though, are neither self-possessed nor responsible. While adults exist in and for themselves, as self-directive and self-conscious beings, young children, especially newborn infants, exist for their families and those who love them. They are not, nor can they in any sense be, responsible for themselves. If being a person is to be a responsible agent, a bearer of rights and duties, children are not persons in a strict sense. They are, rather, persons in a social sense: others must act on their behalf and bear responsibility for them. They are, as it were, entities defined by their place in social roles (for example, mother-child, family-child) rather than beings that define themselves as persons, that is, in and through themselves. Young children live as persons in and through the care of those who are responsible for them, and those responsible for them exercise the children's rights on their behalf. In this sense children belong to families in ways that most adults do not. They exist in and through their family and society.

Treating young children with respect has, then, a sense different from treating adults with respect. One can respect neither a newborn infant's or very young child's wishes nor its freedom. In fact, a newborn infant or young child is more an entity that is valued highly because it will grow to be a person and because it plays a social role as if it were a person.[9] That is, a small child is treated as if it were a person in social roles such as mother-child and family-child relationships, though strictly speaking the child is in no way capable of claiming or being responsible for the rights imputed to it. All the rights and duties of the child are exercised and "held in trust" by others for a future time and for a person yet to develop.

Medical decisions to treat or not to treat a neonate or small child often turn on the probability and cost of achieving that future status—a developed personal life. The usual practice of letting anencephalic children (who congenitally lack all or most of the brain) die can be understood as a decision based on the absence of the possibility of achieving a personal life. The practice of refusing treatment to at least some children born with meningomyelocele can be justified through a similar, but more utilitarian, calculus. In the case of anencephalic children one might argue that care for them as persons is futile since they will never be persons. In the case of a child with meningomyelocele, one might argue that when the cost of cure would likely be very high and the probable lifestyle open to attainment very truncated, there is not a positive duty to make a large investment of money and suffering. One should note that the cost here must include not only financial costs but also the anxiety and suffering that prolonged and uncertain treatment of the child would cause the parents.

This further raises the issue of the scope of positive duties not only when there is no person present in a strict sense, but when the likelihood of a full human life is also very uncertain. Clinical and parental judgment may and should be guided by the expected lifestyle and the cost (in parental and societal pain and money) of its attainment. The decision about treatment, however, belongs properly to the parents because the child belongs to them in a sense that it does not belong to anyone else, even to itself. The care and raising of the child falls to the parents, and when considerable

cost and little prospect of reasonable success are present, the parents may properly decide against life-prolonging treatment.

The physician's role is to present sufficient information in a usable form to the parents to aid them in making a decision. The accent is on the absence of a positive duty to treat in the presence of severe inconvenience (costs) to the parents; treatment that is very costly is not obligatory. What is suggested here is a general notion that there is never a duty to engage in extraordinary treatment and that "extraordinary" can be defined in terms of costs. This argument concerns children (1) whose future quality of life is likely to be seriously compromised and (2) whose present treatment would be very costly. The issue is that of the circumstances under which parents would not be obliged to take on severe burdens on behalf of their children or those circumstances under which society would not be so obliged. The argument should hold as well for those cases where the expected future life would surely be of normal quality, though its attainment would be extremely costly. The fact of little likelihood of success in attaining a normal life for the child makes decisions to do without treatment more plausible because the hope of success is even more remote and therefore the burden borne by parents or society becomes in that sense more extraordinary. But very high costs themselves could be a sufficient criterion, though in actual cases judgments in that regard would be very difficult when a normal life could be expected.[10]

The decisions in these matters correctly lie in the hands of the parents, because it is primarily in terms of the family that children exist and develop—until children become persons strictly, they are persons in virtue of their social roles. As long as parents do not unjustifiably neglect the humans in those roles so that the value and purpose of that role (that is, child) stands to be eroded (thus endangering other children), society need not intervene. In short, parents may decide for or against the treatment of their severely deformed children.

However, society has a right to intervene and protect children for whom parents refuse care (including treatment) when such care does not constitute a severe burden and when it is likely that the child could be brought to a good quality of life. Obviously, "severe burden" and "good quality of life" will be difficult to define and their meanings will vary, just as it is always difficult to say when grains of sand dropped on a table constitute a heap. At most, though, society need only intervene when the grains clearly do not constitute a heap, that is, when it is clear that the burden is light and the chance of a good quality of life for the child is high. A small child's dependence on his parents is so essential that society need intervene only when the absence of intervention would lead to the role "child" being undermined. Society must value mother-child and family-child relationships and should intervene only in cases where (1) neglect is unreasonable and therefore would undermine respect and care for children, or (2) where societal intervention would prevent children from suffering unnecessary pain.[11]

THE INJURY OF CONTINUED EXISTENCE

But there is another viewpoint that must be considered: that of the child or even the person that the child might become. It might be argued that the child has a right not to have its life prolonged. The idea that forcing existence on a child could be wrong is a difficult notion, which, if true, would serve to amplify the foregoing argument. Such an argument would allow the construal of the issue in terms of the perspective of the child, that is, in terms of a duty not to treat in circumstances where treatment would only prolong suffering. In particular, it would at least give a framework for a decision to stop treatment in cases where, though the costs of treatment are not high, the child's existence would be characterized by severe pain and deprivation.

A basis for speaking of continuing existence as an injury to the child is suggested by the proposed legal concept of "wrongful life." A number of suits have been initiated in the United States and in other countries on the grounds that life or existence itself is, under certain circumstances, a tort or injury to the living person.[12] Although thus far all such suits have ultimately failed, some have succeeded in their initial stages. Two examples may be instructive. In each case the ability to receive recompense for the injury (the tort) presupposed the existence of the individual, whose existence was itself the injury. In one case a suit was initiated on behalf of a child against his father alleging that his father's siring him out of wedlock was an injury to the child.[13] In another case a suit on behalf of a child born of an inmate of a state mental hospital impregnated by rape in that institution was brought against the state of New York.[14] The suit was brought on the grounds that being born with such historical antecedents was itself an injury for which recovery was due. Both cases presupposed that nonexistence would have been preferable to the conditions under which the person born was forced to live.

The suits for tort for wrongful life raise the issue not only of when it would be preferable not to have been born but also of when it would be *wrong* to cause a person to be born. This implies that someone should have judged that it would have been preferable for the child never to have had existence, never to have been in the position to judge that the particular circumstances of life were intolerable.[15] Further, it implies that the person's existence under those circumstances should have been prevented and that, not having been prevented, life was not a gift but an injury. The concept of tort for wrongful life raises an issue concerning the responsibility for giving another person existence, namely, the notion that giving life is not always necessarily a good and justifiable action. Instead, in certain circumstances, so it has been argued, one may have a duty *not* to give existence to another person. This concept in-volves the claim that certain qualities of life have a negative value, making life an injury, not a gift; it involves, in short, a concept of human accountability and responsibility for human life. It contrasts with the notion that life is a gift of God and thus similar to other "acts of God" (that is, events for which no man is accountable). The concept thus signals the fact that humans can now control reproduction and that where rational control is possible humans are accountable. That is, the expansion of human capabilities has resulted in an expansion of human responsibilities such that one must now decide when and under what circumstances persons will come into existence.

The concept of tort for wrongful life is transferable in part to the painfully compromised existence of children who can only have their life prolonged for a short, painful, and marginal existence. The concept suggests that allowing life to be prolonged under such circumstances would itself be an injury of the person whose painful and severely compromised existence would be made to continue. In fact, it suggests that there is a duty not to prolong life if it can be determined to have a substantial negative value for the person involved.[16] Such issues are moot in the case of adults, who can and should decide for themselves. But small children cannot make such a choice. For them it is an issue of justifying prolonging life under circumstances of painful and compromised existence. Or, put differently, such cases indicate the need to develop social canons to allow a decent death for children for whom the only possibility is protracted, painful suffering.

I do not mean to imply that one should develop a new basis for civil damages. In the field of medicine, the need is to recognize an ethical category, a concept of wrongful continuance of existence, not a new legal right. The concept of injury for continuance of existence, the proposed analogue of the concept of tort for wrongful life, presupposes that life can be of a negative value such that the medical maxim *primum non nocere* ("first do no harm") would require not sustaining life.[17]

The idea of responsibility for acts that sustain or prolong life is cardinal to the notion that one should not under certain circumstances further prolong the life of a child. Unlike adults, children cannot decide with regard to euthanasia (positive or negative), and if more than a utilitarian justification is sought, it must be sought in a duty not to inflict life on another person in circumstances where that life would be painful and futile. This position must rest on the facts that (1) medicine now can cause the prolongation of the life of seriously deformed children who in the past would have died young and that (2) it is not clear that life so prolonged is a good for the child. Further, the choice is made not on the basis of costs to the parents or to society but on the basis of the child's suffering and compromised existence.

The difficulty lies in determining what makes life not worth living for a child. Answers could never be clear. It seems reasonable, however, that the life of children with diseases that involve pain and no hope of survival should not be prolonged. In the case of Tay-Sachs disease (a disease marked by a progressive increase in spasticity and dementia usually leading to death at age three or four), one can hardly imagine that the terminal stages of spastic reaction to stimuli and great difficulty in swallowing are at all pleasant to the child (even insofar as it can only minimally perceive its circumstances). If such a child develops aspiration pneumonia and is treated, it can reasonably be said that to prolong its life is to inflict suffering. Other diseases give fairly clear portraits of lives not worth living: for example, Lesch-Nyhan disease, which is marked by mental retardation and compulsive self-mutilation.

The issue is more difficult in the case of children with diseases for whom the prospects for normal intelligence and a fair lifestyle do exist, but where these chances are remote and their realization expensive. Children born with meningomyelocele present this dilemma. Imagine, for example, a child that falls within Lorber's fifth category (an IQ of sixty or less, sometimes blind,

subject to fits, and always incontinent). Such a child has little prospect of anything approaching a normal life, and there is a good chance of its dying even with treatment.[18] But such judgments are statistical. And if one does not treat such children, some will still survive and, as John Freeman indicates, be worse off if not treated.[19] In such cases one is in a dilemma. If one always treats, one must justify extending the life of those who will ultimately die anyway and in the process subjecting them to the morbidity of multiple surgical procedures. How remote does the prospect of a good life have to be in order not to be worth great pain and expense?[20] It is probably best to decide, in the absence of a positive duty to treat, on the basis of the cost and suffering to parents and society. But, as Freeman argues, the prospect of prolonged or even increased suffering raises the issue of active euthanasia.[21]

If the child is not a person strictly, and if death is inevitable and expediting it would diminish the child's pain prior to death, then it would seem to follow that, all else being equal, a decision for active euthanasia would be permissible, even obligatory.[22] The difficulty lies with "all else being equal," for it is doubtful that active euthanasia could be established as a practice without eroding and endangering children generally, since, as John Lorber has pointed out, children cannot speak in their own behalf.[23] Thus, although there is no argument in principle against the active euthanasia of small children, there could be an argument against such practices based on questions of prudence. To put it another way, even though one might have a duty to hasten the death of a particular child, one's duty to protect children in general could override that first duty. The issue of active euthanasia turns in the end on whether it would have social consequences that refraining would not, on whether (1) it is possible to establish procedural safeguards for limited active euthanasia and (2) whether such practices would have a significant adverse effect on the treatment of small children in general. But since these are

important to all concerned in symbolic and existential as well as physical terms.

Ambiguous Cases Although for most seriously ill infants there will be either a clearly beneficial option or no beneficial therapeutic options at all, hard questions are raised by the smaller number for whom it is very difficult to assess whether the treatments available offer prospects of benefit—for example, a child with a debilitating and painful disease who might live with therapy, but only for a year or so, or a respirator-dependent premature infant whose long-term prognosis becomes bleaker with each passing day.

Much of the difficulty in these cases arises from factual uncertainty. For the many infants born prematurely, and sometimes for those with serious congenital defects, the only certainty is that without intensive care they are unlikely to survive; very little is known about how each individual will fare with treatment. Neonatology is too new a field to allow accurate predictions of which babies will survive and of the complications, handicaps, and potentials that the survivors might have.[15]

The longer some of these babies survive, the more reliable the prognosis for the infant becomes and the clearer parents and professionals can be on whether further treatment is warranted or futile. Frequently, however, the prospect of long-term survival and the quality of that survival remain unclear for days, weeks, and months, during which time the infants may have an unpredictable and fluctuating course of advances and setbacks.

One way to avoid confronting anew the difficulties involved in evaluating each case is to adopt objective criteria to distinguish newborns who will receive life-sustaining treatment from those who will not. Such criteria would be justified if there were evidence that their adoption would lead to decisions more often being made correctly.

Strict treatment criteria proposed in the 1970s by a British physician for deciding which newborns with spina bifida[16] should receive treatment rested upon the location of the lesion (which influences degree of paralysis), the presence of hydrocephalus (fluid in the brain, which influences degree of retardation), and the likelihood of an infection. Some critics of this proposal argued with it on scientific grounds, such as objecting that long-term effects of spina bifida cannot be predicted with sufficient accuracy at birth.[17] Other critics, however, claimed this whole approach to ambiguous cases exhibited the "technical criteria fallacy."[18] They contended that an infant's future life—and hence the treatment decisions based on it—involves value considerations that are ignored when physicians focus solely on medical prognosis.[19]

---

[15]Uncertainty about the course is partly the consequence of the rapidly expanding ability to save newborns who until recently could not have survived. Neonatal intensive care is a rapidly developing field and long-term follow-up on much of the most modern treatment is not yet available. Limited experience also compromises the ability to assess the effects—especially long-term physical and psychological effects—of medicine's effort to create a womb-like environment for the premature infant. *See* Albert R. Jonsen, *Justice and the Defective Newborn,* in Earl E. Shelp, ed., JUSTICE AND HEALTH CARE, D. Reidel Pub. Co., Boston (1981) at 95.

---

[16]John Lorber, *Early Results of Selective Treatment of Spina Bifida Cystica,* 4 BRIT. MED. J. 201 (1973); John Lorber, *Results of Treatment of Myelomeningocele,* 13 Dev. Med. & Child Neurol. 279 (1971). *See also* Terrence F. Ackerman, *Meningomyelocele and Parental Commitment: A Policy Proposal Regarding Selection for Treatment,* 5 Man & Med. 291 (1980).

[17]John M. Freeman, *The Shortsighted Treatment of Myelomeningocele: A Long-Term Case Report,* 53 PEDIATRICS 311 (1974); Robert Reid, *Spina Bifida: The Fate of the Untreated,* 7 HASTINGS CTR. REP. 16 (Aug. 1977).

[18]Robert M. Veatch, *The Technical Criteria Fallacy,* 7 HASTINGS CTR. REP. 15, 16 (Aug. 1977).

[19]Courts, for example, sometimes automatically assume the priority of the value of a longer life. In the case of Kerri Ann McNulty, a Massachusetts probate judge ruled that corrective surgery had to be done on a month-old infant diagnosed as having congenital rubella, cataracts on both eyes, deafness, congenital heart failure, respiratory problems, and probable severe retardation. After reviewing the medical testimony, the court explicitly eschewed "quality of life" considerations, stating: "I am persuaded that the proposed cardiac surgery is

The decision [to treat or not] must also include evaluation of the meaning of existence with varying impairments. Great variation exists about these essentially evaluative elements among parents, physicians, and policy makers. It must be an open question whether these variations in evaluation are among the relevant factors to consider in making a treatment decision. When Lorber uses the phrase "contraindications to active therapy," he is medicalizing what are really value choices.[20]

The Commission agrees that such criteria necessarily include value considerations. Supposedly objective criteria such as birth weight limits or checklists for severity of spina bifida have not been shown to improve the quality of decisionmaking in ambiguous and complex cases. Instead, their use seems to remove the weight of responsibility too readily from those who should have to face the value questions—parents and health care providers.[21]

Furthermore, any set of standards, when honestly applied, leaves some difficult or uncertain cases. When a child's best interests are ambiguous, a decision based upon them will require prudent and discerning judgment. Defining the category of cases in a way that appropriately protects and encourages the exercise of parental judgment will sometimes be difficult. The procedures the Commission puts forward in the remainder of this chapter are intended to assist in differentiating between the infants whose interests are in fact uncertain and for whom surrogates' decisions (whether for or against therapy) should be honored, and those infants who would clearly benefit from a certain course of action, which, if not chosen by the parents and providers, ought to be authorized by persons acting for the state as *parens patriae.*

POLICY EVALUATION AND RECOMMENDATIONS

The few systematic studies of decisionmaking about seriously ill newborns support the contentions of care professionals before the Commission and elsewhere that such decisionmaking usually adheres to the precepts outlined in this chapter.[22] As shown previously, however, problems of two kinds do occur: (1) parents receive outdated or incomplete information from their physicians and this limits their capacity to act as surrogate decisionmakers,[23] and (2) in what appears to be a limited number of cases, inappropriate decisions are made without triggering a careful reevaluation.[24]

---

not merely a life prolonging measure, but indeed is for the purpose of saving the life of this child, *regardless of the quality of that life.*" In the Matter of Kerri Ann McNulty, No. 1960 (Probate Ct., Essex Co., Mass., Feb. 15, 1978).

[20]Veatch, *supra* note 18, at 15. *But see* Stuart F. Spicker and John R. Raye, *The Bearing of Prognosis on the Ethics of Medicine: Congenital Anomalies, the Social Context and the Law,* in Stuart F. Spicker, Joseph M. Healy, Jr., and H. Tristam Engelhardt, Jr., eds., THE LAW-MEDICINE RELATION: A PHILOSOPHICAL EXPLORATION, D. Reidel Pub. Co., Boston (1981) at 189, 202-05, 212.

[21]Many have noted that diffusion of responsibility often acts to make no one feel responsible. *See, e.g.,* R. B. Zachary, *Commentary: On the Death of a Baby,* 7 J. MED. ETHICS 5, 11 (1981).

[22]*See* notes 46-49 of *Deciding to Forego Life-Sustaining Treatment.*

[23]Hein, *supra* note 6.
> When they [parents] begin to hear both points of view— sometimes it's only that there are excellent adoptive homes for such kids—that's often never raised—that changes the decision. Sometimes they just need to learn more about Down's. Parents have such horrible fantasies about it; it's mongolism and it's something monstrous, they think. This wider process is often nothing more exotic than bringing facts into the discussion.

Testimony of Dr. Norman Fost, transcript of 16th meeting of the President's Commission (Jan. 9, 1982) at 161.

[24]Robertson, *supra* note 8. Perhaps the best-known case, and the only one in which there is an appellate court decision, is the one that has come to be known as the Infant Doe case, in which parents elected to forego treatment of their newborn child who had Down syndrome, tracheoesophageal atresia, and possibly additional anomalies. The course of nontreatment was one "medically recommended" way in which to proceed, according to the opinion of the trial court in an action brought by child welfare authorities on the complaint of some party other than either the physicians or the parents

all small groups, is vital but will be of no avail if the hospital leadership, including the medical director and the chiefs of staff, is opposed.

The remaining membership question is whether patients and families should participate in such group discussions. The family's wishes, resources, and religious orientation are obviously of major importance. The question is whether this information should be presented directly by them or presented to the committee by someone else. While many physicians have paternalistic impulses on this subject, the great majority of patients[43] and parents[44] resent being excluded from discussions about management of a critically or terminally ill patient. When competent patients are under discussion, it is fundamental in American law that "every human being of adult years has a right to determine what shall be done with his own body."[45] Assumptions that relatives cannot tolerate candid discussions or that they will experience long-term guilt are not supported by existing data.[46]

The question, therefore, is not whether to include patient and family in such discussions but whether that involvement should include direct discussion with a group of strangers. In some cases it will be appropriate for relatives to join the discussion (eg, when they insist on it), but that should not preclude the group having an opportunity to discuss the issues among themselves, free of the inhibition that would accompany the presence of patients or relatives. In other cases, family involvement may be unnecessary and/or unwanted by the family. If the primary function of the group is to be advisory to the attending physician, apologies should not be needed for the physician's desire to have a free and uninhibited consultation. A flexible policy would be to invite family members to present their views but not require it.

It is unclear whether physicians could consult such committees without explicit permission from the patient or family. Anyone making such a claim would have to provide some justification for overriding the usual duty to maintain confidentiality. It is possible that a federal or state regulation requiring such consultation could provide this justification, but the matter has not been tested as yet. Considering the profound importance and sensitivity of this area, it would seem prudent, if not required by law, to obtain permission from the patient or family.

As with all committees, the entire membership will not be available for all meetings. There will be times when a majority will not be available. As long as the committee has no regulatory role, there would be no compelling need to formalize quorum requirements. Some HECs provide for consultation with the chairman or any available member of the committee. That person can activate a subcommittee of available members. While every case is unique, as with all areas of medicine there are recurring themes and syndromes, and in some cases the experienced committee person may be able to anticipate a committee consensus accurately. If and when such committees are mandated, such problems as quorum requirements will have to be addressed.

OPEN VS CLOSED MEETINGS, RECORDS, AND ACCOUNTABILITY

The educational functions of ethics committees would be better served if they were open to all interested persons, both for the audience's benefit and so the committee members could get ideas, feelings, and feedback from peers and the community. Many institutional review boards open their meetings to the public, but it is obviously unknown whether such scrutiny has a net positive or negative effect on the quality of review. Case conferences can be developed to promote this purpose, using semifictional data to protect confidential information. Discussion of current cases, however, would be necessarily closed to those who are not officially members of or consultants to the committee. Patient rights of confidentiality would require this, as well as the need for candid discussion.

A related question is whether the substance of discussion in such meetings should be recorded and whether such records should be publicly available in the form of tape recordings, transcripts, minutes, summaries, or notes in the medical record. It is important for there to be accountability for crucial decisions about life and death, and there is broad consensus among mediocolegal experts that the basis for a decision to withdraw life-sustaining treatment should be documented in the medical record.[40] This can be accomplished by a note in the chart by the attending physician documenting that a consultation was obtained and summarizing the key points in that discussion.

Maintaining a permanent, detailed record of the committee's discussion has advantages and disadvantages. On the one hand, it allows for greater accountability, provides a valuable teaching resource, and reduces the possibility for misunderstanding. If one purpose is to provide legal protection for the physician and hospital, it would be essential to have a record of the content of the discussion. On the other hand, there is the risk of inhibiting discussion and possibly increasing the legal liability for members. Such discussions could conceivably be construed as conspiracy to commit homicide,[47] although no such charges have ever been brought. Whether or not records could be protected from discovery proceedings or subpoena in a malpractice or criminal trial is unclear. The need to prepare minutes could unintentionally push the committee toward voting or directing a plan of action rather than confining itself to the more acceptable roles of consultation and advice.

ACCESS AND INDICATIONS FOR CONVENING THE COMMITTEE

The most controversial question confronting an institution considering formation of an ethics committee is the definition of access and jurisdiction. The slow growth of ethics committees nationally, and the modest use of them in institutions where they have had some success, is partly due to resistance and opposition from the medical staff. An extreme view would prohibit or oppose the formation of such committees, usually on the grounds that such a group is less likely to make a good decision than a wise clinician or sensitive family.[48] Others tolerate the existence of such a committee, so long as they are free not to consult it. At the other extreme, some would propose defining cases for which consultation would be mandatory.[49]

At present, most physicians appear unlikely to consult such a group of their own volition, even with the understanding that the committee would have no authority to make decisions. This resistance suggests that hospitals should initially establish a policy of voluntary consultation, with no decision-making authority in the committee. Informal discussion and consensus development may encourage consultation until such review becomes standard through custom or by legal requirement. While mandatory consultation with such committees might be necessary if they are to become an important part of decision making in hospitals, there is no such mandate at present.

It is undesirable for such a committee to be faced with a large volume of cases in the beginning. It is important for the committee to discover and define its own rules, for the members to become comfortable with each other, and for it to gain some early success and esteem in the institution. Consultation on a voluntary basis will minimize the load and allow this development to occur with less pressure.

If a hospital establishes a voluntary committee—with consultation available on an optional basis—there remains the question of access by persons other than the attending physician. While this is in part a political issue to be resolved within the personalities and traditions of each hospital, one purpose of a committee—to minimize the probability of a decision that, in retrospect, may be difficult to justify—would be served by facilitating access to its views. If a house officer, nurse, student, patient, or family member feels sufficiently concerned about a patient's management

Types of Ethics Committee

	Committee Review	
Committee Recommendations	Optional	Mandatory
Optional	A	B
Mandatory	C	D

and cannot obtain satisfaction from discussions with the attending physician, an ethics committee offers a mechanism for intrainstitutional resolution of a potential dispute. Whistle blowers are usually frustrated by the inadequacy of internal review of appeal processes. The celebrated cases involving criminal charges for withholding treatment[50-54] (*California Magazine,* November 1982, pp 79–81, 164-175) were triggered by reports from nurses who thought physicians were making hasty or improper decisions and who felt an inability to seek support within the institution.

While the general policy of the committee might be one of optional consultation, there may be exceptions, cases for which mandatory review would seem prudent. One such category might be handicapped newborns who are not terminally ill but whose interests seem best served by withdrawal of life support. It is this class of patients that has provoked the greatest controversy and stimulated governmental intrusion. Mandatory review would not imply that it is improper to withhold or withdraw treatment from such patients but only that it is a sufficiently weighty decision to justify consultation to reduce the probability of error. There may be no legal authority for mandating review over the objections of the patient or family, although the recent federal statute and subsequent regulations might provide such authority. A proposed statute, which includes standards for jurisdiction, is available in the report of the President's Commission for the Study of Ethical Problems in Medicine.[55]

In summary, consultation can be optional or mandatory with regard to which cases are brought to the committee, and the committee's deliberations can be optional or mandatory with regard to whether they are advisory or action forcing. The policies available are summarized in the Figure. Policy A—"Optional/Optional"—describes the position in most HECs at present. Consultation is voluntary and decisions are not binding. Policy D—"Mandatory/Mandatory"—is seen by some as implied, although not explicit, in the now-inactive federal regulations covering handicapped newborns. This policy has been opposed[56] on the grounds that there is not yet sufficient experience with HECs to warrant giving them such authority. Policy B—"Mandatory/Optional"—is implied by the American Academy of Pediatrics' guidelines[24] and is favored by the President's Commission.[57] It is unlikely that an institution would adopt policy C—"Optional/Mandatory"—which offers consultation on a voluntary basis, but only on the condition that the physician be bound by the committee's decision.

While many correctly point out that a committee cannot be convened at moments of crisis, it is our experience that this concern is overdrawn. The great majority of decisions regarding withdrawal of care can be anticipated days, and often weeks, before a moment of crisis. In truly unexpected emergencies, if there is ambiguity about whether to resuscitate or otherwise treat a dying patient, the prudent course is to avoid making irreversible decisions based on inadequate data or reflection; ie, to maintain life until consultation is available. There will usually be other opportunities to withdraw treatment, if that appears to be the correct course, although it must be conceded that emergency resuscitation sometimes leads to long life, which, in retrospect, should not have been prolonged. Some emergency crises involve situations that are sufficiently similar to al-

low development of policies before the moment of crisis. Examples include the extremely small, nonviable premature infant; live abortuses; anencephalic newborns; and newborns with Down's syndrome. Guidelines do not necessarily dictate behavior in all cases, but they can identify behaviors that are permissible, those that should be forbidden, and those that are sufficiently controversial to warrant consultation.[58] Even in those cases that do not allow for consultation or development of guidelines, post hoc discussion—a "clinical-ethical conference"—can be useful in guiding conduct in future cases.

EFFECT ON LIABILITY

Consultation with an HEC has potential risks and benefits for the hospital and its personnel. Physicians, nurses, and others who participate in decisions to withhold life-sustaining treatment could be charged with civil or criminal offenses, such as negligence and homicide.[7,38,47,50-54] Committee discussion could be construed as conspiracy to commit homicide.[47] Committee members and records of the meeting could be subpoenaed, and a disgruntled member could testify against the attending physician.

We would not view these concerns as arguments discouraging to an attending physician, as they do not present risks different from those that exist without committee consultation. As mentioned earlier, prosecutions can be triggered by disgruntled employees in any case and might be more likely when internal mechanisms for discussion are unavailable. With or without committee consultation, an attending physician must be accountable for a decision to withdraw life-support, which requires, at least, a statement in the chart summarizing the reasons for the decision. We believe the use of a committee is more likely to reduce the risk of litigation and/or prosecution. It provides reassurance and evidence that due care was used in arriving at a decision, and the substance of the consultation is likely to reduce the

chance of a decision that would invite legal attention.

Committee members might incur liability for decisions that they have little ability to affect. They could be liable under child abuse laws for failing to report neglect, although many such statutes only require reporting for patients under the care of the reporter. Such questions may be resolved in part by institutional insurance coverage and assurances that legal services would be provided, but that may not be consoling for the individual involved. If a prosecution were brought, it would most likely be for an egregious case, but a committee member may feel powerless to affect what he considers an egregious decision. We would not consider these risks to be significantly greater than the risks of collaborative care in general. Individuals with serious concerns about liability can obviously choose not to participate in such committees.

CONCLUSIONS

Hospital ethics committees are increasingly becoming a part of decision making involving life support in critically ill patients. Such committees can help promote ethically defensible decisions in three ways: through education, establishment of hospital policies, and consultation and review.

There is adequate experience to justify some optimism in the feasibility and usefulness of such committees, providing they have competent, diverse membership and effective leadership and are supported by opinion leaders in the hospital. It would be desirable for ethics committees to be formed voluntarily, before they are required by law, while the flexibility exists to try alternative procedures. Given the present inexperience and the complex and highly charged cases with which they would deal, it is probable that a mandate for their formation would be associated with unwelcome side effects.

John Robertson and Dan Wikler made many helpful comments and suggestions.

References

[1]Brim OG, Freeman HE, Levine S, et al: *The Dying Patient*. New York, Russell Sage Foundation, 1970, pp 20-26.

[2]*In re* Quinlan, 70 NJ 10, 355 A2d 647, *cert denied*, 429 US 922 (1976).

[3]*Superintendent of Belchertown State School v Saikewicz*, 370 NE2d 417 (Mass 1977).

[4]*In re* Spring, 405 NE2d 115 (Mass 1980).

[5]*Eichner v Dillon*, 426 NYS2d 527 (App Div 1980).

[6]*In re* Storar, 420 NE2d 64 (NY 1981), *rev'g in re* Storar, 433 NYS2d 388 (App Div 1980).

[7]Robertson JA: *The Rights of the Critically Ill*. New York, Bantam Books Inc, 1983.

[8]Arizona HB 2209, July 27, 1983.

[9]Donnelly TR Jr: Nondiscrimination on the basis of handicap, Interim Final Rule (45 CFR 84). *Federal Register* 1983;48(March 17):9630-9632.

[10]Heckler MM: Nondiscrimination on the basis of handicap relating to health care for handicapped infants: Proposed rules. (45 CFR 84). *Federal Register* 1983;48 (July 5):30846-30852.

[11]Nondiscrimination on the basis of handicap: Procedure and guidelines relating to health care for handicapped infants. *Federal Register* (45 CFR 84). 1984;49:1622-1654.

[12]Optimum care for hopelessly ill patients: A report of the Clinical Care Committee of the Massachusetts General Hospital. *N Engl J Med* 1976;295:362-364.

[13]Cohen C: Interdisciplinary consultation on the care of the critically ill and dying: The role of one hospital ethics committee. *Crit Care Med* 1982;10:776-784.

[14]Levine C: Hospital ethics committees: A guarded prognosis. *Hastings Center Rep* 1977; 7:28-30.

[15]Veatch R: Hospital ethics committees: Is there a role? *Hastings Center Rep* 1977;7:22-25.

[16]Bader D: Medical-moral committees: Guarding values in an ambivalent society. *Hosp Prog* 1982, pp 80-83.

[17]Esqueda K: Hospital ethics committees: Four case studies. *Hosp Med Staff* 1978, pp 26-31.

[18]President's Commission for the Study of Ethical Problems in Medicine and Biomedical and Behavioral Research: *Deciding to Forego Life-Sustaining Treatment*. Government Printing Office, 1983, p 164.

[19]President's Commission for the Study of Ethical Problems in Medicine and Biomedical and Behavioral Research: *Deciding to Forego Life-Sustaining Treatment*. Government Printing Office, 1983, pp 160-170, 224-228.

[20]Committee on Bioethics, American Academy of Pediatrics: Treatment of critically ill newborns. *Pediatrics* 1983;72:565-566.

[21]Bioethics committees in hospitals, substitute resolution 70. Adopted by the American Medical Association House of Delegates, Annual Meeting, Chicago, June 17-21, 1984.

[22]Beecher HK: *Research and the Individual*. Boston, Little Brown & Co, 1970.

[23]National Commission for the Protection of Human Subjects in Biomedical and Behavioral Research: *Institutional Review Boards*. Government Printing Office, 1978, p 74.

[24]American Academy of Pediatrics Task Force on Infant Bioethics Committees: Guidelines for infant bioethics committees. *Pediatrics* 1984;72:306-310.

[25]45 CFR 46.

[26]Veatch RM: Generalization of expertise. *Hastings Center Studies* 1973;1:29-40.

[27]Ruddick W (ed): *Philosophers in Medical Centers*. New York, The Society for Philosophy and Public Affairs, 1980.

[28]Delgado R, McAllen P: The moralist as expert witness. *Boston Univ Law Rev* 1982; 62:869-926.

[29]Fost N: Ethical problems in pediatrics. *Curr Probl Pediatr* 1976;6:1-31.

[30]Fost N: Proxy consent for seriously ill newborns, in Smith D (ed): *No Rush to Judgment: Essays on Medical Ethics*. Bloomington, Ind, Poynter Center, 1977, pp 1-17.

[31]Fost N: How decisions are made: A physician's view, in Swinyard C (ed): *Decision Making and the Defective Newborn: Proceedings of a Conference on Spina Bifida and Ethics*. Springfield, Ill, Charles C Thomas Publisher, 1978, pp 220-230.

[32]Youngner SJ, Jackson DL, Coulton C, et al: A national survey of hospital ethics committees, in President's Commission for the Study of Ethical Problems in Medicine and Biomedical and Behavioral Research: *Deciding to Forego Life-Sustaining Treatment*, appendix F. Government Printing Office, 1983, pp 443-449.

[33]Fost N: Putting hospitals on notice. *Hastings Center Rep* 1982;12:5-8.

[34]Annas GJ: Disconnecting the Baby Doe hotline. *Hastings Center Rep* 1983;13:14-16.

[35]Strain JE. The decision to forego life-sustaining treatment for seriously ill newborns. *Pediatrics* 1983;72:572-573.

[36]*American Academy of Pediatrics v Heckler*, No. 83-0774 (D DC April 14, 1983).

[37]*AHA v Heckler*, 585 F Suppl 541 (SDNY 1984).

[38]Robertson JA, Fost N: Passive euthanasia of defective newborn infants: Legal considerations. *J Pediatr* 1976;88:883.

[39]Relman AS: The Saikewicz decision: A medical viewpoint. *Am J Law Med* 1978;4:233-242.

[40]Orders against resuscitation: Selected policy statements, appendix I in President's Commission for the Study of Ethical Problems in Medicine and Biomedical and Behavioral Research: *Deciding to Forego Life-Sustaining Treatment*. Government Printing Office, 1983.

[41]Hospitals and physicians at risk: The need for formal policies for the care of terminally ill patients. *Issues Health Care Technol* 1981, pp 1-5.

[42]Miles SH, Cranford R, Schultz AL: The do-not-resuscitate order in a teaching hospital: Considerations and a suggested policy. *Ann Intern Med* 1982;96:660-664.

[43]Gilbertsen VA, Wangensteen OH: Should the doctor tell the patient the disease is cancer? in *The Physician and the Total Care of the Cancer Patient.* New York, American Cancer Society, 1961.

[44]Ellis HL: Parental involvement in the decision to treat spina bifida cystica. *Br Med J* 1974;1:369-372.

[45]*Schloendorff v Society of New York Hospital,* 105 NE 92 (NY 1914).

[46]Benfield DG, Leib SA, Vollman JH: Grief responses of parents to neonatal death and parent participation in deciding care. *Pediatrics* 1978;62:171.

[47]Robertson JA: Involuntary euthanasia of defective newborns: Legal considerations. *Stanford Law Rev* 1975;27:213.

[48]Duff RS: Counseling families and deciding care in severely defective children: A way of coping with 'medical Vietnam.' *Pediatrics* 1981;67:315-320.

[49]President's Commission for the Study of Ethical Problems in Medicine and Biomedical and Behavioral Research: *Deciding to Forego Life-Sustaining Treatment.* Government Printing Office, 1983, pp 227-228.

[50]Robertson JA: After Edelin: Little guidance. *Hastings Center Rep* 1977;7:15-17.

[51]Robertson JA: Dilemma in Danville. *Hastings Center Rep* 1981;11:5-8.

[52]Towers B: Irreversible coma and withdrawal of life support: Is it murder if the IV line is disconnected? *J Med Ethics* 1982;8:203-205.

[53]Breo DL, Lefton D, Rust ME: MDs face unprecedented murder charge. *Am Med News* 1983; pp 1,13-19,21-22.

[54]Barber v. Sup. Court for the State of California. Court of Appeals, 2nd Appellate District, Division Two, Sup Ct. #A025586, October 12, 1983.

[55]Hospital ethics committees: Proposed statute and national survey, appendix F in President's Commission for the Study of Ethical Problems in Medicine and Biomedical and Behavioral Research: *Deciding to Forego Life-Sustaining Treatment.* Government Printing Office, 1983.

[56]Committee on the Legal and Ethical Aspects of Health Care for Children: Comments and recommendations on the "Infant Doe" proposed regulations. *Law Med Health Care* 1983;11:203-209,213.

[57]President's Commission for the Study of Ethical Problems in Medicine and Biomedical and Behavioral Research. *Deciding to Forego Life-Sustaining Treatment.* Government Printing Office, 1983, p 164.

[58]University of Wisconsin Hospital and Clinics: Guidelines regarding decisions to give, withhold or terminate care, appendix I in President's Commission for the Study of Ethical Problems in Medicine and Biomedical and Behavioral Research: *Deciding to Forego Life-Sustaining Treatment.* Government Printing Office, 1983, pp 513-517.

SELECTED BIBLIOGRAPHY

Barnard, Christian. *Good Life, Good Death: A Doctor's Case for Euthanasia and Suicide.* New York: Prentice-Hall, 1980.

Black, P. M. "Brain Death." *New England Journal of Medicine* 299 (1978): 338–44.

———. "Clinical Problems in the Use of Brain-death Standards." *Achives of Internal Medicine* 143 (1983): 121–23.

Clark, Brian. *Whose Life Is It Anyway?* New York: Avon Books, 1980.

Humphry, Derek. *Let Me Die Before I Wake: Hemlock's Book of Self-Deliverance for the Dying.* New York: Grove Press, 1984.

Jackson, D. L., and S. Younger. "Patient Autonomy and 'Death with Dignity': Some Clinical Caveats." *New England Journal of Medicine* 301 (1979): 404–408.

Kohl, Marvin, ed. *Beneficent Euthanasia.* Buffalo: Prometheus Books, 1975.

Kübler-Ross, Elisabeth. *On Death and Dying.* New York: Macmillan, 1979.

Lo, B., and A. R. Jonsen. "Clinical Decisions to Limit Treatment." *Annals of Internal Medicine* 93 (1980): 764–68.

Maguire, Daniel C. *Death by Choice.* Garden City, N.Y.: Image Books, 1984.

President's Commission for the Study of Ethical Problems in Medicine and Biomedical and Behavioral Research. *Defining Death: Medical, Legal and Ethical Issues in the Determination of Death.* Washington, D.C.: U.S. Government Printing Office, 1981.

———. *Deciding to Forego Life-Sustaining Treatment.* Washington, D.C.: U.S. Government Printing Office, 1983.

Quinlan, Joseph, and Julia Quinlan. *Karen Ann: The Quinlans Tell Their Story.* New York: Bantam Books, 1977.

Rachels, James. *The End of Life: Euthanasia and Morality.* New York: Oxford University Press, 1986.

Rhoden, Nancy K. "Treatment Dilemmas for Imperiled Newborns: Why Quality of Life Counts." *Southern California Law Review* 58, no. 6 (September 1985): 1283–1347.

———, and John D. Arras. "Withholding Treatment from Baby Doe: From Discrimination to Child Abuse." *Health and Society* 63, no. 1 (1985): 18–50.

Robertson, John A. *The Rights of the Critically Ill.* New York: Bantam Books, 1983. Chapters 3 and 4.

Singer, Peter, and Helga Kuhse. *Should the Baby Live? The Problem of Handicapped Infants.* New York: Oxford University Press, 1985.

Steinbock, Bonnie, ed. *Killing and Letting Die.* Englewood Cliffs: Prentice-Hall, 1980.

Trammel, Richard L. "Euthanasia and the Law." *Journal of Social Philosophy* 9 (January 1978): 14–18. (Opposes active euthanasia).

Veatch, Robert M. *Death, Dying, and the Biological Revolution.* New Haven: Yale University Press, 1976.

Walker, A. Earl. *Cerebral Death,* 3rd ed. Baltimore: Urban & Schwarzenberg, 1985.

Wanzer, Sidney H., et al. "The Physician's Responsibility Toward Hopelessly Ill Patients." *New England Journal of Medicine* 310, no. 15 (April 12, 1984): 955–59. See responses in 311, no. 5 (August 2, 1984): 334–36.

CHAPTER 8

Abortion

IS ABORTION MORALLY ACCEPTABLE? In the United States, the discussion of this issue has been especially intense since the Supreme Court legalized abortion in its 1973 *Roe v. Wade* decision. Today around 1.5 million abortions are performed annually in the United States. All too often, there is too much heat and too little light in our contemporary debates. Finally, we may have to agree to disagree about many of the conceptual, metaphysical, and ethical issues raised by the abortion dispute. Yet the brute fact of disagreement may itself have great significance for ethics and public policy. Can philosophy help? Yes, but helping does not always mean reaching definitive solutions. Philosophy can help us make better informed, more reasoned, and fair-minded judgments than we might otherwise have been able to make on such controversial matters. Toward this modest end, we will proceed.

A. STAGES OF FETAL DEVELOPMENT: MEDICAL AND LEGAL PERSPECTIVES

Despite our human predilection for simplistic, black-and-white judgments, making a baby is not an all or nothing affair. It is a developmental process that begins with simplicity itself—a single fertilized egg cell—and proceeds through many stages. Both physically and psychologically, to the extent that psychology depends on neurology, some parts of the developing fetus come into being later than others. The chronicle of this evolution is well told by Andre E. Hellegers in the following selection titled "Fetal Development," in the selections from the 1973 Supreme Court decision, and in the article by Nancy K. Rhoden, which focuses on the problem of live births from late abortions.

Two questions which must be answered in developing an adequately informed position on abortion are these: when does the developing fetus acquire moral standing, and when does it acquire legal standing? Stages of fetal development are highly relevant to each of these questions. Having moral and/or legal standing means being recognized as a proper member of the moral or legal communities, either as a moral or legal agent with duties to self or others or as a moral or legal recipient who is the proper object of such duties owed by self or others. Developing fetuses and newborn infants are obviously too immature to be agents who have duties to others or to themselves. Can they be recipients to whom duties are directly owed by others, some

of which might correlate with rights which they possess?

It is usually thought that one or more properties belonging to an entity entitle it to have moral or legal standing as something to which duties are owed directly. If it lacks the relevant attribute(s), it fails to have such standing. Most people do not recognize rocks, forests, mountain ranges, works of art, or historical sites as having direct moral or legal standing because they lack properties that warrant standing. We may have indirect duties *with respect to* or *involving* them for the sake of the animals or persons who will enjoy or own them, but not duties directly *to them* for their own sakes. Current debates ask whether animals possess properties which entitle them to moral or legal standing as proper recipients of direct duties. Similar debates over infanticide dispute whether and when newborn human infants have acquired characteristics that entitle them to moral or legal standing. Among the properties advanced either to affirm or deny standing to animals or human infants are the following:

a. being alive

b. having a capacity for pleasure or pain (sentience)

c. having desires or interests

d. having a welfare

e. having consciousness

f. having self-consciousness

g. having intelligence or rationality

h. having language capacity

i. being a moral agent

j. being a member of the human species

k. being a person

l. being valued by others

m. having an immortal soul

These same properties are contested in debates over whether fetuses are persons, whether animals and human newborns have rights, and whether we have direct duties to them.

Whether developing human fetuses have standing as proper recipients of moral or legal obligations or as holders of rights depends upon whether they possess the relevant property(s). Which, if any, of the foregoing traits are necessary and/or sufficient for moral or legal standing? Are there others? Why are the ones selected decisive? At which stage of pre- or postnatal development are they acquired?

Consider the following stages of fetal development. At which does the prenatal human fetus have a moral or legal standing which requires others to protect its life?

1. at *conception* when it acquires a complete set of human genes, making it a member of the human species;

2. at *implantation,* 6 to 7 days after conception;

3. at *individuation,* 14 days after conception. Twinning and recombination are possible up to this stage;

4. when the *heart starts beating,* 3 to 4 weeks after conception;

5. when the fetus starts *looking human* (as opposed to looking merely like a vertebrate or mammal) and *all organs* are present in a rudimentary stage, at around 6 weeks;

6. when there is a *reflex response* to pain and tickling stimuli, around 7 weeks;

7. when *brain waves,* emanating from the brain stem, are first detectable, around 8 weeks;

8. when *spontaneous movement* independent of stimulation begins, at 10 weeks;

9. when the *brain has a complete structure,* though with more growing to do, around 12 weeks;

10. at *quickening,* when the mother first feels the fetus's movement, between 12 and 16 weeks. This was the stage selected by common law and by most pre-twentieth-century Roman Catholics.

11. when there is a *10 percent probability of survival* outside of the womb, 20 weeks;

12. at *viability,* when lungs and other organs are developed sufficiently to support independent life, traditionally from 24 to 28 weeks;

13. when *conscious awareness* occurs, probably with the appearance of distinct sleep versus awake brain wave patterns, at around 28 weeks;

14. when the *eyes are reopened* at around 28 to 30 weeks, after being sealed shut since around 13 weeks;

15. at *normal birth,* around 40 weeks;

16. when *self-consciousness, language use,* and *rationality* begin, between 1 and 2 years after birth.

The 1973 Supreme Court Decision

In the United States, the question of the *legal* standing of human fetuses was resolved, at least tentatively, by the Supreme Court in its 1973 decision in the case of *Roe v. Wade.* In the excerpts from that decision which follow, the Court reviews some influential Western attitudes toward abortion and examines the legal position of abortion in common law and in American law. Many Americans will be surprised to learn that abortion was not generally illegal in early America and that restrictive abortion laws were not enacted in most states until the latter half of the nineteenth century. Even then, the purpose of such laws was not to protect what the Court calls "prenatal life." Rather, it was to protect the pregnant woman from the grave hazards of infection in an age prior to the development of antisepsis. Modern medicine has made this rationale for such legislation obsolete.

The Court rejected the contention that fetuses are persons with a right to life from the moment of conception. It refused to call fetuses "persons" at any stage of their prenatal development, indicating that "the unborn have never been recognized in the law as persons in the whole sense" and that "the word 'person,' as used in the Fourteenth Amendment, does not include the unborn." Traditionally, only "rational creatures in being," i.e., surviving independently, have been legally recognized as persons. The Court based a woman's right to an abortion on her constitutional right to privacy which it found in the Fourteenth Amendment, a right which dissenting Justice Rehnquist claimed to be "apparently completely unknown to the drafters of the Amendment."

The 1973 Supreme Court definitely considered stages of fetal development in reaching its decision on abortion, as follows: During the *first trimester,* the first thirteen weeks or so of pregnancy, the states may not regulate the abortion process. The right to have an abortion for any reason during this period is assured by a woman's right to privacy as long as she can find a physician who agrees to carry out the procedure. The same strong right to an abortion on demand for any reason continues through the *second trimester,* during which the developing fetus still has no legal entitlement to protection for its own sake. During the second trimester, the states may regulate the abortion process solely to protect the health of pregnant women. Laws may be enacted that involve fetuses, but the duties they impose are owed solely to the potential mother. The mother's strong but not absolute right to privacy continues to prevail up to the *third trimester,* but then the legal balance shifts to favor the developing fetus. The Court finds that by this time the fetus is sufficiently developed for the states to have a compelling interest in protecting its life for its own sake. Here the fetus acquires legal standing as the proper recipient of direct legal obligations. To have such standing, the Court found, the fetus did not need to be a person. If sufficiently developed, what the Court called "prenatal life," "potential human life," or "fetal life after viability" may not be destroyed on demand. Abortions may still take place during the third trimester, but only "when it is necessary to preserve the life and health of the mother."

Third-trimester fetuses do receive significant direct protection under this Court ruling. Less than one-third of 1 percent of all abortions in the United States are performed during the *third* trimester. To be sure, by this time almost everyone who wants an abortion has already obtained it; yet third-trimester abortions are very hard to get. From 90 to 92 percent of all abortions take place in the *first* trimester and between 7.7 and 9.7 percent during the *second*. As Daniel Callahan has indicated, "over 50 percent of all abortions are performed prior to 8 weeks, over 90 percent prior to 12 weeks, less than 1 percent at more than 20 weeks, and 0.3 percent after 22 weeks."[1]

The Court picked *viability,* the point at which the fetus becomes "potentially able to live outside the mother's womb, albeit with artificial aid," as the essential property which confers legal standing upon developing human fetuses. As Nancy K. Rhoden indicates in her following article, between 1964 and 1974 there was only a 40 to 50 percent chance of survival at 28 weeks. She maintains that developing medical technology, which now allows us to save a percentage of premature infants earlier and earlier, has made untenable the Court's traditional dates of viability at between 24 and 28 weeks.

Our present ability to save third-trimester fetuses—and now, increasingly, late second-trimester fetuses—raises serious conceptual questions about how "abortion" should be defined and about what the "right to an abortion" involves. Should we understand an abortion to be "a procedure which *both* kills the fetus and delivers the pregnant woman of it," or merely to be "a procedure which delivers the pregnant woman of the fetus." Correspondingly, is the moral and/or legal right to an abortion a right to both kill the fetus (what Rhoden calls a "feticide") *and* be delivered of it (what might be called a "deliverance" or in Rhoden's words a "womb-emptying")? Or is it merely the right to be delivered of the fetus in a manner that would be least damaging to it? Until recently, medical procedures employed to empty the womb have necessarily involved feticide; but as medical technology improves, it becomes more practical to separate feticide from deliverance. In the later stages of pregnancy, it is possible to deliver a viable fetus by a cesarean-like procedure called a hysterotomy. As Rhoden notes, it is also possible now to transfer embryos to different wombs; and in the future, artificial gestation at any stage of development may be possible. Rhoden asks if the *Roe v. Wade* decision might have the ironic result of becoming a "right-to-life" decision. Whether this would be undesirable depends, of course, on one's convictions. At present, hysterotomies are much more dangerous to the mother than other abortion procedures, but what if it or other womb-emptying procedures become less or no more dangerous as medicine progresses? Would the right to an abortion then be nothing more than a right to a deliverance, not a right to a feticide? In Georgia and Colorado, courts have already decided that women can be forced to undergo cesarean deliveries if their physicians determine that doing so is necessary to safeguard the lives of their unborn fetuses.[2]

Abortion techniques have changed significantly since the 1973 Supreme Court decision, and this raises new moral and legal problems. Since Rhoden did her research, a self-administered abortifacient for home use between conception and six weeks, RU 486 (antiprogesterone), has been tested and will be available in France and Sweden in the spring of 1987. In the 1970's, first-trimester abortions were performed by what Andre Hellegers called "D & C" (dilation and curettage) or what Rhoden calls "D & E" (dilation and evacuation). This latter procedure involves dilating the cervix of the womb, scraping out its contents, then suctioning out any remnants. It always causes the death of the fetus. Hellegers observed in 1970 that this procedure was too dangerous to the pregnant woman to be used after the twelfth week. Rhoden indicates that today it is being safely used up to and beyond the sixteenth week. She argues that if the

law requires both that the method safest for the mother be used and that viable fetuses be protected, it comes into inescapable conflict with itself during late second-trimester abortions when the safety of a feticidal method coincides with viability. After the sixteenth week or so, Rhoden suggests, abortions are usually performed by instilling into the uterus some abortifacient solution such as saline, prostaglandin, or even urea. These will induce premature labor and cause expulsion. These abortificient methods both are more dangerous to the mother than D & E and result in a significant percentage of live births. As many as 8 percent of the fetuses so aborted may be delivered with signs of life, though severely damaged by the procedure. Fewer live births result from saline infusion alone or from the combination of prostaglandin and saline which is designed to insure feticidal results.

Rhoden asks what we are legally and morally required to do when live births result from abortion attempts. These issues have been especially pressing for physicians since Dr. Kenneth Edelin was convicted of manslaughter in 1974 for not attempting to rescue an allegedly breathing aborted fetus. He was sentenced to one year's probation, but an appeals court later reversed the conviction. In her article Rhoden analyzes the problem of live births from abortion and makes policy recommendations. She presents a wealth of data concerning the physical handicaps, medical complications, and enormous financial costs associated with premature births under the most favorable conditions and resulting from those additional injuries inflicted by failed attempts at feticidal abortion.

Rhoden is persuaded that there is nothing fixed or sacrosanct about viability, which in her view may be pushed back to 20 weeks at the earliest. Yet she thinks that it is symbolically important as a focal point for a workable *compromise* of conflicting interests, rights, and warring factions in a highly pluralistic society. There are legitimate legal and moral interests in protecting the lives of the developed unborn. But we must also consider the rights and welfare of *all* pregnant women, not merely those who are well educated, have regular menstrual periods, are not extremely obese, and who do not have psychological problems that cause them to deny their pregnancies as long as possible. Rhoden is particularly concerned with protecting the disadvantaged, especially very young women. As she says, "Irregular periods, unfamiliarity with their bodies, ignorance about sex, and fear of adults may make even advantaged teenagers overlook or deny pregnancy or delay the decision to abort." In such situations, or where abortion for genetic or birth defects is appropriate, even a 20-week cutoff point would be much too early, she holds. She too is willing to make exceptions beyond her chosen cutoff point.

B. LIBERAL, MODERATE, CONSERVATIVE, AND ULTRACONSERVATIVE PERSPECTIVES ON ABORTION AND PERSONHOOD

The rightness or wrongness of feticidal abortion is one of the most emotional and divisive topics confronting modern civilized societies. Popular rhetoric tends to polarize disputants into extreme "for or against" factions, but rational reflection introduces many complications into the debate. Any developed position on abortion must answer the following questions:

1. At what point of fetal development, if ever, is it morally wrong to abort?

2. At what point, if any, should it be legally wrong to abort?

3. What property(s) possessed by the fetus gives it moral or legal standing, i.e., entitles it to moral or legal protection for its own sake?

4. At what point in fetal development is this property acquired?

5. Are there any legitimate exceptions that permit abortion even after the fetus has acquired
moral standing?

Those who wish to reach an informed judgment must consider the answers given to the
foregoing questions by liberals, moderates, conservatives, and ultraconservatives.

(1) *Liberals* hold that it is not morally
wrong to abort for any reason up to the moment
of natural live birth and that it should not be
illegal to do so. The liberal position denies that
unborn fetuses have any direct moral standing,
either as holders of rights or as proper recipients
of direct obligations. They have no right to life,
and they manifest no properties that would generate a duty to preserve their lives for their own
sakes at any point prior to natural birth. The
usual explanation for this is that fetuses are not
persons. Liberals oppose all legal restrictions on
abortion that are intended to protect fetuses
directly.

In the following selections, the liberal position is represented by the article "On the Moral
and Legal Status of Abortion" by Mary Anne
Warren. With other liberals, she maintains that
paradigm personhood is exemplified by competent adult human beings who are conscious, are
capable of reasoning, engage in self-motivated
activity, can communicate linguistically, and
have a concept of self. As we move further and
further away from this paradigm, the presence of
personhood becomes more and more doubtful.
According to Warren, "All we need to claim, to
demonstrate that a fetus is not a person, is that
any being which satisfies *none* of (these traits) is
not a person." Liberal and conservative notions of
the very nature of personhood are totally dispa-
rate. Conservatives regard *none* of Warren's defining traits as necessary for personhood. They
require only the presence of a complete set of
human genes, but liberals regard this as far from
sufficient. Liberals, moderates, and conservatives
cannot agree on when personhood begins be-

cause they all have radically different concepts
of what constitutes personhood.

In her accompanying "Postscript on Infanticide," Warren explains why the liberal position
on abortion does not commit her to approving
infanticide. Her position on infanticide does not
explain its wrongness in terms of duties owed
directly to newborns or rights held by them. Human newborns are not persons and have no direct moral standing in her view. Infanticide is
wrong only because other people cherish the existence of human infants. It should be prohibited
out of respect for the wishes of those other persons who wish to adopt these infants or who
strongly prefer their preservation and may even
be willing to pay money for their support. She
admits that these two considerations seem on the
surface to make abortion wrong along with infanticide. The difference is that after birth, but
not before, the woman may protect her rights to
privacy, self-determination, the pursuit of happiness, etc. by measures less drastic than the inflic-
tion of death. Warren concedes that if it were
possible to perform an abortion without killing
the fetus, a pregnant woman "would never possess the right to have the fetus destroyed for the
same reasons that she has no right to have an
infant destroyed."

Although the liberal position may be able to
evade the charge of being soft on infanticide in
the manner developed by Warren, conservative
critics reject it partly because they believe there
is something *directly* wrong with killing babies,
and partly because they think that newborn human infants are indeed *persons* as common law
and common sense have always taken them to
be. They predict that killing babies will eventually degenerate into a wholesale slaughter of un-
desirables. They also reject the relevance of a
woman's right to control what happens to her
own body on the grounds that, in the abortion
situation, there are *two* bodies involved.

(2) *Moderates* maintain that somewhere *between* conception and natural birth, fetuses ac-

quire moral standing and abortion becomes morally wrong. Beyond that point, but not before, abortions may be legally proscribed. After fetuses develop some property which warrants moral or legal standing, the duty to protect their lives is strong enough to override most competing rights of the potential mother. Moderates usually recognize some legitimate exceptions beyond their chosen cutoff point, however. Most would allow exceptions to save the life or health of the mother even after the fetus has achieved significant moral standing.

Moderates may give diverse answers to the question of what property gives moral standing. Although it may be personhood, it may be only potential personhood, conscious awareness, viability, upper or lower brain wave activity, a beating heart, etc. It is quite possible for other things besides persons to have moral or legal standing. The moderate 1973 Supreme Court decision assigned standing to fetuses, but not because they are persons. It gave significant legal protection to "fetal life after viability," while refusing to call even third-trimester fetuses "persons." It also recognized that beyond the normal third-trimester cut-off point, exceptions may be made to save the life or health of the mother. If fetuses have lower standing than persons, priority may be given to the mother when her life conflicts with that of the fetus, but this position is difficult to justify if both have *equal* moral or legal standing.

A moderate position is developed by Edward A. Langerak in his following article on "Abortion: Listening to the Middle." He thinks that the "public consensus" on abortion is moderate and that it rejects both liberal and conservative extremes. This consensus shares the two beliefs (1) that something about the fetus itself and not merely about the social effects of abortion makes abortion morally problematic and (2) that late abortions are significantly more problematic than earlier ones.

Langerak rejects the view that abortion is problematic because fetuses are persons. His lib-

eral view of personhood, akin to that of Mary Ann Warren, holds that self-consciousness, the ability to think "I," is the defining trait of personhood. His view is that *potential personhood* confers upon the fetus its claim on life. This is different from mere *possible personhood* in that the former but not the latter has at least a *50–50 chance* of developing into a person. These favorable odds begin at the end of the first trimester; and with the coincident occurrence of *quickening,* the wrongness of abortion is strengthened by the adverse social consequences of destroying a potential person whose presence has begun to manifest itself. Langerak's moderate position thus draws the line at the beginning of the second trimester. He would still permit abortion during the second trimester to preserve the physical or mental health of the mother and during the third trimester only for the physical health of the mother. It is unclear how Langerak would handle the problem of late abortions for fetal defects. He would presumably want to revise current abortion law to prohibit abortion beyond the first trimester while allowing the exceptions mentioned.

Langerak recognizes that the most serious difficulty for the moderate position is that of identifying a point of fetal development that justifiably confers moral standing. Moderates disagree with other moderates as well as with liberals and conservatives about this. We have seen that moderates such as the Supreme Court picked 24 to 28 weeks, Rhoden 20 weeks, and Langerak around 13 weeks, all for different reasons. What are the public policy implications of seemingly unresolvable disagreement? Perhaps a working compromise of competing convictions is all that the law could and should ever give us.

There is no necessary connection between what people believe to be morally wrong and what they believe should be legally prohibited. Though the belief that "We can't legislate morals" is popular, we can and often do enact our moral convictions into law quite successfully when

there is a broad moral consensus, such as on the wrongness of theft or murder. However, when there is a lack of consensus, or when the arguments are inconclusive (as with abortion), we are not being inconsistent if we hold that legal regulations should be different from our own moral convictions. Many prominent public officials often say that they believe certain forms of abortion to be wrong (morally) but that they do not think that they should impose their beliefs (legally) on others. Such persons can make legal but not personal compromises on inescapably controversial issues with perfect consistency.

(3) *Conservatives* hold that it is morally wrong to abort from the very moment of conception, with few exceptions. Some conservatives are unwilling to impose their view by law upon dissenters, but most of them strongly oppose the 1973 Supreme Court decision and actively promote the adoption of conservative abortion statutes or a constitutional amendment. Conservatives hold either that new conceptuses *are persons* in the full metaphysical and moral senses of the term, or that they *may be persons* and should be given the full benefit of the doubt for practical purposes. Since they have full and equal moral standing, they should be accorded the full legal standing of personhood. Conservatives think that abortion is morally equivalent to murder and do not comprehend how anyone who is opposed to murder could favor abortion.

Conservatives allow some legitimate exceptions to their prohibition of abortion from the moment of conception. All are willing to allow abortion to save the life of the mother in life-threatening pregnancies. Some are willing to allow abortions when rape or incest are involved, but they differ in their own ranks about these possible exceptions. Many reject abortion for rape or incest on the grounds that the sins of the parents do not justify the slaughter of their innocent offspring. While allowing abortions to save the life of the mother, conservatives reject abortions to save the mere physical or psychological health of the mother. They also reject abortions

for fetal defects, to protect the mother's career, because of economic hardship to the family, because the fetus is of the wrong sex, because the mother wants to take a trip to Europe, or for any other such reason.

Although conservatives usually insist that the *innocence* of the fetus is an insuperable obstacle to abortion, they are logically bound to reject this if they allow abortion to save the life of the mother. Here the innocence of the fetus is no objection to destroying it. When one or the other but not both may be saved, this exception cannot be justified if both mother and fetus have *equal* moral standing. In medically developed parts of the world, modern cesarean methods may have made some of these problems obsolete. In the past, physicians have often found it necessary to choose between the life of the mother and the life of the infant, as, for example, when the infant's head is too big to pass through the birth canal. Conservatives are always committed *in principle* to giving priority to the mother and allowing a feticidal craniotomy (skull crushing) to remove the fetus. How can they permit this if both mother and fetus are innocent persons with full and equal rights? Oh well, all of us are equal; but apparently some of us are more equal than others! This is the paradox of conservatism.

Many conservatives are very active in promoting the enactment of their position on abortion into law. They are not willing to take an "agree to disagree" approach to abortion. Such an approach will work only as long as the competing sides are willing to leave one another alone, but many conservatives insist upon imposing their views by law upon the rest of the population. Various conservative laws and constitutional amendments have been introduced into Congress by such conservative senators as Jesse Helms (R-North Carolina) and Orrin Hatch (R-Utah). These new laws would have the effect of defining "personhood" for legal purposes as beginning at conception and would give all new conceptuses the full rights and legal standing of personhood. They would outlaw all abortions

except those necessary to save the life of the mother. This legislation is strongly supported by President Ronald Reagan and his administration. Other conservatives would allow exceptions also for rape or incest, but Reagan does not regard these exceptions as legitimate. For a time, conservatives argued that "science proves" that personhood occurs at conception; but after consulting a number of scientists on this and getting little support, they now seldom take that approach. Their real reasons are philosophical and religious, not scientific.[3]

In the following selections, the conservative position is represented in "An Almost Absolute Value in History" by John T. Noonan, Jr. After giving his reasons for rejecting liberal and moderate alternatives, Noonan argues that a new conceptus is a person (or "human," which is his preferred word) with all the rights of humanity. He gives two reasons for thinking that fertilized ova are fully human, even though eggs and sperm before fertilization are not. First, fertilized ova have a higher probability of natural birth (even though, as he admits, at least 20 percent of them will be aborted spontaneously). Next, and most important, they have a complete human genetic code, whereas unmated reproductive cells have only half of such. According to Noonan, "A being with a human genetic code is a man." This is the conservative definition of humanity or personhood. Noonan would still allow abortion to save the life of the mother, on grounds of self-defense. Near the end of his article, he acknowledges the possibility of the ultraconservative Catholic stance on abortion, which permits mother-saving abortions only in certain narrow instances of self-defense but not in all.

(4) *Ultraconservatives* agree with conservatives on all the foregoing points except one. They deny that the mother always has a right to save her own life, holding instead that abortions in self-defense are not always justified. When their lives are in conflict, sometimes the mother and the baby both should be allowed to die, ultraconservatives hold always in principle and some-

times in practice. The official position of the Roman Catholic church is *not* the conservative one which *always* permits therapeutic abortions in self-defense to save the mother's life. Rather it is the ultraconservative one, which in principle *forces both mother and baby to die* rather than saving one innocent at the expense of the other. Ultraconservatives do avoid the paradox of conservatism which holds that both mother and baby are innocent and equal yet gives preference to the mother. Ultraconservatives give preference to *neither* and compel both to die unless the principle of double effect sometimes allows the mother to be saved. Conveniently, this principle does permit saving the mother under some conditions, i.e., where the life-threatening fetus may be aborted without *directly intending* its death and without *directly inflicting* death upon it. As ultraconservatives apply it to abortion, the principle of double effect says, roughly, that it is wrong to intentionally perform a bad act (e.g., directly killing a baby) so that good consequences (e.g., saving a mother) may follow; but it is permissible to perform a good or morally neutral act (e.g., removing a fallopian tube or cancerous uterus) knowing that unintended bad consequences (e.g., the death of a fetus) may follow.

As Susan T. Nicholson explains in the following selection on "The Roman Catholic Doctrine of Therapeutic Abortion," the official position of the Catholic church allows abortions to save the mother when she has cancer of the cervix or when the fetus has implanted itself in a fallopian tube (ectopic pregnancy) on the grounds that in such cases the death of the fetus is not directly intended or inflicted. It is merely the foreseen but unintended result of removing the diseased organs. However, where a pregnant woman has hypertensive heart disease associated with severe renal insufficiency or where the head of the fetus is too large to permit birth, feticidal abortion is prohibited because the death of the fetus is directly intended or inflicted. Too bad for the mother, but in such cases she is not entitled

God knows us as *persons* from the very outset. Unfortunately, this is not what is asserted. Even if the Scriptures are divinely inspired, it is still necessary to distinguish between what they actually say and what we inject into them through our very human interpretations. These Scriptures are perfectly compatible with *either* of the following interpretations: (a) God knows us before birth or from conception as fully ensouled human persons, or (b) God knows us (and those to be aborted spontaneously or otherwise) from conception as possible or potential persons who will be ensouled at some point of later development. Without some such interpretation, this Scripture sheds no light whatsoever on the abortion issue. Yet both interpretations are very human additions to what is actually there in the text. Religious conservatives may prefer (a), but religious moderates and liberals are perfectly entitled to prefer (b). Both sides can agree that God knows everything according to its appropriate mode of being—actualities as actualities and potentialities as potentialities.

The Beginning and the End of Human Life

The preceding chapter, "Death and Dying," suggested that there might be some important correlations between the issues of when life begins and when it ends. When does a developing fetus become a living person? Different concepts of death select the irreversible cessation of various bodily functions (together perhaps with the irreversible cessation of embodied consciousness) as marking the end of human life. The beginning of human life might also be dated from the initial appearance of the same functions, especially if the emphasis is on properties actually possessed rather than on potentialities. If so, the following correlations would result.

(1) Conservative and ultraconservative views that a fetus becomes a living person at conception correlate with the view that life ends only with the irreversible cessation of the func-

tioning of all bodily cells, tissues, or organs. Cells are highly relevant here since the new conceptuses that conservatives designate as persons consist initially of only one living cell. Any human cell (except reproductive) contains a complete set of human genes, and with cloning any cell could in principle be grown into a mature human being. Are we willing to say (a) that every cell in the human body is a person or (b) that no person is dead as long as a single cell lives? If not, we should reject the view that a person exists when there is merely a single fertilized ovum. Moderates and liberals think that conservatives confuse full personhood with what is only a genetic blueprint for the making of a person. They suggest that we would not pay the same thing for the blueprint of a house that we would pay for an actual house. Potential persons no more have the full standing of personhood than potential presidents or husbands have of actual ones. Actual and potential persons are not equals.

Another difficulty with the conservative claim that an entity is a person if it has a complete set of human genes is that even *dead* persons, even dead cells, have complete sets of human genes. Yet they obviously do not have the moral or legal standing of living persons. Surely something more, such as a beating heart, a functioning brain, or consciousness, is required for an entity actually to be a *living* person with the moral and legal standing of personhood. If we are convinced that a genetic human with no beating heart or brain activity is not a living person, why should we believe that a new conceptus with no beating heart or brain activity is a living person?

Significantly, the Roman Catholic church does not claim to know when human life ends, only when it begins. In his 1957 address "The Prolongation of Life," Pope Pius XII asserted that physicians can determine death but that it is not "within the competence of the Church" to do so. Remember that, until the end of the nineteenth century, this church also did not regard as within its competence the ability to determine when hu-

man life begins, and it referred its members to secular authorities like Aristotle or common law for solutions. What is required is a good argument, not the dogmatic assertion of religious faith or authority.

(2) The view that life ends with the irreversible cessation of the flow of all bodily "fluids" such as air and blood is difficult to correlate with a view of when life begins because circulation and breathing first occur at widely separated points. The fetus develops a capacity for circulation at around 3 weeks after conception, but the capacity for breathing begins only around 20 weeks or thereafter. The actuality of breathing begins only with birth, whether premature or normal. The Jewish and American Indian groups that hold this view have usually emphasized the "breath of life," and they presumably think that life begins with the first actual breath and ends with the last. On this view, living personhood arrives fairly late in the development of the fetus, normally only at the time of natural birth. We might wonder, however, if living personhood does not have more to do with what is going on in the human brain than with what is transpiring in the lungs or blood vessels. Those who think so will prefer to adopt one of the next two or three options.

(3) Traditional chest death involves the cessation of both heart and lung function. In the developing fetus, these are widely separated in time. Spontaneous heart function begins at between 3 and 4 weeks, lung capacity at around 20 weeks at the earliest. Nevertheless, those who are attracted to the chest death option might want to give the fetus the benefit of the doubt when the heart begins beating just three weeks or so after conception. In discussing death we recognized that the heart may continue to beat for a time even after all brain stem activity has ceased. Similarly, at the beginning of life, at three weeks the heart is beating independently of all brain control and stimulation. This is precisely why those who are attracted to brain death will want to reject the beginning of heartbeat as the switch-on

point for living personhood. If people can be dead with spontaneously beating hearts, then having one three weeks after conception cannot be sufficient for being a living person.

(4) Whole-brain concepts of death find a counterpoint for the beginning of life at the eighth week of fetal development, when detectable brain wave activity begins in the brain stem though not yet in the upper brain. Some of the reflex responsiveness to stimuli, including pain stimuli, that is controlled by the brain stem also begins around 7 or 8 weeks after conception. Since these reflex responses may also be elicited from comatose adults, there is no convincing reason to believe that consciousness is in any way associated with this stage of brain stem development. At 8 weeks the fetus is consciously aware of nothing, for the upper brain is not sufficiently developed to generate any brain wave activity. For precisely this reason, those who prefer a neocortical or neocortically oriented concept of death will reject any total brain or brain stem concept of the beginning of life.

(5) Neocortical and neocortically oriented concepts of the end of human life correlate with similar counterpoints for the beginning of human life. For these options, a fetus is not a living person merely because it has a set of human genes or has a beating heart or has a functioning brain stem. Life ends and begins with the failure of or initial working of the neocortical brain. But what level of functioning is sufficient? By 12 weeks, neocortical activity is present. It is doubtful that the capacity for conscious awareness is then present, however. Just when it arrives may be uncertain, but very likely it is not present before the appearance of brain wave patterns demarking sleep and wakefulness, at around 28 weeks. To be conscious, one must be awake.[5] If an embodied capacity for conscious experience is necessary for personhood, then the twenty-eighth week of development seems to mark its beginning. Observations of premature infants suggest that they are not capable of wakeful alertness before 30 weeks at the earliest.[6] Liberals

nervous system development, and by chances of survival, they can be summarized as in the accompanying Table.

Throughout the analysis of the beginning of life it is important to bear several factors in mind. First, the understanding of the processes described is the understanding of today. The eliciting of fetal responses depends on the methods available today. Second, it is not a function of science to prove, or disprove, where in this process *human* life begins, in the sense that those discussing the abortion issue so frequently use the word "life," i.e., human dignity, human personhood, or human inviolability. Such entities do not pertain to the science or art of medicine, but are rather a societal judgment. Science cannot prove them; it can only describe the biological development and predict what will occur to it with an accuracy that depends on the stage of development of the particular science. In the ultimate analysis the question is not just to forecast when life begins, but rather: How should one behave when one does not know whether dignity is or is not present in the fetus?

Majority Opinion in Roe v. Wade

Justice Harry Blackmun

The majority opinion in the 1975 Roe v. Wade *case was written by Justice Harry Blackmun, who was appointed to the United States Supreme Court in 1970. Seven of the justices concurred in this decision.*

In this selection from the decision which "legalized abortion" in 1973, the Supreme Court briefly reviews the history of western philosophical and legal stances on abortion. It decided that laws prohibiting abortion violate women's rights to privacy. It concluded (1) that during the first trimester, the state may not regulate abortion, (2) that during the second trimester, abortion may be regulated but not prohibited to protect the health of the mother, and (3) that with the arrival of "viability" at the beginning of the third trimester, abortions may be prohibited except where necessary to preserve the life or health of the mother. It refused to recognize prenatal humans as "persons," preferring "fetal life after viability" for third-trimester fetuses.

I

The Texas statutes that concern us here are Arts. 1191–1194 and 1196 of the State's Penal Code. These make it a crime to "procure an abortion," as therein defined, or to attempt one, except with respect to "an abortion procured or attempted by medical advice for the purpose of saving the life of the mother." Similar statutes are in existence in a majority of the States.

Texas first enacted a criminal abortion statute in 1854. . . .

410 U.S. 116 (1973).

II

Jane Roe, a single woman who was residing in Dallas County, Texas, instituted this federal action in March 1970 against the District Attorney of the county. She sought a declaratory judgment that the Texas criminal abortion statutes were unconstitutional on their face, and an injunction restraining the defendant from enforcing the statutes.

Roe alleged that she was unmarried and pregnant; that she wished to terminate her pregnancy by an abortion "performed by a competent,

licensed physician, under safe, clinical conditions"; that she was unable to get a "legal" abortion in Texas because her life did not appear to be threatened by the continuation of her pregnancy; and that she could not afford to travel to another jurisdiction in order to secure a legal abortion under safe conditions. She claimed that the Texas statutes were unconstitutionally vague and that they abridged her right of personal privacy, protected by the First, Fourth, Fifth, Ninth, and Fourteenth Amendments. By an amendment to her complaint Roe purported to sue "on behalf of herself and all other women" similarly situated. . . .

VI

It perhaps is not generally appreciated that the restrictive criminal abortion laws in effect in a majority of States today are of relatively recent vintage. Those laws, generally proscribing abortion or its attempt at any time during pregnancy except when necessary to preserve the pregnant woman's life, are not of ancient or even of common-law origin. Instead, they derive from statutory changes effected, for the most part, in the latter half of the 19th century.

1. *Ancient attitudes.* These are not capable of precise determination. We are told that at the time of the Persian Empire abortifacients were known and that criminal abortions were severely punished. We are also told, however, that abortion was practiced in Greek times as well as in the Roman Era, and that "it was resorted to without scruple." The Ephesian, Soranos, often described as the greatest of the ancient gynecologists, appears to have been generally opposed to Rome's prevailing free-abortion practices. He found it necessary to think first of the life of the mother, and he resorted to abortion when, upon this standard, he felt the procedure advisable. Greek and Roman law afforded little protection to the unborn. If abortion was prosecuted in some places, it seems to have been based on a concept

of a violation of the father's right to his offspring. Ancient religion did not bar abortion.

2. *The Hippocratic Oath.* What then of the famous Oath that has stood so long as the ethical guide of the medical profession and that bears the name of the great Greek (460(?)–377(?) B.C.), who has been described as the Father of Medicine, the "wisest and the greatest practitioner of his art," and the "most important and most complete medical personality of antiquity," who dominated the medical schools of his time, and who typified the sum of the medical knowledge of the past? The Oath varies somewhat according to the particular translation, but in any translation the content is clear: "I will give no deadly medicine to anyone if asked, nor suggest any such counsel; and in like manner I will not give to a woman a pessary to produce abortion," or "I will neither give a deadly drug to anybody if asked for it, nor will I make a suggestion to this effect. Similarly, I will not give to a woman an abortive remedy."

Although the Oath is not mentioned in any of the principal briefs in this case or in *Doe v. Bolton, post,* p. 179, it represents the apex of the development of strict ethical concepts in medicine, and its influence endures to this day. Why did not the authority of Hippocrates dissuade abortion practice in his time and that of Rome? The late Dr. Edelstein provides us with a theory: The Oath was not uncontested even in Hippocrates' day; only the Pythagorean school of philosophers frowned upon the related act of suicide. Most Greek thinkers, on the other hand, commended abortion, at least prior to viability. See Plato, *Republic,* V, 461; Aristotle, *Politics,* VII, 1335b 25. For the Pythagoreans, however, it was a matter of dogma. For them the embryo was animate from the moment of conception, and abortion meant destruction of a living being. The abortion clause of the Oath, therefore, "echoes Pythagorean doctrines," and "[i]n no other stratum of Greek opinion were such views held or proposed in the same spirit of uncompromising austerity."

Dr. Edelstein then concludes that the Oath originated in a group representing only a small segment of Greek opinion and that it certainly was not accepted by all ancient physicians. He points out that medical writings down to Galen (A.D. 130–200) "give evidence of the violation of almost every one of its injunctions." But with the end of antiquity a decided change took place. Resistance against suicide and against abortion became common. The Oath came to be popular. The emerging teachings of Christianity were in agreement with the Pythagorean ethic. The Oath "became the nucleus of all medical ethics" and "was applauded as the embodiment of truth." Thus, suggests Dr. Edelstein, it is "a Pythagorean manifesto and not the expression of an absolute standard of medical conduct."

This, it seems to us, is a satisfactory and acceptable explanation of the Hippocratic Oath's apparent rigidity. It enables us to understand, in historical context, a long-accepted and revered statement of medical ethics.

3. *The common law.* It is undisputed that at common law, abortion performed *before* "quickening"—the first recognizable movement of the fetus *in utero,* appearing usually from the 16th to the 18th week of pregnancy—was not an indictable offense. The absence of a common-law crime for pre-quickening abortion appears to have developed from a confluence of earlier philosophical, theological, and civil and canon law concepts of when life begins. These disciplines variously approached the question in terms of the point at which the embryo or fetus became "formed" or recognizably human, or in terms of when a "person" came into being, that is, infused with a "soul" or "animated." A loose consensus evolved in early English law that these events occurred at some point between conception and live birth. This was "mediate animation." Although Christian theology and the canon law came to fix the point of animation at 40 days for a male and 80 days for a female, a view that persisted until the 19th century, there was otherwise little agreement about the precise time of formation or animation. There was agreement, however, that prior to this point the fetus was to be regarded as part of the mother, and its destruction, therefore, was not homicide. Due to continued uncertainty about the precise time when animation occurred, to the lack of any empirical basis for the 40–80-day view, and perhaps to Aquinas' definition of movement as one of the two first principles of life, Bracton focused upon quickening as the critical point. The significance of quickening was echoed by later common-law scholars and found its way into the received common law in this country. . . .

5. *The American law.* In this country, the law in effect in all but a few States until mid-19th century was the preexisting English common law. Connecticut, the first State to enact abortion legislation, adopted in 1821 that part of Lord Ellenborough's Act that related to a woman "quick with child." The death penalty was not imposed. Abortion before quickening was made a crime in that State only in 1860. In 1828, New York enacted legislation that, in two respects, was to serve as a model for early anti-abortion statutes. First, while barring destruction of an unquickened fetus as well as a quick fetus, it made the former only a misdemeanor, but the latter second-degree manslaughter. Second, it incorporated a concept of therapeutic abortion by providing that an abortion was excused if it "shall have been necessary to preserve the life of such mother, or shall have been advised by two physicians to be necessary for such purpose." By 1840, when Texas had received the common law, only eight American States had statutes dealing with abortion. It was not until after the War Between the States that legislation began generally to replace the common law. Most of these initial statutes dealt severely with abortion after quickening but were lenient with it before quickening. Most punished attempts equally with completed abortions. While many statutes included the exception for an abortion thought by one or more physicians to be necessary to save the mother's life, that provision

soon disappeared and the typical law required that the procedure actually be necessary for that purpose.

Gradually, in the middle and late 19th century the quickening distinction disappeared from the statutory law of most States and the degree of the offense and the penalties were increased. By the end of the 1950s, a large majority of the jurisdictions banned abortion, however and whenever performed, unless done to save or preserve the life of the mother. The exceptions, Alabama and the District of Columbia, permitted abortion to preserve the mother's health. Three States permitted abortions that were not "unlawfully" performed or that were not "without lawful justification," leaving interpretation of those standards to the courts. In the past several years, however, a trend toward liberalization of abortion statutes has resulted in adoption, by about one-third of the States, of less stringent laws. . . .

It is thus apparent that at common law, at the time of the adoption of our Constitution, and throughout the major portion of the 19th century, abortion was viewed with less disfavor than under most American statutes currently in effect. Phrasing it another way, a woman enjoyed a substantially broader right to terminate a pregnancy than she does in most States today. At least with respect to the early stage of pregnancy, and very possibly without such a limitation, the opportunity to make this choice was present in this country well into the 19th century. Even later, the law continued for some time to treat less punitively an abortion procured in early pregnancy. . . .

VII

Three reasons have been advanced to explain historically the enactment of criminal abortion laws in the 19th century and to justify their continued existence.

It has been argued occasionally that these laws were the product of a Victorian social concern to discourage illicit sexual conduct. Texas, however, does not advance this justification in the present case, and it appears that no court or commentator has taken the argument seriously. . . .

A second reason is concerned with abortion as a medical procedure. When most criminal abortion laws were first enacted, the procedure was a hazardous one for the woman. This was particularly true prior to the development of antisepsis. Antiseptic techniques, of course, were based on discoveries by Lister, Pasteur, and others first announced in 1867, but were not generally accepted and employed until about the turn of the century. Abortion mortality was high. Even after 1900, and perhaps until as late as the development of antibiotics in the 1940's, standard modern techniques such as dilation and curettage were not nearly so safe as they are today. Thus, it has been argued that a State's real concern in enacting a criminal abortion law was to protect the pregnant woman, that is, to restrain her from submitting to a procedure that placed her life in serious jeopardy.

Modern medical techniques have altered this situation. Appellants and various *amici* refer to medical data indicating that abortion in early pregnancy, that is, prior to the end of the first trimester, although not without its risk, is now relatively safe. Mortality rates for women undergoing early abortions, where the procedure is legal, appear to be as low as or lower than the rates for normal childbirth. Consequently, any interest of the State in protecting the woman from an inherently hazardous procedure, except when it would be equally dangerous for her to forgo it, has largely disappeared. Of course, important state interests in the areas of health and medical standards do remain. The State has a legitimate interest in seeing to it that abortion, like any other medical procedure, is performed under circumstances that insure maximum safety for the patient. This interest obviously extends at least to the performing physician and his staff, to the facilities involved, to the availability of after-care,

and to adequate provision for any complication or emergency that might arise. The prevalence of high mortality rates at illegal "abortion mills" strengthens, rather than weakens, the State's interest in regulating the conditions under which abortions are performed. Moreover, the risk to the woman increases as her pregnancy continues. Thus, the State retains a definite interest in protecting the woman's own health and safety when an abortion is proposed at a late stage of pregnancy.

The third reason is the State's interest—some phrase it in terms of duty—in protecting prenatal life. Some of the argument for this justification rests on the theory that a new human life is present from the moment of conception. The State's interest and general obligation to protect life then extends, it is argued, to prenatal life. Only when the life of the pregnant mother herself is at stake, balanced against the life she carries within her, should the interest of the embryo or fetus not prevail. Logically, of course, a legitimate state interest in this area need not stand or fall on acceptance of the belief that life begins at conception or at some other point prior to live birth. In assessing the State's interest, recognition may be given to the less rigid claim that as long as at least *potential* life is involved, the State may assert interests beyond the protection of the pregnant woman alone.

Parties challenging state abortion laws have sharply disputed in some courts the contention that a purpose of these laws, when enacted, was to protect prenatal life. Pointing to the absence of legislative history to support the contention, they claim that most state laws were designed solely to protect the woman. Because medical advances have lessened this concern, at least with respect to abortion in early pregnancy, they argue that with respect to such abortions the laws can no longer be justified by any state interest. There is some scholarly support for this view of original purpose. The few state courts called upon to interpret their laws in the late 19th and early 20th centuries did focus on the State's interest in pro-

tecting the woman's health rather than in preserving the embryo and fetus. Proponents of this view point out that in many States, including Texas, by statute or judicial interpretation, the pregnant woman herself could not be prosecuted for self-abortion or for cooperating in an abortion performed upon her by another. They claim that adoption of the "quickening" distinction through received common law and state statutes tacitly recognizes the greater health hazards inherent in late abortion and impliedly repudiates the theory that life begins at conception.

It is with these interests, and the weight to be attached to them, that this case is concerned.

VIII

The Constitution does not explicitly mention any right of privacy. In a line of decisions, however, . . . the Court has recognized that a right of personal privacy, or a guarantee of certain areas or zones of privacy, does exist under the Constitution. . . .

This right of privacy, whether it be founded in the Fourteenth Amendment's concept of personal liberty and restrictions upon state action, as we feel it is, or, as the District Court determined, in the Ninth Amendment's reservation of rights to the people, is broad enough to encompass a woman's decision whether or not to terminate her pregnancy. The detriment that the State would impose upon the pregnant woman by denying this choice altogether is apparent. Specific and direct harm medically diagnosable even in early pregnancy may be involved. Maternity, or additional offspring, may force upon the woman a distressful life and future. Psychological harm may be imminent. Mental and physical health may be taxed by child care. There is also the distress, for all concerned, associated with the unwanted child, and there is the problem of bringing a child into a family already unable, psychologically and otherwise, to care for it. In other cases, as in this one,

the additional difficulties and continuing stigma of unwed motherhood may be involved. All these are factors the woman and her responsible physician necessarily will consider in consultation.

On the basis of elements such as these, appellant and some *amici* argue that the woman's right is absolute and that she is entitled to terminate her pregnancy at whatever time, in whatever way, and for whtever reason she alone chooses. With this we do not agree. Appellant's arguments that Texas either has no valid interest at all in regulating the abortion decision, or no interest strong enough to support any limitation upon the woman's sole determination, are unpersuasive. The Court's decisions recognizing a right of privacy also acknowledge that some state regulation in areas protected by that right is appropriate. As noted above, a State may properly assert important interests in safeguarding health, in maintaining medical standards, and in protecting potential life. At some point in pregnancy, these respective interests become sufficiently compelling to sustain regulation of the factors that govern the abortion decision. The privacy right involved, therefore, cannot be said to be absolute. . . .

We, therefore, conclude that the right of personal privacy includes the abortion decision, but that this right is not unqualified and must be considered against important state interests in regulation. . . .

Although the results are divided, most of these courts have agreed that the right of privacy, however based, is broad enough to cover the abortion decision; that the right, nonetheless, is not absolute and is subject to some limitations; and that at some point the state interests as to protection of health, medical standards, and prenatal life, become dominant. We agree with this approach. . . .

A. The appellee and certain *amici* argue that the fetus is a "person" within the language and meaning of the Fourteenth Amendment. In support of this, they outline at length and in detail the well-known facts of fetal development. If this suggestion of personhood is established, the ap-

pellant's case, of course, collapses, for the fetus' right to life would then be guaranteed specifically by the Amendment. The appellant conceded as much on reargument. On the other hand, the appellee conceded on reargument that no case could be cited that holds that a fetus is a person within the meaning of the Fourteenth Amendment.

The Constitution does not define "person" in so many words. Section 1 of the Fourteenth Amendment contains three references to "person." The first, in defining "citizens," speaks of "persons born or naturalized in the United States." The word also appears both in the Due Process Clause and in the Equal Protection Clause. "Person" is used in other places in the Constitution: in the listing of qualifications for Representatives and Senators, Art. I, § 2, cl. 2, and § 3, cl. 3; in the Apportionment Clause, Art. 1, § 2, cl. 3; in the Migration and Importation provision, Art. I, § 9, cl. 1; in the Emolument Clause, Art. I, § 9, cl. 8; in the Electors provisions, Art. II, § 1, cl. 2, and the superseded cl. 3; in the provision outlining qualifications for the office of President, Art. II, § 1, cl. 5; in the Extradition provisions, Art. IV, § 2, cl. 2, and the superseded Fugitive Slave Clause 3; and in the Fifth, Twelfth, and Twenty-second Amendments, as well as in §§ 2 and 3 of the Fourteenth Amendment. But in nearly all these instances, the use of the word is such that it has application only postnatally. None indicates, with any assurance, that it has any possible prenatal application.

All this, together with our observation, *supra,* that throughout the major portion of the 19th century prevailing legal abortion practices were far freer than they are today, persuades us that the word "person," as used in the Fourteenth Amendment, does not include the unborn. . . . As we have intimated above, it is reasonable and appropriate for a State to decide that at some point in time another interest, that of health of the mother or that of potential human life, becomes significantly involved. The woman's privacy is no longer sole and any right of privacy she possesses must be measured accordingly.

Texas urges that, apart from the Fourteenth Amendment, life begins at conception and is present throughout pregnancy, and that, therefore, the State has a compelling interest in protecting that life from and after conception. We need not resolve the difficult question of when life begins. When those trained in the respective disciplines of medicine, philosophy, and theology are unable to arrive at any consensus, the judiciary, at this point in the development of man's knowledge, is not in a position to speculate as to the answer.

It should be sufficient to note briefly the wide divergence of thinking on this most sensitive and difficult question. There has always been strong support for the view that life does not begin until live birth. This was the belief of the Stoics. It appears to be the predominant, though not the unanimous, attitude of the Jewish faith. It may be taken to represent also the position of a large segment of the Protestant community, insofar as that can be ascertained; organized groups that have taken a formal position on the abortion issue have generally regarded abortion as a matter for the conscience of the individual and her family. As we have noted, the common law found greater significance in quickening. Physicians and their scientific colleagues have regarded that event with less interest and have tended to focus either upon conception, upon live birth, or upon the interim point at which the fetus becomes "viable," that is, potentially able to live outside the mother's womb, albeit with artificial aid. Viability is usually placed at about seven months (28 weeks) but may occur earlier, even at 24 weeks. The Aristotelian theory of "mediate animation," that held sway throughout the Middle Ages and the Renaissance in Europe, continued to be official Roman Catholic dogma until the 19th century, despite opposition to this "ensoulment" theory from those in the Church who would recognize the existence of life from the moment of conception. The latter is now, of course, the official belief of the Catholic Church. As one brief *amicus* discloses, this is a view strongly held by many non-Catholics as well, and by many physicians. Substantial prob-

lems for precise definition of this view are posed, however, by new embryological data that purport to indicate that conception is a "process" over time, rather than an event, and by new medical techniques such as menstrual extraction, the "morning-after" pill, implantation of embryos, artificial insemination, and even artificial wombs.

In areas other than criminal abortion, the law has been reluctant to endorse any theory that life, as we recognize it, begins before live birth or to accord legal rights to the unborn except in narrowly defined situations and except when the rights are contingent upon live birth. For example, the traditional rule of tort law denied recovery for prenatal injuries even though the child was born alive. That rule has been changed in almost every jurisdiction. In most States, recovery is said to be permitted only if the fetus was viable, or at least quick, when the injuries were sustained, though few courts have squarely so held. In a recent development, generally opposed by the commentators, some States permit the parents of a stillborn child to maintain an action for wrongful death because of prenatal injuries. Such an action, however, would appear to be one to vindicate the parents' interest and is thus consistent with the view that the fetus, at most, represents only the potentiality of life. Similarly, unborn children have been recognized as acquiring rights or interests by way of inheritance or other devolution of property, and have been represented by guardians *ad litem*. Perfection of the interests involved, again, has generally been contingent upon live birth. In short, the unborn have never been recognized in the law as persons in the whole sense.

X

In view of all this, we do not agree that, by adopting one theory of life, Texas may override the rights of the pregnant woman that are at stake. We repeat, however, that the State does have an important and legitimate interest in preserving

and protecting the health of the pregnant woman, whether she be a resident of the State or a nonresident who seeks medical consultation and treatment there, and that it has still *another* important and legitimate interest in protecting the potentiality of human life. These interests are separate and distinct. Each grows in substantiality as the woman approaches term and, at a point during pregnancy, each becomes "compelling."

With respect to the State's important and legitimate interest in the health of the mother, the "compelling" point, in the light of present medical knowledge, is at approximately the end of the first trimester. This is so because of the now-established medical fact, referred to above [p. 551], that until the end of the first trimester mortality in abortion may be less than mortality in normal childbirth. It follows that, from and after this point, a State may regulate the abortion procedure to the extent that the regulation reasonably relates to the preservation and protection of maternal health. Examples of permissible state regulation in this area are requirements as to the qualifications of the person who is to perform the abortion; as to the licensure of that person; as to the facility in which the procedure is to be performed, that is, whether it must be a hospital or may be a clinic or some other place of less-than-hospital status; as to the licensing of the facility; and the like.

This means, on the other hand, that, for the period of pregnancy prior to this "compelling" point, the attending physician, in consultation with his patient, is free to determine, without regulation by the State, that, in his medical judgment, the patient's pregnancy should be terminated. If that decision is reached, the judgment may be effectuated by an abortion free of interference by the State.

With respect to the State's important and legitimate interest in potential life, the "compelling" point is at viability. This is so because the fetus then presumably has the capability of meaningful life outside the mother's womb. State regulation protective of fetal life after viability thus has both logical and biological justifications. If the State is interested in protecting fetal life after viability, it may go so far as to proscribe abortion during that period, except when it is necessary to preserve the life or health of the mother. . . .

XI

To summarize and to repeat:

1. A state criminal abortion statute of the current Texas type, that excepts from criminality only a *lifesaving* procedure on behalf of the mother, without regard to pregnancy stage and without recognition of the other interests involved, is violative of the Due Process Clause of the Fourteenth Amendment.

a. For the stage prior to approximately the end of the first trimester, the abortion decision and its effectuation must be left to the medical judgment of the pregnant woman's attending physician.

b. For the stage subsequent to approximately the end of the first trimester, the State, in promoting its interest in the health of the mother, may, if it chooses, regulate the abortion procedure in ways that are reasonably related to maternal health.

c. For the stage subsequent to viability, the State in promoting its interest in the potentiality of human life may, if it chooses, regulate, and even proscribe, abortion except where it is necessary, in appropriate medical judgment, for the preservation of the life or health of the mother. . . .

This holding, we feel, is consistent with the relative weights of the respective interests involved, with the lessons and examples of medical and legal history, with the lenity of the common law, and with the demands of the profound problems of the present day. The decision leaves the State free to place increasing restrictions on abortion as the period of pregnancy lengthens, so long as those restrictions are tailored to the recognized state interests. The decision vindicates the right of the physician to administer medical treatment

according to his professional judgment up to the points where important state interests provide compelling justifications for intervention. Up to those points, the abortion decision in all its aspects is inherently, and primarily, a medical decision, and basic responsibility for it must rest with the physician. If an individual practitioner abuses the privilege of exercising proper medical judgment, the usual remedies, judicial and intraprofessional, are available. . . .

The New Neonatal Dilemma: Live Births from Late Abortions

Nancy K. Rhoden

Nancy Rhoden is an associate professor of law at Ohio State University, where she specializes in issues in bioethics. She has written extensively about ethical issues in pregnancy and childbirth, and in 1985–86 was a visiting assistant professor of pediatrics at Albert Einstein College of Medicine.

Rhoden explains what is involved in various abortion techniques and in the treatment of premature newborns. She addresses ethically and legally the problem of whether infants born alive from abortion attempts should be saved. She analyzes the meaning and significance of viability and suggests that workable abortion policy will have to reflect a compromise of conflicting interests between "pro-life" and "pro-choice" perspectives.

INTRODUCTION

Suppose a fifteen-year-old girl is pregnant, but due to ignorance, denial, or fear, she does not realize or admit it until after quickening,[1] when she feels her baby kick.[2] She consults a physician, who estimates that she is twenty or twenty-one weeks pregnant,[3] and schedules an abortion. The abortion is performed at what the physician believes to be the twenty-second week of pregnancy, but, as is not uncommon, the estimate is inaccurate by a week or ten days.[4] To the parties' shock

---

*I wish to thank the following for their comments on earlier drafts of this article: John Arras, Nancy Erickson, Ruth Macklin, John Robertson, and Alan Weisbard. I also am grateful to the physicians who took the time to speak with me about these issues.

[1] Quickening usually occurs between 17 and 20 weeks. Reynolds, *Fetal Physiology,* in OBSTETRICAL PRACTICE 78, 95 (S. Aladjem ed. 1980).

[2] This situation is not particularly unusual, especially among teenagers. Interview with Dr. Thomas Kerenyi, Clinical Professor of Obstetrics and Gynecology, Mt. Sinai Medical Center, in New York City (Apr. 8, 1983) [hereinafter cited as Kerenyi interview]. Women who seek late abortions typically are poor, young, and poorly educated. *See infra* note 31 and accompanying text (discussing characteristics of women who seek late abortions).

From *Georgetown Law Journal,* vol. 72, no. 5 (June 1984). Reprinted with permission of the author and the publisher, © 1984 The Georgetown Law Journal Association.

[3] The duration of a pregnancy (or age of the fetus) can be measured either from the first day of the woman's last menstrual period (gestational age) or from the date of conception (conceptional age). *See* Note, Roe v. Wade *and the Traditional Legal Standards Concerning Pregnancy,* 47 TEMP. L.Q. 715, 735-36 (1974). The former, the more commonly used standard of gestational age, will be used here. *See* WILLIAMS OBSTETRICS 923 (16th ed. 1980) (defining full-term pregnancy from date of onset of last menstrual period). By this standard, the average duration of pregnancy is 40 weeks (two weeks longer than duration figured from conception). 47 TEMP. L.Q. at 736 n.148.

[4] *See* Stubblefield, *Abortion vs. Manslaughter,* 110 ARCHIVES OF SURGERY 790, 791 (1975) (discussing medical and legal problems posed by physicians' inability to predict viability with complete accuracy). To estimate gestational age *in utero,* physicians use ultrasonic scanning to measure the biparietal diameter of the fetus' head and then rely on charts which correlate diameter with gestational age. While this is the most accurate method of measurement, it can be inaccurate by a

and dismay, a baby boy emerges showing signs of life. After some agonizing, the doctors rush the infant to the neonatal intensive care unit (N.I.C.U.), where he is resuscitated, intubated, suctioned, placed on a respirator, and treated as aggressively as possible.[5] His extreme prematurity, coupled with damage that the abortion procedure caused, results in various medical problems— respiratory distress syndrome, bone fractures, intraventricular brain hemorrhages, multiple infections, and so on.[6] Despite these problems, the baby lives and after four months in the N.I.C.U. is ready either to go home with the mother, if she chooses to keep him, or to be put up for adoption. Unfortunately, the brain hemorrhages have left him with what will probably be severe to profound retardation, as well as other neurological defects.[7]

This scenario, with its various alternatives of nontreatment of the liveborn infant, death of the infant despite treatment, or a somewhat more favorable prognosis for the infant, has in the past

occurred quite rarely.[8] Even as an infrequent event it raises innumerable moral and legal dilemmas. But recent technological advances in medicine may be increasing the frequency of its occurrence.[9] One technological change concerns abortion procedures. An induced abortion is ordinarily considered a medical procedure with dual functions: removal of the fetus[10] from the woman's body and termination of the fetus' life.[11] Fetal death traditionally has been a necessary and unavoidable consequence of removing the fetus from the womb before it is viable, i.e., capable of surviving outside the womb, albeit with artificial aid,[12] and of tissue destruction that the abortion procedure itself has caused. The feticidal technique of saline amnioinfusion, however, which until recently was the only method of late

---

factor of one to two weeks on either side of the predicted age. *Id. See* Behrman & Rosen, *Report on the Viability and Nonviability of the Fetus,* in RESEARCH ON THE FETUS 12-1, 12-8 app. (National Comm'n for the Protection of Human Subjects of Biomedical and Behavioral Research 1975).

[5] Initial resuscitation may require artificial ventilation with a mask, use of an endotracheal or nasotracheal tube, and external cardiac massage. If the infant has aspirated fluid, it will also have to be intubated and suctioned by mouth-to-tube suction until watery mucus is obtained. *See* Behrman & Rosen, *supra* note 4, at 12-16 (evaluating changes in neonatal survival rates and medical technology from 1965 to 1975).

[6] *See infra* text section III (discussing problems faced by extremely premature infants and techniques doctors use to treat them).

[7] For a description of actual cases of live births, see Kleiman, *When Abortion Becomes Birth: A Dilemma of Medical Ethics Shaken by New Advances,* N.Y. Times, Feb. 15, 1984, at B1, col. 1 (describing case at Beth Israel Medical Center, New York, where fetus believed to be 22 weeks, but which was in fact 25 or 26 weeks, lived, though with severe brain damage); Long, *Aborted Abortion,* Cleveland Plain Dealer, May 8, 1984, at 1-B, col. 1 (describing case at Kettering Medical Center outside Dayton, Ohio where estimate of gestational age was even more inaccurate and where infant eventually went home with her natural parents).

[8] During 1973, there were seven live deliveries and one survival following 5,151 abortions in New York state (live delivery ratio of 1.2 per 1000). Bok, Nathanson, Nathan & Walters, *The Unwanted Child: Caring for the Fetus Born Alive After an Abortion,* 6 HASTINGS CENTER REP. 10, 13-14 (Oct. 1976) [hereinafter cited as Bok].

[9] One recent newspaper article describes six live births at Madison, Wisconsin hospitals in the past 10 months from second-trimester abortions. Cleveland Plain Dealer, Mar. 23, 1983, at 15-A, col. 3. *See infra* notes 48 to 52 and 66 to 77 and accompanying text (discussing studies of rate of live births in late abortions).

[10] This article will use the term "fetus" to refer only to the fetus *in utero,* while the term "abortus" will refer to the fetus *ex utero,* whether it is alive or dead, viable or nonviable. Kass, *Determining Death and Viability in Fetuses and Abortuses,* in RESEARCH ON THE FETUS 11-1 app., 11-2 app. (The National Comm'n for the Protection of Human Subjects of Biomedical and Behavioral Research 1975). The term "abortus" is less cumbersome than the phrase "infant born live from an abortion." It does not imply that the status of the abortus differs from that of an infant born spontaneously.

[11] Definitions of abortion often note the intent to produce a nonviable fetus. *See* CENTER FOR DISEASE CONTROL, ABORTION SURVEILLANCE: ANNUAL SUMMARY 1977 7 (U.S. Dep't of Health, Education and Welfare, Public Health Service 1979) (defining abortion as termination of pregnancy prior to completion of 20th menstrual week of gestation and termination after 20th week intended to produce a nonviable fetus) [hereinafter cited as CDC 1977 REPORT]. This article will use the term "abortion" as meaning a procedure intended both to remove the fetus from the womb and to cause its death.

[12] Kass, *supra* note 10, at 11-6 app.

abortion other than hysterotomy,[13] is no longer the only nonsurgical technique. In the mid-to-late 1970s, the use of prostaglandins became widespread.[14] These substances simply induce premature labor, making live births much more common.[15] Additionally, tremendous advances in neonatal intensive care technology have given physicians the power to save the lives of extremely premature infants who would have been beyond hope only a few years ago.[16] Therefore, as a consequence of technological progress, fetuses now become viable at a significantly earlier point in pregnancy.[17]

While modern medicine has triumphed in saving these premature infants, the availability of this lifesaving technology for a premature infant whose delivery is not spontaneous, but rather is artificially induced, has created a medical, moral, and legal nightmare for the woman having the abortion, the physician and staff performing it, and the society which, although ambivalently, grants the woman the right to abort.[18] Writers on abortion have generally assumed, reasonably

enough, that removing the fetus from the womb ("womb-emptying") would necessarily result in its destruction ("feticide").[19] In the live-birth situation, however, womb-emptying and feticide have diverged; removing the fetus has unexpectedly failed to destroy it. This raises the question of whether the fact of the abortion, and the common justifications for abortion, are relevant to the decision whether to treat such an infant. If they are not, and doctors must try to save infants born from abortions, what is the scope or extent of their duty? Must they always provide treatment, no matter how slim the infant's chances of survival or how dismal its prognosis? This in turn raises the controversial issue of nontreatment of handicapped or "defective" newborns, because extremely premature infants are far more likely than other infants to be mentally retarded or to have other serious problems.[20] While this issue is extraordinarily complex, if we conclude that treatment decisions for abortuses should be similar to treatment decisions for other newborns, how do we resolve the peculiarly thorny problem of abortions for genetic defects, which are necessarily performed after week nineteen?[21]

Additional legal issues include whether the physician must seek parental authorization before treating an infant born from an abortion. If so, what happens if the mother refuses to consent? If treatment is given nonetheless, who should be

---

[13] See infra notes 100 and 101 and accompanying text (discussing abdominal hysterotomy).

[14] See CDC 1977 REPORT, supra note 11, at 4. See infra text Section II (describing various second-trimester abortion techniques).

[15] According to one study, live births may occur in as many as eight percent of second-trimester abortions performed by prostaglandin amnioinfusion. Stubblefield, Noftolm, Frigoletto & Ryan, *Laminaria Augmentation of Intra-Amniotic PG F2d for Midtrimester Pregnancy Termination,* 10 PROSTAGLANDIN 413, 420 (1975) [hereinafter cited as Stubblefield, *Laminaria Augmentation*].

[16] See infra notes 127 to 149 and accompanying text (discussing progress in last decade in saving extremely premature newborns).

[17] Today 50% of liveborn infants weighing less than 1000 grams (2.2 pounds) survive, compared with less than 10% just 20 years ago. Budetti & McManus, *Assessing the Effectiveness of Neonatal Intensive Care,* 20 MED. CARE 1027, 1031 (1982).

[18] According to one doctor: "It makes us all schizophrenic. . . . Nowadays we are asked to terminate a pregnancy that in two weeks doctors on the same floor are fighting to save." Statement of Dr. Richard Hausknecht, Associate Clinical Professor of Obstetrics and Gynecology at Mt. Sinai Hospital, in New York City, as quoted in Kleiman, *supra* note 7.

[19] See Kass, *supra* note 10, at 11-2 app. (explaining terminology). For example, in Roe v. Wade, 410 U.S. 113 (1973), the Supreme Court assumed that even after viability an abortion would terminate the fetus' life. See infra note 184 and accompanying text (quoting *Roe*'s description of hardships caused by undesired pregnancy). Had the Court believed that fetuses could survive an abortion it might have permitted abortions, in the sense of womb emptyings, after viability rather than before. Wikler, *Ought We to Try to Save Aborted Fetuses?,* 90 ETHICS 58, 62 n. 7 (1979) (quoting John Robertson). In the last few years, writers have begun to distinguish these two facets of abortion. *Id.*; Ross, *Abortion and the Death of the Fetus,* 11 PHIL. & PUB. AFF. 232, 234 (1982).

[20] See generally Ross, *Mortality and Morbidity in Very Low Birthweight Infants,* 12 PEDIATRIC ANNALS 32 (1983).

[21] See infra notes 201 to 216 and accompanying text (discussing abortions because of fetal genetic defects).

legally responsible for the costs of intensive care? Could a hospital and physicians who sustain the life of a severely retarded or handicapped infant potentially be liable for the infant's "wrongful birth" or "wrongful life"?[22]

We also must ask how the live-birth dilemma, and the changes in medical technology that it reflects, will affect second-trimester abortions. If a fetus is potentially viable, must physicians use the abortion technique which is least likely to harm it? Alternatively, can an abortion method be chosen precisely because it is feticidal? The ultimate question is whether, as viability occurs earlier in pregnancy, a woman's right to abort will necessarily become more and more circumscribed. In *Roe v. Wade,*[23] the Supreme Court held that the state's interest in potential life becomes compelling when the fetus becomes viable.[24] As viability occurs earlier, therefore, the state's interest in preserving the fetus likewise becomes compelling earlier, with the ironic result that *Roe* soon may become a "right-to-life" decision. Will increasing restriction of the abortion right ultimately eliminate genetic abortions? Is there any limit to the narrowing of the abortion right?

These questions, and many others, are emerging as medical technology doggedly pushes back the time at which a fetus is viable. We have just witnessed the development of techniques for transferring an embryo from one woman's womb to another's.[25] In the future, we could possibly develop techniques to gestate artificially an em-

bryo at any stage of development,[26] or even to transplant a fetus rather than an embryo. The question then may arise as to whether a woman who wishes to have her embryo removed has the right to specify that no one receive it in a transplant or artificially gestate it. These developments, which could render even first-trimester abortions, at least feticidal ones, problematic, are for the future, however. Current difficulties are sufficiently severe in themselves. Therefore, the focus of this article will be limited to issues raised by either existing technology or techniques and refinements reasonably anticipated in the near future. With this limitation, this article will first describe the techniques of abortion and the state of neonatal technology and will ask whether abortuses should be saved. It then will analyze the scope of a physician's duties to a live-born abortus and will consider the special problem of genetic abortions. Finally, it will assess the future of second-trimester abortions.

SECOND-TRIMESTER ABORTION TECHNIQUES

Although today the great majority of abortions are performed during the first twelve weeks of pregnancy, about eight to ten percent of abortions in America are performed between the thirteenth and approximately the twenty-fourth week.[27]

---

[22] *See infra* notes 208 to 221 [not here included] and accompanying text (discussing possible physician liability based on wrongful birth and wrongful life theories when live birth results from abortion).

[23] 410 U.S. 113 (1973).

[24] *Id,* at 163.

[25] *Birth Results from Transferred Embryo,* N.Y. Times, Feb. 4, 1984, at A6, col. 1; NEWSWEEK, Aug. 1, 1983, at 48; *"Prenatal Adoption" is the Objective of New Technique,* N.Y. Times, June 14, 1983, at C1, col. 4. The technique of *in vitro* fertilization, by which a woman's egg cell is fertilized outside her body and then reimplanted, is by now routine. *See The First Test Tube Baby,* TIME, July 27, 1978, at 1 (discussing birth of first child conceived *in vitro*).

[26] *See* Note, *Choice Rights and Abortion: The Begetting Choice Right and State Obstacles to Choice in Light of Artificial Womb Technology,* 51 S. CAL. L. REV. 877 (1978) (discussing potential impact of artificial womb technology on woman's right to opt for abortion and to deny permission for artificial gestation).

[27] CDC 1977 REPORT, *supra* note 11, at 4 (during 1977 more than 90% of abortions performed at less than 13 weeks gestation). *See also* C. TIETZE, INDUCED ABORTION (1979) (reviewing statistics on abortion) [hereinafter cited as TIETZE 1979]. This figure has remained relatively constant. *See* Center for Disease Control, *Abortion Surveillance: Preliminary Analysis, 1979-80—United States,* 32 MORBIDITY & MORTALITY WEEKLY REP., Feb. 11, 1983, at 62 (10% of abortions in 1980 performed after week 13) [hereinafter cited as CDC, *1979-80 Report*].

Since 1973, the percentage of second-trimester abortions has declined significantly.[28] Nonetheless, the number of abortions performed in the United States increases every year.[29] Second-trimester terminations account for nearly 100,000 abortions a year.[30]

Women who seek late abortions generally are poorly educated, have a low socio-economic status, and are very young.[31] One author suggests that this phenomenon "reflects the inexperience of the very young in recognizing the symptoms of pregnancy, their unwillingness to accept the reality of their situation, their ignorance about where to seek advice and help, and their hesitation to confide in adults."[32] In addition to this group, a small but significant number of women have second-trimester abortions after amniocentesis reveals a fetal defect.[33]

The risks of abortion increase substantially as a pregnancy becomes more advanced.[34] There-

fore, safety of the various second-trimester abortion techniques is relevant to the issue of regulation of abortion techniques. Likewise, the techniques differ markedly in their potential for resulting in live births. Accordingly, it is necessary to describe the various procedures, possible complications, and concomitant rates of live births.

One of the oldest techniques for performing second-trimester abortions is the intra-amniotic instillation of hypertonic saline solution.[35] Saline amnioinfusion, like any other technique involving the injection of a substance into the amniotic sac, cannot be performed until the sixteenth menstrual week. Prior to this stage there is insufficient amniotic fluid for successful amniocentesis.[36] The physician injects the saline after withdrawing 50 to 250 milliliters of amniotic fluid. Withdrawal of amniotic fluid prevents a sudden and harmful increase in intra-amniotic pressure and increases the saline concentration to a level sufficient to cause fetal death and expulsion.[37] Within approximately twenty-four to thirty-six hours after instillation, the woman experiences uterine contractions and expels the fetus.[38] Some physicians use augmenting agents, such as laminaria or oxytocin, to stimulate uterine contractions and thereby shorten the instillation-to-abortion time period.[39]

[28]Tietze, *Second Trimester Abortion: A Global View*, in SECOND TRIMESTER ABORTION 1, 3-4 (G. Berger, W. Brenner & L. Keith eds. 1981) [hereinafter cited as Tietze 1981]. In 1972, second-trimester abortions constituted 17.9% of all abortions. CDC, *1979-80 Report*, *supra* note 27, at 62, 63.

[29]The total number of legal abortions passed one million in 1975 and reached 1.27 million in 1977. TIETZE 1979, *supra* note 27, at 20. These figures are derived from surveys undertaken by the Alan Guttmacher Institute, Washington, D.C. Although the Center for Disease Control (CDC) lists the number of abortions in 1977 as 1,079,430, CDC 1977 REPORT, *supra* note 11, at 1, authorities seem to agree that not all abortions performed in this country are reported to the CDC. Tyler, Cates, Shulz, Selik & Smith, *Second-Trimester Induced Abortion in the United States*, in SECOND TRIMESTER ABORTION 13, 15 (G. Berger, W. Brenner & L. Keith eds. 1981) [hereinafter cited as Tyler].

[30]Tyler, *supra* note 29, at 16.

[31]TIETZE 1979, *supra* note 27, at 61; Kerenyi & Den, *Intraamniotic Instillation of Saline and Prostaglandin for Mid-Trimester Abortion*, in PREGNANCY TERMINATION: PROCEDURES, SAFETY, AND NEW DEVELOPMENTS 254, 259 (G. Zatuchni, J. Sciarra & J. Speidel eds. 1978).

[32]TIETZE 1979, *supra* note 27, at 61.

[33]*Id.* at 62. *See generally* Schulman, *Second Trimester Abortion: Techniques and Complications*, in GYNECOLOGY & OBSTETRICS 1 (J. Sciarra ed. 1982) (given particular groups of women who have late abortions, percentage of second-trimester abortions not likely to fall below Sweden's six percent).

[34]Second-trimester abortions are responsible for more than half of the preventable maternal deaths from abortions. Tyler, *supra* note 29, at 16.

[35]Kerenyi, *Hypertonic Saline Instillation*, in SECOND TRIMESTER ABORTION 79 (G. Berger, W. Brenner & L. Keith eds. 1981) [hereinafter cited as Kerenyi, *Saline Instillation.*]

[36]R. Bolognese & S. Corson, INTERRUPTION OF PREGNANCY—A TOTAL PATIENT APPROACH 126 (1975). Amniocentesis is the withdrawing of amniotic fluid.

[37]Kerenyi, *Saline Instillation*, *supra* note 35, at 81.

[38]*Id. See also* R. BOLOGNESE & S. CORSON, *supra* note 36, at 127 (average interval between saline injection and abortion, without early use of oxytocin augmentation, ranges from 30 to 36.5 hours). About 97% of patients expel the fetus within 72 hours. In fewer than one percent of the cases, a second amnioinfusion with hypertonic saline may be necessary after 48 hours because of failure of expulsion. Kerenyi, *Saline Instillation*, *supra* note 35, at 81.

[39]Kerenyi, *Saline Instillation*, *supra* note 35, at 82.

Use of saline is contraindicated in patients with cardiovascular disease, renal disease, sickle cell disease, or other severe anemias.[40] Saline amnioinfusion can cause a number of complications, even in patients with no pre-existing medical conditions. After infusion, virtually every patient demonstrates coagulation alteration.[41] In most cases this reaction is mild and transient, but occasionally severe clotting disorders will occur.[42] Coagulation defects also increase the risk of hemorrhage. Hemorrhage and infection are the most frequent complications of saline abortions[43] and are most likely to occur when an abortion is incomplete.[44] Hypernatremia, involving an excessive increase in the serum sodium level, also may result if saline is inadvertently injected into the patient's vascular system. In mild cases, it simply causes facial flushing, restlessness, thirst, and headache, but severe hypernatremia may induce seizures, coma, or death.[45] In rare cases, uterine injury, including rupture or cervical laceration, may occur.[46] Should the abortion be incomplete,

the physician must remove all fetal parts from the woman's uterus.[47]

Saline infusion is highly feticidal, and therefore live births resulting from use of this abortion technique are rare. One study reports that saline infusion results in a live birth rate of 0.17 per 100 abortions.[48] Another describes no live births in saline-induced abortions between sixteen and nineteen weeks gestation and one live birth in a saline group between twenty and twenty-four weeks gestation, yielding a three percent live-birth ratio in the latter group.[49] Live births associated with saline generally occur when the physician makes an error in the procedure which prevents completion of the saline infusion.[50] Another factor associated with delivery of a live fetus is underestimation of gestational age.[51]

The various risks associated with saline amnioinfusion led physicians to seek alternative abortion methods.[52] In 1973, the Food and Drug Administration approved the use of prostaglandin for intra-amniotic instillation as an abortifacient.[53] The instillation of prostaglandin is similar

---

[40]R. BOLOGNESE & S. CORSON, *supra* note 36, at 126; Kerenyi, *Saline Instillation, supra* note 35, at 85.

[41]R. BOLOGNESE & S. CORSON, *supra* note 36, at 133.

[42]Kerenyi, *Saline Instillation, supra* note 35, at 83.

[43]In one study 96% of all complications suffered by over 4000 patients were due to hemorrhage and/or infection. Berger & Kerenyi, *Control of Morbidity Associated with Saline Abortion,* 9 ADVANCED PLANNED PARENTHOOD 31 (1975). Hemorrhage severe enough to require transfusion has been reported in two to seven percent of patients. Kerenyi, *Saline Instillation, supra* note 35, at 83.

[44]*See* Robins, *Alternatives in Mid-trimester Abortion Induction,* 56 OBSTETRICS & GYNECOLOGY 716 (1980) (excessive blood loss associated with 14 out of 23 incomplete abortions).

[45]Kerenyi, *Saline Instillation, supra* note 35, at 83. *See also* R. BOLOGNESE & S. CORSON, *supra* note 36, at 136 (hypernatremia accounts for majority of deaths associated with saline-induced abortions).

[46]Kerenyi, *Saline Instillation, supra* note 35, at 83. *See* Graham, *Uterine Rupture Occurring During Mid-trimester Abortion,* 59 Obstetrics & Gynecology 625 (1982) (describing one such case and noting factors that may increase risk of rupture).

[47]Kerenyi, *Saline Instillation, supra* note 35, at 84; R. BOLOGNESE & S. CORSON, *supra* note 36, at 134.

[48]Stroh & Hinman, *Reported Live Births Following Induced Abortion: Two and One-Half Years' Experience in Upstate New York,* 126 AM. J. OBSTETRICS & GYNECOLOGY 83 (1976).

[49]Robins, *supra* note 44, at 720.

[50]In one series of 5000 cases, only three fetuses were born with evidence of cardiac or skeletal muscle activity and all three occurred in cases for which the amnioinfusion was not completed because of inadvertent movement. Kerenyi, *Saline Instillation, supra* note 35, at 84.

[51]*Id.*

[52]Because the live birth rate in saline abortions is so low, some authorities believe that despite its potential complications, use of prostaglandins will not replace its use for abortions performed during the 20- to 24-week period. Kerenyi & Den, *supra* note 31, at 254. Saline abortions are now much less common. In 1972, they constituted 10.3% of abortions, and by 1976, they made up only 4.8% TIETZE 1979, *supra* note 27, at 71. By 1980, the dilatation and evacuation method (D & E) had replaced saline as the most widely used abortion method between the 16th and 20th weeks. CDC, *1979-80 Report, supra* note 27, at 63-64.

[53]TIETZE 1979, *supra* note 27, at 68. Prostaglandins are a naturally occurring family of compounds with significant physiological and pharmacological activity. By 1977, prostaglandins were being used for 34% of abortions performed at 16 weeks or later. Tyler, *supra* note 29, at 19-20.

to that of saline, except that amniotic fluid is not ordinarily removed prior to instillation of the prostaglandin.[54] Prostaglandin instillation stimulates smooth muscle contractibility in the uterus, which leads to uterine contractions and fetal expulsion.[55] Use of prostaglandin generally results in a shorter instillation-to-abortion time than does use of saline.[56] Because prostaglandins are rapidly metabolized, however, a second dose may be needed to hasten abortion.[57] Although intra-amniotic use of prostaglandins is by far the most frequently used method, prostaglandins have also been administered vaginally, intramuscularly, and intravenously.[58]

Because prostaglandin generally stimulates contractibility of smooth muscles, it is not recommended for patients with bronchial asthma in whom it may cause bronchial muscle contraction.[59] Additionally, its use is not recommended with patients suffering from pulmonary hypertension, glaucoma, hypertensive disease, and epilepsy.[60] The most frequent side effects associated with prostaglandin are nausea, vomiting, and diarrhea.[61] Patients may also experience chills,

fever, and minor episodes of coughing and shortness of breath, but severe respiratory or cardiovascular complications are rare.[62] Hemorrhages and infections also may occur, especially when the placenta is not expelled within one to two hours following expulsion of the fetus.[63] Theoretically, prostaglandin may be safer than saline because hypernatremia is not a risk with prostaglandin use, and inadvertent intravascular injection of prostaglandin poses less danger than similar injection of saline because prostaglandin metabolizes more quickly.[64] Comparative studies, however, show few differences in complication rates when skilled physicians use saline.[65]

Because prostaglandin instillation does not destroy fetal tissue but merely induces premature labor, it is much more likely to result in live birth than is saline instillation. An early discussion of prostaglandin projected a live-birth rate of approximately 2 per 100 procedures.[66] Writers extrapolating from these rates to the number of abortions performed in 1977 after sixteen weeks gestation estimated that 472 infants were born alive in late abortions and that approximately

---

[54]R. Bolognese & S. Corson, *supra* note 36, at 141.

[55]Kerenyi, *Intra-Amniotic Techniques,* in Abortion and Sterilization: Medical and Social Aspects 359, 367 (J. Hodgson ed. 1981) [hereinafter cited as Kerenyi, *Techniques*]. While physicians do not completely understand the exact manner by which instillation of prostaglandins induces abortion, investigators point to changes in circulating progesterone levels, changes in cell membrane potentials, and direct stimulation of the myometrium. *Id.*

[56]Investigators report mean instillation-to-abortion times ranging from 18 to 32 hours. *Id.* at 368.

[57]*Id.* As with saline instillation, physicians may augment prostaglandins with oxytocin or laminaria. *Id.*; R. Bolognese & S. Corson, *supra* note 36, at 141-42.

[58]Bygdeman, *Prostaglandin Procedures,* in Second Trimester Abortion 89, 95-99 (G. Berger, W. Brenner & L. Keith eds. 1982); Williams Obstetrics, *supra* note 3, at 611.

[59]R. Bolognese & S. Corson, *supra* note 36, at 145; Robins, *supra* note 44, at 717.

[60]Hern, *Mid-Trimester Abortion,* in Obstetrics & Gynecology Ann. 375 (1981).

[61]Kerenyi, *Techniques, supra* note 55, at 368. Use of various prostaglandin analogues may reduce the severity of gastroin-

testinal side effects. R. Bolognese & S. Corson, *supra* note 36, at 145-46; Bygdeman, *supra* note 58, at 95-99.

[62]Kerenyi, *Techniques, supra* note 55, at 368.

[63]*Id.*

[64]Bygdeman, *supra* note 58, at 101.

[65]In one study, the total number of complications and the number of major complications were higher for the prostaglandin group. *Id.* at 102. The death rate was higher, however, with saline plus oxytocin. *Id.* In another study, maternal mortality between 1972 and 1975 was 23 per 100,000 for hypertonic saline and 18 per 100,000 for prostaglandin. Grimes & Cates, *Complication from Legally-Induced Abortion: A Review,* 34 Obstetrics & Gynecology Surv. 177, 188 (1979). The figures are undoubtedly lower today, since mortality from second-trimester abortions has declined from 11.4 deaths per 100,000 procedures in 1972 to 6.5 per procedure in 1977. Tyler, *supra* note 29, at 17. The increasing use of D & E accounts for some of the decline in mortality rates. Cates & Grimes, *Morbidity and Mortality,* in Second Trimester Abortion 163, 172-73 (G. Berger, W. Brenner & L. Keith eds. 1981) [hereinafter cited as Cates & Grimes (Berger)].

[66]Bok, *supra* note 8, at 14.

three percent survived.[67] Other studies showed higher rates of live birth. In one, live births occurred in 3.6 percent of prostaglandin abortions performed between sixteen and nineteen weeks gestation and in 3.4 percent of abortions between twenty and twenty-four weeks' gestation.[68] The rate may be even higher. Experts have stated that prostaglandin is about forty times more likley to produce a live-born abortus than is saline.[69] Moreover, the American College of Obstetricians and Gynecologists, as well as two researchers, have reported that there have been signs of life in as many as seven percent of the fetuses aborted by prostaglandin instillation.[70] Another study reports a live birth rate of eight percent.[71] The possibility of live births may make physicians reluctant to use prostaglandins in abortions performed after the twentieth week. In one institution in New York, use of prostaglandin replaced use of saline for midtrimester abortions in 1974, but in 1975 physicians discontinued using it for pregnancies beyond twenty weeks in order to avoid live births.[72]

At some institutions, physicians have begun combining prostaglandin with saline in an attempt to improve effectiveness and to minimize each agent's dose-related side effects.[73] Although adding saline to prostaglandin reduces the rate of live births,[74] some live births may still occur.[75] Some physicians are also using urea, which causes a lower incidence of gastrointestinal side effects than prostaglandin does. It is, however, a less potent abortifacient and requires augmentation with oxytocin, laminaria, or prostaglandin.[76] Urea instillation, either with or without prostaglandin, may result in live births.[77]

An increasingly common method of second-trimester abortion is dilatation and evacuation (D & E), which requires dilatation of the cervix by means of tapered mechanical dilators and/or laminaria[78] and use of large forceps to evacuate the fetus.[79] Following removal of all fetal and placental tissue, the physician uses suction to ensure that the cavity is completely empty.[80] Additionally, the physician must identify and account for all tissues,[81] because retained fetal parts can lead to infection.[82]

---

[67]Cates & Grimes, *Morbidity and Mortality of Abortion in the United States,* in ABORTION AND STERILIZATION 156, 164 (J. Hodgson ed. 1981) [hereinafter cited as Cates & Grimes (Hodgson)].

[68]Robins, *supra* note 44, at 720 (study based on very small sample).

[69]Cates & Grimes (Berger), *supra* note 65, at 171.

[70]AMERICAN COLLEGE OF OBSTETRICIANS & GYNECOLOGISTS, Tech. Bull. No. 56, METHODS AT MIDTRIMESTER ABORTION 4 (1979); Lee & Baggish, *Live Birth as a Complication of Second Trimester Abortion Induced with Intra-Amniotic Prostaglandin, F2d,* 13 ADVANCES IN PLANNED PARENTHOOD 7 (1978).

[71]Stubblefield, *Laminaria Augmentation, supra* note 15, at 420.

[72]Robins, *supra* note 44, at 717.

[73]Kerenyi, *Techniques, supra* note 54, at 371. By combining these agents, the physician can reduce mean induction-to-abortion time by 15.2 to 20.7 hours. *Id.* at 372.

[74]Kerenyi interview, *supra* note 2.

[75]In one study, two infants were born alive. Kerenyi, *Techniques, supra* note 55, at 372.

[76]*Id.* at 369.

[77]Some of the infants born alive at Madison, Wisconsin hospitals were being aborted with a combination of prostaglandin and urea. Cleveland Plain Dealer, Mar. 23, 1983, at 15-A, col. 3.

[78]Laminaria may be used prior to insertion of mechanical dilators, especially in pregnancies beyond 15 weeks. Schulman, *supra* note 33, at 7. It may also be used alone. Stubblefield, *Midtrimester Abortion by Curretage Procedures: An Overview,* in ABORTION AND STERILIZATION: MEDICAL AND SOCIAL ASPECTS 277, 279-80 (J. Hodgson ed. 1981) [hereinafter cited as Stubblefield, *Curretage Procedures*]. Generally, laminaria is left in place from 8 to 24 hours. Grimes & Cates, *Dilatation and Evacuation,* in SECOND TRIMESTER ABORTION 119, 127 (G. Berger, W. Brenner & L. Keith eds. 1981) [hereinafter cited as Grimes & Cates, *Dilatation*].

[79]Grimes & Cates, *Dilatation, supra* note 78, at 128. To eliminate the need for crushing forceps and fetal dismemberment in pregnancies of 16 weeks or less, physicians can employ a large suction cannula for evacuation of the fetus. Stubblefield, *Curretage Procedures, supra* note 78, at 283-85.

[80]Peterson, *Dilatation and Evacuation: Patient Evaluation and Surgical Techniques,* in PREGNANCY TERMINATION 184, 186 (G. Zatuchni, J. Sciarra & J. Speidel eds. 1978).

[81]*Id.*

[82]*Id.* at 188.

D & E abortions can cause cervical laceration and perforation of the uterus, which are more likely to occur with forcible mechanical dilatation of the cervix than with laminaria distillation.[83] Other possible complications include excessive blood loss,[84] hemorrhage,[85] and pelvic infection.[86] Live birth is not a possibility.[87]

For many years, the conventional medical wisdom was that physicians could not perform these procedures after twelve weeks. Patients seeking abortions between weeks thirteen and fifteen had to wait until week sixteen for performance of an amnioinfusion procedure.[88] In recent years, however, this practice has changed. By 1977, D & E was used in seventy-three percent of all abortions performed between the thirteenth and fifteenth weeks.[89] Sixteen weeks then became the upper limit. While many texts still do not discuss the possibility of using D & E after the sixteenth week,[90] many physicians now perform D & E past this time. In 1980, D & E replaced saline instillation as the most common method of abortion during the sixteen-to-twenty-week interval.[91] Studies also show that it is the safest abortion method through week twenty.[92] It is possible

that D & E will achieve common usage even later in pregnancy. Although few physicians currently use it later than twenty or twenty-one weeks, some recent reports describe excellent results from using D & E for abortions between the twenty-first and twenty-fourth weeks.[93]

D & E has been found to be associated with greater patient comfort and less guilt, anger, and depression than the amnioinfusion methods, which induce a long and painful labor process.[94] It is also more convenient for the woman since it is faster than other methods and does not require overnight hospitalization.[95] Because D & E involves dismemberment and direct contact with fetal parts, some reports describe psychological problems among the staff performing such abortions.[96] D & E may be more convenient for the medical staff than instillation abortions, however, because it can be scheduled[97] and because its lower complication rate results in less physician time spent managing incomplete abortions and

---

[83]Stubblefield, *Laminaria Augmentation, supra* note 15, at 289-91.

[84]*Id.*

[85]*Id.* Hemorrhage requiring transfusion occurs in approximately 0.3% of the cases. Schulman, *supra* note 33, at 7.

[86]Stubblefield, *Curretage Procedures, supra* note 78, at 290-91. To minimize the risk of infection, the physician must ensure that the uterus is completely evacuated of fetal and placental tissue. *Id.*

[87]The Supreme Court in Planned Parenthood Ass'n of Kansas City, Mo., Inc. v. Ashcroft, 103 S.Ct. 2517, 2521 n.7 (1983), recognized that a fetus cannot survive a D & E abortion.

[88]Stubblefield, *Curretage Procedures, supra* note 78, at 278.

[89]CDC 1977 REPORT, *supra* note 11, at 5.

[90]WILLIAMS OBSTETRICS, *supra* note 3, at 603.

[91]CDC, *1979-80 Report, supra* note 27, at 64.

[92]Grimes & Cates, *Dilatation, supra* note 78, at 128. In one study, the total complication rate for D & E was 6%, while that for prostaglandins was 34%. *Id.* at 129. In another study, even when performed at 17 weeks gestation or later, D & E had a lower rate of complications than either prostaglandin

or saline instillation. Cates, Schulz, Grimes, Horowitz, Lyon, Kravitz & Frisch, *Dilatation and Evacuation Procedures,* in SECOND TRIMESTER ABORTIONS, 248 J.A.M.A. 559, 560 (1982) [hereinafter cited as Cates].

[93]Stubblefield, *supra* note 78, at 280. Dr. Stubblefield is skeptical, however, about the wisdom of using D & E after the 21st week. He states that, even though the complication rate may be low, when complications do occur they are devastating. This is in contrast to the more frequent but less serious complications from infusion methods. Interview with Dr. Phillip Stubblefield, Professor of Obstetrics and Gynecology, Harvard Medical School, in Boston (June 6, 1983) [hereinafter cited as Stubblefield interview]. It has recently been observed that a growing number of physicians are developing expertise in performing D & E through the 24th week of pregnancy. Kleiman, *supra* note 7.

[94]Grimes & Cates, *Dilatation, supra* note 78, at 128.

[95]*Id.* at 129–31.

[96]Hern & Corrigan, *What About Us? Staff Reactions to D & E,* 15 ADVANCES IN PLANNED PARENTHOOD 3 (1980). One study suggests that with D & E much of the emotional burden of an abortion shifts from the woman to the physician. Grimes & Cates, *Dilatation, supra* note 78, at 128. Another study reports that an awareness of the advantages of the procedure and provision of internal staff support can minimize staff psychological reactions. Cates, *supra* note 92, at 562.

[97]Grimes & Cates, *Dilatation, supra* note 78, at 131.

performing follow-up care.[98] Moreover, some experts claim that the technical complexities and psychological impact of performing late D & E procedures are balanced by the higher success rate and elimination of the live-birth dilemma.[99]

These procedures are the major ones used for midtrimester abortions. In a few circumstances, where amnioinfusion techniques are unsuccessful or where uterine disease is present, abdominal hysterotomy, a technique similar to a Cesarean section, may be necessary.[100] Because hysterotomy involves surgical removal of the fetus, it does not damage the fetus and may well result in live birth. Hysterotomy is a major surgical procedure, however, and physicians no longer view it as an acceptable method for routine pregnancy termination.[101] Thus, the infusion methods and D & E are the second-trimester abortion techniques of choice.

ADVANCES IN TREATMENT OF PREMATURE NEWBORNS

The second technological change giving rise to the live-birth dilemma is the development of increasingly sophisticated techniques for neonatal intensive care. Until recently, very premature babies seldom survived. But this prognosis has changed dramatically since 1965, with the evolution of perinatal medicine and the development of associated medical technologies.[102] Neonatal intensive care as it exists today involves a team of medical personnel trained in caring for high-risk newborns and adept at operating the various mechanical devices used to assist premature newborns with their life functions.[103]

Infants of very low birth weight[104] face a staggering array of medical problems. The immaturity of their lungs frequently results in respiratory distress syndrome, in which the air sacs in the lungs collapse at the end of expiration due to insufficient surfactant.[105] This syndrome has been associated with fifty to seventy percent of the deaths of premature infants.[106] Recently, however, physicians have been able to prevent lung collapse by employing a continuous distending pressure to keep the alveoli open.[107] Even with this technique, some infants may be too weak to breathe on their own or may experience periods of apnea (cessation of breathing), for which they will require mechanical ventilation. Respirator therapy requires constant monitoring to ensure that the proper amount of pressure and volume are maintained and to prevent adverse side effects of the

---

[98]Cates, *supra* note 92, at 562.

[99]Grimes & Cates, *Dilatation, supra* note 78, at 130. One prominent physician states that he feels physicians who have their patients' best interests at heart should use D & E because this technique is better for the woman both physically and emotionally and because it avoids the live-birth problem. Kerenyi interview, *supra* note 2. Dr. E. Wyman Garrett, a Newark, N.J. obstetrician, has likewise stated that he prefers D & E (and uses it through week 24) both because of its safety and because it cannot result in a live birth, a problem he encountered while performing a saline abortion in 1982. Kleiman, *supra* note 7.

[100]WILLIAMS OBSTETRICS, *supra* note 3, at 607.

[101]*Id.*

---

[102]*See* BUDETTI, MCMANUS, BARRAND & HEINEN, CASE STUDY 10: THE COST AND EFFECTIVENESS OF NEONATAL INTENSIVE CARE (U.S. Off. of Tech. Assessment 1981) (discussing history, utilization, and consequences of neonatal intensive care) [hereinafter cited as BUDETTI]. "Perinatal" is the period around the time of birth, now generally defined as from 20 weeks of gestation up to 28 days of life. This time frame overlaps with the neonatal period, which is the period from the moment of live birth up to, but not including, the moment at which the infant completes the 28th day of life. *Id.* at 7.

[103]*Id.* at 7-8. Because the technology necessary for neonatal intensive care is very expensive, not all hospitals have the most sophisticated level of care. Instead, geographic areas will have a few hospitals with neonatal intensive care units and a transport system which takes high-risk newborns to those centers. *Id.* at 9.

[104]Infants weighing 2500 grams or less are classified as low birth weight infants, those weighing 1500 grams or less are very low birth weight infants. *Id.* at 4.

[105]Behrman & Rosen, *supra* note 4, at 12-19 app.

[106]NEONATOLOGY: PATHOPHYSIOLOGY AND MANAGEMENT OF THE NEWBORN 376 (2d ed. 1981).

[107]*Id.* at 379.

treatment.[108] These side effects include retrolental fibroplasia (a cause of blindness),[109] permanent and sometimes progressive lung damage, intraventricular brain hemorrhages, and necrotizing enterocolitis (an inflammation of the intestinal lining that may be fatal).[110] Despite the complications from these techniques, they nonetheless have dramatically reduced mortality rates. Before their development, sixty-one percent of infants with respiratory distress syndrome died; today, the mortality rate is approximately eleven percent.[111] The impact on the survival of very low birth weight infants is even more striking. In 1965, only ten percent of infants weighing less than 1500 grams and suffering from respiratory distress syndrome survived; by 1979, the survival rate had increased to eighty percent.[112]

Special techniques are also required to feed very low birth weight infants. They often lack the ability to suck, aspiration is a constant threat, and they have a very small stomach capacity.[113] They may be fed through a tube passed into the stomach or by a tube which enters the small intestine.[114] Total intravenous alimentation, another recent development, provides a continuous infusion of fluids, calories, electrolytes, and vitamins.[115] These techniques can produce problems as well as solve them. Excess fluid intake can aggravate problems associated with an overworked heart, while an insufficient amount of fluid and

nutrients may limit growth and allow multiple bone fractures to develop.[116] Immature kidneys may be unable to handle the volume of fluid associated with artificial feeding,[117] and fluctuations in fluid level can likewise increase the risk of intraventricular hemorrhage.

Intraventricular hemorrhage, or bleeding in the brain, is a major cause of neurological handicaps in preterm infants.[118] Until recently, physicians identified such hemorrhages only after symptoms of brain damage appeared. The recent development of computerized tomography (CT scanning) and real-time ultrasound allows noninvasive diagnosis of intraventricular hemorrhages, even when they are clinically silent.[119] Once a CT scan or ultrasound reveals a lesion, physicians may perform lumbar punctures to relieve the buildup of fluid and to prevent dilation of the ventricles.[120] These developments clearly improve the prognosis for premature newborns.

Other medical problems facing premature newborns include frequent infections due to their immature immune system,[121] jaundice,[122] hypoglycemia and hypocalcemia,[123] and other abnor-

---

[108]S. Korones, High Risk Newborn Infants: The Basis for Intensive Nursing Care 216-19 (1981), President's Comm'n for the Study of Ethical Problems in Medicine and Biomedical and Behavioral Research, Deciding to Forego Life-Sustaining Treatment 200-01 n.17 (1983) [hereinafter cited as President's Comm'n].

[109]S. Korones, supra note 108, at 219-20; President's Comm'n, supra note 108, at 200-01 n. 17.

[110]Ismach, The Smallest Patients, Med. World News, Sept. 14, 1981, at 30.

[111]S. Korones, supra note 108, at 233.

[112]Ismach, supra note 110, at 30.

[113]Behrman & Rosen, supra note 4, at 12-19 app.

[114]Id. at 12-19-12-20 app.

[115]Id. at 12-20 app.

[116]President's Comm'n, supra note 108, at 201.

[117]Id.

[118]Id. at 200 n.17. In a preterm baby, the capillaries next to the ventricles are very fragile and can rupture easily, especially when the infant has respiratory distress syndrome. Once there is a hemorrhage in or around the ventricular wall, the blood flows into the cerebral spinal fluid and circulates throughout the ventricular system. S. Korones, supra note 108, at 345-47.

[119]Papille, Burstein, Burstein & Koffler, Incidence and Evolution of Subependymal and Intraventricular Hemorrhage: A Study of Infants with Birth Weights Less Than 1500 Grams, 92 Pediatrics 529, 529 (1978); Levene, Wigglesworth & Dubowitz, Cerebral Structure and Intraventricular Hemorrhage in the Neonate: A Real-Time Ultrasound Study, 56 Archives of Disease in Childhood 416 (1981).

[120]S. Korones, supra note 108, at 347.

[121]President's Comm'n, supra note 108, at 201.

[122]S. Korones, supra note 108, at 284.

[123]Wald, Problems in Metabolic Adaptation: Glucose, Calcium, and Magnesium, in Care of the High Risk Neonate 224, 224 (2d ed. 1979).

malities of blood chemistry.[124] Phototherapy has enhanced greatly physicians' ability to treat jaundice in newborns.[125] In addition, the development of microchemistry techniques to rapidly analyze chemical abnormalities in the newborn's blood has made it possible for doctors to monitor blood glucose, calcium, electrolytes, and liver chemistries and to detect and correct chemical aberrations much sooner.[126]

These developments, along with other new techniques, have produced a marked decrease in mortality for premature infants. Mortality for infants with birth weights of 1001 to 1500 grams has fallen from more than fifty percent in the early-to-middle 1960s to less than twenty percent today.[127] Even the mortality rate for newborns weighing 1000 grams or less has fallen from nearly ninety-four percent in the 1960s to approximately fifty percent.[128] Not only have death rates declined, but the incidence of handicaps in survivors also has decreased. Prior to 1960 about one-fourth of the infants weighing 1500 grams or less suffered from severe neurological or other handicaps.[129] In contrast, recent reports indicate that the rate of severe impairment for newborns with birth weights of 1500 grams or less has declined to about fourteen percent.[130] For infants weighing 1000 grams or less, about thirty percent of survivors formerly had severe handicaps, in contrast to about sixteen percent today.[131] The incidence of

severe retardation in very low birth weight infants similarly has declined from approximately seventeen percent prior to 1965 to eleven percent or less.[132]

Although the handicap rate has decreased, these figures also show that a substantial number of survivors still are severely handicapped. Moreover, survivors may suffer from less serious handicaps. In one study of infants weighing less than 1500 grams at birth, 14.3% had severe developmental delay at one year of age and another 27.5% were impaired moderately or minimally at one year.[133] Also, as survival rates increase among babies weighing less than 1500 grams, and particularly among those infants weighing less than 1000 grams, increased numbers of infants will suffer from problems caused by either extreme prematurity or the treatments such infants receive. One study notes that despite advances in monitoring oxygen levels, present technical skill in administering oxygen still is inadequate to prevent retrolental fibroplasia in the most immature infants, and the level of blind or severely visually impaired survivors could soon approach the level during the "epidemic" of retinopathy from 1942 to 1953, before neonatal intensive care.[134] Finally, for the tiniest of survivors, life is often preserved only at a very high price. In a study of infants weighing between 501 and 750 grams, twenty-seven percent of the survivors were determined to be handicapped upon follow-up.[135] There also is some

---

[124]*See generally* S. KORONES, *supra* note 108, at 268-83 (discussing various hematological disorders which occur during neonatal period).

[125]BUDETTI, *supra* note 102, at 8.

[126]Behrman & Rosen, *supra* note 4, at 12-18.

[127]BUDETTI, *supra* note 102, at 30.

[128]*Id.*

[129]*Id.* at 35.

[130]*Id.* at 36.

[131]*Id.* The authors caution that these studies are not conclusive because of the small number of infants involved. Infants weighing 1500 grams or less totalled only about 1400 patients, and the entire literature on infants weighing 1000 grams or less concerns studies of only about 300 individuals. *Id.*

---

[132]*Id.* at 38.

[133]Sinclair, Torrance, Boyle, Horwood, Saigal & Sackett, *Evaluation of Neonatal-Intensive-Care Programs,* 305 NEW ENG. J. MED. 489, 491 (1981).

[134]Phelps, *Retinopathy of Prematurity: An Estimate of Vision Loss in the United States—1979,* 67 PEDIATRICS 924, 925 (1981).

[135]Orgill, Astbury, Bajak & Yu, *Early Development of Infants 1000 grams or Less at Birth,* ARCHIVES OF DISEASE IN CHILDHOOD 823, 824 (1982). Follow-up was done for most survivors at two years after birth, but researchers studied a few at only one year. Thus, the authors caution that more subtle mental or behavioral handicaps may become apparent in subsequent years. *Id.* at 827. *See also* Hirata, Epcar, Walsh, Mednick, Harris, McGinnis, Sehring & Papedo, *Survival and*

indication that the number of handicaps in infants is increasing and that new technology, which saves infants who otherwise would die and which causes various medical problems, may contribute to this phenomenon.[136]

Just as these improved survival rates have not come without some cost in terms of severely handicapped survivors, they also are not without substantial financial cost. Because of the continuous monitoring required for premature newborns, the large number of personnel necessary, and the highly technological nature of the treatments, neonatal intensive care is one of the most expensive types of medical treatment.[137] One study reports that, through the end of 1978, the cost to produce a survivor among infants weighing between 1000 and 1500 grams was $18,659 and that the cost to produce a survivor for infants weighing less than 1000 grams was $31,621.[138] Another study concludes that for infants weighing less than 1000 grams, the average cost to produce a survivor is $40,287.[139] The authors of this study caution that even this figure greatly underestimates the true cost because it does not include the costs of care to the infants who do not survive.[140] When these costs are taken into account, the figure increases to $61,641 per survivor. Moreover, since only seventy percent of the infants function normally upon follow-up, the authors state that the cost to produce a normal survivor is $88,058.[141] Based on any of these estimates, the conclusion is clear that neonatal intensive care is very costly.

Neonatal intensive care has dramatically altered the lower limits of viability. In 1973, a leading obstetrics text stated that infants generally were not viable below twenty-eight weeks of gestational age and 1000 grams of weight.[142] While this lower limit is clearly obsolete, it is not clear precisely what the lower limit is today. Some writers suggest that infants of less than 700 or 750 grams are, in general, not viable.[143] Studies which look at birth weight in conjunction with gestational age suggest that an infant born at twenty-five weeks or less of gestational age and weighing less than 750 grams has very little chance of survival.[144] Survival rates for even those infants weighing less than 750 grams are increasing, however, albeit much less rapidly than those for larger newborns. Some experts view the prospects for such infants with pessimism:

> During the past three years these "fetal-infants," born after only 23 to 26 weeks of gestation, have constituted 25 percent of babies admitted weigh-

---

Outcome of Infants 501-750 gms: A Six Year Experience, 102 J. PEDIATRICS 741 (1983) (survival rate of 36% with 6 of 18 observed survivors found to be moderately or severely neurologically impaired) [hereinafter cited as Hirata]; Rothberg, Maisels, Bagnato, Murphy, Gifford & McKinley, *Infants Weighing 1000 grams or Less at Birth,* 71 PEDIATRICS 599 (1983) (survival rate of 36%, with severe or moderate neurological deficits in 8 of 23 survivors weighing less than 1000 grams at birth).

[136] *Physical and Mental Disabilities in Newborns Doubled in 25 Years,* N.Y. Times, July 18, 1983, at A1, col. 4. For a moving and highly disturbing account of the way in which attempts to treat extremely premature infants can sometimes result in an unending series of painful and primarily iatrogenic conditions, see R. STINSON & P. STINSON, THE LONG DYING OF BABY ANDREW (1983).

[137] BUDETTI, *supra* note 102, at 19. Costs for neonatal care are similar to the cost of end stage renal disease and coronary bypass surgery. *Id.*

[138] *Id.* at 21.

[139] Pomerance, Ukrainski, Ukra, Henderson, Nash & Meredith, *Cost of Living for Infants Weighing 1,000 Grams or Less at Birth,* 61 PEDIATRICS 908, 909 (1978).

[140] *Id.* In this study, 30 of the 75 infants studied survived. *Id.*

[141] *Id.*

[142] WILLIAMS OBSTETRICS 493 (14th ed. 1973).

[143] Ross, *Mortality and Morbidity in Very Low Birth Weight Infants,* 12 PEDIATRIC ANNALS 32, 38 (1983) (generally infants weighing less than 700 grams at birth not viable). Mortality is nearly 100% for infants under 750 grams. PRESIDENT'S COMM'N, *supra* note 108, at 200.

[144] Philip, Little, Polivy & Lucey, *Neonatal Mortality Risk for the Eighties: The Importance of Birth Weight/Gestational Age Groups,* 68 PEDIATRICS 122, 124-25 (1981). A comprehensive study of viability published in 1975 found that no infant weighing 601 grams or less and born at a gestational age of 25 weeks or less had ever survived. Behrman & Rosen, *supra* note 4, at 12-9 app.

ing less than 1000 grams and almost 10 percent of all very-low-birth-weight infants. Despite great financial costs and major investments of personnel, time and technology, only meager (16 to 30 percent) survival rates are being achieved for such immature infants. It is unlikely that their prognosis will change until more effective means become available to extend their life in utero.[145]

A more recent study, however, reports a neonatal survival rate of forty-two percent for twenty-six infants weighing between 501 and 750 grams.[146] Moreover, an infant born at twenty-two weeks weighing 484 grams has recently survived.[147] Some writers even suggest that neonatal intensive care has so changed the limits of viability that it is arguable whether any lower limit of viability is valid.[148]

Thus, medical developments have dramatically altered the lower limits of viability since 1973, when *Roe v. Wade* was decided. Future developments could alter it even further. At present, fetal lung development is a limiting factor for neonatal survival because an infant whose lungs completely lack surfactant cannot survive. However, researchers are currently attempting to insert artificial surfactant into the lungs of extremely premature infants.[149] If such a technique becomes

feasible, viability could occur even earlier in the gestation period and the chances of an abortus being viable could become even greater than they are today. But even without such developments, a second-trimester abortion using prostaglandin or a combination of agents may well result in the birth of an infant who, if treated aggressively, can potentially survive.

SHOULD INFANTS BORN FROM ABORTIONS BE SAVED?

What should physicians do if a live infant is born from a late abortion? Views on this subject may vary according to one's stance on abortion: Opponents of abortion may stress the live-birth issue and argue that resuscitation is always required, while supporters of abortion may downplay this issue or argue that rescuing such an infant defeats the very purpose of an abortion attempt.[150] Views on this issue, however, need not depend on beliefs about the morality of abortion.[151] Writers on the abortion issue generally assume that removing the fetus from the womb will destroy it. But the very dilemma which the live-birth situation causes is that feticide has not occurred. Therefore, the fact of the abortion attempt may or may not be relevant to the decision how to proceed in live-birth situations.

A. Application of Guidelines to Infants Born From Abortions

Any infant born from a second-trimester abortion would most likely weigh 750 grams or less. Such extreme prematurity carries with it a more highly uncertain prognosis than that resulting from a number of birth defects. Certain defects, such as

---

[145]Hack, Fanaroff & Merkatz, *The Low Birth Weight Infant—Evolution of a Changing Concept,* 301 NEW ENG. J. MED. 1162, 1164 (1979). *See also* Bennett, Robinson & Sells, *Growth and Development of Infants Weighing Less than 800 Grams at Birth,* 71 PEDIATRICS 319 (1983) (mortality rate 80%).

[146]Orgill, *supra* note 135, at 823. *See also* Hirata, *supra* note 135, at 741 (survival rate of 36%).

[147]Wash. Post, Mar. 31, 1983, at A2, col. 2 Survival of another infant with an estimated gestational age of 22 to 23 weeks has been reported. *See* Long, *Supra* note 7.

[148]Campbell, *Which Infants Should Not Receive Intensive Care?,* 57 ARCHIVES OF DISEASE IN CHILDHOOD 569, 569 (1982).

[149]Fujiware, Maeta, Chida, Morita, Watabe & Abe, *Artificial Surfactant Therapy in Hyaline-Membrane Disease,* LANCET, Jan. 12, 1980, at 55. Researchers have isolated human lung surfactant from the amniotic fluid of term infants delivered by Cesarean section, and some believe that the human fetus may become a surfactant donor. Ismach, *supra* note 110, at 33.

[150]Wikler, *Ought We Try to Save Aborted Fetuses?,* 90 ETHICS 58, 58-59 (1979).

[151]*Id.* at 59.

Assessing viability *in utero* is very difficult, and estimations of gestational age may be inaccurate by as much as two weeks. Thus, even with the best attempt to assess gestational age, some pregnancies will be more advanced than expected, such that a fetus believed to be viable in fact may not be. When this occurs, a woman carrying a nonviable fetus will be wrongfully denied an abortion. According to King's proposal, if just one infant has survived at twenty-two weeks, the official time of viability moves to twenty-two weeks. Many women with twenty or twenty-one week pregnancies thus would be prevented from obtaining abortions.[188] Moreover, because the vast majority of fetuses the same age as the most recent miraculous survivor are not viable, such a proposal would deny abortions to a great many women with twenty-two-week pregnancies but nonviable fetuses. In setting the time of viability, we therefore should be medically realistic and not overly influenced by one or two miraculous survivals.

Numerous abortion decisions undoubtedly require this rule of reason regarding viability and technology. It is very likely that the *Roe* Court stated that fetuses were normally viable at twenty-eight weeks because the consensus of the medical profession indicated that forty to fifty percent of fetuses born at twenty-eight weeks survived.[189] The Court clearly was not seeking to protect fetuses with extremely remote chances of survival.[190] Moreover, in *Colautti v. Franklin,* the Court overturned a statute protecting fetuses that "may be viable" on the grounds that there must be a "reasonable likelihood" of "sustained survival

outside the womb."[191] Thus, *contra* King, viability must have its basis in the medical norm rather than in the medical miracle. As viability occurs earlier, states can prohibit abortion of fetuses reasonably likely to survive, but they should not be able to prohibit abortion of fetuses with only very remote chances of survival.

2. Regulation of Abortion Techniques

In postviability abortions, the state's interest in the fetus is compelling. The state constitutionally can require physicians to use the abortion technique least likely to harm the fetus, unless another technique is better for the woman's health.[192] Under *Colautti v. Franklin,* however, maternal health interests must prevail over the state's interest in the fetus.[193] Thus, a feticidal technique can be used if it is merely medically preferable; the state cannot require that use of a feticidal technique be limited to situations where

---

[188]If King's proposal to prohibit abortions of fetuses two weeks younger than the earliest verified survival were adopted, women with 18- or 19-week pregnancies also would be denied abortions.

[189]King, *supra* note 183 at 1679. *See generally* Behrman & Rosen, *supra* note 4, at 12-50-12-51 (charting survival rates between 1964 and 1974).

[190]*Roe,* 410 U.S. at 163 (stating that viability is point at which fetus "has the capability of *meaningful* life outside the mother's womb") (emphasis added).

[191]439 U.S. at 388. Similarly, in Charles v. Cary, 627 F.2d 772 (7th Cir. 1980), numerous provisions of Illinois' abortion statute were challenged, including one that provided that: "The law of this State shall not be construed to imply that any human being aborted alive is not an individual under the 'Criminal Code of 1961' . . . ." The court invalidated this section, stating:

> The meaning of the term 'alive' could include only the most minimal of life signs in a nonviable fetus or it could be limited to the capability of sustained survival. The lack of a precise definition leaves physicians uninformed as to their duties toward the fetus and could deter them from performing abortions for fear of being singled out for prosecution for murder under this ambiguous standard.

Id. at 791. A Nebraska abortion statute was likewise held unconstitutional on the grounds that the definition of viability must "be limited to include only that stage of fetal development in which the potentiality for life is more than mere momentary survival." Schulte v. Douglas, 567 F. Supp. 522, 524 (D. Neb. 1981).

[192]A section of a Missouri statute forbidding the use of abortion procedures fatal to the viable fetus unless alternative procedures posed a greater risk to the health of the woman was upheld in the lower court decision in Planned Parenthood Ass'n of Kansas City, Mo., Inc. v. Ashcroft, 655 F.2d 848, 862-63 (8th Cir. 1981). The Supreme Court similarly implied the constitutionality of this statute on review, 103 S. Ct. 2517, 2521 (1983).

[193]439 U.S. at 400 (1979).

such an abortion method is indispensable to the woman's health.[194]

A question that may arise is whether a technique more likely to be feticidal can be used only when the woman has specific contraindications to an alternative method which is less likely to be feticidal, or whether it can be used simply if it is the statistically safer method. At present, this question may be largely academic because there is little difference in the safety rates of saline and prostaglandin.[195] Yet, it may become important in the near future, if D & E is used one or two weeks later or viability occurs one or two weeks earlier, thereby permitting D & E, which is uniformly feticidal, to be used in postviability abortions.[196] If this occurs, it seems that it would violate the rights of pregnant women, and the medical judgment of physicians, to require that unless there are specific contraindications, a statistically more hazardous abortion procedure must be used so as to protect the fetus. Thus, if D & E becomes statistically safer for post-viability abortions, doctors should be permitted to use it, even if amnioinfusion methods pose no unusual hazard to the woman. Statutes which forbid feticidal procedures unless alternatives are more hazardous must be so construed to avoid usurping the legitimate exercise of medical judgment and subordinating the woman's health to that of the fetus.[197]

Although such statutes protecting the fetus *after* viability are constitutional, there is no doubt that they would be invalid if applied to fetuses *before* viability. Prior to viability, states can regulate abortion only to protect maternal health. Such is not, however, the aim of statutes prohibiting feticidal procedures before viability occurs. Moreover, the Supreme Court has given great weight to technological developments in abortion procedures.[198] Therefore, if D & E were to become the procedure of choice up to the point of viability, the Court should invalidate any regulation which prohibited or hindered its use.[199] Allowing D & E abortions during the period of possible viability may result in the death of a few fetuses that possibly could live. Yet, if feticidal methods must be allowed after viability if they are statistically safer for the woman, there is no doubt that they likewise must be allowed during the time when a physician, in his considered medical judgment, believes that a fetus is not viable.

The principle that states can regulate abortion techniques to protect the fetus after viability, but may not do so before viability, is premised upon a clear distinction between viable and nonviable fetuses and upon the use of viability as an ethical and analytical dividing line. As one can see, viability is not a bright dividing line, and its relevance is practical and symbolic, rather than

---

[194]*Id.* at 397-401.

[195]*See supra* notes 34 to 65 and accompanying text (discussing safety rates and possible complications of saline and prostaglandin abortions).

[196]As noted previously, D & E is being used later and later in pregnancy, with some physicians now using it through the twenty-fourth week. *See supra* notes 91 to 92 and accompanying text. Although the majority in *Ashcroft* expressed doubt that D & E would ever be the method safest for the woman after fetal viability, 103 S. Ct. 2517, 2521 n.7, this skepticism seems unwarranted in light of developments in medical technology. Moreover, the Court of Appeals had found that health reasons could sometimes require the use of D & E after viability. 665 F.2d 865.

[197]Supreme Court decisions such as *Colautti* and *City of Akron,* which emphasize the importance of maternal health concerns and physician discretion, mandate this conclusion. In

holding void for vagueness the postviability requirement that the physician use the least feticidal technique unless an alternative was necessary to preserve the mother's health, the Court in *Colautti* stated:

> [I]t is uncertain whether the statute permits the physician to consider his duty to the patient to be paramount to his duty to the fetus, or whether it requires the physician to make a 'tradeoff' between the woman's health and additional percentage points of fetal survival.

439 U.S. at 400. Likewise, in *City of Akron,* the Court emphasized that abortion is a medical procedure and that physicians must be allowed sufficient latitude to make their best medical judgments. 103 S. Ct. 2481, 2491 (1983).

[198]*See Ashcroft,* 103 S. Ct. at 2521-22 (discussing abortion techniques); *City of Akron,* 103 S. Ct. at 2493-97 (same).

[199]*See Danforth,* 428 U.S. at 77-78 (1976) (invalidating statute which appeared to ban second-trimester saline abortions).

moral. Moreover, as the time of viability shifts, third-trimester regulations inevitably have some impact on late second-trimester abortions. Thus, one must qualify these principles of state regulation.

Truly late abortions, in which the fetus is clearly viable, should be distinguished from those in which the fetus is merely on the threshold of viability. In the former situation, it is appropriate to use the technique best for the fetus unless another method is better for the woman. Such abortions will be performed only to protect the woman's life or health; indeed, feticide may not even be desired. In such abortions, fetuses are likely to be sufficiently developed that they can live without a high risk of serious handicap. Requiring the use of nonfeticidal techniques when the fetus is only at the threshold of viability, however, is a very different proposition. In this instance, there are implicit risks, including: (1) usurpation of medical judgment regarding whether the fetus is viable, causing physicians to feel threatened whenever they judge a borderline fetus not to be viable; (2) excessive restriction of medical discretion to use the method believed best, causing physicians to feel they must justify any use of a more feticidal method; and (3) creation of a situation which gives rise to an increase in the likelihood of a live birth from an abortion. As D & E is increasingly used for abortions of fetuses at the threshold of viability, courts should closely scrutinize any loosely worded regulations that could have a chilling effect on physicians' willingness to perform late second-trimester abortions or their choice of abortion procedure.[200]

3. A Special Problem Revisited: Genetic Abortions

If viability occurs before twenty-two weeks, state authority to protect viable fetuses may threaten genetic abortions. Because genetic abortions cannot be performed before week nineteen or twenty and are often performed around week twenty-two, they involve fetuses which are approaching the threshold of viability. Indeed, defects are sometimes diagnosed only after it is too late to terminate the pregnancy.[201]

The wholesale elimination of genetic abortions undoubtedly would be an unfortunate occurrence. Birth defects cause hardship and suffering to everyone involved.[202] The ability to diagnose such defects *in utero* has been hailed as a major medical advance. Yet some writers argue that under *Roe v. Wade,* we must simply accept the impending demise of genetic abortions. According to King:

> Whether one may kill a human, either because it will enjoy a quality of life below some minimal level or because its parents do not wish a severely handicapped child, is not a question peculiar to the use of viability as a standard. We should treat viable defective fetuses in the same way we treat defective newborns. The problem, in short, should be viewed as one of euthanasia and not one uniquely affecting legal protection of fetuses.[203]

Although defective abortuses must be treated like other defective newborns, it would be inap-

---

[200]This is precisely what the Supreme Court did in *Colautti,* where it held void for vagueness the postviability requirement that a physician use the abortion technique providing the best opportunity for the fetus to be aborted alive, so long as a different technique was not necessary to preserve the mother's life or health. 439 U.S. at 394-400. The Court noted that the choice of an appropriate abortion technique is a complex medical judgment about which experts can disagree and that the uncertainty of the Pennsylvania statute was further exacerbated by the lack of a scienter requirement, such

that criminal liability was possible even in the absence of bad faith on the physician's part. *Id.* at 398, 401. Likewise, in *Schulte v. Douglas,* the court invalidated an abortion statute on the grounds that the statute's broad wording and potential imposition of criminal liability "has had the chilling effect predicted by the court in *Colautti*—physicians are unwilling to perform abortions near the point of viability in the manner indicated by their best medical judgment." 567 F. Supp. at 528.

[201]Stubblefield interview, *supra* note 93.

[202]*See, e.g.,* Strong, *supra* note 170, at 168-69 (describing effect on families of severely handicapped children); Fost, *supra* note 169, at 321 (birth of child with severe defect experienced by parents as calamity).

[203]King, *supra* note 184, at 1686.

propriate to require that viable defective fetuses *in utero* be treated as if they already were independently existing newborns. The Supreme Court has stated that in determining whether an abortion is necessary to preserve a woman's health, a physician may consider emotional and psychological factors as well as strictly physical ones.[204] Even writers who deplore the thought that physicians can perform a postviability abortion to protect a woman's mental health nevertheless recognize that Supreme Court decisions and dicta require this result.[205] Although some state statutes still permit third-trimester abortions only to prevent death or "permanent impairment" to the woman's health,[206] and although some doctors who support abortion believe that they cannot lawfully perform genetic abortions after viability for mental health reasons,[207] there is a strong argument that genetic abortions should be allowed even after viability if continuing the pregnancy will cause a woman severe emotional anguish.

When a pregnant woman learns that her fetus is seriously defective, she is usually devastated. The hardship involved is exacerbated if she is forced to continue the pregnancy. Indeed, the physical hardships of pregnancy and labor normally are balanced against the joyous anticipation of birth. If a genetic defect has been diagnosed, the anticipation is destroyed and only hardship, sorrow, and anguish are left.[208] In arguing that a defective fetus once viable must be treated as if it has been born, King ignores these four months of anguish and treats abortion as truly equivalent to outright infanticide. Although in general we may conclude that by twenty-two or twenty-four weeks a woman has waived her right to abort, discovery of new, material facts regarding the fetus' genetic condition would seem to warrant granting the woman the right to avoid the anguish involved in bearing a severely defective child. Based on Supreme Court dicta, it is unlikely that the Court would allow states to deny this right to a woman whose mental health would suffer if forced to carry a defective fetus to term.[209] While the maternal health exception may preserve the right to genetic abortions in applicable cases, it is not the only reason the right should be sustained. One commentator notes that while most women carrying a severely defective fetus would be sufficiently upset by the diagnosis to qualify for a postviability abortion on mental health grounds, not all women would so qualify. Some women, although extremely unhappy about the situation, may be capable of coping.[210] If mental health is the only reason for treating genetic abortions differently, one should feel comfortable with forcing

---

[204]Doe v. Bolton, 410 U.S. 179, 192 (1973); United States v. Vuitch, 402 U.S. 62, 72 (1971).

[205]Wood & Hawkins, at 415-16 (discussing *Colautti, Doe v. Bolton,* and *Roe*). "State Regulation of Late Abortions and the Physician's Duty of Care to the Viable Fetus," 45 Mo. L. Rev. 394, (1980).

[206]*See* IND. CODE ANN. § 35-1-58.5-2 (Burns 1979) ("substantial permanent impairment of the life or physical health of the pregnant woman"); UTAH CODE ANN. § 76-7-302 (1978) ("serious and permanent damage"). There is little doubt that this requirement is unconstitutional. *See* Margaret S. v. Edwards, 488 F. Supp. 181, 196 (E.D. La. 1980) (Louisiana statute permitting postviability abortions only if necessary to prevent "permanent impairment" to the woman's health unconstitutional). *See also Schulte,* 566 F. Supp. at 525 (Nebraska statute permitting postviability abortions only when necessary to protect a woman "from an *imminent peril* that *substantially endangers* her life or health" unconstitutional) (emphasis in original).

[207]Dr. Phillip Stubblefield, President of the National Abortion Federation from 1982 until May 1984, states that although he would perform a very late abortion for a defect such as anencephaly, which is incompatible with life, he would not perform one for a defect such as Down's Syndrome much past 24 weeks, regardless of the woman's emotional anguish. Stubblefield interview, *supra* note 93.

[208]*See* Adler & Kushnick, *Genetic Counseling in Prenatally Diagnosed Trisomy 18 and 21: Psycho-Social Aspects,* 69 PEDIATRICS 94 (Jan. 1982) (describing parents' trauma at learning of prenatal diagnosis of chromosomal abnormality). This is not to imply that parents cannot derive much joy from raising a handicapped child, but is merely to note that the diagnosis produces serious trauma.

[209]Wood & Hawkins, *supra* note 205, at 415-16 (discussing *Vuitch, Colautti, Doe v. Bolton,* and *Roe*).

[210]*Survey of Abortion Law,* 1980 at Ariz. St. L.J. 67 148-49.

emotionally strong women to carry defective fetuses to term. Yet, this result seems wrong, and it demonstrates the need to preserve genetic abortions on other grounds.

Many foreign countries which allow abortions only up to a particular time make an exception for genetic abortions.[211] In fact, many countries forbid abortion in all circumstances except when the fetus is defective or the mother's life or health is threatened.[212] The basis for such an exception may be the anguish a woman feels at being forced to carry a defective fetus to term,[213] but the exception may also reflect a societal feeling that prevention of birth defects is a legitimate goal.[214] Surveys in the United States in addition show that the vast majority of Americans believe that abortion should be legal if there is a strong chance the fetus is defective.[215] This belief probably is not based solely, or even substantially, on concern for the woman's emotional well-being. Many people simply feel differently about

severely defective fetuses, even at twenty-two to twenty-four weeks, than they do about normal ones.

Widespread availability of methods to detect birth defects in the first trimester would quell much of the ambivalence characterizing the genetic abortion debate.[216] Yet, even if such a development lags behind further changes in the time of viability, the limited significance of viability, the mental anguish involved in forcing a woman to carry a defective fetus to term, and the general desire to prevent birth defects suggests that even if the general abortion right becomes more circumscribed, genetic abortions should be preserved.

4. Retaining the Balance: Establishing Lower Limits Having concluded that genetic abortions should be preserved, what should be the future of other second-trimester abortions? Given the rate of technological advancement, it is possible that in the not-too-distant future fetuses will be viable at around twenty-two weeks.[217] If this occurs, under *Roe* abortions after twenty-two weeks probably will be proscribed. But what if fetuses become viable even before this? Is there no limit to the potential narrowing of the abortion right?

The conclusion that the relevance of viability is practical and symbolic, but not moral, makes it clear that one need not retain the viability standard if it comes into conflict with ethical intuitions.

---

[211]Italy, for example, allows abortion only in the first trimester, but makes an exception for both maternal health risks and fetal defects. 29 INT'L DIG. HEALTH LEGIS 589-91 (1978). *See generally* TIETZE 1979, *supra* note 27, at 9-17 (surveying abortion laws and policies in foreign countries).

[212]*See generally* TIETZE 1979, *supra* note 27, at 15-17 (surveying abortion laws and policies in foreign countries).

[213]Some foreign statutes suggest a concern for the woman's emotional response to the defect, as well as concern for the child's condition. For example, the German Democratic Republic allows abortion until 22 weeks from conception if "imperative grounds exist for presuming that, as a consequence of a hereditary predisposition or harmful influences prior to birth, the child would suffer from irremedial injury to its state of health of such gravity that the pregnant woman *can not be required* to continue the pregnancy to term." TIETZE 1979, *supra* note 27, at 11 (quoting 27 INT'L DIG. HEALTH LEGIS. 562 (1976) (emphasis added).

[214]A statute of the United Kingdom simply states that abortion is permissible if "there is a substantial risk that if the child were born it would suffer from such physical or mental abnormalities as to be seriously handicapped." TIETZE 1979, *supra* note 27, at 10 (quoting 18 INT'L DIG. HEALTH LEGIS. 887 (1967)).

[215]Thompson, *Prenatal Diagnosis and Public Policy,* in GENETIC DISORDERS AND THE FETUS 637, 644 (A. Milunsky ed. 1979) (80% approval where there is strong chance of serious defect); National Opinion Research Center, *Limited Approval of Legal Abortion,* 4 CURRENT OPINION 18 (1976) (same).

[216]Chorionic villi biopsy, the method being tested for detecting genetic disorders in the first trimester, cannot detect neural tube defects such as anencephaly or spina bifida, because discovery of these requires analysis of the amniotic fluid, which can be done only after amniocentesis. Fleischman interview. . . . Thus even when this test becomes widely used, some genetic abortions will still be possible only after amniocentesis.

[217]*See supra* notes 142 to 148 and accompanying text (discussing medical determination of viability). However, some physicians feel that advances in neonatal intensive care are much more likely to improve the chances of saving infants born between 24 and 28 weeks and between 500 and 1000 grams than to make viable infants below these limits. Stubblefield interview, *supra* note 93.

Once viability occurs so early in pregnancy that D & E is the preferred abortion method, the practical import of viability will be lost. Once it occurs so early that it no longer demarcates "late" abortions, its symbolic import disappears as well. To cling to viability as the standard after its import vanishes is like religiously checking the water mark long after the well has run dry. In *City of Arkon,* the Supreme Court recognized that abortion later than week twelve is now safer than childbirth but nevertheless retained the trimester schema.[218] The Court's opinion thereby compels the conclusion that the trimester division was more important than the purported medical justifications for it. The Court likewise can retain the abortion right past the point of viability if viability occurs so early that prohibiting abortions at that point becomes unfair.[219]

This dividing line, of course, will be somewhat arbitrary. There is no escape from the fact that I am trying to make a division in the continuous, ongoing process of fetal development. No precise point is morally obvious, intuitive, or "right." If an exception is made for genetic abortions, the time need not be so late in the pregnancy term to accommodate genetic abortions.[220] With genetic abortions no longer a consideration, arguably there is no problem in following the viability standard wherever it leads; indeed, ninety percent of women who abort do so in the first trimester.[221] It is not unreasonable to expect women to have made this crucial moral decision

by week sixteen. Moreover, society may want to encourage women to abort early, because it is better for their health and more in keeping with society's moral sensibilities.

In an ideal world, permitting abortions up to fourteen or sixteen weeks and making an exception for genetic abortions might be a satisfactory policy, but in this society, the consequences of such restrictions would be unacceptable. To return to the scenario with which this article began, a poor, ill-educated teenager sought the late abortion. Teenagers make up a large proportion of women who seek second-trimester abortions,[221] and minority teenagers comprise a fairly substantial subset of that group.[223] Generally, well-educated women in their twenties and thirties, i.e., women who have regular menstrual periods, are not extremely obese, and do not have a psychological problem causing them to deny their pregnancy, will seek diagnosis of pregnancy and, if they so desire, abort as soon as possible. In contrast, women who have second-trimester abortions often are not in as fortunate a position. Irregular periods, unfamiliarity with their bodies, ignorance about sex, and fear of adults may make even advantaged teenagers overlook or deny pregnancy or delay the decision to abort. Even Sweden, which lacks the extremes of wealth and poverty prevalent in this country, has a second-trimester abortion rate of approximately six percent.[224] When youth is coupled with poverty, poor education, a disrupted family structure, poor nutrition, mistrust of doctors, or inadequate access to medical care, society's choices are to allow late abortions or to force these teenagers to continue unwanted and dangerous pregnancies.[225] Is it fair

---

[218]103 S. Ct. at 2492 n. 11.

[219]The only obstacle to the Court doing this is its repeated assertion that viability is the critical point, *see, e.g., Colautti,* 439 U.S. at 388-89, and its willingness to imply that viability has independent moral significance apart from its demarcation of late abortions from early or midpregnancy ones. But surely the Court's adherence to the balance it found constitutionally required should run deeper than its reliance on statistical medical concepts that, in 1973, simply helped to establish this balance.

[220]*See supra* notes 284 to 291 and accompanying text (discussing amniocentesis technique). [Not here included.]

[221]*See supra* note 27 and accompanying text (discussing percentage of abortions performed after 13 weeks).

---

[222]*See supra* notes 2, 31, and 32 and accompanying text (discussing women who seek late abortions).

[223]Kerenyi interview, *supra* note 2; Stubblefield interview, *supra* note 93.

[224]*See* Schulman, *Second Trimester Abortion: Techniques and Complications,* in GYNECOLOGY AND OBSTETRICS 1 (J. Sciarra ed. 1982).

[225]Pregnancy is more dangerous for teenagers and more likely to result in a low birthweight infant. Paneth, Kiely, Wallenstein, Marcus, Patker & Susser, *Newborn Intensive Care and*

to tell the teenager in the scenario that she must act exactly like a mature, middle-class woman? Allowing states to prohibit abortion at week sixteen would ignore the actual societal conditions in this country and would impose a "higher morality" on a peculiarly vulnerable group which will inevitably be unable to live up to middle-class expectations.[226] Moreover, this group is least prepared to raise children.

Given the difficulties in assessing gestational age, if the time is set at eighteen weeks, many women with sixteen-week pregnancies will be denied abortion.[227] Therefore, no matter how early viability occurs, a reasonable point before which abortions should not be prohibited is twenty weeks. Very few fetuses born before twenty weeks show signs of life. Moreover, D & E is now the most common abortion method in the interval between sixteen and twenty weeks. As its use increases during this interval, the chance of live births will decrease even further. Twenty weeks also marks the midpoint of pregnancy,[228] so that "early" abortions can be divided from "late" ones at the midpoint of fetal development, should viability grow so early that we must find a substitute for the viability standard.[229] Even a twenty-week cutoff will deny abortions to some poverty-stricken and terrified teenagers,[230] and therefore, arguably twenty-two weeks should be the cutoff instead.[231] This standard, too, could be feasible if D & E were commonly used up to that time so as to avoid the live-birth dilemma. Whatever time is ultimately chosen, given the population that seeks late abortions, the Court certainly should never permit states to proscribe abortions prior to twenty weeks.[232]

CONCLUSION

The fact that an infant was born from an abortion is not relevant to the decision whether to resuscitate and treat it. Thus, doctors will at least

---

Neonatal Mortality in Low-Birth-Weight Infants, 307 NEW ENG. J. MED. 149, 150 (1982). Moreover, it has also been noted that the risks inherent in pregnancy are even greater than usual when the pregnancy is unwanted. Cates, *Legal Abortion: The Public Health Record,* 215 SCI. 1586, 1587 (1982).

[226]State restrictions on Medicaid funding of abortions produce essentially the same effect and yet have been held constitutional. *See* Maher v. Roe, 432 U.S. 464 (1977) (upholding Connecticut statute denying Medicaid funds for first-trimester abortions not medically necessary); Harris v. McRae, 448 U.S. 297 (1980) (holding states not required to fund certain medically necessary abortions where federal statute denies Medicaid funds). An early cutoff date clearly would be an outright infringement of the abortion right, however, rather than a mere refusal to provide state funding for it.

[227]*See supra* notes 337 and 338 and accompanying text (discussing use of ultrasonic scanning to determine fetal age). [Not here included.]

[228]Pregnancy duration is most commonly measured from the last menstrual period, making the average pregnancy last 40 weeks. *See supra* note 4 (discussing methods of calculating duration of pregnancy).

---

[229]Because I have been quoted as simply advocating a 20-week cutoff, Kleiman, *supra* note 7, I must emphasize that I am not proposing a firm cutoff of 20 or 22 weeks be adopted immediately. Rather, my argument is that *if* viability grows so early that it no longer supports the balance between the woman's right and the state's interest in the fetus established in *Roe,* the balance should be retained and the viability standard abandoned. Then, and only then, will a firm cutoff have to be selected. Moreover, I do not advocate that 20 weeks necessarily be selected: rather, I simply believe that whatever cutoff is chosen, it definitely should not be any earlier than the twentieth week.

[230]Dr. Phillip Stubblefield does not perform abortions past 22½ weeks and states that he sometimes refers teenagers with more advanced pregnancies to New York City, where abortions will be performed until 24 weeks. Many such teenagers cannot afford to go. Stubblefield interview, *supra* note 93. Because this cutoff denies some teenagers abortions, it is clear that a 20-week cutoff would deny abortions to even more teenagers who are ill equipped to cope with either pregnancy or motherhood. As viability grows earlier, it will become even more important to ensure that teenagers and the poor have ready access to early abortions and are informed of their availability. *See* Kleiman, *supra* note 7.

[231]This later cutoff would have the advantage of denying abortions to a smaller number of women. According to Center for Disease Control statistics, in 1980 only 0.9% of women obtained abortions at 21 weeks or later. CDC, *1979-80 Report, supra* note 27, at 64.

[232]A firm cutoff also will establish a higher degree of certainty for physicians, who under current standards could well be confused about their legal obligation. In fact, one physician

occasionally have an obligation to treat viable live-born abortuses. If we accept the recommendations of the President's Commission regarding treatment decisions, infants so premature that they are at the threshold of viability would be in the category where reasonable parental wishes should be respected. Because infants born from abortions, if viable at all, often will be in this borderline category, decisions not to treat frequently will be ethically acceptable, even though ethics committee review is probably still in order. When treatment is clearly in the infant's best interests, though, parental refusal must be overridden. Treating infants born from abortions is not a particularly satisfying solution to the live-birth dilemma. The ambivalence it reflects has been compared to that involved in requiring medical aid to be given a condemned man injured in a failed execution attempt.[233] Yet, in the few instances where the infant clearly can live, even with some degree of mental or physical handicap, treatment may be the only ethical resolution of the dilemma.

As viability occurs earlier, strict adherence to the viability standard would render the future of second-trimester abortions increasingly grim. We can neither ignore the live-birth dilemma nor pretend that the point of viability lacks practical or symbolic significance. Nevertheless, D & E could eliminate viability's practical import by ensuring no live births; and once viability no longer distinguishes late abortions from early or midpregnancy ones, its symbolic import vanishes as well. It then becomes a dividing line that is both arbitrary and unreasonable. If this occurs, we must abandon the viability standard and choose a cutoff which does not permit live births, but which also does not deny second-trimester abortions to the group most in need of them. If viability grows much earlier, a firm cutoff point will become necessary in order to uphold women's rights to privacy and autonomy and to prevent *Roe v. Wade* from becoming a decision that protects fetuses but not women.

who is greatly concerned about abortion rights stated that he might favor a simple temporal cutoff, because it could avoid the problems of assessing fetal viability and risking a live birth. Stubblefield interview, *supra* note 93.

[233]Robertson, *After Edelin: Little Guidance,* 7 HASTINGS CENTER REP., 15, 17 (June 1977).

On the Moral and Legal Status of Abortion, with Postscript on Infanticide

Mary Anne Warren

Mary Ann Warren studied philosophy at U.C. Berkeley and Harvard and currently teaches at San Francisco State University. She has published on such contemporary moral issues as abortion, affirmative action, animal rights, and the new reproductive technologies. Her books include The Nature of Woman *(Edgepress, 1980) and* Gendercide: The Implications of Sex Selection *(Littlefield, Adams, 1985).*

Warren defends a liberal position on abortion. She argues that fetuses are not persons because they exemplify none of the defining characteristics of personhood. They are not conscious, not capable of reasoning, do not engage in self-motivated activity, cannot communicate linguistically, and do not have a concept of self.

Warren holds that "any being that satisfies none of [these traits] is not a person." In her "Postscript on Infanticide," she argues that her liberal position does not commit her to allowing infanticide because, even if they are not persons, newborn infants are very close to being persons and they are wanted by other people who wish to adopt them or strongly prefer their preservation. Also, after delivery, the right of the mother to protect her life and health are no longer jeopardized by the existence of the infant.

The question which we must answer in order to produce a satisfactory solution to the problem of the moral status of abortion is this: How are we to define the moral community, the set of beings with full and equal moral rights, such that we can decide whether a human fetus is a member of this community or not? What sort of entity, exactly, has the inalienable rights to life, liberty, and the pursuit of happiness? Jefferson attributed these rights to all *men,* and it may or may not be fair to suggest that he intended to attribute them *only* to men. Perhaps he ought to have attributed them to all human beings. If so, then we arrive, first, at Noonan's problem of defining what makes a being human, and, second, at the equally vital question which Noonan does not consider, namely, What reason is there for identifying the moral community with the set of all human beings, in whatever way we have chosen to define that term?

1. ON THE DEFINITION OF "HUMAN"

One reason why this vital second question is so frequently overlooked in the debate over the moral status of abortion is that the term 'human' has two distinct, but not often distinguished, senses. This fact results in a slide of meaning, which serves to conceal the fallaciousness of the traditional argument that since (1) it is wrong to kill innocent human beings, and (2) fetuses are

Reprinted by permission of the author and publisher from *The Monist,* vol. 57, no. 1 (January 1973). "Postscript on Abortion" used with permission of the author and publisher from Joel Feinberg, ed., *The Problem of Abortion,* 2nd ed. (Belmont, Calif.: Wadsworth, 1984). © 1984 by Wadsworth Publishing Company.

innocent human beings, then (3) it is wrong to kill fetuses. For if 'human' is used in the same sense in both (1) and (2) then, whichever of the two senses is meant, one of these premises is question-begging. And if it is used in two different senses then of course the conclusion doesn't follow.

Thus, (1) is a self-evident moral truth,[1] and avoids begging the question about abortion, only if 'human being' is used to mean something like 'a full-fledged member of the moral community.' (It may or may not also be meant to refer exclusively to members of the species *Homo sapiens.*) We may call this the *moral* sense of 'human.' It is not to be confused with what we will call the *genetic* sense, i.e., the sense in which *any* member of the species is a human being, and no member of any other species could be. If (1) is acceptable only if the moral sense is intended, (2) is non-question-begging only if what is intended is the genetic sense.

In "Deciding Who is Human," Noonan argues for the classification of fetuses with human beings by pointing to the presence of the full genetic code, and the potential capacity for rational thought.[2] It is clear that what he needs to show, for his version of the traditional argument to be valid, is that fetuses are human in the moral sense, the sense in which it is analytically true that all human beings have full moral rights. But, in the absence of any argument showing that whatever is genetically human is also morally human, and he gives none, nothing more than genetic humanity can be demonstrated by the presence of the human genetic code. And, as we will see, the *potential* capacity for rational thought can at most show that an entity has the potential for *becoming* human in the moral sense.

2. DEFINING THE MORAL COMMUNITY

Can it be established that genetic humanity is sufficient for moral humanity? I think that there are very good reasons for not defining the moral community in this way. I would like to suggest an alternative way of defining the moral community, which I will argue for only to the extent of explaining why it is, or should be, self-evident. The suggestion is simply that the moral community consists of all and only *people*, rather than all and only human beings,[3] and probably the best way of demonstrating its self-evidence is by considering the concept of personhood, to see what sorts of entity are and are not persons, and what the decision that a being is or is not a person implies about its moral rights.

What characteristics entitle an entity to be considered a person? This is obviously not the place to attempt a complete analysis of the concept of personhood, but we do not need such a fully adequate analysis just to determine whether and why a fetus is or isn't a person. All we need is a rough and approximate list of the most basic criteria of personhood, and some idea of which, or how many, of these an entity must satisfy in order to properly be considered a person.

In searching for such criteria, it is useful to look beyond the set of people with whom we are acquainted, and ask how we would decide whether a totally alien being was a person or not. (For we have no right to assume that genetic humanity is necessary for personhood.) Image a space traveler who lands on an unknown planet and encounters a race of beings utterly unlike any he has ever seen or heard of. If he wants to be sure of behaving morally toward these beings, he has to somehow decide whether they are people, and hence have full moral rights, or whether they are the sort of thing which he need not feel guilty about treating as, for example, a source of food.

How should he go about making this deci-

sion? If he has some anthropological background, he might look for such things as religion, art, and the manufacturing of tools, weapons, or shelters, since these factors have been used to distinguish our human from our prehuman ancestors, in what seems to be closer to the moral than the genetic sense of 'human.' And no doubt he would be right to consider the presence of such factors as good evidence that the alien beings were people, and morally human. It would, however, be overly anthropocentric of him to take the absence of these things as adequate evidence that they were not, since we can imagine people who have progressed beyond, or evolved without ever developing, these cultural characteristics.

I suggest that the traits which are most central to the concept of personhood, or humanity in the moral sense, are, very roughly, the following:

1. Consciousness (of objects and events external and/or internal to the being), and in particular the capacity to feel pain;

2. Reasoning (the *developed* capacity to solve new and relatively complex problems);

3. Self-motivated activity (activity which is relatively independent of either genetic or direct external control);

4. The capacity to communicate, by whatever means, messages of an indefinite variety of types, that is, not just with an indefinite number of possible contents, but on indefinitely many possible topics;

5. The presence of self-concepts, and self-awareness, either individual or racial, or both.

Admittedly, there are apt to be a great many problems involved in formulating precise definitions of these criteria, let alone in developing universally valid behavioral criteria for deciding when they apply. But I will assume that both we and our explorer know approximately what (1)–(5) mean, and that he is also able to determine whether or not they apply. How, then,

should he use his findings to decide whether or not the alien beings are people? We needn't suppose that an entity must have *all* of these attributes to be properly considered a person; (1) and (2) alone may well be sufficient for personhood, and quite probably (1)–(3) are sufficient. Neither do we need to insist that any one of these criteria is *necessary* for personhood, although once again (1) and (2) look like fairly good candidates for necessary conditions, as does (3), if 'activity' is construed so as to include the activity of reasoning.

All we need to claim, to demonstrate that a fetus is not a person, is that any being which satisfies *none* of (1)–(5) is certainly not a person. I consider this claim to be so obvious that I think anyone who denied it, and claimed that a being which satisfied none of (1)–(5) was a person all the same, would thereby demonstrate that he had no notion at all of what a person is—perhaps because he had confused the concept of a person with that of genetic humanity. If the opponents of abortion were to deny the appropriateness of these five criteria, I do not know what further arguments would convince them. We would probably have to admit that our conceptual schemes were indeed irreconcilably different, and that our dispute could not be settled objectively.

I do not expect this to happen, however, since I think that the concept of a person is one which is very nearly universal (to people), and that it is common to both proabortionists and antiabortionists, even though neither group has fully realized the relevance of this concept to the resolution of their dispute. Furthermore, I think that on reflection even the antiabortionists ought to agree not only that (1)–(5) are central to the concept of personhood, but also that it is a part of this concept that all and only people have full moral rights. The concept of a person is in part a moral concept; once we have admitted that *x* is a person we have recognized, even if we have not agreed to respect, *x*'s right to be treated as a member of the moral community. It is true that the claim that *x* is a *human being* is more commonly voiced as part of an appeal to treat *x* decently than is the claim that *x* is a person, but this is either because 'human being' is here used in the sense which implies personhood, or because the genetic and moral sense of 'human' have been confused.

Now if (1)–(5) are indeed the primary criteria of personhood, then it is clear that genetic humanity is neither necessary nor sufficient for establishing that an entity is a person. Some human beings are not people, and there may well be people who are not human beings. A man or woman whose consciousness has been permanently obliterated but who remains alive is a human being which is no longer a person; defective human beings, with no appreciable mental capacity, are not and presumably never will be people; and a fetus is a human being which is not yet a person, and which therefore cannot coherently be said to have full moral rights. Citizens of the next century should be prepared to recognize highly advanced, self-aware robots or computers, should such be developed, and intelligent inhabitants of other worlds, should such be found, as people in the fullest sense, and to respect their moral rights. But to ascribe full moral rights to an entity which is not a person is as absurd as to ascribe moral obligations and responsibilities to such an entity.

3. FETAL DEVELOPMENT AND THE RIGHT TO LIFE

Two problems arise in the application of these suggestions for the definition of the moral community to the determination of the precise moral status of a human fetus. Given that the paradigm example of a person is a normal adult human being, then (1) How like this paradigm, in particular how far advanced since conception, does a human being need to be before it begins to have a right to life by virtue, not of being fully a person as of yet, but of being *like* a person? and (2) To what extent, if any, does the fact that a fetus has the *potential* for becoming a person endow it with

some of the same rights? Each of these questions requires some comment.

In answering the first question, we need not attempt a detailed consideration of the moral rights of organisms which are not developed enough, aware enough, intelligent enough, etc., to be considered people, but which resemble people in some respects. It does seem reasonable to suggest that the more like a person, in the relevant respects, a being is, the stronger is the case for regarding it as having a right to life, and indeed the stronger its right to life is. Thus we ought to take seriously the suggestion that, insofar as "the human individual develops biologically in a continuous fashion . . . the rights of a human person might develop in the same way."[4] But we must keep in mind that the attributes which are relevant in determining whether or not an entity is enough like a person to be regarded as having some of the same moral rights are no different from those which are relevant to determining whether or not it is fully a person—i.e., are no different from (1)–(5)—and that being genetically human, or having recognizable human facial and other physical features, or detectable brain activity, or the capacity to survive outside the uterus, are simply not among these relevant attributes.

Thus it is clear that even though a seven- or eight-month fetus has features which make it apt to arouse in us almost the same powerful protective instinct as is commonly aroused by a small infant, nevertheless it is not significantly more personlike than is a very small embryo. It is *somewhat* more personlike; it can apparently feel and respond to pain, and it may even have a rudimentary form of consciousness, insofar as its brain is quite active. Nevertheless, it seems safe to say that it is not fully conscious, in the way that an infant of a few months is, and that it cannot reason, or communicate messages of indefinitely many sorts, does not engage in self-motivated activity, and has no self-awareness. Thus, in the *relevant* respects, a fetus, even a fully developed one, is considerably less personlike than is the average

mature mammal, indeed the average fish. And I think that a rational person must conclude that if the right to life of a fetus is to be based upon its resemblance to a person, then it cannot be said to have any more right to life than, let us say, a newborn guppy (which also seems to be capable of feeling pain), and that a right of that magnitude could never override a woman's right to obtain an abortion, at any stage of her pregnancy.

There may, of course, be other arguments in favor of placing legal limits upon the stage of pregnancy in which an abortion may be performed. Given the relative safety of the new techniques of artificially inducing labor during the third trimester, the danger to the woman's life or health is no longer such an argument. Neither is the fact that people tend to respond to the thought of abortion in the later stages of pregnancy with emotional repulsion, since mere emotional responses cannot take the place of moral reasoning in determining what ought to be permitted. Nor, finally, is the frequently heard argument that legalizing abortion, especially late in the pregnancy, may erode the level of respect for human life, leading, perhaps, to an increase in unjustified euthanasia and other crimes. For this threat, if it is a threat, can be better met by educating people to the kinds of moral distinctions which we are making here than by limiting access to abortion (which limitation may, in its disregard for the rights of women, be just as damaging to the level of respect for human rights).

Thus, since the fact that even a fully developed fetus is not personlike enough to have any significant right to life on the basis of its personlikeness shows that no legal restrictions upon the stage of pregnancy in which an abortion may be performed can be justified on the grounds that we should protect the rights of the older fetus; and since there is no other apparent justification for such restrictions, we may conclude that they are entirely unjustified. Whether or not it would be *indecent* (whatever that means) for a woman in her seventh month to obtain an abortion just to avoid having to postpone a trip to Europe, it

would not, in itself, be *immoral,* and therefore it ought to be permitted.

4. POTENTIAL PERSONHOOD AND THE RIGHT TO LIFE

We have seen that a fetus does not resemble a person in any way which can support the claim that it has even some of the same rights. But what about its *potential,* the fact that if nurtured and allowed to develop naturally it will very probably become a person? Doesn't that alone give it at least some right to life? It is hard to deny that the fact that an entity is a potential person is a strong prima facie reason for not destroying it; but we need not conclude from this that a potential person has a right to life, by virtue of that potential. It may be that our feeling that it is better, other things being equal, not to destroy a potential person is better explained by the fact that potential people are still (felt to be) an invaluable resource, not to be lightly squandered. Surely, if every speck of dust were a potential person, we would be much less apt to conclude that every potential person has a right to become actual.

Still, we do not need to insist that a potential person has no right to life whatever. There may well be something immoral, and not just imprudent, about wantonly destroying potential people, when doing so isn't necessary to protect anyone's rights. But even if a potential person does have some prima facie right to life, such a right could not possibly outweigh the right of a woman to obtain an abortion, since the rights of any actual person invariably outweigh those of any potential person, whenever the two conflict. Since this may not be immediately obvious in the case of a human fetus, let us look at another case.

Suppose that our space explorer falls into the hands of an alien culture, whose scientists decide to create a few hundred thousand or more human beings, by breaking his body into its component cells, and using these to create fully developed human beings, with, of course, his genetic code.

We may imagine that each of these newly created men will have all of the original man's abilities, skills, knowledge, and so on, and also have an individual self-concept, in short that each of them will be a bona fide (though hardly unique) person. Imagine that the whole project will take only seconds, and that its chances of success are extremely high, and that our explorer knows all of this, and also knows that these people will be treated fairly. I maintain that in such a situation he would have every right to escape if he could, and thus to deprive all of these potential people of their potential lives; for his right to life outweighs all of theirs together, in spite of the fact that they are all genetically human, all innocent, and all have a very high probability of becoming people very soon, if only he refrains from acting.

Indeed, I think he would have a right to escape even if it were not his life which the alien scientists planned to take, but only a year of his freedom, or, indeed, only a day. Nor would he be obligated to stay if he had gotten captured (thus bringing all these people-potentials into existence) because of his own carelessness, or even if he had done so deliberately, knowing the consequences. Regardless of how he got captured, he is not morally obligated to remain in captivity for *any* period of time for the sake of permitting any number of potential people to come into actuality, so great is the margin by which one actual person's right to liberty outweighs whatever right to life even a hundred thousand potential people have. And it seems reasonable to conclude that the rights of a woman will outweigh by a similar margin whatever right to life a fetus may have by virtue of its potential personhood.

Thus, neither a fetus's resemblance to a person, nor its potential for becoming a person provides any basis whatever for the claim that it has any significant right to life. Consequently, a woman's right to protect her health, happiness, freedom, and even her life,[5] by terminating an unwanted pregnancy, will always override whatever right to life it may be appropriate to ascribe to a fetus, even a fully developed one. And thus, in the

absence of any overwhelming social need for every possible child, the laws which restrict the right to obtain an abortion, or limit the period of pregnancy during which an abortion may be performed, are a wholly unjustified violation of a woman's most basic moral and constitutional rights.[6]

POSTSCRIPT ON INFANTICIDE, FEBRUARY 26, 1982

One of the most troubling objections to the argument presented in this article is that it may appear to justify not only abortion but infanticide as well. A newborn infant is not a great deal more person-like than a nine-month fetus, and thus it might seem that if late-term abortion is sometimes justified, then infanticide must also be sometimes justified. Yet most people consider that infanticide is a form of murder, and thus never justified.

While it is important to appreciate the emotional force of this objection, its logical force is far less than it may seem at first glance. There are many reasons why infanticide is much more difficult to justify than abortion, even though if my argument is correct neither constitutes the killing of a person. In this country, and in this period of history, the deliberate killing of viable newborns is virtually never justified. This is in part because neonates are so very *close* to being persons that to kill them requires a very strong moral justification—as does the killing of dolphins, whales, chimpanzees, and other highly personlike creatures. It is certainly wrong to kill such beings just for the sake of convenience, or financial profit, or "sport."

Another reason why infanticide is usually wrong, in our society, is that if the newborn's parents do not want it, or are unable to care for it, there are (in most cases) people who are able and eager to adopt it and to provide a good home for it. Many people wait years for the opportunity to adopt a child, and some are unable to do so even

though there is every reason to believe that they would be good parents. The needless destruction of a viable infant inevitably deprives some person or persons of a source of great pleasure and satisfaction, perhaps severely impoverishing their lives. Furthermore, even if an infant is considered to be unadoptable (e.g., because of some extremely severe mental or physical handicap) it is still wrong in most cases to kill it. For most of us value the lives of infants, and would prefer to pay taxes to support orphanages and state institutions for the handicapped rather than to allow unwanted infants to be killed. So long as most people feel this way, and so long as our society can afford to provide care for infants which are unwanted or which have special needs that preclude home care, it is wrong to destroy any infant which has a chance of living a reasonably satisfactory life.

If these arguments show that infanticide is wrong, at least in this society, then why don't they also show that late-term abortion is wrong? After all, third trimester fetuses are also highly personlike, and many people value them and would much prefer that they be preserved; even at some cost to themselves. As a potential source of pleasure to some family, a viable fetus is just as valuable as a viable infant. But there is an obvious and crucial difference between the two cases: once the infant is born, its continued life cannot (except, perhaps, in very exceptional cases) pose any serious threat to the woman's life or health, since she is free to put it up for adoption, or, where this is impossible, to place it in a state-supported institution. While she might prefer that it die, rather than being raised by others, it is not clear that such a preference would constitute a right on her part. True, she may suffer greatly from the knowledge that her child will be thrown into the lottery of the adoption system, and that she will be unable to ensure its well-being, or even to know whether it is healthy, happy, doing well in school, etc.: for the law generally does not permit natural parents to remain in contact with their children, once they are adopted by another family. But there

The conferral approach to the status of the fetus is not an unusual one,[12] though it is sometimes thought incompatible with an approach that asserts an inherent claim in the fetus itself. But an approach that *confers* claims rubs an approach that *recognizes* inherent claims only if the inherent claim to life is thought to be as serious as an actual person's claim to life. In this case it would be futile (rather than contradictory) to ask what claims society ought to confer on it. However, when the recognized inherent claim is weaker than a normal adult's claim to life, as can be the case with the potentiality principle, one can coherently ask whether society ought, in addition, to confer on the fetus a stronger claim to life.

The argument in favor of such a conferral basically appeals to the social consequences of abortions and infanticide. For example, infants are so similar to persons that allowing them to be killed would generate a moral climate that would endanger the claim to life of even young persons. And older fetuses are so similar to infants that allowing them to be killed without due moral or legal process would endanger infants. Of course there must be a cutoff for this sort of argument. For example, most would agree that preventing the implantation of zygotes would have no discernible effect on our sympathetic capacities toward persons. At what point would abortions begin to have such effects, especially on medical personnel, that it is in society's interest to endow the fetus at that point with a stronger claim to life? This seems largely an empirical question and one not easily answered,[13] though I will suggest some guidelines below.

One difficulty with the conferral approach has always been that the relevant considerations are the interest and sympathies of actual persons, rather than moral claims inherent in the fetus itself. Indeed, the above argument is reminiscent of Kant's view that we ought not beat our dogs merely because beating our dogs might make us more inclined to beat people. Such arguments derive protection for some beings from the rather variable, even capricious, sympathies of other beings. Thus the conferral approach by itself does not account for the belief that something about the fetus itself makes abortion morally problematic; but this belief is accounted for by the potentiality approach.

IMPLANTATION, QUICKENING, VIABILITY, AND BIRTH

My combined approach escapes the problematic implications of the extremes but does it escape the flaw of arbitrary line-drawing that I attributed to those moderate positions that appeal to the stage or "magic moment" approach? Two related considerations show that it does. First, notice that the word "arbitrary" should not be used loosely. For example, there is a certain arbitrariness in making eighteen the age of majority rather than seventeen or nineteen. But the relevant criteria nonarbitrarily imply that, if a legally precise line must be drawn within the continuum of growth, the debate must focus on that time span rather than, say, the span between seven and nine.

Second, I submit that the two criteria I use—important shifts in probabilities and dangerous social consequences—nonarbitrarily suggest four spans (beyond that of conception) for moral and legal line-drawing in a potential person's continuum of growth. Although these criteria imply distinct spans for definite increments in the strength of the claim to life, at no stage does a potential person move from having no claim to having one as strong as an adult.

The first span, as we saw, is that of implantation, when the shift in probabilities of actual personhood signifies a somewhat stronger inherent claim to life, at least from the moral point of view. The recognition of this change is due apart from any consequentialist considerations about the difference between more or less unknowingly preventing implantation and knowingly detaching an implanted embryo. However, the remaining spans are suggested by consequentialist considerations about the psychological and social impact of abortions, considerations in favor of conferring an even stronger claim to life on the fetus.

The second span involves the traditional indicator of "quickening." When the fetus begins making perceptible spontaneous movements (around the beginning of the second trimester), its shape, its behavior, and even its beginning relationship with the mother and the rest of society (every father recalls when he first felt the fetus's movements) all suggest that abortions after this point will have personal and social consequences specifiably more serious than those of earlier abortions.

The third is that of viability, when a fetus is capable of living, with simple medical care, outside the womb (around the end of the second trimester). Recall the "infanticide" trials of physicians who, claiming they were inducing abortions, were charged with participating in premature births and murders. This controversy is only one indication that killing potential persons after viability has social consequences (apart from legal ones) even more serious than abortions soon after quickening.

Finally, consider that allowing infanticide is generally regarded as a *reductio* of those positions that allow it. The aversion to infanticide is shared even by most of those whose criteria for personhood imply that a newborn is still only a potential person and not an actual one. This suggests that most people agree that at birth the potential person attains properties and relationships so close to those of actual persons that the consequences of killing at this point are practically the same as killing young persons.

If these observations are true, they justify conferring on newborns a claim to life as strong as that of adult persons. They also suggest partial wisdom in the Supreme Court's decision allowing states to grant a rather strong claim to life to post-viable fetuses, a claim overridden only by the claim to life or health (I would specify "physical health") of the mother. But the court decision, in effect, mandates the allowing of abortion on demand for all previable fetuses. If my observations about quickening are correct, we should also draw an earlier line, conferring a claim to life on the fetus at the beginning of the second trimester, a claim less strong than that conferred at viability, but one overridden only by such serious claims as that of the mother to mental or physical health.[14] Probably the moral line drawn at implantation should remain outside the legal realm.

I admit the difficulties in legally implementing such an approach, but I doubt that they are insurmountable or as deep as the moral and legal difficulties of alternative approaches. Therefore I believe I have presented a plausible approach to the abortion issue that is coherent, is not arbitrary, and listens well to the considered intuitions of those in the middle.[15]

References

[1]Roger Wertheimer, "Philosophy on Humanity," in *Abortion: Pro and Con,* ed. Robert L. Perkins (Cambridge: Schenkman Publishing Company), p. 127.

[2]For brevity I use "fetus" in a generic sense to refer to unborn humans at any stage of development, including that of zygote, conceptus, and embryo. I assume the fetuses are human beings, genetically defined, and use "person" to refer to those human beings that have as strong a claim to life as a normal adult. I use "as strong a claim" rather than "same claim" because, if very young human beings are persons, their claim to life clearly involves the claim to be nurtured as well as the claim not to be killed, a feature that is not clearly true of a normal adult's claim to life. I use "claim" to life rather than "right" or "prima facie right" because my argument entails that a fetus's (though not a person's) claim to life can be held with varying degrees of strength, and I agree with Joel Feinberg (*Social Philosophy* [Englewood Cliffs: Prentice Hall, 1973], pp. 64-7) that this is a feature of claims rather than rights. Though Feinberg may object to my use of his distinction, I agree with him that the "right" or "valid claim" in a given instance is the strongest of competing claims. For an account of the relationship between claims and rights that I believe is consistent with my argument, see Bertram Bandman's "Rights and Claims" in *Bioethics and Human Rights,* eds. Elsie L. Bandman and Bertram Bandman (Boston: Little Brown and Company, 1978).

[3]One advantage of the potentiality principle is that one need not specify the necessary or sufficient conditions for actual personhood; one need only note that, whatever they are, a potential person will acquire them in the normal course of its development. My own position is that self-consciousness is a necessary and perhaps a sufficient condition for personhood: "The fact that man can have the idea 'I' raises him infinitely above all the other beings

living on earth. By this he is a *person*" (Immanuel Kant, *Anthropology from a Pragmatic Point of View,* trans. Mary J. Gregor, The Hague: Martinus Nijhoff, 1947, p. 9). See also H. Tristram Engelhardt, Jr. ("The Ontology of Abortion," *Ethics,* 84/3 April, 1974, p. 230n): "Only self-conscious subjects can value themselves, and, thus, be ends in themselves, and, consequently, themselves make claims against us." While Joel Feinberg seems to object to thinking of personhood as a property, he does appeal to the fact that persons are "equally centers of experience, foci of subjectivity" (*op. cit.,* p. 93).

⁴Although using the phrase "in the normal course of its development" rather than "in the normal course of events" emphasizes the teleological ("nature's aim") rather than the statistical probability aspect of "normal development," my later argument about probability and claims assumes that even a teleological notion of "normal" has statistical implications: if the natural end of (a) is to become (A) then it is highly probable that, without interference, (a) will become (A). I believe I am referring to what some Thomists call "active, natural potentiality," though I deny potential personhood is as claim-laden as actual personhood.

⁵The class of potential and possible persons must be distinguished from the class (membership unknown) of future persons, namely the class of future actual persons who do not now exist but will in fact exist in the future. One must be careful with analogies between our duties to potential persons and our duties to future persons (for such an analogy, see Werner S. Pluhar, "Abortion and Simple Consciousness," *Journal of Philosophy,* 74/3 March, 1977, p. 167). If there are future persons (as is so likely as to be certain), they will be actual persons whose quality of life will be affected by actions we now perform, while it is debatable whether killing potential persons affects the quality of their lives *as persons.*

⁶A point I argue in reply to Michael Tooley's "Abortion and Infanticide," *Philosophy and Public Affairs* 2/4 (Summer, 1973), pp. 110-16.

⁷Engelhardt, p. 223.

⁸"Abortion, Infanticide, and Respect for Persons," *The Problem of Abortion,* ed. Joel Feinberg (Belmont: Wadsworth Publishing Co., 1973), p. 103.

⁹In this I agree with John T. Noonan, "An Almost Absolute Value in History," *The Morality of Abortion,* ed. John T. Noonan, Jr. (Cambridge: Harvard University Press, 1970), though he seems to argue wrongly that an abortion involves a high probability of killing a person. Instead, it kills a human that had a high probability of becoming a person.

¹⁰Notice that if one uses the potentiality principle to attribute a very strong claim to life for the fetus, one has, in effect, denied the belief that late abortions are significantly more morally problematic than early abortions.

¹¹See Malcolm Potts, Peter Diggory, and John Peel, *Abortion* (Cambridge: Cambridge University Press, 1977), Chap. 2. The highest estimate I have seen, at variance with most others, is 69 percent, by Harvard physiologist John D. Biggers (*Science,* vol. 202, October 13, 1978, p. 198).

¹²See R. B. Brandt, "The Morality of Abortion" (The *Monist,* Vol. 56, 1972, pp. 504-26), for a quasi-Rawlsian development of this approach. See also Ronald M. Green, "Conferred Rights and the Fetus," *Journal of Religious Ethics,* 2/1 (1974), and Benn, *op. cit.*

¹³See Magda Denes, *In Necessity and Sorrow: Life and Death in an Abortion Hospital* (New York: Penguin Books, 1977), for one description of the different social effects of abortions at different stages of pregnancy.

¹⁴Notice that adding the conferred claims approach highly qualifies a possible implication of my defense of the potentiality principle, namely the implication that it is somewhat easier to justify aborting fetuses with defects that lower their probability of attaining their personhood. Any arguments for conferring a stronger claim to life on fetuses at a given point would apply to most defective fetuses as well.

¹⁵Patricia Fauser, James Gustafson, Gary Iseminger, Daniel Lee, and Frederick Stoutland gave me very helpful comments on an earlier draft of this essay.

An Almost Absolute Value in History

John T. Noonan, Jr.

John T. Noonan is Milo Rees Robins Professor of Law and Legal Ethics at the University of California Law School, Berkeley, California, where he has taught since 1967. He is the author of seven books, among them Bribes *(Macmillan, 1984), a study of the history of bribery;* Persons and Masks of the Law *(1976), an analysis of jurisprudence, originally delivered as the Holmes Lectures at Harvard University; and* A Private Choice: Abortion in America in the Seventies *(Free Press, 1979). He is a leading authority on legal ethics, family law, legal history, and jurisprudence. He was appointed on December 17, 1985, to the United States Court of Appeals for the Ninth Circuit.*

Noonan defends a conservative position on abortion, maintaining that full humanhood exists from the moment of conception. He argues that moderate positions can find no satisfactory place to "draw the line" and that anything that has a complete set of human genes is by definition fully human and possesses full human rights.

The most fundamental question involved in the long history of thought on abortion is: How do you determine the humanity of a being? To phrase the question that way is to put in comprehensive humanistic terms what the theologians either dealt with as an explicitly theological question under the heading of "ensoulment" or dealt with implicitly in their treatment of abortion. The Christian position as it originated did not depend on a narrow theological or philosophical concept. It had no relation to theories of infant baptism. It appealed to no special theory of instantaneous ensoulment. It took the world's view on ensoulment as that view changed from Aristotle to Zacchia. There was, indeed, theological influence affecting the theory of ensoulment finally adopted, and, of course, ensoulment itself was a theological concept, so that the position was always explained in theological terms. But the theological notion of ensoulment could easily be translated into humanistic language by substituting "human" for "rational soul"; the problem of knowing when a man is a man is common to theology and humanism.

If one steps outside the specific categories used by the theologians, the answer they gave can be analyzed as a refusal to discriminate among human beings on the basis of their varying potentialities. Once conceived, the being was recognized as man because he had man's potential. The criterion for humanity, thus, was simple and all-embracing: if you are conceived by human parents, you are human.

The strength of this position may be tested by a review of some of the other distinctions offered in the contemporary controversy over legalizing abortion. Perhaps the most popular distinction is in terms of viability. Before an age of so many months, the fetus is not viable, that is, it cannot be removed from the mother's womb and live apart from her. To that extent, the life of the fetus is absolutely dependent on the life of the mother. This dependence is made the basis of denying recognition to its humanity.

There are difficulties with this distinction. One is that the perfection of artificial incubation may make the fetus viable at any time: it may be removed and artificially sustained. Experiments with animals already show that such a procedure is possible. This hypothetical extreme case relates to an actual difficulty: there is considerable elasticity to the idea of viability. Mere length of life is not an exact measure. The viability of the fetus depends on the extent of its anatomical and functional development. The weight and length of the fetus are better guides to the state of its development than age, but weight and length vary. Moreover, different racial groups have different ages at which their fetuses are viable. Some evidence, for example, suggests that Negro fetuses mature more quickly than white fetuses. If viability is the norm, the standard would vary with race and with many individual circumstances.

The most important objection to this approach is that dependence is not ended by viability. The fetus is still absolutely dependent on someone's care in order to continue existence; indeed a child of one or three or even five years of age is absolutely dependent on another's care for existence; uncared for, the older fetus or the younger child will die as surely as the early fetus detached from the mother. The unsubstantial lessening in dependence at viability does not seem to signify any special acquisition of humanity.

A second distinction has been attempted in terms of experience. A being who has had experience, has lived and suffered, who possesses memories, is more human than one who has not. Humanity depends on formation by experience. The fetus is thus "unformed" in the most basic human sense.

This distinction is not serviceable for the embryo which is already experiencing and reacting. The embryo is responsive to touch after eight weeks and at least at that point is experiencing. At an earlier stage the zygote is certainly alive and responding to its environment. The distinction

Reprinted by permission of the author and the publishers from *The Morality of Abortion: Legal and Historical Perspectives,* by John T. Noonan, Jr., Cambridge, Mass.: Harvard University Press, Copyright © 1970 by the President and Fellows of Harvard College.

may also be challenged by the rare case where aphasia has erased adult memory: has it erased humanity? More fundamentally, this distinction leaves even the older fetus or the younger child to be treated as an unformed inhuman thing. Finally, it is not clear why experience as such confers humanity. It could be argued that certain central experiences such as loving or learning are necessary to make a man human. But then human beings who have failed to love or to learn might be excluded from the class called man.

C.   A third distinction is made by appeal to the sentiments of adults. If a fetus dies, the grief of the parents is not the grief they would have for a living child. The fetus is an unnamed "it" till birth, and is not perceived as personality until at least the fourth month of existence when movements in the womb manifest a vigorous presence demanding joyful recognition by the parents.

Yet feeling is notoriously an unsure guide to the humanity of others. Many groups of humans have had difficulty in feeling that persons of another tongue, color, religion, sex, are as human as they. Apart from reactions to alien groups, we mourn the loss of a ten-year-old boy more than the loss of his one-day-old brother or his 90-year-old grandfather. The difference felt and the grief expressed vary with the potentialities extinguished, or the experience wiped out; they do not seem to point to any substantial difference in the humanity of baby, boy, or grandfather.

D   Distinctions are also made in terms of sensation by the parents. The embryo is felt within the womb only after about the fourth month. The embryo is seen only at birth. What can be neither seen nor felt is different from what is tangible. If the fetus cannot be seen or touched at all, it cannot be perceived as man.

Yet experience shows that sight is even more untrustworthy than feeling in determining humanity. By sight, color became an appropriate index for saying who was a man, and the evil of racial discrimination was given foundation. Nor can touch provide the test: a being confined by sickness, "out of touch" with others, does not

thereby seem to lose his humanity. To the extent that touch still has appeal as a criterion, it appears to be a survival of the old English idea of "quickening"—a possible mistranslation of the Latin *animatus* used in the canon law. To that extent touch as a criterion seems to be dependent on the Aristotelian notion of ensoulment, and to fail when this notion is discarded.

E   Finally, a distinction is sought in social visibility. The fetus is not socially perceived as human. It cannot communicate with others. Thus, both subjectively and objectively, it is not a member of society. As moral rules are rules for the behavior of members of society to each other, they cannot be made for behavior toward what is not yet a member. Excluded from the society of men, the fetus is excluded from the humanity of men.

By force of the argument from the consequences, this distinction is to be rejected. It is more subtle than that founded on an appeal to physical sensation, but it is equally dangerous in its implications. If humanity depends on social recognition, individuals or whole groups may be dehumanized by being denied any status in their society. Such a fate is fictionally portrayed in *1984* and has actually been the lot of many men in many societies. In the Roman empire, for example, condemnation to slavery meant the practical denial of most human rights; in the Chinese Communist world, landlords have been classified as enemies of the people and so treated as nonpersons by the state. Humanity does not depend on social recognition, though often the failure of society to recognize the prisoner, the alien, the heterodox as human has led to the destruction of human beings. Anyone conceived by a man and a woman is human. Recognition of this condition by society follows a real event in the objective order, however imperfect and halting the recognition. Any attempt to limit humanity to exclude some group runs the risk of furnishing authority and precedent for excluding other groups in the name of the consciousness or perception of the controlling group in the society.

A philosopher may reject the appeal to the

humanity of the fetus because he views "humanity" as a secular view of the soul and because he doubts the existence of anything real and objective which can be identified as humanity. One answer to such a philosopher is to ask how he reasons about moral questions without supposing that there is a sense in which he and the others of whom he speaks are human. Whatever group is taken as the society which determines who may be killed is thereby taken as human. A second answer is to ask if he does not believe that there is a right and wrong way of deciding moral questions. If there is such a difference, experience may be appealed to: to decide who is human on the basis of the sentiment of a given society has led to consequences which rational men would characterize as monstrous.

The rejection of the attempted distinctions based on viability and visibility, experience and feeling, may be buttressed by the following considerations: Moral judgments often rest on distinctions, but if the distinctions are not to appear arbitrary fiat, they should relate to some real difference in probabilities. There is a kind of continuity in all life, but the earlier stages of the elements of human life possess tiny probabilities of development. Consider for example, the spermatozoa in any normal ejaculate: There are about 200,000,000 in any single ejaculate, of which one has a chance of developing into a zygote. Consider the oocytes which may become ova: there are 100,000 to 1,000,000 oocytes in a female infant, of which a maximum of 390 are ovulated. But once spermatozoon and ovum meet and the conceptus is formed, such studies as have been made show that roughly in only 20 percent of the cases will spontaneous abortion occur. In other words, the chances are about 4 out of 5 that this new being will develop. At this stage in the life of the being there is a sharp shift in probabilities, an immense jump in potentialities. To make a distinction between the rights of spermatozoa and the rights of the fertilized ovum is to respond to an enormous shift in possibilities. For about twenty days after conception the egg may split to

form twins or combine with another egg to form a chimera, but the probability of either event happening is very small.

It may be asked, What does a change in biological probabilities have to do with establishing humanity? The argument from probabilities is not aimed at establishing humanity but at establishing an objective discontinuity which may be taken into account in moral discourse. As life itself is a matter of probabilities, as most moral reasoning is an estimate of probabilities, so it seems in accord with the structure of reality and the nature of moral thought to found a moral judgment on the change in probabilities at conception. The appeal to probabilities is the most commonsensical of arguments, to a greater or smaller degree all of us base our actions on probabilities, and in morals, as in law, prudence and negligence are often measured by the account one has taken of the probabilities. If the chance is 200,000,000 to 1 that the movement in the bushes into which you shoot is a man's, I doubt if many persons would hold you careless in shooting; but if the chances are 4 out of 5 that the movement is a human being's, few would acquit you of blame. Would the argument be different if only one out of ten children conceived came to term? Of course this argument would be different. This argument is an appeal to probabilities that actually exist, not to any and all states of affairs which may be imagined.

The probabilities as they do exist do not show the humanity of the embryo in the sense of a demonstration in logic any more than the probabilities of the movement in the bush being a man demonstrate beyond all doubt that the being is a man. The appeal is a "buttressing" consideration, showing the plausibility of the standard adopted. The argument focuses on the decisional factor in any moral judgment and assumes that part of the business of a moralist is drawing lines. One evidence of the nonarbitrary character of the line drawn is the difference of probabilities on either side of it. If a spermatozoon is destroyed, one destroys a being which had a chance of far less

than 1 in 200 million of developing into a reasoning being, possessed of the genetic code, a heart and other organs, and capable of pain. If a fetus is destroyed, one destroys a being already possessed of the genetic code, organs, and sensitivity to pain, and one which had an 80 percent chance of developing further into a baby outside the womb who, in time, would reason.

The positive argument for conception as the decisive moment of humanization is that at conception the new being receives the genetic code. It is this genetic information which determines his characteristics, which is the biological carrier of the possibility of human wisdom, which makes him a self-evolving being. A being with a human genetic code is man.

This review of current controversy over the humanity of the fetus emphasizes what a fundamental question the theologians resolved in asserting the inviolability of the fetus. To regard the fetus as possessed of equal rights with other humans was not, however, to decide every case where abortion might be employed. It did decide the case where the argument was that the fetus should be aborted for its own good. To say a being was human was to say it had a destiny to decide for itself which could not be taken from it by another man's decision. But human beings with equal rights often come in conflict with each other, and some decision must be made as to whose claims are to prevail. Cases of conflict involving the fetus are different only in two respects: the total inability of the fetus to speak for itself and the fact that the right of the fetus regularly at stake is the right to life itself.

The approach taken by the theologians to these conflicts was articulated in terms of "direct" and "indirect." Again, to look at what they were doing from outside their categories, they may be said to have been drawing lines or "balancing values." "Direct" and "indirect" are spatial metaphors; "line-drawing" is another. "To weigh" or "to balance" values is a metaphor of a more complicated mathematical sort hinting at the process which goes on in moral judgments. All the metaphors suggest that, in the moral judgments made, comparisons were necessary, that no value completely controlled. The principle of double effect was no doctrine fallen from heaven, but a method of analysis appropriate where two relative values were being compared. In Catholic moral theology, as it developed, life even of the innocent was not taken as an absolute. Judgments on acts affecting life issued from a process of weighing. In the weighing, the fetus was always given a value greater than zero, always a value separate and independent from its parents. This valuation was crucial and fundamental in all Christian thought on the subject and marked it off from any approach which considered that only the parents' interests needed to be considered.

Even with the fetus weighed as human, one interest could be weighed as equal or superior: that of the mother in her own life. The casuists between 1450 and 1895 were willing to weigh this interest as superior. Since 1895, that interest was given decisive weight only in the two special cases on the cancerous uterus and the ectopic pregnancy. In both of these cases the fetus itself had little chance of survival even if the abortion were not performed. As the balance was once struck in favor of the mother whenever her life was endangered, it could be so struck again. The balance reached between 1895 and 1930 attempted prudentially and pastorally to forestall a multitude of exceptions for interests less than life.

The perception of the humanity of the fetus and the weighing of fetal rights against other human rights constituted the work of the moral analysts. But what spirit animated their abstract judgments? For the Christian community it was the injunction of Scripture to love your neighbor as yourself. The fetus as human was a neighbor; his life had parity with one's own. The commandment gave life to what otherwise would have been only rational calculation.

The commandment could be put in humanistic as well as theological terms: Do not injure

your fellow man without reason. In these terms, once the humanity of the fetus is perceived, abortion is never right except in self-defense. When life must be taken to save life, reason alone cannot say that a mother must prefer a child's life to her own. With this exception, now of great rarity, abortion violates the rational humanist tenet of the equality of human lives.

For Christians the commandment to love had received a special imprint in that the exemplar proposed of love was the love of the Lord for his disciples. In the light given by this example, self-sacrifice carried to the point of death seemed in the extreme situations not without meaning. In the less extreme cases, preference for one's own interest to the life of another seemed to express cruelty or selfishness irreconcilable with the demands of love.

The Roman Catholic Doctrine of Therapeutic Abortion

Susan T. Nicholson

Susan Nicholson received her Ph.D. in philosophy from the University of Pittsburgh, and she taught philosophy at Chatham College for twelve years. In 1984 she received a law degree from Harvard Law School and is presently practicing in the field of health law with the law firm of Ropes & Gray in Boston.

Nicholson develops a critique of the ultraconservative Roman Catholic position on abortion, which in some instances refuses to permit therapeutic abortion to save the life of the mother. She argues, contrary to ultraconservative assumptions, that in these instances none of the mothers intends the death of her baby, that only the removal of the fetus but not its death is necessary to save the mother, and that the feticidal medical procedures employed to remove the fetus can be described in morally neutral terms.

1. Life-threatening pregnancies present a conflict between the life of the pregnant woman and the life of the fetus. What is the moral thing to do in situations of mortal conflict between two innocent human beings? Roman Catholic moral theology has evolved a detailed response to this question in the context of abortion.

It should be acknowledged that with advances in medical technology, such situations infrequently arise in the United States. Ectopic pregnancy, where the embryo implants and develops outside its normal uterine site, is the exception to this statement. Such pregnancies occur

From Susan T. Nicholson, *Abortion and the Roman Catholic Church* (Knoxville: Religious Ethics, Inc.) Reprinted by permission of the author and The Journal of Religious Ethics, Studies in Religious Ethics, Rutgers University.

frequently—according to one study (Willson *et al.,* 1975:202), at the rate of 1 to every 78 uterine pregnancies. With regard to uterine pregnancies, however, even medical proponents of abortion law liberalization acknowledge that there are few diseases or complications of pregnancy which call for termination of pregnancy in order to save the woman's life. Nevertheless, considerable criticism has been levelled against the traditional Roman Catholic view of what should be done were such situations to arise.

On the basis of the following authoritative statements, one might assume that Catholic doctrine opposes therapeutic abortion. The first statement is from "Casti Connubi," an address by Pope Pius XI (1930:134-5), and the second is from the more recent "Declaration on Abortion"

(1974:257) issued by the Sacred Congregation for the Doctrine of the Faith and confirmed by Pope Paul VI.

> As to the *medical and therapeutic "indication"* to which, using their own words, We may have made reference, Venerable Brethren, however much We may pity the mother whose health and even *life* is gravely imperiled in the performance of the duty allotted to her by nature, nevertheless what could ever be a sufficient reason for excusing in any way the direct murder of the innocent? This is precisely what we are dealing with here. Whether inflicted upon the mother or upon the child, it is against the precept of God and the law of nature: "Thou shalt not kill." The life of each is equally sacred, and no one has the power, not even the public authority, to destroy it. It is of no use to appeal to the right of taking away life, for here it is a question of the innocent, whereas that right has regard only to the guilty; nor is there here question of defense by bloodshed against an unjust aggressor (for who would call an innocent child an unjust aggressor?); again there is no question here of what is called the "law of extreme necessity" which could never extend to the direct killing of the innocent. *Upright and skillful doctors strive most praiseworthily to guard and preserve the lives of both mother and child; on the contrary, those show themselves most unworthy of the noble medical profession who encompass the death of one or the other, through a pretense at practicing medicine or through motives of misguided pity.* (Italics added)

> We must face up to these very serious difficulties: for example, the mother's health, or *even her life*, may be endangered [by pregnancy]. . . .
> Nonetheless we must assert without qualification that *none* of these reasons justifies disposing of the life of another human being, even in its earliest stages. (Italics added)

This assumption, however, is mistaken. While Catholic doctrine does not permit all therapeutic abortions, it does permit *some*. This intriguing distinction among abortions all of which are aimed at preserving the life of the pregnant woman, is the subject of the present chapter. Four obstetrics cases are presented for the purpose of assessing the consistency of the Catholic doctrine of therapeutic abortion. Two of the cases involve situations in which Catholic doctrine permits therapeutic abortion; the other two involve situations in which therapeutic abortion is forbidden. The problem is to determine the difference between the licit and illicit abortions, and whether or not that difference is morally relevant.

Clarification of terminology employed here is in order at this point. The term "fetus" is used to refer to the *conceptus* from fertilization through all subsequent stages of pregnancy. Although the standard medical definition of abortion is the interruption of pregnancy before the fetus is viable (Greenhill and Friedman, 1974:185), it is useful in this study to extend usage of the term to include both the removal of a non-viable fetus and destructive operations in which the death of a viable fetus is a foreseen result.

The term "therapeutic abortion" is used here to refer only to those abortions believed necessary to prevent the "natural" (non-suicidal) death of the woman during pregnancy or shortly thereafter. This is admittedly a departure from common usage, as abortions performed to preserve health and even psychological well-being are frequently called therapeutic. Adoption of this restricted usage is simply for convenience. Since the task is to determine how it is possible to discriminate morally among abortions all of which are undertaken to preserve the woman's life, it is useful to have a term which refers strictly to life-saving abortions.

I. FOUR CASES OF CONFLICT BETWEEN MATERNAL AND FETAL LIFE[1]

2. *Case A.* A woman in early pregnancy has invasive cancer of the cervix. If removal of her uterus (hysterectomy) is promptly performed, she has a good chance of survival. The operation will, of course, result in the death of the fetus, whose development would otherwise be normal.[2]

Case B. A woman has a pre-viable pregnancy

which is developing in one of her fallopian tubes instead of in her uterus. If an operation is not performed to excise the fetus or remove the tube containing the fetus, she may die from a spontaneous tubal abortion or rupture. Although this operation will result in the death of the fetus, it is extremely unlikely that the fetus could survive in any event.[3]

Case C. A woman in early pregnancy is suffering from chronic hypertensive heart disease associated with severe renal insufficiency. If her pregnancy is not terminated, she may die as a result of the increased demands the pregnancy places on her cardiovascular and renal functions. Although termination of the pregnancy will result in the death of the fetus, its chances for survival are slight in any event.[4]

Case D. A woman in prolonged obstructed labor will die unless an operation is performed in which the head of her unborn fetus is crushed (craniotomy). If craniotomy is not performed and the woman dies from uterine rupture or exhaustion, the fetus will in all likelihood die also.[5]

3. According to standard Catholic doctrine, the physician in case A is permitted to remove the cancerous uterus, even though s/he foresees the death of the non-viable fetus as a certain result. Similarly, in the event of a tubal pregnancy, case B, the fallopian tube may be removed, even though the death of the non-viable fetus is foreseen as an inevitable result. In cases C and D, however, the physician may not operate. S/he may not abort the woman with chronic hypertension, and may not perform a craniotomy on a living fetus.[6]

4. Catholic moralists do not justify their judgments on the basis of the probabilities of maternal/fetal survival. It should be observed that it would not be possible to do so. Consider fetal survival, for instance. It might be supposed that abortion of a tubal pregnancy, case B, is permissible because of the extremely slight chance that the fetus could be delivered alive in any event. However, the same may be said of case C, where therapeutic abortion is not permissible.

Nor can it be supposed that maternal mortality is the critical factor. Many women survive tubal pregnancy without the surgical intervention which is licit according to Catholic moral theology.[7] On the other hand, a woman will certainly die if her obstructed labor is not relieved, yet craniotomy—in past times the only way of relieving certain abnormalities of labor—is forbidden by Catholic doctrine.[8] In order to justify the moral discriminations made among these cases, it is evident that appeal must be made to factors other than the chances of maternal/fetal survival.

To account for the moral discriminations among these cases, Catholic moralists invoke the important principle of Catholic moral theology called the Principle of Double Effect. We turn now to an examination of that principle.

II. THE PRINCIPLE OF DOUBLE EFFECT

5. The Principle of Double Effect is used by Catholic moralists to identify those situations in which it is morally permissible to aim at a good effect, even though evil is also a foreseen consequence of one's actions. The principle is aptly termed "Double Effect," as two effects, one good and one bad, are involved. This principle is applied frequently in contemporary Catholic treatment of such topics as abortion, sterilization, prolongation of life, suicide and conduct in war.[9]

The following statement of the Principle of Double Effect by Farraher (1963:71), given equivalent formulations by Callahan (1970:423) and Granfield (1971:127-8) is typical:

> An act having the double effect of a good and an evil consequence is permissible where
>
> (1) the immediate action performed be good or indifferent;
> (2) the foreseen evil effect be not intended in itself;
> (3) the good which is intended be not an effect of the evil;

or by the nature of things (as would be the case if the suppression of the pain could be obtained only by the shortening of life), and if, on the contrary, the administration of narcotics produces two distinct effects, one, the relief of pain and the other, the shortening of life, then the action is lawful; however, it must be determined whether there is a reasonable proportion between these two effects and whether the advantages of the one effect compensate for the disadvantages of the other.

Although in either case the physician may be said to have killed the patient for reasons of mercy, Catholic authorities regard the administration of such pain therapy as distinct from euthanasia.[12] On their view, euthanasia, which is always forbidden, involves an attempt to end suffering with *death as a means.* Again, the Principle of Double Effect is used to forbid those acts in which the bad effect is a means to the good effect, and permit those in which it is not.

A final example comes from Häring. After expressing the standard Catholic doctrine that suicide is immoral, Häring writes that although the Japanese kamikaze pilots could not but lose their lives, they did not commit suicide because "Their direct intention . . . was not self-destruction but a noble military gesture that demanded self-sacrifice." (1973:72).

11. Condition (3), or the means/foresight distinction, is thus the key to understanding many applications of the Double Effect Principle. Reflection upon the four obstetrics cases will show, however, that condition (3) cannot be the key to understanding the application of the Double Effect Principle to therapeutic abortion.

Consider an instance in which therapeutic abortion is licit—case A, for example. This is the case of the pregnant woman with the cancerous cervix. Since removal of her uterus is licit, one would expect that in this instance the operating surgeon does not aim at fetal death either as an end or as a means to the desired end. And indeed this would appear to be true. As stated previously, the end aimed at is manifestly preservation of the woman's life. And the means to this end is not fetal death, but rather removal of the wom-

an's uterus. Death of the non-viable fetus is a by-product of this means. Should the fetus, contrary to expectation, be removed alive, there would be no point in killing it. This may be contrasted with an instance where a person's death is truly aimed at as a means. Imagine a gunman hired to kill a person in order to prevent that person from revealing certain information. Should the victim, contrary to expectation, survive the first attempt upon her/his life, another attempt would be made.

But the same may be said of case C, where therapeutic abortion is illicit. This is the case of the pregnant woman suffering from chronic hypertension. Here it is removal of the fetus, not its death, which is the means to the end of saving the woman's life. Again, there would be no point in killing the fetus should it, contrary to expectation, be removed alive. That the fetus be removed dead rather than alive serves no end of the doctor, or of the woman.

Even in the forbidden case of craniotomy, case D, fetal death is not a means to the desired end. Some Catholic writers have claimed otherwise. For instance, Kenny (1962:192) states in reference to craniotomy that "The person who performs the operation necessarily *wills* the death of the child either as a *means* of saving the mother's life or because he judges it to be the lesser of two evils."

It is not, however, the death of the fetus that is required for the woman's survival, but the narrowing of the fetus' head sufficiently to prevent the hemorrhaging and exhaustion which will bring about her death. That the narrowing of the head and not the death of the fetus is the means to this end is demonstrated by the fact that the fetus would not be killed should it somehow survive the force applied to its skull and be removed alive from the birth canal. Paul Ramsey (1971:21) expresses this point by saying that "the intention of this action is not the killing, not the death of the fetus," but rather the "*incapacitation* of the fetus from doing what it is doing to the life of the mother."

It would appear then that in any abortion

undertaken strictly to prevent the "natural" (non-suicidal) death of the woman during pregnancy or shortly thereafter, the death of the fetus is a foreseen consequence of the means chosen, but is not itself a means to an end. If this conclusion is correct, then all therapeutic abortions satisfy condition (3) of the Principle of Double Effect.

12. It may be noted that this point is obscured by the failure of some Catholic authors to distinguish in a consistent way between the removal of the fetus from the woman's body and its subsequent death. For instance, Gerald Kelly (1955:12) writes that therapeutic abortion in the case of a woman with a cancerous cervix is licit, for "it is the removal of the cancer, *not the death of the fetus,* that saves the woman's life." In other words, Kelly disapproves only of those procedures in which the death of the fetus is the means to the desired end. On the other hand, he writes that the removal of a non-viable fetus as a last resort in a case of *hyperemesis gravidarum* (severe vomiting) is not licit, because the vomiting "is stopped only by the *emptying of the uterus*" (Italics added here and in the above quotation). This suggests the alternative interpretation that Kelly disapproves of those procedures in which the *removal of the fetus* occurs as a means to the end.

In fact, neither view is satisfactory. As I have just argued, the view that a therapeutic abortion is immoral only where *fetal death* is a means to an end is incompatible with making moral distinctions among the four obstetrics cases listed in section 2, distinctions which Kelly himself makes. The second view, that therapeutic abortions are immoral only where *removal of the fetus* is a means to an end, also runs into difficulty. This view presupposes that removal of the fetus is evil, otherwise there would be no reason to condemn its employment as a means to a good end. What makes removal of a non-viable fetus evil, however, is precisely that it results in fetal death. Catholic moralists do not disapprove of removal of a viable fetus for therapeutic reasons. To be consistent, then, any surgical procedure which inevitably results in fetal death should be forbidden as a means. But removal of a cancerous pregnant uterus prior to viability of the fetus is as inevitably associated with fetal death as removal of a non-viable fetus by itself. Consequently, adoption of the second view is again incompatible with the distinctions Kelly and traditional Catholic moralists draw among therapeutic abortions.

13. On the basis of the discussion thus far, we may criticize an interpretation of the Principle of Double Effect provided by Leonard Geddes (1973). Geddes claims that the essence of the Principle of Double Effect is to distinguish between the *intended* and the *merely foreseen* consequences of a voluntary action.[13] Death is an *intended* consequence of an action, Geddes says, where the action aims at death either as an end in itself, or as a means to an end. A killing is *intentional* where death is intended. In voluntary but *non-intentional* killing, on the other hand, death is a foreseen (though not intended) consequence.

There is a broader sense of intended which may be more in accord with ordinary usage than this narrow sense provided by Geddes. Hart (1968:120) suggests that in ordinary usage one does intentionally what one sets out to achieve, either as a means or an end, as well as what is "so immediately and invariably connected with the action done that the suggestion that the action might not have had that outcome would by ordinary standards be regarded as absurd."

Let us examine the possibility that the Principle of Double Effect is meant to distinguish between the intended and merely foreseen consequences of a voluntary action, in one or the other of these two senses of intended. If Hart's broad sense of intended be adopted, it follows that any and all cases of therapeutic abortion would count as intentional killing. That is, the connection between the removal of a cancerous uterus containing a non-viable fetus and the death of the fetus is as close as the connection between crushing the head of the unborn child and the resultant death of that child. To suggest that a six-week fetus might have survived removal of the uterus would by ordinary standards be regarded as absurd. Similarly, one could not, in Hart's interpretation, understand Catholic moral discriminations

which would normally penetrate the thick mucous lining of the uterus instead penetrate the thin wall of the fallopian tube. This "burrowing in" action of the fetus, even in early pregnancy, results in perforation of blood vessels and dissection of muscles in the tube wall. When rupture occurs, the major cause is not the mechanical inability of the wall to stretch sufficiently to accommodate the growing fetus but the erosion of the tubal wall (Woodruff and Pauerstein, 1969:199).

Thus, Bouscaren is able to claim that from the early stages of pregnancy the tube itself is weakened and dangerous, quite apart from any further development of the pregnancy. On this basis Bouscaren concludes that removal of an unruptured pregnant tube constitutes *indirect* killing since the *direct* object of the operation is removal of a pathological organ of the woman's body. This conclusion was inconsistent with a 1902 decree of the Holy Office[17] which explicitly forbade removal of immature ectopic fetuses. Theologians following Bouscaren maintain, however, that the 1902 decree was correctly based upon the medical facts as then known, but is no longer applicable in the light of subsequent medical research (Grisez, 1970a:180; Kelly, 1958: 108-9; Healy, 1956:221-6).

20. We may now return to the criterion of indirect killing proposed by Pius XII (1951b:189) in "Morality in Marriage." It will be recalled that in this address he characterizes fetal killing as indirect if the treatment killing the fetus is required independently of the woman's pregnant condition (Section 19). Now it would clearly be a mistake to conclude from Bouscaren's study that removal of a pregnant fallopian tube is medically indicated independently of pregnancy. Although it is true that at some point prior to rupture the tube becomes dangerous in itself, it is the pregnancy which *causes* the pathological alterations of the tube. Nevertheless, it is possible to see how such a conclusion might be drawn. Bouscaren shows that after a certain point in tubal pregnancy the tube would have to be removed even if the fetus were no longer present. That the tube would have to be removed even if the fetus *were no*

longer present might mistakenly be thought to imply that the tube would have to be removed even if the fetus *had not been present.*

To put the point another way, Bouscaren showed that if the fallopian tube of a non-pregnant woman were to undergo pathological changes similar to those occurring in tubal pregnancy, it would have to be removed. Just as any other part of the body, the fallopian tube is subject to infection and tumors, either of which can cause deterioration similar to that occurring in tubal pregnancy.[18] Consequently there are reasons for removing the fallopian tube of a woman who is not pregnant, just as there are reasons for removing the uterus of a woman who is not pregnant. But the fact that a fallopian tube could deteriorate and require excision as a result of factors other than a tubal pregnancy does not mean that the deterioration is independent of the pregnancy when there *is* one. The fundamental reason for removing a pregnant tube is manifestly *that the tube contains a misplaced fetus.* That particular tube would not be removed at that particular time if the fetus were not present. By contrast, the reason for removing a pregnant cancerous uterus is *that the uterus is cancerous, not that it contains a fetus.*

21. When these confusions have been removed, however, one is left with the following facts. Both pregnant and non-pregnant women may have cancer of the cervix, and the fallopian tubes of either may deteriorate. When such pathological conditions arise, the medical remedy is the same for the non-pregnant women as it is for the pregnant women: remove the diseased organ. The situation is quite different with regard to a pregnant woman suffering from chronic hypertension or an obstructed labor. Although a non-pregnant woman may have chronic hypertension, the medical remedy indicated for her cannot be removal of her fetus, for she doesn't have one. And a non-pregnant woman cannot be in obstructed labor at all.

22. One may hazard a guess that these facts are exploited in application of the Principle of Double Effect to therapeutic abortion. According

to the formulation in section 5, four conditions establish an act as an instance of permissible killing:

(1) That the immediate action performed be good or indifferent;

(2) That the foreseen evil (fetal death) be not intended in itself;

(3) That the good (preservation of the woman's life) which is intended be not an effect of the evil (fetal death); and

(4) That the good (preservation of the woman's life) be commensurate with the evil (fetal death) foreseen.

It should be clear from previous discussion that conditions (2)-(4) fail to distinguish permissible from non-permissible cases of therapeutic abortion. That leaves condition (1) as a possible basis for distinguishing among therapeutic abortions. It has been argued that it is impossible to distinguish among therapeutic abortions in terms of the temporal priority of their good and bad effects. Adoption of another sense of immediate, however, may provide a solution to the problem.

Observe that removal of a diseased organ from a *non*-pregnant woman cannot result in fetal death. Instead removal is unambiguously life-preserving, and thus has positive moral value. Suppose, now, that one were to describe "the immediate action performed" in removal of a pregnant cancerous uterus or pregnant fallopian tube as *the removal of a diseased organ of the woman's body*. Suppose further that one were to transfer the positive moral value such operations acquire in ordinary contexts to the special context of pregnancy. If this were done, some therapeutic abortions would satisfy condition (1) of the Principle of Double Effect whereas others wouldn't. Specifically, therapeutic abortion in cases A and B would satisfy this condition, while therapeutic abortion in cases C and D would not. "Crushing the head of a fetus," or "removal of a non-viable fetus" are comparable descriptions of immediate actions whose consequences always include the bad effect of loss of life. Consequently, the distinc-

tion comes to this: In the case of permissible therapeutic abortion there exists a description of what the surgeon does such that, considered under this description, the surgeon's action in *other* contexts is solely life-preserving. In the case of illicit therapeutic abortion no comparable description is available.

23. Consideration of the following case suggests a more precise formulation of this conclusion. Suppose a woman in early pregnancy suffering from chronic hypertension (case C) also has benign uterine tumors. According to the preceding analysis, removal of her non-viable fetus is illicit. However, the presence of uterine tumors in non-pregnant women is an indication for hysterectomy. Consequently, it might appear licit to terminate her pregnancy by hysterectomy.

In analyzing this case, however, it must be observed that uterine tumors are usually a threat to health but not to life. Consequently, while Catholic moralists would describe fetal killing as indirect if a hysterectomy were performed to rid the woman of uterine tumors, they would probably not consider the gain to health from ridding her body of tumors to be commensurate with loss of fetal life. Certainly this would be true where the benefit to her health was small.

We may now formulate more precisely the difference between licit and illicit therapeutic abortions. Licit abortions meet the following conditions:

(1′) fetal death occurs as a result of medical procedures employed to modify *life-threatening* conditions which can occur apart from pregnancy and which, if they did occur apart from pregnancy, would necessitate employment of similar procedures (for brevity of exposition, procedures which satisfy this description will hereafter be referred to as *standard procedures*);

(2) the foreseen evil effect is not intended in itself;

(3) the good which is intended is not an effect of the evil;

(4) the good intended is commensurate with the evil foreseen.

On this interpretation, the only difference between licit and illicit therapeutic abortions is that the licit ones involve *standard procedures* whereas the illicit ones do not. That is, in a licit therapeutic abortion fetal death occurs as a result of a standard medical procedure, as defined above; in illicit therapeutic abortion, it does not. We may refer to the distinction embodied in (1′) as the *standard/non-standard procedures* distinction. Our investigation suggests, then, that it is not the means/foresight distinction but the standard/non-standard procedures distinction which accounts for the orthodox Catholic doctrine of therapeutic abortion.

24. That the standard/non-standard procedures distinction has no moral relevance should be evident. Therapeutic abortions satisfying condition (1′) involve medical procedures which are exclusively life-preserving in ordinary contexts but which in the context of pregnancy have both life-preserving and life-destroying consequences. Removal of a cancerous uterus, for instance, has a positive value in ordinary contexts *because* its foreseen consequences are exclusively life-preserving. Thus in appraising its moral value in the context of pregnancy, it cannot be considered *apart from* its foreseen consequences which in this case include fetal death. That is, it is morally irrelevant that removal of a cancerous uterus has purely beneficial effects in *other* contexts when in the context in question it has the same foreseen effects as any procedure of therapeutic abortion. However, on the assumption that Catholic moralists *do* employ the Double Effect Principle to make such spurious distinctions, sense can be made of application of the principle to a number of cases.

25. Consider, for example, the striking illustration of the doctrine presented in Häring's (1970) discussion of abortion. Häring describes an incident recounted to him by a gynecologist who removed a benign uterine tumor from a woman four months pregnant. On the womb the

doctor encountered numerous very thin and fragile varicose veins which bled profusely, and whose bleeding was only aggravated by suturing. Two means of preventing the woman's death from loss of blood were available: (1) removal of the bleeding uterus with the fetus inside; (2) removal of the fetus from the uterus, whereupon the bleeding would be stopped by contraction of the uterus. Death of the fetus would result in either case. Thinking that the fetus could not be saved in any event and that preservation of the woman's fertility was desirable, the gynecologist chose the latter course. He was later told by "a noted Catholic moral theologian" (unidentified by Häring) that the course he chose was objectively wrong. According to the gynecologist, "I would have been allowed to remove the bleeding uterus with the fetus itself," he said, "but was not permitted to interrupt the pregnancy while leaving the womb intact. This latter," he said, "constituted an immoral termination of pregnancy, though done for the purpose of saving the mother, while the other would have been a lawful direct intention and action to save life" (1970:136).

It is instructive to note the similarity between the sanctioned removal of the uterus containing the fetus and the forbidden removal of the fetus from the uterus. Both procedures have the negative and undesired effect of fetal death; both have the positive and desired effect of preservation of maternal life. In neither case is the negative effect the means to the positive one. The procedures are similar in their physical aspects except that the first involves the removal of an additional piece of tissue. That variation in physical detail, however, allows description of what the surgeon does in terms of a standard medical procedure which in other contexts lacks the negative effect of fetal death (although it does of course have the negative effect of loss of fertility). That is, in the second case the surgeon removes a non-viable fetus, whereas in the first case he removes a dangerously hemorrhaging uterus.

26. Still another striking application of the Principle of Double Effect confirms this interpretation and illustrates the extraordinary detail of

which the Catholic analysis is capable. In an extremely rare type of ectopic pregnancy a fetus which has been growing in the fallopian tube will, after spontaneous abortion or rupture of the tube, pass into the abdominal cavity. The fetus may reimplant on the external surface of the bowel, ovary, uterus, or liver, or in the lining of the body wall, and continue to grow. This condition is known as secondary abdominal pregnancy, and as in tubal pregnancy, the chances of fetal survival are slight (Greenhill and Friedman, 1974:359).

The morality of intervention in such cases is also considered in Bouscaren's study. As mentioned earlier, Bouscaren concludes that it is licit under the Principle of Double Effect to remove an unruptured fallopian tube containing a non-viable fetus. This conclusion rests upon the medical finding that the tube undergoes deterioration prior to rupture. On the other hand, a fetus growing in the abdominal cavity presents a rather different problem. As Bouscaren (1944:164) queries, "Where, in this case, is the dangerous organ which must be the *direct object of the operation*?" In his view, to remove the fetus while leaving intact the tissues or organs to which the fetus is attached would be a direct attack upon the fetus. Yet an abdominal pregnancy is dangerous not so much because of changes in the tissue but because it will probably terminate in a spontaneous abortion involving severe hemorrhage. Hence it is not possible to describe the tissues as themselves diseased. Bouscaren is thus led to conclude that although it would have been permissible to operate while the fetus was growing in the fallopian tube, once the fetus has moved into the abdominal cavity an attempt to remove it cannot be justified.[19]

It seems peculiar that the morality of killing a misplaced fetus depends solely upon the fetus' location in the woman's body, when this factor is not significantly related either to its life-chances or to the threat that it poses to the woman's life. Nevertheless this is to be expected in an approach which fixes on whether or not the fetus is killed by a standard medical procedure.

In qualifying his condemnation of abortion in secondary abdominal pregnancy, Bouscaren only reinforces this point. Bouscaren states that in the crisis of spontaneous detachment of the placenta and consequent hemorrhaging, it is permissible to kill the fetus in the process of *attending to the hemorrhage*. That is, the physician may treat the hemorrhage by ligation of the maternal blood vessels. The by-product of this procedure is the death of the fetus through deprivation of its blood supply. The physician may not, however, remove the fetus from its site in the abdominal cavity prior to such hemorrhage. By thus waiting to act until a hemorrhage occurs, the physician again insures that he kill the fetus only through the use of a standard medical procedure—that is, one which would also be indicated were hemorrhaging to occur in a non-pregnant woman.[20]

27. In this connection, it is interesting to note a discussion by Kelly (1958:84-89) on the general problem of hemorrhaging in inevitable spontaneous abortion. The problem Kelly poses is whether or not ergot preparations may be used when it is foreseen that their use will very likely shear off the placenta and thus hasten the death of the fetus. Kelly concludes that the use of ergot is morally permissible in such cases provided nothing can be done to save the fetus and control the hemorrhaging. The point here is that Kelly's conclusion is based on the fact that as ergot acts to produce uterine contractions, its principal use is to stop uterine hemorrhaging regardless of pregnancy. In prescribing ergot in an inevitable spontaneous abortion, then, the physician is employing the medical treatment indicated by the condition—uterine hemorrhaging—with the death of the fetus simply an unavoidable by-product of the uterine contractions induced by the drug.

Had ergot been found to control hemorrhaging in pregnant women through the expulsion of the fetus rather than through the production of uterine contractions, it is clear that Kelly's conclusion would have had to have been different. That is, should ergot lack hemorrhage-controlling capacity in non-pregnant women, its use to control hemorrhage in pregnant women would not be standard medical procedure, and condition (1')

of the Principle of Double Effect would not be satisfied.

Although Kelly does not consider the question explicitly, he implies disapproval of the use of ergot to expel the fetus of a woman whose life was threatened by a non-hemorrhaging pregnancy. Again, the use of ergot in this case would not be standard medical procedure as the term is used here, since ergot would not be used on a non-hemorrhaging, non-pregnant woman.

28. If the interpretation of the Principle of Double Effect offered here is correct, it follows that the fallopian tube *must* be removed along with the fetus in a licit tubal abortion, even though it might be medically possible to remove the fetus while leaving the tube intact. According to *Ethical and Religious Directives for Catholic Health Facilities* (1971:section 16):

> In extrauterine pregnancy the dangerously affected part of the mother (e.g., cervix, ovary, or fallopian tube) may be removed, even though fetal death is foreseen, provided that: (a) the affected part is presumed already to be so damaged and dangerously affected as to warrant its removal, and that (b) *the operation is not just a separation of the embryo or fetus from its site within the part* (which would be a direct abortion from a uterine appendage), and that (c) the operation cannot be postponed without notably increasing the danger to the mother. (My italics)

Moreover, the directives require that the uterine appendage be "so damaged and dangerously affected as to warrant its removal." By this time it should be apparent why a physician might have to delay surgically treating an ectopic pregnancy. Once sufficient damage has been done to the uterine appendage (by the fetus, of course) the condition of the appendage is life-threatening in itself. Only at that point can the operation be described as a medical procedure indicated by the dangerous condition of the organ itself.[21]

29. On this interpretation of the Principle of Double Effect, it should also be clear why abortion on psychiatric grounds is illicit. There is first of all the requirement of proportionality; whether or not preservation of the pregnant woman's mental health, rather than her physical life, can be commensurate with fetal death. One gains the impression, in the context of Catholic discussions of abortion, that no good except the preservation of the life of one human being can be considered proportional to another human being's death. (On the other hand, in the context of war Catholic moralists have allowed other values, such as the defense of property or a way of life, to be commensurate with the death of innocent human beings.) Even if the preservation of the woman's mental health were to be treated as proportional to the death of the fetus, however, it is doubtful that any abortion for psychiatric reasons could be considered indirect.[22]

To be indirect, the abortion would have to occur as a result of a procedure which would be indicated were similar symptoms of mental distress to appear in a non-pregnant woman. If drugs used in treating psychiatric disorders are also abortifacient, then their use on a mentally disturbed pregnant woman would constitute an indirect abortion. The vast majority of abortions performed on psychiatric grounds, however, clearly falls outside this category. By no stretch of the imagination can the administration of prostaglandins, or the performance of vacuum aspirations, saline abortions and hysterotomies, be considered standard psychiatric treatment for non-pregnant women.

30. Summarizing then: Abortionists who follow Catholic manuals of medical ethics control hemorrhaging or remove cancerous uteruses and diseased fallopian tubes; the gynecologist of Häring's account should have removed a hemorrhaging uterus. Ignored in this accounting of what the physician does is the fact that in each case he deliberately kills what is, on Catholic doctrine, one of his patients and an innocent human being. At this point it is difficult to suppress the suspicion that a necessary condition of licit killing in Catholic moral theology is that it be possible to represent the fatal act as something other than killing. By requiring that therapeutic abortions

satisfy condition (1'), Catholic doctrine insures that what the surgeon does be describable as a completely innocuous procedure necessitated by conditions unrelated to pregnancy. Such moralizing exploits the variety of descriptions by which it is always possible to refer to one and the same set of events, ignoring the fact that any and all therapeutic abortions could equally well be described as an attempt to save life or as a destruction of innocent human life.

To conclude this chapter: We have described the orthodox Roman Catholic doctrine which forbids some therapeutic abortions while permitting others, and have examined the important Principle of Double Effect with reference to which this doctrine is justified. It was shown that all therapeutic abortion satisfy the 2nd and 4th conditions of the Double Effect Principle. Condition (3), which distinguishes among acts according to whether their evil effects are a means to the good end or are only foreseen consequences, is the key to many applications of the Double Effect Principle. It was argued, however, that the doctrine of therapeutic abortions cannot be accounted for by reference to the means/foresight distinction. In no therapeutic abortion is fetal death aimed at as a means. Additional formulations of the distinction between licit and illicit killing found in papal documents and the writings of moral theologians were rejected as irreconcilable with the doctrine of therapeutic abortion.

Our investigation revealed, however, that the moral judgments made concerning therapeutic abortion may be understood in terms of the standard/non-standard procedures distinction. That is, licit therapeutic abortions involve the use of medical procedures indicated by life-threatening conditions whose occurrence in non-pregnant women requires similar treatment; illicit therapeutic abortions do not.

Moreover, therapeutic abortions involving standard procedures may be construed as satisfying condition (1) of the Double Effect Principle, while those involving non-standard procedures may be construed as violating that condition.

Finally, it was suggested that the standard/non-standard procedures distinction is without moral relevance. Consequently, it would appear that the orthodox Roman Catholic doctrine of therapeutic abortion is internally inconsistent.

Notes

[1]These cases are intended to be medically accurate. However, the reader should be alerted to the fact that there are aspects of the cases concerning which medical authorities themselves disagree.

[2]Treatment of invasive cancer of the cervix complicated by pregnancy is discussed in Lapid *et al.* (1965). Three alternative therapies—hysterectomy, irradiation, and irradiation combined with hysterotomy—are outlined for women in the first or second trimester of pregnancy, and each is described as fatal to the fetus. The authors state that in most cases the cancer does not disturb the course of gestation. The opinion that it is very unlikely that the cancer would have adverse effects upon the fetus was confirmed in conversation with Dr. John Josimovich, Professor of Obstetrics and Gynecology at the University of Pittsburgh. Dr. Josimovich also remarked that death of the woman prior to viability of the fetus was unlikely with this variety of slow-growing cancer.

[3]Tubal pregnancy accounts for the vast majority of ectopic pregnancies (Willson *et al.*, 1975:202). Fetal mortality is nearly 100% (Gompel and Silverburg, 1969:388; Woodruff

and Pauerstein, 1969:196). The profuse hemorrhage and shock associated especially with tubal rupture is a life-threatening situation for the woman requiring emergency care given with the utmost dispatch (Greenhill and Friedman, 1974:359).

[4]Dack *et al.* (1965:52) places the fetal mortality rate at close to 100%, due to placental dysfunction and increased incidence of preeclampsia (hypertensive disorder peculiar to pregnancy). See also Willson *et al.* (1975:198).

[5]The extremely slight chance of salvaging a live fetus from a woman who died in an obstructed labor is confirmed by Dr. John Josimovich, Professor of Obstetrics and Gynecology at the University of Pittsburgh, and by Dr. Thomas Allen, Director of Women's Health Services, Pittsburgh, Pa. It should be noted that craniotomy has been superseded by cesarian section. With the exception of the presence of hydrocephalus (enlargement of the fetal head caused by excessive cerebrospinal fluid), craniotomy on a living fetus is virtually obsolete (Hellman *et al.*, 1971:1140-41). That such operations were performed in the past, however, is indicated by pronouncements concerning craniotomy issued by the Holy Office in

1884 and 1889 (Kelly, 1958:69-70). In previous centuries when the maternal mortality rate from cesarian section approached 100% (Danforth, 1966;672), cutting up the fetus was the only means of saving the life of a woman unable to deliver vaginally.

[6]The following Catholic texts of medical ethics were consulted: Healy (1956); Kelly (1958); Kenny (1962); McFadden (1967); Niedermeyer (1961); O'Donnell (1959); Häring (1973). Except for Häring, who explicitly acknowledged his departure from orthodox doctrine, there was unanimity of opinion concerning the four obstetrics cases described above.

[7]A tubal pregnancy may spontaneously abort rather than rupture the fallopian tube. While some spontaneous tubal abortions require emergency care, others (at early stages of pregnancy) occur without symptoms, and the products of conception are absorbed (Woodruff and Pauerstein, 1969:192 4).

[8]Craniotomy should be distinguished from the less drastic procedure of tapping the skull of a hydrocephalic fetus to drain off the excess fluid. Since an intraventricular tap is the same operation which would be performed if the child were born and gave hope of survival, Catholic moralists approve this procedure on a hydrocephalic fetus (McFadden, 1967:192).

[9]One can acquaint oneself with application of the Principle of Double Effect to a variety of moral problems by scanning "Notes on Moral Theology" which have appeared in the Catholic journal *Theological Studies* over the past 20 years, and the texts of medical ethics cited in note 6.

[10]While these are the judgments required by standard Catholic doctrine and imposed upon Catholic hospitals by the *Ethical and Religious Directives for Catholic Health Facilities* (1971), it should be acknowledged that in the last decade some Catholic moralists have expressed dissatisfaction with them (See, e.g., Curran, 1970; Häring, 1973). Several writers have undertaken to reexamine the Double Effect Principle, proposing reinterpretations which have the effect of liberalizing traditional judgments concerning therapeutic abortion (Fuchs, 1971; Grisez, 1970a, 1970b; Knauer, 1967; Van der Marck, 1967; Van der Poel, 1968). With the exception of Grisez (whose very modest revision of the Double Effect Principle will be examined in the next chapter) [not here included], these critics suggest abandonment of condition (3) and the adoption of an underlying ethical theory which is thoroughly teleological. These recent developments in Catholic moral theology will not be considered here because (1) a teleological ethical theory is not, in my opinion, acceptable; and (2) the criticism offered in this chapter of the application of the Double Effect Principle to therapeutic abortion is quite independent of the more general criticism of Double Effect found in recent Catholic literature. For a comprehensive review of that literature, see McCormick (1973).

[11]This account of the direct/indirect distinction is also invoked in "Declaration on Abortion" (1974:254).

[12]See, e.g., section 29 of the *Ethical and Religious Directives for Catholic Health Facilities* (1971). "It is not euthanasia to give a dying person sedatives and analgesics for the alleviation of pain, when such a measure is judged necessary, even though they may deprive the patient of the use of reason, or shorten his life."

[13]Geddes bases his interpretation of the Principle of Double Effect on a reading of the principle by Anscombe (1961).

[14]The Holy Office in 1884 responded negatively to the question of whether or not a craniotomy could be performed to save the life of the mother, where without the operation, *both* mother and child would die. The doctrine has been consistently taught since that time (Grisez, 1970a, 179-80).

[15]It is noteworthy that [a section not presented here] *defines* abortion as any procedure which has as its sole immediate effect the termination of pregnancy before viability. This definition—encountered elsewhere in the Catholic literature, but not outside it—appears to be motivated by a desire that the prohibition of abortion be *exceptionless*. Terminations of previable pregnancies which are considered licit in Catholic doctrine—such as removal of a pregnant fallopian tube—are simply not called abortions.

[16]Grisez (1970a:182) refers to this formulation as "what is probably the clearest statement of the concept of *indirect* abortion to be found in the entire Catholic tradition."

[17]The Holy Office is the division of pontifical government entrusted with the doctrine of faith and morals.

[18]A number of such conditions are described in Woodruff and Pauerstein (1969).

[19]A fact not mentioned by Bouscaren is that the placenta may attach to a vital organ such as the liver. Removal of the woman's liver (with the fetus attached) is obviously not a standard medical procedure; it would be fatal to the woman. On the other hand, removal of the fetus while leaving the liver intact is not a standard medical procedure either; it could not be performed on a non-pregnant woman.

[20]"We must wait until the child is viable (at least with the aid of the most modern incubator methods) or until the crisis of dangerous hemorrhage makes intervention necessary, in which case the removal of the fetus is incidental and indirect" (Bouscaren, 1944:165). *Ethical and Religious Directives for Catholic Health Facilities* (1971:section 14) makes a similar point regarding treatment of hemorrhage which occurs before viability: "Procedures that are designed to empty the uterus of a living fetus still effectively attached to the mother are not permitted; procedures designed to stop hemorrhage (as distinguished from those designed precisely to expel the living and attached fetus) are permitted insofar as necessary, even if fetal death is inevitably a side effect." To wait until such procedures may be employed is, of course, to increase the risk of death for the woman.

[21]See, e.g., Healy (1956:224). "It may be that in most cases where an ectopic pregnancy is found, the removal of the tube at once is required to avert existing and grave danger from the mother. But this is not true in all cases. In some few cases at least there is no grave danger to the mother when the ectopic is first discovered. In these few cases the immediate removal of the tube is not licit. The diseased tube may not be excised until it is a source of grave danger to the mother. To excise the

tube before this time would indirectly shorten the life of the ectopic fetus without a sufficient reason, and this would be illicit."

[22]Paul Ramsey (1971:17) appears to make the suggestion that Catholic doctrine could consider abortions performed on psy-

chiatric grounds as indirect, and hence permissible, if only psychiatric predictions were more reliable. This suggestion indicates, I believe, a misunderstanding of the manner in which the Double Effect Principle has been applied to therapeutic abortion.

References

Anscombe, G. E. M., 1961, "War and murder." Pp. 45–62 in Walter Stein (ed.), *Nuclear Weapons: A Catholic Response.* New York: Sheed and Ward.

Bouscaren, T. Lincoln, 1944, *Ethics of Ectopic Operations,* 2nd ed. Milwaukee: Bruce Publishing Co.

Callahan, Daniel, ed., 1969, *The Catholic Case for Contraception.* New York: Macmillan; 1970. *Abortion: Law, Choice and Morality.* New York: Macmillan.

Curran, Charles E., 1970, *A New Look at Christian Morality.* Notre Dame, Indiana: Fides Publishers.

Dack, Simon, *et al.,* 1965, "Heart disease." Pp. 1–63 in Joseph J. Rovinsky and Alan F. Guttmacher (eds.), *Medical, Surgical and Gynecologic Complications of Pregnancy,* 2nd. ed. Baltimore: Williams and Wilkins Co.

Danforth, David N., ed., 1966, *Textbook of Obstetrics and Gynecology.* New York: Harper and Row.

"Declaration on procured abortion"; 1974, Issued by the Sacred Congregation for the Doctrine of the Faith. *The Pope Speaks* 19:250–262.

Ethical and Religious Directives for Catholic Health Facilities, 1971, Washington, D.C.: Department of Health Affairs, United States Catholic Conference.

Farraher, Joseph J., 1963. "Notes on Moral Theology." *Theological Studies* 24:53–105.

Fuchs, Joseph, 1971, "The absoluteness of moral terms." *Gregorianum* 52:415–458.

Geddes, Leonard, 1973, "On the intrinsic wrongfulness of killing innocent people." *Analysis* 33:93–97.

Gompel, Claude, and Silverberg, S. G., 1969, *Pathology in Gynecology and Obstetrics.* Philadelphia: Lippincott and Co.

Granfield, David, 1971, *The Abortion Decision,* rev. ed. New York: Doubleday and Co.

Greenhill, J. P., and Friedman, Emanuel A., 1974, *Biological Principles and Modern Practice of Obstetrics.* Philadelphia: W. B. Saunders Company.

Grisez, Germain G., 1970a, *Abortion: The Myths, the Realities and the Arguments.* New York: Corpus Books; 1970b, "Toward a consistent natural-law ethics of killing." *American Journal of Jurisprudence* 15: 64–96.

Häring, Bernard, 1970, "A theological evaluation." Pp. 123–145 in John T. Noonan, Jr. (ed.), *The Morality of Abortion.* Cambridge, Mass.: Harvard University Press; 1973, *Medical Ethics.* Notre Dame, Indiana: Fides Publishers.

Hart, H. L. A., 1968, "Intention and punishment." Pp. 113–135 in *Punishment and Responsibility: Essays in the Philosophy of Law.* New York: Oxford University Press.

Healy, Edwin F., 1956, *Medical Ethics.* Chicago: Loyola University Press.

Hellman, Louis M., *et al.,* 1971, *Williams Obstetrics,* 14th ed. New York: Appleton-Century-Crofts.

Huser, Roger J., 1942, *The Crime of Abortion in Canon Law.* Washington, D.C.: Catholic University of America Press.

Kelly, Gerald, 1955, *Medico-Moral Problems,* Part I. St. Louis: The Catholic Hospital Association; 1958, *Medico-Moral Problems.* St. Louis: The Catholic Hospital Association.

Kenny, John P., 1962, *Principles of Medical Ethics,* 2nd ed. Westminster, Maryland: The Newman Press.

Knauer, Peter, 1967, "The hermeneutic function of the principle of the double effect." *Natural Law Forum* 12:132–162.

Lapid, Louis S., *et al.,* 1965, "Carcinoma of the cervix." Pp. 349–358 in Joseph J. Rovinski and Alan F. Guttmacher (eds.), *Medical, Surgical, and Gynecologic Complications of Pregnancy,* 2nd ed. Baltimore: Williams and Wilkins Co.

McCormick, Richard A., 1973, *Ambiguity in Moral Choice.* The 1973 Pere Marquette Theology Lecture.

McFadden, Charles J., 1967, *Medical Ethics,* 6th ed. Philadelphia: F. A. Davis.

Niedermeyer, Albert, 1961, *Compendium of Pastoral Medicine,* trans. by Fulgence Buonanno. New York: Joseph P. Wagner, Inc.

O'Donnell, Thomas J., 1959, *Morals in Medicine.* Westminster, Maryland: The Newman Press.

Ramsey, Paul, 1971, "The morality of abortion." Pp. 3–27 in James Rachels (ed.), *Moral Problems.* New York: Harper and Row.

Van der Marck, William, 1967, *Toward a Christian Ethic: A Renewal of Moral Theology.* Westminster, Maryland: Newman Press.

Van der Poel, Cornelius, 1968, "The principle of double effect." Pp. 186–210 in Charles Curran (ed.), *Absolutes in Moral Theology.* Washington, D.C.: Corpus Books.

Willson, J. Robert, *et al.,* 1975, *Obstetrics and Gynecology,* 5th ed. St. Louis: C. V. Mosby Co.

Woodruff, J. Donald, and Pauerstein, Carl J., 1969, *The Fallopian Tube: Structure, Function, Pathology and Management.* Baltimore: Williams and Wilkins Co.

Papal Addresses

Pius XI, 1930, "Casti connubi." Pp. 129–140 in Raziel Abelson (ed.), *Ethics and Metaethics*. New York: St. Martin's Press, 1963.

Pius XII, 1951a, "The apostolate of the midwife." Pp. 160–176 in Vincent A. Yzermans (ed.), *The Major Addresses of Pope Pius XII,* Vol. I. St. Paul: North Central Publishing Co., 1961;

1951b, "Morality in marriage." Pp. 185–190 in Vincent A. Yzermans (ed.), *The Unwearied Advocate: Public Addresses of Pope Pius XII,* Vol. III. St. Cloud, Minnesota: Vincent A. Yzermans, 1954; 1957, "Anesthesia: three moral questions: address of Pius XII to a symposium of the Italian society of anesthesiology." *The Pope Speaks* 4 (1957–8): 33–49.

Abortion and the Concept of a Person

Jane English

Before her tragic death in a mountain climbing accident on the Matterhorn in 1978 at age 31, Jane English taught at the University of North Carolina in Chapel Hill.

English insists that we have no concept of a "person" that is sharp enough to solve the problem of abortion, but she contends that the conservative position is indefensible even if we assume personhood from conception onward. She argues that sometimes we are justified in killing innocent *persons in self-defense and that the ethic of killing in self-defense can be extended beyond killing to save one's life and physical health to saving one's mental health and even one's career.*

The abortion debate rages on. Yet the two most popular positions seem to be clearly mistaken. Conservatives maintain that a human life begins at conception and that therefore abortion must be wrong because it is murder. But not all killings of humans are murders. Most notably, self defense may justify even the killing of an innocent person.

Liberals, on the other hand, are just as mistaken in their argument that since a fetus does not become a person until birth, a woman may do whatever she pleases in and to her own body. First, you cannot do as you please with your own body if it affects other people adversely.[1] Second, if a fetus is not a person, that does not imply that you can do to it anything you wish. Animals, for example, are not persons, yet to kill or torture them for no reason at all is wrong.

At the center of the storm has been the issue of just when it is between ovulation and adult-

From the *Canadian Journal of Philosophy,* vol. V, no. 2, October 1975. Reprinted with permission.

hood that a person appears on the scene. Conservatives draw the line at conception, liberals at birth. In this paper I first examine our concept of a person and conclude that no single criterion can capture the concept of a person and no sharp line can be drawn. Next I argue that if a fetus is a person, abortion is still justifiable in many cases; and if a fetus is not a person, killing it is still wrong in many cases. To a large extent, these two solutions are in agreement. I conclude that our concept of a person cannot and need not bear the weight that the abortion controversy has thrust upon it.

I

The several factions in the abortion argument have drawn battle lines around various proposed criteria for determining what is and what is not a person. For example, Mary Anne Warren[2]

lists five features (capacities for reasoning, self-awareness, complex communication, etc.) as her criteria for personhood and argues for the permissibility of abortion because a fetus falls outside this concept. Baruch Brody[3] uses brain waves. Michael Tooley[4] picks having-a-concept-of-self as his criterion and concludes that infanticide and abortion are justifiable, while the killing of adult animals is not. On the other side, Paul Ramsey[5] claims a certain gene structure is the defining characteristic. John Noonan[6] prefers conceived-of-humans and presents counterexamples to various other candidate criteria. For instance, he argues against viability as the criterion because the newborn and infirm would then be non-persons, since they cannot live without the aid of others. He rejects any criterion that calls upon the sorts of sentiments a being can evoke in adults on the grounds that this would allow us to exclude other races as non-persons if we could just view them sufficiently unsentimentally.

These approaches are typical: foes of abortion propose sufficient conditions for personhood which fetuses satisfy, while friends of abortion counter with necessary conditions for personhood which fetuses lack. But these both presuppose that the concept of a person can be captured in a strait jacket of necessary and or sufficient conditions.[7] Rather, "person" is a cluster of features, of which rationality, having a self concept and being conceived of humans are only part.

What is typical of persons? Within our concept of a person we include, first, certain biological factors: descended from humans, having a certain genetic makeup, having a head, hands, arms, eyes, capable of locomotion, breathing, eating, sleeping. There are psychological factors: sentience, perception, having a concept of self and of one's own interests and desires, the ability to use tools, the ability to use language or symbol systems, the ability to joke, to be angry, to doubt. There are rationality factors: the ability to reason and draw conclusions, the ability to generalize and to learn from past experience, the ability to

sacrifice present interests for greater gains in the future. There are social factors: the ability to work in groups and respond to peer pressures, the ability to recognize and consider as valuable the interests of others, seeing oneself as one among "other minds," the ability to sympathize, encourage, love, the ability to evoke from others the responses of sympathy, encouragement, love, the ability to work with others for mutual advantage. Then there are legal factors: being subject to the law and protected by it, having the ability to sue and enter contracts, being counted in the census, having a name and citizenship, the ability to own property, inherit, and so forth.

Now the point is not that this list is incomplete, or that you can find counterinstances to each of its points. People typically exhibit rationality, for instance, but someone who was irrational would not thereby fail to qualify as a person. On the other hand, something could exhibit the majority of these features and still fail to be a person, as an advanced robot might. There is no single core of necessary and sufficient features which we can draw upon with the assurance that they constitute what really makes a person; there are only features that are more or less typical.

This is not to say that no necessary or sufficient conditions can be given. Being alive is a necessary condition for being a person, and being a U.S. Senator is sufficient. But rather than falling inside a sufficient condition or outside a necessary one, a fetus lies in the penumbra region where our concept of a person is not so simple. For this reason I think a conclusive answer to the question whether a fetus is a person is unattainable.

Here we might note a family of simple fallacies that proceed by stating a necessary condition for personhood and showing that a fetus has that characteristic. This is a form of the fallacy of affirming the consequent. For example, some have mistakenly reasoned from the premise that a fetus is human (after all, it is a human fetus rather than, say, a canine fetus), to the conclusion that it is *a* human. Adding an equivocation on "being," we

get the fallacious argument that since a fetus is something both living and human, it is a human being.

Nonetheless, it does seem clear that a fetus has very few of the above family of characteristics, whereas a newborn baby exhibits a much larger proportion of them—and a two-year-old has even more. Note that one traditional anti-abortion argument has centered on pointing out the many ways in which a fetus resembles a baby. They emphasize its development ("It already has ten fingers . . .") without mentioning its dissimilarities to adults (it still has gills and a tail). They also try to evoke the sort of sympathy on our part that we only feel toward other persons ("Never to laugh . . . or feel the sunshine?"). This all seems to be a relevant way to argue, since its purpose is to persuade us that a fetus satisfies so many of the important features on the list that it ought to be treated as a person. Also note that a fetus near the time of birth satisfies many more of these factors than a fetus in the early months of development. This could provide reason for making distinctions among the different stages of pregnancy, as the U.S. Supreme Court has done.[8]

Historically, the time at which a person has been said to come into existence has varied widely. Muslims date personhood from fourteen days after conception. Some medievals followed Aristotle in placing ensoulment at forty days after conception for a male fetus and eighty days for a female fetus.[9] In European common law since the Seventeenth Century, abortion was considered the killing of a person only after quickening, the time when a pregnant woman first feels the fetus move on its own. Nor is this variety of opinions surprising. Biologically, a human being develops gradually. We shouldn't expect there to be any specific time or sharp dividing point when a person appears on the scene.

For these reasons I believe our concept of a person is not sharp or decisive enough to bear the weight of a solution to the abortion controversy. To use it to solve that problem is to clarify *obscurum per obscurius*.

II

Next let us consider what follows if a fetus is a person after all. Judith Jarvis Thomson's landmark article, "A Defense of Abortion,"[10] correctly points out that some additional argumentation is needed at this point in the conservative argument to bridge the gap between the premise that a fetus is an innocent person and the conclusion that killing it is always wrong. To arrive at this conclusion, we would need the additional premise that killing an innocent person is always wrong. But killing an innocent person is sometimes permissible, most notably in self defense. Some examples may help draw out our intuitions or ordinary judgments about self defense.

Suppose a mad scientist, for instance, hypnotized innocent people to jump out of the bushes and attack innocent passers-by with knives. If you are so attacked, we agree you have a right to kill the attacker in self defense, if killing him is the only way to protect your life or to save yourself from serious injury. It does not seem to matter here that the attacker is not malicious but himself an innocent pawn, for your killing of him is not done in a spirit of retribution but only in self defense.

How severe an injury may you inflict in self defense? In part this depends upon the severity of the injury to be avoided: you may not shoot someone merely to avoid having your clothes torn. This might lead one to the mistaken conclusion that the defense may only equal the threatened injury in severity; that to avoid death you may kill, but to avoid a black eye you may only inflict a black eye or the equivalent. Rather, our laws and customs seem to say that you may create an injury somewhat, but not enormously, greater than the injury to be avoided. To fend off an attack whose outcome would be as serious as rape, a severe beating or the loss of a finger, you may shoot; to avoid having your clothes torn, you may blacken an eye.

Aside from this, the injury you may inflict should only be the minimum necessary to deter

or incapacitate the attacker. Even if you know he intends to kill you, you are not justified in shooting him if you could equally well save yourself by the simple expedient of running away. Self defense is for the purpose of avoiding harms rather than equalizing harms.

Some cases of pregnancy present a parallel situation. Though the fetus is itself innocent, it may pose a threat to the pregnant woman's well-being, life prospects or health, mental or physical. If the pregnancy presents a slight threat to her interests, it seems self defense cannot justify abortion. But if the threat is on a par with a serious beating or the loss of a finger, she may kill the fetus that poses such a threat, even if it is an innocent person. If a lesser harm to the fetus could have the same defensive effect, killing it would not be justified. It is unfortunate that the only way to free the woman from the pregnancy entails the death of the fetus (except in very late stages of pregnancy). Thus a self defense model supports Thomson's point that the woman has a right only to be freed from the fetus, not a right to demand its death.[11]

The self defense model is most helpful when we take the pregnant woman's point of view. In the pre-Thomson literature, abortion is often framed as a question for a third party; do you, a doctor, have a right to choose between the life of the woman and that of the fetus? Some have claimed that if you were a passer-by who witnessed a struggle between the innocent hypnotized attacker and his equally innocent victim, you would have no reason to kill either in defense of the other. They have concluded that the self defense model implies that a woman may attempt to abort herself, but that a doctor should not assist her. I think the position of the third party is somewhat more complex. We do feel some inclination to intervene on behalf of the victim rather than the attacker, other things equal. But if both parties are innocent, other factors come into consideration. You would rush to the aid of your husband whether he was attacker or attackee. If a hypnotized famous violinist were attacking a skid row

bum, we would try to save the individual who is of more value to society. These considerations would tend to support abortion in some cases.

But suppose you are a frail senior citizen who wishes to avoid being knifed by one of these innocent hypnotics, so you have hired a bodyguard to accompany you. If you are attacked, it is clear we believe that the bodyguard, acting as your agent, has a right to kill the attacker to save you from a serious beating. Your rights of self defense are transferred to your agent. I suggest that we should similarly view the doctor as the pregnant woman's agent in carrying out a defense she is physically incapable of accomplishing herself.

Thanks to modern technology, the cases are rare in which a pregnancy poses as clear a threat to a woman's bodily health as an attacker brandishing a switchblade. How does self defense fare when more subtle, complex and long-range harms are involved?

To consider a somewhat fanciful example, suppose you are a highly trained surgeon when you are kidnapped by the hypnotic attacker. He says he does not intend to harm you but to take you back to the mad scientist who, it turns out, plans to hypnotize you to have a permanent mental block against all your knowledge of medicine. This would automatically destroy your career which would in turn have a serious adverse impact on your family, your personal relationships and your happiness. It seems to me that if the only way you can avoid this outcome is to shoot the innocent attacker, you are justified in so doing. You are defending yourself from a drastic injury to your life prospects. I think it is no exaggeration to claim that unwanted pregnancies (most obviously among teenagers) often have such adverse life-long consequences as the surgeon's loss of livelihood.

Several parallels arise between various views on abortion and the self defense model. Let's suppose further that these hypnotized attackers only operate at night, so that it is well known that they can be avoided completely by the considerable inconvenience of never leaving your house after

dark. One view is that since you could stay home at night, therefore if you go out and are selected by one of these hypnotized people, you have no right to defend yourself. This parallels the view that abstinence is the only acceptable way to avoid pregnancy. Others might hold that you ought to take along some defense such as Mace which will deter the hypnotized person without killing him, but that if this defense fails, you are obliged to submit to the resulting injury, no matter how severe it is. This parallels the view that contraception is all right but abortion is always wrong, even in cases of contraceptive failure.

A third view is that you may kill the hypnotized person only if he will actually kill you, but not if he will only injure you. This is like the position that abortion is permissible only if it is required to save a woman's life. Finally we have the view that it is all right to kill the attacker, even if only to avoid a very slight inconvenience to yourself and even if you knowingly walked down the very street where all these incidents have been taking place without taking along any Mace or protective escort. If we assume that a fetus is a person, this is the analogue of the view that abortion is always justifiable, "on demand."

The self defense model allows us to see an important difference that exists between abortion and infanticide, even if a fetus is a person from conception. Many have argued that the only way to justify abortion without justifying infanticide would be to find some characteristic of personhood that is acquired at birth. Michael Tooley, for one, claims infanticide is justifiable because the really significant characteristics of person are acquired some time after birth. But all such approaches look to characteristics of the developing human and ignore the relation between the fetus and the woman. What if, after birth, the presence of an infant or the need to support it posed a grave threat to the woman's sanity or life prospects? She could escape this threat by the simple expedient of running away. So a solution that does not entail the death of the infant is available. Before birth, such solutions are not available because of the biological dependence of the fetus on the woman.

Birth is the crucial point not because of any characteristics the fetus gains, but because after birth the women can defend herself by a means less drastic than killing the infant. Hence self defense can be used to justify abortion without necessarily thereby justifying infanticide.

III

On the other hand, supposing a fetus is not after all a person, would abortion always be morally permissible? Some opponents of abortion seem worried that if a fetus is not a full-fledged person, then we are justified in treating it in any way at all. However, this does not follow. Non-persons do get some consideration in our moral code, though of course they do not have the same rights as persons have (and in general they do not have moral responsibilities), and though their interests may be overridden by the interests of persons. Still, we cannot treat them in any way at all.

Treatment of animals is a case in point. It is wrong to torture dogs for fun or to kill wild birds for no reason at all. It is wrong Period, even though dogs and birds do not have the same rights persons do. However, few people think it is wrong to use dogs as experimental animals, causing them considerable suffering in some cases, provided that the resulting research will probably bring discoveries of great benefit to people. And most of us think it all right to kill birds for food or to protect our crops. People's rights are different from the consideration we give to animals, then, for it is wrong to experiment on people, even if others might later benefit a great deal as a result of their suffering. You might volunteer to be a subject, but this would be supererogatory; you certainly have a right to refuse to be a medical guinea pig.

But how do we decide what you may or may not do to non-persons? This is a difficult problem, one for which I believe no adequate account exists. You do not want to say, for instance, that torturing dogs is all right whenever the sum of its effects on people is good—when it doesn't warp

the sensibilities of the torturer so much that he mistreats people. If that were the case, it would be all right to torture dogs if you did it in private, or if the torturer lived on a desert island or died soon afterward, so that his actions had no effect on people. This is an inadequate account, because whatever moral consideration animals get, it has to be indefeasible, too, It will have to be a general proscription of certain actions, not merely a weighing of the impact on people on a case-by-case basis.

Rather, we need to distinguish two levels on which consequences of actions can be taken into account in moral reasoning. The traditional objections to Utilitarianism focus on the fact that it operates solely on the first level, taking all the consequences into account in particular cases only. Thus Utilitarianism is open to "desert island" and "lifeboat" counterexamples because these cases are rigged to make the consequences of actions severely limited.

Rawls' theory could be described as a teleological sort of theory, but with teleology operating on a higher level.[12] In choosing the principles to regulate society from the original position, his hypothetical choosers make their decision on the basis of the total consequences of various systems. Furthermore, they are constrained to choose a general set of rules which people can readily learn and apply. An ethical theory must operate by generating a set of sympathies and attitudes toward others which reinforces the functioning of that set of moral principles. Our prohibition against killing people operates by means of certain moral sentiments including sympathy, compassion and guilt. But if these attitudes are to form a coherent set, they carry us further: we tend to perform supererogatory actions, and we tend to feel similar compassion toward person-like non-persons.

It is crucial that psychological facts play a role here. Our psychological constitution makes it the case that for our ethical theory to work, it must prohibit certain treatment of non-persons which are significantly person-like. If our moral rules allowed people to treat some person-like non-persons in ways we do not want people to be treated, this would undermine the system of sympathies and attitudes that makes the ethical system work. For this reason, we would choose in the original position to make mistreatment of some sorts of animals wrong in general (not just wrong in the cases with public impact), even though animals are not themselves parties in the original position. Thus it makes sense that it is those animals whose appearance and behavior are most like those of people that get the most consideration in our moral scheme.

It is because of "coherence of attitudes," I think, that the similarity of a fetus to a baby is very significant. A fetus one week before birth is so much like a newborn baby in our psychological space that we cannot allow any cavalier treatment of the former while expecting full sympathy and nurturative support for the latter. Thus, I think that anti-abortion forces are indeed giving their strongest arguments when they point to the similarities between a fetus and a baby, and when they try to evoke our emotional attachment to and sympathy for the fetus. An early horror story from New York about nurses who were expected to alternate between caring for six-week premature infants and disposing of viable 24-week aborted fetuses is just that—a horror story. These beings are so much alike that no one can be asked to draw a distinction and treat them so very differently.

Remember, however, that in the early weeks after conception, a fetus is very much unlike a person. It is hard to develop these feelings for a set of genes which doesn't yet have a head, hands, beating heart, response to touch or the ability to move by itself. Thus it seems to me that the alleged "slippery slope" between conception and birth is not so very slippery. In the early stages of pregnancy, abortion can hardly be compared to · murder for psychological reasons, but in the latest stages it is psychologically akin to murder.

Another source of similarity is the bodily continuity between fetus and adult. Bodies play a surprisingly central role in our attitudes toward persons. One has only to think of the philosophical literature on how far physical identity suffices

Ethics and Reproduction

Issues relating to reproduction are shrouded in mystery and emotion. On the one hand, we must guard against allowing these elements to obscure clear and careful critical thinking. On the other hand, it would be a mistake to ignore the emotional aspects altogether, for they have power to influence actions and reactions even when we are not consciously aware of them. Resolving reproductive issues requires coming to grips with our embodiment, and this is bound to arouse deep emotion.

SOME TRUTHS ABOUT CHILDBEARING

It is beyond the scope of this textbook to investigate in detail the reasons people have children, but some general and obvious truths should be kept in mind as reference points for our thinking throughout this chapter:

(1) Not every pregnancy is planned.
Indeed, until the last quarter century (with the advent of contraceptive pills and other relatively safe and convenient forms of birth control), it is probably safe to say that the planned pregnancy was more the exception than the rule. People tra-

ditionally viewed children as a "gift" from God and/or nature, and the timing of pregnancy was perceived to be not totally under one's control. (Or, at least, the price of control—sexual abstinence—was higher than people were generally willing to pay.)

Even when one parent was pleased at the prospect of having a child, sometimes the other was not. Indeed, this failure of couples to agree continues today. Tales abound of the wife who ceased taking "the pill" without consulting her husband in order to get pregnant when she suspected that he would not agree to having a child otherwise.

Furthermore, every form of contraception or birth control has a failure rate, even if only a fraction of 1 percent. Thus unplanned pregnancies will still occur, even with the most careful "precautions."

(2) Not every "unwanted" child is unloved and abused. The assumption is often made, in contemporary discussions of childbearing, that the child who was not planned is at greatly increased risk of rejection and abuse. However, empirical studies do not bear out this dire prediction. Child abuse appears to be largely a *learned* pattern of parenting. The parents who

react to their children with outbursts of physical or emotional violence are those whose parents reacted in this way *to them.* These parents generally have the same desire to have children as the rest of the population. The problem arises when the inevitable frustrations of parenting occur; abusive parents know of no other way to cope with these except by violence.

Putting the same point another way, the process of pregnancy and the appealing nature of the newborn child generally stir up emotions of acceptance and love of the child, even if he or she was not initially planned or "wanted." Many parents who were anything but enthusiastic when they first learned of the pregnancy come to love and value the child as much as or more than their children who were planned and "wanted" from the beginning.

If there were reason to believe that any development in the medical management of reproduction was responsible for an increase in the risk of child abuse, this would be a strong reason *not* to support that step. But more evidence must be presented of such a danger than merely the assumption that a lack of initial enthusiasm will lead to rejection and/or mistreatment of the child.

(3) When pregnancy is welcomed, the couple's motivation is often vague, complex, and ambivalent.   Even in this era of birth "control" and family "planning," reproductive decisions are not made on a totally rational basis.

To begin with, one does not choose a mate wholly on the basis of his or her contribution to one's reproductive potential. This may be a factor, as when a young man says, "I want my daughters to have her golden hair and my sons to have her big blue eyes." But this is rarely, if ever, a major factor in the choice of a mate. One is generally more interested in what the partner can do to satisfy *one's own needs* than in what he or she can contribute to the creation of one's children.

(4) One significant element in the motivation for having children is to fulfill the expectations of others.   The parents of a young couple often announce explicitly that they want and expect to be provided with grandchildren. Other, more subtle influences are also present: Madison Avenue advertising portrays the family with one son and one daughter as the cultural norm; conversations at the workplace and on social occasions revolve around parenting experiences. All these forces influence a couple's thinking and emotions about childbearing.

(5) Another significant element in the motivation for having children is narcissistic—a bid to achieve a kind of immortality by perpetuating one's name, genes, personality traits, and/or (through enculturation) beliefs and values.   We do not have children wholly to satisfy the expectations of others. We also have certain self-oriented goals in mind. Some of these are morally questionable—for example, the "stage mother" who pushes her child into theatrical activities not because the child has expressed an independent interest in them but because *she* always wanted to be an actress and never succeeded; or the businessman who insists that his son take over the family business, without consideration as to whether the son would find it personally fulfilling. It is not clear, however, that *any* element of self-oriented motivation, no matter how small, is enough to "spoil" the moral value of a decision to become a parent. Parents who have a deep affection for their child in her own right, yet also look forward to personal gratifications from parenthood, would not necessarily be morally condemnable. The challenge will be to ascertain which of such motives, and what level of strength, moves beyond the boundary of moral acceptability.

(6) Uncertainty and risk are inherent in childbearing.   Traditionally, one could not know the sex of one's child until birth. Congenital

would back out of an already established relationship on the basis of genetic risk? The upshot, then, is that prior knowledge of carrier status has little influence on the selection of a mate. The most it can do is alert the couple to initiate prenatal diagnosis, when available.

The dangers of carrier screening are, first and foremost, a threat to autonomy. The cost of genetic diseases to society makes it desirable to mandate screening to couples at risk, and perhaps even to mandate that carriers not mate reproductively. Even if there are not mandatory screening programs, there may still be informal pressures from families and friends of couples in at-risk populations.

If people were totally rational about reproductive decisions, perhaps they would take these matters into account; but, as we saw in the initial "basic truths about childrearing," emotion and mixed motives often replace rational calculation in this domain of decision-making.

GENETIC ENGINEERING AND GENE THERAPY

Genetic engineering techniques raise many of the same issues as other reproductive technologies we have been considering—but they are multiplied in their importance corresponding to the vast increase in both power for benefit and potential for harm which genetic manipulation promises.

Genetic engineering offers the potential for astounding benefits to humanity. In agriculture, there is the possibility, for example, for enhancing the efficiency of food plants in assimilation of nitrogen, thus reducing the necessity for application of expensive (and polluting) nitrogen fertilizers. Further, enhanced resistance to disease and harm from climactic conditions could be bred into plants or imparted to them from outside. One genetic engineering product currently being tested, called "Ice Minus," consists of a bacterium which is claimed to make strawberry plants resistant to frost when it is sprayed on the field.

In industry, there is a possibility of employing biological agents to clean up environmental contaminants and pollutants. The first recombinant life form to receive a patent in the United States was a bacterium which neutralizes oil spills.

The most dramatic applications of these technologies occur, however, in medicine. Several genetically engineered products are already in use, including human insulin (which offers an alternative to pork and beef insulin previously administered), human growth hormone, and hepatitis B vaccine. The advent of more exotic forms of medical treatment is not far in the future. Possibilities include *gene therapy* (the introduction of a functioning gene into a cell in which its defective counterpart is inactive) and *gene surgery* (a technique in which not only is a normal gene added but defective genes are excised or their functioning suppressed). Grobstein and Flower focus on the former of these in their article "Gene Therapy: Proceed with Caution," since it is the technology more likely to be developed in the very near future.

Scientific Self-Regulation

Genetic engineering is one of the few areas (perhaps the only one) in the history of science in which the scientists themselves halted the progress of their research until considerations of safety could be studied. In 1974, when the biological community was on the verge of developing techniques for working with recombinant DNA, Berg et al. published a letter in *Science* urging a voluntary moratorium on this research until the hazards could be definitively ascertained. A moratorium of several years ensued while the scientific community and national governments around the world debated this issue. The research resumed in 1976, when the National Institutes of Health (and parallel agencies in other countries) issued guidelines for recombinant DNA research.[4]

DOCTRINAIRE OBJECTIONS

"We would be playing God."—The General Secretaries of three national religious groups (i.e., the National Council of Churches, the Synagogue Council of America, and the U.S. Catholic Conference) wrote a letter to the President's Commission for the Study of Ethical Problems in Medicine and Biomedical and Behavioral Research expressing distress about theological implications of proposed manipulations of genetic structures. In response, the President's Commission sought testimony from a wide variety of theologians to determine what basis there might be for serious objection to genetic research. No basis for objection was found other than the bare slogan itself.

"We have no business unravelling the mysteries of life."—This objection is reminiscent of medieval objections to autopsy. If this attitude were to prevail, the advances of modern medicine would have been impossible. The objection assumes that awe and any sense of mystery at the workings of nature would inevitably be destroyed by knowledge about the mechanics of it. But this is not necessarily the case.[5]

"We would be dethroning humans from their status in the scheme of things."—A view that humans stand apart from the rest of nature is a strongly held tenet of Western culture. One of its roots is in the Judaic and Christian tradition.[6]

"Manipulation of genetic structures represents an arrogant interference with nature."—It must be admitted that an antagonistic view towards nature has sometimes been expressed—undoubtedly in part a heritage from the religious view that humans are given "dominion" over nature. John Stuart Mill, for example, states such an attitude in his essay "Nature":

"the ways of nature are to be conquered, not obeyed; . . . her powers are often toward man in the position of enemies, from whom he must wrest, by force and ingenuity, what little he can for his own use."[7]

But this attitude is not inevitable in connection with genetic manipulation. It is possible to proceed with research and treatment in this area while retaining respect for the "wisdom" and power of nature and thus not overreaching in attempts to control it.

"It is wrong to create new life forms."—The reply to this objection is to point out that we do this already in cases that are not considered objectionable. Plant hybrids like the grapefruit and animal hybrids like the mule are examples in which the genetic structure of distinct forms of life were altered. The only difference introduced is that genetic engineering is performed from "inside," through direct manipulation of genetic material, rather than from "outside" by selective breeding.

"It is wrong to breach species barriers."—This, too, is already done on a macro level. The mule is a cross between two species. One suspects that the root of this objection is a worry that animal–human hybrids may be developed. This possibility would, indeed, be disturbing—leading us to examine the fundamental question of what characteristics are uniquely human.

In general, would the wrong in creating such hybrids lie

(a) in bestowing some but not all of these human characteristics on the creature?

(b) in depriving of his or her full humanity the 100 percent human who *might have been*?

(c) extrinsically, in the way these hybrids might be treated (enslaved, etc.)? If this last, the objection should be with the mode of treatment, not necessarily with the mode of "production."

VALID GENERAL CONCERNS

Dramatic developments in genetics are on the horizon; and they will lead to some dramatic alterations in our *concepts* of life, the human, parenting, family relationships, etc. One concern which must be borne in mind is that success in

this area may reinforce a "fix-it" attitude towards nature, which can lead us to expect too much of medical and biological science. Further, parental attitudes and expectations may well be changed—and not always in healthy directions. When genetic selection (and, eventually, gene surgery) is possible before birth, will an "imperfect" child be regarded as unacceptable, as a "mistake," and rejected by parents and/or society? How will this selection alter our attitude towards handicaps and other "imperfections" in the existing population?

Recall the truths about childbearing with which this chapter began. In evaluating new developments, we must not expect clearer patterns of motives and emotions than the *status quo ante*. On the other hand, we must keep in mind the elements of emotion and mystery which attend reproduction. We cannot expect people to be wholly rational or altruistic in their reaction to new developments (any more than they have been in the past in reaction to "natural" elements). We must guard against changes which would stimulate undesirable emotional reactions.

UNCERTAINTIES

Several kinds of uncertainties will remain with us, to be resolved piece by piece as scientific knowledge in this area expands.

Occurrence Uncertainty   We cannot be certain in advance what all the consequences of genetic manipulations will be. Genetic engineering and therapy techniques are not different in *kind* from other maneuvers, but they are significantly different in degree—especially when we come to heritable changes which may affect all future generations. Genetic engineering makes selective changes in complex systems which are far from fully understood. Our experience with ecosystems should have taught us to be *cautious*

here: small changes can have major effects. One theory of the origin of Acquired Immune Deficiency Syndrome (AIDS) furnishes a tragic example here. In this view, a small change in a virus which had previously infected green monkeys in Central Africa led to a catastrophic disease which is threatening to devastate hundreds of thousands of people around the world. Similarly, curing Johnny's growth deficiency by administering genetically engineered growth hormone could trigger cancer in Johnny, or his offspring, or *their* offspring. These dangers are lessened if we concentrate on somatic cell therapy rather than manipulating germ cells. But, as Grobstein and Flower point out in their essay on genetic therapy, the benefits of germ cell therapy in rooting out heritable genetic diseases in the next generations make it a compelling candidate for development.

Conceptual Uncertainty   A second kind of uncertainty with which we must deal is unclarity about the concepts which figure in this area of study. Questions which arise include the following:

What is "human"?

What is a "species"?

What is a "new form of life"?

Evaluative Uncertainty   Finally, uncertainties in value and ethical issues will remain with us. Is it appropriate, for example, to use genetic engineering techniques to decrease susceptibility to some toxic substance in the workplace, or would it be more appropriate to take steps to *remove* the substance from the environment? How important to our long-term survival as a species is *genetic diversity*?

At the very least, what seems to be needed is a continuing review body to foster public discussion of these issues. Grobstein and Flower make the case for such a body, and they also suggest some guidelines to shape its discussions.

Notes

[1] *Griswold v. Connecticut,* 381 U.S. 479 (1964).

[2] Joseph Fletcher, "Humanness," in *Humanhood: Essays in Biomedical Ethics,* Joseph Fletcher, ed. (Buffalo: Prometheus Books, 1979), p. 16.

[3] *Ibid.,* p. 17.

[4] An absorbing account of these events is found in Sheldon Krimsky, *Genetic Alchemy* (Cambridge, Mass.: The M.I.T. Press, 1982).

[5] Cf. Richard Selzer (*Mortal Lessons,* Touchstone Books, 1978, pp. 25–26) on the sense of awe experienced by a sensitive surgeon at each incision:

> One enters the body in surgery, as in love, as though one were an exile returning at last to his hearth, daring uncharted darkness in order to reach home. Turn sideways, if you will, and slip with me into the cleft I have made. Do not fear the yellow meadows of fat, the red that sweats and trickles where you step. Here, give me your hand. Lower between the beefy cliffs. Now rest a bit upon the peritoneum. All at once, gleaming, the membrane parts . . . and you are *in.* It is the stillest place that ever was. As though suddenly you are struck deaf. Why, when the blood sluices fierce as Niagara, when the brain teems with electricity, and the numberless cells exchange their goods in ceaseless commerce—why is it so quiet? Has some priest in charge of these rites uttered the command "Silence"? This is no silence of the vacant stratosphere, but the awful quiet of ruins, of rainbows, full of expectation and holy dread. Some of you shall know surgery as a Mass served with Body and Blood, wherein disease is assailed as though it were sin.

[6] The religious roots of this attitude are dramatically expressed in the following passage (Psalm 8:3–9):

> When I consider thy heavens, the work of thy fingers, the moon and the stars, which thou hast ordained;
> What is man, that thou are mindful of him? and the son of man, that thou visitest him?
> For thou hast made him a little lower than the angels, and hast crowned him with glory and honour.
> Thou madest him to have dominion over the works of thy hands; thou has put all things under his feet;
> All sheep and oxen, yea, and the beasts of the field; the fowl of the air, and the fish of the sea, and whatsoever passeth through the paths of the seas.
> O Lord our Lord, how excellent is thy name in all the earth!

[7] John Stuart Mill, *Nature and Utility of Religion,* George Nakhnikian, ed. (Indianapolis: Bobbs-Merrill Library of Liberal Arts, 1958), p. 14.

A Criticism of Moral Conservatism's View of In Vitro Fertilization

Richard M. Zaner

Richard M. Zaner is currently Ann Geddes Stahlman Professor of Medical Ethics in the Department of Medicine at Vanderbilt University School of Medicine. He holds secondary appointments in philosophy, the Graduate Department of Religion, and the Schools of Divinity and Nursing. He is a senior research associate in the Vanderbilt Institute for Public Policy Studies. Involved in the medical humanities since 1971, Professor Zaner is a founding member of the Journal of Medicine and Philosophy *and is on the editorial board of numerous other journals. He is the author of numerous books and articles, including* The Context of Self *(Ohio University Press, 1981) and has just completed a new study titled* Chance and Morality: Ethics in the Clinical Context *(unpublished). He wishes to thank the staff of The Center for Fertility and Reproductive Research, Vanderbilt University School of Medicine, for their cooperation and helpfulness in his efforts to understand the problems faced by patients suffering from infertility, and those of researchers and physicians.*

Zaner outlines a wide range of arguments offered by those who take a conservative position on in vitro fertilization and embryo transfer. These arguments are parallel to, and in many cases overlap with, the positions on abortion which we labelled "conservative" and "ultraconservative" in Chapter 8. Zaner challenges both the logic of these arguments and their specific application to public policy issues regarding in vitro

fertilization. He claims that at the root of many of these arguments is a form of moral absolutism which breeds moral intolerance and attempts to discredit the motives of those who disagree.

It must be noted that Zaner's own argument contains an error of logic. In the third paragraph of the section titled "On 'Slopes,' 'Noses,' or 'Wedges,'" he describes both "affirming the antecedent" of a conditional and "denying the consequent" as logical fallacies. Actually, both of these are deductively valid inferences. The fallacies associated with conditionals are "denying the antecedent" and "affirming the consequent." You should consider how seriously these errors damage his argument as a whole.

In a recent article, Hans O. Tiefel argues for "a more cautious or conservative position" on in vitro fertilization/embryo transfer (IVF/ET) for human beings [1]. His argument is not merely against recommendations for federal support for such programs but is to provide a "decisive" moral objection to this technology itself—whether used therapeutically or for purely research purposes [2]. His major point concerns the supposed "unknown risks" to the offspring. A subsidiary but also key point is that the requirements of informed consent cannot be fulfilled with regard to the offspring.

A good deal of research into animal and human reproductivity has been conducted, with much evidence collected over the past decade from clinical applications of IVF/ET [2–6]. Nonetheless, Tiefel contends, "nobody knows for sure" about possible damages that may result to the infant-product of this technology. Because of this, we are obliged to make moral judgments in the absence of certain knowledge, and this means that an "ethics of risk" is needed. This ethics is guided by two main principles. (1) Every child is owed "a fair chance at physical and mental health," which requires that no parent should "take chances" with the health of any child-to-be. (2) Without clear and certain knowledge, and in the absence of informed consent from such an infant, no risk taking can be tolerated. His conclusion is that only total "abstinence" from IVF/ET is justified ethically.

Tiefel's main argument is derived from Leon Kass's earlier argument. Kass urged that in these prospective experiments on the unconceived and

From *Perspectives in Biology and Medicine*, vol. 27, no. 2 (1984): 201–212. © 1984 by The University of Chicago Press. Reprinted with permission of the author and publisher.

the unborn, "it is not enough to know of any grave defects; one needs to know that there will be no such defects—or at least no more than there are without the procedure." He concluded, "The general presumption of ignorance is caution. When the subject-at-risk cannot give consent, the presumption should be abstention" [7]. Tiefel cites and agrees with Kass's principle: "One cannot ethically choose for the would-be-child the unknown hazards that he must face and simultaneously choose to give him life in which to face them" [7].

Parents otherwise unable to bear children have nonetheless earnestly desired to utilize IVF/ET. Like Kass before him, Tiefel regards these desires as unobjectionable in themselves. However, one cannot justify the use of this technology simply by appealing to these desires. To accede to them, Tiefel believes, is to endorse a most unfortunate "ethical relativism." This would devastate medicine: "If one lets go of objective and universal values to defer to dubious patient choice, one also relinquishes the heart of medicine, whose life is the objective value of healing and doing no harm" [1].

Thus, IVF/ET cannot be ethically justified by reference either to the future child or to the parents' desires. The claims of such moral conservatism require careful scrutiny, for they are expressive not only of a prominent view among some ethicists working within medicine but also of a widely held view in our society today.

THE QUESTION OF RISK TO OFFSPRING

Even though the likelihood of possible but unknown risks is the major concern, it is quite diffi-

cult to tell just which risks concern Tiefel. At one point he asserts that one must have a "wide conception" of risk: "Mental or physical, emotional or social, possible or actual, detracting from the health or worth of any or all parties" [1].

This "wide conception," however, is not helpful, and not only because it is so sweepingly general and vague. The idea would also commit Tiefel to being opposed to many if not most "natural" pregnancies. After all, it is hardly unreasonable to point out that parents could not possibly know, in advance of initiating a pregnancy, what emotional, social, mental, or other actual or possible "risks" might occur and which would compromise the health or worth of the planned offspring. Or, since a parent knows full well that any offspring, whether "naturally" or "technologically" conceived, will by the mere fact of being human have to face any number of "unknown risks" in life, it follows that Tiefel would apparently have to regard any parent as unethical.

As the wide conception leads to such absurdities and vague generalities, what alternatives does Tiefel give for understanding just what risks must concern us? Although he is surprisingly silent on this issue, one can suppose that there are two sorts: those which might occur because of the technical procedures themselves; and those arising from the purposes and actions of the technicians, researchers, and/or physicians.

1. Which risks should be of concern in the first case? Tiefel at one point cites evidence [8] that there seems to be no pattern of increased congenital defects due to the procedures. Yet, he contends that "there is no guarantee" that such a pattern will not emerge. Nor is there a guarantee that many or most abnormalities present before birth will be expelled spontaneously. Given this "factual uncertainty," hence no guarantee of certainty, IVF/ET must be abandoned. However, the logic of Tiefel's argument at this point, it must be emphasized, would require him to be completely opposed to *any* medical procedure which could not offer such a guarantee. This implication is surely unacceptable since it would require the

abandonment of most if not all medical procedures—there simply is little, if any, such certainty in medicine.

While Tiefel is content to leave the crucial issue of risk definition so unclear, Kass was not. Also concerned about possible unknown damages from technological manipulations of the pre-implanted embryo, Kass was considerably more specific. He mentioned "gross [physical] deformities," "species differences in sensitivity to the physical manipulations," "possible teratogenic agents in a culture medium," "mental retardation," and "sterility" [7].

As reported by Edwards, however, experiments with animals had clearly demonstrated that no embryopathic effect could be ascribed to the researcher's manipulations, the culture medium, and so on. So far as humans are concerned, Edwards reported, "the two most serious risks were [i.e., by 1971] known to be hyperstimulation of the ovary and multiple births. No anomalies other than a low birth weight in multi-pregnancies have occurred in children as a result of these treatments" [3]. Moreover, it has been shown not only that the preimplanted embryo is highly resistant to malformations but also that "the fetuses of non-human primates are less resistant than human fetuses" in response to various cultures and manipulations [3]. In general, then, there seems no evidence that IVF/ET has resulted in any increase in number or type of abnormality [5, 6].

Kass's specific concerns were thus addressed directly. The evidence available does not now seem to support the concerns which he expressed—even though it was surely legitimate to worry about these at the time Kass wrote. So far as the question of "certainty" is concerned in such research and clinical applications, Jones's judgment seems the most balanced and warranted: while "abnormalities will undoubtedly be associated with this process, it now seems unlikely that the risk will be substantially greater than the risk following normal fertilization" [6].

2. This brings up the possibility of understanding risk in the second sense: concerns about

the purposes and actions of the researcher/physicians using these technical procedures, and those of infertile couples. As this opens up some genuinely murky and sensitive regions, it is essential to be most cautious.

Tiefel remarks with plain dismay that "a survey of the literature yields no medical researcher who thinks that this is one procedure that should not be used. None of the medical experts rejects this risky procedure" [1]. This should hardly be surprising, however, since Kass's specific concerns have indeed been responded to directly. What is surprising is Tiefel's continued dismay, and it is this which must be examined.

At one point he makes it quite clear just what concerns him: if we do not protect embryos and fetuses, he believes that they will then "tend" to be ranked with the lower animals. With that, we have opened a veritable "Pandora's box" of evils—and just that, he contends, is inherent to IVF/ET. This "tendency," it seems perfectly clear, is not at all connected with possible risks from the technical procedures; if it were, he could be charged with simply ignoring or underestimating the scientific evidence at hand, or perhaps with asking what cannot be delivered ("guarantees of certainty"). This tendency, on the contrary, is one which he believes is to be found with the *users* of IVF/ET: parents and clinicians who select it to resolve infertility. The issue, then, seems principally a matter of distrust and fear of what these persons might do with this technology.

He suggests, for instance, that the physician's obligation to succeed without mishap, or to avoid research mistakes, may well create a conflict of interest with a flawed fetus. Presumably, this would tend to motivate the physician toward abortion: there is "an inherent impetus to jettison any problem pregnancy" [1]. However, as he gives no reasons for the claim of "conflict of interest" or for this supposedly "inherent impetus," we are left with the only credible conclusion: he simply does not believe such physicians can be trusted with the power of such technology.

This conclusion receives direct support from Tiefel's subsequent argument: "the greatest hazard to the unborn may not lie in the vicissitudes of pregnancies as such or in close monitoring but in the physician's desire for a perfect child" [1]. Given this "desire," the point seems to be, the physician will "tend" (or be "impelled") to "jettison" anything less than "perfection." In somewhat different terms, the real fear here is the Pandora's box supposedly inherent in such technologies. Once the camel's nose is under the tent, there is no way to keep it from carrying off the whole thing. In short, what concerns him is the "slippery slope": once the first step is allowed, there is no way to prevent sliding down to the horrors at the bottom. The only effective way to stop what this argument contends is "inevitable" is to ensure that not even the first step be permitted. The argument, it needs to be stressed, focuses not on the procedure but on those who use it. I return to this shortly.

About the parents, Tiefel is equally explicit. He asserts, without detectable reason, that to accede to a couple's desire to have their own biologic child is a "quicksand" of "shifting individual preferences," an "ethical relativism" to be avoided at all costs. Such "dubious patient choices" should not be permitted. Indeed, he goes so far as to condemn one parent's desire to have his own biologic child: "Pride is never a good reason for becoming a parent, not only because one never knows how children will turn out but because the motive is self-serving" [1]. As was already mentioned, the fact that "one never knows" about a child's future would imply that not even "natural pregnancies" should be permitted. Beyond that, to regard pride in every form as merely "self-serving" seems hardly warranted. To condemn this parent, much less to condemn him and others like him to a condition of childlessness, is little short of plain arrogance.

It is equally unwarranted, finally, to assert without argument that acceding to a couple's desire to resolve their infertility by IVF/ET is equivalent to endorsing "ethical relativism." After all, to act on behalf of what a patient honestly believes

is his or her own good could more readily be understood as benevolence. It need hardly be pointed out that the very part of the moral norms of medical practice which Tiefel himself stresses—that is, acting on behalf of the patient's best interests—is precisely what is involved here. To be sure, a patient might not know what these best interests actually are in a given situation. But then one is obliged to give sound reasons for such a claim. In any case, the kind of infertility for which IVF/ET is an appropriate response is neither commonly debilitating nor mentally incapacitating. Hence, it can hardly be claimed that such persons do not and cannot know their own best interests, nor is there any reason to suppose that Tiefel is in any better position to know this than are the parents.

Regarding individual preferences as a shifting quicksand, patient choices as dubious, and physicians as being unwittingly driven by an inherent impetus to achieve perfection, it is quite evident that what concerns Tiefel is not unknown risks stemming from the procedures of IVF/ET but, rather, his considerable distrust of the persons involved.

3. A final possible sense of risk deserves brief comment. Walters suggests that some ethicists object to IVF/ET on the grounds that no laboratory or clinical experiments are capable of providing the amount or kind of evidence needed to assuage moral concern. They have concluded that "the risks of clinical IVF research are not only unknown but unknowable" [2]. If this were Tiefel's, or even Kass's, concern, there would obviously be no possible response. There is no answer to a demand for certainty, since medicine is a science or discipline incorporating an element of "necessary fallibility" [9].

Tiefel does not argue for unknowable risks, however. Rather, he contends that "the morally crucial answer to the question of risk to the would-be child thus requires a great number of births and much time" [1]. Therefore, *only* further factual investigations are appropriate for satisfying his concern. Now, not only does this

stance (contra the abstention Tiefel argues for) require such research, but, in fact, the evidence to date gives far greater weight to IVF/ET than to Tiefel's claims.

THE QUESTION OF "CONSENT" AND "MORAL STATUS"

The appeal to unknown risks seems mainly a straw man. To ask for certainty is to ask for what cannot be given and would forbid any clinical trial, any experimentation and scientific research—since the very point of these is to find out or make known what is yet unknown, often in the context of some risk.

In any event, even if there were no more risks from IVF/ET than from "normal" procreation, the moral conservative is still opposed. Part of the reason has to do with the moral status of the embryo as "human" from "conception" onward. Kass [7, 10] and Ramsey [11, 12] make informed consent a central issue here; Tiefel apparently agrees with this, but makes moral status the main one.

Kass, for instance, would require that the subject-at-risk give its consent; this is not possible; therefore, IVF/ET is ethically unjustified. For Tiefel, human life "begins at conception," and the embryo is therefore "human life"; since this gives it full human status for all moral purposes, consent would surely be required.

Edwards's quick response to this issue is worth repeating: it is "unrealistic in practice because it leads to total negation—even to denying a mother a sleeping pill, a Caesarian section, or an amniocentesis for fear of disturbing the child." For that matter, he caustically remarks, "fetuses are not asked beforehand about their own conception or even their abortion" [3]. Since this is patently true regardless of the specific mode of procreation, "natural" or otherwise, insistence on consent would forbid any pregnancy whatever. It is, of course, quite pointless to demand consent from embryos, fetuses, and newborns, but it is also obvious that this is not expected. What we

do expect is that others (parents, health professionals, teachers, etc.) will act responsibly on behalf of their best interests.

The same clearly applies to clinical IVF; perhaps even more stringently (although a case would have to be made for this), in view of the still tentative status of the procedures. Still, this is far short of the abstention Kass, Ramsey, and Tiefel demand and is a precaution which could reasonably be encouraged for any parent: to be more thoughtful about bringing children into the world even in "natural" ways.

Although Tiefel asserts (without argument) that life begins at conception, he later maintains that the "problem is not when life begins but when it should have human status, when it should be important and count as one of us" [1]. Of course, one wants to recognize that human life is a matter of continuous development through a sequence of stages. The issue, then, concerns whether this development at any one stage is sufficient to make a difference, that is, exhibits a moral status requiring all the protections (goods, rights, etc.) which are recognized for any clearly moral human being.

One such stage is the preembryonic. Since the union of the spermatozoon and ovum is necessary to initiate the development of a new individual, this stage does not make the difference sought for. Fertilization may seem morally significant since at its completion a zygote is formed and, it would appear, a distinctively human individual is initiated. Strictly speaking, of course, this is not necessarily the case. Fertilization might result in two (or more) such individuals. It might also result in such severe chromosomal abnormalities as to preclude subsequent development. It may even result in a hydatidiform mole. Indeed, even normal development shows that fertilization results, first, in a cell mass which ultimately divides into the embryoblast and the trophoblast. While the former becomes the fetus, the latter becomes not a "child" but the extraembryonic membranes, placenta, and umbilical cord. Of course, the trophoblastic derivatives are quite as much "alive" and "human" as the embryoblast and have the same genetic composition as the fetus. Hence, this stage does not make the moral difference that Tiefel and others are seeking.

Conception, the stage initiating pregnancy marked by the implantation of the blastocyst, however, may be the difference which makes a moral difference. Throughout the entire process there is one and the same organism. However, as Eike-Henner Kluge emphasizes, "it is one and the same only in the sense that it is one continually growing aggregate of matter that develops according to a genetically fixed plan. This continuation, however, does not mean continued identity—any more than the continuation of protein molecules when ingested and assimilated by us entails that we have become the cow that we have eaten" [13]. The crucial difference, then, is this "identity": at what point of development can it be said credibly that "one and the same" human individual is present? For Kluge, this point comes only with the adequate formation of the central nervous system, especially the brain, for only then is there an adequate support for the sorts of complex neural activities which can serve as the biologic foundation for distinctively human rationality, for "personhood."

Others would locate this morally significant point at "viability" (the Supreme Court), while still others would push this point further. Throughout such discussions, however, several issues tend to be obscured, issues which must give one pause at the very idea of trying to establish one or another "point" as somehow morally significant. Suppose a point were agreed on; what then? In the first place, it would be implied that *prior* to that point the developing human life would be *excluded* from "protectable humanity" [1]. Presumably, then, for such stages there would be no argument against many if not all types of research manipulations. But surely this permissiveness could not be tolerated even by Tiefel. In the second place, since IVF/ET procedures occur

at the *preconception* stages (and if we take Tiefel at his own words), they should be of no concern to him at all, as "human moral status" has not yet been achieved, according to him.

In the third place, supposing such a point were agreed on, we need to establish just what this implies. Here Tiefel's claim simply begs the question. Simply because the fertilized ovum (for instance) does not yet have that moral status in no way implies that it *thereby* is excluded from protectable humanity, much less *thereby* ranked with the lower animals. And even if the latter were the case (which is dubious), not even that would necessarily imply that any and all clinical or laboratory manipulations would be justified ethically.

In many respects, this anxiety about finding differences which make a moral difference itself seems suspect. What underlies it, certainly in Tiefel's case, is this "fear" about a "tendency" by the researchers and physicians to abuse and misuse their powers. Once again, that is, we are in the face of the slippery slope argument, and it is this which must be squarely confronted.

ON "SLOPES," "NOSES," OR "WEDGES"

This argument has exercised many persons, including ethicists. Its appeal is familiar and seems quite powerful. It is essentially a hypothetical, conditional argument: "if . . . then . . . ." It postulates that "if" something is once done, or a course of action initiated, however innocuous this bare beginning might be, "then" certain highly unacceptable results will occur. Since these are unacceptable, the initial step is unacceptable. Or, to accept the initial step will "tend" inevitably to bring the host of horrors in its wake.

Often the argument includes one or another conditional qualifier: "tendency," "might occur," "unknown risks," and the "inevitability" of the bad

results. Despite these qualifiers, however, the logical force of the argument is the appeal to necessity, otherwise there would be no compelling reason for the abstention.

Logically, of course, the argument is plainly fallacious. If the first step is accepted, the evil at the slope's bottom is inevitable. This is a version of affirming the antecedent, and from this no conclusion whatever follows. In some versions (e.g., Tiefel's), the logical fallacy of denying the consequent is also committed: the evils which will result must be rejected; therefore, not even the first step should be permitted. Again, no conclusion follows.

Even so, the argument continues to be used, and this presents a curious problem. If it is maintained merely that the initiation of a course of action might occur, then they might not occur; while this implies great caution at every stage, it hardly implies abstention. If the argument appeals to necessity, it is a clear fallacy. In either case the conclusion argued for simply does not follow. Why, then, its remarkable appeal?

At its root is a certain psychological observation, coupled with an appeal to fear: once people become accustomed to something they find it easier, perhaps even attractive, not only to do it again and again (developing a habit) but also to engage in a different but related activity which, however, is bad. Examples include welshing on a promise, not telling the truth, fudging on getting consent, etc. The focus of the "argument," then, is on the people doing the action, not on the action itself (nor the technical means required by the action).

The slippery slope, in other words, works (to the extent that it does work) primarily as a misanthropic exercise: it moves from the psychological likelihood that some persons might be tempted to engage in such actions, to the very different presumption that all persons (within a certain class, e.g., IVF/ET clinicians) will inevitably engage in such actions. That is to say, the slippery slope has its force mainly in distrust of

persons—they are not able to resist the temptations to continue each step down the slippery slope all the way to the bottom. For each step down differs so little from the prior one that we are easily duped; the first was okay, so the second seems okay as well. . . .

In fact, of course, not even the psychological observation is necessarily accurate. Some people do indeed resist such temptations (for instance, I should imagine that Tiefel would). This being true, the appeal to fear loses its force as well. The move from a psychological observation (which is itself dubious in many cases) about only some person's presumable tendency or temptability (without telling which people are that way) to the strongest possible moral prohibition does not hold up. Hence, the "argument" is not an argument at all but an illicit appeal to distrust, suspicion, and fear—and the basis for these is at least open to question.

The acceptance of the initial step, then, by no means implies that one must accept the evil consequences; it does not even mean that these particular consequences are in any way related to the initial step. But even if Tiefel were in some way correct about such potential dangers of the Pandora's box, this would hardly signify a muting of our moral awareness; it would suggest, on the contrary, a remarkable heightening and sharpening of it—as the presence of danger of any sort does. To the extent that the slippery slope is legitimate, it leads to the very opposite of what those who use it wish us to believe.

CAN IVF/ET BE "THERAPEUTIC"?

A final point remains to be considered. The moral conservative urges that the only sense in which IVF/ET can be considered therapeutic is with regard to the parents. Tiefel argues, however, that accepting the validity of this is equivalent to giving over to "dubious patient choice" and "ethical relativism." Kass argues that this procedure can be considered a "cure for infertility" (as Edwards believes) [3] only if infertility were incorporated into the "medical model" as a "disease."

However, Kass insists, infertility is precisely *not* a disease. It "is not life threatening or crippling, nor does it lead to detectable bodily damage" [7]. Moreover, even if a successful pregnancy and birth are obtained, the infertility still remains. Hence, IVF/ET can be considered at most the "symptom" of a disease. In that case, however, it would have to be understood strictly as a process occurring solely within or to an individual. But infertility is not that; it is, rather, a "condition that is located in a marriage, in union of two individuals" [7].

Since infertility is not a disease, IVF/ET cannot be conceived as a therapy. What is in fact "treated" is the woman's, or the couple's, "desire" to bear a child. And, however unobjectionable in itself, to treat this desire requires a "clear medical therapeutic purpose," and infertility simply does not present such a purpose for Kass, even less so if there is a risk of damage to the would-be child (from whom, of course, no consent is possible).

On this issue, Paul Ramsey seems even more extreme. He believes that IVF/ET is focused solely on the "product" and "is therefore manufactured by biological technology, not medicine." Such technological manipulations in effect reduce the child to the status of a mere "prosthesis for his mother's condition" [11, 12].

Setting aside the questions of risk and consent, which have already been dealt with, we are left with the issue of "treating" the "desires" of the couple. Is infertility a treatable condition, and is IVF/ET a "therapeutic" procedure for it?

To this, Edwards's direct response bears repeating. There are many examples of clinical conditions which remain even after treatment, which only modifies their expression. He lists insulin, false teeth, and spectacles; patients with these conditions "want" (desire) to be nondiabetic, to eat properly, to see. Physicians quite appropriately respond to these desires by treating the symptomatic expressions. "In fact," he points out, "most medical treatment, particularly on consti-

tutional or genetic disorders, is similarly symptomatic in nature," and infertility is precisely like those [3]. To refuse to respond to a couple's desire to have a child, when otherwise they could not, is in effect to require that they accept their childlessness. This attitude "assumes that a doctor or someone else is sufficiently authoritative to decide on the problems of the couple." On this, however, "there is no reason to believe that ethical advice from outsiders about their condition is sounder than their own judgment of it" [3].

I doubt that Kass, Ramsey, or Tiefel would disagree with Edwards about diabetes, bad eyesight, or poor teeth. I doubt indeed that they would disagree that a severely burned person's desire to have some cosmetic surgery is legitimate, even though this would leave the underlying condition as it was. In short, the argument against IVF/ET glosses over a key distinction, that between *trivial* and *nontrivial* desires.

One response to the plight of infertile persons is adoption. It need not be belabored, however, that adoption can hardly be given as the avenue for all would-be parents. This is so whatever the intrinsic values of adoption, and even if there were fewer difficulties than there now are, for many people, in finding adoptable children and being accepted as appropriate adoptive parents. In any case, even to recommend adoption to such persons, it is worth emphasizing, one has to suppose that their "desire" for a child is hardly trivial!

Unless one were prepared to argue that *every* desire to have one's own biologic child (even by "natural" means) is trivial—which seems outrageous—the point about desire is simply another straw man. To insure that no clearly trivial desire should be taken seriously by medicine is doubtless a sound point. But that is to say no more than what has been long known and practiced in medicine generally and seems particularly true of IVF/ET programs.

Of course, a fuller discussion of this issue would have to be more specific on the distinction between trivial and nontrivial desires. However

difficult that may be, it seems only reasonable to believe that the desires in question are hardly, and certainly not universally, trivial. Where they are not trivial, it is perfectly acceptable (perhaps even obligatory) for physicians to utilize the means provided by clinical IVF/ET.

A CONCLUDING WORD

Tiefel, it can be supposed, would still demur, for he wants deliberately to contend that to respect even (I suppose) serious desires for such couples is to give in to ethical relativism. There is no middle road between absolute relativism and absolute paternalism. As I have suggested, this commits him to a fundamental kind of misanthropy, to being systematically suspicious of (at least) IVF/ET physicians and infertile parents. His paternalism is most stringent; "children are gifts of God to which believers have no claims, either before or after birth" [1]. This means that God alone can decide the issues with which IVF/ET teams merely imagine they have to grapple. Hence, the "universal and objective" moral norms he believes lie at the heart of medicine are, in truth, God's unalterable norms. From this perspective, it must by definition be true that letting individuals decide is most "dubious" indeed.

It should also be pointed out, however, that his view presupposes a radically privileged source of knowledge, namely, of God's purported purposes. It presupposes not only that Tiefel has such access but that others of us have as well. Otherwise, the view he espouses is simply by definition unassailable: any opinion to the contrary would be merely one more "dubious" individual opinion.

That feature is troublesome enough, but not as serious as the problem his view necessarily creates: that of basic ethical disagreement and even, at times, serious ethical conflict. Must those who disagree with him (as he clearly suggests, in the case of patients) be regarded as "dubious"? Could his view tolerate even the modest admission that not every patient (e.g., Tiefel himself) is ipso facto

"dubious"? I suspect that at the core of his view is a kind of moral intolerance toward any opposing view, and it is precisely for this reason that the mere presence of a dissenting view (e.g., by IVF/ET physicians) presents such harsh issues for him, even though he says nothing about the problem of moral disagreement.

In any event, a number of things seem quite evident. First, the concern about potential damage to the offspring of IVF/ET seems clearly unfounded. Second, the question of consent, while it has an obvious and significant place in many situations (e.g., for the would-be parents), cannot be legitimately required of the potential offspring itself. Third, the attempt to assign a special, morally privileged status to one or another stage of human development is at best problematic and at worst arbitrary. Fourth, the argument that IVF/ET is not therapeutic for the couple does not stand up to analysis, as the discussion of "desire" trades on a gloss of a key distinction between desires which are genuine and those which are merely trivial. Making that distinction, however, suggests that IVF/ET is an appropriate medical response to a couple's infertility. Finally, the nub of moral conservatism turns out to be at once highly questionable, an exercise in "playing God" in far more dangerous ways than anything in the current medical armamentarium, and a viewpoint which seems incapable of accommodating moral disagreement. Hence, this viewpoint presents a kind of intolerance which the facts of human life, and of medicine, cannot support.

References

[1]TIEFEL, H. O. Human in vitro fertilization: a conservative view. *JAMA* 247:3235–3242, 1982.

[2]WALTERS, L. Human in vitro fertilization: a review of the ethical literature. *Hastings Cent. Rep.* 9:23–42, 1979.

[3]EDWARDS, R. G. Fertilization of human eggs in vitro: morals, ethics and the law. *Q. Rev. Biol.* 40:3–26, 1974.

[4]LOPATA, A.; JOHNSTON, I. W.; HOULT, I. J.; and SPEIRS, A. L. In vitro fertilization in the treatment of human infertility. In *Bioregulators of Reproduction,* edited by G. JAGIELLO and H. J. VOGEL. New York: Academic Press, 1981.

[5]CRAFT, I.; MCLEOD, F.; GREEN, S.; et al. Human pregnancy following oocyte and sperm transfer to the uterus. *Lancet,* pp. 1031–1033, 1982.

[6]JONES, H. W., JR. The ethics of in vitro fertilization: 1982. *Fertil. Ster.* 37:146–149, 1982.

[7]KASS, L. R. Babies by means of in vitro fertilization: unethical experiments on the unborn? *N. Engl. J. Med.* 285:1174–1179, 1971.

[8]BIGGERS, J. D. In vitro fertilization and embryo transfer in human beings. *N. Engl. J. Med.* 304:336–342, 1981.

[9]GOROVITZ, S., and MACINTYRE, A. Towards a theory of medical fallibility. *J. Med. Philos.* 1:51–71, 1976.

[10]KASS, L. E. Making babies—the new biology and "old" morality. *Public Interest* 26:32–33, 1972.

[11]RAMSEY, P. Shall we "reproduce"? I. The medical ethics of in vitro fertilization. *JAMA* 220:1347, 1972.

[12]RAMSEY, P. Shall we "reproduce"? II. Rejoinders and future forecast. *JAMA* 220:1480–1483, 1972.

[13]KLUGE, E-H. *The Practice of Death.* New Haven, Conn.: Yale Univ. Press, 1975.

Surrogate Mothers: Not So Novel After All

John A. Robertson

A biographical sketch of John A. Robertson is given on page 502.
   Robertson surveys the potential benefits and harms of allowing surrogate mother arrangements. He disagrees with Krimmel's basis for opposition (see essay, pages 658–64) and maintains that no objectionable

new moral element is introduced into childbearing by such a practice. As a lawyer, Robertson is especially interested in what the role of the state should be with regard to such arrangements. A variety of state reactions are possible, from outlawing such practices at one extreme to facilitating and even financing them at the other. Robertson argues for a middle ground here.

All reproduction is collaborative, for no man or woman reproduces alone. Yet the provision of sperm, egg, or uterus through artificial insemination, embryo transfer, and surrogate mothering makes reproduction collaborative in another way. A third person provides a genetic or gestational factor not present in ordinary paired reproduction. As these practices grow, we must confront the ethical issues raised and their implications for public policy.

Collaborative reproduction allows some persons who otherwise might remain childless to produce healthy children. However, its deliberate separation of genetic, gestational, and social parentage is troublesome. The offspring and participants may be harmed, and there is a risk of confusing family lineage and personal identity. In addition, the techniques intentionally manipulate a natural process that many persons want free of technical intervention. Yet many well-accepted practices, including adoption, artificial insemination by donor (AID), and blended families (families where children of different marriages are raised together) intentionally separate biologic and social parenting, and have become an accepted thread in the social fabric. Should all collaborative techniques be similarly treated? When, if ever, are they ethical? Should the law prohibit, encourage, or regulate them, or should the practice be left to private actors? Surrogate motherhood—the controversial practice by which a woman agrees to bear a child conceived by artificial insemination and to relinquish it at birth to others for rearing—illustrates the legal and ethical issues arising in collaborative reproduction generally.

From *The Hastings Center Report*, vol. 13, no. 5 (October 1983). Reprinted by permission of the author and publisher. © The Hastings Center, 360 Broadway, Hastings-on-Hudson, New York 10706.

AN ALTERNATIVE TO AGENCY ADOPTIONS

Infertile couples who are seeking surrogates hire attorneys and sign contracts with women recruited through newspaper ads. The practice at present probably involves at most a few hundred persons. But repeated attention on *Sixty Minutes* and the *Phil Donahue Show* and in the popular press is likely to engender more demand, for thousands of infertile couples might find surrogate mothers the answer to their reproductive needs. What began as an enterprise involving a few lawyers and doctors in Michigan, Kentucky, and California is now a national phenomenon. There are surrogate mother centers in Maryland, Arizona, and several other states, and even a surrogate mother newsletter.

Surrogate mother arrangements occur within a tradition of family law that gives the gestational mother (and her spouse, if any) rearing rights and obligations. (However, the presumption that the husband is the father can be challenged, and a husband's obligations to his wife's child by AID will usually require his consent.)[1] Although no state has legislation directly on the subject of surrogate motherhood, independently arranged adoptions are lawful in most states. It is no crime to agree to bear a child for another, and then relinquish it for adoption. However, paying the mother a fee for adoption beyond medical expenses is a crime in some states, and in others will prevent the adoption from being approved.[2] Whether termination and transfer of parenting rights will be legally recognized depends on the state. Some states, like Hawaii and Florida, ask few questions and approve independent adoptions very quickly. Others, like Michigan and Kentucky, won't allow surrogate mothers to terminate and assign rearing rights to another if a fee

wanted to have the child, but find that they are unable to provide for it because of some unfortunate circumstances that develop after conception.

Second, even if surrogate mother arrangements were to be classified as a type of adoption, not all offerings of children for adoption are necessarily moral. For example, would it be moral for parents to offer their three-year-old for adoption because they are bored with the child? Would it be moral for a couple to offer for adoption their newborn female baby because they wanted a boy?

Therefore, even though surrogate mother arrangements may in some superficial ways be likened to adoption, one must still ask whether it is ethical to separate the decision to create children from the desire to have them. I would answer no. The procreator should desire the child for its own sake, and not as a means to attaining some other end. Even though one of the ends may be stated altruistically as an attempt to bring happiness to an infertile couple, the child is still being used by the surrogate. She creates it not because she desires it, but because she desires something from it.

To sanction the use and treatment of human beings as means to the achievement of other goals instead of as ends in themselves is to accept an ethic with a tragic past, and to establish a precedent with a dangerous future. Already the press has reported the decision of one couple to conceive a child for the purpose of using it as a bone marrow donor for its sibling (*Los Angeles Times,* April 17, 1979, p. 1-2). And the bioethics literature contains articles seriously considering whether we should clone human beings to serve as an inventory of spare parts for organ transplants[4] and articles that foresee the use of comatose human beings as self-replenishing blood banks and manufacturing plants for human hormones.[5] How far our society is willing to proceed down this road is uncertain, but it is clear that the first step to all these practices is the acceptance of the same principle that the Nazis attempted to use to justify their medical experiments at the Nuremberg War Crimes Trials: that human beings may be used as means to the achievement of other goals, and need not be treated as ends in themselves.[6]

But why, it might be asked, is it so terrible if the surrogate mother does not desire the child for its own sake, when under the proposed surrogate mother arrangements there will be a couple eagerly desiring to have the child and to be its parents? That this argument may not be entirely accurate will be illustrated in the following section, but the basic reply is that creating a child without desiring it fundamentally changes the way we look at children—instead of viewing them as unique individual personalities to be desired in their own right, we may come to view them as commodities or items of manufacture to be desired because of their utility. A recent newspaper account describes the business of an agency that matches surrogate mothers with barren couples as follows:

> Its first product is due for delivery today. Twelve others are on the way and an additional 20 have been ordered. The "company" is Surrogate Mothering Ltd. and the "product" is babies.[7]

The dangers of this view are best illustrated by examining what might go wrong in a surrogate mother arrangement, and most important, by viewing how the various parties to the contract may react to the disappointment.

WHAT MIGHT GO WRONG

Ninety-nine percent of the surrogate mother arrangements may work out just fine; the child will be born normal, and the adopting parents (that is, the biological father and his wife) will want it. But, what happens when, unforeseeably, the child is born deformed? Since many defects cannot be discovered prenatally by amniocentesis or other means, the situation is bound to arise.[8] Similarly, consider what would happen if the biological father were to die before the birth of the child. Or if the "child" turns out to be twins or triplets. Each of these instances poses an inevitable situation

where the adopting parents may be unhappy with the prospect of getting the child or children. Although legislation can mandate that the adopting parents take the child or children in whatever condition they come or whatever the situation, provided the surrogate mother has abided by all the contractual provisions of the surrogate mother arrangement, the important point for our discussion is the attitude that the surrogate mother or the adopting parent might have. Consider the example of the deformed child.

When I participated in the Surrogate Parent Foundation's inaugural symposium in November 1981, I was struck by the attitude of both the surrogate mothers and the adopting parents to these problems. The adopting parents worried, "Do we have to take such a child?" and the surrogate mothers said in response, "Well, we don't want to be stuck with it." Clearly, both groups were anxious not to be responsible for the "undesirable child" born of the surrogate mother arrangement. What does this portend?

It is human nature that when one pays money, one expects value. Things that one pays for have a way of being seen as commodities. Unavoidable in surrogate mother arrangements are questions such as: "Did I get a good one?" We see similar behavior with respect to the adoption of children: comparatively speaking, there is no shortage of black, Mexican-American, mentally retarded, or older children seeking homes; the shortage is in attractive, intelligent-looking Caucasian babies.[9] Similarly, surrogate mother arrangements involve more than just the desire to have a child. The desire is for a certain type of child.

But, it may be objected, don't all parents voice these same concerns in the normal course of having children? Not exactly. No one doubts or minimizes the pain and disappointment parents feel when they learn that their child is born with some genetic or congenital birth defect. But this is different from the surrogate mother situation, where neither the surrogate mother nor the adopting parents may feel responsible, and both

sides may feel that they have a legitimate excuse not to assume responsibility for the child. The surrogate mother might blame the biological father for having "defective sperm," as the adopting parents might blame the surrogate mother for a "defective ovum" or for improper care of the fetus during pregnancy. The adopting parents desire a normal child, not *this* child in any condition, and the surrogate mother doesn't want it in any event. So both sides will feel threatened by the birth of an "undesirable child." Like bruised fruit in the produce bin of a supermarket, this child is likely to become an object of avoidance.

Certainly, in the natural course of having children a mother may doubt whether she wants a child if the father has died before its birth; parents may shy away from a defective infant, or be distressed at the thought of multiple births. Nevertheless, I believe they are more likely to accept these contingencies as a matter of fate. I do not think this is the case with surrogate mother arrangements. After all, in the surrogate mother arrangement the adopting parents can blame someone outside the marital relationship. The surrogate mother has been hosting this child all along, and she is delivering it. It certainly *looks* far more like a commodity than the child that arrives in the natural course within the family unit.

A DANGEROUS AGENDA

Another social problem, which arises out of the first, is the fear that surrogate mother arrangements will fall prey to eugenic concerns.[10] Surrogate mother contracts typically have clauses requiring genetic tests of the fetus and stating that the surrogate mother must have an abortion (or keep the child herself) if the child does not pass these tests.[11]

In the last decade we have witnessed a renaissance of interest in eugenics. This, coupled with advances in bio-medical technology, has created a host of abuses and new moral problems.

For example, genetic counseling clinics now face a dilemma: amniocentesis, the same procedure that identifies whether a fetus suffers from certain genetic defects, also discloses the sex of a fetus. Genetic counseling clinics have reported that even when the fetus is normal, a disproportionate number of mothers abort female children.[12] Aborting normal fetuses simply because the prospective parents desire children of a certain sex is one result of viewing children as commodities. The recent scandal at the Repository for Germinal Choice, the so-called "Nobel Sperm Bank," provides another chilling example. Their first "customer" was, unbeknownst to the staff, a woman who "had lost custody of two other children because they were abused in an effort to 'make them smart.'"[13] Of course, these and similar evils may occur whether or not surrogate mother arrangements are allowed by law. But to the extent that they promote the view of children as commodities, these arrangements contribute to these problems. There is nothing wrong with striving for betterment, as long as it does not result in intolerance to that which is not perfect. But I fear that the latter attitude will become prevalent.

Sanctioning surrogate mother arrangements can also exert pressures upon the family structure. First, as was noted earlier, there is nothing technically to prevent the use of surrogate mother arrangements by single males desiring to become parents. Indeed, single females can already do this with AID or even without it. But even if legislation were to limit the use of the surrogate mother arrangement to infertile couples, other pressures would occur: namely the intrusion of a third adult into the marital community.[14] I do not think that society is ready to accept either single parenting or quasi-adulterous arrangements as normal.

Another stress on the family structure arises within the family of the surrogate mother. When the child is surrendered to the adopting parents it is removed not only from the surrogate mother, but also from her family. They too have interests to be considered. Do not the siblings of that child have an interest in the fact that their little baby brother has been "given" away?[15] One woman, the mother of a medical student who had often donated sperm for artificial insemination, expressed her feelings to me eloquently. She asked, "I wonder how many grandchildren I have that I have never seen and never been able to hold or cuddle."

Intrafamily tensions can also be expected to result in the family of the adopting parents due to the asymmetry of relationship the adopting parents will have toward the child. The adopting mother has no biological relationship to the child, whereas the adopting father is also the child's biological father. Won't this unequal biological claim on the child be used as a wedge in child-rearing arguments? Can't we imagine the father saying, "Well, he is my son, not yours"? What if the couple eventually gets divorced? Should custody in a subsequent divorce between the adopting mother and the biological father be treated simply as a normal child custody dispute? Or should the biological relationship between father and child weigh more heavily? These questions do not arise in typical adoption situations since both parents are equally unrelated biologically to the child. Indeed, in adoption there is symmetry. The surrogate mother situation is more analogous to second marriages, where the children of one party by a prior marriage are adopted by the new spouse. Since asymmetry in second marriage situations causes problems, we can anticipate similar difficulties arising from surrogate mother arrangements.

There is also the worry that the offspring of a surrogate mother arrangement will be deprived of important information about his or her heritage. This also happens with adopted children or children conceived by AID,[16] who lack information about their biological parents, which could be important to them medically. Another less popularly recognized problem is the danger of half-sibling marriages,[17] where the child of the surrogate mother unwittingly falls in love with a half sister or brother. The only way to avoid these problems is to dispense with the confidentiality of parental records; however, the natural parents may not always want their identity disclosed.

The legalization of surrogate mother ar-

rangements may also put undue pressure upon poor women to use their bodies in this way to support themselves and their families. Analogous problems have arisen in the past with the use of paid blood donors.[18] And occasionally the press reports someone desperate enough to offer to sell an eye or some other organ.[19] I believe that certain things should be viewed as too important to be sold as commodities, and I hope that we have advanced from the time when parents raised children for profitable labor, or found themselves forced to sell their children.

While many of the social dilemmas I have outlined here have their analogies in other present-day occurrences such as divorced families or in adoption, every addition is hurtful. Legalizing surrogate mother arrangements will increase the frequency of these problems, and put more stress on our society's shared moral values.[20]

A TALE FOR OUR TIME

An infertile couple might prefer to raise a child with a biological relationship to the husband, rather than to raise an adopted child who has no biological relationship to either the husband or the wife. But does the marginal increase in joy that they might therefore experience outweigh the potential pain that they, or the child conceived in such arrangements, or others might suffer? Does their preference outweight the social costs and problems that the legalization of surrogate mothering might well engender? I honestly do not know. I don't even know on what hypothetical scale such interests could be weighed and balanced. But even if we could weigh such interests, and even if personal preference outweighed the

costs, I still would not be able to say that we could justify achieving those ends by these means; that ethically it would be permissible for a person to create a child, not because she desired it, but because it could be useful to her.

Edmond Cahn has termed this ignoring of means in the attainment of ends the "Pompey syndrome":[21]

I have taken the name from young Sextus Pompey, who appears in Shakespeare's *Antony and Cleopatra* in an incident drawn directly from Plutarch. Pompey, whose navy has won control of the seas around Italy, comes to negotiate peace with the Roman triumvirs Mark Antony, Octavius Caesar, and Lepidus, and they meet in a roistering party on Pompey's ship. As they carouse, one of Pompey's lieutenants draws him aside and whispers that he can become lord of all the world if he will only grant the lieutenant leave to cut first the mooring cable and then the throats of the triumvirs. Pompey pauses, then replies in these words:

Ah, this thou shouldst have done,
And not have spoke on't!
In me 'tis villainy;
In thee't had been good service.
Thou must know tis not my profit that does lend
    mine honour;
Mine honour, it. Repent that e'er thy tongue
Hath so betrayed thine act; being done unknown;
I should have found it afterwards well done,
But must condemn it now. Desist, and drink.

Here we have the most pervasive of moral syndromes, the one most characteristic of so-called respectable men in a civilized society. To possess the end and yet not be responsible for the means, to grasp the fruit while disavowing the tree, to escape being told the cost until someone else has paid it irrevocably; this is the Pompey syndrome and the chief hypocrisy of our time.

References

[1]See Philip J. Parker, "Motivation of Surrogate Mothers: Initial Findings," *American Journal of Psychiatry* 140:1 (January 1983), 117-18; see also Doe v. Kelley, Circuit Court of Wayne County Michigan (1980) reported in 1980 Rep. on Human Reproduction and Law II-A-1.

[2]See, e.g., C.M. v. C.C., 152 N.J. Supp. 160, 377 A.2d 821 (1977);

"Why She Went to 'Nobel Sperm Bank' for Child," *Los Angeles Herald Examiner,* Aug. 6, 1982, p. A9; "Womb for Rent," *Los Angeles Herald Examiner,* Sept. 21, 1981, p. A3.

[3]See also Richard McCormick, "Reproductive Technologies: Ethical Issues" in *Encyclopedia of Bioethics,* edited by Walter Reich, Vol. 4 (New York: The Free Press, 1978) pp. 1454, 1459; Robert

Snowden and G. D. Mitchell, *The Artificial Family* (London: George Allen & Unwin, 1981), p. 71.

4See, e.g., Alexander Peters, "The Brave New World: Can the Law Bring Order Within Traditional Concepts of Due Process?" *Suffolk Law Review* 4 (1970), 894, 901-02; Roderic Gorney, "The New Biology and the Future of Man," *UCLA Law Review* 15 (1968), 273, 302; J. G. Castel, "Legal Implications of Biomedical Science and Technology in the Twenty-First Century," *Canadian Bar Review* 51 (1973), 119, 127.

5See Harry Nelson, "Maintaining Dead to Serve as Blood Makers Proposed: Logical, Sociologist Says," *Los Angeles Times*, February 26, 1974 p. II-1; Hans Jonas, "Against the Stream: Comments on the Definition and Redefinition of Death," in *Philosophical Essays: From Ancient Creed to Technological Man* (Chicago: University of Chicago Press, 1974), pp. 132 40.

6See Leo Alexander, "Medical Science under Dictatorship," *New England Journal of Medicine* 241:2 (1949), 39; United States v. Brandt, Trial of the Major War Criminals, International Military Tribunal: Nuremberg, 14 November 1945-1 October 1946.

7Bob Dvorchak, "Surrogate Mothers: Pregnant Idea Now a Pregnant Business," *Los Angeles Herald Examiner*, December 27, 1983, p. A1.

8"Surrogate's Baby Born with Deformities Rejected by All," *Los Angeles Times*, January 22, 1983, p. 1-17; "Man Who Hired Surrogate Did Not Father Ailing Baby," *Los Angeles Herald Examiner*, February 3, 1983, p. A-6.

9See, e.g., Adoption in America, Hearing before the Subcommittee on Aging, Family and Human Services of the Senate Committee on Labor and Human Resources, 97th Congress. 1st Session (1981), p. 3 (comments of Senator Jeremiah Denton) and pp. 16-17 (statement of Warren Master, Acting Commissioner of Administration for Children, Youth and Families, HHS).

10Cf. "Discussion: Moral, Social and Ethical Issues," in *Law and Ethics of A.I.D. and Embryo Transfer* (1973) (comments of Himmelweit); reprinted in Michael Shapiro and Roy Spece, *Bioethics and Law* (St. Paul: West Publishing Company, 1981), p. 548.

11See, e.g., Lane (Newsday), "Womb for Rent," *Tucson Citizen* (Weekender), June 7, 1980, p. 3; Susan Lewis, "Baby Bartering? Surrogate Mothers Pose Issues for Lawyers, Courts," *The Los Angeles Daily Journal*, April 20, 1981; see also Elaine Markoutsas, "Women Who Have Babies for Other Women," *Good Housekeeping* 96 (April 1981), 104.

12See Morton A. Stenchever, "An Abuse of Prenatal Diagnosis," *Journal of the American Medical Association* 221 (1972), 408; Charles Westoff and Ronald R. Rindfus, "Sex Preselection in the United States: Some Implications," *Science* 184 (1974), 633, 636; see also Phyllis Battelle, "Is It a Boy or a Girl"? *Los Angeles Herald Examiner,* Oct. 8, 1981, p. A17.

13"2 Children Taken from Sperm Bank Mother," *Los Angeles Times,* July 14, 1982; p. 1-3; "The Sperm-Bank Scandal," *Newsweek* 24 (July 26, 1982).

14See Helmut Thielicke, *The Ethics of Sex,* John W. Doberstein, trans. (New York: Harper & Row, 1964).

15According to one newspaper account, when a surrogate mother informed her nine-year-old daughter that the new baby would be given away, the daughter replied: "Oh, good. If it's a girl we can keep it and give Jeffrey [her two-year-old half brother] away." "Womb for Rent," *Los Angeles Herald Examiner,* Sept. 21, 1981, p. A3.

16See, e.g., Lorraine Dusky, "Brave New Babies"? *Newsweek* 30 (December 6, 1982). Also testimony of Suzanne Rubin before the California Assembly Committee on Judiciary, Surrogate Parenting Contracts, Assembly Publication No. 962, pp. 72-75 (November 19, 1982).

17This has posed an increasing problem for children conceived through AID. See, e.g., Martin Curie-Cohen, et al., "Current Practice of Artificial Insemination by Donor in the United States," *New England Journal of Medicine* 300 (1979), 585-89.

18See e.g., Richard M. Titmuss, *The Gift Relationship: From Human Blood to Social Policy* (New York: Random House, 1971).

19See, e.g., "Man Desperate for Funds. Eye for Sale at $35,000," *Los Angeles Times,* February 1, 1975, p. II-1; "100 Answer Man's Ad for New Kidney," *Los Angeles Times,* September 12, 1974, p. I-4.

20See generally Guido Calabresi, "Reflections on Medical Experimentation in Humans," *Daedalus* 98 (1969), 387-93; also see Michael Shapiro and Roy Spece, "On Being 'Unprincipled on Principle': The Limits of Decision Making 'On the Merits,'" in *Bioethics and Law,* pp. 67-71.

21Edmond Cahn, "Drug Experiments and the Public Conscience," in *Drugs in Our Society,* edited by Paul Talalay (Baltimore: The Johns Hopkins Press, 1964), pp. 255, 258-61.

Genetic Choice

Michael D. Bayles

Michael D. Bayles is professor of philosophy at the University of Florida. He was formerly the director of the Westminster Institute for Ethics and Human Values in London, Canada; and he has taught at the University of Western Ontario, the University of Kentucky, Brooklyn College, and the University of Idaho. He has been a fellow at Harvard Law School, the Hastings Center, and the National Humanities Center. Among his books are

Morality and Population Policy (University of Alabama Press, 1980) and Professional Ethics (Wadsworth, 1981).

Bayles discusses three methods which allow people some choice about the genetic constitution of their offspring: (a) techniques of sex preselection, (b) carrier screening, and (c) prenatal diagnosis. He analyzes the value issues underlying decisions to make use of each method, as well as key ethical principles applicable to each. Further, he examines the case for and against the adoption of public policies with regard to these methods.

This [essay] considers issues raised by methods developed in the last two decades that provide people some choice of the genetic features of their children. For the most part, these methods enable people to choose not to have children with certain features.

Three types of methods of genetic choice are available. One type enables people to increase the chances of having a child of a specific sex. Another type, carrier screening, enables people to determine whether they are likely to transmit deleterious genetic features to offspring. The third type, prenatal diagnosis, can be used to determine whether a fetus has some specific characteristic and then abort it if that is desirable. Not all the conditions that can be detected by prenatal diagnosis are genetic; some of them result from drugs, maternal illness, or other causes.

SEX PRESELECTION

Case 2.1   Jeremiah and Katharine have two daughters, ages six and nine. Katharine is thirty-four years old. Jeremiah would like to have a son; indeed, he wants one very much. Katharine would like another child but does not especially care whether it is a boy or girl. However, she does not want to have more than one more child, and plans to be sterilized after the birth of the next child, whether Jeremiah likes it or not. The risks of having a child with Down syndrome are increasing as Katharine gets older; besides, she would like to go back to nursing, which she gave up when their older daughter was born.

Jeremiah reads a newspaper story describing a patented process that makes it possible to select with considerable accuracy the sex of a child at conception. The process involves taking semen from the husband and separating the male-determining sperm from the female determining sperm. The process destroys most of the female-determining sperm. Physicians at the clinic then artificially inseminate the woman with the male sperm. This process cannot be used to produce females, but Jeremiah is only interested in having a boy. Katharine agrees to the treatment; after the third month, she is pregnant. Jeremiah is joyous, because he is sure that this time he will have a son. Now and then, though, Katharine notices him sitting quietly with a worried look. She finally asks him what is wrong, and he says that he sometimes has doubts that this child will be a son, and he does not know what he will do if it is not.

In recent years, several methods in addition to the one just described have been developed to increase the chances of conceiving a child of a particular sex.[1] One technique involves injecting the woman with antibodies against male- or female-determining sperm. Animal sperm have been separated by using a medium of varying viscosity. Two methods that do not involve medical intervention have been suggested. One is to time intercourse to occur two days before ovulation in order to have a girl, or at ovulation for a boy. Another technique recommends a different timing, a vinegar douche, shallow penetration, and

---

From Michael D. Bayles, *Reproductive Ethics,* © 1984, pp. 33–51. Reprinted by permission of the author and Prentice-Hall, Inc., Englewood Cliffs, New Jersey.

[1]For more details, see M. Ruth Netwig, "Technical Aspects of Sex Preselection," in *The Custom-Made Child? Women-Centered Perspectives,* ed. Helen B. Holmes, Betty B. Hoskins, and Michael Gross (Clifton, N.J.: The Humana Press, Inc., 1981), pp. 181–86.

no female orgasm in order to have a girl; and opposite conditions for a boy. These two methods have not been well established; indeed, they recommend contrary timing of intercourse. A more accurate method, which is not yet possible, would be to ascertain the sex of embryos in IVF before transfer. Existing methods are not as accurate as IVF would be; at best, they increase the probability of a child being of one sex or another.

One rather different method for reliably determining the sex of the fetus now exists: prenatal diagnosis. At about sixteen weeks, amniotic fluid is withdrawn from the womb, fetal cells are cultured, and the sex is determined by chromosomal analysis. Some new techniques of recovering fetal cells may allow this procedure to be performed at an earlier date. To ensure the desired sex of the child, a woman must abort a fetus of the unwanted sex.

Sex Preference

Considerable evidence exists that many men and women, like Jeremiah, desire male children. Indeed, many prefer to have a male child first, and then a female. But is it rational to desire a child of a particular sex? A preference for one sex over the other, for its own sake, is simply sexism. It implies that one sex is intrinsically more valuable than another, but good reasons can be and have been given against this view by many authors, so such a desire is irrational.

Most people would not admit to such a pure sex preference but claim that the desire for a child of a particular sex is instrumental to fulfilling other desires. However, there are strong reasons for believing that many of the most common instrumental reasons are unsound and probably mask an irrational sexism. Reasons often given in the past for instrumentally preferring children of one sex (particularly males) are to inherit, to carry on the family name, and to have workers. But none of these reasons are relevant in the modern Western world. Today, male and female children inherit equally. Females can carry on the family name if they want; they need not change their names when they marry. Few jobs exist that women cannot fulfill as well as men (and of course they are generally better than men at some jobs).

One might reply that someone like Jeremiah need not be sexist or irrational to want a boy. He has two daughters, and he would simply like to have a boy as well. Had he had two boys, he might have wanted a girl. But why would two daughters and one son be preferable to three daughters? Someone like Jeremiah might respond that he would like a son so that he could have certain pleasures in child rearing—such as fishing and playing ball with him. But that too is probably a sexist assumption. As the father of two daughters, I have fished and played ball with them, watched my daughter play on a ball team, and gone camping and hiking with them, as well as cooked, cleaned house, done laundry, and engaged in various other so-called women's activities with them.

There may be some activities that are strongly sex-related in that members of one sex are generally better at them than members of the other sex. For example, perhaps most women have a greater aptitude for ballet than men. Recognition of such differences in role aptitude is not sexist, but the assumption that no members of the other sex can perform the same roles well or that one set of such roles is preferable to the other is sexist. Thus, a desire to have a male (female) child because of a preference for one set of "sex-linked" roles in sexist. Nor can one argue that variety is desired. Were children allowed to develop freely their own interests and talents, children of the same sex would probably exhibit as much diversity as children of opposite sexes.

Consequently, an instrumental preference for a child of one sex or the other is also often irrational. However, in some cases it is reasonable to desire a child of one sex rather than another for instrumental reasons. Undoubtedly, the most serious reason concerns X-linked genetic diseases, such as hemophilia. Only males exhibit the disease; females can only be carriers. Thus, if a woman is a carrier of such a disease, it would be rational to desire female children. Ironically, this

is not the sex preference most people express. In this case, sexism is not involved. The preference here is not for a female child, but for a healthy child, and a female has a significantly better chance of being healthy.

Ethical Analysis

We can assume that sexism is wrong. Arguments to this effect have been offered by many authors, and the history of sexism clearly shows the misery and unfortunate consequences it has wrought. Nonetheless, sexism is still prevalent in society. That sex preselection on the basis of intrinsic and most instrumental sex preference expresses an unethical sexist attitude is sufficient for holding that it is wrong. Its practice would probably reinforce sexist attitudes both in those who practice it and in others.

Two other general social consequences are often thought likely to result from sex preselection. First, evidence exists that most people who want a child of each sex prefer to have a male first, and that first-born children are apt to achieve more than later-born children.[2] If couples used sex preselection to have a male child first, and males were thus on average better social achievers than females, this would tend to reinforce sexist attitudes. Second, if sex preselection resulted in more males than females, the sex imbalance could have undesirable social consequences, such as insufficient mates. There might be good results as well. Population growth might decrease, because people often have more children in an attempt to have some of each sex. A better balance of male/female companionship among the elderly might result. The elderly population is now disproportionately female since women live longer than men; were there considerably more males than females born, the elderly population would be more evenly balanced between the sexes. Younger

women would be in short supply and might have more social opportunities. (Of course, more younger men might then lack mates and be lonely.) However, most of these projections about the consequences of a sex imbalance are mere speculation. They are not well enough founded to support an ethical principle.

In sum, sex preselection on the basis of intrinsic sex preference is always wrong, and so is most sex preselection on the basis of instrumental sex preference. One should accept an ethical principle condemning sex preselection as the expression of irrational desires and as reinforcing sexism in society. Unlike the irrational desire for genetic offspring, these irrational desires might have further untoward consequences if people act on them. However, sex preselection for clearly rational instrumental reasons, for example, to avoid offspring with sex-linked genetic diseases, constitutes an ethically permissible and desirable exception. Jeremiah's intrinsic desire for a son is the expression of a sexist attitude, and he and Katharine are ethically wrong to try to have a son.

Policy Analysis

Although most sex preselection is ethically wrong, policies to prevent its practice are not acceptable. Laws to prohibit sexism are justifiable in many areas, but sex preselection presents special problems. It would be impossible to enforce such a prohibition in practice if timing methods were effective. Any effort to prevent the use of timing methods would involve an unacceptable governmental intrusion into people's private lives. The best that could be done would be to prohibit the use of artificial insemination techniques for sex preselection by fertility clinics and others. Such a step would not effectively prevent such sex preselection, because people would lie about their reasons or an underground business would develop, so it would be pointless to restrict fertility clinics.

Should a sex imbalance result and the consequences be highly undesirable, then some social policy might be necessary and possible. The pol-

---

[2]Roberta Steinbacher, "Futuristic Implications of Sex Preselection," in *The Custom-Made Child? Women-Centered Perspectives,* ed. Helen B. Holmes, Betty B. Hoskins, and Michael Gross (Clifton, N.J.: The Humana Press, Inc., 1981), p. 188.

icy would not consist in prohibiting sex preselection, but in encouraging it! Incentives, such as extra tax deductions, could be offered for having children of a particular sex, or for having them first. Such policies might also reinforce sexism and would be acceptable only if the consequences of unfettered sex preselection were quite bad. Indeed, it might be wise not to accept them even then but merely to increase efforts at educating people not to be sexists.

Regardless of the ethics of abortion, the use of prenatal diagnosis and abortion for most sex selection is ethically wrong simply as sex preselection. However, that does not provide a reason for a policy against its use or withholding information about the sex of the fetus after amniocentesis. People may also simply be curious about the fetus's sex.

CARRIER SCREENING

Case 2.2   Louis and Miriam are in their early twenties. They have been married about a year but have not yet had any children. Both want to have their life together fairly well-adjusted before taking on parental responsibilities. They hear about a program at a clinic in their city to screen Jewish couples for carrier status of the recessive gene for Tay-Sachs disease. Miriam is especially concerned about it, because a friend of hers has recently given birth to a child with Tay-Sachs. The child faces a general neurological deterioration and almost certain death before school age. Her friend is going through emotional turmoil. Louis is less enthusiastic about having the tests. "After all," he says, "the disease results from recessive genes, so there is no chance of a child of ours having the defect unless both of us are carriers. Even then, the odds are only one in four. Why not simply have prenatal diagnosis done during pregnancy to determine whether the fetus has the disease? Even if both of us are carriers, we could go ahead and conceive and use prenatal diagnosis to find out if the baby is normal."

This case concerns one of the usual forms of carrier screening, that for a recessive autosomal (non-sex chromosomal) gene which is rare but more frequently found in a specific population. For recessive conditions, both parents must be carriers before there is a chance a child will have the condition. That is, to have a recessive disease, a child must inherit an affected gene from each parent. In this case, Tay-Sachs is found with a much higher frequency among Ashkenazi Jews—those from Eastern Europe—than others. A slightly more prevalent form of carrier screening is for defects in blood—sickle cell anemia among blacks, and beta-thalassemia among people of Mediterranean origin. Most carrier screening is relatively inexpensive and accurate and involves analysis of a small blood sample. Carrier testing is possible for a few other genetic conditions, and the number continues to grow. A few conditions are caused by dominant genes; with them, only one parent need be a carrier, but that parent will also suffer from the defect or disease. Most dominant disorders are detected in spontaneous mutants.

Value Analysis

Louis's and Miriam's differing attitudes towards carrier screening center on the value of the knowledge that will be gained. The primary outcome of genetic testing is knowledge—knowing whether a person is a carrier or has a condition. Knowledge can be desired either intrinsically or instrumentally. When knowledge is intrinsically valued, a person simply wants to know something for its own sake, out of curiosity. When knowledge is desired instrumentally, it is valued because of its consequences, usually because it enables one to take some action.

Information obtainable from genetic screening is primarily of instrumental value. Some people may simply be curious about their genetic constitution, but that is not the usual reason for having the tests. People desire knowledge about carrier status in order to relieve their anxiety

about having a child with a defect, and to enable them to take action to avoid having such a child. When tests are done to find out whether a newborn or adult actually has a disease, the people involved desire the knowledge in order to treat or ameliorate the condition. Sometimes the fear of finding out about a disease may be greater than any alleviation of anxiety. For example, Huntington disease results from a dominant gene and does not become manifest until later in life, usually between the ages of thirty and fifty. The disease involves progressive mental deterioration and uncontrollable physical movements. Woody Guthrie, the musician, died of it. The worry and anxiety of knowing that one has such a disease can be overwhelming, and the suicide rate amongst people who have it is high. Many people would rather not know whether or not they have it. The same may be true of some carrier screening, for some people have a lower self-image when they discover they are carriers. Thus, the bad consequences of genetic information can sometimes outweigh the good ones, and the information is not then instrumentally valuable.

The desire for genetic information is rational because it is surely rational to want to avoid having a child with a defect. One aspect of that desire is to avoid begetting (conceiving) a child with a significant handicap. Generally, a significant handicap is one that decreases the value of life to the person who lives it. The life of a child with a handicap can be of value but it is still rational to desire not to conceive such a child. Handicaps are by definition undesirable characteristics, and it is rational to avoid them. One might object that one also avoids the existence of the person, not merely the handicap. Yet, it is precisely the fact that no person exists that makes it quite rational to avoid begetting such a person. One would not, except under the most unusual circumstances, make a radio using a defective speaker even if that radio would have some value. Another aspect of the desire to avoid begetting a child with a significant handicap is to avoid the suffering of oneself and others. Handicapped children place greater burdens on their parents and siblings in terms of time, effort, and financial resources than do normal children.

Another relevant value pertains to risk taking. With recessive traits, one out of four children will have the deleterious disease. With dominant traits, one out of two children of an affected parent will have it. Other conditions have varying degrees of risk. Thus, attitudes about risk are important for making decisions. Unfortunately, no known method exists for showing that an attitude toward risk is rational or irrational. Some people are gamblers and risk-takers while others are cautious. No evidence exists that people would generally adopt one attitude rather than another were they fully informed of the facts. However, even if attitudes towards risk can rationally vary, they are not equally acceptable when the well-being of others depends on the decision. It may be reasonable to take significant risks with one's own life, for example, by riding a motorcycle, but it is unreasonable or ethically inappropriate to take significant risks with another person's life.

Ethical Analysis

Suppose Miriam talks Louis into going to the clinics to find out more about the test for Tay-Sachs. What information should Louis obtain and evaluate in order to give his informed consent to the procedure? This question is quite important in programs that involve mass screening; large-scale programs are apt to process people routinely without adequately explaining matters to them.

The point of having the test is to gain information. If Louis is to decide whether that information is worthwhile, he needs to be informed of all the relevant facts. How much will the tests cost? Sometimes the information obtainable is not worth the expense of obtaining it. Another important question is, What precisely does the procedure entail? Louis also needs to know what he can do with the test results. As such knowledge is only instrumentally valuable, he needs to know what options the information gives him. In the case of

Tay-Sachs, as Louis already knows, if both he and Miriam are carriers, prenatal diagnosis can be performed to determine whether a fetus actually has the disease. Another option would be to use artificial insemination by a noncarrier donor or to use a noncarrier surrogate mother. Louis should also want to know how bad the disease is, as well as the chances that someone of his background is a carrier. In short, Louis needs to be advised of the chances that he is a carrier, the nature of the test, the nature of the disease, and all the available options for action should both he and Miriam be carriers. With less than this information, he could not make a rational decision whether or not to have the test.

It might be argued that Louis has a duty to undergo the test, that he has a duty to discover whether he is at risk of having a child with a severe genetic disease or defect. After all, his ignorance could result in the birth of a child with a serious handicap; the child would suffer the consequences of Louis's action more than Louis.

Whether Louis has a duty to have the test depends on whether he and Miriam would have a duty not to have an affected child if it were revealed that both are carriers. If they would not have such a duty, they do not have a duty to find out that they are carriers and at risk of having such a child. Two factors are relevant to whether carriers have a duty to avoid having an affected child—the value of the life to the child and the effects of its life on others. Both of these factors must then be considered in light of variable risks of having an affected child.

The principle of avoiding risk to the unborn is that it is prima facie wrong to take a substantial risk of a significant defect or handicap to an unborn child. A number of reasons support this principle. First, since the child does not exist, failure to reproduce does not harm it, and . . . there is no duty to reproduce. Second, such a handicapped individual would lack an equal opportunity with others in society. For their own interests, parents would have deliberately brought into existence a person lacking equality

of opportunity. Third, if the handicap would be so severe that life would not be of value to the individual, misery would have been inflicted on that person. Consequently, while other considerations might outweigh the prima facie wrongness of risking a significant handicap that would still leave life of value, nothing short of averting a large-scale disaster could justify bringing into existence someone whose life was of no value to that person.

The principle regarding risk to the unborn deliberately does not specify degrees of risk and handicap, only that they be substantial and significant. The two considerations must be balanced against one another. The greater the handicap, the less the risk should be; and vice versa. At this point, what makes life valuable, and thus what constitutes a significant handicap, is not fully specified. . . . The crucial elements of a valuable life are pleasant experiences and the fulfillment of interests, both of which can be detrimentally affected by pain or lack of physical or mental abilities.

The principle regarding risk to the unborn has been justified solely by consequences for the child. However, effects on others, primarily the parents and siblings, are also relevant. The principle regarding burdens to others states that the burdens a child's life will place on others constitute an ethically relevant reason not to bring an unborn child into existence. In deciding whether to reproduce, couples should consider whether they would enjoy raising a child, as well as possible harmful effects on existing siblings. Since there is no duty to reproduce and the unborn child does not exist, it would not be harmed by not being brought into existence; but existing people might be. Thus, even if the child's life might be of value to it, the burden to others is a relevant reason for not reproducing.

***Case* 2.3**   Nathaniel and Olive are very much in love. A year or so after their marriage, they consider having a child. However, in their situation, they think it best to talk to a genetic

counselor first. Both have mildly expressed sickle cell disease, but they lead reasonably normal lives and their few attacks are under control.

The counselor tells them that pregnancy for a woman with sickle cell disease is rather risky. About half of such pregnancies result in spontaneous abortion or stillbirth, and the maternal death rate is very high.[3] Nathaniel and Olive are quite lucky that their sickle cell anemia is not severe. Ten percent of people born with the disease die by the age of ten, and many others live with great pain and are severely handicapped. Given that both of them have the disease, each of their children is also certain to have it.

This case presents an issue of risk taking. Unlike the problems of Louis and Miriam where the risk is whether a child will have the disease, in this case the risk pertains to the severity of the disease. For carriers of recessive conditions (like Louis and Miriam), the risk is one in four that their children will have the disease, and often this cannot be determined by prenatal diagnosis. The ethical questions in all of these cases are whether the principle regarding risk to the unborn applies, and whether other reasons for having a child outweigh it if it does.

In the case of Nathaniel and Olive, the principle clearly applies; a child of theirs is certain to have a life-threatening disease. The question is whether good reasons exist that outweigh the prima facie wrongness of their begetting a child together. Couples like Nathaniel and Olive may consider taking such a risk to have a child. One must here distinguish the desires to have genetic offspring, to bear offspring, and to rear them. As we have seen, the desire to beget offspring for its own sake is not rational. It is the only desire that need be frustrated if Nathaniel and Olive are to have a child without this risk of defect. If Olive were artificially inseminated with the sperm of a noncarrier donor, she could bear a child and they

[3]Robert M. Veatch, *Case Studies in Medical Ethics* (Cambridge, Mass.: Harvard University Press, 1977), p. 182.

could both rear it. She would even have begotten the child, but not with Nathaniel. Similarly, Nathaniel could beget a child by a noncarrier surrogate mother without risk of sickle cell disease. He could even beget by a noncarrier ovum and have the embryo transferred to Olive. Consequently, only the couple's desire to beget a child with each other supports reproduction in the usual manner. As a subclass of the desire to have genetic offspring, the desire to have genetic offspring with a specific person is also irrational. It surely does not override the principle of avoiding risk to the unborn. Thus, the risk is not one that may ethically be taken.

In general, then, the desire for genetic offspring cannot override the principle of avoiding risk to the unborn. It is not, however, always clear that the principle of risk applies. Suppose a couple is at risk of having a child with a disease like galactosemia, which can result in cataracts, mental retardation, and digestive disorders. The effects of galactosemia can be controlled by diet, primarily by avoiding milk and milk products, but this can cause considerable difficulty for parents, especially in preparing meals for a large family. With treatment, such a disease does not result in significant handicap to the individual, although it is a significant bother. Thus, the principle of risk to the unborn does not pertain, or at least has little weight. However, couples might decide not to risk such a child because of the burdens to them.

Another ethical issue that arises in carrier screening concerns confidentiality. Suppose Louis were tested and found to be a carrier of Tay-Sachs. Then each of his siblings has a 50 percent chance of being a carrier as well. Ethically, it seems clear, Louis should inform his brothers and sisters that they should also be tested. Suppose, though, he refuses to do so. May a physician suggest screening to the siblings without Louis's consent? One might suggest that his brothers and sisters need never know that Louis is a carrier; Louis's physician could simply tell them that they should be screened. But that would not work. Either Louis's siblings would know it was his doctor or they

would ask why the doctor thought they should be screened. The same problem would arise were the information given to their family physicians, supposing the testing center could find out who the doctors were.

The ethical conflict is between Louis's claim to confidentiality and his siblings' claim to have information important to them. The two values must be weighed. To do so, one must clarify the situation and consider the two values or desires as affecting oneself. Louis's fear of disclosure is irrational; being a carrier does not significantly affect his health, and he is not at fault for being a carrier. Even if the claim of confidentiality is weighted heavily, in this situation the value of the information is greater than that of confidentiality. Consequently, an acceptable principle of confidentiality would allow an exception for such a case. But the exception would extend only to Louis's siblings, who should ethically keep the information confidential.

A final difficulty that arises from carrier screening pertains to truth telling. Sometimes carrier screening is not performed until after the birth of an affected child. In that case, carrier screening might indicate that the putative father is not the genetic father. Should the counselor tell the man that he is not a carrier and so there is no risk in a subsequent conception? This would clearly indicate that he was not the father. Some counselors confronted with this situation lie and say that the defect was due to a spontaneous mutation so that there is no risk in a subsequent pregnancy.[4]

Although this type of situation cannot be avoided, the ethical situation can be clarified in advance. The purpose of screening is to obtain information, and prior to the screening the putative father should be told what types of information might be obtained. Prior to consent, he should be advised that information of nonpaternity might be discovered. At that point, he can decide whether he wishes to risk finding out that

information. Although a child might suffer should a putative father discover he was not the biological father and legally contest his paternity and obligation to support, this consideration is not stronger for handicapped than for normal children. Granted, the burden on a handicapped child may be greater than on a normal one, but the burden on the putative father is also greater, both emotionally and financially. Securing the putative father's consent beforehand will not make the discovery any easier for him or the child, and will probably make his decision to be tested more difficult, but it clarifies the duty of the physician to inform.

Policy Analysis

The primary policy issue in carrier screening concerns legally compulsory screening. Most mandatory screening is for treatable diseases in infants, but in the early 1970s a number of states enacted laws requiring all blacks to be screened for carrier status for sickle cell disease. Sometimes the legislatures were probably confused as to what they were requiring, thinking that the tests were for the disease rather than the carrier state. Are there circumstances in which mandatory screening is acceptable?

Two related reasons might support compulsory screening for carrier status. (1) Screening might decrease the number of children born with handicapping diseases. (2) This decrease might save public funds for the care of handicapped individuals. Mandatory carrier screening will not contribute significantly to either goal. Both of these possible benefits depend on people avoiding birth of handicapped children. Screening itself only provides information enabling people to avoid giving birth to such children. At a minimum, one would also have to ensure that most couples at risk were counseled as to how they could avoid such births. For the policy to be effective, the couples would then have to act to avoid such births.

The question is whether a compulsory screening program would be more effective than

---

[4]"Genetic Screening," *Encyclopedia of Bioethics* (1978), 2, 571.

a voluntary one. Little reason exists to think that it would be. Although counseling does have some effect in decreasing the number of children couples have, depending on the severity of the disease anywhere from 35 to 75 percent have the same number they planned to have before counselling.[5] Since most of these people were voluntarily counseled, it is unlikely the success rate would be as high among people screened involuntarily. If no significant reduction in births of defective children is achieved, there will be little or no financial savings either. Because of this, and because a mandatory program is an infringement of people's freedom, compulsory screening is not acceptable. Nonetheless, a voluntary program is supportable. Such a program is likely to be more effective because participants will be motivated to avoid the birth of children with defects (the primary reason for coming), and it will increase their freedom to control their reproductive activity.

One might ask at what age such screening should be offered. Many of the mandatory carrier programs screened newborn children. However, the main purpose of carrier screening is to provide information for reproductive decisions—decisions that newborn children do not confront. In a voluntary program, there is no reason for age restrictions. Voluntary programs should, however, be aimed at people before their reproductive attitudes are set. This means that, at the least, general education about genetics and reproduction should begin in elementary school. Actual screening and information about contraception and parenting should occur before reproductive years—in junior high school.

PRENATAL DIAGNOSIS

Prenatal diagnosis includes a variety of techniques designed to provide information about whether a fetus has a defect. The following techniques are currently used. (1) Maternal blood serum can be tested. Such tests for alpha-fetoprotein can determine whether the fetus is likely to have neural tube defects (those in the spine or brain). (2) Ultrasound can be used to picture the fetus. (3) Fetoscopy, which involves inserting a needle-like instrument into the womb, enables physicians to visualize the fetus. (4) Amniocentesis, the most frequent type of prenatal diagnosis, involves using a needle to withdraw some of the amniotic fluid in the womb; the fluid can then be used for a variety of tests. Fetal cells in the fluid are often cultured and the chromosomes examined for defects. Amniocentesis is not usually performed until the fourteenth to sixteenth week of pregnancy, and culturing fetal cells then takes several weeks. Amniocentesis enables tests to be performed to discover most chromosomal anomalies, the most common being Down syndrome, as well as an increasing number of rare metabolic errors. One can also use amniocentesis with fetoscopy to obtain samples of fetal blood to test for sickle-cell anemia and other blood disorders.

So far as is known, all of these techniques are reasonably safe when performed by experienced physicians. At first, there was much concern about the safety of amniocentesis, but subsequent study has shown that the primary risk is inducing a spontaneous abortion in about 0.5 to 1.0 percent of the cases. The type of amniocentesis which involves drawing samples of fetal blood from the placenta has a somewhat higher risk of spontaneous abortion than drawing amniotic fluid. Ethically, these spontaneous abortions differ even from abortions for medical indications; there is no desire or intent to cause fetal death or knowledge that the fetus will die. Ultrasound, a relatively new technique, has been shown to be safe at the levels used, although it is so new that no information exists about its possible long-term effects. Safety is not currently a major issue in prenatal diagnosis.

People undergo prenatal diagnosis for basically the same reasons as carrier screening—to relieve anxiety about defects of the fetus, and to avoid the birth of a significantly handicapped

[5]"Genetic Diagnosis and Counseling," *Encyclopedia of Bioethics* (1978), 2, 563.

child. In 95 percent or more of the instances of amniocentesis, the fetus is discovered not to have the defect in question. If a defect is found, then avoiding the birth of a child involves a second trimester abortion, around twenty weeks' gestation.

Much of the concern and ethical argument about prenatal diagnosis has centered around the abortion issue. . . . It should be noted, however, that prenatal diagnosis decreases rather than increases the number of abortions.[6] Some women at risk would have an abortion rather than continue the pregnancy. Prenatal diagnosis usually shows that no defect is present, so these women are able to continue the pregnancy without fear of the specific defect. Other women have an abortion because the fetus is discovered to have a defect. However, as the number of those who would have had an abortion but are reassured is greater than the number who have an abortion, prenatal diagnosis decreases the number of abortions. Also, some women at risk of having children with defects will become pregnant only if amniocentesis is available.

Case 2.4   Paula is in her late twenties and her husband Quincy is a year or two older. Paula is pregnant for the first time and goes to the genetics clinic to request prenatal diagnosis for Down syndrome, a chromosomal abnormality causing mental retardation. She works in an institution for mentally retarded persons and is anxious about having a child with Down syndrome. The general incidence of Down syndrome is low for someone Paula's age, less than one-half of one percent, although it increases rapidly for women over thirty-five years old and is about two percent for women over forty. Nor is there a history of the condition in her family. Consequently, the genetics clinic denies her request because there is no medical indication for prenatal diagnosis.

---

[6]See Aubrey Milunsky, ed., *Genetic Disorders and the Fetus* (New York: Plenum Press, 1979), Chapters 5–7.

After a normal pregnancy, Paula delivers a child with Down syndrome.

Ethical Analysis

This case raises the issue of access to prenatal diagnosis. The primary medical indications for it are advanced maternal age (where the risk of a number of chromosomal anomalies is higher), previous spontaneous abortion or birth of a child with a defect, family history of defects, or carrier screening indicating that there is a higher than normal risk of a child with a defect. Should prenatal diagnosis be denied to women who, like Paula, want it even though there is no medical indication? The arguments for offering the service in these cases are that the normal risk of a defect is about one in two hundred, so there is always some risk of a defective fetus. If no defect is found, anxiety is relieved. In Paula's case, because she works with retarded persons, the anxiety was probably greater than for many other women without medical indications.

The arguments against offering prenatal diagnosis in such cases are these: First, a small risk of spontaneous abortion exists and that risk is not worth taking unless there is an above average risk of defect. However, should the genetics unit make this decision about risk, or should Paula? Paula bears the consequences—either a defective child or the loss of a normal one if a spontaneous abortion occurs. The difference between the risk of a defect in her case and the so-called risk cases is certainly less than two percent. That does not seem like a great enough difference simply to take the decision out of Paula's hands.

Second, there are considerations of cost. If Paula is paying, it is her decision to spend her money on the screening. Cost considerations primarily apply if the government is paying for the procedure. The government might conclude that performing the tests on someone in Paula's situation is not cost-effective; that is, the costs of the test will be greater than money saved by not having to provide for defective children whose birth

would be averted. One might reply that many other medical procedures do not save money, and the costs of Paula's anxiety and worry as well as the suffering of any defective children should also be taken into account. Nevertheless, given finite resources, the government might reasonably decide not to fund prenatal diagnosis unless patients are in a class for which it is cost-effective; it simply cannot afford to provide all possible medical tests for everyone who wants them.

A third reason against offering Paula the test is a shortage of resources. This point concerns a lack of facilities, usually laboratories, to perform the tests. If there is a shortage, then tests should be reserved for the high risk patients most apt to benefit by avoiding the birth of a defective child. This concern has been a real one in Canada, where some centers have had to consider raising the maternal age indication from thirty-five to thirty-seven because of lack of facilities for providing tests for all women thirty-five years of age or more who requested them. Even so, if there is laboratory room and Paula is not depriving anyone else of access, this reason has no force.

Another reason has been offered for denying prenatal diagnosis even for women at risk. The suggestion is that if adequate treatment exists for the condition, then prenatal diagnosis should not be offered. An example would be galactosemia. The objection to providing the test for this condition is basically the objection against the use of abortion for this reason. Its soundness therefore depends on the ethics of abortion. If abortion at this stage is not prima facie morally wrong, then the principle of burdens to others supports a decision to abort an affected infant. Even if abortion is a prima facie wrong, consideration of burdens to others might outweigh its wrongness. Consequently, prenatal diagnosis can be denied due to the availability of treatment only if abortion for the proffered reason is ethically wrong. As we shall see in Chapter 3 [not here included], abortion for such reasons is not ethically wrong, so there is no basis for denying prenatal diagnosis.

Another issue that arises in prenatal diagnosis is withholding information. One example has already been broached earlier, namely, withholding the sex of the fetus to prevent a woman aborting for sex preselection. However, other reasons also arise. For example, whenever a chromosomal analysis is performed from amniocentesis, most other major chromosomal anomalies are discovered. Thus, the fetus might be found to have XYY chromosomes. Some evidence indicates that males with an extra Y chromosome (which determines male sex) are more likely to be violent and to become inmates of prisons or institutions for the insane. However, the vast majority of XYY men are not violent or insane, and the evidence of greater risk is uncertain. If parents are told of this characteristic, it might adversely alter the way they raise the child if they decide to continue the pregnancy. Yet the purpose of prenatal diagnosis is to discover information; this is why the woman wants the diagnosis. To withhold information seems contrary to the very purpose of prenatal diagnosis.

As in carrier screening, these difficulties can be clarified by advance agreement. Before prenatal diagnosis is performed, a woman can be advised that all sorts of information might be gained, that the significance of some of it is ambiguous, and that she can have all information gained or only selected parts. In short, it can be agreed in advance what type of information will be imparted. It is up to the woman to decide what information is worth having and what is not. Even if it would be ethically wrong for her to have an abortion for sex preselection or an XYY condition, that is a matter for ethical and policy conditions for abortion, not for information from prenatal diagnosis. Not all women want the information in order to decide about abortion; some of them are simply curious about the sex of the fetus.

Another aspect of agreements prior to prenatal diagnosis should be considered. When prenatal diagnosis began, a number of centers refused to provide it unless the woman agreed to have an abortion should a defect be found. Otherwise, it was claimed, the risks were not worth

enzyme in people who have the disease. Second-trimester amniotic fluid samples from a number of at-risk pregnancies were tested for this enzyme. In the first 69 monitored pregnancies that resulted in full-term live births, however, comparison of actual outcome with the predicted outcome indicated an unacceptably high rate of both false positives and false negatives. Indeed, the overall results were not statistically better than chance.[7] The basis and validity of this method has been called into question.[8]

Other methods of detecting CF prenatally look encouraging, although false positive and false negative rates remain too high.[9] Rapid advances in fields such as biochemistry, cell biology, and molecular biology (particularly employing recombinant DNA technology) are being incorporated into research protocols. Following an April 1982 conference the Cystic Fibrosis Foundation was optimistic that the collaborative efforts of researchers, aided by the cooperation of the CF clinical community in providing samples for study, will ultimately result in reliable CF screening methods.[10] Of course, it is not possible to predict how soon such tests will be available.

As research into CF tests proceeds, experts are establishing the scientific criteria an acceptable test must meet. For example, screening will need to differentiate possible heterogeneity in the genetic defect responsible for CF. . . . An incomplete understanding of the heterogeneity of the genetic defect that causes hyperphenylalaninemia

led to confusion and misleading test results in the early stages of PKU screening. In addition, the enormity of the potential demand for CF screening makes it important that the tests that are developed can be automated.

Ethical Issues During Research

As with all research, studies of prospective CF tests require careful attention to ethical issues. Investigators must comply with specific procedures intended to protect human subjects, including prior review and approval of the study by an Institutional Review Board.[11] Issues of concern in CF screening include the selection of subjects, the disclosure of results to participants, and the monitoring, oversight, and funding of adequate pilot studies.

Subject Selection and Disclosure of Results   Blood samples for experimental newborn screening can be readily obtained in large numbers by obtaining proper consent for the use of samples already collected from most newborns during PKU screening. In contrast, investigating a CF prenatal test requires recruiting women to have amniocenteses they would not otherwise undergo.[12] In the early stages of such research, fluid samples from women who have had amniocentesis because of their increased risk for other biochemical or chromosomal defects are useful. However, this group is not representative of the potential target population for CF prenatal screening. Ultimately, research on women known to carry the CF gene (that is, women who have already borne a child with CF) is required.

When research subjects risk injury—and

Transport in Cystic Fibrosis Fibroblasts Not Different from Normal, 304 NEW ENG. J. MED. 1 (1981).

[7]*Heterozygote Detection and Prenatal Diagnosis: Conference Report,* New York, March 30-April 2, 1982, Cystic Fibrosis Foundation, Rockville, Md., mimeo. (n.d.).

[8]B. R. Branchini *et al., 4-Methylumbelliferylguanidinobenzoate Reactive Plasma "Protease" in Cystic Fibrosis in Albumin,* 1 LANCET 619 (1982).

[9]Henry L. Nadler, Phyllis Rimbelski, and Kathi Hanna Mesirow, *Prenatal Detection of Cystic Fibrosis,* 2 LANCET 1226 (1981).

[10]*Heterozygote Detection and Prenatal Diagnosis: Conference Report, supra* note 7, at i.

---

[11]45 CFR 46.

[12]A small number of women at increased risk for CF may be candidates for amniocentesis because of "advanced maternal age" or other reasons. However, the overlap is not likely to be sufficient to avoid some women having to undergo amniocentesis solely for research purposes.

amniocentesis carries a small risk—it is preferable that those who bear the burdens of research also benefit from it to the greatest possible extent. As a group, those with an increased risk for bearing children with CF stand to gain the most from development of a screening test. Indeed, the eagerness to advance research in this area is one incentive for women to participate in the research; the provision of a cytogenetic analysis of the amniotic fluid, including identification of the sex of the fetus, at no cost to the subjects could be another benefit. However, the most desirable benefit for subjects is information about whether they are carrying a child with CF. Yet reporting the results of experimental CF tests to the subjects could have scientific as well as ethical ramifications.

CF cannot be definitively diagnosed in an aborted fetus; prenatal test results can be verified only by performing a sweat test on an infant after birth. Establishing the sensitivity and specificity of a prenatal test depends, therefore, on subjects continuing their pregnancies to term. If a significant portion of the participants in a CF prenatal study were to terminate their pregnancies, research goals could not be met—and thus all the women who participated in order to advance research would have undergone amniocentesis pointlessly.

The importance of refraining from actions based on unproven test results is not solely a matter of scientific concern, however. If the accuracy of test results is unknown, then actions based upon them may cause rather than prevent harm. The harm that could result from false positive results varies with the type of test. Parents who are told that their newborn may have CF are likely to suffer considerable anxiety until a sweat test can be done; this test may also be associated with minor inconvenience or expense. In contrast, a "positive" result in a prenatal study might lead a couple to terminate a pregnancy.

In light of the tentative nature of the results and the need to continue pregnancies to evaluate the test, one approach would be to withhold test results. The strongest case for withholding data is when researchers lack evidence of the test's accuracy. As research results begin to approach a level that is scientifically valid, however, the question of disclosure of test results becomes more difficult, and turns in part on the level of proof demanded of the test. Researchers may believe that a test should have a very low false positive rate before it forms the basis for clinical decisions. On the other hand, the parents participating in the research, many of whom have had a child with CF and are eager to have an unaffected baby, may be willing to act upon much less conclusive data; some would prefer to abort what may be a normal pregnancy rather than risk bearing a child with CF. Despite specific warnings that results are for research purposes and not for clinical decisions, some women may nonetheless make decisions about their pregnancies on the basis of preliminary CF test results.

Clearly, the degree of certainty required for scientific conclusions can differ from that considered sufficient for personal decisionmaking. Once evidence of some increase in the ability of the test to detect CF accumulates, withholding test results precludes subjects from exercising personal value judgments. Therefore, subjects should be informed in advance of participation whether results will or will not be disclosed. If results are reported, their limitations should be fully explained to the subjects.

Assuring Adequate Pilot Studies If limited trials of possible CF screening tests are successful, larger-scale pilot studies will be needed; their scope will depend on the numbers required to obtain statistically valid data. In addition to ascertaining how well a test works from a scientific or statistical perspective, pilot studies should also evaluate other aspects of the screen, such as cost-effectiveness, measures to educate professionals and the public about the test, and laboratory performance.

The promising research into CF screening tests that is under way gives particular urgency to

the Commission's recommendation that researchers, along with government, industry, and other funding and regulatory sources, begin now to identify their respective roles in adequate premarket testing of new screening methods.

PLANNING PROGRAMS FOR CARRIER AND PRENATAL TESTING

If a carrier and/or prenatal test proves acceptable in pilot studies, planners will need to identify who to screen and in what setting. Both the likely benefits and harms to potential screenees and the relative costs and benefits to society will need to be evaluated. Outside a research setting, screening programs ought to be introduced only if they seem likely to offer a net benefit to those being screened. The benefits of carrier and prenatal tests differ and will be influenced by the order in which the tests become available. Clearly, families who have a child with CF view the tests differently from those who do not.

Assessing Potential Benefit and Harm

Prenatal diagnosis for CF is likely to be developed either in conjunction with the discovery of a carrier test or in advance of it, depending upon the method that first proves successful (for example, biochemical or recombinant DNA). The availability of a prenatal test would eliminate some of the difficulties that arise when only carrier testing is available; in the latter case, test results may be used to select mates or to decide whether to forego childbearing but not to determine the outcome of a particular pregnancy. The contrasting experiences of screening for sickle-cell anemia (before the recent development of a means of prenatal diagnosis) and Tay-Sachs disease are illustrative. Some potential sickle-cell screenees found that the availability of carrier screening without

prenatal diagnosis was more harmful than helpful since they did not wish to make decisions based on carrier status alone. With Tay-Sachs disease, the simultaneous availability of a carrier test and prenatal diagnosis (and selective abortion) led some carrier couples to try to have children rather than forego reproduction entirely.

Although the experiences with sickle-cell and Tay-Sachs screening are instructive, neither is perfectly analogous to CF testing.[13] Like sickle-cell anemia, CF can be variable and is susceptible to some palliative treatment; although not as rapidly lethal as Tay-Sachs, CF is usually a very burdensome condition. Moreover, there are sociocultural as well as individual differences in the assessment of the benefits of prenatal diagnosis based on the importance people attach to health and to medicine generally and on their attitudes toward abortion.

In this way, the potential for CF screening is a precursor of the many difficult issues of risk and benefit that will increasingly arise in various types of genetic testing. The expanding capability to detect conditions and even predilections toward diseases prenatally—including, perhaps, some that occur later in life—underscores the importance of individuals freely choosing whether to participate in screening.

Deciding Who and When to Screen

Careful consideration will need to be given to the relative advantages and disadvantages of the two possible approaches to CF screening: prospective and retrospective testing. A prospective program would extend to the general population or some segment of it (for example, couples considering

---

[13]One reason for the greater acceptance of Tay-Sachs screening is the seriousness of the disorder itself; after a few months of normal development, affected infants begin to undergo a tragic degeneration, followed by death at a very young age. In contrast, the clinical effects of sickle-cell anemia vary considerably; patients can reach adulthood with symptoms ranging from quite mild to very severe.

childbearing). It would require extensive educational efforts to provide information about CF to people who are unacquainted with the disease. A retrospective program would be limited to families that include someone with CF. These candidates would already have some familiarity with the condition.

There are several ways that prospective screening could be organized. It could be provided in a community-based or mass screening program in which community resources are used to inform people about the disease and the test and in which screening is made widely available. Some experts have questioned this approach for diseases with a low incidence, however, arguing that the anxiety and stigmatization that can result from such a mass screening effort can outweigh the benefits when the likelihood that an individual screenee will produce an affected child is small.[14] This question will need to be addressed in the planning of a CF program, especially in deciding whether to screen populations with a very low incidence of the disease. CF is very rare in American blacks, for example. Just as individuals without eastern Jewish heritage are not screened for Tay-Sachs disease and Caucasians are not screened for sickle-cell anemia, CF screening of American blacks is probably inappropriate. In the past, screening for PKU was discontinued in predominantly black cities (such as Washington, D.C.) because PKU is so rare in blacks that the costs of screening were seen to outweigh the benefits.

In defining the target population a decision will also have to be made about whether to offer screening to people who are unmarried or not of reproductive age. The U.S. experience with sickle-cell screening of schoolchildren—about whom confidentiality was often difficult to maintain—sounds a warning about screening a population in which the benefits are so remote that they are likely to be outweighed by the harm, including the risk of breach of confidence. The young children screened for sickle-cell could do nothing with the information, and serious problems of stigmatization and confusion over the meaning of carrier status injured those screened and gave the whole effort a bad name.[15]

Alternatively, it is at least theoretically possible to obtain nearly as complete an identification of at-risk cases through screening solely married couples and people planning marriage as through general screening.[16] Initially, most Tay-Sachs screening involved only married couples because the programs' organizers (which typically included rabbis and other leaders in the Jewish community) did not want to risk having carrier status influence marital choices (and saw no need for such an influence, since amniocentesis was available for carrier-carrier couples). This policy reflected an understandable sensitivity to the risk that the label "carrier" might stigmatize a person in the eyes of others (including prospective mates and their families) as well as lead to a loss of self-esteem. Since children would not need the information to make reproductive decisions, there was no reason to risk the stigma.[17]

Although concerns over the possible harm of stigmatization are important, they must be weighed against the value of early screening. Many people may wish to know their carrier status prior to marriage (though not all of them may have thorough premarital medical examinations) and some do not wait until marriage to conceive

[14]Madeleine J. Goodman and Lenn E. Goodman, *The Overselling of Genetic Anxiety,* 12 HASTINGS CTR. REP. 20 (Oct. 1982); Arno G. Motulsky, *Brave New World? Current Approaches to Prevention, Treatment and Research of Genetic Diseases Raise Ethical Issues,* 185 SCIENCE 653 (1974).

[15]Ernest Beutler *et al., Hazards of Indiscriminate Screening for Sickling* (Letter), 285 NEW ENG. J. MED. 1485 (1971).

[16]Arno G. Motulsky, George R. Fraser, and Joseph Felsenstein, *Public Health and Long-Term Genetic Implications of Intrauterine Diagnosis and Selective Abortion,* J BIRTH DEFECTS: ORIGINAL ARTICLE SERIES (No. 5, 1971) at 22.

[17]This strict policy in the early Tay-Sachs programs has been relaxed in light of demands for the test from unmarried individuals, particularly those with a Tay-Sachs victim in the family.

children. This raises the question of whether people would generally regard it as desirable for decisions about dating, marriage, and reproduction to be made (at least in part) on genetic grounds. The outcome of the balancing process in the case of CF screening will depend upon facts about the test and the auspices and procedures for implementing it. The benefits of administrative efficiency in screening easily accessible populations (such as schoolchildren) will need to be weighed against all the harms, including nonphysical risks to individuals and society.

The alternative to a community-based program would be physician-based screening. If both prenatal and carrier tests were available, obstetricians could provide screening. All pregnant women could be offered the heterozygote test, partners of carriers could be screened, and "carrier couples" could be offered prenatal diagnosis. One drawback of this approach is that some couples or individuals, particularly those who would not want prenatal diagnosis, may wish to know whether they are carriers before marrying or conceiving a child. An obstetrics-based screening program would be inadequate in these cases. Screening offered as part of more generalized medical care (internists, gynecologists, and family practitioners) might be more responsive to this demand, but would still exclude a large number of potential screenees who do not receive regular medical care. Physician-based screening would require improved understanding of genetic diseases among physicians who are not specialists in genetics.[18]

If retrospective instead of prospective screening were used (for example, if a prenatal test were developed before a cost-effective means of carrier screening), the physician-based rather than the community-based approach would have to be employed. In terms of reducing the incidence of CF, the impact of retrospective screening would be much less than large-scale prospective screening.

> Under a scheme of prospective diagnosis the case reduction is 100% (i.e. no cases with the disease are born), as opposed to the less effective reduction which can be achieved with retrospective diagnosis (i.e. following birth of an affected child). Considering only the economic aspects, the saving to society by not having to bear the high costs of supporting patients with cystic fibrosis for the relatively large number of years which they can now survive will probably be substantially greater than the continuing costs of the programs for premarital screening, for intrauterine diagnosis and for selective abortion once the use of automated devices is introduced.[19]

As the Commission has noted throughout this Report, however, the fundamental value of genetic screening and counseling lies in its potential for providing individuals with information they consider beneficial for autonomous decision-making. Therefore, although societal impact and cost-effectiveness are relevant considerations, the benefits and harms that could accrue to individual screenees deserve special consideration if retrospective CF screening is being contemplated.

Distributing Benefits

The potential demand for CF screening is so large that even if a rather sizable portion of it does not materialize an enormous demand for genetic counselors and other health care personnel and services could still be engendered. Since CF tests should not be offered unless support services are adequate, program objectives must either provide for the expansion of needed resources, especially

---

[18]In a 1974 survey of a random sample of pediatricians, obstetricians/gynecologists, and family physicians, nearly three-quarters of the group reported that no courses in genetics had been available during their medical training. The study found that the medical profession as a whole is not ready to accept the importance of genetic disease, but that readiness could be increased if physicians had greater knowledge of human genetics. Committee for the Study of Inborn Errors of Metabolism, GENETIC SCREENING: PROGRAMS, PRINCIPLES AND RESEARCH, National Academy of Sciences, Washington (1975) at 161-64.

---

[19]Motulsky, Fraser, and Felsenstein, *supra* note 16, at 24.

trained personnel, or limit screening initially in a manner that would distribute it equitably.

An important objective, therefore, for those with responsibility for genetic screening programs will be to guarantee that needed resources, or the means of generating them in an orderly fashion, are available as screening is offered. Because the National Genetic Diseases Act was replaced by the Omnibus Reconciliation Act of 1981, greater responsibility for adequate preparation now rests with the states (from funds provided in block grants for maternal and child health programs) and with voluntary and professional organizations.[20] The states that had the strongest and best developed programs before 1981 may have the best chance of receiving non-Federal funds because successful programs typically develop local supporters who help lobby for grants. Conversely, where there has been little effort to date, the medical and lay communities may be unable to articulate the need for programs convincingly, even though the unmet need in such localities may actually be greater than elsewhere and the ability of preliminary programs to generate funds from other sources is usually less. Private organizations and government agencies should therefore pay particular attention to developing services in those areas.

Without knowing the type of test that might first become available, it is impossible to predict precise resource demands. A multiphasic test that uses several technologies (as in tests for neural tube defects done with blood samples after AFP testing, for example) would require different resources than a single biological assay. Nevertheless, it should be possible to begin to analyze the impact that large-scale CF screening, as well as other forms of genetics services, could have on the health care system.

A rough approximation of the number of tests an obstetrics-based system would involve can be calculated as follows: screening 3.3 million pregnant women (the approximate number of live births each year[21]) would yield about 165,000 carriers (assuming a carrier frequency of 5%); if the partner of each carrier is then screened, about 8250 couples who are carriers would be identified. Theoretically, therefore, the capability to perform more than 3.4 million carrier tests and 8250 prenatal tests annually would be needed even under the narrowest form of prospective screening (that is, obstetrics-based). Of course, not all women obtain medical care early enough in pregnancy for prenatal diagnosis, and some pregnant women or their partners may choose not to undergo the carrier or prenatal test, so that demand will not be fully realized. Still, trying to meet even part of that demand would put a considerable strain on the health care system.

Alternatively, a mass screening program to detect carriers that was targeted, for example, at Caucasians of reproductive age could create a demand for many millions of tests in a short period of time. Large numbers of trained counselors and other public health personnel would be required, in addition to widespread public education and community involvement.

Involving and Educating the Public

The generalized nature of the population at risk for cystic fibrosis in the United States has implications for the types of public education programs and local involvement in screening that will be suitable for this disease. A mass screening program will not be able to rely on any preexisting subgroups in the population affected who have special interest in the tests, as has been done with other genetic diseases. Planners would need to

---

[20]The voluntary groups include disease-based foundations, such as the Cystic Fibrosis Foundation, and umbrella groups, such as the National Foundation-March of Dimes. The American Society of Human Genetics provides leadership in professional activities relating to medical genetics.

[21]As this figure does not include miscarriages, the total number of women screened could be even higher, depending on when the miscarriages occurred in relation to the timing of a prenatal test.

turn to a larger and more diverse range of organizations and individuals, both locally and nationally, to achieve public participation. They will have to be very resourceful in identifying how members of the public can become informed about the availability and objectives of the screening and participate in planning local programs.

Although it may seem obvious that realistic goals for the program should be understood by the public, difficulties have arisen in the past when this has not occurred. Enthusiasm for mandatory PKU screening legislation, for example, was propelled in part by misguided notions that the test would significantly reduce the burden on public institutions for the mentally retarded when in fact less than 1% of the institutionalized retarded had PKU.[22]

PLANNING A NEWBORN SCREENING PROGRAM

Assessing Benefits and Harms

The value of the most widely used neonatal genetic test—for PKU—is that early diagnosis and treatment averts serious disease complications. For cystic fibrosis, however, it is not clear that a diagnosis in the neonatal period would usually affect outcome or even alter therapy. CF is not always recognized at the first sign of symptoms but some delay in arriving at a correct diagnosis has not been thought to affect the outcome of treatment adversely.

Families with a child who has CF should already be aware of the possibility of a subsequent CF birth, and therefore newborn screening would primarily benefit those who are not aware they are carriers. The possible benefits of mass newborn CF screening (if an effective method is developed) are that it could eliminate some of the costs, frustration, parental anxiety, and harm of incorrect diagnoses and therapies. Physicians are now studying the possibility that the prognosis for CF patients improves if treatment is begun before the onset of clinical signs. In addition, prospective newborn screening would provide the parents of a CF child with an earlier warning that they are CF carriers and, therefore, that any other children they conceive have a 25% chance of having cystic fibrosis. On the other hand, presymptomatic identification of CF may generate needless psychosocial problems within families since infants who would otherwise still be regarded as "normal" would instead be seen as sick and at risk for developing CF symptoms at any moment.

Distributing Benefits

In newborn screening, concerns about equity and access to services will probably be most acute in relation to follow-up tests. If the screening protocol relied on sweat testing as a confirmatory diagnostic measure, then present limitations in the reliability of such tests not done in specialized centers will be a serious concern.[23] In deciding whether and how to implement widespread newborn screening, the feasibility of upgrading test performance in areas now inadequately served must be considered, either through specialized laboratories or through providing equitable access for patients from these areas to centers that perform the diagnostic tests reliably.

Protecting Autonomy

A basic ethical consideration underlying any CF screening program should be the protection of individual autonomy. Although considerable public interest has been shown in the development of a test, some individuals are likely to choose not to

---

[22]GENETIC SCREENING: PROGRAMS, PRINCIPLES AND RESEARCH, *supra* note 18, at 24.

[23]*Problems in Sweat Testing,* Report of a Conference, Hilton Head, S.C., Feb. 6-7, 1975, Cystic Fibrosis Foundation, Rockville, Md., mimeo. (n.d.).

be screened for CF, and their ability to make that choice must be safeguarded.

The need to assure the option of refusing a CF newborn test underscores the importance of informed consent in newborn screening generally. Although most states' mandatory genetic screening statutes provide that parents may object to screening (in some cases, specifically on religious grounds), these provisions are usually ineffective since parents seldom learn about the test until after it has been performed.[24] Some people have concluded that "informed consent" ought not to be necessary for a procedure that offers great benefit and little risk.[25] According to this argument, parental autonomy in decisionmaking about newborn screening is grounded in a principle of beneficence, which holds that parents are the people most well suited to act in the best interests of an infant. When, the argument goes, it would be generally agreed that children's best interests lie in being screened, parental consent is superfluous. But even if this case could be made for certain established screening programs—and the Commission is not wholly persuaded that it could—it certainly does not apply to a condition like CF, in which the benefits of the screening test are not clear-cut and in which parents, therefore, may choose not to participate.

Moreover, informed consent is more than just a legal formality—one more piece of paper to sign. It is a process of shared decisionmaking between patients and providers.[26] It can play an educational role—both in telling a pediatrician something about new parents' values and beliefs

and in informing the parents about the usefulness of obtaining evaluations even for apparently "well" children, about their mutual responsibility (along with physicians and nurses) for their child's health, and even about probability and genetics. In addition, a process of this sort, in which parents are informed and their permission is sought for CF newborn screening, is a reminder to health care professionals and legislators of the importance of informed consent more generally.

The availability of a neonatal CF test suitable for mass screening could stimulate both a more scrupulous enforcement of the current "permissible refusal" provisions of existing laws and, even more important, lead to a reevaluation of the wisdom of mandatoriness in all newborn genetic screening. As a practical matter, a CF screen is likely to be performed on the same blood sample now obtained for other newborn tests and the need to obtain informed consent for the CF test may encourage simultaneous consent for other tests. Since parents, excited about the recent birth of their child, may prefer not to contemplate the remote possibility that their infant has a serious disease, physicians should consider initiating discussions about these tests prior to delivery, at which time the genetic screening programs can be placed in the context of other medical information relevant to the impending birth.

ADEQUATE EVALUATION

It is particularly important that appropriate plans for evaluation be a stated objective of initial CF screening efforts. First, since testing for CF will probably involve a much larger program than any previous genetic carrier screening efforts, careful monitoring will be needed to determine whether it is reaching its objectives. The specific questions to be answered in follow-up studies will depend on whether the screening involves prenatal, carrier, and/or newborn tests. In any event, the scientific, epidemiological, and psychosocial effects of screening all deserve careful attention.

---

[24]Ruth Faden *et al.*, *A Survey to Evaluate Parental Consent as Public Policy for Neonatal Screening*, 72 AM. J. PUB. HEALTH 1347 (1982).

[25]Ruth R. Faden, Neil A. Holtzman, and A. Judith Chwalow, *Parental Rights, Child Welfare, and Public Health: The Case of PKU Screening*, 72 AM. J. PUB. HEALTH 1396 (1982).

[26]President's Commission for the Study of Ethical Problems in Medicine and Biomedical and Behavioral Research, MAKING HEALTH CARE DECISIONS, U.S. Government Printing Office, Washington (1982).

Second, screening for cystic fibrosis is likely to provide a preview of what will in the future be an increasingly important part of health care. The lessons of CF screening can augment those of previous programs—for PKU and other newborn screening for inborn metabolic errors, for trait carriers and affected fetuses of Tay-Sachs and sickle-cell anemia, and for chromosomal anomalies in the fetus.

The ethical imperative for adequate evaluation flows from the principle of beneficence—the promotion of the well being of those who participate in genetic screening and counseling. Moreover, follow-up studies not only provide a basis for an overall evaluation of the test; they also enhance autonomy by contributing important information for the informed consent process. Appraisal of the screening once it has become more widely available will, therefore, be needed.

The Commission believes that for some screening programs evaluation is likely to be most effective if coordinated on a national basis, whether the evaluation is done by private bodies (with or without support from a Federal agency), by state agencies, or by a Federal health agency such as the Centers for Disease Control. As described in Chapter One, this model was followed by the United Kingdom in its large-scale study of AFP testing. Public and private funding should be made available for such follow-up. The important role that state health agencies can play in this field is well illustrated by the activities of the Commission on Hereditary Disorders in Maryland, which for nearly a decade has overseen and promoted the development of screening programs in that state. The legislation that established that body provides a valuable model for other states.

CONCLUSION

Within the next decade screening for cystic fibrosis may be possible. This could be of great benefit. If adequate preparation for its introduction is not made, however, it could also create serious problems. The technical aspects of such preparation are not the primary concern of this Commission; they rest with the Food and Drug Administration and with the process of peer review at Federal and private funding agencies and in scientific journals.

The likelihood of a huge demand for CF screening—of carriers, of pregnant women, or of newborns—merits attention to more than merely technical issues and to more than just CF testing, however. The possible demand for millions—or tens of millions—of tests in a short period of time, and the consequent need for follow-up diagnostic studies and counseling, is daunting in itself. Moreover, it is merely the harbinger of a still greater demand: the ability to screen for genetic conditions is certain to affect not only health care but also areas as varied as environmental control and occupational and product safety, as it becomes possible to determine personal susceptibility to particular disorders or to the risk of passing them on to offspring.

In this Report the Commission has reached a number of conclusions about what might be termed "ethical preparedness" for genetic screening and counseling. It believes that the guidance set forth here, in conjunction with that provided by other groups,[27] establishes a solid starting point for resolving the issues—of autonomy, confidentiality, equity, knowledge, well-being, and the like—that will arise when various types of CF testing become feasible. Some of these issues concern benefits and risks to individuals, others the welfare of the entire society, and still others a combination of both. Some of the problems are concrete—such as protecting the confidentiality

---

[27] *See, e.g.,* GENETIC SCREENING: PROGRAMS, PRINCIPLES AND RESEARCH, *supra* note 18; M. Lappé *et al., Ethical and Social Issues in Screening for Genetic Disease,* 286 NEW ENG. J. MED. 1129 (1972); Tabitha M. Powledge and John Fletcher, *Guidelines for the Ethical, Social, and Legal Issues in Prenatal Diagnosis,* 300 NEW ENG. J. MED. 168 (1979); Council on Scientific Affairs, *Council Report: Genetic Counseling and Prevention of Birth Defects,* 248 J.A.M.A. 221 (1982).

of screening results. Others, which are harder to address, are more abstract—such as correcting the notion that genetic measures can, or should, be used to make the outcome of each pregnancy a "normal" person, much less a "perfect" one.

The Commission recognizes that it is unlikely that all problems can be avoided—or even that they can all be anticipated at the moment. But it encourages continued attention to this area by government officials, as well as by people knowledgeable about relevant scientific, ethical, social, and legal concerns. This call for attention is not meant to raise an alarm, merely to point to some steps that should be taken—and, in partic-

ular, some ethical concerns that need to be addressed—to ensure that the burgeoning capabilities of medical genetics achieve their great potential for good. This field holds the promise of increasing people's options and letting them make choices informed and free of the constraints of ignorance. By educating people about their own particular inherited makeup, genetic screening and counseling—if employed with care and with attention to the issues addressed in this Report—can increase respect for the great diversity of human beings that rests in part on their genetic heritage.

Gene Therapy: Proceed with Caution

Clifford Grobstein and Michael Flower

Clifford Grobstein is professor of biological science and public policy at the University of California, San Diego. He is a member of the National Academy of Sciences and the Institute of Medicine.

Michael Flower is visiting assistant professor of biology at Lewis and Clark College, Portland, Oregon. He teaches courses in science, technology, and human values.

The authors review the recent history of both research leading towards gene therapy and the public policy discussions it has engendered. While acknowledging that there are sufficient risks to warrant societal reviews of future developments, they do not see insuperable ethical barriers to continuing the search for gene therapy techniques—even in germ cells. They offer guidelines for societal oversight of initial tests of gene therapies, as well as for their long-term implementation. With regard to the shorter term, they state four basic principles to be promulgated as a basis for review.

On February 6, 1984, a new page was added to the short but contentious history of gene therapy in human beings when the Recombinant DNA Advisory Committee (RAC) of the National Institutes of Health (NIH) approved a recommendation for final guidelines for agency oversight of this controversial form of research and therapy. The guidelines were hurried along in response to concerns that at least two researchers from the

From *The Hastings Center Report*, vol. 14, no. 2 (April 1984). Reprinted by permission of the authors and publisher. © The Hastings Center, 360 Broadway, Hastings-on-Hudson, New York 10706.

University of California, San Diego and San Francisco campuses, will be submitting research protocols for gene therapy in human beings before the end of 1984. They illustrate the dramatic shift in attitudes that has taken place in this country toward recombinant DNA research on human beings.

Seven years ago, in March 1977, the National Academy of Sciences sponsored a forum in Washington, D.C., on research with recombinant DNA. The Great Hall of the Academy was brightly floodlit for televising the event. The hall was packed. As the first session began, uninvited

demonstrators marched down the aisle waving placards and charts denouncing the proceedings. "Recombinant DNA scientists have unlocked the mystery of life itself," said Jeremy Rifkin, a leader of the demonstration and now president of the Foundation on Economic Trends. Biologists, he predicted, will now be able "to create new plants, new strains of animals, and even genetically alter the human being on this earth." Rifkin went on to warn, "Wait until the Protestants, the Jews and the Catholics, the Methodists, the Presbyterians and the Baptists all over America start to realize the long-range implications of what you gentlemen are doing."[1]

Seven years later, in November 1983, the National Institute for Child Health and Human Development (NICHHD) held a public forum on gene therapy in Bethesda, Maryland, and the tone was altogether different. Invitations had gone out to many groups and individuals, including the 200 signers of Rifkin's recent petition to ban all germ-line therapy, but the audience far from filled the large auditorium.

At the morning session, the presentations were authoritative and informative, but added little new hard information for those who had been following the field. During the afternoon session, one speaker calmly discussed the ethical issues in gene therapy from a religious perspective. Questions from the floor were temperate and thoughtful and little or no rancor erupted. Clearly, gene therapy in human beings was seen as offering substantial potential medical benefit, and a process of policy formation was under way to understand and minimize the possible risks of the procedure.

Gene therapy refers to the process of introducing a properly functioning gene to correct the effect of a defective one in order to cure hereditary diseases that are caused by gene mutations. Researchers hope that one day gene therapy will cure inherited disorders such as thalassemia and sickle cell anemia; Tay-Sachs, a disease of the central nervous system that usually leads to death at an early age; and Lesch-Nyhan disease—a painful neurological disorder that generally attacks children and causes them, among other things, to mutilate themselves. At present there are no effective cures for these diseases though, in some, palliative treatments may relieve symptoms for a time. The only permanent "treatment" now available is prevention where possible—screening and counseling couples at risk for Tay-Sachs, beta thalassemia and sickle-cell anemia; and avoiding conception or aborting fetuses that may be affected.

Though gene therapy has not been effectively attempted so far in treating human beings, researchers have reported some success in introducing genes in mouse studies. In one experiment, for example, researchers reported introducing into preimplantation mouse zygotes a gene for the production of growth hormone in rats.[2] The "supermice" born with the new rat gene grew far faster and larger than their brothers and sisters. This is a model not for therapy but for possible improvement of livestock.

GUIDELINES FOR CLINICAL TRIALS

The ethical and other issues raised by such gene transfer to humans relate to two cases: somatic therapy, which affects only the person being treated, and more controversial germ-line therapy, which involves changes that can be passed on to future generations.

There is a growing consensus that gene therapy addressed to somatic or general body cells (and not affecting sperm, eggs, or germ line cells able to give rise to them) can and should be attempted, so long as clinical trials meet rigorous stipulations. Though the nature of these stipulations has been discussed, no set of recommendations has yet been adopted or promulgated by any agency with authority. Investigators are therefore left in doubt as to how IRBs and or other reviewers will react to a particular proposal for a clinical trial of a given genetic therapy.

The following cautionary guidelines have been consolidated from several sources:[3]

(a) Only a disease that drastically reduces the quality or duration of life should be a candidate for somatic gene therapy.

(b) A clinical trial should be conducted only if there is no alternative established therapy that is likely to yield as good or better results.

(c) Investigators should be able to identify the nature of the selected genetic defect as well as the course of events leading to symptoms.

(d) There should be evidence that the planned procedure for modifying the specific genetic defect is regularly safe and efficacious in comparable animal studies. This should include a demonstration that the new gene has been inserted in proper target cells; that it remains there; that it is expressed appropriately (in other words, produces proper quantities of its product); and that it does no harm to target cells or, inadvertently, to nontarget cells.

(e) All established procedures for the ethical conduct of human clinical trials should be followed.

(f) The protocol should be so planned that even if therapy is not achieved its subsequent success will be more likely, i.e. "shots in the dark" should not be attempted.

Such possible guidelines for initiating a clinical trial indicate that gene transfer to somatic cells must not only meet standard ethical and scientific criteria for human experimentation; additional safeguards must be provided—because of the novelty of the technique and the large uncertainties about the nature of its effects on the complex human genome. A case in point is the guideline that would emphasize that "regularly safe and efficacious" results must be achieved in animal studies, demonstrating that the inserted gene is incorporated at a proper place, remains there, and functions without harming intended targets or, inadvertently, nontargets. This stipulation reflects uneasiness generated by recent findings that genes do not go to the right place in the genome of animals, that they are not necessarily stable in their new site, and that they can cause harm to the cells or the animal when improperly inserted. Such findings may mean that successful human gene therapy is still fairly far off, and, at least initially, may be quite restricted in application.[4]

DANGERS OF GERM-LINE THERAPY

To date all effort leading toward human gene therapy has focused on somatic cells. If human somatic gene therapy is medically demonstrated and accepted, however, a powerful rationale will exist to extend gene transfer to germ-line cells as well. If, for example, somatic cell therapy were fully effective in treating betathalassemia, an individual still having a double recessive germ-line defect could lead a normal life. But if reproductive health includes the probability of having genetically normal offspring, that individual could claim an ethical right not to be deprived of germ-line repair since, without it, all offspring would at least be carriers and, were two double recessive individuals to marry, all offspring would develop the disease. Although somatic cell therapy might be provided in each generation, the argument to rid the lineage of the defective genes once and for all might prove compelling.

At present, both technical uncertainties and serious ethical and social issues surround the deliberate application of gene therapy to germ-line cells. The technical uncertainties include generally low and variable efficacies of gene transfer in animals by most procedures used so far. For example, at present only a small percentage of microinjected mouse zygotes survive the required technical manipulations and emerge as genetically transformed mice.[5] Moreover, whether inserted genes will express themselves can depend

on the site of insertion, which is difficult to control so far.[6] If more were known about the relationship between the site of insertion and the expression of inserted genes, we might better understand how to proceed. Without that knowledge there are serious practical obstacles to precise gene therapy.

There are also disturbing reports of inserted gene sequences altering the function of neighboring genes.[7] In two cases, the inserted genes produced a mutation that in the homozygous state resulted in embryonic death.[8] Until these matters are clarified, human germ-line therapy is likely to be regarded as too risky to undertake. Results of this kind call for caution even in somatic gene therapy, if there is any likelihood that germ-line cells can become an inadvertent target.

Despite this need for caution, John Fletcher of the National Institutes of Health has cogently argued that, with certain provisos, gene transfers to human germ-line cells would be as acceptable ethically as transfer to human somatic cells.[9] Such provisos, at least for the time being, might include stipulations that the procedures will cause no harm, that their objective is limited to medically necessary goals, and that they do not violate generally acceptable ethical principles.

Unfortunately, what constitutes a legitimate medical objective has never been fully defined—witness the controversies over sex change surgery—and it is possible to imagine extra-medical objectives for germ-line therapy, such as elimination of characteristics currently judged to be undesirable. Furthermore, since animal experiments have shown that effective gene transfer to the germ-line requires early embryonic intervention, Fletcher's argument assumes we can resolve the knotty issue of the status of the early human embryo as a subject of experimentation.

THE POLICY PROCESS

In November 1981, the National Institutes of Health informed Martin Cline, a professor at the University of California at Los Angeles, that funding for several of his research projects would be discontinued as a result of what was judged to be premature work with human gene therapy. Cline had inserted genes into the bone marrow of two terminally ill patients, in Italy and Israel, who were suffering from thalassemia. Although he had approval from groups abroad, the proposed trial was still under review by the Human Subjects Use Committee and the Recombinant DNA Biosafety Committee at UCLA. NIH also informed Cline that any future applications by him for grants involving recombinant DNA research and human experimentation would require more stringent review than normal at both UCLA and NIH. In addition, he was required to provide written assurance that he was conforming with federal regulations.[10]

The Cline incident indicates that mechanisms put in place in the last decade or two can make and enforce judgments about the readiness of gene transfer for clinical trials. However, institutional review boards, which oversee human experimentation, and committees to oversee recombinant DNA research are neither specifically charged, nor necessarily well constituted, to undertake the broad and continuing deliberation that human gene transfer now requires. Fortunately, a policy process for overseeing gene therapy has already been proposed, though its initiation is proceeding slowly.

Some options that are now being considered were enumerated in the recent report of the President's Commission for the Study of Ethical Problems in Medicine and Biomedical and Behavioral Research.[11] One—a proposal to establish a President's Commission on the Human Applications of Genetic Engineering—was incorporated into the NIH reauthorization bill, passed by the House of Representatives in November 1983, and is slated for Senate consideration this year.

These options have been referred to as a "means of oversight," a good term because it implies a perspective beyond that of the immediate actors (the physician and the patient), yet leaves open the manner of implementation. Oversight is not synonymous with regulation. As the Presi-

dent's Commission wisely noted, the immediate need is to widen awareness, and deepen deliberation, about the issues that are raised by human gene transfer.

Although oversight at the federal level has advantages, it is not the only possibility. Oversight might be provided at the quasi-federal level (for example, by the National Academy of Sciences complex) or entirely in the private sector by relevant professional groups, by a foundation-supported ad hoc mechanism, by consumer-oriented organizations, or by a religious consortium. Moreover, there is no reason why several oversight mechanisms might not function independently or in collaboration. If the objective is to increase awareness and understanding, a multiplicity of oversight efforts may even be preferable. Obviously, however, these efforts must converge toward public action if actual regulatory control is considered necessary.

Despite the multiplicity of possible oversight mechanisms, attention has focused mainly on a federal commission. In part, this is because of our recent reliance on federal commissions to deal with biomedical issues that raise significant ethical questions. The National Commission, which focused on human experimentation, and the President's Commission, which examined a broad range of bioethical issues including gene transfer, are widely regarded as having had a constructive impact. Thus, establishing similar commissions seems attractive.

The recent report of the President's Commission, although surveying other options and eschewing a stated preference, details a concept of a new commission devoted to gene therapy and assigns to it a "forcing function," requiring federal agencies to respond to commission recommendations. A commission very like that described by the President's Commission, but without a forcing function, would be established by the pending legislation passed by the House in November. Most witnesses at the 1982 hearings on gene therapy conducted by Congressman Albert Gore endorsed this kind of mechanism.[12] It was also viewed favorably by a group assembled by the

Institute of Medicine late last spring to discuss the continuing need for an ethics commission.[13] A new and special federal mechanism is not uniformly accepted, however. Jeremy Rifkin regards such a commission as a legitimization of eugenics and oppose it on that count. Others suggest that existing groups can fulfill at least part of the need.

In June 1983, a working group of the RAC, responding to the President's Commission's report, proposed that "the membership of the RAC be modified to include adequate representation to deal credibly with these issues," since "there is currently no other national body that deals with ethical issues in the biomedical field." RAC proposed to expand its expertise by adding experts in the ethical issues of using human subjects.

In December the working group suggested that a committee, composed of nine members, be formed to conduct an initial review of federally funded proposals submitted to the RAC, which would then be reviewed by the whole RAC. The committee would include those with expertise in basic science, clinical medicine, law, and ethics, as well as liaison members from the Food and Drug Administration and the Office of Protection from Research Risks. The working group also recommended revising the language of the NIH guidelines for research review to specifically include "deliberate transfer of recombinant DNA or DNA derived from recombinant DNA into human subjects." On February 6, 1984, the RAC accepted the recommendations of the working group. If NIH approves the recommendations as expected, future federally funded research protocols for gene therapy in human beings will be subject first to review by an institutional review board to assure protection of human subjects; then by the special committee of the RAC, which would review proposals for the consequences to society; and finally by the entire RAC.[14]

Members of the FDA staff also see a role for their agency. In the future the FDA will regulate DNA used in gene therapy just as it now reviews drugs and biologic or medical devices, whether the research is funded by the public or private sector.

THE SEARCH FOR PRINCIPLES

What results can we hope for from any oversight mechanism? Clearly, there are near-term and longer-term tasks, either to complete or to initiate. In the immediate future there is a need to establish and promulgate guidelines for clinical trials of various somatic gene therapies. Presumably such guidelines would, at least initially, take the form of an advisory to existing institutional review boards. However, there might also be need for preliminary and continuing evaluation of the effectiveness of institutional review boards in carrying out this new function.

Also in the near-term, an oversight body might consider drafting a first-round set of principles that could be promulgated provisionally. Such principles are appropriate provided they: (1) derive from apparent consensus; (2) relieve significant anxiety; or (3) delimit the area requiring detailed deliberation. The following set of principles is suggested to initiate discussion.

Principle A As an extension of existing charters of human rights that guarantee voluntary participation and informed consent in human experimentation, *no genetic intervention shall be attempted on any human being with the intention or reasonable expectation that it will reduce either somatic or germ-line potential.* However worded, the principle is intended to assuage fears that gene transfer will become a tool of tyrannical malevolence to denigrate human beings for political or social purposes.

Principle B *Any human genetic modification that is intended or may reasonably be expected to alter germ-line cells shall not be attempted without special review and sanction by a body suitably constituted to evaluate not only technical risks of effects on the human gene pool but political, social, and moral impacts as well.* However worded, the principle is intended to affirm the special problems raised by germ-line modification and to assure the most careful deliberation about any proposal with eugenic objectives.

Principle C *Except as demonstrably required under Principles A, B, or other comparable principles, no restriction shall be placed on research intended to increase understanding of human heredity and its expression.* However worded, the principle is intended to affirm the primacy of free conduct of research, unless it endangers fundamental human rights.

Principle D *Principles regarding human genetic therapy should be incorporated not only into national policy but into international covenants.* However worded, the principle should affirm that the collective human gene pool knows no national boundaries but is the biological heritage of the entire human species.

A third near-term objective should be to establish an information clearinghouse for both the general public and specialized scholars. This resource should be used to enlarge the informed audience about gene therapy and facilitate public discourse at all levels, through both formal and informal education channels.

LONG-TERM OVERSIGHT

Beyond immediate concerns, the oversight body will need to anticipate imminent new uses of gene transfer, and provide clarifying evaluations well before a "decision crunch." It will also need to evaluate on a continuing basis the "large issues" that lie ahead, for example, gene pool shifts, which are already occurring both spontaneously and as indirect consequences of cultural factors such as advanced medical technology. Such background information is necessary in order to evaluate the direct consequences of gene therapy or other deliberate genetic interventions. Closely tied to these questions is the issue of positive eugenics and control of human evolution.

These large issues will need to be closely watched as biotechnologies advance—biotechnologies that include not only genetic intervention but alteration in the developmental processes of early embryos as well. One already noted suc-

cessful experimental approach involves the transfer of genes into germ-line cells in order to study their effects in very early embryos. The embryonic stages to which the transfers were made are the same ones exposed to manipulation during external human fertilization. Early stage animal embryos also have been the subject of successful manipulations—removal and transplantation of a cell nucleus, fusion of cells from several embryos or different genotypes into one individual, separation of cells of one embryo to produce several individuals of identical genotype (twinning), and extension of external development to the early stages of organ formation.

These developmental technologies, as in the case of gene transfer, are currently part of the armamentarium of basic research. However, preliminary discussions have taken place about the possible medical uses to which such techniques might be put.[15] In a few instances, developmental interventions are being introduced, in combination with genetic technologies, to improve animal production.[16] Some are also part of popular culture, often the basis of literary and film scenarios as well as speculative and sometimes sensational treatment in press reports of new research advances.

Such emergent technologies raise social and ethical issues comparable to, and often overlapping, those of gene transfer. And while many of the technologies may never come to pass, others are at least as likely as is gene therapy. To evaluate their potential, as well as their socioethical dimension, requires that we view them in light of other emergent technologies that clearly are changing fundamental attitudes and may drastically alter the human future. The demands of nuclear and space technologies may move genetic and developmental technologies from limited medical application to the wider goal of species survival on earth or in extraterrestrial migration.

This agenda should also be the subject of deliberative oversight, preferably by the same mechanism as gene transfer. Such an agenda will profitably occupy us into the far future, for specific cases and issues will continue to be defined as the vast technological wave already unleashed reaches its crest in the next century.

Acknowledgment

The studies leading to the publication of this paper were supported by NSF grant PRA-8020679.

References

[1]Academy Forum, *Research With Recombinant DNA* (Washington, D.C.: National Academy of Sciences, 1977), pp. 19, 21.

[2]R.D. Palmiter, R.L. Brinster, R.W. Hammer, M.E. Trumbauer, M.G. Rosenfeld, N.C. Birnberg and R.M. Evans, "Dramatic Growth of Mice that Develop from Eggs Microinjected with Metallothionein—Growth Hormone Fusion Genes," *Nature* 300 (1982), 611-15.

[3]T. Friedmann and R. Roblin, "Gene Therapy for Human Genetic Disease?" *Science* 175 (1972), 949-55; K.E. Mercola and M.J. Cline, "The Potentials of Inserting New Genetic Information," *New England Journal of Medicine* 303 (1980), 1297-1300; and W.F. Anderson and J.C. Fletcher, "Gene Therapy in Human Beings: When is it Ethical to Begin?" *New England Journal of Medicine* 303 (1980), 1293-97.

[4]T. Friedmann, *Gene Therapy: Fact and Fiction in Biology's New Approaches to Disease* (Cold Spring Harbor, N.Y.: Cold Spring Harbor Laboratory, 1983).

[5]J.W. Gordon and F.H. Ruddle, "Integration and Stable Germ Line Transmission of Genes Injected into Mouse Pronuclei," *Science* 214 (1981), 1244-46; F. Costantini and E. Lacy, "Introduction of a Rabbit Beta-Globin Gene into the Mouse Germ Line," *Nature* 294 (1981), 92-94; T.A. Stewart, E.F. Wagner and B. Mintz, "Human Beta-Globin Gene Sequences Injected into Mouse Eggs, Retained in Adults and Transmitted to Progeny," *Science* 217 (1982), 1046-48; and Palmiter, et al., "Dramatic Growth of Mice . . . ."

[6]A.C. Spradling and G.M. Rubin, "The Effect of Chromosomal Position on the Expression of the Drosophila Xanthine Dehydrogenase Gene," *Cell* 34 (1983), 47-57; G.S. McKnight, R.H. Hammer, E.A. Kuenzel and R.L. Brinster, "Expression of the Chicken Transferrin Gene in Transgenic Mice," *Cell* 34 (1983), 335-41; and E. Lacy, S. Roberts, E.P. Evans, M.D. Burtenshaw and F.D. Costantini, "A Foreign Beta-Globin Gene in Transgenic Mice: Integration at Abnormal Chromosomal Positions and Expression in Inappropriate Tissues," *Cell* 34 (1983), 343-58.

[7]H.E. Varmus, N. Quintrell and S. Ortiz, "Retroviruses as Mutagens: Insertion and Excision of a Nontransforming Provirus Alter Expression of a Resident Transforming Provirus," *Cell* 25 (1981), 23-6; N. Jenkins, N. Copeland, B. Taylor and B. Lee, "Dilute (d) Coat Colour Mutation of DBA/2J Mice is Associated with the Site

along, having just been bitten by the insect in question and thus suffering from a life-threatening condition which can be alleviated only if she is given Kent's potion immediately. His ownership of the potion does not seem as strong a basis for refusing her claim in this situation as the parallel claim for Ian. (It might, however, be a basis for insisting that she compensate him for using his supply of the potion or perhaps that she replace it as soon as she is well enough to carry out the work of preparing a new batch.) Here a genuine question of justice is presented: her urgent need is in competition with his ownership right. Which of these should be the decisive basis for distributing the resource?

Air is abundant; but if the output from an industrial plant or from numerous autos pollutes the atmosphere, then *clean air* will be unavailable to other beings who want and need it. Thus the issue of environmental pollution is (at least in part) a question of justice. Although nobody *owns* the atmosphere, claims are made to it which may come into conflict; and, when they do conflict, distributive justice enters the picture.

All this is relevant to medical ethics because health services are a resource to which there can be competing claims. Both Mark and Norelle require immediate hospitalization, but only one hospital bed is currently available. Both Oscar and Pearl want to consult a specific physician, but she has only one empty appointment. Both Quincy and Ruth have diseases which no drugs have yet been developed to treat, but the pharmaceutical corporation is only prepared to fund one research initiative to develop a new medication. Scott and Teresa will die unless they both receive heart transplants, but only one heart is available for transplantation. Deciding which of these competing claims to grant involves questions of justice.

Most of the examples presented thus far involve *micro*allocation decisions—i.e., deciding between specific competing claims made by particular individuals. Should Earl or Farah get the one remaining apple? (Or, perhaps, would it be more just to divide it between them?) Should Ian or Judy get to eat the special dish which Ian prepared? Should Kent get to keep his potion, or should it be administered to Lola?

There are related decisions, however, that bring up parallel issues on a larger, social scale—decisions which typically arise before specific competing claims have arisen and which may obviate conflict. Whoever planted the apple tree in Earl and Farah's backyard might have decided to plant two trees instead of just one; and, if he had done so, presumably there would be lots more apples available. Then the situation of Earl and Farah would become parallel to that of Adam and Benita, in which no problem of justice obtains. Ian and Kent might each have decided to make a double portion of their respective concoctions; if they had done so, the claims of Judy and Lola, respectively, might not conflict with their own plans. The hospital which Mark and Norelle need to enter might have been built with more beds, and the physician whom Oscar and Pearl want to consult might have established longer office hours; if so, then the conflicts described earlier would not have arisen.

But these *macro*allocation decisions, which pertain to distributions on a wider social level, also involve trade-offs between competing claims. In many cases, what are involved here are (at least in part) anticipated future claims. Thus the hospital board may have had to decide whether to build additional inpatient beds or construct an outpatient diagnostic facility. Or they may have chosen to increase present charges (and thus conflict with the desire of patients to spend their money in other ways) in order to fund expansion. Extending the physician's office hours might conflict with her own priorities for allocation of her time between work, family responsibilities, leisure activities, community service, continuing professional education, etc.

Decisions by Default

Some macroallocation decisions are made explicitly, as when the hospital board votes on whether to initiate an expansion program. Others are

made implicitly by default, as would happen if the hospital were to remain the same size because the issue of possible expansion were never placed on the board's agenda for decision. It seems clear that the board is no less responsible for the second decision than for the first. They have responsibility for providing adequate services; and failure to recognize the need is no defense for failure to meet this responsibility.

Microallocation decisions may also be made tacitly by default. A patient with a failing heart may be declared to be "end stage" without the possibility of heart transplant or other exotic last-ditch effort to sustain life even being considered. This situation amounts to a microallocation decision because it reduces the competition for these resources. Here again, making the decision by default does not seem to diminish responsibility for having made it. If this patient would stand a good chance of being restored to meaningful life by the therapy, it would be negligent practice to fail to consider therapy as a possibility. If, on the other hand, the treatment offers no realistic hope of benefit, then to avoid such a futile attempt is appropriate (and perhaps even courageous in today's era of pro-technological zeal).

Similarly, the society as a whole can be said to make macroallocation decisions—and to bear responsibility for them. Some are made explicitly, as when Congress acted in 1972 to take over the funding of renal dialysis and transplantation, thus making this resource available to virtually all who would profit from it. Others are made tacitly and by default, as when Congressional decision about funding for heart transplants is repeatedly postponed and referred for further study. When (and if) the artificial heart is perfected, will Congress allocate the billions of dollars necessary for making it available to all who need it, or will Congress do nothing (i.e., decide by default) and let all these people die? Furthermore, when nothing is done to relieve the plight of the "medically indigent"—i.e., some 25 million Americans who have no health insurance and are not covered by Medicare or Medicaid programs—we must also say that an allocation

decision has been made by default. We will amine these public policy issues in greater d shortly, but first a preliminary matter must be discussed.

Fundamental Criteria of Justice

How should we go about deciding how to allocate the one remaining apple between Earl and Farah?

(1) The solution that comes most readily to mind is to divide it evenly between them. This reflects one fundamental principle of justice—*equality*. Each individual has an equal *prima facie* claim to the resource.

From a Kantian viewpoint, this would be seen as a reflection of the moral obligation to treat all members of the moral community as ends in themselves and never merely as means. To deny Earl's claim in order to satisfy Farah's would be to treat him merely as a means to her happiness, and vice versa if Farah's claim were denied.

An act utilitarian would view this judgment as a prediction that equal division would maximize the happiness of both parties. But what if it were clear that it did *not* maximize happiness in a given case? An act utilitarian would regard a continued requirement of equal division as an unjustified side constraint on their pursuit of the moral goal. Thus the principle of justice is often viewed as an inherently deontological principle. Childress, in the second of his selections in this chapter, regards the demand of justice as a rival to utilitarian "social worth" criteria. Young, in his selection on this issue, also treats justice as logically independent of utilitarian considerations, although he attempts to reconcile them insofar as possible. Yet we must decide which should prevail when act utility cannot be reconciled with claims of justice.

Rule utilitarians and minimizing utilitarians, by contrast, could justify a principle of equality even in many situations in which specific acts of justice would not immediately maximize happiness or minimize unhappiness; their

ould be that a *policy* of equal division
uce more satisfactory (and/or less
expectations on the part of all parties
ative policies if universally acted upon
d. This argument would, of course,
evaluated critically. If it does not hold
e would become a deontological princi-
, too.

(2) An act utilitarian might argue for some
ner basis of allocation. For example, suppose
we realized that the use Earl would make of the
apple, if all of it were given to him, would have
better social consequences than would result
from dividing it between him and Farah. The example is somewhat fanciful, but imagine that he
is a neo-Newton and that he would study the
shape of the apple and thereby discover new
truths about the nature of the planets. On this
view, it would be more appropriate to give the
whole apple to him. In general, if it were determined that more good would result from giving
him the whole apple than from having the two
share it, act utilitarians would reject the notion
of equal division.

For rule utilitarians and minimizing utilitarians, the difference of good or harm to the individual and to society would have to be
sufficiently great to outweigh the negative effects
of violating the *policy* of equality; but the logic of
the position would be essentially the same.
When benefits to society only are being considered, criteria of this type are labelled as *social
worth* or *future contribution* criteria of justice—
resources are allocated in accordance with the
future social contributions they are likely to promote.

(3) Other theorists have argued for back-
ward-looking criteria of allocation instead of (or,
perhaps, in addition to) the forward-looking social contribution criteria. Suppose, although the
apple orchard was a cooperative enterprise and
no one person in the group *owned* the fruit, it
happened that Farah had worked much longer
and harder on planting and cultivating the trees
than Earl. It might seem only fair, as a reward for
her past contributions, to give priority to her de-

mand for the one remaining apple. Further, even
if her contribution were not to the apple orchard
but instead to some other aspect of the life of the
community which was significantly greater than
any contribution made by Earl, we might still
consider that she had a stronger claim than Earl
to be rewarded by being given the apple. Criteria
of this sort are called criteria of *past contribution,
merit,* or *desert* (i.e., what is deserved).

A deontological foundation for these criteria
is found in Chapter 1 in Ross's Duties of Gratitude—here elevated to a social level. Rule utilitarian justifications of these standards would
emphasize their effectiveness as incentives for
persons to behave in ways that will serve the social good.

(4) Ross's Duties of Reparation are also
sometimes elevated to a social level, where they
become principles of *compensatory justice.* In
Chapter 4, we saw the relevance of this to medical experimentation, but it also must be considered when scarce medical resources are being
allocated.

(5) Another element of justice is *procedural
justice.* The manner in which a decision is made
is important—partly because a just procedure is
more likely to lead to a just result, partly because
a just procedure itself acknowledges the dignity
of the parties, and partly because those affected
are less likely to be unjustly harmed if fair procedural policies are being followed. In the law, the
set of procedures called *due process* are an
expression of procedural justice. In the area of
health care allocation, procedural justice is often
addressed through the recommendation that allocation decisions be made by a committee
rather than by any single individual. Robert
Young makes some suggestions along these lines
in his selection in this chapter.

In the myriad allocation systems which are
at work in our society, all these criteria (and others as well) are employed at various times. Egalitarian principles are greatly respected, and they
play a dominant role. Thus, for example, we offer
universal public education in order to provide all
citizens an equal opportunity for self-develop-

ment. However, we do not insist on giving every student the same grade. Here we consider it appropriate to acknowledge merit criteria. Further, we establish systems of scholarships and other financial aid in order to encourage those who show outstanding promise for making future contributions to society. This is an acknowledgement of social worth criteria.

Macroallocation and Public Policy

The issue of allocation of health care resources is a complex one. Several interrelated questions must be considered; and, furthermore, it is difficult to decide which of these questions is fundamental and thus should be dealt with first. We shall survey several of these questions here; but bear in mind that, in order to develop a policy solution concerning allocation of health care resources, one would probably have to move back and forth between these questions until a set of answers is reached that is coherent and results in a stable equilibrium between our intuitions concerning the several issues.

A. WHAT IS THE GOAL?

The first task is to try to clarify what we are trying to achieve in a just health care system.

1. Nonexclusionary Policies and Conduct Denial of access to health care facilities and services on grounds, for example, of race or sex or national origin is obviously unjust. So also are differences in the way persons are treated within the institution—whether this is a matter of separate (and inevitably unequal) facilities within the institution for different sexes or racial groups or differences in the demeanor of personnel towards people of different backgrounds.

2. Availability of Services The problem of discrimination is not by any means the whole issue of justice in health care, however. Some rural areas in our country have no health

services personnel or facilities available to them at all. People must travel miles to see a physician, often further still if they need to be hospitalized. For certain kinds of care—especially skilled nursing home care—there is a shortage of facilities nearly everywhere, as witnessed by long waiting lists for admission. Not all claims to resources can be met, and thus a question of justice is involved.[1]

3. Access to Services Even if health services are generally available in an area, they do not do the individual any good if he lacks the means of access to them. Three elements are primary here:

a. money—when, for example, a physician or hospital requires payment in advance;

b. transportation—which can be an especially acute problem for the disabled;

c. time—when, for example, a public clinic requires patients to wait for long periods to be seen. People may be unable to be away from their family responsibilities for the larger portion of a day in order to see a physician. People who are marginally employed may not be able to afford to take an entire day off from work to see a doctor; indeed, in some cases, unsympathetic employers may fire them for such an absence.

If we could assume that the amount of money one possesses is an accurate indication of the social contributions one has made in the past, then the role of money as a barrier to access would not be objectionable to a proponent of desert criteria. However, those who favor either egalitarian or social worth criteria would object; and even proponents of desert criteria would disapprove of transportation and time serving as barriers to access.

4. Use of Services Most descriptive analyses of health care allocation focus on the use of services.[1] The assumption is that justice has not been achieved, even if availability and

access have been assured, as long as rates of use vary. But many factors influence an individual's decision to seek medical care, including personal and cultural beliefs about disease and the sick role. Hence we are moving beyond questions of allocation (and therefore of justice) if we take maximizing or equalizing patterns of use as our social goal.

5. Results of Services   Suppose we were to achieve strict equality in availability, access, and even use of health care services. It would not follow that everyone would be brought to the same level of health as a result. Some people are naturally healthy and thus have little need of health care services. Others have serious and/or chronic health problems which require extensive health care services, and even these will not restore them to a state of perfect health; the most they can hope for is to "make the best of a bad situation."

This strict equality gives rise to a paradox for the issue of justice in health care. To achieve equality in availability and access will result in unequal use and, more serious, in radical inequalities in the resulting health status. This last difference cannot be eliminated entirely no matter what we do. We can restore the unhealthy to a somewhat higher level of functioning in many cases—but only by devoting a large proportion of health services to them. We cannot equalize *all* these things at once, therefore. The question is, then, Which of these should be the goal of allocation policies?

B. BASIC ALLOCATIVE STRUCTURE

Once we have achieved agreement on the goal, an obvious next step is to consider what the ideal basic structure of health care organization would be; and, in particular, what role the government should play in this structure. As Tom Beauchamp and James Childress put this question, "To what

extent should the government be in the health allocation business at all, instead of leaving the allocation of such goods to the marketplace?" (Beauchamp and Childress, 1st ed., page 189)*[2] There are several possibilities, including the following:

1. Laissez Faire   This is the possibility of leaving the allocation of health services to the marketplace. In the extreme version, which we shall call *(a) the commodity viewpoint,* health services would be regarded as no different, from a moral viewpoint, than any other goods and services in the society. As we rely on private enterprise to provide the food, clothing, shelter, transportation, and consumer goods in our society, so we would rely on it for health services. The basis of exchange for these services would be economic, as it is for other commodities. Just as the baker need not give you a cookie unless you have the money to pay for it, the physician or clinic would not be expected to provide health care services unless payment was forthcoming. It might seem initially that this is the existing structure of health care in the United States, but we will introduce some important exceptions and qualifications to this characterization shortly.

The first qualification to note in a strict market view is the degree to which health services are *(b) driven by professional norms and values.* In contrast to the overt profit motive of providers of most (other) goods and services, professionals profess (both to the general public and to initiates into the profession) that goals of service are primary and that the economic benefits of professional practice ought never to be the dominant focus of attention. We might question the

---

*Questions from Beauchamp and Childress's *Principles of Biomedical Ethics,* first or second edition, will be brought in throughout this discussion. Edition and page numbers will be included at each reference. See note 2 at the end of the chapter for full bibliographic information.

extent to which these norms are honored in practice by members of the profession, but it cannot be denied that they form part of both the self-image and the public image of the profession. It is these norms which have fostered a tradition of charity care by professionals and institutions in the past.

2. *Moral Suasion*   Perhaps injustices in allocation could be corrected through moral appeals to professionals to increase the extent and direction of individual charity care, as well as to root out exclusionary policies and conduct. Cynics will not have much confidence in the effectiveness of such moral appeals, but their role must not be dismissed without consideration.

3. *Private Subsidies*   Another important qualification to a pure market operation in health care is the role of private subsidies in supporting health care research and services. The various (a) *charitable organizations* which sponsor fund drives, telethons, and the like contribute a vital margin of support for health care efforts. We cannot, however, count on private subsidies to provide more than a small fraction of the needed funds. It would be unrealistic to rely on voluntary charitable contributions to provide for the full measure of needed research and services.

Another form of private subsidy which was widely practiced in the past is (b) *"cost shifting."* Charges to paying patients and their fiscal agents were set at a rate that would cover uncollectible expenses of the professional or institution. This form of subsidy has the moral demerit that it is both involuntary and generally covert. Patients and their agents are currently showing their unwillingness to continue this form of subsidy by insisting on cost containment measures which disallow this practice. For example, in many areas of the country, health insurance carriers select a limited panel of "preferred providers" on the basis of competitive bids. For the patient/client, the incentive to seek health care from

these sources is that a higher percentage of the charges will be reimbursed than if he or she consulted other providers not on the preferred list; the advantage to the carrier is a discounted charge. But, in order to arrive at a competitive discounted rate to offer the carriers, providers must sacrifice cost shifting.

4. *Government Subsidies*   A less hidden form of subsidy which works within a fundamentally market-driven system of allocation is the government subsidy for health care services for certain populations. Funded through one form or another of taxation, chief examples are the Medicare program (which is funded entirely by the federal government) and the Medicaid program (which is funded by a combination of federal and state resources). The President's Commission for the Study of Ethical Problems in Medicine and Biomedical and Behavioral Research recommends that this remain the approach to providing health care for the needy:

> When equity occurs through the operation of private forces, there is no need for government involvement, but the ultimate responsibility for ensuring that society's obligation is met, through a combination of public and private sector arrangements, rests with the Federal government.[3]

5. *Governmental Manipulation*   Further governmental involvement comes in various forms of manipulation of an essentially private market system. It may be achieved in any or all of the several following ways:

- statutory law
- court rulings
- bureaucratic regulation

For example, courts have ruled that any hospital with an emergency department must treat any patient who presents herself in a life-threatening condition, regardless of the patient's ability to pay. In most states, the obligation extends only to

stabilizing the patient, at which point the hospital may transfer patients who are unable to pay to another facility (generally a public institution). This process is popularly called "dumping." Texas is an exception, having recently passed "anti-dumping" legislation which prohibits this practice. An example of bureaucratic regulations would be the implementation of DRG's (Diagnosis Related Groups) as the mechanism for reimbursement for Medicare patients.

Governmental manipulation has been exerted on several fronts to foster competition between health care professionals and institutions. Federal legislation requires that employers offer a choice between health insurance plans (including HMO membership) whenever approved alternatives exist in the area. Federal employees' health insurance plans have been used as models to implement this requirement. The Federal Trade Commission required professional associations to drop their traditional ban on advertising, claiming that it was "in restraint of trade."

6. Nationalization of the Health Care System The most direct way the government might become involved is by taking over and managing the health services system. The Veterans' Administration health care system provides one example of this in the United States. Britain and most Western European countries have organized virtually their entire health care system in this way (as well as certain other segments of the economy). A variety of models are possible here, ranging from total central management such as that found in the U.S. Postal Service to predominantly local control such as that found in the American public education system.

C. PRIORITIES AMONG ENDS

"If the government is involved in the allocation and distribution of health care, as our government is, how much of its budget should be allocated for health [oriented measures] and how

much for other social goods, such as housing, education, culture, and recreation?" (Beauchamp and Childress, 2nd ed., page 204)

Health is clearly not the *only* good. One important issue of macroallocation is the determination of how health should rank among the various social goods which compete for society's resources. Several concrete questions arise here:

a. Should health expenditures be the absolute first priority; or

b. should the first dollar to be spent for health measures be allocated only after, for example, education or defense spending needs are met; or

c. should a balance be struck among various competing needs, funding a proportionate share of several or all of them, as funds allow?

d. Should there be control of how much individuals are permitted to spend for health measures? If so, how much of the Gross National Product (GNP) should the government (and other control forces) *permit* to be spent for health measures?

This is the locus of much of the current debate about cost containment in health care. Many commentators voiced alarm a few years ago when expenditures for health care first exceeded 10 percent of the GNP. As this proportion continues to climb (although at a slower rate than in previous years), pressure mounts for radical cost containment measures.

D. PRIORITIES AMONG MEANS

Even if the general amount to be devoted to health-oriented measures is determined, there are still significant allocation decisions to be made. As Beauchamp and Childress phrase it, "What are the most effective and efficient ways to protect and promote life and health (or to prevent death and disability)?" (Beauchamp and Childress, 1st ed., page 189)

A number of approaches are possible here (as well as various combinations of these), including

1. nonmedical approaches, such as improving sanitation, and improving the general standard of living;
2. prevention, such as promoting life-style changes, health education, vaccination, and health screening for early detection;
3. primary care, for example, item 4 plus a mixture of 2, 5, 6 and continuity of care;
4. rescue strategies—acute care;
5. rehabilitation;
6. chronic care;
7. research.

In the first of his selections in this chapter, James Childress discusses this stage in the allocation debate. He presents the case for giving priority to preventive measures as well as bringing up some ethical questions raised by this approach.

E. SPECIFIC EMPHASES

"Which categories of illness or disease should receive priority in the allocation of public resources if it is not possible to fund maximal research and therapy in all areas? For example, should heart disease have priority over cancer?" (Beauchamp and Childress, 2nd ed., page 205)

This is the issue addressed by Franz Ingelfinger in his selection in this chapter. He raises three questions:

1. whether focus on a specific disease is the most efficient way to foster medical progress, or whether it would be more effective in the long run to put these funds into basic research;
2. whether the choice of which diseases to focus funding upon should be made on the basis of "political" considerations or on the basis of "scientific reasons";

3. whether the focus on killer diseases is consistent with our emphasis, in care of the individual patient, on "a philosophy that emphasizes the quality of life rather than mere existence."

Friedrich raises similar questions in connection with the artificial heart technology in his following selection, "One Miracle, Many Doubts."

F. STRATEGIES

"Different strategies may compromise various values or principles, and this compromise should be acknowledged in formulating public policies." (Beauchamp and Childress, 1st ed., page 191)

Childress notes several such conflicts in his selection on macroallocation, notably the conflict between effective preventive measures and the principle of *liberty*. Ingelfinger's third question is another example of this sort of conflict.

More generally, we must examine the implications of the various allocation strategies we consider. For example, there are a variety of ways to structure payment to physicians and hospitals. The most prominent are listed in the following table:

Paying the Doctor	Paying the Hospital
Fee-for-service	Cost-plus reimbursement
Capitation	Capitation
Salary	Fixed sum
Case payments	Case payments (e.g., DRG's)
Scholarships with service requirements	Construction grants with service requirements

Each of these offers economic incentives for certain sorts of behavior. For example, fee-for-service and cost-plus reimbursement (which have, until recently, been the dominant structures in the U.S. health care system) reward aggressive

styles of practice. The more procedures performed, the greater the reimbursement; and, assuming that a margin of profit is built into each charge, the more one profits. In contrast, a capitation fee (in which the doctor is paid a fixed sum for providing whatever health care a given patient might need) rewards *not* doing procedures. The less one does, the more of the fixed capitation sum remains as profit.

These incentives are not, of course, irresistible. If following the incentive in a given case is not in the best interests of the patient, professional codes and ethical principles alike would mandate that it be resisted. The danger is, however, that (especially in marginal cases) the economic incentive would subtly and imperceptibly color the practitioner's perception, preventing her from fully appreciating countervailing factors.

One way to counter the impact of these influences is through a mechanism such as peer review. The question to consider is what combination of influences, checks, and balances is the most appropriate structure.

Microallocation

Allocation decisions on an individual level are heavily influenced by macroallocation decisions. If health services resources were made available in abundance and the means of access to them were guaranteed to all, then few competing claims would arise.

But the need for microallocation decisions can never be eliminated entirely. There will always be some resources which are in limited supply, even with the most generous macroallocation policies imaginable. For example, as new technologies, drugs, etc. are developed, their supply will inevitably be limited until they become fully established and tested. The artificial heart furnishes a current example of this. Also, the supply of some resources is limited by forces outside human control—for example, even if we retrieved all usable cadaver organs, there still

might not be enough to meet the total need for transplants. Furthermore, it is highly unlikely that such a generous macroallocation policy will be forthcoming.

Hence microallocation decisions will continue to arise, and guidelines for them need to be developed. The same fundamental principles of justice which guided macroallocation decisions can operate here, although certain modifications are necessary. Half a heart would not do anybody any good, so if only one donor heart is available and two people have need of it, dividing it into equal shares is *not* an adequate solution. James Childress contends, in his following selection on microallocation, that the principle of equality is to give each candidate an *equal chance* to receive the resource—say, by means of a lottery.

Childress maintains that a principle of "first come, first served" is equivalent to a lottery, since the timing of when disease strikes is largely a matter of chance (sometimes called the "natural lottery"). This equivalence can be questioned, however. In the principle "first come, first served," we are talking not about the time of onset of the disease, but rather about the time of presentation for treatment; and this is influenced by factors other than the "natural lottery." It is well established that persons in lower socio-economic groups tend to delay seeking medical help until their diseases have progressed further than the diseases of those who are economically better off.[4] (This pattern is undoubtedly influenced by the barriers to access described earlier.) And, if the site of decision-making is a referral center (e.g., a dialysis or transplant unit), further delays may be introduced for some patients as a result of the sort of primary care initially available to them. A physician in a busy inner-city clinic is unlikely to be as prompt or as aggressive in seeking a referral site as a physician in private practice who has had a long-term relationship with the patient.

Before you read the philosophical discussions of microallocation that follow, it might be interesting and useful for you to grapple with

these problems on your own. In the following exercise, you will be provided first with a list of criteria often recommended or used in making microallocation decisions about which individuals will receive—and which will not receive— scarce (often lifesaving) medical resources. You should decide which of these criteria, if any, you wish to apply; why you select those you do; and why you reject the other options. Next, you will be provided with a set of patient profiles and asked to select a candidate using your chosen criteria.

(1) Criteria for Allocating Scarce Medical Resources

You may want to adopt the NO TREATMENT option (i.e., that none should live when not all can live); but if you decide to treat *some,* then principles of selection will have to be adopted. You may choose any one of, or any combination of, the following. None of the lists is complete. Feel free to add anything you consider significant.

A. Medical Criteria   Such as

1. likelihood of benefit or success;
2. increased life expectancy;
3. absence of other medical complications, such as diabetes, cancer, or heart disease;
4. psychiatric suitability—i.e., ability to understand and willingness to follow medical procedures; emotional stability; cooperativeness; motivation;
5. tissue matching (in case of organ or tissue transplants).

B. Random Selection Criteria

1. lotteries;
2. first come, first served.

C. Constituency Criteria

1. area of residence;

2. some social worth criteria from (E) below— e.g., Catholic and Jewish hospitals might give priority to Catholics and Jews, respectively;
3. the progress-of-science factor (in research hospitals);
4. children (for children's hospitals);
5. veterans (for veterans' hospitals);
6. ability to pay.

D. Present and/or Future Quality of Life Criteria   *Degrees* of some of the following, as self-reported or as independently determined. (Note: These all pertain to the value of the person's life *to himself or herself.*)

1. consciousness or self-consciousness;
2. autonomy;
3. moral insight and commitment;
4. rationality, knowledge, intelligence;
5. love, desirable emotions;
6. happiness;
7. uniqueness.

E. Social Worth Criteria   (Note: These all pertain to the value of the person's life *to others.*)

1. age;
2. sex;
3. marital status;
4. number of dependents;
5. ages of dependents;
6. income;
7. net economic worth (including insurance policies);
8. educational background;
9. occupation;
10. past performance;
11. future potential;

12. political affiliation;

13. religious affiliation;

14. race;

15. physical beauty or ugliness (of patient or spouse);

16. criminal record;

17. charitable contributions;

18. spouse's financial status;

19. monetary cost of therapy to society;

20. possible contribution to progress of science.

(2) Patient Profiles

The following eight patients are candidates for a heart transplant. Without a new heart, each will probably die in a few weeks. Only one heart is available. Who should receive it? Remember that, as a consequence of your decision, one person will live and seven others—each of whom might have lived if your decision had been different—will die.

Patient 101   is a 42-year-old white male. He is married and has two young children. He works as an inspector at an electronics firm with a salary of $25,000 per year. His wife does not work, but they own their own home in the suburbs. He has been relatively athletic; he was the high scorer on the company bowling team the year before his illness felled him. His immediate family is extremely close and supportive; they have unselfishly nursed him back to health after both of his previous cardiac arrests. In general, his life has been satisfactory and content, if unspectacular. The probability of successful treatment is estimated by the transplant team at 50 percent (a bit higher than average due to his athletic background and the absence of complicating conditions). His life expectancy, if treatment is successful, is estimated at 20 years.

102   is a 25-year-old white male. He has a B.A. degree in art and has sold several paintings to local galleries. The patient has a criminal record consisting of several arrests for homosexual solicitation. At present, he is unmarried but lives with (and provides some financial support for) another young male. His only sources of income are from prostitution and the selling of his art work. His art work has been so well received that the California Institute of the Arts (the premier art institute in the nation) has offered him a fellowship, with a substantial stipend, to encourage his artistic talents. The probability of successful treatment is rated at 65 percent. (The chance of rejection of the foreign material is reduced due to the fact that the patient has a compromised immune system. He has tested positive for AIDS antibodies, although he cannot be said to have the disease—as yet). His life expectancy, if treatment is successful, is estimated at 8–10 years (due to the strong possibility that he will develop AIDS in the next several years).

103   is a 47-year-old Eurasian female neurosurgeon. She has pioneered surgical techniques and is affiliated with a prestigious teaching hospital where she supervises surgical training of medical students. She is married with no dependents. She is currently involved in her second malpractice suit in connection with her innovative surgical advances. She has collected numerous awards for outstanding success in orchid growing. In the course of her illness, she suffered a stroke affecting the left side of her brain, thus impairing her communication skills. The probability of successful treatment is estimated at 25 percent (due to her compromised cardiovascular system). Due to the same factors, her life expectancy, if treatment is successful, is estimated at only 10 years.

104   is a 72-year-old black male with nine children and fifty-four grandchildren. He has had only a sixth-grade education but has worked his way up through the ghetto—holding odd jobs to successfully provide for his family. His children and grandchildren are no longer de-

pendent on him financially, but they are emotionally. He is loved very much by his family and friends in the neighborhood. The patient said he wanted to be placed on the artificial heart because "I don't know what my grandchildren would do without me. They just love to sit around and listen to me tell stories about the old days. I love each and every one of them very much, and I'm sure they feel the same way about me." The probability of successful treatment is estimated at 40 percent (due to physical systems compromised because of his advanced age). His life expectancy, if treatment is successful, is estimated at 5 years.

105   is a 65-year-old white male. He is professor emeritus of literature at Harvard University. His area of specialty and the topic of most of his numerous publications is Russian literature. He has also authored a best-selling novel, which was widely acclaimed by the critics. He is currently in the process of writing the long-awaited sequel to that novel. He is married but has no children; and his only surviving relatives in addition to his wife are his wife's invalid mother and unmarried sister who live with his wife and him. The probability of successful treatment is estimated at 45 percent. His life expectancy, if treatment is successful, is estimated at 10 years.

106   is an extremely bright, 22-year-old nursing student. She has no children yet, but she and her husband have just learned that she is pregnant. The pregnancy reduces the probability of successful treatment to 35 percent, and her illness increases the possibility of a spontaneous abortion to nearly 50 percent. If the treatment is successful, and if no added complications from the pregnancy arise, she has a life expectancy of nearly 40 years, which she plans to spend in hospital nursing practice.

107   is a 27-year-old philosophy graduate student who is regarded as intelligent (al-

though not brilliant) by his teachers. He is rated as a good teacher and a promising research scholar. The probability of successful treatment is 45 percent. His life expectancy if treatment is successful is 35 years. He is married and has one infant son.

108   is 46-year-old priest who has worked for the past 18 years among a tribe of South American Indians. Due to the necessity of medical follow-up to treatment, he will not be able to continue this work and will find it necessary to transfer to a parish ministry (at which he has been much less successful in the past). He has no personal family ties. His life expectancy if treatment is successful is 15 years; the probability of successful treatment is 45 percent.

If you have been tempted to make heavy use of social worth criteria, as many people are when they first become involved in this exercise, you will want to pay special attention to a number of objections to their use in the following selections. Both Young and Childress criticize standard social worth criteria. Childress argues for a lottery approach, whereas Young supports various utilitarian considerations in hopes of achieving "the best possible use of scarce resources consistent with fairness." After you have read their arguments, think back to the exercise you just completed and try to determine which candidate each author would choose. Would you do things differently now that you have read their arguments?

Consider especially these two objections to social worth criteria. First, social worth criteria are unworkable because we have no objectively valid way to measure social worth. A recent defender of social worth criteria has claimed that "random selection has no place in scarce medical resource allocation except when our primitive techniques for social value rating fail to distinguish among candidates in any way."[5] The problems are that all available theoretical techniques

are primitive and that in practice human biases are too intrusive. In theory as well as in practice, people tend to select candidates who are most like themselves or most like those they admire. The difficulty is that in a highly pluralistic society we are not all alike and do not all admire the same kinds of people. This is not likely to change. During the 1960's, citizen selection committees—often called "God squads"—were actually deciding who would live (or die) by being given (or not given) slots on kidney machines which then were very scarce. The committees employed mainly social worth criteria. Critics have characterized the efforts of the selection committee operating at the Swedish Hospital in Seattle, Washington, in the 1960's as "the bourgeoisie sparing the bourgeoisie" and have remarked that "the Pacific Northwest is no place for a Henry David Thoreau with bad kidneys."[6] How much social worth did you assign to the philosopher in the preceding exercise? How do you suppose that compares with the worth we, the authors of this text, assigned to him?

A second serious difficulty with social worth criteria is that their application is unjust in the sense that it fails to recognize all the candidates as having equal basic human rights and human dignity or individual worth. To put the point in terms of rights, it fails to ascribe an equal right to life to all but assumes instead that one's right to life varies with such social worth criteria as the degree of education, productiveness, promise, age, sex, marital status, number of dependents, or race. That broad classes of individuals have been discriminated against with respect to such an essential condition of a worthwhile life as life itself becomes readily apparent when the track record of the kidney machine committees of the 1960's is examined. During this period, "patients were predominantly white (91 percent), male (75 percent), married (79 percent) and in age groups 35–54 years (59 percent)."[7] Given the way our society tends to measure social worth, it is doubtful that we could do any better today.

The proponent of social worth criteria

might reply that the fact that these criteria are not well developed is not a reason to abandon them, but rather a reason to work at making them more precise and workable. The alternative of a choice by lottery can also be objected to on at least two grounds. First, it appears to be more a way of *avoiding* the admittedly difficult task of making a decision than an ethical technique for decision-making. Ordinarily, it is only when the choice at issue is ethically *unimportant* that we consider deciding it by lot. "Since nobody really cares which restaurant we go to tonight, let's flip a coin to decide." As a way of making choices when the moral stakes are high, however (as they certainly are in microallocation decisions), a lottery does not seem appropriate. Second, this technique has the unfortunate connotation that we are gambling with human lives, which is morally unseemly. Are we really acknowledging the intrinsic value of human life by placing it at risk on the basis of such a "frivolous" method of decision-making as a lottery?

Donor Organs

As the success of organ transplantation increases, the scarcity of donor organs becomes a cause for concern. Some sources of limitation on the supply are inevitable. Only so many people are going to die each year with organs intact and sufficiently healthy to be transplanted. We would not want to reverse current trends in highway safety in order to increase the supply. It has been suggested that we might breed clones of ourselves as a source for "spare parts"—but this would be fraught with both technological and ethical difficulties.

What could be changed, however, is the situation of donatable organs that "go to waste" because the family of a brain-dead potential donor is unable or unwilling to make a decision to authorize donation. It is this situation that Caplan addresses in his selection that follows. He once endorsed a policy of presumed consent, in which the law would require usable organs to be har-

vested unless the patient had previously taken action to register a desire *not* to be a donor or the family took the initiative to object to donation. Now, however, he favors a policy of required request, which provides either that individuals indicate their willingness to be donors or that the family members be asked. There are at least two

other issues of justice which arise in connection with transplants: the invasion of privacy which may arise in searching through medical records for compatible living donors for certain organs and tissues and the question of macroallocation which arises from the enormous cost of widespread organ transplant programs.

Notes

[1]See, for example, President's Commission for the Study of Ethical Problems in Medicine and Biomedical and Behavioral Research, *Securing Access to Health Care: The Ethical Implications of Differences in the Availability of Health Services,* Vol. 1, Report (Washington, D.C.: U.S. Government Printing Office, 1983), Chapter 2.

[2]Tom Beauchamp and James Childress, *Principles of Biomedical Ethics* (New York: Oxford University Press, 1st edition—1979; 2nd edition—1983).

[3]President's Commission for the Study of Ethical Problems in Medicine and Biomedical and Behavioral Research, *Securing Access to Health Care: The Ethical Implications of Differences in*

the Availability of Health Services, Vol. 1: Report (Washington, D.C.: U.S. Government Printing Office, 1983), p. 5.

[4]Ibid., p. 74.

[5]Marc D. Basson, "Choosing Among Candidates for Scarce Medical Resources," *The Journal of Medicine and Philosophy* 4, no. 3 (1979): 331.

[6]David Sanders and Jesse Dukeminier, Jr., "Medical Advance and Legal Lag: Hemodialysis and Kidney Transplantations," *U.C.L.A. Law Review* 15, no. 2 (February 1968): 378.

[7]Quoted in Paul Ramsey, *The Patient As Person* (New Haven: Yale University Press, 1970), p. 250, n. 12.

Haves and Have-Nots in the World of Disease

Franz J. Inglefinger

Franz J. Inglefinger (1910–1980) taught in the department of medicine of Boston University and was the distinguished editor of The New England Journal of Medicine *between 1967 and 1977.*

Inglefinger indicates that on a broad societal level we provide support and funding for medical research and patient care for an elect group of diseases such as cancer, cardiovascular disease, sickle-cell disease, and multiple sclerosis. These are usually quick killer diseases by comparison with the diseases that we neglect to fund, such as arthritis, asthma, and ulcerative colitus, which disable and kill slowly. To the extent that we participate in this skewed allocation process through government or medical charities, Inglefinger suggests that we are making "the assumption—intrinsically arrogant—that the disease one man has can be identified as more important than that which lays another low."

Just as there are haves and have-nots among people, universities and nations, so are there among diseases. Prominent haves, for obvious reasons,

Reprinted by permission of *The New England Journal of Medicine,* vol. 287 (December 7, 1972), pp. 1198–1199. Copyright 1972 Massachusetts Medical Society.

are cancer and cardiovascular disease, and their "conquest" is one of those unassailable goals profitable for the politician seeking votes or the specialty organization collecting money. As a result, not only are cancer and cardiovascular disease between them responsible for the deaths of 70

per cent of us, but in addition, we are never allowed to forget it.

Lately there are some new haves—sickle-cell disease, multiple sclerosis, Cooley's anemia, hemophilia, cystic fibrosis, and sudden-infant-death syndrome, for example. Each of these has been designated by our government as worthy of special attention, along with concomitant financial benefits. Yet none is a have disease by virtue of its high prevalence; each enjoys its status because of the activities of pressure groups, often but not invariably organized on an ethnic basis.

The record of the present administration suggests that the next four years will see a relatively fixed ceiling imposed in health expenditures. Thus, an obligatory by-product of establishing have diseases is the creation of have-nots. Every dollar more for cancer is to a certain extent a dollar less for arthritis. The question, then, that deserves much more discussion than it is receiving is whether or not a system of have and have-not diseases is really in the interest of the people's health. The issue not only is practical but also has its psychologic, political, social, and moral aspects.

"Let's knock them down, one by one," is appealing and often successful strategy. Furthermore, the atomic bomb and the moon shots are persuasive models of accomplishments, achieved by targeted and systematically organized efforts. So, for that matter, was the development of methods to manufacture, distribute, and test penicillin once Fleming had discovered that agent. The unanswered and probably unanswerable question is whether the have diseases possess penicillin equivalents, whether the knowledge that has accrued about them is ready for exploitation, or whether much more innovation is first necessary. A decade ago federal funds were earmarked for research in cystic fibrosis, but the results were nil. The field was not sufficiently prepared to make gainful use of the extra funds it was obliged to accept. Today, the situation may be different; indeed, certain prophylactic programs applicable to cardiovascular disease appear to be in a stage of development that would warrant special support. But it is a safe bet that not all the have diseases are ready for the moonshot approach. Some of these diseases need more basic research, the type of research that thrives on communality, on opportunity for haphazard pollination, and on the promotion of work not tied to some specific end point.

The coexistence of haves and have-nots is always a source of trouble, but their purposeful creation in a democracy compounds the trouble. Those that are deprived struggle to better their position. Thus, a constant effort is made to secure favored treatment, specially allocated funds, or perhaps a new National Institute of Health for this or that medical specialty or subspecialty. Such efforts are inappropriate or even unseemly in that they rely on public-relations technics to promote arguments that usually are of the "my disease is more important than yours—yah, yah!" variety. Such artificial build-ups appear unnecessary, for progress and its support are usually self-generating when a real need exists and a discipline is prepared: witness the immunologic advances made in response to the widespread use of organ transplantation. It is a truism that there always will be haves and have-nots, but their selection for political rather than scientific reasons is demoralizing.

Even the have diseases may not be entirely happy with their favored status. Bickering breaks out over the proper management of the funds that suddenly have to be expended on something. Rivalry among researchers is fostered as each seeks a good share of the public largesse, and claims of breakthroughs become so common that the daily newspaper wedges them among the ads for hats and bras. Even sickle-cell-anemia programs, which in part were idealistically conceived, are now beset by warnings, disputes, and resentment, once again showing that havingness is not the same as happiness.

The big haves are haves because they are killers; the big have-nots—arthritis, asthma, ulcerative colitis and Crohn's disease of the intestine,

for example—just cause suffering, although once in a while they too are lethal. It is a remarkable paradox that care of the individual patient is currently dominated by a philosophy that emphasizes the quality of life rather than mere existence. Death is preferred by many to prolonged suffering, especially when prognosis appears hopeless. But health care for the nation appears to be motivated by concepts that are directly polar. The big have diseases—i.e., cancer and cardiovascular disorders—enjoy support because they are so deadly. Patients whose limbs ache or whose joints are stiff and swollen—complaints that ¼ of our adult population have[1]—must in contrast be content with the fact that they suffer from a have-not disease. So must the many patients who chronically fight for breath because of emphysema or asthma, or whose life is made miserable by day-in, day-out diarrhea. It is time that national health care adopted the values of individual health care and realized that it is more important to live a certain way than to die a certain way.

At times, over-riding reasons may exist for directing funds for health into specific channels.

The body of information about a certain disease may be such as to justify an intensive and targeted campaign of research and development. Threats against the public health must be met. Because of empirical or humanitarian convictions, one may wish to select for special attention diseases that are prevalent or serious or both. But the general practice of creating a caste system of diseases for reasons that usually are not scientific surely suffers from too many disadvantages to warrant its continuance. It is difficult to believe that the public health will in the long run benefit from a system that creates a category of have-nots even as it favors the haves, that discourages the free-roaming scientific idea, that fosters among rival groups a dependence on advertising rather than on achievement, and that tends to emphasize the mode of death at the expense of the mode of life. Even the basic philosophy underlying have and have-not classes of diseases is distasteful, for it rests on the assumption—intrinsically arrogant—that the disease one man has can be identified as more important than that which lays another low.

Notes

[1] A Study of Health Practices and Opinions: Final report (Contract No FDA 66–193). Conducted for Food and Drug Administration, Department of Health, Education, and Welfare. Philadelphia, National Analysts, Inc., June 1972.

Priorities in the Allocation of Health Care Resources

James F. Childress

James F. Childress is Commonwealth Professor of Religious Studies and professor of medical education at the University of Virginia. Before assuming this position, he was professor of Christian ethics at the Kennedy Institute Center for Bioethics at Georgetown University.

Childress maintains that our public policies should promote equal access of medical care and insists that the most efficacious way to improve the nation's health is through preventive health care rather than through crisis intervention health care. He indicates that our current macroallocation policies emphasize the latter rather than the former, however. He suggests that, in making macroallocations, we need to take into account

(1) the symbolic value of rescue efforts, (2) the duty of compensatory justice which gives priority to identified lives in danger, (3) the duty of distributive justice which requires equality of access to medical care, and (4) the principle of liberty which allows individuals to choose their own lifestyles.

"Public policy is whatever governments choose to do or not to do."[1] An adequate definition would also stress that public policy is purposive action and, indeed, a course or pattern of action or inaction by government officials. As such, public policies typically involve one or more of the following actions: allocation and distribution of benefits (e.g., goods and services) and burdens (e.g., taxation) and regulation (e.g., prohibition and control of an activity). While these categories are by no means fully distinct and exhaustive, I shall concentrate on the allocation of resources for and within health care. Furthermore, I shall emphasize the *content* of public policies not the *processes* by which they are formulated and implemented.[2] I shall also avoid some broad and important questions of social ethics about the structure of the health care system in the United States (e.g., whether the current mix of public and private is desirable). While answers to some policy questions may imply proposals for the structure of the health care system, I shall limit my attention and analysis to policies of allocation of resources for and within health care.

Another preliminary comment about my approach is necessary. How should we do ethics in relation to public policy? On the one hand, we could proceed by developing a systematic theory of justice or rights that could provide a basis for priorities in the allocation of health care resources. *A Theory of Justice* by John Rawls could be a model.[3] On the other hand, we could proceed by examining existing practices, institutions, and policies to determine their underlying principles and values. Then we could use these principles and values to illuminate priorities in allocation. Perhaps we would discover a plurality of principles and values, differently weighted in different

policies, and possibly even incoherently stated and inconsistently applied. This second way of doing ethics is close to Albert Jonsen and Lewis Butler's vision of "public ethics."[4] It has the advantages of concreteness and immediate relevance to policy, but it lacks the critical distance of the first approach.

I do not want to overemphasize the differences between these two approaches, much less to suggest that they are mutually exclusive or exhaust the possibilities. But my approach in this paper is closer to the second one, since I do not defend the principles and values that I invoke. Instead, I examine the way several principles and values such as equality, liberty, effectiveness and efficiency in the promotion of health can illuminate our choices in the allocation of health care resources.

Our society affirms many principles and values that may come into conflict when we try to formulate public policies. For instance, the effective and efficient promotion of health may come into conflict not only with the principle of liberty (which I shall discuss later in connection with preventive health care) but also with the ideals of providing medical care "to each according to his needs" and providing equal access to medical care.[5] Let me describe the latter conflict. Rick Carlson contends that five major variables influence health, and he ranks them according to their importance: (1) environment, (2) lifestyle, (3) society, (4) genetics, and (5) medical care. Medical care is the lowest on this list of influences on health and he gives it approximately 6 per cent weight.[6] If his position is sound, to concentrate resources on *medical* care is to misallocate them. One does not have to agree with the "therapeutic nihilists" such as Ivan Illich that medical care is pernicious (e.g., because it creates an attitude of dependence that leads individuals to abdicate their responsibility for their own health or be-

From *Soundings: An Interdisciplinary Journal,* vol. 62 (Fall 1979): 256–74. Reprinted by permission of the author and publisher.

cause there is an increase in iatrogenic diseases) in order to concede that medical care is relatively ineffective in the promotion of health.[7] While medical care may have other values such as reducing insecurity in crises of life, Paul Starr is right: "If one wishes to *equalize health, equalizing medical care* is probably not the most effective strategy."[8] But the promotion of health is not society's only goal. As long as medical care is perceived as important to health or at least increases our sense of security, perhaps we ought to promote *equal access* to it. Despite the apparent oddity of arguing for equal access to what is ineffective, the principle of equality may indicate that such a policy is morally defensible and even mandatory. This conflict between the promotion of health and the promotion of equal access to medical care is only one of the many conflicts that we encounter in trying to formulate allocative policies.

I want to concentrate on one major question in the allocation of resources for and within health care.[9] ... Within the area of health care (once we have determined its budget), how much time, energy, money, etc., should we allocate for prevention and how much for rescue or crisis medicine? ...

This is only one of several questions that could be raised and profitably discussed about allocative decisions within the health care budget. For example, another very important question concerns *basic research* vs. *applied research*. In response to Ivan Illich, who claims that modern medicine is a major threat to health, Dr. Lewis Thomas replies that we do not really have modern medicine yet.[10] Medicine has "hardly begun as a science." Most diseases cannot be prevented because we do not understand their mechanisms. Until we have more basic research, he contends, we will simply develop more and more "half-way technologies," such as transplanted and artificial organs, that merely compensate for the incapacitating effects of certain diseases whose course we can do little about. A "half-way technology" is designed to "make up for disease, or to postpone death." Usually it is very expensive and requires

an expansion of hospital facilities. By contrast, a "high technology" based on an understanding of disease mechanisms is very simple and inexpensive. Compare the treatment of polio by half-way technologies such as iron lung and support systems with the simple and inexpensive high technology—the polio vaccine.

I want to concentrate on prevention and crisis or rescue medicine. Although this conflict rarely emerges in a clear and manageable form in debates about public policy, it is present and needs identification and analysis so that we can appreciate the "trade-offs" that we frequently, if unwittingly, make. *Prevention* includes strengthening individuals (e.g., through vaccines), changing the environment, and altering behavioral patterns and lifestyles. As I have indicated, many recent commentators insist that the most effective and efficient way to improve the nation's health is through *prevention,* since our current emphasis on rescue medicine now produces only marginal returns. DHEW's *Forward Plan for Health,* Fiscal Years 1977–81, holds: "Only by preventing disease from occurring, rather than treating it later, can we hope to achieve any major improvement in the Nation's health."[11]

This recommendation is at odds with our current macroallocation policies. For example, in 1976 expenditures for health amounted to 11.4% of the federal budget. When that amount (42.4 billion dollars) is assigned to four major determinants of health (human biology, lifestyle, environment, and the health care system), the results are striking: 91% went to the health care system, while 3% went to human biology, 1% to lifestyle, and 5% to environment.[12]

Nevertheless, the evidence for the effectiveness and efficiency of a preventive strategy to reduce morbidity and premature mortality by concentrating on human biology, lifestyle, and environment is by no means conclusive. The appropriate mix of preventive and rescue strategies will depend in part on the state of knowledge of causal links. Despite the dramatic example of polio, some other conditions such as renal failure are

not the result of a single disease or factor. As a consequence, prevention appears to be only a remote possibility. In some cases prevention (which might involve extensive and expensive screening in order to identify a few persons at risk) may be less cost-effective than therapy after the disease has manifested itself. As Thomas suggests, our uncertainty in these areas is an argument for increased research.

Even if a preventive program (at least in certain areas) would be more effective and efficient, its implementation would not be free of moral, social, and political difficulties. Effectiveness and efficiency, or utility, are not the only relevant standards for evaluating policies of allocation of resources within health care (which is defined broadly and includes more than medical care). I shall concentrate on (1) the symbolic value of rescue efforts (what is symbolized about both the victim and the rescuer), (2) the duty of compensatory justice generated by the principle of fairness, (3) the principle of equal access, and (4) the principle of liberty.

(1) Our society often favors rescue or crisis intervention over prevention because of our putative preference for known, identified lives over statistical lives. The phrase "statistical lives" (Thomas Schelling) refers to unknown persons in possible future peril.[13] They may be alive now, but we do not know which ones of them will be in future peril. Mining companies often are willing to spend vast sums of money to try to rescue trapped miners when they will spend little to develop ways to prevent such disasters even if they could save more lives *statistically* in the long run. At 240 million dollars a year, we could save 240 lives of workers at coke ovens. We do not know which ones will be saved, and we are not likely as a society to respond enthusiastically to this expenditure. But we cannot ignore statistical lives in a complex, interdependent society, particularly from the standpoint of public policy.

The principle of equality is not violated by including statistical lives in public policy deliberations. It is not merely a matter of sacrificing present persons for future persons, for there are two different distinctions to consider: On the one hand, the distinction between *known* and *unknown* persons; on the other hand, the distinction between *present* and *future* peril.[14] Existing and known persons who may not be in present danger may be in future danger if certain preventive measures are not taken. Thus, preventive measures may aid existing persons who are at risk and not merely future persons.

Following Max Weber, it is possible to distinguish between "goal-rational" (*zweckrational*) and "value-rational" (*wertrational*) conduct.[15] Conduct that is "goal-rational" involves instrumental rationality—reasoning about means in relation to ends. Conduct that is "value-rational" involves matters of value, virtue, character, and identity that are not easily reduced to ends, effects, or even rules of right conduct. There is thus an important distinction between *realizing* a goal and *expressing* a value, attitude or virtue. In the context of debates about prevention and rescue intervention, the "goal-rational" approach concentrates on effectiveness and efficiency in statistical terms, while the "value-rational" approach focuses on the values, attitudes, and virtues that policies express.

This distinction between "value-rational" and "goal-rational" conduct may illuminate the 1972 congressional decision to make funds available for almost everyone who needed renal dialysis or transplantation. This decision followed widespread publicity in the media about particular individuals who were dying of renal failure. One patient was even dialyzed before the House Ways and Means Committee. Now we have a program that costs over 500 million dollars annually, and by the early 1980's the cost is expected to be more than 1 billion dollars each year. Some argue that this decision was an attempt to preserve society's cherished myth that it will not sacrifice individual lives in order to save money. Of course, we make those sacrifices all the time (e.g., when

we fail to pass and enforce some safety measures). But society's myth is not as threatened when the sacrificed lives are statistical rather than identified. Hence, decisions to try to rescue identified individuals have symbolic value. It has been said that the Universalists believe that God is too good to damn men, and the Unitarians believe that man is too good to be damned. Similarly, the symbolic value argument suggests that rescue attempts show that individuals are "priceless" and that society is "too good" to let them die without great efforts to save them. This is society's myth. And, so the argument goes, when Congress acted to cover the costs of renal dialysis, it acted in part to preserve this myth, for the "specific individuals who would have died in the absence of the government program were known."[16] They were identified lives. The policy was "value-rational," if not "goal-rational."

Insofar as this argument focuses on the way rescue interventions symbolize the value of the victims, it encounters difficulties as a basis for allocative decisions. Consider two possibilities: *(a)* we keep the same total lifesaving budget but withdraw resources from *preventive* efforts in order to put them in *rescue* efforts so that we can gain the symbolic value of crisis interventions. As Charles Fried argues, "surely it is odd to symbolize our concern for human life by actually doing less than we might to save it," by saving fewer lives than we might in a maximizing strategy. *(b)* Another possibility is to keep the same prevention budget but to take resources from other areas of the larger budget so that we can increase crisis interventions. In this case, however, "we symbolize our concern for human life by spending more on human life than in fact it is worth."[17]

The symbolic value argument focuses not only on the symbolic value of the victims, but also on what is symbolized about the agents: the virtue and character of the society and its members, what is sometimes called "agent-morality." Conduct that is "value-rational," in contrast to "goal-rational," may thus be based on an answer to the questions "who are we?" or "who shall we be?" Allocation policies may be thought of as ways for the society to define and to express its sense of itself, its values, and its integrity. From this standpoint, it is possible to argue that rescue efforts should be important, if not dominant, in allocative decisions. As Lawrence Becker notes, "we have (rationally defensible) worries about the sort of moral character represented by people who propose to stand pat and let present victims die for the sake of future possibilities. One who can fail to respond to the call for help is not quite the same sort of character as one who can maximize prevention."[18] Although "agent-morality" has strong appeal, and no doubt influences many of our decisions, it is difficult to determine how much weight it should have in our policy deliberations.

(2) In some situations the principle of fairness can generate a duty of *compensatory justice* that assigns priority to identified lives in present danger. In such situations society has an obligation to try to rescue individuals even though it departs from a strategy that would save more lives in the long run. These situations involve some unfairness because of an inequality in the distribution of risks which the society has assigned, encouraged, or tolerated. Suppose that a person who has worked in a coal mine under terrible conditions that should have been corrected is trapped in a cave-in or comes down with a disease related to his working conditions. Fairness requires greater expenditures and efforts for him in order to equalize his risks. Likewise, if society fails to correct certain environmental conditions that may interact with a genetic predisposition to cause some diseases, it may have a duty of compensatory justice. A policy of compensatory justice in health-related matters, of course, faces numerous practical difficulties, such as identifying causation. But it is important to underline the point that the principle of fairness can generate a duty of compensatory justice that sets limits on utility and efficiency in some situations. Those

who argue that individuals voluntarily choose to bear risks and thus waive any claim to compensatory justice need to show that the individuals in question really understand the risks and voluntarily assume them (e.g., do the workers in an asbestos factory have an opportunity to find other employment, to relocate, etc.?). But even the voluntary assumption of risks should not always be construed as a waiver of a claim to compensatory justice when the person is injured (e.g., research-related injuries).[19]

(3) If we include statistical lives in a preventive strategy, while allowing for compensatory justice, we still face difficult questions about *distributive justice,* particularly the principle of equality or equal access. It is not enough to maximize aggregate health benefits. Our policies should also meet the test of distributive justice, which is, indeed, presupposed by compensatory or corrective justice. For example, consider a program to reduce hypertension (high blood pressure) which affects approximately 24 million Americans and poses the risk of cardiovascular disease. In order to reduce the morbidity and mortality from cardiovascular disease, Weinstein and Stason propose an anti-hypertensive program on the basis of cost-effectiveness analysis. They recommend the intensive management of known hypertensives instead of public screening efforts. As they recognize, this proposal appears to be disadvantageous to the poor who would probably be unaware of their hypertensive condition because of their limited access to medical care. This inequity might be diminished by Weinstein and Stason's proposal to give target screening in black communities priority over community-wide screening since hypertension is more common among blacks than among whites, and by selective screening in low-income communities.[20]

The formal principle of equality, or justice, is "treat similar cases in a similar way." Of course, such a formulation does not indicate the relevant similarities. When we discuss equal access to medical care, we most often consider medical need, in contrast to geography, finances, etc., as the relevant similarity that justifies similar treatment. Suppose we decide that an effective and efficient strategy to improve the nation's health will not permit us to do all we could do in rescue or crisis medicine. A decision to forego the development of some technology or therapy may condemn some patients to continued ill health and perhaps to death. Can such a policy be justified?

One possible approach that still respects the formal principle of justice and excludes arbitrary distinctions (e.g., geography and finances) between patients would exclude "entire classes of cases from a priority list." According to Gene Outka, it is more "just to discriminate by virtue of categories of illness, for example, rather than between rich ill and poor ill."[21] Society could decide not to allocate much of its budget for treatment of certain diseases that are rare and noncommunicable, involve excessive costs, and have little prospect for rehabilitation. The relevant similarity under conditions of scarcity would not be medical need but category of illness. While certain forms of treatment would not be developed and distributed for some categories of illness, care would be provided. Patients would not be abandoned.

For allocation of funds for research into the prevention and treatment of certain diseases, it is important to consider such criteria as the pain and suffering various diseases involve, their costs, and the ages in life when they are likely to occur.[22] Applying some criteria such as pain and suffering, we might decide to concentrate less on killer diseases such as some forms of cancer and more on disabling diseases such as arthritis. Thus, says Franz Ingelfinger, national health expenditures would reflect the same values that individuals express: "it is more important to live a certain way than to die a certain way."[23]

One danger of such an approach to priorities among diseases should be noted: a decision about which diseases to treat may in fact conceal a decision about which population groups to treat since some diseases may be more common among

some groups.[24] Injustice may result from these priorities.

(4) The principle of *liberty* also poses some moral, social, and political difficulties for an effective and efficient preventive strategy. Mounting evidence indicates that a key determinant of an individual's health is his or her *lifestyle.* Leon Kass argues that health care is the individual's duty and responsibility, not a right.[25] And Lester Breslow offers seven rules for good health that are shockingly similar to what our mothers always told us! The rules, based on epidemiological evidence, are: don't smoke, get seven hours sleep each night, eat breakfast, keep your weight down, drink moderately, exercise daily, and don't eat between meals. At age 45, one who has lived by 6 of these rules has a life expectancy eleven years longer than someone who has followed fewer than 4.[26] In his book, *Who Shall Live?,* Victor Fuchs contrasts the states of Utah and Nevada which have roughly the same levels of income and medical care, but are at the opposite ends of the spectrum of health. For example, mortality for persons ages 20–59 is approximately 39% higher in Nevada than in Utah. Fuchs asks, "What, then, explains these huge differences in death rates? The answer almost surely lies in the *different lifestyles* of the residents of the two states. Utah is inhabited primarily by Mormons, whose influence is strong throughout the state. Devout Mormons do not use tobacco or alcohol and in general lead stable, quiet lives. Nevada, on the other hand, is a state with high rates of cigarette and alcohol consumption and very high indexes of marital and geographical instability. The contrast with Utah in these respects is extraordinary."[27]

On the one hand, we have increasing evidence that individual behavioral patterns and lifestyles contribute to ill health and premature mortality. On the other hand, we have the liberal tradition that views lifestyles as matters of private choice, not to be interfered with except under certain conditions (e.g., harm to others).

Each person has what Charles Fried calls a *life plan* consisting of aims, ends, values, etc. That life plan also includes a *risk budget,* for we are willing to run certain risks to our health and survival in order to realize some ends.[28] We do not sacrifice all our other ends merely to survive or be healthy. Our willingness to run the risk of death and ill health for success, friendship, and religious convictions discloses the value of those ends for us and gives our lives their style. Within our moral, social, and political tradition, the principle of liberty sets a presumption against governmental interference in matters of lifestyle and voluntary risk-taking. But that presumption may be overridden under some conditions. Let me make a few points about those conditions which are similar to just war criteria:

1. An important goal is required to override liberty. One goal is *paternalistic:* to protect a person even when his actions do not harm anyone else. This is rarely a sufficient justification for interference with liberty. Usually we require that restrictions of liberty be based, at least in part, on the threat of harm to others or to the society (e.g., compulsory vaccinations). We have difficulties with purely paternalistic arguments in requiring seatbelts, etc. Another goal might be to *protect the financial resources of the community.* If we get national health insurance, we can expect increased pressure to interfere with individual liberty. Why? People simply will not want to have their premiums or taxes increased to pay for the *avoidable afflictions* of others. They will charge that such burdens are unfair.

2. To override the presumption against interfering with liberty, we need strong evidence that the behavior or lifestyle in question really contributes to ill health. This second standard must be underlined because there is a tendency to use a term like "health" which has the ring of objectivity to impose other values without articulating and defending those values. In Camus' novel, *The Plague,* a doctor and a priest fighting the plague in an Algerian city engage in the following conversation. The priest says to the doctor: "I see that

you too are working for the salvation of mankind." "That is not quite correct," the doctor replies, "Salvation is too big a word for me. I am working first of all for man's health." The danger is that "salvation" or "morality" or a certain style of life will be enforced in the name of health although it has little to do with health and more to do with the legislation of morality.

3. Another condition for overriding the presumption against interfering with liberty is that the interference be the *last resort*. Other measures short of interference such as changing the environment should be pursued and sometimes continued even when they are less effective and more costly than measures that restrict liberty.

4. A fourth condition is a reasonable assurance that the restriction will have the desired result as well as a net balance of good over evil.

5. Even when we override the principle of liberty, it still has an impact. It requires that we use the least restrictive and coercive means to reduce risk-taking. For example, information, advice, education, deception, incentives, manipulation, behavior modification, and coercion do not equally infringe liberty. In addition to choosing the least restrictive and coercive means, we should evaluate the means on other moral grounds.

These considerations and others come into play when we try to determine whether (and which) incursions into personal liberty are justified. To allocate resources to prevention rather than to rescue is not a simple matter, for successful prevention may infringe autonomy and other moral principles. . . .

Notes

[1]Thomas R. Dye, *Understanding Public Policy*, second edition (Englewood Cliffs, N.J.: Prentice-Hall, Inc., 1975), p. 1.

[2]For an examination of *processes* in "tragic choices," see Guido Calabresi and Philip Bobbitt, *Tragic Choices* (New York: W. W. Norton & Co., 1975), particularly their emphasis on openness and honesty in processes of allocation.

[3]John Rawls, *A Theory of Justice* (Cambridge: Harvard University Press, 1971). For instance, Ronald M. Green accepts Rawls' theory, with some modifications, and develops its implications for health care policy. "Health Care and Justice in Contract Theory Perspective," in *Ethics and Health Policy*, edited by Robert M. Veatch and Roy Branson (Cambridge: Ballinger Publishing Co., 1976), chap. 7.

[4]Albert R. Jonsen and Lewis H. Butler, "Public Ethics and Policy Making," *The Hastings Center Report*, Vol. 5, No. 4 (August 1975): 19–31.

[5]There is some confusion between the *needs-principle* and the *equal-access-principle* perhaps even in Gene Outka's fine discussion in "Social Justice and Equal Access to Health Care," *The Journal of Religious Ethics*, Vol. 2, No. 1 (1974): 11–32. As Weale notes, it is possible to satisfy needs up to an equal level in a society without satisfying needs as such. For example, providing extra police protection for an individual who is at grave risk may give him the same level of security as his fellow-citizens, but the need for security by this individual and the whole community may still not be met. The satisfaction of needs, including the need for health care, thus must be distinguished from the provision of equal access to what society provides to meet those needs. See Albert Weale, *Equality and Social Policy* (London: Routledge and Kegan Paul, 1978). I discuss Outka's position in relation to this distinction in "A

Right to Health Care?" *The Journal of Medicine and Philosophy* 4 (June 1979), where I also examine other issues of relevance to priorities in the allocation of resources for and within health care.

[6]Rick J. Carlson, "Alternative Legislative Strategies for Licensure: Licensure and Health." Paper presented at the Conference on Quality Assurance in Hospitals, Boston University, Program on Public Policy for Quality Health Care, Nov. 21–22, 1975. Quoted by Walter J. McNerney, "The Quandary of Quality Assessment," *The New England Journal of Medicine*, Vol. 295, No. 27 (Dec. 30, 1976): 1507. See also Carlson, *The End of Medicine* (New York: Wiley, 1975).

[7]See Ivan Illich, *Medical Nemesis: The Expropriation of Health* (London: Calder and Boyara, 1975).

[8]Paul Starr, "The Politics of Therapeutic Nihilism," *The Hastings Center Report*, Vol. 6, No. 5 (October 1976): 24–30.

[9]There are at least three important priority questions regarding resources for and within health care: (1) What resources (time, energy, money, etc.) should be put into health care and into other social goods such as education and defense? (2) Within the area of health care, how much of the budget should go for prevention and how much for rescue or crisis medicine? (3) Within either preventive care or rescue medicine, who should receive scarce resources when we cannot meet everyone's needs? For a similar list of priority questions, see Gene Outka, "Social Justice and Equal Access to Health Care," *The Journal of Religious Ethics*, Vol. 2, No. 1 (1974): 29, fn. 2.

[10]Lewis Thomas, "Rx for Illich," *The New York Review of Books* (Sept. 16, 1976): 3–4, and *The Lives of a Cell: Notes of a Biology Watcher* (New York: The Viking Press, 1974), pp. 31–36.

[11]U.S. Department of Health, Education, and Welfare. Public Health Service. *Forward Plan for Health: FY 1977–81* (DHEW Publication No. (OS) 76–50024), p. 15. Cf. Marc LaLonde, *A New Perspective on the Health of Canadians: A Working Document* (Ottawa, Canada: The Government of Canada, 1974).

[12]These categories and figures are presented in Michael S. Koleda, et al., *The Federal Health Dollar: 1969–1976* (Washington, D.C.: National Planning Association, Center for Health Policy Studies, 1977).

[13]Thomas Schelling, "The Life You Save May Be Your Own," *Problems in Public Expenditure Analysis,* edited by Samuel B. Chase, Jr. (Washington, D.C.: The Brookings Institution, 1966), pp. 127–66. Cf. Warren Weaver, "Statistical Morality," *Christianity and Crisis,* Vol. XX, No. 24 (Jan. 23, 1961): 210–213.

[14]Charles Fried, *An Anatomy of Values: Problems of Personal and Social Choice* (Cambridge: Harvard University Press, 1970), pp. 224f. Fried's argument is important for much of this section of the paper.

[15]See Max Weber, *Max Weber on Law in Economy and Society,* edited and annotated by Max Rheinstein and translated by Edward Shils and Max Rheinstein (New York: Simon and Schuster, 1967), p. 1. The translators use the term "purpose-rational" for "zweckrational."

[16]Richard Zeckhauser, "Procedures for Valuing Lives," *Public Policy* Vol. 23 (Fall 1975): 447–48. Contrast Richard A. Rettig, "Valuing Lives: The Policy Debate on Patient Care Financing for Victims of End-Stage Renal Disease," The Rand Paper Series (Santa Monica, Cal.: The Rand Corporation, 1976).

[17]Fried, *An Anatomy of Values,* p. 217.

[18]Lawrence C. Becker, "The Neglect of Virtue," *Ethics* 85 (January 1975): 110–22. See also, Lewis H. LaRue, "A Comment on Fried, Summers, and the Value of Life," *Cornell Law Review* 57 (1972): 621–31 and Benjamin Freedman, "The Case for Medical Care, Inefficient or Not," *The Hastings Center Report* 7 (April 1977): 31–39.

[19]For a fuller discussion of compensatory justice, see James F. Childress, "Compensating Injured Research Subjects: The

Moral Argument," *The Hastings Center Report* 6 (December 1976): 21–27. Cf. also Charles Fried, *An Anatomy of Values,* p. 220.

[20]See Milton C. Weinstein and William B. Stason, "Allocating Resources: The Case of Hypertension," *The Hastings Center Report* 7 (October 1977): 24–29; "Allocation of Resources to Manage Hypertension," *The New England Journal of Medicine* 296 (1977): 732–739; and *Hypertension: A Policy Perspective* (Cambridge: Harvard University Press, 1976). Recent data indicate that "the stroke death rate, when adjusted for age changes in the population, has declined 36.1 percent since 1962, with more than two-thirds of that drop occurring since 1972, the year a major, continuing national campaign was begun to identify and treat those suffering from high blood pressure." B. D. Colen, "Deaths Caused by Strokes Fall Sharply in U.S.," *The Washington Post,* Feb. 23, 1979, A 1, A 9.

[21]Gene Outka, "Social Justice and Equal Access to Health Care," p. 24.

[22]Conrad Taeuber, "If Nobody Died of Cancer. . . ." *The Kennedy Institute Quarterly Report,* Vol. 2, No. 2 (Summer 1976): 6–9.

[23]F. J. Ingelfinger, "Haves and Have-Nots in the World of Disease," *The New England Journal of Medicine* 287 (December 7, 1972): 1199.

[24]Jay Katz and Alexander Morgan Capron, *Catastrophic Diseases: Who Decides What?* (New York: Russell Sage Foundation, 1975), p. 178.

[25]Leon Kass, "Regarding the End of Medicine and the Pursuit of Health," *The Public Interest,* No. 40 (Summer 1975): 39.

[26]See Nedra B. Belloc and Lester Breslow, "Relationship of Physical Status and Health Practices," *Preventive Medicine* 1 (1972): 409–21, and Nedra B. Belloc, "Relationship of Health Practices and Mortality," *Preventive Medicine* 2 (1973): 67–81.

[27]Victor R. Fuchs, *Who Shall Live?: Health, Economics and Social Choice* (New York: Basic Books, 1974), p. 52. (Italics added.)

[28]Fried, *An Anatomy of Values,* part III, chapters 10–12.

One Miracle, Many Doubts

Otto Friedrich

Otto Friedrich is a writer for Time *magazine.*

    Friedrich calls our attention to the enormous monetary costs of organ transplants and of medical technologies such as dialysis machines and artificial hearts and points out that only a comparatively small number of persons are having their lives saved by these extraordinary expenditures. In the early 1970's, we faced the question of whether we would make kidney dialysis available to all who needed it; Congress said yes at a cost now of over 2 billion dollars per year. The new technology of artificial hearts will force us to make a similar decision in the next few years. Will we allocate the billions needed for this, or will we just decide to let

these people die? Friedrich indicates that we could save far more lives in a much more equitable distribution of societal resources if we put that money into such things as preventive care, immunization, regular examinations, nutrition, and developing a healthier life style. He suggests that our society must eventually deal with the question "How high a price for modern medicine is too high a price?"

The dying heart was an ugly yellowish color when Dr. William DeVries finally cut it loose, tore it out of the Mercurochrome-stained chest cavity, and put it to one side. For the next three hours, while a nearby heart-lung bypass machine kept the unconscious patient alive—and while a tape in the background eerily played Mendelssohn and Vivaldi—DeVries' sure hands carefully stitched into place a grapefruit-size gadget made of aluminum and polyurethane. At 12:50 p.m. last Monday, the Jarvik-7 artificial heart newly sewn inside William J. Schroeder began beating steadily, 70 beats to the minute. When Schroeder opened his eyes 3½ hours later in the intensive-care unit, DeVries bent over his patient and whispered assurances, "The operation is all through. You did really well. Everything is perfect."

So, for only the second time in history, a human heart had been permanently replaced by a machine. Like a landing on the moon or a close-up photograph of Saturn's rings, it was an event that seized the world's imagination, arousing once again a sense of shuddering awe at the incredible powers of technology, a sense that almost anything is possible, almost anything that can be imagined can be done.

Though nobody could predict how long the aging and diabetic Schroeder would survive—his only predecessor, Dr. Barney Clark, died after a courageous 112-day struggle last year—he was reported at week's end to be doing "beautifully." But even if Schroeder dies soon, there will be more such operations, and even more complicated ones, in the near future.

The Humana Hospital Audubon in Louisville, where the operation took place, has received

permission from the Food and Drug Administration to perform another five artificial-heart implants. One candidate is now in the hospital for evaluation, but will most likely be turned down. At the same time, two Southern girls are scheduled for complex variations of organ replacements this month. Cynthia Bratcher, 6, of Scottsville, Ky., will be taken to Birmingham for an operation that will install a second heart inside her. Meanwhile, Mary Cheatham, 17, of Fort Worth, will go to Pittsburgh for simultaneous transplanting of heart and liver. (The first recipient of such a double transplant, Stormie Jones, 7, of Cumby, Texas, is still doing well after ten months.)

In what should be a time for congratulations and rejoicing, it may seem carping to raise questions about the value of such spectacular operations, yet that is exactly what a number of medical experts were doing last week. They did so because they feel serious doubts about the whole course of high-technology medicine, doubts about cost, ethics, efficiency and simple justice.

On a narrow technical level, this is partly a continuing debate about the comparative merits of transplanted human hearts *vs.* mechanical hearts (not to mention animal hearts like the one that kept Baby Fae alive for three dramatic weeks). When Dr. Christiaan Barnard began performing some of the world's first heart transplants in 1967, such efforts usually ended in failure and death because the patient's immune system rejected the implanted heart. But the development in 1980 of the antirejection drug cyclosporin has brought a drastic change. More than 200 heart transplants a year are now being performed in the U.S. alone, and the survival rate is about 80% for one year, 50% for five years. "I love life," says Dr. Barnard, now 62, retired, and contemplating a

third marriage (to a 21-year-old Cape Town model), "but I certainly wouldn't go for an artificial heart. A transplant, yes, but I don't fancy being attached to a machine for whatever life I have left." On a more philosophical level, some experts challenge the very idea of artificial and transplanted organs. Dr. Lewis Thomas, president emeritus of the Memorial Sloan-Kettering Cancer Center and the thoughtful author of *The Lives of a Cell,* warns that such procedures represent an "insupportably expensive, ethically puzzling, halfway technology." Says Kenneth Vaux, professor of ethics in medicine at the University of Illinois: "We are going to have to decide as a society what we want from our biomedical projects. What kind of a person are we seeking to create? A collection of interchangeable parts you can continually change when those parts fail? An artificial person? We are going to have to temper our ambitions and learn to accept the inevitability of disease, the inevitability of death itself."

Colorado Democratic Governor Richard Lamm, 49, who created a furor last spring by declaring that "we've got a duty to die and get out of the way with all of our machines and artificial hearts, so that our kids can build a reasonable life," reasserted that view last week. Said he: "High-tech medicine is really the Faustian bargain, where for a few extra days of life, we have to pay the price that could bankrupt the country."

Pay the price—the argument keeps coming back to that. When people are sick, they and their families hardly question the price; somebody will have to pay—the insurance company, the Government, the hospital. Humana, for one, is waiving all heart implant fees for Schroeder and other pioneering patients, though this may serve primarily to give the institution a commanding leadership in the field of artificial hearts. But somebody does eventually have to pay.

Dr. Thomas Starzl, a noted transplant surgeon at the University Health Center in Pittsburgh, argues that "the cost of transplants is no higher than the cost of dying from severe diseases of vital organs." A patient can run up expenses of $250,000 before getting a liver transplant, Starzl points out. Nevertheless, the prices of organ transplants remain staggering: heart transplants cost somewhere between $100,000 and $200,000 (Clark's hospital bill was $200,000, not counting $9,000 for the artificial heart, $7,400 for its pump, and the $3,000 or so per year that it would have cost him to run the system if he had survived). The prices for other organs are comparable. A liver transplant costs $135,000, and a year of rehabilitation treatment can double that. Bone-marrow transplants run to $60,000.

Organ transplants are by no means the only miracle cures provided by high-tech medicine. A hemophiliac's Autoplex injections, which stimulate blood coagulation, can cost up to $100,000 to keep him alive for three months. Dialysis machines for kidney patients, which pump the blood through an artificial cleansing device, cost nearly $20,000 per year.

If there were only a few desperately ill patients to be saved, extraordinary meansures could be organized to save them. At one of the Humana press conferences last week, a young woman named Theresa Garrison sat wearing a T shirt that said HELP US HELP AMIE LIVE. Amie Garrison, 5, of Clarksville, Ind., was born without bile ducts, which drain bile out of the liver, and she will die unless she gets a liver transplant. A country-and-western band has so far helped raise $20,000, but the Garrisons also need publicity to find a liver donor. Both Indiana Senators are assisting. To further promote Amie's cause, the Garrisons hope she can join President Reagan in lighting the national Christmas tree next week.

But there are at least 150 other Amies around the country who are hoping for liver transplants, and the need for other organs runs into many thousands. Medical insurance firms generally decline payment for such operations on the ground that they are still experimental, though Blue Cross of California has paid between $95,000 and $100,000 for each of two heart transplants this

year. The prospect of the Federal Government taking over the financing is none too cheering either, since the Social Security system is already staggering under a burden of an estimated $85 billion in annual medical costs.

The only real precedent for a federal intervention is Congress's decision in 1972 to pay 80% of the ruinous cost of kidney transplants and dialysis for anyone whose kidneys fail. Congress expected to pay nearly $140 million for 5,000 to 7,000 dialysis patients. The first year's bill came to $241 million for 10,300 patients. In a decade, the number of patients has soared to 82,000—including dying cancer victims and nursing-home octogenarians—at a cost of $2 billion, which accounts for 10% of all medicare payments for physicians.

Heart replacements could run considerably higher than that (some guesses go as high as $40 billion). The number who could benefit from artificial or transplanted hearts is usually estimated at 50,000 per year, possibly 75,000. Multiplying 50,000 cases by an average cost of, say, $150,000 per operation comes to a breathtaking total of $7.5 billion annually.

In theory, even such a cost is quite feasible in a trillion-dollar economy. For the Federal Government, the gigantic bill would represent only about 3% of the budget deficit, the price of three Trident submarines, or about half of what is spent annually on bridge and highway repair. And until fairly recently, the ideal of good medical care for every citizen was proclaimed to be a top national priority. "The fulfillment of our national purpose," Congress rather grandly declared in 1966, "depends on promoting and assuring the highest level of health attainable for every person."

Realistically, however, the question is not how much the U.S. could theoretically afford to spend but how it should apportion the resources available for medicine. Those resources, though not unlimited, are enormous. After a generation of rising costs, the U.S. now spends more than $1 billion every day on health care, 10.8% of the gross national product. Once a country spends

more than 10% of G.N.P. on health, says Robert Rushmer, a professor of bioengineering at the University of Washington who has studied medical costs in Europe, it begins imposing restrictions on who gets what. "We have to come to grips with the fact that our technical abilities have outstripped our social, economic and political policies," says Rushmer.

"But where has all the money gone?" asks one of Rushmer's colleagues, James Speer, a professor of biomedical history at Washington. "We are not living all that much longer. These expenditures can't be understood in the health of people, but in the creation of a very large industry." Harvey Fineberg, dean of Harvard's School of Public Health, attributes fully one-third of the past decade's increase in Medicare costs to the increased use of high-tech medicine, particularly surgical and diagnostic procedures. "I don't mean to downplay the bravery of this individual," Fineberg says of last week's artificial-heart recipient, "but someone has to speak up for the thousands of people whose names are not on everybody's lips, who are dying just as surely as Mr. Schroeder, and whose deaths are preventable."

Rina Spence, president of Emerson Hospital in Concord, Mass., estimates that the bill for Schroeder's operation represents 790 days of hospital care at her hospital, or full treatment for 113 patients for an average stay of a week. "That's what is in the balance," she says sternly.

In terms of the poor, the comparisons look even worse. "We are not giving basic medical care to people in the inner cities," says Tom Preston, chief of cardiology at the Pacific Medical Center in Seattle. A liver transplant of the kind that little Amie Garrison needs would finance a year's operation by a San Francisco inner-city clinic that provides 30,000 office visits in that time. Says Harmon Smith, a professor of moral theology at Duke: "I don't understand the fascination with these absurd, bizarre experiments when we have babies born every day in the U.S. who are brain-damaged because of malnutrition. It is a serious indictment of our society." Barton Bernstein, a his-

torian at Stanford, takes a similar but broader view: "Changing the conditions of poverty would improve health more than all the medical innovations we are going to get in the next decade."

Among those who criticize the financial inefficiency of spectacular surgical experiments, the most common prescription is a greater emphasis on preventive medicine—immunization, examination, nutrition—and not just medicine but a healthier way of living. "Control smoking, alcohol, handguns, overeating and seat belts," says Speer, "and that would be a new world." Sensible though such suggestions are, they are highly colored by wishful thinking.

What is far more likely, since overall demand exceeds overall ability to pay, is some form of rationing or restriction. "There is no question that we face rationing," says Morris Abram, the New York attorney who served from 1979 to 1983 as chairman of the President's commission on medical ethics. But Gregory Pence, who teaches ethics at the University of Alabama Medical School, offers a warning: "Medical costs are uncontrollable because we lack moral agreement about how to deny medical services. Deciding how to say 'no,' and to say it with honesty and integrity, is perhaps the most profound, most difficult moral question our society will face in coming years. But face it we must, for the alternative is disastrous."

Triage is the French military term for the battlefront procedure by which overworked surgeons reject some casualties as too lightly wounded to require treatment, reject others as too badly wounded to be saved, and concentrate their limited resources on the remainder. No matter how it is done, triage is a cruel procedure, perhaps an immoral one, but generally recognized as necessary.

Nobody likes to admit that triage is already being employed in high-tech medicine. When a Long Island hospital was accused last summer of posting color-coded charts next to patients who could be allowed to die, its official loudly denied the district attorney's accusations and the matter was allowed to drop.

But there are many ways of practicing triage. One of the simplest, quite possibly illegal, is by age. One reason both Barney Clark and William Schroeder wanted artificial hearts was that they were both over 50, the unofficial cutoff point for heart transplants. Schroeder had been rejected three times. A more ambiguous standard is the idea that doctors should decide on their own who is best suited for high-tech treatment. But who should get preference—the most sick or the least sick?

The British National Health Service practices triage by delay. For example, it provides heart transplants (110 this year) entirely at government expense, but there are waiting lists of up to a year for all such complex surgery. Though the principle of first come, first served is fair in its random way, rather like a London bus queue, the delay inevitably kills off a certain number of applicants.

And then there is the old tradition of triage by money. A wealthy Briton who does not want to wait in the National Health Service queue can have a private transplant operation for a reported $13,000. In the U.S. too, and in most of the world, money may not buy health, but it certainly helps.

Ever since the coming of the welfare state two generations ago, there has been an increasing repugnance to the idea of the rich enjoying essential services that are denied to the poor. But that same period has seen a drastic change both in the meaning of essential services and in the way people die. At the turn of the century, most people died fairly quickly of infectious diseases, primarily influenza and pneumonia. Now that those diseases can be cured with drugs, the chief killers are slow degenerative diseases, notably heart ailments and cancer. At the turn of the century, most people died at home, cheaply. Today more than 70% die in expensively equipped hospitals, and it is estimated that half of an average person's lifetime medical expenses will occur during his last six months.

What quantity and quality of hospital care people have a right to expect lies at the center of the problem, particularly since 90% of the bills

available for transplant in France in the late 1970s, today live donors make up less than 10 percent of the donor pool. (Live donors constitute nearly a third of the donor pool in the United States, Britain, and other nations with public policies of voluntarism based upon donor cards.)

Second, French physicians note that, despite a public policy allowing strong presumed consent, doctors are not willing to remove organs from cadavers without the consent of family members. Strong presumed consent exists only on paper in France. In practice French physicians find it psychologically intolerable to remove tissues from a body without obtaining the permission of next-of-kin.

In the view of both physicians and nurses, however, the French public strongly supports organ transplantation. The physicians I spoke with reported consent rates of between 90 and 95 percent when permission was sought to remove solid organs. In practice French physicians believe strongly in allowing family members to retain the right to object to organ removal. But few family members actually do object, indicating that a public policy of weak presumed consent is compatible with the moral values of both health professionals and the public in France.

Even if French physicians are only willing to participate in a system whose governing philosophy is one of weak presumed consent, why, given the low rate of refusal, are a larger number of organs not available for transplant? The answer is illuminating for its policy implications for the United States.

France, unlike the United States, does not have a cadre of highly trained personnel to handle the process of organ procurement. Health professionals, usually nurses, must bear the burdens of inquiring about objections to organ removal, locating a suitable recipient, and arranging the removal of organs. French hospital administrators, physicians, and nurses all reported that this process was both time-consuming and costly. Given the growing concern in France over the rising costs of health care there is a reluctance to devote

scarce medical resources to organ procurement. French transplant surgeons also noted that, at present, there were severe limits both in terms of personnel and hospital space on the number of transplants of all types that can now be performed. One surgeon noted that "if we had your resources and facilities for transplantation we would be much more aggressive in pursuing organ donors." Limits on the availability of transplant services in France seem to dampen the ardor with which organ procurement is undertaken.

Moreover, the French, like their American counterparts, find it psychologically difficult to approach grieving family members about the prospect of organ procurement even if only to ascertain whether the family objects to what is usually described in the consent process as a routine, customary, and legally sanctioned practice. Busy emergency room personnel are loathe to take the time necessary to fully discuss the subject of transplantation with distraught family members. In sum, despite the existence on paper of a strong version of presumed consent, health care professionals in France are only willing to operate within the boundaries of weak presumed consent. And while this approach has helped to increase the supply of available cadaver kidneys to the point where few live donations are utilized, economic, organizational, and psychological factors limit the willingness of French medical personnel to ask about objections to removing kidneys and other solid organs for transplantation.

The French experience with strong presumed consent legislation holds important lessons for those, such as myself, who believe that our system of organ procurement must be changed. The French physicians' unwillingness to act upon the authority granted them by the state to remove organs regardless of the wishes of family members parallels the unwillingness of American physicians to remove organs solely on the basis of the legal authority granted by donor cards. As organ procurement specialists know all too well, donor cards are almost never viewed by hospital administrators and physicians as ade-

quate authorization for allowing organ retrieval. The permission of family members is always sought prior to organ removal whether or not a donor card or other legal document can be found.

On the other hand, the practical experience obtained by the French with a version of weak presumed consent does not support the sorts of concerns raised by the Sadlers about presumed consent. French physicians are impressed with the fact that objections have been raised by less than 10 percent of the families who have been given the opportunity to refuse consent. The French press has not reported any dissatisfaction on the part of the public with presumed consent. And French physicians were uniformly relieved to be able to decrease their earlier dependence on live donors. A policy of weak presumed consent appears to have produced a significant amount of social good while allowing for family choice and autonomy in an atmosphere of mutual respect.

The organizational, financial, and psychological factors at work in the French system of organ procurement are also present in the United States. Unlike the French, we have a large number of highly trained and proficient specialists available in the field of organ procurement, but constant pressures to reduce costs in combination with an increasingly litigious atmosphere in medicine make it unlikely that the modest reforms of the present voluntary system proposed by the Sadlers and others[9] will lead to significant improvement in the supply of cadaver organs.

THE PRIMACY OF THE FAMILY

One key factor emerges from both the French and the American experience: the major obstacle to organ procurement is the failure to ask family members about organ donation. French physicians are entitled by law to take tissues without asking anyone but are unwilling to do so. American physicians are entitled by the Uniform Anatomical Gift Act to take tissues from those who sign donor cards but they are unwilling to do so.

Whether or not one believes that the wishes of the family should supersede either the wishes of the public, as in France, or the wishes of the individual, as in the United States, in fact both countries always treat the family as the final authority insofar as the disposition of the dead is concerned.

The respect accorded family members' wishes in these two large and medically sophisticated nations would seem to dictate the kind of public policy change that has the greatest chance of alleviating the shortage in cadaver donors. The French experience indicates that the only practical policy options are those that recognize and respect the role of family members in participating in decisions about cadaver donation. The weak version of required request acknowledges the role of family members, while at the same time ensuring that an optimal environment exists for eliciting organ donations.

Physicians, nurses, or other hospital personnel should be required to inquire whether available family members will give their consent to organ donation. This could be accomplished by modifying the current legal process for declaring death in all states to include a provision requiring that a request concerning organ donation be made to available family members by a party not connected with the determination of death. When family members are not available, organs would be removed only if a donor card or other legal document were present. Or, hospital accreditation requirements could be revised to include a provision mandating that at death the families of potential donors be approached about their willingness to consent.

LINKING REQUEST AND CONSENT

A public policy of weak required request could be merged with a further change in our current procurement policy. We could modify the consent process from the present system of opting in to

one of opting out along the lines of the weak presumed consent approach used in Scandinavia and, de facto, in France. But weak required request need not be linked to any version of presumed consent. If, as the Sadlers apparently believe, there is something coercive about family members being asked to opt out of donations rather than being asked to opt in, our society might wish to see what the effects are of merely modifying the present emphasis on voluntarism to include required request.

In considering the alternatives of presumed consent or required request, four combinations of request and consent are possible:

Request	Consent
Optional	Opt in
Required	Opt out

The current system of donor cards is, in practice, an optional-opt-in approach. While sound moral arguments can be mounted in favor of the strongest alternative approach—a required-opt-out system—I believe that public and professional consensus could be achieved for a required-opt-in policy.

The Sadlers note that many philosophers, theologians, and social theorists have emphasized the importance of encouraging altruism on the part of every individual within a society. But, as those involved in blood donation in this country learned through years of hard-won efforts to improve the frequency with which blood is given, altruism is not sufficient to assure adequate supplies of necessary medical resources. People must be asked to act if their altruistic motivations are to make a significant difference in helping those in need.

Cadaver organ donation is, whether we like it or not, a family matter. Families should be given every opportunity to act upon their desire to transform the tragedy of death into the gift of life. But they must be asked. If our society were to institute a policy of weak required request, those who are, according to the public opinion polls, willing to give would have a maximal opportunity to do so. We should not allow our concern for the rights and values of the individual to blind us to policy options that can accommodate both individual autonomy and community good.

References

[1]G. Kolata, "Organ Shortage Clouds New Transplant Era," *Science* 221 (July 1, 1983); 32-33.

[2]R. W. Evans, "Organ Scarcity and Issues of Distribution: An Overview," paper presented at a conference; "The Future of Technology in a New Payment Environment," American Enterprise Institute, Washington, D.C., January 24, 1984.

[3]T. D. Overcast, R. W. Evans, et al., "Problems in the Identification of Potential Organ Donors," JAMA (March 23-30, 1984), 1559-62.

[4]See A. L. Caplan, "Public Policy and Organ Transplantation," Testimony to New York State Assembly Health Committee, April 26, 1984, and, "Morality Dissected: A Plea for Reform of Current Policies With Respect to Autopsy," *Human Pathology*, December, 1984.

[5]Evans, op. cit.

[6]A. J. Matas and F. J. Veith, "Presumed Consent for Organ Retrieval," *Theoretical Medicine* 5 (1984), 155-66.

[7]P. Safar, Hearings on Organ Transplants before the Subcommittee on Investigations and Oversight, Committee on Science and Technology, U. S. House of Representatives, April 23, 1983, Washington, D.C., pp. 653-59.

[8]I would like to thank Claire Ambroselli at INSERM and the personnel at Hopital Necker and Hotel Dieu for providing information.

[9]J. M. Prottas, "Obtaining Replacements: The Organizational Framework of Organ Procurement," Hearings on Organ Transplants before the Subcommittee on Investigations and Oversight of the Committee on Science and Technology, U. S. House of Representatives, April 1983, pp. 714-51.

Some Criteria for Making Decisions Concerning the Distribution of Scarce Medical Resources

Robert Young

Robert Young is a reader in philosophy at La Trobe University, Melbourne, Australia. He is author of Freedom, Responsibility and God *and* Personal Autonomy: Beyond Negative and Positive Liberty *(1986). He has also written various pieces in professional journals and anthologies on ethics, social and political philosophy, and the philosophy of religion.*

Young develops criteria for the allocation of scarce medical resources to specific individuals which he believes will combine "the maximum possible benefits consistent with the recognition that all are equally deserving of respect and fair consideration." His combination of utility with justice involves the proposal that all people can have equal worth without having an equally valid claim on the use of scarce medical resources. The validity of such claims may vary, Young suggests, with such factors as the probability of success of treatment, varying life expectancy, degree of prolongation of treatment, resources consumed in treatment, and dependence of others on the patient.

I. MORAL PHILOSOPHY AND THE SPECIFICITY OF MEDICAL DECISIONS

There is evidence of growing dissatisfaction among moral philosophers with the excessive importance placed on what is usually referred to as meta-ethics. While such meta-ethical reflection (or, as I should prefer, reflection on the foundations of ethical judgments) is not unimportant, it is liable when pursued as an end in itself to become a 'dead-end.' At least some moral philosophers have started to re-emphasize that serious moral reflection begins at the point where moral decisions have to be made in response to genuine and perplexing moral problems. It has seemed, furthermore, to such moral philosophers, that acknowledgement of this truth should lead to a recognition that neglect of pressing moral and social problems, and the failure to make use of the resources of their own privileged vantage point in

contributing to the resolution of these problems, represents a condemnation of the practice of philosophy in general and of moral philosophy in particular.

In this essay I want to discuss some moral problems associated with the necessity of making decisions concerning the distribution of scarce medical resources. Foremost among these problems are those which stem from the costliness and shortness of supply of medical remedies for fatal or seriously disabling ailments, especially when the number of medically eligible patients exceeds the number whose treatment can be managed. For example, the number of persons seeking admittance to a kidney dialysis program at any time currently exceeds the available facilities. Likewise, the number seeking kidney transplantations at any time presently exceeds the number of suitable organs available under donation schemes.

These (and other comparable) facts give rise to the moral problems which must be faced by those deciding who shall receive the scarce resources available and who shall miss out.

It may be thought that one should first attend to another associated problem of priorities,

namely the problem of distribution of total medical resources and the ranking one should give in that distribution to the procedures referred to in relation to fatal and seriously disabling ailments. I will allude to this associated problem toward the end of the essay. I relegate it to this position because I'm not convinced that the issues it raises are as difficult of resolution.

It is my contention that it will be a measure of the value of doing moral philosophy that one be able to lay down decision rules or guidelines which would enlighten those actually confronted with these medical decisions. The professional moral philosopher, of course, is only rarely, if ever, going to be in on the decision-making as regards the distribution of scarce medical resources. But he can make a contribution in advance of the specific moral problems being confronted. This contribution consists in the formulating of decision rules or guidelines that will be relevant to the solution of these real moral problems, because even though the professional moral philosopher may not be involved in applying the guidelines, he has at least one significant advantage as regards the opportunity to develop them. Namely, he has at his disposal a far greater measure of the required freedom, opportunity and resources than does, e.g., a typical medical practitioner. None of my remarks are intended to suggest that moral philosophers have superior capacities as moral agents, nor that non-professionals cannot do what I have suggested professionals should do. What I have been trying to stress is that what should be distinctive of moral philosophical activity is the formulation of decision rules or guidelines for resolving real medical distribution problems, because the absence of such guidelines seems likely to lead to 'decisions' being taken in ways that are *ad hoc* and (because ill-thought-out), unfair. Far better that decision-taking be informed by guidelines having a carefully considered conceptual base.

What I shall, therefore, try to do in this paper is to offer some proposals on the decision-proce-dure which might justifiably be employed by medical decision-makers faced with the problem of allocating scarce medical resources. I will seek to do this in two ways. Firstly, I shall critically consider some proposals which have been made elsewhere. Secondly, I shall formulate some principles and some decision rules as suggestions on the implementation of these principles, in accordance with the sort of moral position I would defend. (This position is roughly that the demands of justice have priority over those for the maximization of utility (or any other teleologically oriented notion) *except when* the overwhelming importance of bringing about such consequences can be achieved at the cost of only a *trivial* injustice.) The principles are to be accorded more moral weight than the suggestions for implementing them, but I do not attempt to place the members of either group in any ordering signifying moral importance. (This would be the task of those who might formulate a super decision rule.) Each decision-maker has *at least* to try to utilize as many principles and adopt as many suggestions for their implementation as is possible, given that the overall task is to achieve the optimal use of scarce medical resources that is consistent with a concern for fairness.

2. A CRITICAL ASSESSMENT OF RESCHER'S CRITERIA FOR USE AT THE FIRST STAGE

Where decision procedures for allocating the available equipment, vital organs, skilled personnel and so on have been established, a two-stage screening process has commonly been adopted. First, it has customarily been the task of medical staff to decide *on medical grounds* those who should be streamed through to the second-stage, where a selection panel makes the final assessment and matches up as fairly as possible available supply with demand.

Nicholas Rescher, who is one of the few philosophers to have proposed some decision criteria for the allocation of scarce medical resources, has suggested there are three criteria of relevance at the initial screening stage.[1] He introduces 'the constituency factor', 'the progress-of-science factor' and 'the prospect-of-success factor'.

According to the first criterion a medical institution is justified in considering for exotic medical lifesaving therapy only persons within its own constituency, provided this constituency itself rests on a defensible basis. This is not strictly a medical criterion, but, because the issue will largely take care of itself, I do not think one need dispute placing this criterion among those appropriate to the first stage. Specialized hospitals such as those for children, the armed services and so on are unlikely to receive applications from those outside their constituencies. Distance from the institution is likely also to operate as a factor excluding potential applicants. Nevertheless, one can see the pitfalls of allowing a strictly nonmedical consideration in at this stage, though, if it is recalled that those in rural communities or depressed urban areas with poor facilities may well be placed at a severe disadvantage if the constituency factor is over-rigidly applied.

Rescher's second suggested factor seems to me to be of even more dubious merit. I do not dispute his contention that it may be important for the progress of medical science and *a fortiori* a potential benefit to many future sufferers to determine how effective a certain life-preserving treatment is in relation to certain specific characteristics of the history (medical or otherwise) of those selected for treatment. Clearly, of course, those chosen with the progress of medical science specifically in mind will *have* to be selected automatically at the second stage.

Quite apart from the serious epistemological difficulties attaching to the task of deciding in advance what research leads are justifiably to be followed up given scarcity, there is a further consideration against giving this kind of favored

treatment. Namely, that it seems likely that the information yielded in this way could be obtained without introducing such discriminatory methods of selection. Surely the same information could be obtained by co-ordinating the information derived from the regular functioning of selection procedures in institutions on a nation-wide or international basis. No doubt this would require soliciting some useless information. But it seems preferable that redundant information be collected and stored than that unnecessarily discriminatory variables be allowed to influence selection of whose lives shall be saved. There is too much at stake to allow that to happen.

Rescher's third suggestion does seem to have more to recommend it. If some treatment were highly successful with a particular category of person this would be significant as a medical consideration. Knowledge of such a fact could be derived from the information collected and stored in the manner already spoken of. There is a related point which Rescher does not discuss. It is that if a person has a record of refusing to follow (or perhaps has some inability to follow) medical instructions, this should, I would urge, be taken into account in assessing the likelihood of treatment succeeding in his case. (I presume, of course, that if his inability to follow instructions can be overcome, steps would be taken, in the event of his being selected for treatment, to ensure that it was overcome.) The justification for taking success rates into account is that when scarcity is a pre-eminent consideration one should seek to achieve optimum benefits from the deployment of available resources, and when the ingredients for success are known they ought not to be ignored.

In general I think that only the last of Rescher's criteria can bear much weight as concerns medical decision making. What I propose to do now is to advocate the first of the principles I said I would outline. I shall use capital letters: (A), (B), (C), and so on to identify these principles of medical decision-making. I shall also make some suggestions for implementing the principles,

these decision rules or suggestions being identified as (S1), (S2), (S3) and so on. I have already indicated my agreement with Rescher's 'the prospect-of-success' factor which I shall dub (A) and which reads:

> (A) In a situation of scarcity, priority should be given to treating those who fall within a category for which there is reliable evidence (antecedently available) of a markedly higher rate of successful treatment.

I also made a suggestion (S1) that evidence as to a person's capacity and willingness to follow the medical instructions he is given would also need to be considered.

Though it would no doubt lead to more work for those making decisions at the second-stage, I would urge the following new principle:

> (B) Medical staff operating at the first screening should err on the side of liberality in streaming people through to the second stage. In practice this will mean that deliberations should be confined to what are pretty clearly medical considerations.

The justification for this is tied up with a suggestion I shall make here though it has to do chiefly with the second-stage.

(S2) The committee at the second-stage should be drawn from a wide cross-section of thoughtful members of the community in an endeavour to rule out any biases that members of a single profession may share.

If the first-stage selection process is made on grounds that are similar to those at the second, the attempt to iron out biases will be defeated. Studies have shown that estimates of social worthiness sometimes lurk in apparently objective medical and psychiatric evaluations.[2] Medical professionals like anyone else can no doubt be influenced or swayed by personal reactions to a patient.

Further, I would suggest (S3) that there is, therefore, a case for having a *panel* of medical professionals (decision-makers) at the first stage as one way of eliminating the effect on an individual's assessment of the personableness of a candidate.

A further point is that what pass for 'medical' grounds at this initial screening are arguably not always such at all. For example, upper or lower age limits applied across-the-board to applicants for haemodialysis could hardly be said to constitute medical grounds for rejection *in every particular case,* even if *on the whole* their employment would be medically justifiable. It is clear then, I think, that it would be better for the medical screeners to take as liberal a view of their task as is feasible.

3. A CRITICAL ASSESSMENT OF SOME PROPOSED CRITERIA FOR USE AT THE SECOND-STAGE

The problems at the second-stage bulk larger. In selecting patients with fatal or seriously disabling illnesses who are to be given treatment unable to be made available to all, it is incumbent upon us to come up with criteria which are fair. Four sorts of criterion have been advanced, though at least two of them can be easily dismissed.

First, it has sometimes been suggested that certain rules could be announced in advance based on statistical medical probabilities which would be rigidly enforced. I have already referred to age limits. Those over forty five years of age and children might be excluded by the application of a criterion based on statistical probabilities.

(S4) Such facts as that children on prolonged dialysis do not find it easy to endure the demanding treatment or do not always come to pubertal maturity are obviously to be taken into account.

Nevertheless, like upper age limits, these are only statistically grounded and to that extent are apt to operate with an arbitrariness inconsistent with fairness. More significant still, criteria like age limits are unlikely to be sufficient in themselves. As I've already argued, success rates connected with such criteria should be taken into

account. But since there would remain problems of selection after rigid enforcement of criteria like those based on age, other criteria would still be needed to complete the sorting-out process.

Secondly, it is conceivable that someone might urge that scarcity will lead to unfairness whatever one does to minimize it, hence, taking serious cognizance of the 'equality of all men' should lead to our adopting the view that if not all can be given the needed treatment, none should be given it. In like vein it has sometimes been said that in deciding how to choose which passengers in an overcrowded and leaky lifeboat should be jettisoned to improve the odds of survival for those left, it is fairer that all should stay aboard if none are willing heroically to volunteer. Perhaps someone might urge similar inaction when confronted with the moral dilemmas confronting those charged with allocating scarce medical therapy.

It is not necessary to labor the disanalogies between the cases like, for example, the fact that those in the lifeboat *might* make such a decision, whereas in the medical dilemma it is not the candidates themselves who make the allocation decisions. This need not be labored, simply because the advocacy of inaction is morally grotesque and irresponsible in the medical case. One might say that the hope of rescue remains open in the lifeboat case but not in the medical ones we're envisaging. This may be true, too, but it is the overriding concern to bring about the best use of available resources that leads to condemnation of the failure to save some when some could be saved. Nobody espousing an ethic like that I have previously said I support can support such moral inertia as this view would license.

The third proposal which warrants consideration is that involving random patient selection. Two methods are available: a straight-out lottery method and a 'first-come-first-served' kind. The latter is really a form of on-going lottery and since there would need to be numbers of lotteries if the former method were employed, the two methods can be regarded as one for our purposes.[3] Ramsey

claims that equality of worth as a human being mandates the randomizing of selection, given that selection is required if not all are to perish. He further contends that we have no way of knowing accurately how to estimate societal worth as between individuals (which he takes to be the only alternative to his procedure).

I shall take this up when the fourth possibility is canvassed later. Ramsey thinks that the 'exceptions' to his ruling principle are justified if, and only if, a community and its members have (or have been reduced to) a single focus or goal under some extraordinary circumstance. Thus, one might support the giving of penicillin in war conditions to sufferers from venereal disease rather than to victims of battle wounds. The justification would be the need to achieve restoration of the largest number to fighting conditions in the shortest possible time. One might ask what would be the effect (in terms of encouraging more abuse) of such a policy, but Ramsey's point is not without force. An even more powerful illustration is to be found in what Ramsey calls the 'morality of triage' (literally, sorting according to quality) in disaster medicine. In such circumstances the victims most in need of help are often left unattended, because first priority is given to those who can quickly be restored to a measure of health which would enable them to do such things as bury the dead and so prevent epidemics, or to carry out makeshift medicine. Thus it might be that one should treat injured doctors first.

Now these putative exceptions to the ruling principle of randomization themselves cast doubt on that principle because they show we are unprepared to avoid facing difficult but inescapable decisions by appealing to the simplicities of a lottery. Furthermore, such a selection procedure is repugnant to those who like myself believe that morally right actions are to be evaluated in terms of their justice *and* their contribution to the maximization of human well-being. Even if a lottery method were a just one, it would still be inferior to method no more unjust which achieved a grea product of human well-being.

Furthermore, the proponent of the lottery scheme must tread warily if he is not to lay himself open to the charge of begging the question. He assumes all claims to the scarce medical resources are equally valid—but that is just what is disputed by advocates of the fourth scheme I will now consider. If a case can be made out which shows that not all claims need be equally valid, the lottery scheme loses whatever support it commands.

At the outset I should point out that I think Ramsey and others who have attacked the fourth method have confused themselves a little by fastening on to the idea that the basis for the method is that of 'societal worth'. Perhaps some have advocated related views which have used such a notion but if so it is unfortunate, I think. Deliberation about the identity of the recipients of scarce medical resources would be pointless if worth were the basis for distribution for the simple reason that men have equal worth.[1] Now it might be retorted that I am simply shifting ground to a conception of merit. But I would stoutly resist this suggestion. What I am claiming is needed is a method which is at the same time as fair as possible and makes the best possible use of scarce medical resources. The measure of 'the best possible use' I have indicated I am appealing to is that maximization of overall human well-being consistent with fairness. Hence I want to avoid talk of 'worth' or 'merit.' I shall speak of the fourth method simply as 'the comparative approach'.

Previously I noted that the degree of success likely with certain categories of patient should be taken into account wherever it can reliably be estimated. This principle, (A), remains relevant when dealing with individual cases. Indeed, it obviously is already taken into account.

At the simplest illustrative level, care is taken when doing organ transplants to minimize the possibility of rejection and this is no doubt associated with the desire to avoid unnecessary loss of valuable resources (as well as with the obvious concern for the patient).

Now there is a related consideration which leads to the third of the principles I wish to put forward. (It has also been pointed out by Rescher in the article cited previously.) It is

(C) A person's life expectancy subsequent to successful treatment should be taken into account. Where a person's age or general medical condition provides grounds for belief that he will be able to benefit from treatment only for a short time, this must count heavily against his candidature in a situation of scarcity.

It is for this reason, for example, that sufferers from systemic diseases like diabetes are normally ruled out of consideration for haemodialysis programs. There may be occasions when principle (A) and principle (C) are difficult to reconcile, though I suspect that (A) would allow some through to the second-stage who would then unfortunately be unable to overcome the presumption underlying (C) despite the likelihood of successful treatment.

A fourth principle is as follows:

(D) Other things being equal, preference will be given to those candidates who will not require a disproportionate share of the available scarce resources.

Candidates who require a prolonged or indefinitely greater number of years of treatment will have to be assessed against those with potentially reversible conditions who would need less access to the resources.

(S5) The claims of children are apt to be relatively discounted by the operation of this criterion.

Even so, there may be a recognition that during the child's lifetime adequate facilities per capita will be made available and hence the child's presently receiving treatment may not deprive others in the future even though the child's demand on resources will be large.

(S6) Putting this possibility on one side, it remains true that the thing cuts the other way, of course, when the treatment, even though scarce, is of a once-for-all kind.

Transplants, the implanting of 'pacemakers' and so on come into this category. Because they should be able to benefit for a far greater period of time, children should have their claims on such resources more favorably assessed.

The mention of children provides an appropriate occasion for introducing the next proposed principle.

(E)   The degree of dependence of others on the candidate is to be accounted a critical consideration.

This dependence may most obviously be that of familial relationship, but may also perhaps consist in a relationship in which one member (such as a social worker, clergyman or the like) provides significant emotional support for others. The loss of a mother or of a father is a stringent one for young children. Thus other things being equal or indecisive a mother with young dependents ought to be given preference over a middle-aged spinster. I stress again this is not a judgment that has anything to do with human worth or merit. Here again the claims of children for certain kinds of treatment are no doubt weaker than those of adults with dependents.

Should dependents be nearly at an age and position of independence this must be weighed against a candidate.

(S7) Where a relationship could satisfactorily be entered into by another this assumes importance.

Thus where one person's financial position renders others (outside of the family or outside of the emotionally supportive roles referred to above) dependent upon them, provided another employer, or the state's welfare arm could satisfactorily take over such a role, the significance of such a circumstance would be pretty minimal, I suggest. The fact that others can sometimes assume a role previously occupied by a different person may well, of course, be significant in assessing the importance of nonfinancially based relationships. If, for example, a person could (and would be willing to) remarry, this would need to be taken into account (if it could be reliably established). This seems to me to be one of the few possible circumstances in which sex might be a pertinent consideration. Opportunities for remarriage may well be significantly different as between persons of different sex (whose other differentia are less prominent).[5]

(S8) Perhaps it would be appropriate to suggest here that in at least some situations occasioned by the scarcity of medical resources, the family organization may contain within itself the capacity to resolve the problem.

Parents or siblings often are able to provide healthy organs with a higher likelihood of successful transplantation into another member of the family than would be the case with an organ from a non-relative. Under other circumstances maybe the donor would be less willing. (I pass no moral judgment on the fact, though I believe it to be an important one in moral psychology, that we are usually more willing to do things for those who stand in special relationships to us such as being mothers, lovers and so on, than we are for those who do not.)

The availability of such a willing donor ought to be sufficient for triggering off the release of any further requisite resources such as skilled personnel, theater facilities and so on.

Nicholas Rescher and others have claimed that comparisons as between potential recipients of scarce medical resources should take into account the potential future contributions and the past services rendered of seekers of such resources. He rightly notices that these criteria would, if invoked, give rise to the exercise of judgment concerning difficult and often intangible matters and also that this constitutes no ground for shirking the task if it is demanded of us. Should we invoke such criteria? I think that if we do they ought not to be given any special emphasis since such emphasis appears likely to lead away from an egalitarian conception of human worth. The only justification I can see for drawing upon such criteria is (once again) that their employment may be necessary for the achievement

of the best possible use of scarce resources consistent with fairness.

Rescher has written:

> One popular article states that 'the most difficult standard would be the candidate's value to society', and goes on to quote someone who said: 'You can't just pick a brilliant painter over a labourer. The average citizen would be quickly eliminated.' But what if it were not a brilliant painter but a brilliant surgeon or medical researcher that was at issue? One wonders if the author of the *obiter dictum* that one 'can't just pick' would still feel equally sure of his ground. (p. 32 of the reprinting in J. Rachels and F. Tillman, *op. cit.*)

It is not necessary to quibble with the final sentence in order to retort to Rescher's question: 'What if it *were* a surgeon or medical researcher of brilliance?' I personally cannot see that the brilliance of the contribution such a person had made or could make should cut any ice at all *unless* all other grounds were indecisive as between him and another candidate. Later on in the paper, Rescher indicates his attachment to 'perfectionist' sentiments[6] when he contends that a civilized society has an obligation to promote the furtherance of positive achievements in cultural and related areas even though this imposes additional burdens. Such a view seems to me to furnish insecure foundations for the distribution of scarce resources and I would be unwilling to give it entrance at any earlier stage as a criterion *in competition with* those already advanced above.

(S9) Thus the supposed dilemma: greatest future contribution vs. greatest future burdens imposed on others, should in my view always be resolved in favor of the latter horn.

If an individual's death would lead to society being forced to take up the burden in a way that would not be especially detrimental to the deceased's dependents, one could perhaps argue for the former horn being taken. But when that is not feasible, the obligation to prevent injury or harm should take over because it is clearly a more stringent one than that of providing aid.[7]

It will probably be obvious without my saying it that I would rate the past-services-rendered factor as even less important than the prospective one I have been discussing. Rescher thinks considerations of *equity* demand its being taken into account. The notion of 'equity' is far from clear in the context, but I pass over that. The criterion seems unlikely always to be helpful even if we have to invoke it (being unable to decide on all other relevant criteria concerning who comes off comparatively as the one most likely to maximize the benefits of receiving the treatment). How would one weigh a man's valor in war against another's significant peacetime contributions allowing that each had been singularly unsuccessful in the other period (of peace or war respectively)? The criterion, furthermore, seems unfairly loaded against those whose scope for having made past contributions is strictly limited, namely the young.

Let us assume for the sake of argument that we *are* to take social contributions into account. It is worth pondering one particular point apt to be neglected in assessing such contributions. Namely, what importance should we attach to a man's moral conduct?

(S10) I would suggest that if such contributions were to be taken into account, a fair working principle would seem to be that any seriously detrimental effects a man's conduct had on the liberty and welfare of others should be used to discount any other contributions he made which were of value.

The rapist, the murderer with psychopathic tendencies, the wife-basher, the child-beater, the fomenter of racial strife, the willful industrial polluter and so on would all lose points gained on other scores.

Naturally, (S11) if a man undergoes a permanent transformation in these matters he must be re-evaluated.

It is worth asking what we should do if we admit these sorts of consideration when a man preferred for treatment partly because of his social consciousness and moral uprightness becomes morally depraved and anti-social. Ought he to be

taken off the treatment in the event of its being of a continuous nature?

(S12) Should a decision be made to take moral conduct into account, the possibility of removal from the treatment program for certain kinds of behavior deemed to flout reasonable standards of other-regardingness, should be broached prior to the commencement of treatment.

If his subsequent behavior is such as reasonably to be under his control and should his being confronted with the previously broached possibility of removal from the program fail to bring him to his senses, I believe it would be justifiable to re-allocate the resources to another.

There is an important point which I think should be made at this stage which stems from the rather inegalitarian nature of western society. It is that it seems unlikely that those who will have to come before selection committees of the sort being envisaged, will be drawn from the advantaged groups of our society. One finds it hard to believe, for example, that the brilliant surgeon wouldn't receive favored treatment from his colleagues which would circumvent his having to compete for selection for the scarce resources. Likewise the statesman, the large asset-holding capitalist entrepreneur and so on seem certain to be shielded from such procedures. Even allowing that the expenses if borne privately would be enormous, and that for this and other reasons (such as the need for sterile conditions, constant attendance of skilled personnel and so on) the scarce medical resources that have been our concern must be largely under institutional control, the inegalitarian nature of our society seems almost certain to operate to the advantage of the wealthy and powerful as already happens in other spheres.

No doubt the decisions will not be easy even when all pertinent information is available, but if my arguments to date have had some force, the five chief considerations will be those I have labelled (A) to (E), namely: the probability of success of the treatment; the need for liberality rather than stringency in the first-stage screening; the life expectancy of the patient (assuming recovery); the degree of prolongation of treatment or the proportion of available resources needed to effect a successful treatment; and the nature and extent of the dependence of others on the candidate.

As previously noted the principles have deliberately been left unordered *morally*. I want to stress again, too, that the principles have not been put forward for the purpose of establishing that one human is more *worthy* or deserving of treatment than another, but rather with a view to bringing into existence the maximum possible benefits consistent with the recognition that all are equally deserving of respect and fair consideration.

4. WHERE BEST TO CONCENTRATE ONE'S SCARCE RESOURCES

In this final section I want briefly to give some attention to a further issue connected with the distribution of medical resources. In one obvious sense the total funds available for medical purposes are restricted and to that extent 'scarce.' The question arises whether less funds should be given at the desperate end of treatment (like dialysis or transplantation) rather than at the possibly curative stages.

(S13) It seems to me that it would be more effective to concentrate research and funds at the stage where detection and eradication of causes is possible.

The egalitarianism I have been urging as crucial to the resolution of the issues raised by scarcity of medical resources supplies such an answer. The simple, the preventative and so on are more fundamental and should be given priority over the spectacular, the costly and the virtuoso performance. Naturally not all medical treatment can be of this form, but wherever it is possible to develop

and use therapies applicable at earlier stages resources should be channelled into these kinds of treatment. The medical researchers often allege, of course, that there is 'spinoff' value from more exotic investigations and treatments—this was frequently said in the heyday of heart transplantations.

Nevertheless, (S14) if the benefits of medical resources can be spread more widely by focussing on the less spectacular but more fundamental (and where this assumption doesn't hold I would be happy to waive my suggestion), the moral philosopher should oppose the directing of funds into the more publicity-gaining ventures.[8]

(S15) Similar principles of egalitarianism seem to me to suggest that more of our total resources ought to be directed toward medical needs and away from other fields less concerned with the promotion of human well-being.

Cutting back defense budgets would, for example, be an obvious first step. No doubt medical needs cannot be given *carte blanche* within national budgets but neither should they be relegated to become a mere after-thought (along with aid to developing countries, anti-pollution measures, the eradication of poverty and the halting of the decay of our major cities!).

At the heart of all that I have been advocating and suggesting is the moral conviction that we must move toward an egalitarian society (preferably on an international scale) in which primary human *needs* for adequate nourishment, housing, health care, education, meaningful employment and so on must be given top priority. The moral philosopher must help show the way to understanding our obligation to promote the satisfaction of such needs in the fairest and best possible ways. It seems to me, as I indicated above (see (S13)), that in a world of scarcity the more fundamental, preventative and cause-eradicating tasks should be preferentially fostered.

It is important, though, that I end on a note related to the present less satisfactory situation. That is, one of scarcity in which difficult and perplexing medical decisions must be confronted.

I have sought to show that the moral philosopher can have something to say about the decisions, rules, principles and guidelines appropriate to such medical decisions. It goes without saying that he ought also to publicize them outside the confines of his own discipline and solicit public comment upon and criticism of them. It would be arrogant to claim that my deliberations counted for more than those of just one moral philosopher. Nevertheless, I do not believe that it would be arrogant to say that the contribution of moral philosophers on a wider scale to the sort of issues I have tackled, will be a measure of the value of pursuing moral philosophy.[9]

Notes

[1]'The Allocation of Exotic Medical Lifesaving Therapy', *Ethics,* vol. 79, 1969, pp. 173–180. It has been reprinted in J. Rachels and F. Tillman (eds.) *Philosophical Issues: A Contemporary Introduction* (New York, Evanston, San Francisco and London, 1972) pp. 27–33.

[2]Cf. P. Ramsey *The Patient as Person* (New Haven and London, 1970) p. 248f.

[3]Ramsey, *ibid.,* has advocated this procedure. See, e.g. pp. 252–259. G. E. M. Anscombe's remarks in 'Who is Wronged?' *The Oxford Review* no. 5, 1967, pp. 16–17 strongly suggest that she would be in sympathy with a 'first-come-first-served' basis. In her view, provided resources are used to supply human need, it is not morally wrong to withhold help from several and give it to one, presuming it is not given to the one for some morally bad reason such as his being wealthier.

[4]There is an excellent discussion of this matter in G. Vlastos 'Justice and Equality' in R. B. Brandt (ed.) *Social Justice* (Englewood Cliffs, N. J., 1962) pp. 31–72. See, too, B. Williams 'The Idea of Equality' reprinted in his *Problems of the Self* (Cambridge, 1973).

[5]Like sex, intelligence also seems to be a largely irrelevant factor. Selection committees would need to guard, therefore, against the possibility that the more intelligent and articulate might be better equipped to present their case in a persuasive way, just as they would need to guard against sex-based discrimination (no matter how unwitting) when sexual differences were not to the point.

[6]Cf. J. Rawls' terminology in *A Theory of Justice* (Oxford, 1972). One might equally speak of 'elitism'.

[7]Cf. P. Foot 'The Problem of Abortion and the Doctrine of the Double Effect' *The Oxford Review,* no. 5, 1967, pp. 5–15 (esp. 11ff).

[8]Ramsey, *op. cit.,* pp. 269, 271, details several incidents from the period of the heart transplant boom which reveal rather disturbingly how mundane heart operations and research into the causes, prevention and cure of coronary ills were pushed off the stage because of the concentration on what now can be seen to have been relatively a futile pursuit.

[9]I should like to thank my colleague, Barry Wilkins, and the editors of *Theory and Decision,* W. Leinfellner and E. Booth, for helping me to make improvements to the paper.

Who Shall Live When Not All Can Live?

James F. Childress

A biographical sketch of James F. Childress is given on page 715.

Childress advocates a two-stage selection process for allocating scarce medical resources to specific individuals: first the use of medical criteria, then the use of random selection criteria. He gives at least six important arguments for the use of random selection criteria. (1) They best express a commitment to equality of human dignity by providing equality of opportunity. (2) They best promote trust between physician and patient. (3) They would be selected as the fairest methods by impartial choosers of allocation procedures. (4) They would best ease the psychological strain on those rejected and on those who must explain to them why they have been rejected. (5) They would eliminate the need for a committee to make social worth judgments. (6) They would prompt those in positions of economic and political power to make medical resources available to everyone to insure that they would not be excluded.

Who shall live when not all can live? Although this question has been urgently forced upon us by the dramatic use of artificial internal organs and organ transplantations, it is hardly new. George Bernard Shaw dealt with it in *The Doctor's Dilemma:*

Sir Patrick: Well, Mr. Savior of Lives: which is it to be? that honest decent man Blenkinsop, or that rotten blackguard of an artist, eh?

Ridgeon: It's not an easy case to judge, is it? Blenkinsop's an honest decent man; but is he any use? Dubedat's a rotten blackguard; but he's a genuine source of pretty and pleasant and good things.

Sir Patrick: What will he be a source of for that poor innocent wife of his, when she finds him out?

Ridgeon: That's true. Her life will be a hell.

Sir Patrick: And tell me this. Suppose you had this choice put before you: either to go through life and find all the pictures bad but all the men and women good, or go through life and find all the pictures good and all the men and women rotten. Which would you choose?[1]

A significant example of the distribution of scarce medical resources is seen in the use of penicillin shortly after its discovery. Military officers had to determine which soldiers would be treated—those with venereal disease or those wounded in combat.[2] In many respects such decisions have become routine in medical circles. Day after day physicians and others make judgments and decisions "about allocations of medical care to various segments of our population, to various types of hospitalized patients, and to specific individuals,"[3] for example, whether mental illness or cancer will receive the higher proportion of available funds. Nevertheless, the dramatic

From *Soundings: An Interdisciplinary Journal,* vol. 53 (Winter 1970): 339–55. Reprinted by permission of the author and publisher.

forms of "Scarce Life-Saving Medical Resources" (hereafter abbreviated as SLMR) such as hemodialysis and kidney and heart transplants have compelled us to examine the moral questions that have been concealed in many routine decisions. I shall not attempt [here] to show how a resolution of SLMR cases can help us in the more routine ones that do not involve a conflict of life with life. Rather I shall develop an argument for a particular method of determining who shall live when not all can live. No conclusions are implied about criteria and procedures for determining who shall receive medical resources that are not directly related to the preservation of life (e.g., corneal transplants) or about standards for allocating money and time for studying and treating certain diseases.

Just as current SLMR decisions are not totally discontinuous with other medical decisions, so we must ask whether some other cases might, at least by analogy, help us develop the needed criteria and procedures. Some have looked at the principles at work in our responses to abortion, euthanasia, and artificial insemination.[4] Usually they have concluded that these cases do not cast light on the selection of patients for artificial and transplanted organs. The reason is evident: in abortion, euthanasia, and artificial insemination, there is no conflict of life with life for limited but indispensable resources (with the possible exception of therapeutic abortion). In current SLMR decisions, such a conflict is inescapable, and it makes them morally perplexing and fascinating. If analogous cases are to be found, I think that we shall locate them in moral conflict situations.

ANALOGOUS CONFLICT SITUATIONS

An especially interesting and pertinent one is *U.S. v. Holmes*.[5] In 1841 an American ship, the *William Brown,* which was near Newfoundland on a trip from Liverpool to Philadelphia, struck an iceberg. The crew and half the passengers were able to

escape in the two available vessels. One of these, a longboat, carrying too many passengers and leaking seriously, began to founder in the turbulent sea after about twenty-four hours. In a desperate attempt to keep it from sinking, the crew threw overboard fourteen men. Two sisters of one of the men either jumped overboard to join their brother in death or instructed the crew to throw them over. The criteria for determining who should live were "not to part man and wife, and not to throw over any woman." Several hours later the others were rescued. Returning to Philadelphia, most of the crew disappeared, but one, Holmes, who had acted upon orders from the mate, was indicted, tried, and convicted on the charge of "unlawful homicide."

We are interested in this case from a moral rather than a legal standpoint, and there are several possible responses to and judgments about it. The judge contended that lots should have been cast, for in such conflict situations, there is no other procedure "so consonant both to humanity and to justice." Counsel for Holmes, on the other hand, maintained that the "sailors adopted the only principle of selection which was possible in an emergency like theirs—a principle more humane than lots."

Another version of selection might extend and systematize the maxims of the sailors in the direction of "utility"; those are saved who will contribute to the greatest good for the greatest number. Yet another possible option is defended by Edmond Cahn in *The Moral Decision.* He argues that in this case we encounter the "morals of the last days." By this phrase he indicates that an apocalyptic crisis renders totally irrelevant the normal differences between individuals. He continues,

> In a strait of this extremity, all men are reduced—or raised, as one may choose to denominate it—to members of the genus, mere congeners and nothing else. Truly and literally, all were "in the same boat," and thus none could be saved separately from the others. I am driven to conclude that otherwise—that is, if none sac-

rifice themselves of free will to spare the others—they must all wait and die together. For where all have become congeners, pure and simple, no one can save himself by killing another.[6]

Cahn's answer to the question "who shall live when not all can live" is "none" unless the voluntary sacrifice by some persons permits it.

Few would deny the importance of Cahn's approach, although many, including this writer, would suggest that it is relevant mainly as an affirmation of an elevated and, indeed, heroic or saintly morality that one hopes would find expression in the voluntary actions of many persons trapped in "borderline" situations involving a conflict of life with life. It is a maximal demand that some moral principles impose on the individual in the recognition that self-preservation is not a good that is to be defended at all costs. The absence of this saintly or heroic morality should not mean, however, that everyone perishes. Without making survival an absolute value and without justifying all means to achieve it, we can maintain that simply letting everyone die is irresponsible. This charge can be supported from several different standpoints, including society at large as well as the individuals involved. Among a group of self-interested individuals, none of whom volunteers to relinquish his life, there may be better and worse ways of determining who shall survive. One task of social ethics, whether religious or philosophical, is to propose relatively just institutional arrangements within which self-interested and biased men can live. The question then becomes: which set of arrangements—which criteria and procedures of selection—is most satisfactory in view of the human condition (man's limited altruism and inclination to seek his own good) and the conflicting values that are to be realized?

There are several significant differences between the *Holmes* and SLMR cases, a major one being that the former involves *direct* killing of another person, while the latter involve only *permitting* a person to die when it is not possible to save all. Furthermore, in extreme situations such

as *Holmes,* the restraints of civilization have been stripped away, and something approximating a state of nature prevails, in which life is "solitary, poor, nasty, brutish and short." The state of nature does not mean that moral standards are irrelevant and that might should prevail, but it does suggest that much of the matrix that normally supports morality has been removed. Also, the necessary but unfortunate decisions about who shall live and die are made by men who are existentially and personally involved in the outcome. Their survival too is at stake. Even though the institutional role of sailors seems to require greater sacrificial actions, there is obviously not assurance that they will adequately assess the number of sailors required to man the vessel or that they will impartially and objectively weigh the common good at stake. As the judge insisted in his defense of casting lots in the *Holmes* case: "In no other than this [casting lots] or some like way are those having equal rights put upon an equal footing, and in no other way is it possible to guard against partiality and oppression, violence, and conflict." This difference should not be exaggerated, since self-interest, professional pride, and the like obviously affect the outcome of many medical decisions. Nor do the remaining differences cancel *Holmes's* instructiveness.

CRITERIA OF SELECTION FOR SLMR

Which set of arrangements should be adopted for SLMR? Two questions are involved: Which standards and criteria should be used? and, Who should make the decision? The first question is basic, since the debate about implementation, e.g., whether by a lay committee or physician, makes little progress until the criteria are determined.

We need two sets of criteria, which will be applied at two different stages in the selection of recipients of SLMR. First, medical criteria should be used to exclude those who are not "medically

acceptable." Second, from this group of "medically acceptable" applicants, the final selection can be made. Occasionally in current American medical practice, the first stage is omitted, but such an omission is unwarranted. Ethical and social responsibility would seem to require distributing these SLMR only to those who have some reasonable prospect of responding to the treatment. Furthermore, in transplants such medical tests as tissue and blood typing are necessary, although they are hardly fully developed.

"Medical acceptability" is not as easily determined as many nonphysicians assume, since there is considerable debate in medical circles about the relevant factors (e.g., age and complicating diseases). Although ethicists can contribute little or nothing to this debate, two proposals may be in order. First, "medical acceptability" should be used only to determine the group from which the final selection will be made, and the attempt to establish fine degrees of prospective response to treatment should be avoided. Medical criteria, then, would exclude some applicants but would not serve as a basis of comparison between those who pass the first stage. For example, if two applicants for dialysis were medically acceptable, the physicians would *not* choose the one with the *better* medical prospects. Final selection would be made on other grounds. Second, psychological and environmental factors should be kept to an absolute minimum and should be considered only when they are without doubt critically related to medical acceptability (e.g., the inability to cope with the requirements of dialysis, which might lead to suicide).[7]

The most significant moral questions emerge when we turn to the final selection. Once the pool of medically acceptable applicants has been defined and still the number is larger than the resources, what other criteria should be used? How should the final selection be made? First, I shall examine some of the difficulties that stem from efforts to make the final selection in terms of social value; these difficulties raise serious doubts about the feasibility and justifiability of the utili-

tarian approach. Then I shall consider the possible justification for random selection or chance.

Occasionally criteria of social worth focus on past contributions, but most often they are primarily future-oriented. The patient's potential and probable contribution to the society is stressed, although this obviously cannot be abstracted from his present web of relationships (e.g., dependents) and occupational activities (e.g., nuclear physicist). Indeed, the magnitude of his contribution to society (as an abstraction) is measured in terms of these social roles, relations, and functions. Enough has already been said to suggest the tremendous range of factors that affect social value or worth. (I am excluding from consideration the question of the ability to pay, because most of the people involved have to secure funds from other sources, public or private, anyway. Legislation in 1972 provided payment for most persons who need kidney dialysis or transplantation.) Here we encounter the first major difficulty of this approach: How do we determine the relevant criteria of social value?

The difficulties of quantifying various social needs are only too obvious. How does one quantify and compare the needs of the spirit (e.g., education, art, religion), political life, economic activity, technological development? Joseph Fletcher suggests that "some day we may learn how to 'quantify' or 'mathematicate' or 'computerize' the value problem in selection, in the same careful and thorough way that diagnosis has been."[8] I am not convinced that we can ever quantify values, or that we should attempt to do so. But even if the various social and human needs, in principle, could be quantified, how do we determine how much weight we will give to each one? Which will have priority in case of conflict? Or even more basically, in the light of which values and principles do we recognize social "needs"?

One possible way of determining the values that should be emphasized in selection has been proposed by Leo Shatin.[9] He insists that our medical decisions about allocating resources are al-

ready based on an unconscious scale of values (usually dominated by material worth). Since there is really no way of escaping this, we should be self-conscious and critical about it. How should we proceed? He recommends that we discover the values that most people in our society hold and then use them as criteria for distributing SLMR. These values can be discovered by attitude or opinion surveys. Presumably if 51 percent in this testing period put a greater premium on military needs than technological development, military men would have a greater claim on our SLMR than experimental researchers. But valuations of what is significant change, and the student revolutionary who was denied SLMR in 1970 might be celebrated in 1990 as the greatest American hero since George Washington.

Shatin presumably is seeking criteria that could be applied nationally, but at the present, regional and local as well as individual prejudices tincture the criteria of social value that are used in selection. Nowhere is this more evident than in the deliberations and decisions of the anonymous selection committee of the Seattle Artificial Kidney Center, where such factors as church membership and Scout leadership have been deemed significant for determining who shall live.[10] As two critics conclude after examining these criteria and procedures, they rule out "creative nonconformists, who rub the bourgeoisie the wrong way but who historically have contributed so much to the making of America. The Pacific Northwest is no place for a Henry David Thoreau with bad kidneys."[11]

Closely connected to this first problem of determining social value is a second one. Not only is it difficult if not impossible to reach agreement on social value, but it is also rarely easy to predict what our needs will be in a few years and what the consequences of present actions will be. Furthermore it is difficult to predict which persons will fulfill their potential function in society. Admissions committees in colleges and universities experience the frustrations of predicting realization of potential. For these reasons, as someone

has indicated, God might be a utilitarian, but we cannot be. We simply lack the capacity to predict very accurately the consequences which we then must evaluate. Our incapacity is never more evident than when we think in societal terms.

Other difficulties make us even less confident that such an approach to SLMR is advisable. Many critics raise the specter of abuse, but this should not be overemphasized. The fundamental difficulty appears on another level: the utilitarian approach would in effect reduce the person to his social role, relations, and functions. Ultimately it dulls and perhaps even eliminates the sense of the person's transcendence, his dignity as a person that cannot be reduced to his past or future contribution to society. It is not at all clear that we are willing to live with these implications of utilitarian selection. Wilhelm Kolff, who invented the artificial kidney, has asked: "Do we really subscribe to the principle that social standing should determine selection? Do we allow patients to be treated with dialysis only when they are married, go to church, have children, have a job, a good income and give to the Community Chest?"[12]

The German theologian Helmut Thielicke contends that any search for "objective criteria" for selection is already a capitulation to the utilitarian point of view which violates man's dignity.[13] The solution is not to let all die, but to recognize that SLMR cases are "borderline situations" which inevitably involve guilt. The agent, however, can have courage and freedom (which, for Thielicke, come from justification by faith) and can

> go ahead anyway and seek for criteria for deciding the question of life or death in the matter of the artificial kidney. Since these criteria are . . . questionable, necessarily alien to the meaning of human existence, the decision to which they lead can be little more than that arrived at by casting lots.[14]

The resulting criteria, he suggests, will probably be very similar to those already employed in American medical practice.

He is most concerned to preserve a certain *attitude* or *disposition* in SLMR—the sense of guilt

that arises when man's dignity is violated. With this sense of guilt, the agent remains "sound and healthy where it really counts."[15] Thielicke uses man's dignity only as a judgmental, critical, and negative standard. It only tells us how all selection criteria and procedures (and even the refusal to act) implicate us in the ambiguity of the human condition and its metaphysical guilt. This approach is consistent with his view of the task of theological ethics: "to teach us how to understand and endure—not 'solve'—the borderline situation."[16] But ethics, I would contend, can help us discern the factors and norms in whose light relative, discriminate judgments can be made. Even if all actions in SLMR should involve guilt, some may preserve human dignity to a greater extent than others. Thielicke recognizes that a decision based on any criteria is "little more than that arrived at by casting lots." But perhaps selection by chance would come the closest to embodying the moral and nonmoral values that we are trying to maintain (including a sense of man's dignity).

THE VALUES OF RANDOM SELECTION

My proposal is that we use some form of randomness or chance (either natural, such as "first come, first served," or artificial, such as a lottery) to determine who shall be saved. Many reject randomness as a surrender to nonrationality when responsible and rational judgments can and must be made. Edmond Cahn criticizes "Holmes' judge" who recommended the casting of lots because, as Cahn puts it, "the crisis involves stakes too high for gambling and responsibilities too deep for destiny."[17] Similarly, other critics see randomness as a surrender to "non-human" forces which necessarily vitiates human values. Sometimes these values are identified with the process of decision-making (e.g., it is important to have persons rather than impersonal forces determining who shall live). Sometimes they are identified

with the outcome of the process (e.g., the features such as creativity and fullness of being that make human life what it is are to be considered and respected in the decision). Regarding the former, it must be admitted that the use of chance seems cold and impersonal. But presumably the defenders of utilitarian criteria in SLMR want to make their application as objective and impersonal as possible so that subjective bias does not determine who shall live.

Such criticisms, however, ignore the moral and nonmoral values that might be supported by selection by randomness or chance. A more important criticism is that the procedure that I develop draws the relevant moral context too narrowly. That context, so the argument might run, includes the society and its future and not merely the individual with his illness and claim upon SLMR. But my contention is that the values and principles at work in the narrower context may well take precedence over those operative in the broader context, both because of their weight and significance and because of the weakness of selection in terms of social worth. As Paul Freund rightly insists, "The more nearly total is the estimate to be made of an individual, and the more nearly the consequence determines life and death, the more unfit the judgment becomes for human reckoning. . . . Randomness as a moral principle deserves serious study."[18] Serious study would, I think, point toward its implementation in certain conflict situations, primarily because it preserves a significant degree of *personal dignity* by providing *equality* of opportunity. Thus it cannot be dismissed as a "nonrational" and "nonhuman" procedure without an inquiry into the reasons, including human values, which might justify it. Paul Ramsey stresses this point about the *Holmes* case:

> Instead of fixing our attention upon "gambling" as the solution—with all the frivolous and often corrupt associations the word raises in our minds—we should think rather of *equality* of opportunity as the ethical substance of the relations of those individuals to one another that

might have been guarded and expressed by casting lots.[19]

The individual's personal and transcendent dignity, which on the utilitarian approach would be submerged in his social role and function, can be protected and witnessed to by a recognition of his equal right to be saved. Such a right is best preserved by procedures which establish equality of opportunity. Thus selection by chance more closely approximates the requirements established by human dignity than does utilitarian calculation. It is not infallibly just, but it is preferable to the alternatives of letting all die or saving only those who have the greatest social responsibilities and potential contribution.

This argument can be extended by examining values other than individual dignity and equality of opportunity. Another basic value in the medical sphere is the relationship of trust between physician and patient. Which selection criteria are most in accord with this relationship of trust? Which will maintain, extend, and deepen it? My contention is that selection by randomness or chance is preferable from this standpoint too.

Trust, which is inextricably bound to respect for human dignity, is an attitude of expectation about another. It is not simply the expectation that another will perform a particular act, but more specifically that another will act toward him in certain ways—which will respect him as a person. As Charles Fried writes:

> Although trust has to do with reliance on a disposition of another person, it is reliance on a disposition of a special sort: the disposition to act morally, to deal fairly with others, to live up to one's undertakings, and so on. Thus to trust another is first of all to expect him to accept the principle of morality in his dealings with you, to respect your status as a person, your personality.[20]

This trust cannot be preserved in life-and-death situations when a person expects decisions about him to be made in terms of his social worth, for such decisions violate his status as a person. An applicant rejected on grounds of inadequacy in social value or virtue would have reason for feeling that his "trust" had been betrayed. Indeed, the sense that one is being viewed not as an end in himself but as a means in medical progress or the achievement of a greater social good is incompatible with attitudes and relationships of trust. We recognize this in the billboard which was erected after the first heart transplants: "Drive Carefully. Christiaan Barnard Is Watching You." The relationship of trust between the physician and patient is not only an instrumental value in the sense of being an important factor in the patient's treatment. It is also to be endorsed because of its intrinsic worth as a relationship.

Thus the related values of individual dignity and trust are best maintained in selection by chance. But other factors also buttress the argument for this approach. Which criteria and procedures would men agree upon? We have to suppose a hypothetical situation in which several men are going to determine for themselves and their families the criteria and procedures by which they would want to be admitted to and excluded from SLMR if the need arose.[21] We need to assume two restrictions and then ask which set of criteria and procedures would be chosen as the most rational and, indeed, the fairest. The restrictions are these: (1) The men are *self-interested.* They are interested in their own welfare (and that of members of their families), and this, of course, includes survival. Basically, they are not motivated by altruism. (2) Furthermore, they are *ignorant* of their own talents, abilities, potential, and probable contribution to the social good. They do not know how they would fare in a competitive situation, e.g., the competition for SLMR in terms of social contribution. Under these conditions which institution would be chosen—letting all die, utilitarian selection, or the use of chance? Which would seem the most rational? the fairest? By which set of criteria would they want to be included in or excluded from the list of those who will be saved? The rational choice in this setting (assuming self-interest and ignorance

of one's competitive success) would be random selection or chance since this alone provides equality of opportunity. A possible response is that one would prefer to take a "risk" and therefore choose the utilitarian approach. But I think not, especially since I added that the participants in this hypothetical situation are choosing for their children as well as for themselves; random selection or chance could be more easily justified to the children. It would make more sense for men who are self-interested but uncertain about their relative contribution to society to elect a set of criteria that would build in equality of opportunity. They would consider selection by chance as relatively just and fair.[22]

An important psychological point supplements earlier arguments for using chance or random selection. The psychological stress and strain among those who are rejected would be greater if the rejection is based on insufficient social worth than if it is based on chance. Obviously stress and strain cannot be eliminated in these borderline situations, but they would almost certainly be increased by the opprobrium of being judged relatively "unfit" by society's agents using society's values. Nicholas Rescher makes this point very effectively:

> a recourse to chance would doubtless make matters easier for the rejected patient and those who have a specific interest in him. It would surely be quite hard for them to accept his exclusion by relatively mechanical application of objective criteria in whose implementation subjective judgment is involved. But the circumstances of life have conditioned us to accept the workings of chance and to tolerate the element of luck (good or bad): human life is an inherently contingent process. Nobody, after all, has an absolute right to ELT [Exotic Lifesaving Therapy]— but most of us would feel that we have "every bit as much right" to it as anyone else in significantly similar circumstances.[23]

Although it is seldom recognized as such, selection by chance is already in operation in practically every dialysis unit. I am not aware of any unit that removes some of its patients from kidney machines in order to make room for later applicants who are better qualified in terms of social worth. Furthermore, very few people would recommend it. Indeed, few would even consider removing a person from a kidney machine on the grounds that a person better qualified *medically* had just applied. In a discussion of the treatment of chronic renal failure by dialysis at the University of Virginia Hospital Renal Unit from November 15, 1965 to November 15, 1966, Dr. Harry Abram writes: "Thirteen patients sought treatment but were not considered because the program had reached its limit of nine patients."[24] Thus, in practice and theory, natural chance is accepted, at least within certain limits.

My proposal is that we extend this principle (first come, first served) to determine who among the medically acceptable patients shall live or that we utilize artificial chance such as a lottery or randomness. "First come, first served" would be more feasible than a lottery since the applicants make their claims over a period of time rather than as a group at one time. This procedure would be in accord with at least one principle in our present practices and with our sense of individual dignity, trust, and fairness. Its significance in relation to these values can be underlined by asking how the decision can be justified to the rejected applicant. Of course, one easy way of avoiding this task is to maintain the traditional cloak of secrecy, which works to a great extent because patients are often not aware that they are being considered for SLMR in addition to the usual treatment. But whether public justification is instituted or not is not the significant question; it is rather what reasons for rejection would be most acceptable to the unsuccessful applicant. My contention is that rejection can be accepted more readily if equality of opportunity, fairness, and trust are preserved, and that they are best preserved by selection by randomness or chance.

This proposal has yet another advantage since it would eliminate the need for a committee to examine applicants in terms of their social value. This onerous responsibility can be avoided.

Finally, there is a possible indirect consequence of widespread use of random selection

which is interesting to ponder, although I do *not* adduce it as a good reason for adopting random selection. It can be argued, as Professor Mason Willrich of the University of Virginia Law School has suggested, that SLMR cases would practically disappear if these scarce resources were distributed randomly rather than on social worth grounds. Scarcity would no longer be a problem because the holders of economic and political power would make certain that they would not be excluded by a random selection procedure; hence they would help to redirect public priorities or establish private funding so that life-saving medical treatment would be widely and perhaps universally available.

In the framework that I have delineated, are the decrees of chance to be taken without exception? If we recognize exceptions, would we not open Pandora's box again just after we had succeeded in getting it closed? The direction of my argument has been against any exceptions, and I would defend this as the proper way to go. But let me indicate one possible way of admitting exceptions, while at the same time circumscribing them so narrowly that they would be very rare indeed.

An obvious advantage of the utilitarian approach is that occasionally circumstances arise that make it necessary to say that one man is practically indispensable for a society in view of a particular set of problems it faces (e.g., the president when the nation is waging a war for survival). Certainly the argument to this point has stressed that the burden of proof would fall on those who think that the social danger in this instance is so great that they simply cannot abide by the outcome of a lottery or a first come, first served policy. Also, the reason must be negative rather than positive; that is, we depart from chance in this instance not because we want to take advantage of this person's potential contribution to the improvement of our society, but because his immediate loss would possibly (even probably) be disastrous (again, the president in a grave national emergency). Finally, social value (in the negative sense) should be used as a standard of exception in dialysis, for example, only if it would provide a reason strong enough to warrant removing another person from a kidney machine if all machines were taken. Assuming this strong reluctance to remove anyone once the commitment has been made to him, we would be willing to put this patient ahead of another applicant for a vacant machine only if we would be willing (in circumstances in which all machines are being used) to vacate a machine by removing someone from it. These restrictions would make an exception almost impossible.

While I do not recommend this procedure of recognizing exceptions, I think that one can defend it while accepting my general thesis about selection by randomness or chance. If it is used, a lay committee (perhaps advisory, perhaps even stronger) would be called upon to deal with the alleged exceptions, since the doctors or others would in effect be appealing the outcome of chance (either natural or artificial). This lay committee would determine whether this patient was so indispensable at this time and place that he had to be saved even by sacrificing the values preserved by random selection. It would make it quite clear that exception is warranted, if at all, only as the "lesser of two evils." Such a defense would be recognized only rarely, if ever, primarily because chance and randomness preserve so many important moral and nonmoral values in SLMR cases.[25]

Notes

[1]George Bernard Shaw, *The Doctor's Dilemma* (New York, 1941), pp. 132–33.

[2]Henry K. Beecher, "Scarce Resources and Medical Advancement," *Daedalus* (Spring 1969), 279–80.

[3]Leo Shatin, "Medical Care and the Social Worth of a Man," *American Journal of Orthopsychiatry,* 36 (1967), 97.

[4]Harry S. Abram and Walter Wadlington, "Selection of Patients for Artificial and Transplanted Organs," *Annals of Internal Medicine,* 69 (September 1968), 615–20.

[5]*United States v. Holmes,* 26 Fed. Cas. 360 (C.C.E.D. Pa. 1842). All references are to the text of the trial as reprinted in Philip E. Davis, ed., *Moral Duty and Legal Responsibility: A Philosophical-Legal Casebook* (New York, 1966), pp. 102–18.

[6]*The Moral Decision* (Bloomington, Ind., 1955), p. 71.

[7]For a discussion of the higher suicide rate among dialysis patients than among the general population and an interpretation of some of the factors at work, see H. S. Abram, G. L. Moore, and F. B. Westervelt, "Suicidal Behavior in Chronic Dialysis Patients," *American Journal of Psychiatry,* 127 (1971): 1119–1204. This study shows that even "if one does not include death through not following the regimen the incidence of suicide is still more than 100 times the normal population."

[8]Joseph Fletcher, "Donor Nephrectomies and Moral Responsibility," *Journal of the American Medical Women's Association,* 23 (December 1968), 1090.

[9]Leo Shatin, pp. 96–101.

[10]For a discussion of the Seattle selection committee, see Shana Alexander, "They Decide Who Lives, Who Dies," *Life,* 53 (November 9, 1962), 102. For an examination of general selection practices in dialysis see "Scarce Medical Resources," *Columbia Law Review* 69:620 (1969) and Abram and Wadlington.

[11]David Sanders and Jesse Dukeminier, Jr., "Medical Advance and Legal Lag: Hemodialysis and Kidney Transplantation," *UCLA Law Review* 15:367 (1968), 378.

[12]"Letters and Comments," *Annals of Internal Medicine,* 61 (August 1964), 360. Dr. G. E. Schreiner contends that "if you really believe in the right of society to make decisions on medical availability on these criteria you should be logical and say that when a man stops going to church or is divorced or loses his job, he ought to be removed from the programme and somebody else who fulfills these criteria substituted. Obviously no one faces up to this logical consequence" (G. E. W. Wolstenholme and Maeve O'Connor, eds., *Ethics in Medical Progress: With Special Reference to Transplantation.* A Ciba Foundation Symposium [Boston, 1966], p. 127).

[13]Helmut Thielicke, "The Doctor as Judge of Who Shall Live and Who Shall Die," *Who Shall Live?* ed. by Kenneth Vaux (Philadelphia, 1970), p. 172.

[14]Ibid., pp. 173–74.

[15]Ibid., p. 173.

[16]Thielicke, *Theological Ethics,* Vol. 1, *Foundations* (Philadelphia, 1966), p. 602.

[17]Cahn, op. cit., p. 71.

[18]Paul Freund, "Introduction," *Daedalus* (Spring 1969), xiii.

[19]Paul Ramsey, *Nine Modern Moralists* (Englewood Cliffs, N.J., 1962), p. 245.

[20]Charles Fried, "Privacy," in *Law, Reason, and Justice,* ed. by Graham Hughes (New York, 1969), p. 52.

[21]My argument is greatly dependent on John Rawls's version of justice as fairness, which is a reinterpretation of social contract theory. Rawls, however, would probably not apply his ideas to "borderline situations." See "Distributive Justice: Some Addenda," *Natural Law Forum,* 13 (1968), 53. For Rawls's general theory, see "Justice as Fairness," *Philosophy, Politics and Society* (Second Series), ed. by Peter Laslett and W. G. Runciman (Oxford, 1962), pp. 132–57 and *A Theory of Justice* (Cambridge, Mass., 1971).

[22]Occasionally someone contends that random selection may reward vice. Leo Shatin (op. cit., p. 100) insists that random selection "would reward socially disvalued qualities by giving their bearers the same special medical care opportunities as those received by the bearers of socially valued qualities. Personally I do not favor such a method." Obviously society must engender certain qualities in its members, but not all of its institutions must be devoted to that purpose. Furthermore, there are strong reasons, I have contended, for exempting SLMR from that sort of function.

[23]Nicholas Rescher, "The Allocation of Exotic Medical Lifesaving Therapy," *Ethics,* 79 (April 1969), 184. He defends random selection's use only after utilitarian and other judgments have been made. If there are no "major disparities" in terms of utility, etc., in the second stage of selection, then final selection could be made randomly. He fails to give attention to the moral values that random selection might preserve.

[24]Harry S. Abram, M.D., "The Psychiatrist, the Treatment of Chronic Renal Failure, and the Prolongation of Life: II" *American Journal of Psychiatry* 126:157–67 (1969), 158.

[25]I read a draft of this paper in a seminar on "Social Implications of Advances in Biomedical Science and Technology: Artificial and Transplanted Internal Organs," sponsored by the Center for the Study of Science, Technology, and Public Policy of the University of Virginia, Spring 1970. I am indebted to the participants in that seminar, and especially to its leaders, Mason Willrich, Professor of Law, and Dr. Harry Abram, Associate Professor of Psychiatry, for criticisms which helped me to sharpen these ideas. Good discussions of the legal questions raised by selection (e.g., equal protection of the law and due process) which I have not considered can be found in "Scarce Medical Resources," *Columbia Law Review,* 69:620 (1969); "Patient Selection for Artificial and Transplanted Organs," *Harvard Law Review,* 82:1322 (1969); and Sanders and Dukeminier, op. cit.

SELECTED BIBLIOGRAPHY

Aaron, Henry J., and William B. Schwartz. *The Painful Prescription: Rationing Hospital Care.* Washington, D.C.: Brookings Institution, 1984.

Alexander, Shana. "They Decide Who Lives, Who Dies: Medical Miracle Puts a Moral Burden on a Small Committee." *Life* vol. 9 (November 1962): 102ff. Reprinted in Robert Hunt and John Arras, eds. *Ethical Issues in Modern Medicine.* Palo Alto, Calif.: Mayfield Publishing Co., 1977. Pp. 409–24.

Bayer, Ronald, Arthur L. Caplan, and Normal Daniels, eds. *In Search of Equity: Health Needs and the Health Care System.* New York: Plenum Press, 1983.

Calabresi, Guido, and Philip Bobbit. *Tragic Choices: The Conflicts Society Confronts in the Allocation of Tragically Scarce Resources.* New York: W. W. Norton and Company, 1978.

Daniels, Norman. *Just Health Care.* Cambridge: Cambridge University Press, 1985.

Encyclopedia of Bioethics. Warren T. Reich, ed. New York: Macmillan/Free Press, 1978.
  "Health Care"
    "III. Right to Health-Care Services," by Albert R. Jonsen
    "IV. Theories of Justice and Health Care," by Roy Branson
  "Health Insurance," by Stefan A. Riesenfeld
  "Justice," by Joel Feinberg
  "Kidney Dialysis and Transplantation," by Renee C. Fox and Judith P. Swazey
  "Life—I. Value of Life" by Peter Singer
  "Rationing of Medical Treatment," by James F. Childress
  "Social Medicine," by George A. Silver
  "Technology—III. Technology Assessment," by LeRoy Walters

Enthoven, Alain C. *Health Plan: The Only Practical Solution to the Soaring Cost of Medical Care.* Reading, Mass.: Addison-Wesley, 1980.

Fried, Charles. "Rights and Health Care—Beyond Equity and Efficiency." *New England Journal of Medicine* 293 (1975): 241–45.

Fuchs, Victor R. *Who Shall Live? Health, Economics, and Social Choice.* New York: Basic Books, 1974.

Graber, Glenn C., Alfred D. Beasley, and John A. Eaddy. *Ethical Analysis of Clinical Medicine.* Baltimore: Urban and Schwarzenberg, 1985. Especially Chapter 5.

Hiatt, Howard H. "Protecting the Medical Commons: Who Is Responsible?" *New England Journal of Medicine* 293 (1975): 235–41.

Outka, Gene. "Social Justice and Equal Access to Health Care." *The Journal of Religious Ethics* 2 (Spring 1973): 11–32.

Pellegrino, Edmund D. "Medical Morality and Medical Economics." *Hastings Center Report* 8 (August 1978): 8–12.

President's Commission for the Study of Ethical Problems in Medicine and Biomedical and Behavioral Research. *Securing Access to Health Care* (Washington, D.C.: U.S. Government Printing Office, 1983).
  Vol. I—Report; Vol. II—Appendices: Sociocultural and Philosophical Studies; Vol. III—Appendices: Empirical, Legal, and Conceptual Studies.

Ramsey, Paul. *The Patient as Person.* New Haven: Yale University Press, 1970. Chapters 4, 5, 6, 7.

Relman, Arnold S. "The New Medical-Industrial Complex." *New England Journal of Medicine* 303, no. 17 (October 23, 1980): 963–70.

Starr, Paul. *The Social Transformation of American Medicine.* New York: Basic Books, 1982.

Veatch, Robert M., and Roy Branson. *Ethics and Health Policy.* Cambridge, Mass.: Ballinger Publishing Company, 1976.

Winslow, Gerald R. *Triage and Justice.* Berkeley: University of California Press, 1982.